The
Restaurant Guide
2010

AA Lifestyle Guides

Please contact
Advertisement Sales: advertisingsales@theaa.com
Editorial Department: lifestyleguides@theaa.com

AA Media Limited would like to thank the following photographers, companies and picture libraries for their
assistance in the preparation of this book.
Abbreviations for the picture credits are as follows: (t) top; (b) bottom; (l) left; (r) right; (c) centre; (AA) AA
World Travel Library.
Front cover: (t) Andrew Fairlie at Gleneagles, Auchterarder, Scotland, photography by A Donaldson;
(bl) Royal Garden Hotel, London, photography by N Clutton; (br) Photodisc.
Back cover: (l) Malmaison, Manchester; (c) The Latymer, Pennyhill Park, Bagshot; (r) Photodisc.
Every effort has been made to trace the copyright holders, and we apologise in advance for any accidental
errors. We would be happy to apply any corrections in the following edition of this publication.

Typeset/Repro: Keenes, Andover
Printed by Trento Srl, Italy.
This directory is compiled by AA Lifestyle Guides; managed in the Librios Information
Management System and generated by the AA establishment database system.

AA Restaurant Guide edited by Andrew Turvil, assisted by Fiona Griffiths

Restaurant descriptions have been contributed by the following team of writers:
Fiona Griffiths, David Hancock, Julia Hynard, Felicity Jackson, Denise Laing, Mike Pedley,
Carina Simon, Allen Stidwill, Mark Taylor, Stuart Taylor, Andrew Turvil

Published by AA Publishing, a trading name of AA Media Limited,
whose registered office is Fanum House, Basing View, Basingstoke, Hampshire RG21 4EA.
Registered number 06112600.
A CIP catalogue for this book is available from the British Library.
ISBN: 978-0-7495-6283-0
A03986

Maps prepared by the Mapping Services
Department of AA Publishing.

Maps © AA Media Limited 2009.

 This product includes
mapping data licensed from
Ordnance Survey® with the permission of the
Controller of Her Majesty's Stationery Office.
© Crown copyright 2009.
All rights reserved.
Licence number 100021153.

 Land &
Property
Services.
This is based upon Crown
Copyright and is reproduced
with the permission of Land &
Property Services under delegated authority from
the Controller of Her Majesty's Stationery Office.
© Crown copyright and database rights 2009
Licence number 100,363. Permit number 90027

Republic of Ireland mapping based on
© Ordnance Survey Ireland/Government of Ireland
Copyright Permit number MP000109

Information on National Parks in England
provided by the Countryside Agency
(Natural England).
Information on National Parks in Scotland
provided by Scottish Natural Heritage.
Information on National Parks in Wales provided
by The Countryside Council for Wales.

Contents

Welcome to the Guide

Welcome to the 17th edition of the AA Restaurant Guide. The AA has over one hundred years of experience of seeking out, assessing and recommending the best places to eat and sleep around the country. And for seventeen years the booming restaurant sector has had its own guide to focus on finding the best places to eat, from country inns on wild moors to city-centre hotels handy for a spot of retail therapy, and from lively bistros on local high streets to first-class Indians in London or Glasgow. And, of course, the increasing number of destination restaurants of international standing.

It's been a vibrant seventeen years for the restaurant business: the rise of the celebrity chef, fusion cooking, the renaissance of the pub as a serious foodie contender, molecular gastronomy, to name but a few of the headline-grabbing developments to the UK dining scene. The world of restaurants does not stand still and within these pages you'll find lots of newcomers to the guide for 2010. Whatever your budget or personal preference, and for whichever occasion, you're sure to find what you're looking for.

The AA inspectors have a vast amount of experience within the hospitality industry and restaurants are visited regularly to ensure that Rosettes are awarded at the right levels and that standards are being maintained. A five-Rosette meal is going to be staggeringly good, may possibly blow your mind (will certainly blow a fair bit of cash) and will leave a lasting impression, undoubtedly. That does not mean, however, that you won't find lots of thrilling and memorable experiences further down the Rosette ladder; sparklingly fresh seafood, perhaps, eaten on the banks of a loch, or a simply chargrilled steak in a thrusting metropolitan brasserie. The lower ranked places have much to offer and every restaurant in this book is being recommended.

A good restaurant experience is not only about the food – everything and anything can affect how it goes, from the effectiveness of the service, the price you pay, to the reason you're there in the first place. If your proposal of marriage is refused perhaps you won't go back, if it's accepted you'll probably return on the same date every year without fail. The restaurant can't control your destiny, but everything else is down to them – the chef, the manager and the waiting staff. If the food is not up to scratch or what is promised is not delivered, tell them about it. If the service is unacceptably slow or careless, tell them about it. They may well assume everything is hunky-dory until you point it out. Give the restaurant a chance to rectify any mistakes by complaining about poor food and service at the time.

Le Crunch

Every year restaurants close during the year-long life of the guide. It's always been an economically fragile business, but this year we can expect more closures than usual. The economic downturn, the credit crunch, whatever you call it, has already caused problems for chefs such as Antony Worrall Thompson and Jean-Christophe Novelli, and even Tom Aikens, the proud holder of 5 Rosettes, wobbled in the economic conditions. The Gordon Ramsay empire has had a tough year, too, and had to close a few of its foreign outposts to consolidate the company's position; Prague, LA and Paris were sacrificed.

Previous recessions, such as the early 1990s, hit the restaurant trade hard, and this one looks particularly bad. The restaurant scene, though, is a little different this time around. Eating out is something more people are doing more regularly than ever before, and even in a harsh economic climate eating out won't be cut out of everyone's life entirely. There are customers out there. Certainly most restaurants will find their footfall reduced – people will eat out less often or spend a little less when they do – and there will be casualties. And some of these casualties may prove to be surprising.

The silver lining is that the weak pound will encourage many UK residents to holiday at home and make it good value for people to come here from abroad, thus UK holiday destinations are likely to do rather well over the life of this guide. Restaurants that are geographically situated to take advantage of increased UK tourist numbers could do okay. A holiday in the UK is often a family affair, so restaurants that appeal to families are in a strong position. The details at the bottom of each entry give information on what concessions are made to children, whether there is a full children's menu or if smaller portions of the main dishes are available. Many restaurants could do better when dealing with children. Parents often just require flexibility – a small portion of fish without the sauce, for example, rather than a plate of frozen nuggets out of the freezer.

Value for money (that doesn't necessarily mean cheap) is something most of us look for at all times, regardless of the economic situation, but those restaurants that are perceived as good value will clearly do better than somewhere considered over-priced. A restaurant is only value for money, though, if standards are maintained – cutting corners in an attempt to save the bottom line can be a fatal mistake.

The next year is likely to be a roller-coaster ride for many restaurateurs, but as customers, there are many, many great restaurants to discover and perhaps a few bargains to be found along the way.

Menus with a local flavour

One of the biggest changes (and a definite improvement) to UK restaurants over recent years has been the increased use of local and regional produce. There have been chefs who have championed the specialities of their regions for many years, such as Nigel Haworth in Lancashire, or Raymond Blanc growing his own in his Oxfordshire garden, but whereas a few years ago they were in the minority, now a significant number of restaurants featured within these pages flag up their use of produce from the surrounding areas.

Many of the dishes described in this guide mention the breed of animal, sometimes the farm from whence it came, they name-check the harbour where the fish was landed and indicate where the vegetables are grown. This has two important results. Firstly, it demonstrates to the customer that the food is being sourced with care, that the chef is proud of what he is cooking and that the kitchen pays attention to detail. Secondly, it can bring a regional identity to the menu.

In Scotland, for example, it might be seafood from the local coastline and lochs, or in Wales lamb from the hills, and in the West Country everything from fresh fish to local cheeses. And ever-increasing numbers of places are growing their own vegetables, salads, fruits and herbs.

Such a regional identity makes sense on many levels, from low transportation costs, freshness and as an antidote to the corporate blandness of menus that read the same from Land's End to John O'Groats.

Thank you for choosing this guide

I hope you enjoy many fantastic meals and memorable experiences in the restaurants within these pages. This book reflects the amazing diversity of restaurants we have in the UK and the talents of the people who work in them.

Good eating

Andrew Turvil
Editor

How to Use the Guide

1 MAP REFERENCE

The atlas section is at the back of the Guide. The map page number is followed by the National Grid Reference. To find a location, read the first figure horizontally and the second figure vertically within the lettered square. For Central London and Greater London, there is a 13-page map section starting on page 216.

2 PLACE NAME

Restaurants are listed in country and county order, then by town and then alphabetically within the town. There is an index by restaurant at the back of the book and a similar one for the Central & Greater London sections on pages 218-221.

3 RESTAURANT NAME

4 ⊛ THE AA ROSETTE AWARD

Entries have been awarded one or more Rosettes, up to a maximum of five. See page 8.

5 FOOD STYLE

Food style of the restaurant is followed by a short summary statement.

6 PHOTOGRAPHS

Restaurants are invited to enhance their entry with up to two photographs.

7 CHEF(S) AND OWNER(S)

The names of the chef(s) and owner(s) are as up-to-date as possible at the time of going to press, but changes in personnel often occur, and may affect both the style and quality of the restaurant.

8 PRICES

Prices are for fixed lunch (2 courses) and dinner (3 courses) and à la carte dishes. Service charge information (see also opposite). Note: Prices quoted are a guide only, and are subject to change.

---

2 EVERSLEY Map 5 SU76 **1**

3 The New Mill Riverside Restaurant

4 ⊛ ⊛ Modern European ⚑ NOTABLE WINE LIST **19**

HAMPSHIRE

Beautiful setting for well-crafted, modern food

☎ 0118 973 2277 📠 0118 932 8780
New Mill Rd RG27 0RA
e-mail: info@thenewmill.co.uk
web: www.thenewmill.co.uk
dir: Off A327 2m S of Arborfield Cross. N of village follow brown signs. Approach from New Mill Rd

There is something romantic about mills and this one (not so new at 400 years-plus) is idyllically situated in lush green gardens and still has a working waterwheel. It's full of character on the inside, too, with low ceilings, old beams, grand fireplaces and flagstone floors; the dining areas include a conservatory with views over the water and a large patio. The cooking is in the modern vein, with good British produce delivered in broadly European preparations; thus twice-baked Barkham Blue soufflé with peashoot salad and walnut dressing might precede pan-fried sea bass with cassoulet of haricot beans and Toulouse sausage. The lunchtime table d'hôte is exceptionally good value.

Chef Colin Robson-Wright **Owner** Cindy & John Duffield **Times** 12-2/7-10 Closed 1-2 Jan, Mon **Prices** Fixed L 2 course £15, Fixed D 3 course £25, Starter £9.95-£12.50, Main £17.25-£23.95, Dessert £7.75-£8.50, Service optional, Groups min 8 service 10% **Wines** 150 bottles over £20, 10 bottles under £20, 10 by glass **Notes** Tasting menu available, Sunday L, Vegetarian available, Dress restrictions, Smart casual, Civ Wed 150, Air con **Seats** 80, Pr/dining room 32 **Children** Portions **Parking** 60

9 NOTES

Additional information e.g. availability of vegetarian dishes, civil weddings, air conditioning etc.

---

10 DIRECTIONS

Directions are given if supplied.

11 PARKING DETAILS

On-site parking is listed if applicable, then nearby parking.

12 CHILDREN

Menu, portions, age restrictions etc.

13 NUMBER OF SEATS

Number of seats in the restaurant, followed by private dining room (Pr/dining room).

14 NUMBER OF WINES

Number of wines under and over £20, and available by the glass.

15 DAILY OPENING AND CLOSING TIMES

Daily opening and closing times, the days of the week it is closed and seasonal closures. Note that opening times are liable to change without notice. It is wise to telephone in advance.

16 DESCRIPTION

Description of the restaurant and the food.

17 E-MAIL ADDRESS AND WEBSITE

18 VEGETARIAN MENU

V Indicates a vegetarian menu. Restaurants with some vegetarian dishes available are indicated under Notes.

19 NOTABLE WINE LIST

⚑ NOTABLE WINE LIST Indicates notable wine list (See p18-19).

20 LOCAL AND REGIONAL PRODUCE

🐾 Indicates the use of local and regional produce. More than 50% of the restaurant food ingredients are produced within a 50-mile radius. Suppliers are mentioned by name on the menu.

All establishments take major credit cards, except where we have specified otherwise.

All information is correct at the time of printing but may change without notice. Details of opening times and prices may be omitted from an entry when the establishment has not supplied us with up-to-date information. This is indicated where the establishment name is shown in *italics*.

Service Charge

We ask restaurants the following questions about service charge (their responses appear under Prices in each entry):

- Is service included in the meal price, with no further charge added or expected?
- Is service optional – charge not automatically added to bill?
- Is service charge compulsory, and what percentage?
- Is there a service charge for larger groups, minimum number in group, and what percentage?

Many establishments automatically add service charge to the bill but tell the customer it is optional.

Smoking Regulations

From July 2007 smoking was banned in all enclosed public places in the United Kingdom and Ireland. A hotel or guest accommodation proprietor can designate one or more bedrooms with ventilation systems where the occupants can smoke, but communal areas must be smoke-free. Communal areas include the interior bars and restaurants in pubs and inns.

Facilities for Disabled Guests

The Disability Discrimination Act (access to Goods and Services) means that service providers may have to consider making adjustments to their premises. For further information see disability.gov.uk/dda.

The establishments in this Guide should all be aware of their responsibilities under the Act. Always phone in advance to ensure that the establishment you have chosen has appropriate facilities. See also holidaycare.org.uk.

Website Addresses

Where website addresses are included they have been supplied and specified by the respective establishment. Such websites are not under the control of AA Media Limited and as such AA Media Limited has no control over them and will not accept any responsibility or liability in respect of any and all matters whatsoever relating to such websites including access, content, material and functionality. By including the addresses of third-party websites the AA does not intend to solicit business or offer any security to any person in any country, directly or indirectly.

How the AA Assesses for Rosette Awards

The AA's Rosette award scheme was the first nationwide scheme for assessing the quality of food served by restaurants and hotels. The Rosette scheme is an award, not a classification, and although there is necessarily an element of subjectivity when it comes to assessing taste, we aim for a consistent approach throughout the UK. Our awards are made solely on the basis of a meal visit or visits by one or more of our hotel and restaurant Inspectors, who have an unrivalled breadth and depth of experience in assessing quality. They award Rosettes annually on a rising scale of one to five.

So what makes a restaurant worthy of a Rosette Award?
For our Inspectors, the top and bottom line is the food. The taste of a dish is what counts, and whether it successfully delivers to the diner the promise of the menu. A restaurant is only as good as its worst meal. Although presentation and competent service should be appropriate to the style of the restaurant and the quality of the food, they cannot affect the Rosette assessment as such, either up or down. The summaries below indicate what our Inspectors look for, but are intended only as guidelines. The AA is constantly reviewing its award criteria, and competition usually results in an all-round improvement in standards, so it becomes increasingly difficult for restaurants to reach award level. For more detailed Rosette criteria, please visit theAA.com.

◉ One Rosette
- Excellent restaurants that stand out in their local area
- Food prepared with care, understanding and skill
- Good quality ingredients
Around 50% of restaurants have one Rosette.

◉◉ Two Rosettes
- The best local restaurants
- Higher standards
- Better consistency
- Greater precision apparent in the cooking
- Obvious attention to the quality and selection of ingredients
About 40% of restaurants have two Rosettes.

◉◉◉ Three Rosettes
- Outstanding restaurants demanding recognition well beyond local area
- Selection and sympathetic treatment of highest quality ingredients
- Timing, seasoning and judgement of flavour combinations consistent
- Excellent intelligent service and a well-chosen wine list
Around 10% of restaurants have three Rosettes.

◉◉◉◉ Four Rosettes
Dishes demonstrate:
- intense ambition
- a passion for excellence
- superb technical skills
- remarkable consistency
- appreciation of culinary traditions combined with desire for exploration and improvement
- Cooking demands national recognition
Twenty-six restaurants have four Rosettes.

◉◉◉◉◉ Five Rosettes
- Cooking stands comparison with the best in the world
- Highly individual
- Breathtaking culinary skills
- Setting the standards to which others aspire
- Knowledgeable and distinctive wine list
Seven restaurants have five Rosettes.

AA Chefs' Chef 2009-2010

This is the annual poll of all the chefs in The Restaurant Guide. Around 2,000 of the country's top chefs were asked to vote to recognise the achievements of one of their peers from a shortlist chosen by the AA's team of Inspectors.

Marcus Wareing

This year's AA Chefs' Chef Award goes to 39-year-old Marcus Wareing, chef-patron at his eponymous restaurant, Marcus Wareing at The Berkeley.

For any chef or restaurateur, getting positive feedback from customers confirms you're on the right track, while winning the favour of restaurant critics and inspectors helps bring customers through the door. Gaining the recognition of your peers, on the other hand, is surely the icing on the cake of any career.

The Chefs' Chef Award comes at a time when Wareing has spread his wings and broken from his long-time collaborator, Gordon Ramsay. His restaurant continues to go from strength-to-strength.

Marcus Wareing became chef-patron at The Berkeley in 2003 and finally took over the running of the restaurant on his own terms in September 2008, changing the name from Pétrus to Marcus Wareing at The Berkeley.

Wareing was born in Lancashire in 1970, his career starting at The Savoy, where he arrived in 1988 aged just eighteen to work under Anton Edelmann. The classical grounding gained there and under Albert Roux at Le Gavroche, which he joined the following year, is evident in his style of modern European cooking, which is refined, intelligent and shows an extraordinary eye for detail. ▷

No longer part of the Ramsay group, as Wareing puts it, "my name is on the door for the first time, but I remain in familiar surroundings with the same loyal and dedicated team around me".

AA Chefs' Chef *continued*

Wareing's long-term working relationship with Ramsay began in 1993 when he bagged the job as sous–chef at the newly opened Aubergine, part of the A-Z group. The head chef was one Gordon Ramsay.

Wareing went on to open L'Oranger for the A-Z group as Ramsay left Aubergine amid controversy to open his own eponymous restaurant in Royal Hospital Road. In 1999 Ramsay opened Pétrus in its original site in St James's and Wareing was installed as chef-patron, where he remained as the restaurant moved to The Berkeley, and he also oversaw the Ramsay group's move into The Savoy.

This career spent working within first-rate fine-dining restaurants has given Wareing the perfect platform to develop and perfect his own brand of contemporary cooking. "I am determined to make this London's finest restaurant", as he puts it, a goal many might argue he has already achieved. This award goes to show the respect there is for him within the industry. Marcus Wareing at The Berkeley is a remarkable 5-Rosetted restaurant with a charm and confidence all of its own. Flavours pack a punch and luxuries abound on menus that reflect the finely judged skills of the AA Chefs' Chef of the Year. The set-lunch menu is remarkably good value at £35 for three courses and everything from the highly polished service to the copious delights of the bonbon trolley make for a stunningly memorable experience. □

PREVIOUS WINNERS

Michael Caines
Gidleigh Park, Chagford, Devon
p121

Andrew Fairlie
Andrew Fairlie @ Gleneagles, Scotland
p526

Germain Schwab
Winteringham Fields (former chef), Lincolnshire

Raymond Blanc
Le Manoir aux Quat' Saisons, Great Milton, Oxfordshire
p359

Shaun Hill
Walnut Tree Inn, Abergavenny, Monmouthshire, Wales
p557

Heston Blumenthal
The Fat Duck, Bray, Berkshire
p50

Jean-Christophe Novelli

Gordon Ramsay
Restaurant Gordon Ramsay, London SW3
p269

Rick Stein
The Seafood Restaurant, Padstow, Cornwall
p87

Marco Pierre White
Marco Pierre White's Yew Tree Inn, Highclere, Hampshire,
p178

Kevin Viner

Philip Howard
The Square, London
p305

On The Menu

Pan-fried veal sweetbread with Swiss chard, roasted ceps and celeriac, Sauternes jus

Dorset turbot with frogs' legs with lemon confit, caper and golden raisin purée and jus rôti

Rhug Farm Welsh suckling pig, cooked for 24 hours, with braised chicory and pommes mousseline

Raspberry and milk chocolate gâteau with basil and Eton mess

AA Lifetime Achievement Award 2009-2010

Raymond BLANC

It is 25 years since Raymond Blanc picked up the keys to Le Manoir and embarked on an epic journey to fulfil his vision of a centre of excellence, which seems like a fitting time for the AA Lifetime Achievement Award to go to this Frenchman who has done so much for British food. He spoke to Andrew Turvil... ▷

IT TAKES A PARTICULAR type of courage to put the roof over your head on the line to kick-start your dream, and any financial advisor worth their salt would advise against such action, but that's what Raymond Blanc did in 1977 when he and his wife mortgaged their house to open their first restaurant, Les Quat' Saisons in Oxford. And that was at a time when the interest rates really made your eyes water. But the restaurant was a success.

"We won lots of awards at this tiny, humble place", says Blanc, but he wanted more. "I wanted a small place, somewhere cottagey which we could call a home from home, somewhere with a big garden, where we could connect with our soul." The search was on to find somewhere to fulfil this dream.

But you know what estate agents are like; they showed him an old stone manor in Great Milton. "We ended up falling in love with it immediately. There was something so beautiful about it... the Oxford stone... the garden", says Blanc,

> **"I wanted a small place, somewhere cottagey which we could call a home from home, somewhere with a big garden, where we could connect with our soul."**

"I put my heart into it, and by God I needed to". It was a hugely ambitious project, to restore such a large and magnificent house.

"There was huge, serious decay. It cost about three times more than we expected, put us on the back foot. There were a few moments that were rather scary." But with such a beautiful manor house at its core, Blanc's ambition couldn't fail to be realised, and in 1984 Le Manoir aux Quat' Saisons opened its doors for the first time.

From the outset, Blanc was determined to create a fine dining experience that wasn't stuffy or exclusive. He wanted Le Manoir to be the sort of place where ordinary people would feel comfortable – even if they did need to save up to go there.

"I didn't want a temple or a shrine", he says, "luxury is something for people to aspire to. I wanted to undo the tie a little

> **"I didn't want a temple or a shrine... I wanted to undo the tie a little bit so the guests could breathe."**

bit so the guests could breathe. Eating out is not about suffering, it is about celebration. But eating out in England was a social occasion, it was not about the food. I wanted working class people - like me - to come here... that is the most wonderful thing on earth."

This egalitarian approach was radical for the time – some might argue it still is today – and extended to an inclusive attitude towards children. "I really wanted to welcome children, because I'm French. But I had to fight the food writers, my staff, everybody. It was never a problem as you can make a friend or foe of a child in two seconds."

The wisdom Blanc has been passing on over many years is essentially a straightforward message, the clue to which is in the name he chose for his business – the seasons. He believes that farming motivated by yield and a food industry based on heavy processing and aggressive marketing resulted in the UK food industry losing its way. "Society valued cheapness and shelf life and forgot that our land is our gold. They created a monster. The biggest mistake was separating food from culture. The foundation is missing," he says. "I am not blaming that generation; we didn't think there would be consequences but of course there have been terrible consequences."

But the green shoots of recovery can be seen as many British chefs are finally working with farmers – "to enrich each other", as Blanc puts it – and he believes that the key is in "reinventing the regions". Reading the entries in this guidebook you will see that more and more chefs understand the importance of provenance and are not only buying and cooking carefully sourced, high quality produce, but are putting the facts on the menu to inform the customer. Twenty-five years ago, though, the breed of pig or lamb got no mention, the British chefs didn't think the customer needed to know, or cared, but things are changing. For Blanc, of course, it's always been only natural to make the connection between farmers and the food on the plate, following the seasons, and using carefully sourced produce. He supported the work of groups like the Soil Association and the Marine Conservation Society. "Today", he says, "chefs are selecting their foods more knowledgeably, more carefully – connecting with the farmers."

Twenty-five years on and the vision of a luxurious centre of excellence has been realised. Blanc sees himself as a benevolent autocrat, the architect of the vision. Since Le Manoir opened its doors, hundreds of British chefs have passed through the kitchen and have gone on to help the UK become recognised internationally – and to help the nation connect to a food culture after many decades in the wilderness. "Restaurant kitchens are much more professional these days. Our chefs are being trained to be managers, and British chefs now believe in themselves. They have embraced multiculturalism. Now Britain has a cuisine very much of its own right." Like any good leader, Blanc surrounds himself with a talented team and brings the best out of them. Perhaps the key to his success has been this desire to share his values and to ensure they are passed down. Le Manoir's current 35 managers and sub-managers are part of a team that

> **"Today, chefs are selecting their foods more knowledgeably, more carefully – connecting with the farmers."**

is rooted in these ideals. Many have been at Le Manoir for years, including executive head chef Gary Jones, who has been part of the team for 14 years.

A walk in the gardens – connecting to the seasons, you might say – is a must for any visitor and M Blanc reckons that guests should allow 5 or 6 hours for the whole Manoir experience. Strolling through the grounds, sitting on a bench in the Japanese Tea garden, admiring the bronze sculptures that pepper the gardens is a magical experience before or after a meal, or both. The bedrooms and suites, too, are all part of the experience and the vision.

"I wanted to create a modern classic," says Blanc. And because of his attention to every detail and his ability to get the very best out of people, he's done just that. But more than that, he has trained and inspired a generation of British chefs with his passion and values, and together they have made a huge impact on the food culture of this country.

As he says himself, "I think it is okay to say, just for one minute, 'you done alright Raymond'." □

AA Restaurants of the Year

Potential Restaurants of the Year are nominated by our team of full-time Inspectors based on their routine visits. In selecting a Restaurant of the Year, we look for somewhere that is exceptional in its chosen area of the market. Whilst the Rosette awards are based on the quality of the food alone, Restaurant of the Year takes into account all aspects of the experience.

ENGLAND

PURNELL'S ⊛⊛⊛
BIRMINGHAM
PAGE 426

Glynn Purnell's eponymous restaurant in one of Birmingham's conservation areas delivers compellingly modern and skilfully prepared food. The cool and contemporarily converted warehouse displays enigmatic photographs of Birmingham landscapes, further enhancing the local flavour. The fixed-price carte and tasting menu is based on first-rate produce, a great deal of it local, and both lunch and dinner include excellent breads, amuse-bouche and petits fours (peanut cream lollipop, for example). Presentation is superb and technical dexterity evident in a starter of chicken liver parfait with home-cured beef, confit of pineapple, jelly of the same fruit, and a port reduction. Main-course brill cooked in coconut milk with Indian lentils and cumin and toffee carrots reflects the multi-cultural heritage of the city, or there might be daube of beef with mijoté of snails, summer radishes and mushroom milk. The finale is no less impressive: dark chocolate torte with warm chocolate mousse and passionfruit sorbet.

LONDON

CORRIGAN'S MAYFAIR ⊛⊛⊛
LONDON W1
PAGE 285

Richard Corrigan is a chef who puts the quality of the produce at the centre of everything and consequently his restaurant sparkles like the water in Galway Bay. There is a refreshing simplicity to this Irishman's cooking, but it is not unrefined. His newest outpost in the heart of Mayfair (he also owns Bentley's Oyster Bar & Grill in Swallow Street) is a space displaying the same kind of satisfying richness as the food – comfortable arctic blue leather banquettes and chairs, natural oak flooring and white linen-clad tables. The menu brings us the best of Britain and Ireland, but is a pragmatic selection, so Medjool dates partner beetroot and wild watercress and octopus carpaccio is invigorated with Clementine and almond. First-class langoustines make a fine starter with spiced chick pea purée, while main-course breast of pheasant is poached in butter and served with chestnuts, bacon and game toast. Desserts can be as comforting as rhubarb and custard or as modern as quince tart with golden raisins and Sauternes ice cream.

SCOTLAND

PLUMED HORSE ❀❀❀

EDINBURGH
PAGE 498

WALES

Y POLYN ❀❀

NANTGAREDIG, CARMARTHENSHIRE
PAGE 547

The brain-child of chef-proprietor Tony Borthwick, the Plumed Horse makes the most of its relocation from Castle Douglas to Leith by using locally landed fish and seafood. The rather sedate looking Georgian building sits in the middle of a mainly residential area and, once inside, the grandeur of its heritage comes to the fore via the many sympathetically restored original features and is enhanced by the formal table settings. Service is professional and genuinely friendly. Imaginative cooking is executed with precision and plenty of land-based local produce joins that sparkling seafood on the menu. Start perhaps with a twice-baked parmesan and truffle soufflé with tomato and cucumber salad before moving onto fillet of monkfish with curry spices, gratin of Jerusalem artichokes, green beans and orange and vermouth sauce before pushing the boat out with fudge and ginger parfait, ginger beer, vanilla, lime and 'Sailor Jerry' sorbet.

A black-beamed, whitewashed pub in the Towy Valley, Y Polyn was once a tollhouse (its name meaning 'The Pole', probably referred to the barrier that once stretched across the road). It is these days a friendly, attractively rustic restaurant rather than a pub, with farmhouse furniture and a quarry-tiled floor, but it is still possible to pop in for a pint. The daily-changing menus offer heart-warming, rustic food based on top-notch produce and everything from bread to ice cream is made on the premises. Start with crispy pig's ear salad with capers and red onion, or smooth chicken liver parfait with a plum and apple chutney of good bite. Carefully timed John Dory on local samphire with hollandaise is a well-judged main course, while Welsh lamb daube caters for heartier appetites. Good pastry distinguishes a nectarine frangipane tart, served warm, with rich vanilla ice cream. Don't miss the excellent home-made breads.

Make more of your money with the AA

■ Attractive rates on savings accounts

■ A range of fixed term and easy access accounts

■ Joint and single account options

**To open a savings account and
start making more of your money call**

0845 603 6589* quoting ref AA Guides

See our full range of savings accounts at **theAA.com/savings**

Lines are open between 8am and 8pm, Monday to Saturday.

Savings

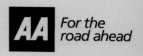

AA Wine Awards

The AA Wine Award

The annual AA wine award, sponsored again by T&W Wines, attracted a huge response from our AA recognised restaurants with over 1,000 wine lists submitted for judging. Three national winners were chosen – The Old Bridge Hotel, Huntingdon, England, The Cross at Kingussie, Scotland, and The Bell at Skenfrith, Wales. The Old Bridge Hotel at Huntingdon was selected as the Overall Winner, and a member of their wine team wins an all-expenses-paid trip to Willi Opitz's vineyards at Illmitz in Austria's Burgenland.

All 2,000 or so Rosetted restaurants in last year's guide were invited to submit their wine lists. From these the panel selected a shortlist of around 170 establishments who are highlighted in the guide with the Notable Wine List symbol.

The shortlisted establishments were asked to choose wines from their list (within a budget of £70 per bottle) to accompany a menu designed by Martin Lam, owner of Ransome's Dock, London, the 2009 England and Overall Winner.

The final judging panel included Simon Numphud, AA Hotel Services Manager, Martin Lam, proprietor of Ransome's Dock, Trevor Hughes, Managing Director of T&W Wines (our sponsor), Brian St Pierre from Decanter magazine and Fiona Sims, an independent wine journalist. The judges' comments are shown under the award winners on page 19.

Notable Wine Lists

What makes a wine list notable?
We are looking for high-quality wines, with diversity across grapes and/or countries and style, the best individual growers and vintages. The list should be well presented, ideally with some helpful notes and, to reflect the demand from diners, a good choice of wines by the glass.

What disappoints the judges are spelling errors, wines under incorrect regions or styles, split vintages (which are still far too common), lazy purchasing (all wines from a country from just one grower or negociant) and confusing layouts. Sadly, many restaurants still do not pay much attention to wine, resulting in ill considered lists.

To reach the final shortlist, we look for a real passion for wine, which should come across to the customer, a fair pricing policy (depending on the style of the restaurant) an interesting coverage (not necessarily a large list), which might include areas of specialism, perhaps a particular wine area, sherries or larger formats such as magnums.

The AA Wine Awards are sponsored by T&W Wines Ltd, 5 Station Way, Brandon, Suffolk, IP27 0BH
Tel: 01842 814414
email: contact@tw-wines.com
web: www.tw-wines.com

Old Bridge Hotel, Huntingdon - Winning Wine Selection

Menu	Wine selection	Price
Canapés – Parmesan cheese shortbreads, anchovy palmiers	1998 Pol Roger	£69 per bottle
Appetiser – Lincolnshire smoked eel fillets with horseradish and buckwheat blini	1983 Riesling Vendage Tardive, Fredric Emile Trimbach	£54 per bottle
Starter – Seared scallops with celeriac and parsley mash and grilled chorizo picante	1998 Kistler Chardonnay, Sonoma Coast, USA	£69 per bottle
Main course – Grilled saddle and fillet of Elwy Valley lamb, braised lentils with aromatic vegetables and wilted spinach	2002 Giaconda Pinot Noir, Beechworth, Australia	£70 per bottle
Cheese – Lincolnshire Poacher, mature Comté, Kirkham's Lancashire, fig chutney and oatcakes	2004 Amarone Allegrini, Veneto, Italy	£57 per bottle
Dessert – Prune and Armagnac soufflé with Armagnac custard	1996 Grand Cuvee No7, Trockenbeerenauslese, Alois Kracher, Austria	£40 per half bottle
Coffee and Petits Fours	1980 Folie Blanch, Domaine Boingeres, Bas Armagnac	£9.90 per measure

WINNER FOR ENGLAND AND OVERALL WINNER

The Old Bridge Hotel ◉◉

Huntingdon, Cambridgeshire Page 73

Not only does this handsome old inn boast a superb wine list, but it's gone a step further by opening a fantastic on-site wine shop, with 24 bottles open for tasting each day.

The 18th-century ivy-clad building stands smack beside the old stone bridge over the River Ouse, with a glorious terrace to make the most of the riverside setting. There's a classic-looking bar for sandwiches and a pint of Adnams, while The Terrace Restaurant, with its bold murals and big windows, is the place to head to for some interesting and accomplished modern cooking, combining rustic European cuisine with modern British dishes.

Judges' comments: An exceptional list full of passion and knowledge, it exudes personality and quirkiness in equal measure. Sensitive mark ups mean it offers excellent value for money with high quality selections throughout.

WINNER FOR SCOTLAND

The Cross at Kingussie ◉◉◉

Kingussie, Highland Page 517

A textile mill it may once have been, but there's nothing tweedy about David and Katie Young's classy restaurant with rooms. The stone building sits in four idyllic acres of grounds, with the Gynack Burn bubbling by a delightful terrace. The mill has been lovingly restored, its rough stone walls and heavy beams blending seamlessly with modern artworks and natural wood tables with quality glassware in the spacious dining room. Wild mushrooms are foraged locally and Scotland's finest materials are showcased in compact daily-changing menus of modern British dishes, while the wine list balances serious quality with fair pricing.

Judges' comments: A list that has a good sense of humour combined with a real passion for wine, its personal approach draws you in and overall it ticks all the right boxes. Good quality choices throughout combine with some food matching suggestions.

WINNER FOR WALES

The Bell at Skenfrith ◉◉

Skenfrith, Monmouthshire Page 559

Sitting beside the River Monnow in glorious Monmouthshire countryside, this beautifully restored 17th-century inn impresses on many counts. It oozes all the charming allure of an old Welsh inn, with slate walls, oak beams and blazing log fires, yet offers all the modern-day comforts of a chic country hotel, with sumptuous sofas and beautifully appointed bedrooms. A commitment to local produce, as evidenced by the list of suppliers on the daily menus and ingredients from The Bell's own organic kitchen garden, results in some seriously good cooking that displays great technical skill. A large walk-in wine cellar and excellent list completes the picture.

Judges' comments: This list was difficult to put down. Beautifully presented, with personal tasting notes to give you a good feel for each wine, exceptionally well priced, plus a stunning list of Cognacs.

In the HEAT of the KITCHEN

By Fiona Griffiths

Right across the country chefs are inviting diners into their kitchens, but what is the experience of eating at a 'chef's table' really like – both for the customer and chef?

It's Saturday night at South Lodge in Lower Beeding, West Sussex, and we're all dressed up for dinner.

We ask a receptionist the way to the hotel's new restaurant, The Pass, and he offers to show us. We follow him through some very inconspicuous wooden double doors, just to the left of reception, and suddenly we're confronted with the strangest sight.

We're in the hotel's kitchen; to our right some 10 or 12 chefs are working away, chopping, pan-frying, plating up dishes, while on our left are several rather stylish dark-wood tables, with raised banquette seating and smart chairs in green leather, and at each table people are eating.

Of course, I already knew that The Pass was a 22-cover restaurant actually inside the South Lodge's kitchen, but I wasn't prepared for quite how bizarre the experience of dining there would be.

Live action

A waiter swiftly appeared and led us to our table between another table of two, with a couple deep in conversation, and a party of four all avidly watching the chefs at work just a few metres away.

The wall-length banquette is certainly the best seat in the house, with a direct view of the pass - the part of the kitchen where dishes are collected by the waiting staff, and from which the restaurant takes its name.

Those with their backs to the action don't have to miss out, as their chairs swivel and there are TV screens set in the wall showing live footage from different corners of the kitchen.

South Lodge is by no means the first to invite people back-of-house to dine and watch their food being prepared.

Such is the British public's appetite for watching chefs at work, that more and more restaurants across the country have been putting "chef's tables" in the kitchen for six or eight diners - but this is a supersized version.

Matt Gillan, who switched from head chef at the hotel's Camellia Restaurant to take the helm at The Pass, admits it actually all started as a bit of joke.

"When we were designing the new kitchen [as part of a major refurbishment of the hotel] we were going to put a chef's table in," he explains.

"There was a meeting to discuss the plans and after a few hours everyone was getting tired and it got a bit jokey, and our executive chef Lewis Hamblet said why don't we just put a restaurant in the kitchen? It was meant as a joke, but then our managing director thought it would be something really different."

So the kitchen plans were rejigged, and Gillan and his team began an exciting journey into the unknown.

"Because we hadn't seen a restaurant in a kitchen - we'd only come across chef's ▷

Left and above: Taking the chef's table concept to a new level – The Pass is a whole restaurant actually inside the kitchen

tables before - it was hard to imagine what it would be like. It only became daunting when we came back after all the work was finished and saw the tables - that's when we started imagining people sitting there watching us, and we began to wonder what we were supposed to do, whether we were meant to watch what we said and what we did.

"But we haven't changed the way we work at all."

I'm surprised when I hear Gillan say this, because when I dined at The Pass I was amazed by how quiet it was. I assumed the chefs had deliberately toned down the shouting and swearing that I'd come to understand - from watching TV programmes and reading chef biographies - is the norm in restaurant kitchens

But Gillan has a good explanation for the lack of fireworks.

"Most kitchens have really noisy extraction systems which is why you get a lot of raised voices, but in the new kitchen we've got a state-of-the-art extraction system which is just so quiet, there's no need to shout."

I must admit I would've preferred a bit more chaos, but one thing I couldn't fault was the food, which has been awarded three Rosettes in this year's guide.

At dinner Gillan offers a choice of a seven (£68) or a nine-course (£78) tasting menu, with a nine-course vegetarian menu, too, and the option to mix and match between the three.

Feeling ambitious (and, more importantly, very hungry), we went for the nine-course menu with a flight of wines

(£55) to match.

It was a true gourmet experience, with the roast frogs' legs, snails, bacon bonbon, parsley sauce and blackened onions; and fillet of John Dory, tortellini of oxtail, baby gem, caper and lemon being particular highlights.

However, Gillan believes The Pass is booked up on Friday and Saturday nights at least a week in advance not because of his cooking, but because people are "intrigued to find out whether it'll be like on TV".

He adds: "There is a danger of it becoming gimmicky, but at the end of the day we're chefs, not performers. We're aiming our standards high and the purpose of The Pass is to deliver good food - it's not theatre."

Of course, if you choose to eat at a chef's table, it certainly enhances the experience if your host is a bit of a showman, and Jason Hornbuckle at Lewtrenchard Manor in Devon is exactly that.

The Purple Carrot - his own interpretation of the chef's table (named after the original colour of carrots) - is a private dining room just off the hotel's kitchen, with a beautiful granite-topped table seating up to eight.

Hornbuckle wears a microphone and talks you through the preparation of each dish as you watch him and his team on three plasma screens (he also talks about the produce and throws in a few jokes), or you can wander out of The Purple Carrot and lean on a counter into the kitchen to chat to the chefs.

"I wanted to do something a little bit different to the chef's tables which have been done before and make it a more personal experience," explains Hornbuckle.

"So I let the guests have as much input into the menu as they want, I introduce the team, and I'm microphoned up so I'm talking about the produce, and the combination of flavours and why I feel they work together.

"I judge what level of input people want - how interested they are about food. If it's a business thing they're obviously not so interested in my team, but most people want to see the workings of a kitchen - to get a feeling of real people in real jobs."

Best of both worlds

With The Purple Carrot, Hornbuckle feels he's come up with the perfect formula.

"You get a sense of privacy because you're in your own room, and you don't get the cooking smells so you can dress up and your clothes aren't going to smell at the end of the evening. But you're also

Left: The charismatic Jason Hornbuckle, chef-patron at Lewtrenchard Manor.

Opposite: The Purple Carrot chef's table is just off the main kitchen at Lewtrenchard.

close enough to the kitchen that you do feel you're in the kitchen," he says.

I have to agree. The whole experience was truly memorable - not just the seven-course tasting menu (£95), including a bold-flavoured squid and chorizo ragout with goats' cheese salsa, and a silky smooth ballotine of foie gras with smoked raisin and apple salad - but the matching flight of wine (£40) and the banter between ourselves and the staff.

Admittedly, we didn't witness any shouting or swearing, but that's not typical of most professional kitchens according to Hornbuckle.

"What people see on TV is places where the staff are a nightmare.

"A normal kitchen during a normal service is a well oiled machine. People are trained well, they know their job,

❝ I wanted to do something a little bit different to the chef's tables and make it a more personal experience ❞

know their product, and there doesn't need to be all this shouting."

The Ramsay effect
So is there any restaurant kitchen where you can witness a bit of Ramsay-esque belligerence over dinner?

Perhaps Gordon Ramsay at Claridge's might be worth a try (if you can get in, as the chef's table is booked up daily for lunch and dinner about six months in

advance).

Gordon Ramsay at Claridge's was the first restaurant in the group to install a chef's table back in 2001, and head chef Mark Sargeant recalls being extremely nervous about the whole idea - which Ramsay had picked up from Charlie Trotter's in Chicago.

"Within the first week of opening we had the first chef's table - I think in the country, let alone in the group. ▷

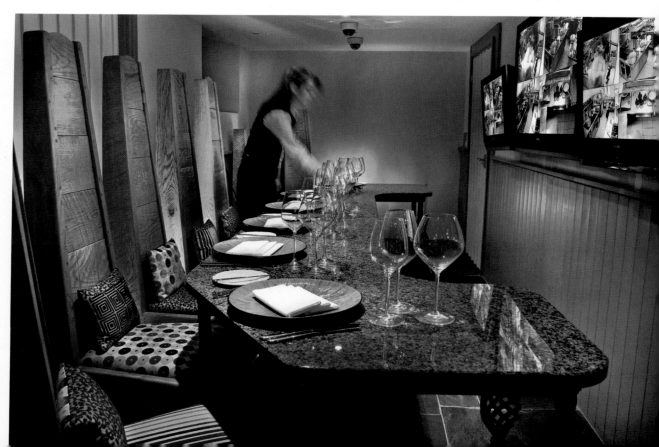

"I was 28 and opening at Claridge's was the most significant thing Gordon had done at that stage in his career, so I was under pressure to say the least. Then suddenly to have customers in the kitchen, well, the colourful language we normally use when we're under pressure, I thought I'm just not going to be able to do it," says Sargeant.

"By the end of our first night I had a massive hole in my lip where I'd been biting it so much trying not to swear and lose my temper.

"I remember asking the customers at the chef's table whether they'd enjoyed it, and they were thrilled and delighted, but they said there was one problem - they were expecting more shouting and swearing.

"So from then on we started acting normally."

You might well expect to hear some raised voices and a bit of bad language in a Gordon Ramsay kitchen, but you perhaps wouldn't imagine that sometimes it's the guests who cause a scene.

Below: Ear plugs at the ready – the chef's table at Gordon Ramsay at Claridge's.

At Pennyhill Park in Bagshot, Surrey, head chef Michael Wignall and his team aren't fazed in the slightest by having customers in the kitchen - that is until they start getting loud and annoying.

"You don't really think about it unless they get really drunk and start hassling you, which has happened a few times," says Wignall.

I'm happy to say we didn't fit into that category when we dined at Pennyhill's chef's table, although we were a little tipsy after making our way through the 10-course tasting menu (£78) with a different wine to match nearly every course (£27 a head for the wine flight).

The Latymer restaurant at Pennyhill Park has just gained four Rosettes under Wignall's stewardship, and it showed in such creative and winning combinations as loin of Lakeland hare, Hereford snails, glazed comté and broad beans, and vanilla marinated organic salmon with an oyster beignet, ruby grapefruit, champagne and oyster jelly.

Here, the glass-topped, eight-seater chef's table is enclosed in a glass-panelled room near the pot wash.

Wignall concedes it's not the best position, but there are cameras dotted around the kitchen, including one over the pass, thus diners can watch live footage of the chefs at work on a big screen.

"The chef's table gets booked up three to four weeks in advance on Friday and Saturday nights. I think people like the exclusivity of it - you feel extra special," says Wignall.

"It's not everyone's cup of tea - some people will look at it and say 'I'd rather have the noise of other people around me in the restaurant' - but everyone who has tried it has loved it.

Below: Michael Wignall at Pennyhill Park. "When people are at the chef's table it doesn't make any difference to the way my team work. People want to see the atmosphere of the kitchen – not to see a load of robots."

Opposite: The glitzy chef's table at Pennyhill Park. The glass-topped table changes colour, as does the room lighting, and the glass walls can be switched to opaque for privacy.

"If you come on a Saturday night it can be quite eventful because we treat it just as a normal service, so people get shouted at and things get thrown."

Start them young

Naturally, eating in the kitchen of a top restaurant is expensive (dining at Gordon Ramsay at Claridge's will set you back around £800 for a party of six), but there's one chef's table you can book for a mere £21 a head.

For that price you'll get five courses - with a few extras thrown in - and a prime position near the hot plate.

"As soon as word got round about the chef's table, we had a month-long

> *I think people like the exclusivity of it – you feel extra special*

waiting list," says Shane Guildford, a chef lecturer at South Cheshire College in Crewe.

Guildford, who looks after the college's three kitchens, plus the training restaurant and bar, came up with the idea of a chef's table to "generate some business and excitement"- and, as the first college in the country to have one, it's certainly worked.

"It's gone extremely well and the students absolutely love it. They get their names on the menu and they tend to raise their game a bit which is really good for them," Guildford says.

"They also benefit from it confidence-wise because they're interacting with the customer, which is certainly great preparation for the future." □

Top *of the*

Chops

By Fiona Griffiths

A new kind of meat has been finding its way onto the nation's menus lately.

From gastro-pubs to fine dining restaurants, mutton has become the new lamb in slow-cooked dishes like stews, curries and pies.

Of course, mutton isn't exactly a 'new' meat; it comes from older sheep, and while ordering it in a restaurant remains quite a novelty, it was actually a staple part of our diet for centuries, until lamb began to take precedence after the Second World War.

So why is mutton - a meat which has been much maligned in the past for being fatty, tough, and of inferior quality to lamb - making such a dramatic comeback?

Why do so many of the country's top chefs now regard it as a premium meat, in the same league, even, as venison?

Well, it's largely down to the Mutton Renaissance Campaign.

Instigated by Prince Charles in 2004 and coordinated by the Academy of Culinary Arts and the National Sheep Association (NSA), its aim was to help sheep farmers by creating value for their older animals.

John Thorley, director of pastoral alliance at the NSA, explains: "The Prince of Wales was distraught at the extremely low prices being paid to farmers for sheep which were carrying good quality meat, but had finished their breeding life. He wanted to do something which would raise the profile of mutton, get people to understand what its qualities are, and to get better prices back to the farmers. ▷

"There's still some distance to go but we're definitely on track. The poor image mutton had when we started the campaign is being dispelled and people are now talking about it with the kind of enthusiasm we would never have dreamt of five or six years ago."

A major focus of the campaign has been to drive up production standards for mutton to give chefs and consumers confidence in the meat's quality.

So all mutton sold under the Renaissance banner comes from sheep which are at least two years old and have been reared on a natural, forage-based diet such as grass and heather.

Renaissance mutton must also be hung for a minimum of two weeks, which is paramount to producing tender meat.

In 2006 the Mutton Renaissance Club was formed with the aim of uniting every

❝ *[the mutton chop] was so popular, we physically couldn't make enough of it* ❞

part of the supply chain, from farmers to abattoir operators and chefs, to share information, ideas and expertise.

Mutton movers and shakers

John Williams, executive chef at The Ritz and chairman of the Academy of Culinary Arts, says: "One thing we've proven is that if chefs and farmers get together you can actually successfully raise the standard and quality of a product. The quality of mutton has definitely been raised and people are starting to look at mutton as a nice piece of meat now,

whereas only a few years ago they wouldn't even have entertained the thought of mutton."

Although some chefs have reported good results from roasting or even grilling mutton, most agree that long, slow cooking is key to getting the best out of the meat.

Mark Hix, owner of Hix Oyster and Chop House in Smithfield Market and director of food at Brown's Hotel in Mayfair, uses mutton as old as five years in dishes like Scotch broth, mutton and turnip pie, Lancashire hotpot and mutton chop curry.

"If you get mutton from a younger animal you can get away with roasting some cuts, but it's perfect for slow cooking. Mutton has so much more flavour than lamb and through slow cooking you get a lot of that almost gamey flavour into the sauce," says Hix.

"We put the mutton chop curry on two months into opening The Albemarle [at Brown's Hotel] and it was so popular, we physically couldn't make enough of it."

Return of the Native

Down at the Walnut Tree in Abergavenny, South Wales, Shaun Hill's Irish stew with mutton has also been a big seller.

"It's not just the flavour that appeals to people, but the notion of it taking you back to Dickensian times when people ate these things on a regular basis," says Hill.

"It also makes you understand how some of the trimmings like mint sauce and redcurrant jelly came about; they went perfectly with mutton because it's a stronger meat than more delicate lamb."

When Hill - in his role as consultant chef - was asked to serve mutton at the relaunch of Fortnum & Mason in late 2007, he found that the meat is so old-fashioned, none of the chefs at the famous London store knew how to cook it.

"Prince Charles agreed to open the refurbished store and he particularly wanted mutton," Hill explains.

"None of the cooks there had ever cooked mutton before because it's just off the radar. I think that's the main problem ▷

Left: John Williams shows off the mutton dish he prepared for the Mutton Renaissance Club launch dinner at The Ritz, hosted by Prince Charles

Right: Mark Hix demonstrates mutton chop curry and Scotch broth at a Mutton Renaissance masterclass at Brown's Hotel, Mayfair

the meat has - people aren't used to handling it anymore and it does handle differently to lamb."

Acclaimed Irish chef Richard Corrigan has resurrected a mutton dish which dates back even further than Dickensian times at his new London restaurant, Corrigan's Mayfair.

"I've got a 17th century cookbook which a customer gave me many years ago, and that's where I found this lovely recipe for a steamed mutton and oyster pudding. I put it on the menu shortly after we opened and it was a huge success," says Corrigan.

"Mutton takes braising incredibly well and it's the only meat to put into Irish stew. It's a completely different product to lamb because of the extra mature feeling of the meat and the extra flavour.

"When I think of mutton, believe it or not, I think of venison."

Cass Titcombe, executive chef at Canteen - with restaurants, known for their traditional British cooking, at London's Spitalfields Market, Baker Street and the Royal Festival Hall - uses leg and shoulder of mutton in a spicy mutton pie as a seasonal special.

"Because of the cuts we use, it really benefits from long, slow cooking. I love it because it has a great strong taste, robust enough to stand up well to those other flavours," says Titcombe.

"I think it's a particularly masculine meat, which is probably why it sells more at Spitalfields, with all the City workers, than at Baker Street or the Royal Festival Hall where we sell more fish and vegetarian food."

Mutton v lamb
Although diners at Canteen may find spicy mutton pie (or mutton and

Left: Hywel Jones at Lucknam Park is pushing the boundaries with mutton

❝When I think of mutton, believe it or not, I think of venison ❞

vegetable pie, or Lancashire hotpot) on the menu as late as June, at The Ritz John Williams prefers to serve it (in a navarin perhaps, a cottage pie, Scotch broth or a mutton pudding) only during the official season from October to March.

"That's a personal preference though," says Williams.

"People are certainly using it much longer, but we have great lamb in spring, so when spring arrives I just want to use spring lamb."

At The Royal Oak in Paley Street, Berkshire, head chef Dominic Chapman puts mutton on as a special at every opportunity.

"If a supplier or a local farmer offers me mutton I'll usually bite their arm off for it. When a sheep is a little bit older it's developed more fat and more flavour, and it's absolutely delicious," says Chapman.

"Depending on the cut and the age of the meat, you don't have to stew it for hours and hours either.

"I've grilled mutton chops and served them with béarnaise sauce, and the last time we had it on was for Sunday lunch. I bought five legs of mutton and roasted them, and although the meat tasted a lot stronger than your usual leg of lamb, people adored it."

Another big fan of mutton is Hywel Jones, executive chef at Lucknam Park Hotel in Wiltshire.

A keen supporter of the campaign, Jones has been experimenting with cooking Renaissance mutton in different ways, including in a water bath at a low temperature, with the finished product served pink.

That particular dish is still in development, but braised fillet of mutton, and mutton Champvallon (cutlets baked between layers of onions and sliced potatoes) have proven a real hit with diners at the hotel's new Brasserie.

"Mutton is one of those things which has been overlooked for so long, and yet the flavour you get out of it is fantastic," says Jones.

"We're in the middle of the countryside, with a big emphasis on local producers and farmers, so it fits in well with our ethos, and at the end of the day, the Mutton Renaissance Campaign is all about supporting farmers." □

A BRIEF HISTORY OF MUTTON

Right up until the 1940s sheep in Britain were reared for their fleeces and fattened for slaughter at the age of five or more.

The resulting mutton was prized for its texture and flavour, and was the nation's meat of choice for centuries.

During the Second World War, however, many sheep farmers were away fighting and much of the expertise to produce the best mutton was lost from the countryside.

With the constrained supply of fresh food, some of the worst examples of mutton were served up to entrenched communities during the blackouts – further helping to damage mutton's reputation.

Imports of mutton and lamb from New Zealand increased after the war to maintain year-round supplies, while at home, rationing and the post-war food shortages put new pressure on the food chain.

With the need to feed the population quickly and efficiently, lamb that could be born, raised, finished and slaughtered in four to six months seemed far more logical and economically attractive when compared to mutton roaming the hillsides for two or more years.

The final nail in the coffin for British mutton was the decline of the wool trade with the advent of modern textiles, as farmers no longer saw value in keeping their sheep on the land for their fleeces.

English vines

English *wines*

By Susy Atkins

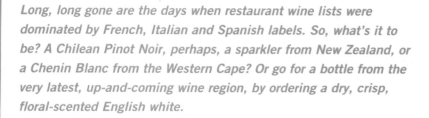

Long, long gone are the days when restaurant wine lists were dominated by French, Italian and Spanish labels. So, what's it to be? A Chilean Pinot Noir, perhaps, a sparkler from New Zealand, or a Chenin Blanc from the Western Cape? Or go for a bottle from the very latest, up-and-coming wine region, by ordering a dry, crisp, floral-scented English white.

England? Yes, English wine is finally making it onto more restaurant wine lists, and there's no reason to panic. Forget the awful, cidery plonk of ten years ago, quality is up, up and away, as the 2009 wine awards season attested. The big three international wine competitions (the International Wine Challenge, Decanter World Wine Awards and the International Wine & Spirit Competition) together handed out over 100 gongs to English and Welsh wine, and that included a first-ever IWC gold for a still white, and two Decanter golds for high-quality local sparklers. And these are international competitions, I stress, so the wines were up against the cream of Europe and those trendy New World regions too. You can't really argue with results like that.

So as English wine starts to take us by storm, let's get a few facts straight. This is English wine, NOT British wine. There's an important distinction. British wine is usually made from imported grape concentrate (from, say, Cyprus) while English wine is made from grapes grown in English vineyards. With English wine, you should expect a light, delicate, aromatic style - characteristics that are becoming its trademark.

A growing business

This is no longer a tiny, cottage industry. Today England has over 115 wineries, and over 400 vineyards. Most of these are in the south of England, although there are commercial vineyards as far north as Leeds and York. The average ▷

Left: Three Choirs Vineyard, Gloucestershire

annual production is 2 million bottles, although anyone who sat through the rainy summers of 2007 and '08 won't be surprised to hear these vintages fell way short of that figure. Still, in a good year (like 2006), a whopping 3.5 million bottles is nearer the mark. Plantings, at just over 3000 acres, are the highest ever.

Pick a dry white and you should also be able to spot some of that distinctive quality don't expect to fall over after a couple of glasses. English wine tends to be lower in alcohol than many, weighing in at around 10-11%, or so, compared to 13 or 14% for many of today's table wines.

That's the whites, anyway. The sparklers are considered especially fine, with lean, mineral freshness, incisive lemon and lime fruit and a toasty hint that forms after long lees ageing - the traditional

> ❝ We all know the difference between a Spanish strawberry and an English one, and our wines also have unique English fruit styles ❞

of decent English wine, namely a fresh scent that mingles white blossom with chopped lemon and a hint of nettles and grass. On the palate, expect crisp, racy acidity, citrus and apple flavours and a whistle-clean finish, often bone-dry. And or Champagne method, used for most fine English fizz. English sparklers have become so impressive in recent years that several Champagne houses are said to be sniffing round our vineyards, with a view to making an investment, much as

they did in Australia, New Zealand and California twenty years ago. I reckon it can only be a matter of time before we see a Champagne producer making an English sparkling wine.

It's our cool climate they are after. Lighter, more subtle, scented wines are created when the temperature doesn't get too high - look at the wines of the relatively northern (and not too distant) Loire, Mosel and, of course, Champagne itself. Global warming has meant that England - and southern England in particular - can ripen grapes just that little bit more than it used to, and juicy, fruity flavours of citrus and apple have started to creep in. Bob Lindo, of the Camel Valley winery in Cornwall, says: "We all know the difference between a Spanish strawberry and an English one, and our wines also have unique English fruit styles." I know what he means - nothing tastes like English wine, not even the more grapey, lightly honeyed German whites they are often compared to.

The red route

Now for the reds. There are a few palatable English red wines, in my view, but only a handful, and those are made in the soft, light, crunchy red-berry style, a bit like simple Beaujolais. Fine, if you like that kind of thing - and actually, chilled a little and served with cold meats, salads and mild cheeses, an English red makes a perfectly acceptable glassful. But I'll stick my neck out here and say that England will never produce a wide range of truly impressive reds - unless global warming accelerates at an even more alarming rate than predicted. No, when it comes to ▷

Left: Tenterden Vineyard in Kent

Right: Pinot noir grapes (used for Champagne production) at Ridgeview Wine Estate in East Sussex

serious, award-winning English wine, the whites and sparklers are what it's all about, save the odd, rare, pleasing pink or honeyed dessert wine.

The white grapes used tend to be fairly obscure varieties, and those which ripen easily and early on in the season – Madeleine Angevine, Bacchus, Seyval Blanc – although Pinot Noir is often grown for the base wine to make fizz. Reds are often from an early-ripening clone of

wine at home, and near £25 to enjoy it in a restaurant? Well, a lot more so than in the past, for sure, as all local food and drink enjoys a new popularity and understanding. Put it this way, if you are going to make a point of ordering the local beef, seafood or strawberries, you will probably pay a bit extra for a glass of the wine made up the road, rather than the Southern French or Californian house wine.

6 *If you haven't got an English wine on your list, then you should be ashamed of yourself!* 9

Pinot Noir, also, the varieties Rondo and Germany's Dornfelder are pressed into service. If you're stuck on super-rich, ripe Cabernet Sauvignon, Shiraz and Viognier - all grapes which need very hot sun to ripen - then England may not be the wine region for you.

Keeping down costs

Another problem might be the price of English wine. There are few, if any, economies of scale in an industry made up of small wineries, little tracts of land, and where the cool climate means relatively low crops, even in good years. This is not Italy, or Australia, which regularly turn out vast oceans of wine from huge plains of vines. Matthew Bernstein, who founded Kenton vineyard in Devon 5 years ago, explains: "There has been a sea change in the past ten years in the English wine industry. The knowledge and professionalism have increased and climate change has made a difference, but now the big issue is economics. Our vineyards are relatively small, so the question is what price you put on your wine to make a profit."

And is the consumer willing to pay around £8-£10 a bottle to drink the

Bob Lindo - whose Bacchus white won that IWC gold medal in Spring 2009 - feels strongly that English wine should be on restaurant wine lists. This is a man who has no trouble selling all his Cornish sparklers and whites each year, but nonetheless he challenges narrow-minded restaurateurs. "If you haven't got an English wine on your list, then you should be ashamed of yourself! It's just like having English cheeses - you should be stocking them, not to be patriotic, but because people are genuinely looking for local food and drink nowadays."

Left: A selection of wines from Three Choirs Vineyards in Gloucestershire

Right: Harvest time at Camel Valley Winery in Cornwall

A local flavour

An increasing number of restaurants, especially rural ones, do now stock a wine or two from a local winery, typically offering a light English white by the glass as an aperitif. A few others have gone further, in particular Hugh Fearnley-Whittingstall's Canteen restaurants in Axminster and Bath, which feature predominantly English wines throughout the list, together with English ales, ciders, apple juices and liqueurs. And certainly this makes perfect sense when the menu makes a point of its local produce. Interestingly, at the Canteen in Axminster, the English sparkling wines continue to outsell the Champagnes on the list.

So, let's say you are keen to try an English wine next time you dine out, and you are lucky enough to find some on the list. What are the best matches? Bob Lindo recommends English sparkling wine with "top-notch fish and chips"; sparkling pink with oriental food, or a nettley, lemon-fresh Bacchus with white fish, ideally "a piece of turbot with Cornish new potatoes and green beans".

Here to stay

Julia Trustram-Eve, managing director of English Wine Producers, has her own favourites: "Asparagus with dry whites made from Bacchus, and medium-dry whites with gently flavoured cheeses like Wensleydale." One of my star matches is a pairing of fine English sparkling wine with sushi, especially sushi with fish and prawn wrapped inside. The scented, gently yeasty fizz is lovely with the soft rice, while the crisp, cool-climate acidity acts like a squeeze of lemon over the whole mouthful. Eclectic? Certainly. But English wine is here to stay, and pairing it with world cuisine is only the natural next step. □

Susy Atkins is an award-winning wine writer and broadcaster. She is the wine editor of *Delicious* magazine, has a regular column in *The Sunday Telegraph* and can be seen on BBC1's *Saturday Kitchen*.

The Top Ten Per Cent

Each year all the restaurants in the AA Restaurant Guide are awarded a specially commissioned plate that marks their achievement in gaining one or more AA Rosettes. The plates represent a partnership between the AA and Villeroy & Boch two quality brands working together to recognise high standards in restaurant cooking.

Restaurants awarded three, four or five AA Rosettes represent the Top Ten Per Cent of the restaurants in this Guide. The pages that follow list those establishments that have attained this special status

Villeroy & Boch
1748

The Villeroy & Boch
LOOk
Style your life

www.villeroy-boch.com

A reflection of your good taste. An expression of your originality.
That's the beauty of NewWave Caffè from Villeroy & Boch.

For a brochure and complete list of stockists call 020 8875 6060 or email brochure@villeroy-boch.co.uk

Villeroy & Boch
260
1748-2007

Villeroy & Boch
1748

5 ROSETTES

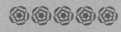

LONDON
**Marcus Wareing at
The Berkeley**
The Berkeley, Wilton Place,
Knightsbridge, SW1
020 7235 1200

Restaurant Gordon Ramsay
68 Royal Hospital Road,
SW3
020 7352 4441

Tom Aikens
43 Elystan Street, SW3
020 7584 2003

**Sketch
(Lecture Room & Library)**
9 Conduit Street, W1
0870 777 4488

ENGLAND
BERKSHIRE
The Fat Duck
High Street, BRAY,
SL6 2AQ
01628 580333

NOTTINGHAMSHIRE
**Restaurant Sat Bains
with Rooms**
Lenton Lane,
NOTTINGHAM, NG7 2SA
0115 986 6566

OXFORDSHIRE
Le Manoir aux Quat' Saisons
GREAT MILTON,
OX44 7PD
01844 278881

4 ROSETTES

LONDON
Foliage
Mandarin Oriental Hyde Park,
66 Knightsbridge, SW1
020 7235 2000

The Capital
Basil Street, SW3
020 7589 5171

The Greenhouse
27a Hay's Mews, W1
020 7499 3331

**Hélène Darroze at
The Connaught**
Carlos Place, W1
020 3147 7200

Hibiscus
29 Maddox Street, W1
020 7629 2999

Maze
London Marriott Grosvenor
Hotel,10-13 Grosvenor
Square, W1
020 7107 0000

Pied à Terre
34 Charlotte Street, W1
020 7636 1178

The Square
6-10 Bruton Street, W1
020 7495 7100

LONDON, GREATER
Chapter One
Farnborough Common,
Locksbottom,
BROMLEY, BR6 8NF
01689 854848

ENGLAND
BERKSHIRE
Waterside Inn
Ferry Road, BRAY, SL6 2AT
01628 620691

The Vineyard at Stockcross
Stockcross, NEWBURY,
RG20 8JU
01635 528770

BUCKINGHAMSHIRE
**Oak Room at
Danesfield House**
Henley Road,
MARLOW, SL7 2EY
01628 891010

CAMBRIDGESHIRE
Midsummer House
Midsummer Common,
CAMBRIDGE, CB4 1HA
01223 369299

CHESHIRE
**Simon Radley at The
Chester Grosvenor**
Chester Grosvenor & Spa,
Eastgate, CHESTER,
CH1 1LT
01244 324024

CUMBRIA
L'Enclume
Cavendish Street, CARTMEL,
LA11 6PZ
01539 536362

DERBYSHIRE
Fischer's Baslow Hall
Calver Road, BASLOW,
DE45 1RR
01246 583259

DEVON
Gidleigh Park
CHAGFORD, TQ13 8HH
01647 432367

GLOUCESTERSHIRE
Le Champignon Sauvage
24 Suffolk Road,
CHELTENHAM, GL50 2AQ
01242 573449

RUTLAND
Hambleton Hall
Hambleton, OAKHAM,
LE15 8TH
01572 756991

SURREY
**The Latymer
Pennyhill Park Hotel & Spa**
London Road, BAGSHOT,
GU19 5EU
01276 471774

WILTSHIRE
Whatley Manor
Easton Grey, MALMESBURY,
SN16 0RB
01666 822888

JERSEY

Bohemia Restaurant
The Club Hotel & Spa,
Green Street, ST HELIER,
JE2 4UH
01534 880588

SCOTLAND

CITY OF EDINBURGH

Restaurant Martin Wishart
54 The Shore, Leith,
EDINBURGH, EH6 6RA
0131 553 3557

HIGHLAND

The Boath House
Auldearn, NAIRN, IV12 5TE
01667 454896

PERTH & KINROSS

Andrew Fairlie @ Gleneagles
AUCHTERARDER, PH3 1NF
01764 694267

NORTHERN IRELAND

CO BELFAST

Deanes Restaurant
36-40 Howard Street,
BELFAST, BT1 6PF
028 9033 1144

REPUBLIC OF IRELAND

DUBLIN

Restaurant Patrick Guilbaud
Merrion Hotel, 21 Upper
Merrion Street, DUBLIN
01 676 4192

3 ROSETTES

LONDON

EC1

Club Gascon
57 West Smithfield
020 7796 0600

EC2

Rhodes Twenty Four
Tower 42, Old Broad Street
020 7877 7703

N7

Morgan M
489 Liverpool Road,
ISLINGTON
020 7609 3560

NW1

Odette's
130 Regent's Park Road
020 7586 8569

York & Albany
127-129 Parkway
020 7388 3344

SW1

Nahm
The Halkin Hotel,
Halkin Street
020 7333 1234

One–O–One
Sheraton Park Tower,
101 Knightsbridge
020 7290 7101

Roussillon
16 St Barnabas Street
020 7730 5550

Zafferano
15 Lowndes Street
020 7235 5800

SW3

Rasoi Restaurant
10 Lincoln Street
020 7225 1881

SW4

Trinity Restaurant
4 The Polygon,
Clapham Old Town
020 7622 1199

SW7

Ambassade de l'Ile
117-119 Old Brompton Road
020 7373 7774

SW17

Chez Bruce
2 Bellevue Road,
Wandsworth Common
020 8672 0114

W1

Alain Ducasse
The Dorchester,
53 Park Lane
020 7629 8866

The Albemarle
Brown's Hotel,
Albemarle Street
020 7518 4004

Arbutus Restaurant
63-64 Frith Street
020 7734 4545

L'Autre Pied
5-7 Blandford Street
020 7486 9696

Corrigan's Mayfair
28 Upper Grosvenor Street
020 7499 9943

Galvin at Windows
London Hilton on Park Lane,
Park Lane
020 7208 4021

Le Gavroche Restaurant
43 Upper Brook Street
020 7408 0881

**Gordon Ramsay at
Claridge's**
Brook Street
020 7499 0099

The Landau
The Langham London,
Portland Place
020 7965 0165

Locanda Locatelli
8 Seymour Street,
020 7935 9088

Murano
20 Queen Street
020 7592 1222

Rhodes W1 Restaurant
Great Cumberland Place
020 7616 5930

Roka
37 Charlotte Street
020 7580 6464

Texture Restaurant
34 Portman Street
020 7224 0028

**Theo Randall,
InterContinental London**
1 Hamilton Place,
Hyde Park Corner
020 7318 8747

3 ROSETTES

W1 CONTINUED

Umu
14-16 Bruton Place
020 7499 8881

W4
La Trompette
5-7 Devonshire Road,
CHISWICK
020 8747 1836

W6
The River Café
Thames Wharf,
Rainville Road
020 7386 4200

W8
Min Jiang
Royal Garden Hotel
2-24 Kensington High Street
020 7361 1988

W11
The Ledbury
127 Ledbury Road,
NOTTING HILL
020 7792 9090

Notting Hill Brasserie
92 Kensington Park Road
020 7229 4481

WC1
Pearl Restaurant & Bar
Renaissance
Chancery Court,
252 High Holborn
020 7829 7000

WC2
L'Atelier de Joël Robuchon
13-15 West Street
020 7010 8600

Clos Maggiore
33 King Street,
COVENT GARDEN
020 7379 9696

LONDON, GREATER
The Glasshouse
14 Station Road,
KEW, TW9 3PZ
020 8940 6777

The Bingham
61-63 Petersham Road,
RICHMOND-UPON-THAMES,
TW10 6UT
020 8940 0902

ENGLAND
BERKSHIRE
L'ortolan
Church Lane, SHINFIELD,
RG2 9BY
01189 888 500

BRISTOL
Casamia Restaurant
38 High Street,
WESTBURY-ON-TRYM
BS9 3D2
0117 959 28840

BUCKINGHAMSHIRE
Hartwell House Hotel,
Restaurant & Spa
Oxford Road,
AYLESBURY, HP17 8NR
01296 747444

Aubergine at
The Compleat Angler
Macdonald Compleat Angler,
Marlow Bridge, MARLOW,
SL7 1RG
01628 484444

The Hand & Flowers
126 West Street,
MARLOW, SL7 2BP
01628 482277

CHESHIRE
The Church Green
Higher Lane, LYMM,
WA13 0AP
01925 752068

CORNWALL &
ISLES OF SCILLY
Restaurant Nathan Outlaw
Marina Villa Hotel,
17 Esplanade,
FOWEY, PL23 1HY
01726 833315

Well House Hotel
St Keyne, LISKEARD,
PL14 4RN
01579 342001

The Seafood Restaurant
Riverside, PADSTOW,
PL28 8BY
01841 532700

Driftwood
Rosevine, PORTSCATHO,
TR2 5EW
01872 580644

Hotel Tresanton
Lower Castle Road,
ST MAWES, TR2 5DR
01326 270055

CUMBRIA
Rampsbeck
Country House Hotel
WATERMILLOCK, CA11 0LP
017684 86442

Gilpin Lodge Country House
Hotel & Restaurant
Crook Road,
WINDERMERE, LA23 3NE
015394 88818

Holbeck Ghyll Country
House Hotel
Holbeck Lane,
WINDERMERE, LA23 1LU
015394 32375

The Samling
Ambleside Road,
WINDERMERE, LA23 1LR
015394 31922

DERBYSHIRE
The Old Vicarage
Ridgeway Moor,
RIDGEWAY, S12 3XW
0114 247 5814

DEVON
The New Angel
2 South Embankment,
DARTMOUTH, TQ6 9BH
01803 839425

The Horn of Plenty
GULWORTHY, PL19 8JD
01822 832528

The Masons Arms
KNOWSTONE, EX36 4RY
01398 341231

Lewtrenchard Manor
LEWDOWN, EX20 4PN
01566 783222

Corbyn Head Hotel &
Orchid Restaurant
Sea Front, TORQUAY,
TQ2 6RH
01803 213611

The Elephant Bar &
Restaurant
3/4 Beacon Terrace,
TORQUAY, TQ1 2BH
01803 200044

DORSET
Sienna Restaurant
36 High West Street,
DORCHESTER, DT1 1UP
01305 250022

Summer Lodge
Country House Hotel,
Restaurant & Spa
EVERSHOT, DT2 0JR
01935 482000

CO. DURHAM
Seaham Hall Hotel
The White Room Restaurant
Lord Byron's Walk,
SEAHAM, SR7 7AG
0191 516 1400

GLOUCESTERSHIRE
Lower Slaughter Manor
LOWER SLAUGHTER,
Cheltenham, GL54 2HP
01451 820456

Lords of the Manor
UPPER SLAUGHTER,
Cheltenham, GL54 2JD
01451 820243

5 North Street
5 North Street,
WINCHCOMBE, GL54 5LH
01242 604566

HAMPSHIRE
Le Poussin at
Whitley Ridge Hotel
Beaulieu Road,
BROCKENHURST,
SO42 7QL
01590 622354

36 on the Quay
47 South Street,
EMSWORTH, PO10 7EG
01243 375592

Chewton Glen Hotel & Spa
Christchurch Road,
NEW MILTON, BH25 6QS
01425 275341

JSW
20 Dragon Street,
PETERSFIELD, GU31 4JJ
01730 262030

Avenue Restaurant
Lainston House Hotel,
Sparsholt, WINCHESTER,
SO21 2LT
01962 863588

HEREFORDSHIRE
Castle House
Castle Street, HEREFORD,
HR1 2NW
01432 356321

HERTFORDSHIRE
Auberge du Lac
Brocket Hall Estate,
WELWYN, AL8 7XG
01707 368888

KENT
The West House
28 High Street,
BIDDENDEN, TN27 8AH
01580 291341

Apicius
23 Stone Street,
CRANBROOK, TN17 3HF
01580 714666

Rowhill Grange – Truffles
Rowhill Grange Hotel & Spa,
DARTFORD, DA2 7QH
01322 615136

Read's Restaurant
Macknade Manor,
FAVERSHAM, ME13 8XE
01795 535344

Thackeray's
TUNBRIDGE WELLS,
TN1 1EA
01892 511921

LANCASHIRE
Northcote
Northcote Road,
LANGHO, BB6 8BE
01254 240555

The Longridge Restaurant
104-106 Higher Road,
LONGRIDGE, PR3 3SY
01772 784969

LINCOLNSHIRE
Harry's Place
17 High Street,
Great Gonerby,
GRANTHAM, NG31 8JS
01476 561780

MERSEYSIDE
Fraiche
11 Rose Mount,
Oxton Village,
BIRKENHEAD, CH43 5SG
0151 652 2914

NORFOLK
Morston Hall
Morston, Holt,
BLAKENEY, NR25 7AA
01263 741041

The Neptune Inn &
Restaurant
85 Old Hunstanton Road,
HUNSTANTON, PE36 6HZ
01485 532122

NORTHAMPTONSHIRE
Equilibrium
Fawsley Hall, Fawsley,
DAVENTRY, NN11 3BA
01327 892000

3 ROSETTES

CONTINUED

SHROPSHIRE
Old Vicarage Hotel and Restaurant
BRIDGNORTH, WV15 5JZ
01746 716497

La Bécasse
17 Corve Street,
LUDLOW, SY8 1DA
01584 872325

SOMERSET
Bath Priory Hotel, Restaurant & Spa
Weston Road, BATH,
BA1 2XT
01225 331922

Little Barwick House
Barwick Village,
YEOVIL, BA22 9TD
01935 423902

SUFFOLK
The Bildeston Crown
104 High Street,
BILDESTON, IP7 7EB
01449 740510

Drake's Restaurant
The Clock House,
High Street, RIPLEY,
GU23 6AQ
01483 224777

SUSSEX, EAST
Newick Park Hotel & Country Estate
NEWICK, BN8 4SB
01825 723633

SUSSEX, WEST
Queens Room at Amberley Castle Hotel
AMBERLEY, BN18 9LT
01798 831992

West Stoke House
Downs Road, West Stoke,
CHICHESTER, PO18 9BN
01243 575226

Ockenden Manor
Ockenden Lane,
CUCKFIELD, RH17 5LD
01444 416111

Gravetye Manor Hotel
EAST GRINSTEAD,
RH19 4LJ
01342 810567

The Camellia Restaurant at South Lodge Hotel
Brighton Road, LOWER
BEEDING, RH13 6PS
01403 891711

The Pass
South Lodge Hotel
LOWER BEEDING,
RH13 6PS
01403 891711

TYNE & WEAR
Jesmond Dene House
Jesmond Dene Road,
NEWCASTLE UPON TYNE,
NE2 2EY
0191 212 3000

WARWICKSHIRE
Mallory Court Hotel
Harbury Lane,
Bishop's Tachbrook,
ROYAL LEAMINGTON SPA,
CV33 9QB
01926 330214

WEST MIDLANDS
Purnell's
55 Cornwall Street,
BIRMINGHAM, B3 2DH
0121 212 9799

Simpsons
20 Highfield Road,
Edgbaston,
BIRMINGHAM, B15 3DU
0121 454 3434

WIGHT, ISLE OF
Robert Thompson
The Hambrough
Hambrough Road,
VENTNOR, PO38 1SQ
01983 856333

WILTSHIRE
The Bybrook at the Manor
CASTLE COMBE, SN14 7HR
01249 782206

Lucknam Park
COLERNE, SN14 8AZ
01225 742777

The Harrow at Little Bedwyn
LITTLE BEDWYN, SN8 3JP
01672 870871

YORKSHIRE, NORTH
Burlington Restaurant
The Devonshire Arms
Country House Hotel & Spa,
Bolton Abbey,
SKIPTON, BD23 6AJ
01756 718111

Samuel's at Swinton Park
MASHAM, Ripon, HG4 4JH
01765 680900

Judges Country House Hotel
Kirklevington, YARM,
TS15 9LW
01642 789000

YORKSHIRE, WEST
Box Tree
35-37 Church Street,
ILKLEY, LS29 9DR
01943 608484

Anthony's Restaurant
19 Boar Lane,
LEEDS, LS1 6EA
0113 245 5922

JERSEY
Ocean Restaurant at the Atlantic Hotel
Le Mont de la Pulente,
ST BRELADE, JE3 8HE
01534 744101

Grand Jersey
The Esplanade,
ST HELIER, JE4 8WD
01534 722301

Longueville Manor Hotel
ST SAVIOUR, JE2 7WF
01534 725501

SCOTLAND
ABERDEENSHIRE
Darroch Learg Hotel
Braemar Road,
BALLATER, AB35 5UX
013397 55443

ARGYLL & BUTE
Isle of Eriska
ERISKA, PA37 1SD
01631 720371

Airds Hotel and Restaurant
PORT APPIN, PA38 4DF
01631 730236

DUMFRIES & GALLOWAY
Knockinaam Lodge
PORTPATRICK, DG9 9AD
01776 810471

EDINBURGH
The Kitchin
78 Commercial Quay, Leith,
EDINBURGH, EH6 6LX
0131 555 1755

Norton House Hotel
Ingliston, EDINBURGH,
EH28 8LX
0131 333 1275

Number One,
The Balmoral Hotel
Princes Street, EDINBURGH,
EH2 2EQ
0131 557 6727

Plumed Horse
50-54 Henderson Street,
Leith, EDINBURGH,
EH6 6DE
0131 554 5556

FIFE
Cellar Restaurant
24 East Green,
ANSTRUTHER, KY10 3AA
01333 310378

Peat Inn
ST ANDREWS, KY15 5LH
01334 840 206

The Road Hole Restaurant
Old Course Hotel Golf Resort
& Spa, ST ANDREWS,
KY16 9SP
01334 474371

The Seafood Restaurant
The Scores, ST ANDREWS,
KY16 9AS
01334 479475

GLASGOW
Hotel du Vin Bistro at
One Devonshire Gardens
1 Devonshire Gardens,
GLASGOW, G12 0UX
0141 339 2001

HIGHLAND
Kinloch Lodge
Sleat, ISLE ORNSAY,
IV43 8QY
01471 833214

The Three Chimneys
COLBOST, Isle of Skye
IV55 8ZT
01470 511258

Inverlochy Castle Hotel
Torlundy, FORT WILLIAM,
PH33 6SN
01397 702177

Abstract Restaurant
Glenmoriston Town House
Hotel,
Ness Bank, INVERNESS,
IV2 4SF
01463 223777

The Cross at Kingussie
Tweed Mill Brae,
Ardbroilach Road,
KINGUSSIE, PH21 ILB
01540 661166

Ullinish Country Lodge
STRUAN, Isle of Skye,
IV56 8FD
01470 572214

PERTH & KINROSS
Kinnaird
Kinnaird Estate, DUNKELD,
PH8 0LB
01796 482440

SCOTTISH BORDERS
The Horseshoe Inn
EDDLESTON, Peebles,
EH45 8QP
01721 730225

SOUTH AYRSHIRE
Glenapp Castle
BALLANTRAE, KA26 0NZ
01465 831212

Lochgreen House
Monktonhill Road,
Southwood
TROON, KA10 7EN
01292 313343

STIRLING
Roman Camp Country
House Hotel
CALLANDER, FK17 8BG
01877 330003

WEST DUNBARTONSHIRE
Martin Wishart at
Loch Lomond
Cameron House on Loch
Lomond,
BALLOCH, G83 8QZ
01389 722504

WALES
CEREDIGION
Ynyshir Hall
EGLWYSFACH, Machynlleth,
SY20 8TA
01654 781209
CONWY
Tan-y-Foel Country House
Capel Garmon,
BETWS-Y-COED, LL26 0RE
01690 710507

Bodysgallen Hall and Spa
LLANDUDNO, LL30 1RS
01492 584466

MONMOUTHSHIRE
Walnut Tree Inn
Llandewi Skirrid,
ABERGAVENNY, NP7 8AW
01873 852797

NEWPORT
The Crown at Celtic Manor
Coldra Woods,
NEWPORT, NP18 1HQ
01633 410262

POWYS
Carlton Riverside
Irfon Crescent,
LLANWRTYD WELLS,
LD5 4SP
01591 610248

REPUBLIC OF IRELAND
CO KILDARE
The Byerley Turk
The K Club,
STRAFFAN
01 601 7200

CO MONAGHAN
Restaurant at Nuremore
CARRICKMACROSS
042 966 1438

England

BEDFORDSHIRE

BOLNHURST
Map 12 TL05

The Plough at Bolnhurst

Modern British NEW

Rustic, modern food in a restored medieval pub

☎ 01234 376274
Kimbolton Rd MK44 2EX
e-mail: theplough@bolnhurst.com
dir: Please telephone for directions

Rescued and beautifully restored with style by Martin and Jayne Lee, the Plough is a striking medieval building that oozes charm and character, with fine old timbers, stripped boards and big log fires. Like the fresh, contemporary décor, Martin's inventive food is bang up-to-date, the open-to-view kitchen delivering exciting and gutsy modern British dishes prepared from the best British produce. Kick off proceedings with potted shrimp risotto, move on to lamb shoulder with cannellini bean purée, chorizo and black cabbage, or whole grilled lemon sole with parsley butter, and round off with lemon tart or a plate of Neal's Yard cheeses. The lunch board set menu is a steal.

Chef Martin Lee **Owner** Martin Lee, Jayne Lee, Michael Moscrop **Times** 12-2.30/6.30-9.30 Closed 27 Dec-14 Jan, Mon, D Sun **Prices** Fixed L 2 course £13, Starter £5.25-£7.25, Main £12.95-£24.95, Dessert £5-£6, Service optional **Wines** 80 bottles over £20, 42 bottles under £20, 12 by glass **Notes** Sunday L, Vegetarian available **Seats** 80, Pr/dining room 40 **Children** Portions **Parking** 30

FLITWICK
Map 11 TL03

Menzies Flitwick Manor

Modern British

Georgian manor house with confident kitchen

☎ 0871 472 4016 📠 01525 718753
Church Rd MK45 1AE
e-mail: flitwick@menzies-hotels.co.uk
dir: M1 junct 12, follow Flitwick after 1m turn left into Church Rd. Manor 200 yds on left

Standing in peaceful grounds, this handsome manor house is the place to go for a touch of cosseting and luxury. The house retains many original features and is furnished throughout with antiques and fine art, while the restaurant is equally well turned out in its best whites, with fine views over parkland and manicured lawns. Modern British dishes form the backbone of the menu, based around intelligent combinations of flavours; start with home-cured sea trout with shallot confit and lentil vinaigrette, following on with slow-roasted Middlewhite pork with Savoy cabbage and bacon and an apple purée, and finishing with sticky toffee pudding with honeycomb and caramel.

Times 12-2.30/7-9.30

LUTON
Map 6 TL02

Wernher Restaurant

Modern European

Modern food in a quintessentially British stately home setting

☎ 01582 734437 📠 01582 485438
Luton Hoo Hotel, Golf and Spa, The Mansion House LU1 3TQ
e-mail: reservations@lutonhoo.com
dir: M1 junct 10 signed Luton Airport. Take 3rd exit at Kidneywood rdbt onto A1081 towards Harpenden. Turn left after 0.5m to Luton Hoo

Transformed into a luxury hotel with an 18-hole golf course and stunning spa in 2007, this magnificent country retreat stands in 1,000 acres of parkland and gardens that were originally designed by 'Capability' Brown. The elegance and grandeur of the Great Hall epitomises the style of this impressive mansion, so expect sweeping staircases, fine sculptures, marble walls, beautiful tapestries and grand chandeliers throughout the public rooms. Exotic marble panel work and richly coloured fabrics adorn the elegant Wernher Restaurant, named after a former owner of Luton Hoo. Modern British food is cooked with flair and passion and the well-balanced menu may offer pan-fried scallops with pickled fennel to start, followed by a tasting of pork (ham hock tortellini, herb-crusted loin, pressed belly) with celeriac fondant and honey jus, and pomegranate parfait with exotic fruit salsa and raspberry jelly. Service throughout is well drilled and friendly. There are other dining options in the hotel, including a brasserie in the former stables.

Chef Kevin Clark **Owner** Elite Hotels **Times** 12.30-2/7-10 Closed L Sat **Prices** Fixed D 3 course £42, Starter £6-£9.50, Main £18-£34, Dessert £6-£8.50, Service optional **Wines** 338 bottles over £20, 18 by glass **Notes** Sunday L, Vegetarian available, Dress restrictions, Jacket & tie, Civ Wed 200 **Seats** 80, Pr/dining room 120 **Children** Portions, Menu **Parking** 150

WOBURN
Map 11 SP93

The Inn at Woburn

Modern British

Seamless blend of old and modern in lovely market town

☎ 01525 292292 📠 01525 290432
George St MK17 9PX
e-mail: enquiries@theinnatwoburn.com
dir: 5 mins from M1 junct 13. Follow signs to Woburn. Inn in town centre at x-rds, parking to rear via Park St

Named after chef Olivier Bertho, the restaurant of this lovely 18th-century coaching inn sits at the heart of the handsome Georgian market town of Woburn. The beamed Tavistock bar and lounge is a great place for that fine British institution of afternoon tea, or for a snifter before dinner in Olivier's restaurant, which has the clubby comfort of an upscale country house, with its chocolate leather seats, wood floors, muted earthy tones and sprays of lillies in antique vases. Typical starters include pan-fried scallops in a black pepper bread crust with white pudding, pancetta and chervil oil, followed by a paupiette of lemon sole filled with crab soufflé and served with vegetable tempura and bisque foam. Finish with the lush comfort of brioche bread-and-butter pudding with rum and raisins and vanilla custard.

Times 12-2.30/6-10.15

Paris House Restaurant

◉◉ French V

Classical French cooking in a historic English park

☎ 01525 290692   ▤ 01525 290471
Woburn Park MK17 9QP
e-mail: gail@parishouse.co.uk
web: www.parishouse.co.uk
dir: M1 junct 13. From Woburn take A4012 Hockliffe, 1m out of Woburn village on left

The half-timbered extravaganza of Paris House looks as if it has sat among the deer-speckled pastures of Woburn Park since Tudor times. Not a bad guess, but no cigar, as it is actually a Victorian pastiche, built in 1878 for the Paris Exhibition (hence the name) and relocated by the 9th Duke of Bedford to his Woburn Estate. The French moniker could equally be a clue to where the kitchen's heart lies since it became a restaurant in the early 1980s. Chef-patron Peter Chandler knows the classical French repertoire like the back of his ladle after 12 years working for the Roux brothers, so expect refined but unpretentious dishes such as seared scallops in ginger butter with spinach and tomato concasse, followed by a classic combination of corn-fed chicken breast stuffed with a mousse of chicken, morels and truffles in a rich Madeira sauce.

Chef Peter Chandler **Owner** Mr P Chandler
Times 12-2/6.30-10 Closed 26 Dec, 1-17 Jan, Mon, D Sun
Prices Fixed L 2 course £20-£30, Fixed D 3 course £25-£55, Service optional **Wines** 80 bottles over £20, 8 by glass **Notes** ALC 3 course £55, Gastronomic menu 5 courses £60, Sunday L, Vegetarian menu **Seats** 48, Pr/dining room 16 **Children** Portions, Menu **Parking** 24

BERKSHIRE

ASCOT   Map 6 SU96

Hyperion at Macdonald Berystede Hotel & Spa

◉ Modern European

Elegant dining room offering contemporary cuisine

☎ 01344 623311 & 0844 8799 104 ▤ 01344 872301
Bagshot Rd, Sunninghill SL5 9JH
e-mail: general.berystede@macdonald-hotels.co.uk
dir: M3 junct 3/A30, A322 then left onto B3020 to Ascot or M25 junct 13, follow signs for Bagshot. At Sunningdale turn right onto A330

With Ascot racecourse just a short canter away, it's no surprise that the interior of this turreted Victorian neo-Gothic fantasy celebrates its historic horse racing heritage. If you're not there for the gee gees, the Macdonald Berystede hotel is fully up to speed with 21st-century leisure facilities and its Hyperion Restaurant, named after a superstar Derby-winning racehorse, has an inviting roof terrace for outdoor dining with views over the immaculate grounds. The food is modern British with international influences: expect dishes such as veal carpaccio with rocket salad and sesame and ginger dressing to precede fillet of pork, carrot dauphinoise, baby vegetables and morel jus.

Chef Nick Fischer **Owner** Macdonald Hotels
Times 12.30-2/7-9.45 Closed L Sat **Prices** Food prices not confirmed for 2010. Please telephone for details.
Wines 40 bottles over £20, 40 bottles under £20, 12 by glass **Notes** Sunday L, Vegetarian available, Civ Wed 150, Air con **Seats** 100, Pr/dining room 24 **Children** Portions, Menu **Parking** 120

BRACKNELL   Map 5 SU86

Rowans at Coppid Beech

◉ European, Pacific Rim

Alpine atmosphere and modern food by the Thames

☎ 01344 303333   ▤ 01344 301200
John Nike Way RG12 8TF
e-mail: sales@coppidbeech.com
web: www.coppidbeech.com
dir: From M4 junct 10 follow A329(M) (Bracknell/Wokingham) to 1st exit. At Rdbt take 1st exit to Binfield (B3408); hotel 200yds on right

Of striking Swiss chalet design, set beside a dry-ski slope, an ice rink and toboggan run, this unique hotel looks and feels like an Alpine resort by the Thames. Rowans is the fine dining venue, a traditional restaurant with heavy drapes, linen-clothed tables with gleaming glassware, a lofty timbered ceiling with crystal chandeliers, and attentive service from uniformed staff. Expect an extensive menu listing imaginative, modern European dishes from grilled squid with harissa and lime aïoli to seafood linguine or rib-eye steak with béarnaise, finishing with chocolate mousse cake with peppered pineapple.

Rowans at Coppid Beech

Chef Paul Zolik **Owner** Nike Group Hotels Ltd
Times 12-2/7-9.45 Closed L Sat **Prices** Fixed L 2 course £15-£20, Fixed D 3 course £25-£31.50, Starter £6.75-£10.50, Main £12.50-£29.50, Dessert £6.50-£8.50, Service optional **Wines** 61 bottles over £20, 7 bottles under £20, 11 by glass **Notes** Sunday L, Vegetarian available, Dress restrictions, Smart casual, Civ Wed 300, Air con **Seats** 120, Pr/dining room 20 **Children** Portions, Menu **Parking** 350

BRAY   Map 6 SU97

The Fat Duck

◉◉◉◉◉ **– see page 50**

Hinds Head

◉◉ British ◔

The best of British pub food - Blumenthal style

☎ 01628 626151   ▤ 01628 623394
High St SL6 2AB
e-mail: info@hindsheadhotel.co.uk
dir: M4 junct 8/9, at rdbt take exit to Maidenhead Central, next rdbt take exit Bray & Windsor, after 0.5m take B3028 to Bray

Heston Blumenthal has always looked forwards and backwards in his thirst for culinary understanding (and sideways, you might say), and the Hinds Head - the Fat Duck's boozy younger sibling - represents the journey back to classic recipes that fit perfectly into the pub setting. Once a royal hunting lodge, the building retains its oak panelling and beams, plus roaring fires and comfortable seating. Top-notch produce is used in dishes that are cooked simply and delivered in an unfussy manner, with several recipes echoing the pub's Tudor roots. Guinea fowl terrine with spiced apples, or a pea and ham soup full of fabulous flavours, are typical starters. Main-course oxtail and kidney pudding with braised cabbage and bacon is an excellent version, and the triple-cooked chips are a must. For dessert, lardy cake with whisky ice cream is a stunning dish, fitting for a pub and a reminder of the pedigree of this particular hostelry.

Chef Clive Dixon **Owner** Heston Blumenthal & James Lee
Times 11-2.30/6.30-9.30 Closed 25-26 Dec, D 1 Jan
Prices Starter £6.35-£12.95, Main £12.90-£29.90, Dessert £5.85-£7.80, Service added but optional 12.5%
Wines 69 bottles over £20, 10 bottles under £20
Notes Tasting menu available 7 course, Sunday L, Vegetarian available, Air con **Seats** 100, Pr/dining room 22 **Children** Portions, Menu **Parking** 40

The Fat Duck

Modern British V NOTABLE WINE LIST

World class innovation and creativity

☎ 01628 580333   📠 01628 776188
High St SL6 2AQ
dir: M4 junct 8/9 (Maidenhead) take A308 towards Windsor, turn left into Bray. Restaurant in centre of village on right

Our television screens have seen a lot more of Mr Blumenthal over the course of the year as he's served up a series of historical feasts and battled to revive a chain of roadside restaurants. His relaxed manner and easy charm work well on the telly and he makes the most of his time on the box to get across his philosophy. A chef's statement on the website aims to do the same. He wants us to understand, amongst other things, the physiological and psychological complexities of taste and to appreciate that he values tradition whilst embracing innovation. Head to the posh Thames-side village of Bray to see for yourself. It will set you back a few quid, but will leave an impression that will linger longer in the memory than just about anything else you might spend the one hundred and thirty pounds on (that's the cost of the tasting menu). The disarming unpretentiousness of the place, both outside and in, makes the experience all the more enjoyable; staff work like a finely-tuned Swiss watch as they engage with the customers with charm and professionalism. You can tell it's an old building but everything inside is comfortably contemporary with some bright modern artworks adding a bit of individuality; tables are a little close together, but not so much as to cause anxiety. The carte and tasting menu are available lunch and dinner (no bargain lunch here, I'm afraid) and the latter seems to be the popular choice, customers deciding, most likely, that you only live once. The obvious thing each of the procession of courses has in common is they are based on superb produce. Snail porridge is Hereford snails, beautifully cooked, with shaved Jabugo ham, fennel lightly dressed in walnut oil and parsley purée mixed with oatmeal - a divine combination that does not defy good sense, simply teases with its name. If you're expecting a bit of science, roast foie gras 'Benzaldehyde', with almond fluid gel, cherry and almond chamomile, will not disappoint, but it makes sense when informed the chemical compound is a component of the scent of almonds; the dish is a delight to eat, full of thrilling flavours. Sounds of the Sea is a lot of fun, served up with an i-Pod to deliver aural stimulation alongside the tuna, mackerel, halibut and three types of seaweed. There's more, of course, plenty more, and it's all world class, even the wine list, and as you head out onto the pavement you'll have an even greater understanding of what makes Heston tick.

Chef Heston Blumenthal **Owner** Fat Duck Ltd **Times** 12-1.45/7-9.45 Closed 2 wks at Xmas, Mon, D Sun **Prices** Tasting menu fr £130, Service added but optional 12.5% **Wines** 500 bottles over £20, 13 by glass **Notes** ALC 3 course £98, Vegetarian menu, Air con **Seats** 40 **Children** Portions **Parking** Two village car parks

Waterside Inn

French

A gastronomic Thames-side legend delivering classic French cuisine

☎ 01628 620691 📠 01628 784710
Ferry Rd SL6 2AT
e-mail: reservations@waterside-inn.co.uk
dir: M4 junct 8/9, A308 (Windsor) then B3028 to Bray. Restaurant clearly signed

The gourmet-magnet village of Bray is rarely out of the news these days, but it is fitting to remember that the Waterside Inn is where the fuss all started. The venerable Roux brothers put the timeless Thames-side spot on the culinary map in 1972 and the Waterside is still in the business of serving timeless, world-class food cooked with passion and skill, under the guidance of Alain Roux, who took over the helm from his father Michel in 2001. Alain closed the restaurant for three months at the start of 2009 to install a new state-of-the-art kitchen, so expect even more streamlined preparation and service, plus the theatre of a new rôtisserie for spit-roasting suckling pig, duck and chicken. On the service front, the Waterside is a benchmark against which all others may be judged: you're in polished, professional hands before you're even out of the car, with the luxury touch of valet parking (a necessity, at any rate, given the limited space). Well-drilled staff offer faultless standards of skills and knowledge as well as chatty and completely un-snooty service. On a balmy day, head straight for the romantic waterside terrace to sip bubbly and nibble canapés, while watching fish splash and the odd boat scull by. Inside, the interior has the plush, homely comfort of a bourgeois - if rather upmarket - French country auberge in lush hues of green and gold, with hand-painted floral frescoes and walls of mirrors that create an expansive feeling of space; most tables get a river view through vast picture windows that open up the garden-like room to the Thames. The cooking and service are defiantly, classically French so expect the very best in opulent ingredients from the UK, France and further afield, and a cerebral approach to balance and understanding of flavours. The depth of your pockets will decide whether you go for a fixed-price lunch, five-course Menu Exceptionnel, or eye-watering à la carte options. Whichever you choose, long-standing favourites sit alongside dishes that make an effort to move with the times; all are prepared with the highest levels of skill and exceptional clarity of flavour. To start, shining sushi-grade tuna tartare is served with a fondue of confit peppers, coulis of gem lettuce and caviar. Next, loin of venison in a pastry crust with wild mushrooms, Hermitage wine sauce and blackcurrant vinegar is a triumphant balance of ingredients and flavour. At dessert, a classic apple tarte Tatin with cinnamon ice cream is as good as it gets. The wine list is an outstanding piece of work that waves the flag for aristocrats of the Gallic wine world; prices start at 'cor blimey'.

Chef Michel Roux, Alain Roux
Owner Michel Roux & Alain Roux
Times 12-2/7-10 Closed Mon, L Tue, D Tue (ex Jun-Aug) **Prices** Fixed L 2 course fr £39.50, Fixed D 4 course £109.50, Starter £28-£56, Main £47.50-£68, Dessert £27-£37.50, Service included
Wines 650 bottles over £20, 14 by glass
Notes Fixed D 5 course £93.50, Sunday L, Vegetarian available, Dress restrictions, Smart casual, Civ Wed 70, Air con **Seats** 75, Pr/dining room 8
Children Menu **Parking** 20

BRAY *continued*

The Riverside Brasserie

◉◉ French

Brasserie dining beside the Thames

☎ 01628 780553 📠 01628 674312
Bray Marina, Monkey Island Ln SL6 2EB
e-mail: info@riversidebrasserie.co.uk
dir: Off A308, signed Bray Marina

Expect wooden floors, an open-to-view kitchen, a relaxed atmosphere, and unpretentious yet accomplished brasserie fare at this contemporary, no-frills eatery in a unique location right beside the Thames in Bray Marina. A pit-stop for boaters, it draws the summer crowds for leisurely alfresco lunches on the waterside decked terrace. Come for clean, well-presented dishes prepared from top-notch ingredients, from starters like crispy pork belly salad with rocket and fennel, or chilled gazpacho, followed by skate wing with brown butter, lemon and capers, or rib-eye steak with roasted bone marrow and triple-cooked chips. Classic puddings include lemon tart or strawberry millefeuille, or opt for the plate of British cheeses.

Chef Phil Boardman **Owner** Alfie Hitchcock
Times 12-3/6.30-10 Closed Mon-Thu (Oct-Mar), L Fri (Oct-Mar) **Prices** Food prices not confirmed for 2010. Please telephone for details. **Wines** 20 bottles over £20, 3 bottles under £20, 6 by glass **Seats** 60 **Children** Portions, Menu **Parking** 30

Waterside Inn

◉◉◉◉ – *see page 51*

The Crab at Chieveley

◉◉ Modern French NEW

Friendly seafood restaurant with international style

☎ 01635 247550 📠 01635 247440
Wantage Rd RG20 8UE
e-mail: info@crabatchieveley.com
web: www.crabatchieveley.com
dir: M4 junct 13, towards Chieveley. Left into School Rd, right at T-junct, 0.5m on right

Once a downland pub, this 600-year-old building is now a hotel and award-winning seafood restaurant. Choose from the informal oyster and caviar bar or the formal fine dining area, where there's an eclectic mix of all things maritime and equestrian - fishing nets complete with scallop and oyster shells are attached to the ceiling beams. The cooking is deceptively simple but very precise, allowing well-defined flavours to shine through. Daily deliveries ensure the freshest lobsters, crabs, oysters, scallops, langoustines and prawns, as well as less glamorous (but equally delicious) fish such as mackerel and sardines. Dishes include squid and lemongrass risotto with sweet chilli and crayfish salsa, or hot fruits de mer (half a lobster, oysters, mussels and scallops) with garlic butter.

Chef Dave Horridge, Jamie Hodson **Owner** Steve Hughes
Times 12-2.30/6-9.30 Closed D 25 Dec **Prices** Fixed L 2 course fr £15.95, Fixed D 3 course fr £19.95, Starter £8-£11, Main £20-£39.95, Dessert £6-£14, Service added but optional 10% **Notes** Sunday L, Vegetarian available **Seats** 100, Pr/dining room 14 **Children** Portions **Parking** 80

Malik's

◉◉ Traditional Indian

Precision Indian cooking in rural Berkshire

☎ 01628 520085 📠 01628 529321
High St SL6 9SF
dir: M4 junct 7, take A4 towards Maidenhead, 2m

Not all Britain's quality Indian restaurants are in the big cities, as is evidenced by Malik's, which inhabits an old ivy-covered coaching inn in a picture-postcard Berkshire village. Stylish monochrome shots of Indian spices decorate the walls, while tables are traditionally attired in smart white linen and topped with candles. The staff are both attentive and knowledgeable, and the food scores highly for forthright, accurate seasoning and notable freshness. Duck breast cooked in the tandoor, alight with green chillies and coriander, and served with a red-hot dipping sauce, is a first course to ignite the taste buds, while mains might include the superb sikandari lamb, marinated over 2 days and cooked on the bone in a tomato-based sauce of impressive subtlety, accompanied by marinated chickpeas. Cinnamon-poached pear and traditional gulab jamun with vanilla ice cream round things off well.

Chef Malik Ahmed, Shapon Miah **Owner** Malik Ahmed
Times 12-2.30/6-11 Closed 25-26 Dec, L Eid festival **Prices** Fixed D 3 course fr £30, Main £7.50-£16, Dessert £3.50-£5.50, Service added but optional 10% **Wines** 39 bottles over £20, 11 bottles under £20, 7 by glass **Notes** Sunday L, Vegetarian available, Dress restrictions, Smart dress **Seats** 70, Pr/dining room 30 **Children** Portions **Parking** 26

The Inn on The Green

◉◉ Modern European

Modern classics at a stylish restaurant with rooms

☎ 01628 482638 ▤ 01628 487474
The Old Cricket Common SL6 9NZ
e-mail: reception@theinnonthegreen.com
dir: From Marlow or Maidenhead follow Cookham Dean
signs. In Cookham Dean turn into Hills Lane; into National
Trust road by War Memorial

An unexceptional mock-Tudor pub on the outside, the Inn
on the Green is a different kettle of fish inside. A rambling
series of interconnected dining areas is done out in
contrasting styles: the Lamp room - named for its
splendid chandelier - has a rustic-chic blend of bare
brick and rich burgundy walls and toffee-brown leather
seats; the Stublie goes for an Alpine log cabin vibe with
floor-to-ceiling wood-panels, then there's an airy
conservatory leading to the canopied courtyard. There's a
sound classical basis to the creative modern European
cooking with a twist of oriental spice, as in tempura of
Cornish squid with aïoli and rocket salad, or Asian-spiced
Gloucestershire Old Spot pork belly with a stirfry of carrot
apple and pak choi. End back in rural Berkshire with
apple and blackberry crumble with crème anglaise.

Chef Garry Hollihead **Owner** Andy Taylor, Mark Fuller &
Garry Hollihead **Times** 1-4/7-10 Closed Mon, L Tue-Sat, D
Sun **Prices** Starter £4.95-£8.95, Main £8.95-£15.95,
Dessert £4.95-£7.50, Service added but optional 12.5%
Wines 40 bottles over £20, 4 bottles under £20, 10 by
glass **Notes** Sunday L, Vegetarian available, Civ Wed 100,
Air con **Seats** 60, Pr/dining room 35 **Children** Portions
Parking 50

The Pot Kiln

◉ Traditional British, European ✍

Hearty country cooking in rural Berkshire pub

☎ 01635 201366 ▤ 01635 201366
RG18 0XX
e-mail: info@potkiln.org
web: www.potkiln.org
dir: From Yattendon follow Frilsham signs, cross over
motorway. Approx 0.25m pub on right

TV chef and presenter Mike Robinson's red brick country
pub in the back lanes of Berkshire is a bit tricky to find
for first-timers, but once there, you'll quickly settle into
the relaxed rustic ambience of the L-shaped dining room
and dinky, stripped-out bar. Nods to the kitchen's
hunting, shooting and fishing ethos are all around in the
prints and stuffed deers' heads on the terracotta walls,
as the menu is built on simple English country cooking,
with a clear inclination for meat and game. Mike's
marksmanship supplies much of the venison, and
mushrooms are often foraged by the kitchen team.
Modern, gutsy flavours appear in dishes such as game
terrine of ham hock, pigeon, venison, black pudding and

pheasant, and slow-braised shoulder of Peasemore lamb
with champ and pearl barley and leek broth.

Chef Mike Robinson **Owner** Mike & Katie Robinson
Times 12-2.30/7-9.30 Closed 25 Dec, Tue (Winter only), D
Sun **Prices** Fixed L 2 course fr £14.50, Starter £5.50-
£6.95, Main £12.50-£16.50, Dessert £5.75, Service added
but optional 10% **Wines** 51 bottles over £20, 8 bottles
under £20, 6 by glass **Notes** Tasting menu available,
Sunday L, Vegetarian available **Seats** 48, Pr/dining room
16 **Children** Portions **Parking** 70

The Bear Hotel

◉◉ Modern British

**Ambitious modern cooking in historic hotel with
contemporary makeover**

☎ 01488 682512 ▤ 01488 684357
41 Charnham St RG17 0EL
e-mail: info@thebearhotelhungerford.co.uk
web: www.thebearhotelhungerford.co.uk
dir: M4 junct 14, follow A338/Hungerford signs. 3m to
T-junct turn right onto A4 over 2 rdbts. Hotel 500yds on
left

One of the most historic inns in the country, with origins
in the 13th century and reputedly once the property of
Henry VIII. Real fires and striking black beams abound
but refurbishment has seen this ancient building
transformed into a contemporary and stylish hotel, with
the fresh, white-painted restaurant featuring vibrant
modern artwork and tables set with crisp white linen and
polished silver cutlery. Seasonal menus showcase British
cooking, with subtle, modern twists, and locally-sourced
produce with an accomplished, crowd-pleasing brasserie-
style repertoire of simple dishes; from classics like grilled
rump steak with chunky chips to Thai-spiced fish stew,
saddle of lamb with white bean and garlic purée, and
plum tarte Tatin with star anise, vanilla custard and
home-made ice cream.

Chef Philip Wild **Owner** The Bear Hungerford Ltd
Times 12-3/7-9.30 Closed D Sun **Prices** Food prices not
confirmed for 2010. Please telephone for details.
Wines 24 bottles over £20, 26 bottles under £20, 8 by
glass **Notes** Sunday L, Vegetarian available, Civ Wed 80
Seats 50, Pr/dining room 18 **Children** Portions
Parking 68

Black Boys Inn

◉◉ Modern

A corner of France in the English countryside

☎ 01628 824212
Henley Rd SL6 5NQ
e-mail: info@blackboysinn.co.uk
dir: M40 junct 4, A404 towards Henley, then A4130.
Restaurant 3m from Henley-on-Thames & Maidenhead

The Black Boys may look every inch the 16th-century
country village inn from the outside, but indoors it has
morphed into a contemporary restaurant with rooms.
Ancient beams, well-trodden floorboards and a huge
wood-burning stove blend with the modern rustic chic of
bare wood tables, log piles and scuffed leather
armchairs. After years spent with Gallic luminaries, chef
Simon Bonwick cooks with a style that is deeply-rooted in
old-school French cuisine bourgeoise, jazzed up with
lighter modern touches. It's the sort of place that laps up
local produce, but also ships it in from Parisian markets
and Cornish harbours to ensure peerless quality. Tuna
tartare is paired with a saffron and liquorice dressing in
a visually-striking cube, then comes main-course roasted
Middlewhite pork loin with a fat sausage of the same
rare-breed meat and braised haricots blancs.

Chef Marc Paley **Owner** Adrian & Helen Bannister
Times 12-2/7-9 Closed 1 wk Xmas, D Sun **Prices** Starter
£5.50-£9.95, Main £13.50-£20.50, Dessert £5.95-£9.95,
Service optional **Wines** 105 bottles over £20, 6 bottles
under £20, 32 by glass **Notes** Sunday L, Vegetarian
available **Seats** 45, Pr/dining room 12 **Parking** 45

The Castle Inn

◉◉ Traditional British, French

Traditional dining in handsome village pub

☎ 0118 934 0034 ▤ 0118 934 0334
Church Hill RG10 0SJ
e-mail: info@castlerestaurant.co.uk
dir: M4 junct 10, A329(M) towards Reading (E). Take 1st
exit to Winnersh/Wokingham. Continue for 1m, at
Sainsbury's turn left into Robin Hood Lane & continue
further 1.5m. Go straight when approaching sharp left
bend towards St Nicholas Church

Once used as a wash house by monks, this Grade II listed
16th-century inn is owned by the village church opposite.
Occupying a quintessential English setting overlooking
the second oldest bowling green in Britain, its original
wattle-and-daub plastering and oak panels inside are
complemented by a modern décor with warm chocolate
colours throughout. The upstairs gallery room boasts
views of the church and the rolling countryside, and
there's a small but lively bistro-style bar. Local produce
is used to produce classic French and British dishes, with
daily specials chalked up on the board. Generous portions
of old favourites include beef, stilton and suet pudding

continued

HURST *continued*

with horseradish mashed potatoes, while crème brûlée might be flavoured with pistachio.

Chef Jerome Leopold **Owner** Amanda Hill
Times 12-2/6-9.30 **Prices** Fixed L 2 course £10.95, Fixed D 3 course £15.95, Starter £5-£8.50, Main £10-£17, Dessert £6-£7, Service optional, Groups min 10 service 10% **Wines** 38 bottles over £20, 15 bottles under £20, 6 by glass **Notes** Early evening menu 6-7.30pm, Sunday L, Vegetarian available **Seats** 80, Pr/dining room 40 **Children** Portions **Parking** 43

LAMBOURN Map 5 SU37

The Hare Restaurant

◎◎ Modern European

Confident cooking in stunning countryside

☎ 01488 71386
RG17 7SD
e-mail: cuisine@theharerestaurant.co.uk
dir: M4 junct 14, A338 towards Wantage, left onto B4000 towards Lambourn, restaurant 3m on left

Set in outstanding countryside, this smart old inn is located on the edge of Lambourn - horseracing country. The three dining rooms boast a bright, contemporary and stylish décor, with slate floors, exposed beams, rustic wooden tables, and comfortable leather sofas by the log fire. In the summer months, the south facing terrace is ideal for alfresco dining. This is a relaxing and informal setting in which to sample some ambitious cooking that combines British with modern European influences. Sensibly compact menus (including a menu du jour) are well balanced, using top-notch ingredients and interesting combinations; perhaps chicken and mushroom terrine with piccalilli, or rack of lamb with couscous and pepper tian served with Provençale vegetables.

Chef Damien Lenaff **Owner** John Kirby **Times** 12-2/7-9.30 Closed 2 wks Jan, 2 wks summer, Tue after BH, Mon, D Sun **Prices** Fixed L 2 course £20, Fixed D 3 course £26, Starter £7-£8.50, Main £16-£22, Dessert £6.50-£8.50, Service optional, Groups min 10 service 10% **Wines** 70 bottles over £20, 6 bottles under £20, 6 by glass **Notes** Sunday L, Vegetarian available **Seats** 50, Pr/dining room 24 **Children** Portions **Parking** 30

MAIDENHEAD Map 6 SU88

Fredrick's Hotel Restaurant Spa

◎◎ Modern British, French

Modern British cooking in an opulent spa hotel

☎ 01628 581000   🖹 01628 771054
Shoppenhangers Rd SL6 2PZ
e-mail: reservations@fredricks-hotel.co.uk
dir: From M4 junct 8/9 take A404(M), then turning (junct 9A) for Cox Green/White Waltham. Left on to Shoppenhangers Rd, restaurant 400 mtrs on right

Not far from Windsor Castle and Wentworth and Sunningdale golf courses, Fredrick's is a grand hotel in the modern style, which is to say that spa therapies and beauty treatments are on offer amid the enveloping sense of grande luxe. The dining room has a restrained palatial air, with polished silver accoutrements, gleaming glassware and crisp white napery all adding to the elevated tone. A la carte or fixed-price menus are showcases for a gentle style of modern British cooking. Confit salmon with jumbo shrimps and curried lentils might open proceedings, while main courses aim for the stars with tender-textured Gressingham duck breast, served with cherries and cinnamon and impressive ginger and spring onion mash, or cod fillet with lobster and pak choi. Finish with forthrightly rich banana praline parfait.

Chef Brian Cutler **Owner** R Takhar **Times** 12-2.30/7-10 Closed 24-30 Dec, L Sat **Prices** Fixed L 2 course £18.95, Fixed D 3 course £38.95, Starter £9.50-£14.50, Main £16.50-£23.50, Dessert £9.95, Service optional **Wines** All bottles over £20, 6 by glass **Notes** Sunday L, Vegetarian available, Dress restrictions, Smart casual, Civ Wed 120, Air con **Seats** 60, Pr/dining room 140 **Children** Portions **Parking** 90

The Royal Oak at Paley Street

◎◎ British ♦NOTABLE WINE LIST

Old-fashioned inn with classy cooking

☎ 01628 620541
Paley St, Littlefield Green SL6 3JN
e-mail: royaloakmail@aol.com
dir: M4 junct 8/9. Take A308 towards Maidenhead Central, then a A330 to Ascot. After 2m, turn right onto B3024 to Twyford. Second pub on left

On the outskirts of Maidenhead is a traditional whitewashed inn with celebrity connections. Owner Nick Parkinson, son of Michael, is making his mark in a pub full of oak beams, polished wooden floors and roaring log fires. The dining room is refined yet unfussy, so bare tables are set with quality glassware, and modern furniture and original artwork give it a classy feel. Service is friendly and unstuffy. The kitchen, led by chef Dominic Chapman (whose previous employers include Heston Blumenthal), turns out well-known classic dishes with a touch of contemporary flair. Traditional pub snacks such as scotch eggs or roll mops will keep you going, or get stuck into a full meal, starting with macaroni cheese with ham hock followed by oxtail and kidney pie. Round things off with a cooked to order chocolate fondant with vanilla ice cream. A serious wine list includes an impressive range of champagnes.

Chef Dominic Chapman **Owner** Nick Parkinson **Times** 12-3/6-12 Closed 25 Dec, 1 Jan, D Sun **Prices** Fixed L 2 course fr £15.50, Starter £6.50-£9.50, Main £12.50-£22.50, Dessert £6.50-£7, Service optional **Wines** 250 bottles over £20, 25 bottles under £20, 20 by glass **Notes** Sunday L, Vegetarian available, Air con **Seats** 50 **Children** Portions **Parking** 70

NEWBURY Map 5 SU46

Donnington Valley Hotel & Spa

◎◎ Modern British ♦NOTABLE WINE LIST

Wine-themed restaurant in golfing hotel with spa

☎ 01635 551199   🖹 01635 551123
Old Oxford Rd, Donnington RG14 3AG
e-mail: general@donningtonvalley.co.uk
dir: M4 junct 13, A34 towards Newbury. Take immediate left signed Donnington Hotel. At rdbt take right, at 3rd rdbt take left, follow road for 2m, hotel on right

Set amid attractive grounds that also incorporate an 18-hole golf course, this wine-themed restaurant is part of a

continued on page 56

The Vineyard at Stockcross

Modern British V

Creative, compelling cooking in top-drawer venue

☎ 01635 528770 📄 01635 528398
Stockcross RG20 8JU
e-mail: general@the-vineyard.co.uk
dir: M4 junct 13/A34 Newbury bypass southbound, take 3rd exit signed Hungerford/Bath road interchange. Take 2nd exit at 1st and 2nd rdbts signed Stockcross, 0.6 mile on right

Don't go searching for the vines in the grounds as the vineyard referenced in the name is inspired by the owner's winery in sunny California. It is, though, the perfect opportunity to explore the wines of the West Coast of the USA, and avoid the trials of Terminal 5, by delving into the magnificent list of Californian wines; there's a second list covering the rest of the world which is no slouch either. The place is a blend of Californian and Mediterranean styles, with a sweeping gravel driveway, a luxurious spa, and, undoubtedly the star attraction, a restaurant of international repute. Art and sculpture also figure large, the centrepiece being the contemporary 'Fire and Water' sculpture out front. John Campbell's cooking is as individual as the setting. The split-level dining room is linked by a sweeping staircase with a balustrade fashioned as if it were a grapevine snaking between the spaces, and, with tables smartly set with white linen and muted, mellow tones throughout, it is a classy setting for an inspirational chef at the top of his game. Tasting, carte and (exceedingly good value) lunch menu showcase Campbell's cooking, which puts the emphasis on flavour, working with first-class produce and, although refined, complex and innovative, it has seen a highly successful, slightly more measured approach of late. Organic salmon mi-cuit, for example, is a beautifully presented first course, topped with a piece of foie gras and perfectly partnered with a vanilla and apple purée. Deftly handled flavours are evident in a main course dish of turbot, where the lemongrass foam is judged to a tee, and accompanying pork belly, langoustines and mushrooms bring the dish to a satisfying crescendo. The creative thinking and technical proficiency extends to desserts such as sweet cucumber and mango consommé poured over vanilla pannacotta, with a cucumber sorbet and pea shoots. Service is out of the top drawer, confident and informed, and all the extras (bread, pre-starter etc.) confirm the Vineyard to be a compelling, dynamic restaurant of the highest order.

Chef John Campbell, Peter Eaton
Owner Sir Peter Michael
Times 12-2/7-9.30 **Prices** Fixed L 2 course fr £19, Fixed D 3 course £42-£68, Tasting menu fr £95, Service optional

Wines 3000 bottles over £20, 60 bottles under £20, 50 by glass **Notes** Sunday L, Vegetarian menu, Civ Wed 120, Air con **Seats** 86, Pr/dining room 120 **Children** Portions, Menu **Parking** 100

NEWBURY *continued*

stylish contemporary hotel that also boasts a state-of-the-art spa and impressive conference facilities. A raised gallery overlooks the central dining area and the wine theme extends to a mighty list of some 300 well chosen bottles. When it comes to food, the emphasis is firmly on fresh produce, locally sourced and simply prepared. Expect mains such as venison loin, pancetta, Savoy cabbage, beetroot, celeriac and buttered mash or pan-fried brill with chive mash, pak choi, shallot, scallop and saffron vinaigrette, and finish with pineapple carpaccio with coconut pannacotta and Malibu reduction.

Chef Kelvin Johnson **Owner** Sir Peter Michael
Times 12-2/7-10 **Prices** Fixed L 2 course £19-£22, Fixed D 3 course £27-£30, Starter £7-£12, Main £14-£24, Dessert £7-£9.50, Service optional **Wines** 190 bottles over £20, 34 bottles under £20, 30 by glass **Notes** Sunday L, Vegetarian available, Dress restrictions, Smart casual, Civ Wed 85, Air con **Seats** 120, Pr/dining room 130 **Children** Portions, Menu **Parking** 150

Regency Park Hotel

French, European

Contemporary and relaxed setting and appealing brasserie-style menu

☎ 01635 871555 📠 01635 871571
Bowling Green Rd, Thatcham RG18 3RP
e-mail: info@regencyparkhotel.co.uk
dir: M4 junct 13, follow A339 to Newbury for 2m, then take the A4 (Reading), the hotel is signed

Set within a smart hotel within easy reach of the M4, the Watermark Restaurant has views over an attractive landscaped water garden. It's an airy, modern restaurant, with large windows, crisp linen, and a brasserie-style menu full of European flavours and some British favourites. Seasonal ingredients are used to good effect in dishes such as a starter of pressed confit of duck, ham hock and wild mushrooms, served with a chicory and green bean salad in a walnut dressing. Move on to a 28-day aged sirloin steak or pan-fried monkfish with chorizo risotto and herb and mussel sauce. Chocolate fondant with prune and Armagnac ice cream is a fine finish.

Times 12.30-2/7-10 Closed L Sat

River Bar Restaurant

Modern European

Delightful riverside restaurant serving good food

☎ 01635 528838 📠 01635 523406
Newbury Manor Hotel, London Rd RG14 2BY
e-mail: enquiries@newbury-manor-hotel.co.uk
web: www.riverbarrestaurant.co.uk
dir: M4 junct 13, A34 Newbury, A4 Thatcham, 0.5m on right opposite Swan Pub

The restaurant at this splendidly refurbished Grade II listed Georgian house, surrounded by 9 acres of mature woodland and water meadows, is just a short stroll along herringbone brick paths, over wooden bridges, through the herb gardens and past the pond. The conservatory-style River Bar has full-length windows providing great views across the jetty and River Kennet, giving plenty of opportunity to watch both woodland and water wildlife in action. Here the emphasis is on quality ingredients and the straightforward preparation of classic cuisine, such as chicken liver and foie gras parfait accompanied by fig and date chutney and brioche, followed by a main course of glazed salmon, saffron mash, Provençal ratatouille and watercress pesto.

Chef David Horridge, John Harrison **Owner** Heritage Properties & Hotels **Times** 12-2.30/6-10 **Prices** Fixed D 3 course £20, Starter £5-£8.95, Main £14.50-£25, Dessert £5-£6, Service optional **Wines** 29 bottles over £20, 15 bottles under £20, 12 by glass **Notes** Sunday L, Vegetarian available, Civ Wed 100 **Seats** 48, Pr/dining room 40 **Parking** 80

The Vineyard at Stockcross

– see page 55

The Elephant at Pangbourne

British, French

Great food served in unique, colonial-style setting

☎ 0118 984 2244 & 07770 268359 📠 0118 976 7346
Church Rd RG8 7AR
e-mail: reception@elephanthotel.co.uk
dir: A4 Theale/Newbury, right at 2nd rdbt signed Pangbourne. Hotel on left

This hotel brings some of the opulence of the Empire to the village of Pangbourne with beautiful hand-crafted Indian furniture alongside rich rugs and warm red wall coverings. Sip a cocktail in the lounge before moving on to the elegant Christoph's Restaurant, with its large windows giving panoramic views of the grounds and local church; the elephant theme is continued with carved elephant tea light holders on the tables. The kitchen team uses good local and seasonal produce to create well-refined dishes. Expect starters such as pressed terrine of rabbit with roast garlic, thyme, Serrano ham and pickled mushrooms, followed by cider-braised belly of rare breed pork, bubble-and-squeak, sage jus and rhubarb purée. There's the more informal bistro-style BaBar, too.

Times 12-2.30/7-9

Acqua Restaurant & Bar

Modern British **NEW**

Modern cooking on the banks of the Thames

☎ 0118 925 9988 📠 0118 939 1665
Crowne Plaza Reading, Caversham Bridge, Richfield Av RG1 8BD
e-mail: info@cp-reading.co.uk
dir: M4 junct 11, take the Inner Distribution Rd to Caversham

An impressive hotel delightfully positioned on the banks of the River Thames and ideally located for Reading town centre and the many local business parks. The light and spacious restaurant mixes contemporary elegance with stunning views across the River Thames. The kitchen caters for a wide range of tastes but the cornerstone is local, seasonal produce and high quality ingredients. The broad menu takes in salads and classic grills alongside dishes such as seared scallops with crab bisque, chervil and parmesan followed by braised pig's cheeks with chorizo and haricot cassoulet, black pudding and quail's egg. Dessert could be pear crumble soufflé with prune ice cream and poached pear.

Chef Paul Riley **Owner** Pedersen Hotels
Times 12-2.30/6.30 **Prices** Starter £5.80-£8.50, Main £10.50-£18.50, Dessert £1.75-£7.50, Service optional **Wines** 16 bottles over £20, 23 bottles under £20, 11 by glass **Notes** Vegetarian available, Air con **Seats** Pr/dining room 20 **Children** Portions, Menu

Cerise Restaurant at The Forbury Hotel

French, Mediterranean

Smart brasserie dining at stylish townhouse hotel

☎ 08000 789789 & 0118 952 7770 📠 0118 929 0740
The Forbury Hotel, 26 The Forbury RG1 3EJ
e-mail: reservations@theforburyhotel.co.uk
dir: M4 junct 11/A33 towards town centre, then right onto A329. Follow station signs & continue forward over flyover. At traffic lights bear left into Watlington St & continue to Forbury Rd. Take left turns into Blagrove St, Valpy St and at War Memorial. Hotel on the left

The Forbury is a contemporary hotel with a bit of swagger. Among the dining options is this brasserie and bar with its hip and happening vibe. There's a sumptuous cocktail lounge with a superb list, and a dining room done out in a stylishly modern way with splashes of cerise and clothless wooden tables. The menu has a modern European accent, so lobster and salmon ravioli is flavoured with a chervil emulsion and lemon as a starter, and roasted saddle of rabbit comes with black pudding, cauliflower and Armagnac. Desserts include the intriguingly titled 'elements of forced rhubarb'. Eden is the hotel's fine-dining option, open for lunch and dinner Thursday and Friday, and dinner only on Saturday.

Chef Daniel Galmiche & Craig Teasdale **Owner** Toby Hunter **Times** 12-3/7-10.30 **Prices** Fixed L 2 course £14, Starter £7.50-£11.50, Main £13.50-£19, Dessert £7-£7.50, Service added but optional 12.5% **Wines** 200 bottles over £20, 3 bottles under £20, 13 by glass **Notes** Vegetarian available, Air con **Seats** 60, Pr/dining room 35 **Children** Portions, Menu **Parking** 18

Forburys Restaurant

 French, European

An enclave of France in Reading's modern Forbury Square development

☎ 0118 957 4044 📠 0118 956 9191
1 Forbury Square RG1 3BB
e-mail: forburys@btconnect.com
dir: In town centre, opposite Forbury Gardens

This swish contemporary restaurant occupies the ground floor of a striking glass office building designed by the

architect who created Canary Wharf. The expansive dining room has huge floor-to-ceiling windows overlooking Forbury Square, and a clean-cut chic décor of blond-wood floors and plenty of chocolate-brown leather. For a buzzier ambience, the Market and à la carte menus are also served in the stainless steel and leather wine bar. Cooking is emphatically French, with classic flavour combinations, but not to a degree that stops the kitchen going off-piste into more inclusive modern British territory; raw materials are the best the UK has to offer. Eye-catching dishes include seared Cornish hand-dived scallops with celeriac purée and lentils, mains such as an assiette of pig's head cooked three ways with Roscoff onions and sauce soubise, and Amadei bitter chocolate fondant with dark chocolate ice cream to finish.

Chef Gavin Young **Owner** Xavier Le-Bellego
Times 12-2.15/6-10 Closed 26-28 Dec, 1-2 Jan, Sun **Prices** Fixed D 3 course £19, Tasting menu £49, Starter £6.95-£11.50, Main £12.95-£22.50, Dessert £6.50-£8.50, Service optional, Groups min 4 service 12.5% **Wines** 145 bottles over £20, 9 bottles under £20, 15 by glass **Notes** Vegetarian available, Air con **Seats** 80, Pr/dining room 16 **Children** Portions **Parking** 40

Malmaison Reading

Modern European

Contemporary brasserie dining in rejuvenated former Great Western Rail hotel

☎ 0118 956 2300 & 956 2302 📠 0118 956 2301
Great Western House, 18-20 Station Rd RG1 1JX
e-mail: reading@malmaison.com
dir: Next to Reading station

Malmaison have stylishly revamped the former Great Western Railway Hotel into a chic, contemporary hotel, yet the décor reflects its long-standing relationship with the railway in the form of railway memorabilia in the public areas. There's a chic, funky feel to the brasserie-style restaurant, which fuses the atmosphere of a nightclub with the exciting energy of a trendy restaurant, with movie-style lighting, a glass wine wall and black tiled flooring. The cooking style is equally modern, but classically based and delivering clear and precise dishes packed with flavour, so seared chorizo comes with squid and chick peas in a salad, pan-fried lemon sole with clams and garlic, and blueberries in a steamed pudding.

Chef Andrew Holmes **Owner** Malmaison H & V Group **Times** 12-2.30/6-11 Closed L Sat **Prices** Fixed L 2 course fr £14.50, Fixed D 3 course fr £16.50, Starter £4.50-£7.95, Main £10.95-£18.50, Dessert £4.95-£8.50, Service added but optional 10% **Wines** 234 bottles over £20, 16 bottles under £20, 18 by glass **Notes** Sunday L, Vegetarian available, Civ Wed 35, Air con **Seats** 64, Pr/dining room 14 **Children** Portions, Menu **Parking** NCP across road

L'ortolan

French V

Fine dining in stylish listed building

☎ 0118 988 8500 📠 0118 988 9338
Church Ln RG2 9BY
e-mail: info@lortolan.com
web: www.lortolan.com
dir: From M4 junct 11 take A33 towards Basingstoke. At 1st rdbt turn left, after garage turn left, 1m turn right at Six Bells pub. Restaurant 1st left (follow tourist signs)

The pretty red-brick former vicarage - duly listed to preserve its character - dates back to the 17th-century and is these days a destination restaurant. Alan Murchison's highly acclaimed French cooking is the star attraction, even overshadowing the beautiful setting amid peaceful grounds. Chocolate and caramel tones

create a modern, sophisticated feel on the inside, and you can see Alan and his team in action - glimpsed through a fish tank. There's a stylish champagne bar and conservatory lounge, plus chef's table and private dining rooms, and the service is slick and personable. The cooking is rooted in French classicism, but is modern, light, highly creative and does not shy away from influences from further afield (some Asian flavours, for example). Top-notch seasonal ingredients shine through and presentation really catches the eye. A starter from the carte of a foie gras and pain d'epice 'sandwich' comes with smoked duck and pineapple chutney, while a main course from the Du Jour menu might be bouillabaisse - a refined and impressive dish with a superb piece of red mullet and subtly flavoured saffron potatoes. Finish with pain perdu with apple galette and vanilla ice cream. Everything, from the excellent breads, amuse-bouche (celeriac and apple soup, perhaps), pre-dessert and petits fours, is made with flair and attention to detail.

Chef Alan Murchison **Owner** Alan Murchison Restaurants Ltd **Times** 11.45-2/7-10 Closed 2 wks Xmas/New Year, Mon/Sun **Prices** Fixed L 3 course fr £26, Fixed D 3 course fr £38, Tasting menu £69, Service added but optional **Wines** 350 bottles over £20, 10 bottles under £20, 10 by glass **Notes** Tasting menu 7 course, Vegetarian menu, Dress restrictions, Smart casual, Civ Wed 62 **Seats** 64, Pr/dining room 22 **Children** Portions, Menu **Parking** 45

READING *continued*

Millennium Madejski Hotel Reading

◉ British, International

Contemporary cuisine in striking, modern stadium complex

☎ 0118 925 3500 ▤ 0118 925 3501
Madejski Stadium RG2 0FL
e-mail: sales.reading@millenniumhotels.co.uk
dir: 1m N from M4 junct 11. 2m S from Reading town centre

Part of the impressive Madejski Stadium complex, home to both Reading FC and London Irish Rugby team, Cilantro is this stylish hotel's buzzy, contemporary fine-diner. There's leather seating in the bar area and mood lighting throughout, while white, black and red walls are joined by an eye-catching wall of wine bottles that conceals the kitchen. French-inspired cooking with modern interpretations fits the bill, driven by quality produce; perhaps Brixham red mullet, pan roasted and served with Alsace bacon and a shellfish risotto and jus, or maybe Cornish lamb noisette, delivered with foie gras gratin, pomme Anna and cherry vine tomatoes.

Times 7–10 Closed 25 Dec, 1 Jan, BHs, Sun, L all week

SHINFIELD Map 5 SU76

L'ortolan

◉◉◉ – *see page 57*

SONNING Map 5 SU77

The French Horn

◉◉ British, French **V**

Classical dining on the Thames

☎ 0118 969 2204 ▤ 0118 944 2210
RG4 6TN
e-mail: info@thefrenchhorn.co.uk
dir: From Reading take A4 E to Sonning. Follow B478 through village over bridge, hotel on right, car park on left

The renowned French Horn enjoys an idyllic setting beside the serene waters of the Thames, and the elegant, glass-fronted dining room opens on to a delightful terrace which overlooks attractive grounds and the willow-fringed river. Take a drink in the cosy bar, where a spit-roast duck turns above the fire, and peruse the classic English and French menu, which delivers some innovative touches that perfectly suit the opulent and formal setting of the well-appointed dining room. A typical meal might kick off with an open raviolo of tiger prawns and mushrooms with a shellfish sauce, followed by rack of lamb with mint sauce and redcurrant jelly, or whole Dover sole, with dark chocolate marquise with spiced banana ice cream or bread-and-butter pudding to finish.

Chef G Company **Owner** Emmanuel Family
Times 12-2.15/7-9.45 Closed 26-30 Dec **Prices** Fixed L 2 course £24, Fixed D 3 course £35.50, Starter £9.50-£130,
Main £24-£39.50, Dessert £9.50, Service included
Wines 450 bottles over £20, 14 by glass **Notes** Sunday L, Vegetarian menu, Dress restrictions, No shorts or sleeveless shirts **Seats** 70, Pr/dining room 24
Children Portions **Parking** 40

STREATLEY Map 5 SU58

Cygnetures

◉◉ British, International

Fine-dining hotel restaurant with a gorgeous Thames-side vista

☎ 01491 878800 ▤ 01491 872554
The Swan at Streatley, High St RG8 9HR
e-mail: sales@swan-at-streatley.co.uk
web: www.swanatstreatley.co.uk
dir: Follow A329 from Pangbourne, on entering Streatley turn right at lights. Hotel on left before bridge

The 17th-century Swan at Streatley is the very image of bucolic English charm, and it is supposedly the place where Jerome K Jerome settled in to write *Three Men in a Boat*. The hotel is now a very contemporary affair that does a brisk trade in weddings, conferences and pampering sessions in its spa complex, but those unbeatable Thames-side views are still an integral element of the dining experience in Cygnetures restaurant. Inside, the décor is clean-cut and minimal: sailing images hang from white walls and a single flower at each table injects a note of colour. Modern European cooking is the order of the day, built on a foundation of classic French technique, in dishes such as scallops with squid and sauce noir, or lamb cutlets with smoked anchovy beignet and crêpe Parmentier.

Owner John Nike Group **Times** 12.30-2/7-10 **Prices** Food prices not confirmed for 2010. Please telephone for details. **Wines** 89 bottles over £20, 31 bottles under £20, 18 by glass **Notes** Sunday L, Vegetarian available, Dress restrictions, Smart casual, Civ Wed 150 **Seats** 70, Pr/dining room 130 **Children** Portions, Menu **Parking** 130

WINDSOR Map 6 SU97

The Dining Room

◉ Modern British, French

Modern cooking beside the Thames

☎ 01753 609988 & 609900 ▤ 01628 609942
Oakley Court Hotel, Windsor Rd, Water Oakley SL4 5UR
e-mail: reservations@oakleycourt.com
dir: M4 junct 6 to Windsor. At rdbt right onto A308. Hotel 2.5m on right.

This stunning Victorian Gothic mansion is set in 35 acres of landscaped gardens on the banks of the Thames. In the 1960s it was the setting for the St Trinian's films and such famous Hammer Horror productions as *Dracula*. These days it earns its crust as a country-house hotel and there's nothing scary about the traditional oak-panelled restaurant, with its well-spaced tables and beautiful views of the gardens. The style of cooking is modern European with French influences, using high-quality local ingredients. Ginger biscuit-crusted venison loin, for example, with wild berry and potato gâteau, confit of pear, root vegetable purée and cassis jus, followed by vanilla pannacotta with praline mousse and tempura strawberry.

Chef Darran Kimber **Owner** Heuston Hospitality
Times 12-2/7-9.30 Closed L Sat **Prices** Fixed L 2 course fr £33.50, Fixed D 3 course fr £65, Starter £9.50-£16, Main £18-£32, Dessert £9.50-£12, Service optional **Wines** 40 bottles over £20, 4 bottles under £20, 7 by glass **Notes** Sunday L, Vegetarian available, Dress restrictions, Smart casual, Civ Wed 200, Air con **Seats** 110, Pr/dining room 25 **Children** Portions, Menu **Parking** 180

Mercure Castle Hotel

◉◉ Modern European

Contemporary dining in the heart of Windsor

☎ 0870 4008300 & 01753 851577
▤ 01753 841149/856930
High St SL4 1LJ
dir: M25 junct 13 take A308 towards town centre then onto B470 to High St. M4 junct 6 towards A332, at rdbt first exit into Clarence Rd, left at lights to High St

Right in the heart of Windsor, this 16th-century former coaching inn enjoys fine views of the castle. The elegant modern restaurant is decorated in shades of aubergine and soft beige, and offers comprehensive modern international cuisine that makes the most of seasonal produce, sourced from a range of suppliers countrywide. Cooking is thoughtful and innovative with a variety of classical dishes and modern interpretations on the seasonally-changing menus, complemented by an extensive wine list. Seared scallops, for example, with rhubarb compôte, champagne foam and caviar to start, followed with braised halibut, celeriac purée, salsify and red wine jus. Finish with toasted oat and whisky parfait and raspberry sorbet.

Times 12-2.30/6.30-9.45

Sir Christopher Wren's House Hotel & Spa

◉◉ Modern British

Elegant restaurant with riverside views

☎ 01753 861354 📠 01753 860172
Thames St SL4 1PX
e-mail: reservations@windsor.wrensgroup.com
dir: Telephone for directions

Standing beneath the ramparts of Windsor Castle, this hotel enjoys a spectacular setting, overlooking the River Thames at Eton Bridge. Once the family home of Sir Christopher Wren, the main house holds a unique place in British heritage and the hotel's Strok's restaurant has those amazing views. It's worth the trip to watch the sun set behind the riverbank trees from the champagne terrace. Inside, the style is contemporary with a touch of traditional elegance and service is formal but friendly enough. The menu changes seasonally with classical influences underpinning the modern approach. Perhaps choose pressed foie gras, brioche, apple and grape chutney followed by beef fillet with Lyonnaise potatoes, asparagus and carrot purée.

Chef Stephen Boucher **Owner** The Wrens Hotel Group **Times** 12.30-2.30/6.30-10 **Prices** Food prices not confirmed for 2010. Please telephone for details. **Wines** 60 bottles over £20, 8 bottles under £20, 8 by glass **Notes** Pre-theatre D available, Sunday L, Vegetarian available, Dress restrictions, Smart casual preferred, Civ Wed 100, Air con **Seats** 65, Pr/dining room 100 **Children** Portions **Parking** 14, Riverside train station

BRISTOL

BRISTOL Map 4 ST57

Bells Diner

◉◉ Modern European

Innovative cooking in Bristol's Bohemian quarter

☎ 0117 924 0357 📠 0117 924 4280
1-3 York Rd, Montpellier BS6 5QB
e-mail: info@bellsdiner.com
web: www.bellsdiner.com
dir: Telephone for further details

A grocery shop in a former life, the intimate restaurant of today retains some of the original shop fittings in the front room, with the rear dining area having a more contemporary feel. Inventive European cooking is the order of the day with appealing flavour combinations delivered via both cutting edge and traditional cooking techniques. The presence of a tasting menu lays bare the serious intentions of the kitchen. Start with a mackerel ballotine, perfectly partnered with pickled beetroot, cucumber sorbet and horseradish cream, and for main course, perhaps, Gressingham duck, with pear jelly, pumpkin, pommes Anna, baby leek and 12-year-old balsamic. Inventive desserts include banana soufflé with a toffee sauce and vanilla ice cream, or go for the selection of artisan British cheeses with grapes, biscuits and walnut bread.

Times 12-2.30/7-10.30 Closed 24-30 Dec, Sun, L Mon & Sat

Bordeaux Quay

◉◉ European 🍃

Sleek continental cooking in the redeveloped docklands

☎ 0117 906 5550 & 943 1200 📠 0117 906 5567
V-Shed, Canons Way BS1 5UH
e-mail: info@bordeaux-quay.co.uk
dir: Canons Rd off the A4

The venue on the city docks was built in 1926 as a warehouse, with a flat roof area from which cranes hoisted cargoes off the container ships. It's quite as much of a hive of activity today, set amid the bars and cafés that many a redeveloped harbour-front now boasts. There's a ground-floor bistro with waterside seating, and upstairs a more luxurious restaurant and wine bar. Classical continental modes are brought to bear on the seasonally informed menus, with everything from breads

to ice creams produced in-house. A game risotto is correctly textured and bursting with meaty, red-wine flavour, while loin of venison makes a handsome main course, coming with celeriac, turnips and greens, and chocolate pot garnished with candied orange peel and biscotti is the real thing, full of rich, dark bitterness.

Chef Liz Payne, Barny Haughton **Owner** Barny Haughton **Times** 12.30-3/6-10 Closed Mon, L Sat, D Sun **Prices** Fixed L 2 course fr £19.50, Starter £5.50-£12.50, Main £11.50-£23.50, Dessert £6-£7, Service added but optional 10% **Wines** 140 bottles over £20, 20 bottles under £20, 30 by glass **Notes** Sunday L, Vegetarian available **Children** Portions

The Bristol Marriott Royal

◉ Modern

Imaginative British cooking in spectacular dining room

☎ 0117 925 5100 📠 0117 925 1515
College Green BS1 5TA
e-mail: bristol.royal@marriotthotels.co.uk
dir: Next to cathedral by College Green

A fine example of Victorian ambition, the gloriously imposing hotel occupies a prestigious city centre site overlooking the cathedral and harbour. The Palm Court restaurant is spectacular: a classical extravaganza of sandstone walls, balconies, statues and a stained glass wall. West Country produce is to the fore in the menu of mostly British-inspired dishes with some contemporary touches. Start with a tian of Cornish crab with crème fraîche, Keta (salmon caviar), and pickled cucumber, then perhaps roast rump of Welsh lamb with ratatouille, spinach and tapenade sauce, and finishing with warm apple tarte Tatin, given a local flavour in its pairing with Westons Organic Cider ice cream.

Casamia

◉◉◉ – see page 60

City Café

◉◉ Modern European NEW

Confident cooking in a modern restaurant in Bristol centre

☎ 0117 910 2700 📠 0117 910 2727
City Inn Bristol, Temple Way BS1 6BF
e-mail: bristol.citycafe@cityinn.com
dir: M4 junct 19, M32 to Bristol, follow signs to Temple Meads Station. Hotel on right after underpass

In the thick of the action in Bristol's bustling centre and close by Temple Meads railway station, this contemporary hotel's City Café restaurant offers a choice of memorable settings. On a fine day, take a seat outdoors on the terrace overlooking the avenues of mature trees in Temple Gardens, or in any weather, go for the stylish dining room with its polished wooden floors and crisp white linen clothed tables. The kitchen has a serious approach to local sourcing, and turns out confident well-executed modern European dishes. Chicken and crayfish soufflé

continued

BRISTOL *continued*

with a caramelised apple galette and Madeira jus makes a refined starter, followed by Somerset lamb cutlets wrapped in basil and filo pastry with potato dauphinoise and a tomato and basil jus.

Chef Matthew Lord **Owner** City Inn Ltd
Times 12-2.30/6-10.30 **Prices** Fixed L 2 course £9.95, Fixed D 3 course £16.50, Starter £4.95-£6.95, Main £9.95-£19.95, Dessert £5.50-£5.95, Service optional **Wines** 36 bottles over £20, 12 bottles under £20, 29 by glass **Notes** Sunday L, Vegetarian available, Dress restrictions, Smart casual, Civ Wed 50, Air con **Seats** 72, Pr/dining room 28 **Children** Portions, Menu **Parking** 45, 35 spaces next to hotel

Culinaria

◉◉ Mediterranean

Excellent bistro cooking amid cheerful informality

☎ 0117 973 7999
1 Chandos Rd, Redland BS6 6PG
dir: Please telephone for directions

Stephen and Judy Markwick's bistro-cum-deli is based on sound principles - local seasonal food, cooked in an unfussy manner - and serves the community well by offering takeaway dishes (fresh or frozen) alongside produce in the deli. The dining area is contemporarily styled, but refreshingly plain, and there are even a couple

of tables in the small courtyard garden. Judy leads the service team, which goes along nicely and fits the relaxed mood of the place. The weekly-changing menu delivers sound, confident cooking, with game terrine (pheasant, venison and partridge), for example, preceding pan-fried fillet of brill with a crab and prawn risotto, and rhubarb fool or West Country cheeses to finish.

Chef Stephen Markwick **Owner** Stephen & Judy Markwick
Times 12-2.30/6.30-10 Closed Xmas, New Year, BHs, 4 wks during year, Sun-Wed **Prices** Fixed L 2 course £15.50, Starter £7-£8.50, Main £15.50-£17.75, Dessert £6-£6.75, Service optional **Wines** 13 bottles over £20, 20 bottles under £20, 6 by glass **Notes** Vegetarian available **Seats** 30 **Children** Portions **Parking** On street

Ellipse Bar & Restaurant

◉ Modern British

Stylish modern hotel dining on the riverside

☎ 0117 933 8200 & 929 1030 📠 0117 929 2030
Mercure Brigstow Bristol, 5-7 Welsh Back BS1 4SP
e-mail: h6548@accor.com
dir: M32, follow signs for Bristol Temple Meads train station. At rdbt turn into Victoria St. Continue over Bristol bridge turn left and immediately left and then left again onto Welsh Back, hotel on left

This modern, purpose-built hotel has an enviable position on the riverside at the heart of the old city, with the smart Ellipse Restaurant opening directly onto a cobbled

sidewalk in one of Bristol's most fashionable and popular areas. The lobby leads into the open-plan bar and restaurant, all stylishly appointed and comfortably furnished, and there's a mezzanine level, too. The kitchen's modern approach suits the setting, with a sensibly concise menu running from crab and prawn cakes with light blue cheese dressing to roast breast of duck with a roasted fig and Anya potatoes, finishing with chocolate and cherry trifle.

Chef Luke Trott **Owner** Accor Hotel **Times** 11-5/6-9.45 Closed 25 Dec **Prices** Food prices not confirmed for 2010. Please telephone for details. **Wines** 26 bottles over £20, 15 bottles under £20, 11 by glass **Notes** Sunday L, Vegetarian available, Civ Wed 70 **Seats** 65, Pr/dining room 50 **Children** Portions **Parking** NCP

Glass Boat Restaurant

◉ Modern British 🍃

Comforting cooking in a unique riverside setting

☎ 0117 929 0704 📠 0117 927 7006
Welsh Back BS1 4SB
e-mail: bookings@glassboat.co.uk
dir: Moored below Bristol Bridge in the old centre of Bristol

This beautiful 1920s barge of polished walnut, maple and Burmese teak spent its working life along the Severn Estuary before retiring to the waterfront of Bristol's historic docks. Moored close to Bristol Bridge, it has a

Casamia

| BRISTOL | Map 4 ST57 |

Modern Italian, Mediterranean **NEW**

Highly inventive modern cooking in Bristol suburbs

☎ 0117 959 2884
38 High Street, Westbury Village, Westbury-on-Trym BS9 3DZ
e-mail: spiglesias@blueyonder.co.uk
dir: Please telephone for directions

Behind wrought-iron gates on Westbury Village High Street in the northern suburbs of Bristol is a family-run restaurant which has truly embraced generational changes. Mum and dad (Susan and Paco) have run it for years as a successful Italian trattoria, but now sons Jonray and Peter are in the kitchen (mum and dad are front-of-house) and the menu has evolved into something rather special - highly original contemporary cooking

based on their Italian roots with French and Spanish overtones. The restaurant is simply and comfortably decorated, with well-spaced linen-clad tables, and whitewashed walls hung with pictures of Italian scenes, while the service is both professional and cheerful. This is a world of froths, foams and powders, of exciting flavour combinations and eye-catching presentations. Salmon with fennel and lemon is a starter with the wow factor: superb fish, cooked mi-cuit with fennel as confit and purée, some dried mushroom dust, raisins and confit lemon, and if it all sounds very busy, note the dish works a treat. Roast quail – beautifully tender – with celery root, grapes and hazelnut is equally creative, the grapes in the form of a jelly and the nuts wafer-thin, and dark chocolate ice cream comes with a beetroot sorbet in a thrilling finish. The set-lunch menu is excellent value, the carte prices won't scare the horses, and there's a tasting menu if you want to push the boat out, while everything from the amuse-bouche to the excellent coffee demonstrate this is a restaurant on top form.

Chef Peter & Jonray Sanchez-Iglesias **Owner** Paco & Susan Sanchez-Iglesias **Times** 12.30-2.30/7-10 Closed Sun, Mon, L Tue **Prices** Fixed L 2 course £15, Fixed D 3 course £28, Service optional, Groups min 6 service 10% **Wines** 30 bottles over £20, 8 bottles under £20, 20 by glass **Notes** Vegetarian available, Dress restrictions, Smart casual, Tasting menus 6 & 10 course fr £30 **Seats** 45 **Parking** On street

special charm: glass walls all around open up a bustling backdrop for lunch and make for a uniquely romantic setting for candlelit dinner à deux. The kitchen deals in straightforward British and European cooking and doesn't stint on portions. Enticing menus offer good value, especially at lunch. Recommendations include a nicely creamy honey-roasted parsnip soup, followed by roasted salmon fillet with bubble-and-squeak and smoked bacon in a velvety soubise sauce. Finish, perhaps, with white chocolate bread-and-butter pudding.

Chef Neil Davis **Owner** Arne Ringer
Times 12-2.30/6.30-11 Closed 24-26 Dec, 1 Jan, Sun, L Sat **Prices** Fixed L 2 course fr £10, Fixed D 3 course fr £27.95, Starter £5.25-£9.95, Main £9.95-£18.50, Dessert £7.25, Service added but optional 10% **Wines** 100 bottles over £20, 40 bottles under £20, 8 by glass **Notes** Pre-theatre menu 2 or 3 course £12.50-£17.50, Vegetarian available, Civ Wed 120, Air con **Seats** 120, Pr/dining room 40 **Parking** NCP Queen Charlotte St

Goldbrick House

◉◉ Modern British, European

Modern city-centre dining in vibrant atmosphere

☎ 0117 945 1950 📄 0117 945 2660
69 Park St, West End BS1 5PB
e-mail: info@goldbrickhouse.co.uk
web: www.goldbrickhouse.co.uk
dir: M32, follow signs for city centre. Left side of Park St, going up the hill towards museum

This stylish foodie bolt-hole spreads a variety of dining and drinking options around 4 floors in a converted Georgian townhouse and Victorian factory. The first-floor champagne and cocktail bar is the place to sharpen the appetite with a rhubarb caiprissima before moving downstairs to the main restaurant. Here, period features blend well with eye-catching porcelain tile chandeliers in a funky, contemporary setting. The cuisine is tailored to the bustling city-centre ambience with an intelligent Mediterranean-tinged modern European style and a few home-grown British classics for good measure. Expect locally sourced produce and well-matched flavours - perhaps pan-fried squid with the zing of chilli and lime, chorizo and rocket to wake the taste buds, then haunch of venison served with winter greens, pumpkin and a rich jus.

Chef Mark Stavrakakis **Owner** Dougal Templeton, Alex Reilley, Mike Bennett **Times** 12-3/6-10.30 Closed 25-26 Dec, 1 Jan, Sun **Prices** Fixed L 2 course £10, Fixed D 3 course £27.50, Starter £4.50-£11.95, Main £12.95-£25.95, Dessert £3.95-£6.50, Service added but optional 10% **Wines** 36 bottles over £20, 18 bottles under £20, 12 by glass **Notes** Early evening D menu 6-7pm, Vegetarian available, Civ Wed 100 **Seats** 180, Pr/dining room 20 **Children** Portions, Menu **Parking** On street, NCP

Hotel du Vin Bristol

◉ Modern European

Relaxed and friendly atmosphere and French-style bistro cooking

☎ 0117 925 5577 📄 0117 925 1199
The Sugar House, Narrow Lewins Mead BS1 2NU
e-mail: info.bristol@hotelduvin.com
dir: From M4 junct 19, M32 into Bristol. At rdbt take 1st exit & follow main road to next rdbt. Turn onto other side of carriageway, hotel 200yds on right

The Bristol outpost of one of Britain's most innovative hotel groups is located in a converted 18th-century sugar refinery close to the city centre. Expect heavy wooden floors, rustic tables, hop garlands at huge windows, a wine themed décor, and a bustling, informal atmosphere. The brasserie-style menu is well balanced and chock full of local produce, all carefully prepared to create simple, full-flavoured dishes. Choose from 'simple classics' like confit duck leg with pomme purée and Puy lentils; braised pig's cheeks with swede purée and black pudding, or sea bream, spinach, artichokes and crayfish gremolata, finishing with crème brûlée. The wine list is a highlight.

Chef Marcus Lang **Owner** Hotel du Vin Ltd
Times 12-2/6-10 **Prices** Starter £4.95-£7.25, Main £13.50-£17.50, Dessert £5.50-£6.75, Service added but optional 10% **Wines** 400 bottles over £20, 15 bottles under £20, 10 by glass **Notes** Sunday L, Vegetarian available, Civ Wed 70, Air con **Seats** 85, Pr/dining room 72 **Children** Portions, Menu

No. 4 Restaurant & Bar

◉ Modern European

Bright modern hotel dining in smart Clifton

☎ 0117 973 5422 📄 0117 946 7092
Rodney Hotel, 4 Rodney Place, Clifton BS8 4HY
e-mail: info@numberfourrestaurant.co.uk
web: www.numberfourrestaurant.co.uk
dir: M5 junct 19, follow signs across Clifton Bridge. At mini rdbt turn onto Clifton Down Rd. Hotel 150yds on right

Full of original Georgian features, this sensitively refurbished townhouse hotel in Clifton exudes style. Outdoor dining in a sheltered garden will be a lure on sunny days, and the No 4 restaurant has a relaxed, modern feel with lots of designer touches. A Mediterranean approach imbues dishes such as grilled trout with roasted vine tomatoes and a warm rocket salad to start, followed perhaps by lightly fried breast and wing of chicken served with parmesan mash and a fricassée of chorizo, tomato and coriander. Finish with the mega-rich bitter chocolate torte with orange and hazelnut syrup.

Chef David Jones **Owner** Hilary Lawson **Times** 6-10 Closed Xmas, Sun, L all week **Prices** Fixed D 3 course £15.99-£25.99, Starter £3.95-£6.95, Main £11.95-£14.95, Dessert £4.95-£5.95, Service added 10% **Wines** 7 bottles over £20, 15 bottles under £20, 5 by glass **Notes** Vegetarian available **Seats** 35, Pr/dining room 35 **Children** Portions **Parking** 10

The Restaurant@ Cadbury House

◉◉ Modern British 🍃

Clean modern cooking in relaxed, stylish contemporary hotel

☎ 01934 834343 📄 01934 834390
Cadbury House Hotel, Frost Hill, Congresbury BS49 5AD
e-mail: info@cadburyhouse.com
dir: M5 junct 20, left at rdbt, turn onto B133 at next rdbt towards Congresbury. Continue through village of Yatton for 4m, hotel is on left after village

The new kid in town has certainly found his feet very quickly, helped, no doubt, by the head chef's F-word experience after a 4-year stint in the Ramsay empire. The unfussy modern cooking is based on seasonal local ingredients - most of which come from within a 30-mile radius. OK, the fish comes all of seventy miles from Torbay, but it is slippery fresh each day. The stylish restaurant is as modern and relaxed as the cooking and service. Start with a main course in miniature: rump of local Cleve lamb comes with wild garlic mash, roasted cherry tomatoes and shallot rings, followed by tender braised pork belly with ham hock ravioli. And how could you resist a modern take on the knickerbocker glory to finish - a tall glass of broken chocolate brownie, lavender ice cream and fudge sauce.

Chef Richard Wilcox, Mark Veale **Owner** Nick Taplin **Times** 6.30-9.30 Closed L Mon-Sat **Prices** Food prices not confirmed for 2010. Please telephone for details. **Wines** 24 bottles over £20, 12 bottles under £20, 10 by glass **Notes** Sunday L, Vegetarian available, Dress restrictions, Smart casual, Civ Wed 140, Air con **Seats** 80, Pr/dining room 80 **Children** Portions, Menu **Parking** 350

BRISTOL *continued*

riverstation

◉ Modern European

Buzzy, contemporary dining on the waterfront

☎ 0117 914 4434 📄 0117 934 9990
The Grove BS1 4RB
e-mail: relax@riverstation.co.uk
dir: On the dock side in central Bristol

This former river police station occupies a prime spot on the city's regenerated waterfront. A chic, contemporary décor and an abundance of glass, wood and steel sets it apart from its neighbours. Downstairs there's a popular café serving light meals and hot and cold snacks, while upstairs the light, airy restaurant caters to a smarter crowd lured by the buzzy ambience and the confident cooking. The menu offers good quality ingredients, simply prepared and with a strong leaning towards the Mediterranean and France. Try roast quail, pearl barley risotto, hazelnuts, tarragon and fried quails' eggs to start, then tuck into fillet of wild sea bass with wilted spinach, roast salsify, brown shrimp and caper vinaigrette.

Chef Tom Green **Owner** J Payne & P Taylor
Times 12-2.30/6-10.30 Closed Xmas, 1 Jan, D Sun (except BH) **Prices** Fixed L 2 course £12.50, Fixed D 3 course £22-£35, Starter £5-£11, Main £12.50-£18.50, Dessert £4.50-£5.50, Service optional, Groups min 8 service 10% **Wines** 56 bottles over £20, 12 bottles under £20, 10 by glass **Notes** Sunday L, Vegetarian available **Seats** 120, Pr/dining room 26 **Children** Portions, Menu **Parking** Pay & display, meter parking opposite

BUCKINGHAMSHIRE

AMERSHAM	Map 6 SU99

The Artichoke

◉◉ Modern French

Smart high-street restaurant with refined cooking

☎ 01494 726611 📄 01494 726611
9 Market Square, Old Amersham HP7 0DF
e-mail: info@theartichokerestaurant.co.uk
dir: M40 junct 2. 1m from Amersham New Town

The 16th-century house in the market square of old Amersham was forced to close temporarily after a fire spread from a neighbouring building. Of course, every cloud has a silver lining, and for Laurie and Jacqueline Gear the fire has meant a chance to refurbish their restaurant. Laurie also made good use of his forced sabbatical by undertaking stages in various kitchens, including the cutting-edge Noma in Copenhagen. His cooking is based around top-quality produce, much of it local, and follows an intelligently refined modern French path. The new menu sees saddle of Manor Farm hare paired with bitter chocolate in a ravioli and served with celeriac purée and watercress, followed by a fillet of line-caught Cornish sea bass with chick peas, gremolata, clams, roasted Piedmont pepper and aubergine. The creativity continues at dessert stage with a hot blackberry soufflé with Granny Smith sorbet and blackberry sauce.

Chef Laurie Gear **Owner** Laurie & Jacqueline Gear **Times** 12-3/6.30-11 Closed 1 wk Xmas, 1 wk Apr, Sun, Mon **Prices** Fixed L 2 course £18.50, Fixed D 3 course £38, Main £14-£20, Service added but optional 12.5% **Wines** 76 bottles over £20, 5 bottles under £20, 8 by glass **Notes** Tasting menu 7 course, Vegetarian available **Seats** 25 **Children** Portions **Parking** On street, nearby car park

AYLESBURY	Map 11 SP81

Hartwell House Hotel, Restaurant & Spa

◉◉◉ – *see below*

Hartwell House Hotel, Restaurant & Spa

AYLESBURY	Map 11 SP81

British 🏅 🍷

Luxurious dining in outstanding stately home

☎ 01296 747444 📄 01296 747450
Oxford Rd HP17 8NR
e-mail: info@hartwell-house.com
dir: 2m SW of Aylesbury on A418 (Oxford road)

During his exile from the French throne, King Louis XVIII was lucky enough to call Hartwell House 'chez moi' for 5 years from 1809. Make no mistake, this stately Jacobean and Georgian pile is the real deal, bedecked with decorative ceilings and oak panelling and liberally strewn with antiques and paintings throughout. It is, perhaps, no wonder that ownership of the property passed to the National Trust in 2008. But that's not to say that dining here is a stuffy exercise in formality: service is friendly and pleasantly free of solemnity, while the high-ceilinged, neo-classical restaurant makes an elegant backdrop for the talented kitchen's elaborate creations. Technically brilliant cooking goes hand in hand with diligently-sourced seasonal and local ingredients here - some as local as Hartwell's own gardens and orchards. Duck parfait combined with pan-fried duck liver, rhubarb purée and ginger brioche is a typical starter, followed by sea bass and langoustine ravioli with a fennel shellfish sauce and tarragon crushed new potatoes. Dessert might Tango you with orange in three guises - a light-as-air soufflé, orange tiramisù and ice cream.

Chef Daniel Richardson **Owner** Historic House Hotels **Times** 12.30-1.45/7.30-9.45 **Prices** Fixed L 2 course £22.95, Fixed D 3 course £29.95, Tasting menu £65, Starter £8.50-£11, Main £22-£27, Dessert £8-£9, Service included **Wines** 300 bottles over £20, 11 bottles under £20, 10 by glass **Notes** Sunday L, Vegetarian available, Dress restrictions, Smart casual, No jeans, tracksuits/trainers, Civ Wed 60 **Seats** 56, Pr/dining room 30 **Children** Portions **Parking** 50

BLETCHLEY — Map 11 SP83

The Crooked Billet

◉ Modern, Traditional ☺

Popular village pub serious about its food and wine

☎ 01908 373936 ▤ 01908 631979
2 Westbrook End, Newton Longville MK17 0DF
e-mail: john@thebillet.co.uk
dir: M1 junct 14 follow A421 towards Buckingham. Turn left at Bottledump rdbt to Newton Longville. Restaurant on right as you enter the village

The combined talents of John Gilchrist, a former Sommelier of the Year, and his wife (and head chef) Emma, have put this traditional 17th-century thatched and beamed village pub firmly on the local culinary map. There may be original beams and inglenook fireplaces in the refurbished bar and restaurant but the real attraction is the food and wine. Simple British cooking using quality local seasonal ingredients ranges from traditional pub dishes and sandwiches at lunchtime to more innovative evening meals, perhaps roast quail with wild mushroom risotto, halibut with champagne and lemon velouté sauce, and banana and chocolate parfait. The cheeseboard is particularly noteworthy, as is the large selection of wines by the glass.

Chef Emma Gilchrist **Owner** John & Emma Gilchrist
Times 12.30-2.30/7-10 Closed 25 Dec, L Mon, D Sun
Prices Fixed L 2 course £12-£16, Fixed D 3 course £19-£27, Starter £4.50-£9, Main £10-£20, Dessert £5-£7, Service optional, Groups min 6 service 12% **Wines** 250 bottles over £20, 20 bottles under £20, 30 by glass **Notes** Tasting Menu 8 course, Sunday L, Vegetarian available **Seats** 70, Pr/dining room 16 **Children** Portions **Parking** 30

BUCKINGHAM — Map 11 SP63

Villiers Hotel Restaurant & Bar

◉◉ Modern British

Modern brasserie cooking in stylish old coaching inn

☎ 01280 822444 ▤ 01280 822113
3 Castle St MK18 1BS
e-mail: reservations@villiershotels.com
web: www.villiers-hotel.co.uk
dir: Town centre - Castle Street is to the right of Town Hall near main square

A hotel and coaching inn for 450 years, the Villiers is designed around the cobbled courtyard which once stabled 150 horses. With an atmospheric bar for drinks before dinner, the restaurant has a contemporary look and feel, with marble floors and two fish tanks which are seemingly popular with guests of all ages. The simple modern cooking to match provides some classics with a few twists along the way: pan-fried scallops with black pudding, cauliflower purée and pea shoots, followed, perhaps, by roasted fillet of sea bream with brandade potatoes, garden greens and horseradish sauce. Finish with warm pear frangipane tart and pear cider sorbet. A selection of pasta dishes are available as both starters and mains.

Chef Paul Stopps **Owner** Oxfordshire Hotels Ltd
Times 12-2.30/6-9.30 **Prices** Fixed L 2 course £10-£14.95, Fixed D 3 course £18.95-£23.95, Starter £4.25-£6.95, Main £8.95-£17.50, Dessert £5.95-£7.95, Service optional, Groups min 6 service 10% **Notes** Sunday L, Vegetarian available, Civ Wed 150, Air con **Seats** 70, Pr/dining room 150 **Children** Portions **Parking** 52

BURNHAM — Map 6 SU98

Gray's Restaurant

◉ British, European

Elegant woodland setting for French-influenced classic cuisine

☎ 0844 736 8603 & 01628 600150 ▤ 01628 603994
Burnham Beeches Hotel, Burnham Beeches, Grove Rd SL1 8DP
e-mail: burnhambeeches@corushotels.com
web: www.corushotels.com
dir: off A355, via Farnham Royal rdbt

Burnham Beeches is an elegant Georgian mansion set in 10 acres of mature gardens on the fringes of ancient woodland, originally built as a hunting lodge for Windsor Park and where poet Thomas Gray wrote his elegy. Gray's Restaurant, with its oak-panelled walls and sash windows, affords lovely views and provides attentive service from a courteous team. A typical selection of dishes from the seasonal British menu with French influences might be smoked salmon tartar with a light horseradish cream mousse to start, followed by roast guinea fowl on celeriac rösti with tomato and parsley jus. To finish, perhaps apple tarte Tatin with toffee and maple sauce and caramel ice cream, or a plate of British cheeses.

Chef John Dickson **Owner** Corus Hotels
Times 12-2/7-9.30 **Prices** Fixed L 2 course fr £18, Fixed D 3 course £26-£42, Starter £7-£10, Main £15-£30, Dessert £7-£10 **Wines** 19 bottles over £20, 5 bottles under £20, 6 by glass **Notes** Sunday L, Vegetarian available, Dress restrictions, Smart casual, Civ Wed 120 **Seats** 70, Pr/dining room 120 **Children** Portions, Menu **Parking** 150

The Grovefield House Hotel

◉◉ Traditional Mediterranean

Refurbished country-house hotel with ambitious cooking

☎ 01628 603131 ▤ 01628 668078
Taplow Common Rd SL1 8LP
e-mail: gm.grovefield@classiclodges.co.uk
dir: From M4 left on A4 towards Maidenhead. Next rdbt turn right under railway bridge. Straight over mini rdbt, garage on right. Continue for 1.5m, hotel on right

Once the country retreat of John Fuller of the Fuller brewing family, Grovefield House has recently undergone

continued

BURNHAM *continued*

an all-encompassing £2 million refurbishment. The hotel, set in 7 acres of grounds and with some parts dating from the Edwardian era, has been brought fully into the 21st century but retains a classic English style. Hamilton's Restaurant is a light and airy space with well-appointed white-clothed tables, and views over the well-manicured gardens. Service comes from a friendly, well-trained team, and the menu is modern British and based around locally sourced, seasonal produce. A light and fresh twice-baked Oxford Blue soufflé comes with poached pears as a starter, while main-course Aylesbury duck is cooked 2 ways (confit leg and duck breast) and served with fondant potato, spring greens and a sloe gin sauce. A well-made iced cherry parfait rounds things off nicely

Chef Imad Nazzak **Owner** Classic Lodges Ltd **Times** 12-2.30/7-9.30 Closed L Sat **Prices** Fixed L 2 course £26, Fixed D 3 course £35, Service optional **Wines** 37 bottles over £20, 28 bottles under £20, 4 by glass **Notes** Sunday L, Vegetarian available, Dress restrictions, No T-shirts, trainers, Civ Wed 150 **Seats** 60, Pr/dining room 50 **Children** Portions, Menu **Parking** 150

The Bedford Arms Hotel

 Modern International

Pastoral charm in the Chilterns

☎ 01923 283301 📠 01923 284825
WD3 6EQ
e-mail: contact@bedfordarms.co.uk
dir: M25 junct 18/A404 towards Amersham, after 2m turn right & follow signs for hotel

The early Victorian redbrick inn in the Chilterns is full of pastoral charm. Despite being panelled in oak, the dining room maintains an air of homeliness, with smartly laid tables turned out in their best. Fixed-price menus offer plenty of choice, with a mix-and-match culinary approach in tune with the times. Angus beef tartare glazed in ginger and soy, dressed with wasabi cream, is one way to begin, and might be succeeded by turbot with mussels, tomato and capers, or rack of lamb with a tian of red pepper and feta. Finish with fig tarte Tatin served with lavender ice cream and a hazelnut tuile.

Chef Christopher Cloonan **Owner** Arthur & Celia Rickett **Times** 12-2.30/7-9.30 Closed 26 Dec-5 Jan **Prices** Fixed D 3 course £25, Service optional **Wines** 21 bottles over £20, 20 bottles under £20, 10 by glass **Notes** Sunday L, Vegetarian available, Civ Wed 80 **Seats** 55, Pr/dining room 24 **Children** Portions **Parking** 60

Annie Baileys

 Modern British

Ever-popular rural restaurant with classic brasserie-style dishes

☎ 01494 865625 📠 01494 866406
Chesham Rd, Hyde End HP16 0QT
e-mail: david@anniebaileys.com
dir: Off A413 at Great Missenden. On B485 towards Chesham

The Victorian landlady Annie Bailey must have been quite a character as her name still graces this popular country restaurant a century and a half later. Inside it's a relaxed and friendly place with a blend of country-cottage cosiness and sunny Mediterranean colours, great for dining and drinking year-round - by the warm glow of a fire in winter, or in a delightful secluded sun-trap courtyard in summer. The food also hankers for Mediterranean climes, with a simple brasserie-style menu of old favourites - the risotto of the day might feature wild mushrooms, followed by duck confit and garlic mash, or lemon sole and crab linguine with shallot and dill sauce.

Chef Malcolm Nolan **Owner** Open All Hours (UK) Ltd **Times** 12-2.30/7-9.30 Closed D Sun **Prices** Fixed L 2 course £10-£12.50, Fixed D 3 course £15-£22.95, Starter £4.50-£7.50, Main £9.95-£16.95, Dessert £4.50-£5.95, Service optional **Wines** 10 bottles over £20, 20 bottles under £20, 16 by glass **Notes** Sunday L, Vegetarian available **Seats** 65, Pr/dining room 34 **Children** Portions **Parking** 40

Nags Head Inn

 Traditional British, French NEW

Charming pub offering simple, unfussy food

☎ 01494 862200 & 862945 📠 01442 862685
London Rd HP16 0DG
e-mail: goodfood@nagsheadbucks.com
dir: North from Amersham on A413 sign posted Great Missenden, left at Chiltern Hospital on to London Road (1m south of Great Missenden)

Located in the valley of the River Misbourne in the Chiltern Hills, this 15th-century pub has had many famous visitors over the years, including various Prime Ministers stopping off on their journeys to Chequers.

Children's author Roald Dahl was a local and many of his prints adorn the walls of this recently refurbished pub, which retains its original oak beams and large inglenook fireplace as well as a new bar and stylish new furnishings. The food is simple but well done, with a good use of local and seasonal produce. A starter of pan-fried king scallops wrapped in Parma ham with parsnip purée could be followed by confit leg of Barbary duck served with a sweet-and-sour orange jus.

Chef Alan Bell, Howard Gale & Claude Paillet **Owner** Alvin, Adam & Sally Michaels **Times** 12-2.30/6-9.30 Closed 25 Dec, D Sun & 31 Dec **Prices** Starter £4.95-£12.95, Main £12.95-£22.50, Dessert £4.95-£7.50, Service optional, Groups min 6 service 10% **Wines** 80 bottles over £20, 28 bottles under £20, 12 by glass **Notes** Sunday L, Vegetarian available, Dress restrictions, Smart casual **Seats** 60 **Children** Portions **Parking** 35

Green Dragon

 Modern, Traditional

Refined rustic food in a picturesque village setting

☎ 01844 291403
8 Churchway HP17 8AA
e-mail: enquiries@greendragonhaddenham.co.uk
web: www.greendragonhaddenham.co.uk
dir: From M40 take A329 towards Thame, then A418. Turn 1st right after entering Haddenham

A traditional pub in a picture-postcard village, The Green Dragon dates back to the 17th-century. It maintains the best period elements whilst meeting 21st-century expectations. Wooden tables are laid as you place your order, and the central bar area is the main focus of the dining room. There are plenty of menu options and a flexibility about the ordering process; the à la carte is for the more adventurous, whilst there is lots for traditionalists and a regularly-changing blackboard menu. Start with one of the kitchen's signature dishes - smoked haddock Scotch egg with wilted chive butter - then perhaps a classic suet pudding (venison and wild mushrooms), served with creamed potatoes and curly kale. Sticky toffee pudding and praline ice cream covers all bases for dessert.

Green Dragon

Chef Derek Muircroft **Owner** Oak Tree Inns Limited
Times 12-2.30/6.30-9.30 Closed 26 Dec **Prices** Fixed D 3
course fr £13.95, Starter £7-£9, Main £8.50-£16.95,
Dessert £6-£8, Service optional **Wines** 7 bottles over £20,
16 bottles under £20, 15 by glass **Notes** Sunday L,
Vegetarian available **Seats** 50 **Children** Portions
Parking 20

IVINGHOE — Map 11 SP91

The King's Head

🌐 Modern British, French **V**

**Charming inn with bags of character and traditional
dining**

☎ 01296 668388   📠 01296 668107
Station Rd LU7 9EB
e-mail: info@kingsheadivinghoe.co.uk
web: www.kingsheadivinghoe.co.uk
dir: From M25 junct 20 take A41 past Tring. Turn right
onto B488 (Ivinghoe), hotel at junct with B489

The 17th-century King's Head is the quintessential
English village inn, festooned with ivy outside, and
packed inside with period character thanks to ancient
beams, huge inglenooks and a sprinkling of antiques.
Candlelight sets the scene for dinner, nudging up the
romance factor, and, for a sense of occasion, roasted
Aylesbury duckling is carved at the table. Classic and
modern, French and English influences rub shoulders on
a well-balanced menu. Starters might deliver seared
scallops with a herb salad, deep-fried capers and sultana
vinaigrette, then a pavé of cod with bacon and cabbage,
smoked haddock and parsley brandade and cep velouté is
a typical main course. Crêpes Suzette flambéed at the
table finish the meal with a theatrical flourish.

Chef Jonathan O'Keeffe **Owner** G.A.P.J. Ltd
Times 12-3/7-10 Closed 27-30 Dec, D Sun **Prices** Fixed L
2 course £19, Starter £8-£13, Main £18-£28, Dessert £6,
Service added but optional 12.5% **Wines** 80 bottles over

£20, 8 bottles under £20, 4 by glass **Notes** Sunday L,
Vegetarian menu, Dress restrictions, No jeans, trainers or
shorts, Air con **Seats** 55, Pr/dining room 40
Children Portions **Parking** 20, On street

LONG CRENDON — Map 5 SP60

The Angel Restaurant

🌐 Modern Mediterranean, Pacific Rim 🍴 ☕

Gastro-pub with an affable atmosphere

☎ 01844 208268   📠 01844 202497
47 Bicester Rd HP18 9EE
e-mail: angelrestaurant@aol.com
dir: M40 junct 7, beside B4011, 2m NW of Thame

A wattle-and-daub wall, exposed timbers and inglenook
are ample testament to the 17th-century pedigree of this
welcoming gastro-pub in a postcard-pretty village.
Choose between a spacious conservatory, cosy bar and a
heated sun terrace for alfresco dining. A daily delivery of
fish and seafood gives the chef a chance to show off his
creativity on a menu that takes British classics and gives
them a Mediterranean or Pacific Rim twist. A starter of
roast quail comes wrapped in pancetta atop flavoursome
black pudding and a mustard-dressed salad, while mains
might be a mildly curried slab of cod with spinach and
potato saag aloo. Look out for interesting wines by the
glass on the blackboard.

Chef Trevor Bosch **Owner** Trevor & Annie Bosch
Times 12-3/7-10 Closed D Sun **Prices** Fixed L 2 course
£14, Fixed D 3 course £24.95, Starter £4.95-£8.25, Main
£14.95-£28.75, Dessert £4.50, Service optional, Groups
min 8 service 10% **Wines** 58 bottles over £20, 29 bottles
under £20, 12 by glass **Notes** Tasting menu 5 course
Mon-Fri, Sunday L, Vegetarian available, Air con
Seats 75, Pr/dining room 14 **Children** Portions
Parking 30

MARLOW — Map 5 SU88

Aubergine at the Compleat Angler

🌐🌐🌐 — *see page 68*

Bowaters

🌐🌐 Modern British

**Modern British food served in a charming Thames-side
setting**

☎ 0844 879 9128 & 01628 484444   📠 01628 486388
**Macdonald The Compleat Angler, Marlow Bridge
SL7 1RG**
e-mail: compleatangler@macdonald-hotels.co.uk
dir: M4 junct 8/9 or M40 junct 4. A404 to rdbt, take
Bisham exit, 1m to Marlow Bridge, hotel on right

Picture a balmy summer's evening on a lawn by the side
of the River Thames, glowing candles reflected in the lazy
water, the distant roar of the weir at Marlow - that's the
quintessentially English scene at the handsome Georgian
Compleat Angler hotel. The historic Bowaters restaurant
is a suave affair with its comfortable pastel shades and

high-backed chairs pulling together contemporary and
classic strands - and you get those river views come rain
or shine. The kitchen's modern British style delivers
clearly-defined flavours thanks to skilful technique;
menus change with the seasons, offering simple
combinations and good-looking dishes, as in a starter of
Loch Fyne smoked haddock with squid ink ravioli and
creamed leeks, or a main course of pan-fried wild sea
bass with fondant potatoes, girolles and red wine sauce.
Bowaters restaurant is one of a brace of dining options
here, the other being Aubergine (see entry).

Chef David Smith **Owner** Macdonald Hotels
Times 12.30-2/7-10 **Prices** Fixed L 2 course £15-£21,
Fixed D 3 course £35, Service added but optional 12.5%
Wines 115 bottles over £20, 5 bottles under £20, 13 by
glass **Notes** Sunday L, Vegetarian available, Civ Wed 100
Seats 90, Pr/dining room 40 **Children** Portions, Menu
Parking 100

The Hand & Flowers

🌐🌐🌐 — *see page 66*

Oak Room at Danesfield House

🌐🌐🌐🌐 — *see page 67*

The Vanilla Pod

🌐🌐 Modern British, French **V**

Historic house offering imaginative modern cuisine

☎ 01628 898101   📠 01628 898108
31 West St SL7 2LS
e-mail: contact@thevanillapod.co.uk
dir: From M4 junct 8/9 or M40 junct 4 take A404, A4155
to Marlow. From Henley take A4155

Discreetly tucked away in an elegant townhouse, once
owned by the poet and critic TS Eliot, this small,
unassuming building has been transformed into a stylish
dining venue. Rich colours and clean lines create a
contemporary and luxurious feel, which complement the
beamed walls and ceiling, and the atmosphere is warm
and welcoming, with polite, professional and
knowledgeable service. Modern cooking combines British
style and French influences, with a deft touch and well-
judged ingredients, in dishes such as terrine of cured
salmon with vanilla and lime pickled cucumber, followed
by rump of lamb with red wine and garlic purée, or roast
cod with Bourbon vanilla infused white beans, and spiced
bread ice cream and fig tart for pudding.

Chef Michael Macdonald **Owner** Michael & Stephanie
Macdonald **Times** 12-2.30/7-11 Closed 24 Dec-3 Jan, 25
May-3 Jun, 24 Aug-2 Sep, Sun-Mon **Prices** Fixed L 2
course £15.50, Fixed D 3 course £40, Tasting menu £50,
Service optional **Wines** 102 bottles over £20, 6 bottles
under £20, 15 by glass **Notes** ALC £40, Tasting menu 8
course, Vegetarian menu, Dress restrictions, Smart
casual, Air con **Seats** 28, Pr/dining room 8 **Parking** On
West Street

The Hand & Flowers

British, European

Classy cooking in stylish yet unpretentious pub

☎ 01628 482277   📄 01628 401913
126 West St SL7 2BP
e-mail: theoffice@thehandandflowers.co.uk
web: www.thehandandflowers.co.uk
dir: M40 junct 4/M4 junct 8/9 follow A404 to Marlow

Tom and Beth Kerridge's whitewashed pub on the outskirts of Marlow could be considered the model modern restaurant. From its informal and unpretentious appearance (flagstone floors, beams and exposed stone walls meet neutral colours, leather banquettes and cloth-less, smartly-set tables) and its intelligently straightforward food, The Hand & Flowers hits the spot with consistency. The informed and enthusiastic service also helps to set the tone of the place. Tom's CV reveals a past spent working in some serious kitchens, including The Capital and Adlard's in Norwich, and it is clear with what arrives on the plate that he has both considerable technical skill and the confidence to keep things relatively simple. The food takes a broadly modern British direction, with classical French cooking at the root of much of it, and the seasonally-changing menu is based around first-class produce. Somerset smoked eel is partnered with beetroot Royale and caper salad in a starter of well-judged and deftly handled flavours, followed by a main course such as saddle of Thames Valley lamb with bacon, pearl barley and laverbread. Flavour is to the fore once again with desserts, so thyme pannacotta is enriched with heather honey, honeycomb and whisky, and apple tart comes with caramel ice cream. There's a three-dish bar menu available at lunchtime, and the patio is an option in the milder months.

Chef Tom Kerridge **Owner** Tom & Beth Kerridge **Times** 12-2.30/6.30-9.30 Closed 24-26 Dec, L 31 Dec, D 1 Jan **Prices** Starter £6.50-£9.50, Main £15.50-£19.50, Dessert £7.50, Service optional, Groups min 6 service 10% **Wines** 63 bottles over £20, 3 bottles under £20, 10 by glass **Notes** Vegetarian available **Seats** 50 **Children** Portions **Parking** 30

Oak Room at Danesfield House

Modern European 🍷 NOTABLE WINE LIST

Grand Chiltern pile with outstanding cooking

☎ 01628 891010   🖷 01628 890408
Henley Rd SL7 2EY
e-mail: reservations@danesfieldhouse.co.uk
web: www.danesfieldhouse.co.uk
dir: M4 junct 4/A404 to Marlow. Follow signs to Medmenham and Henley. Hotel is 3m outside Marlow

With its broad, whitewashed façade, crenellated roofline and twin towers, Danesfield looks like a particularly opulent Victorian seaside hotel. In fact, it's the Thames that it overlooks in landlocked Buckinghamshire, with further vistas of the Chilterns beyond. High, oak-beamed ceilings and magisterial fireplaces abound within, and in the Oak Room (where the panelling is limed white), the house boasts one of the most outstanding restaurants of the Home Counties. Service is delivered by a highly skilled team who are justly proud of their environment, and the sizeable kitchen brigade is testament to the absolute seriousness of the culinary intentions. The style of cooking is unmistakably now, with all the jellies, foams, purées and sorbets in unexpected places we have come to anticipate, but the depth and clarity of flavour on show here, the clever juxtapositions and contrasts, are something else. Smoked haddock risotto achieves astonishing richness and profundity, and is matched with a pungent but not oversweet beetroot sorbet and smoothly fiery horseradish velouté. Main course might be sautéed sweetbreads of Limousin veal, gently browned and buttery, accompanied by cauliflower purée and perfectly judged anchovy tortellini, which add their forthrightly savoury note without unbalancing the dish. A fish dish to conjure with might be poached brill fillet, served with caraway-spiked creamed cabbage, bacon gnocchi scented with the same spice, onion purée and a foaming sauce flavoured with the earthiness of yeast. Textural counterpoints are the hallmark of desserts such as praline mousse with hazelnut cake, yogurt and tarragon sorbet, Pernod cream and a crunchy tuile. With stunning amuse-bouche (a combination of pink champagne jelly and granita with passionfruit froth fascinatingly mimics the effervescence of champagne itself) and fruity pre-desserts, as well as excellent breads, the whole package is delivered, along with an unblemished degree of customer satisfaction.

Chef Adam Simmonds
Times 12-2/7-9.30 Closed 16 Aug-1Sep, 20 Dec-5 Jan, BHs, Sun-Mon, L Tue
Prices Fixed L 2 course £25, Tasting menu £75, Service added but optional

12.5% **Wines** 400 bottles over £20, 20 by glass **Notes** ALC 3 course £55, Sunday L, Dress restrictions, Smart casual, Civ Wed 100 **Seats** 30, Pr/dining room 14 **Children** Portions **Parking** 100

Aubergine at the Compleat Angler

MARLOW Map 5 SU88

Modern French

Impressive cooking in fine-dining restaurant overlooking the Thames

☎ 0844 879 9128 & 01628 484444 📠 01628 486388
Macdonald Compleat Angler, Marlow Bridge SL7 1RG
e-mail: aubergineca@londonfinedininggroup.com
web: www.auberginemarlow.com
dir: M4 junct 8/9 or M40 junct 4. A404 to rdbt, take Bisham exit, 1m to Marlow Bridge, hotel on right

The Macdonald Compleat Angler has landed a big fish in its association with Aubergine in Chelsea. The modern French style of the London restaurant where Gordon Ramsay made his name has arrived at this idyllic spot overlooking Marlow weir on the River Thames. Aubergine is very much the theme in the dining room with the image of the fruit appearing on plates and cutlery, and the colour adding richness to the space. It is a stylish, contemporary room, the scene completed by the smartly turned out waiting staff who deliver polished and formal service. High quality seasonal produce passes through the kitchen and is handled with precision and skill. Pithivier of quail is immaculately constructed, glazed to a beautiful golden colour, and is served with spinach, girolles and a Madeira jus as a starter. Main-course fillet of John Dory is perfectly cooked (good crisp skin) with a fricassée of girolles and watercress, and clementine soufflé with dark chocolate sauce rises to the occasion for dessert. Incidentals such as bread, amuse-bouche and pre-dessert show this is a serious restaurant firing on all cylinders.

Chef Miles Nixon **Owner** London Fine Dining Group **Times** 12-3/7-11.30 Closed Mon, D Sun **Prices** Fixed L 3 course fr £28.50, Fixed D 3 course fr £55, Service added but optional 12.5% **Wines** 50+ bottles over £20, 4 bottles under £20, 6 by glass **Notes** Gourmand menu 7 course from £77, Sunday L, Vegetarian available, Dress restrictions, Smart casual, Air con Seats 49, Pr/dining room 120 **Children** Portions **Parking** 100

Waldo's Restaurant, Cliveden

Rosettes not confirmed at time of going to press

TAPLOW Map 6 SU98

Modern British V 🏛

Creative kitchen team at historic venue

☎ 01628 668561 📠 01628 661837
Cliveden Estate SL6 0JF
e-mail: reservations@clivedenhouse.co.uk
dir: M4 junct 7, A4 towards Maidenhead for 1.5m, onto B476 towards Taplow, 2.5m, hotel on left

Cliveden is a stately home that positively defies adjectival description. It's a grand house, certainly, handsomely Italianate in style, built of impressive proportions; suffice to say it would blow the socks off any visiting American tourist. It is a jewel in the National Trust crown. The hotel's flagship restaurant is Waldo's, named after the sculptor of the famous *Fountain of Love* in the sweeping driveway, and as we go to press a new chef has taken command of the kitchen. Chris Horridge joins from The Bath Priory (in the eponymous city) and he's arrived with his brigade of chefs and a toque full of ambition and ground-breaking ideas. Maintaining the nutritional content of the ingredients is a core aim of the kitchen and time is made for investigating new techniques. The format is two 10-course tasting menus (although the kitchen is flexible enough to offer a simpler four courses if that suits the customer), which come as 'With' or 'Without' - the latter delivering the full recommended daily amounts of vitamins and minerals with virtually no sugar, gluten or dairy produce; the former is a little heavier but still light by today's standards. Expect clean flavours, tip-top produce, exciting combinations and dishes that are a delight to eat: scallops poached in coconut oil with whipped shallot and capers, then red mullet, kohlrabi and a spot of orange, and chocolate and carrot seed ice with carrot cake and peanut infusion to finish.

Chef Chris Horridge **Owner** von Essen Hotels **Times** 7-9.30 Closed Xmas, New Year, 2 wks Aug, Sun-Mon, L all week **Prices** Food prices not confirmed for 2010. Please telephone for details. **Wines** All bottles over £20, 10 by glass **Notes** Vegetarian menu, Dress restrictions, Jacket & tie, Civ Wed 120, Air con **Seats** 28, Pr/dining room 12 **Parking** 60

Berry's at Taplow House Hotel

◎◎ Modern British 🕯️

Architectural, horticultural and culinary interest combined

☎ 01628 670056 📠 01628 783985
Berry Hill SL6 0DA
e-mail: reception@taplowhouse.com
dir: M4 junct 7 towards Maidenhead, at lights follow signs to Berry Hill

An intriguing-looking mansion on the Berks-Bucks border, Taplow House is a dramatically contrasting mix of white- and red-brick façades with crenellations. The original house that stood here was built in the Elizabethan era, but this is the Georgian phoenix that rose from the ashes of a 17th-century fire. It's all rather splendid, from a garden that features Europe's tallest tulip trees, to the high-windowed dining room with its swagged curtains and chandelier. Here, a gentle style of country-house cooking is offered, with ingredients such as foie gras (in a terrine with chicken) or brandy (in the sauce for a crab soufflé) adding richness and depth. Mains might include roast monkfish with squid-ink risotto and desserts banana and pistachio parfait and caramel sauce.

Chef Neil Dore **Owner** Taplow House Hotel Ltd
Times 12-2/7-9.30 Closed L Sat **Prices** Fixed L 2 course £15, Fixed D 3 course £25, Service added but optional 12.5% **Wines** 36 bottles over £20, 8 bottles under £20, 10 by glass **Notes** Sunday L, Vegetarian available, Dress restrictions, Smart casual, Civ Wed 90, Air con **Seats** 40, Pr/dining room 90 **Children** Portions, Menu **Parking** 100

The Terrace Dining Room, Cliveden

◎◎ Mediterranean, French

Fine dining in famous country house

☎ 01628 668561 📠 01628 661837
Cliveden Estate SL6 0JF
e-mail: reservations@clivedenhouse.co.uk
dir: M4 junct 7, A4 towards Maidenhead for 1.5m, onto B476 towards Taplow, 2.5m, hotel on left

There will always be a sense of occasion when you dine in one of England's finest country houses, spiked with a whiff of distant scandal for anyone old enough to remember the Profumo affair. The sun-washed Terrace Dining Room looks through 6 French windows over a classical parterre garden to the distant Thames, while Waterford chandeliers, wood panelling and oil paintings combine in an elegant setting. The kitchen delivers what you'd expect of a top-ranking country house: imaginative interpretations of classic French cuisine, with correctly formal service to match. Starters might combine a smoked mackerel pot with an unusual chilled organic poached egg, pancetta and walnut salad. Next up, a spot-on rack of lamb comes with gratin dauphinoise and root vegetables. The hotel is also home to Waldo's (see entry).

Times 12-2.30/7-9.30

Waldo's Restaurant, Cliveden
— see opposite

The Plough Wavendon

◎◎ Modern French NEW 📖

Creative European cooking in stylish setting

☎ 01908 587576
72 Walton Rd MK17 8LW
e-mail: info@theploughwavendon.com
web: www.theploughwavendon.com
dir: M1 junct 13, 7m from central Milton Keynes

The Plough Wavendon

This 16th-century former coaching inn and bake house is these days a smart and contemporary restaurant, the setting for some serious cooking using good local ingredients. The interior is light and open, tastefully decorated in neutral tones with high-backed chairs and dark-wood tables, while outside is an impressively large terrace for alfresco dining. The food is as well presented as the restaurant, with plenty of modern ideas and sound technical skill on display. Diver-caught scallops are cooked beautifully and served with Scottish black pudding, beetroot reduction and cauliflower purée in an enjoyable starter, and English rose veal comes in a classic combination with dauphinoise potatoes, vegetable panaché and red wine jus. Cheeses are British and dessert comes with a wine recommendation - Clos Dady Sauternes, 2003, for the crème brûlée, for example.

Chef Grant Hawthorne **Owner** Jon Todd
Times 12-2.30/5.30-10.30 Closed 1 Jan, Mon, L 26 Dec, D 25 Dec **Prices** Fixed L 2 course £21-£24, Fixed D 3 course £26-£29, Starter £7-£11, Main £16-£29, Dessert £7-£11, Service optional, Groups min 6 service 10% **Wines** 290 bottles over £20, 3 bottles under £20, 15 by glass **Notes** Tasting menu 7-9 course, Pre-theatre menu, Sunday L, Vegetarian available, Dress restrictions, Smart casual **Seats** 48 **Children** Portions **Parking** 30

See advert below

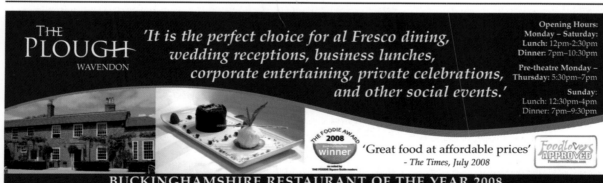

WOOBURN COMMON
Map 6 SU98

Chequers Inn

◉ British, French

High comfort values in both furnishings and food

☎ 01628 529575 📠 01628 850124
Kiln Ln HP10 0JQ
e-mail: info@chequers-inn.com
dir: M40 junct 2, A40 through Beaconsfield Old Town
towards High Wycombe. 2m from town left into Broad Ln.
Inn 2.5m on left

A brick-built 17th-century inn featuring dangerously
comfy sofas in the flagstoned bar, and a smartly attired
restaurant with swagged drapes and good pictures,
overlooking a pretty patio. Expect some refined Anglo-
French cooking. Star of the show at dinner might be
chargrilled rib-eye with Savoy cabbage and bacon,
truffled pomme purée and red wine jus, or sea bass with
crushed potatoes and chorizo, preceded perhaps by
grilled tiger prawns with celeriac remoulade and crayfish,
and rounded off with something like prune and almond
tart with clotted cream. A fixed-price specials menu
represents a simpler route.

Chef Tony Sharman **Owner** PJ Roehrig
Times 12-2.30/7-9.30 Closed D 25 Dec, 1 Jan
Prices Fixed L 2 course £13.95-£21.95, Fixed D 3 course
£23.95-£27.95, Starter £4.75-£9.75, Main £10.95-
£18.95, Dessert £5.95-£6.95, Service optional **Wines** 36
bottles over £20, 25 bottles under £20, 11 by glass
Notes Sunday L, Vegetarian available **Seats** 60, Pr/dining
room 60 **Children** Portions **Parking** 50

CAMBRIDGESHIRE

BABRAHAM
Map 12 TL55

The George Inn

◉ Modern British, International

**Georgian coaching inn with simple but effective
cooking**

☎ 01223 833800
High St CB22 3AG
e-mail: stevelythall@btinternet.com
web: www.georgeinn-babraham.co.uk
dir: At junct of A11 & A1307 take A1307 towards
Cambridge. Turn left after 200mtrs

Built as a coaching inn during the Georgian era to serve
travellers on the London to Norwich route, the sensitively
restored George can be found in a pretty village about 3
miles south of Cambridge. A pair of dining-rooms, one of
which opens out on to a terrace in summer, are decorated
in understated contemporary style. Simple but effective
dishes are the order of the day, from seafood platters
with lime and wasabi mayonnaise to monkfish tail
modishly wrapped in pancetta, served with sauté
potatoes, roasted wild garlic and thyme cream sauce.
Finish with rhubarb and ginger brûlée, which comes with
oven-fresh oatmeal flapjacks.

Chef Ian Kyle **Owner** S L Lythall **Times** 11.30-3/5.30-11
Closed D Sun (winter) **Prices** Fixed L 2 course £13.95,
Fixed D 3 course £17.95, Starter £5.50-£7.25, Main
£12.95-£18.95, Dessert £4.95-£6.20, Service optional,
Groups min 10 service 10% **Wines** 17 bottles over £20,
21 bottles under £20, 8 by glass **Notes** Sunday L,
Vegetarian available, Civ Wed 40 **Seats** 115, Pr/dining
room 40 **Children** Portions, Menu **Parking** 40

CAMBOURNE
Map 12 TL35

The Cambridge Belfry

◉◉ Modern

Modern British cuisine in a setting to match

☎ 01954 714995
Back St CB3 6BW
e-mail: cambridge@marstonhotels.com
dir: Telephone for directions

Sitting at the gateway to Cambourne Business Park and
village, this modern hotel boasts great views over a large
lake. The aptly named Bridge Restaurant is a
contemporary space with sleek lines, polished tiles, and
dramatic splashes of deep red. Expect a modern British
menu with a few international flavours. Try the crispy
Oriental duck pancake with sweet chilli sauce to start,
before main-course slow-roasted loin of lamb served with
sweet potato dauphinoise and roasted root vegetables, or
luxury fish pie with salmon, smoked haddock and tiger
prawns accompanied by a mixed salad and slices of
ciabatta. Save room for the sticky toffee pudding with
butterscotch sauce. Service is relaxed but attentive.

Times 12.30-2.30/7.30-9 Closed L Sat

CAMBRIDGE
Map 12 TL45

Best Western Cambridge Quy Mill Hotel

◉ Modern European

**Watermill and miller's house serving traditional dishes
with a modern twist**

☎ 01223 293383 📠 01223 293770
Newmarket Rd, Stow Cum Quy CB5 9AG
e-mail: cambridgequy@bestwestern.co.uk
dir: exit A14 at junct 35, E of Cambridge, onto B1102 for
50yds. Entrance opposite church

This 19th-century former watermill and miller's house,
set in 11 acres of riverside meadowland, has been
transformed into a stylish hotel. The main building is

Grade II listed and is set in open countryside on the
outskirts of Cambridge. The restaurant has been created
from the dining room, kitchen and buttery of the old
miller's house, while the private dining room retains the
waterwheel behind glass. More casual dining is available
in the lounge, bars, conservatory and, in summer, outside
on the terrace. The menu features traditional dishes
prepared with good-quality ingredients and presented in
a modern context. Try slow-roasted belly of pork,
braised apricots and red cabbage, black pudding potato mash
and Calvados cream sauce, followed by caramelised
lemon tart with raspberry and cassis compôte and clotted
cream.

Chef Josh Fox **Owner** David Munro **Times** 12-2.30/7-9.45
Closed 24-31 Dec **Prices** Fixed L 2 course £18, Fixed D 3
course £19, Starter £5-£6.50, Main £12.95-£18.95,
Dessert £5-£6.50, Service optional, Groups min 8 service
10% **Wines** 23 bottles over £20, 11 bottles under £20, 11
by glass **Notes** Sunday L, Vegetarian available, Dress
restrictions, Smart dress/smart casual - no shorts (men),
Civ Wed 80 **Seats** 48, Pr/dining room 80
Children Portions, Menu **Parking** 90

Graffiti at Hotel Felix

◉◉ Modern British

**Vibrant modern brasserie dining in a boutique Victorian
mansion**

☎ 01223 277977 📠 01223 277973
Whitehouse Ln CB3 0LX
e-mail: help@hotelfelix.co.uk
web: www.hotelfelix.co.uk
dir: M11 junct 12. From A1 N take A14 turn onto A1307.
At City of Cambridge sign turn left into Whitehouse Ln

Victorian mansion on the outside, sleek and chic 21st-
century boutique hotel inside: Hotel Felix is a clever fusion
of period elegance with the stripped-out style, neutral
tones and silky wooden floors of self-consciously modish
décor. The Graffiti restaurant is an exercise in understated
chic: clean lines, sensual textures, soft-focus colours and
eye-catching modern art; a terrace for alfresco aperitifs
and sunny day dining completes the stylish package. On
the brasserie-style menu is vibrant modern British fare
with a clear Mediterranean leaning. Starters might include
ham hock terrine with spicy home-made piccalilli and a
warm potato and shallot salad; loin of venison comes next
atop creamed curly kale and potato rösti, with a fine,
flavoursome jus. Valrhona chocolate tart with marinated
berries and grappa sabayon ends on an indulgent note.

Graffiti at Hotel Felix

Chef Nick Parker **Owner** Jeremy Cassel
Times 12-2/6.30-10 **Prices** Fixed L 2 course fr £12.95,
Starter £5.25-£6.75, Main £15.50-£18.75, Dessert £5.25-
£7.95, Service added but optional 10%, Groups min 10
service 10% **Wines** 37 bottles over £20, 14 bottles under
£20, 14 by glass **Notes** Sunday L, Vegetarian available,
Civ Wed 75 **Seats** 45, Pr/dining room 60 **Children** Portions
Parking 90

Hotel du Vin Cambridge

◉ Modern British V ✏

Bistro cooking in a medieval building

☎ 01223 227330 📄 01223 227331
15-19 Trumpington St CB2 1QA
e-mail: info.cambridge@hotelduvin.com
dir: M11 junct 11 Cambridge S, pass Trumpington Park &
Ride on left. Hotel 2m on right after double rdbt

The building harks back to medieval times, and has been
sensitively converted to make the Cambridge branch of
the celebrated vinous hotel group. Bare wooden floors and
rough-cast walls set a pleasingly rustic tone in the bistro
dining room, and the menus tack to the successful,
refreshingly straightforward Anglo-French culinary style
that is the chain's hallmark. Escargots in garlic butter or
a brown shrimp cocktail might start you off, while mains
run a gamut from haunch of venison with polenta, plum
tomatoes and wild mushrooms to herb-crusted halibut
with spring onions in Pommery mustard sauce. A side
order of bubble-and-squeak will fill any gaps.

Chef Jonathan Dean **Owner** MWB **Times** 12-2/6-10
Prices Fixed L 2 course fr £15.50, Starter £4.95-£7.75,
Main £11.75-£19.75, Service added but optional 10%
Wines 400 bottles over £20, 30 bottles under £20, 15 by
glass **Notes** Sunday L, Vegetarian menu **Seats** 76, Pr/
dining room 24 **Children** Portions **Parking** On street,
Lyons Yard NCP

Midsummer House

◉◉◉◉ — *see page 72*

Restaurant Alimentum

see below

Restaurant 22

◉ Modern British

**Consistent and accomplished cooking in an intimate
setting**

☎ 01223 351880 📄 01223 323814
22 Chesterton Rd CB4 3AX
e-mail: aandstommaso@restaurant22.co.uk
dir: Telephone for directions

With the look of a private house - which is precisely what
it once was - this former Victorian residence is now home
to a candlelit restaurant. The monthly-changing menu
draws on good quality produce, locally sourced where
possible. Chicken breast served with whole, braised baby
leeks and chestnut mushrooms in nut-brown butter and
sweetcorn purée is a good ensemble piece from the fixed
price menu, which offers an optional fish course. Desserts
can be intriguing: gin and tonic on a plate, and chocolate
delice with salted caramel and brioche ice cream. The
tables are close together, adding to the homely feel, and
the atmosphere is relaxed.

continued on page 73

Restaurant Alimentum

Rosettes not confirmed at time of going to press

CAMBRIDGE Map 12 TL45

Modern European ✏

Stylish restaurant with keen ethical principles

☎ 01223 413000
152-154 Hills Rd CB2 8PB
e-mail: info@restaurantalimentum.co.uk
dir: Opposite Cambridge Leisure Park

Named after the Latin word for food, Alimentum is an
ambitious restaurant and a valuable addition to the
Cambridge restaurant scene. A new chef as we go to
press has resulted in the suspension of rosettes pending
inspections. This is a restaurant that goes the extra mile
to source ethical produce, which includes making sure all
farms are visited and probing questions are asked about
the use of antibiotics and attitudes towards GM. Housed
in a smart building opposite the city's Leisure Park, the
sleek and stylish design is making quite a statement, too.
The cooking is modern European and based on those
carefully sourced ingredients. Potato and garlic soup with
deep-fried quail's egg might precede braised Denham
Estate venison neck with buttered mash, cabbage and
bacon, finishing with a pineapple and lime salad with a
French meringue and mango sorbet. Good quality breads
and a reasonably priced wine list add to the appeal.

Chef Mark Poynton **Owner** John Hudgell **Times** 12-3/6-10
Closed 24-31 Dec **Prices** Fixed L 2 course £13.50-£15.50,
Fixed D 3 course £18.50, Starter £7.50-£8.95, Main
£16-£19.95, Dessert £6.95-£8.95, Service added but
optional 12.5% **Wines** 83 bottles over £20, 8 bottles
under £20, 40 by glass **Notes** Pre-theatre D Mon-Fri
6-7pm, Sunday L, Vegetarian available, Dress
restrictions, Smart casual, Air con **Seats** 62, Pr/dining
room 34 **Children** Portions, Menu **Parking** NCP Cambridge
Leisure Centre (3 min walk)

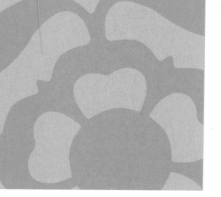

Midsummer House

French, Mediterranean ⚑ NOTABLE WINE LIST

Creative cooking of the highest order

☎ 01223 369299 📠 01223 302672
Midsummer Common CB4 1HA
e-mail: reservations@
midsummerhouse.co.uk
web: www.midsummerhouse.co.uk
dir: Park in Pretoria Rd, then walk
across footbridge. Restaurant on left

It is a curious quirk of the British
gastronomic map that, with a captive
audience of gourmet academics, well-
heeled visiting parents and scrums of
tourists, our major university towns
have so few top-flight restaurants.
Happily, Midsummer House has chef
Daniel Clifford's relentless pursuit of
innovation and perfection as an
exception to prove the rule. The modest
Victorian villa beside the River Cam is
English to the core, but a distinctly
Gallic sheen infuses this enterprise,
from slickly attentive French waiters, to
a strong showing of French wines and
the unmistakably classical French
technique that underpins the kitchen's
exuberant culinary style. The
conservatory extension dining room,
modishly minimal with pristine white
walls and Indian slate floors, overlooks
a delightfully-fragrant walled herb
garden with river views; diners are kept
well apart at capacious tables dressed
in white linen. You might choose to
arrive here via the sophisticated
upstairs bar and river-view terrace for
alfresco aperitifs. Clifford's cooking is
full of twists and turns, foams and
essences, constantly thrilling and
surprising with off-the-wall contrasts in
texture and curveball flavour
combinations. Of course, you can't pull
off this kind of wizardry without the
basics of top quality ingredients, hyper-
advanced technique and a committed,
talented kitchen team all singing in
tune. One ingredient - perhaps cod,
sweetbread, turbot or pig's trotter -
introduces each dish on fixed-price
lunch, à la carte or tasting menus;
these terse descriptions listing
ingredients with few adjectives do little
to prepare you for the wow factor that
arrives with each plate. Langoustine is
grilled and lightly coated in sesame
seeds alongside tortellini of moist king
crab and a purée of sweet-and-sour
swede. Main courses bring on more
revelatory arrays - slow-roasted belly
pork comes with superb Savoy cabbage
and a crisp potato tube filled with
braised pork and an apple and shallot
foam. Desserts end on the same note,
for example a pear and fennel delice
that is served with black olives
marinated in a vanilla syrup, and a
cannelloni filled with fennel mousse and
olive oil ice cream.

Chef Daniel Clifford **Owner** Midsummer
House Ltd **Times** 12-1.30/7-9.30
Closed 2 wks late Aug, 2 wks from 25
Dec, 1 wk Etr, Sun & Mon, L Tue
Prices Fixed L 2 course £24, Service
added but optional 12.5% **Wines** 900
bottles over £20, 12 by glass **Notes** ALC
3 course £60, Vegetarian available
Seats 54, Pr/dining room 16
Children Portions **Parking** On street

CAMBRIDGE *continued*

Chef Martin Cullum, Seb Mansfield **Owner** Mr A & Mrs S Tommaso **Times** 7-9.45 Closed 25 Dec & New Year, Sun-Mon, L all week **Prices** Fixed D 3 course £27.95, Service optional **Wines** 40 bottles over £20, 30 bottles under £20, 4 by glass **Notes** Vegetarian available, Air con **Seats** 26, Pr/dining room 14 **Children** Portions **Parking** On street

The Tickell Arms

◉◉ Traditional French NEW 🍷 👐

Classical French cooking in an English country setting

☎ 01223 833128   🖷 01223 835907
1 North Rd, Whittlesford CB22 4NZ
e-mail: dine@thetickell.co.uk
dir: M11 junct 10, turn E onto the A505, within 1m follow signpost to Whittlesford, left off A505

The 17th-century inn has barely changed over the years, with the exception of the large conservatory extension that affords views of a duck pond and luxurious garden to lunchtime and summer evening diners. Classical music plays in rooms that retain a slightly lived-in, but elegant, feel. The daily-changing menus deal in French dishes constructed from fresh East Anglian produce, overlaid with the occasional homage to English recipes of times gone by. Expect therefore a chaudrée, rather than a chowder, of smoked fish, packed with flavour and creamy richness. Bourne Wood venison is sensitively timed and comes dressed with a reinterpretation of a plum 'catchup' from Hannah Glasse's 18th-century cookery book, and the crème brûlée is scented with rosewater. An extensive menu of fine English cheeses, home-baked breads and top-notch incidentals indicate the unwavering attention to detail.

Chef Michael Burgoyne **Owner** Michael Burgoyne **Times** 12-2.30/7-9.30 Closed Mon, D Sun **Prices** Fixed L 2 course £23.50-£27.95, Fixed D 3 course £33.95-£35.95, Starter £4.50-£9, Main £12.95-£16, Dessert £5.95-£6.95, Service added but optional 12.5% **Wines** 150 bottles over £20, 20 bottles under £20, 9 by glass **Notes** Chef's table, 12 course tasting menu, Sunday L, Vegetarian available, Civ Wed 120 **Seats** 60 **Parking** 25

DUXFORD   Map 12 TL44

Duxford Lodge Hotel

◉ British, European

Cambridgeshire country house steeped in world war history

☎ 01223 836444   🖷 01223 832271
Ickleton Rd CB22 4RT
e-mail: admin@duxfordlodgehotel.co.uk
web: www.duxfordlodgehotel.co.uk
dir: M11 junct 10, onto A505 to Duxford. 1st right at rdbt, hotel 0.75m on left

The country-house hotel, which was built in the early part of the last century, is steeped in the history of the world wars, when it served as an officers' mess. In the 1940s, it was a magnet for visiting dignitaries, when Sir Winston Churchill might have rubbed shoulders with Bing Crosby, had their bookings coincided. The restaurant is done out in pastel colours, and offers ambitious modern dining in either fixed-price or à la carte format. Expect wild rabbit and apricot boudin to begin, and then chargrilled fillet steak with stilton sauce, or roast salmon with buttered spinach and saffron cream, to follow on.

Chef Jason Burridge **Owner** Mr Hemant Amin **Times** 12-2/7-9.30 Closed 24 Dec-2 Jan, L Mon, Fri, Sat **Prices** Fixed L 2 course £13.95, Fixed D 3 course £27.50, Starter £9.50-£11.25, Main £14.50-£24.95, Dessert £6.25-£6.95, Service optional **Wines** 19 bottles over £20, 16 bottles under £20, 6 by glass **Notes** Sunday L, Vegetarian available, Dress restrictions, Smart dress/smart casual, Civ Wed 46, Air con **Seats** 45, Pr/dining room 24 **Children** Portions **Parking** 30

ELY   Map 12 TL58

The Anchor Inn

◉ Modern British

Riverside inn serving imaginatively presented local produce

☎ 01353 778537   🖷 01353 776180
Sutton Gault, Sutton CB6 2BD
e-mail: anchorinn@popmail.bta.com
dir: Signed off B1381 in Sutton village, 7m W of Ely via A142

Uneven tiled floors, antique pine furniture and roaring fires in winter add a timeless, welcoming charm to this historic inn. Dating back to 1650, it was originally built to provide shelter for workers digging the New Bedford River

---

(as part of the mass draining of the Fens), but now offers accommodation and fine sustenance for a more discerning audience. The cooking takes a modern British approach with a subtle nod to Europe; supreme of guinea fowl, perhaps, served with fondant potatoes and a broad bean and chorizo cassoulette, or fillet of sea bass teamed with a warm salad of creamed leeks, new potatoes and almond pesto.

Times 12-3.30/7-11

HINXTON   Map 12 TL44

The Red Lion Inn

◉ Modern British NEW

Good food in charming village inn

☎ 01799 530601   🖷 01799 531201
32 High St CB10 1QY
e-mail: info@redlionhinxton.co.uk

Set in the pretty village of Hinxton, this privately-owned 16th-century inn achieves the right balance between 'gastro' and 'pub'. The Grade II listed bar oozes character with its low ceilings, open fire, wooden floor and Chesterfield sofas making for a charming setting to savour the 4 local real ales. The restaurant meanwhile is rustic with lofty ceilings, dry-pegged oak rafters and high-backed settles. In warmer months, the walled garden overlooked by a dovecote and village church clock tower, offers guests a quintessentially English setting. The food mixes contemporary and traditional dishes using local produce. A starter of lamb's sweetbreads with fried red onions, red chicory and endive salad with mustard dressing might be followed by honey-glazed duck breast with fondant potato, steamed broccoli and peach-infused jus.

Times 12-2/6.45-9

HUNTINGDON   Map 12 TL27

WINE AWARD WINNER

The Old Bridge Hotel

◉◉ Modern British 🍷

Charming hotel with high standards and versatile dining options

☎ 01480 424300   🖷 01480 411017
1 High St PE29 3TQ
e-mail: oldbridge@huntsbridge.co.uk
dir: From A14 or A1 follow Huntingdon signs. Hotel visible from inner ring road

The brilliant wine list and new in-house wine shop alone (24 bottles open for tasting each day) make this 18th-century ivy-clad townhouse hotel a worthy destination. It stands smack beside the old stone bridge over the River Ouse and a glorious terrace makes the most of the riverside setting. There's a classic-looking bar for sandwiches and a pint of Adnams, while the lively and informal Terrace Restaurant, with its bold murals and big windows, serves more formal lunches and dinners. The

continued

HUNTINGDON *continued*

kitchen produces interesting modern cooking to a high standard, combining rustic European cuisine with modern British dishes, so expect a strong French or Italian accent. Kick off a meal with tortellini of Portland crab with leeks and crab sauce, move on to pan-fried pigeon with butternut squash risotto, chorizo and curly kale, and finish with apricot bread-and-butter pudding with clotted cream ice cream. The wine list is a treat.

Chef Simon Lodge **Owner** J Hoskins **Times** 12-2/6.30-10 **Prices** Fixed L 2 course £15.50, Starter £5.95-£9.95, Main £13.95-£24.50, Dessert £5.95-£7.50, Service optional **Wines** 350 bottles over £20, 50 bottles under £20, 35 by glass **Notes** Sunday L, Vegetarian available, Civ Wed 80, Air con **Seats** 100, Pr/dining room 60 **Children** Portions, Menu **Parking** 60

KEYSTON   Map 11 TL07

Pheasant Inn

◉ British, French ⭐ 📖 ✋

Unfussy seasonal cooking in comfortable country inn

☎ 01832 710241 📄 01832 710340
Village Loop Rd PE28 0RE
e-mail: info@thepheasant-keyston.co.uk
dir: 0.5m off A14, clearly signed, 10m W of Huntingdon, 14m E of Kettering

A thatched, beamed 16th-century inn set in a sleepy farming village, The Pheasant makes the most of its rural location. Old farming equipment and wallpaper depicting hunting scenes add to this traditional country feel, as does the fact the pub backs on to its own vegetable garden. This connection with its farming roots continues with the produce used in the kitchen, much of it coming from just a few miles from the pub. The 3 distinct dining areas are comfortable, intimate and relaxed with well-spaced, polished wooden tables and pine settles having a suitably rustic appeal. The food is unpretentious British and French cooking: grilled calves' heart salad with pickled shallots and watercress might be followed by medallions of pork with red cabbage, new potatoes and prune and sherry sauce.

Chef Jay Scrimshaw, Liam Goodwill **Owner** Jay & Taffeta Scrimshaw **Times** 12-2.30/6-9.30 Closed D Sun **Prices** Fixed L course £18.50, Fixed D 3 course £18.50, Starter £5.50-£8.50, Main £12-£19.50, Dessert £5-£8, Service optional, Groups min 10 service 10% **Wines** 60 bottles over £20, 20 bottles under £20, 12 by glass **Notes** Sunday L, Vegetarian available **Seats** 80, Pr/dining room 30 **Children** Portions, Menu **Parking** 40

LITTLE WILBRAHAM   Map 12 TL55

Hole in the Wall

◉ Modern British ✋

Fine old country pub with modern approach in the kitchen

☎ 01223 812282
2 High St CB21 5JY
e-mail: jenniferleeton@btconnect.com
dir: A14 junct 35. A11 exit at The Wilbrahams

At the end of a hard day's work local farm workers used to collect their barrels of beer through a hole in the wall of the main bar, as only the gentry were allowed inside. That was some time ago, thankfully. Now, all are welcome at this attractive 15th-century pub, where inside copious exposed beams and open fires help to retain the traditional atmosphere. Fresh, seasonal local produce is used to good effect in lively modern British dishes with a bit of a twist, with flavour very much to the fore. Try home-made game sausage with pickled red cabbage, apple purée and redcurrant jus, or cod fishcake with white bean, chorizo and pork belly stew, cavolo nero and saffron aïoli. Finish with slow-baked pear with oaty topping and clotted cream custard.

Chef Christopher Leeton **Owner** Christopher & Jennifer Leeton, Stephen Bull **Times** 12-2/7-9 Closed 2 weeks in Jan & 2 weeks in Oct, Mon (except L BH), D Sun, 26 Dec, 1 Jan **Prices** Starter £3.50-£8.50, Main £11.50-£17, Dessert £5.95-£8.50, Service optional **Wines** 15 bottles over £20, 26 bottles under £20, 12 by glass **Notes** Sunday L, Vegetarian available **Seats** 65 **Children** Portions **Parking** 30

MADINGLEY   Map 12 TL36

Three Horseshoes Restaurant

◉ Italian

Modern Italian dining in quintessential English village pub

☎ 01954 210221 📄 01954 212043
High St CB3 8AB
e-mail: 3hs@btconnect.co.uk
dir: M11 junct 13, turn left, then next right and continue to end of road, and at mini-rdbt turn right

A picturesque 16th-century thatched inn with a large garden overlooking the village cricket pitch, this popular gastro-pub has a decidedly Mediterranean feel inside. Cooking is rustic Italian with bold flavours and a good use of seasonal produce. The daily-changing menu may include the likes of risotto of Bottisham Smokery haddock flavoured with chives, parmesan and Vermouth, followed by a chargrilled leg of Cornish lamb with sheep's milk ricotta gnudi, tomato and balsamic sauce and garlic braised cime di rape. To finish, try the comice pear and almond tart with clotted cream.

Chef Richard Stokes **Owner** Richard Stokes **Times** 12-2/6.30-9.30 Closed 1-2 Jan **Prices** Starter £6-£14, Main £12-£22, Dessert £5-£9, Service added but optional 10%, Groups min 8 service 10% **Wines** 100

bottles over £20, 20 bottles under £20, 12 by glass **Notes** Sunday L, Vegetarian available **Seats** 65 **Children** Portions **Parking** 50

PETERBOROUGH   Map 12 TL19

Best Western Orton Hall Hotel

◉ British

Historic setting for modern cuisine

☎ 01733 391111 📄 01733 231912
The Village, Orton Longueville PE2 7DN
e-mail: reception@ortonhall.co.uk
dir: off A605 E, opposite Orton Mere

Set in 20 acres of parkland, this rambling country-house hotel dates from the 17th century and was once home to the Marquis of Huntly. It retains a wealth of original features, including terracotta floors, stained-glass windows and some fine oak panelling in the elegant restaurant. Cooking is bang up-to-date, with a modern British menu listing the likes of seared scallops with lime risotto, local estate venison with parsley mash, poached sole with ginger foam, and white rum pannacotta with mango and kiwi salsa. The on-site pub, Ramblewood Inn, offers an alternative, informal dining venue.

Chef Kevin Wood **Owner** Abacus Hotels **Times** 12.30-2/7-9.30 Closed 25 Dec, L Mon-Sat **Prices** Fixed D 3 course £23-£35, Service optional **Wines** 23 bottles over £20, 42 bottles under £20, 6 by glass **Notes** Sunday L, Civ Wed 150 **Seats** 34, Pr/dining room 40 **Parking** 200

ST NEOTS   Map 12 TL16

The George Hotel & Brasserie

◉ Modern British ✋

Stylish, bustling brasserie in Georgian coaching inn

☎ 01480 812300 📄 01480 813920
High St, Buckden PE19 5XA
e-mail: mail@thegeorgebuckden.com
dir: Off A1, S of junct with A14

This George is very Georgian indeed, the sort of place where you can easily picture carriages pulling up for the night. A top-to-toe makeover in 2004 remodelled the interior in a chic metropolitan style with a fun 'famous George' theme in its twelve bedrooms (Gershwin, Orwell, Eliot and Best - you get the idea). The ground-floor brasserie is a slice of London. Brown leather stools perch at a long metal bar, while polished and unclothed wooden tables gleam beneath sparkling glassware - an appropriate setting for a menu of modern British cuisine. Try sautéed lamb's kidneys with rösti potato cake, black pudding and shallot grain mustard sauce or spiced lamb shank casserole with cannellini beans, garden herbs and lemon couscous.

Chef Ray Smikle **Owner** Richard & Anne Furbank **Times** 12-2.30/7-9.30 **Prices** Starter £5.50-£9, Main £11.50-£22, Dessert £5.50-£7.50, Service optional **Wines** 35 bottles over £20, 35 bottles under £20, 16 by glass **Notes** Sunday L, Vegetarian available, Dress restrictions, Smart dress, Civ Wed 40 **Seats** 60, Pr/dining room 30 **Children** Portions **Parking** 25

STILTON Map 12 TL18

Bell Inn Hotel

British, French 🍷

Modern British cuisine in delightful 16th-century surroundings

☎ 01733 241066   📠 01733 245173
Great North Rd PE7 3RA
e-mail: reception@thebellstilton.co.uk
dir: A1(M) junct 16, follow Stilton signs. Hotel in village centre

Famous for being the birthplace of stilton cheese, the inn is steeped in history - Dick Turpin was a regular guest by all accounts - and many original features remain. Extra accommodation has been built around the old courtyard, blending into the ageless original stone. A consistently good standard of traditional British favourites, as well as internationally influenced dishes is served in the historic setting of the bar and bistro, and beamed first-floor Galleried Restaurant. In summer, you can also eat outside in the attractive courtyard. Typical starters might include chicken liver parfait with pear and thyme chutney and walnut toast, followed by main-course braised Suffolk pork belly served with fondant potato, wilted spinach purée, and sweet-and-sour red onions.

Chef Robin Devonshire **Owner** Mr Liam McGivern **Times** 12-2/7-9.30 Closed 25 Dec, 31 Dec, L Mon-Sat, D Sun **Prices** Fixed D 3 course fr £30.95, Starter £4.95-£8.95, Main £12.25-£17.45, Dessert fr £5.75, Service optional **Wines** 30 bottles over £20, 30 bottles under £20, 10 by glass **Notes** Sunday L, Vegetarian available, Dress restrictions, Smart casual, Civ Wed 90, Air con **Seats** 60, Pr/dining room 20 **Parking** 30

WISBECH Map 12 TF40

The Moorings

Modern, Traditional 🍷

Contemporary brasserie-style restaurant with grill-inspired dining

☎ 01945 773391   📠 01945 772668
Crown Lodge Hotel, Downham Rd, Outwell PE14 8SE
e-mail: office@thecrownlodgehotel.co.uk
dir: 5m SE of Wisbech on A1122, 1m from junct with A1101, towards Downham Market

The Crown Lodge Hotel lies a little off the beaten track on the tranquil banks of Welle Creek in rural Cambridgeshire. The Moorings restaurant is a contemporary open-plan brasserie-style affair that takes top-quality produce and lets it speak for itself. After all, the fish here comes from the source who supplies Her Maj at Sandringham, and meat comes from a butcher who raises his own animals to ensure quality. The kitchen's modern approach is gloriously simple and avoids cluttering the plate with too many flavours. A nicely-spicy duck rillette with plum chutney might precede an oven-baked partridge wrapped in pancetta with lentil casserole, sage-roasted new potatoes and green beans, or one of the chargrilled specialities.

Chef Mick Castell **Owner** Mr W J Moore **Times** 12-2.30/6-10 Closed 25-26 & 31 Dec, 1 Jan **Prices** Starter £4.90-£7, Main £9-£22, Dessert £5-£6, Service optional **Wines** 13 bottles over £20, 44 bottles under £20, 9 by glass **Notes** Sunday L, Vegetarian available, Dress restrictions, Smart casual, Air con **Seats** 40, Pr/dining room 35 **Children** Portions **Parking** 50

CHESHIRE

ALDERLEY EDGE Map 16 SJ87

The Alderley Restaurant

@@ British V 🍷

Innovative cuisine in country-house hotel with stunning views

☎ 01625 583033   📠 01625 586343
Alderley Edge Hotel, Macclesfield Rd SK9 7BJ
e-mail: sales@alderleyedgehotel.com
dir: A538 to Alderley Edge, then B5087 Macclesfield Rd

Set on the edge of the town, this former cotton merchant's house stands in its own grounds with views

across to the Welsh mountains. Recently refurbished with the old split-level floor having been levelled, giving diners improved views of the Cheshire countryside, the smart, airy conservatory restaurant has been known to play host to celebrity footballers; little wonder, given the contemporary, innovative approach taken by the kitchen team. A creative use of flavours and locally-sourced ingredients feature in an imaginative menu, with main courses such as fillet of Horseshoe Farm beef, braised smoked ox cheek, truffle potato espuma and horseradish jelly, while desserts could include a comice pear tarte Tatin with peanut croquant and 12-year-old balsamic ice cream.

Chef Chris Holland **Owner** J W Lees (Brewers) Ltd **Times** 12-2/7-10 Closed 1 Jan, L 31 Dec, D 25-26 Dec **Prices** Fixed L 2 course fr £14.95, Fixed D 2 course fr £29.95, Starter £8.95-£11, Main £22.95-£24.95, Dessert £8.25, Service optional **Wines** 450+ bottles over £20, 30 bottles under £20, 7 by glass **Notes** Tasting menu available, Sunday L, Vegetarian menu, Dress restrictions, Smart casual, Civ Wed 150, Air con **Seats** 80, Pr/dining room 150 **Children** Portions, Menu **Parking** 82

CHESTER Map 15 SJ46

La Brasserie at The Chester Grosvenor & Spa

Modern International

Classy brasserie cooking in Chester's ancient heart

☎ 01244 324024   📠 01244 313246
Eastgate CH1 1LT
e-mail: hotel@chestergrosvenor.co.uk
dir: A56 follow signs for city centre hotels. Opposite Town Hall on Northgate St

The black-and-white timbered Chester Grosvenor is a culinary destination in the North West, what with the presence of Simon Radley in his eponymous restaurant in the hotel (see entry). La Brasserie offers something different - a classy brasserie experience with a varied menu of French classics, British favourites, and some international flavours. Art deco mirrors hang above black leather banquettes and sleek granite tabletops are smartly set with quality appointments. Grilled scallops with piquillo peppers, chorizo and fried beans supplies the flavours of Southern Europe, while corned beef hash cake with home-made baked beans, runny egg and ketchup offers a touch of British comfort. Runny chocolate tart is a star turn at dessert.

Chef Simon Radley, Bradley Lean **Owner** Grosvenor - Duke of Westminster **Times** 12-10.30 Closed 25-26 Dec **Prices** Fixed L 2 course fr £14.95, Starter £7.95-£13.95, Main £14.95-£26.95, Dessert £5.25-£5.95, Service optional, Groups min 8 service 12.5% **Wines** 40 bottles over £20, 5 bottles under £20, 11 by glass **Notes** Vegetarian available, Civ Wed 120, Air con **Seats** 80, Pr/dining room 250 **Children** Portions, Menu **Parking** 250, NCP attached to hotel

CHESTER *continued*

Doubletree by Hilton Chester

◎◎ Modern British NEW

Accurate Modern British cooking in stylish country house

☎ 01244 408800 📠 01244 320251
Warrington Rd, Hoole Village CH2 3PD

Set in extensive grounds, this notable 18th-century house has been sympathetically restored and retains many period features including a Grade II listed conservatory. Behind the elegant period exterior, The Orchid Restaurant boasts a vibrant, minimalist décor with quality modern art on the walls, well-spaced booths and chairs finished in white leather. Smart uniformed staff are knowledgeable and discreet, with the finer points of service observed at all times. The food is modern British in essence with some French and Eastern influences and the best seasonal produce is used in dishes like roasted breast of wood pigeon with baby beets, watercress, pistachio and champagne vinaigrette, followed by monkfish baked with bresaola, celeriac, baby fennel and a red wine reduction.

Times 8am-10.30pm **Prices** Food prices not confirmed for 2010. Please telephone for details.

Langdale Restaurant

◎◎ Traditional British

Magnificent Georgian country-house hotel with fine dining

☎ 01244 335262 📠 01244 335464
Rowton Hall Country House, Whitchurch Rd, Rowton CH3 6AD
e-mail: reception@rowtonhallhotelandspa.co.uk
dir: M56 junct 12, A56 to Chester. At rdbt left onto A41 towards Whitchurch. Approx 1m, follow hotel signs

Whether you're up for the gee gees at Chester races or a spot of down-time and de-stressing in the swish health and beauty spa, this handsome Georgian mansion in 8 acres of lovely gardens should fit the bill. The interior blends period elegance, in the shape of acreages of oak panelling and Robert Adam fireplaces, with a smart line in contemporary style. The Langdale restaurant is a neatly turned-out venue for the kitchen team's uncomplicated output of modern dishes that focus sensibly on a few core ingredients to keep flavours clear and fresh. Kick off with smoked trout terrine with dill and cucumber salsa, and follow with well-balanced mains such as grilled sea bass fillet with wilted spinach and saffron cocottes.

Chef Matthew Hawnes **Owner** Mr & Mrs Wigginton **Times** 12-2/7-9.30 **Prices** Fixed L 3 course £13-£18.50, Fixed D 3 course £19.95-£26.50, Starter £3.50-£9.50, Main £9.50-£22.50, Dessert £3.50-£9.50, Service optional **Notes** Sunday L, Vegetarian available, Dress restrictions, Casually elegant, Civ Wed 170, Air con **Seats** 70, Pr/dining room 30 **Children** Portions, Menu **Parking** 200

Oddfellows

◎ Modern British NEW

Sound cooking in stylish Georgian house

☎ 01244 400001
20 Lower Bride St CH1 1RS
e-mail: reception@oddfellows.biz
dir: Please telephone for directions

Surrounded by quality designer shops and just a few minutes from Chester Rows, old meets new in this stylish renovated Georgian mansion. The upper ground floor comprises a walled garden with ornamental moat, Arabic tents and a roofed patio. Enjoy an aperitif in the cocktail bar before moving to the elegant fine-dining restaurant where the accurate, unfussy modern British cooking majors on local produce. A starter of seared scallops with grilled boudin noir and celeriac purée might be followed by slow-cooked shoulder of lamb with braised faggot and pease pudding. There's a good choice of wines by the glass.

Chef Mark Fletcher **Owner** Oddfellows **Times** 12-10 **Prices** Fixed L 2 course fr £12.50, Fixed D 3 course fr £14.50, Starter fr £6, Main fr £15, Dessert fr £5 **Notes** Fixed L & D available Mon-Thu, Vegetarian available

Simon Radley at The Chester Grosvenor

◎◎◎◎ — *see opposite page*

CREWE	Map 15 SJ75

The Brasserie

◎ Modern European

Contemporary brasserie in modern wing of stately home

☎ 01270 253333 📠 01270 253322
Crewe Hall, Weston Rd CW1 6UZ
e-mail: crewehall@qhotels.co.uk
dir: M6 junct 16, follow A500 to Crewe. Last exit at rdbt onto A5020. 1st exit next to Crewe. Crewe Hall 150 yds on right

A glass walkway at this stately Grade I listed Jacobean mansion is a sort of time tunnel that transports you from a hushed world of Victorian (yes, those makeover pioneers redecorated after a fire) oak panelling, plasterwork, stained glass and marble fireplaces into the lively modern wing. A cocktail in the revolving bar is de rigueur before you take a seat for skilled modern European fare produced in a modish open kitchen. The menu roams widely from exotic-tinged starters like crab and ginger fishcakes with Thai jelly and chilli jam, through grills of rib-eye steak, tuna or salmon, then diverts into France for daube of beef with pickled red cabbage and dauphinoise potatoes. The Ranulph (see entry) is the more formal dining option.

Chef Andrew Hollinshead **Owner** Q Hotels **Times** all day **Prices** Fixed L 2 course £11.50, Starter £2.90-£8.90, Main £8.90-£18.50, Dessert £5.90-£7.50, Service

optional **Wines** 31 bottles over £20, 9 bottles under £20, 10 by glass **Notes** Sunday L, Vegetarian available, Civ Wed 280, Air con **Seats** 140 **Children** Portions, Menu **Parking** 500

Hunters Lodge Hotel

◎ British, European

Traditional dining surrounded by glorious Cheshire countryside

☎ 01270 539100 📠 01270 500553
Sydney Rd, Sydney CW1 5LU
e-mail: info@hunterslodge.co.uk
dir: 1m from Crewe station, off A534

Originally a farmhouse, this family-run hotel set in 16 acres of delightful Cheshire countryside has been extended and modernised and now offers well-equipped bedrooms and extensive leisure facilities. British dishes, showing plenty of influences from mainland Europe, are served in the spacious, beamed restaurant, using locally-sourced seasonal produce. Main courses such as well-flavoured braised shoulder of lamb with asparagus, oven-dried tomatoes and onion polenta, or breast of Gressingham duck with cabbage, bacon and fondant potato, might precede chocolate and honey soufflé with shortbread and chocolate sauce. Informal meals are served in the popular bar.

Chef David Wall **Owner** Mr A Panayi **Times** 12-2/7-9.30 Closed BHs, D Sun **Prices** Fixed D 3 course £19.95, Starter £4.95-£7.95, Main £10.95-£22.95, Dessert £6.95, Service optional **Wines** 26 bottles over £20, 27 bottles under £20, 21 by glass **Notes** Sunday L, Vegetarian available, Civ Wed 130 **Seats** 60, Pr/dining room 30 **Children** Portions, Menu **Parking** 200

The Ranulph

◎◎ Modern European NEW

Fine dining amidst a touch of Jacobean splendour

☎ 01270 253333 📠 01270 253322
Crewe Hall, Weston Rd CW1 6UZ
e-mail: crewehall@qhotels.co.uk
web: www.qhotels.co.uk
dir: M6 junct 16 follow A500 to Crewe. Last exit at rdbt onto A5020. 1st exit next rdbt to Crewe. Crewe Hall 150yds on right

The ever-so-stately Crewe Hall dates from the 17th century and was re-built after a fire in the Victorian era

continued on page 78

Simon Radley at The Chester Grosvenor

CHESTER   Map 15 SJ46

Modern French V  NOTABLE WINE LIST

Innovative and highly skilled cooking in top city hotel

☎ 01244 324024   📄 01244 313246
Chester Grosvenor & Spa, Eastgate CH1 1LT
e-mail: hotel@chestergrosvenor.co.uk
dir: City centre (Eastgate St) adjacent to Eastgate Clock & Roman walls

The Duke of Westminster, owner of this Grade II listed, black-and-white timbered hotel dating from 1865, flies high in the UK's rich list, and his peers would doubtless feel very much at home at this piece of 5-star luxury in historic Chester. The dining options include La Brasserie (see entry) and the jewel in the crown, Simon Radley at the Chester Grosvenor. The restaurant, formerly the Arkle, was named after its executive chef in 2008 after more than 10 years of loyal service, and it continues to go from strength to strength. The room is designed to sooth and pamper, with comfortable cushioned chairs, crisp white linen tablecloths and an understated elegance. Everything from the formal service to the impressive wine list, running to an imposing 1,000 bins, identifies this as the premier fine dining venue in the region. There's the de rigueur tasting menu, eight courses starting with an amuse-bouche - perhaps of wood smoke pepper whip

with saffron and grissini - and including saddle of roe deer with onion 'study', Iberico pork and hazelnut along the way. This is cooking displaying a high degree of technical skill, creativity and a light touch; complex, certainly, but combinations catch the eye and the top quality ingredients are not lost in the process. Warm scallop and fennel pannacotta with poached oysters and caviar is a first course of refinement and well-judged flavours, and Challans duck comes in an inventive dish alongside hazelnut and crispy skin granola, Cheshire honey, duck titbits and haricots blancs.

Chef Simon Radley, Ray Booker
Owner Grosvenor - Duke of Westminster
Times 7-9.30 Closed 25-26 Dec, 1 wk Jan, Sun-Mon, L all week (except Dec)
Prices Food prices not confirmed for 2010. Please telephone for details.
Wines 600 bottles over £20, 5 bottles under £20, 15 by glass **Notes** Tasting menu 8 course, Vegetarian menu, Dress restrictions, Smart dress, no jeans, shorts or sportswear, Civ Wed 120, Air con **Seats** 45, Pr/dining room 240
Parking 250, NCP attached to hotel

CREWE *continued*

by the chap who designed London's Charing Cross Station. Today it is a state-of-the-art hotel popular for weddings and conferences, so expect plenty of character and original features alongside first-class facilities. The brasserie (see entry) displays the modern face of the hotel, while The Ranulph restaurant provides a touch of opulence and tradition with rich fabrics, formally laid tables and even hand-painted wallpaper bearing the Crewe Hall crest. The modern European cooking sees rillette of duck with foie gras and home-made chutney preceding sea bass with herb gnocchi and roasted butternut squash, and pear tarte Tatin with caramel ice cream to finish. Service is unobtrusive and efficient.

Chef Andrew Hollinshead **Owner** Q Hotels **Times** 12-3/7-10 Closed Mon-Wed, L Thu-Sat, D Sun **Prices** Starter £10, Main £22, Dessert £7, Service optional **Wines** 40 bottles over £20, 10 bottles under £20, 21 by glass **Notes** Sunday L, Dress restrictions, Smart casual, Civ Wed 280 **Seats** 40, Pr/dining room 280 **Children** Portions, Menu **Parking** 500

Mere Court Hotel & Conference Centre

◉ Modern British

Fine dining with fine views

☎ 01565 831000 📄 01565 831001
Warrington Rd, Mere WA16 0RW
e-mail: sales@merecourt.co.uk
web: www.merecourt.co.uk
dir: A50, 1m W of junct with A556, on right

Originally built in 1903 as a wedding present for a lucky couple (the toaster was yet to be invented), this fine Arts and Crafts-style house is set amid well-tended gardens. There are views over the lake and parkland from the elegant high-beamed dining room, which boasts oak panelling and formally dressed tables. The cooking is modern British with plenty of Mediterranean flavours and local produce to the fore. Start with a classic moules marinière with lightly toasted bread, or sautéed lamb's liver and sweetbreads with a focaccia bruschetta and balsamic jus. Main-courses might include braised ox cheek with carrot purée and Lyonnaise potatoes.

Times 12-2/7-9.30 Closed L Sat

The Church Green

◉◉◉ *– see below*

Rookery Hall

◉◉ Modern British

Accomplished cooking in luxurious restaurant with views

☎ 01270 610016 📄 01270 626027
Main Rd, Worleston CW5 6DQ
e-mail: rookeryhall@handpicked.co.uk
dir: B5074 off 4th rdbt, on Nantwich by-pass. Hotel 1.5m on right

Built in 1816, Rookery Hall Hotel is located 15 minutes from the M6 and within easy reach of Chester and Manchester. Set in 38 acres of gardens and wooded parkland, its striking tower gives this Georgian mansion

---

The Church Green

Modern British **NEW**

Seriously good cooking in a stylish village pub

☎ 01925 752068
Higher Lane, WA13 0AP
dir: M6 junct 20/M56 junct 9. Follow signs to Lymm on B5158 for 1.5m. Right at T-junct onto A56 towards Altrincham for approx 0.5m. The Church Green is on right.

Aiden Byrne has made a name for himself heading up the kitchens of some pretty smart gaffs, including most recently The Grill at the Dorchester. He's on the TV a fair bit, too, including a stint on Masterchef, and his cookbook, *Made in Great Britain* reveals his passion for good British food. With his partner, Sarah, who also has considerable experience in hospitality, he's opened his own venture in an attractive village with good

connections (M6 etc.). The pub is next to the Lymm dam and church, so ideal for a pre- or post-prandial stroll. A neutral colour scheme sees plenty of natural wood and open brickwork, and tables run through into a conservatory to the side of the building. Sarah runs front-of-house with charm and her young team are all fully briefed on the menu and wine list; the atmosphere is unstuffy with just the right degree of refinement. Aiden has taken his fine dining background and tweaked it a little to present modern British dishes of considerable appeal. The cooking is based on excellent produce (much of it local), attractively presented and served in generous portions, perhaps to suit local appetites. Start with pan-fried scallops, for example (four not three), in a fashionable pairing with pork belly, some caramelised baby onions and a wonderfully flavoured reduction sauce, then perhaps main-course braised veal breast with perfectly poached lobster tail and a suitably tart apple purée.

Chef Aiden Byrne **Owner** Aiden Byrne **Times** 12-3/6-9.30 **Prices** Starter £6.50-£11.50, Main £12.50-£23, Dessert £4-£6.95, Service charge optional **Wines** 42 bottles over £20, 14 bottles under £20, 13 by glass **Notes** Sunday L, Vegetarian available, Dress restrictions, Smart casual preferred **Seats** 50 **Children** Portions

the look of a French château. The sandstone walls, polished wood paneling and sumptuous leather seats give the elegant restaurant a luxurious feel, whilst fabulous views over the rolling Cheshire countryside can be glimpsed through the windows. Modern British cooking with a heavy French accent brings on seared scallops with grilled Bury black pudding, apple and sage compôte, followed by fillet of Yorkshire beef, dauphinoise potatoes, roast beetroot and a shallot and wild mushroom cream. Warm chocolate fondant with white chocolate sorbet and griottine cherry syrup completes the picture.

Chef John Badley **Owner** Hand Picked Hotels
Times 12-2/7-9.30 Closed L Sat **Prices** Food prices not confirmed for 2010. Please telephone for details.
Wines 160 bottles over £20, 20 bottles under £20, 16 by glass **Notes** Sunday L, Vegetarian available, Dress restrictions, Smart casual, no jeans or trainers, Civ Wed 200 **Seats** 90, Pr/dining room 60 **Children** Portions, Menu **Parking** 100

PECKFORTON — Map 15 SJ55

1851 Restaurant at Peckforton Castle

@@ Modern British NEW 🖐

Inventive cuisine in a (Victorian) medieval castle

☎ 01829 260930 📄 01828 261230
Stone House Ln CW6 9TN
e-mail: info@peckfortoncastle.co.uk
dir: 15m from Chester, situated near Tarporley

Peckforton has to be seen to be believed. A Victorian vanity project and then some, it was built in the 1840s when local landowner and parliamentarian John Tollemache decided what was missing in his life was a minutely detailed medieval castle. The edifice that rose above the villages of Peckforton and Beeston has a grain store, a chapel, a gatehouse and even a keep. Peacocks strut their stuff in the grounds these days, as the Naylor family has transformed the place into what is surely its most fitting role yet - as a lavish country hotel. In the 1851 Restaurant, the place also has a fine-dining venue to suit the surroundings. Steve Ramsden is a former pupil of Gary Rhodes, and brings a dynamic culinary intelligence to the modern British cooking on offer. Scallops with cauliflower purée may be a tried-and-tested dish, but smoke the cauliflower and it becomes an altogether edgier, more distinctive proposition. Duck from a local farmer is presented as sliced breast and confit leg, alongside home-made spicy black pudding and a jus that cleverly combines lentils, apple and vanilla. With incidentals all up to the mark, this is assuredly one to watch.

Chef Stephen Ramsden **Owner** Naylor Family
Times 12-9/6-9 **Prices** Fixed L 2 course fr £10.95, Fixed D 3 course £25.95-£28.95, Starter £5.95-£8.50, Main £15.95-£19.95, Dessert £4.95-£8.95, Service optional **Wines** 21 bottles over £20, 12 bottles under £20, 9 by glass **Notes** Sunday L, Vegetarian available, Civ Wed 180, Air con **Seats** 60, Pr/dining room 165 **Children** Portions

---

PRESTBURY — Map 16 SJ87

White House Restaurant

@ Modern British

Bistro cooking with a loyal local following

☎ 01625 829336 📄 01625 829336
SK10 4DG
e-mail: enquiries@thewhitehouseinprestbury.com
dir: Village centre on A538 N of Macclesfield

The white-fronted restaurant is to be found in the heart of the village, and retains a loyal, enthusiastic following. Smartly decorated with a light touch, it also has a conservatory extension. The cooking may be characterised as modern bistro, with a perhaps over-extended menu choice. 'To commence,' as the menu has it, there might be onion soup with stilton beignets, or succulent grilled scallops with tomato and chorizo salsa. Continue with balsamic-glazed lamb with sweet potato gratin, and finish with properly textured vanilla pannacotta with poached fruits in a red wine syrup.

Times 12-2/6-9 Closed 25 Dec, 1 Jan, Mon, D Sun

PUDDINGTON — Map 15 SJ37

Macdonald Craxton Wood

@ Modern British

Smart hotel with wide-ranging menu

☎ 0151 347 4000 & 0844 879 9038 📄 0151 347 4040
Parkgate Rd, Ledsham CH66 9PB
e-mail: info@craxton.macdonald-hotels.co.uk
dir: from M6 take M56 towards N Wales, then A5117/ A540 to Hoylake. Hotel on left 200yds past lights

Approached via a tree-lined drive, this smart hotel stands amid 27 acres of mature woodland and well-tended gardens. Located on the outskirts of Chester, it offers excellent leisure facilities and an impressive conservatory lounge and bar. Its restaurant boasts fine garden views and a menu with a broad range of dishes - seared Loch Fyne scallops, perhaps, with cauliflower purée and crisp pancetta could be followed by roast tenderloin and caramelised belly of free-range British pork with dauphinoise potatoes and mushroom cream. Finish with pear and walnut pudding and walnut praline ice cream.

Chef Rob Pritchett **Owner** Macdonald Hotels Plc
Times 12.30-2/7-9.30 Closed L Sat **Prices** Starter £5-£12.50, Main £12.50-£25, Dessert £5-£8, Service included **Notes** Vegetarian available, Dress restrictions, No jeans, Civ Wed 300, Air con **Seats** 56, Pr/dining room 40 **Children** Portions, Menu **Parking** 200

RAINOW — Map 16 SJ97

The Highwayman

@ British 🖐

Traditional inn with modern approach to food and service

☎ 01625 573245
Macclesfield Rd SK10 5UU
dir: From Macclesfield take B5470 towards Whaley Bridge. Restaurant between Rainow & Kettleshulme

This 17th-century country pub hits the spot at any time of year: on a good day you get fabulous views over Lancashire and Cheshire from outdoor tables; when the weather does its worst, move indoors and it's a cosy old-style inn with a modern makeover. Stone-flagged floors, crackling open fires and low ceilings work well with comfy leather sofas and chunky wooden tables in the lounge bar and dinky dining room. Service is modern in its chatty, clued-up approach and the kitchen's fuss-free attitude does a sterling job with quality local ingredients. The menu mixes pub classics such as beer-battered haddock and chips or lamb shank, slow-braised in Guinness and treacle, with more inventive choices such as Goosnargh duck breast served with pain d'épice rhubarb crumble, crispy confit wing, Savoy cabbage and spring onion potato cake.

Chef Tim Finney, Richard Finney **Owner** Kristiane Harrison
Times 12-2.30/6-9 **Prices** Starter £3.95-£6.95, Main £9.95-£16.95, Dessert £4.95-£7.50, Service optional, Groups min 6 service 10% **Wines** 9 bottles over £20, 19 bottles under £20, 7 by glass **Notes** Sunday L, Vegetarian available **Seats** 50, Pr/dining room 24 **Children** Portions **Parking** 22

SANDIWAY — Map 15 SJ67

Nunsmere Hall Country House Hotel

@@ British, European 🖐

Country-house elegance in a Cheshire forest

☎ 01606 889100 📄 01606 889055
Tarporley Rd, Oakmere CW8 2ES
e-mail: reservations@nunsmere.co.uk
dir: M6 junct 18, A54 to Chester, at x-rds with A49 turn left towards Tarporley, hotel 2m on left

The expansive Victorian mansion is set within Cheshire's Delamere Forest, with landscape gardens and a 60-acre

continued

SANDIWAY *continued*

lake to contemplate. Sir Aubrey Brocklebank designed the first Queen Mary ocean-liner in what is now the drawing room here. The rich red colour-scheme of the dining room is fully in keeping with the surrounding opulence, and the modern British food offers good clarity of flavours based on well-sourced seasonal produce. Seared scallops with champ, pea purée and pancetta is a fine modern classic, as is the pairing of fillet and braised shin of local beef with roast vegetables in a cep and truffle sauce, and the gin and tonic sorbet and orange 'pastel' that accompany thickly based rhubarb cheesecake are sensational.

Chef Craig Malone **Owner** Prima Hotels **Times** 12-2/7-10 **Prices** Fixed L 2 course fr £15.95, Fixed D 3 course fr £29.50, Tasting menu £55-£88.50, Starter £8.50-£13.95, Main £18.50-£28, Dessert £4.50-£8.50, Service added but optional 10% **Wines** 140 bottles over £20, 12 bottles under £20, 8 by glass **Notes** Sunday L, Vegetarian available, Dress restrictions, No jeans, trainers or shorts, Civ Wed 100 **Seats** 60, Pr/dining room 45 **Children** Portions **Parking** 80

TARPORLEY   Map 15 SJ56

Macdonald Portal Hotel

◉◉ Modern British

Sophisticated country-club setting serving contemporary cuisine

☎ 0844 879 9082
Cobbiers Cross Ln CW6 0DJ

A plush new hotel in the verdant Cheshire countryside, the Macdonald Portal hit the ground running when it opened with 2 golf courses and a full line-up of health, fitness and beauty treats. Named after the earl who built nearby Beeston Castle, the sleek Ranulf Restaurant is the venue for the kitchen's output of uncomplicated modern dishes, led by well-sourced materials in intelligent combinations that let the essential flavours work in harmony. Pan-seared West Coast scallops with minted pea mousse and crispy pork belly might start things off, followed by herb-crusted rack of Highland lamb with confit shoulder, black pudding, ratatouille, and thyme jus.

WILMSLOW   Map 16 SJ88

Stanneylands Hotel

◉◉ Modern British

Country-house hotel dining close to Manchester airport

☎ 01625 525225   ▤ 01625 537282
Stanneylands Rd SK9 4EY
e-mail: enquiries@stanneylandshotel.co.uk
dir: from M56 at airport turn off, follow signs to Wilmslow. Left into Station Rd, onto Stanneylands Rd. Hotel on right

Set in mature gardens boasting some fine specimen trees and based around an original 1920s house, this traditional country-house hotel is handy for Manchester Airport and the city centre. The elegant panelled

restaurant is a popular venue for locals and visitors alike. Relax over a drink in one of the modern lounges before tucking into a starter of Herdwick mutton salad with green beans, cucumber, mint and sheep's cheese. Follow on with poached line-caught sea bass with lobster ravioli, crushed new potatoes and lobster bisque, or pan-fried beef fillet with stout-braised ox cheek, cauliflower purée and beef jus.

Chef Thomas Ludecke **Owner** Mr L Walshe **Times** 12.30-2.30/7-9.30 **Prices** Food prices not confirmed for 2010. Please telephone for details. **Wines** 108 bottles over £20, 31 bottles under £20, 6 by glass **Notes** Vegetarian available, Dress restrictions, Smart casual, Civ Wed 100 **Seats** 60, Pr/dining room 120 **Children** Portions, Menu **Parking** 110

CORNWALL & ISLES OF SCILLY

BODMIN   Map 2 SX06

Trehellas House Hotel & Restaurant

◉ Modern European

Celebrating the best of Cornish produce in an old farmhouse setting

☎ 01208 72700   ▤ 01208 73336
Washaway PL30 3AD
e-mail: enquiries@trehellashouse.co.uk
dir: Take A389 from Bodmin towards Wadebridge. Hotel on right 0.5m beyond road to Camelford

The old farmhouse on the Bodmin to Wadebridge road has served time as a courthouse in its past. Now a characterful hotel, it takes on a cosy, even slightly quaint, atmosphere in the evenings, when candles are lit in the slate-floored restaurant, and a menu of assured country cooking is offered. Start perhaps with Cornish scallops, served with lemon butter and a herb salad, before considering haunch of local venison with creamed potatoes and spinach, in a jus of garlic, shallots, red wine and thyme. The parfait of white chocolate and hazelnut has just the right texture, and is full of flavour, not least from its accompanying black cherry compôte. Wines include the pride of Cornwall, Camel Valley Vineyard.

Chef Tim Parsons **Owner** Alistair & Debra Hunter **Times** 12-2/6.30-9 **Prices** Fixed L 2 course £10, Starter £6.95-£11.75, Main £14.75-£47.25, Dessert £5.50-£7.95, Service included **Wines** 7 bottles over £20, 24 bottles under £20, 6 by glass **Notes** Sunday L, Vegetarian available **Seats** 40 **Children** Portions, Menu **Parking** 25

BOSCASTLE   Map 2 SX09

The Wellington Hotel

◉ Modern British ♨

Imaginative cooking in popular Cornish fishing village

☎ 01840 250202   ▤ 01840 250621
The Harbour PL35 0AQ
e-mail: info@boscastle-wellington.com
dir: A30/A395 at Davidstowe follow Boscastle signs. B3266 to village. Right into Old Rd

The devastating Boscastle floods put one of north Cornwall's most touristy fishing villages in the headlines for all the wrong reasons in 2004. Even the 'Welly', despite its foursquare solidity, with a battlemented turret that gave it the original name of the Bos Castle hotel, took a battering. Six years on, it's fully back on its feet, and thanks to the BBC's 'Changing Rooms' makeover team the Waterloo restaurant has a sharp contemporary look with black leather high-backed chairs and black table linen set against dove-grey walls – the perfect setting for chef Scott's imaginative cooking. Local sourcing is taken seriously and forms the backbone of enticing daily-changing menus. Cornish bouillabaisse with rouille and garlic oil might get things rolling, followed by herb-baked cod with roast fennel, crispy potato cake and dill butter.

Chef Scott Roberts **Owner** Paul Roberts **Times** 6.30-9.30 Closed Thu **Prices** Starter £6-£8.50, Main £11-£20, Dessert £6-£8.50, Service optional **Wines** 20 bottles over £20, 48 bottles under £20, 8 by glass **Notes** Tasting menu available with advance notice **Seats** 35, Pr/dining room 28 **Children** Portions, Menu **Parking** 15

BUDE   Map 2 SS20

The Castle Restaurant

◉ Modern European **NEW**

Relaxed bistro with sound cooking and great views

☎ 01288 350543
The Wharf EX23 8LG
e-mail: enquiries@thecastlerestaurantbude.co.uk
dir: Please telephone for directions

Housed in an historic castellated building with sea views, this restaurant shares its home with a museum and art gallery. The simple bistro style of unclothed wooden tables, local artwork and open kitchen is matched by the uncomplicated cooking and relaxed, friendly service. Dishes on the chalkboard menu let ingredients speak for themselves and there is a lightness of touch in the kitchen. A meal starting with sautéed chicken liver bruschetta with rocket, crispy red onions and balsamic, followed by sea bass fillet with grilled potatoes, braised celery and blood orange hollandaise, could finish with a classic crème brûlée.

Chef Kit Davis **Owner** Kit Davis **Times** 12-2.30/6-9.30 Closed D Sun **Prices** Fixed L 2 course £11.50-£13, Fixed D 3 course £22-£35, Starter £4-£10, Main £12-£25, Dessert £5-£7, Service optional **Wines** 4 bottles over £20, 15 bottles under £20, 7 by glass **Notes** Sunday L, Vegetarian available, Civ Wed 120 **Seats** 40, Pr/dining room 25 **Children** Portions, Menu **Parking** Parking nearby

CALLINGTON — Map 3 SX36

Langmans Restaurant

Modern British

Well presented modern British food served in a relaxed atmosphere

☎ 01579 384933
3 Church St PL17 7RE
e-mail: dine@langmansrestaurant.co.uk
dir: From the direction of Plymouth into town centre, left at lights and second right into Church St

With crisp white table linen and crystal glassware, this stylish, intimate restaurant, housed in a Grade II listed former bakery, exudes a friendly and relaxed atmosphere. Staff are personally trained by the owner and it shows from the warm welcome to the personable yet unobtrusive service. The menu of seasonal and often organic dishes changes every 4 to 6 weeks and may include Jerusalem artichoke soup with ceps purée and confit duck to start followed by fillet of Cornish beef, red wine sauce and dauphinoise potatoes topped off with a decadent trio of puddings featuring banana and praline iced parfait, chocolate tower and pistachio mousse and rhubarb crumble with stem ginger ice cream. There's a tasting menu at dinner, plus a good selection of wines by the glass.

Chef Anton Buttery **Owner** Anton & Gail Buttery
Times 7.30 Closed Sun-Wed, L all week **Prices** Tasting menu fr £35, Service optional **Wines** 49 bottles over £20, 28 bottles under £20, 11 by glass **Notes** Tasting menu available 6 courses, Vegetarian available, Dress restrictions, Smart casual preferred **Seats** 24 **Parking** Town centre car park

CONSTANTINE — Map 2 SW72

Trengilly Wartha Inn

Traditional British, International

Country inn serving good Cornish produce

☎ 01326 340332 ▤ 01326 340332
Nancenoy TR11 5RP
e-mail: reception@trengilly.co.uk
dir: Follow signs to Nancenoy, left towards Gweek until 1st sign for inn, left & left again at next sign, continue to inn

Secreted away in a tranquil wooded valley along a creek off the Helford River, this buzzy country pub is a bit of a foodie hotspot. There's a cosy bistro kitted out with blond wood furniture made by local artisans and a lively bar where daily specials are chalked up on boards. The kitchen has a cracking line in skilfully-prepared food based on fresh, local materials, with an eclectic mix of global influences. You couldn't find a starter more local than Falmouth River mussels, done marinière-style with garlic and white wine; next, mains might include a whole baked red mullet with oriental vegetable and rainbow chard stock and dauphinoise potatoes. The wine list punches above its weight, so make sure to give it serious attention.

Chef Nick Tyler, Richard Penna **Owner** William & Lisa Lea
Times 12-3/7-12 Closed 25 Dec **Prices** Food prices not confirmed for 2010. Please telephone for details.
Wines 27 bottles over £20, 113 bottles under £20, 15 by glass **Notes** Sunday L, Vegetarian available **Seats** 25, Pr/dining room 16 **Children** Portions, Menu **Parking** 30

FALMOUTH — Map 2 SW83

Falmouth Hotel

Modern British **V**

Grand seaside hotel with seasonal menu

☎ 01326 312671 & 0800 44 888 44 ▤ 01326 319533
Castle Beach TR11 4NZ
e-mail: reservations@falmouthhotel.com
dir: A30 to Truro then A390 to Falmouth. Follow signs for beaches, hotel on seafront near Pendennis Castle

This grand old Victorian lady has it all. A glorious beachfront location, with 5 acres of gardens with views to the Pendennis headland to stroll around, and when the British weather does its worst, there are comfy lounges with vast picture windows and ample leisure and beauty facilities. The food is served beneath chandeliers and amid the period elegance of the Trelawney Restaurant. The kitchen chooses well from the brimming West Country larder to produce uncomplicated and well-executed fixed-price menus and daily specials. Start with chicken and red pepper terrine with sweetcorn relish and melba toast, then pan-fried Newlyn sea bass with cucumber and dill potato salad, braised fennel and salsa verde.

Chef Paul Brennan **Owner** Richardson Hotels of Distinction **Times** 12.30-2/7-9.30 Closed L Sat
Prices Food prices not confirmed for 2010. Please telephone for details. **Wines** 21 bottles over £20, 29 bottles under £20, 7 by glass **Notes** Sunday L, Vegetarian menu, Dress restrictions, Smart casual, no sportswear, Civ Wed 250 **Seats** 150, Pr/dining room 40 **Children** Portions, Menu

The Flying Fish Restaurant Bar

Modern British

Seductive sea views and sub-tropical gardens

☎ 01326 312707 ▤ 01326 211772
St Michael's Hotel and Spa, Gyllyngvase Beach, Seafront TR11 4NB
e-mail: info@stmichaelshotel.co.uk
dir: Please telephone for directions

The Gulf Stream microclimate allows for sub-tropical gardens at St Michael's Hotel, complete with gracefully ruffling palms; ask the head gardener for your botanical crash-course. In the restaurant, seductive sea views are best enjoyed from the open-air terrace on light evenings, and the food mixes traditional British modes with continental influences. Expect local mussels in cider and parsley cream, with tiger prawn linguini or maybe a pair of lamb chops with celeriac purée and a wholegrain mustard and rosemary jus, to follow. There are fine West Country cheeses on offer too.

Chef Emma Barry **Owner** Nigel & Julie Carpenter
Times 12-2/7-9 **Prices** Food prices not confirmed for 2010. Please telephone for details. **Wines** 13 bottles over £20, 19 bottles under £20, 12 by glass **Notes** Sunday L, Dress restrictions, Smart casual, Civ Wed 100 **Seats** 90, Pr/dining room 30 **Children** Portions, Menu **Parking** 30

Harbourside Restaurant

Modern British

Regionally based cooking with sweeping harbour views

☎ 01326 312440 ▤ 01326 211362
The Greenbank, Harbourside TR11 2SR
e-mail: sales@greenbank-hotel.co.uk
web: www.greenbank-hotel.co.uk
dir: Approaching Falmouth from Penryn, take left along North Parade. Follow sign to Falmouth Marina and Greenbank Hotel

The restaurant of the Greenbank Hotel is a triumph of airiness and light, gently lit with ceiling spots in the evenings, but benefiting primarily from wide-screen views of Falmouth harbour. As seems only natural, fish and seafood are the strong suits, with baked smoked haddock served with smoked mussels, spring onion mash, a poached egg and mustard sauce among the main-course options, preceded perhaps by a Cornish seafood basket with Marie Rose dressing and pickled lemon, or crab risotto balls with pickled beetroot and tomato relish. Local cheeses are an appropriate way to finish, or try apple crumble cake with cinnamon yogurt and clotted cream.

Times 12-2/7-9.30 Closed L Sat

FALMOUTH *continued*

Penmere Manor Hotel

Modern French, European NEW V

Georgian hotel with local produce to the fore

☎ 01326 211411 📠 01326 317588
Mongleath Rd, Falmouth TR11 4PN
e-mail: reception@penmere.co.uk
dir: Please telephone for directions

Set in five acres of well tended grounds, Penmere dates from 1820 and is these days a comfortable hotel with new owners looking to raise the bar. The restaurant changes its menus with the seasons and includes plenty of local produce. France and the Mediterranean are the focus of the food, with local goats' cheese, Gevrik, served on toast as a starter with wild mushrooms, young spinach leaves and balsamic, and John Dory as a main course with saffron potatoes, broad beans and lemon beurre blanc. Pre-dinner drinks can be taken in the lounge (where a pianist plays) or on the terrace.

Chef Joe Lado Devesa **Owner** Nick Moore **Times** 7-9.30 Closed 21-26 Dec, L all week **Prices** Fixed D 3 course £25, Starter £5.50-£8, Main £15-£18, Dessert £5.50-£7, Service optional **Wines** 20 bottles over £20, 16 bottles under £20, 9 by glass **Notes** Sunday L, Vegetarian menu, Civ Wed 70, Air con **Seats** 80, Pr/dining room 40 **Children** Portions, Menu **Parking** 60

The Terrace Restaurant

Modern International

Super views across Falmouth Bay and classy eye-catching food

☎ 01326 313042 📠 01326 319420
The Royal Duchy Hotel, Cliff Rd TR11 4NX
e-mail: info@royalduchy.co.uk
dir: on Cliff Rd, along Falmouth seafront

Views from the stripy lawns of this grand seafront hotel sweep clear across Falmouth Bay to historic Pendennis Castle. The Royal Duchy consistently comes up with the goods, thanks to its relaxed and welcoming style, comforting surroundings, and cheery, switched-on staff. In the dining room, chandeliers and live music courtesy of a tinkling grand piano hark back to the glamour of a bygone age, while the kitchen's focus is on bringing

Cornwall's excellent produce to the table. A repertoire of classic and modern dishes shows a sound command of simple flavour combinations, in starters such as ballotine of ham hock with vegetables à la Grecque, and a main course of slow-roasted rack of pork with butter beans and bacon and Madeira sauce. Puddings are also a strong suit - try bitter chocolate tart with coffee and Muscovado parfait and crème fraîche.

Chef Dez Turland **Owner** Brend Hotel Group **Times** 12.30-2/6.30-9 Closed L Mon-Sat **Prices** Fixed L 3 course fr £16.50, Fixed D 4 course fr £35, Service optional **Wines** 16 by glass **Notes** Sunday L, Vegetarian available, Dress restrictions, Smart casual, Civ Wed 150, Air con **Seats** 100, Pr/dining room 24 **Children** Portions, Menu **Parking** 40

Restaurant Nathan Outlaw

| **FOWEY** | **Map 2 SX15** |

Modern British V

Refined, confident cooking with sea views

☎ 01726 833315 📠 01726 832779
Marina Villa Hotel, 17 Esplanade PL23 1HY
e-mail: info@marinavillahotel.com
dir: Please telephone for directions

On entering the hotel and heading downstairs to the restaurant you might be expecting a basement setting. Far from it. Restaurant Nathan Outlaw has superb terraces overlooking the harbour and out to sea and even in bad weather you can take it all in through the large windows. The building hugs the hillside and was once the holiday home of the Bishop of Truro; these days it's a destination restaurant. There's a small bar or those terraces for pre-dinner drinks and a dining room with a

smart and contemporary look. Nathan may hail from Kent but he is flying the Cornish flag for local produce and supports many of the small, artisan producers the county has to offer. Expect refined, intelligent and creative cooking. Appealing combinations such as a starter of salt cod with oxtail with pickled walnuts and watercress are imaginative and highly successful. Main-course plaice appears in partnership with mustard, capers and coco beans, while desserts such as poached peach with an ice cream of the same fruit and toasted brioche are equally well crafted and attractively presented. Service fits the bill, too.

Chef Nathan Outlaw **Owner** Mr S Westwell **Times** 12-2/7-9.30 Closed Mon (Tue out of season), L Tue (in season) Wed-Fri & Sun **Prices** Fixed L 2 course £30, Fixed D 4 course £55-£85, Starter £10-£14, Main £24-£28, Dessert £10-£14, Service included **Wines** 65 bottles over £20, 15 bottles under £20, 10 by glass **Notes** Tasting menu available, Vegetarian menu, Civ Wed 45 **Seats** 40 **Parking** Car Park

The Fowey Hotel

Modern European **V**

Super views and elegant dining

☎ 01726 832551 📠 01726 832125
The Esplanade PL23 1HX
e-mail: info@thefoweyhotel.co.uk
dir: A30 to Okehampton, continue to Bodmin. Then B3269 to Fowey for 1m, on right bend left junct then right into Dagands Rd. Hotel 200mtrs on left

The Fowey Hotel's kitchen puts a firm emphasis on its use of locally-sourced and seasonal produce, and with fresh Cornish fish and seafood turning up on the doorstep, expect plenty of piscine pleasures. Take seared Cornish scallops and hogs pudding with leeks and butternut squash coulis to start, then perhaps a pan-seared turbot fillet partnered with crushed potatoes and smoked bacon velouté. Flipping to the carnivorous side, the menu runs to the likes of brioche-crusted rack of lamb with dauphinoise potatoes in a mint and balsamic jus, with perhaps a glazed lemon tart with raspberry compôte and crème fraîche or West Country cheeses to finish. Marvellous marine views are the backdrop, as the handsome Victorian hotel perches above the River Fowey estuary in landscaped gardens.

Chef Mark Griffiths **Owner** Keith Richardson
Times 12-3/6.30-9 **Prices** Food prices not confirmed for 2010. Please telephone for details. **Wines** 14 bottles over £20, 29 bottles under £20, 7 by glass **Notes** Vegetarian menu, Dress restrictions, Smart casual, No torn denim, trainers, shorts **Seats** 60 **Children** Portions, Menu **Parking** 13

Hansons

British, French

Accomplished cuisine in ornate family-friendly surroundings

☎ 01726 833866 📠 01726 834100
Fowey Hall Hotel, Hanson Dr PL23 1ET
e-mail: info@foweyhall.com
dir: Into town centre, pass school on right, 400yds turn right onto Hanson Drive

This grand Victorian château-style pile was the inspiration for Toad Hall in the children's classic *Wind in the Willows*, so it is rather fitting that the modern luxury hotel has a strong family focus. The ethos here is that families should be able to enjoy themselves in opulent, stylish surroundings with good food to boot. Hansons restaurant is a thoroughly adult space once the kids are tucked up for the night, all oak panels and floors, and gilt mirrors that make for a romantic setting by candlelight. The kitchen aims high, using choice Cornish produce as the backbone of its contemporary country-house cuisine. Dishes such as steamed organic salmon with squid ink risotto, candied lemon and scallop foam start things rolling, while mains might feature local grey mullet with tiger prawns, cauliflower and truffle foam and rock samphire. High-class comfort food, such as warm ginger cake with crème caramel and carrot sorbet, appears at dessert.

Chef John Mijatovic **Owner** Andrew Davis
Times 12-2.15/7-10 **Prices** Fixed D 3 course £39.50, Tasting menu £64.50, Service optional **Wines** 70 bottles over £20, 18 bottles under £20, 12 by glass **Notes** Tasting menu 7 course, Sunday L, Vegetarian available, Civ Wed 50 **Seats** 60, Pr/dining room 20 **Children** Portions, Menu **Parking** 35

The Old Quay House

British, French

Fresh local produce served in waterfront location with views of Fowey estuary

☎ 01726 833302 📠 01726 833668
28 Fore St PL23 1AQ
e-mail: info@theoldquayhouse.com
web: www.theoldquayhouse.com
dir: From A390 through Lostwithiel, take left onto B3269 to Fowey town centre, on right next to Lloyds TSB bank

The setting is just perfect: a former custom-house on the quay that has been beautifully restored and transformed into a stylish boutique hotel. The architect-designed interior brings contemporary style to the historic setting, and views from the stylish restaurant are amazing. Accomplished cuisine relies on classic French technique but with some British and European influences. The emphasis is firmly on fresh, locally-sourced produce, with seasonally-changing menus and regular specials. Try cumin-roasted lamb shank with pumpkin tagine and preserved lemon, sea bass with roasted root vegetables, smoked bacon and rocket and tarragon oil, and crème brûlée with vanilla shortbread. The terrace, on the old quay itself, juts out into the harbour and is a great place for drinks, as is the chic 'Q' Bar.

Chef Ben Bass **Owner** Jane & Roy Carson
Times 12.30-2.30/7-9 Closed L Mon to Fri (Oct to May) **Prices** Fixed D 3 course fr £35, Starter £5-£10, Main £14-£21, Dessert £5-£8, Service optional **Wines** 15 bottles over £20, 15 bottles under £20, 5 by glass **Notes** Sunday L, Vegetarian available, Civ Wed 40 **Seats** 38

Restaurant Nathan Outlaw

— see opposite

Cormorant Hotel and Riverview Restaurant

Modern British

Fine modern British food with sumptuous river views

☎ 01726 833426 📠 01726 833426
PL23 1LL
e-mail: relax@cormoranthotel.co.uk
dir: A390 onto B3269 signed Fowey. In 3m left to Golant, through village to end of road, hotel on right

The setting could hardly be more sumptuous, with the Cormorant perched as it is above the River Fowey. Enjoy broad, expansive views from the aptly named restaurant, or get even closer by means of a terrace in benevolent weather. Well-drilled service, crisp napery and a light, airy feel add gloss to proceedings, and so does the adventurous cooking. Flair and consistency distinguish dishes such as tenderly sautéed lamb's kidneys with mushrooms, smoked bacon and a poached quail's egg, or flavourful tenderloin of local pork with creamed spinach and leeks and crisp potato rösti. Glazed lemon tart combines richness and citric zing for a simply effective finale.

Chef Martin Adams **Owner** Mrs Mary Tozer
Times 12.30-2.30/6.30-9.30 Closed L Mon, Tue (summer) **Prices** Fixed D 3 course £30-£40, Starter £7-£12, Main £12-£27, Dessert £7-£10, Service optional, Groups min 7 service 12% **Wines** 41 bottles over £20, 30 bottles under £20, 8 by glass **Notes** Sunday L, Vegetarian available, Dress restrictions, Smart casual, no shorts **Seats** 30 **Children** Portions **Parking** 16, On street, Public car park

New Yard Restaurant

◉◉ Modern British 🌱

Solid commitment to local food in an 18th-century stable yard

☎ 01326 221595 📠 01326 221440
Trelowarren, Mawgan TR12 6AF
e-mail: info@trelowarren.com
dir: 5m from Helston

The historic 1,000-acre Trelowarren estate at the heart of the Lizard Peninsula has been run by the same family for 600 years, and is taking on the 21st century with a sound eco-friendly ethos. A carriage house in the stable yard has been converted into a bright and breezy restaurant, where there's a cosy real fire and tables are made of local ash. The kitchen takes the concepts of sustainability and food miles very seriously, after all, 90% of the ingredients on your plate will have come from within a 10-mile radius. Lobster risotto infused with Menallack vintage cheese and truffle oil might start things off, followed by Trelowarren pheasant wrapped in smoked bacon, stuffed with thyme and citrus farce. Try treacle tart with rich vanilla ice cream and citrus syrup for pudding, or go for the excellent Cornish artisan cheeses.

Chef Greg Laskey **Owner** Sir Ferrers Vyvyan
Times 12-2/7-9.30 Closed Mon (mid Sep-Whitsun), D Sun
Prices Fixed L course £16.25, Fixed D 3 course £24.95, Starter £6.20-£8.50, Main fr £11.95, Dessert £6.15-£7.25, Service optional **Wines** 29 bottles over £20, 28 bottles under £20, 4 by glass **Notes** Sunday L, Vegetarian available, Dress restrictions, Smart dress, smart casual **Seats** 45 **Children** Portions, Menu **Parking** 20

The Well House Hotel

◉◉◉ – *see below*

Barclay House

◉ Modern British **NEW** 🌱

Imaginative cooking with splendid estuary views

☎ 01503 262929 📠 01503 262632
St Martin's Rd PL13 1LP
e-mail: info@barclayhouse.co.uk
dir: 1st house on left on entering Looe from A38

The views across the East Looe River estuary from Barclay's bright and modern restaurant are quite something, and in summer, the doors open out onto the terrace for aperitifs. A relaxed atmosphere prevails, with wooden tables and colourful original local art, but the daily-changing menu - which reflects exactly what's best and in season locally from sea and land - catches the eye and imagination. Take a trio of local Looe day-boat fish served with capers, home-grown parsley and brown butter, or from land, perhaps Trenent Farm (at Looe) fillet steak with crispy-fried Cornish hen's egg, leek julienne and black pepper oil.

Chef Benjamin Palmer **Owner** Malcolm, Graham & Gill Brooks **Times** 12-2/7-9 Closed 24-26 Dec, Sun in winter, L winter by arrangement only **Prices** Food prices not confirmed for 2010. Please telephone for details. **Wines** 35 bottles over £20, 17 bottles under £20, 13 by glass **Notes** ALC prices L only, Sun L summer only, Sunday L, Vegetarian available, Dress restrictions, Smart casual, Civ Wed 120 **Seats** 45 **Children** Portions, Menu **Parking** 25

The Well House Hotel

Modern European **V**

Culinary hideaway in a tranquil valley

☎ 01579 342001 📠 01579 343891
St Keyne PL14 4RN
e-mail: enquiries@wellhouse.co.uk
dir: A38 to Liskeard and A390 to town centre, then take B3254 to St Keyne 3m. In village take left fork at church signed St Keyne. Hotel 0.5m on left

The Well House was built by a Victorian tea tycoon to hide away in idyllic seclusion in the Looe Valley. As you toast his excellent eye for a plum location with afternoon tea on the terrace, taking in the quintessentially English view of verdant hills and meadows all around, it's hard to imagine that crowds are queuing to get into the Eden Project a short drive away. It's the perfect bolthole for a restful gastronomic getaway too, with a resolutely country-house ambience courtesy of relaxed and friendly staff. The excellent canapés served in the bar are the first hint that dining here is a cut or two above the ordinary. Sculptures and fine art blend well with the white and neutral tones of the smart contemporary restaurant. Modern European cooking with the emphasis on prime local, seasonal produce is the key here: Tom Hunter is a young Master Chef who channels his passion and skills well without straying too far into avant-garde territory. Technique and presentation are at a high level throughout in an intelligently-conceived repertoire; expect sharp, clearly-defined flavours and well-judged combinations. A creamy white onion risotto comes with the nutty bite and texture of toasted almonds and herb butter, while a main course of halibut is partnered with young kale, crispy bacon and 5 types of wild mushroom.

Chef Tom Hunter **Owner** Richard Farrow
Times 12-3/6.30-10 **Prices** Fixed L 2 course £18.50, Fixed D 3 course £37.50, Tasting menu £42.50, Service optional **Wines** 79 bottles over £20, 39 bottles under £20, 6 by glass **Notes** Tasting menu 6 course, Sunday L, Vegetarian menu, Dress restrictions, Smart casual, Civ Wed 30 **Seats** 26, Pr/dining room 34 **Children** Menu **Parking** 30

Trelaske Hotel & Restaurant

◉ Modern, Traditional British ◐

Locally sourced produce in verdant Cornwall

☎ 01503 262159   📠 01503 265360
Polperro Rd PL13 2JS
e-mail: info@trelaske.co.uk
dir: Over Looe bridge signed Polperro. After 1.9m signed on right

The white-fronted hotel hides within 4 acres of verdant grounds in the hinterland between Looe and Polperro. Produce is conscientiously locally sourced within a 30-mile radius, with fruit, vegetables and herbs coming largely from the hotel's own garden. Large windows allow diners generous views of the big Cornish picture. Modern British cooking with some old favourites brings on wild boar terrine with crab-apple jelly and pickled walnuts, baked turbot with roasted tomatoes in lemon and herb oil, or pork fillet wrapped in Cornish coppa (cured pork neck) with caramelised pear and Calvados sauce. Desserts include a pleasingly light and zestily sauced orange and date pudding.

Chef Ross Lewin **Owner** Ross Lewin & Hazel Billington **Times** 12-2/7-9 **Prices** Fixed D 3 course £29, Service optional **Wines** 11 bottles over £20, 23 bottles under £20, 32 by glass **Notes** Sunday L, Vegetarian available, Dress restrictions, Smart casual **Seats** 70 **Children** Portions, Menu **Parking** 60

MARAZION   Map 2 SW53

Mount Haven Hotel & Restaurant

◉◉ Modern British

Modern British cooking in stylish hotel with wonderful views

☎ 01736 710249   📠 01736 711658
Turnpike Rd TR17 0DQ
e-mail: reception@mounthaven.co.uk
dir: From centre of Marazion, up hill E, hotel 400yds on right

Overlooking St Michael's Mount and the bay, this hotel has an enviable position. To make the best of it, take pre-dinner drinks on the west-facing terrace and keep your fingers crossed for a spectacular sunset (they're common round these parts). Inside the décor is a chic mixture of Eastern culture and Western comfort. The light and airy dining room, overlooking the garden, features white walls, tables and crockery. The style of cooking is modern British, based on fresh local produce, especially seafood, with starters such as soused mackerel, fennel and cucumber and main courses like John Dory with samphire, quail's eggs and gnocchi, or duo of spring lamb, rosemary mash and butternut squash.

Times 12-2.30/6.30-10.30 Closed mid Dec-mid Feb

MAWGAN PORTH   Map 2 SW86

Bedruthan Steps Hotel

◉ Modern British ◐

Vibrant cooking with panoramic ocean views

☎ 01637 860555 & 860860   📠 01637 860714
TR8 4BU
e-mail: stay@bedruthan.com
dir: From A39/A30 follow signs to Newquay Airport. Turn right at T-junct to Mawgan Porth. Hotel at top of hill on left

Cornwall is blessed with many restaurants that take maximum advantage of the soothing sea views, and this one is no exception. The dining-room at this friendly hotel faces out over the bay, and looks all the better when, aperitif in hand, you watch the sun slipping slowly below the horizon. Contemporary design and vibrant, multi-layered cooking set the tone, with dishes ranging from potted salmon terrine with sorrel and green chutney, through slow-roast pork belly with black pudding stovie, buttered kale, and apple brandy and sage jus, to a finale of baked rice pudding with a compôte of rhubarb, orange and ginger.

Chef Adam Clark **Owner** Mrs Stratton & Mrs Wakefield **Times** 12-2/7.30-9.30 Closed Xmas **Prices** Food prices not confirmed for 2010. Please telephone for details. **Wines** 53 bottles over £20, 23 bottles under £20, 16 by glass **Notes** Sunday L, Dress restrictions, Smart casual, no beach wear, Civ Wed 200 **Seats** 200, Pr/dining room 150 **Children** Portions, Menu **Parking** 100

MAWNAN SMITH   Map 2 SW72

Budock Vean - The Hotel on the River

◉ Traditional British **V**

Peacefully situated hotel using good Cornish produce

☎ 01326 252100 & 250288   📠 01326 250892
TR11 5LG
e-mail: relax@budockvean.co.uk
dir: from A39 follow tourist signs to Trebah Gardens. 0.5m to hotel

With a private foreshore to Helford River, and an 18-hole golf course, the 65 acres of gardens and parkland that surround this tranquil hotel are quite glorious. Comforting British dishes with a few international flavours are served in the traditional candlelit restaurant, the daily-changing dinner menu featuring carefully sourced Cornish produce, including Newlyn crab, served with avocado, crème fraîche and wasabi dressing, and locally-landed lemon sole with nut brown butter. Alternatives may take in duck with Puy lentils and port wine jus, pork tenderloin with mustard mash and Madeira, with vanilla and coconut pannacotta for pudding.

Chef Darren Kelly **Owner** Barlow Family **Times** 12-2.30/7.30-9 Closed 3 wks Jan, L Mon-Sat **Prices** Starter £7.95-£18.75, Main £14.25-£32.50, Dessert £6, Service optional **Wines** 52 bottles over £20, 42 bottles under £20, 7 by glass **Notes** Fixed D 5 courses £33.50, Sunday L, Vegetarian menu, Dress restrictions, Jacket & tie, Civ Wed 60, Air con **Seats** 100, Pr/dining room 40 **Children** Portions, Menu **Parking** 100

Meudon Hotel

◉ Traditional British ◐

Country-house hotel serving regional produce

☎ 01326 250541   📠 01326 250543
TR11 5HT
e-mail: wecare@meudon.co.uk
dir: from Truro A39 towards Falmouth at Hillhead (Anchor & Cannons) rdbt, follow signs to Maenporth Beach. Hotel on left 1m after beach

Set in a peaceful, sub-tropical valley on the south Cornish coast, this Victorian mansion is made up of two 300-year old coastguard cottages and has been in the same family for 5 generations. The delightful conservatory restaurant features an exotic fruiting vine, and every table has a view of the magical 8-acre garden that sweeps down to the private beach at Bream Cove. The kitchen creates regional, seasonal dishes using the best locally-sourced West Country ingredients, including seafood deliveries coming daily from Newlyn, oysters from Helford and cheese from a farm 2 miles away. Local smoked mackerel, trout and salmon come as a starter on a soused cucumber salad, with yogurt and horseradish dressing, followed by pan-cooked Cornish pork tenderloin with cider, thyme and exotic mushrooms.

Chef Alan Webb **Owner** Mr Pilgrim **Times** 12.30-2/7.30-9 Closed Jan **Prices** Fixed L course £18.50, Fixed D 3 course £35-£39.50, Service optional **Wines** 80 bottles over £20, 39 bottles under £20, 5 by glass **Notes** Sunday L, Vegetarian available, Dress restrictions, Smart dress **Seats** 60 **Children** Portions, Menu **Parking** 30

Trelawne Hotel

◉ Modern British ◐

Imaginative British cooking and magnificent views

☎ 01326 250226   📠 01326 250909
TR11 5HS
e-mail: info@trelawnehotel.co.uk
dir: A39 to Falmouth, right at Hillhead rdbt signed Maenporth. Past beach, up hill and hotel on left

Situated in a designated Area of Outstanding Natural Beauty, this small, family-run hotel is surrounded by attractive gardens and enjoys superb views over Falmouth Bay. Imaginative modern British menus, priced from two to four courses, are served in the spacious restaurant, with dishes such as sliced smoked haunch of venison with Parma ham and pine nuts to start, and steamed fillet of sea bass with smoked salmon and dill dressing as a main course. Quality local produce is organic where possible, and all the meats and vegetables come from local farms.

Chef Martin Jones, Oliver Wyatt **Owner** G P Gibbons **Times** 7-9 Closed 30 Nov-20 Feb, L all week **Prices** Fixed D 3 course £28.50, Service optional **Wines** 11 bottles over £20, 44 bottles under £20, 5 by glass **Notes** Vegetarian available, Dress restrictions, Smart casual **Seats** 30 **Children** Portions, Menu **Parking** 20

MOUSEHOLE — Map 2 SW42

The Cornish Range Restaurant with Rooms

◉◉ Modern British

The best local seafood in charming village restaurant

☎ 01736 731488
6 Chapel St TR19 6SB
e-mail: info@cornishrange.co.uk
web: www.cornishrange.co.uk
dir: From Penzance 3m S to Mousehole, via Newlyn. Follow road to far side of harbour

Among the winding streets of this picturesque village, a former pilchard factory, sturdily built of granite, is these days earning its crust as a charming restaurant with rooms specialising in seafood from nearby Newlyn. The dining room is pleasantly decorated with a seafaring theme, so local seascapes adorn the walls and blue is the predominant colour. It maximises its usefulness to the community by opening for brunch (a locally-smoked kipper, perhaps) and by producing an imaginative children's menu. A starter of game terrine with chestnut beignets and cranberry jam shows seafood is not the only ace up its sleeve, while roast cod fillet with succotash and monkfish scampi highlights the quality of the seafood. Alfresco eating in the sub-tropical garden is a delight.

Chef Keith Terry **Owner** Chad James & Keith Terry
Times 10-2.15/6-9.30 **Prices** Fixed D 2 course £14.95-£15.95, Starter £4.95-£8.95, Main £10.95-£25.50, Dessert £5.95-£6.95, Service optional **Wines** 13 bottles over £20, 19 bottles under £20, 6 by glass
Notes Vegetarian available **Seats** 60 **Children** Portions, Menu **Parking** Harbour car park

NEWQUAY — Map 2 SW86

Sand Brasserie

◉ Modern British 🍴

Modern dining with superb ocean views

☎ 01637 872211 📠 01637 872212
Headland Hotel, Fistral Beach TR7 1EW
e-mail: office@headlandhotel.co.uk
dir: A30 onto A392 towards Newquay, follow signs to Fistral Beach, hotel is adjacent

The aptly-named Headland Hotel is a grand old Victorian lady with cracking views over Fistral beach from its perch on a craggy outcrop. The perfect backdrop, then, for dining on the sunny terrace of the Sand Brasserie with waves lashing the rocks below, or inside where a vibrant modern colour palette adds a sleek note to the period grandeur. Its modern British menus list local suppliers upfront and major on sea-fresh local fish and shellfish, so smoked Cornish fish - perhaps gurnard, monkfish and red mullet - with apple and horseradish is a typical starter, followed by something meaty like West Country chicken Wellington with sautéed potatoes, tomato and basil.

Chef Chris Wyburn-Ridsdale **Owner** John & Carolyn Armstrong **Times** 12.30-2/7-9.45 Closed 25-26 Dec, L Mon-Sat **Prices** Starter £4.95-£6.95, Main £9.95-£14.95, Dessert £3.95-£5.95, Service optional **Wines** 79 bottles over £20, 51 bottles under £20, 13 by glass **Notes** Sunday L, Vegetarian available, Civ Wed 200 **Seats** 250, Pr/dining room 40 **Children** Portions, Menu **Parking** 200

PADSTOW — Map 2 SW97

Margot's

◉ British

Friendly family-run bistro with a genuine local flavour

☎ 01841 533441
11 Duke St PL28 8AB
e-mail: enquiries@margots.co.uk
dir: Please telephone for directions

Margot's is a charming little bistro - nine tables probably counts as little - down a side street in thriving Padstow. It is family run, informal and advisable to book. Local paintings hang on the walls and local produce fills the menu; expect plenty of fresh seafood and vegetables and salads from nearby growers. The waters around here are brimming with mackerel (no sustainability issues around

this fish) which might pop up on the menu with cucumber and caper berries. A meaty main course is braised lamb shank with spring onion mash and rosemary sauce. Service is genuinely friendly and the chef-proprietor likes to pop out of his kitchen from time to time, and might even bring your food to the table.

Times 12-2/7-9 Closed Nov, Jan, Sun-Mon

The Metropole

◉ Modern British 🍴

Modern British cooking and fabulous sea views

☎ 01841 532486 📠 01841 532867
Station Rd PL28 8DB
e-mail: info@the-metropole.co.uk
dir: M5/A30 past Launceston, follow signs for Wadebridge and N Cornwall. Then take A39 and follow signs for Padstow

Perched on the brow of a hill overlooking Padstow, this elegant Victorian-inspired hotel offers the most spectacular views across the Camel estuary. Built in 1904, it was once a favourite haunt of the Prince of Wales in the 1930s and it still retains that bygone charm, whilst being thoroughly up-to-date at the same time. The café bar offers lighter snacks, but for the full experience eat in the restaurant with its wonderful views. Modern British dishes take in grilled mackerel, potato salad and shallot and caper dressing, followed by brill poached in red wine with a wild mushroom risotto and a red wine butter sauce.

Chef Adam Warne **Owner** Richardson Hotels Ltd
Times 6.30-9.00 Closed L Mon-Sat **Prices** Fixed D 3 course £30, Service included **Wines** 21 bottles over £20, 26 bottles under £20, 8 by glass **Notes** Sunday L, Dress restrictions, No jeans, shorts, swimwear, trainers **Seats** 70 **Children** Portions, Menu **Parking** 40

Paul Ainsworth at No. 6

◉◉ Modern British 🍴

Exciting modern cooking using the best local produce

☎ 01841 532093 📠 01841 533941
6 Middle St PL28 8AP
e-mail: enquiries@number6inpadstow.co.uk
dir: A30 follow signs for Wadebridge then sign to Padstow

No. 6 is the latest jewel in Padstow's gastronomic crown; a Georgian townhouse, once a smugglers' den and now a smart, contemporary dining room with simple, whitewashed walls, wooden tables and high quality glassware. Service is efficient, slick and knowledgeable, the atmosphere relaxed and informal. Paul Ainsworth (who previously worked for Gordon Ramsay) shows his pedigree in accomplished, attractively presented modern dishes that use top-notch ingredients, including an abundance of fish from local day boats. Expect crubeens (pig's trotter), pickled beetroot and horseradish salad to start, and perhaps line-caught Cornish mackerel, cockles, chorizo and chickpeas for main course. A typical dessert could be pineapple, warm vanilla rice and coconut sorbet.

Chef Paul Ainsworth **Owner** Paul Ainsworth
Times 12-2.30/6.30-10 Closed 23-26 Dec, 3-26 Jan, Mon, L Sun (out of season), D Sun **Prices** Fixed L 2 course £10, Starter £5-£10, Main £12-£20, Dessert £5-£7, Service optional, Groups min 8 service 10% **Wines** 40 bottles over £20, 6 bottles under £20, 11 by glass **Notes** Sunday L, Vegetarian available, Dress restrictions, Smart casual **Seats** 40, Pr/dining room 24 **Children** Portions **Parking** Harbour car park and on street

St Petroc's Hotel and Bistro

French, Mediterranean

Rick Stein's bustling seafood bistro

☎ 01841 532700 ▦ 01841 532942
4 New St PL28 8EA
e-mail: reservations@rickstein.com
dir: Follow one-way around harbour, 1st left, establishment 100yds on right

Sitting a short stride uphill from its fish suppliers in Padstow's photogenic harbour, the bistro outpost of Rick Stein's empire is a more casual alternative to the Seafood Restaurant (see entry). A jaunty interior pairs bright modern paintings by local artists with crisp white walls and plenty of bare wood, while cheery staff serve up in professional, unstuffy style. Fish clearly gets pole position on a menu built around classic bistro influences mingling with a straightforward modern repertoire. Kick off with tender warm pigeon breasts with sautéed potatoes and walnut oil-dressed watercress salad, then move on to vibrantly-fresh grilled sea bass, finishing with a sticky toffee pudding with clotted cream.

Chef Paul Harwood, David Sharland **Owner** R & J Stein
Times 12-2/7-10 Closed 25-26 Dec, 1 May, D 24 Dec
Prices Fixed L course £17.50, Starter £6.65-£7.50, Main £12.25-£19.95, Dessert £4.45-£5.90, Service optional **Wines** 22 bottles over £20, 9 bottles under £20, 14 by glass **Notes** Sunday L, Vegetarian available, Air con **Seats** 54 **Children** Portions, Menu **Parking** Car park

The Seafood Restaurant

⚘⚘⚘ – **see below**

Treglos Hotel

Modern British

Victorian hotel with gorgeous views over the Bay

☎ 01841 520727 ▦ 01841 521163
Constantine Bay PL28 8JH
e-mail: stay@treglos-hotel.com
dir: At St Merryn x-rds take B3276 towards Newquay. In 500mtrs right to Constantine Bay, follow brown signs

A late Victorian house overlooking Constantine Bay and one of Cornwall's many sumptuous beaches, Treglos has been in the ownership of the Barlow family for the past 40 years or so. An autumnal palette of greens and browns has been brought to bear on the dining room, which makes the most of those fine marine views. A dress code applies, gentlemen. Good seafood might include grilled sardines in tomato and caper sauce, followed by accurately cooked Newlyn monkfish with spring greens. Finish with lemon syllabub or sticky toffee pudding with butterscotch sauce and clotted cream.

Times 7.15-9.15 Closed Jan-Feb, L all week except by arrangement

The Seafood Restaurant

International Seafood

Rick Stein's famous restaurant

☎ 01841 532700 ▦ 01841 532942
Riverside PL28 8BY
e-mail: reservations@rickstein.com
dir: Follow signs for town centre. Restaurant on riverside

It should be easy enough, but it clearly isn't or everybody would be doing it. Maybe it is the location right on the harbour. Maybe it is the personality and determination of Rick Stein. And what is 'it'? 'It' is serving the very best seafood in an uncomplicated way, never following fad or fashion but not standing still either, cooking the freshest fish and shellfish with passion and still managing to, after nearly 35 years, give an experienced inspector the best piece of brill she's ever had. Every coastal town should have a restaurant like this...few do. The entrance by the quayside is via a conservatory with a distinctly designer look, hinting that behind the brick and granite façade is a restaurant of real class. The centrepiece of the room is a mosaic and stainless steel-topped circular bar counter. It's a smartly unpretentious space, with linen-clad tables and splashes of colour coming from contemporary artworks. The menu isn't exactly cheap, but the produce (as discussed) is spot-on and, if you really want to push the boat out, there's a tasting menu, too. Shrimp and samphire risotto is a dish that relies on much more than sparklingly fresh seafood, and it is a triumph in the art of risotto making: just the right degree of bite and creaminess and wonderful flavours and textures. Turbot with hollandaise (on the bone) is simplicity itself, served with some mixed vegetables, while braised fillet of brill is given an earthy richness in a dish with black truffle, mushrooms and truffle oil. Desserts are not neglected (pannacotta with rhubarb compôte) and the wine list does great justice to the fruits of the sea.

Chef Stephane Delourme, David Sharland **Owner** R & J Stein **Times** 12-2/7-10 Closed 25-26 Dec, 1 May, D 24 Dec **Prices** Fixed L course £28.50, Tasting menu £65, Starter £10-£22, Main £17.50-£44, Dessert fr £8.35, Service optional **Wines** 156 bottles over £20, 5 bottles under £20, 21 by glass **Notes** Vegetarian available, Air con **Seats** 120 **Children** Portions, Menu **Parking** Pay & display opposite

The Bay Restaurant

◉◉ Modern British ◔

Contemporary restaurant with fabulous views

☎ 01736 366890 & 363117 ▤ 01736 350970
Hotel Penzance, Britons Hill TR18 3AE
e-mail: table@bay-penzance.co.uk
dir: from A30 pass heliport on right, left at next rdbt for town centre. 3rd right onto Britons Hill. Hotel on right

A stylishly redesigned Edwardian building with a bright, contemporary restaurant that doubles as a gallery displaying work by local artists. Peruse the paintings and take in the mesmerising views across Mount's Bay from the light and airy dining room, the modern feel enhanced by stripped floors, polished wooden tables, and doors leading out to a decked area for summer alfresco dining. The focus on style is also apparent in the kitchen's competent, modern approach to cooking fresh Cornish produce. Dishes offered from the sea, land and garden might include steamed mussels in a garlic, shallot and cider cream sauce, followed by monkfish with butterbean and chorizo stew, or roast venison with roasted root vegetables and a dark chocolate jus. Choose a plate of local cheeses or warm almond pudding with saffron ice cream for dessert.

Chef Ben Reeve, Katie Semmens, Roger Hosken **Owner** Yvonne & Stephen Hill **Times** 11-2/6.15-11 Closed L Sat **Prices** Fixed L 2 course fr £11.50, Fixed D 3 course fr £28, Service optional, Groups min 8 service 10% **Wines** 15 bottles over £20, 16 bottles under £20, 10 by glass **Notes** Tasting menu available 7 course, Vegetarian available, Dress restrictions, Smart casual, no shorts, Air con **Seats** 60, Pr/dining room 12 **Children** Portions, Menu **Parking** 13, On street

Harris's Restaurant

◉ Modern European

Simple, freshly cooked food in a charming little restaurant

☎ 01736 364408
46 New St TR18 2LZ
e-mail: contact@harrissrestaurant.co.uk
dir: Located down narrow cobbled street opposite Lloyds TSB & the Humphry Davy statue

Local produce, especially fish from Newlyn and estate game, feature on the modern European menu at this cosy, well-established restaurant tucked away down a narrow street in the town centre. A spiral metal staircase links the upstairs bar, where light lunches are served, with the attractive downstairs restaurant. Food is simply prepared using quality ingredients and unfussy presentation ensures key flavours shine through. Duck terrine, for instance, with a well made green tomato chutney to start, followed by fresh, moist monkfish with wild mushroom risotto and a light white wine sauce. Finish with a zesty lemon tart with a smooth and intensely flavoured white chocolate ice cream.

Chef Roger Harris **Owner** Roger & Anne Harris **Times** 12-2/7-9.30 Closed 3 wks winter, 25-26 Dec, 1 Jan, Sun-Mon (winter), L Mon **Prices** Starter £5.50-£8.50, Main £10.50-£27.50, Dessert £6.95-£7.95, Service added but optional 10% **Wines** 27 bottles over £20, 17 bottles under £20, 6 by glass **Notes** Light L & D menu £8.50-£14.95, Vegetarian available, Dress restrictions, Smart casual **Seats** 40, Pr/dining room 20 **Parking** On street, local car park

The Navy Inn

◉ Modern British ◔

Penzance local with an ambitious kitchen

☎ 01736 333232
Lower Queen St TR18 4DE
e-mail: keir@navyinn.co.uk
dir: In town centre, follow Chapel St for 50yds, right into Queen St to end

If you're strolling the promenade and feeling peckish, then head for this brightly-painted pub just back from the seafront. The rewards on arrival are the glorious views across Mount's Bay, a contemporary, nautical-themed interior replete with wooden floors, log fires and fat candles on scrubbed tables, and a changing menu that champions Cornish produce, notably fresh local fish and game. In a warm, friendly and comfortable atmosphere tuck into a classic pub dish or opt for something more adventurous, perhaps roast John Dory with lemon couscous and a tomato herb butter sauce, or pan-fried venison with black peppercorn dressing. For pudding, try the lemon and pistachio parfait with basil ice cream.

Chef Keir Meikle **Owner** Keir Meikle **Times** 12-10 Closed D 25 Dec **Prices** Starter £2.95-£6.95, Main £8.95-£18.50, Dessert £4.95-£6.50, Service optional **Wines** 12 bottles over £20, 19 bottles under £20, 10 by glass **Notes** Sunday L, Vegetarian available **Seats** 54 **Children** Portions, Menu **Parking** Free parking on promenade

The Summer House

◉◉ Mediterranean

Mediterranean cooking in Cornish townhouse

☎ 01736 363744 ▤ 01736 360959
Cornwall Ter TR18 4HL
e-mail: reception@summerhouse-cornwall.com
dir: into Penzance on A30. Along harbour past open-air bathing pool onto Promenade at Queens Hotel. Right immediately after hotel, restaurant 30mtrs on left

Set in a quiet lane 50 metres from the sea, The Summer House is an enchanting Grade II Regency house converted into a small townhouse hotel. Sympathetically converted with a Mediterranean theme, the delightful restaurant spills out into a tropical walled garden, where dinner and drinks are served on summer evenings. The philosophy is simple - great food, beautiful surroundings and an informal, happy atmosphere. Chef-patron Ciro Zaino has clearly found inspiration in Cornwall's fine larder, providing a daily-changing menu that includes a wide range of fish and seafood. Start with warm fennel soup with wild rocket purée and follow with Cornish sea bass pan-fried with Pernod. Round things off with rich, moist chocolate cake with cinnamon ice cream.

Times 7-9.30 Closed Nov-Feb, Mon-Thu, L all week

The Victoria Inn

◉ Modern British ◔

Simply great food in a friendly village inn

☎ 01736 710309
TR20 9NP
e-mail: enquiries@victoriainn-penzance.co.uk
dir: A30 to Penzance, A394 to Helston. After 2m turn right into Perranuthnoe, pub is on right on entering the village

A wood-burning fire, cosy nooks in the bar and some great food make this ancient village pub in an unspoilt Cornish coastal village a great base for exploring the area. Add into the equation a chef who trained with Raymond Blanc and Michael Caines with a passionate belief in buying the finest local produce and enough self-confidence to treat it with care and simplicity, and the result is earthy, flavoursome dishes that pack a real punch. Daily specials don't miss a trick when it comes to showcasing the best fish, seafood and seasonal ingredients. For main course perhaps slow-roasted belly of St Buryan pork with champ potato, black pudding and apple and bayleaf sauce, and to finish, the choice of West Country artisan cheeses, such as Kenwyn Goat and rind-washed Keltic Gold, is too good to pass over.

Chef Stewart Eddy **Owner** Stewart & Anna Eddy **Times** 12-2/6.30-9.30 Closed 25-26 Dec, 1 Jan, 1st wk Jan, Mon (off season), D Sun **Prices** Starter £4.95-£9.50, Main £10.50-£18, Dessert £6-£6.50, Service optional **Wines** 10 bottles over £20, 20 bottles under £20, 8 by glass **Notes** Sunday L, Vegetarian available **Seats** 60 **Children** Portions, Menu **Parking** 10, On street

Kota Restaurant with Rooms

◉ British, Pacific Rim

Modern British and Asian cooking by the sea

☎ 01326 562407 ▤ 01326 562407
Harbour Head TR13 9JA
e-mail: kota@btconnect.com
dir: B3304 from Helston into Porthleven, Kota on harbour head opposite slipway

This 18th-century former corn mill occupies prime position on Harbour Head in the Cornish fishing port of Porthleven. You may have suspected that Kota isn't a Cornish word: in fact it is Maori for shellfish, and when you know that little clue, the focus of this relaxed bistro-style restaurant with rooms becomes clear. Modern British cooking is given a light Asian twist, with a clear emphasis on locally sourced, organic ingredients. Fish and seafood, of course, form the backbone of the menu

belly, soy ginger, cider apple purée and coriander and mains such as pan-fried turbot with samphire, local cockles and mussels and cider saffron sauce.

Chef Jude Kereama **Owner** Jude & Jane Kereama **Times** 12-2/5.30-9.00 Closed 25 Dec, Jan, Sun (off season), L Sun-Thu **Prices** Fixed L 2 course £14, Fixed D 2 course £14, Starter £4.50-£8.50, Main £11.50-£18.95, Dessert £4.50-£5.50, Service optional, Groups min 6 service 10% **Wines** 30 bottles over £20, 23 bottles under £20, 13 by glass **Notes** Tasting menu available (pre-order), Sun L summer & BHs, Vegetarian available **Seats** 40 **Children** Portions, Menu **Parking** On street

---

PORTLOE — Map 2 SW93

The Lugger Hotel

⚜ Modern European

- -

Excellent seafood in harbour hotel with stunning views

☎ 01872 501322 & 501238 📠 01872 501691
TR2 5RD
e-mail: office@luggerhotel.com
dir: A390 to Truro, B3287 to Tregony, A3078 (St Mawes Rd), left for Veryan, left for Portloe

Once a 16th-century inn, The Lugger sits on the beautiful Roseland Peninsula at the foot of a valley in Portloe with its picturesque cove and tiny harbour. Now a luxury hotel, the modern restaurant offers superb harbour views and in warmer weather the sun terrace is just the ticket.

Carefully prepared fresh local produce is the order of the day here, with seafood delivered direct from the boats. Subject to availability you could start with Helford oysters or Falmouth Bay scallops, then go for St Ives grilled fillet of gurnard with confit saffron potato, wilted baby spinach and parsley salsa or Cornish lobster with garlic, lime and parsley butter.

Chef Didier Bienaime **Owner** Oxford Hotels **Times** 12-2.30/7-9.30 **Prices** Starter £8.50-£15, Main £12.50-£70, Dessert £7.50-£15, Service optional **Wines** 31 bottles over £20, 8 bottles under £20, 8 by glass **Notes** Sunday L, Vegetarian available, Civ Wed 60 **Seats** 54 **Parking** 24

PORTSCATHO — Map 2 SW83

Driftwood

⚜ ⚜ ⚜ — **see below**

PORTWRINKLE — Map 3 SX35

Whitsand Bay Hotel & Golf Club

⚜ Modern British **V** ✋

- -

Luxurious setting for seasonal Cornish produce

☎ 01503 230276 📠 01503 230329
PL11 3BU
e-mail: whitsandbayhotel@btconnect.com
dir: A38 from Exeter over River Tamar, left at Trerulefoot rdbt onto A374 to Crafthole/Portwrinkle. Follow hotel signs

Steeped in history and standing high on a cliff with fabulous views across Whitsand Bay, this imposing Victorian stone hotel includes among its facilities an 18-hole cliff-top golf course. Original features abound inside, notably the sweeping staircase, the splendid oak panelling and some fine stained-glass windows. The elegant dining room exudes a restrained air of luxury and offers a modern British menu that champions seasonal Cornish produce, from duck terrine with plum chutney and baked local brill with parsley sauce to roast venison with celeriac purée and cauliflower cream.

Chef Tony Farmer **Owner** Chris, Jennifer, John, Tracey & Paul Phillips **Times** 12-2/7-9 **Prices** Fixed L 2 course £14.50, Fixed D 3 course £29.95, Service optional **Wines** 20 bottles over £20, 28 bottles under £20, 5 by glass **Notes** ALC fixed menu £29.95, Sunday L, Vegetarian menu, Dress restrictions, Smart dress, no jeans, T-shirts, Civ Wed 90, Air con **Seats** 70 **Children** Portions, Menu **Parking** 90

Driftwood

PORTSCATHO — Map 2 SW83

Modern European

Accomplished cooking in a stunning coastal location

☎ 01872 580644 📠 01872 580801
Rosevine TR2 5EW
e-mail: info@driftwoodhotel.co.uk
dir: 5m from St Mawes off the A3078, signposted Rosevine

From its Cornish cliff-top location, this contemporary New England-style hotel offers visitors some of the most stunning views across the English Channel. The minimalist, chic and modern decor works in perfect harmony with the blue-horizon views, while the crashing waves can be heard as you sip aperitifs on the garden terrace. The smart dining room, with its neutral tones, continues the relaxed theme and there are plenty of

windows to take in those views of the bay. Expect skilful cooking with an equally light, contemporary tone, driven by prime quality produce from the abundant local larder (unsurprisingly featuring fresh fish and shellfish from local waters). Start with hand-dived scallops, endive and orange, pistachio and red wine shallots and follow with sea bass, grilled leeks, buckwheat crêpe and wild mushrooms and red wine emulsion. Round off a memorable meal with chilled chocolate fondant and malted milk ice cream.

Chef Christopher Eden **Owner** Paul & Fiona Robinson **Times** 7-9.30 Closed mid Dec-mid Feb, L all week **Prices** Fixed D 3 course £40, Tasting menu £55, Service optional **Wines** 50 bottles over £20, 7 bottles under £20, 6 by glass **Notes** Vegetarian available **Seats** 34 **Parking** 20

ROCK Map 2 SW97

The St Enodoc Hotel

◉◉ Modern British, European 🍴

Cornish views and a local flavour

☎ 01208 863394 📠 01208 863970
The St Enodoc Hotel PL27 6LA
e-mail: info@enodoc.co.uk
dir: M5/A30/A39 to Wadebridge. B3314 to Rock

The spectacular views across the water towards Padstow remain timeless, but change has come to the St Enodoc in the form of Nathan Outlaw. His restaurant in Fowey (see entry for Restaurant Nathan Outlaw) has made waves in the south west and beyond, and here he has opened the Seafood & Grill, a reasonably priced restaurant that has broad appeal and an informal atmosphere. Start with pea and mint soup or some local Porthilly mussels cooked in Cornish Blonde (a wheat beer brewed by Truro-based Skinners), then move on to a dry-aged Cornish beef chop, fish pie, or a whole lemon sole with caper and lemon sauce. Finish with chocolate tart or Cornish cheeses.

Chef Ben Harmer **Owner** Linedegree Ltd
Times 12.30-2.30/7-10 Closed 2 mths (late Dec - early Feb) **Prices** Food prices not confirmed for 2010. Please telephone for details. **Wines** 35 bottles over £20, 15 bottles under £20, 10 by glass **Notes** Sunday L, Vegetarian available, Dress restrictions, Smart casual, Air con **Seats** 55, Pr/dining room 30 **Children** Portions, Menu **Parking** 60

RUAN HIGH LANES Map 2 SW93

Fish in the Fountain

◉ British, Mediterranean 🍴

Country-house hotel making good use of local produce

☎ 01872 501336 📠 01872 501151
The Hundred House Hotel TR2 5JR
e-mail: enquiries@hundredhousehotel.co.uk
dir: On A3078 towards St Mawes, hotel 4m after Tregony on right, just before Ruan High Lanes

The Hundred House Hotel is a Georgian country house in the heart of the stunning Roseland Peninsula, with 3 acres of elegant gardens, including a croquet lawn. The elegant Fish in the Fountain Restaurant is open for dinner only and offers a sensibly concise daily-changing menu of 3 choices per course. The focus is on sound British cooking with plenty of Mediterranean influences, making good use of Cornwall's abundant seafood, as well as prime local meat, game and poultry and home-grown salads. Start, perhaps, with Cornish country vegetable soup, followed by grilled fillets of wild sea bass served with cracked black pepper butter, and finish with garden-fresh rhubarb fool.

Chef Richard Maior-Barron **Owner** Richard Maior-Barron
Times 6.45-8 Closed Jan-Feb, L all week **Prices** Fixed D 3 course £30, Service optional **Wines** 7 bottles over £20, 33

bottles under £20, 4 by glass **Notes** Vegetarian available, Dress restrictions, Smart casual **Seats** 24 **Children** Portions **Parking** 15

ST AGNES Map 2 SW75

Valley Restaurant

◉ Traditional British 🍴

Enjoyable local food in peaceful setting

☎ 01872 562202 📠 01872 552700
Rose-in-Vale Hotel, Mithian TR5 0QD
e-mail: reception@rose-in-vale-hotel.co.uk
dir: Take A30 S towards Redruth. At Chiverton Cross rdbt take B3277 signed St Agnes. In 500mtrs turn at tourist info sign for Rose-in-Vale. Into Mithian, right at Miners Arms, down hill

Set in a secluded wooded valley, this Grade II listed Georgian manor house is an oasis of calm and tranquillity and an ideal place to relax. The light and airy Valley Restaurant follows the theme with friendly and attentive service, formal table settings and views across the well-tended gardens. The traditional British cooking is governed by the seasons and the menus change daily to make the best of the local produce - meat and vegetables from local farms, fish landed nearby. A starter of locally smoked chicken breast with herb croûtons might be followed by chargrilled medallions of Cornish beef fillet with caramelised red onion and béarnaise sauce.

Chef Colin Hankins, Nick Cassidy **Owner** James & Sara Evans **Times** 12-2/7-9 Closed L Mon-Wed (winter) **Prices** Fixed D 3 course £25-£45, Service included **Wines** 10 bottles over £20, 25 bottles under £20, 5 by glass **Notes** Sunday L, Vegetarian available, Dress restrictions, Smart dress, Civ Wed 100 **Seats** 80, Pr/dining room 12 **Children** Portions **Parking** 50

ST AUSTELL Map 2 SX05

Austell's

◉◉ Modern British 🍴

Contemporary dining utilising local produce

☎ 01726 813888
10 Beach Rd PL25 3PH
e-mail: brett@austells.net
dir: From A390 towards Par, 0.5m after Charlestown rdbt at 2nd lights turn right. Left at rdbt. Restaurant 600yds on right

With 6 golf courses and the Eden Project a mere 20 minute-drive away, Austell's occupies an enviable position on the approach road to the tranquil beach at Carlyon Bay. The chic, contemporary dining area is raised and allows a view of the chefs in the open kitchen. Chef Brett counts The Ivy, The Waldorf and The Four Seasons on his CV and this pedigree shines through in his seasonal, uncomplicated British food. Local produce is a benchmark of the kitchen and the frequently-changing menu could start with a carpaccio of local beef, smoked tomato, rocket and shaved parmesan salad with port and truffle dressing and be followed by pan-fried fillet of

silver mullet with creamed potato, green beans, crab and roast pepper sauce.

Chef Brett Camborne-Paynter **Owner** J & S Camborne-Paynter **Times** 11.30-3/7-10.30 Closed 25, 26 Dec & 1-15 Jan, Mon, L Sun-Thu **Prices** Fixed D 3 course £29.95, Service optional **Wines** 34 bottles over £20, 7 bottles under £20, 7 by glass **Notes** Vegetarian available **Seats** 48 **Children** Portions **Parking** 30

Carlyon Bay Hotel

◉ Modern, Traditional 🍴

West Country produce and fantastic sea views

☎ 01726 812304 📠 01726 814938
Sea Rd, Carlyon Bay PL25 3RD
e-mail: info@carlyonbay.co.uk
web: www.carlyonbay.com
dir: From St Austell, follow signs for Charlestown. Carlyon Bay signed on left, hotel at end of Sea Rd

Sitting on the cliff-top above St Austell, this splendid art deco hotel is set in 250 acres of grounds, including a championship golf course. The contemporary restaurant is bright and cheerful, furnished with bold artwork and comfortable high-backed leather chairs; a spot where diners can enjoy fabulous sea views. The menu features modern British cuisine prepared from top-quality West Country produce, especially fish and shellfish from the Cornish coast. Starters might include an interesting mix of Cornish shellfish salad with Thai fragrant scents, or you could take a more occidental route via braised cannon of spring lamb with wild garlic and olives, tapenade mash and basil oil. Finish with chocolate and raspberry tart or Callestick Cornish ices.

Chef Paul Leakey **Owner** PR Brend Hoteliers Ltd
Times 12-2/7-9.30 **Prices** Fixed D 3 course fr £37, Starter £6-£10, Main £14-£25, Dessert £6-£8, Service optional **Wines** 115 bottles over £20, 66 bottles under £20, 27 by glass **Notes** Sunday L, Dress restrictions, Smart dress, Civ Wed 140, Air con **Seats** 180, Pr/dining room 70 **Children** Portions, Menu **Parking** 60

ST IVES
Map 2 SW54

Alba Restaurant

◉ Modern European V

Former lifeboat house with sea views and local produce on the menu

☎ 01736 797222 📠 01736 798937
Old Lifeboat House, Wharf Rd TR26 1LF
e-mail: albarestaurant@aol.com
web: www.thealbarestaurant.com
dir: 1st building on St Ives harbour front, opposite new lifeboat house

As a former lifeboat station a good position on the quay is a given, and Alba's large windows make the best of the picturesque, harbourside setting. The first-floor dining room has the best of the views, alongside some bold modern art, and comfortable suede chairs and banquettes at white-clothed tables. The food is based on excellent local produce, including fish and shellfish from the day boats, and herbs, mushrooms and seaweed from a local forager. Tender pigeon breast with pissaladière, sautéed wild mushrooms, peas and pigeon jus demonstrates the lively modern European style of the food, and vanilla pannacotta with blueberries is a well-made finish.

Chef Grant Nethercott **Owner** Harbour Kitchen Co Ltd **Times** 12-2/6-9.45 Closed 25-26 Dec **Prices** Fixed L 2 course £13.50, Fixed D 3 course £16.50, Starter £4.95-£8.95, Main £11.50-£18.95, Dessert £5.25-£7.95, Service optional, Groups min 6 service 10% **Wines** 24 bottles over £20, 50 bottles under £20, 30 by glass **Notes** Fixed price menus before 7 in season or 7.30 rest of year, Vegetarian menu, Air con **Seats** 60 **Children** Portions, Menu

Boskerris Hotel

◉ Modern British NEW

Delightful seaside boutique hotel with a modern menu of local produce

☎ 01736 795295
Boskerris Rd, Carbis Bay TR26 2NQ
e-mail: reservations@boskerrishotel.co.uk
dir: From Exeter take A30 until A3074 towards St Ives. On entering Carbis Bay take 3rd on right

The Boskerris is a modern beach-house style hotel on the fringes of arty St Ives, full of light and infused with the essence of summer. White walls, pale wood floors and pastel shades of the Mediterranean open onto a decking terrace with magical views over Carbis Bay to Godrevy lighthouse and the wide ocean beyond. The airy restaurant has a touch of clean-cut Riviera glamour, and a simple concise menu that suits the relaxed vibe with its modern dishes founded on excellent Cornish produce. Warm Cornish duck breast with celeriac remoulade and fig jam might start things off, followed by fillet of John Dory with caramelised cherry tomato and fennel, potato gnocchi and salsa verde.

Times 7-9pm

Garrack Hotel & Restaurant

◉ Modern British ☺

Relaxed hotel dining with seafood playing a starring role

☎ 01736 796199 & 792910 📠 01736 798955
Burthallan Ln, Higher Ayr TR26 3AA
e-mail: aarest@garrack.com
dir: Exit A30 for St Ives, then from B3311 follow brown signs for Tate Gallery, then brown Garrack signs

The ivy-shrouded Garrack Hotel has been run by the same family for over 40 years - and you can understand why: the location, perched in a tranquil spot above Porthmeor Beach is one that no-one would readily give up. The smartly-decorated L-shaped restaurant has great views across gardens to St Ives and offers a good variety of contemporary dishes from the modern British palette, with the odd splash of exotic colour. Fresh local fish and seafood is a strength, in starters such as St Ives Bay crab gratin with sesame and parmesan crust, or local mussels with leeks, saffron, white wine and cream. Meat appears as whole roasted stuffed partridge with herb mash, spiced chutney and natural pan juices.

Chef Neil O'Brien **Owner** Kilby family **Times** 12.30-2/6-9 Closed 5 days Xmas, L Mon-Sat **Prices** Fixed D 3 course £25, Starter £7-£9, Main £14-£22, Dessert £4.95-£7.95, Service optional **Wines** 21 bottles over £20, 56 bottles under £20, 8 by glass **Notes** Early D 6-7pm 2 course £12.95, Sunday L, Vegetarian available, Dress restrictions, Smart casual **Seats** 40 **Children** Portions, Menu **Parking** 36

Porthminster Beach Restaurant

◉ Modern International V

Global cooking right on the beach

☎ 01736 795352 📠 01736 795352
Porthminster TR26 2EB
e-mail: pminster@btconnect.com
dir: On Porthminster Beach, beneath the St Ives Railway Station

This art deco former deckchair store, right on Porthminster Beach, is these days a St Ives institution. The views over sand and sea - best enjoyed from the large terrace - will, like the menu, reflect the seasons. Modern Pan-Asian and European influences are very much in evidence, and the development of the kitchen's own garden is bearing fruit (and veg), but it's the seafood that's the star of the show. Start with Cornish oysters, or wild mushroom ravioli with sage, Cornish ricotta and black truffle, before pan-fried halibut with crab polonaise, parsnip purée, pea velouté and yuzu jelly, and finish with chocolate pannacotta with Amaretto foam. The room is simply decorated, with splashes of colour coming from Anthony Frost's artworks, and service maintains the relaxed and unpretentious vibe.

Chef M Smith, Isaac Anderson **Owner** Jim Woolcock, David Fox, Roger & Tim Symons, M Smith **Times** 12-3.30/6 Closed 25 Dec, Mon (Winter) **Prices** Starter £5-£9.50, Main £12.95-£19.50, Dessert

£4.95-£6.50, Service optional **Wines** 13 bottles over £20, 15 bottles under £20, 9 by glass **Notes** Sunday L, Vegetarian menu **Seats** 60 **Children** Portions **Parking** 300yds (railway station)

Sands Restaurant

◉ Traditional Mediterranean

Tranquil beachside hotel with traditional dining

☎ 01736 795311 📠 01736 797677
Carbis Bay Hotel, Carbis Bay TR26 2NP
e-mail: carbisbayhotel@btconnect.com
dir: A3074, through Lelant. 1m, at Carbis Bay 30yds before lights turn right into Porthrepta Rd to sea & hotel

In a peaceful location with access to its own white sand beach, this family-run hotel offers impressive views across Carbis Bay. Built in 1894 by Cornish architect Sylvanus Trevail, the hotel offers a traditional style of European cooking in the light and airy, refurbished restaurant. Seasonality and local produce are the cornerstones of the menu, which could include megrim sole with caramelised lemon and caper butter sauce or braised beef casserole with button mushrooms, onions, red wine sauce and baby leeks. Finish with one of the home-made desserts or a selection of Cornish cheeses.

Chef Paul John Massey **Owner** Mr M W Baker **Times** 12-3/6-9 Closed 3 wks Jan **Prices** Food prices not confirmed for 2010. Please telephone for details. **Wines** 15 bottles over £20, 20 bottles under £20, 8 by glass **Notes** Sunday L, Vegetarian available, Dress restrictions, Smart casual, Civ Wed 150 **Seats** 150, Pr/dining room 40 **Children** Portions, Menu **Parking** 100

The Wave Restaurant

◉ Modern Mediterranean ☺

Modern Mediterranean cooking close to St Ives harbour

☎ 01736 796661
17 St Andrews St TR26 1AH
e-mail: lcowling2000@yahoo.com
dir: Just outside town centre, 100yds from parish church

Tucked away in a quiet street behind the harbour, this contemporary two-room restaurant has a distinctly cosmopolitan feel to it. Bright and uncluttered with local art on the walls, the service is friendly and informal. In keeping with the cheery feel of the place, the menu offers vibrant Mediterranean cooking with occasional Asian touches. Good use is made of local, seasonal produce,

continued

ST IVES *continued*

including lots of locally-caught fish, in dishes such as pan-fried squid with chorizo, red pepper salsa and fresh rocket, followed by sea bass fillets with chargrilled asparagus, lemon risotto cake and tomato, vanilla and crab dressing.

Chef S M Pellow **Owner** Mr & Mrs Cowling, Mr & Mrs Pellow **Times** 6-9.30 Closed end Nov-beg Mar, Sun, L all week **Prices** Fixed D 3 course fr £16.95, Starter £4.95-£7.95, Main £13.95-£19.95, Dessert £5.75-£6.95, Service optional **Wines** 4 bottles over £20, 20 bottles under £20, 8 by glass **Notes** Fixed D 6-7.15pm, Vegetarian available, Dress restrictions, Smart casual, no swimwear or bare chests **Seats** 50 **Children** Portions, Menu **Parking** Station car park

ST MAWES	Map 2 SW83

Hotel Tresanton

@@@ – *see below*

Idle Rocks Hotel

@@ Modern European

Modern cuisine in picturesque fishing port

☎ 01326 270771 📠 01326 270062
Harbour Side TR2 5AN
e-mail: reception@idlerocks.co.uk
dir: From St Austell A390 towards Truro, left onto B3287 signed Tregony, through Tregony, left at T-junct onto A3078, hotel on left on waterfront

On the edge of the harbour wall in the pretty fishing village of St Mawes, on the Roseland Peninsular, sea views don't get much closer than this. The split-level Water's Edge restaurant is decorated in contemporary shades of blue, gold and sand, with picture windows that give everyone a glimpse of the water. The terrace is a great place to eat in summer. The talented kitchen makes use of the rich availability of local Cornish produce, including early season fruit and vegetables, fish and meat, to produce innovative, modern dishes based on classic techniques. Expect the likes of lobster-stuffed pasta with a nage of scallops, cucumber and ginger to start, followed by roast pigeon with stuffed cabbage, Umbrian lentils and caramelised salsify with red wine sauce.

Times 12-3/6.30-9

SALTASH	Map 3 SX45

The Farmhouse

@ Modern British **NEW** 🍃

Country club fine dining in an original farmhouse

☎ 01752 854664 & 854661
China Fleet Country Club PL12 6LJ
e-mail: sales@china-fleet.co.uk
dir: Please telephone for directions or see website

Part of the main China Fleet Country Club complex, though, as the name implies, set in an original farmhouse; the restaurant is off to one side and quiet enough for an intimate dinner for two. The club's fine-dining option, it retains much of its old-style charm, the light, airy room formally attired in clothed tables. The cooking takes a modern approach, driven by the abundant local larder of quality, seasonal ingredients and delivered with accuracy and flair. So, poached Torbay sole is served with tagliatelle, rocket, and ginger and lemongrass butter, and roast loin of West Country venison with Tamar Valley blackberry and thyme-roasted potatoes.

Chef Marc Slater **Owner** In Trust Ownership **Times** 12-3/7-9 Closed 24 Dec-1 Jan, L Mon-Sat **Prices** Fixed D 3 course £30-£35, Service optional **Wines** 6 bottles over £20, 23 bottles under £20, 4 by glass **Notes** Sunday L, Vegetarian available, Civ Wed 200, Air con **Seats** 60, Pr/dining room 200 **Children** Portions, Menu **Parking** 400

Hotel Tresanton

ST MAWES	Map 2 SW83

Modern British, Mediterranean 🍃

Simple but accomplished cooking in a stylish seafront hotel

☎ 01326 270055 📠 01326 270053
Lower Castle Rd TR2 5DR
e-mail: info@tresanton.com
dir: On the waterfront in town centre

Tresanton is fashioned from a straggle of old houses set at different levels on the St Mawes waterfront. In the 1940s, it became a yachting club, but was restored and relaunched in the 1990s by Olga Polizzi as a boutique hotel. The views over the sea towards Falmouth are exquisite, and the place makes the most of the breezy freshness of its surroundings with a daylight-filled dining room, where a restful beige colour scheme is featured in

tongue-and-groove walls and a mosaic-tiled floor. Attentive and knowledgeable staff are eager to please, and so is the food, which tacks to a modern European course, with local produce very much to the fore. Simple but effective presentation marks dishes such as thick beetroot and horseradish tortellini with goats' cheese and shredded sage, or Cornish crab with apple, celery and cucumber. Main courses give equal shakes to fish, meat and vegetarian options, and may take in herb-crusted brill with new potatoes, spinach and asparagus, or duck confit with boulangère potatoes, green beans and tomato. This being the West Country, you can expect clotted cream to crop up somewhere, and here it serves in a soft-textured tart with sharply flavoured raspberry sorbet.

Chef Paul Wadham **Owner** Olga Polizzi **Times** 12-2.30/7-9.30 **Prices** Fixed L 2 course £25, Fixed D 3 course £42, Service optional **Wines** 114 bottles over £20, 8 by glass **Notes** Sunday L, Vegetarian available, Civ Wed 50 **Seats** 50, Pr/dining room 45 **Children** Menu **Parking** 30

SCILLY, ISLES OF

BRYHER
Map 2 SW81

Hell Bay

◉◉ Modern British

Stunning location, stunning food

☎ 01720 422947 📠 01720 423004
TR23 0PR
e-mail: contactus@hellbay.co.uk
dir: Helicopter from Penzance to Tresco, St Mary's. Plane from Southampton, Bristol, Exeter, Newquay or Land's End

There's a real sense of adventure on the trip to Hell Bay. Take the helicopter, light aircraft or ferry over to St Mary's, then a short boat ride to the smallest of the inhabited islands of the Scillies, and, finally, a Land Rover to take you up the sandy track to the hotel. The reward is two-fold: the beauty of the island - dramatic and romantic - and a stay at the relaxed and charmingly unpretentious hotel with its skilful kitchen team. Local artworks add to the sense of place and the dining room is dominated by tones of blue and cream. The menu is sensibly concise and the cooking shows a high degree of skill. The fruits of the sea are put to good use in a British spin on the assiette of seafood: a seared scallop, piece of battered cod and a fishcake served with tartare sauce. Main-course slow-roasted pork belly comes with sweet potato dauphinoise, Bryher spinach and superb warm apple and pine nut chutney, while a trio of chocolate desserts sees first-class pastry in a dark chocolate tart, plus a luxurious chocolate mousse and iced parfait.

Chef Glenn Gatland **Owner** Tresco Estate
Times 12-2/6.30-9.30 Closed Nov-Feb **Prices** Fixed D 3 course fr £35, Service optional **Wines** 32 bottles over £20, 17 bottles under £20 **Notes** Sunday L, Vegetarian available, Dress restrictions, No jeans, T-shirts in eve **Seats** 75, Pr/dining room 20 **Children** Portions, Menu

TRESCO
Map 2 SV81

The Island Hotel

◉◉ British

Refined cuisine in wonderful location

☎ 01720 422883 📠 01720 423008
TR24 0PU
e-mail: islandhotel@tresco.co.uk
dir: 20 minutes from Penzance to St Mary's by helicopter, then small boat to island

Guests arriving at the quay or heliport are transported by tractor-drawn charabanc to the island's only hotel, a delightful colonial-style building set in beautifully tended gardens by the shore. Furnished in contemporary style, the light-and-airy restaurant enjoys stunning sea views and forms an elegant backdrop for displays of original art. Carefully prepared, imaginative modern British cuisine is the order of the day, drawing inspiration from international sources and local ingredients, particularly seafood. Fish-lovers will not be able to resist Cornish

seafood tempura with lemon mayonnaise, perhaps preceded by steamed mussels in garlic, white wine and cream, with white chocolate mousse with cocoa snaps for dessert, or maybe a plate of West Country cheeses.

Times 12-2.30/7-9 Closed 2 Nov-1 Mar, L all week

New Inn

◉ British

Old world island inn with modern food in a choice of lovely settings

☎ 01720 422844 📠 01720 423200
TR24 0QQ
e-mail: newinn@tresco.co.uk
dir: Ferry or helicopter from Penzance; 250yds from harbour (private island, contact hotel for details)

The dreamy isle of Tresco is close to the mainland and yet so far with its car-free tranquillity, exotic gardens and sandy turquoise bays. The New Inn is practically on the beach and fuses quaint old-world character with a beachcomber-chic, New England-style décor in its light and airy restaurant. Whether you go for the restaurant, the Driftwood Bar, the bistro-style Pavilion or sit outside in the sun, the menus and daily specials are the same. Quality local ingredients - fish and seafood in particular - drive the cooking in an old favourites repertoire. Salmon fishcakes with chive fish cream and spinach might start you off, followed by plump scallops with garlic butter, parsley and first-rate chips.

Chef Peter Marshall **Owner** Mr R Dorrien-Smith
Times 12-2.15/6-9 Closed L all week **Prices** Food prices not confirmed for 2010. Please telephone for details.
Wines 18 bottles over £20, 13 bottles under £20, 13 by glass **Notes** Vegetarian available **Seats** 40
Children Portions, Menu

TALLAND BAY
Map 2 SX25

Terrace Restaurant at Talland Bay Hotel

◉◉ Modern British

Idyllic Cornwall coast location and refined cuisine

☎ 01503 272667
PL13 2JB
e-mail: reception@tallandbayhotel.co.uk
dir: Signed from x-rds on A387 between Looe and Polperro

You can set off along the Cornish coastal path with glorious sea views all the way from the end of the garden in this welcoming family-run hotel. All that sea air is sure to sharpen the appetite, so the oak-panelled dining room is at hand to take care of dining by mellow evening candlelight, with those gorgeous bay views over soaring Monterey pines in the exotic gardens. The kitchen's modern British repertoire delivers some good old favourites with updated interpretations sprinkled here and there. Straightforward, simply-presented dishes might include a goats' cheese fondant with beetroot, figs and pain d'épice, then seared halibut with thyme gnocchi, spinach, red onions and fish jus with rosemary.

End with chocolate fondant with gingerbread ice cream, confit orange and orange syrup.

Chef Steve Buick **Owner** Mr & Mrs G Granville
Times 12.30-2/7-9 Closed L Mon-Sat (Oct-mid Apr)
Prices Fixed L 2 course £15.50, Starter £6-£9.50, Main £14.50-£22.75, Dessert £4.75-£6, Service optional
Wines 50 bottles over £20, 20 bottles under £20, 12 by glass **Notes** Sunday L, Vegetarian available, Dress restrictions, Smart casual minimum **Seats** 40 **Parking** 20

TRURO
Map 2 SW84

Alverton Manor

◉◉ Traditional British

Innovative cooking in stately surroundings

☎ 01872 276633 📠 01872 222989
Tregolls Rd TR1 1ZQ
e-mail: reception@alvertonmanor.co.uk
web: www.alvertonmanor.co.uk
dir: From Truro bypass take A39 to St Austell. Just past church on left

Formerly a convent, this impressive Grade II listed sandstone property stands in 6 acres of grounds within walking distance of the city centre. The original gothic windows and ornate wooden staircases remain, but this is now a modern hotel which combines comfort with character. The dining room is elegant, and the service is on the ball. Innovative modern cooking is driven by quality produce from local suppliers, allotments and small growers. They rear their own Devon Red cattle, keep their own bees, and have sourced free-range eggs, lamb, chicken and pork. Dishes to impress include Cornish red mullet soup with green olive tapenade and pan-fried calves' liver with peppered home-cured pancetta, bubble-and-squeak rösti and thyme juices.

Owner Mr M Sagin **Times** 11.45-1.45/7-9.15 Closed L Mon-Sat **Prices** Fixed L 2 course £14.95, Fixed D 3 course £31.50, Starter £18, Main £20, Dessert £9, Service optional **Wines** 80 bottles over £20, 40 bottles under £20, 15 by glass **Notes** Sunday L, Vegetarian available, Dress restrictions, Smart casual, Civ Wed 80 **Seats** 30, Pr/dining room 80 **Children** Portions, Menu **Parking** 80

TRURO *continued*

Bustophers Bar Bistro

◎ Modern British **NEW** ✋

Buzzy, contemporary setting for well-crafted cooking

☎ 01872 279029 📠 01872 271940
62 Lemon St TR1 2PN
e-mail: info@bustophersbarbistro.com
dir: Located on right, past Plaza Cinema up the hill

On the town's attractive Lemon Street, this cracking
venue - a contemporary wine bar/bistro - has broad
appeal. The big zinc-topped bar, open-plan kitchen,
glass-roofed atrium and polished tables create a
modishly upbeat atmosphere, while the terrace is the
place to go when the sun is shining. The cooking suits
the surroundings; an accomplished, simply prepared,
crowd-pleasing repertoire driven by fresh local,
seasonal and traceable produce (a roll-call of suppliers
comes with the menu). Take straightforward classics
like River Fal moules marinière and frites or Shepherd's
pie, to the more modern duo of Primrose Herd (St
Austell) pork belly and loin with herb-crushed potatoes
and Savoy cabbage.

Chef Rob Duncan **Owner** Simon & Sue Hancock
Times 12-2.30/5.30-9.30 Closed 25-26 Dec, 1 Jan
Prices Fixed L 2 course £12, Fixed D 3 course £15, Starter
£5-£10, Main £7-£20, Dessert £4-£7, Service optional,
Groups min 8 service 10% **Wines** 68 bottles over £20, 17
bottles under £20, 19 by glass **Notes** Pre-theatre menu
available, Sunday L, Vegetarian available, Air con
Seats 110, Pr/dining room 30 **Children** Portions, Menu
Parking Moorfield NCP at rear of property

Probus Lamplighter Restaurant

◎◎ Modern British ✋

Produce is king at this reputable old-timer

☎ 01726 882453 📠 01726 882938
Fore St, Probus TR2 4JL
e-mail: maireadvogel@aol.com
dir: 5m from Truro on A390 towards St Austell

This small oak-beamed restaurant has been pleasing its
regulars for over 50 years now with its simply cooked
local produce and unhurried friendly service. Run by a
husband-and-wife team, the décor in the 300-year old
restaurant is simple with comfy sofas and candlelit
service adding to the relaxed atmosphere. The quality of
the modern British cooking is down to chef Robert Vogel's
use of local, seasonal quality produce carefully prepared
and straightforwardly presented. So foie gras is partnered
with beetroot pancakes and a port wine sauce to start,
followed by a well thought-out Gressingham duck breast
with confit leg, pumpkin and apple mousse and cider
sauce. Try not to fill up on the good home-made breads to
leave room for a rich but light sticky toffee pudding with
Guinness ice cream and clotted cream.

Chef Robert Vogel **Owner** Robert & Mairead Vogel
Times 7-10 Closed Sun-Mon, L all week **Prices** Fixed D 3
course £29.90 **Wines** 16 bottles over £20, 17 bottles

under £20, 6 by glass **Notes** Vegetarian available, Dress
restrictions, Smart casual **Seats** 32, Pr/dining room 8
Children Portions **Parking** On street & car park

Tabb's

◎◎ Modern British ✋

**Contemporary dining in former pub championing local
produce**

☎ 01872 262110
85 Kenwyn St TR1 3BZ
dir: Down hill past train station, right at mini rdbt,
200yds on left

Black slate floors and lilac walls, complemented by high-
backed leather chairs in cream and lilac and white linen-
clothed tables, create a stylish, contemporary vibe at this
chic modern restaurant on fashionable Kenwyn Street.
Husband-and-wife-team Nigel and Melanie Tabb run the
place with great care and attention to detail, with
everything made in-house, from the bread to the ice
creams and petits fours, to furnish an appealing menu
that champions local seasonal produce and suppliers, in
particular fish and game. Cooking takes an innovative
modern approach, yet dishes are simple and unfussy,
taking in smoked haddock soup with chilli and Devon
blue relish for a starter, and main dishes like ray wing
with polenta, cockles and chive butter sauce, and mutton
with celeriac mash, sweetbreads and onion gravy.

Chef Nigel Tabb **Owner** Nigel & Melanie Tabb
Times 6.30-9.30 Closed 25 Dec, 1 Jan, 1 wk Jan, Sun,
Mon, L all week **Prices** Fixed D 2 course £18.50, Starter
£6.50-£9.75, Main £14.75-£21.50, Dessert £6.50, Service
optional **Wines** 26 bottles over £20, 11 bottles under £20,
6 by glass **Notes** Vegetarian available **Seats** 30
Children Portions **Parking** 200yds

Trenython Manor

◎ Modern British

The flavour of Cornwall in magnificent Italianate setting

☎ 01726 814797 📠 01726 817030
Castle Dore Rd PL24 2TS
e-mail: enquiries@trenython.co.uk
dir: A390/B3269 towards Fowey, after 2m right into
Castledore. Hotel 100mtrs on left

Sweeping staircases and colonnades, Italian marble and
carved oak panelling make this Italian-designed English
country-house a hotel with a difference. Built in 1872, it
sits in a 24-acre estate between the picturesque ports of
Fowey and Charlestown with beautiful views of St Austell
Bay. The menu changes daily with a selection of specials
available. Dishes are created with contemporary flair
using fresh Cornish seafood and produce from local
farms wherever possible. Cornish crab cake, for example,
comes with Thai-spiced salad to start, then perhaps local
pork sausages with mashed potato, seasonal vegetables
and onion gravy. Light bites are available in the bar at
lunchtime.

Times 12-2.30/7-9.30

Nare Hotel

◎ Traditional British

Seaside hotel with fabulous views over the bay

☎ 01872 501279 📠 01872 501856
Carne Beach TR2 5PF
e-mail: office@narehotel.co.uk
dir: from Tregony follow A3078 for approx 1.5m. Left at
Veryan sign, through village towards sea & hotel

The Nare Hotel is a relaxed country house by the sea with
breathtaking views across Gerran's Bay. It proudly states
that it is not a designer hotel, but that's not to say it isn't
very smart indeed, and old-fashioned service from lovely
staff is heartfelt and genteel. There are two dining
options, and you get those gorgeous views wherever you
choose to eat. The jaunty nautically-themed Quarterdeck
restaurant injects a contemporary note, with a teak inlaid
deck and yachting prints, and a more contemporary
brasserie-style menu. If you go for the five-course table
d'hôte in the formal dining room, expect straightforward,
classic cooking, starting with, perhaps, a game terrine
with Cumberland sauce and fresh fig from the hors
d'oeuvre trolley; a fish course of bream with sauce vierge
precedes a veal escalope with sage sauce and Jerusalem
artichokes.

Chef Richard James **Owner** T G H Ashworth
Times 12.30-2.30/7.30-10 Closed L Mon-Sat **Prices** Food
prices not confirmed for 2010. Please telephone for
details, Service optional **Wines** 300 bottles over £20, 200
bottles under £20, 18 by glass **Notes** Fixed D 5 course
£45, Sunday L, Vegetarian available, Dress restrictions,
Jacket and tie, Air con **Seats** 75 **Children** Portions, Menu
Parking 70

The Brasserie

◎ Modern European ✋

**Beachside surfer-chic hotel with modern brasserie
dining**

☎ 01637 860543 📠 01637 860333
The Hotel & Extreme Academy TR8 4AA
e-mail: life@watergatebay.co.uk
dir: A30 onto A3059, follow Airport/Watergate Bay signs

Newquay's Victorian Watergate Hotel has reinvented itself
in recent years, morphing into one of Cornwall's top
surfer-chic hangouts. It's right on a superb private
beach, where the Extreme Academy watersports centre
provides adrenaline-based thrills, but you can just chill
out and take in the stylish luxury beachcomber ambience.
Sea views form the backdrop for the Brasserie's modern
British and European repertoire of dishes built from
quality Cornish produce. Daily menus offer straight-up
fare in the vein of parmesan-crusted fillets of Cornish
mackerel with shaved fennel and lemon salad, then cod,
salmon and haddock fishcakes with chunky chips and
'mushed' peas.

Chef Tom Bradbury **Owner** Watergate Bay Hotel Ltd **Times** 6.45-9.30 Closed L all week **Prices** Fixed D 3 course fr £27.50, Service optional **Wines** 28 bottles over £20, 13 bottles under £20, 9 by glass **Notes** Vegetarian available, Civ Wed 40, Air con **Seats** 120 **Children** Portions, Menu **Parking** 45

Fifteen Cornwall

◉ Modern British, Italian ☺

Freshest fish and seafood with views of the rolling surf

☎ 01637 861000
On The Beach TR8 4AA
e-mail: restaurant@fifteencornwall.co.uk
web: www.fifteencornwall.co.uk
dir: M5 to Exeter & join A30 westbound. Exit Highgate Hill junct, following signs to airport and at T-junct after airport, turn left & follow road to Watergate Bay

Like its siblings, the Cornish branch of Jamie O's restaurant group features natural materials in the design, including a reclaimed tree-trunk reception desk, and plenty of pink. As elsewhere, the place is about helping youngsters who have had poor starts in life to reclaim their own potential with a career in the restaurant industry. The word 'industry' doesn't seem quite right, though, as you gaze out over the sandy beaches, the wet-suited surfers and the crystal-clear sea. Impeccably fresh seafood is the winner, from a serving of sardines with candied beetroot and chive crème fraîche, to mains such as the 'amazing' (it says so on the menu) fish stew, an aïoli-dressed riot of lobster, squid, brill, monkfish, sea bass and pollock.

Chef Neil Haydock **Owner** Cornwall Foundation of Promise **Times** 12-3/6.15-9.45 **Prices** Fixed L fr £26, Tasting menu £50, Starter £6.50-£9, Main £17-£22, Dessert £6, Service optional **Wines** 90 bottles over £20, 3 bottles under £20, 10 by glass **Notes** Tasting menu only served evenings, Vegetarian available, Air con **Seats** 100, Pr/dining room 12 **Children** Portions, Menu **Parking** In front of restaurant

ZENNOR   Map 2 SW43

The Gurnard's Head

◉◉ Modern British

Roadside inn with appealing modern menu

☎ 01736 796928
Treen TR26 3DE
e-mail: enquiries@gurnardshead.co.uk
dir: 6m W of St Ives by B3306

The winding coast road south-west from St Ives is a spectacular journey across open moors with the sea as a backdrop, and The Gurnard's Head, a four-square roadside inn, offers a lot more than mere refreshment along the route. It combines a country atmosphere - log fires, solid wood floors and tables - with modern cooking in both bar and dining areas. Good local produce meets modern British and European sensibilities on the carte, so venison carpaccio with horseradish, beetroot and spring onion is alongside parsnip soup with onion fritter as starters. Main-course local mackerel is given a

European flavour with chorizo, Puy lentils and rocket, and desserts such as prune parfait with Earl Grey prunes come with dessert wine suggestions. Service gets the tone of friendly efficiency just right.

Chef Robert Wright **Owner** Charles & Edmund Inkin **Times** 12-2.30/6.30-9.30 Closed 24-25 Dec **Prices** Starter £4.50-£7.50, Main £9.50-£16, Dessert £4.50-£6, Service optional **Wines** 63 bottles over £20, 8 bottles under £20, 24 by glass **Notes** Sunday L, Vegetarian available **Seats** 50 **Children** Portions **Parking** 40

CUMBRIA

ALSTON   Map 18 NY74

Lovelady Shield Country House Hotel

◉◉ Modern British

Family-run country-house hotel with innovative cuisine

☎ 01434 381203   📠 01434 381515
CA9 3LF
e-mail: enquiries@lovelady.co.uk
web: www.lovelady.co.uk
dir: 2m E of Alston, signed off A689 at junct with B6294

Picture a grand old Georgian house in the middle of nowhere among the wild fells of the North Pennines. Lovelady Shield is the perfect place to get lost in - provided, of course, that you find it in the first place, secreted away at the end of a long, wooded drive. Relax in lots of comfy lounges, or sip a pre-dinner drink before settling into an elegant room surrounded by antiques and paintings. The cooking here is essentially modern British with excursions to the continent and further afield. Daily-changing menus showcase some interesting combinations and high quality ingredients, including starters such as spiced confit mutton samosa with redcurrant and mint chutney; pheasant might follow, as a grilled breast, ravioli of confit leg with wild mushrooms, baby carrots and truffle foam, then finish with an inventive medley of beetroot set cream, parsnip ice cream and warm carrot cake.

Chef Barrie Garton **Owner** Peter & Marie Haynes **Times** 12-2/7-8.30 Closed L Mon-Sat **Prices** Fixed D 4 course £41.50, Service optional **Wines** 98 bottles over £20, 29 bottles under £20, 6 by glass **Notes** Sunday L, Vegetarian available, Dress restrictions, No jeans or shorts, Civ Wed 40 **Seats** 24, Pr/dining room 10 **Children** Portions, Menu **Parking** 20

AMBLESIDE   Map 18 NY30

Drunken Duck Inn

◉◉ Modern British, European ☺

Superb local produce in a glorious Lakeland setting

☎ 015394 36347   📠 015394 36781
Barngates LA22 0NG
e-mail: info@drunkenduckinn.co.uk
web: www.drunkenduckinn.co.uk
dir: Take A592 from Kendal, follow signs for Hawkshead (from Ambleside), in 2.5m sign for inn on right, 1m up hill

This Lake District country pub deserves its popularity. The 400-year-old coaching inn has been run with unstuffy flair by the same family for over thirty years. It's still a real pub, albeit a tad gentrified with its leather club chairs and foot-wide oak boards. Its own Barngate Brewery ales are pulled at a black slate bar, but it is the three stylish dining areas that are the main focus for modern brasserie-style cuisine. Local produce suppliers are name-checked on a menu of accomplished cooking: pepper-crusted carpaccio of beef, with redcurrants and rocket to start, then breast of duck with roast sweet potato, confit garlic risotto and duck jus; the tone continues with tempting puddings, such as dark chocolate pannacotta with pistachio ice cream and mint jelly.

Chef Luke Shaw, Jim Metcalfe **Owner** Stephanie Barton **Times** 12-4/6-9.30 Closed 25 Dec **Prices** Starter £5.50-£14, Main £12.95-£25, Dessert £5-£10, Service optional **Wines** 155 bottles over £20, 25 bottles under £20, 17 by glass **Notes** Sunday L, Vegetarian available **Seats** 60 **Children** Portions **Parking** 40

AMBLESIDE *continued*

The Log House

◉ Modern Mediterranean

Norwegian log-house restaurant with flavour-driven modern fare

☎ 015394 31077
Lake Rd LA22 0DN
e-mail: nicola@loghouse.co.uk
dir: M6 junct 36. Situated on A591 on left, just beyond garden centre

The authentic Norwegian Log House was imported in the late 19th century as the home and studio of the artist Alfred Heaton Cooper, who pined for the fjords after returning to make a better living out of well-heeled Lake District tourists. Nowadays, the interior of the split-level restaurant and bar has been remodelled to suit contemporary aesthetics, with smart lightwood floors and terracotta-washed walls. The kitchen works with the seasons' bounty and applies classic techniques in a Mediterranean-inflected modern repertoire. Scallops and sticky pork millefeuille might start off proceedings, then roasted loin of Vale of Lune lamb with crème fraîche mash, salsa verde and lamb jus.

Chef Heath Calman **Owner** Nicola & Heath Calman
Times 5-9.30 Closed 7 Jan-7 Feb, Mon, L all week
Prices Fixed D 3 course £17.50, Starter £4.95-£8.95, Main £11.95-£19.95, Dessert £5.50-£6.95, Service optional **Wines** 32 bottles over £20, 31 bottles under £20, 5 by glass **Notes** Chef's choice menu available, Vegetarian available **Seats** 40 **Children** Portions, Menu **Parking** 3, Pay & display opposite

Rothay Manor

◉ Traditional British **V** 🕲

Lakeland country dining in family-run hotel

☎ 015394 33605   📠 015394 33607
Rothay Bridge LA22 0EH
e-mail: hotel@rothaymanor.co.uk
web: www.rothaymanor.co.uk
dir: In Ambleside follow signs for Coniston (A593). Manor 0.25m SW of Ambleside opposite rugby pitch

The low-slung, white-fronted building has been in the same family ownership for over 40 years, and is fitted out with all the facilities of the modern hotel. Interiors are traditional and comfortable, and there is an acre-and-a-half of landscaped gardens to wander in. A whole range

of eating options includes children's and diabetic menus. Dinner is a fixed-price deal of up to five courses, with a soup or sorbet after the starter, and English cheeses after the dessert. You might begin with mussels served in a creamy sauce with winter veg and garlic bread, and choose a main such as wild mallard braised in damson gin, with red cabbage, Anna potatoes and Cumberland sauce. Classical French desserts include tarte Tatin or crêpe Suzette.

Chef Jane Binns **Owner** Nigel Nixon
Times 12.30-1.45/7.15-9 Closed 3-28 Jan, L 1 Jan, D 25 Dec **Prices** Fixed L 2 course £17-£18, Fixed D 3 course £40, Starter £5-£6, Main £8-£12, Dessert £5, Service optional **Wines** 123 bottles over £20, 48 bottles under £20, 9 by glass **Notes** ALC L only, Sunday L, Vegetarian menu, Dress restrictions, Smart casual, Air con **Seats** 65, Pr/dining room 34 **Children** Portions, Menu **Parking** 35

Appleby Manor Country House Hotel

◉ Modern British

Good cooking in relaxed country-house hotel

☎ 017683 51571   📠 017683 52888
Roman Rd CA16 6JB
e-mail: reception@applebymanor.co.uk
dir: M6 junct 40/A66 towards Brough. Take Appleby turn, then immediately right. Continue for 0.5m

The garden has picked up a gong for being blooming lovely and it can be fully appreciated from the dining room, plus there are distant views of the countryside beyond. Dine in the conservatory or the oak-panelled part of the dining room and choose from a menu of accomplished dishes, featuring interesting combinations and lots of regional produce. Sweetcorn and lemon broth or lobster ravioli, served with a shrimp bisque and flavoured with tarragon, might precede main-course pot-roasted Lakeland beef brisket with a blue cheese and peppercorn pithivier. Finish with the local champion, sticky toffee pudding, or cheeses from the trolley.

Times 12-2/7-9 Closed 24-26 Dec

The Pheasant

◉ Modern British

Accomplished cooking in cosy coaching inn

☎ 017687 76234   📠 017687 76002
CA13 9YE
e-mail: info@the-pheasant.co.uk
dir: M6 junct 40, take A66 (Keswick and North Lakes). Continue past Keswick and head for Cockermouth. Signed from A66

With its rural position within well-tended gardens on the western side of Bassenthwaite Lake, this 16th-century coaching inn is brimful of character and charm. There are comfy lounges for afternoon tea and an attractive bar with polished walls, oak settles and log fires, but it's the dining room that's the real draw, where you can sample a menu of modern British dishes conjured from the top-notch local Cumbrian ingredients. Pan-fried breast of wood pigeon with sautéed wild mushrooms and pancetta is a typical starter, while mains might include seared cannon of Lakeland lamb with haggis beignet, winter root vegetable purée, fondant potato and lamb jus.

Chef Malcolm Ennis **Owner** Trustees of Lord Inglewood
Times 12-1.30/7-9 Closed 25 Dec **Prices** Fixed L 2 course £20-£22.95, Fixed D 3 course £33.25-£35.95, Service optional, Groups min 8 service 10% **Wines** 60 bottles over £20, 19 bottles under £20, 12 by glass **Notes** Sunday L, Vegetarian available, Dress restrictions, Smart casual, No jeans, T-shirts, trainers **Seats** 45, Pr/dining room 12 **Parking** 40

Hazel Bank Country House

◉ British, European

Sound cooking in Victorian house with stunning Lakeland views

☎ 017687 77248   📠 017687 77373
Rosthwaite CA12 5XB
e-mail: enquiries@hazelbankhotel.co.uk
dir: A66 Keswick, follow B5289 signed Borrowdale, turn left before Rosthwaite over humpback bridge

Reached over a humpback bridge and down a long and winding drive flanked by rhododendrons, this splendid Victorian Lakeland house is set in 4 acres of beautiful gardens to the front and side. With its own woodlands and pretty little streams to the back of the house, Hazel

Bank also overlooks some of England's highest mountain peaks. The elegant dining room has a friendly, informal dinner party atmosphere, starting with pre-dinner drinks in front of the real fire in the lounge. Traditional British dishes with European influences feature local ingredients, and may include a lemon sole fillet with saffron and caper sauce, followed by caramelised apple Tatin with a Calvados cream.

Times 7 Closed 25-26 Dec, L all week

Leathes Head Hotel

🏵 Modern British

Sound cooking in restaurant with fabulous views

☎ 017687 77247 📠 017687 77363
CA12 5UY
e-mail: enq@leatheshead.co.uk
dir: 3.75m S of Keswick on B5289, set back on the left

The Borrowdale Valley has been described as the most beautiful valley in England and that is a claim few will dispute on arriving at this former Edwardian gentleman's residence. Now a family-run hotel, it welcomes guests with comfy lounges for pre-dinner drinks, plus a traditionally decorated restaurant that makes the most of the stunning fell views. Take your seat for some flavourful, unpretentious cuisine using well-sourced ingredients. Home-made goulash soup with yogurt and mint might kick things off, then perhaps baked fillet of cod with a ginger, lemon and spring onion butter sauce, and chilled lemon curd syllabub with Cumberland flapjack to finish.

Times 7.30-8.15 Closed mid Nov-mid Feb

BRAITHWAITE Map 18 NY22

The Cottage in the Wood

🏵🏵 Modern European **V**

Excellent food and service in dramatic Lake District setting

☎ 017687 78409
Whinlatter Pass CA12 5TW
e-mail: relax@thecottageinthewood.co.uk
dir: M6 junct 40, A66 signed Keswick. 1m after Keswick take B5292 signed Braithwaite, hotel in 2m

This delightful restaurant with rooms deep in Whinlatter Forest looks down the valley to dramatic vistas of the Skiddaw mountain range. The former 17th-century coaching inn is looking spruce after a recent refurbishment to its restaurant, adding on a light and airy conservatory and extending its outdoor terrace. The experienced chef-patron is always striving to improve and comes up with some lively ideas. The appealing menus offer wonderful flavour combinations with European and Mediterranean influences, but no unnecessary fuss. Cream of cumin, roasted butternut squash, feta and spinach starts off with well-balanced flavours; next up, perfectly-cooked loin of local lamb is roasted with herbs and served with celeriac gratin and a glossy merlot jus. A very British combination of apple cake, raspberry coulis

and vanilla ice cream makes a simple, effective conclusion.

Chef Liam Berney **Owner** Liam & Kath Berney
Times 12-2.30/6.30-9 Closed Jan, Mon, D Sun
Prices Fixed L 2 course fr £23.50, Service included, Groups min 8 service 10% **Wines** 20 bottles over £20, 20 bottles under £20, 6 by glass **Notes** Sunday L, Vegetarian menu **Seats** 36 **Children** Portions **Parking** 16

BRAMPTON Map 21 NY56

Farlam Hall Hotel

🏵 Modern British **V** 🕤

Elegant dining in a traditional setting

☎ 016977 46234 📠 016977 46683
Hallbankgate CA8 2NG
e-mail: farlam@relaischateaux.com
web: www.farlamhall.co.uk
dir: On A689, 2.5m SE of Brampton (not in Farlam village)

Farlam Hall is a comfortingly old-fashioned sort of place that prides itself on first-class service from a family-run team of local people. Those great makeover enthusiasts, the Victorians, remodelled an older house to reflect their tastes, leaving us with a huge dining room where floor-to-ceiling windows overlook the garden and ornamental lake. The time-warp ambience is boosted by friendly waitresses in long black skirts, floral-patterned plates, silver cutlery and gleaming crystal laid out on damask tablecloths. Not so the food: modern English country house menus are kept concise to allow best use of local, seasonal produce. To start, spiced slow-cooked pork comes with caramelised apples, cherry tomatoes and West Cumbrian pancetta; next, perhaps red mullet on griddled aubergine and vine tomatoes with basil and sweet chilli reduction, and to finish, a raspberry Elizabeth crunch.

Chef Barry Quinion **Owner** Quinion & Stevenson Families
Times 8-8.30 Closed 24-30 Dec, L all week **Prices** Fixed D 4 course £42-£44, Service optional **Wines** 43 bottles over £20, 10 bottles under £20, 11 by glass **Notes** Vegetarian menu, Dress restrictions, Smart dress, No shorts **Seats** 40, Pr/dining room 20 **Children** Portions **Parking** 25

CARTMEL Map 18 SD37

Aynsome Manor Hotel

🏵 British 🕤

Long-standing Lakeland hotel with comfortingly traditional approach

☎ 015395 36653 📠 015395 36016
LA11 6HH
e-mail: aynsomemanor@btconnect.com
dir: M6 junct 36, A590 signed Barrow-in-Furness towards Cartmel. Left at end of road, hotel before village

Dating originally from the reign of George II, Aynsome once belonged to wealthy clergy, but all may now experience its deeply traditional, oak-panelled interiors and typically Lakeland atmosphere. Local suppliers are proudly listed on the menu, and the kitchen looks after its clientele well with comforting country-house cooking. Smoked mackerel pâté or pea and ham soup might be typical starters, followed by baked sea bass with caramelised baby onions or breast of Holker pheasant with wild mushrooms and Puy lentils in Madeira. Sticky toffee pudding with luxuriously velvety butterscotch sauce is the favoured way to finish.

Chef Gordon Topp **Owner** P A Varley **Times** 7 (1pm Sun) Closed 25-26 Dec, 2-28 Jan, L Mon-Sat, D Sun (ex residents) **Prices** Fixed D 3 course £26-£27, Service optional **Wines** 25 bottles over £20, 60 bottles under £20, 6 by glass **Notes** Sunday L, Vegetarian available, Dress restrictions, Smart dress **Seats** 28 **Children** Portions, Menu **Parking** 20

L'Enclume

🏵🏵🏵🏵 – *see page 98*

Rogan & Company Bar & Restaurant

🏵🏵 British **NEW**

Confident modern cooking in relaxed village setting

☎ 015395 35917 & 07813 347475
Devonshire Square LA11 6PZ
e-mail: reservations@roganandcompany.co.uk
dir: From M6 junct 36 follow signs for A590. Turn off at sign for Cartmel village

Simon Rogan's second venture, located near the trickling stream in the pretty village of Cartmel, is a different kettle of fish from L'Enclume, (see entry) which is just around the corner. Spread over two floors, there is a stylish bar (an appealing blend of old and new), a first-floor restaurant, plus a private dining room and courtyard. Occupying a 16th-century building that was formerly an antique shop, this is Rogan's version of casual dining, and very good value it is, too. Seasonality and local produce dominate the menu, which takes in classic British dishes with plenty of modern European flourishes and a few flavours from farther afield. Butternut squash soup with nutmeg crème fraîche and sage proves to be a divine combination of flavours, and

continued on page 99

L'Enclume

Modern French — NOTABLE WINE LIST

Exhilarating, innovative cuisine to stir a quiet Lakeland village

☎ 015395 36362
Cavendish St LA11 6PZ
e-mail: info@lenclume.co.uk
web: www.lenclume.co.uk
dir: Follow signs for A590 W, turn left for Cartmel before Newby Bridge

As a blacksmiths forge, over 700 years old, the building must have seen plenty of sparks fly, but never like this - who could have imagined this humble old forge in the sleepy village of Cartmel would be at the epicentre of 21st-century culinary goings on? The stillness of the locale gives a good first feeling, and the plainness of the whitewashed building may not linger in the memory, but the food...the food will leave a lasting impression. Simon Rogan is a chef striving for perfection, an innovator who seeks out ingredients such as wild flowers that have been lost in the past and looks to deliver exciting and unusual flavour combinations. He is a relentless researcher, experimenter and tester, constantly striving to thrill his customers with glorious tastes and textures, and he is not without a whimsical side, as seen in the naming of some of the dishes. The restaurant with rooms has been sensitively converted, leaving plenty of reminders

of its antiquity in the craggy beams, flagstones and stone walls, whilst bringing in contemporary furniture (tables are clothless), abstract artworks and spotlights to create a thoroughly confident and almost minimalist space. It is all very civilised, and the service - bright, alert, informed and well structured - fits the bill. There's a choice of three menus, each a multiple taster, and Menu 3 with 17 items is just over twice as long as Menu 1. Whichever one you go for, you're going to get superb produce, an awful lot of it from the local area, in an array of complex, inventive, highly creative and beautifully presented dishes. The menu requires explanation (staff will help) but you can just dive in and wait to be amazed. Cod 'yolk' crispies is a brandade of cod with a yolk inside, served with a luscious bacon cream - a brilliant dish of earthy, natural flavours. Surf and turf is a little different to what you'll get in the local pub - what comes are four (a generous portion given the number of dishes to come) pork belly and eel fritters full of superb flavour, topped with a lovage cream and sitting on a sweetcorn purée. Sticky tacky pudding remains a signature dessert; a deconstructed version with wonderfully defined flavours. This is world class cooking, boldly innovative without being overly heavy or rich; dairy produce is used with a careful hand and heavy stock and sauces are eschewed in favour of lighter, more natural flavours.

(See Rogan & Company, for Simon's take on casual dining).

Chef Simon Rogan **Owner** Simon Rogan, Penny Tapsell **Times** 12-1.30/6.30-9.30 Closed L Mon & Tue **Prices** Fixed L course £25, Service optional, Groups min 8 service 10% **Wines** 356 bottles over £20, 4 bottles under £20, 10 by glass **Notes** Fixed D 8, 13 or 17 course £50-£90, Vegetarian available, Air con **Seats** 50, Pr/dining room 8 **Parking** 7

CARTMEL *continued*

another starter of smoked ham hock cannelloni with lentils and runny yogurt shows good technical skills. Cumbrian rib steak with béarnaise sauce and thick-cut chips is a simple and appealing main course, and desserts extend to warm cinnamon cake with Granny Smith sorbet.

Chef Simon Rogan, Adam Wesley **Owner** Simon Rogan & Penny Tapsell **Times** 12-2.30/6.30-9 **Prices** Food prices not confirmed for 2010. Please telephone for details. **Notes** Sunday L, Vegetarian available, Air con **Seats** 100, Pr/dining room 24 **Children** Menu **Parking** On street

---

CROSTHWAITE
Map 18 SD49

The Punchbowl Inn at Crosthwaite

⊚ Modern British V

Historic, elegantly refurbished inn with refined cooking

☎ 015395 68237 📠 015395 68875
Lyth Valley LA8 8HR
e-mail: info@the-punchbowl.co.uk
web: www.the-punchbowl.co.uk
dir: 6m from Kendal

This character-packed place combines the classic features of a traditional inn - open fireplaces, slate floors - with stylish contemporary touches and modern facilities. Sibling to The Drunken Duck, Ambleside (see entry), and standing next to the parish church in the unspoilt Lyth Valley, The Punchbowl is surrounded by beautiful Lakeland countryside. Imaginative menus in both the elegant restaurant and rustic-style bar focus on traditional British and regional dishes with some modern touches and a slight French accent. Good seasonal produce is used, much of it from the surrounding area; baked Cumbrian cheddar cheese and spring onion soufflé with wilted spinach and parmesan cream, followed by slow-cooked belly of pork with confit root vegetables and apple jus.

Chef Jonathon Watson **Owner** Paul Spencer, Richard Rose **Times** 12-6/6-9.30 **Prices** Starter £3.95-£8.95, Main £13.95-£17.95, Dessert £4.50-£8.50, Service optional, Groups min 10 service 10% **Wines** 58 bottles over £20, 15 bottles under £20, 14 by glass **Notes** Sunday L, Vegetarian available, Vegetarian menu, Civ Wed 45 **Seats** 30 **Children** Portions **Parking** 40

ELTERWATER
Map 18 NY30

Purdeys

⊚ Modern, Traditional British 🍃

Enjoyable dining in a mill-styled restaurant

☎ 015394 37302 & 38080 📠 015394 37694
Langdale Hotel & Country Club LA22 9JD
e-mail: purdeys@langdale.co.uk
web: www.langdale.co.uk
dir: M6 junct 36, A591 or M6 junct 40, A66, B5322, A591

Thirty-five acres of prime Lakeland countryside with woodlands and waterways enfold this modern hotel, dotted with artefacts such as a cannon used to test explosives as a reminder that the site was once a Victorian gunpowder works. Purdeys restaurant is designed in the style of an old mill with high barn-like rafters, oak floors, walls of local stone and views over the walled garden to a working waterwheel. There's plenty of thought and imagination in the kitchen's British cuisine, which plumps for local materials, prepared and presented with care. The revamped menu offers starters such as roast quail with smoked bacon and mushroom fricasée, while mains include roast rump of Cumbrian lamb with rösti potatoes, ratatouille and basil jus.

Chef Graham Harrower **Owner** Langdale Leisure **Times** 6.30-9.30 Closed L Group L booking essential **Prices** Starter £6-£11.50, Main £12.50-£25, Dessert £7.50-£9.50, Service optional **Wines** 22 bottles over £20, 40 bottles under £20, 9 by glass **Notes** Vegetarian available, Dress restrictions, Smart casual, Civ Wed 60 **Seats** 80, Pr/dining room 40 **Children** Portions, Menu **Parking** 50

GLENRIDDING
Map 18 NY31

The Inn on the Lake

⊚ Modern European V

Traditional restaurant with stunning Lakeside views

☎ 017684 82444 📠 017684 82303
Lake Ullswater CA11 0PE
e-mail: info@innonthelakeullswater.co.uk
dir: M6 junct 40, A66 Keswick, A592 Windermere

In 15 acres of grounds with lawns sweeping down to the shores of Lake Ullswater, The Inn on the Lake Hotel enjoys one of the most spectacular settings in the Lake District. The restored grand Victorian hotel comes complete with

---

its own traditional pub in the grounds - the Ramblers Bar. The traditional restaurant offers diners fabulous views over the water and local ingredients come to the fore in the modern cooking. Take king scallop salad with pancetta lardons, Caesar dressing, pea shoots and tomato foam, followed by steamed loin of lamb with tarragon, fondant potato, aubergine caviar and sauce ravigote. End with warm treacle tart and vanilla ice cream.

Chef Fraser Soutar **Owner** Charles & Kit Graves **Times** 12.30-2/7-9 Closed L Sat **Prices** Food prices not confirmed for 2010. Please telephone for details. **Wines** 38 bottles over £20, 12 bottles under £20, 8 by glass **Notes** Sunday L, Vegetarian menu, Dress restrictions, Smart casual, Civ Wed 110 **Seats** 100, Pr/dining room 40 **Children** Portions, Menu **Parking** 100

GRANGE-OVER-SANDS
Map 18 SD47

Clare House

⊚ Modern British

Country-house cooking and great views

☎ 015395 33026 & 34253 📠 015395 34310
Park Rd LA11 7HQ
e-mail: info@clarehousehotel.co.uk
dir: From M6 take A590, then B5277 to Grange-over-Sands. Park Road follows the shore line. Hotel on left next to swimming pool

In June 2009, the Read family marked their 40th anniversary in Clare House, a relaxing country-house hotel bracketed by the Lakes and the sea. You can see why they have put down deep roots here: the grand old Victorian mansion sits in gorgeous gardens with spectacular views over Morecambe Bay, and inside it's every inch the gentleman's residence. The period character of the dining room, all high ceilings, plasterwork and burnished mahogany furniture is the perfect setting for a repertoire that is equally at home with traditional country-house fare and more modern dishes, as in a smoked haddock and spring onion risotto with butter and parmesan, followed by roast loin of Gloucestershire Old Spot pork with slow-cooked belly and herb jus.

Chef Andrew Read, Mark Johnston **Owner** Mr & Mrs D S Read **Times** 6.45-7.15 Closed Dec-Apr, L all week **Prices** Fixed D 4 course £30, Service optional **Wines** 7 bottles over £20, 30 bottles under £20, 2 by glass **Notes** Fixed price D 5 course £30, Vegetarian available **Seats** 32 **Children** Portions, Menu **Parking** 16

GRASMERE
Map 18 NY30

Grasmere Hotel
Traditional European

Traditional country-house hotel with good food

☎ 015394 35277 📄 015394 35277
Broadgate LA22 9TA
e-mail: enquiries@grasmerehotel.co.uk
dir: Off A591 close to village centre

Tradition runs through the very core of this small-scale Victorian Lakeland hotel. With an acre of lovely gardens and an original water feature called the River Rothay running through, it is looking spruce after a refurb in 2006. The interior still centres around period wood panelling and a grand staircase, while the dining room has an amazing acanthus chandelier dangling from a vaulted ceiling. Dining here is an old-school experience: pre-dinner drinks and banter in the lounge before everyone takes their seats for the day's four-course menu. The classic country-house fare is all cooked from scratch using fresh local materials: expect smoked salmon and tuna fishcakes with a lime and chilli dressing, then a pause for soup or sorbet, before locally-caught Hawkshead trout baked in white wine.

Times 7 Closed Jan-early Feb, L all week

Rothay Garden Hotel & Restaurant
Modern European V

Superb fell views and attentive staff

☎ 015394 35334 📄 015394 35723
Broadgate LA22 9RJ
e-mail: stay@rothaygarden.com
dir: From N M6 junct 40, A66 to Keswick, then S on A591 to Grasmere. From S M6 junct 36 take A591 through Windermere/Ambleside to Grasmere. At N end of village adjacent to park

On the edge of tourist hotspot Grasmere village, this hotel and restaurant sits in a couple of acres of riverside gardens and has a pleasing combination of stylish design and luxurious comfort. Friendly staff provide attentive service in the chic lounge bar and elegant candlelit restaurant, informally set and with great views across the Lakeland fells. The menu changes daily and goes in for the likes of seared scallops with a haddie sausage, celeriac roulade and sauce rouille, followed, perhaps, by roast loin of Lakeland lamb served with a mini shepherd's pie, rösti potato, summer greens and a rosemary jus. Finish off with sticky toffee pudding, toffee sauce and cinder toffee ice cream or perhaps a selection of Cumbrian farmhouse cheeses.

Rothay Garden Hotel & Restaurant

Chef Andrew Burton **Owner** Chris Carss
Times 12-1.45/7-9.30 Closed 25-26 Dec, 1 Jan
Prices Fixed L course £19.50, Fixed D 4 course £42.50, Service optional **Wines** 113 bottles over £20, 30 bottles under £20, 15 by glass **Notes** Sunday L, Vegetarian menu, Dress restrictions, Smart casual, No jeans or T-shirts **Seats** 60 **Children** Portions **Parking** 35

Wordsworth Hotel
Modern British

Skilful modern country-house cooking in traditional Lakeland hotel

☎ 015394 35592 📄 015394 35765
LA22 9SW
e-mail: enquiry@thewordsworthhotel.co.uk
web: www.thewordsworthhotel.co.uk
dir: From Ambleside follow A591 N to Grasmere. Hotel in town centre next to church

The Earl of Cadogan's Victorian hunting lodge makes a splendid traditional Lakeland hotel wrapped in a couple of acres of gardens, and surrounded by the elemental beauty of the high fells. Literary pilgrims might work up an appetite on a short stroll via the neighbouring churchyard, where Wordsworth is buried, to his former home at Dove Cottage. A conservatory extension brings an airy, summery tone to the traditionally-styled Prelude Restaurant, where the kitchen follows the seasons assiduously in its use of prime local produce, combined creatively in a repertoire of French-inflected modern dishes. Dinner might begin with roast king scallops with ratatouille and courgette fritters, then move on to best end of new season's lamb with minted tagliatelle, spring vegetables and garden pea cappuccino.

Owner Mr Gifford **Times** 12.30-2/7-9.30 **Prices** Fixed L 2 course fr £12.50, Fixed D 4 course fr £39.50, Service added but optional 10% **Wines** 50 bottles over £20, 22 bottles under £20, 10 by glass **Notes** Sunday L, Vegetarian available, Dress restrictions, Smart casual, jacket preferred, Civ Wed 100, Air con **Seats** 65, Pr/dining room 18 **Children** Portions, Menu **Parking** 50

HAWKSHEAD
Map 18 SD39

Queen's Head Hotel
British, International

Charming old-world inn serving contemporary food

☎ 015394 36271 & 0800 137263 📄 015394 36722
Main St LA22 0NS
e-mail: enquiries@queensheadhotel.co.uk
dir: Village centre

A strikingly atmospheric 16th-century Lakeland hostelry built to provide hospitality to travellers on the Windermere to Penrith coaching route, tradition reigns supreme in the rambling interior. Famous for its antique beams, settles and wooden furniture, roaring log fires, and hand-pumped ales, the food on the other hand is bang-up-to-date. Expect hearty, uncomplicated dishes prepared from quality local ingredients. Tuck into scallops with pea purée and crispy pancetta, calves' liver with roasted shallot jus, slow-roasted lamb shoulder, and summer berry Eton mess.

Chef Vincent Mumbuma **Owner** Anthony Merrick
Times 12-2.30/6.15-9.30 **Prices** Starter £3.95-£7.25,

Main £10.25-£18.50, Dessert £3.25-£5.75, Service optional **Wines** 20 bottles over £20, 40 bottles under £20, 14 by glass **Notes** Sunday L, Vegetarian available, Dress restrictions, Smart casual, Air con **Seats** 38, Pr/dining room 20 **Children** Portions, Menu **Parking** NCP permits issued

HOWTOWN   Map 18 NY41

Sharrow Bay Country House Hotel

@@@ British, International ♨ NOTABLE WINE LIST

Gracious country-house setting for modern British food

☎ 017684 86301   ▤ 017684 86349
Sharrow Bay CA10 2LZ
e-mail: info@sharrowbay.co.uk
dir: M6 junct 40. From Pooley Bridge right fork by church towards Howtown. Right at x-rds, follow lakeside road for 2m

Sharrow Bay blazed a trail for fine dining at a time when most of it went on in the well-heeled south of England, and was one of the first places that offered the ambience we now know as country-house hotel. It's still all as grandly well-maintained as it ever was, with splendid public rooms that look like something out of an interiors magazine, bright with floral displays and flickering candles in the evenings. Add to these attractions seductive views over Ullswater and cooking of high refinement, and it's hard to argue. The classical French mode of earlier eras has given place to a modern British style, as in a main course of well-timed turbot fillets with shrimp risotto, a sautéed scallop and a tempura-battered oyster, garnished with spears of asparagus.

Times 1-8pm **Prices** Food prices not confirmed for 2010

IREBY   Map 18 NY23

Overwater Hall

@@ Modern British

Fine country house with creative cooking

☎ 017687 76566   ▤ 017687 76921
CA7 1HH
e-mail: welcome@overwaterhall.co.uk
dir: A591 at Castle Inn take road towards Ireby. After 2m turn right at sign

The elegant Overwater Hall stands in 18 acres of grounds flanked by Skiddaw and surrounding fells. There are two comfortable sitting rooms and a mahogany-panelled bar where pre-dinner drinks and canapés are served, while the well-proportioned dining room possesses plenty of Georgian grandeur. Tables are smartly set and service is knowledgeable and on the formal side. The menu is ambitious with lots of inter-courses along the way. Start with terrine of three confit (chicken, duck and guinea fowl) layered with foie gras and served with home-made mango chutney, before tournedos of beef with creamed wild mushrooms, oxtail pie, fondant potato, carrot purée and Marsala sauce.

Chef Adrian Hyde **Owner** Adrian & Angela Hyde, Stephen Bore **Times** 7-8.30 Closed 1st 2 wks Jan **Prices** Fixed D 4 course £40-£50, Service optional **Wines** 46 bottles over £20, 18 bottles under £20, 9 by glass **Notes** Vegetarian available, Dress restrictions, Smart casual **Seats** 30 **Children** Portions **Parking** 15

KENDAL   Map 18 SD59

Best Western Castle Green Hotel in Kendal

@@ Modern British, European ♨

Ambitious cooking in modern Lakeland hotel

☎ 01539 734000   ▤ 01539 735522
Castle Green Ln LA9 6RG
e-mail: reception@castlegreen.co.uk
web: www.castlegreen.co.uk
dir: M6 junct 37, A684 towards Kendal. Hotel on right in 5m

Not far from the M6 and the town centre, this contemporary hotel enjoys a peaceful Lakeland setting with castle views. The bright-and-airy Greenhouse restaurant is decorated in muted shades that provide a perfect foil for the dramatic scenery outside the large plate-glass windows. The ambitious cooking is showcased on the modern British menu, using local

produce wherever possible and there is a good value five-course tasting menu on offer. Daily specials complement the good-value carte, offering starters like slow-cooked pork belly with quail's eggs and carrots, followed by a fillet of beef, braised shin, horseradish mash, shallots and red wine sauce. Finish with rosemary pannacotta, green figs and cardamom.

Chef Justin Woods **Owner** James & Catherine Alexander **Times** 12-2/6-10 **Prices** Fixed D 3 course £27.95, Service included **Wines** 23 bottles over £20, 27 bottles under £20, 12 by glass **Notes** Vegetarian available, Dress restrictions, Smart casual, Civ Wed 100, Air con **Seats** 80, Pr/dining room 200 **Children** Portions, Menu **Parking** 200

KESWICK   Map 18 NY22

Dale Head Hall Lakeside Hotel

@ Modern British

Country-house dining in stunning spot

☎ 017687 72478   ▤ 017687 71070
Lake Thirlmere CA12 4TN
e-mail: onthelakeside@daleheadhall.co.uk
dir: 5m from Keswick on A591

Stroll across the garden of Dale Head Hall and you can skim a stone into Lake Thirlmere, or dip a toe into the chilly water if you're inclined - the hotel is set just back from the water's edge. Trees are all around and Helvellyn looms large behind the hotel, which dates originally from the 16th century. In the traditionally decorated, beamed restaurant, the daily-changing dinner menu might offer home-cured gravad lax with chive and potato salad with a sweet mustard and dill dressing, followed by roast beef with Yorkshire pudding and roast potatoes. Choose between cheese or dessert to finish (maybe lemon and raspberry syllabub with hazelnut shortbread).

Times 7.30-8 Closed Jan, L all wk

Highfield Hotel & Restaurant

@@ Modern European

Ambitious cooking in friendly Lakeland hotel with marvellous views

☎ 017687 72508   ▤ 017687 80234
The Heads CA12 5ER
e-mail: info@highfieldkeswick.co.uk
dir: M6 junct 40, A66, 2nd exit at rdbt. Left to T-junct, left again. Right at mini-rdbt. Take 4th right

'Restaurant with a view' is a common boast, but in the case of this lovely Lakeland country-house hotel the
continued

KESWICK *continued*

reality far outweighs expectations. The grand old slate-built house is just a short stroll from the centre of Keswick, and comes with many of the features beloved of the Victorians, including turrets and bay windows from which the views extend down the Borrowdale Valley to Derwentwater and the fells beyond. While the hotel goes for comforting tradition, the cooking takes a modern approach in its creative, dinner-only menus. Quality local ingredients are put to good use in dishes such as collop of Cumbrian venison with roast root vegetables or roast loin of Cumbrian fell lamb with rosemary and garlic, crushed new potatoes and port wine jus.

Chef Gus Cleghorn **Owner** Howard & Caroline Speck **Times** 6.30-8.30 Closed Jan-Early Feb, L all week **Prices** Fixed D 3 course £29.50, Service optional **Wines** 22 bottles over £20, 41 bottles under £20, 7 by glass **Notes** Vegetarian available, Dress restrictions, Smart casual, Air con **Seats** 40 **Children** Portions **Parking** 20

Lyzzick Hall Country House Hotel

@ European

Quality cooking accompanied by superb Lakeland views

☎ 017687 72277 🖹 017687 72278
Under Skiddaw CA12 4PY
e-mail: info@lyzzickhall.co.uk
dir: M6 junct 40 onto A66 to Keswick. Do not enter town, keep on Keswick by-pass. At rdbt 3rd exit onto A591 to Carlisle. Hotel 1.5m on right

The views over Lakeland hills are mightily impressive, and this hotel, perched on the foothills of Skiddaw, makes a superb bolthole for exploring the area. The décor is traditional but not at all chintzy - this is an elegant place and nothing seems to be too much trouble for the staff. The kitchen uses good quality produce (some of it local) in a range of accomplished dishes based on English and European traditions. A classic cream of carrot, orange and coriander soup might be followed by braised lamb shank with mash potato and rosemary and thyme sauce (with a wild berry sorbet in-between).

Times 12-2/7-9 Closed Jan

Swinside Lodge

@@ British, European V

Delightful country house with indulgent food and friendly service

☎ 017687 72948 🖹 017687 73312
Grange Rd, Newlands CA12 5UE
e-mail: info@swinsidelodge-hotel.co.uk
web: www.swinsidelodge-hotel.co.uk
dir: M6 junct 40, A66, left at Portinscale. Follow to Grange for 2m ignoring signs to Swinside & Newlands Valley

Away from the madding crowds that descend on the Lake District, yet just a short stroll from the shores of Derwentwater is this lovely intimate Georgian house. Tradition is the watchword here, and guests gather in cosy lounges for pre-dinner nibbles and apéritifs before taking a seat in the small-scale dining room. Interesting four-course dinners serve up technically-accomplished modern British dishes that change daily and make fine use of local farmers' and kitchen garden produce. Everything is home-made - canapés, breads, sorbets, ice creams and petits fours. A dainty starter of saffron-rubbed monkfish, smoked trout and grilled salmon might lead on to a perfectly-cooked rosemary-roasted loin of lamb atop confit shoulder with potato fondant and kumquat chutney.

Chef Clive Imber **Owner** Mike & Kath Bilton **Times** 7-10.30 Closed 25 Dec, L all week **Prices** Fixed D 4 course £40, Service optional **Wines** 19 bottles over £20, 11 bottles under £20, 6 by glass **Notes** Vegetarian menu **Seats** 14 **Children** Portions **Parking** 12

| **KIRKBY LONSDALE** | **Map 18 SD67** |

Hipping Hall

@@ Modern British, French V

Wisteria-clad country house in the verdant North West

☎ 015242 71187 🖹 015242 72452
Cowan Bridge LA6 2JJ
e-mail: info@hippinghall.com
dir: 8.5m E of M6 junct 36 on A65

Bounded on all sides by some of England's most verdant beauty - from the Trough of Bowland to the Eden Valley - Hipping Hall is an enviably sited country-house hotel. The dining-room, a 15th-century hall complete with minstrels' gallery and tapestries, may sound haughtier than it is, but the whole place is on a human scale, and run with

the human touch. New chef Michael Wilson maintains the style of his predecessor in cooking that juxtaposes flavours and textures to impressive effect. Start with seared mackerel, adorned with braised baby gem, beetroot and pear remoulade and a sardine dressing, and follow up with roast breast of Goosnargh duck with the confit leg, Umbrian lentils, parsnip purée, kale and a vanilla jus. A five-course tasting menu (with all the intermediary bits) is another possibility.

Chef Michael Wilson **Owner** Andrew Wildsmith **Times** 12-2/7-9.30 Closed 3-8 Jan, L Mon-Thu **Prices** Fixed L 3 course fr £29.50, Fixed D 3 course £49.50-£60, Tasting menu £60, Service optional **Wines** 12 bottles over £20, 10 bottles under £20, 4 by glass **Notes** Sunday L, Vegetarian menu **Seats** 30 **Parking** 14

The Sun Inn

@ Modern British 🕭

Old market town inn with contemporary restaurant

☎ 015242 71965 🖹 015242 72485
6 Market St LA6 2AU
e-mail: email@sun-inn.info
dir: From A65 follow signs to town centre. Inn on main street

Lovingly restored by dedicated owners Mark and Lucy Fuller, this 17th-century inn overlooks St Mary's Church in the heart of this ancient market town. Brimming with charm and character, with old beams, oak floors, stone walls lined with bright modern art, roaring log fires and a contemporary-styled dining room, The Sun has a strong local following for tip-top cask ales and some hearty modern British cooking. Quality local ingredients are used to good effect, with the kitchen delivering dishes with simple combinations and clear flavours, as seen in pan-fried chicken livers and mushrooms on toasted brioche, tender beef medallions with caramelised shallots and a rich, tasty red wine jus, and an indulgent baked chocolate and orange cheesecake with vanilla pod ice cream.

Chef Sam Carter **Owner** Lucy & Mark Fuller **Times** 12-2.30/7-9 Closed L Mon **Prices** Starter £3.95-£5.95, Main £10.95-£15.95, Dessert £4.95-£6.95, Service optional **Wines** 8 bottles over £20, 23 bottles under £20, 7 by glass **Notes** Sunday L, Vegetarian available **Seats** 36 **Children** Portions, Menu **Parking** On street & nearby car park

NEAR SAWREY Map 18 SD39

Ees Wyke Country House

Modern, Traditional

Splendid Lakeland views and tip-top country-house cooking

☎ 015394 36393
LA22 0JZ
e-mail: mail@eeswyke.co.uk
web: www.eeswyke.co.uk
dir: On B5285 on W side of village

The views from this Georgian country house over Esthwaite Water and the surrounding countryside are the very essence of Lakeland beauty. No wonder Beatrix Potter came here to holiday, helping to spawn a huge tourism industry. Cossetting log fires crackle through the colder months, and in summer you can sit out with a drink and watch sheep grazing the fells before taking a seat for classic country-house dinners. British and European flavours mingle on an interesting menu - perhaps apple and almond black pudding with red onion marmalade, sliced duck and sweet chilli sausage, before noisettes of local lamb with wine jus, mint and garlic. Pudding - maybe Yorkshire rhubarb crumble with orange and pine nuts - is served the English way, before superbly-kept regional cheeses.

Chef Richard Lee **Owner** Richard & Margaret Lee
Times 7.30 **Prices** Food prices not confirmed for 2010. Please telephone for details, Service included **Wines** 41 bottles over £20, 29 bottles under £20, 5 by glass **Notes** Fixed D 5 course £33.00, Vegetarian available **Seats** 16 **Parking** 12

NEWBY BRIDGE Map 18 SD38

Lakeside Hotel

Modern British V

Accomplished cooking in elegant Lakeside restaurant

☎ 015395 30001 📠 015395 31699
Lakeside, Lake Windermere LA12 8AT
e-mail: sales@lakesidehotel.co.uk
dir: M6 junct 36 follow A590 to Newby Bridge, straight over rdbt, right over bridge. Hotel within 1m

Originally a 17th century coaching inn, this welcoming family-run hotel on the shores of Lake Windermere is surrounded by archetypal Lake District countryside of fells, forests and crystal clear streams. Dinner is served in the graceful, oak-panelled Lakeview restaurant, with the modern John Ruskin's brasserie giving a more informal alternative. The confident cooking is in the modern British vein, using plenty of regional produce in skillfully prepared, creative dishes. Take seared hand-dived scallops with lemon emulsion, cauliflower pannacotta, beetroot and red amaranth cress, followed by fillet of wild sea bass with artichoke purée, shin of beef, razor clams and creamed leek. Pineapple tarte Tatin with yogurt sorbet rounds things off.

Chef Richard Booth **Owner** Mr N Talbot
Times 12.30-2.30/6.45-9.30 Closed 23 Dec-15 Jan
Prices Fixed L 2 course £18-£25, Fixed D 3 course £33-£37, Service included **Wines** 190 bottles over £20, 15 bottles under £20, 12 by glass **Notes** Sunday L, Vegetarian menu, Dress restrictions, Smart casual, no jeans, Civ Wed 80, Air con **Seats** 70, Pr/dining room 30 **Children** Portions, Menu **Parking** 200

PENRITH Map 18 NY53

The Martindale Restaurant

Traditional British

Plenty of fine Cumbrian produce in hunting lodge-style hotel

☎ 01768 868111 📠 01768 868291
North Lakes Hotel & Spa, Ullswater Rd CA11 8QT
e-mail: nlakes@shirehotels.com
dir: M6 just off junct 40

Handy for the M6 at Penrith, the North Lakes Hotel is an eye-catching contemporary complex with top-class spa and leisure facilities. The striking interior design goes for a modern hunting lodge look, with high timber-beamed ceilings, wooden floors, baronial fireplaces and clever use of Lakeland stone and slate. The style works well in the Martindale Restaurant, where the kitchen team turn out a nice line in simple, unfussy dishes using well-sourced Cumbrian produce. Thornby Moor goats' cheese 'stumpies' with ginger and chilli jam is a typical starter, followed by old favourites such as Cumberland sausage with leek mash and onion sauce.

Chef Mr Mike Haddow **Owner** Shire Hotels Ltd
Times 12.15-1.45/7-9.15 Closed L Sat-Sun **Prices** Food prices not confirmed for 2010. Please telephone for details. **Wines** 41 bottles over £20, 17 bottles under £20, 14 by glass **Notes** Vegetarian available, Dress restrictions, Smart casual, Civ Wed 200 **Seats** 112 **Children** Portions, Menu **Parking** 120

SEASCALE Map 18 NY00

Cumbrian Lodge

British, Mediterranean

Chic modern restaurant with globally-influenced bistro dining

☎ 019467 27309 📠 019467 27158
58 Gosforth Rd CA20 1JG
e-mail: cumbrianlodge@btconnect.com
dir: From A595 onto B5344, hotel on left after 2m

The owners of this lovely sky-blue Victorian restaurant with rooms have really got things right after a top-to-toe refurbishment. The interior is stylish in a neutral modern vein, particularly in the sophisticated chic of the dining room, where cool hues of caramel and white rub along with modern art and deep blue glassware on crisp linen-clothed tables, and there are delightful thatched garden buildings for sheltered alfresco dining throughout the year. The bistro-style menu majors in traditional British dishes, but takes its influences from around the globe, ranging from hot and spicy lamb kofte, to classically Gallic moules marinière, and main courses such as oven-baked local lamb with creamed onion and caper sauce and chive mashed potatoes.

Chef R Hickson, C Brown **Owner** David J Morgan
Times 12-2/6.30-9.30 Closed Xmas, New Year, BHs, Sun, L Mon & Sat **Prices** Food prices not confirmed for 2010. Please telephone for details. **Wines** 17 bottles over £20, 19 bottles under £20, 15 by glass **Notes** Vegetarian available **Seats** 32 **Parking** 17

TEBAY — Map 18 NY60

Westmorland Hotel

◉ Modern British ◐

Friendly modern hotel overlooking rugged moorland

☎ 015396 24351 📄 015396 24354
Near Orton CA10 3SB
e-mail: reservations@westmorlandhotel.com
dir: Signed from Westmorland Services between M6 junct 38 & 39

Put prejudice aside and hot foot it to Tebay motorway services in Cumbria for delicious local produce. The family who own the services also run the Westmoreland Hotel, just a mile away from the M6 but with dramatic views of the Howgill fells. The kitchen stocks its larders with produce from the local farming community, while Herdwick lamb and Galloway beef come from the hotel's own farm a further 3 miles away (it's quite an enterprise). The well-thought-out modern menu offers the likes of terrine of ox tongue wrapped in Cumbrian air-dried ham, served with pickled radish, beetroot, baby leeks and toasted brioche, then the farm's own lamb chump comes with crushed peas and baby lettuce. Don't leave without paying a visit to the excellent deli and farm shop to stock up with prime local produce.

Chef Bryan Parsons **Owner** Westmorland Ltd
Times 6.30-9 **Prices** Starter £4.95-£6.95, Main £12.95-£18.95, Dessert £5.50-£6.50, Service optional **Wines** 4 bottles over £20, 32 bottles under £20, 8 by glass **Notes** Set menus can be provided for pre-booked groups, Vegetarian available, Dress restrictions, Smart casual, No jeans or T-shirts, Civ Wed 120, Air con **Seats** 100, Pr/dining room 40 **Children** Portions, Menu **Parking** 60

TEMPLE SOWERBY — Map 18 NY62

Temple Sowerby House Hotel & Restaurant

◉◉ Modern British ◐

Intimate setting for ambitious cooking

☎ 017683 61578 📄 017683 61958
CA10 1RZ
e-mail: stay@templesowerby.com
dir: 7m from M6 junct 40, midway between Penrith & Appleby, in village centre

Temple Sowerby House is a tranquil Georgian and Victorian bolthole overlooking the eponymous village green and Pennine fells in the northern Lake District's Eden Valley. In fine weather, the terrace is an irresistible spot to take in the views over pre-dinner drinks, before moving indoors to the homely restaurant, a cheery, well-lit space with large picture windows that look onto a peaceful walled garden. The cooking takes top-notch local seasonal produce along two main routes - modern British and classic French - but with some innovations and excellent presentation. To start, 'pork' comes as a pressing of ham hock and crisp belly rillettes with home-made piccalilli and sage toast, then pan-fried halibut is matched with a cassoulet of white beans, smoked bacon

and cabbage and lemon risotto. Chatty and attentive staff work hard to create a warm and relaxed ambience throughout.

Chef Ashley Whittaker **Owner** Paul & Julie Evans
Times 7-9 Closed 8 days Xmas, L all week **Prices** Fixed D 3 course £35.50, Service optional **Wines** 30 bottles over £20, 10 bottles under £20, 7 by glass **Notes** Vegetarian available, Dress restrictions, Smart casual preferred, Civ Wed 40 **Seats** 24, Pr/dining room 24 **Parking** 20

WATERMILLOCK — Map 18 NY42

Macdonald Leeming House

◉ Modern British

Accomplished Lakeland cooking on the shore of Ullswater

☎ 0870 4008131 📄 017684 86443
CA11 0JJ
e-mail: leeminghouse@macdonald-hotels.co.uk
dir: M6 junct 40, continue on A66 signed Keswick. At rdbt follow A592 towards Ullswater, at T-junct turn right, hotel 3m on left

Standing in over 20 acres of wooded grounds, the hotel is superbly located on the shore of Ullswater, with the fells looming all around. Interiors are all about high refinement, with ornately decorated lounges and the Regency restaurant offering comfort and civility in equal measure. A change of guard in the kitchens in 2009 has seen some modifications to the menu style, but the ground-note is still modern British cooking with an adventurous touch. That new 'old favourite', ham hock terrine with piccalilli, is brought off with aplomb, and comes as a satisfyingly thick slab, while main courses deal in the likes of salmon, pan-roasted and served with beetroot risotto, horseradish foam and crackling made from the skin.

Chef Gary Fothersgill **Owner** Macdonald Hotels
Times 12-2/6.30-9 **Prices** Fixed L 2 course fr £15, Fixed D 3 course £25, Starter £8.95-£12.95, Main £13.50-£16.95, Dessert £7.50-£8.50, Service optional **Wines** 75 bottles over £20, 11 bottles under £20, 13 by glass **Notes** Sunday L, Vegetarian available, Dress restrictions, Smart casual, No jeans or T-shirts, Civ Wed 80 **Seats** 60, Pr/dining room 24 **Children** Portions, Menu **Parking** 50

Rampsbeck Country House Hotel

◉◉◉ – *see opposite page*

WINDERMERE — Map 18 SD49

Best Western Burn How Garden House Hotel

◉ Modern British **V**

Traditional dining a short walk from Lake Windermere

☎ 015394 46226 📄 015394 47000
Back Belsfield Rd, Bowness LA23 3HH
e-mail: info@burnhow.co.uk
dir: Exit A591 at Windermere, following signs to Bowness. Pass Lake Piers on right, take 1st left to hotel entrance

Two minutes' walk from Lake Windermere, this elegant Victorian hotel is an oasis of tranquillity despite its close proximity to the bustling village of Bowness. The light and airy restaurant is a relaxed affair with large windows overlooking the leafy gardens. Choose from a menu of hearty British fare with the odd nod to more exotic climes. Starters might include a salmon, crab and smoked haddock fishcake with light curry sauce and lemon pickle, while mains are along the lines of best end of Herdwick lamb with saffron fondant potato, parsnip purée and mint sauce.

Chef Jane Kimani **Owner** Michael Robinson
Times 6.30-8.30 Closed Xmas, L all week **Prices** Food prices not confirmed for 2010. Please telephone for details. **Notes** Vegetarian menu **Seats** 40 **Children** Portions, Menu **Parking** 28

Burlington's Restaurant

◉◉ Modern British ◐

Spectacular views and traditional dining

☎ 015394 42137 📄 015394 43745
The Beech Hill Hotel, Newby Bridge Rd LA23 3LR
e-mail: reservations@beechhillhotel.co.uk
web: www.beechhillhotel.co.uk
dir: M6 junct 36, A591 to Windermere. Left onto A592 towards Newby Bridge. Hotel 4m from Bowness-on-Windermere

The beautiful oak-panelled restaurant set within a stylish hotel is perched up high allowing unrivalled views across Lake Windermere and over to Coniston Old Man. Traditional French and British dishes appear on the 'Classic' menu, while the 'Gourmet' delivers some contemporary flourishes. Choose from the latter and you get incidentals such as an iced apple spritzer. The place settings are formally laid on white linen cloths and service is friendly without being intrusive. Start with hot-smoked salmon Niçoise salad with salsa verde, followed by Holker Hall pheasant served with a bread and gruyère pudding. Saturdays also offer entertainment in the form of a resident jazz band.

Chef Christopher Davies **Owner** Mr & Mrs E K Richardson
Times 7-9 Closed L all week, D 25 Dec **Prices** Fixed D 3 course £29.95-£39.95, Service optional **Wines** 25 bottles over £20, 36 bottles under £20, 7 by glass **Notes** 5 course gourmet menu £39.95 to £44.95, Dress restrictions, Smart casual, no denim or trainers, Civ Wed 130 **Seats** 130, Pr/dining room 90 **Children** Portions, Menu **Parking** 60

Rampsbeck Country House Hotel

Modern British, French

Self-assured cooking of a high order by Ullswater

☎ 017684 86442 📠 017684 86688
CA11 0LP
e-mail: enquiries@rampsbeck.co.uk
web: www.rampsbeck.co.uk
dir: M6 junct 40, A592 to Ullswater, T-junct turn right at lake's edge. Hotel 1.25m

Fans of Coronation Street may find themselves assailed by a sense of déjà vu on arriving at the Rampsbeck; the hotel has been used for location filming in several episodes. It's a highly comforting, welcoming, 18th-century former farmhouse that is the very image of a Lakeland country retreat, with Ullswater shimmering nearby. The dining room is done in restful tones, with deep red cloths and a pale coffee-coloured carpet, and staff who inspire confidence with a polished, formal, but customer-centred approach. Andrew McGeorge has been at the stoves long enough to have crafted a very self-assured style of country-house cooking, notable in dishes such as seared mullet with crab risotto and lime dressing, braised veal cheek with roasted sweetbreads and ceps purée in a foie gras and thyme emulsion, and plum soufflé with cinnamon milkshake and green apple sorbet to finish. Incidentals, including the brilliant canapés, fine breads and petits fours, all give notice that this is one of Cumbria's destination restaurants.

Chef Andrew McGeorge
Owner Blackshaw Hotels Ltd
Times 12-1.45/7-9 Closed 4-27 Jan, L booking only **Prices** Fixed L 2 course £23-£25, Fixed D 3 course £43-£45, Service optional **Wines** 44 bottles over £20, 59 bottles under £20, 6 by glass
Notes Sunday L, Vegetarian available, Dress restrictions, Smart casual, no jeans or shorts preferred, Civ Wed 65
Seats 40, Pr/dining room 15
Children Portions **Parking** 30

WINDERMERE *continued*

Cedar Manor Hotel & Restaurant

◉ Modern British 🍴

Candlelit dining in romantic setting

☎ 015394 43192 📄 015394 45970
Ambleside Rd LA23 1AX
e-mail: info@cedarmanor.co.uk
dir: From A591 follow signs to Windermere. Hotel on left just beyond St Mary's Church at bottom of hill

A traditional country retreat within the Lake District National Park, this former Victorian gentleman's residence boasts a peaceful location despite being a short walk from the town centre. The Gothic-style manor house retains many period features and takes its name from a 200-year-old Indian cedar tree in the mature garden. The candlelit restaurant is relaxed and cosy in a modern country-house style with white linen, crystal glassware and silver cutlery. As much locally sourced produce as possible is used in classic British dishes with a hint of European influence, such as ham hock terrine with home-made grape chutney and toasted brioche, followed by wild sea bass with new potatoes, fine green beans, Savoy cabbage, shiitaki mushrooms, caper dressing and fennel cream.

Chef Roger Pergl-Wilson **Owner** Caroline & Jonathan Kaye **Times** 6.30-8.30 Closed Xmas & 6-25 Jan, L all week **Prices** Fixed D 4 course £24.95-£28.95, Starter £6.25,

Main £12.95-£18.95, Dessert £6.25-£7.95, Service optional **Wines** 14 bottles over £20, 16 bottles under £20, 7 by glass **Notes** Vegetarian available, Dress restrictions, Smart casual, no mountain wear **Seats** 22 **Children** Portions **Parking** 12

Fayrer Garden Hotel

◉◉ Modern British, Traditional

Traditional country-house dining with lake views

☎ 015394 88195 📄 015394 45986
Lyth Valley Rd, Bowness on Windermere LA23 3JP
e-mail: lakescene@fayrergarden.com
dir: M6 junct 36, A591. Past Kendal, at rdbt left onto B5284 signed Crook Bowness & Ferry, 8m, left onto A5074 for 400yds

The Edwardian gentleman who built his Lake District residence in 5 acres of lovely gardens and grounds

perched above Lake Windermere certainly had an eye for a prime location. The elegant hotel still has the feel of a posh country house with sumptuous fabrics and drapes adding an air of understated contemporary luxury to its recently refurbished lounges and bar. The Terrace Restaurant has a backdrop of garden and lake views to go with its keenly-priced five-course, daily-changing menus. Local, seasonal ingredients are to the fore in the kitchen's repertoire of traditional British dishes spiked here and there with a few modern twists. Confit of Pooley Bridge chicken leg with spring onion crushed potato and thyme jus might start, followed by suprême of Barbary duck with apple braised red cabbage, roast sweet potato purée and apricot coulis.

Times 7-8.30 Closed 1st 2wks Jan, L all week

Gilpin Lodge Country House Hotel & Restaurant

◉◉◉ – **see below**

Gilpin Lodge Country House Hotel & Restaurant

WINDERMERE	**Map 18 SD49**

Modern British V

Elegant hotel with first-class food

☎ 015394 88818 📄 015394 88058
Crook Rd LA23 3NE
e-mail: hotel@gilpinlodge.co.uk
web: www.gilpinlodge.co.uk
dir: M6 junct 36 & A590, then B5284 for 5m

The setting amid tall trees and sweeping lawns instantly soothes away the stresses of the real world. Perhaps it's the 20 acres of woodland, moors and award-winning gardens, or maybe it's the sheer luxury and comfort of the immaculately decorated and furnished house, which dates from 1901. This is Lake District living at its very best, with the kind of attention to detail such a family-run place can offer. Food is placed high on the agenda

and the arrival of a new chef has not dinted the desire to seek the best local produce, much of it organic. There are four dining rooms to choose from, each different in feel and design, but each stylish and comfortable, plus a champagne bar and terraces and patios for when the weather is fine. Lunch and dinner menus are full of both classical and modern ideas, with appealing combinations based on sound principles. Sautéed scallops, extremely good hand-dived specimens, come in a thrillingly successful partnership with curry oil, smoked bacon and cauliflower purée - a starter of real pedigree. Main-course best end and braised shoulder of Herdwick lamb from nearby Borrowdale is served with garlicky potato mousseline and rosemary jus, and a dessert of lemon bavarois comes with a strongly flavoured lime granité, shortbread and lemon anglaise.

Chef Russell Plowman **Owner** The Cunliffe Family **Times** 12-2/6.30-9.15 **Prices** Fixed L 2 course £20-£25, Fixed D 4 course £52, Starter £6-£9, Main £9-£20, Dessert £6.50-£7.50, Service optional **Wines** 235 bottles over £20, 1 bottles under £20, 15 by glass **Notes** Tasting menu with wine, Sunday L, Vegetarian menu, Dress restrictions, Smart Casual **Seats** 60, Pr/dining room 20 **Parking** 40

The Hideaway at Windermere

Modern, Traditional British NEW

Intimate and relaxed dining in Lakeland restaurant with rooms

☎ 015394 43070 📄 015394 48664
Phoenix Way LA23 1DB
e-mail: eatandstay@thehideawayatwindermere.co.uk
web: www.thehideawayatwindermere.co.uk
dir: M6 junct 36/A5391. Pass sign to Windermere Village, then take 2nd left into Phoenix Way. Restaurant on right

The Hideaway is a fine example of a Lakeland Victorian house, with many original features lovingly restored by the owners. The dining room is split between two light, airy and elegantly decorated rooms, while the food, based around good local produce, is presented in an unfussy fashion and sees some traditional British ideas alongside a few international influences. Reg Johnson's Goosnargh duck liver paté is served with home-made chutney and chunky slices of toasted apricot and sunflower bread, while 6oz fellbred beef is perfectly cooked and comes with mushroom, shallot and Cognac cream sauce. Traditional desserts include hot sticky toffee pudding.

Chef Richard Gornall **Owner** Richard & Lisa Gornall **Times** 12-2.30/6.30-11 Closed Mon-Tue, L Wed-Sat **Prices** Fixed D 3 course £16.50-£24.50, Starter £4.95-£8.95, Main £9.95-£19.95, Dessert £3.95-£8.95, Service optional, Groups min 10 service 10% **Wines** 6 bottles over £20, 28 bottles under £20, 4 by glass **Notes** Sunday L, Vegetarian available, Dress restrictions, Smart casual, no sportswear or trainers **Seats** 30, Pr/dining room 12 **Parking** 15

Holbeck Ghyll Country House Hotel

⦿⦿⦿ — see below

Jerichos At The Waverley

Modern British NEW

Traditional British cooking using the finest local produce

☎ 015394 42522 & 07885 544503 📄 015394 88899
College Rd LA23 1BX
e-mail: info@jerichos.co.uk
dir: M6 junct 36. A591 to Windermere. 2nd left towards Windermere then 1st right onto College Rd. Restaurant 300mtrs on right

After a decade at Jerichos in Windermere centre, chef-proprietor Chris Blaydes has relocated to a new venue in a discreet Victorian house that was once a Temperance Hotel. This restaurant with rooms has a good contemporary vibe from its stripped pine floors and jazz-themed art on white walls blending nicely with the Victorian bits. On the culinary front, it's business as usual at the stoves: Chris is still cooking with confidence in an unfussy modern style. His approach is to keep things simple and showcase the seasonality, quality and provenance of the raw materials. Chargrilled breast of wood pigeon with grilled black pudding, caramelised onions and mustard sauce is typical of the bold flavour combinations you can expect, followed by slow-roasted Gloucestershire Old Spot belly pork, colcannon, sage and mustard butter and port wine sauce. To finish, there might be bitter chocolate tart with added kick from a chocolate fondue.

Chef Chris Blaydes, Tim Dalzell **Owner** Chris & Jo Blaydes **Times** 7-9.30 Closed 1st 2 wks Nov, 24-26 Dec, 1 Jan, last 3 wks Jan, D Thu **Prices** Starter £4.50-£10.50, Main £15.50-£25, Dessert £6.25-£8, Service optional, Groups min 6 service 10% **Wines** 32 bottles over £20, 32 bottles under £20, 8 by glass **Notes** Vegetarian available **Seats** 28 **Children** Portions **Parking** 13

Holbeck Ghyll Country House Hotel

Modern British V

Breathtaking views and classy cooking

☎ 015394 32375 📄 015394 34743
Holbeck Ln LA23 1LU
e-mail: stay@holbeckghyll.com
dir: 3m N of Windermere on A591, right into Holbeck Lane (signed Troutbeck), hotel 0.5m on left

In an area hardly lacking attractive country houses enjoying breathtaking views, Holbeck remains a class act. The beautiful and peaceful grounds are all you might expect and the 19th-century former hunting lodge is the epitome of Lakeland charm and comfort. A walk in the grounds will build up an appetite, then before dinner order an aperitif and sink into a big comfy sofa in one of the lounges and gaze into a crackling fire. The views from the restaurant are - you guessed it - breathtaking. There are two dining rooms, one rich with glorious oak panelling, the other a more contemporary room with doors leading onto the terrace; both are elegant and stylish. Local food is put centre stage on the menu and the cooking does justice to the fine, seasonal produce. Start, perhaps, with rillette of rabbit with crostini and truffle cream vinaigrette and move onto a stunning roasted brill with apple, potato, braised gem lettuce and cider foam. The likes of cherry clafloutis with almond ice cream, cherries and cherry sorbet are a tempting finale, but the star of the show may prove to be the fantastic cheese selection that might include Cooleeny Farmhouse, Hawes Wensleydale and Celtic Promise alongside some French classics. The wine list has something to suit all budgets with some nice half bottles and glasses also available.

Chef David McLaughlin **Owner** David & Patricia Nicholson **Times** 12.30-2/7-9.30 **Prices** Fixed L 2 course fr £23.50, Fixed D 4 course fr £55, Service optional **Wines** 264 bottles over £20, 19 bottles under £20, 14 by glass **Notes** Gourmet menu £75, Sunday L, Vegetarian menu, Dress restrictions, Smart casual, No jeans or T-shirts, Civ Wed 65 **Seats** 50, Pr/dining room 20 **Children** Portions, Menu **Parking** 34

The Samling

Modern British V

Impressive dining in Lakeland hillside retreat

☎ 015394 31922   📠 015394 30400
Ambleside Rd LA23 1LR
e-mail: info@thesamlinghotel.co.uk
dir: On A591 towards Ambleside. 1st on right after Low
Wood Hotel. 2m from Windermere

The combination of the location on a wooded hillside with views down to Lake Windermere and the charm of the white-painted 18th-century house is a winning one. Add to that the indefatigably tasteful interior and a lasting impression is guaranteed. The hotel is part of a 67-acre estate, and inside the emphasis is firmly on rest and relaxation - the comfortable drawing room and small library catch the eye, while staff are enthusiastic, clearly happy to be on duty and are knowledgeable about the food and wine. The two small dining areas are kitted out with quality glassware and crockery and provide a stylish backdrop to some lively, creative cooking. Tip-top, fresh seasonal produce, much of it local, combine with a lightness of touch and precise flavours in well-executed modern dishes with a keen eye on presentation. Take a loin and braised shoulder of Herdwick mutton served with langoustine and Jerusalem artichoke, for instance, or perhaps a fillet of John Dory teamed with kipper tortellini and caper berries, while an assiette 'taste of blood orange' - parfait, mousse, terrine and sorbet - offers a fitting finale. Peripherals like canapés and petits fours hold form, too, and there's a menu gourmand with wine suggestions.

Chef Nigel Mendham **Owner** von Essen Hotels
Times 12.30-2/7-9 Closed L Mon-Sun (ex bookings)
Prices Food prices not confirmed for 2010. Please telephone for details. **Wines** 97 bottles over £20, 15 by glass **Notes** Gourmand tasting menu, Vegetarian menu, Civ Wed 20 **Seats** 22 **Children** Portions, Menu **Parking** 15

The Macdonald Old England Hotel & Spa

Windermere, Cumbria, England

The Old England Hotel sits proudly on the shores of Windermere surrounded by rolling hills and the gentle beauty of the Lake District. The award winning 2 AA Rosettes Vinand Restaurant, headed by Executive Head Chef, Mark Walker has an unrivaled location with views over the garden and lake, serving classical English cuisine with modern, international overtones. Following a £10 million investment the Old England has been transformed into one of the leading hotels in the north of England with 106 bedrooms and suites, a luxury spa including pool, gym and treatment rooms. The restaurant and public areas including the Terrace and lounge, which also serve light meals and afternoon teas, have all been refurbished with contemporary décor to create a relaxing ambience.

Tel: 0844 879 9144   email: groups.oldengland@macdonald-hotel.co.uk   www.macdonaldhotels.co.uk/oldengland

WINDERMERE *continued*

Lindeth Fell Country House Hotel

◉ Modern British

Traditional English cooking in a tranquil Lakeland haven

☎ 015394 43286 & 44287 ▤ 015394 47455
Lyth Valley Rd, Bowness-on-Windermere LA23 3JP
e-mail: kennedy@lindethfell.co.uk
dir: 1m S of Bowness-on-Windermere on A5074

As Lakeland views go, the one from the dining room at this elegant country-house hotel is hard to beat. The magnificent seven-acre grounds, full of colourful rhododendrons and azaleas, stretch away to Lake Windermere below and the mountains in the distance - a beautiful sight. It's a very English scene too, and the food at the Lindeth Fell follows the same path. Home-made soups (tomato, apple and celery for example), roast meats (perhaps loin of Lakeland lamb with honeyed shallots and rosemary gravy), and English puddings (how about pear and ginger sponge pudding with custard?) are all specialties of the house.

Times 12.30-1.45/7.30-9 Closed 3 wks in Jan

Lindeth Howe Country House Hotel

◉◉ Modern British ✋

Accomplished food and Lakeland views in the former home of a famous author

☎ 015394 45759 ▤ 015394 46368
Lindeth Dr, Longtail Hill LA23 3JF
e-mail: hotel@lindeth-howe.co.uk
dir: 1m S of Bowness onto B5284, signed Kendal and Lancaster. Hotel 2nd driveway on right

Beatrix Potter associations are strong in this delightful country-house hotel. With its secluded gardens perched on a leafy hillside with to-die-for views over Lake Windermere, you can see why the Potter settled here after many happy holidays. The light conservatory-style restaurant basks in those views as a backdrop to its modern country-house cooking. A new chef has brought a touch of Gallic flair to this sleepy part of the Lakes, so Beatrix's bunnies better watch out or they might appear in a starter of sweet-cured rabbit carpaccio with cider dressing to kick off a traditional five-course dinner. Mains might feature a pan-fried Cumbrian beef fillet with steak and mushroom pudding, sweet fondant potatoes and ale jus, while desserts often come in threes, as in a trilogy of star anise crème brûlée, mulled wine jelly and Amaretto ice cream.

Chef Marc Guibert **Owner** Lakeinvest Ltd
Times 12-2.30/7-9 **Prices** Fixed L 2 course £10-£19, Fixed D 4 course £30-£38.50, Service optional **Wines** 29 bottles over £20, 37 bottles under £20, 8 by glass **Notes** Sunday L, Vegetarian available, Dress restrictions, Smart casual, no jeans or sleeveless T-shirts **Seats** 70, Pr/dining room 20 **Children** Portions, Menu **Parking** 50

Linthwaite House Hotel

◉◉ Modern British Ⓥ ✋

Elegant hotel dining with modern, classy food

☎ 015394 88600 ▤ 015394 88601
Crook Rd LA23 3JA
e-mail: stay@linthwaite.com
dir: M6 junct 36. A591 towards The Lakes for 8m to large rdbt, take 1st exit (B5284), 6m, hotel on left. 1m past Windermere Golf Club

A former Edwardian gentlemen's residence, dating back to 1901, Linthwaite has superb views across its 14 acres of hilltop grounds and out over Lake Windermere. There's a genuine warmth and hospitality here and restaurant service is professional without being stuffy. There's not a hint of the chintz often found in country-house hotels - furnishings are contemporary, the linen is crisp and the tables well-spaced out. The food is similarly modern and the best dishes are often the simplest, letting the great local quality produce speak for itself. Smoked haddock ravioli, creamed leeks and mustard beurre blanc is well-executed and can be followed by a pot roasted breast of Cartmel Valley pheasant, creamed Savoy and chestnuts, turnip gratin and roasting juice. Apple tarte Tatin, Calvados caramel sauce and vanilla ice cream provides a perfect finish.

Chef Richard Kearsley **Owner** Mike Bevans **Times** 12.30-2/7-9.30 Closed Xmas & New Year (ex residents) **Prices** Fixed L 2 course £15.95, Fixed D 4 course £50, Service optional **Wines** 100 bottles over £20, 10 bottles under £20, 13 by glass **Notes** Sunday L, Vegetarian menu, Dress restrictions, Smart casual, Civ Wed 64 **Seats** 64, Pr/dining room 16 **Children** Portions, Menu **Parking** 40

Miller Howe Hotel

◉◉ Modern British ▮NOTABLE WINE LIST

Skilful modern cooking in a much-loved Lakeland hotel

☎ 015394 42536 ▤ 015394 45664
Rayrigg Rd LA23 1EY
e-mail: lakeview@millerhowe.com
dir: M6 junct 36. Follow the A591 bypass for Kendal. Enter Windermere, continue to mini rdbt, take left onto A592. Miller Howe is 0.25m on right

Along with Sharrow Bay (see entry, Howtown), Miller Howe was one of the places that put the Lake District on the gastronomic map a generation ago. Perched above Lake Windermere, with head-turning views of the Langdale Pikes range, the place has been gently updated by its present owners, and features some fine contemporary artworks, as well as the relaxing dining room with its lovely lakeside views. Andy Beaton's food evinces a high degree of technical skill and a sensitivity to the seasons, in dishes such as seared scallops with strong goats' cheese glaze, citrus confit and fennel purée, a courageous pairing of roast cod and braised short rib of beef, served with creamed leeks and capers, and desserts like spiced peanut parfait with super-rich chocolate genoise.

Times 12.30-1.45/6.45-8.45

The Samling

◉◉◉ – *see opposite page*

Storrs Hall Hotel

◉◉ Modern British Ⓥ

Accomplished, imaginative cuisine in luxurious country surroundings

☎ 015394 47111 ▤ 015394 47555
Storrs Park LA23 3LG
e-mail: storrshall@elhmail.co.uk
web: www.elh.co.uk/hotels/storrshall
dir: on A592 2m S of Bowness, on Newby Bridge road

An elegant Georgian mansion on the shores of Lake Windermere. Tick. Landscaped gardens with views across the lake and wild fells all around. Tick. Antiques, oil paintings and plush furnishings in the elegant interior. Tick. Storrs Hall certainly has all the elements of a classic country-house hotel, and the skilled cooking in the Terrace Restaurant completes a classy package. The kitchen uses quality seasonal produce imaginatively in its ambitious repertoire of sharply-presented contemporary cuisine. A well-made pressing of Gers foie gras and free range chicken with pain d'épice makes a visually-striking starter, followed by sea bass with coriander tagliatelle, ceps, pea purée and fish velouté. Tried and tested flavour combinations round things up with a dark chocolate terrine, fleur de sel wafers, mandarin sorbet and decadent gold leaf.

Chef Will Jones **Owner** English Lakes Hotels
Times 12.30-2/7-9 **Prices** Fixed L 3 course £19.75-£22.75, Fixed D 3 course fr £42.50, Service included

continued

WINDERMERE *continued*

Wines 149 bottles over £20, 21 bottles under £20, 6 by glass **Notes** Tasting menu and themed eves available, Sunday L, Vegetarian menu, Dress restrictions, Smart casual, no jeans or trainers, Civ Wed 90 **Seats** 64, Pr/dining room 40 **Children** Portions **Parking** 50

Vinand Restaurant at the Old England Hotel & Spa

◎◎ Classic British, International

Stylish modern dining and stunning lake views

☎ 0870 400 8130 📠 015394 43432
The Macdonald Old England Hotel & Spa, Church St, Bowness LA23 3DF
e-mail: general.oldengland@macdonald-hotels.co.uk
web: www.macdonald-hotels.co.uk
dir: Through Windermere to Bowness, straight across at mini-rdbt. Hotel behind church on right

Traditionally decorated with modern trappings, the Old England stands on the shore of Lake Windermere and has stunning views across the lake and surrounding woodland. The hotel was refurbished to the tune of £10m over the last couple of years and it shows in the beautifully furnished, spacious Vinand Restaurant. The cooking makes great use of quality local produce such as fell bred lamb or Gressingham Duck to produce innovative and refined dishes. Start, perhaps, with Cartmel rabbit Wellington with crushed peas, celeriac purée, radish and sherry vinaigrette, moving on to 24-hour cooked pork belly with oxtail risotto, air-dried Cumbrian ham, tripe and onion soubise, white chocolate, cauliflower purée and baby turnips.

Chef Mark Walker **Owner** Macdonald Hotels & Resorts **Times** 6.30-9 Closed L all week **Prices** Fixed D 3 course £30, Starter £8.50-£14.50, Main £17.50-£24, Dessert £7.95-£8.50, Service optional **Wines** 76 bottles over £20, 6 bottles under £20, 18 by glass **Notes** Vegetarian available, Dress restrictions, Smart casual Jacket prefered No denim/vests, Civ Wed 150 **Seats** 170, Pr/dining room 60 **Children** Portions, Menu **Parking** 100

See advert on page 108

DERBYSHIRE

ASHBOURNE   Map 10 SK14

Callow Hall

◎◎ Modern British, French

Innovative British cuisine in country-house hotel close to Peak District

☎ 01335 300900 📠 01335 300512
Mappleton Rd DE6 2AA
e-mail: reservations@callowhall.co.uk
dir: A515 through Ashbourne towards Buxton, left at Bowling Green pub, then 1st right

This ivy-clad Victorian country-house hotel is surrounded by 44 acres of garden, woods and fields overlooking the Bentley Brook and vale of the River Dove. Situated at the gateway to the Peak District National Park, and just 5 minutes' drive from the centre of Ashbourne, this family-run hotel is an ideal retreat. There are lots of period features, most notably in the William Morris dining room with its warm red décor. The traditional British menus use local and home-produced food, including home baking, smoking and curing, to create full-flavoured dishes, such as Callow Hall smoked organic Scottish salmon with dressed Devon crab, crispy leek, stem ginger and lime. Follow with roast loin and rack of lamb with an individual moussaka and rosemary and honey glaze.

Times 12.30-1.30/7.30-9 Closed 25-26 Dec, L Mon-Sat, D Sun (ex residents)

The Dining Room

◎◎ Modern British 🍃

A virtuoso culinary one-man band

☎ 01335 300666
33 St John St DE6 1GP
dir: On A52 (Derby to Leek road)

Bursting with character, the Dining Room is a destination restaurant for this part of Derbyshire. The building itself dates back to the early years of the reign of James I, as the low-beamed ceilings attest, and the original cast-iron range and wood-burning stove are fully in keeping. Peter Dale cooks single-handedly for a mere half-dozen tables, producing modern British food with outstanding clarity of flavours, using seasonal local produce (see the back of the menu) in a truly unique style. Home-smoked Loch Duart salmon is partnered with pink grapefruit, fennel, cucumber, apple and wild rice 'krispies', while the main course of local beef that's aged for 60 days, accompanied by ox cheek braised for 16 hours, indicates that patience is a virtue. Desserts must be ordered upfront and the fabulous selection of British and Irish cheeses has won awards.

Chef Peter Dale **Owner** Peter & Laura Dale **Times** 12.30-7.30 Closed 2 wks 26 Dec, 1 wk Sep, 1 wk Mar, Sun-Mon **Prices** Fixed L 2 course £21-£22, Starter £10, Main £20, Dessert £7, Service optional **Wines** 35 bottles over £20, 10 bottles under £20, 3 by glass **Notes** Tasting menu 16 course Sat D £45, Dress restrictions, Smart casual **Seats** 16 **Children** Portions **Parking** Opposite restaurant (evening)

ASHFORD-IN-THE-WATER   Map 16 SK16

Riverside House Hotel

◎◎ Modern French

Fine dining in opulent surroundings on the Wye

☎ 01629 814275 📠 01629 812873
Fennel St DE45 1QF
e-mail: riversidehouse@enta.net
dir: off A6 (Bakewell/Buxton road) 2m from Bakewell, hotel at end of main street

Its setting on the banks of the River Wye in one of Derbyshire's most picturesque villages fits this elegant Georgian country house like a glove. The former shooting lodge is the consummate small-scale country house, set in landscaped grounds and brimming with character. The Riverside Room restaurant is a delightful setting, with an inglenook that was part of the original kitchen and an ambience of posh dinner party chic thanks to classy fabrics, antique tables and chairs. It's clear that a steady hand in the kitchen guides the output with imagination and intelligence: beautifully-presented dishes range from a starter of quail, served as smoked breast, confit leg and egg, to a precisely-timed main course of pan-fried sea bass with smoked Toulouse sausage and potato gnocchi. To finish, try a flavoursome pain perdu with cherry sauce and ice cream.

Chef John Whelan **Owner** Penelope Thornton
Times 12-2.30/7-9.30 **Prices** Food prices not confirmed
for 2010. Please telephone for details. **Wines** 200 bottles
over £20, 26 bottles under £20, 32 by glass **Notes** ALC L
only, Sunday L, Vegetarian available, Dress restrictions,
Smart casual, Jacket & tie preferred, Civ Wed 32
Seats 40, Pr/dining room 30 **Parking** 25

BAKEWELL
Map 16 SK26

Monsal Head Hotel

◉ Modern British **NEW**

Down-to-earth cooking in a scenic hotspot

☎ 01629 640250 ▯ 01629 640815
Monsal Head DE45 1NL

The Monsal Head Hotel is onto a winner with its to-die-for
location overlooking Monsal Dale at the heart of the Peak
District National Park. The flagstoned Stable Bar's array
of a dozen or so real ales is enough to set real ale fans'
hearts aflutter, plus there's classic pub fodder to refuel
after fresh air exertions. There is some overlap between
bar and restaurant menus, but if you're after more
ambitious cooking, the Longstone Restaurant provides a
menu of satisfyingly hearty dishes. Substantial portions
of simple tried-and-tested combinations are sure-fire
crowd pleasers. Double-baked goats' cheese soufflé with
mixed leaves, toasted hazelnuts, green beans and sweet
pepper coulis might start, then oregano and garlic
marinated roast rump of lamb, with olive and feta
couscous and rich tomato jus.

Times 6pm

Piedaniel's

◉ French, European

**Impeccably served traditional French-European cuisine
in peaceful setting**

☎ 01629 812687
Bath St DE45 1BX
dir: From Bakewell rdbt in town centre take A6 Buxton
exit. 1st right into Bath St (one-way)

Tucked down a side street in the centre of town, the
restaurant enjoys views over its own pretty cottage
garden, while natural light and tones of white and green
dominate in the room. Whitewashed exposed-brick walls,
beams, simply laid, white-clothed tables and comfortable
high-backed chairs make for a pleasingly civilised space,
and a hands-on, friendly approach pervades the place. M.
Piedaniel's French heritage is detectable in the food on
the plate: lightly pan-fried lamb cutlets come with silky
tarragon sauce and minted crushed potatoes in a dish of
clear, uncomplicated flavours, and white chocolate
gâteau (iced white chocolate on a sticky brownie base) is
a good finish.

Chef E Piedaniel **Owner** E & C Piedaniel **Times** 12-2/7-10
Closed Xmas & New Year, 2 wks Jan, 2 wks Aug, Mon, D
Sun **Prices** Fixed L 2 course £10, Fixed D 3 course £24,
Starter £5, Main £14-£17.50, Dessert £5, Service

included **Wines** 6 bottles over £20, 23 bottles under £20,
10 by glass **Notes** Sunday L, Vegetarian available
Seats 50, Pr/dining room 16 **Children** Portions
Parking Town centre

The Square

◉ Modern British

Creative cooking in the home of Bakewell pudding

☎ 01629 812812 ▯ 01629 812309
The Rutland Arms Hotel, The Square DE45 1BT
e-mail: enquiries@rutlandarmsbakewell.co.uk
web: www.rutlandarmsbakewell.co.uk
dir: On A6 in Bakewell centre opposite war memorial.
Parking opposite side entrance

Built during the reign of George III, the Rutland Arms lies
on the outskirts of the Chatsworth Estate, between the
spa towns of Matlock and Buxton. Inside is a clock-
fancier's heaven, with every half-hour marked with
melodious chiming. Amid the colourful interiors, the
restaurant has been relaunched as The Square, but with
décor still in keeping, and the commitment to Peak
District produce unwavering. Start with creamy-textured
wild mushroom risotto topped with quail, and go on to
pollock on roasted salsify, or rabbit served three ways -
seared loin, confit leg and in a puff-pastry pie. Round
things off with sweet mascarpone, served with mango
jelly and blueberry foam.

Chef Greg Wallace **Owner** David Donegan
Times 12-2.30/7-9.30 **Prices** Fixed L 2 course £15,
Fixed D 3 course fr £27.95, Service optional **Notes** Sunday
L, Vegetarian available, Dress restrictions, Smart casual
Seats 50, Pr/dining room 30 **Children** Menu **Parking** 25

BASLOW
Map 16 SK27

Cavendish Hotel

◉◉ Modern British ✋

Skilful cooking in luxurious coaching inn

☎ 01246 582311 ▯ 01246 582312
Church Ln DE45 1SP
e-mail: info@cavendish-hotel.net
web: www.cavendish-hotel.net
dir: M1 junct 29 follow signs for Chesterfield. From
Chesterfield take A619 to Bakewell, Chatsworth & Baslow

Overlooking the Chatsworth Estate, this splendid inn
dates back to the 18th century and offers visitors a sense
of luxury and history in equal measure. The antiques and
original artworks are a reminder that the Duke and
Duchess of Devonshire had a hand in the design. Guests
can dine in the more informal conservatory Garden Room
where food is served all day, or in the elegant Gallery
Restaurant. The cooking style gets the balance of flavours
spot on, shows good technique and offers some
interesting twists on classic dishes, all accompanied by
excellent service. A starter of home-smoked duck breast
with cranberry and port dressing, followed by line-caught
Brixham sea bass with Cornish crab potato cake and
ginger beurre blanc show the style.

Chef Martin Clayton **Owner** Eric Marsh
Times 12.30-2.30/6.30-10 **Prices** Fixed L 2 course
£29.50, Fixed D 3 course £38.50, Service added 5%
Wines 38 bottles over £20, 10 bottles under £20, 11 by
glass **Notes** Sunday L, Vegetarian available, Dress
restrictions, No trainers, T-shirts **Seats** 50, Pr/dining
room 16 **Children** Portions **Parking** 40

Fischer's Baslow Hall

◉◉◉◉ *– see page 112*

Fischer's Baslow Hall

Modern European 🍽

Sumptuous manor house offering high-impact cooking

☎ 01246 583259 📄 01246 583818
Calver Rd DE45 1RR
e-mail: reservations@fischers-baslowhall.co.uk
dir: From Baslow on A623 towards Calver. Hotel on right

Unless you're in on the secret, you could be forgiven for thinking you were pitching up at a classical Restoration manor house, with its gabled façade, mullioned windows and balustraded entrance. In fact, Baslow Hall, built on the edge of the Chatsworth estate, is a painstaking Edwardian pastiche of the 17th-century manner. Sweep up the chestnut-lined drive, and take time to look at the magnificent gardens, before progressing to the lavishly appointed dining-room that is Fischer's. Elegant table settings, log fires and an intimate ambience provide a backdrop for the stylish modern European cooking, which uses plenty of local produce, underpinned by classical French techniques. Dishes are highly inventive, built around outstanding combinations that leave you eager to explore the next one. A seven-course Prestige Menu, with cheeses as an optional extra, is the way to do so comprehensively. Textures of foie gras is a signature starter, in which the liver is presented three ways - pan-fried, cured and warm - with accompaniments such as spiced cherries and 'cappuccino' dressing. Foamy sauces are a preferred method of presentation, as with the potato version that comes with poached turbot, alongside a leek terrine and hazelnut emulsion. Local venison is served in the form of roasted loin, with a glazed chicory tart, red cabbage, parsnip purée and a juniper-scented jus, and meals end with high-impact desserts such as pistachio terrine with chocolate 'soil' and green tea sorbet. Imaginative amuse-bouche and pre-desserts are all part of the deal. Home-baked breads include beautifully light ciabatta, while coffee comes with a phalanx of moreish petits fours.

Chef Max Fischer, Rupert Rowley
Owner Mr & Mrs M Fischer
Times 12-2/7-8.30 Closed 24-26 Dec, 31 Dec, L Mon, D Sun (ex residents)
Prices Fixed L 2 course fr £23, Fixed D 3 course fr £68, Tasting menu £63, Service optional **Wines** 119 bottles over £20, 1 bottles under £20, 5 by glass
Notes Sunday L, Vegetarian available, Dress restrictions, Smart casual, no jeans, sweatshirts, trainers, Civ Wed 38
Seats 38, Pr/dining room 20
Children Portions **Parking** 38

BASLOW *continued*

Rowley's Restaurant & Bar

◎◎ Modern British

Informal pub offshoot of Fischer's Baslow Hall

☎ 01246 583880
Church Ln DE45 1RY
e-mail: info@rowleysrestaurant.co.uk
dir: A619/A623 signed Chatsworth, Baslow edge of Chatsworth estate.

The team behind the four-Rosette Fischer's at Baslow Hall just up the road have diversified into a country pub setting that operates as an all-day bar venue, as well as serving hand-pumped ales to local regulars in a stone-flagged bar. The three dining areas offer a mix of trad and modern British food, with the emphasis on local supply-lines, whether you're in the market for a light bite or the full works. A meal that steers a course from smoked haddock ravioli with wilted spinach to oxtail suet pudding with celeriac mash gives an accurate impression of the style, but consider too baked goats' cheese with pickled beetroot and hazelnuts in mulled wine vinaigrette, followed by basil-crusted halibut with piperade and courgette 'linguini'. Illy coffee and chocolates make for an invigorating finish.

Chef Richard Barber **Owner** Susan & Max Fischer, Rupert Rowley **Times** 12-2.30/6-8.45 Closed 2-7 Jan, D Sun **Prices** Starter £5-£8, Main £14-£25, Dessert £4.50-£6, Service optional **Wines** 16 bottles over £20, 16 bottles under £20, 10 by glass **Notes** Sunday L, Vegetarian available **Seats** 64, Pr/dining room 18 **Children** Portions, Menu **Parking** 17, On street

Devonshire Arms-Beeley

◎◎ Modern British NEW ⊘

Stylish country inn with seriously good food

☎ 01629 733259 📠 01629 734542
Devonshire Square DE4 2NR
e-mail: enquiries@devonshirebeeley.co.uk
dir: 6m N of Matlock & 5m E of Bakewell, located off B6012

Driving through the dinky village of Beeley on the Derbyshire Chatsworth Estate, the Devonshire Arms is one of those quintessentially English honey-hued stone inns that makes you want to screech to a halt for an impromptu pitstop. Inside, solid country inn credentials

are present and correct in the cosy bar: exposed stone nooks and crannies, old oak beams and a fine choice of real ales. Then there's the startlingly colourful, chic modern brasserie. Yes, quite a surprise. The contemporary posh pub menu hits fine dining status with ease, in a starter of crispy king scallop 'petit déjeuner' - a play on breakfast that marries the scallops with black and white puddings, streaky bacon, quail egg and mushroom duxelle. A main course might be home-cured spiced pork belly with red cabbage, prune purée and potato fondant; leave room for Mrs Hill's lemon tart (the chef's mum's recipe).

Chef Alan Hill **Owner** Duke of Devonshire **Times** 12-9.30 **Prices** Starter £3.95-£12.95, Main £9.95-£23.95, Dessert £5.95-£6.95, Service optional **Wines** 120 bottles over £20, 30 bottles under £20, 20 by glass **Notes** Sunday L, Vegetarian available **Seats** 60 **Children** Portions

Priory Restaurant

◎ Modern British

Fine dining at a medieval priory with huge grounds

☎ 01332 832235 📠 01332 833509
Marriott Breadsall Priory, Hotel & Country Club, Moor Rd DE7 6DL
e-mail: allayne.broom@marriotthotels.com
dir: M1 junct 25, A52 to Derby, then follow Chesterfield signs. Right at 1st rdbt, left at next. A608 to Heanor Rd. In 3m left then left again

Breadsall Priory - the oldest hotel in the Marriott chain - dates from the 13th century, but fits firmly in the 21st-century idiom of luxurious country-house hotel with 400 acres of well cared for grounds complete with an ornamental lake and golf course. The exposed beams and archways of the medieval priory's wine cellar, jazzed up with a cheery contemporary colour scheme, make a fittingly atmospheric venue for an uncomplicated modern repertoire founded on the best local, seasonal produce to hand. Seared cod cheeks come with a warm salad of pancetta, black pudding and parsnip purée in a typical opener, followed by a signature dish of mini beef Wellington, lamb cutlet and pork fillet with sage mousse, served with fondant potato and red wine sauce.

Chef Karl J Kenny **Owner** Royal Bank of Scotland **Times** 1-2/7-10 Closed L Mon-Sat (private functions only) **Prices** Starter £5.95-£9.50, Main £14.50-£19.95, Dessert £5.50-£6.25, Service optional **Wines** 40 bottles over £20, 20 bottles under £20, 10 by glass **Notes** Sunday L, Vegetarian available, Dress restrictions, Shirt with collar, long trousers required, Air con **Seats** 104 **Children** Portions, Menu **Parking** 200

Best Western Lee Wood Hotel

◎ British, International

Conservatory dining in a country-house setting

☎ 01298 23002 📠 01298 23228
The Park SK17 6TQ
e-mail: leewoodhotel@btinternet.com
dir: M1 junct 24, A50 towards Ashbourne, A515 to Buxton. From Buxton town centre follow A5004 Long Hill to Whaley Bridge. Hotel approx 200mtrs beyond University of Derby campus

This Georgian townhouse hotel is perfectly placed for delving into the Georgian delights of Buxton, or pulling on the hiking boots and hitting the open-air of the Derbyshire Peaks. Two generations of the Millican family have run the hotel with cheery hands-on style, providing a fine choice of British classics and cuisine with a wider European accent in the conservatory-style Elements restaurant. Pan-seared red mullet with fennel remoulade and ratatouille dressing shows the style, and main courses offer fish in the form of pan-seared sea bass with coriander and chorizo risotto in poached clam essence, or meaty options such as smoked loin of Chatsworth venison with parsnip rösti, pickled beetroot jelly and Jerusalem artichoke purée.

Times 12-2.15/7.15-9.30

The Old Post Restaurant

◎ British, European

Converted shop with skilful, bold cooking

☎ 01246 279479 📠 01246 205925
43 Holywell St S41 7SH
e-mail: theoldpostrestaurant@btopenworld.com
dir: M1 junct 29, follow town centre & central parking signs. Pass crooked spire church on left, park in Holywell Cross Car Park. Restaurant opposite

In a characterful old hodgepodge of listed 15th- and 18th-century buildings that have seen service as a butcher's, grocer's, Victorian laundry, and latterly, the post office that left behind its name, this intimate little restaurant is near Chesterfield's centre, and just a short drive from the wide-open spaces of the Peak district. It is now the venue for chef Hugh Cocker's confident modern European cooking. Local produce drives dishes that are

continued

CHESTERFIELD *continued*

elegant and big on flavour - try hot and sour mussel and crayfish soup with spinach and ricotta tortellini for starters, while main courses might feature roast wild boar with goats' cheese gnocchi, dauphinoise potatoes, spiced red cabbage, caramelised pear and crab apple sauce.

Chef Hugh Cocker **Owner** Hugh & Mary Cocker **Times** 12-2/7-9.30 Closed 26 Dec, 1 Jan, Mon, L Tue, Sat, D Sun **Prices** Fixed L 2 course £13.25, Fixed D 4 course £28.50, Starter £6-£7.80, Main £17.50-£22.95, Dessert £6.50-£7.55, Service optional **Wines** 5 bottles over £20, 24 bottles under £20, 4 by glass **Notes** Early bird D Tue-Fri 6-7.15pm 2-3 course £13.25-£16.95, Sunday L, Vegetarian available, Dress restrictions, Smart casual **Seats** 24 **Parking** Car park opposite

---

DARLEY ABBEY   Map 11 SK33

Darleys Restaurant

⚯⚯ Modern British V

Modern British cooking by the water's edge

☎ 01332 364987 🖨 01332 364987
Hashams Ln, Darley Abbey DE22 1DZ
e-mail: info@darleys.com
dir: A6 N from Derby (Duffield road). Right in 1m into Mileash Ln, to Old Lane, right, over bridge. Restaurant on right

Refurbishment at the start of 2009 has produced a more contemporary feel at Darley's, with glitzy lighting and a restful combination of pinks and browns throughout. It's all a far cry from the days when the place was a canteen for cotton-mill workers. The decked alfresco area that overlooks the Derwent weir remains an irresistible prospect on sunny days. A refreshingly straightforward approach to modern British cooking involves walnut-crusted crottin goats' cheese with beetroot carpaccio to start, with perhaps crisp-skinned sea bass topped with deep-fried carrot threads, or rack of lamb with split-pea sauce and a boudin of black pudding and sweet potato, to follow. Dessert inventions might include a risotto brûlée with tea-soaked apricots and blood-orange sorbet.

Chef Jonathan Hobson, Mark Hadfield **Owner** Jonathan & Kathryn Hobson **Times** 12-2/7-10 Closed BHs, 1st 2 wks Jan, D Sun **Prices** Fixed L 2 course fr £15.95, Starter £6-£8, Main £17-£22, Dessert £6.50-£7.50, Service optional **Wines** 42 bottles over £20, 41 bottles under £20, 15 by glass **Notes** Sunday L, Vegetarian menu, Air con **Seats** 70 **Children** Portions **Parking** 12

DERBY   Map 11 SK33

Cathedral Quarter Hotel

⚯ Modern British NEW

Exciting modern repertoire in a luxurious Victorian hotel

☎ 01332 546080
16 St Mary's Gate DE1 3JR
e-mail: opulence@cathedralquarterhotel.com
dir: Follow brown signs to Cathedral Quarter. Hotel on one way road

The foursquare redbrick hotel near Derby's fine cathedral has more the air of a municipal library from the outside, but presents quite a different impression within. A magnificent staircase sweeps up to the first floor, where the Opulence restaurant is situated. A panelled room with discreet lighting, gathered curtains and space between tables, it forms an elegant context for the up-to-the-minute culinary goings on. Smoked eel with celeriac remoulade, supported by flavours of apple and vanilla, is one possible opener, then main-course lamb in three manifestations - the loin, the beautifully tender braised neck, a portion of sweetbreads - alongside chestnuts and crushed peas. Desserts are quite as inventive as the rest, with a substance called 'raspberry paper' appearing as a garnish for lemon sabayon tart with pine-nuts and crème fraîche.

Times 12-2/7-9.30 Closed Sat, D Sun

Masa Restaurant

⚯⚯ Modern British V

Immaculate cuisine in converted chapel

☎ 01332 203345 🖨 01332 349191
The Old Chapel, Brook St DE1 3PF
e-mail: enquiries@masarestaurantwinebar.com
dir: 8m from M1 junct 25. Brook St off inner ring road near BBC Radio Derby

The faithful of Derby flock to this stylishly-converted old Wesleyan chapel and worship at the altar of good food. The restaurant has period character in spades on the chapel's soaring galleries, above the buzzing wine bar, and it all has a sharp contemporary style with chestnut-hued floors and bold blocks of deep purple and white. The immaculately-prepared cuisine sticks to simple tried-and-tested combinations in a menu of clear flavours and balanced dishes. Ballotine of foie gras with poached figs and parsnip crisps is a top-quality starter, followed by pink breast and confit leg of duck with braised red cabbage, caramelised pear and five spice velouté.

Chef José Vega **Owner** Didar & Paula Dalkic **Times** 12-2.30/6-9.30 Closed 26 Dec-1 Jan, Mon-Tue **Prices** Fixed L 3 course £18, Fixed D 3 course £22, Starter £5.50-£8.50, Main £12.50-£22, Dessert £5.95-£7.45, Service added but optional 10% **Wines** 20 bottles over £20, 24 bottles under £20, 20 by glass **Notes** Tasting menu 5 course, Sunday L, Vegetarian menu, Dress restrictions, Smart casual, black tie when specified, Air con **Seats** 120 **Children** Portions **Parking** On street (Pay & display), Car park Brook St

---

FROGGATT   Map 16 SK27

The Chequers Inn

⚯ Traditional British ☘

Popular country inn serving heart-warming food to fuel Peak District walkers

☎ 01433 630231 🖨 01433 631072
S32 3ZJ
e-mail: info@chequers-froggatt.com
dir: On A625 between Sheffield & Bakewell, 0.75m from Calver

Tucked in acres of woodland beneath panoramic Froggatt Edge, the convivial Chequers Inn dates back to the 16th century and offers oodles of historic charm. When you've been hoofing around the Derbyshire Peaks, there's plenty to catch the eye on a hearty refuelling menu of old favourites and modern British classics. As well as pub grub staples, such as pot-roasted lamb shanks, haddock in beer batter and local sausages with parsley mash, the daily specials menu might offer roast loin of ling with wilted gem lettuce and broad beans, and for dessert, go for a rhubarb crème brûlée with ginger.

Chef Philip Ball **Owner** Jonathan & Joanne Tindall **Times** 12-2/6-9.30 Closed 25 Dec **Prices** Starter £4.95-£6.50, Main £9.95-£15, Dessert £4.50-£6.50, Service optional **Wines** 11 bottles over £20, 29 bottles under £20, 9 by glass **Notes** Sunday L, Vegetarian available **Seats** 90 **Children** Menu **Parking** 50

GRINDLEFORD   Map 16 SK27

The Maynard

⚯⚯ Modern British

Stylishly renovated hotel with imaginative food

☎ 01433 630321 🖨 01433 460445
Main Rd S32 2HE
e-mail: info@themaynard.co.uk
dir: M1/A619 into Chesterfield, onto Baslow, A623 to Calver right into Grindleford

Walking from the glorious natural beauty of the Peak District National Park into the Maynard is like entering the pages of a style magazine. The handsome Victorian building has been stylishly reworked with a hip boutique hotel décor, and a voguish dining room packed with funky modern art on the walls and ceiling. The cooking too takes a contemporary line, juggling classics with imagination and a hint of the Orient here and there in its simple flavour combinations; materials are local and organic as far as possible. Among starters might be sesame and wasabi-crusted tuna cake with sweet lemon and coriander salad; follow with mustard-glazed gurnard fillet with creamed cauliflower and braised leek gratin.

Chef Ben Hickinson **Owner** Paul Downing **Times** 12-2/7-9 Closed L Sat **Prices** Food prices not confirmed for 2010. Please telephone for details. **Wines** 6 bottles over £20, 8 bottles under £20, 4 by glass **Notes** Vegetarian available, Dress restrictions, Smart casual, Civ Wed 140, Air con **Seats** 50, Pr/dining room 140 **Children** Portions, Menu **Parking** 60

HATHERSAGE
Map 16 SK28

George Hotel

◉◉ Modern British

Accomplished modern cooking in traditional coaching inn

☎ 01433 650436 🖹 01433 650099
Main Rd S32 1BB
e-mail: info@george-hotel.net
dir: In village centre on junction of A625/B6001

A 500-year-old coaching inn on a former turnpike route, Charlotte Brontë reputedly stayed here whilst writing Jane Eyre. Located in the heart of the picturesque town of Hathersage, the pub retains many original features, although the contemporary George's restaurant has recently been refurbished with cool colours, wooden floors and a decidedly modern feel. The food is also contemporary, with an emphasis on the best ingredients and bold flavours. Starters might include crab, coriander and lime fishcakes with crispy squid and mango chutney, followed by imaginative mains such as sirloin of Castlegate beef with cannelloni of 12-hour braised shin, fondant potato, red wine sauce and roasted garlic foam. Finish with baked ginger parkin with roasted plum sorbet, plum compôte and clotted cream.

Chef Helen Heywood **Owner** Eric Marsh
Times 12-2.30/7-10 Closed D 25 Dec **Prices** Fixed L 2 course £28, Fixed D 3 course £35, Service included
Wines 28 bottles over £20, 19 bottles under £20, 8 by glass **Notes** 'Early bird' menu Mon-Fri 6.30-7.30pm, Sunday L, Vegetarian available, Civ Wed 45 **Seats** 45, Pr/dining room 80 **Children** Portions **Parking** 45

The Plough Inn

◉ British, European ◐

Good honest food in a traditional inn

☎ 01433 650319 🖹 01433 651049
Leadmill Bridge S32 1BA
e-mail: sales@theploughinn-hathersage.co.uk
web: www.theploughinn-hathersage.co.uk
dir: 1m SE of Hathersage on B6001. Over bridge, 150yds beyond at Leadmill

The 16th-century Plough has led an interesting life as a corn mill, lead smelting house and farm, but surely it has found its vocation as charming country inn. The 9 acres of grounds on the banks of the River Derwent in the heart of the Peak District are well worth exploring and the menu, a mix of traditional British and modern European dishes, has broad appeal. Top-quality produce comes from local suppliers and you can choose to eat in the traditional bar or the more intimate dining room. Expect starters such as home-smoked trout fillet with horseradish crème fraîche, followed by roast fillet of beef, shallots, bacon, mushrooms and real ale sauce, and treacle tart for dessert.

Chef Robert Navarro **Owner** Robert & Cynthia Emery
Times 11.30-2.30/6.30-9.30 Closed 25 Dec **Prices** Fixed L 2 course fr £16.25, Fixed D 3 course £20.05-£29.95, Starter £4.95-£9.95, Main £11.95-£24.50, Dessert £4.50-£7.95, Service optional **Wines** 27 bottles over £20, 22 bottles under £20, 14 by glass **Notes** Sunday L, Vegetarian available, Dress restrictions, Smart Casual, Air con **Seats** 40, Pr/dining room 24 **Children** Portions **Parking** 40

HIGHAM
Map 16 SK35

Santo's Higham Farm Hotel

◉ Modern ◐

Modern cuisine in a romantic setting

☎ 01773 833812 🖹 01773 520525
Main Rd DE55 6EH
e-mail: reception@santoshighamfarm.demon.co.uk
dir: M1 junct 28, A38 towards Derby, then A61 to Higham, left onto B6013

As its name might suggest, this lovely hotel is a rustic conversion of a stone-built 15th-century farmhouse and crook barn, with sweeping views over the Amber Valley. The restaurant has an easy-going ambience with its exposed stone walls, rich red suede chairs and oil-filled candles on crisp white linen-clothed tables. The kitchen keeps things uncomplicated and puts a strong emphasis on local produce: expect starters such as venison terrine with kumquat marmalade to precede roast monkfish with spring cabbage, potato and clam casserole, or jellied pork hock with home-made flat bread and beetroot relish. End with fresh strawberries paired with champagne sorbet and a black pepper tuile.

continued

HIGHAM *continued*

Chef Raymond Moody **Owner** Santo Cusimano
Times 12-2/7-9.30 Closed L Mon-Sat, D Sun **Prices** Food
prices not confirmed for 2010. Please telephone for
details. **Wines** 26 bottles over £20, 23 bottles under £20,
3 by glass **Notes** Sunday L, Vegetarian available, Dress
restrictions, Smart casual, Civ Wed 70 **Seats** 50, Pr/
dining room 34 **Children** Portions **Parking** 100

See advert on page 115

HOPE   Map 16 SK18

Losehill House Hotel & Spa

◉ Modern British **NEW** ☺

Imaginative cooking in an idyllic Peak District location

☎ 01433 621219   📄 01433 622501
Edale Rd S33 6RF
e-mail: info@losehillhouse.co.uk
dir: Enter Hope, follow signs to Edale. Opp church turn
right at brown sign. Hotel is 1.5 miles on left

Tucked away down a quiet leafy lane with glorious wide-
open vistas all around, this stylishly-renovated country
house makes a perfect base for striking out into the fresh
air of the Peak District National Park. After a day
stomping around the hills and dales, an aperitif on the
hotel's terrace amid the sheep-freckled scenery should
set you up for dinner with a view in the Orangery
restaurant. Delicate wrought-iron seats, pale wood floors
and warm butterscotch walls combine in a light feminine
décor, while efficient service is a strong point. On the
culinary front, the kitchen proudly sources the best the
region has to offer and shows good technique in its
unpretentious modern British dishes. Sautéed tiger
prawns with carrot and courgette ribbons and lemongrass
cream might precede marinated rump of Derbyshire lamb
with dauphinoise potatoes and cep jus.

Chef Darren Goodwin **Owner** Paul & Kathryn Roden
Times 12-2.30/7-9 **Prices** Fixed L 2 course £13–£16,
Fixed D 3 course £30-£40, Service optional **Wines** 6 by
glass **Notes** Daily changing table d'hote menu, Sunday L,
Vegetarian available, Civ Wed 80 **Seats** 50, Pr/dining
room 12 **Parking** 20

MATLOCK   Map 16 SK35

The Red House Country Hotel

◉ Traditional British

Traditional cooking in relaxed country-house hotel

☎ 01629 734854
Old Rd, Darley Dale DE4 2ER
e-mail: enquiries@theredhousecountryhotel.co.uk
dir: off A6 onto Old Rd signed Carriage Museum, 2.5m N
of Matlock

With good views down the Derwent Valley, this privately-
owned country house dates from 1891 and has
delightfully manicured grounds as well as lots of original
Victorian features inside and out. The views can be

enjoyed from the attractive dining room, which is situated
within the elegant former drawing room with its oak floor
and formal table settings. Service is both friendly and
professional. The food is pleasingly simple, mostly
traditional British, and presented in a no-nonsense style:
duck and pistachio terrine is full of clear flavours and
main-course salmon is pan-fried and served with pea
purée, pancetta and mint oil. Finish with almond mousse
or British cheeses and biscuits.

Chef Alan Perkins **Owner** David & Kate Gardiner **Times**
7-8.30 Closed 25-29 Dec, 1st 2 wks Jan, L all week
Prices Fixed D 4 course £26.50-£29.50, Service optional
Wines 14 bottles over £20, 15 bottles under £20, 6 by
glass **Notes** Vegetarian available, Dress restrictions,
Smart casual **Seats** 30 **Parking** 15

Stones Restaurant

◉◉ Modern British **NEW** **V**

**Confident cooking in a stylish basement overlooking
Matlock**

☎ 01629 56061
1c Dale Rd DE4 3LT
e-mail: info@stones-restaurant.co.uk
web: www.stones-restaurant.co.uk
dir: Please telephone for directions

With its intimate basement setting overlooking Matlock
and the River Derwent, Stones has an interior stylishly
accessorised with abstract canvasses and upholstered
church pews. Textures of bare wood and exposed brick
work well with its warm earthy tones of chocolate, cherry,
caramel and cream - shades to remind you that you're
here to eat. The kitchen team knows its way around the
modern British repertoire, confidently picking and
choosing from the world's flavours in well-judged
combinations. Robust dishes kick off with confit duck and
roasted monkfish cheek with braised Puy lentils and a
light garlic foam; next off, an assiette of pork gives pig
four ways: belly, black pudding, fillet and cheek, with
cabbage and bacon and an apple purée. The meal ends
strongly with blackberry pannacotta with lemon ice
cream.

Stones Restaurant

Chef Kevin Stone **Owner** Kevin Stone, Jade Himsworth,
Katie Temple **Times** 12-2/6.30-9 Closed D Sun
Prices Fixed L 2 course £13.95, Fixed D 3 course £15.95-
£21, Starter £5.50-£8, Main £14.90-£17.90, Dessert
£5.25-£11.95, Service optional **Wines** 12 bottles over
£20, 17 bottles under £20, 7 by glass **Notes** Early D
6.30-7.30pm, Sunday L, Vegetarian menu **Seats** 30
Children Portions, Menu **Parking** Matlock train station

MELBOURNE   Map 11 SK32

The Bay Tree

◉ Modern British

Eclectic modern cooking in the heart of the village

☎ 01332 863358   📄 01332 865545
4 Potter St DE73 8HW
e-mail: enquiries@baytreerestaurant.co.uk
dir: Telephone for directions

Located in the centre of the village of Melbourne, this
popular restaurant has been attracting praise since it
first opened its doors 22 years ago. The 17th-century
building has been extended to create a bar for pre-dinner
drinks or the champagne breakfasts available most
mornings. The smart, airy dining room has timber floors
and contemporary artwork on the walls. The modern menu
has an international flavour with local produce used to
create exotic dishes such as tea-smoked rabbit and green
pea risotto and breast of duckling with a black cherry
sauce.

Times 10.30-3/6.30-10.30

The Old Vicarage

Modern British NOTABLE WINE LIST

Memorable dining in striking house and gardens

☎ 0114 247 5814
Ridgeway Moor S12 3XW
e-mail: eat@theoldvicarage.co.uk
web: www.theoldvicarage.co.uk
dir: Please telephone for directions

Tessa Bramley has written cookbooks and countless articles in magazines and newspapers, appeared on many TV shows and is a Fellow of the Institute of Master Chefs of Great Britain. And for over 20 years her strong principles and considerable cooking skills have been on display at this charming country house, built for a very lucky reverend in 1846, the garden designed by a renowned Victorian horticulturalist. Approach down the splendid sweeping gravel drive and take in the rolling lawns and majestic trees. The house is full of character and Victorian features, handsome rather than grand, and traditionally decorated and furnished, but not at all preserved in aspic. Bright and sunny in summer and warm and cosy in winter, the dining room has well-spaced tables, dressed in their best whites, and the conservatory dining area has lovely garden views and opens out on to the terrace. The kitchen puts the sourcing of its produce at the top of the agenda, so the best local suppliers

are sought with some of the vegetables, fruits and herbs coming from the Vicarage's own kitchen garden, and the seasons guide the way. The fixed-price four-course menu, plus a tasting and lunch option, reveal dishes based on clear flavours, displaying plenty of invention and showing considerable skill in the delivery. Saddle of hare, for example, on star anise-spiced red cabbage with a mulled pear compôte and a gin and tonic jelly might precede thyme-roasted fillet of locally-reared Charolais beef with grain mustard mash with pancetta and sautéed goose liver. Finish with baked chocolate pudding with chocolate fudge sauce and English custard, or go for the impressive selection of British cheeses, all hand-made by traditional methods.

Chef T Bramley, N Smith
Owner Tessa Bramley
Times 12.30-2.30/6.30-10 Closed 10 days Xmas/New Year, 2 wks Aug & BHs, Sun & Mon, L Sat **Prices** Fixed L 2 course £30, Fixed D 4 course £60, Service optional **Wines** 600+ bottles over £20, 24 bottles under £20
Notes Tasting menu 7 course, Vegetarian available, Civ Wed 50
Seats 40, Pr/dining room 20
Children Portions **Parking** 18

MORLEY · Map 11 SK34

The Morley Hayes Hotel - Dovecote Restaurant

Modern British

Converted 18th-century farmstead serving creative modern cooking

☎ 01332 780480 📠 01332 781094
Main Rd DE7 6DG
e-mail: enquiries@morleyhayes.com
dir: 4m N of Derby on A608

Morley Hayes Hotel started life as an 18th-century farmstead attached to Morley Manor, which traces its origins back to the Domesday Book. It has entered the 21st century as a contemporary hotel built of Pennine stone reclaimed from railway tunnels, plus there's an 18-hole championship golf course. No prizes for guessing what the purpose of the Dovecote restaurant was before it was turned into an atmospheric dining room with a vaulted roof, massive exposed beams and bare brickwork walls. Sip a cocktail in the piano bar while you mull over the dinner options on the broad-ranging menus of modern English and European dishes. Confit duck leg with Barry Fitch black pudding and celeriac remoulade might precede hare Wellington with chicken mousse, glazed turnips and pickled pears.

Chef Nigel Stuart **Owner** Robert & Andrew Allsop/Morley Hayes Leisure Ltd **Times** 12-2/7-9.30 Closed 1 Jan, L Sat, Mon **Prices** Fixed L 2 course fr £14.45, Starter fr £5.25, Main fr £13.25, Dessert fr £5.95, Service optional **Wines** 25 bottles over £20, 15 bottles under £20, 12 by glass **Notes** Sunday L, Vegetarian available, Dress restrictions, Smart casual, Civ Wed 80, Air con **Seats** 100, Pr/dining room 24 **Children** Portions, Menu **Parking** 250

RIDGEWAY · Map 16 SK48

The Old Vicarage

🏵🏵🏵 – see page 117

RISLEY · Map 11 SK43

Risley Hall

European

Ancient manor house with modern amenities

☎ 0115 939 9000 📠 0115 939 7766
Derby Rd DE72 3SS
e-mail: enquiries@risleyhallhotel.co.uk
dir: M1 junct 25, Sandiacre exit into Bostock Ln. Left at lights, hotel on left in 0.25m

The original country manor here was built all of a millennium ago, although the Baronial Hall that is one of its interior splendours is a relative stripling at 500 years old. The full contemporary package of spa treatments, swimming pool and weddings is offered, but without a trace of corporate anonymity. In these venerable surroundings, the ground-floor Abbey restaurant is the scene for some straightforward cooking of the chicken liver parfait, poached salmon with hollandaise, and

tiramisù variety, accompanied by a useful listing of wines by the glass.

Times 12-6.30/7-10.30

ROWSLEY · Map 16 SK26

East Lodge Country House Hotel

🏵🏵 Modern British V 🖐

Classical and modern mix in the Peak District

☎ 01629 734474 📠 01629 733949
DE4 2EF
e-mail: info@eastlodge.com
web: www.eastlodge.com
dir: On A6, 5m from Matlock & 3m from Bakewell, at junct with B6012

A sweeping, tree-lined drive leads up to a handsome, greystone Lodge in the Peak District, not far from the spa town of Matlock. It was once the hunting lodge of Haddon Hall. Ten acres of grounds tempt guests to wander, but not too far when Simon Bradley's cooking is at hand. A Favourites menu (perhaps prawn cocktail followed by liver and bacon) is supplemented by the seasonally changing carte, which mixes classical and modern ideas productively. A delightful, exactly flavoured terrine of guinea-fowl, ham hock and artichoke is a great opener, and locally-shot pheasant with chipolatas and Madeira might be one way of proceeding, or there could be brill served with a crab fritter and linguini. Vegetarians have their own menu.

Chef Simon Bradley **Owner** Elyzian Hospitality Ltd
Times 12-2/7-9.30 **Prices** Fixed L 2 course £19.50, Fixed D 3 course £36, Service optional **Notes** Sunday L, Vegetarian menu, Dress restrictions, Smart casual, no jeans or trainers, Civ Wed 66, Air con **Seats** 50, Pr/dining room 36 **Children** Portions, Menu **Parking** 40

The Peacock at Rowsley

🏵🏵 Modern British V 🖐

Ambitious cooking at a chic hotel

☎ 01629 733518 📠 01629 792671
Bakewell Rd DE4 2EB
e-mail: reception@thepeacockatrowsley.com
web: www.thepeacockatrowsley.com
dir: A6, 3m before Bakewell, 6m from Matlock towards Bakewell

Built in 1642 as a dower house for the Haddon Hall estate, who recently spruced up the handsome stone building, this fine small hotel cleverly fuses the antique

and modern. Step inside to find a cool, trendy interior where original features and period furnishings blend effortlessly with contemporary boutique-hotel styling. With glorious garden views the elegant restaurant follows the theme, backed by impeccable service, a relaxed atmosphere, and well-balanced modern menus. Expect highly accomplished, flavourful dishes with some exciting combinations that testify to the kitchen's ambition and technical skill. Dishes reflect good use of local seasonal produce - venison loin with pancetta, sweet potato and sloe gin, lemon sole with brandade ravioli, green olive and lemon dressing and Pernod cream.

Chef Daniel Smith **Owner** Rutland Hotels **Times** 12-2/7-9 Closed D 24-26 Dec **Prices** Food prices not confirmed for 2010. Please telephone for details. **Wines** 35 bottles over £20, 20 bottles under £20, 15 by glass **Notes** Sunday L, Vegetarian menu, Civ Wed 20 **Seats** 40, Pr/dining room 20 **Children** Portions, Menu **Parking** 25

THORPE · Map 16 SK15

Izaak Walton Hotel

🏵🏵 Modern European

Modern cooking in hotel with strong fishing theme

☎ 01335 350555 📠 01335 350539
Dovedale DE6 2AY
e-mail: reception@izaakwaltonhotel.com
dir: A515 onto B5054, to Thorpe, continue straight over cattle grid & 2 small bridges, 1st right & sharp left

Named after the famous author of *The Compleat Angler*, this restored 17th-century farmhouse has outstanding views across the Derbyshire Peaks and boasts its own 2-mile stretch of the River Dove overlooking the Dovedale Valley (excellent fishing by all accounts). The fishing theme continues in the bar which features angling memorabilia and pictures; bar meals are served here. The traditional restaurant has outstanding views of Thorpe Cloud in the Peak District National Park. Confident contemporary cooking is exemplified in dishes like breast of wood pigeon with baby cress, toasted hazelnuts and port reduction followed by braised halibut, crushed potatoes, spinach, girolles and truffle foam. Finish with dark chocolate marquise, praline ice cream, hazelnut biscuit and caramel sauce.

Chef James Harrison **Owner** Mrs Bridget Day
Times 12.30-2.30/7-9 **Prices** Fixed L 3 course fr £23.95, Fixed D 3 course fr £35, Service optional **Wines** 40 bottles over £20, 25 bottles under £20, 4 by glass **Notes** Sunday L, Vegetarian available, Dress restrictions, Smart casual, Civ Wed 80 **Seats** 100, Pr/dining room 20 **Children** Portions, Menu **Parking** 80

DEVON

ASHBURTON · Map 3 SX77

Agaric

◎ Modern British

Stylish restaurant with rooms with intimate feel

☎ 01364 654478
30 North St TQ13 7QD
e-mail: eat@agaricrestaurant.co.uk
dir: Opposite town hall. Ashburton off A38 between Exeter & Plymouth

Agaric is a restaurant with rooms, the rooms being in a converted townhouse all of two doors up the road. A courtyard garden and stylish little bar to the rear add to the restaurant's charms, while the large shop-front windows throw plenty of light on the subject. Nick Coiley once cooked alongside the legendary Joyce Molyneux in Dartmouth, and there is a refreshing honesty about his style. A pairing of scallops and brill is well-served by spiced chickpeas, olive oil and coriander as a first course, while main courses offer the likes of leg of spring lamb with thick asparagus and a filo case of cream cheese and chives. Lemon polenta cake with clotted cream ice-cream and raspberry sorbet is a pleasing finish.

Chef Nick Coiley **Owner** Mr N Coiley & Mrs S Coiley
Times 12-2/7-9.30 Closed 2 wks Aug, Xmas, 1 wk Jan, Sun-Tue, L Sat **Prices** Fixed L 2 course £12.95-£14.95, Starter £4.95-£8.95, Main £14.95-£18.95, Dessert £5.95-£6.95, Service optional **Wines** 16 bottles over £20, 9 bottles under £20, 4 by glass **Notes** Vegetarian available **Seats** 30 **Children** Portions **Parking** Car park opposite

ASHWATER · Map 3 SX39

Blagdon Manor Hotel & Restaurant

◎◎ Traditional British V ♨

Solid cooking in secluded country house hotel

☎ 01409 211224 📠 01409 211634
EX21 5DF
e-mail: stay@blagdon.com
dir: From A388 towards Holsworthy, 2m N of Chapman's Well take 2nd right towards Ashwater. Next right by Blagdon Lodge. Hotel 2nd on right

Located on the borders of Devon and Cornwall within easy reach of the coast, and set in its own beautifully kept gardens, this small and friendly country-house hotel offers a charming home-from-home atmosphere. A Grade

II listed Devon longhouse dating back to the 16th century, the hotel retains many original features, including a freshwater well. The main restaurant is candlelit and cosy, and leads through to the light and airy conservatory extension. The traditional British cuisine makes the most of high-quality local produce, as in a pan-fried mackerel fillet with beetroot and horseradish risotto, black pudding and crisp sage leaves, followed by pan-fried sea bass and roasted scallop with soft green herb velouté. Finish with caramelised vanilla rice pudding with apple jam, prune and Armagnac ice cream.

Chef Stephen Morey **Owner** Stephen & Liz Morey
Times 12-2/7-9 Closed 1-31 Jan, Mon (ex residents), L Tue, D Sun **Prices** Fixed L 2 course £17, Fixed D 3 course £35, Service optional **Wines** 20 bottles over £20, 5 bottles under £20, 6 by glass **Notes** Sunday L, Vegetarian menu, Dress restrictions, Smart casual **Seats** 24, Pr/dining room 16 **Parking** 12

AXMINSTER · Map 4 SY29

Fairwater Head Country House Hotel

◎ Modern, Traditional ♨

Relaxing country-house hotel dining with stunning views

☎ 01297 678349 📠 01297 678459
Hawkchurch EX13 5TX
e-mail: info@fairwaterheadhotel.co.uk
dir: A358 into Broom Lane at Tytherleigh, follow signs to Hawkchurch & hotel

The motto 'East or West home is best' inscribed above the reception area fireplace neatly sums up the comforting ambience of this delightfully tranquil Edwardian country house hotel in 2 acres of gardens amid rolling Devon countryside. The Garden restaurant overlooks the Axe Valley through vast picture windows, providing a bucolic backcloth to the kitchen's repertoire of modern and traditional British and European cuisine. Expect cooking with focus and elegant presentation, starting with confit leg of Barbary duck with white bean casserole, pea shoots and sesame soya sauce reduction before spanking-fresh grilled fillet of Cornish hake with crushed potatoes, Avruga caviar and chive butter sauce. Plans are afoot as we go to press to refurbish the dining room with a more contemporary brasserie style.

Chef Mike Reid **Owner** Adam & Carrie Southwell
Times 12-2/7-9 Closed Jan, L Mon & Tue **Prices** Fixed L 2 course fr £12.50, Fixed D 2 course £24.50, Fixed D 4 course £29.50, Service optional **Wines** 33 bottles over £20, 27 bottles under £20, 6 by glass **Notes** Sunday L, Vegetarian available, Dress restrictions, Smart casual, Civ Wed 50 **Seats** 60, Pr/dining room 18 **Children** Portions, Menu **Parking** 40

BEESANDS · Map 3 SX84

The Cricket Inn

◎ Modern British **NEW**

Top-notch seafood at an inn on the shore

☎ 01548 580215
TQ7 2EN
e-mail: enquiries@thecricketinn.com
dir: From Kingsbridge follow A379 towards Dartmouth, at Stokenham mini-rdbt turn right for Beesands

This quaint seaside inn sits on the sea front just behind the sea wall on the shingle beach, giving it unrivalled views over Start Bay. On the South West Coastal Path, and dating back to 1867, the inn has been recently refurbished but still maintains the traditional elements of a fishing inn with black-and-white photos of the old village and fishing memorabilia hanging on the walls. Diver-caught scallops are brought in by one of the locals, as are crabs and lobsters from pots in the bay. Starters include crab cocktail and Thai-style fishcakes, while main courses run to hand-dived scallops with local black pudding and pea and mint purée, or Start Bay dressed lobster.

Chef Alex Jones **Owner** Nigel & Rachel Heath
Times 12-3/6-9 **Prices** Starter £5-£8, Main £8.50-£20, Dessert £3-£6, Service optional **Wines** 8 bottles over £20, 19 bottles under £20, 9 by glass **Notes** Sunday L, Vegetarian available **Seats** 65, Pr/dining room 40 **Children** Portions, Menu

BIDEFORD · Map 3 SS42

Yeoldon Country House Hotel

◎ British

Accomplished cooking in peaceful country-house hotel

☎ 01237 474400 📠 01237 476618
Durrant Ln, Northam EX39 2RL
e-mail: yeoldonhouse@aol.com
dir: A39 from Barnstaple over River Torridge Bridge. At rdbt right onto A386 towards Northam, then 3rd right into Durrant Lane

Set in a tranquil location overlooking attractive grounds and the River Torridge, this charming Victorian country-house hotel boasts an elegant ground floor restaurant with impressive views from the large windows. There's an intelligent simplicity to the cooking style, the accomplished kitchen delivering well-executed, honest, unpretentious British dishes using fresh, local produce. On the daily-changing menu you might spot smoked haddock and potato soup flavoured with saffron and chives, followed by pan-fried Barbary duck breast with light raspberry jus, and finishing with lemon and Amaretto torte with lemon meringue ice cream.

Chef Brian Steele **Owner** Brian & Jennifer Steele
Times 7-8 Closed Xmas, Sun, L all week **Prices** Fixed D 3 course £32.50, Service included **Wines** 7 bottles over £20, 32 bottles under £20, 4 by glass **Notes** Vegetarian available, Civ Wed 60 **Seats** 30 **Children** Portions **Parking** 30

The Masons Arms

◎ Traditional British

Characterful village inn near one of Devon's loveliest beaches

☎ 01297 680300   📄 01297 680500
EX12 3DJ
e-mail: reception@masonsarms.co.uk
dir: Village off A3052 between Sidmouth and Seaton

Close to beautiful Branscombe beach, The Masons Arms is brimming with old-world charm. Back in 1360 it was a cider house with a single tiny bar and since then it has expanded into nearby cottages to create a busy bar and restaurant with a relaxed, welcoming atmosphere, and the added attractions of blazing open fires in winter and plenty of outdoor seating in summer. The menu features produce from within a 10-mile radius of the village, including lobsters landed a few hundred feet from the back door. Expect starters such as Dartmouth Freedom Farm approved smoked salmon with lime, cucumber and coriander relish, or a main course of pan-fried West Country pork tenderloin with cider beurre blanc and baby apple fritter.

Chef S Garland, A Deam **Owner** Mr & Mrs C Slaney
Times 12-2/7-9 **Prices** Fixed D 3 course £29.95, Service optional **Wines** 22 bottles over £20, 28 bottles under £20, 10 by glass **Notes** Sunday L, Vegetarian available, Dress restrictions, No shorts or jeans **Seats** 70, Pr/dining room 20 **Parking** 45

Northcote Manor

◎◎ Modern British 🏅

Accomplished cooking in historic country house

☎ 01769 560501   📄 01769 560770
EX37 9LZ
e-mail: rest@northcotemanor.co.uk
dir: M5 junct 27 towards Barnstaple. Left at rdbt to South Molton. Do not enter Burrington village. Follow A377, right at T-junct to Barnstaple. Entrance after 3m, opp Portsmouth Arms railway station and pub

A long list of the great and good have chosen to live in this lovely 18th-century wisteria-draped manor house, and it's easy to see why: its bucolic setting in a vast estate among rolling North Devon hills is enough to make anyone put down roots. The smartly-refurbished dining room has bright oil-painted murals adding a dash of colour to the understated caramel and honey colour scheme. The Devon larder is thoroughly pillaged for top-drawer raw materials by a team that believes in putting together unfussy dishes that are well executed, simply presented and show mature combinations of natural flavours. Expect the likes of guinea fowl sausage with wilted spinach and garlic cream sauce to precede roasted saddle of wild Devon venison with fondant potato, parsnip purée, fig compôte and its own juices. For

dessert, fresh strawberries are highlighted as a soufflé, a sorbet and oven-baked with strawberry and cassis sauce.

Times 12-2/7-9

Gidleigh Park

◎◎◎◎ – *see opposite page*

Mill End

◎◎ Modern British 🍷

Impressive food in peaceful riverside setting

☎ 01647 432282   📄 01647 433106
TQ13 8JN
e-mail: info@millendhotel.com
dir: From A30 turn on to A382. Establishment on right before Chagford turning

Occupying an attractive waterside location, this 18th-century working water mill sits by the River Teign and offers 6 miles of angling. Once the home of Sir Frank Whittle, inventor of the jet engine, it is more like a family home than a hotel, with guests encouraged to relax and enjoy the surroundings. The restored water wheel of the flour mill turns just outside the dining room, which has a decided air of understated elegance. The cooking style is modern and the kitchen utilises the best of local produce. Take off with a starter of smoked salmon, mussel and coriander risotto with lightly poached egg, followed by a main course of pan-roasted fillet of St Ives brill with baby fennel, champ and a white wine cream.

Chef Jay Allen **Owner** Keith Green **Times** 12-2/7-9 Closed L Mon-Sat (except by appointment) **Prices** Fixed D 4 course £42, Service optional, Groups min 8 service 10% **Wines** 41 bottles over £20, 16 bottles under £20, 7 by glass **Notes** Sunday L, Vegetarian available, Dress restrictions, No jeans, trainers **Seats** 42 **Parking** 20

22 Mill Street Restaurant & Rooms

◎◎ Modern European **V**

Contemporary dining in Dartmoor village

☎ 01647 432244
22 Mill St TQ13 8AW
e-mail: info@22millst.com
web: www.22millst.com
dir: Please telephone for directions

Tucked away down a lane close to the centre of this Dartmoor village in the foothills of the National Park, the bijou 22 Mill Street is a smart restaurant with rooms. Contemporary artworks adorn the walls of the cosy lounge and dining room, and the smart, modern style of the place suits the up-to-date food. There are tasting and vegetarian menus to bolster the carte, with local produce featuring heavily. From the carte, roasted breast of wood pigeon, hazelnut gnocchi, buttered spinach and sherry caramel shows the modern European influences at play, while main-course baked fillet of halibut, poached langoustines, celeriac and roasted cumin oil is a dish with well-judged flavours. Save room for cinnamon doughnuts, William pear and mascarpone, or the selection of British cheeses.

Chef John Hooker **Owner** Helena King **Times** 12-4/6.30-10 Closed Mon, D Sun **Prices** Fixed L 2 course £14.95, Fixed D 3 course £42, Tasting menu £50, Service optional **Wines** 50 bottles over £20, 10 bottles under £20, 8 by glass **Notes** Tasting menu 7 course, Sunday L, Vegetarian menu **Seats** 28, Pr/dining room 14 **Children** Portions **Parking** On street

Jan and Freddies Brasserie

◎ Modern European 🍷

Brasserie dining in a relaxed atmosphere

☎ 01803 832491
10 Fairfax Place TQ6 9AD
e-mail: info@janandfreddiesbrasserie.co.uk
dir: Fairfax Place runs parallel to S Embankment. Restaurant faces Hawley Rd

Just a stone's throw from the River Dart, this lively modern bar and brasserie has a funky modern look with its buffed wooden tables and snazzy coloured lighting reflected in lots of mirrors. Relaxed and friendly service suits the casual mood, as does the food which majors on unpretentious modern British dishes prepared with top-

continued on page 123

Gidleigh Park

Modern European V · NOTABLE WINE LIST

First-class country-house fine dining in beautiful Dartmoor hotel

☎ 01647 432367 · 📄 01647 432574
TQ13 8HH
e-mail: gidleighpark@gidleigh.co.uk
dir: From Chagford Sq turn right at Lloyds TSB into Mill St, after 150yds right fork, across x-rds into Holy St. Restaurant 1.5m

It's probably not long enough to appear on a list of great car journeys of the world, but the one-and-a-half-mile drive along the country lane from Chagford to Gidleigh Park should be considered for inclusion simply because of the anticipation generated as you wait for the house to come into view. It's in quite some spot - the black-and-white mock-Tudor hotel stands in idyllic gardens with the River Teign tumbling through the grounds. A pre- or post-prandial stroll in the 54 acres of grounds is something you shouldn't miss out on even if the weather isn't on your side; saunter among delightful terraced gardens and beech woods, on manicured lawns and beside the riverbank, but rest assured you can still enjoy the views from the inside if it is blowing a hoolie outside. The house is impeccably turned-out and luxuriously finished without losing its charm and comforting appeal. There are three dining rooms, each with a slightly different style - one is a rather more contemporary room, another is a light space with access out on to the garden terrace and the third is oak panelled and traditional in style. Michael Caines's cooking is based on first-class seasonal produce and classical principles, with lots of luxury, intricate presentations and plenty of creative touches. Prices are as high as you might expect given the setting and the style of food. Canapés start the ball rolling (including a delicious crab custard) before, from the à la carte menu, a first-course pan-fried langoustines with rigatoni and black truffle, and main-course Hatherleigh venison with braised pork belly, red cabbage and a fig and chestnut purée. A plate of rhubarb, featuring mousse, crumble and sorbet, is an outstanding finish, although strictly speaking that will be the superb petits fours.

Chef Michael Caines MBE
Owner Andrew and Christina Brownsword **Times** 12-2/7-9.45
Prices Fixed L 2 course £38, Fixed D 3 course £105, Tasting menu £120, Service optional **Wines** 750 bottles over £20, 11 by glass **Notes** Tasting menu 7 course, Vegetarian menu, Dress restrictions, Shirt with collar, no jeans or sportswear, Civ Wed 52 **Seats** 52, Pr/dining room 22 **Children** Portions, Menu **Parking** 30

The New Angel Restaurant & Rooms

DARTMOUTH   Map 3 SX85

French 🍃

Fresh seafood and quality meats at the river's edge

☎ 01803 839425   📠 01803 839505
2 South Embankment TQ6 9BH
e-mail: info@thenewangel.co.uk
dir: Town centre, on water's edge

Perched right on the harbour-front, with all but edible views across the Dart, the New Angel has long been a destination restaurant in the area - not least because its presiding genius, John Burton-Race, has had one of the more visible TV chef careers. It's very much a restaurant of two halves, the ground floor a merry bustle with kitchen open to view, upstairs a more sedate space, with a nice contrast between the smart table coverings and uncovered floor. Fish and seafood are sourced from boats that tie up a few feet away, and the cooking mostly has an uncomplicated feel, with dishes that are not overworked. Dressed crab is bound with red pepper and almonds and served in a lightly spiced crab nage, while main-course fish might be roasted brill with new potatoes and béarnaise. Meat-eaters are by no means neglected, and might be glad of South Devon beef rib with bordelaise beans in red wine (served for two). Desserts are no mere afterthought, as may be gleaned from the delectable warm pineapple tart,

daringly glazed in white chocolate, with a vibrant coconut sorbet.

Chef John Burton-Race
Owner Clive Jacobs
Times 12-2.30/6.30-10 Closed Jan
Prices Fixed L 2 course £19.50-£24.50, Fixed D 3 course fr £29.50, Starter £7.50-£15.50, Main £18.50-£28, Dessert £9, Service optional, Groups min 10 service 12.5% **Wines** 150 bottles over £20, 32 bottles under £20, 8 by glass **Notes** Sunday L, Vegetarian available, Dress restrictions, Smart casual, Air con **Seats** 80, Pr/dining room 6 **Children** Portions **Parking** 6, Dartmouth central car park

DARTMOUTH *continued*

quality local ingredients. Twice-baked Devon cheese soufflé with pear and celery salsa gets things started, while pan-fried local pollock with confit fennel and prawn risotto, or fore-rib of Blackawton beef with blue cheese croquettes and wild mushroom fricassée are typical of main courses.

Chef Richard Hilson **Owner** Jan & Freddie Clarke **Times** 12.30-2/6.30-9 Closed Xmas, Sun, L Mon **Prices** Fixed D 3 course £21.95-£29.95, Starter £4.95-£8.95, Main £14.95-£19.95, Dessert £5.95-£6.95, Service optional **Wines** 16 bottles over £20, 22 bottles under £20, 10 by glass **Notes** Vegetarian available **Seats** 40 **Parking** On street

The New Angel Restaurant & Rooms

◉◉◉ *– see opposite page*

River Restaurant

◉◉ Modern British

Skilful cooking in stylish waterfront hotel restaurant

☎ 01803 832580 🖹 01803 835040
The Dart Marina Hotel, Sandquay Rd TQ6 9PH
e-mail: info@dartmarinahotel.com
dir: A3122 from Totnes to Dartmouth. Follow road which becomes College Way, before Higher Ferry. Hotel sharp left in Sandquay Rd

Located on the banks of the River Dart, this stylish and unpretentious waterfront hotel is a truly special place to stay. It is also a popular dining destination with two restaurants offering a choice of styles. The Wildfire Bistro is a more informal rendezvous, whilst the main River Restaurant with its elegant modern décor gives superb views across the busy river and the chance to dine alfresco in summer. The skilled kitchen delivers accomplished cuisine, using carefully sourced, high quality ingredients. Expect starters like duck liver and foie gras terrine with celeriac remoulade and smoked sultana reduction, followed by fillet of gilt head bream, braised baby gem, tempura oyster and citrus beurre blanc.

Chef Mark Streeter **Owner** Richard Seton **Times** 12-2/6-9 **Prices** Fixed L 2 course £12-£18, Fixed D 3 course £32-£42, Service optional **Notes** Sunday L, Vegetarian available, Dress restrictions, Smart casual, Air con **Seats** 80 **Children** Portions

The Seahorse

◉◉ Seafood NEW

Top-notch fish and seafood on the River Dart

☎ 01803 835147
5 South Embankment TQ6 9BH
e-mail: enquiries@seahorserestaurant.co.uk
dir: Please telephone for directions

Fishworks founder Mitch Tonks' Seahorse has bagged a plum spot overlooking the River Dart estuary right in the heart of town. While children fish for crabs out front and yachts to-and-fro, expect to tuck into some seriously good seafood. The dining room is traditionally done out, with dark lacquered tables and an open-plan kitchen bringing the space to life. Look out for the splendid picture of a John Dory - a reminder that seafood is king here. The freshness of the fish and seafood is second to none, selected from whatever was landed in the morning, and it is cooked with skill and without over-complication. So, what better way to start than Dartmouth crab with mayonnaise and cucumber? Perhaps smoked cods roe crostini, then maybe a seafood stew with saffron and thyme or the Menorcan-influenced lobster 'caldereta', using local crustacea of course. A delectable pannacotta with sweet sherry and figs shows the kitchen can handle the fruits of the land as well. The impressive wine list has been wisely chosen to complement the menu.

Chef Mat Prowse & Mitch Tonks **Owner** Mat Prowse & Mitch Tonks **Times** 12-3/6-10 Closed 3 wks Jan, BH Mon, Mon-Tue (Winter), Mon (Summer), L Wed (Winter), Tue (Summer), D Sun **Prices** Fixed L 2 course £15, Starter £5-£11, Main £12-£30, Dessert £3.50-£9.50, Service optional **Wines** 109 bottles over £20, 14 bottles under £20, 6 by glass **Notes** Sunday L, Vegetarian available, Air con **Seats** 40 **Children** Portions **Parking** On street

EGGESFORD　　　　　Map 3 SS61

Fox & Hounds Country Hotel

◉ Traditional British NEW 🐾

Unfussy food in former coaching inn

☎ 01769 580345
EX18 7JZ
e-mail: relax@foxandhoundshotel.co.uk
dir: M5 junct 27, A361 towards Tiverton. Take A396 signed Tiverton/Bickleigh. Then take A3072 to Crediton. Then A377 towards Barnstaple. In 14m pass Eggesford Station, hotel just beyond on left

Located in the beautiful Taw Valley in the heart of Devon, this former coaching inn has been much extended to provide comfortable accommodation. There is a strong fishing and hunting theme at this hotel, with the River Taw accessed from the rear of the hotel. Meals can be taken in the bar with its crackling fire or in the more formal restaurant. Sound techniques in the kitchen means cooking is assured with an emphasis on local produce, including trout or salmon caught within 100 yards of the pub. Start with pan-seared scallops with sesame oil, lime and coriander, following on with home-made steak and kidney pudding made with Exmoor chuck steak and lambs' kidneys.

Chef Alex Pallatt **Owner** Nick & Tara Culverhouse **Times** 12-2.30/6.30-9 **Prices** Fixed L 2 course £10, Fixed D 3 course £20-£25, Starter £5-£7, Main £9-£17, Dessert £5-£8 **Wines** 19 bottles under £20, 8 by glass **Notes** Sunday L, Vegetarian available, Civ Wed 120 **Seats** 60, Pr/dining room 120 **Children** Portions, Menu **Parking** 60

EXETER　　　　　Map 3 SX99

Barton Cross Hotel & Restaurant

◉ British, French

Sound cooking in engaging 17th-century thatched hotel

☎ 01392 841245 🖹 01392 841942
Huxham, Stoke Canon EX5 4EJ
e-mail: bartonxhuxham@aol.com
dir: 0.5m off A396 at Stoke Canon, 3m N of Exeter

This 17th-century thatched longhouse has bags of character and a pretty, rural location, plus a restaurant in an impressive room with a huge inglenook fireplace and a minstrels' gallery. Cob walls and low beams are a constant reminder of the antiquity of the building, parts of which actually date from the 14th century, while the food is rather more modern. Roast scallops (good quality) with sweetcorn purée, crispy bacon and basil oil is a starter firmly rooted in the 21st century, and main-courses extend to breast of pheasant on a blue cheese mash with cider and wild mushroom sauce.

Times 6.30-mdnt Closed Sun, L Mon

EXETER *continued*

Best Western Lord Haldon Country House Hotel

◉ British, European

Ambitious cooking in elegant country house

☎ 01392 832483 📄 01392 833765
Dunchideock EX6 7YF
e-mail: enquiries@lordhaldonhotel.co.uk
dir: From M5 junct 31 or A30 follow signs to Ide, continue through village for 2.5m, left after red phone box, 0.5m, pass under stone bridge, left

The setting in verdant Devon countryside and views over the Exe Valley are English to a tee. The hotel is a fine-looking country house, with a large open archway leading into an attractive courtyard from which the Courtyard Restaurant takes its name, and where you can dine alfresco if the weather permits. The cooking is broadly modern European and based around good British produce. Dinner begins with canapés before a starter such as roast beetroot, asparagus and goats' cheese terrine and main-course rack of Devonshire lamb with a piquant mint syrup, warm salad Niçoise and Madeira jus.

Chef Paul Rutledge **Owner** Pullman Premier Leisure **Times** 12-2/7-8.45 Closed L Mon-Sat **Prices** Food prices not confirmed for 2010. Please telephone for details. **Wines** 2 bottles over £20, 36 bottles under £20, 6 by glass **Notes** Sunday L, Vegetarian available, Dress restrictions, Smart casual, Civ Wed 120 **Seats** 60, Pr/dining room 25 **Children** Portions, Menu **Parking** 120

Michael Caines at ABode Exeter

◉◉ Modern European V ✋

Contemporary cooking in cosmopolitan hotel with cathedral views

☎ 01392 223638 📄 01392 223639
Cathedral Yard EX1 1HD
e-mail: tablesexeter@michaelcaines.com
dir: Town centre, opposite cathedral

Located on Exeter's beautiful Cathedral Yard with stunning views of the city's magnificent 11th-century gothic cathedral, ABode Exeter occupies the former Royal Clarence hotel. This was the first in the chain of ABode's boutique hotels and it offers several dining options, from the informal Café Bar to the lively Well House Tavern. The modern dining room is relaxed and airy with contemporary art on the walls, dark-wood floor and crisp white linen.

The kitchen is committed to local produce and seasonality, which is anchored by some skilful cooking. Cannelloni of Start Bay crab, braised fennel, sauce vierge and shellfish bisque is an appealing starter, followed by roast saddle and loin of local lamb, confit shoulder, fondant potato, onion and thyme purée with tapenade sauce. Rum and raisin soufflé with rum and raisin ice cream is one of several tempting desserts.

Chef Tony Williams-Hawkes **Owner** Michael Caines & Andrew Brownsword **Times** 12-2.30/7-10 Closed Sun, D Xmas **Prices** Fixed L 2 course fr £14.50, Tasting menu £58, Starter £12-£15.50, Main £21-£24, Dessert £7.50-£8.50, Service added but optional 12%, Groups min 10 service 12.5% **Wines** 158 bottles over £20, 8 bottles under £20, 8 by glass **Notes** Early D menu Mon-Fri 6-7pm 2 course £14.50, Vegetarian menu, Dress restrictions, Smart casual, Civ Wed 50, Air con **Seats** 70, Pr/dining room 80 **Children** Portions, Menu **Parking** Mary Arches St car park

No 21

◉ Modern European

Contemporary bistro with cathedral views

☎ 01392 210303
21a Cathedral Yard EX1 1HB
e-mail: restaurant@21cathedralyard-exeter.co.uk
dir: Opposite cathedral

A real gem of a location in the heart of Exeter, right in Cathedral Yard overlooking the superbly-carved 12th-century façade of the cathedral, plus a modern and uncluttered interior with chunky unclothed oak tables and splashes of contemporary art make No 21 a popular spot. It starts with breakfast and stays busy through the day, but it is evening service that brings out the true depth of the pedigree modern European cooking on offer here. Integrity and class shine through in a starter of ham hock and chicken terrine with piccalilli and pickled chestnut mushrooms, and mains such as mixed seafood and shellfish in shrimp bisque, served with silky basil mash and orange-poached fennel.

Chef Andrew Shortman **Owner** Andrew Shortman **Times** 9-5/6-9.30 Closed 25-26 Dec, 1 Jan, D all week except for private dining **Prices** Fixed D 3 course £20-£40, Service optional **Wines** 6 bottles over £20, 20 bottles under £20, 4 by glass **Notes** Private dining for 12+ people only, Sunday L, Vegetarian available, Air con **Seats** 56, Pr/dining room 18 **Children** Portions

The Olive Tree Restaurant

◉ Modern British NEW

Confident cooking in a smart Exeter hotel

☎ 01392 272709 📄 01392 491390
Queens Court Hotel, 6-8 Bystock Ter EX4 4HY
e-mail: enquiries@queenscourt-hotel.co.uk
dir: Leave dual carriageway at junct 30 onto B5132 Topsham Rd towards city centre. Hotel 200yds from station

Built in 1840, this handsome townhouse hotel occupies three terraced buildings on a quiet leafy Exeter square

that was once the home of wealthy merchants. The charming Olive Tree restaurant betrays a hankering for Mediterranean climes in more than just its name: Venetian masks, olive oil bottles and flickering candles all add to the intimate Italian-led vibe, and dishes arrive with lots of smiles from lovely staff. Cooking here, however, is firmly in the Modern British vein, and has plenty of guts and depth, with well-developed flavours and unfussy presentation. A starter of home-smoked mackerel is served with wholegrain mustard-infused potato salad, mackerel mousse and herb oil. Next comes seasonal comfort in honey-glazed pork belly with sweet potato purée, chilli-roasted salsify and lemongrass jus. Dessert might be pannacotta with raspberry sorbet.

Chef Darren Knockton **Owner** C F & B H Bowring **Times** 12-2/7-9.30 Closed Xmas, L Sun **Prices** Starter £5.50-£6.25, Main £14.95-£17, Dessert £5.45-£6.45, Service optional **Wines** 8 bottles over £20, 15 bottles under £20, 7 by glass **Notes** Vegetarian available, Civ Wed 60 **Seats** 24, Pr/dining room 16 **Children** Portions **Parking** Public car park in front of hotel

| GULWORTHY | Map 3 SX47 |

The Horn of Plenty

◉◉◉ *– see opposite page*

| HAYTOR VALE | Map 3 SX77 |

Rock Inn

◉ British

Wild Dartmoor scenery at a classic country inn serving accomplished British food

☎ 01364 661305 📄 01364 661242
TQ13 9XP
e-mail: reservations@rockinn.co.uk
dir: From A38 at Drum Bridges, onto A382 to Bovey Tracey. In 2m take B3387 towards Haytor for 3.5m, follow brown signs

After a day in the elemental wilderness of Dartmoor, this beamed and flagstoned 18th-century inn is an oasis of civility sheltering below the Haytor Rocks. A strong seam of tradition runs through the Rock Inn, from its genuinely friendly service to the classic British food based on super local produce, such as delicious Dartmoor lamb. Starters might include a fresh crab tart with tomato and tarragon dressing, and Devon beef appears as a main course with roasted vine tomatoes, new potatoes and wild mushroom jus. Lemon tart with ginger ice cream turns up at dessert, or you could go for a platter of Devon cheeses. It's nice to see West Country wines from Manstree Estate near Exeter and the Camel Valley featuring on the menu too.

Chef Sue Beaumont Graves **Owner** Mr C Graves **Times** 12-2.15/6.30-9 Closed 25-26 Dec **Prices** Food prices not confirmed for 2010. Please telephone for details. **Wines** 44 bottles over £20, 26 bottles under £20, 11 by glass **Notes** Vegetarian available, Dress restrictions, No jeans **Seats** 75 **Children** Portions, Menu **Parking** 25

The Horn of Plenty

GULWORTHY
Map 3 SX47

Modern International 🖐

Serious cuisine amidst stunning Devon countryside

☎ 01822 832528 📠 01822 834390
PL19 8JD
e-mail:
enquiries@thehornofplenty.co.uk
dir: From Tavistock take A390 W for 3m. Right at Gulworthy Cross. In 400yds turn left, hotel in 400yds on right

The setting in the Tamar Valley is idyllic, with the creeper-covered Victorian country house perfectly placed to take in the spectacular Devon vista. There are five acres of grounds to explore, too, including soaring mature trees, walled gardens and wild orchards. Then there is the hotel itself - elegantly decorated in a traditional manner with a restaurant of serious class. The chic dining room has panoramic views through large windows and makes the perfect setting for the refined and intelligent cooking of Peter Gorton. Drawing on the very best of local and regional produce, including vegetables and fruits from the hotel's kitchen garden, Peter produces a menu of well-judged modern dishes, influences drawn from mainland Europe and beyond. Goats' cheese, for example, is baked in an Indian pastry with balsamic mushrooms and served with kale pesto and red pepper sauce, while saddle of venison comes on a tangle of greens and creamy rosemary and garlic polenta. Steamed ginger sponge pudding with caramel sauce, clotted cream and vanilla ice cream makes for a splendid finale. The wine list is equally well constructed, offering an extensive selection plus a good range of ports and digestifs.

Chef Peter Gorton & Edward Wagy **Owner** Mr & Mrs P Roston, Peter Gorton **Times** 12-4/7-12 Closed 24-26 Dec **Prices** Fixed L course £26.50, Fixed D 3 course £47, Service included, Groups min 10 service 10% **Wines** 115 bottles over £20, 20 bottles under £20, 11 by glass **Notes** Sunday L, Vegetarian available, Dress restrictions, Smart casual, Civ Wed 150, Air con **Seats** 60, Pr/dining room 12 **Children** Portions, Menu **Parking** 20

HOLBETON   Map 3 SX65

The Dartmoor Union Inn

◎ Modern British 🍷

Soothing village inn with accomplished cooking

☎ 01752 830460   🖷 01752 830461
Fore St PL8 1NE
dir: Village signposted off A379 W of A3121 junct, follow brown signs

The inn has been cleverly modernised to create a soothing place with a dark wood bar, small pictures on the walls and a relaxed ambience. Seasonally oriented cooking is the name of the game, and the production is a few cuts above the country-pub norm. Start with spice-roasted scallops in chilli butter, or parmesan-topped seafood risotto, and go on to Markstone Farm beef fillet garnished with crisp-cooked Parma ham and red wine sauce, or slow-roast pork belly with plum confit and cumin oil. A simpler bar menu includes baguettes and a proper ploughman's lunch.

Chef Nicholas Hack **Owner** Simon Rattray
Times 12-2.30/6-11 **Prices** Fixed L 2 course £10, Fixed D 2 course £15-£25, Starter £4.50-£7.95, Main £9.50-£19.95, Dessert £5.50-£6.50, Service optional **Wines** 12 bottles over £20, 20 bottles under £20, 10 by glass **Notes** Vegetarian available **Children** Portions, Menu **Parking** 12

HONITON   Map 4 ST10

Combe House - Devon

◎◎ Modern British V 🍷

Fine dining in stunning Elizabethan manor

☎ 01404 540400   🖷 01404 46004
Gittisham EX14 3AD
e-mail: stay@thishotel.com
web: www.thishotel.com
dir: Off A30 1m S of Honiton, follow Gittisham Heathpark signs

Combe House is up there with the very best of the UK's historic country house hotels. The pedigree of this Grade I listed many-gabled Elizabethan mansion is beyond question: oak panelling, walk-in fireplaces, ancestral oils and fine antiques are taken as read, and it all sits in 3,500 acres of Devon's lush landscape. The kitchen makes good use of the local larder on the fixed-price menus, including herbs, fruits and vegetables from their own walled garden, and the three dining areas are elegantly and comfortably furnished. Classical preparations and creative modern British ideas combine to produce refined and well-flavoured dishes such as crab ravioli with pak choi, lemongrass and ginger velouté, followed by roast breast and confit leg of partridge with honey-roasted salsify, braised red cabbage and fondant potato. Finish with an exemplary tarte Tatin and vanilla ice cream.

Chef Hadleigh Barrett, Stuart Brown **Owner** Ken & Ruth Hunt **Times** 12-2/7-9.30 Closed 2 wks end Jan **Prices** Fixed L 3 course £29-£34, Fixed D 3 course fr £45, Service optional **Wines** 88 bottles over £20, 2 bottles under £20, 8 by glass **Notes** Sunday L, Vegetarian menu, Dress restrictions, Smart casual, Civ Wed 100 **Seats** 60, Pr/dining room 48 **Children** Portions, Menu **Parking** 35

The Holt Bar & Restaurant

◎ British NEW

Skilful cooking of local produce in buzzy pub-restaurant

☎ 01404 47707
178 High St EX14 1LA
e-mail: enquiries@theholt-honiton.com
dir: Please telephone for directions

Owned by the Otter Brewery, this modern, rustic-style pub-restaurant on Honiton's High Street is the place to come for a cracking pint, a buzzy, welcoming atmosphere, and some assured, punchy cooking using great local produce and home-smoked fish and meats. At simple, unclothed tables tuck into excellent tapas dishes or some appealing choices on the daily-changing menu; take a delicious ham hock terrine with pea bubble-and-squeak and deep-fried quail's egg, well-cooked John Dory fillets with smoked salmon potato cake and a well-balanced coriander butter sauce, and a zesty lemon tart with fruit coulis.

Chef Mike Bowditch **Owner** Jo & Angus McCaig
Times 12-2/7-10 Closed Sun-Mon **Prices** Starter £5-£6.50, Main £12.50-£15.50, Dessert £5.50 **Notes** Vegetarian available

Home Farm Restaurant & Hotel

◎ Modern British

Imaginative modern English cuisine in former farmhouse

☎ 01404 831278   🖷 01404 831411
Wilmington EX14 9JR
e-mail: info@thatchedhotel.co.uk

Originally a 16th-century thatched farmhouse, this attractive hotel and restaurant still has the original cobbled courtyard, as well as pretty gardens. The cottage-style restaurant, while retaining many original features, has a light and contemporary feel and an intimate atmosphere. The cooking is an interesting blend of modern influences with skilfully presented, imaginative flavour combinations. Start with West Country cured ham and wild garlic salad in a filo basket, followed by chargrilled venison steak served on a nettle risotto with nutmeg spinach, broad beans and red wine jus. Finish with caramelised sweet poached local rhubarb and crème anglaise.

Times 12-2/7-9

HORNS CROSS   Map 3 SS32

The Hoops Inn & Country Hotel

◎ British, French 🏴 🍷

Gastro-pub fare at an ancient inn

☎ 01237 451222   🖷 01237 451247
EX39 5DL
e-mail: sales@hoopsinn.co.uk
dir: A39 from Bideford towards Clovelly/Bude, through Fairy Cross & Horns Cross, restaurant on right

Genuinely friendly and welcoming 13th-century thatched inn surrounded by glorious natural gardens and within walking distance of the North Devon coast. Former smuggling connections, and a ghost, add to the atmosphere created by low beams, log fires, and a series of rambling, recently refurbished bars and dining rooms. Locally sourced produce is at the heart of the operation and a mature approach to cooking results in honest, unfussy dishes cooked with care and accuracy. The modern British menu has some French and Spanish influences, and may take in fish and shellfish cassoulet, venison with dauphinoise and cherry jus, and vanilla pod crème brûlée.

Chef M Somerville & Jo Winter **Owner** Gerry & Dee Goodwin **Times** 12-2/6-11 **Prices** Fixed L 2 course £15-£29, Fixed D 2 course £15-£29, Starter £5.50-£9, Main £10-£20, Dessert £4.95-£6.95, Service optional **Wines** 98 bottles over £20, 132 bottles under £20, 20 by glass

Notes Sunday L, Vegetarian available, Dress restrictions, Smart casual **Seats** 90, Pr/dining room 16 **Children** Portions, Menu **Parking** 100

The Quay

◉◉ Modern British

Unpretentious food with Damien Hirst's Brit art for company

☎ 01271 868090 & 868091 ▤ 01271 865599
11 The Quay EX34 9EQ
e-mail: info@11thequay.com
dir: Follow signs for harbour and pier car park. Restaurant on left before car park

Maverick artist Damien Hirst's expedition into the culinary world is thankfully more easy to digest than pickled sharks and diamond-crusted skulls. As its name might suggest, the Quay sits on the harbour in Ilfracombe, a handsome building of red brick and stone. Ascending from the ground-floor bar, the Atlantic room looks through huge windows over the ocean, beneath a ceiling designed to look like an upturned boat. As a bonus, the place is liberally sprinkled with Hirst's seashell artworks. The other option is the Harbourside room, which - you may have seen this coming - overlooks the harbour, and comes with the artist's 'Modern Medicine' artworks as visual entertainment. The kitchen has its feet on the ground, dealing in modern British cooking with punchy flavours, and unaffected presentation. Local fish is a strong suit, so kick off with local crab claws with chilli and roast garlic mayonnaise, and move on to king prawn and smoked haddock pie.

Chef Lawrence Hill-Wickham **Owner** Simon Browne & Damien Hirst **Times** 10-3/6-9 Closed 25-26 Dec, 2-25 Jan, Mon & Tue **Prices** Starter £5-£9, Main £12-£28, Dessert £5-£8, Service optional **Wines** 50 bottles over £20, 30 bottles under £20, 29 by glass **Notes** Vegetarian available **Seats** 32, Pr/dining room 26 **Parking** Pier car park 100yds

Ilsington Country House Hotel

◉◉ Modern European

Traditional dining in Dartmoor country-house hotel

☎ 01364 661452 ▤ 01364 661307
Ilsington Village TQ13 9RR
e-mail: hotel@ilsington.co.uk
web: www.ilsington.co.uk
dir: A38 to Plymouth, exit at Bovey Tracey. 3rd exit from rdbt to Ilsington, then 1st right, pass village shop, hotel on right

Ilsington certainly ticks all the right boxes for a country-house hotel break. It's a friendly family-run place with the wide-ranging vistas you'd expect from its lofty perch on the elemental slopes of Dartmoor. In fact the scenery is so lovely that a new restaurant with full-length windows was built in 2006 specifically to bask in the views across the moor to Haytor Rocks. The kitchen is driven by a classical French ethos that seeks to draw full flavours from well-sourced local materials. Smoked ham and wood pigeon croquettes with chickpea cassoulet, chorizo and root vegetables in Madeira and garlic jus shows the style. Pan-fried red mullet with smoked haddock risotto, caramelised fennel and red pepper essence might follow.

Chef Mike O'Donnell **Owner** Hassell Family **Times** 12-2/6.30-9 **Prices** Fixed L 2 course £15.95-£16.95, Fixed D 3 course £33.95-£35, Service included **Wines** 31 bottles over £20, 40 bottles under £20, 9 by glass **Notes** Sunday L, Vegetarian available, Dress restrictions, Shirt with a collar (smart casual) no shorts, Air con **Seats** 75, Pr/dining room 70 **Children** Portions **Parking** 60

Decks Restaurant

◉ Modern British ✤

Hearty modern cooking with superb sea views

☎ 01271 860671
Hatton Croft House, Marine Pde EX39 4JJ
e-mail: decks@instow.net
dir: From Barnstaple follow A38 to Bideford. Follow signs for Instow, restaurant at far end of seafront

There's a jaunty nautical theme (the clue is in the name) to this light and airy beachfront restaurant. A ship's mast runs through the ceiling into the upstairs restaurant, where a wall of windows means that everyone gets superb views over the Torridge estuary to pretty Appledore and the dunes of Braunton Burrows. The menu matches the cheerful ambience and sticks to simple, clearly-conceived dishes built on locally-sourced fish and seafood and West Country meat. Expect tried-and-tested combinations, such as tomato and red pepper compôte soup, or rack of Exmoor lamb with root vegetables and dauphinoise potatoes.

Chef Lee Timmins **Owner** Lee Timmins **Times** 12-2.30/7-9.30 Closed 25-26 Dec, 1 Jan, Sun-Mon, L ex by appointment **Prices** Starter £5-£12, Main £12.95-£31, Dessert £5-£8, Service optional **Wines** 18 bottles over £20, 21 bottles under £20, 10 by glass **Notes** Vegetarian available, Dress restrictions, Smart casual, Air con **Seats** 50 **Children** Portions, Menu **Parking** On street; beach car park

The Masons Arms

KNOWSTONE Map 3 SS82

Modern British

Exemplary food in the middle of Exmoor

☎ 01398 341231
EX36 4RY
e-mail: dodsonmasonsarms@aol.com
dir: Signed from A361, turn right once in Knowstone

Located midway between the market towns of South Molton and Tiverton, just off the southern borders of Exmoor, The Masons Arms sits opposite the parish church of St Peter's in the heart of the village. The church was mainly built in the 13th century and the inn was built by the same builders around the same time; the clue is in the name. With a population of around 220, this rural village is as picture postcard as they come and the thatched pub may be more of a dining destination these days but it oozes rustic character and charm. Duck as you enter the low doorway and step into the beamed bar with its enormous fireplace. The restaurant occupies the more contemporary rear extension with its magnificent views of the rolling hills of Exmoor. Hand-painted murals adorn the apex ceiling here, offering a complete contrast to the traditional bar areas of the original inn. Mark Dodson had made a name for himself long before he arrived here with his wife and children; he was head chef at the venerable Waterside Inn at Bray (see entry) and his cooking displays utter confidence and impeccable skills. His modern take on British and French classics has justifiably attracted foodies from far and wide and a use of top drawer ingredients is evident at every stage. Take a starter risotto of smoked haddock and poached egg with grain mustard sauce, and to follow, perhaps roulade of pork belly, braised red cabbage and apple compôte.

Chef Mark Dodson **Owner** Mark & Sarah Dodson
Times 12-2/7-9 Closed 1st wk Jan, Mon, D Sun
Prices Starter £8.50-£12, Main £16-£20.50, Dessert £7.50-£8.75, Service optional **Wines** 30 bottles over £20, 12 bottles under £20, 9 by glass **Notes** Sunday L, Vegetarian available **Seats** 28 **Children** Portions **Parking** 10

Lewtrenchard Manor

LEWDOWN Map 3 SX48

Modern British

Exemplary modern food in idyllic country house

☎ 01566 783222 📠 01566 783332
EX20 4PN
e-mail: info@lewtrenchard.co.uk
dir: Take A30 signed Okehampton from M5 junct 31. 25m, exit at Sourton Cross. Follow signs to Lewdown, then Lewtrenchard

It's hard not to be charmed by the quintessential Englishness of the historic Jacobean manor house and its peaceful position in a quiet valley on the edge of Dartmoor. Surrounded by idyllic gardens and peaceful parkland, the magnificent house was once the home of the celebrated hymn writer and novelist Reverend Sabine Baring-Gould of 'Onward Christian Soldiers' fame. The timeless interior oozes understated charm and wonderful period detail, complete with oak panelling, beautifully ornate ceilings, stained-glass windows, large fireplaces, period furnishings and family portraits. The candlelit, panelled dining room overlooks the pretty colonnaded courtyard and provides the perfect setting for alfresco dining. The new 'Purple Carrot' private dining room captures the passion of the kitchen on camera with its flat screen TVs and viewing areas into the kitchen itself. The kitchen takes a thoroughly modern approach with the focus on top quality fresh local produce, much grown in the garden, and seasonality. Deceptively simple dishes conceal a flair and confidence with the main ingredient taking centre stage. Take braised pork cheek with star anise, parsley mash and piccalilli vegetables, or perhaps tart of lamb's kidneys with sautéed loin and liver, sweetbread beignet and broccoli purée, while a chocolate and hazelnut praline with purée of prunes and white chocolate ice cream will certainly catch the eye at dessert.

Chef Jason Hornbuckle **Owner** Von Essen Hotels
Times 12-1.30/7-9 Closed L Mon **Prices** Fixed L 2 course £15, Fixed D 3 course £55, Tasting menu fr £95, Service optional **Wines** 234 bottles over £20, 5 bottles under £20, 13 by glass **Notes** The Chef's Table in the Purple Carrot (8 course), Sunday L, Vegetarian available, Dress restrictions, L smart casual, D no jeans or T-shirts, Civ Wed 100 **Seats** 45, Pr/dining room 22 **Children** Portions, Menu **Parking** 40

KNOWSTONE — Map 3 SS82

The Masons Arms

@@@ — *see opposite page*

LEWDOWN — Map 3 SX48

Lewtrenchard Manor

@@@ — *see opposite page*

LIFTON — Map 3 SX38

Arundell Arms

@@ Modern British V

Old coaching inn with local flavours on the menu

☎ 01566 784666 📠 01566 784494
Fore St PL16 0AA
e-mail: reservations@arundellarms.com
web: www.arundellarms.com
dir: Just off A30 in Lifton, 3m E of Launceston

Outdoor activities such as shooting and fishing are on the agenda for many of the guests at this reassuringly unchanged 18th-century coaching inn on the edge of Dartmoor. Low ceilings above, stone flags underfoot and classic country chintz make for a relaxed atmosphere, while a huge open log fire keeps out the chill after a day on the moors. Classic combinations that won't scare the horses form the backbone of the accomplished kitchen's output, and naturally West Country produce features prominently. A starter of Falmouth Bay scallops with tempura cauliflower and sweet chilli dressing might precede a main course of Devon beef fillet with oxtail pudding, root vegetables and Madeira.

Chef Steven Pidgeon **Owner** Anne Voss-Bark
Times 12.30-2.30/7.30-10 Closed 27 Dec, D 24-26 Dec
Prices Fixed D 4 course £46, Service optional **Wines** 37 bottles over £20, 3 bottles under £20, 7 by glass
Notes Sunday L, Vegetarian menu, Dress restrictions, Smart casual, Civ Wed 80 **Seats** 70, Pr/dining room 24
Children Portions, Menu **Parking** 70

Tinhay Mill Guest House and Restaurant

@ British, French V

Delightful restaurant with rooms offering local produce

☎ 01566 784201 📠 01566 784201
Tinhay PL16 0AJ
e-mail: tinhay.mill@talk21.com
dir: From M5 take A30 towards Okehampton/Launceston. Lifton off A30 on left. Follow brown tourist signs. Restaurant at bottom of village near river

This charming restaurant with rooms occupies what was once two 15th-century mill cottages. The interior is traditional with thick whitewashed walls, beamed ceilings, a log fire and a separate lounge bar with the comfort of leather sofas. Chef-proprietor and cookery writer Margaret Wilson has long been a champion of local produce, used to good effect in dishes such as Cornish mushrooms filled with local crab and cream cheese; and pork tenderloin cooked with brandy, crushed green peppercorns and cream. Dessert might be a warm chocolate fondant pudding with warm chocolate fudge sauce.

Chef Margaret Wilson **Owner** Mr P & Mrs M Wilson
Times 7-9.30 Closed 2 wks Xmas & New Year, 3 wks Feb & Mar, Sun & Mon (ex residents), L all week
Prices Starter £5.25-£8.50, Main £13.50-£22.50, Dessert £5.50-£8, Service optional, Groups min 8 service 10%
Wines 12 bottles over £20, 11 bottles under £20, 4 by glass **Notes** Vegetarian menu, Dress restrictions, Smart casual, no T-shirts or trainers **Seats** 24, Pr/dining room 24 **Parking** 10

LYDFORD — Map 3 SX58

Dartmoor Inn

@@ Modern British

Stylish and original country inn with first-class food

☎ 01822 820221 📠 01822 820494
EX20 4AY
e-mail: info@dartmoorinn.co.uk
dir: On A386 (Tavistock to Okehampton road)

If the moor represents the untamed nature of the elements, the Dartmoor Inn embodies the endeavours of mankind. It is a charming country inn, certainly, but the inn represents the passions and hard work of its proprietors, who have fashioned an idyllic retreat amid the natural beauty of the moorland. There's a small bar (a fire blazes in the cool months) where real ales and high class pub classics are on offer, and a restaurant made up of a series of rooms where original features and contemporary styles are interwoven - there's a decidedly New England or Swedish look to the spaces, and the tables are laid with crisp white linen. The Swedish influence extends to the boutique shop, which sells glassware, plus jewellery and more. The menu is based on seasonal ingredients, sourced locally, and turned into intelligently uncomplicated dishes. Kick off with corned beef terrine with mustard dressing, followed by pan-fried lamb's kidneys, bacon, black pudding and red wine sauce. Meringues with lemon curd and passionfruit sauce is a dessert with a superb combination of textures and tastes. Special promotion nights are a popular feature.

Times 12-2.15/6.30-9.30 Closed Mon, D Sun

LYNMOUTH — Map 3 SS74

Tors Hotel

@ Modern, Traditional European

Sound cooking and fantastic views over land and sea

☎ 01598 753236 📠 01598 752544
EX35 6NA
e-mail: torshotel@torslynmouth.co.uk
dir: M5 junct 23 (Bridgwater). Continue 40m on A39 through Minehead. Hotel at base of Countisbury Hill on left

You couldn't ask for a better view over Lynmouth and the sea than the one from Tors Hotel, sitting up on the wooded hillside in peace and tranquillity amid five acres of grounds. The smartly decorated restaurant has a

continued

LYNMOUTH *continued*

colonial feel and faces south to benefit from those great views. Local produce is a feature of the menu, which delivers straightforward and attractively presented dishes. Start with timbale of white crab with citrus dressing and a rocket and chive mayonnaise, moving onto roast loin of pork stuffed with apricot, orange and thyme and finished with the roasting juices, then apple pie with cinnamon ice cream and green apple sorbet.

Times 7-9 Closed 3 Jan-4 Feb (wknds only in Feb), L all week

LYNTON Map 3 SS74

Lynton Cottage Hotel

◉◉ Modern British V ✱

Stunning clifftop views and skilfully cooked food

☎ 01598 752342 📠 01598 754016
North Walk EX35 6ED
e-mail: enquiries@lynton-cottage.co.uk
dir: M5 junct 27, follow A361 towards Barnstaple. Follow signs to Lynton A39. In Lynton turn right at church. Hotel on right

Breathtaking views of the dramatic North Devon coastline would be reason enough to dine at this historic cliff-top country house, and lesser restaurants might be happy to let the views bring in the punters for indifferent food. Luckily, chef Matthew Bailey is passionate about the kitchen's output at every stage: his maturity shines through in well-conceived, elegantly constructed and judiciously balanced dishes of genuine integrity. In the elegant dining room, interesting, boldly-coloured artwork from local artists fights for diners' attention, but it's a one-sided struggle as the eye is continually drawn to the ragged cliffs below. Until, that is, the food arrives: expect Devon's finest local, organic and seasonal produce, accurate cooking and eye-catching modern presentation; wild sea bass with pak choi and sweet-and-sour damson dressing shows the style. The finale is a dish of genuine class - a vanilla pannacotta with Italian prunes served three ways - a sorbet, purée, and light mousse.

Chef Matthew Bailey **Owner** Allan Earl, Heather Biancardi **Times** 12-2.30/7-9.30 Closed Dec & Jan **Prices** Food prices not confirmed for 2010. Please telephone for details. **Wines** 12 bottles over £20, 8 bottles under £20, 4 by glass **Notes** Vegetarian menu **Seats** 40 **Children** Portions **Parking** 18

MORETONHAMPSTEAD Map 3 SX78

The White Hart Hotel

◉ British, International

Traditional British alongside modern European in Devon coaching inn

☎ 01647 441340 📠 01647 441341
The Square TQ13 8NQ
e-mail: enquiries@whitehartdartmoor.co.uk
dir: Please telephone for directions

Set in the heart of Dartmoor, and proudly flying the Union and St George's flags above the entrance, the White Hart opened in the 17th century as a coaching inn. Solid, foursquare interiors include a restaurant with undressed tables and bare-boarded floor, while the cooking majors on traditional British fare, such as soused mackerel with potato salad and sirloin steak with a mini-cottage pie, alongside more obviously European influences. Brixham crab linguini is vibrantly spiced with chilli, ginger and coriander. Chicken breast might come with a very assured mushroom and spinach risotto and tarragon jus, and well-textured white chocolate mousse is teamed with crumbled honeycomb and raspberry sorbet.

Owner Hart Inns Limited **Times** 12-2.30/6-9 **Prices** Starter £4.95-£6.50, Main £10.95-£18.95, Dessert £5.95-£7.95, Service optional **Wines** 15 bottles over £20, 15 bottles under £20, 15 by glass **Notes** Sunday L, Vegetarian available, Civ Wed 100 **Seats** 62 **Children** Portions, Menu **Parking** Public car park 100mtrs

---

NEWTON ABBOT Map 3 SX87

Sampsons Farm & Restaurant

◉ British ✱

Fresh local produce in a charming farmhouse hotel

☎ 01626 354913 📠 01626 332673
Preston TQ12 3PP
e-mail: info@sampsonsfarm.com
dir: M5/A380/B3195 signed Kingsteignton. Pass Ten Tors Inn on left & take 2nd rd signed B3193 to Chudleigh. At rdbt 3rd exit, left after 1m

Sampsons Farm is a true slice of Devon, a medieval thatched farmhouse that has been run by the same hands-on family for over 30 years. Low beams, gentle lighting and crackling log fires make for a cosily romantic restaurant, with art by Devon-based artist Sarah Bell to provide visual entertainment. The owners are passionately committed to buying local wherever possible so fish is fresh from the boats in Brixham and meat is sourced from Devon farms. The modern menu offers pressed terrine of Bickington lamb with minted new potato salad, followed by brill with parsnip purée and honey and aniseed sauce, or caramelised breast of Crediton duck with porcini risotto and spicy rhubarb.

Chef Tony Carr **Owner** Nigel Bell **Times** 12-2/7-9 Closed 25-26 Dec **Prices** Fixed L 2 course £14.95-£19.95, Fixed D 2 course £19.95-£29.95, Starter £5-£9, Main

---

£14.50-£23, Dessert £4.50-£7.50 **Wines** 6 by glass **Notes** Dress restrictions, No jeans **Seats** 36, Pr/dining room 20 **Children** Portions, Menu **Parking** 20

NEWTON POPPLEFORD Map 3 SY08

Moore's Restaurant & Rooms

◉◉ Modern British ✱

Stylish village restaurant serving imaginative dishes

☎ 01395 568100 📠 01395 568092
6 Greenbank, High St EX10 0EB
e-mail: info.moores@btconnect.com
dir: On A3052 in village centre

Located in the centre of pretty Newton Poppleford, this friendly restaurant is run by the Moores, a husband-and-wife team. Formerly two cottages, one of which doubled as a grocer's store, it boasts several bedrooms as well as an intimate dining room with wide windows that overlook the village and a neutral décor that's easy on the eye. Dishes are imaginative and full of flavour, making use of good quality, locally sourced ingredients wherever possible, including Mr Moore's very own catch of the day. Seared scallops are a typical starter, served with pea purée, with roast chump of Gatcombe Farm lamb to follow, accompanied by sea salt baked Pink Fir potatoes and wild mushroom sauce. Round off with Baileys bread-and-butter pudding with Devonshire clotted cream.

Chef Jonathan Moore **Owner** Jonathan & Kate Moore **Times** 12-1.30/7-9.30 Closed 25-26 Dec, 1st 2 wks in Jan, Mon, D Sun **Prices** Fixed L 2 course £14.95, Fixed D 3 course £22.45-£27.50, Service optional **Wines** 19 bottles over £20, 12 bottles under £20, 6 by glass **Notes** Sunday L, Vegetarian available **Seats** 32, Pr/dining room 12 **Children** Portions **Parking** 2, On street & free car park behind church

---

PLYMOUTH Map 3 SX45

Artillery Tower Restaurant

◉ British ✱

Confident cooking in historic maritime building

☎ 01752 257610
Firestone Bay PL1 3QR
dir: 1m from city centre & rail station

One of the oldest complete military buildings on Plymouth's seafront, this 16th-century stone tower once protected the deep water passage at the north of Plymouth Sound, between Drake's Island and the main waterfront. The restaurant is simply furnished with wooden tables set against stone walls in a round room with sea views. Local produce dominates the menu with the main ingredient taking centre stage; an impressive starter of seared scallops with belly pork and apple, perhaps, followed by roast Devon duck breast with prunes marinated in Armagnac.

Chef Peter Constable **Owner** Peter Constable **Times** 12-2.15/7-9.30 Closed Xmas & New Year, Sun-Mon, L Sat **Prices** Fixed L 2 course fr £31, Fixed D 3

course fr £41, Groups min 8 service 6% **Wines** 60 bottles over £20, 30 bottles under £20, 6 by glass **Seats** 40, Pr/dining room 16 **Children** Portions **Parking** 20, (Evening only)

Barbican Kitchen

◎ Modern British ⓒ

The Tanner Brothers' stylish brasserie serving contemporary food

☎ 01752 604448 📄 01752 604445
Blackfriars Distillery, 60 Southside St PL1 2LQ
e-mail: info@barbicankitchen.com
dir: On Barbican, 5 mins walk from Bretonside bus station

The ancient Plymouth Gin distillery, where the Pilgrim Fathers spent their last night before sailing off to the New World, makes a super location for this fun and funky brasserie in the heart of Plymouth's historic Barbican quarter. An eye-catching interior of bold colour contrasts, wooden floors and bare rafters is alive with a buzz of conviviality. The open kitchen provides a touch of culinary theatre as the team rustles up forthright, sharply-executed dishes, such as Barbican fishcakes with tomato salsa, or a garlic and thyme roast pork fillet with Devon cider mash.

Chef Lee Holland, C & J Tanner **Owner** Christopher & James Tanner **Times** 12-3/5-10 Closed 25-26 & 31 Dec **Prices** Starter £3.95-£7.95, Main £7.95-£16.95, Dessert £4.95-£5.50, Service included **Wines** 16 bottles over £20, 22 bottles under £20, 13 by glass **Notes** Pre-theatre menu 2 course £9.95, 3 course £13.95, Sunday L, Vegetarian available, Civ Wed 60, Air con **Seats** 80 **Children** Portions, Menu **Parking** Drakes Circus, Guildhall

Best Western Duke of Cornwall Hotel

◎ British, European **V**

Classic Victorian hotel on a grand scale

☎ 01752 275850 📄 01752 275854
Millbay Rd PL1 3LG
e-mail: enquiries@thedukeofcornwall.co.uk
dir: City centre, follow signs 'Pavilions', hotel road is opposite

This is one of those imposing Victorian hotels built during the good times - right in the heart of the city, with everything on a grand scale - and these days it is very much part of the skyline. The dining room is no less impressive: chandeliers hang from the high ceilings, well-spaced, smartly laid tables fill the room, and paintings with gilded frames adorn the walls. The food takes a less grand approach, keeping things relatively simple and delivering dishes such as local asparagus with puff pastry and hollandaise sauce, grilled sea bass with clam and mussel marinière, and raspberry and lemon soufflé with coconut.

Chef Darren Kester **Owner** W Combstock, J Morcom **Times** 7-10 Closed 26-31 Dec, L all week **Prices** Starter £5.95-£8, Main £12.95-£18.50, Dessert £5.95-£6.50 **Wines** 50% bottles over £20, 50% bottles under £20, 8 by glass **Notes** Vegetarian menu, Civ Wed 300 **Seats** 80, Pr/dining room 30 **Children** Portions, Menu **Parking** 40

Bistro Bacchanalia

◎ Traditional British

Relaxed, friendly atmosphere in contemporary harbourside bistro

☎ 01752 254879 📄 01752 254879
Dolphin House, Sutton Harbour PL4 0DW
e-mail: bb@suttonharbour.net
dir: From A38 follow signs at Marsh Mill to City Centre, then to Barbican. Left to Sutton Wharf

This light and airy modern bistro offers waterside dining in pole position at the heart of Plymouth's historic Sutton Harbour. A jaunty New England-style décor of polished wooden floors and tables makes an aptly nautical setting for the bistro's unfussy food. You're in the right spot for the catch of the day here too, as the fish comes flapping-fresh from the fish market just across the harbour. Try a warm crab and cheddar cheese tartlet, then pan-fried sea bass with sautéed potatoes, chorizo, wilted rocket and red wine shallots. A white chocolate fudge cake might catch the eye for pudding, and there are heaps of wines by the glass.

Chef Chris Whitehead **Owner** Bruce & Lesley Brunning **Times** 12-2/7-9.30 Closed 25 Dec, 1 Jan, Sun **Prices** Starter £4.50-£6.25, Main £11.50-£17.95, Dessert £5.95-£8.50, Service optional **Wines** 24 bottles over £20, 12 bottles under £20, 16 by glass **Notes** Vegetarian available **Seats** 90 **Parking** 200 yds

Langdon Court Hotel & Restaurant

◎ British **V**

Contemporary cuisine in impressive Tudor setting

☎ 01752 862358 📄 01752 863428
Down Thomas PL9 0DY
e-mail: enquiries@langdoncourt.com
dir: From A379 at Elburton, follow brown tourist signs

Once owned by Henry VIII and home to his 6th wife, Katherine Parr (one who kept her head), this splendid Grade II listed manor house is situated in beautiful Devon countryside. Formal gardens and a path lead to the beach and coastal footpaths. Expect local produce, including excellent seafood, in both the contemporary bistro-bar and the elegantly formal restaurant. Seared Brixham scallops, perhaps, with crispy Parma ham and baby leaves, or a bouillabaisse made with locally caught fish, followed by marinated breast of Creedy Carver chicken with a pea risotto. Finish with a tangy lemon tart.

Chef Carl Smith **Owner** Emma & Geoffrey Ede **Times** 12-2.30/6.30-9.30 **Prices** Fixed D 4 course £25-£35, Starter £5.95-£8.95, Main £15.95-£21.95, Dessert £3.95-£7.25, Service included **Wines** 10 bottles over £20, 36 bottles under £20, 8 by glass **Notes** Tasting menu available, Sunday L, Vegetarian menu, Dress restrictions, Smart casual, Civ Wed 100 **Seats** 60, Pr/dining room 100 **Children** Portions **Parking** 80

Tanners Restaurant

◎◎ Modern British **V** ⓒ

Contemporary cuisine in restored medieval house

☎ 01752 252001 📄 01752 252105
Prysten House, Finewell St PL1 2AE
e-mail: enquiries@tannersrestaurant.com
dir: Town centre. Behind St Andrews Church on Royal Parade

It may be housed in Plymouth's oldest surviving domestic building, dating back to the 1490s, but Tanner's is firmly rooted in the present. The house was a hundred years old when Drake saw the Armada, and its medieval character remains in the flagstone walls hung with oil canvases,

continued

PLYMOUTH continued

the slate floors and the beams. The Tanner brothers, though, are 21st-century restaurateurs; James does a fair bit of TV work and they've a couple of books out. The style of cooking is modern and not overly complex, making full use of the plentiful West Country larder, so the seasonally-changing menu might see glazed Vulscombe goats' cheese in a dish with roasted figs and beetroot with port dressing, or a salad of Brixham crab with parmesan and apple. Bodmin venison loin, red cabbage, orange-glazed carrots and bitter chocolate jus is a typical main course. The brothers also have a popular brasserie in the city - the Barbican Kitchen (see entry).

Chef Christopher & James Tanner **Owner** Christopher & James Tanner **Times** 12-2.30/7-9.30 Closed 25, 31 Dec, 1st wk Jan, Sun & Mon **Prices** Fixed L 2 course £14, Fixed D 3 course £35, Tasting menu £45, Service optional, Groups min 8 service 10% **Wines** 40 bottles over £20, 20 bottles under £20, 8 by glass **Notes** Tasting menu 6 course, Vegetarian menu, Dress restrictions, Smart casual preferred, no trainers **Seats** 45, Pr/dining room 26 **Children** Portions **Parking** On street, church car park next to restaurant

See advert below

ROCKBEARE   Map 3 SY09

The Jack In The Green

@@ Modern British V ✋

Relaxed pub with seriously impressive food

☎ 01404 822240   📄 01404 823445
EX5 2EE
e-mail: info@jackinthegreen.uk.com
dir: 3m E of M5 junct 29 on old A30

Over the years this place has extended from the original pub and now has plenty of space to accommodate its many fans, including a new courtyard and beer garden. The interior is still reassuringly pubby and people do come just for a drink, though food is very much at the heart of the operation. Tables are unclothed and simply laid, and there are log fires in winter and leather sofas for relaxing. Specials with understated descriptions are

chalked on the board; it's the food on the plate that does the talking. Devon produce is treated with respect, as demonstrated in a sensitively cooked dish of skate with mash and spinach, and for a touch of the exotic, try a perfect pannacotta of coconut and lemongrass.

Chef Matthew Mason, Craig Sampson **Owner** Paul Parnell **Times** 12-2/6-9.30 Closed 25 Dec-1 Jan **Prices** Fixed L 2 course £18.95, Fixed D 3 course £25, Starter £4.95-£7.25, Main £11.50-£23.50, Dessert £5.95-£8.50, Service optional **Wines** 40 bottles over £20, 60 bottles under £20, 12 by glass **Notes** Sunday L, Vegetarian menu, Dress restrictions, Smart casual, Air con **Seats** 80, Pr/dining room 60 **Children** Portions, Menu **Parking** 120

SALCOMBE   Map 3 SX73

Soar Mill Cove Hotel

@@ Modern British ✋

Seaside dining in a friendly family-run hotel

☎ 01548 561566   📄 01548 561223
Soar Mill Cove, Marlborough TQ7 3DS
e-mail: info@soarmillcove.co.uk
dir: A381 to Salcombe, through village follow signs to sea

A family-run hotel in beautiful south Devon, Soar Mill Cove is the name of the setting as well as the venue. Indeed, it's what you will be looking out over, through full-drop windows, once you take your place in the restaurant. All tables face outwards, and if you can tear

your gaze away, there's some good local artwork on the walls. Tables are highly polished, and so is the service. The bracing, unfussy cooking, with seafood a strong suit, sees lightly cooked red mullet playing a starring role in a tomato and fennel soup, which you might follow with lobster, partnered with queen scallops, in a saffron sauce. Meat shows up well too though, as in a breast and confit leg of Gressingham duck with red cabbage and a slightly over-sweet, but otherwise textbook, orange sauce. Crème brûlée scented with lavender ends things on a note of refinement.

Chef I Macdonald **Owner** Mr & Mrs K Makepeace & family **Times** 7.15-9 Closed Jan, L all week **Prices** Fixed D 3 course fr £29, Service optional **Wines** 40 bottles over £20, 11 bottles under £20, 4 by glass **Notes** Vegetarian available, Civ Wed 150 **Seats** 60 **Children** Portions, Menu **Parking** 25

Tides Reach Hotel

◉ Modern British

Traditional British fare in beautiful beach setting

☎ 01548 843466 📠 01548 843954
South Sands TQ8 8LJ
e-mail: enquire@tidesreach.com
dir: Take cliff road towards sea and Bolt Head

Located at the water's edge of a picturesque cove called South Sands in the delightful South Hams area of Devon, this friendly hotel enjoys splendid views over Salcombe Estuary. The famous sub-tropical gardens at Overbecks are close by on the hill above the hotel. The conservatory-style Garden Room Restaurant offers a daily-changing, traditional British menu with a modern touch or two, featuring top-quality local produce, especially fish and seafood. Expect hand-picked Salcombe crab, or smoked Exmoor venison to start, with mains such as rib of prime south Devon beef, or line-caught local sea bass. For dessert, try baked gooseberry cheesecake.

Times 7-9 Closed Dec-Jan, L all week

SHALDON   Map 3 SX97

ODE

◉ Modern British 🌿

Top-quality local and organic produce in coastal village

☎ 01626 873977
21 Fore St TQ14 0DE
e-mail: info@odetruefood.co.uk
dir: Cross bridge from Teignmouth then 1st left into Fore St

The owners of ODE believe in true food values and are passionate about sourcing only the finest seasonal raw ingredients. The same ethos applies to the interior of this three-storey Georgian townhouse in the picturesque coastal village of Shaldon, which has been refurbished with environmentally-friendly materials by local craftsmen. The innovative menu offers broadly modern British dishes based on traditional French preparations and supported by occasional flavours from around the world, all using regional meats, line-caught fish and organic fruit and vegetables. Choose seared diver-caught Start Bay scallops and Paignton crab salad with saffron and lemon aïoli, followed by breast of Crediton ducked cooked under vacuum with clove, sweet-and-sour soy sauce and pearl barley. Finish with the fine choice of West Country artisan cheeses.

Chef Tim Bouget **Owner** Tim & Clare Bouget **Times** 12-1.30/7-9.30 Closed 25 Dec, BHs, Mon-Tue, L Wed, D Sun **Prices** Fixed L 2 course £17.50, Starter £6-£12.50, Main £16-£22, Dessert £5.50-£9.50, Service optional, Groups min 6 service 10% **Wines** 15 bottles over £20, 8 bottles under £20, 5 by glass **Notes** Vegetarian available **Seats** 24 **Parking** Car park 3 mins walk

SIDMOUTH   Map 3 SY18

Riviera Hotel

◉ Modern British

Dine in Regency splendour with splendid Lyme Bay views

☎ 01395 515201 📠 01395 577775
The Esplanade EX10 8AY
e-mail: enquiries@hotelriviera.co.uk
web: www.hotelriviera.co.uk
dir: From M5 junct 30 take A3052 to Sidmouth. Situated in centre of Esplanade

The bay-fronted Riviera Hotel is the Regency jewel in the crown of Sidmouth's historic Esplanade, and in summer there's nowhere finer than its sunny terrace for dining alfresco with lovely views over the russet cliffs of Lyme Bay. Inside, traditional comfort and elegance sets the tone in the restaurant, where a daily-changing menu follows the seasons and balances traditional fare with forays into modern innovative dishes. Vegetarians are well catered for with a separate menu. Expect starters such as pan-fried baby squid with tomato and mango salad and a balsamic reduction, followed by poached maize-fed chicken stuffed with red pepper mousse and served with apricot potato cake and tarragon velouté. Leave room for pudding - perhaps a hot chocolate fondant with cherry compôte and clotted cream.

Chef Matthew Weaver **Owner** Peter Wharton **Times** 12.30-2/7-9 **Prices** Starter £8.50-£12, Main £20.50-£29, Dessert £6-£6.95 **Wines** 45 bottles over £20, 30 bottles under £20, 4 by glass **Notes** Fixed L 5 course £27, Fixed D 6 course £38.50, Sunday L, Vegetarian available, Air con **Seats** 85, Pr/dining room 65 **Children** Portions, Menu **Parking** 26

The Salty Monk

◉◉ Modern British 🌿

Contemporary cooking in historic building

☎ 01395 513174
Church St, Sidford EX10 9QP
e-mail: saltymonk@btconnect.com
web: www.saltymonk.co.uk
dir: From M5 junct 30 take A3052 to Sidmouth, or from Honiton take A375 to Sidmouth, left at lights in Sidford, 200yds on right

Originally a Salt House used by the Benedictine Monks who traded salt at Exeter Cathedral, this smart restaurant with rooms dates from the 16th century. The lounge and bar are full of charm and character while the light and airy restaurant at the rear has a more modern feel and lovely views over the award-winning gardens. The two owners both cook, using fresh local produce and many of the suppliers are listed on the menu. They create some very enjoyable dishes with well-defined flavours, such as a warm salad of Brixham lobster and locally smoked wild boar bacon, followed by loin of local veal and home-made faggot served with pan-fried calves' liver and dauphinoise potatoes.

Chef Annette & Andy Witheridge **Owner** Annette & Andy Witheridge **Times** 12-1.30/6.30-9.30 Closed 3 wks Jan, 2 wks Nov, L Mon-Wed **Prices** Fixed D 3 course £39.50-£45, Service optional, Groups min 15 service 10% **Wines** 24 bottles over £20, 56 bottles under £20, 10 by glass **Notes** Vegetarian available, Dress restrictions, Smart casual **Seats** 55, Pr/dining room 14 **Children** Portions **Parking** 18

Victoria Hotel

◉ Traditional

Victorian splendour and appealing menu at seafront hotel

☎ 01395 512651 📠 01395 579154
The Esplanade EX10 8RY
e-mail: info@victoriahotel.co.uk
dir: At western end of The Esplanade

The grand old Victoria is a large, smart hotel in an elevated position at the end of the promenade, surrounded by well-tended gardens and enjoying fine views over the bay. The interior retains its period character and the restaurant - a large room with high ceilings and ornate plaster mouldings - is traditionally decorated. The menu is similarly traditional but with modern influences; potted

continued

SIDMOUTH *continued*

duck rillette, for example, with figs, home-made bread and dressed leaves, then a sorbet or salad, followed by a main course such as breast of guinea fowl with fondant potato, peas, baby gems and bacon.

Times 1-2/7-9

| SOUTH BRENT | Map 3 SX66 |

Glazebrook House Hotel & Restaurant

@ British 🕙

Relaxed country-house dining in a tranquil setting

☎ 01364 73322 📠 01364 72350
TQ10 9JE
e-mail: enquiries@glazebrookhouse.com
dir: From A38, between Ivybridge & Buckfastleigh exit at South Brent, follow hotel signs

The former home of an 18th-century gentleman is these days a welcoming country house hotel. On the edge of Dartmoor National Park and standing in four acres of pretty gardens, the hotel is beautifully maintained and classic in style. The restaurant is elegantly done out in natural tones with white linen-clad tables, and is a pleasingly understated and refined space. The menu focuses on local produce and follows a broadly British path. Grilled goats' cheese and warm baby beetroot is served with a walnut salad in an appealing first course, while next up might be fillet of West Country beef with caramelised shallots and Madeira sauce.

Chef David Merriman **Owner** Dave & Caroline Cashmore **Times** 7-9 Closed 2 wks Jan, 1 wk Aug, Sun, L all week **Prices** Fixed D 3 course £15-£19.50, Starter £4.50-£6.50, Main £16.50-£20.50, Dessert £4.50-£4.95, Service optional **Wines** 13 bottles over £20, 19 bottles under £20, 8 by glass **Notes** Vegetarian available, Civ Wed 80 **Seats** 60, Pr/dining room 12 **Children** Portions **Parking** 40

| STRETE | Map 3 SX84 |

The Kings Arms

@ Modern British

Foodie pub with fine sea views and an emphasis on fresh local fish

☎ 01803 770377 📠 01803 771008
Dartmouth Rd TQ6 0RW
e-mail: kingsarms_devon_fish@hotmail.com
dir: A379 coastal road from Dartmouth to Kingsbridge, 5m from Dartmouth

The splendidly ornate cast-iron balcony fronting this Victorian pub suggests tradition through and through, but inside a makeover has brought in a clean-cut contemporary look in keeping with its well-earned reputation as a foodie venue majoring in super fresh fish. The owners have teamed up with a local boat that fishes exclusively for the pub, so you may even be watching supplies being caught as you take in the stunning views of Start Bay that are a scenic backdrop to the food. The

kitchen knows there's no need to mess about with fish and seafood this good: simply prepared dishes kick off with Start Bay chilli spider crab bisque, or seared scallops with Puy lentils and Pedro Ximenez syrup. Mains might include bream and fennel braised with white rum and lime, crispy pancetta and apple and vanilla syrup.

Chef Rob Dawson **Owner** Rob Dawson & Virgina Heath **Times** 12-2/6.30-9 **Prices** Starter £6-£10, Main £10-£17, Dessert £6-£8, Service optional **Wines** 26 bottles over £20, 10 bottles under £20, 11 by glass **Notes** Sunday L, Vegetarian available **Seats** 30 **Children** Portions, Menu **Parking** Patron only parking 200yds

---

| TAVISTOCK | Map 3 SX47 |

Bedford Hotel

@ Modern British 🕙

Best of local produce served in a landmark hotel

☎ 01822 613221 📠 01822 618034
1 Plymouth Rd PL19 8BB
e-mail: enquiries@bedford-hotel.co.uk
dir: M5 junct 31, A30 (Launceston/Okehampton). Then A386 to Tavistock, follow town centre signs. Hotel opposite church)

In a former life this impressively castellated building was a residence of the Dukes of Bedford and it will come as no surprise that it's the oldest in town. The elegant Woburn Restaurant serves a seasonal, largely traditional menu, making good use of regional produce and adding a few interesting international touches along the way. Ashmoor goats' cheese turns up in a ravioli with roasted red peppers (accompanied by a basil pesto and red pepper consommé), while roasted Gressingham duck comes with orange and rhubarb pudding and rosemary jus. Sunday lunch is eaten in the thoroughly modern surroundings of Gallery 26.

Chef Matt Carder **Owner** Warm Welcome Hotels **Times** 12-2.30/7-9.30 Closed L Mon-Sat **Prices** Fixed L 3 course fr £16.95, Starter £5.25-£6.95, Main £13.95-£21, Dessert £5.25-£7.50, Service optional **Wines** 5 bottles over £20, 12 bottles under £20, 6 by glass **Notes** Sunday L, Vegetarian available, Dress restrictions, Smart casual, no jeans **Seats** 55, Pr/dining room 24 **Children** Portions, Menu **Parking** 48

| THURLESTONE | Map 3 SX64 |

Thurlestone Hotel

@ Modern, Traditional British

Good modern cooking with dramatic sea views

☎ 01548 560382 📠 01548 561069
TQ7 3NN
e-mail: enquiries@thurlestone.co.uk
dir: A38 take A384 into Totnes, A381 towards Kingsbridge, onto A379 towards Churchstow, onto B3197 turn into lane signed to Thurlestone

The modern-looking white hotel has been in the Grose family for over a century, and is still run with the personal touch. The full-length windows of the dining room are

designed to afford the most generous sea views, and there are fine clifftop walks hereabouts to enable you to prime your appetite. The daily-changing menus are based on traditional techniques, given a gentle modern spin. Rabbit and Parma ham terrine with apricot chutney is chunky and satisfying, and good fish dishes might include well-timed sea bream with roasted vegetables and herb butter. Crediton duckling confit with Savoy cabbage and pancetta might be a meat option, with positively flavoured but not over-sweet, white chocolate pannacotta and hazelnut ice cream to finish.

Chef H Miller **Owner** Grose Family **Times** 12.30-2.30/7.30-9 Closed L Mon-Sat **Prices** Fixed D 3 course £18.50, Service optional **Wines** 113 bottles over £20, 40 bottles under £20, 8 by glass **Notes** Fish tasting menu, Sunday L, Vegetarian available, Dress restrictions, Jacket, Civ Wed 150, Air con **Seats** 150, Pr/ dining room 150 **Children** Portions, Menu **Parking** 120

| TORQUAY | Map 3 SX96 |

Corbyn Head Hotel & Orchid Restaurant

@@@ – *see opposite page*

The Elephant Restaurant and Brasserie

@@@ – *see page 136*

Grand Hotel

@ Modern NEW

Fine local ingredients cooked with aplomb in characterful sea view hotel restaurant

☎ 01803 296677 📠 01803 213462
Torbay Rd TQ2 6NT
e-mail: reservations@grandtorquay.co.uk
dir: M5 junct 31, follow signs for Torquay. At the Penn Inn rdbt follow signs for seafront

Grand by name and by nature, this lordly Edwardian hotel sits smack in the middle of Torquay's seafront. Agatha Christie once had her own suite in the hotel, and the whiff of Empire still lingers in its grand lounges and public rooms. The Gainsborough restaurant is its fine dining venue, a spacious buzzy place with a soothing décor and efficient staff keeping things purring along smoothly. The kitchen team thinks local with its sourcing of produce, and deals in straightforward modern dishes, cooked with care to intensify flavours and presented without affectation. Slow-roast pork belly is served with white bean purée, chorizo and a cider reduction in a typical starter, followed by roast Exmoor venison, carrot purée, Anna potatoes and sloe gin jus.

Chef Richard Hunt **Owner** Keith Richardson **Times** 12.30-2.30/7-9.30 Closed L Mon-Sat **Prices** Fixed L 2 course fr £10.95, Fixed D 3 course fr £25, Starter £5.25-£7.95, Main £12.95-£17.95, Dessert fr £5.95 **Wines** 60 bottles over £20, 27 bottles under £20, 5 by glass **Notes** Sunday L, Vegetarian available, Dress restrictions, No shorts at D, Civ Wed 250 **Seats** 180, Pr/ dining room 200 **Children** Portions, Menu **Parking** 26, Station car park opposite

Corbyn Head Hotel & Orchid Restaurant

TORQUAY   Map 3 SX96

Modern British V

Superb views combine with first-class cooking

☎ 01803 296366 & 213611
📄 01803 296152
Sea Front TQ2 6RH
e-mail: dine@orchidrestaurant.net
web: www.orchidrestaurant.net
dir: Follow signs to Torquay seafront, turn right on seafront. Hotel on right with green canopies

There's an undeniable Riviera touch to this hotel with its jaunty lines and green canopied façade, and the views alone, stretching from Torquay to Berry Head at Brixham, are worth the visit. The formal fine-dining Orchid restaurant not only gets those amazing vistas framed in large half-moon picture windows from its first-floor vantage point, but the room is easy on the eye too, done out in creamy toffee hues with plush velvet seats and well-distanced linen-clothed tables. An unmistakably Gallic accent is present both in the politely correct service and the techniques at the foundations of the refined modern cuisine. The pick of local produce appears in dishes of elegant simplicity, showing the confident restraint of a mature kitchen team. Textures and flavours are in perfect balance in a tian of cock crab with sweetcorn velouté and Avruga caviar; next, a main course of

pork medallions, black pudding fritter, parsley potatoes and Dijon foam produces well-rested meat and well-paired ingredients. At dessert, kaffir lime leaves lend an Asian edge to a textbook crème brûlée, cleverly accompanied by a creamy coconut sorbet. All the peripheral bits and pieces such as amuse-bouche, breads and petits fours are produced with the same care as main courses, and the detailed wine list lays out an impressive spread with plenty of choice by the glass.

Chef Daniel Kay, Marc Evans
Owner Rew Hotels Ltd
Times 12.30-2.30/7-9.30 Closed 2 wks Jan, 2 wks Nov, 1 wk Apr, Sun-Mon, L Tue **Prices** Fixed L 2 course £20.95, Fixed D 3 course £37.95, Service optional **Wines** 47 bottles over £20, 65 bottles under £20, 11 by glass
Notes Vegetarian available, Vegetarian menu, Dress restrictions, Smart casual, Air con **Seats** 26 **Children** Portions, Menu **Parking** 50

TORQUAY *continued*

No 7 Fish Bistro

⊛ Mediterranean, European NEW

Unpretentious, friendly seafood bistro above the harbour

☎ 01803 295055
7 Beacon Ter TQ1 2BH
e-mail: paul@no7-fish.com
dir: Close to Royal Torbay Yacht Club & Imperial Hotel

With something of a Mediterranean feel, No. 7 Fish Bistro is in a terrace of properties overlooking Torquay's harbourside. Wooden floors, hardwood chairs and walls decked out with seafaring memorabilia and specials blackboards create a relaxed atmosphere. It's an unpretentious sort of place, family-run, with the freshest of daily-caught fish from local boats and markets driving the menu. Staff circulate a huge platter for diners to view before ordering. Simple treatment and presentation ensure the main ingredients are centre-stage; monkfish baked with black pepper and sea salt, or more Mediterranean-sounding sea bass (whole) grilled or roasted with olive oil, herbs and garlic. Non-fish eaters are also accommodated.

Chef Graham, Jill, Oliver & Paul Stacey **Owner** Graham & Jill Stacey **Times** 12.15-1.45/6-9.30 Closed 2 wks Xmas & New Year, Sun-Mon (Nov-May, also Sun Jun & Oct) **Prices** Starter £5.50-£9.75, Main £12.75-£25, Dessert £5-£6.50, Service optional, Groups min 6 service 10% **Wines** 20 bottles over £20, 16 bottles under £20, 12 by glass **Notes** Vegetarian available, Air con **Seats** 38 **Parking** Car park opposite

Orestone Manor Hotel & Restaurant

⊛ Modern British

Beguiling country house serving West Country produce

☎ 01803 328098 ▤ 01803 328336
Rockhouse Ln, Maidencombe TQ1 4SX
e-mail: info@orestonemanor.com
dir: From Teignmouth take A379, through Shaldon towards Torquay. 3m take sharp left into Rockhouse Lane. Hotel signed

With glorious views of the coastline and countryside from the stylish lounges and sun-trapped terrace of this delightful colonial-style country-house hotel, on warm summer days, you could almost believe you were in the Med. The elegant restaurant, decorated in bold colours, offers an innovative menu that takes full advantage of the wonderful seasonal, local larder, including fresh seafood and herbs, fruits and vegetables from Orestone's kitchen garden. Expect punchy flavours from dishes like thyme-roasted scallops served with braised leeks and caper butter, or perhaps pan-roasted duck accompanied by creamed potatoes, Chantenay carrots and beurre noisette.

Times 12-2/7-9 Closed 2-26 Jan

The Normandy Arms

⊛⊛ British, Mediterranean

Welcoming village pub with cooking that's getting seriously good

☎ 01803 712884 ▤ 01803 712734
Chapel St, Blackawton TQ9 7BN
e-mail: peter.alcroft@btconnect.com
dir: From Totnes follow A3188 for 9m, take A3122 (Dartmouth road). Right into Blackawton

The Normandy Arms retains the feel of a proper village pub, with slate floors, wooden tables and log-burning fires a cheering prospect in winter. Cooking is in the hands of the talented Peter Alcroft, who trained in the capital but has returned triumphantly to his roots. Dishes display a real understanding of flavour, respecting the quality of raw materials, thus a breakfast-themed starter dish comprises a cake of excellent black pudding with crushed potato and bacon, alongside a poached egg, in a glorious grain mustard sauce. Seasonal game makes for a fine main course, accompanied classically by a mixture of Savoy cabbage, chestnuts and bacon in a slightly sweet, but earthy, red wine jus. If you're in the market for fish, the must-have main course is a seafood medley en bouillabaisse with saffron potatoes and rouille.

Chef Peter Alcroft **Owner** Peter Alcroft, Sharon Murdoch **Times** 12-2/6.30-11 Closed 25-26 Dec, 2 wks winter

The Elephant Restaurant and Brasserie

Modern British 🍃

Contemporary harbourside restaurant with first-class food

☎ 01803 200044 ▤ 01803 202717
3-4 Beacon Ter TQ1 2BH
e-mail: info@elephantrestaurant.co.uk
dir: Follow signs for Living Coast, restaurant opposite

A certain Basil Fawlty has landed Torquay with a culinary reputation that is quite at odds with the Elephant's classy act. Behind its canary yellow Georgian façade the Elephant offers two levels of dining: a ground-floor brasserie is quite literally, the entry level, or ascend to the upstairs fine-dining restaurant - The Room. The brasserie offers a relaxed setting for sound, straightforward cooking at keen prices; braised beef with truffle and marrowbone bread pudding or good old fish and chips. Upstairs you get bay views and food of serious merit. At the helm is an accomplished chef who has served time under some of Europe's legendary names, and now delivers a punchy menu showcasing elegant technique and ambitious combinations. The sheer quality of West Country ingredients shines through in dishes such as a pan-roasted fillet of halibut on parsnip purée with spring onion and verjus butter sauce, or Devon beef filled with truffle and bone marrow with Jerusalem artichoke and cep mousse and shallot tart.

Chef Simon Hulstone **Owner** Peter Morgan, Simon Hulstone **Times** 7-9.30 Closed Jan, Sun-Mon, L all week **Prices** Fixed D 3 course £45, Service optional, Groups min 8 service 10% **Wines** 36 bottles over £20, 15 bottles under £20, 9 by glass **Notes** Tasting menu available, Vegetarian available, Air con **Seats** 24 **Parking** Opposite restaurant

period, Mon, L Tue-Sat, D Sun in winter **Prices** Starter £4.50-£7.95, Main £11.95-£18.95, Dessert £5.75-£6.95, Service optional **Wines** 12 bottles over £20, 26 bottles under £20, 6 by glass **Notes** Sunday L, Vegetarian available **Seats** 42 **Children** Portions, Menu **Parking** 4, On street

---

TWO BRIDGES   Map 3 SX67

Prince Hall Hotel

◉◉ British, European

Assured cooking in the heart of Dartmoor

☎ 01822 890403   📠 01822 890676
PL20 6SA
e-mail: info@princehall.co.uk
dir: On B3357 (Ashburton to Tavistock road), 1m E of Two Bridges junct with B3212

Approached by a beech-lined drive and surrounded by open moorland, tors and rivers, this traditional country-house hotel is set in the heart of Dartmoor National Park. Originally built as a private residence in 1787, it benefits from views across to the West Dart river. The stylish, intimate restaurant is hung with paintings from local artists, combining contemporary décor with country-house character. The kitchen impresses with well prepared, skilfully presented dishes using carefully sourced local produce. To start there might be ravioli of Brixham lobster and salmon with buttered baby spinach, chive beurre blanc and shellfish coulis, followed by roasted marinated rack of lamb with aromatic stirfry vegetables, horseradish and sesame potatoes, soy and lemongrass jus. To finish iced mocha parfait with coffee ice cream, cinnamon doughnut and espresso syrup hits the spot.

Chef Raoul Ketelaars **Owner** Fi & Chris Daly
Times 12-3/7-8.30 **Prices** Fixed L 2 course £12-£19, Fixed D 3 course £25-£37, Service optional, Groups min 10 service 10% **Wines** 15 bottles over £20, 20 bottles under £20, 6 by glass **Notes** Monthly tasting menu, Sunday L, Vegetarian available, Dress restrictions, Smart casual, Civ Wed 50 **Seats** 24 **Children** Portions **Parking** 12

Two Bridges Hotel

◉ Modern British **V**

Scenic moorland spot offering fine dining

☎ 01822 890581   📠 01822 890575/892306
PL20 6SW
e-mail: enquiries@twobridges.co.uk
dir: 8m from Tavistock on B3357, hotel at junct with B3312

This country house is a wonderful riverside retreat right in the heart of the Dartmoor National Park. It provides a choice of lounges and a traditional-style restaurant with oak panelling, linen tablecloths, great views and a young staff providing attentive service that is formal but very friendly. The seasonally-changing menu offers skilfully cooked British dishes, using quality local produce, with an emphasis on game. Start with salad of Torbay crabmeat with crème fraîche, Bloody Mary sorbet and crayfish. Venison is particularly good here so try the loin with port wine sauce, or go for sirloin of Dartmoor beef with wild mushroom ravioli, roast garlic dauphinoise and smoked bacon jus.

Chef Michael Palmer **Owner** Warm Welcome Hotels
Times 12-2/6.30-9.30 **Prices** Fixed L 2 course fr £14.95, Starter £5.50-£7.95, Main £14.95-£21.50, Dessert £5.50-£7.50, Service optional **Wines** 6 bottles over £20, 12 bottles under £20, 6 by glass **Notes** Sunday L, Vegetarian menu, Dress restrictions, Smart casual, No jeans, Civ Wed 120 **Seats** 85 **Children** Portions, Menu **Parking** 150

WOODBURY   Map 3 SY08

The Atrium Restaurant

◉ British

Golf and motor-racing themes in an expansive West Country retreat

☎ 01395 233382 & 234735   📠 01395 233384
Woodbury Park Hotel, & Golf, Woodbury Castle EX5 1JJ
e-mail: enquiries@woodburypark.co.uk
dir: M5 junct 30, take A376/A3052 towards Sidmouth, turn right opposite Halfway Inn onto B3180 towards Budleigh Salterton to Woodbury Common, hotel signed on right

Over 500 acres of Devon landscape surrounds the Woodbury Park Hotel, incorporating a PGA championship golf course. The place was formerly owned by Formula One ace Nigel Mansell, and still houses his collection of racing cars and trophies. In the glass-roofed restaurant, the walls are done in simmering claret, and the service is genuine and helpful, rather than austerely formal. The cooking scores some palpable hits, as in quail from the local estate, served gently pink and dressed with pesto. Grilled turbot might appear on truffled mash, with a wild mushroom and baby carrot fricassée, and meals conclude with the likes of bread-and-butter pudding or spiced blackberry mille-feuille.

Chef Matthew Pickett **Owner** Sue & Robin Hawkins
Times 12.30-2.30/6.30-9.30 Closed L Mon-Sat
Prices Starter £5.50-£9.50, Main £14.50-£22.95, Dessert

£5.50-£8.95, Service optional **Wines** 13 bottles over £20, 26 bottles under £20, 12 by glass **Notes** Sunday L, Vegetarian available, Dress restrictions, Smart casual, Civ Wed 150, Air con **Seats** 120, Pr/dining room 180 **Children** Portions **Parking** 350

WOOLACOMBE   Map 3 SS44

Watersmeet Hotel

◉ European

Rugged coastline setting for fine local cuisine

☎ 01271 870333   📠 01271 870890
Mortehoe EX34 7EB
e-mail: info@watersmeethotel.co.uk
dir: M5 junct 27. Follow A361 to Woolacombe, right at beach car park, 300yds on right

Once an Edwardian gentleman's residence, this elegant country-house hotel overlooks Woolacombe Bay, with steps leading right down to the beach. The Pavilion Restaurant has magnificent panoramic views across the waters of the bay to Hartland Point and Lundy Island. So expect candlelit dinners with spectacular sunsets (hopefully). Good-quality local produce, particularly fresh fish, is used to create well-balanced dishes such as Devon blue cheese and sun-blushed tomato roulade to start, followed by a medley of sea and shellfish with prawn sauce and wilted spinach. Save room for a fresh strawberry and clotted cream meringue dessert.

Times 12-2/7-8.30

YEALMPTON   Map 3 SX55

The Seafood Restaurant

◉ Seafood

Local catch served up in nautical setting

☎ 01752 880502   📠 01752 881058
Market St PL8 2EB
e-mail: enquiries@theseafood-restaurant.co.uk
web: www.theseafood-restaurant.co.uk
dir: A379 8m from Plymouth. A38 from Exeter, take A3121 through Ermington, turn right onto A379 towards Plymouth

This engaging restaurant has a nautical, beach hut style with whitewashed wood-panelled walls adorned with photographs of local fishing boats and harbours. The atmosphere is relaxed and informal, with attentive staff. There is a small bar area for pre-dinner drinks and an open-plan kitchen allows diners to watch the activity. Well-spaced, white-clothed tables and huge white plates give the restaurant a modern feel. Fish is clearly the main focus here, but not exclusively; Cornish red mullet with ratatouille and Serrano ham foam is a typical starter, and next up comes roast halibut with an octopus salad and bacon dressing, or lamb rump with spring vegetables and a thyme and mint jus. A gastro-pub, The Rose and Crown (just across the lane), has the same owners.

Times 12-2/6.30-9.30 Closed Sun & Mon

DORSET

BEAMINSTER — Map 4 ST40

BridgeHouse

◎ Modern British 🌿

Mixing traditional and modern in a medieval house

☎ 01308 862200 🖹 01308 863700
3 Prout Bridge DT8 3AY
e-mail: enquiries@bridge-house.co.uk
web: www.bridge-house.co.uk
dir: From A303 take A356 towards Dorchester. Turn right onto A3066, 200mtrs down hill from town centre

The stone-built former priest's house is 7 centuries old, and offers comfortable guest rooms and a range of dining possibilities, encompassing a conservatory, outdoor eating in a walled garden and the appealing, low-ceilinged Georgian dining room. A gentle style of rural cooking is on offer, with much use of traditional Dorset recipes. Watercress soup with a poached egg and a swirl of cream is a comforting opener, while mains deal in loin of lamb wrapped in Denhay ham and leeks, with artichoke gratin and saffron potatoes, in red wine jus. Go for variations on rhubarb for dessert, or perhaps red summer fruits marinated in Cointreau and black pepper, with clotted cream.

Chef Mrs Linda Paget, Mr Stephen Pielesz **Owner** Mark and Joanna Donovan **Times** 12-2.30/6.30-9.30 **Prices** Starter £6.50-£7.50, Main £19.50-£28, Dessert £6.25, Service added but optional 10%, Groups min 10 service 10% **Wines** 55 bottles over £20, 21 bottles under £20, 15 by glass **Notes** Sunday L, Vegetarian available, Civ Wed 50 **Seats** 36, Pr/dining room 30 **Children** Portions, Menu **Parking** 20

BOURNEMOUTH — Map 5 SZ09

Blakes@ Best Western The Connaught Hotel

◎ Modern British

Friendly, relaxed hotel restaurant serving imaginative cuisine

☎ 01202 298020 🖹 01202 298028
30 West Hill Rd, West Cliff BH2 5PH
e-mail: dining@theconnaught.co.uk
web: www.theconnaught.co.uk
dir: Please telephone for directions

Conveniently close to the beaches and the town centre, this friendly and relaxed, privately-owned hotel stands on the West Cliff and was built as a gentleman's residence in 1901. Blakes is an unpretentious-styled restaurant and delivers simply cooked and presented dishes from locally-sourced ingredients. Typical dishes may include ballotine of free-range chicken with red onion confit to start, with roast cod with mussel fricassée, or 28-day aged rib-eye steak with hand-cut chips and Café de Paris butter, for main course. Finish with iced banana parfait with toffee sauce.

Chef Jon Underwood, Thomas Lhermenier **Owner** Franklyn Hotels Ltd **Times** 6.30-9 Closed L Mon-Sat **Prices** Food prices not confirmed for 2010. Please telephone for details. **Wines** 6 bottles over £20, 24 bottles under £20, 9 by glass **Notes** Sunday L, Vegetarian available, Dress restrictions, Smart casual, no jeans or T-shirts, Civ Wed 150, Air con **Seats** 80, Pr/dining room 16 **Children** Menu **Parking** 66

Chine Hotel

◎ Modern British, European

Seaside hotel with sumptuous gardens

☎ 01202 396234 🖹 01202 391737
Boscombe Spa Rd BH5 1AX
e-mail: reservations@chinehotel.co.uk
dir: From M27, A31, A338 follow signs to Boscombe Pier. Boscombe Spa Rd is off Christchurch Rd near Boscombe Gardens

The Chine might be said to enjoy the best of two different worlds. It's a majestic house set in 3 acres of mature gardens, with stained-glass windows and burnished wood panelling within, and yet is also only a couple of minutes from Bournemouth's sandy beaches. Huge picture windows in the dining room look out over Poole Bay, with tables so arranged that no-one misses out. Shortish menus keep things simple, but the cooking shows care and thought, from seared scallops with carrot and ginger purée and a blood orange reduction, to slow-roast leg of lamb in port with rosemary potatoes and pancetta, and chocolate fondant with whisky ice cream to finish.

Chef Carl Munroe **Owner** Brownsea Haven Properties Ltd **Times** 12.30-2/7-9 Closed L Sat **Prices** Fixed L 2 course fr £12.50, Fixed D 3 course fr £25.95, Service optional **Wines** 21 bottles over £20, 8 bottles under £20, 10 by glass **Notes** Sunday L, Vegetarian available, Dress restrictions, No jeans, T-shirts or trainers at D, Civ Wed 120, Air con **Seats** 150, Pr/dining room 120 **Children** Portions, Menu **Parking** 55

Hermitage Hotel

◉ British

Unpretentious cooking in seafront hotel

☎ 01202 557363 🖷 01202 559173
Exeter Rd BH2 5AH
e-mail: info@hermitage-hotel.co.uk
dir: Follow A338 (Ringwood-Bournemouth) & signs to pier, beach & BIC. Hotel directly opposite

Occupying a splendid spot, this smart hotel is close to the seafront and opposite the pier right in the heart of Bournemouth. The lounge is suitably grand and the well-appointed dining room offers a regularly-changing menu featuring plenty of local produce. Among starters, local oysters and mussels come respectively with shallot vinegar and lemon and white wine, garlic and cream. Dishes can be as simple as avocado and pink grapefruit cocktail or as imaginative as pan-seared fillet of line-caught sea bass with spiced Puy lentils, wilted spinach and fennel cream sauce. The menu is sensibly concise - 6 or so dishes at each course - with bitter chocolate tart with clotted cream an indulgent finish.

Chef Paul Groves **Owner** Mr P D Oram
Times 12.30-2/6.15-9 Closed L Mon-Sat **Prices** Food prices not confirmed for 2010. Please telephone for details. **Wines** 12 bottles over £20, 40 bottles under £20, 8 by glass **Notes** Vegetarian available, Dress restrictions, No T-shirts or shorts, Air con **Children** Portions, Menu **Parking** 69

Highcliff Grill

◉ Modern British NEW

Contemporary dining with great views in a traditional hotel

☎ 01202 557702 🖷 01202 293155
Marriott Highcliff Hotel, St Michael's Rd, West Cliff BH2 5DU
e-mail: reservations.bournemouth@marriotthotels.co.uk
dir: Take A338 dual carriageway through Bournemouth, then follow signs for International Centre to West Cliff Rd, then 2nd R

Fashioned from an old Victorian seaside hotel dining room, the contemporary Highcliff Grill (in the smart though traditional Marriott Hotel) blows away any preconceived stuffy-and-starchy expectations, and, as its name suggests, there are cracking views over Bournemouth's coastline. Clean modern lines and colours

are the thing with banquette seating and chairs providing the comforts in a white-linen-free zone. The cooking continues the theme, modern but without over embellishment, taking its cue from quality ingredients on a crowd-pleasing repertoire. Gurnard fillet, for example, is served with braised fennel and a fragrant shellfish sauce, then maybe aged rib-eye steak and treacle tart for dessert.

Chef Eugene Cartwright **Owner** Marriott Hotels
Times 6-9.30 Closed L all week **Prices** Starter £5.50-£8.50, Main £9.50-£23.50, Dessert £5.95-£7.95, Service included **Wines** 43 bottles over £20, 13 bottles under £20, 13 by glass **Notes** Sunday L, Vegetarian available, Civ Wed 250, Air con **Seats** 80, Pr/dining room 14 **Children** Portions, Menu **Parking** 100

Langtry Restaurant

◉ Modern

Edwardian setting for some contemporary cooking

☎ 0844 3725 432 🖷 01202 290115
Langtry Manor, 26 Derby Rd, East Cliff BH1 3QB
e-mail: lillie@langtrymanor.com
dir: On East Cliff, at corner of Derby & Knyveton Roads

Built as a country house by Edward VII in 1877 for the actress Lillie Langtry, this stately manor brims with history and original features abound in the magnificent dining hall. A unique dining venue, oozing character with high ceilings, huge stained glass windows and Tudor tapestries, a grand fireplace, and a minstrels' gallery, it also hosts weekend gourmet Edwardian banquets. Sit on velvet chairs at linen-draped tables and choose from the seasonal carte, perhaps starting with pear and pork terrine with blue vinney fondue, followed by lamb rump with fondant potato and olive jus, with banana tarte Tatin with butterscotch sauce to finish.

Chef Matthew Clements **Owner** Mrs P Hamilton-Howard
Times 12-2/7-9 Closed L all week **Prices** Fixed D 3 course fr £32, Service optional **Wines** 25 bottles over £20, 30 bottles under £20, 5 by glass **Notes** Vegetarian available, Dress restrictions, Smart casual, Civ Wed 100 **Seats** 60, Pr/dining room 16 **Children** Portions, Menu **Parking** 20

The Print Room & Ink Bar & Brasserie

◉ Classic Brasserie ✆

Classic dishes served in busy brasserie

☎ 01202 789669 🖷 01202 554246
The Print Room & Ink Bar, & Brasserie, Richmond Hill BH2 6HH
e-mail: info@theprintroom-bournemouth.co.uk
dir: Town centre - located in landmark art deco listed Daily Echo newspaper building

An impressively huge art deco room is the venue for this restaurant and brasserie-style grand café housed in the Daily Echo's former print room. The brasserie is light and spacious with double-height windows, hanging lanterns lit with church candles and a mix of banquette seating and tables and chairs on the chequerboard-tiled floor. And with dining booths, brown-leather seating and a long zinc-topped bar, you can see why it has been described as the South Coast's answer to London's Wolseley. There's an authentic charcuterie bar, patisserie counter and partially open kitchen, plus an extensive menu offering breakfast and afternoon tea, with the main menu kicking off at noon and running until late. Expect classics like bouillabaisse with aïoli and garlic toast followed by Chateaubriand with pommes cocotte, turned vegetables, game chips and claret jus.

continued

BOURNEMOUTH *continued*

Chef Simon Trepess **Owner** Andy Price **Times** 12-5/5-11 Closed D 25-26 Dec, 1 Jan **Prices** Starter £4.50-£8.50, Main £8.75-£39, Dessert £5-£7.50, Service added but optional 10%, Groups min 8 service 10% **Wines** 80 bottles over £20, 40 bottles under £20, 14 by glass **Notes** Sunday L, Vegetarian available **Seats** 170, Pr/dining room 14 **Children** Portions, Menu **Parking** NCP - 100yds

The Upper Deck

◉ Modern British **NEW**

Panoramic sea views and modern cuisine at seaside hotel

☎ 01202 433093 🖷 01202 424228
Grange Hotel, 57 Overcliffe Dr, Southbourne BH6 3NL
e-mail: info@grangehotelbournemouth.co.uk
dir: Telephone for directions

The name is a big clue; housed in a new extension of this hotel and fashioned like a ship's upper deck, the restaurant comes with panoramic windows offering superb sea views. It's a modern open-plan space, decked out with black leather seating, unclothed tables and contemporary lighting, plus an intimate bar and a fantastic deck terrace to take in the sea air while you eat. The accomplished cooking sails a traditional course with a few modern twists and a focus on fresh seafood. Halibut might come with glazed Welsh rarebit, braised peas, beans and pancetta, or go for the show-boating fruits de mer platter, though there's plenty to keep meat-eater's happy here, too.

Chef Matthew Jones **Owner** Kay & Gordon Blakey **Times** 12-2/6-9 Closed Mon, D Sun **Prices** Fixed L 2 course £14.95-£16.95, Starter £5.25-£7.50, Main £10.50-£55, Dessert £5.50-£6.50, Service optional, Groups min 8 service 10% **Wines** 18 bottles over £20, 22 bottles under £20, 9 by glass **Notes** Sunday L, Vegetarian available, Dress restrictions, Smart casual, Civ Wed 60, Air con **Seats** 58 **Children** Portions

West Beach

◉◉ Modern

Buzzy beachfront setting for modern cooking

☎ 01202 587785 🖷 01202 298208
Pier Approach BH2 5AA
e-mail: enquiry@west-beach.co.uk
web: www.west-beach.co.uk
dir: 100yds W of the pier

Bournemouth has left behind its blue-rinse image and rebranded itself as a funky seaside hangout, snapping at the heels of über-cool Brighton along the coast. And right on the prom by the pier, not quite with its toes in the sands of the superlative beach, but as close as it gets when you're dining out on the wooden deck terrace, is this easy-going seafood-oriented modern restaurant. Inside, the stripped-out beachcomber-chic pastel shades and bleached wood almost fool you into thinking you could be in Oz, except that's Poole Bay out there through the vast floor-to-ceiling windows. Chefs are at work in the open kitchen, taking daily deliveries of fresh fish to create bright and simple, clearly-flavoured dishes. Start with Studland ceviche scallops, chargrilled red capsicum salsa and baby avocado, then perhaps whole baked sea bass with roast beetroot glazed with wild flower and vanilla honey.

Chef Ese Kousin **Owner** Andrew Price **Times** 9-5.30/6-10 Closed D 26 Dec, 1 Jan **Prices** Fixed L 2 course fr £12.90, Starter £5.50-£9.50, Main £7-£39.50, Dessert £3.50-£7.50, Service optional, Groups min 10 service 10% **Wines** 65 bottles over £20, 16 bottles under £20, 12 by glass **Notes** Tasting menu available, Sunday L, Vegetarian available, Dress restrictions, No bare feet or bikinis, Air con **Seats** 90 **Children** Portions, Menu **Parking** NCP 2 mins

Riverside Restaurant

◉ Seafood, International 🍷

The pick of local seafood in a great waterside setting

☎ 01308 422011 🖷 01308 458808
West Bay DT6 4EZ
e-mail: artwatfish@hotmail.com
web: thefishrestaurant-westbay.co.uk
dir: A35 Bridport ring road, turn to West Bay at Crown rdbt

A mile outside Bridport, on the Dorset coast at West Bay, this restaurant has been in the same family ownership since the swinging sixties. It's all bang up-to-date these days of course, and majors on impeccably fresh fish and seafood, lightly sauced and presented without undue fuss, as feels only right. Bountiful bouillabaisse, brill with spinach and sorrel sauce, and a sizeable portion of monkfish with ratatouille, chickpeas and chorizo are what to expect, as is warm, friendly service. Meat-eaters might opt for braised venison with pancetta, sauced in red wine and thyme. Treat yourself to buttermilk pannacotta with honeycomb to finish.

Chef N Larcombe, G Marsh, A Shaw **Owner** Mr & Mrs A Watson **Times** 12-2.30/6.30-9 Closed 30 Nov-14 Feb, Mon (ex BHs), D Sun **Prices** Fixed L 2 course £10-£16, Starter £4.50-£12.50, Main £11.50-£30, Dessert £4.25-£6, Service optional, Groups min 8 service 10% **Wines** 23 bottles over £20, 35 bottles under £20, 10 by glass **Notes** Sunday L, Vegetarian available **Seats** 70, Pr/dining room 30 **Children** Portions, Menu **Parking** Public car park close by

CHRISTCHURCH
Map 5 SZ19

Captain's Club Hotel

⊛⊛ Modern European

Contemporary riverside restaurant focusing on locally-sourced ingredients

☎ 01202 475111 📠 01202 490111
Wick Ferry, Wick Ln BH23 1HU
e-mail: enquiries@captainsclubhotel.com
web: www.captainsclubhotel.com
dir: Hotel just off Christchurch High St, towards Christchurch Quay

Built in 2007, this striking, contemporary-designed hotel stands on the edge of the River Stour. Step inside the boutique-styled interior to find chic bedrooms, a dramatic curved bar, deep sofas in swish lounges, and Tides Restaurant, a stylish dining space with a modern maritime theme and fabulous river views. Expect modern British cooking from a kitchen delivering simply cooked and presented dishes using top-notch ingredients, including plenty of local fish and seafood. Menus evolve with the seasons, a summer meal perhaps kicking off with succulent scallops served with earthy pork confit and a smooth pea purée, followed by moist, seared sea bass with rich ratatouille, crisp parmesan gnocchi and intensely flavoured bouillabaisse. To finish, there may be local gooseberries served with a creamy pannacotta. Service is slick, friendly and professional.

Chef Andrew Gault **Owner** Platinum One Hotels Ltd **Times** 12-2.30/7-10 **Prices** Fixed L 3 course £16-£25, Fixed D 3 course £25-£35, Starter £5-£8, Main £12-£22, Dessert £6-£7, Service optional **Wines** 90 bottles over £20, 35 bottles under £20, 14 by glass **Notes** Sunday L, Vegetarian available, Civ Wed 100, Air con **Seats** 72, Pr/dining room 44 **Children** Portions, Menu **Parking** 41

Christchurch Harbour Restaurant

⊛⊛ Traditional

Stylishly refurbished hotel restaurant with modern European cuisine

☎ 01202 483434 📠 01202 479004
95 Mudeford BH23 3NT
e-mail: christchurch@harbourhotels.co.uk
dir: A35/A337 to Highcliffe. Right at rdbt, hotel & restaurant 1.5m on left

After a multi-million pound makeover in 2008, this elegant Regency gentleman's residence came away with a spa and all mod cons to take on the 21st century. What hasn't changed are the superb views overlooking the mouth of the River Avon, seen in all their glory from the Harbour restaurant's Riviera-chic alfresco terrace. The menu offers a mixed bag of contemporary Anglo-Mediterranean ideas built around tried-and-tested flavour combinations - how about chicory tarte Tatin with home-made goats' cheese and soft herbs for starters, followed by rump and cutlet of Dorset lamb with redcurrant jelly, courgettes, pine nuts and yellow chanterelles. Desserts might offer spiced apple cake with apple risotto and toffee apple.

Chef Kevin Hartley **Owner** Harbour Hotels Group **Times** 12-2.30/6.30-9.30 **Prices** Starter £5.95-£8.95, Main £12.95-£18.95, Dessert £4.95-£5.50, Service optional **Notes** Sunday L, Vegetarian available, Civ Wed 120, Air con **Seats** 80, Pr/dining room 100 **Children** Portions, Menu **Parking** 70

Crooked Beam Restaurant

⊛ Modern British

Genuinely friendly welcome and plenty of old world charm

☎ 01202 499362
Jumpers Corner, 2 The Grove BH23 2HA
e-mail: info@crookedbeam.co.uk
web: www.crookedbeam.co.uk
dir: Situated on corner of Barrack Road A35 and The Grove

Yes, there are an awful lot of beams in the cosy interior of this super little neighbourhood restaurant, and at 300 years old and counting, the historic Crooked Beam is one of the oldest in Dorset. You get genuine service with a smile here from a sincere couple who work their socks off making everything on site and have recently opened a deli down the road selling home-made cakes, bread and biscuits as well as some of the restaurant dishes. Chef-proprietor Simon Hallam uses the best quality local produce in simple but effective dishes. The no-nonsense menu delivers vine tomato soup to start, and main courses such as well-cooked and rested pork tenderloin with bubble-and-squeak cake, nicely balanced by grain mustard sauce and a quenelle of apple purée. Much-lauded desserts might offer a raspberry crème brûlée with pistachio shortbread.

Chef Simon Hallam **Owner** Simon & Vicki Hallam **Times** 12-2/7-11 Closed Mon, L Sat, D Sun **Prices** Fixed L 2 course £12.95, Fixed D 3 course £21.95, Starter £4.95-£7.50, Main £14-£21, Dessert £5.95-£6.95, Service optional, Groups min 10 service 10% **Wines** 4 bottles over £20, 28 bottles under £20, 6 by glass **Notes** Sunday L, Vegetarian available, Dress restrictions, Smart casual, Air con **Seats** 80, Pr/dining room 20 **Children** Portions **Parking** 10, On street

CHRISTCHURCH *continued*

Kings Rhodes Brasserie

◉◉ Modern British NEW

Tapas-style or full dishes in a chic seaside setting

☎ 01202 483434 & 588938 📄 01202 479004
The Kings Hotel, 18 Castle St BH23 1DT
e-mail: restaurant@kings-rhodes.co.uk
web: www.kings-rhodes.co.uk
dir: Exit A35 onto Christchurch High St. Turn left at rdbt, restaurant 20m on left

Simple, flavour-packed eating is the ethos that launched a thousand brasseries in the 20th century, and Gary Rhodes' modern take on the theme can be found in the stylishly-renovated Kings Hotel. It's a delicious exercise in understated modish décor, all dark hardwood floors, muted colours, classy fabrics, and well-spaced linen-swathed tables laid with designer cutlery. The cooking stays simple and honest and true to the Rhodes brasserie style, while voguish tapas-style dishes encourage guests to share. Meat from the New Forest turns up, as does fish from Mudeford Quay and specialist French foods come from the Parisian Rungis market. A couple of starters from the tapas menu might yield roast parsnip soup with blue cheese crostini, and a cassoulet-style fried baby squid with white beans, air-dried cherry tomatoes and chorizo dressing. Resonant depth of flavour comes next in slow-roast belly pork with black pudding and three mustard sauce.

Chef James Watson **Owner** Harbour Hotels Group
Times 10-3/5.30-9.30 Closed 25-26 Dec **Prices** Fixed L course £15, Fixed D 3 course £16.50, Starter £4.95-£8.50, Main £9.50-£19.95, Dessert £6-£7, Service optional **Wines** 13 bottles over £20, 13 bottles under £20, 12 by glass **Notes** Sunday L, Vegetarian available, Air con **Seats** 70, Pr/dining room 50 **Children** Portions **Parking** 7

The Lord Bute & Restaurant

◉◉ British, European

Fine dining in historic surroundings

☎ 01425 278884 📄 01425 279258
179-185 Lymington Rd, Highcliffe-on-Sea BH23 4JS
e-mail: mail@lordbute.co.uk
web: www.lordbute.co.uk
dir: Follow A337 to Lymington, opposite St Mark's churchyard in Highcliffe

Named for an erstwhile resident and 18th-century Prime Minister, the Lord Bute Hotel sits behind the original entrance lodges of Highcliffe Castle, a stone's throw from the beach. Portraits of the many distinguished visitors to the castle welcome you in the entrance hall, and you can sip an aperitif out on the patio before settling into the stylish restaurant's high-backed black and gold chairs to the sounds of a live pianist or jazz band. Top-notch Dorset ingredients are the foundations of the kitchen's output; ambitious modern British food with an unmistakable French accent appears in a starter of braised chicken leg stuffed with pistachio and basil and served with butter bean and wild mushroom cassoulet and red wine foam, then perhaps Dorset brill wrapped around scallops with asparagus tips, smoked salmon and chervil cream.

Chef Kevin Brown **Owner** S Box & G Payne
Times 12-2/7-9.30 Closed Mon, L Sat, D Sun **Prices** Fixed L 3 course fr £16.95, Fixed D 3 course fr £31.95, Service optional **Wines** 28 bottles over £20, 32 bottles under £20, 6 by glass **Notes** Sunday L, Vegetarian available, Dress restrictions, Smart casual, no jeans or T-shirts, Air con **Seats** 95 **Children** Portions **Parking** 50

Rhodes South

◉◉ Modern British NEW

Eco-friendly quayside restaurant with stylish modern British cuisine

☎ 01202 483434 & 400950 📄 01202 479004
95 Mudeford BH23 3NJ
e-mail: reservationenquiries@rhodes-south.co.uk
dir: A35/A337 to Highcliffe. Right at rdbt, hotel & restaurant 1.5m on left

The Gary Rhodes brand has taken a contemporary eco-friendly slant with this classy new venture in the grounds of the Christchurch Harbour Hotel. The Baufritz-designed timber and glass building is the UK's first carbon positive restaurant, and makes the most of its waterside spot with glorious views over Mudeford Quay through floor-to-ceiling windows. The interior makes a subtle design statement with dark wood, black slatted chairs and white linen, while a feature window opens onto the world of the kitchen for diners' entertainment. The menu reflects the location with its fish and seafood choices, but deals equally in local meat and game dishes, with solid foundations in French technique as you'd expect from the Rhodes stable. Pan-fried red mullet is teamed interestingly with duck confit hash, fresh grapes and sauce Véronique to start, then perhaps pan-fried black bream taken upmarket with foam-capped lobster champ potatoes and lobster sauce.

Chef Darryl Wilder **Owner** Harbour Hotels Ltd
Times 12-2.30/6.30-10 Closed Xmas, Sun, Mon
Prices Fixed L 2 course £19.50, Starter £6.80-£12, Main £16-£22, Dessert £7-£8.50, Service optional **Wines** 55 bottles over £20, 2 bottles under £20, 13 by glass **Notes** Vegetarian available, Air con **Seats** 60 **Children** Portions **Parking** 40

Splinters Restaurant

@@ British, International

Family-run favourite with modern classics on the menu

☎ 01202 483454 🖨 01202 480180
12 Church St BH23 1BW
e-mail: eating@splinters.uk.com
dir: Directly in front of Priory gates

Look for the neat pastel-green frontage along the cobbled street leading to Christchurch Priory: this is Splinters Restaurant, a characterful Christchurch institution that deserves its place as a favourite local dining venue. Inside is a warren of separate dining areas with intimate booths and quiet corners for a romantic dinner à deux. Relax with an aperitif and canapés to nibble in the attractive bar-lounge, where a spiral staircase leads to the upstairs areas. A small kitchen team delivers a menu of modern classics, built on excellent local produce and daily deliveries of fish. Sea-fresh seared scallops with parsnip and vanilla purée, vermouth and saffron foam is a fine starter, followed by, perhaps, roast rump of Hampshire lamb with lamb breast gratin, rosemary and truffle polenta, pea and mint purée.

Chef Paul Putt **Owner** Paul & Agnes Putt
Times 11-2/7-10 Closed 26 Dec, 1-10 Jan, Sun-Mon
Prices Fixed L 2 course fr £11.95, Fixed D 3 course fr £25.95, Service included, Groups min 8 service 10%
Wines 105 bottles over £20, 37 bottles under £20, 5 by glass **Notes** ALC 2-3 course £31.95-£38.95, Vegetarian available, Dress restrictions, Smart casual **Seats** 42, Pr/dining room 30 **Children** Portions

---

CORFE CASTLE Map 4 SY98

Mortons House Hotel

@@ Traditional British

Fine Elizabethan manor with ambitious kitchen team

☎ 01929 480988 🖨 01929 480820
East St BH20 5EE
e-mail: stay@mortonshouse.co.uk
dir: In village centre on A351

Built in the shape of an 'E' to honour Queen Elizabeth I, this Tudor manor is nowadays a beautifully appointed hotel with attractive grounds and a serious restaurant. The large, panelled drawing room has bags of character, and furnishings and fabrics are traditional. Tables in the two dining areas are formally laid with crisp white-linen tablecloths and Villeroy and Boch crockery, and the service is both professional and affable. The chef takes good British produce, much of it local, to create dishes of some complexity, with the addition of the occasional Asian flavour. Confit of honey-glazed pork belly comes with langoustine and lime and chilli dressing as a starter, followed by roast wood pigeon with seared foie gras, truffled mash, braised salsify, chanterelles and thyme jus. Home-made bread demonstrates the seriousness of the enterprise, along with amuse-bouche (asparagus velouté, perhaps) and petits fours.

Chef Ed Firth **Owner** Mrs Hageman, Mr & Mrs Clayton
Times 12-1.45/7-9 **Prices** Fixed L 2 course £25-£30, Fixed D 3 course £30-£35, Service optional, Groups min 20 service 10% **Wines** 40 bottles over £20, 5 bottles under £20, 4 by glass **Notes** Sunday L, Vegetarian available, Dress restrictions, Smart casual preferred, Civ Wed 60 **Seats** 60, Pr/dining room 22 **Children** Portions, Menu **Parking** 40

CORFE MULLEN Map 4 SY99

The Coventry Arms

@ Modern British

Country pub with robust and refined menu of British favourites

☎ 01258 857284
Mill St BH21 3RH
dir: A31, 2m from Wimborne

The name of this popular village pub, a converted 15th-century watermill, idyllically situated by the river, has been changed with the 'Chop & Ale' moniker added to reflect alterations to the menu and range of beers. Inside,

it remains full of rustic, old-world charm with its original flagstone floors, large open fireplace, low ceilings and exposed beams. There's a choice of distinctive drinking and dining areas, and the fishing paraphernalia reflects the interests of the proprietor. The menu starts with a list of ales and ciders and moves on to an appealing range of mostly British dishes, such as devilled lambs' kidneys, rock oysters, a choice of steaks with various sauces, and braised belly pork with sage mash, green beans and port gravy.

Times 12-2.30/6-9.30

CRANBORNE Map 5 SU01

La Fosse at Cranborne

@ British **V** ✋

Well-judged traditionally based cooking in Thomas Hardy country

☎ 01725 517604
London House, The Square BH21 5PR
e-mail: lafossemail@gmail.com
dir: M3, M27 W to A31 to Ringwood. Left onto B3081 to Verwood, then Cranborne (5m)

A 16-century farmhouse that was once part of the Cranborne estate, in the midst of Thomas Hardy country, La Fosse has forged an elevated local reputation for itself, maintained and built on by its new owners, the Hartstones. The old-world cosiness of the restaurant, with its fine inglenook fireplace and stove, is a suitable setting for the cooking, which mixes English tradition (pan haggerty, piccalilli, pears poached in dandelion and burdock) with more contemporary flourishes. Strips of the estate's superb beef make a great starter in a salad with watercress and a well-judged oyster sauce dressing, and a seafood main course that pairs sea bass with crab manages richness and lightness all at once.

Chef Mark Hartstone **Owner** Mr & Mrs Hartstone
Times 12-3/6.30-9.30 Closed L Mon-Tue & Thu-Sat, D Tue-Thu & Sun **Prices** Fixed L 2 course £19.95, Fixed D 3 course £24.95, Service optional **Notes** Sunday L, Vegetarian menu **Seats** 25 **Children** Portions **Parking** On street

---

DORCHESTER Map 4 SY69

Sienna

@@@ – see page 144

Sienna

DORCHESTER	Map 4 SY69

Modern British

Pint-sized restaurant showcasing giant talent

☎ 01305 250022
36 High West St DT1 1UP
e-mail: browns@siennarestaurant.co.uk
dir: Near top of town rdbt in Dorchester

The Browns' high-street restaurant might look like a teashop from the outside, but that wholly belies the seriousness of its intent. Catering for just 15 covers, it's a classic two-hander, run out front by Elena Brown with grace and skill, while Russell cooks up a storm out back. The restful décor, with its eponymous colour scheme, helps to ensure a harmonious experience throughout. That is helped by cooking of rare directness and integrity - no head-scratching concept food here - and there is a palpable determination to get each dish absolutely right. It takes skill to make a starter of roast breast and confit leg of pigeon with broad beans so ethereally light, but so it is. Fish main courses, such as a double-bill of impeccable John Dory and the sweetest scallops, gently supported with a light-touch herb butter sauce, show up well, too. The invention doesn't flag at dessert stage, either, as witness in a stunning caramelised peach and tonka bean cheesecake with almond praline and peach sorbet. Incidentals such as bread, canapés and petits fours are all up to snuff.

Chef Russell Brown **Owner** Russell & Elena Brown **Times** 12-2/7-9 Closed 2 wks Feb/Mar, 2 wks Sep/Oct, Sun-Mon **Prices** Fixed L 2 course £21.50, Fixed D 3 course £39, Tasting menu £48.50, Service optional **Wines** 20 bottles over £20, 15 bottles under £20, 7 by glass **Notes** Tasting menu 6 course, Vegetarian available, Air con **Seats** 15 **Parking** Top of town car park, on street

---

Summer Lodge Country House Hotel, Restaurant & Spa

EVERSHOT	Map 4 ST50

Modern British

Sumptuous country-house chic in the depths of Dorset

☎ 01935 482000   📠 01935 482040
DT2 0JR
e-mail: summer@relaischateaux.com
web: www.summerlodgehotel.com
dir: 1.5m off A37 between Yeovil and Dorchester

The picturesque hotel in the heart of Dorset, partly designed by local author and architect Thomas Hardy (yes, that Thomas Hardy), offers the ideal rural retreat for getting away from it all. A former dower house, the luxurious hotel boasts delightful grounds and gardens and a sumptuous lounge with open fire. The design of the split-level restaurant is all about fabrics, fabrics and more fabrics. Soft furnishings are as tactile as they come and provide an impressive level of comfort representing an antithesis to the ubiquitous modern chic minimalism so often employed by refurbished country-house hotels these days. A conservatory area gives views of the 4-acre walled garden. Carefully presented dishes and assured cooking exhibit the kitchen's fine pedigree, with local Dorset produce used in abundance. The tasting menu, available with matching wines, may offer cannelloni of Cornish brill, tomato purée, samphire and champagne, while from the carte comes first-class loin of venison, served with Puy lentils, celeriac purée, a 'confit' of baby carrots and a truffle jus. The wine list has an excellent geographical spread and the sommelier offers sound advice.

Chef Steven Titman **Owner** Red Carnation Hotels **Times** 12-2.30/7-9.30 **Prices** Fixed L 2 course £22, Tasting menu £75-£125, Starter £13.50-£17.95, Main £21.50-£34.95, Dessert £9.50-£12.95, Service included, Groups min 12 service 12.5% **Wines** 1500 bottles over £20, 15 bottles under £20, 15 by glass **Notes** Tasting menu 8 course with selected wine, Sunday L, Vegetarian available, Dress restrictions, No shorts, T-shirts or sandals, Jackets pref, Civ Wed 30, Air con **Seats** 60, Pr/dining room 20 **Children** Portions, Menu **Parking** 60

EVERSHOT — Map 4 ST50

The Acorn Inn

◎ Traditional British

Picturesque village inn of literary legend focusing on local produce

☎ 01935 83228 📠 01935 83707
28 Fore St DT2 0JW
e-mail: stay@acorn-inn.co.uk
dir: 2m off A37, between Dorchester and Yeovil. In village centre

Thomas Hardy fans will be delighted to know that this 16th-century mellow stone Dorset coaching inn was the inspiration for 'The Sow and Acorn' in *Tess of the D'Urbervilles*. It certainly looks the essence of Wessex, nestling among the buxom hills of Hardy country, and you can picture the great author's cider-fuelled rustics among its exposed beams, flagstone floors, oak panelling and open fires. Stick with the bar menu if you prefer pubby cosiness, or trade up to more ambitious fare in the snug restaurant. Whichever you choose, the kitchen tries to source its materials from within a 25-mile radius, and serves hearty portions of modern British dishes that are easy on the eye. Smoked haddock and grain mustard chowder with poached egg and croûtons might precede roast breast of Barbary duck with red wine, black cherry and cinnamon sauce.

Chef Justin Mackenzie **Owner** Red Carnation Hotels **Times** 12-2/7-9 **Prices** Starter £4.50-£6.95, Main £10.95-£17.95, Dessert £4.95-£6.50, Service included **Wines** 13 bottles over £20, 13 bottles under £20, 8 by glass **Notes** Sunday L, Vegetarian available, Dress restrictions, Smart casual **Seats** 45, Pr/dining room 65 **Children** Portions **Parking** 40

Summer Lodge Country House Hotel, Restaurant & Spa

◎◎◎ — *see opposite page*

FARNHAM — Map 4 ST91

The Museum Inn

◎ Modern British

Gastro-pub with accomplished cooking and contemporary vibe

☎ 01725 516261 📠 01725 516988
DT11 8DE
e-mail: enquiries@museuminn.co.uk
dir: 12m S of Salisbury, 7m N of Blandford Forum on A354

The father of modern archaeology General Augustus Lane Fox Pitt Rivers had this solid inn of red brick and thatch built to put up visitors to his nearby museum. In the buzzy bar, the original stone-flagged floors and inglenook are still in place, but a tasteful makeover has lightened the tone, particularly in the Shed, a separate light-and-airy barn-like dining room. Wherever you choose to eat, service is low-key and relaxed, and you choose from the same menu. The cooking relies on the integrity of top-drawer locally-sourced produce: well-executed dishes in a modern British vein might include game terrine with tomato and courgette chutney, then black bream in a parsley and hazelnut crust with creamed cauliflower, sautéed ratte potatoes and leeks.

Chef Patrick Davy **Owner** David Sax **Times** 12-2/7-9.30 Closed D 25 Dec **Prices** Starter £6.50-£9.50, Main £14.50-£23.50, Dessert £6.50-£8, Service optional **Wines** 120 bottles over £20, 28 bottles under £20, 12 by glass **Notes** Sunday L, Vegetarian available **Seats** 80, Pr/dining room 30 **Children** Portions **Parking** 20

MAIDEN NEWTON — Map 4 SY59

Le Petit Canard

◎ Modern British, French

Impressive unfussy cooking in a pretty village restaurant

☎ 01300 320536 📠 01300 321286
Dorchester Rd DT2 0BE
e-mail: craigs@le-petit-canard.co.uk
web: www.le-petit-canard.co.uk
dir: In centre of Maiden Newton, 8m W of Dorchester

In summer this small but perfectly formed cottage restaurant becomes a focal point of the village when it is ablaze with flowers. Inside, exposed brickwork, low beams and a softly-lit palette of restful colours set a romantic tone, bolstered by the engaging charm with which husband-and-wife-team Cathy and Gerry Craig run their consistently impressive enterprise. Cathy runs front-of-house with plenty of smiles and a helpful approach, while Gerry's cooking evolves constantly to keep an edge of vitality to his repertoire of French and Asian-inflected modern British dishes. Perennial favourites include Dorset crab risotto with spring onions, parmesan and coriander, or roast breast of Barbary duck with oriental chilli and five spice sauce. Finish with a classic dark chocolate tart with vanilla ice cream.

Chef Gerry Craig **Owner** Mr & Mrs G Craig **Times** 12-2/7-9 Closed Mon, L all week (ex 1st & 3rd Sun in month), D Sun **Prices** Fixed D 3 course £31-£34, Service optional **Wines** 17 bottles over £20, 14 bottles under £20, 6 by glass **Notes** Sunday L, Vegetarian available, Dress restrictions, Smart casual preferred **Seats** 28 **Parking** On street/village car park

POOLE Map 4 SZ09

Harbour Heights Hotel

@ @ Modern British, French 🐾

Modern bistro with unbeatable harbour views

☎ 01202 707272 📠 01202 708594
Haven Rd, Sandbanks BH13 7LW
e-mail: enquiries@harbourheights.net
dir: From A338 follow signs to Sandbanks, restaurant on
left past Canford Cliffs

Built in the 1920s and completely renovated in 2003, this
popular hotel occupies a prominent and lofty position and
has spectacular views over Poole Harbour and Brownsea
Island. Floor-to-ceiling picture windows ensure diners at
the hotel's contemporary, open-plan brasserie don't miss
out. Expect skilfully prepared dishes conjured from quality
local ingredients. Start with native lobster ravioli with
tomato fondue and shellfish bisque, perhaps followed by
line-caught Weymouth sea bass with hot pot of white
beans and chorizo, or roast loin of local venison with
vanilla scented mashed potato, salsify purée with
elderflower, juniper, liquorice red wine sauce. Finish with
vanilla pannacotta with pear sorbet and cinnamon
shortbread.

Chef Stephane Jouan **Owner** FJB Hotels
Times 12-2.30/7-9.30 **Prices** Fixed L 2 course £15-
£19.50, Fixed D 2 course £20-£30, Starter £8.75-£10.95,
Main £15.50-£21.50, Dessert £4.80-£7, Service optional
Wines 155 bottles over £20, 6 bottles under £20, 28 by
glass **Notes** Sunday L, Vegetarian available, Dress
restrictions, Smart casual, Civ Wed 120, Air con **Seats** 90,
Pr/dining room 120 **Children** Portions, Menu **Parking** 80

Haven Hotel

@ @ Modern British **V** 🐾

Poole Bay setting for fine dining

☎ 01202 707333 📠 01202 708796
161 Banks Rd, Sandbanks BH13 7QL
e-mail: reservations@havenhotel.co.uk
dir: Follow signs to Sandbanks Peninsula; hotel next to
Swanage ferry departure point

Standing at the southernmost point of the Sandbanks
peninsular, this building overlooks the magnificent sweep
of Poole Bay. Once the home of radio pioneer Marconi, it
is now a well-established hotel with a waterside
restaurant, La Roche. Diners can choose from a seasonal
menu that features top-notch local produce, especially
fish and seafood, and, wherever possible, food from
sustainable sources, while enjoying breathtaking views.
Typical starters might include Poole Harbour rock oysters
with shallot vinegar, and main courses such as brill with
gnocchi, Dorset crab and purple sprouting broccoli, or
South Coast lobster grilled with garlic butter, Jersey Royal
potatoes and green salad. For more informal dining there
is also the Seaview Restaurant, and, in summer, alfresco
on the terrace.

Chef Damian Clisby **Owner** Mr J Butterworth
Times 12-2/7-9 Closed Xmas **Prices** Fixed L 2 course
£15-£22, Fixed D 3 course £20-£28, Starter £5-£12, Main
£14-£24, Dessert £6-£12, Service optional **Wines** 82
bottles over £20, 8 bottles under £20, 12 by glass
Notes Sunday L, Vegetarian menu, Dress restrictions, No
shorts or beach wear, Civ Wed 99, Air con **Seats** 80, Pr/
dining room 156 **Children** Portions, Menu **Parking** 90

Hotel du Vin Poole

@ Modern British, French NEW

**European bistro classics in a Georgian townhouse near
the waterfront**

☎ 01202 685666 📠 01202 665709
Thames St BH15 1JN
dir: A350 into town centre follow signs to Channel Ferry/
Poole Quay, left at bridge, 1st left is Thames St

Hotel du Vin have once again injected their designer
pizzazz into a handsome old building: this time an
elegant Georgian townhouse just off Poole's harbourfront
has got the masculine leather and wood makeover that is
the signature of the HDV chain. In its previous
incarnation as the Mansion House, the building had the
air of a gentleman's club, and the facelift has swept in a
more Gallic tone, a buzzier vibe and a more open, lighter
feel in the bistro. Wine buffs can salivate over the
expertly-chosen, French dominated list while youthful,
helpful staff serve modern bistro dishes, starting with a
hearty mutton broth with barley and parsley; the quality
of the raw materials shines in a main course roast breast
of wood pigeon with petits pois and red wine jus.

Chef Darren Rockett **Owner** Hotel Du Vin
Times 12.30-2/7-10 **Prices** Fixed D 3 course fr £37,
Service optional **Wines** 95 bottles over £20, 40 bottles
under £20, 10 by glass **Notes** Vegetarian available, Dress
restrictions, Smart casual, Civ Wed 35, Air con **Seats** 85,
Pr/dining room 36 **Children** Portions, Menu **Parking** 46

Sandbanks Hotel

@ Traditional European **V**

Vibrant beachside brasserie

☎ 01202 707377 & 709884 📠 01202 708885
15 Banks Rd, Sandbanks BH13 7PS
e-mail: reservations@sandbankshotel.co.uk
dir: From Poole or Bournemouth, follow signs to
Sandbanks Peninsula. Hotel on left along peninsula

The attractive terrace and garden have direct access to a
wonderful Blue Flag beach at this enviably positioned
waterside hotel, which is popular with both leisure and
business guests. Dining options include the informal and
vibrant Sand Brasserie, which draws the crowds for its
beachside position, and the new octagonal Sea View
Restaurant, which affords panoramic views across Poole
Bay and the Purbeck Hills. In the Brasserie, expect
modern variations on classical themes: a starter of

seared pigeon with chorizo and cannellini beans for example, followed by line-caught sea bass with baby spinach and curried mussels, and apple and frangipane tart with Calvados ice cream.

Sandbanks Hotel

Chef Paul Harper **Owner** Mr J Butterworth
Times 12-3/6-10 Closed Mon-Tue, D Sun **Prices** Fixed L 2 course £18, Fixed D 3 course £25, Starter £6.50-£9.50, Main £13.50-£19, Dessert £6-£6.90, Service optional **Wines** 73 bottles over £20, 10 bottles under £20, 17 by glass **Notes** Sunday L, Vegetarian menu, Dress restrictions, No jeans, smart casual, Civ Wed 80, Air con **Seats** 65, Pr/dining room 25 **Children** Portions, Menu **Parking** 130

PORTLAND — Map 4 SY67

The Bluefish Restaurant

◉ Modern European 🍃

Flavourful cooking a stone's throw from Chesil Beach

☎ 01305 822991   🖹 01305 822203
15-17a Chiswell DT5 1AN
e-mail: thebluefish@tesco.net
dir: Take A354 by Chesil Bank, off Victoria Square in Portland, over rdbt towards Chesil Beach, next to 72hr free car park

Below the stunning shingle bank that forms Chesil Beach is this simple and unpretentious restaurant. It's on the ground floor of a sturdy property built from the famous local Portland stone. Dine in one of the two interconnecting dining rooms under twinkling lights from ceiling spots and tea-lights dotted around, or go alfresco in the summer. Great food is prepared with minimal fuss for maximum benefit. With the sea just a stone's throw away, the modern European menu offers plenty of fish and seafood, but there are good meat choices, too. Expect baked Serrano ham with spinach, duck egg and parmesan cream, followed by fillet of local cod with citrus and fennel risotto and aubergine caviar.

Chef Luciano Da Silva **Owner** Jo Da Silva
Times 12-3/6.45-9 Closed Mon & Tue, L Wed-Fri, D Sun (in Winter) **Prices** Fixed L 2 course £10, Fixed D 3 course £20-£23, Starter £4.50-£9.95, Main £10.50-£19, Dessert £5.50-£6.50, Service optional, Groups min 8 service 10% **Wines** 2 bottles over £20, 12 bottles under £20, 9 by glass **Notes** Sunday L, Vegetarian available **Seats** 45 **Children** Portions **Parking** 72-hr free car park

SHAFTESBURY — Map 4 ST82

The Byzant

◉ Modern British 🍃

Appealing menu in picture-postcard Dorset

☎ 01747 853355   🖹 01747 851969
Best Western Royal Chase Hotel, Royal Chase Roundabout SP7 8DB
e-mail: royalchasehotel@btinternet.com
dir: On rdbt at A350 & A30 junction (avoid town centre)

A busy country hotel in picture-postcard Dorset dates partly from Tudor times, and was once a monastery. Guests are well looked after by a small team of friendly staff, and the Byzant restaurant, which is divided into two separate areas, makes for elegant surroundings. Duck liver parfait is luxuriously smooth and comes with red onion marmalade and brioche, and a main course like pork loin medallions on bubble-and-squeak with a black pudding and bacon fritter, sauced with cider, makes the most of traditional British components. Pannacotta is gently enriched with white chocolate, sauced with dark chocolate and garnished with strawberries, to make a satisfying finale.

Chef Charlie Patterson **Owner** Travel West Inns
Times 12-2/7-10 **Prices** Starter £4.95-£7.95, Main £8.95-£19.95, Dessert £4.95-£7.95, Service included **Wines** 20 bottles over £20, 37 bottles under £20, 6 by glass **Notes** Sunday L, Vegetarian available, Civ Wed 150 **Seats** 49, Pr/dining room 150 **Children** Portions, Menu **Parking** 101

Le Chanterelle

◉ French, British NEW

Ambitious Anglo-French cooking

☎ 01747 852821
Sherborne Causeway SP7 9PX
e-mail: lamb_chef@yahoo.co.uk
dir: On A30 from Shaftesbury to Yeovil

The 18th-century character of this former cottage has been retained following refurbishment, with exposed stone walls and a large fireplace enhancing the atmosphere. Le Chanterelle is a welcoming, family-run restaurant, with a highly committed team in the kitchen producing an ambitious menu from scratch. Everything from the bread to the pre-dessert is made with passion and flair, and inspiration is drawn from both Britain and France. Hand-dived scallop tarte Tatin, creamed leeks, crispy sorrel and tarragon and crayfish oil, and ballotine of wood pigeon stuffed with foie gras, confit of the legs,

creamed ceps fricassee and morel jus are two typically complex dishes which border on the overpowering, with too many flavours. Cheese is taken seriously with an excellent local and French selection.

Chef Ryan Lamb **Owner** Susan Lamb **Times** 12-3/7-9.30 Closed Mon-Tue **Prices** Food prices not confirmed for 2010. Please telephone for details. **Wines** 35 bottles over £20, 15 bottles under £20, 9 by glass **Notes** Sunday L, Dress restrictions, Smart casual **Seats** 32 **Children** Portions

La Fleur de Lys Restaurant with Rooms

◉◉ French, European

Smart restaurant with rooms serving imaginative Anglo-French dishes

☎ 01747 853717   🖹 01747 853130
Bleke St SP7 8AW
e-mail: info@lafleurdelys.co.uk
dir: Junct A350/A30

This welcoming town-centre restaurant with rooms offers modern Anglo-French cuisine in a charming setting. The elegant L-shaped dining room is softly lit for dinner, with tables clothed in linen and laid with classy Villeroy & Boch china. Soundly-sourced seasonal ingredients are used to good effect in well-presented dishes, with some imaginative combinations. A hot scallop tartlet is paired with a rich and lemony sorrel sauce to start, then a nicely pink saddle of Dorset lamb is served on spinach and chanterelles in a creamy thyme sauce. Dessert delivers an unusual, but successful, take on a crème brûlée - prepared with lemon and pistachios.

Chef D Shepherd & M Preston **Owner** D Shepherd, M Preston & M Griffin **Times** 12-2.30/7-10.30 Closed 3 wks Jan, L Mon & Tue, D Sun **Prices** Fixed L 2 course £23-£24, Fixed D 3 course fr £29, Starter £7-£11, Main £18-£26, Dessert £6-£9, Service optional **Wines** 180 bottles over £20, 20 bottles under £20, 8 by glass **Notes** Sunday L, Vegetarian available, Dress restrictions, Smart casual, No T-shirts or dirty clothes **Seats** 45, Pr/dining room 12 **Children** Portions **Parking** 10

SHERBORNE — Map 4 ST61

Eastbury Hotel

◉◉ Modern British

Assertive cooking in a well-run townhouse hotel

☎ 01935 813131 📠 01935 817296
Long St DT9 3BY
e-mail: enquiries@theeastburyhotel.com
dir: 5m E of Yeovil, follow brown signs for The Eastbury Hotel

A townhouse hotel in the heart of Sherborne, the Eastbury adopts a gently traditional approach. The principal room for dining is the conservatory, which looks out over a dramatically lit lawn and walled kitchen garden, the latter supplying some of the vegetables. Otherwise, West Country produce is what it's about, in a cooking style that is gutsy and assertive, with high-impact flavours, but a lightness of touch too - an impressive balancing act. Seared pigeon breast in a lasagne with celeriac and wild mushrooms is an enterprising first course, and could be followed by plaice fillets wadded with potato and basil mousse, on a fricassée of artichokes and sprouting broccoli. Finish with pineapple, sliced carpaccio-thin, topped with iced mango and coconut jelly, and dressed in passionfruit syrup. The range of excellent home-made breads is fully worthy of mention too.

Chef Brett Sutton **Owner** Mr & Mrs P King
Times 12-2/7-9.30 **Prices** Fixed L 2 course £12-£18, Fixed D 3 course £33, Service optional **Wines** 61 bottles over £20, 30 bottles under £20, 12 by glass **Notes** Vegetarian available, Civ Wed 80 **Seats** 40, Pr/dining room 12 **Children** Portions, Menu **Parking** 20

The Grange at Oborne

◉ Modern British NEW

Confident cooking in country-house hotel with gardens

☎ 01935 813463 📠 01935 817464
Oborne DT9 4LA
e-mail: reception@thegrange.co.uk
dir: From A30 turn left at sign & follow road through village to hotel

Just one mile from the historic town of Sherborne, this privately-owned hotel occupies a 200-year-old country house with attractive gardens. The candlelit restaurant is comfortably appointed with views of the floodlit garden and fountain from the large Georgian windows. In the kitchen, locally sourced produce is used with care and the

seasonal menu might include salmon and prawn terrine with home-cured gravad lax, cucumber and dill relish, citrus mascarpone, followed by pan-fried medallions of wild boar, roasted garlic, spinach, creamed potato, juniper and port wine sauce. Finish with one of the comforting puddings from the dessert trolley.

Chef Nick Holt **Owner** Mr & Mrs K E Mathews
Times 12-1.30/7-9 Closed D Sun **Prices** Fixed L 2 course £20-£28, Fixed D 3 course £34-£39, Service optional **Wines** 18 bottles over £20, 24 bottles under £20, 5 by glass **Notes** Sunday L, Vegetarian available, Dress restrictions, Smart casual, Civ Wed 120 **Seats** 30, Pr/dining room 120 **Children** Portions **Parking** 50

The Green

◉ Modern British

Laid-back stylishness near Sherborne Abbey

☎ 01935 813821 📠 01935 813821
3 The Green DT9 3HY
e-mail: green.restaurant@tiscali.co.uk
dir: A30 towards Milborne Port, at top of Greenhill turn right at mini rdbt. Restaurant located on the left

A laid-back but stylish atmosphere has been created here, with aged oak tables and wide-boarded oak floors in an attractive greystone building not far from the abbey. A lengthy list of local suppliers furnishes the kitchen with everything from Creedy Carver ducks to Somerset cider brandy, and the modern British cooking has an eye for bright combinations. Ilminster salsify, spinach, new potatoes and roasted red pepper dressing make a great mix of accompaniments for a main-course fillet of brill, and nice contrasts of sweet and sharp, in the forms of Longburton wild honey and rhubarb, enliven a pannacotta dessert.

Chef Michael Rust **Owner** Michael & Judith Rust
Times 12-2/7-9 Closed 2 wks Jan,1 wk Jun,1 wk Sep, BHs, Xmas, Sun-Mon **Prices** Fixed D 3 course £32.50, Starter £4.75-£7, Main £8.50-£14.95, Dessert £2.75-£6.50, Service optional, Groups min 10 service 10% **Wines** 19 bottles over £20, 31 bottles under £20, 12 by glass **Notes** Vegetarian available **Seats** 40, Pr/dining room 25 **Parking** On street, car park

TARRANT MONKTON — Map 4 ST90

The Langton Arms

◉ Modern British

Modern cooking in attractive village pub

☎ 01258 830225 📠 01258 830053
DT11 8RX
e-mail: info@thelangtonarms.co.uk
dir: exit A354 for Tarrant Hinton towards Tarrant Monkton, continue through ford, pub directly ahead

Occupying a peaceful spot close to the village church, this attractive thatched 17th-century inn comprises a small bar-restaurant and an airy conservatory in a converted stable overlooking beautiful countryside that Thomas Hardy made famous. The contemporary cuisine

takes in Mediterranean and oriental influences, and locally smoked produce features prominently on the menu. Start with smoked haddock, prawn and leek gratin and move on to herb-crusted fillet of cod with wilted spinach and a Noilly Pratt velouté or rump of marinated lamb, chargrilled and served with parsnip purée and red wine sauce. Desserts include Grand Marnier crème brûlée.

Chef Siôn Harrison **Owner** Barbara & James Cossins
Times 12-2.30/7-12 Closed 25 Dec **Prices** Fixed L 2 course £14-£30, Fixed D 3 course £18-£40, Starter £4.95-£13, Main £9.95-£30, Dessert £4.95-£7.50, Service optional **Wines** 10 bottles over £20, 15 bottles under £20, 7 by glass **Notes** Sunday L, Vegetarian available, Civ Wed 60 **Seats** 40, Pr/dining room 24 **Children** Portions, Menu **Parking** 100

WAREHAM — Map 4 SY98

Kemps Country House

◉ Traditional International

Country-house dining in the heart of Thomas Hardy country

☎ 0845 8620315 📠 0845 8620316
Kemps Country House, East Stoke BH20 6AL
e-mail: info@kempscountryhouse.co.uk
web: www.kempshotel.com
dir: A352 between Wareham and Wool

Surrounded by unspoilt Dorset countryside, this charming former Victorian rectory has been sympathetically refurbished to a high standard. Dinner is served in the delightful, spacious restaurant, adjoining the conservatory which overlooks the garden; alfresco dining is available in the summer, while welcoming log fires protect against the chill at colder times of the year. The table d'hôte dinner menu delivers fine dining, country-house style dishes, starting, perhaps, with a garden pea risotto, parmesan and pea shoots, following on with some Dorset lamb (roast rump with Provençal vegetables, mashed potato and rosemary sauce), while classic peach Melba is an appealing finale.

Times 12-3/6.30-9.30

WEYMOUTH
Map 4 SY67

Moonfleet Manor

◎◎ Modern British

Vibrant cooking in a peaceful coastal hotel

☎ 01305 786948 📠 01305 774395
Fleet DT3 4ED
e-mail: info@moonfleetmanor.com
dir: A354 from Dorchester, right into Weymouth at Manor Rdbt, right at next rdbt, left at next rdbt, up hill (B3157) then left, 2m towards sea

Overlooking Chesil Bay, this charming Georgian house at the end of the village of Fleet is especially popular with families, with children actively welcomed throughout the sea-facing hotel. The airy restaurant is a relaxed and informal venue staffed by a friendly and attentive waiting team, who deliver appealing dishes of acclaimed modern British cuisine. Start with a carpaccio of monkfish with marinated crayfish tails, cucumber and avocado salad, before tucking into roasted breast of guinea fowl with an open ravioli of wild mushrooms and asparagus, pea purée and thyme foam, and desserts such as warm ginger bread pudding with caramel sauce and lemongrass ice cream.

Times 12.30-2/7-9.30

Perry's Restaurant

◎ British, French

Fresh seafood and more by the harbour

☎ 01305 785799 📠 01305 787002
4 Trinity Rd, The Old Harbour DT4 8TJ
e-mail: perrysrestaurant@hotmail.co.uk
dir: On western side of old harbour - follow signs for Brewers Quay

The harbourside location defines the character of Perry's and gives easy access to wonderfully fresh seafood landed by small day boats. The menu is not exclusively given over to the fruits of the sea, with meat and vegetarian dishes much more than mere footnotes. Service is helpful but not pushy, and the room is comfortably furnished with plenty of Georgian features. Warm salmon mousse with lemon, caper and dill sauce is a well-judged first course, and main-course fillets of turbot with a lemon and butter sauce and a crab cake displays good balance of flavours. The excellent wine list is well worth exploring.

Chef Andy Pike **Owner** Matt & Liz Whishaw
Times 12-2/7-9.30 Closed 25-27 Dec, 1 Jan, Mon (winter), L Mon (summer), D Sun (winter) **Prices** Fixed L 2 course fr £12.95, Starter £4.95-£8.50, Main £11.95-£19.95, Dessert £5.50-£7.95, Service optional, Groups min 8 service 10% **Wines** 132 bottles over £20, 42 bottles under £20, 12 by glass **Notes** Sunday L, Vegetarian available **Seats** 60, Pr/dining room 36 **Children** Portions **Parking** On street or Brewers Quay car park (200yds)

WIMBORNE MINSTER
Map 5 SZ09

Les Bouviers Restaurant with Rooms

◎◎ Traditional French

Restaurant with rooms offering a taste of France

☎ 01202 889555 📠 01202 639428
Arrowsmith Rd, Canford Magna BH21 3BD
e-mail: info@lesbouviers.co.uk
dir: 1.5m S of Wimborne on A349, turn left onto A341. In 1m turn right into Arrowsmith Rd. 300yds, 2nd property on right

This smart restaurant with rooms is ideally placed to take in the pick of local Dorset farm produce and fish landed in nearby Poole harbour. Five acres of peaceful grounds, landscaped with a lake and stream, give the impression that you are deep in the countryside, yet Wimborne and Bournemouth are only a short drive away. Bold tones of burgundy and gold and a fair sprinkling of modern art make for an opulently eclectic country-house ambience. A clear French influence with hints of the Mediterranean drives the kitchen's style on a repertoire of fixed-price menus offering a wide choice. Expect multi-faceted dishes like pan-fried scallops with spiced butternut squash purée, dried Parma ham and a balsamic reduction, or venison loin in a herb crust with fondant potato, braised shallots and carrot tarte Tatin.

Chef James Coward **Owner** James & Kate Coward
Times 12-2.15/7-9.30 Closed D Sun **Prices** Fixed L 2 course £16.95-£18.95, Fixed D 4 course £29.95-£31.95, Tasting menu £68, Service optional, Groups min 7 service 10% **Wines** 100+ bottles over £20, 100+ bottles under £20, 24 by glass **Notes** Tasting menu 7 course (incl wine), Sunday L, Vegetarian available, Dress restrictions, No jeans or shorts, Civ Wed 100, Air con **Seats** 50, Pr/dining room 150 **Children** Portions, Menu **Parking** 50

See advert below

CO DURHAM

BEAMISH — Map 19 NZ25

Beamish Park Hotel

Modern International

Inventive food against a thoroughly modern backdrop

☎ 01207 230666 ▤ 01207 281260
Beamish Burn Rd NE16 5EG
e-mail: reception@beamish-park-hotel.co.uk
web: www.beamish-park-hotel.co.uk
dir: A1 junct 63 onto A693 Stanley. Exit rdbt onto A6076, hotel 2m on right

Close by Beamish's famous open air museum, this modern hotel enjoys great hillside views. The conservatory dining room is a sight to see, with a modern brasserie feel, the walls stacked high with diverting pictures and some fabulous furry curtains. Classic dishes underpin the imaginative menus, and the kitchen is provisioned by its own garden as well as by blue-chip local suppliers. Home-made black pudding with a poached egg and spicy gravy is one way to set about the menu, or head towards the outer shores where rice dough balls with peanuts, watermelon and tomato chilli jam await. An up-to-date spin on fish, chips and mushy peas chimes well with the surroundings, while cakes such as rhubarb or lemon, served with ice creams of one sort or another, make for a fine finish.

Chef Christopher Walker **Owner** William Walker
Times 12-2.30/7-10.30 **Prices** Starter £4.95-£8.50, Main £10-£18, Dessert £5.25-£7, Service optional **Wines** 7 bottles over £20, 17 bottles under £20, 7 by glass **Notes** Sunday L, Vegetarian available, Dress restrictions, Smart casual preferred, Civ Wed 100, Air con **Seats** 70, Pr/dining room 150 **Children** Portions **Parking** 100

DARLINGTON — Map 19 NZ21

Hansard's

British NEW V

Contemporary cooking in 12th-century castle hotel

☎ 01325 485470 ▤ 01325 462257
Best Western Walworth Castle Hotel, Walworth DL2 2LY
e-mail: enquiries@walworthcastle.co.yk
dir: A1 junct 58, follow A68 Corbridge for 1m. At rdbt keep left for 1m

Located within a 12th-century castle, Walworth Castle Hotel is set in the rolling countryside of the Tees valley, just to the west of Darlington and close to the A1(M) in County Durham. The comfortable rooms are matched by the sensitively refurbished 16th-century dining room, which offers contemporary dishes in a traditional setting. A starter of roast duckling breast with parsnip purée and fresh fig dressing might be followed by poached fillet of cod with prawns, boulangère potatoes and broccoli. Finish with a trio of rhubarb. More informal dining is offered in the pubbier Farmer's Bar.

Chef Steven Myers, Claire Wilson **Owner** Chris Swain & Rachel Swain **Times** 12-2/7-9.30 Closed L Mon-Sat **Prices** Food prices not confirmed for 2010. Please telephone for details. **Wines** 11 bottles over £20, 25 bottles under £20, 5 by glass **Notes** Sunday L, Vegetarian menu, Civ Wed 120 **Seats** 45, Pr/dining room 20 **Children** Portions, Menu

Headlam Hall

British, French

Modern cooking served in a Jacobean hall

☎ 01325 730238 ▤ 01325 730790
Headlam DL2 3HA
e-mail: admin@headlamhall.co.uk
dir: 8m W of Darlington off A67

Headlam Hall is the archetypal Jacobean manor house, surveying its expansive Cumberland estate across lovely walled gardens. Of course, like many a country house it has moved with the times and offers modern diversions with its 9-hole golf course and spa complex. The restaurant spreads itself around four areas with different moods, encompassing an Orangery conservatory, a stately panelled room, and a Victorian-style space with bold green walls and gilt mirrors. The hall's own gardens supply produce in season for menus based around French and British classics spiced up with flashes of innovative ambition. Expect the likes of pink bream fillet with lemon and sun-blushed tomato couscous and red pepper oil, then crispy breast of Gressingham duck with duck leg hash, carrot purée and black cherry sauce.

Chef Austen Shaw, David Hunter **Owner** J H Robinson
Times 12-2.30/7-9.30 Closed 25-26 Dec **Prices** Fixed L 2 course £12-£20, Starter £5-£9, Main £12-£25, Dessert £4-£6, Service optional **Wines** 25 bottles over £20, 30 bottles under £20, 10 by glass **Notes** Sunday L, Vegetarian available, Dress restrictions, Smart casual, No shorts, Civ Wed 150 **Seats** 70, Pr/dining room 30 **Children** Portions, Menu **Parking** 70

DURHAM — Map 19 NZ24

Bistro 21

Modern British, European V

Stylish bistro with appealing menu

☎ 0191 384 4354 ▤ 0191 384 1149
Aykley Heads House, Aykley Heads DH1 5TS
e-mail: admin@bistrotwentyone.co.uk
web: www.bistrotwentyone.co.uk
dir: Off B6532 from Durham centre, pass County Hall on right & Dryburn Hospital on left. Turn right at double rdbt into Aykley Heads

A rustic French provincial look - whitewashed walls, wooden and stone floors, an inner courtyard and a vaulted bar - sums up this cracking bistro set in a restored 18th-century former farmhouse. Cooking is modern bistro-style and dishes are simple but accurately cooked with clean, clear flavours. Take a pigeon breast salad with spiced pears or fried squid with chilli jam to start, with fishcakes with chips and parsley cream, slow-cooked pork belly with green lentils and braised chicory, or best end of lamb with ratatouille for main course. Puddings like Pimms jelly with spearmint ice cream and summer pudding complete the picture.

Chef Tom Jackson **Owner** Terence Laybourne
Times 12-2/7-10.30 Closed 25 Dec, 1 Jan, BHs, D Sun
Prices Fixed L 2 course fr £15, Fixed D 3 course fr £18, Starter £5.50-£10.50, Main £14.50-£22, Dessert £6-£8.50, Service added but optional 10% **Wines** 48 bottles over £20, 13 bottles under £20, 7 by glass **Notes** Early D menu available, Vegetarian menu **Seats** 55, Pr/dining room 20 **Children** Portions **Parking** 11

ROMALDKIRK Map 19 NY92

Rose & Crown Hotel

◉◉ Traditional British

Cosy upmarket country inn in a quintessentially English setting

☎ 01833 650213 📠 01833 650828
DL12 9EB
e-mail: hotel@rose-and-crown.co.uk
dir: 6m NW of Barnard Castle on B6277

The Rose & Crown is one of those exemplary inns that works on all levels. First, there's its setting in a chocolate box Teesdale village complete with stocks, water pump and Saxon church. Fancy a pint? Then the cosy, creaky bar serves well-kept ale next to a crackling log fire. But it's true to say that most guests are here for the food, served in either an informal brasserie ambience or a handsome oak-panelled restaurant, romantically candlelit and decked with starched white linen and gleaming silvery cutlery. Dishes are simply conceived and showcase clear-flavoured classic British cuisine with regional influences. A four-course dinner might typically start with Cotherstone cheese soufflé with gazpacho sauce, then slot in a courgette and sweet pear soup, before a main course of pan-fried mallard breast with creamed celeriac tartlet and green peppercorn sauce. Go for home-made Amaretto ice cream or Northumberland cheeses to finish.

Chef Chris Davy, Andrew Lee **Owner** Mr & Mrs C Davy **Times** 12-1.30/7.30-9 Closed Xmas, L Mon-Sat **Prices** Fixed L course £17.95, Fixed D 4 course £30-£36, Service optional **Wines** 46 bottles over £20, 20 bottles under £20, 14 by glass **Notes** Sunday L, Vegetarian available **Seats** 24 **Children** Portions **Parking** 24

SEAHAM Map 19 NZ44

The Ozone Restaurant

◉ Modern Thai, Pacific Rim NEW

Pan-Asian restaurant in stylish hotel

☎ 0191 5161400 📠 0191 516 1410
Seaham Hall Hotel, Lord Byron's Walk SR7 7AG
e-mail: info@seaham-hall.co.uk
dir: Leave A1018 onto A19 at rdbt take 2nd exit onto B1285/Stockton Rd. Turn left at Lord Byron Walk in 0.3m turn right

Seaham Hall's elegant 19th-century façade and stylish interior is only half the story: the Oriental-inspired 'Serenity Spa' and Pan-Asian Ozone Restaurant bring a bit of Feng Shui to the North East. There are three kitchens in the hotel (see entry below), and this one delivers Pan-Asian cooking and sees East and West combined in some genuine fusion dishes. The dining room is glamorously decorated in tones of red and orange, tables are bare wood, and an open kitchen brings energy to the space. There is a day menu (aromatic duck leg with wraps and hoisin sauce) and in the evening a Pan-Asian 'tapas' menu with lots of tantalising dishes such as soy- and ginger-cured salmon with pear and cress salad and horseradish crème fraîche; Malaysian seafood laksa with salmon, tuna, tiger prawns and jasmine rice; and seared scallops with cauliflower and saffron purée, cauliflower tempura and cumin foam.

continued

Seaham Hall Hotel - The White Room Restaurant

SEAHAM Map 19 NZ44

Modern British V 🌿

Top-end dining in luxury spa hotel

☎ 0191 516 1400 📠 0191 516 1410
Lord Byron's Walk SR7 7AG
e-mail: reservations@seaham-hall.co.uk
dir: A19 at 1st exit signed B1404 Seaham and follow signs to Seaham Hall

Seaham Hall has changed quite a bit since Lord Byron got married here back in 1815. He'd recognise the splendid Georgian façade, but we can only imagine what he'd make of the lavish spa facilities. It is the epitome of the modern makeover, with the original style of the building remaining intact whilst all around are the latest hi-tech facilities and elegant 21st-century designer flourishes. The White Room Restaurant is the headliner amongst the dining options, and under chef Kenny Atkinson, it is a star attraction in the North East. Handsome floor-to-ceiling windows give views over the beautiful grounds and the room is elegant simplicity itself, with neutral and natural tones and smartly laid tables helping to create a timeless space that is perfect for the business of fine dining. The staff show passion for the food and formality in the delivery. The cooking is based on sound classical principles and is elevated by the technical ability and creative intuition of the chef; broadly modern British, the fixed-price carte and tasting menus draw on first-class produce and show a distinct regional flavour. A stunning first course sees a brace of terrines, Anjou quail and foie gras and ham hock with parsley, with crystal clear flavours, perfectly partnered by a silky smooth apple purée, powdered hazelnuts, celeriac remoulade, fried quail's egg and crisp piece of pancetta. North Sea halibut is a super-fresh piece of fish, with creamed heritage potatoes and Shetland mussels, while desserts such as a tasting of dark Valrhona chocolate and banana includes a stellar chocolate fondant and an excellent banana parfait. Attention to detail runs through the operation and the wines on the magnificent tome are stored in the original cellar.

Chef Kenny Atkinson **Owner** von Essen Hotels **Times** 12-3/7-10 Closed L Mon-Tue **Prices** Fixed L 2 course £21.50-£60, Fixed D 3 course £60, Tasting menu £80, Service optional **Wines** 700+ bottles over £20, 6 bottles under £20, 7 by glass **Notes** Sunday L, Vegetarian menu, Dress restrictions, Smart casual, Civ Wed 42, Air con **Seats** 42, Pr/dining room 30 **Children** Portions **Parking** 145

SEAHAM *continued*

Chef Martin Moore **Owner** von Essen Hotels
Times 11-5/6-9 Closed 25 Dec, D Sun-Mon, 25-26 Dec, 1
Jan **Prices** Fixed L 2 course £17, Fixed D 3 course £20-
£25, Starter £4.50-£6.50, Main £9.10-£15, Dessert
£4.50-£6, Service optional **Wines** 10 bottles over £20, 3
bottles under £20, 5 by glass **Notes** Sunday L, Vegetarian
available, Dress restrictions, Smart casual, no robes after
6pm, Civ Wed 100, Air con **Seats** 60 **Children** Portions
Parking 200

Seaham Hall Hotel - The White Room Restaurant

@@@ – *see page 151*

see page 151

SEDGEFIELD	Map 19 NZ32

Best Western Hardwick Hall Hotel

@ Modern British NEW V ☺

Basement restaurant in a venerable Durham location

☎ 01740 620253   🖶 01740 622771
TS21 2EH
e-mail: info@hardwickhallhotel.co.uk
dir: Please telephone for directions

The hall traces its lineage back to a manor house built
here in the 1430s. In its time, it has been a maternity
hospital, but was returned to its best role as a hotel by
the present owners in the 1960s. In the basement is the
Ha Ha restaurant, named after the sunken garden
boundary rather than any commitment to unrelenting
jollity, although a good time is in the offing on the
culinary front. Low ceilings and a bare wood floor, bistro
tables and discreet music create a welcoming ambience
for the soundly based modern British cooking. Start with
marinated salmon and celeriac remoulade, or more
robustly with a suet pudding of pork belly, prunes and
apple in a cider jus, with something like monkfish teamed
with a confit duck spring roll to follow.

Chef Craig Stephenson **Owner** Ramside Estates
Times 7-9.30 **Prices** Starter £4.50-£6.95, Main £10.95-
£21.95, Dessert £5, Service optional **Notes** Sunday L,
Vegetarian menu, Dress restrictions, Smart casual, Civ
Wed 200 **Seats** 90, Pr/dining room 15 **Children** Portions,
Menu **Parking** 250

ESSEX	

BRENTWOOD	Map 6 TQ59

Marygreen Manor

@@ Modern European V

International cuisine in Tudor hall

☎ 01277 225252   🖶 01277 262809
London Rd CM14 4NR
e-mail: info@marygreenmanor.co.uk
dir: M25 junct 28, onto A1023 over 2 sets of lights, hotel
on right

Set in the baronial hall of 16th-century Marygreen Manor,
the Tudors restaurant is decorated in grand style with
barley-twist columns, high beamed ceiling and coats of
arms. The warm interior is the perfect setting for Modern
European dishes that centre around confident classics
based on quality seasonal produce. Warm oysters,
smoked duck breast, asparagus and oyster foam is a
typical starter, while mains might include saddle of lamb
or steak and kidney pudding with minestrone vegetables.
Finish your meal with chocolate fondant with hot
chocolate and chocolate tuile. The food is complemented
by a sound wine list, and you can tuck into afternoon tea
or a snack in the tranquil gardens or conservatory.

Chef Mr Majid Bouroute **Owner** Mr S Bhattessa
Times 12.30-2.30/7.15-10.15 Closed D Sun & BHs
Prices Fixed L 2 course £13.50-£16.50, Fixed D 3 course
£39.50, Starter £10.50, Main £25.50, Dessert £8.50,
Service added but optional 12% **Wines** 80 bottles over
£20, 21 bottles under £20, 7 by glass **Notes** Tasting
menu 6 course, Sunday L, Vegetarian menu, Dress
restrictions, No jeans or trainers, Civ Wed 60, Air con
Seats 80, Pr/dining room 85 **Children** Portions
Parking 100

CHELMSFORD	Map 6 TL70

County Hotel

@ Modern British NEW ☺

Town centre hotel serving seasonal British cuisine

☎ 01245 455700   🖶 01245 492762
29 Rainsford Rd CM1 2PZ
e-mail: kioftus@countyhotelgroup.co.uk
dir: Off Chelmsford ring road close to town centre and
A12 junct 18

Situated within easy walking distance of the railway
station and town centre, this family-owned hotel has a
contemporary style. The light and airy dining room has a
conservatory feel and the sunny terrace is perfect for al
fresco dining. Simply decorated walls are paired with
contemporary artwork and fresh flowers inject a splash of
colour. The unfussy British cuisine makes the best of
seasonal, locally-sourced produce and cooking is
accurate. Start with beef carpaccio with rocket, parmesan
and horseradish dressing and follow it with lemon-
roasted spatchcock chicken with Savoy cabbage.

Chef Steven Cansell **Owner** Richard & Ginny Austin
Times 12-2.30/6-10 **Prices** Fixed L 2 course £15.50-£19.95,

Fixed D 3 course £19.95-£27.50, Starter £4.50-£7.95, Main
£11.95-£17.95, Dessert £5.50, Service included **Wines** 55
bottles over £20, 15 bottles under £20, 6 by glass
Notes Sunday L, Vegetarian available, Air con **Seats** 64, Pr/
dining room 50 **Children** Portions, Menu **Parking** 70

COGGESHALL	Map 7 TL82

Baumann's Brasserie

@ British, French

Buzzy brasserie in historic building

☎ 01376 561453   🖶 01376 563762
4-6 Stoneham St CO6 1TT
e-mail: food@baumannsbrasserie.co.uk
dir: A12 from Chelmsford, exit at Kelvedon into
Coggeshall. Restaurant in centre opposite clock tower

Chef-proprietor Mark Baumann has done a brisk trade in
this buzzy brasserie since it was set up in 1986 with
renowned brasserie-meister Peter Langan. On a sunny
day, tables on the pavement outside this 16th-century
timbered house offer a continental touch; inside, it's like
eating in a bijou art gallery with antique chairs and
tables clothed in white damask. A wide-ranging menu
offers gutsy, interesting dishes based on French and
British cuisine with a few global twists. Check out the
'Billingsgate Best' section for daily fresh fish. Rillettes of
ham hock with ginger shallot marmalade and plum sauce
is typical of starters, and might be followed by whole
roasted sea bass with lemon, garlic and thyme and
champagne sauce.

Chef Mark Baumann, Tony Turner **Owner** Baumann's
Brasserie Ltd **Times** 12-2/7-9.30 Closed 2 wks Jan, Mon-
Tue **Prices** Food prices not confirmed for 2010. Please
telephone for details. **Wines** 20 bottles over £20, 24
bottles under £20, 11 by glass **Notes** Sunday L,
Vegetarian available, Air con **Seats** 80 **Children** Portions
Parking Opposite

White Hart Hotel

@ Modern European

Modern classics in a splendid medieval inn

☎ 01378 561654   🖶 01378 561789
Market End CO6 1NH
e-mail: 6529@greeneking.co.uk

The 15th-century inn is one of the assets of this Essex
market town. Its timbered interiors are host to a
traditional pub, as well as a smartly appointed restaurant
on two floors, with carefully mounted pictures and

exposed brickwork. The cooking draws influences from around Europe for some modern classic dishes such as monkfish swaddled in Parma ham with pea and mint risotto. Start perhaps with cured venison carpaccio with wild horseradish cream and redcurrant dressing, and build up to a good version of crème brûlée that has a correctly brittle top and plenty of vanilla kick.

Prices Food prices not confirmed for 2010. Please telephone for details

COLCHESTER   Map 13 TL92

Best Western Rose & Crown Hotel

◉◉ Traditional, International

Contemporary dining in a traditional Tudor building

☎ 01206 866677 🖹 01206 866616
East St CO1 2TZ
e-mail: info@rose-and-crown.com
dir: From A12 take exit to Colchester North onto A1232

The black and white half-timbered Rose & Crown is a pedigree 14th-century posting inn brought into the new millennium with a contemporary look. Exposed beams and timbered walls blend with vibrant colours, unclothed rosewood tables, polished wooden floors and contemporary prints in the smart East Street Grill restaurant. The kitchen turns out an eclectic menu inflected with Mediterranean and oriental influences, as in starters of lime-scented crab cakes or Parma ham-wrapped scallops. Mains might offer red wine braised lamb shanks with rosemary mash and minted jus. In the bar there's a classic array of crowd-pleasing pubby staples - calves' liver and bacon, or Lancashire hotpot, for example.

Chef Venu Mahankali **Owner** Bremwell Limited
Times 12-2/7-9.45 Closed 27-30 Dec, D Sun
Prices Starter £3.95-£6.95, Main £9.95-£18.95, Dessert £3.75-£5.95, Groups min 5 service 10% **Wines** 12 bottles over £20, 19 bottles under £20, 6 by glass **Notes** Sunday L, Vegetarian available, Civ Wed 150 **Seats** 80, Pr/dining room 50 **Children** Portions **Parking** 60

Juniper

◉ Modern British 🕭

Trendy health spa with an orangery-style restaurant

☎ 01206 734301 🖹 01206 734512
Clarice House, Kingsford Park, Layer Rd CO2 0HS
e-mail: colchester@claricehouse.co.uk
dir: SW of town centre on B1026 towards Layer

It's fair to say that most guests have pampering health and beauty treatments high on the agenda at the luxurious Clarice House health spa, but all that detoxing doesn't exclude indulgence in some serious food too. The light-flooded orangery-style restaurant goes for a chic colonial look with its bamboo chairs, cool magnolia colour scheme and conservatory roof, and the kitchen deals in an inventive modern British repertoire. Lobster and salmon ravioli is teamed with Bloody Mary tartare and lobster broth in a suitably indulgent starter, while main courses might bring pot-roasted chicken with Aspall's organic cider stock, broad beans en gelée and potato millefeuille.

Chef Paul Boorman **Owner** Clarice House (Colchester) Ltd
Times 7-9 Closed 25-26 Dec, 1 Jan, Sun-Wed, L all week
Prices Fixed D 3 course £30, Service optional **Wines** 14 bottles over £20, 19 bottles under £20, 10 by glass
Notes Monthly pudding club, Vegetarian available, Dress restrictions, Smart casual, Civ Wed 50, Air con **Seats** 60 **Parking** 100

The North Hill Hotel

◉ Modern British NEW

Well-prepared food in a newly-refurbished Colchester bistro

☎ 01206 574001
51 North Hill CO1 1PY
e-mail: info@northhillhotel.com
web: www.northhillhotel.com
dir: Follow signs for town centre. Up North Hill, hotel on right

The Grade II listed Georgian North Hill Hotel is quite a find at the heart of historic Colchester. It is looking spruce after a recent refurbishment, cream-painted outside and with a clean modern look indoors; staff are praised by guests for their genuinely friendly welcome. The Green Room bistro has been given a smartly contemporary makeover and serves modern British cuisine to match. There's plenty of local produce on the menu, including local rare breed meat and well-sourced fish. Take smoked mackerel pâté with yogurt piccalilli to start, followed by free-range Blythburgh pork chop with black pudding, honey apples, sage sauce and good hand-cut chips. Finish with a classic treacle tart served with Jersey cream.

Chef John Riddleston **Owner** Rob Brown
Times 12-2.30/6-9.30 **Prices** Fixed L 2 course £9.95-£12.95, Starter £3.95-£6.95, Main £8.95-£16.95, Dessert £4.50-£5.50, Service optional **Wines** 13 bottles over £20,

21 bottles under £20, 13 by glass **Notes** Sunday L, Vegetarian available **Seats** 45 **Children** Portions **Parking** NCP opposite

DEDHAM   Map 13 TM03

milsoms

◉◉ International 🏅🍷 🕭

Global cooking in buzzy brasserie

☎ 01206 322795 🖹 01206 323689
Stratford Rd CO7 6HN
e-mail: milsoms@milsomhotels.com
web: www.milsomhotels.com
dir: 7m N of Colchester, just off A12

This contemporary brasserie has a relaxed feel with its split-level dining room and appealing use of natural fabrics, stone, wood and leather. Eat inside or out - the terrace is available all year thanks to heaters and a gigantic 'sail' above. Informality is the order of the day - there is a no-booking policy and you write up your own order on the notepads provided. The extensive brasserie-style menu takes a global sweep but uses plenty of local produce. A starter of crab and chilli linguine might be followed by Greek lamb burger with houmous, tzatziki and chips. Finish with a traditional bread-and-butter pudding and 'proper' custard.

Chef Stas Anastasiades, Sarah Norman, Ben Rush
Owner Paul Milsom **Times** 12-9.30 **Prices** Starter £4.90-£6.95, Main £9.50-£16.95, Dessert £5.65-£6.40, Service optional **Wines** 34 bottles over £20, 16 bottles under £20, 11 by glass **Notes** Vegetarian available, Air con **Seats** 80, Pr/dining room 24 **Children** Portions, Menu **Parking** 60

DEDHAM *continued*

Le Talbooth Restaurant

@@ Modern British 🌐 🍴

Seasonal cooking in picture postcard location

☎ 01206 323150 📠 01206 322309
Gun Hill CO7 6HP
e-mail: talbooth@milsomhotels.com
web: www.milsomhotels.com
dir: 6m from Colchester: follow signs from A12 to
Stratford St Mary, restaurant on left before village

Run by the same family for more than 50 years, this
riverside restaurant occupies part of a beautiful Tudor
house on the River Stour and was once painted by
Constable. Set amidst immaculate lawns with a
picturesque bridge, the former weaver's cottage and toll
booth boasts old beams, leather chairs, striking artwork
and smart table settings. There's a terrace for all-
weather alfresco dining beside the river, complete with
sail canopy and heaters. The food matches the setting,
with its emphasis on superior seasonal ingredients, local
whenever possible. Think lobster and potato salad with
truffle mayonnaise and Sévruga caviar, and perhaps
navarin of lamb with confit shoulder, boulangère
potatoes, spinach and baby vegetables.

Chef Ian Rhodes, Tom Bushell **Owner** Paul Milsom
Times 12-2/7-9 Closed D Sun (Oct-Apr) **Prices** Starter
£8.25-£14.75, Main £16.95-£28.95, Dessert £7-£8.50,
Service included **Wines** 560 bottles over £20, 38 bottles
under £20, 10 by glass **Notes** Sunday L, Vegetarian
available, Dress restrictions, Smart casual, No jeans, Civ
Wed 50 **Seats** 75, Pr/dining room 34 **Children** Portions
Parking 50

FELSTED Map 6 TL62

Reeves Restaurant

@ Modern British

Ambitious cooking in a charming old cottage

☎ 01371 820996 📠 01371 820100
Rumbles Cottage, Braintree Rd CM6 3DJ
e-mail: reevesrestaurant@tiscali.co.uk
dir: A120 E from Braintree, B1417 to Felsted

The village of Felsted has plenty of attractive old
buildings and this 16th-century property can be counted
among them. Originally a cottage, a myriad of exposed
oak beams combine with large windows and tables set
with crisp linen cloths and fresh flowers to create a
traditional and attractive setting. The menus offer a
range of creative dishes inspired by the head chef's
worldwide travel with the McLaren racing team. Smoked
eel and crispy pork belly comes with baby beetroot and
horseradish crème fraîche in a contemporary starter,
while main-course tea-smoked breast of Gressingham
duck is partnered with orange and fennel salad, crushed
new potatoes and pomegranate syrup. Everything from
breads to petits fours is made on the premises.

Times 12-2/7 Closed Mon-Wed

GREAT CHESTERFORD Map 12 TL54

The Crown House

@ Modern British 🍴

Traditional cooking in a peaceful village setting

☎ 01799 530515 📠 01799 530683
London Rd CA10 1NY
e-mail: stay@thecrownhouseonetel.net

The Georgian façade of this old coaching inn does not tell
the whole story - parts of the building date back to even
older times. Much of the original character has been
retained after sympathetic restoration, and public rooms
include an attractive lounge bar, oak-panelled restaurant
and a conservatory. Terrace dining is an option in the
summer, between the main house and the walled garden.
Sound cooking from good-quality produce delivers simple
dishes with excellent flavours. Expect the likes of duck
liver paté with apple and black grape chutney, drizzled
with Cumberland sauce, and to follow braised partridge
and venison casserole, or monkish and salmon with a
lemon beurre blanc.

Chef David Ostle **Owner** F D Ebdon **Times** 12-2/7-9
Prices Fixed L 2 course £11.50-£15.50, Fixed D 3 course
£20, Starter £5.50-£8.50, Main £13.50-£18.50, Dessert
£5.50-£7.50, Service optional **Wines** 20 bottles over £20,
32 bottles under £20, 4 by glass **Notes** Sunday L,
Vegetarian available, Civ Wed 50 **Seats** 60, Pr/dining
room 28 **Children** Portions **Parking** 30

HARWICH Map 13 TM23

The Pier at Harwich

@@ British, Seafood

Quayside hotel restaurant with plenty of piscine appeal

☎ 01255 241212 📠 01255 551922
The Quay CO12 3HH
e-mail: pier@milsomhotels.com
web: www.milsomhotels.com
dir: A12 to Colchester then A120 to Harwich Quay

The truly nautical Harbourside Restaurant is located on
the first floor of the contemporary-styled Pier Hotel and
certainly has the wow factor to draw the crowds -
stunningly fresh fish and seafood landed on the quay
opposite and wonderful views over the Stour and Orwell
estuaries. The setting is stylish, note the leather chairs
and the polished pewter bar, and the service is relaxed
and professional. Fish and seafood are the stars of the
extensive menu; take a simply prepared and presented
plate of hot smoked salmon with hollandaise, horseradish
and beetroot relish, roast cod on leek mash with shrimp
sauce, and sea bass with basil oil dressing. Meat-eaters
will not be disappointed with pan-fried sirloin steak
served with fat chips. For informal bistro-style food, try
the Ha'penny downstairs.

Chef Chris Oakley **Owner** Paul Milsom **Times** 12-2/6-9
Closed D 25 Dec **Prices** Fixed L 2 course £18, Starter
£6.35-£9, Main £15.50-£31.50, Dessert £5.95-£6.95,
Service added 10% **Wines** 82 bottles over £20, 25 bottles
under £20, 6 by glass **Notes** Sunday L, Vegetarian
available, Dress restrictions, Smart casual, Civ Wed 50,
Air con **Seats** 80, Pr/dining room 16 **Children** Portions,
Menu **Parking** 20, On street, pay & display

MANNINGTREE   Map 13 TM13

The Mistley Thorn

◎◎ International ✪

Great use of local produce in bustling bistro with rooms

☎ 01206 392821   📄 01206 390122
High St, Mistley CO11 1HE
e-mail: info@mistleythorn.co.uk
web: www.mistleythorn.co.uk
dir: From A12 take A137 for Manningtree & Mistley

Right in the centre of the historic coastal village of Mistley with panoramic views down the Stour Estuary, The Mistley Thorn was built as a coaching inn circa 1723. Now a smart and bustling restaurant with rooms, the bistro-style dining room has a light and airy New England feel to it with its terracotta tiled floors, exposed beams and tongue and groove walls. The food is simple, seasonal and locally sourced with seafood a speciality. Mersea oysters are available all year round and Colchester natives when they're in season. The Oyster Bar might also offer whole cracked Norfolk crabs, Harwich lobster and house-cured organic salmon. Elsewhere on the menu, Heirloom tomato and Ticklemore goats' cheese salad might be followed by a seafood stew of shellfish with local wild bass or peppered rib-eye steak with wild rocket, onion strings and hand-cut chips.

Chef Sherri Singleton, Chris Pritchard **Owner** Sherri Singleton, David McKay **Times** 12-2.30/6.30-9.30 **Prices** Fixed L 2 course £11.95-£13.95, Fixed D 3 course £13.95-£16.95, Starter £3.95-£7.95, Main £8.95-£16.95, Dessert £4.75-£6.50, Service optional, Groups min 8 service 10% **Wines** 22 bottles over £20, 19 bottles under £20, 17 by glass **Notes** Sunday L, Vegetarian available **Seats** 75, Pr/dining room 28 **Children** Portions, Menu **Parking** 7

TOLLESHUNT KNIGHTS   Map 7 TL91

The Camelot Restaurant at Five Lakes

◎ Modern British

Fine-dining restaurant in a resort hotel

☎ 01621 868888   📄 01621 869696
Five Lakes Hotel, Colchester Rd CM9 8HX
e-mail: enquiries@fivelakes.co.uk
web: www.fivelakes.co.uk
dir: M25 junct 28, then on A12. At Kelvedon take B1024 then B1023 to Tolleshunt Knights, clearly marked by brown tourist signs

This modern resort hotel is set in 320 acres of countryside and boasts two 18-hole golf courses plus a spa and country club. With all those exercise opportunities on site, there's no reason not to treat yourself to dinner at The Camelot Restaurant. Themed around the legend of King Arthur, The Camelot serves up modern British and European food based around locally sourced ingredients. Kick off with seared scallops with Jerusalem artichoke purée, beetroot salad and hazelnut butter, following on with a perfectly cooked, tender duck breast, served classically with Savoy cabbage and smoked bacon, parsnip purée and creamed potatoes.

Times 7-10 Closed 26, 31 Dec, 1 Jan, Sun-Mon

GLOUCESTERSHIRE

ALMONDSBURY   Map 4 ST68

Quarterjacks Restaurant

◎ Modern British Ⅴ

Relaxed, brasserie-style dining in modern Nordic-style hotel

☎ 01454 201090   📄 01454 201593
Aztec Hotel & Spa, Aztec West BS32 4TS
e-mail: quarterjacks@shirehotels.com
dir: M5 junct 16/A38 towards city centre, hotel 200mtrs on right

Conveniently placed close to the motorway links north of Bristol, the Aztec Hotel is a modern, Nordic-style building featuring vaulted ceilings, stone-flagged floors and open fires throughout the contemporary-styled public rooms. Expect a relaxed brasserie atmosphere in Quarterjacks restaurant and a popular monthly-changing menu that ranges from light simple salads to robust Spanish flavours. Using fresh local produce, simply prepared dishes may include mussel, leek and saffron soup, chicken, pea and ham hock pie, and ginger pudding with mascarpone cream. The terrace provides the perfect space for alfresco summer dining.

Chef Mike Riordan **Owner** Shire Hotels **Times** 12.30-2/7-10 Closed L Sat **Prices** Fixed L 2 course fr £14.50, Starter £6-£8.50, Main £12-£22, Dessert £6-£7.50, Service optional **Wines** 25 bottles over £20, 10 bottles under £20, 12 by glass **Notes** Sunday L, Vegetarian menu, Civ Wed 160 **Seats** 80, Pr/dining room 40 **Children** Portions, Menu **Parking** 200

ALVESTON   Map 4 ST68

Carriages at Alveston House Hotel

◎ Modern European **NEW** ✪

Seasonal produce in a refurbished period house hotel

☎ 01454 415050   📄 01454 415425
Davids Ln BS35 2LA
e-mail: info@alvestonhousehotel.co.uk
dir: On A38, 3.5m N of M4/M5 interchange. M5 junct 16 northbound or junct 14 southbound

Alveston House is a fine period country-house hotel a few miles north of Bristol. Newly refurbished in a contemporary style, Carriages Restaurant offers a friendly, welcoming atmosphere, a good value market menu and a changing carte with a good emphasis on fresh seasonal produce. Unfussy dishes are simply prepared with good attention to detail and resulting flavour combinations are sound. Typical dishes include tempura king prawns with sweet chilli sauce to start, followed by beef fillet with bubble-and-squeak and Madeira sauce, and lemon curd and orange meringue parfait.

Chef Ben Halliday **Owner** Julie Camm **Times** 12-1.45/7-9.30 **Prices** Starter £4.75-£7, Main £13.50-£21, Dessert £4.75-£5.50, Service optional **Wines** 11 bottles over £20, 28 bottles under £20, 5 by glass **Notes** Vegetarian available, Civ Wed 75, Air con **Seats** 75, Pr/dining room 40 **Children** Portions, Menu **Parking** 60

ARLINGHAM   Map 4 SO71

The Old Passage Inn

◎◎ Seafood

Seafood restaurant with river and forest views

☎ 01452 740547   📄 01452 741871
Passage Rd GL2 7JR
e-mail: oldpassage@ukonline.co.uk
web: www.theoldpassage.com
dir: M5 junct 13/A38 towards Bristol, 2nd right to Frampton-on-Severn, over canal, bear left, follow to river

The fast-flowing River Severn and the wooded hills of the Forest of Dean make a fine backdrop at this secluded

continued

ARLINGHAM *continued*

seafood restaurant with rooms. In fine weather the garden terrace is the obvious place to dine; check the tide tables and you might even be treated to the surreal sight of surfers riding the Severn Bore as it surges by. The menu deals almost exclusively in fish and seafood, brought in fresh from Pembrokeshire or Cornwall, while the restaurant's salt water tanks guarantee fighting-fresh lobsters. The kitchen sticks to rule number one of fish and seafood excellence: don't mess about with it. Thus, dishes are kept simple, presented attractively and blend tradition, in the form of beer battered fish, hand-cut chips, mushy peas and tartare sauce, with Mediterranean climes, as in a Provençal-style fish soup with croûtons, gruyère and saffron mayonnaise. Mains might include roast monkfish with braised little gems, baby onions, wild mushrooms and oxtail jus.

Chef Mark Redwood **Owner** Sally Pearce
Times 12–2/6.30-9.30 Closed 25 Dec, Mon, D Sun
Prices Fixed L 2 course fr £15, Tasting menu £55, Starter £7.50–£12, Main £16–£45, Dessert £7.50–£9, Service optional **Wines** 53 bottles over £20, 36 bottles under £20, 15 by glass **Notes** Shell fish tasting menu, Sunday L, Vegetarian available, Air con **Seats** 60, Pr/dining room 12 **Children** Portions **Parking** 40

BARNSLEY
Map 5 SP00

The Village Pub

◉◉ Modern British ✋

Cotswold inn with deserved reputation for good food

☎ 01285 740421 📠 01285 740929
GL7 5EF
e-mail: info@thevillagepub.co.uk
dir: 4m from Cirencester, on B4425 to Bibury

A traditional Cotswolds country inn in the desirable village of Barnsley, this popular gastro-pub is a favourite with locals but brings in punters from far and wide for its good food. There are 5 beautifully restored and refurbished dining rooms, each decorated in a different style, plus flagged and oak-boarded floors, exposed timbers and 3 open fireplaces. The rooms are filled with antique furniture, oil paintings, window settles and polished candlelit tables, or go for the heated terrace. Well kept local real ales, an extensive wine list and locally produced soft drinks complement the unfussy, modern food. Top-notch local produce is used in dishes such as smoked duck breast salad with roasted beets and sherry vinegar dressing, to be followed, perhaps, by roasted cod and Niçoise salad. Finish with Rum Baba with roasted peaches and zabaglione ice cream.

Chef Graham Grafton **Owner** Tim Haigh & Rupert Pendered **Times** 12–2.30/7-9.30 **Prices** Starter £5–£8, Main £11.50–£18, Dessert fr £6, Service optional **Wines** 29 bottles over £20, 19 bottles under £20, 11 by glass **Notes** Sunday L, Vegetarian available **Seats** 100, Pr/dining room 16 **Children** Portions **Parking** 40

BIBURY
Map 5 SP10

Bibury Court

◉◉ British

Confident modern cooking in stunning country-house hotel

☎ 01285 740337 & 740324 📠 01285 740660
GL7 5NT
e-mail: info@biburycourt.com
web: www.biburycourt.com
dir: On B4425 between Cirencester & Burford; hotel behind church

Tucked away behind a beautiful Cotswold village in a picture-postcard spot on the River Coln, this grand 17th-century country-house hotel stands in 6 acres of grounds. With traditional wood panelling, log fires, comfy sofas and antique furniture, it overflows with historic charm and character. A confident kitchen uses fine seasonal and local ingredients to create modern, classically-based dishes with excellent flavour combinations. Hearty dishes might include the likes of Loch Duart salmon and herb fishcake with pea purée, soft poached hen's egg, rapeseed oil hollandaise, followed by a main course of slow-roast Gloucestershire Old Spot pork belly served with butternut squash, a cider fondant, roast apples and sage. Eat in the more informal conservatory at lunch and the formal restaurant at dinner.

Times 12–2/7-9

Swan Hotel

◉ International ✋

Relaxed dining in picturesque setting

☎ 01285 740695 📠 01285 740473
GL7 5NW
e-mail: info@swanhotel.co.uk
dir: 9m S of Burford A40 onto B4425. 6m N of Cirencester A4179 onto B4425. In town centre by bridge

Cut into the hillside across from the River Coln, beautiful riverside gardens and a trout farm, this classic Cotswold-stone building enjoys an idyllic, picture-postcard setting. The appealing first impressions continue throughout the interior, all sumptuous fabrics and furnishings and fine period furniture. Equally pleasing are seasonal modern British menus served in the traditional Gallery Restaurant, which draw on locally-sourced ingredients. Dishes are well balanced, simply cooked and presented and may include ham hock and barley broth, roast

venison with thyme and port glaze, and passionfruit soufflé with mandarin sorbet. The popular café-bar serves meals all day.

Chef Chris Hutchings **Owner** Pamela & Michael Horton **Times** 12–2.30/7-9 Closed L Mon-Sun **Prices** Food prices not confirmed for 2010. Please telephone for details. **Notes** Sunday L, Vegetarian available, Dress restrictions, Smart casual, no jeans or trainers, Civ Wed 90 **Seats** 60, Pr/dining room 30 **Children** Portions **Parking** On street

---

BOURTON-ON-THE-WATER
Map 10 SP12

The Dial House Hotel & Restaurant

◉◉ Modern British **NEW V**

High quality cooking in historic Cotswold setting

☎ 01451 822244 📠 01451 810126
The Chestnuts, High St GL54 2AN
e-mail: info@dialhousehotel.com
dir: Located just off the A429

Built in 1698, this is the oldest building in picturesque Bourton-on-the-Water. The intimate restaurant's décor combines a contemporary style with the historic setting to great effect. The small kitchen team, led by Jamie Forman, turns out dish after dish of refreshingly simple food and impresses with some excellent flavour combinations. A wild mushroom risotto is perfectly cooked and topped with a small layer of duck confit, while Gloucestershire beef served with root vegetables, pomme mousseline and truffle jus is tender and has good depth of flavour. Light and airy caramel soufflé, with a jug of hot chocolate sauce and home-made vanilla ice cream, keeps up the standard to the finish.

Chef Jamie Forman **Owner** Elaine & Martyn Booth **Times** 12–2/6.30-9.30 **Prices** Fixed L 2 course £12–£20, Fixed D 3 course £30–£40, Starter £7.25–£12, Main £14.25–£23, Dessert £6.50–£7, Service added but optional 10% **Wines** 35 bottles over £20, 8 bottles under £20, 9 by glass **Notes** Tasting menu available, Sunday L, Vegetarian menu, Dress restrictions, Smart casual **Seats** 26, Pr/dining room 16 **Children** Portions **Parking** 16

BUCKLAND — Map 10 SP03

Buckland Manor

◎◎ Traditional British, French

Ancient manor-house setting overlooking the Vale of Evesham

☎ 01386 852626 📄 01386 853557
WR12 7LY
e-mail: info@bucklandmanor.com
web: www.bucklandmanor.com
dir: 2m SW of Broadway. Take B4632 signed Cheltenham, then take turn for Buckland. Hotel through village on right

With grandiose views over the proverbially lush Vale of Evesham, Buckland is a Cotswold manor house from the original mould, built of honey-coloured stone, with commanding fireplaces, panelled walls and fine oil paintings within. In the 16th century, the Lord Mayor of London owned it. The air of refinement extends to jacket-and-tie order for male diners, and a formal style of service in the small dining room that seems entirely in keeping. The country-house culinary style tends to concentrate the inventive flourishes in first courses such as lobster ravioli with sautéed langoustines and (sparingly served) lemongrass velouté, while mains are in the more traditional mould of beef fillet with rösti, girolles and Madeira, or corn-fed chicken with morel cream and pasta. Finish with chocolate truffle mousse and candied kumquats.

Buckland Manor

Chef Matt Hodgkinson **Owner** Buckland Manor Country House Hotel Ltd **Times** 12.30-1.45/7.30-9 **Prices** Fixed L 2 course £15, Starter £7.25-£13.50, Main £25.50-£29.50, Dessert £9, Service optional **Wines** 574 bottles over £20, 7 bottles under £20, 35 by glass **Notes** Pre-theatre D available, Sunday L, Vegetarian available, Dress restrictions, Jacket & tie **Seats** 40 **Parking** 30

CHARINGWORTH — Map 10 SP13

The John Greville Restaurant

◎ Modern International

Medieval manor with appealing menu

☎ 01386 593555 📄 01386 593353
Charingworth Manor GL55 6NS
e-mail: charingworthmanor@classiclodges.co.uk
dir: M40 exit at signs for A429/Stow. Follow signs for Moreton-in-Marsh. From Chipping Camden follow signs for Charingworth Manor

Dating back to the early 14th century, Charingworth Manor lies in a 55-acre estate in magnificent Cotswold countryside. Now a country-house hotel, it still retains beams showing the original medieval decoration. The small, traditional restaurant, which has a beamed ceiling and warm rag-rolled walls, is divided into separate areas. Its slightly formal setting is offset by the relaxed and welcoming hospitality and service. The menu offers a good range of dishes using simply prepared local produce; start, perhaps, with smoked salmon and smoked haddock fishcake with wild chilli jam and lemongrass sauce, followed by chicken breast with herb mash and fricassée of mushrooms.

Times 12-2/7-9.30

See advert below

CHELTENHAM — Map 10 SO92

Le Champignon Sauvage

◎◎◎◎ – *see opposite page*

The Cheltenham Regency Hotel

◎ Modern, Traditional NEW V

Finely crafted food in quiet Cotswold setting

☎ 01452 713226 & 0845 194 9867
Staverton Rd GL51 0ST
e-mail: gm@cheltenhamregency.co.uk
dir: 1m from A40 Cheltenham

A couple of miles outside Cheltenham, and only a little way from the M5, the hotel is on the fringe of the Cotswolds, with its straggle of tranquil villages and gently undulating hills. Equipped for business custom and registered for weddings and partnership ceremonies, the place aims to keep everyone happy. Recently refurbished, the dining room has well-spaced tables, comfortable chairs and an attentive yet relaxed style of service. Locally raised meats and Cornish fish and seafood are the main attractions, and preparations are simple, but with well-judged flavours and textures. Start with cream of Jerusalem artichoke soup, rich and concentrated, before proceeding to herb-coated brill with crab, fennel, roasted parsnip and champagne foam. The simplest of desserts, maybe iced honey parfait, can be the highlight of a meal.

Chef Robin Dudley **Owner** Dorian Charlton
Times 12-2/7-9.30 **Prices** Fixed L 2 course £15-£30, Fixed D 3 course £30-£40, Starter £4.95-£8.95, Main £11.95-£19.95, Dessert £4.95-£9.50, Service included **Wines** 8 bottles over £20, 8 bottles under £20, 8 by glass **Notes** Sunday L, Vegetarian menu **Seats** 80 **Children** Portions **Parking** 140

The Daffodil

◎ Modern British, Mediterranean NEW

Brasserie cooking in a former art deco cinema

☎ 01242 700055 🖷 01242 700088
18-20 Suffolk Pde, Montpellier GL50 2AE
e-mail: daffodilrest@cs.com
dir: S of town centre, just off Suffolk Rd, near Cheltenham Boys' College

Once an art deco cinema, in the era when Mary Pickford and Rudolf Valentino were box-office gold, the place has to be seen to be believed. The sweeping entrance staircase with original mosaic tiles, period film posters, old vending machines and even an antique projector are all still on view, and where once you might have been gazing in wonder at the silver screen, there is now an open-to-view bustling kitchen. TV design guru Laurence Llewelyn-Bowen had a hand in the décor, with stylish leather booths all part of the experience. A menu of modern European brasserie dishes features some adept and appetising cooking; crispy duck salad with plum and hoisin dressing before slow-roast pork belly with a pan-roasted cutlet, served with apple and celeriac mash.

Bramley apple cheesecake with pecan and caramel sauce makes for a happy ending.

Chef Mark Davidson **Owner** Mark Stephenson & James McAlpine **Times** 12-2.30/6-10.30 Closed Sun **Prices** Fixed L 2 course £13.50, Fixed D 3 course £15.50 **Notes** Fixed price menu Mon-Fri until 7.30pm, Vegetarian available **Seats** 150

The Greenway Hotel

◎◎ Modern British V

Ambitious cooking and understated elegance in a fine period property

☎ 01242 862352 🖷 01242 862780
Shurdington GL51 4UG
e-mail: info@thegreenway.co.uk
web: www.the-greenway.co.uk
dir: 3m S of Cheltenham on A46 (Stroud) & through Shurdington

The creeper-covered Elizabethan manor on the outskirts of Cheltenham is part of the fabric of this part of the Cotswolds, and with its views over the original sunken garden and the surrounding hills beyond, there is no better place to appreciate what this region has to offer. Inside there's just the right balance between traditional and contemporary, with well-appointed tables in the restaurant, plus subtle lighting and discreetly attentive service. The menu deals in creative modern British ideas, with plenty of contemporary touches and presentations. Slow-braised pig's trotter with Wiltshire hare and hazelnut farce and celeriac as purée and crisps is a compelling first course, while main-course Brixham brill is cooked sous-vide, and served with young leeks, ham crisp and prawn and tomato butter. Desserts are a strength: witness a banana roasted with rum and served with bergamot parfait, walnut mascarpone and caramel ice cream.

Chef Paul Mottram **Owner** von Essen Hotels
Times 12-2.30/7-9.30 **Prices** Fixed L 2 course £16.50-£18, Fixed D 3 course £45, Tasting menu £65, Service optional **Wines** 150 bottles over £20, 6 bottles under £20, 10 by glass **Notes** ALC 3 course £48.50, Tasting menu 6 course, Sunday L, Vegetarian menu, Dress restrictions, Smart casual, No jeans, T-shirts or trainers, Civ Wed 45 **Seats** 46, Pr/dining room 22 **Children** Portions **Parking** 50

Hotel du Vin Cheltenham

◎ British, European

Chic hotel with lively menu of French-focused dishes

☎ 01242 588450 🖷 01242 588455
Parabola Rd GL50 3AQ
e-mail: info.cheltenham@hotelduvin.com
dir: Please telephone for directions

From Brighton to Edinburgh, the HDV chain of boutique hotels with lively French-style bistros is a winning formula. In the smart Montpelier district of the town, the building is a suitably handsome Georgian pile, and inside big and bold artworks and original features blend to create a pleasingly contemporary vibe; a centrepiece chandelier is made of wine glasses. Nicotine-coloured walls and dark-wood tables set the scene for good bistro cooking with a touch of class, as in cod brandade with tartare sauce before roast chicken jardinière, or pollock with leeks and mussel sauce. Service is tip-top, and do make use of the sommelier.

Chef Jon Parsons **Owner** MWB **Times** 12-2/6.30-10.30 Closed L 31 Dec **Prices** Starter £4.50-£6.95, Main £11.50-£19.50, Dessert £5.75-£8.50, Service added but optional 10% **Wines** 450 bottles over £20, 20 bottles under £20, 20 by glass **Notes** Plats du jour 1 course plus glass wine or coffee £10.95, Sunday L, Vegetarian available, Air con **Seats** 92, Pr/dining room 22 **Children** Portions **Parking** 23

Monty's Brasserie

◎◎ Modern International

Confident cooking in stylish, contemporary setting

☎ 01242 227678 🖷 01242 224359
George Hotel, 41 St Georges Rd GL50 3DZ
e-mail: info@montysbraz.co.uk
dir: M5 junct 11, follow signs to town centre. At lights (TGI Fridays) turn left onto Gloucester Rd. Straight on, turn right at lights, Monty's 0.75m on left

A refit has given this Regency dandy a new set of clothes. Seen from outside the George still belongs in the 1840s, but once you're inside, it's a brave new world of contemporary clean-cut style. The buzzy Monty's Brasserie takes a similar modern line with toffee-hued leather seats and warm claret walls, lots of wood and unclothed tables, and a relaxed, informal vibe. The kitchen team knows its way around the modern brasserie repertoire, treating prime ingredients with confident simplicity. Oriental influences pop up here and there, as in a simple starter of Thai crispy duck served with chilli and sesame oil dipping sauce and wafer-thin pancakes for wrapping. Fish is a strong suit, with mains offering pan-fried sea bass with spring greens, creamed potato, artichoke and cockle popcorn.

Chef Rob Owen **Owner** Jeremy Shaw **Times** 12-2/6-10 Closed 25-26 Dec **Prices** Food prices not confirmed for 2010. Please telephone for details. **Wines** 35 bottles over £20, 14 bottles under £20, 7 by glass **Notes** Sunday L, Vegetarian available, Air con **Seats** 40, Pr/dining room 32 **Children** Portions, Menu **Parking** 30

Le Champignon Sauvage

Modern

Innovative French cooking of considerable class

☎ 01242 573449 📄 01242 254365
24-28 Suffolk Rd GL50 2AQ
e-mail: mail@
lechampignonsauvage.co.uk
dir: S of town centre, on A40, near
Cheltenham College

While many renowned chefs are rarely to be seen in their kitchens - busy as they are with other commitments such as appearing on TV or overseeing the expansion of their empires - that's not the case with David Everitt-Matthias. He's a hands-on chef, always at the stoves, never missing a beat. The terrace building in the popular Montpelier part of the town is the setting for some thrillingly good cooking, with France, both modern and classical, as the focal point. For food of such undoubted quality, the setting is refreshingly unpretentious, with a cheerful yellow and blue colour scheme, bold modern artworks and well dressed, well spaced tables. After more than 20 years as a team (they opened in 1987), Helen has perfected the role of gracious host as adeptly as David has refined his culinary skills. The fixed-price carte is available for lunch and dinner, plus there's a set lunch menu and set dinner option midweek. First-class seasonal produce is treated with respect and although deeply creative and innovative, the cooking is precise without being precious and at its core is a feeling for the produce itself from the humble to the refined. A pre-starter of curried almond and coconut mousse with coconut foam along with excellent breads (glistening brioche with bacon and shallots among them) set the standard before a first course of celeriac lasagne with megrim sole, cockles and sea beet, or there is the seldom seen kid, in a terrine with ham hock. Main-course Cinderford lamb with its gayette and lentils braised with Morteau sausage is a dish with robust and deftly balanced flavours and textures, and bitter chocolate and olive tart with fennel ice cream is a dessert of impeccable contemporary credentials.

Chef David Everitt-Matthias
Owner Mr & Mrs D Everitt-Matthias
Times 12.30-1.30/7.30-8.30 Closed 10 days Xmas, 3 wks Jun, Sun-Mon
Prices Fixed L 2 course £25-£30, Fixed D 3 course £30-£50, Service optional
Wines 97 bottles over £20, 45 bottles under £20, 6 by glass **Notes** Air con
Seats 40 **Parking** Public car park (Bath Rd)

CHELTENHAM *continued*

The Royal Well Tavern

◉ Modern British NEW

Remodelled town-centre pub with well-conceived bistro menu

☎ 01242 221212
5 Well Place GL50 3DN
dir: Please telephone for directions

Opening in 2008, the Tavern has been fully refurbished to look like a classic British pub, albeit one with comfortable banquette seating, quality wooden tables and artfully lit and framed pictures on the walls. Chef Humphrey Fletcher comes with a distinguished London-based CV under his belt, and a mission to combine modern British cooking with classical French bistro fare, in a style that showcases fine home produce with the minimum of elaboration. That translates as a rustic salad of lamb's sweetbreads, duck hearts and a poached egg, followed perhaps by accurately timed fillet of bream with ratte potatoes, fennel, delicious brown shrimps and gremolata dressing. Steak frites with beurre maître d'hôtel is a crowd-pleasing alternative.

Times 10-3/5-11

Hicks' Brasserie

◉ Modern British

Brasserie-style dining in cool and contemporary surroundings

☎ 01386 840330 ▤ 01386 840310
Cotswold House, The Square, High St GL55 6AN
e-mail: hicks@cotswoldhouse.com
dir: 1m N of A44 between Moreton-in-Marsh & Broadway on B4081

This relaxed brasserie is the more informal baby brother of first-class Juliana's Restaurant (see entry) at the slick Cotswold House Hotel. The same kitchen turns out the food so you can be sure of top-level attention to detail and quality raw ingredients. The metro-chic décor is astonishingly hip: take in the swish marble-topped bar, modern artwork, ivory and ox-blood walls, banquettes and polished-wood tables and you could be in London. The same modern vibe drives the menu in a repertoire of crowd-pleasing old favourites tweaked for added interest. Parmesan and spinach risotto cake with celery and apple salad is a typical starter, followed by a nicely medium rare pan-fried tuna steak with Mexican crushed potato, mixed peppers and salsa dressing.

Owner Concorde Hotel Management **Times** 12-3/6-9:45
Prices Fixed L 2 course £14.95-£17.95, Fixed D 3 course £19.50-£21, Starter £4.95-£6.95, Main £10.75-£24.50,

---

Dessert £5.50-£9.50, Service optional, Groups min 8 service 10% **Wines** 13 bottles over £20, 10 bottles under £20, 9 by glass **Notes** Sunday L, Vegetarian available, Air con **Seats** 50, Pr/dining room 14 **Children** Portions, Menu **Parking** 26

Juliana's Restaurant, Cotswold House

see below

The Kings Hotel

◉ Modern British

Cotswold inn with contemporary style

☎ 01386 840256 & 841056 ▤ 01386 841598
The Square GL55 6AW
e-mail: info@kingscampden.co.uk
web: www.kingscampden.co.uk
dir: Please telephone for directions

Juliana's Restaurant, Cotswold House

Rosettes not confirmed at time of going to press

Modern British V ✧

Fine Georgian hotel with a first-class restaurant

☎ 01386 840330 ▤ 01386 840310
Cotswold House, The Square, High St GL55 6AN
e-mail: reception@cotswoldhouse.com
dir: 1m N of A44 between Moreton-in-Marsh & Broadway on B4081

The honey-hued tones of this Regency townhouse blend seamlessly into chocolate-box pretty Chipping Campden. But, rather like a sober judge wearing lingerie beneath his robes, there's something altogether different going on inside this house. The interior is straight from the pages of a design magazine: rich tones of chocolate, caramel and ivory, opulent fabrics and touchy-feely textures blend with period elegance in a one-off blend of antique and

cutting edge features. The main dining room, Juliana's, continues the theme, with a cosmopolitan décor guaranteed to appeal to city slickers who want a trip out to the country. The kitchen displays a penchant for full-on earthy flavours delivered in architecturally perfect packages. An impeccable roll-call of well-sourced ingredients includes a starter of confit duck foie gras, port wine figs, fig chutney and fig sorbet, and continues with an inventive riff on Warwickshire rabbit - its loin, rack, pastilla of the leg, rarebit rabbit with rhubarb, black pepper caramel and trompette noir mushrooms. The high level of care and attention concludes with a dessert of marinated poached pineapple with coconut porridge, coconut sorbet and sesame seed crisp. As we went to press we heard there was a change of chef here. Please see theaa.com for the latest information.

Owner Concorde Hotel Management **Times** 7-10 Closed Sun-Mon, L all week **Prices** Fixed D 3 course £39.50-£49.50, Service added but optional 10% **Wines** 150 bottles over £20, 10 by glass **Notes** Vegetarian

menu, Dress restrictions, Smart casual, Civ Wed 96, Air con **Seats** 40, Pr/dining room 96 **Children** Portions **Parking** 25

This Georgian Cotswold stone inn in the town's historic centre is a focal point for locals and visitors alike. Choose between the boldly-painted light and airy bar, a casual contemporary brasserie, or the relaxed restaurant overlooking the square. Here, stylish chocolate and cream leather seating and modern art mix with ancient gnarled beams and an inglenook fireplace and there's a friendly buzz fostered by down-to-earth staff. The kitchen's emphasis is on quality ingredients, thoughtfully put together and presented well; the wide-ranging menu has something for everyone, from a simple but high-quality chicken salad to braised filled leg of rabbit with thyme mash. Delicious desserts, such as chocolate and orange tart with clotted cream are not to be missed.

Chef Gareth Rufus **Owner** Sir Peter Rigby **Times** 12-2.30/6.30-9.30 **Prices** Fixed L 2 course £12.50, Fixed D 3 course fr £19.50, Starter £4.95-£8.95, Main £7-£22, Dessert £5.75-£6.50, Service optional **Wines** 47 bottles over £20, 13 bottles under £20, 10 by glass **Notes** Tasting events & chef master classes, Sunday L, Vegetarian available, Civ Wed 60 **Seats** Pr/dining room 20 **Children** Portions, Menu **Parking** 8

Three Ways House

⊛ Modern British

Welcoming home of the famous Pudding Club

☎ 01386 438429 🖹 01386 438118
Chapel Ln, Mickleton GL55 6SB
e-mail: reception@puddingclub.com
dir: On B4632, in village centre

The Cotswold home of the famous Pudding Club, the hotel dates from 1870 and has lots of period charm, though the refurbished restaurant has a more contemporary style, with its attractive blue décor, crisp linen and armchair seats. The menu features regional British cuisine and traditional dishes with a modern lightness, using the best of fresh produce, much of it from local suppliers. Try smoked duck breast poached in Earl Grey tea for starters, followed by braised blade of beef served with horseradish rösti and a selection of vegetables. The famous Pudding Club was founded in 1985 (even the hotel bedrooms have pudding themes) and at least three puddings with custard are always on offer, though other desserts are available; a trio of steamed puddings includes an excellent version with coconut and raspberry jam.

Chef Mark Rowlandson **Owner** Simon Coombe & Peter Henderson **Times** 12-2.30/7-9.30 Closed L Mon-Sat **Prices** Fixed L 2 course £20-£25, Fixed D 3 course £35-

£40, Service optional **Wines** 36 bottles over £20, 22 bottles under £20, 15 by glass **Notes** Sunday L, Vegetarian available, Civ Wed 80, Air con **Seats** 80, Pr/ dining room 70 **Children** Portions, Menu **Parking** 37, On street parking

---

CLEARWELL   Map 4 SO50

Tudor Farmhouse Hotel & Restaurant

⊛⊛ Modern British 🍃

Romantic converted farm with well judged modern cooking

☎ 01594 833046 🖹 01594 837093
High St GL16 8JS
e-mail: info@tudorfarmhousehotel.co.uk
dir: Off A4136 onto B4228, through Coleford, turn right into Clearwell, hotel on right just before War Memorial Cross

Exposed stonework, oak beams, wall panelling and wonderful inglenook fireplaces enhance the intimate and relaxed atmosphere at this 13th-century converted farm deep in the Forest of Dean. With a new chef at the stove cooking has moved up a gear; the innovative modern British menu changes with the seasons and utilises high quality local ingredients, including Welsh lamb and beef. Dishes are simply prepared allowing flavours to shine through, as seen in a well-textured ballotine of confit chicken with pistachios and chopped Parma ham, served with a spicy red onion relish and Dijon mustard cream, and a perfectly-cooked fillet of turbot served with a crispy crab beignet and a strong crab butter sauce. A rich, creamy white chocolate and raspberry crème brûlée rounds things off nicely.

Chef Blaine Reed **Owner** Colin & Hari Fell **Times** 12-2/7-9 Closed 24-27 Dec **Prices** Fixed L 2 course fr £16.50, Fixed D 3 course fr £32.50, Service optional **Wines** 22 bottles over £20, 24 bottles under £20, 8 by glass **Notes** Sunday L, Vegetarian available **Seats** 36, Pr/dining room 22 **Children** Portions, Menu **Parking** 30

The Wyndham Arms Hotel

⊛ Modern British

Ancient hostelry serving up classic gastro-pub dishes

☎ 01594 833666 🖹 01594 836450
GL16 8JT
e-mail: stay@thewyndhamhotel.co.uk
dir: Off B4228, in village centre on B4231

Sandwiched between the Wye Valley and the Forest of Dean the Wyndham Arms is a quintessential village inn with 6 centuries of history. True to type, it comes complete with all the gnarled oak beams, flagstone floors, exposed red brick walls and crackling log fire in an inglenook fireplace that you might expect. Unwind in the down-to-earth conviviality of the bar, where there's a wide-ranging fuss-free menu, or the Old Spot Restaurant offering a modern British carte based around local materials treated simply. Try local chicken and walnut terrine with pear and ginger chutney and follow with casserole of local mutton with juniper, red wine and root vegetables.

Times 12-2/6.30-9 Closed 1st wk Jan

COLN ST ALDWYNS   Map 5 SP10

The New Inn at Coln

⊛⊛ Modern European

Contemporary food in sensitively modernised village inn

☎ 01285 750651 🖹 01285 750657
GL7 5AN

Tucked away in a sleepy village setting the ancient New Inn looks a picture with its Cotswold stonework covered in creepers, open fields at the back and the River Coln meandering through nearby meadows. Refurbished and revitalised in recent years and now owned by Hillbrooke Hotels, the sensitive make-over has created light, bright and welcoming spaces using natural colours and smart contemporary furniture while maintaining the heart and soul of the building. At dinner, choose from a modern menu that focuses on high quality local and seasonal produce, a typical meal perhaps taking in pan-seared scallops with Niçoise salad to start, with steamed hake with beetroot risotto and leek and horseradish cream for main course. For pudding, try the pecan and date tart with coconut ice cream. Simpler dishes are available in the bar and on the terrace.

Times 12-2/7-9

CORSE LAWN
Map 10 S083

Corse Lawn House Hotel

British, French **V**

Attractive Queen Anne house with skilful kitchen team

☎ 01452 780771   📄 01452 780840
GL19 4LZ
e-mail: enquiries@corselawn.com
web: www.corselawn.com
dir: 5m SW of Tewkesbury on B4211, in village centre

The Grade II listed Queen Anne house sits back from the village green behind a pond that was once a coach wash in the days of horse-drawn transport. It has been home to the Hine family since 1978, and in many ways - entirely good ones - it is the antithesis of the modern, hip hotel, with genteel old-school standards of friendly service from uniformed staff and exemplary cuisine. The kitchen sources the finest local materials, with an especially keen eye for seasonal fish and game, and everything from the bread to petits fours is made in-house. Classic French and English culinary influences are the mainstay of the extensive menu, but flashes of modernity blend seamlessly with old favourites. Sharp technique from a long-standing kitchen team delivers precise flavours in starters such as baked queen scallops with Provençal stuffing, while main-course traditional roast woodcock comes with game gravy.

Chef Andrew Poole **Owner** Hine Family **Times** 12-2/7-9.30 Closed 24-26 Dec **Prices** Fixed L 2 course £15.50-£22.50, Fixed D 3 course £32.50, Starter £4.95-£10.95, Main £12.95-£18.95, Dessert £5.95-£6.95, Service optional **Wines** 400 bottles over £20, 39 bottles under £20, 10 by glass **Notes** Sunday L, Vegetarian menu, Civ Wed 70 **Seats** 50, Pr/dining room 28 **Children** Portions, Menu **Parking** 60

EBRINGTON
Map 10 SP14

The Ebrington Arms

Modern British **NEW**

Village inn with great British food

☎ 01386 593223   & 593378
GL55 6NH
e-mail: claire.alexander@mac.com
web: www.theebringtonarms.co.uk
dir: Take B4035 from Chipping Campden towards Shipston on Stour. After 0.5m turn left signed Ebrington

Pubs may be under threat across the country, but the Ebrington Arms has all the right attributes for a long and prosperous future: fabulous Cotswold stone exterior (it dates from 1640), atmospheric bar and dining area with loads of original features from flagstone flooring to roaring open fires, local ales and good, unpretentious, home-made food from a daily-changing menu. Crab cakes with wilted spinach and mustard sauce is a typical starter, and main courses might include line-caught sea bass with Ebrington wild garlic and lemon risotto, or home-cooked ham with free-range eggs from the village and home-cut chips. Classic desserts such as sticky toffee pudding make a fine finish to a meal.

Chef James Nixon, Andrew Knight **Owner** Claire, Jim Alexander **Times** 12-2.30/6.30-9.30 Closed 25 Dec, Mon (except BHs), D Sun **Prices** Starter £5-£6.50, Main £9.50-£16, Dessert £5-£5.95, Service optional, Groups min 6 service 10% **Wines** 7 bottles over £20, 20 bottles under £20, 8 by glass **Notes** Sunday L **Seats** 50, Pr/dining room 30 **Children** Portions **Parking** 13

LOWER SLAUGHTER
Map 10 SP12

Lower Slaughter Manor

– *see below*

Lower Slaughter Manor

LOWER SLAUGHTER
Map 10 SP12

Modern **V**

Exemplary cooking in chic manor house

☎ 01451 820456   📄 01451 822150
GL54 2HP
e-mail: info@lowerslaughter.co.uk
dir: Off A429, signed 'The Slaughters'. 0.5m into village on right

There is a timeless elegance about this wonderful manor house, which dates back to the 17th century, and its imposing presence makes it very much the centrepiece of this famous Cotswold village. Set within ample grounds with beech trees, manicured lawns and a secluded walled garden, it's an idyllic retreat. Inside, the levels of comfort and quality are immediately evident, with crackling log fires warming the many sumptuous lounges. The dining room is an elegant space that suitably complements the excellent cuisine on offer. The chic restaurant is intimate and sophisticated, and the stunning private dining room has sculptured coving and an impressive pillared fireplace. Accomplished modern British cuisine includes the likes of bresaola of home-cured Hereford beef with piccalilli, baby pear and dressed salad, or roasted pumpkin, chilli and coriander tortellini with butternut squash velouté, toasted pumpkin seeds and truffle dressing. Main courses make good use of wonderful produce and might include pan-fried breast of free-range Cotswold duck with confit duck leg and foie gras, red cabbage and glazed root vegetables. Finish with glazed lemon thyme tartlet and raspberry smoothie ice cream.

Chef David Kelman **Owner** von Essen Collection **Times** 12-2.30/7-9.30 **Prices** Fixed L 2 course £19.50, Starter £9.50-£13, Main £19.50-£37.50, Dessert £8.50-£10.50, Service optional **Wines** All bottles over £20, 6 by glass **Notes** Sunday L, Vegetarian menu, Dress restrictions, Smart, no jeans or trainers, Civ Wed 70

Seats 55, Pr/dining room 20 **Children** Portions, Menu **Parking** 30

Washbourne Court Hotel

◎◎ Modern British, French

Inventive cooking by the River Eye

☎ 01451 822143 📄 01451 821045
GL54 2HS
e-mail: info@washbournecourt.co.uk
dir: Off A429, village centre by river

The setting could do service in a TV costume drama. A 17th-century riverside inn in a pretty Cotswold village has low-slung beamed interiors with crooked ceilings and a magnificent fireplace, although by the time you reach the dining room, you know you've moved into the present day. Mirrored walls and box light fittings form the backdrop for modern European cooking of great imagination. Start with seared scallops on a purée of butternut squash, paired with chicken wing confit and red wine shallots, before going on to accurately cooked loin of local venison with braised red cabbage and Ventrèche bacon, served with quince, wild mushrooms and port sauce. A beautifully caramelised tarte Tatin has excellent flaky pastry and comes with boldly flavoured prune and Armagnac ice cream. Extras are all up to the mark, including the pre-dinner nibbles served in the bar.

Times 12.30-2.30/7-9.30

Mulberry Restaurant

◎◎ Modern British V

Modern cooking in a 16th-century inn

☎ 01608 650501 📄 01608 651481
Manor House Hotel, High St GL56 0LJ
e-mail: info@manorhousehotel.info
web: www.cotswold-inns-hotels.co.uk/manor
dir: Off A429 at south end of town

The house was bequeathed to the Dean and Chapter of Westminster in 1539 by Henry VIII, when it was a traditional coaching inn. Today, it offers the best of both worlds, with bags of period atmosphere alongside contemporary comforts and an enterprising style of modern cooking. That might translate as red mullet in tomato consommé with fennel salad, or thickly flavourful onion and thyme soup garnished with pig cheek raviolo, to begin, and then sea bass served on a slate tile with baby vegetables and a lobster claw. Fine British cheeses with walnut bread, quince and figs are one way to finish, or there may be pannacotta with spiced kumquats, caramelised hazelnuts and biscotti.

Chef Matt Pashley **Owner** Michael & Pamela Horton **Times** 12-2.30/7-9.30 **Prices** Fixed D 3 course £37.50, Service added but optional 10% **Wines** 53 bottles over £20, 26 bottles under £20, 8 by glass **Notes** Tasting menu 7 course, Sunday L, Vegetarian menu, Dress restrictions, Smart casual, no jeans, shorts or trainers, Civ Wed 120 **Seats** 65, Pr/dining room 120 **Children** Portions **Parking** 32

Redesdale Arms

◎ British

Relaxed dining in historic Cotswold inn

☎ 01608 650308 📄 01608 651843
High St GL56 0AW
e-mail: info@redesdalearms.co.uk

The fine old Cotswold-stone inn has stood for centuries in bustling Moreton and today offers a relaxed blend of traditional features and modern comforts. Eat in the bar or the conservatory restaurant and, when the weather allows, go for the courtyard garden. The light and airy dining room is relaxed and unstuffy, with varnished oak tables and walls hung with modern art; wood panelling and oak floorboards are a reminder of the heritage of the place. The menu focuses on local, seasonal produce, with

---

the straightforward approach successfully delivering traditional favourites such as beef Wellington or Devonshire mussels (seafood comes up from Brixham), to the more globally inspired tiger prawns in tempura batter with chicory salad and chilli and mango salsa.

The Wild Garlic Restaurant

◎◎ Modern British 🍸

Relaxing atmosphere and top-quality ingredients

☎ 01453 832615
Heavens Above, 3 Cossack Square GL6 0DB
e-mail: info@wild-garlic.co.uk
dir: M4 junct 18. A46 towards Stroud. Enter Nailsworth, turn left at rdbt and then an immediate left. Restaurant opposite Britannia Pub

In a quiet corner of a charming Cotswold town, this restaurant with rooms serves a sensibly short menu reflecting the best of what is in season. Chef-patron, and former head chef of nearby Calcot Manor, Matthew Beardshall, has settled into running his own venture and his hands-on approach, both with front-of-house staff and in the kitchen, ensures standards are kept high. The modern and stylish restaurant is housed in the former blacksmith's quarters. Tables and chairs are hand-made by local craftsmen, as are the stained glass panels. The unpretentious menu may feature rabbit and mushroom pie, fillet of halibut, garlic and mussel broth, and toffee soufflé and banana and lime ice cream to finish. Extras such as home-baked bread and infused dipping oil and a pre-dessert granité are all of a high standard. Service is welcoming with no airs and graces.

Chef Matthew Beardshall **Owner** Matthew Beardshall **Times** 12-2/7-9 Closed 1st 2 wks Jan, Mon-Tue, D Sun **Prices** Starter £3.95-£7.95, Main £11.50-£15.95, Dessert £4.25-£6.25, Service optional **Wines** 21 bottles over £20, 20 bottles under £20, 6 by glass **Notes** Sunday L, Vegetarian available **Seats** 45 **Children** Portions **Parking** NCP, parking on street

Three Choirs Vineyards

◎◎ Modern British 🍸

Tuscan-style vineyard views and summer terrace dining

☎ 01531 890223 📄 01531 890877
GL18 1LS
e-mail: ts@threechoirs.com
dir: 2m N of Newent on B4215, follow brown tourist signs

There are few better ways to sample the wares from one of Britain's leading vineyards than sitting on the vine-covered terrace of this converted farmhouse; the setting is idyllic and the views across the 100-acre estate are wonderful. As you look out across the vines, sipping a glass of fumé, you could be in Burgundy or Tuscany and the Mediterranean-inspired food certainly fits the vibe on warm summer days. Using fresh local ingredients, simply

continued

NEWENT *continued*

prepared and well-executed dishes may take in mosaic of rabbit loin, confit leg, chicken liver and caramelised figs with tomato chutney, seared bream on wilted spinach with a light parmesan velouté, and iced chocolate and honeycomb parfait. Huge picture windows in the light and airy restaurant make the most of the vineyard views.

Chef Darren Leonard **Owner** Three Choirs Vineyards Ltd **Times** 12-2/7-9 Closed Xmas, New Year **Prices** Fixed L 2 course fr £19.50, Fixed D 3 course fr £36.95, Starter £5.50-£9.95, Main £16-£19.95, Dessert £5.50-£7.50, Service optional, Groups min 10 service 10% **Wines** 20 bottles over £20, 34 bottles under £20, 12 by glass **Notes** Sunday L, Vegetarian available **Seats** 50, Pr/dining room 20 **Children** Portions, Menu **Parking** 50

NORTHLEACH   Map 10 SP11

The Puesdown Inn

◉◉ Modern British

Stylish coaching inn with appealing modern menu

☎ 01451 860262   📠 01451 861262
Compton Abdale GL54 4DN
e-mail: inn4food@btopenworld.com
dir: On A40 (Cheltenham-Oxford), 7m from Cheltenham, 3m W of Northleach

The unusual monicker of this stylish Cotswold coaching inn comes from the ancient English for 'windy ridge'. Its elevated location on the A40 - the Old Salt Way - has been a roadside pitstop for travellers since as long ago as 1236. The current hands-on owners have given the venerable old place a loving restyle, but nothing too radical, mind - no sterile stripped-out minimalism - just warm hues, squashy sofas and log fires to foster an inviting, laid-back ambience. A daily menu takes well-sourced local and seasonal produce along the modern British route to skilfully-cooked, eye-catching dishes that might include baked scallops with black pudding, tiger prawns and Pernod jus, or roast local partridge with rösti potato, glazed apples and brandy sauce. To finish, there might be an olive oil and orange cake with seasonal berries and crème fraîche.

Chef John Armstrong **Owner** John & Maggie Armstrong **Times** 10-3/6-11 Closed 1 wk Jan, D Sun-Mon **Prices** Fixed L 2 course £10-£18.75, Fixed D 3 course £23.50-£28.50, Starter £5-£8.50, Main £10.50-£17, Dessert £5.50-£6.25, Service optional, Groups min 8 service 10% **Wines** 19 bottles over £20, 16 bottles under £20, 11 by glass **Notes** Sunday L, Vegetarian available **Seats** 48, Pr/dining room 24 **Children** Portions **Parking** 80

PAXFORD   Map 10 SP13

Churchill Arms

◉ Modern British

Enjoyable food in charming Cotswold pub

☎ 01386 594000   📠 01386 594005
GL55 6XH
e-mail: mail@thechurchillarms.com
dir: 2m E of Chipping Campden

An unpretentious Cotswold-stone pub with inglenook fireplace, beams, oak flooring and flagstones, the Churchill Arms has plenty of rustic charm and relaxed informality, with an assortment of wooden furniture, a collection of prints, and chalkboards for both food and wine. Food is ordered at the bar in the traditional fashion. Expect attractively presented, modern dishes that might include sautéed lamb's kidneys with a tartlette of creamed leeks, pancetta and prunes, followed by grilled pork chop with a herb and parmesan crust, served with lentils with apple and mustard. Finish with triple chocolate torte with raspberry parfait.

Times 12-2.30/7-9.30 Closed 25 Dec

SOUTHROP   Map 5 SP10

The Swan at Southrop

◉◉ British, European Ⓥ ✪

Anglo-Mediterranean cooking in a creeper-clad Cotswold inn

☎ 01367 850205   📠 01367 850517
GL7 3NU
e-mail: info@theswanatsouthrop.co.uk
web: www.theswanatsouthrop.co.uk
dir: Please telephone for directions

A painstakingly preserved early 17th-century Cotswold inn, smothered in creepers, is unexpectedly light and airy inside, and yet retains all its period charm. Log fires make for a cosy wintertime ambience, and the service could hardly be more efficient and welcoming. 'Turf-to-table cooking' is what's on offer, with some splashes of Mediterranean sunshine illuminating the impeccable local produce. Crab linguini is alive with chilli flakes and fine flavour, while a ballotine of chorizo-stuffed squid makes an unusual and enjoyable main dish, served with peperonata and garlic-roast potatoes. Belly pork confit is cooked crisp, and accompanied by field mushrooms and artichokes, and the must-have dessert is surely the

chargrilled peach, dosed with Amaretto and served with salty butterscotch ice cream.

Chef Sebastian Snow **Owner** Sebastian & Lana Snow **Times** 12-3/6-10 Closed 25 Dec, D Sun **Prices** Fixed L 2 course £13, Fixed D 3 course £17, Starter £6-£9, Main £12-£18, Dessert £5-£6, Service optional **Wines** 80 bottles over £20, 22 bottles under £20, 16 by glass **Notes** Sunday L, Vegetarian menu **Seats** 70, Pr/dining room 24 **Children** Portions, Menu

---

STONEHOUSE   Map 4 SO80

Stonehouse Court

◉ British, Mediterranean

Modern British style in Elizabethan manor, plus ghost

☎ 0871 871 3240   📠 0871 871 3241
Bristol Rd GL10 3RA
e-mail: info@stonehousecourt.co.uk
dir: M5 junct 13/A419 (Stroud). Straight on at 2 rdbts, under rail bridge. Hotel 100yds on right

Set in 6 acres of attractive gardens overlooking the Stroud Canal, Stonehouse is an Elizabethan manor house. Gutted by fire in 1908, and haunted evidently by the ghost of a love-lorn butler, it also features the elegantly panelled Henry's Restaurant, complete with open-air terrace. Modern British cooking of some distinction takes in roasted aubergine risotto with anchovy Caesar salad, pistachio-crusted lamb with creamed potatoes, and baked lemon sole filled with sole and langoustine mousse, in vermouth butter sauce. Finish with lemon tart, or plum crumble with clotted cream.

Times 12-3/7-10 Closed L Sat

STOW-ON-THE-WOLD   Map 11 SP12

Fosse Manor

◉◉ Modern British

Accomplished cooking in elegant country-house hotel

☎ 01451 830354   📠 01451 832486
GL54 1JX
e-mail: enquiries@fossemanor.co.uk
dir: From Stow-on-the-Wold take A429 S for 1m

A private residence until the 1950s, when it was changed into a nursing home, Fosse Manor has been a hotel for thirty years. Set back from the A429, this sophisticated and comfortable country-house hotel was once a rectory and it stands in 5 acres of tranquil grounds. Behind the mellow stone exterior is a blend of contemporary and traditional décor. The Modern British cuisine is underpinned by classical techniques, with an emphasis on local produce. Try a starter of Donnington smoked trout fishcake with poached Burford Brown egg and hollandaise, followed by Cotswold chicken breast with celeriac and potato gratin, truffled beans and Madeira sauce. Finish with iced banana parfait with chocolate sorbet and toffee sauce.

Times 12-2/7-9

The Kings Head Inn

◎ Traditional British

Charming village-green inn serving accomplished traditional food

☎ 01608 658365 🖹 01608 658902
The Green, Bledington OX7 6XQ
e-mail: kingshead@orr-ewing.com
dir: On B4450, 4m from Stow-on-the-Wold

Facing the village green with its meandering brook, the rambling, stone-built 15th-century Kings Head is the quintessential Cotswold pub. Expect crackling log fires, wonky floors, head-cracking low beams and pints of Hooky on tap in the bar, an informal dining room decked out with solid oak tables on flagstones, and a clutch of contemporary-styled bedrooms. Fresh local produce, including beef from the family farm, feature on ever-changing menus, which mix classic dishes with more innovative choices: potted shrimps with lemon butter, crayfish and rocket linguini, and lamb cutlets with redcurrant and mint salsa, and chocolate caramel brownie.

Times 12-2/7-9.30 Closed 25-26 Dec

The Old Butcher's

◎◎ Modern British

Uncomplicated modern British food in informal surroundings

☎ 01451 831700
Park St GL54 1AQ
e-mail: info@theoldbutchers.com
dir: Please telephone for directions

As the name announces, this used to be a butcher's shop, but is now a bustling, modern restaurant with white walls, a relaxed approach and some seating out front. Crisply written menus advertise a style of uncomplicated modern British food that makes the most of fresh ingredients. Parma ham is used to wrap up a hare terrine that comes with fig chutney and toasted sourdough, while the quality of fish can be little short of amazing, especially when simply presented like the roasted plaice that comes with capers and lemon. Slow-cooking is as ever the best method for good pork, which might be the tender belly, served with its crackling and a bean and chorizo salad. Properly oozy chocolate fondant with vanilla ice cream on crushed pistachios is a memorable finale.

Chef Peter Robinson **Owner** Louise & Peter Robinson **Times** 12-2.30/6-9.30 Closed Mon, D Sun **Prices** Fixed L 2 course fr £12, Starter £5-£8.50, Main £10.50-£16.50, Dessert £4-£5.50, Service optional **Wines** 55 bottles over £20, 19 bottles under £20, 14 by glass **Notes** Sunday L, Vegetarian available, Air con **Seats** 45 **Children** Portions **Parking** On street

The Royalist Hotel

◎◎ Modern European

Modern British cooking in a 10th-century inn

☎ 01451 830670 🖹 01451 870048
Digbeth St GL54 1BN
e-mail: info@theroyalisthotel.com
dir: Off A436

They (quite literally) don't come any older than this. With a construction date of AD 947, the Royalist is Britain's earliest surviving inn. The millennium-old timbers, medieval frieze and the leper pit in the cellars are attractions enough in themselves, but the place wouldn't be in the guide unless there were also gastronomic reason for stopping by. And that there is in plenty. The cooking is considerably more modern than the surroundings, with the likes of seared scallops accompanied by squid ink risotto, or partridge breast with soused vegetables and redcurrant jus, to start, followed by mackerel with clams and baby leeks in shellfish bisque. Finish with an apple muffin, served with clotted cream ice cream and cider granita.

Times 12-2.30/7-9.30

STROUD Map 4 SO80

Burleigh Court Hotel

◎◎ Modern British

Classical country-house style

☎ 01453 883804 🖹 01453 886870
Burleigh, Minchinhampton GL5 2PF
e-mail: info@burleighcourthotel.co.uk
dir: 2.5m SE of Stroud, off A419

This listed Cotswold stone manor house - nestled into the steep hillside with stunning views over the Golden Valley - dates back to the 18th century and is set in beautifully maintained terraced gardens designed by Clough

Williams-Ellis. The hotel remains true to its classical country-house roots, with an oak-panelled bar and elegant restaurant that provides a formal setting for modern British cuisine. The menus make the most of the freshest local produce, with many herbs and vegetables home grown, while the cooking keeps things accurate, simple and fresh. Think confit belly of Gloucestershire Old Spot pork served with celeriac purée, glazed apples and a sage jus, or perhaps a rhubarb and mascarpone cheesecake finish, accompanied by vanilla ice cream and stem ginger syrup.

Times 12-2/7-9 Closed 24-26 Dec

TETBURY Map 4 ST89

Calcot Manor

◎◎ Modern British ★

Charming 14th-century Cotswold retreat with vibrant modern cuisine

☎ 01666 890391 🖹 01666 890394
Calcot GL8 8YJ
e-mail: reception@calcotmanor.co.uk
dir: M4 junct 18, A46 towards Stroud. At x-roads junct with A4135 turn right, then 1st left

The Cistercian monks who built this medieval English farmhouse would no doubt have approved of the food now served at Calcot Manor, but the pampering pleasures on offer in its sleek health spa might sit uneasily with a hairshirt mindset. Contemporary rustic chic is the order of the day in this effortlessly elegant hotel that offers two eating venues: the light-bathed main Conservatory Restaurant, or the more casual pubby-style Gumstool Inn for simple classics. The succinct modern British menu offers lively flavour combinations that wring the most out of carefully-sourced local produce. Try Jerusalem artichoke soup with truffle oil and a pesto-topped croûton to start, then watch your fillet of aged beef being roasted in the wood-burning oven then served un-fussily with creamy béarnaise sauce and crispy potato rösti.

continued

TETBURY *continued*

Chef Michael Croft **Owner** Richard Ball (MD) **Times** 12-2/7-9.30 **Prices** Fixed L 2 course fr £19, Starter £8.35-£17.40, Main £17.95-£21, Dessert £8.35, Service optional **Wines** 6 bottles under £20, 12 by glass **Notes** Sunday L, Vegetarian available, Civ Wed 100, Air con **Seats** 100, Pr/dining room 16 **Children** Portions, Menu **Parking** 150

The Trouble House

◉◉ Traditional French 🕭

Classy yet hearty food in relaxed inn

☎ 01666 502206
Cirencester Rd GL8 8SG
e-mail: info@troublehouse.co.uk
dir: 1.5m outside Tetbury on A433 towards Cirencester

Hard beside the busy Tetbury to Cirencester road, this isolated and unassuming Cotswold-stone pub continues to draw discerning foodies for robust, full-flavoured dishes prepared from quality local seasonal produce. Expect wooden floors, open fires, pastel-coloured walls and rustic, unclothed tables in the relaxed, contemporary-styled bar and dining room. Choose from a short, regularly-changing menu, order at the bar in typical, informal pub style and perhaps tuck into an intensely flavoured red mullet soup, a carefully prepared and presented roast partridge with confit leg, fondant potatoes and thyme jus, rounding off

with a traditional coffee crème brûlée. Home-made breads and chocolate truffles, and a handful of quality bar meals complete the pleasing picture.

Chef Martin Caws **Owner** Martin & Neringa Caws **Times** 12-2/7-9.30 Closed 1st wk Jan & BHs, Mon, D Sun **Prices** Starter £5-£9.50, Main £13.95-£18.90, Dessert £5-£5.50, Service optional, Groups min 8 service 10% **Wines** 41 bottles over £20, 32 bottles under £20, 12 by glass **Notes** Sunday L, Vegetarian available **Seats** 50 **Children** Portions **Parking** 25

Thornbury Castle

◉◉ Modern British

Up-to-date cooking in a majestic Tudor castle

☎ 01454 281182 📠 01454 416188
Castle St BS35 1HH
e-mail: info@thornburycastle.co.uk
dir: M5 junct 16, N on A38. 4m to lights, turn left. Follow brown Historic Castle signs. Restaurant behind St Mary's church

The only Tudor castle in England open as a hotel, Thornbury is a magnificent edifice, within which the enamoured Henry VIII and Anne Boleyn once sauntered, before that unpleasantness took place. So majestic is it that the restaurant is composed of a trio of rooms, in which oak panelling and fine portraits set the elevated

tone. Admirably resisting the tendency to pastiche medieval banqueting, the menu offers a much more contemporary take on country-house cooking, with some nice combinations. A salad of firm globe artichoke and potato is served in tomato vinaigrette with a poached egg as a simple enough opener, or there may be red mullet with mascarpone and soused vegetables. Continue with impressive rump of lamb, accompanied by sumptuously textured pomme mousseline and Savoy cabbage in red wine jus, and round things off with an exquisitely refreshing ensemble of mango bavarois, pineapple salsa and orange sorbet.

Thornbury Castle

Times 11.45-2/7-9

Lords of the Manor

◉◉◉ — *see below*

Lords of the Manor

Modern British 🍷

Gutsy modern European cooking in a stylishly-refurbished country house

☎ 01451 820243 📠 01451 820696
GL54 2JD
e-mail: enquiries@lordsofthemanor.com
dir: Follow signs towards The Slaughters 2m W of A429. Hotel on right in centre of Upper Slaughter

At the heart of a blue-chip Cotswold hamlet, this caramel-coloured stone former rectory presents an image of country-house tradition as English as green wellies and Burberry headscarves. At least from the outside, that is: in 2008 the designers were let loose with a £1.5 million budget to give the old girl a more chic, modern look. Nothing too radical, mind, just enough in the way of

bold colours, contemporary fabrics, touchy-feely textures and up-to-date furnishings to blend subtly with the antiques, mullioned windows and grand fireplaces dotted around its warren of rooms. The dining room has vibrant modern art on ivory walls, comfy high-backed chairs and exuberant displays of flowers. Service delivers a serious level of polish and proficiency, to go with food that pulls out all the stops for intense flavour and precise presentation. Chef Matt Weedon uses top-notch local, seasonal produce as the solid foundation for gutsy modern cooking, underpinned by outstanding classically-based technical skills. Simple flavours leap from the plate in a menu packed with inventive vitality that consistently hits the high notes. A riff on crab might appear among starters, as Cornish white crab meat, brown meat bavarois, crab beignet, ginger beer jelly, crab tuile and lemon dressing. Next, a tasting plate of rabbit, presented as a mini rack with mustard crust, liver, kidney and loin demonstrates strong technical skills. Decadent desserts might turn up a praline mousse with walnut

croquant, Pedro Ximenez jelly and dark chocolate sorbet. Top-drawer Tuscan heavyweights feature on a superlative choice of Italian wines.

Chef Matt Weedon **Owner** Empire Ventures **Times** 12-2.30/7-9.30 **Prices** Fixed D 4 course £55-£59.95, Tasting menu £65, Service added but optional 10% **Wines** 385 bottles over £20, 4 bottles under £20, 12 by glass **Notes** Tasting menu 7 course, Sunday L, Vegetarian available, Dress restrictions, Smart casual, no trainers or jeans, Civ Wed 50 **Seats** 50, Pr/dining room 30 **Children** Portions, Menu **Parking** 40

WICK Map 4 ST77

Oakwood

◉◉ Modern British ✿

Stylish cooking in a stone lodge in the Cotswolds

☎ 0117 937 1800 📠 0117 937 1813
The Park, Bath Rd BS30 5RN
e-mail: info@presort.com
dir: Just off A420

A majestic Jacobean country house in the Cotswolds near Bath is home to The Park hotel and golfing resort. Even if you're not the golfing sort, the place has plenty to ponder, with 240 acres of parkland to explore, and fine interiors, including the converted stone Masonic lodge that forms the Oakwood restaurant. The menus are written with appealing simplicity, and furnish cooking of some flair. A tartlet of braised leeks, walnuts and Roquefort, dressed in aïoli, might start a meal, while main courses run a gamut from roast brill with sweet peppers, capers, tomatoes and basil, to noisettes of lamb with sprouting broccoli, roasted hazelnuts and lemon. The trendy tonka bean gets an outing at dessert stage, in a rich cream offset with tart Granny Smith apple and blackcurrant sorbet.

Chef Mark Treasure **Owner** TP Resort Ltd
Times 12-2.30/7-9.30 Closed L Mon-Sat **Prices** Fixed L 2 course £15.75, Fixed D 3 course £29.95, Service added but optional 12.5% **Wines** 49 bottles over £20, 15 bottles under £20, 8 by glass **Notes** Sunday L, Vegetarian available, Civ Wed 130 **Seats** 36, Pr/dining room 130 **Children** Portions, Menu **Parking** 250

WINCHCOMBE Map 10 SP02

5 North Street

◉◉◉ *— see below*

Wesley House

◉◉ Modern European

Stylish restaurant in pretty Cotswold town

☎ 01242 602366 📠 01242 609046
High St GL54 5LJ
e-mail: enquiries@wesleyhouse.co.uk
web: www.wesleyhouse.co.uk
dir: In centre of Winchcombe

Tucked away in the heart of this small Cotswold town, Wesley House is a charming half-timbered property named after the Methodist preacher who once stayed here in the 18th century. Oozing traditional character, with beamed ceilings, exposed stone, and open fireplaces, the restaurant also incorporates a stylish glass atrium with unique modern lighting and stunning floral displays. Seasonal variations ring the changes on the modern

continued

---

5 North Street

WINCHCOMBE Map 10 SP02

Modern European V

Cotswold star serving straightforwardly brilliant food

☎ 01242 604566 📠 01242 603788
5 North St GL54 5LH
e-mail: marcusashenford@yahoo.co.uk
dir: 7m from Cheltenham

Just off the high street, the Ashenfords' small but perfectly formed restaurant is a major player in the highly dynamic Cotswold dining scene. The style is determinedly unpretentious, with amiable service and well-spaced, unclothed tables and a sober colour scheme. Marcus's simple but effective cooking utilises produce of palpable quality, achieving excellent combinations and fantastic depth of flavour. Like the surrounding décor, it's all about quiet understatement, and all the more effective for that.

High standards are consistently hit from one visit to the next, and within each meal. A range of four fixed-price menus enables you to decide on a budget, with the seven-course Gourmet option a succession of surprises. A brace of fat, tenderly caramelised scallops is topped with light cauliflower purée, with an expertly judged dressing of mango and vanilla in support. Alongside them comes a glass of richly dark crab consommé containing pieces of the white meat. So far, so stunning, but dinner may proceed with meltingly soft best end of local lamb, accompanied by the rolled, slow-cooked breast, served with rosemary carrots, mash, and an opulent lamb stock reduction. The form dessert is a serving of white chocolate and basil crème brûlée, intense passionfruit sorbet and chocolate ice cream studded with gooey marshmallow. All incidentals, from the superlative breads to the petits fours, are equally up to snuff.

Chef Marcus Ashenford **Owner** Marcus & Kate Ashenford
Times 12.30-1.30/7-9 Closed 1st 2 wks Jan, 1 wk Aug, Mon, L Tue, D Sun **Prices** Fixed L 2 course £21.50, Fixed D 3 course £34-£44, Tasting menu £65, Service optional **Wines** 60 bottles over £20, 12 bottles under £20, 6 by glass **Notes** Gourmet menu 7 course £55, Tasting menu 10 course, Sunday L, Vegetarian menu **Seats** 26 **Children** Portions, Menu **Parking** On street, pay & display

WINCHCOMBE *continued*

British menus with Mediterranean influences, and look out for special offers at lunch. Start with terrine of confit duck with grape chutney and follow with roast halibut with mussel stew or pork loin with apple sauce. Finish with warm almond sponge with caramelised pear compôte and vanilla ice cream.

Wesley House

Chef Martin Dunn **Owner** Matthew Brown **Times** 12-2/7-9 Closed D Sun **Prices** Food prices not confirmed for 2010. Please telephone for details. **Wines** 65 bottles over £20, 20 bottles under £20, 15 by glass **Notes** Sunday L, Vegetarian available, Civ Wed 60, Air con **Seats** 70, Pr/dining room 24 **Children** Portions **Parking** In the square

---

WOTTON-UNDER-EDGE   Map 4 ST79

Orangery Restaurant

◉ Modern British NEW ✿

Inspiring conservatory setting

☎ 01454 263000 🖹 01454 263001
Tortworth Court Four Pillars, Tortworth GL12 8HH
e-mail: tortworth@four-pillars.co.uk
web: www.four-pillars.co.uk
dir: M5 junct 14. Follow B4509 towards Wotton. Turn right at top of hill onto Tortworth Rd, hotel 0.5m on right

The Tortworth Estate shop with its produce from surrounding farms is the source of much of what appears on the menu at the Orangery Restaurant. There are over 30 acres of grounds surrounding this imposing gothic manor, including an arboretum and beautifully manicured lawns. The Orangery is a fabulous free-standing construction of ornate curved glass dating from 1899, which has been impeccably restored and fitted out as a restaurant. Dishes are refreshingly straightforward, such as confit magret - good crisp skin and soft-textured meat - in a starter with braised butter beans, and main-course roasted Cornish turbot with dill tagliatelle and

mussels. Finish with vanilla pannacotta invigorated with passionfruit, pineapple and orange.

Chef Nigel Jones **Owner** Four Pillars **Times** 12-2.30/7-10 Closed Sun-Mon, L Sat **Prices** Fixed L 2 course fr £15.95, Starter £5.25-£9.95, Main £13.95-£22.95, Dessert £5.95-£7.95, Service included **Wines** 22 bottles over £20, 24 bottles under £20, 12 by glass **Notes** Vegetarian available, Dress restrictions, Smart casual, Civ Wed 120 **Seats** 90, Pr/dining room 12 **Children** Portions **Parking** 150

GREATER MANCHESTER

MANCHESTER   Map 16 SJ89

Abode Manchester

◉◉ Modern European

Exciting food and a cool vibe

☎ 0161 200 5678 & 247 7744 🖹 0161 247 7747
107 Piccadilly M1 2DB
e-mail: reservationsmanchester@abodehotels.co.uk
dir: in city centre, 2 mins walk from Piccadilly station

Victorian cotton merchants had a few bob back in the day, and one of their former warehouses has been transformed into something a bit special: a glamorous and hip hotel with a basement restaurant and bar. Today's equivalent of those cotton merchants can unwind in the chic champagne bar or eat at dark-wood tables in the moodily-lit restaurant, where fine glassware and crockery add a touch of refinement. Michael Caines' food is broadly modern European, and the grazing menu (alongside a carte and tasting options) gives the chance to get a real taste of the place. North Western produce figures on the menu, so pan-fried Cheshire sirloin steak comes with celeriac as purée and remoulade, roasted shallots and Madeira sauce. Finish with passionfruit parfait with coconut foam. There's an all-day café-bar, too.

Times 12-2.30/6-10 Closed 1 Jan, Sun

City Café

◉ Modern European NEW ✿

Contemporary European cooking in the bustling heart of Manchester

☎ 0161 242 1020 & 242 1000 🖹 0161 242 1001
City Inn Manchester, One Piccadilly Place, 1 Auburn St M1 3DG
e-mail: manchester.citycafe@cityinn.com

This stylish modern restaurant has a prime location in a landmark development at the heart of Manchester. If you're seriously into people-watching as you eat, the outdoor terrace overlooking the constant bustle of Piccadilly Place is made for you; otherwise, the smart restaurant is a softly stylish venue for interesting modern European cuisine prepared by a confident kitchen that clearly seeks out quality, seasonal ingredients. Starters might offer delicately cured salmon with gribiche sauce and a warm crab cake, followed by a fillet of cod with

crisp rösti potato and fish cream sauce. End with a classic almond pannacotta.

Chef Kevin Fawkes **Owner** City Inn Ltd **Times** 12-2.30/5.30-10 **Prices** Food prices not confirmed for 2010. Please telephone for details. **Wines** 44 bottles over £20, 13 bottles under £20, 29 by glass **Notes** Sunday L, Vegetarian available, Dress restrictions, Smart casual, Civ Wed 120, Air con **Seats** 114, Pr/dining room 130 **Children** Portions, Menu **Parking** 24, NCP Piccadilly Place

---

The Dining Rooms@ Worsley Park

◉ British

Country club serving modern British/European food

☎ 0161 975 2000 🖹 0161 799 6341
Walkden Rd, Worsley M28 2QT
e-mail: anna.collier@marriotthotels.com
dir: M60 junct 13, over 1st rdbt take A575. Hotel 400yds on left

This hotel and country club is situated in over 200 acres of attractive parkland, complete with championship golf course, that was formerly the Duke of Bridgwater's estate. The stylish Dining Rooms are divided into 3 chic sections, each one light and airy and decorated in modern style, with well-spaced tables and good views of the courtyard. The cooking style is modern British/European with the emphasis on regional and national top-quality ingredients. Simply yet attractively presented dishes might include a starter of crayfish soup with tarragon sour cream, a main course of spring rack of Yorkshire lamb with hazelnut crust, cabbage and carrots and red wine sauce, and, to finish, a light and rich Worsley sticky toffee pudding with vanilla ice cream.

Chef Sean Kelly **Owner** Marriott Hotels **Times** 1-3/5-10 Closed L Mon-Sat **Prices** Food prices not confirmed for 2010. Please telephone for details. **Wines** 40 bottles over £20, 27 bottles under £20, 20 by glass **Notes** Fixed L 4 course fr £18.95, Sunday L, Vegetarian available, Dress restrictions, Smart casual, Civ Wed 200, Air con **Seats** 140, Pr/dining room 14 **Children** Portions, Menu **Parking** 250

The French

◉◉ French

Lovingly preserved Edwardian hotel in the city centre

☎ 0161 236 3333 🖹 0161 932 4100
The Midland Hotel, Peter St M60 2DS
e-mail: midlandsales@qhotels.co.uk
dir: Please telephone for directions

The Midland Hotel was built in the Edwardian era for the railway company of the same name. Its arched façade, grandiose scale and beautifully restored interiors create a thoroughly convincing mood of bygone opulence, and the French restaurant, with its patterned red walls and distant waft of piano music, will have you all but adjusting your spats. Naturally, the cooking brings things gently up to date, with the likes of golden-seared scallops with Cumbrian pork confit and apple sauce to start, followed by something fashionable like a pairing of halibut and braised oxtail with fondant potato, or honey-roasted duck with beetroot tarte fine and orange purée. Execution of dessert soufflés such as raspberry, which comes with a matching ice cream, is flawless. Don't miss the superb petits fours with coffee.

Chef Paul Beckley **Owner** QHotels **Times** 7-11 Closed BHs, Sun-Mon, L all week **Prices** Starter £7.95-£14.95, Main £22.95-£29.95, Dessert £7.95, Service optional **Wines** 57 bottles over £20, 1 bottles under £20, 18 by glass **Notes** Dress restrictions, Smart casual, No sportswear, Civ Wed 50, Air con **Seats** 55 **Children** Portions **Parking** NCP behind hotel

Greens

◉ Modern Vegetarian V ✆

Well-established vegetarian restaurant

☎ 0161 434 4259 📠 0161 448 2098
43 Lapwing Ln, Didsbury M20 2NT
e-mail: simoncgreens@aol.com
dir: Telephone for directions, or see website

No spirit-sapping nut cutlets or stodgily virtuous beanburgers on the menu at Greens, thank you very much. This Mancunian haven of vegetarianism in trendy Didsbury offers an eclectic and tempting alternative to dead animals in a buzzy bistro-like restaurant. Unusually for a vegetarian restaurant, chef Simon Rimmer is actually a carnivore which certainly seems to work fine here and his TV experience makes him aware of the visual impact of each dish. So expect appealing looking dishes full of verve and flavour: pumpkin, pine nut and feta salad smacks nicely of the Mediterranean, deep-fried oyster mushrooms with plum sauce and Chinese pancakes hails from further east, while a homely main course of Cheshire cheese sausage with mustard mash comes with tomato chutney and a full-flavoured beer gravy.

Chef Simon Rimmer **Owner** Simon Connolly & Simon Rimmer **Times** 12-2/5.30-10.30 Closed BHs, L Mon **Prices** Fixed D 2 course fr £13.95, Starter £4-£6, Main £9.95-£11.25, Dessert £4.50-£5.50, Service optional, Groups min 6 service 10% **Wines** 6 bottles over £20, 16 bottles under £20, 6 by glass **Notes** Sunday L, Vegetarian menu **Seats** 48 **Children** Portions, Menu **Parking** On street

Harvey Nichols Second Floor Restaurant

◉ Modern European ⬧ NOTABLE WINE LIST

Trendy dining for designer shoppers, overlooking Exchange Square

☎ 0161 828 8898 📠 0161 828 8815
21 New Cathedral St M1 1AD
e-mail: secondfloor.reservations@harveynichols.com
dir: Just off Deansgate, town centre. 5 min walk from Victoria Station, on Exchange Sq

Floor-to-ceiling windows give diners great views of the city at this stylish and contemporary bar and brasserie located on the second floor of this trendy department store. With its black marble floor, crisp linen-clothed tables, swanky lighting and slick service, it draws sophisticated shoppers from the adjoining upmarket food hall for unfussy modern European dishes. The constantly evolving menu may take in chicken and foie gras terrine with quince purée and pear chutney, venison loin with smoked mash potato, celeriac purée, poached pear and sloe sauce, and banana crème brûlée with toffee spring roll.

Chef Alison Seagrave **Owner** Harvey Nichols **Times** 12-3/6-10.30 Closed 25-26 Dec, 1 Jan, Etr Sun, D Sun-Mon **Prices** Fixed L 2 course £30, Fixed D 3 course £40, Service added but optional 10% **Wines** 100+ bottles over £20, 30 bottles under £20, 20 by glass **Notes** Tasting menu 6 course, Sunday L, Vegetarian available, Air con **Seats** 50 **Children** Portions, Menu **Parking** Under store, across road

Lowry Hotel, The River Restaurant

◉◉ Modern British ✆

Stylish dining in a sophisticated, contemporary setting

☎ 0161 827 4000 & 827 4041 📠 0161 827 4001
50 Dearmans Place, Chapel Wharf, Salford M3 5LH
e-mail: hostess@roccofortehotels.com
dir: Telephone for directions

The River Restaurant is the gastronomic hub of Manchester's upscale, city-centre Lowry Hotel. It's a stylish, fashionable venue, as befits its centre-stage location, overlooking the River Irwell through a soaring wall of glass. The clean-cut designer décor ticks all the right boxes, with leather banquettes, crisp, white linen-clad tables, wooden flooring, and bright artwork to jazz up the neutral tones; clued-up, obliging staff complete the package with slick service. The kitchen has recently re-thought its menu and settled on a simplified, back-to-basics repertoire of British brasserie fare, carefully prepared and presented without fuss. To start, clam and lobster chowder is poured from a jug over fennel and basil ravioli, followed by seared scallops with cauliflower risotto, pine nuts and raisins. Treacle tart with prune and Armagnac ice cream wraps things up very satisfyingly. The wine list is worth a serious once-over.

Chef Oliver Thomas **Owner** Sir Rocco Forte & family **Times** 12-2.30/6-10.30 **Prices** Fixed L 2 course £14, Fixed D 3 course £21, Starter £6.75-£13.50, Main £15.75-£32.75, Dessert £7.50, Service added but optional 10% **Wines** 100 bottles over £20, 10 bottles under £20, 8 by glass **Notes** Sunday L, Civ Wed 108, Air con **Seats** 108, Pr/dining room 20 **Children** Portions, Menu **Parking** 100, NCP

Malmaison Manchester

◉ British, French

Contemporary dining in trendy boutique hotel

☎ 0161 278 1000 📠 0161 278 1002
1-3 Piccadilly M1 1LZ
e-mail: manchester@malmaison.com
dir: From M56 follow signs to Manchester, then to Piccadilly

Set in a former warehouse, the Manchester member of the Malmaison group of boutique hotels brings a touch of cool and somewhat theatrical style to the centre of the city. The restaurant marries art deco with booth-style seating, while the accomplished brasserie-style cooking suits the surroundings, majoring on flavour rather than fussy presentation. The seasonally-changing carte offers a grill selection as well as a Homegrown & Local menu. Mutton and barley broth is a comforting start before a fishy main course such as baked sea bass with braised fennel and confit tomato. Confit of Goosnargh chicken leg with sautéed spinach and red wine jus comes under the local banner.

continued

MANCHESTER *continued*

Chef Kevin Whiteford **Owner** Malmaison Limited **Times** 12-2.30/6-11 **Prices** Fixed L 2 course fr £14.50, Fixed D 3 course fr £16.50, Starter £4.50-£7.50, Main £11-£20, Dessert £4.95-£8.50, Service added but optional 10% **Wines** 173 bottles over £20, 19 bottles under £20, 21 by glass **Notes** Sunday L, Vegetarian available, Air con **Seats** 85, Pr/dining room 10 **Children** Portions **Parking** NCP 100 mtrs

Moss Nook

⊚ Modern International V

Traditional haute cuisine not far from the airport

☎ 0161 437 4778   📠 0161 498 8089
Ringway Rd, Moss Nook M22 5NA
e-mail: enquiries@mossnookrest.co.uk
dir: 1m from airport at junction of Ringway with B5166

A long-established traditional restaurant just a short onward journey from Manchester Airport, Moss Nook sticks to doing what it does well. Fresh flowers, crisp table linen, lots of silverware and crystal decanters offer a vision of period style, and the pergola terrace is popular in the summer. Twice-baked Swiss cheese soufflé is thoughtfully offset with a rocket salad, while main courses bring on moistly flaky poached hake on spinach with a richly buttery sauce, or grilled loin of venison sauced with red wine and wild mushrooms. To finish, the pear brûlée presented in a copper pan, with cassis sorbet and an array of fruits, comes highly recommended.

Chef Kevin Lofthouse **Owner** P & D Harrison **Times** 12-1.30/7-9.30 Closed 1 wk Jan, Sun & Mon, L Sat **Prices** Fixed L 2 course £15, Fixed D 3 course £36.50-£45, Starter £8.75-£14, Main £19.50-£24, Dessert £6.75-£7.25 **Wines** 100 bottles over £20, 10 bottles under £20, 8 by glass **Notes** Fixed L 5 course £21, Fixed D 7 course £38.50, Vegetarian available, Vegetarian menu, Dress restrictions, No jeans, trainers, Air con **Seats** 72 **Parking** 30

Signatures

⊚ Modern British

Mezzanine restaurant with city skyline views

☎ 0844 879 9088   📠 0870 194 2237
Macdonald Manchester Hotel, London Rd M1 2PG
e-mail: sales.manchester@macdonald-hotels.co.uk
dir: Please telephone for directions

Located high above the Manchester streets with great views of the city skyline, Signatures Restaurant in this smart modern hotel is bright by day, intimate by night. The menus offer an ever-growing range of organic foods, grass-fed beef and fish; salmon, kippers and haddock are supplied by the Loch Fyne Oysters company. Classic dishes are prepared with flair and imagination in the open kitchen, and might include seared Scottish king scallops with herb risotto and lemon and chive dressing to start, with main courses such as roast breast of corn-fed free-range chicken, Parmentier potatoes, sautéed morels, spring greens and lemon thyme velouté.

Chef Stuart Duff **Owner** Macdonald Hotels **Times** 6-10 **Prices** Fixed D 3 course £20-£24, Starter £5-£9, Main £11-£20, Dessert £4-£7, Service optional **Wines** 27 bottles over £20, 4 bottles under £20, 13 by glass **Notes** Vegetarian available, Dress restrictions, Smart casual **Seats** 40 **Children** Portions, Menu **Parking** 80, Fee for parking

---

OLDHAM   Map 16 SD90

White Hart Inn

⊚⊚ Modern, Traditional British 🕯

Impressive cooking in a venerable Lancashire inn

☎ 01457 872566   📠 01457 875190
51 Stockport Rd, Lydgate OL4 4JJ
e-mail: bookings@thewhitehart.co.uk
dir: M62 junct 20, A627, continue to end of bypass, then A669 to Saddleworth. Enter Lydgate turn right onto Stockport Rd. White Hart Inn 50yds on left

On the windswept A6050 opposite St Anne's church stands the White Hart, a venerable old inn that retains much of its Georgian charm. That said, the restrained modern styling in the restaurant has been sensitively applied, and there's an oak-beamed function room to cater for larger parties. The fixed-price Restaurant Menu comes into operation in the latter part of the week, and aims for clearly defined, honest flavours and presentations, rather than the frills of haute cuisine. Results are nonetheless impressive, ranging from rabbit rillettes with spiced pear chutney to mains such as poached halibut with crab and broad bean risotto, or Goosnargh duck, both breast meat and a confit leg, with Puy lentils and blackcurrants. North Country cheeses are proudly served for the savoury-toothed. The rest might set about lime pannacotta with mango sorbet.

Chef Paul Cookson **Owner** Mr C Brierley **Times** 12-2.30/6-9.30 Closed 26 Dec, 1 Jan, L Mon-Sat, D Tue & Sun **Prices** Fixed D 3 course £19.95, Service optional **Wines** 120 bottles over £20, 45 bottles under £20, 15 by glass **Notes** Fixed D 5 course £26.95, Sunday L, Vegetarian available, Civ Wed 140, Air con **Seats** 45, Pr/dining room 220 **Children** Portions, Menu **Parking** 75

ROCHDALE   Map 16 SD81

Nutters

⊚⊚ Modern British V 🏆 🕯

Technically skilful cooking using the best of Lancashire

☎ 01706 650167
Edenfield Rd, Norden OL12 7TT
e-mail: enquiries@nuttersrestaurant.com
dir: From Rochdale take A680 signed Blackburn. Edenfield Rd on right on leaving Norden

Confident flavour combinations rule at Andrew Nutter's eponymous restaurant housed in Wolstenholme Manor. If the gothic arches, 19th-century building and 6 acres of well-maintained parkland look familiar, that's probably because the building has been used for various TV and film shoots over the years. Service at the linen-clad tables is relaxed and friendly as befits a family-run restaurant. Prettily presented dishes show off the kitchen's high technical skills and local produce leads the way. Start perhaps with fillet of brill with a summer savoury crumb, sweetcorn pancake and a citrus yogurt dressing. Move on to loin of lamb with sticky shallot, pak choi fricassée, its own mini Lancashire hotpot and rosemary jus and finish with toffee apple and pear tart with flapjack ice cream. Afternoon tea, with or without champagne and strawberries, is also served.

Chef Andrew Nutter **Owner** Mr A Nutter, Mr R Nutter, Mrs K J Nutter **Times** 12-2/6.30-9.30 Closed 1-2 days after Xmas and New Year, Mon **Prices** Fixed L 2 course £13.95, Starter £4.80-£9.50, Main £16.95-£22, Dessert £6.50-£7.50, Service optional, Groups min 10 service 10% **Wines** 141 bottles over £20, 23 bottles under £20, 9 by glass **Notes** Gourmet menu 6 course £36, afternoon tea special Tue-Sat, Vegetarian menu, Dress restrictions, Smart casual, Civ Wed 120, Air con **Seats** 143, Pr/dining room 30 **Children** Portions, Menu **Parking** 100

The Peacock Room

◉ Modern British

Enjoyable dining in relaxed setting

☎ 01706 368591   🖷 01706 365177
The Crimble Hotel, Crimble Ln, Bamford OL11 4AD
e-mail: crimble@thedeckersgroup.com
dir: M62 junct 20 onto A627(M). Along Roch Valley Way, left at lights (B6222) & again at pub

Sitting in the grounds of the Crimble Hotel, which started life as a farm in the 17th century, The Peacock Room is a stunningly ornate space, with a mirrored ceiling, chandeliers, bronze statuettes and boldly patterned carpets and fabrics. The art deco look, inspired by the glamour of 1930s ocean liners, continues in the small bar, with its mullioned windows, gold ceiling mouldings and rich red drapes. The cooking is modern British, using the best of seasonal, regional ingredients. Start with smoked haddock and spinach tart with hollandaise, followed by rack of lamb with Provençale vegetables, fondant potato and red wine and black olive sauce. Melting chocolate pudding with black cherry compôte and vanilla ice cream makes a comforting finale.

Times 12-2.30/6.30-10 Closed Mon, L Sat

WIGAN   Map 15 SD50

Laureate Restaurant

◉ Modern British

Modern food in a conservatory restaurant with great views

☎ 01257 472100   🖷 01257 422401
Macdonald Kilhey Court, Chorley Rd, Standish WN1 2XN
e-mail: general.kilheycourt@macdonald-hotels.co.uk
dir: M6 junct 27, through village of Standish. Take B5239, left onto A5106, hotel on right

The Kilhey Court Hotel and Spa occupies an impressive Victorian-style country-house hotel convenient for Liverpool and Manchester. Set in 10 acres of private grounds, it has spectacular views of Worthington Lake, and a split-level restaurant in a large and airy conservatory. Take in the fabulous garden views through full-length windows whilst perusing the seasonal menu, which features some modern ideas and combinations. Dry-cured organic Scottish salmon, for example, comes with Morecambe Bay shrimps and mustard oil, and might be followed by loin of Perthshire venison with braised red cabbage, honey roast parsnips and juniper berry jus.

Chef Colin Cannon **Owner** Macdonald Hotels
Times 12.30-2.30/6.30-9.30 Closed L Sat **Prices** Food prices not confirmed for 2010. Please telephone for details. **Wines** 24 bottles over £20, 16 bottles under £20, 13 by glass **Notes** Vegetarian available **Seats** 80, Pr/dining room 22 **Children** Portions, Menu **Parking** 300

HAMPSHIRE

ALTON   Map 5 SU73

Alton Grange Hotel

◉◉ Modern European

Contemporary cuisine in a family-run country hotel

☎ 01420 86565   🖷 01420 541346
London Rd GU34 4EG
e-mail: info@altongrange.co.uk
web: www.altongrange.co.uk
dir: 300yds from A31 on A339

Handily placed for visits to Winchester and Jane Austen's house at Chawton, Alton Grange sits in 2 acres of pleasant gardens with rolling Hampshire countryside all around. It is a welcoming, family-run place that has a strong local following for its two dining venues. For simple food Muffins brasserie fits the bill, but the bar is raised a notch or two in the main Truffles restaurant, where Tiffany lamps, oriental bits and bobs and bold colours make for an intimate, traditional setting. Top quality seasonal ingredients underpin accurately-cooked classic British cuisine with modern flourishes. Flavour combinations draw on a tried and tested repertoire, as in a starter of chicken liver parfait with fig chutney and granary toast, while main-course Barbary duck breast with honey-roasted parsnips gets an oriental twist with pak choi and ginger-scented duck jus.

Chef David Heath **Owner** Andrea & David Levene
Times 12-2/7-9.30 Closed 24 Dec-3 Jan, ex 31 Dec
Prices Fixed L 2 course £19.50-£25.95, Fixed D 3 course £25.95-£30, Service added but optional 10% **Wines** 40 bottles over £20, 18 bottles under £20, 12 by glass **Notes** Sunday L, Vegetarian available, Dress restrictions, No shorts or jeans, Civ Wed 100 **Seats** 45, Pr/dining room 18 **Children** Portions **Parking** 40

The Anchor Inn

◉ British 🍃

Atmospheric country inn serving modern English classics

☎ 01420 23261
Lower Froyle GU34 4NA
e-mail: info@anchorinnatlowerfroyle.co.uk
dir: Leave A31 at exit for Bentley, follow signs for Lower Froyle. Inn on left

This gastro-pub with rooms is cousin to The Peat Spade Inn (see entry) and part of the Miller's Collection of small luxury inns and hotels. It displays the mini-group's unique country-inn styling; cosy bars have bags of atmosphere, as does the dining room which retains plenty of original features while period furnishings and prints hint at a bygone era. But it's not all interior styling over substance. The kitchen's accessible English menu keeps things simple and seasonal. Think traditional classics like Cumberland sausage with champ and onion gravy, and salt-beef hash with pickled cabbage and mustard sauce. Puddings follow suit, perhaps spotted dick and custard.

Chef Kevin Chandler **Owner** The Millers Collection
Times 12-2.30/7-9.30 **Prices** Starter £5.50-£9.50, Main £10.50-£18.90, Dessert £5.95, Service optional **Wines** 58 bottles over £20, 8 bottles under £20, 9 by glass
Notes Sunday L, Vegetarian available, Civ Wed 30
Seats 70, Pr/dining room 14 **Children** Portions
Parking 36

ANDOVER   Map 5 SU34

Esseborne Manor

◉ Modern British V

Timeless country-house setting with appealing menu

☎ 01264 736444   🖷 01264 736725
Hurstbourne Tarrant SP11 0ER
e-mail: info@esseborne-manor.co.uk
web: www.esseborne-manor.co.uk
dir: Halfway between Andover & Newbury on A343, just 1m N of Hurstbourne Tarrant

Set back from the A343 and surrounded by rolling farmland high above the beautiful Bourne Valley stands this beautiful Victorian house. Originally a country retreat and retaining that feel of a private home, this stylish country-house hotel is elegantly decorated, the intimate dining room adorned with rich fabrics, linen-clothed tables and upholstered chairs. In keeping with the setting, cooking is traditional British and European with occasional modern flourishes and makes good use of quality local seasonal ingredients. Start with pheasant terrine with plum chutney, then a sorbet appears before main courses such as Angus beef fillet with red wine jus, with dark chocolate fondant with vanilla ice cream a typical dessert.

Chef Anton Babarovic **Owner** Ian Hamilton
Times 12-2/7-9.30 **Prices** Fixed L 2 course £12, Fixed D 3 course £18, Starter £5-£8, Main £12-£28, Dessert £7-£9, Service optional **Wines** 90 bottles over £20, 42 bottles under £20, 11 by glass **Notes** Fixed menu with wine available 2, 3 or 4 course £25-£35, Sunday L, Vegetarian menu, Dress restrictions, Smart dress, Civ Wed 100 **Seats** 35, Pr/dining room 80 **Children** Portions **Parking** 40

BARTON-ON-SEA   Map 5 SZ29

Pebble Beach

◉ French, Mediterranean

Cliff-top restaurant serving good, fresh produce with a touch of French flair

☎ 01425 627777   🖷 01425 610689
Marine Dr BH25 7DZ
e-mail: mail@pebblebeach-uk.com
dir: A35 from Southampton onto A337 to New Milton, turn left down Barton Court Ave to clifftop

A lofty cliff-top position gives unbroken sea views from the ample terrace of Pebble Beach clear across Christchurch Bay to the chalk-white Needles on the Isle of Wight. When the weather is doing its worst, full-length windows provide the same outlook from inside a rather glitzy split-level dining room with a white baby grand, wrought-iron railings and high stools at the oyster bar where you can watch the action in the open kitchen. With head chef Pierre Chevillard at the helm, French influences are clear. Fresh local shellfish come by the platter, or try a double-baked smoked haddock and mature cheese soufflé, then steamed brill topped with shrimps, tomato compôte and spinach with a garlicky jus. An impeccable iced raspberry parfait filled with warm raspberries and meringue served on crunchy praline makes a fine finale.

Chef Pierre Chevillard **Owner** Mike Caddy
Times 11-2.30/6-11 Closed D 25 Dec & 1 Jan
Prices Starter £4.95-£9.90, Main £12.95-£34, Dessert £6.50-£17.90, Service optional, Groups min 10 service 10% **Wines** 74 bottles over £20, 31 bottles under £20, 16 by glass **Notes** Sunday L, Vegetarian available, Dress restrictions, Smart casual, no beachwear, Air con
Seats 90 **Children** Portions **Parking** 20

BASINGSTOKE   Map 5 SU65

Audleys Wood

◉◉ European

Modern cooking in relaxing Hampshire countryside

☎ 01256 817555   🖷 01256 817500
Alton Rd RG25 2JT
e-mail: info@audleyswood.com
dir: M3 junct 6. From Basingstoke take A339 towards Alton, hotel on right

The red-brick Victorian mansion was built in the gothic renaissance style and was born again as a hotel in 1989. The attractive grounds can be glimpsed through large windows in the impressive vaulted Gallery Restaurant, where wooden tables are dressed with candles and hyacinths. Service is refined but not too stiff. The eye-catching menu sees some modern classics alongside a few more adventurous combinations: pressed ham hock terrine, for example, with real depth of flavour and accompanied by toasted brioche and date and fig relish. Main-course braised ox cheek and tail is dressed with a fashionable foam (horseradish) and dessert might be not one, not two, but three brûlées (raspberry, maple syrup and traditional vanilla).

Times 12.30-2/7-9.45 Closed L Sat, BHs (booking only)

The Hampshire Court Hotel

◉ Modern British

Smart, modern hotel restaurant with appealing menu

☎ 01256 319700   🖷 01256 319730
Centre Dr, Great Binfields Rd, Chineham RG24 8FY
e-mail: hampshirecourt@qhotels.co.uk
dir: M3 junct 6, A33 towards Reading. Right at Chineham centre rdbt onto Great Binfields Rd. Hotel 400mtrs on left

Well placed for the M3 (J6) and the town centre, this striking modern hotel is built around 8 tennis courts and successfully caters for the needs of both leisure and business guests. The contemporary restaurant overlooks the centre court and a decked terrace, and offers swift and attentive service at smart linen-dressed tables. Monthly menus list traditional British dishes with a modern twist and the food is honestly cooked using quality ingredients. Typical choices may include pressed ham terrine with apple compôte, roast pork belly with apple and sage jus, clam linguini, chargrilled rib-eye steak with béarnaise sauce, and sticky toffee pudding.

Chef James Parsons, Ali Bensarda **Owner** QHotels
Times 12-2/7-9.30 Closed L Sat **Prices** Starter £4.50-£8, Main £12.50-£23.50, Dessert £5-£7.50, Service optional **Wines** 13 bottles over £20, 11 bottles under £20, 13 by glass **Notes** Vegetarian available, Dress restrictions, Smart casual, no shorts or swimwear, Civ Wed 200
Seats 200, Pr/dining room 170 **Children** Portions, Menu **Parking** 200

Vespers

◉ International

Smart and stylish modern hotel dining

☎ 01256 796700   🖷 01256 796701
Apollo Hotel, Aldermaston Roundabout RG24 9NU
e-mail: admin@apollo-hotels.co.uk
dir: From M3 junct 6 follow ring road N & signs for Aldermaston/Newbury. Then follow A340 (Aldermaston) signs, at rdbt take 5th exit onto Popley Way. Hotel entrance 1st left

Situated in the well-appointed Apollo Hotel, Vespers is the fine-dining option here - there's also a brasserie for more informal fare. An airy, modern and stylish room of clean lines, Vespers comes with banquette seating or tub chairs, large mirrors and prints and tables dressed in their best whites. It's only open for dinner and serves a modern menu of well-balanced dishes; take free-range chicken breast served with a lemon and rosemary risotto and a girolle cream sauce, while for chocoholics, a dark chocolate tart with Grand Marnier sorbet is the only way to finish.

Times 12-2/7-10 Closed Xmas, New Year, Sun, L Sat

BAUGHURST   Map 5 SU56

The Wellington Arms

◉◉ Modern British ◉

High quality, honest cooking using local and home-grown ingredients

☎ 0118 982 0110
Baughurst Rd RG26 5LP
e-mail: info@thewellingtonarms.com
dir: M4 junct 12 follow Newbury signs on A4. At rdbt left signed Aldermaston. Through Aldermaston. Up hill, at next rdbt 2nd exit, left at T-junct, pub 1m on left

In a former life this intimate pub-restaurant was the Duke of Wellington's hunting lodge. It seats around twenty-five, somewhat cosily, with an open fireplace at one end and a blackboard menu at the other. Attention to detail shines through in the friendly and attentive service while the owners' commitment to high quality, often home grown, produce is second to none. The simple menu - which is chalked up daily - uses honey from bees kept in the Wellington's fields, herbs from the pub's garden and on-site free range chickens also make an appearance. What they can't make or create themselves comes from reputable local suppliers within a 5-mile radius wherever possible. The result is an honest, crowd-pleasing menu of dishes such as a roast rack of home-reared pork with crackling, bashed butternut squash and Oak House apple sauce, plus the odd foray into culinary alchemy with vanilla and honey jelly with Persian fairy floss and a jug of pouring cream.

Chef Jason King **Owner** Simon Page & Jason King
Times 12-2.30/6.30-9.30 Closed Mon, L Tue, D Sun
Prices Fixed L 2 course fr £15, Starter £5.50-£9, Main £10.50-£17.50, Dessert fr £5.50, Service added but optional 10% **Wines** 51 bottles over £20, 8 bottles under £20, 9 by glass **Notes** Sunday L, Vegetarian available
Seats 25 **Children** Portions **Parking** 25

BEAULIEU   Map 5 SU30

Beaulieu Hotel

◉ Modern British, European

Classic country-house cuisine in the depths of the New Forest

☎ 023 8029 3344   🖷 023 8029 2729
Beaulieu Rd SO42 7YQ
e-mail: beaulieu@newforesthotels.co.uk
dir: On B3056 between Lyndhurst & Beaulieu. Near Beaulieu Rd railway station

Set among the open heathlands of the New Forest where the ponies roam free, this enchanting country-house hotel makes a great base for exploring a beautiful part of Hampshire. The cosily traditional restaurant overlooks forest and heath and deals in classic country-house cooking with tried-and-tested flavour combinations and simple presentation. You might kick off with the likes of pan-fried pigeon breast with orange pine nut salad and port syrup, followed by Barbary duck breast with garlic champ and redcurrant jus. Give way to temptation and round it off with Sicilian lemon pannacotta with honey and lemon sauce.

Chef Michael Mckell Owner New Forest Hotels plc
Times 7-9 Prices Fixed D 3 course £21.50-£27.50,
Service optional Wines 32 bottles over £20, 29 bottles
under £20, 2 by glass Notes Sunday L, Civ Wed 60
Seats 40, Pr/dining room 60 Children Portions, Menu

The Montagu Arms Hotel

◎◎ British, European

Old-world charm and accomplished cooking

☎ 01590 612324 ▤ 01590 612188
Palace Ln SO42 7ZL
e-mail: reservations@montaguarmshotel.co.uk
dir: From M27 junct 2 take A326 & B3054 for Beaulieu

Located in the heart of the New Forest National Park in
sight of the river and the Palace House, The Montagu
Arms Hotel dates back to 1742. The traditional
character of this fine English country house is on
display throughout, from the old brick fireplaces, which
bring forth natural warmth in winter, to the oak
paneling in the Terrace Restaurant. Overlooking a rear
courtyard with well-kept gardens, smartly dressed
tables await and knowledgeable staff complete the fine-
dining atmosphere (there's a less formal approach
found at the hotel's Monty's Bar and Brasserie). The
accomplished cooking lets local, seasonal and organic
ingredients do the talking; take slow-cooked oxtail and
celeriac 'lasagne' with celeriac purée, spinach and
horseradish cream, or perhaps honey-roast Beaulieu
Estate partridge with sweet-and-sour cabbage,
boulangère potatoes and game jus. Finish with
raspberry soufflé with rice pudding ice cream and
raspberry sauce.

Chef Matthew Tomkinson Owner Greenclose Ltd, Mr
Leach Times 12-2.30/7-9.30 Prices Food prices not
confirmed for 2010. Please telephone for details.
Wines 200+ bottles over £20, 9 bottles under £20, 12 by
glass Notes Sunday L, Dress restrictions, Smart casual,
Civ Wed 60 Seats 60, Pr/dining room 32 Children Portions
Parking 45

Macdonald Botley Park, Golf & Country Club

◎ British, European

Simple, honest cooking in relaxed hotel

☎ 01489 780888 & 0870 194 2132 ▤ 01489 789242
Winchester Rd, Boorley Green SO32 2UA
e-mail: botleypark@macdonald-hotels.co.uk
dir: M27 junct 7, A334 towards Botley. At 1st rdbt left,
past M&S store, over next 5 mini rdbts. At 6th mini rdbt
turn right. In 0.5m hotel on left

This large country hotel is only 15 minutes from
Southampton Airport and within easy reach of the M3. Set
in 176-acres of landscaped gardens with an 18-hole
championship golf course, there is a traditional feel to
the restaurant, with formal yet friendly service. The light-
and-airy dining room is contemporary in style with wood
panelling and decorated mirrors. It all creates a
comfortable setting for the unpretentious cooking. A
starter of smoked haddock linguine and braised leeks
could be followed by peppered duck breast with fondant
potato and stir-fried vegetables. For a more casual dining
experience, relax in the Swing and Divot Sports Bar
overlooking the 18th green.

Chef Matt Wallace Owner Macdonald Hotel Group
Times 12.30-2.30/7-9.45 Closed L Sat Prices Food prices
not confirmed for 2010. Please telephone for details.
Wines 48 bottles over £20, 20 bottles under £20, 14 by
glass Notes Sunday L, Vegetarian available, Civ Wed 200,
Air con Seats 70, Pr/dining room 250 Children Portions,
Menu Parking 200

The Three Tuns

◎◎ British, European

**A pretty village inn serving classic pub grub alongside
more ambitious dishes**

☎ 01425 672232 & 07850 713406
Ringwood Rd BH23 8JH
e-mail: threetunsinn@btconnect.com
web: www.threetunsinn.com
dir: On A35 at junct for Walkford/Highcliffe follow
Bransgore signs, 1.5m, restaurant on left

Picture this: a postcard-perfect 17th-century thatched
pub festooned with a riot of flowers and with a sun-
drenched south facing garden in the heart of the New
Forest; inside, low-beamed ceilings, bare wood tables
and red-brick fireplaces. A popular place? You had better
believe it, and the busy buzzy vibe just adds to its cosy
charm. And there's something for everyone here, from
regularly changing blackboard specials, to an eclectic
menu that runs from a simple ploughman's to classic
pub grub like pan-fried calves' liver with bacon and
mash, and more ambitious restaurant-style dishes. If you
want to put the kitchen through its paces, try ham soup
with mustard ice cream for starters, then twice-cooked
rabbit with polenta, winter greens and golden raisins.

Chef Colin Nash Owner Nigel Glenister
Times 12-2.15/6.30-9.15 Closed 25 Dec, D 31 Dec
Prices Starter £4.95-£7.95, Main £7.95-£18.95, Dessert
£5-£7.95, Service optional Wines 2 bottles over £20, 21
bottles under £20, 11 by glass Notes Sunday L,
Vegetarian available, Dress restrictions, Smart casual,
Air con Seats 60, Pr/dining room 50 Children Portions
Parking 50

BROCKENHURST Map 5 SU30

Balmer Lawn Hotel

◉ Modern British

Fine dining at a grand New Forest hotel

☎ 01590 623116 & 625725 🖹 01590 623864
Lyndhurst Rd SO42 7ZB
e-mail: info@balmerlawnhotel.com
web: www.balmerlawnhotel.com
dir: Take A337 towards Brockenhurst, hotel on left after 'Welcome to Brockenhurst' sign

There are echoes of the Raj in this grandiose pavilion-style Victorian hunting lodge deep in the New Forest. Prime ministers and presidents have stayed during its fascinating history; now it's a friendly family-owned hotel refurbished in a classy style blending modern interior aesthetics with period character. The Beresfords restaurant shares the same understated contemporary chic, with its high-backed leather seats at bare dark-wood tables and restful mustard colour scheme. The kitchen deals in modern British cuisine with an impressive showing of local produce. Pan-fried breast of woodpigeon with morel and wheatgerm risotto and liquorice and parmesean tuile is a typical starter, with main courses such as New Forest venison with beetroot, blackberries and balsamic beetroot jus.

Chef Gavin Barnes **Owner** Mr C Wilson
Times 12.30-2.30/7-9.30 **Prices** Fixed L 2 course fr £9.95, Fixed D 3 course fr £25, Starter £4.50-£9.50, Main £11.50-£19.50, Dessert £4.50-£8.95, Service optional, Groups min 10 service 12.5% **Wines** 26 bottles over £20, 24 bottles under £20, 18 by glass **Notes** Sunday L, Vegetarian available, Dress restrictions, Smart casual, no jeans or trainers, Civ Wed 120, Air con **Seats** 80, Pr/dining room 100 **Children** Portions, Menu **Parking** 100

Carey's Manor Hotel

◉◉ Modern British

Carefully-sourced produce cooked up in the heart of the New Forest

☎ 01590 623551 🖹 01590 622799
SO42 7RH
e-mail: stay@careysmanor.com
dir: M27 junct 2, follow Fawley/A326 signs. Continue over 3 rdbts, at 4th rdbt right lane signed Lyndhurst/A35. Follow A337 (Lymington/Brockenhurst)

Located deep in the heart of the beautiful New Forest National Park, Carey's Manor has 3 restaurants to choose from. The Blaireaus bistro offers French cuisine, while Thai cooking is the order of the day in the Zen Garden Restaurant, but if it's fine dining you are looking for, head to the Manor Restaurant. Top-notch ingredients - much of them local, free-range and organic - are used to create British dishes with French and European influences. Expect starters such as orange-cured air-dried duck on celeriac and apple salad with aged balsamic, followed by pan-roasted pork fillet and crispy belly on lavender and potato fondant with Savoy cabbage, apple syrup and root vegetable jus.

Times 12-2/7-10 Closed L Mon-Sat

Le Poussin at Whitley Ridge Hotel

BROCKENHURST Map 5 SU30

Modern British, French 🍃

Refined cooking using local produce in the heart of the New Forest

☎ 01590 622354 🖹 01590 622856
Beaulieu Rd SO42 7QL
e-mail: info@whitleyridge.co.uk
web: www.whitleyridge.co.uk
dir: From Brockenhurst, 1m along Beaulieu Rd

This delightful, secluded country-house hotel and its grounds are within the boundaries of the New Forest, and it originally earned its crust in the 18th century as a Royal hunting lodge. It first became a hotel under the auspices of the Conan Doyle family. Country-style parquet flooring and linen draped tables together with chandeliers, elegant mirrors and high ceilings help create a restaurant that pleases the eye, while large bay windows give views over the grounds - there are lakes as well as a walled vegetable garden. The kitchen, led by Alex Aitken, produces classical dishes with modern panache and supports the local larder with evangelical zeal, utilising top-notch stuff from local farmers and producers. The cooking is based on sound classical techniques and takes on halibut roasted on the bone and served with parsley purée and wild mushrooms, and fillet of veal with new season asparagus and morels. Service is formal and attentive and the sommelier should be singled out for special praise.

Chef Alex Aitken, Neil Duffet **Owner** A & C Aitken
Times 12-2/6.30-9.30 **Prices** Fixed L 2 course fr £17.50, Fixed D 3 course £35, Starter £9.50-£14.95, Main £21-£27.50, Dessert £8.50-£14, Service added but optional 12.5% **Wines** 300 bottles over £20, 30 bottles under £20, 30 by glass **Notes** Tasting menu 8 course, Sunday L, Vegetarian available, Dress restrictions, Smart casual, Civ Wed 45 **Seats** 50, Pr/dining room 24 **Children** Portions **Parking** 30

New Park Manor Hotel & Spa

◎◎ Modern

Royal connections and confident modern cooking

☎ 01590 623467 📄 01590 622268
Lyndhurst Rd SO42 7QH
e-mail: info@newparkmanorhotel.co.uk
dir: On A337, 8m S of M27 junct 1

Once the favoured hunting lodge of King Charles II, this well presented hotel in the heart of the New Forest, enjoys a tranquil setting and comes complete with its own equestrian centre, croquet lawn and spa. With sofas and log fires, the public areas are exceedingly comfortable. The restaurant is split into two smaller rooms, with high ceilings and original features - some of which date back to the 15th century - but it's refreshingly informal and large windows provide views of the paddock with its roaming ponies. The food is predominantly modern British with some French influences, based on quality seasonal produce and good technical skills. Oxtail and leek ravioli, for example, with fondant potato and spinach mousse, followed by pan-fried fillet of gilt-head bream, saffron-infused Parisienne potatoes and cockle velouté, with pear and gingerbread tarte Tatin to finish.

Chef Mark Speller **Owner** von Essen Hotels
Times 12-2/7-9 **Prices** Fixed L 2 course £15, Fixed D 3 course £42, Starter £5.50-£7.50, Main £9.50-£13.50, Dessert £4.50-£6.50, Service optional **Wines** 70 bottles over £20, 10 bottles under £20, 16 by glass **Notes** Sunday L, Vegetarian available, Dress restrictions, Smart casual, no jeans or trainers, Civ Wed 80 **Seats** 65, Pr/dining room 16 **Children** Portions, Menu **Parking** 70

Le Poussin at Whitley Ridge Hotel

◎◎◎ – see opposite page

Rhinefield House

◎◎ Modern British 🍃

Imaginative cooking in stylish hotel with stunning grounds

☎ 01590 622922 📄 01590 622800
Rhinefield Rd SO42 7QB
e-mail: info@rhinefieldhousehotel.co.uk
web: www.rhinefieldhousehotel.co.uk
dir: M27 junct 1, A337 to Lyndhurst, then A35 W towards Christchurch. 3.5m, left at sign for Rhinefield House. Hotel 1.5m on right

A forest hotel situated at the end of a long drive in 40 acres, Rhinefield House is a magnificent 19th-century building; an engaging mixture of Tudor and Gothic architecture with some fascinating features - carvings by Grinling Gibbons and a huge Elizabethan-style fireplace. Enjoy a stroll through the beautiful ornamental gardens before dinner in the elegant, richly furnished Armada restaurant. A small kitchen brigade delivers an imaginative, well-balanced menu featuring well-executed modern British dishes prepared from the best seasonal ingredients that the New Forest has to offer. Follow, perhaps, confit duck rillettes, served with orange compôte and a mustard dressing, with a richly flavoured saddle of venison with celeriac purée, braised red cabbage and quince syrup, and, to finish, a creamy crème brûlée. There is also a relaxed brasserie and a delightful terrace for alfresco dining.

Chef David Kinnes **Owner** Hand Picked Hotels Ltd
Times 12.30-2/7-9.30 **Prices** Fixed L 3 course fr £24.50, Fixed D 3 course fr £45, Service optional **Wines** 100+ bottles over £20, 2 bottles under £20, 15 by glass **Notes** Sunday L, Vegetarian available, Dress restrictions, Smart casual preferred, Civ Wed 130 **Seats** 58, Pr/dining room 12 **Children** Portions, Menu **Parking** 150

Simply Poussin

◎◎ Modern

Courtyard dining at the younger sibling of Le Poussin

☎ 01590 623063 📄 01590 623144
The Courtyard, Brookley Rd SO42 7RB
e-mail: info@simplypoussin.co.uk
dir: Village centre, through archway between two shops on High St

Enter via a small, welcoming courtyard, with the conservatory restaurant entrance to the right, in the baby sibling of Le Poussin (see entry). Well-spaced big tables on a wooden floor, with bright white walls, create an airily refreshing ambience, which is helped along by clued-up staff who keep their eye on the ball. The cooking keeps things up-to-date, with some assured bistro-style dishes, ranging from a modern combination of belly pork and prawns with stir-fried pak choi in ginger syrup dressing, to best end of lamb, simply served with buttery fondant potato, runner beans and confit garlic. Liquid-centred hot chocolate fondant with mint and vanilla ice cream delivers fabulous flavour contrasts. Good breads and a small but perfectly formed wine list complete the picture.

Times 12-2/6.30-9.45 Closed Sun-Mon

BROOK Map 5 SU21

Briscoe's

◎◎ Modern English

New Forest haven with an ambitious team in the kitchen

☎ 023 8081 2214 📄 023 8081 3958
Bell Inn SO43 7HE
e-mail: bell@bramshaw.co.uk
dir: M27 junct 1 onto B3079, hotel 1.5m on right

Dating from 1782, this handsome brick inn is located in the heart of the New Forest and is part of the Bramshaw Golf Club, specialising in golfing breaks and conferences. Period features have been retained in the cosy bar and in Briscoe's Restaurant, where old-fashioned charm and character blend well with chic modern colours. Expect a sound modern approach to cooking traditional dishes from an ambitious brigade that show great promise. Dishes are well executed and make good use of locally-sourced ingredients; warm scallop mousse with caviar crème fraîche, followed by trio of pork (fillet wrapped in Parma ham, confit belly, black pudding beignet) with wholegrain mustard sauce, and apple and rhubarb crumble tart with pistachio ice cream to finish.

Chef Scott Foy **Owner** Crosthwaite Eyre Family
Times 7-9.30 Closed L all week **Prices** Fixed D 3 course £35, Service optional **Wines** 65 bottles over £20, 25 bottles under £20, 13 by glass **Notes** Vegetarian available, Dress restrictions, No jeans, T-shirts, trainers or shorts **Seats** 50, Pr/dining room 40 **Children** Portions, Menu **Parking** 40

BURLEY — Map 5 SU20

Moorhill House

Traditional

Enjoyable New Forest hotel dining

☎ 01425 403285 ≣ 01425 403715
BH24 4AG
e-mail: moorhill@newforesthotels.co.uk
dir: Exit A31 signed Burley Drive, through village, turn right opposite cricket pitch

The Edwardian gentleman who built his residence here on the fringes of a pretty village in the New Forest picked a gorgeous spot. The hotel's Burley Restaurant spills onto a patio area overlooking sprawling gardens and lawns in fair weather - an idyllic setting for three-course menus of uncomplicated modern British cooking. You might start with chicken ballotine stuffed with apricots and chestnuts, and follow with seared pork tenderloin with fondant potato, bramley apple compôte and sage café crème. All desserts are made in-house - coffee and brandy iced parfait with toffee sauce, perhaps.

Chef Ben Cartwright **Owner** New Forest Hotels
Times 12-2/7-9 **Prices** Fixed D 3 course £21.50-£30, Service optional **Notes** Sunday L, Dress restrictions, Smart casual, Air con **Seats** 60, Pr/dining room 40

CADNAM — Map 5 SZ21

Bartley Lodge

Traditional British

Traditional cooking in former hunting lodge

☎ 023 8081 2248 ≣ 023 8081 2075
Lyndhurst Rd SO40 2NR
e-mail: reservations@newforesthotels.co.uk
dir: M27 junct 1, A337, follow signs for Lyndhurst. Hotel on left

Despite being only minutes from the M27, Bartley Lodge occupies a quiet spot in picturesque grounds. Built in 1759 as a hunting lodge for the founder of the New Forest Hounds, this fine building is now a comfortable and friendly hotel. A host of charming period features include hand-crafted oak panelling, a minstrels' gallery and a magnificent fireplace. Wonderful views over the garden can be enjoyed from the elegant Crystal Restaurant, which offers a traditionally based menu with influences from France, the Mediterranean and Asia. Kick off with salad of smoked duck breast with rocket, orange and soused vegetables, followed by pan-fried breast of chicken with Puy lentils, chorizo and a mushroom cassoulet.

Chef John Lightfoot **Owner** New Forest Hotels plc
Times 12.30-2.30/7-9 Closed L Mon-Sat **Prices** Fixed D 3 course £21.50-£27.50, Service optional **Wines** 16 bottles over £20, 25 bottles under £20, 2 by glass **Notes** Sunday L, Vegetarian available, Civ Wed 80 **Seats** 60 **Children** Portions, Menu **Parking** 60

DENMEAD — Map 5 SU61

Barnard's Restaurant

Modern British

Friendly neighbourhood restaurant

☎ 023 9225 7788 ≣ 023 9225 7788
Hambledon Rd PO7 6NU
e-mail: mail@barnardsrestaurant.co.uk
dir: A3M junct 3, B1250 into Denmead. Opposite church

Sandie and David Barnard run this small country restaurant opposite the church in pretty Denmead with upbeat charm and hands-on friendliness. Two dining areas vary in ambience: the front room goes for lemon walls, unclothed dark wood tables and high-backed chairs, while the rear area has exposed red brick walls, and overlooks a gravelled outdoor patio. The key to the cooking here is sourcing incredibly good local ingredients. Not only do the flavours work really well together, but unfussy dishes look great and are excellent value for money. Pan-fried Scottish scallops are spot-on with a mild lime and chilli dressing, followed by grilled fillet of bream with sautéed new potatoes and a sauce of vine-ripened tomatoes, garlic, herbs and olive oil.

Chef David Barnard, Sandie Barnard **Owner** Mr & Mrs D Barnard **Times** 12-1.30/7-9.30 Closed 25-26 Dec, New Year, Sun-Mon, L Sat **Prices** Fixed L 2 course £10-£12, Fixed D 3 course £13-£15, Starter £5.30-£7.95, Main £10.50-£20, Dessert £5.30-£5.50, Service optional **Wines** 8 bottles over £20, 20 bottles under £20, 8 by glass **Notes** Vegetarian available **Seats** 40, Pr/dining room 34 **Children** Portions **Parking** 3, Car park opposite

DOGMERSFIELD — Map 5 SU75

Seasons

French, European V

Elegant dining with superb views

☎ 01252 853000 ≣ 01252 853010
Four Seasons Hotel Hampshire, Dogmersfield Park, Chalky Ln RG27 8TD
e-mail: reservations.ham@fourseasons.com
dir: M3 junct 5 onto A287 Farnham. After 1.5m take left to Dogmersfield, hotel 0.6m on left

This plush conversion of a Georgian manor house in 500 acres of prime Hampshire countryside is the Four Seasons group's first foray into English country house territory. Expect a no-expense-spared, full-on contemporary pampering package, including a ritzy spa in the Grade II

listed 18th-century stable block. French windows frame views over the primped grounds of Dogmersfield Park from the stylish restaurant. The elaborate French-based cooking makes forays into wider European idioms, is executed with panache and presented flamboyantly - as in hand-dived Portland scallops in an apple, lime and vanilla vinaigrette, with butternut squash and orange purée, followed with loin of venison dusted with dried orange, and served with celeriac purée, cranberry compôte and smoked chocolate sauce.

Chef Cyrille Pannier **Owner** Four Seasons Hotels & Resorts **Times** 12.30-2.30/6-10.30 Closed D Sun-Mon **Prices** Starter £12-£18, Main £27-£38, Dessert £9.50-£12, Service added but optional 12.5% **Wines** 167 bottles over £20, 17 by glass **Notes** Tasting menu weekdays, Sunday L, Vegetarian menu, Dress restrictions, Smart casual, Civ Wed 250, Air con **Seats** 100, Pr/dining room 24 **Children** Portions, Menu **Parking** 100

DROXFORD — Map 5 SU61

Bakers Arms

British NEW

Unpretentious country pub serving simple and generous local food

☎ 01489 877533
High St SO32 3PA
e-mail: adam@thebakersarmsdroxford.com

This white-painted country dining pub on the main road through the village looks much like any other from the outside, but the savvy Hampshire locals are drawn here by its accessible and generous cooking that keeps things local, seasonal, simple and fresh. There's a friendly community buzz, with the local store and post office parked on the side and Droxford's Bowman ales on tap. True the inside may have been opened-up and modernised, but there's still bags of unpretentious charm and warmth here. A blackboard menu over the fire and cottagey furniture hint at its accomplished dining-pub credentials, with accessible British cooking driven by local produce. Think classics like Droxford Gloucestershire Old Spot sausages with a traditional mash and onion gravy accompaniment, while slow-cooked duck leg might offer a more modern spin with pearl barley and chorizo.

Chef Richard Harrison **Owner** Adam & Anna Cordery **Times** 12-2/7-9 Closed Mon, D Sun **Prices** Food prices not confirmed for 2010. Please telephone for details.

EAST TYTHERLEY — Map 5 SU22

The Star Inn Tytherley

Modern British

Traditional inn with serious attitude to food

☎ 01794 340225
SO51 0LW
e-mail: info@starinn.co.uk
dir: Romsey A3057 N, left onto B3084, then left to Awbridge, Kents Oak, through Lockerley on right

Tucked away in East Tytherley, the smallest village in the

Test Valley, this 16th-century former coaching inn is a cosy place with a pretty courtyard garden overlooking the village cricket green. Exposed beams, log fires, tub chairs, leather Chesterfields and warm colours add to the traditional atmosphere. The dining room follows the relaxed country restaurant theme, with its lightwood tables and pine-clad walls adorned with country prints. The kitchen's style is to give a modern twist to traditional dishes using local seasonal ingredients, including meat and freshly caught fish. Everything from the flavoured breads to the delicious biscuits or petits fours at the end of the meal is made in the kitchen. Expect main dishes such as braised belly pork, sage polenta, celeriac purée, haricot bean, smoked bacon and garlic casserole, and finish with baked white chocolate cheesecake with maple syrup.

Chef Justin Newitt **Owner** Alan & Lesley Newitt **Times** 11-2.30/6-11 Closed Mon, D Sun **Prices** Food prices not confirmed for 2010. Please telephone for details. **Wines** 16 bottles over £20, 16 bottles under £20, 7 by glass **Notes** Sunday L, Vegetarian available, Dress restrictions, Smart casual **Seats** 36, Pr/dining room 12 **Children** Portions, Menu **Parking** 60

EMSWORTH   Map 5 SU70

Fat Olives

◉◉ British, Mediterranean

Family-run brasserie by the sea with good, honest cooking

☎ 01243 377914
30 South St PO10 7EH
e-mail: info@fatolives.co.uk
dir: In town centre, 1st right after Emsworth Square, 100yds towards the Quay. Restaurant on left with public car park opposite

Simple honest cooking is on the menu at this husband-and-wife run brasserie by the sea now in its 10th year of business. Just a short walk from picturesque Emsworth harbour, the restaurant's interior is as unpretentious as the food with its intimate dining room of pale magnolia walls, stripped wooden floors and furniture and un-dressed tables. The local and seasonal ingredients from land and sea are allowed to speak for themselves without over embellishment. Start, perhaps, with seared scallops with a carrot and cumin salad, sherry vinegar dressing, then maybe partridge with bubble-and-squeak and parsley sauce. Warm pecan and date sponge, caramel sauce and praline ice cream is a comforting way to finish. Alfresco dining is an option in the warm months.

Chef Lawrence Murphy **Owner** Lawrence & Julia Murphy **Times** 12-1.45/7-9.15 Closed 2 wks Xmas, 2 wks Jun, Sun-Mon & Tue after a BH **Prices** Fixed L 2 course £16.75, Starter £5.50-£8.25, Main £14.75-£22.95, Dessert £5.95-£6.95, Service optional, Groups min 10 service 10% **Wines** 36 bottles over £20, 10 bottles under £20, 7 by glass **Notes** Vegetarian available **Seats** 28 **Parking** Opposite restaurant

36 on the Quay

◉◉◉ – *see below*

36 on the Quay

EMSWORTH   Map 5 SU70

Modern French

Vibrant modern cooking by the waterside

☎ 01243 375592 & 372257   ▤ 01243 375593
47 South St PO10 7EG
e-mail: info@36onthequay.com
dir: Please telephone for directions

'On the Quay' is right. The cream-painted building sits right across the road from the harbour front in the picturesque town of Emsworth. Within is a simple and compact bar area with bare wood floor, while the restaurant itself is done in marine blue, and offers bay-window views of the water. Service is very much hands-on, in a gently formal way that enhances the whole experience. Ramon Farthing aims high, producing dishes that are technically skilled, essentially French in their

orientation, but embellished with many modern ideas. Complexity is all, but is brought off well, as in a starter that combines seared scallops with pea-shoots, apple crisps, a 'dust' of Serrano ham, passionfruit dressing and beetroot syrup, a courageous medley of sweet, salt and savoury flavours that shows great balance. New season's lamb noisettes are more traditionally accompanied by dauphinoise, roasted shallots and confit tomatoes, with strips of the liver and rosemary sauce. Desserts bring the curtain down with a flourish, perhaps in the form of chocolate-coated peanut parfait with mini-doughnuts of butterscotch and an incredibly intense espresso foam.

Chef Ramon Farthing **Owner** Ramon & Karen Farthing **Times** 12-2/7-10 Closed 1 wk end Oct, 25-26 Dec, 1st 3 wks Jan, 1 wk end May, Sun, Mon **Prices** Fixed L 2 course fr £20.95, Fixed D 3 course fr £46.95, Service optional **Wines** 15 bottles over £20, 10 bottles under £20, 7 by glass **Notes** Dress restrictions, Smart casual, no shorts

Seats 45, Pr/dining room 12 **Children** Portions **Parking** 6, Residents only, car park nearby

EVERSLEY — Map 5 SU76

The New Mill Riverside Restaurant

Modern European

Beautiful setting for well-crafted, modern food

☎ 0118 973 2277   ▤ 0118 932 8780
New Mill Rd RG27 0RA
e-mail: info@thenewmill.co.uk
web: www.thenewmill.co.uk
dir: Off A327 2m S of Arborfield Cross. N of village follow brown signs. Approach from New Mill Rd

There is something romantic about mills and this one (not so new at 400 years-plus) is idyllically situated in lush green gardens and still has a working waterwheel. It's full of character on the inside, too, with low ceilings, old beams, grand fireplaces and flagstone floors; the dining areas include a conservatory with views over the water and a large patio. The cooking is in the modern vein, with good British produce delivered in broadly European preparations; thus twice-baked Barkham Blue soufflé with peashoot salad and walnut dressing might precede pan-fried sea bass with cassoulet of haricot beans and Toulouse sausage. The lunchtime table d'hôte is exceptionally good value.

Chef Colin Robson-Wright **Owner** Cindy & John Duffield **Times** 12-2/7-10 Closed 1-2 Jan, Mon **Prices** Fixed L 2 course £15, Fixed D 3 course £25, Starter £9.95-£12.50, Main £17.25-£23.95, Dessert £7.75-£8.50, Service optional, Groups min 8 service 10% **Wines** 150 bottles over £20, 10 bottles under £20, 10 by glass **Notes** Tasting menu available, Sunday L, Vegetarian available, Dress restrictions, Smart casual, Civ Wed 150, Air con **Seats** 80, Pr/dining room 32 **Children** Portions **Parking** 60

HIGHCLERE — Map 5 SU45

Marco Pierre White's Yew Tree Inn

British, French

Stylish dining pub close to Highclere Castle

☎ 01635 253360   ▤ 01635 255035
Hollington Cross, Andover Rd RG20 9SE
e-mail: info@theyewtree.net
dir: M4 junct 13, A34 S, 4th junct on left signed Highclere/Wash Common, turn right towards Andover A343, Yew Tree Inn on right

Marco's country seat near Newbury is a class act, as you might hope considering his reputation and experience. The Yew Tree is a whitewashed 17th-century inn with head-grazing ancient beamed ceilings and log fires, and yes, you can get a good pint of Black Sheep, but it's more of a restaurant than a pub. Stick to the tables in the bar for a posh pubby feel, or go through to the formal dining room where there's food-themed art on the walls and well-dressed tables. Marco's fingerprints are all over the Anglo-French menu in brasserie-style dishes that sound simple but are raised to a higher level by razor-sharp technique. There's haddock and chips with pea purée and tartare sauce, Shepherd's pie, or braised oxtail and kidney pudding; more ritzy touches include fillet of venison 'Pierre Koffmann' in a bitter chocolate sauce, and desserts include rice pudding or clafoutis of cherries.

Chef Neil Thornley **Owner** The Yew Tree (Highclere) Ltd **Times** 12-2.30/6-9.30 **Prices** Fixed L 2 course £15.50-£19.95, Starter £7.50-£12.50, Main £13.50-£19.50, Dessert £7.50, Service included **Wines** 58 bottles over £20, 12 bottles under £20, 10 by glass **Notes** Sunday L, Vegetarian available **Seats** 90 **Children** Portions **Parking** 40

LYMINGTON — Map 5 SZ39

Stanwell House

Modern European

Contemporary style and choice of two restaurants

☎ 01590 677123   ▤ 01590 677756
14-15 High St SO41 9AA
e-mail: enquiries@stanwellhouse.com
web: www.stanwellhouse.com
dir: M27 junct 1, follow signs to Lyndhurst into Lymington centre & High Street

This Georgian former coaching inn on the High Street is a stylish and contemporary boutique hotel with a brace of restaurants; one a smart bistro and the other a seafood restaurant, and if indecision is in the air you can choose from either menu if you sit in the conservatory. The bistro, overlooking the terrace, offers a fixed-price menu that goes from carpaccio of beef with rocket, parmesan and cracked black pepper dressing to chargrilled sirloin steak frites, while the seafood restaurant makes the best of the local resources to deliver lemon sole with a lemon caper butter, or a full seafood platter.

Chef Mr Stuart White **Owner** Mrs V Crowe, Mr R Milton **Times** 12-3/6-10 **Prices** Fixed L 2 course fr £10, Fixed D 3 course fr £26.45, Tasting menu £39.95, Service included **Wines** 55 bottles over £20, 18 bottles under £20, 8 by glass **Notes** Sunday L, Vegetarian available, Civ Wed 70 **Seats** 70, Pr/dining room 18 **Children** Portions **Parking** Public car park or on street

LYNDHURST
Map 5 SU30

The Glasshouse

Modern British

Chic New Forest trend-setter

☎ 023 8028 3677 & 023 8028 6129 📄 023 8028 2940
**Best Western Forest Lodge, Pikes Hill, Romsey Rd
SO43 7AS**
e-mail: forest@newforesthotels.co.uk
web: www.newforesthotels.co.uk
dir: M27 junct 1 signed Lyndhurst A337, after 3m turn
right into Pikes Hill

Within the heart of the New Forest, the Forest Lodge hotel
boasts the estimably chic Glasshouse restaurant, a place
of black-clothed tables, discreet lighting and
knowledgeable, unobtrusive service. Special events add
to the scope of the operation, and Richard Turner's
cooking is aspirational, attractively presented and
founded on sound technique. Ham hock and foie gras
terrine with Burley cider jelly and remoulade dressing
indicates a finely balanced, classical approach, but then
along comes roasted goats' cheese with pistachio
crumble, spiced Puy lentils, onion 'linguini' and tomato
foam to overturn expectations. West Country cheeses are
worth a look, as an alternative to desserts such as glazed
fruits in Cointreau sabayon with clotted cream ice cream.

Chef Richard Turner **Owner** New Forest Hotels
Times 12-2.30/7-9.30 Closed Mon, D Sun **Prices** Food
prices not confirmed for 2010. Please telephone for
details. **Wines** 31 bottles over £20, 10 bottles under £20,
8 by glass **Notes** Sunday L, Vegetarian available, Dress
restrictions, Smart dress, Civ Wed 90, Air con **Seats** 40,
Pr/dining room 10 **Parking** 60

See advert below

MILFORD ON SEA
Map 5 SZ29

One Park Lane

Modern British V

Fine dining in magnificent Victorian mansion with
stunning sea views

☎ 01590 643044 📄 01590 644490
Westover Hall Hotel, Park Ln SO41 0PT
e-mail: info@westoverhallhotel.com
dir: From M27 junct 1 take A337 then B3058. Hotel just
outside centre of Milford, towards clifftop

The 19th-century industrialist Alexander Siemens brought
electricity to England and built this gorgeous seaside
mansion on the edge of the New Forest, overlooking the
Needles and the Isle of Wight. When you have got over the
amazing stained-glass windows, oak panelling and
intricate ceiling friezes, take in the fantastic sea views
from the classy country house-style restaurant. The
kitchen delivers cleverly-executed modern takes on
classics, shot through with flashes of innovation. Dishes
are pretty as a picture and built on quality local and
seasonal produce. Dinner might begin with a terrine of
foie gras, smoked duck, shiitake mushrooms and free-
range chicken with parsnip purée; next, a sorbet, followed
by locally-caught sea bass with watercress cream, pan-
roasted scallops and warm crab brandade on mash and
oxtail jus.

Chef Denis Rhoden **Owner** David & Christine Smith
Times 12-2/7-9 **Prices** Fixed L 2 course £15, Fixed D 4
course fr £42, Starter £6-£10, Main £21-£26, Dessert £7-
£9, Service optional **Wines** 60 bottles over £20, 11 bottles
under £20, 11 by glass **Notes** Gourmet menu available,
Sunday L, Vegetarian menu, Civ Wed 50 **Seats** 40, Pr/
dining room 10 **Children** Portions **Parking** 60

NEW MILTON
Map 5 SZ29

Chewton Glen Hotel & Spa

– see page 180

Chewton Glen Hotel & Spa

NEW MILTON Map 5 SZ29

Traditional British V NOTABLE WINE LIST

Immaculate cooking in internationally renowned country-house hotel

☎ 01425 275341 📄 01425 272310
Christchurch Rd BH25 6QS
e-mail: reservations@chewtonglen.com
web: www.chewtonglen.com
dir: Off A35 (Lyndhurst) turn right through Walkford, 4th left into Chewton Farm Rd

From the croquet lawn to the iron gated-entrance, and from the luxurious spa to the elegant restaurant, Chewton Glen must be the quintessential English country hotel. Set in well-manicured grounds, guests have enjoyed impeccable English hospitality here since the 18th century, and the service remains suitably immaculate. Warming log fires, afternoon teas and traditional country-house furnishings set the tone, whilst fine views from the lounges and bar confirm, if ever you could doubt it, that this is England. The stylish restaurant has those wonderful garden views, while the elegant conservatory, with its impressive tented ceiling, brings diners even closer to the splendour of the garden. The menu is fiercely seasonal and uses as much local produce as possible, with suppliers duly named. The food is rooted in the classics and cooking is precise with bold flavours and stunning presentation. Among starters, perhaps, dressed Cornish crab with salmon ceviche, grapefruit purée, avocado and coriander, while a main course of Laverstoke Park pork fillet comes with Savoy cabbage, parsley root purée, Jerusalem artichokes and Madeira jus. Hot Valrhona chocolate fondant with kaffir lime leaf ice cream is a creative finish. The impressive wine list runs to more than 500 bins.

Chef Luke Matthews
Owner Chewton Glen Hotels Ltd
Times 12.30-1.45/7.30-9.30
Prices Fixed L course £24.50, Fixed D 3 course £65, Service included **Wines** 750 bottles over £20, 13 bottles under £20, 18 by glass **Notes** Sunday L, Vegetarian menu, Dress restrictions, Jackets preferred, no denim, Civ Wed 60, Air con
Seats 120, Pr/dining room 120
Children Portions, Menu **Parking** 150

ODIHAM
Map 5 SU75

St John Restaurant

Modern NEW

Classic French cuisine in a stylish setting

☎ 01256 702697
83 High St RG29 1LB
e-mail: info@stjohn-restaurant.co.uk
dir: Please telephone for directions

In the centre of lovely Odiham, 2 huge picture windows fronting a listed red-brick building look into the sort of stylishly revamped interior you'd expect to see in a cosmopolitan city eatery. The kitchen deals in classic French cuisine, cooked confidently using well-sourced local materials, and offered in options ranging from a great value lunchtime market menu, through to à la carte and a full-on 'menu découverte'. You might start with pan-fried scallops with fennel salad and apple and ginger purée, and follow with roasted cannon of venison with pommes Anna, saffron and onion purée, and peppered cabbage with bitter chocolate sauce.

Chef Steven James **Owner** Mr R Evans
Times 12-2.15/6-9.30 Closed Sun **Prices** Tasting menu £45, Starter £6.50-£11.75, Main £18.95-£25, Dessert £6.50 **Notes** Early bird menu Mon-Fri before 8pm, 2 courses £14.95, Vegetarian available **Seats** 55

OLD BURGHCLERE
Map 5 SU45

The Dew Pond Restaurant

Modern British, French

Country restaurant with fine views and modern cooking

☎ 01635 278408
RG20 9LH
dir: Telephone for details

The Dew Pond lies on a narrow lane at the foot of Watership Down, embraced by the sheep-freckled folds of rural Hampshire - hard to believe, then, that the busy A34 is not far away. Inside the 16th-century country-house restaurant a brace of dining rooms comes with ancient oak beams, cool pastel shades and a mini gallery of colourful artwork. The modern British repertoire is founded on meat, game and cheeses from nearby farms, skilfully prepared with an eye to full flavours. Fixed-price, dinner menus offer a wealth of ideas: seared diver scallops with chorizo, sauté potatoes and pea shoots, perhaps, before a main course of roasted rump and crispy confit shoulder of new season's lamb with a rosemary and red wine reduction.

Times 7-9.30 Closed 2 wks Xmas & New Year, 2 wks Aug, Sun-Mon, L served by appointment only

PETERSFIELD
Map 5 SU72

Annie Jones Restaurant

Modern European

Confident cooking in a market town setting

☎ 01730 262728
10 Lavant St GU32 3EW
e-mail: info@anniejones.com
dir: From A3 into town centre, following Winchester direction. Restaurant is in Lavant St (the road leading to rail station)

Many towns the size of Petersfield would kill for a restaurant like Annie Jones - hands-on owners, vibrant atmosphere, brimming with character, and serving bold and confident food. Red walls, wooden floor, high-backed leather chairs and simply dressed tables set the scene inside, while there is a great terrace for when the Hampshire climate is kind. Mixed olives and home-made focaccia make a good beginning, and the toffee soufflé married with banana and praline parfait is a definite hit. In between, expect roast belly of Hampshire pork with roasted butternut squash, bacon and apple compôte or saddle of rabbit with Serrano ham and truffled macaroni cheese.

Chef Steven Ranson **Owner** Steven Ranson, Jon Blake
Times 12-2/6-late Closed 4 wks per yr, Mon, L Tue, D Sun
Prices Fixed D 3 course £38, Service added but optional 12.5% **Wines** 6 bottles over £20, 26 bottles under £20, 6 by glass **Notes** Tasting menu 7 course, early bird Tue-Thu 6-7.30pm, Sunday L, Vegetarian available **Seats** 32 **Children** Portions **Parking** On street or Swan Street car park

Frederick's Restaurant, Langrish House

Modern International

Historic setting for accomplished cooking

☎ 01730 266941   📠 01730 260543
Langrish GU32 1RN
e-mail: frontdesk@langrishhouse.co.uk
dir: From Petersfield A272 towards Winchester, turn left into Langrish & follow brown hotel signs

The Talbot-Ponsonby family have called Langrish House their home for seven generations. Built in the 17th century by Royalist prisoners taken at the Battle of Cheriton, it sits just outside Petersfield in lovely gardens surrounded by rolling South Downs countryside. Frederick's restaurant takes its name from a nautical great uncle who played tennis in a Victorian skirt (don't ask!). It's a cosy place with an open fire in winter, and you can also eat in the atmospheric old vaults below. A modern menu with international influences offers duck rillettes, prune and orange-infused compôte, toasted brioche and watercress to start, and plump fillets of butter-poached halibut in a herb crust with a fricassée of ceps, leeks and chestnuts as a typical main course.

Chef Peter Buckman **Owner** Mr & Mrs Talbot-Ponsonby
Times 12-2/7-9.30 **Prices** Fixed L 2 course £16.95, Fixed D 3 course £35.95, Service optional **Wines** 15 bottles over £20, 13 bottles under £20, 2 by glass **Notes** Sunday L, Vegetarian available, Dress restrictions, Smart casual, Civ Wed 60 **Seats** 24, Pr/dining room 20 **Children** Portions **Parking** 100

JSW

⊛⊛⊛ — see page 182

PORTSMOUTH & SOUTHSEA
Map 5 SU60

8 Kings Road

Modern French, European

Modern French cooking in a stunning Victorian building

☎ 08451 303234 & 023 9285 1698   📠 023 9286 2729
8 Kings Rd, Southsea PO5 3AH
e-mail: info@8kingsroad.co.uk
web: www.8kingsroad.co.uk
dir: M27 junct 12/M275/A3 left at rdbt onto Kings Road

Money may make the world go round, but it didn't stop this grand old Victorian bank from being remodelled into an atmospheric restaurant. It has a definite wow factor, with a mezzanine dining area, cascading chandeliers hanging from sky-high ceilings and expanses of wood panelling; live jazz and soul adds rhythm on Friday nights. The modern French cooking is more in tune with la Marseillaise. Classical roots and fresh ingredients - particularly locally-caught fish - are the cornerstones of the kitchen's output. You could start with Scottish mussels in a chorizo, coconut and coriander sauce, then move on to free range chicken breast with Savoy cabbage, lardons, silverskin onions, sautéed potatoes and wild mushrooms. Finish with a classic crème brûlée with berry compôte.

continued on page 183

JSW

Modern British **V**   NOTABLE WINE LIST

Confident cooking in understated restaurant with rooms

☎ 01730 262030
20 Dragon St GU31 4JJ
e-mail: jsw.restaurant@btconnect.com
web: www.jswrestaurant.com
dir: A3 to town centre, follow one-way system to College St which becomes Dragon St, restaurant on left

Everything about this restaurant with rooms is pleasingly understated, from the plain white exterior to the simple, yet classic food delivered by the kitchen. A beautifully restored 17th-century former coaching inn with large oak beams and generously sized, linen-clad tables, the dining room is an attractive space, smart yet unpretentious. Service is by a professional, well trained team who display good knowledge of the menu and the 700-strong wine list. The food has a confidence about it, with sound classical techniques underpinning the use of top quality produce on the sensibly concise fixed-price carte (there's a tasting menu, too). The chef proprietor is so hands-on he might even have caught the brill that turns up in a fricassée with mussels and carrot purée. The presentation of dishes allows the food to speak for itself, but technique is good and the balance of flavours key: scallops with butternut squash purée is a well-judged starter, slow-cooked lamb with root vegetables and Hampshire hotpot a fine main course, and mango mousse with passionfruit and pineapple a well-crafted finish. The reasonably priced wine list is worth exploring.

Chef Jake Watkins **Owner** Jake Watkins **Times** 12-1.30/7-9.30 Closed 2 wks Jan & summer, Sun-Mon **Prices** Fixed L 2 course £15-£28.50, Fixed D 2 course fr £19.50, Tasting menu £40-£50, Service optional, Groups min 10 service 10% **Wines** 556 bottles over £20, 14 bottles under £20, 10 by glass **Notes** Tasting menu 8 course, Vegetarian menu **Seats** 58, Pr/dining room 18 **Parking** 19

PORTSMOUTH & SOUTHSEA *continued*

Chef James Harrison **Owner** James Harrison **Times** 6-11 Closed 26-27 Dec, 1-3 Jan, L Mon-Sat, D Sun **Prices** Starter £4-£8, Main £10-£20, Dessert £4-£7, Service optional, Groups min 6 service 10% **Wines** 135 bottles over £20, 15 bottles under £20, 10 by glass **Notes** Sunday L, Vegetarian available, Dress restrictions, Smart casual, Air con **Seats** 80, Pr/dining room 32 **Children** Portions, Menu **Parking** On street

---

ROTHERWICK	Map 5 SU75

Oak Room Restaurant

◎◎ Modern British 🍃

Smart formal dining in opulent country-house surroundings

☎ 01256 764881 📠 01256 768141
Tylney Hall Hotel RG27 9AZ
e-mail: sales@tylneyhall.com
dir: M3 junct 5 take A287 (Newnham). From M4 junct 11 take B3349 (Hook), at sharp bend left (Rotherwick), left again & left in village (Newnham) 1m on right

Tradition and well-drilled service are the watchwords in this handsome red-brick Victorian country house. Tylney Hall is the classic rural retreat, set in 66 acres of parkland which include Gertrude Jekyll-designed gardens, waterfalls, ornamental lakes and woodland walks. Once inside, you're greeted with vast expanses of oak panelling and fancy plasterwork - indeed, the ceiling in the Italian lounge came from the Grimaldi Palace in Florence. Culinary endeavours focus on the glass-domed Oak Room restaurant, where the cooking is in a contemporary vein, but on the whole eschews foams and fireworks, preferring a solid focus on top-notch British produce, with a fair showing of luxury ingredients. Dishes are built on uncomplicated classical roots with intelligent modern twists. So a delicate chicken and langoustine roulade with tomato coulis might precede the more robust

flavours of braised brill fillet with glazed crab, spring onion and ginger and decadent desserts such as a double chocolate tart.

Chef Stephen Hine **Owner** Elite Hotels **Times** 12.30-2/7-10 **Prices** Fixed L 2 course fr £18, Fixed D 3 course fr £37, Starter fr £12.50, Main fr £24, Dessert fr £10, Service included **Wines** 350 bottles over £20, 2 bottles under £20, 10 by glass **Notes** Sunday L, Vegetarian available, Dress restrictions, Jacket & tie at D, no jeans, Civ Wed 100 **Seats** 80, Pr/dining room 100 **Children** Portions, Menu **Parking** 150

SHEDFIELD	Map 5 SU51

Broadstreet Restaurant and Bar

◎ Modern British

Country club hotel with uncomplicated modern dining options

☎ 01329 833455 📠 01329 834411
Marriott Meon Valley Hotel & Country Club, Sandy Ln SO32 2HQ
e-mail: gareth.bowen@marriotthotels.co.uk
dir: Please telephone for directions

This classy modern country hotel has the full leisure and pampering package, with 2 championship courses and its own golfing academy, plus tennis courts and a health and beauty spa. The Zest café and restaurant is the more casual of its 2 dining venues - a stylish space with oxblood leather seating, pale wood and exposed stone walls - while the upscale Broadstreet restaurant is the fine-dining option. The kitchen majors on simple, unfussy cooking using good quality ingredients in dishes such as London-cured smoked salmon with beetroot, horseradish and dill, and grilled spatchcock poussin rubbed with thyme, garlic and lemon.

Chef Gareth Bowen, Jamie Welch **Owner** Marriott International **Times** 6-10 Closed Sun-Mon, L Tue-Sat **Prices** Fixed D 3 course fr £22.50, Starter £5-£9, Main £10.50-£25, Dessert £5-£7.50, Service included **Wines** 28 bottles over £20, 24 bottles under £20, 17 by glass **Notes** Vegetarian available, Dress restrictions, Smart casual, Civ Wed 80, Air con **Seats** 65, Pr/dining room 20 **Parking** 200

SOUTHAMPTON	Map 5 SU41

Legacy Botleigh Grange Hotel

◎ Traditional British, Mediterranean **V**

Formal dining in well positioned hotel

☎ 0870 832 9950 📠 0870 832 9951
Grange Rd, Hedge End SO30 2GA
e-mail: res-botleighgrange@legacy-hotels.co.uk
dir: On A334, 1m from M27 junct 7

Botleigh Grange Hotel is in an idyllic position, and its all only 1 mile from Junction 7 of the M27 motorway. A traditional hotel set in stunning grounds with 2 lakes, the driveway to the house is flanked by the magnificent Highland cattle that graze freely in the grounds. The

restaurant is light and airy with a glass domed ceiling and views overlooking the immaculate gardens. The modern European dishes include crayfish and crab linguine with creamy lemon, dill and tomato sauce, followed by tenderloin of pork stuffed with chorizo and wrapped in Parma ham.

Chef Stephen Lewis **Owner** David K Plumpton **Times** 12.30-2.30/7-9.45 **Prices** Fixed L 2 course £17.95-£21.95, Fixed D 3 course £21.50-£35, Starter £4.75-£6.95, Main £12.50-£16.50, Dessert £4.95-£7.50, Service optional **Wines** 2 bottles over £20, 10 bottles under £20, 7 by glass **Notes** Sunday L, Vegetarian menu, Civ Wed 200 **Seats** 80, Pr/dining room 350 **Children** Portions, Menu **Parking** 300

Vatika

◎◎ British, Indian **NEW**

Vibrant Indian spicing in English country vineyard

☎ 01329 830405
Botley Rd, Shedfield SO32 2HL
e-mail: info@vatikarestaurant.co.uk
dir: M27 junct 7 through Botley towards Wickham. M27 junct 10, A32 through Wickham towards Bishops Waltham. Turn left into Wickham Rd towards Vineyard

This classy restaurant puts a new spin on the concept of 'Going for an Indian'. First off, you don't often come across a location like this, on the delightful Wickham Vineyard in deepest Hampshire. Vatika - meaning 'Vineyard' in Sanskrit and Hindi - is the latest venture from Atul Kochhar of Benares fame (see entry); his cuisine here, overseen by protégé Jitin Joshi who heads up the kitchen, might best be described as 'Indlish' - creative modern British food with a clear Indian influence. The team clearly has a strong understanding of the Indian arsenal of spices and herbs, sharp technical skills and lively imagination to pull off a classy act. Innovative dishes look the part and are named after their two main ingredients, as in a starter of 'mackerel_grape', the fish served as an accurately cooked medallion and raw marinated slivers with grape chutney and parsley pesto. 'Prawn_turnip' delivers Tandoori tiger prawn tails with Goan-style turnips and tamarind glaze. To end, 'date_milk' is a light sponge with sticky caramel foam, tandoori dates and milk kewra jam.

Chef Jitin Joshi **Owner** Atul Kochhar **Times** 12-2.30/6.30-9.30 Closed Mon-Tue **Prices** Fixed L 2 course fr £19.50, Fixed D 3 course fr £40, Service added but optional 12.5% **Wines** 60 bottles over £20, 11 bottles under £20, 14 by glass **Notes** Tasting menu & vegetarian tasting menu available, Sunday L, Vegetarian available, Dress restrictions, Smart casual, Air con **Seats** 45 **Children** Portions, Menu **Parking** 25

SOUTHAMPTON *continued*

White Star Tavern, Dining and Rooms

Modern British **NEW**

Modern British dining in Southampton's restaurant district

☎ 023 8082 1990
28 Oxford St SO14 3DJ
e-mail: reservations@whitestartavern.co.uk
dir: Please telephone for directions

Southampton has never been known as a destination for good eating, but in recent years gentrified Oxford Street, just a stone's throw from the busy docks, has turned into something of a restaurant quarter. In the heart of things is the White Star Tavern, named after the Southampton-based White Star Line shipping company - owner of the ill-fated Titanic. Dine in the lively bar area or in the more peaceful surrounds of the restaurant, or even outside if the weather permits. The modern British menu offers the likes of treacle-cured salmon tartar with pickled cucumber and dill, Lymington day boat sole with caper butter, lemon and minted new potatoes, and local venison with red cabbage and prune, parsnip drop scone and a bitter chocolate jus.

Chef J Hayward **Owner** Matthew Boyle
Times 12-2.30/6-9.30 Closed 25-26 Dec **Prices** Starter £4.50-£9, Main £10-£21, Dessert £5-£8, Service optional, Groups min 6 service 10% **Wines** 22 bottles over £20, 14 bottles under £20, 14 by glass **Notes** Sunday L, Vegetarian available, Air con **Seats** 40, Pr/dining room 10 **Children** Portions **Parking** On street or 2 car parks nearby

---

The Greyhound

Modern British

Popular gastro-pub on the River Test

☎ 01264 810833 📠 0870 891 2897
31 High St SO20 6EY
e-mail: enquiries@thegreyhound.info
dir: 9m NW of Winchester, 8m S of Andover. Off A303

The Greyhound may look like a thoroughbred 15th-century village inn on the outside, but indoors it's a classy modern gastro-pub. The history-steeped bar and more contemporary lounge both have inglenook fireplaces, old beams and timbers, bare floorboards and angling paraphernalia hung around as a reminder that you're in fishing country here in the Test Valley, between Winchester and Salisbury. Simplicity is the key to the kitchen's approach, delivering cracking modern fodder with care, finesse and thoughtful composition. Fresh linguine with seared scallops, tomato, olives and spring onions hits the mark to start, followed by braised noisette of Cornish salt-marsh lamb with fondant potato, crushed peas and braising juices.

Chef Norelle Oberin **Owner** Tim Fiducia **Times** 12-2/7-9 Closed 25-26 Dec, 31 Dec & 1 Jan, D Sun **Prices** Starter £6-£8, Main £12.50-£20, Dessert £6-£8 **Wines** 60 bottles

over £20, 20 bottles under £20, 8 by glass **Notes** Sunday L, Vegetarian available **Seats** 52 **Children** Portions **Parking** 20

Peat Spade Inn

British

Good food in Test Valley village pub

☎ 01264 810612
Longstock SO20 6DR
dir: 1.5m N of Stockbridge on A3057

The Peat Spade is a gem of a dining pub with bedrooms located in a tranquil village close to the River Test, the fly-fishing capital of the world. A small seating area near the bar leads round to the dining area which has wooden tables with lit candles, and walls covered with old school pictures, and leading off this is the rod room where the ceiling is home to a selection of, yes, fishing rods. The seasonal menu delivers classic English dishes, using excellent local ingredients and straightforwardly presented. Start with chicken liver and foie gras parfait with home-made chutney, and follow on with pork belly, black pudding and a nicely tart apple sauce. Finish with treacle tart and clotted cream.

Times 12-2/6.30-9.30 Closed 3 wks Feb/Mar & 25-26 Dec, D Sun

Old House Hotel & Restaurant

Modern British

Georgian splendour and impressive cuisine

☎ 01329 833049 📠 01329 833672
The Square PO17 5JG
e-mail: enquiries@oldhousehotel.co.uk
dir: In centre of Wickham, 2m N of Fareham at junct of A32 & B2177

History is quite literally built into the fabric of this handsome early-Georgian townhouse, in the shape of timbers within the restaurant that were salvaged from the American civil war battleship *Chesapeake*. Bare boards, bare tables and art by Bill Crozier set the scene in the three eating areas, one of which looks onto the village square. A straightforward menu of modern British and continental dishes changes with the seasons - there is proudly-named local produce in a starter of Moor Farm rabbit with pickled Stockbridge Wood blewits and sweet mustard sabayon, then South Coast sea bass and lobster

---

with lemon and green onion risotto, sautéed leeks, lobster foam and brandy bisque. End with spiced pear tarte Tatin with citrus pannacotta and red wine syrup.

Chef James Parsons **Owner** Mr J R Guess
Times 12-2.30/7-9.30 Closed D Sun **Prices** Fixed L 3 course fr £16.45, Fixed D 3 course £25, Starter £5.50-£8.50, Main £15.50-£24, Dessert £5-£8, Service optional, Groups min 8 service 10% **Wines** 72 bottles over £20, 24 bottles under £20, 12 by glass **Notes** Tasting menu available, Sunday L, Vegetarian available, Dress restrictions, Smart casual, Civ Wed 80, Air con **Seats** 85, Pr/dining room 14 **Children** Portions **Parking** 12, Street parking

---

Avenue Restaurant

– see opposite page

The Black Rat

Modern British

Relaxed, unbuttoned dining in character-packed surroundings

☎ 01962 844465
88 Chesil St SO23 0HX
e-mail: reservations@theblackrat.co.uk
dir: M3 junct 9/A31 towards Winchester & Bar End until T-junct. Turn right at traffic lights, restaurant 600yds on left

Don't be put off by the somewhat shabby appearance of this former pub, because inside it's a whole different, sympathetically refurbished, world. Purely an eating pub (there's only a small bar upstairs for pre-dinner drinks), there are two cosy dining rooms brimming with original features. Think beams, wooden floors, exposed brickwork and an inglenook fireplace, along with chunky bare wood tables matched with old church chairs. The food is modern British and mostly based around seasonal ingredients. Rabbit and saffron pappardelle makes a satisfying start to lunch, followed by wonderfully meaty braised Blackface mutton with pearl barley and spring vegetables, and a light hazelnut polenta cake with roasted plum and crème fraîche sorbet to finish.

Chef Chris Bailey **Owner** David Nicholson
Times 12-2.15/7-9.30 Closed 2 wks Etr, 2 wks Xmas & New Year, L Mon-Fri **Prices** Starter £6.25-£7, Main £16.50-£20, Dessert £6.50-£7.50, Service optional, Groups min 10 service 10% **Wines** 40 bottles over £20, 25 bottles under £20, 6 by glass **Notes** Sunday L, Vegetarian available **Seats** 40, Pr/dining room 14 **Parking** Car park opposite

The Chesil Rectory

◉◉ Modern British

Great British cooking in historic building

☎ 01962 851555
1 Chesil St SO23 0HU
e-mail: enquiries@chesilrectory.co.uk
dir: S from King Alfred's statue at bottom of The Broadway, cross small bridge, turn right, restaurant on left, just off mini rdbt

The oldest house in Winchester (built 1450, it says on an old beam above the window) was taken over by a new team in October 2008 and so began the latest adventure for the house at 1 Chesil Street. A refurbishment has lost none of the atmospheric charm of the old building - dark beams, inglenook fireplaces - whilst adding some well chosen items such as vintage chandeliers, stylish chairs and green leather banquettes. Chef Damian Brown's menus are firmly focused on Britain, both in terms of the quality produce used and the style and manner of the cooking. Bury black pudding, for example, in a starter with a poached egg and piquant devilled sauce, or how about Greenfield pork belly perfectly pointed with an apple and vanilla compôte? Un-clothed tables and professional, friendly and passionate service complete the picture. Finish with a simply perfect burnt Cambridge cream.

Chef Damian Brown **Owner** Mark Dodd, Damian Brown, Iain Longhorn **Times** 12-2.30/6-9.30 Closed 1 wk Xmas, 1 wk Aug, Mon, D Sun **Prices** Fixed L 2 course £14.95, Fixed D 3 course £19.95, Starter £4.50-£7.95, Main £11.95-£15.50, Dessert £6, Service optional, Groups min 10 service 10% **Wines** 50+ bottles over £20, 10 bottles under £20, 9 by glass **Notes** Sunday L, Vegetarian available, Civ Wed 30 **Seats** 75, Pr/dining room 14 **Parking** NCP Chesil Street

Hotel du Vin Winchester

◉◉ Traditional, International

Busy bistro in popular, city-centre, boutique-chain hotel

☎ 01962 841414 ▤ 01962 842458
14 Southgate St SO23 9EF
e-mail: info@winchester.hotelduvin.co.uk
dir: M3 junct 11, follow signs to Winchester town centre, located on left

A charming central-city town house hotel dating back to 1715, with wine the dominant theme throughout the bustling French-style bistro and bar, and the comfortable, wine company sponsored bedrooms. This was the first of the group. Expect an elegantly refurbished interior mixed with a relaxed easy style, shown to best effect in the bustling, French-style bistro and bar. Here, bare boards, an eclectic mix of polished tables and chairs, and wine memorabilia crowding the walls, form the backdrop for a modern, Mediterranean-influenced menu that utilises locally-sourced produce. Expect simple, light, clean-cut, well-presented classics with some creative touches: succulent scallops with pea purée and crispy pancetta, rich seared calves' liver with smooth pomme purée and a well-balanced red wine jus, and apple tarte Tatin with subtly flavoured cinnamon ice cream. Knowledgeable staff apply Gallic commitment, and the wine list is a delight.

Chef Marcela Morales **Owner** MWB **Times** 12-1.45/7-10 **Prices** Starter £4.50-£6.75, Main £10.95-£16.50, Dessert £2.50-£6.75, Service added but optional 10% **Wines** 90% bottles over £20, 10% bottles under £20, 10 by glass **Notes** Sunday L, Vegetarian available, Dress restrictions, Smart casual, Civ Wed 60 **Seats** 65, Pr/dining room 48 **Children** Portions, Menu **Parking** 40, NCP Tower St

Avenue Restaurant

◉◉◉

| WINCHESTER | Map 5 SU42 |

Modern British V ▤ ⌖

Imaginative modern cooking in a historic house

☎ 01962 776088 ▤ 01962 776672
Lainston House Hotel, Woodman Ln, Sparsholt SO21 2LT
e-mail: enquiries@lainstonhouse.com
dir: 2.5m NW off A272, road to Stockbridge, signed

The house has many stories to tell, virtually from the moment of its construction in the late 17th century. Barely had the place been finished than Charles II looked in with one of his mistresses. Owned successively by courtiers and members of parliament over the years, it has been a hotel since 1981. Don't miss the medieval chapel ruins in the grounds. Inside, all is both smart and relaxing, with the Avenue restaurant an intimate space adorned with characterful portraits on oak-panelled walls. In summer months, bag a table on the terrace, where the receding avenue of lime trees was inspired by a poetic work written here by Sir John Evelyn. Sir John might have found further inspiration had he been living in the era of Andrew MacKenzie, whose cooking style lends a thoroughly modern sensibility to the produce of a group of carefully cultivated Food Heroes. Portland lobster makes a grand opener, served with mango salsa and a Bloody Mary sorbet, while mains might bring on rump of miraculously tender Casterbridge beef, accompanied by cep ravioli, carrot purée and a version of salsa verde made with Hampshire watercress. Crunchy rosemary tuiles and a piece of delectable honeycomb are the garnishes for a honeycomb parfait dessert, a superbly rendered essay in textural contrasts. Fine Anglo-Irish cheeses are on offer too.

Chef Andrew MacKenzie **Owner** Exclusive Hotels **Times** 12-2/7-10 **Prices** Fixed L 2 course fr £21.50, Fixed D 3 course fr £35.50, Starter £10.50-£16.50, Main £18.50-£28, Dessert £10.50, Service optional **Wines** 200 bottles over £20, 200 by glass **Notes** Sunday L, Vegetarian menu, Dress restrictions, Smart dress, Civ Wed 200 **Seats** 60, Pr/dining room 120 **Children** Portions, Menu **Parking** 200

WINCHESTER continued

Hutton's Brasserie & Bar

◉ Modern European

Sound, modern cooking in a contemporary setting

☎ 01962 709988   📠 01962 840862
The Winchester Hotel, Worthy Ln SO23 7AB
e-mail: info.winchester@pedersenhotels.com
dir: M3 junct 9, at rdbt take 3rd exit (A34/Newbury).
0.5m, right & follow A33/Basingstoke signs. 1st left onto
B3047 to Winchester. Hotel 2m on right

Located in the heart of the city, the smart, modern
brasserie and bar in this refurbished hotel boasts walnut
floors, leather banquette seating, and a stunning feature
wall. Contemporary European cuisine is the order of the
day, accompanied by efficient, friendly service. Start with
open ravioli of crab and tiger prawn with wilted rocket
and lemongrass butter sauce, and for main course try
confit pork belly with smoked bacon and cannellini bean
casserole, braised butternut squash and Madeira jus, or
perhaps crispy fillet of sea bass with fennel risotto,
roasted cherry tomatoes and pea foam. Finish with a
dessert of caramelised pear tarte Tatin, toffee ripple ice
cream and pear crisp.

Chef Paul Bentley **Owner** Pedersen Hotels
Times 12.30-2/7-9.30 **Prices** Fixed L 2 course £15.95-
£16.95, Fixed D 3 course £25-£26, Starter £6-£10, Main
£9-£20, Dessert £5-£8, Service optional **Wines** 15 bottles
over £20, 25 bottles under £20, 9 by glass **Notes** Sunday
L, Vegetarian available, Dress restrictions, Smart casual,
Civ Wed 180, Air con **Seats** 80, Pr/dining room 40
Children Portions, Menu **Parking** 70

The Running Horse

◉ Modern International

Hearty British food served in relaxed gastro-pub

☎ 01962 880218   📠 01962 886596
88 Main Rd, Littleton SO22 6QS
e-mail: runninghorseinn@btconnect.com
dir: 3m from city centre, 2m off A34

A short canter from the M3, this whitewashed village pub
is situated on the western outskirts of Winchester and is
ideal for business or pleasure (or both, if that's possible).
Locals and residents mingle in the bar and the friendly
atmosphere, combined with high quality cuisine, makes
this a valuable local resource. Warm colours, clean lines,
flagstone floors, leather sofas and a marble-topped bar
characterise the interior, and you can choose from
blackboard menus in the restaurant, bar and alfresco
terrace. The varied choice of accomplished dishes might
include twice-baked cheese soufflé or rump of lamb,
dauphinoise potatoes, red cabbage and rosemary jus.
Locally brewed beers and a comprehensive wine list
complete the package.

Chef Julien Lubeda **Owner** Light Post Ltd
Times 11-3/5.30-11 **Prices** Starter £4.95-£7.50, Main
£10-£20, Dessert £5.95-£7, Service optional, Groups min
6 service 10% **Wines** 9 bottles over £20, 17 bottles under

£20, 10 by glass **Notes** Sunday L, Vegetarian available
Seats 48 **Children** Portions, Menu **Parking** 42

The Winchester Royal

◉ Traditional

Modern menu in the heart of historic Winchester

☎ 01962 840840   📠 01962 841582
St Peter St SO23 8BS
e-mail: winchester.royal@forestdale.com
dir: Take one-way system through Winchester, turn right
off St George's Street into St Peter Street. Hotel on right

Built in the 16th century, this building was a bishop's
house, a private residence and a Benedictine convent
before becoming a hotel 160 years ago. Right in the
centre of Winchester, the stylish Conservatory Restaurant
overlooks a beautiful walled garden. The cuisine is
traditional English but with a few modern twists, and
based around good quality produce, with a menu that
changes monthly. Chicken liver parfait with home-made
mustard seed chutney might kick things off, then lamb
shank with shallot compôte and smoked bacon, finishing
with apple and thyme crumble, mascarpone and caramel
sauce for dessert.

Chef Michael LePoidevin **Owner** Forestdale Hotels
Times 12-2/7-9.30 **Prices** Starter £5.50-£6.75, Main
£14-£18.50, Dessert £5.50-£6.50, Service optional
Wines 11 bottles over £20, 24 bottles under £20, 7 by
glass **Notes** Sunday L, Vegetarian available, Civ Wed 120,
Air con **Seats** 95, Pr/dining room 30 **Children** Portions,
Menu **Parking** 50

HEREFORDSHIRE

HEREFORD · Map 10 SO53

Castle House

◉◉◉ — *see opposite page*

KINGTON · Map 9 SO25

The Stagg Inn and Restaurant

◉◉ Modern British 🍃

Friendly, quality-driven gastro-pub

☎ 01544 230221   📠 01544 231390
Titley HR5 3RL
e-mail: reservations@thestagg.co.uk
dir: Between Kington & Presteigne on B4335

The Stagg is perfectly placed to hunt down the very best
of the Welsh Marches' marvellous produce - after all, wild
venison, duck and pheasant comes from local shoots,
organic fruit, veg and fish is farmed nearby, and the
owners keep their own rare breed pigs. Despite the foodie
focus, it is still a proper roadside pub whose engine room
is a rustic bar alive with a convivial buzz of local
drinkers; the smart dining areas are simply kitted out
with bare farmhouse tables. In keeping with the general
lack of pretension, the waffle-free menu lays out an
admirable choice of classic dishes; the cooking is

technically spot-on, gutsy stuff with clear flavours in
starters such as baked pressed pig's head with onion
purée, and a main course of Herefordshire beef fillet with
watercress purée and dauphinoise potato. Standards are
still tip-top at dessert - perhaps a lemon tart with cassis
sorbet.

Chef S Reynolds, M Handley **Owner** Steve & Nicola
Reynolds **Times** 12-3/6.30-9.30 Closed 1st 2wks Nov,
1wk Jan, Mon, D Sun **Prices** Starter £4.20-£8.50, Main
£14.50-£18.50, Dessert £6-£7.50, Service optional
Wines 44 bottles over £20, 28 bottles under £20, 8 by
glass **Notes** Sunday L, Vegetarian available **Seats** 70, Pr/
dining room 30 **Children** Portions **Parking** 22

LEDBURY · Map 10 SO73

Feathers Hotel

◉ Modern British 🍃

Modern combinations in an Elizabethan setting

☎ 01531 635266   📠 01531 638955
High St HR8 1DS
e-mail: mary@feathers-ledbury.co.uk
dir: M50 junct 2. Ledbury on A449/A438/A417. Hotel on
main street

The majestic, four-storeyed Elizabethan inn is hard to
miss on the high street, and draws in a loyal clientele to
both the Fuggles Brasserie (named after a variety of
hops) and the rather fancier weekend venue, Quills.
Simple presentation and sensitive cooking characterise
dishes such as sautéed scallops with new potatoes and
black truffle dressing. Poultry from nearby Madgetts Farm
might be cold-poached chicken breast stuffed with sun-
blushed tomatoes, shallots and herbs, or a main course
of duck with thyme-buttered courgettes and a chestnut
potato cake. Firmly set pannacotta with poached prunes
and apricot sorbet is a good finishing combination.

Chef Susan Isaacs **Owner** David Elliston
Times 12-2/7-9.30 **Prices** Starter £4.50-£12.50, Main
£14.50-£25, Dessert £5-£10, Service added but optional
10% **Wines** 45 bottles over £20, 57 bottles under £20, 10
by glass **Notes** Sunday L, Vegetarian available, Civ Wed
100, Air con **Seats** 55, Pr/dining room 60
Children Portions **Parking** 30

Verzon House Bar, Brasserie & Hotel

◉◉ Modern British, European

Quality local produce in modern, stylish surroundings

☎ 01531 670381 🖷 01531 670830
Hereford Rd, Trumpet HR8 2PZ
e-mail: info@theverzon.com
dir: M5 junct 8, M50 junct 2 (signed Ledbury/A417).
Follow signs for Hereford (A438). Hotel on right

Far-reaching views of the Malvern Hills can be enjoyed from the extensive grounds at this large, elegant Georgian country house. Its Brasserie restaurant is a modish affair with stylish fixtures and fittings and contemporary natural tones, while service is formal yet friendly. The accomplished kitchen seeks out high-quality local, seasonal produce and delivers accomplished modern British dishes with eye-catching presentation. Take a terrine of Cornish crab and Wye Valley smoked salmon with toasted brioche to start, while honey-and-thyme roasted breast of Madgetts Farm free-range duck served with sweet potato mash and balsamic roasted beetroot and shallots, or perhaps, shallow pan-fried Cornish scallops accompanied by cannellini beans, roasted red peppers, caramelised garlic and deep-fried parsley might catch the eye at mains.

Times 12-2/7-9.30

ROSS-ON-WYE   **Map 10 SO52**

The Bridge at Wilton

◉◉ Modern British, French 🥂

Accomplished cooking on the banks of the Wye

☎ 01989 562655 🖷 01989 567652
Wilton HR9 6AA
e-mail: info@bridge-house-hotel.com
web: www.bridge-house-hotel.com
dir: Off junct A40 & A49 into Ross-on-Wye, 300yds on left

Facing Ross-on-Wye across a lovely medieval bridge, this small-scale restaurant with rooms opens into a lush walled garden on the banks of the River Wye where you can watch the fish jump as you sip a glass of wine. Rustic chic reminiscent of a French country auberge sets the tone indoors, with creaky dark oak floorboards underfoot and modern paintings by a local artist on cool cream walls. The kitchen keeps things simple, producing clear flavours; it helps, of course, that local produce, including vegetables and herbs from the hotel's own garden, forms the backbone of the menu, with suppliers proudly credited for each dish, as in a starter of twice-baked Hereford hop cheese soufflé with May Hill rhubarb purée and beetroot dressing. Mains might offer best end of Phocle Green pork teamed with black pudding fritter, honey-roast apple and clove jus.

Chef James Arbourne **Owner** Mike & Jane Pritchard **Times** 12-2/7-9 **Prices** Starter £7-£12, Main £18-£23, Dessert £7-£10, Service optional **Wines** 27 bottles over £20, 27 bottles under £20, 4 by glass **Notes** Dress restrictions, Smart casual **Seats** 40, Pr/dining room 26 **Parking** 40

Castle House

HEREFORD   **Map 10 SO53**

Modern British 🥂

Adventurous cooking in contemporary luxury

☎ 01432 356321 🖷 01432 365909
Castle St HR1 2NW
e-mail: info@castlehse.co.uk
web: www.castlehse.co.uk
dir: City centre, follow signs to Castle House Hotel

A grand marble-pillared entrance flanked by potted bay trees greets you at this grand Georgian townhouse hotel. The town centre bustle and amazing cathedral with its world-class attractions, the Mappa Mundi and Chained Library, are but a short stroll away, while Castle house bathes in delicious tranquillity amid lovingly landscaped gardens. Inside, the designers have been at work, putting together an opulent interior of heavy-swagged drapes, antiques and rich textures. The plush restaurant has topiary-themed artworks on mustard walls, tables are draped with floor-length pleats of linen and laid with gleaming silver and crystal, and there are lovely views into the garden; if the weather is on your side, it's a treat to eat out on the terrace overlooking the castle moat. The menu delivers subtly inventive combinations underpinned by sound classical foundations and presented with eye-catching flair. Chef Claire Nicholls is a local girl who stays true to her roots in sourcing excellent materials from the Marches and from the hotel owner's farm. Seared scallops have spring onion and parmesan gnocchi and watercress emulsion for company in a typically elegant starter. Local meat is showcased in a main-course fillet of Hereford beef with mushroom and pancetta sausage, carrot fondant and asparagus. Indulgence is the name of the game at dessert in artfully-presented creations such as pistachio and hazelnut parfait, dark chocolate brownie and candied orange salad.

Chef Claire Nicholls **Owner** David Watkins **Times** 12-2/7-10 **Prices** Tasting menu £49, Starter £4-£9, Main £9-£20, Dessert £3.50-£7, Service optional **Wines** 9 by glass **Notes** Tasting menu 7 course, Sunday L, Vegetarian available, Civ Wed 40, Air con **Seats** 30 **Children** Portions **Parking** 12

ROSS-ON-WYE *continued*

Glewstone Court

◉ Modern British, French 🍃

Fine Georgian house with local produce dominating the menu

☎ 01989 770367 🖷 01989 770282
Glewstone HR9 6AW
e-mail: glewstone@aol.com
web: www.glewstonecourt.com
dir: From Ross Market Place take A40/A49 (Monmouth/ Hereford) over Wilton Bridge. At rdbt left onto A40 (Monmouth/S Wales), after 1m turn right for Glewstone. Hotel 0.5m on left

Owned and run by the same family for more than twenty years, Glewstone Court is located just 3 miles from Ross-on-Wye in a wonderfully unspoilt corner of Herefordshire. Set amongst fruit orchards within an Area of Outstanding Natural Beauty, this listed Georgian country house overlooks the Wye Valley and retains many original features. The restaurant is decorated in a contemporary style - local artists exhibit on the walls - while the cooking is traditionally based. The French-influenced menu showcases the best of local produce, including on the Marches tapas platter featuring local smoked fish and charcuterie and a main course of fillet of Hereford beef grilled to order.

Chef Christine Reeve-Tucker, Richard Jefferey, Tom Piper **Owner** C & W Reeve-Tucker **Times** 12-2/7-10 Closed 25-27 Dec **Prices** Fixed L 2 course £10, Starter £4.50-£8.95, Main £12.95-£19.95, Dessert £5.75-£7.50, Service optional, Groups min 8 service 10% **Wines** 18

bottles over £20, 18 bottles under £20, 6 by glass **Notes** Sunday L, Vegetarian available, Dress restrictions, No baseball caps or mobile phones, Civ Wed 65 **Seats** 36, Pr/dining room 40 **Children** Portions, Menu **Parking** 28

Harry's

◉ Modern European

Ambitious cuisine in an elegant Georgian hotel

☎ 01989 763161 🖷 01989 768330
Chase Hotel, Gloucester Rd HR9 5LH
e-mail: res@chasehotel.co.uk
dir: M50 junct 4 A449, A440 towards Ross-on-Wye

The Chase Hotel is a creeper-swathed Georgian country house in 11 acres of landscaped gardens amid a lush Herefordshire landscape, yet just a short stroll from the town centre. Elegant high ceilings and ornate plasterwork make a fine foil for the ivory and honey hues, high-backed black and caramel leather seats and pale silk drapes of the clean-cut contemporary-styled Harry's restaurant. Knowledgeable staff deliver amiable, well-paced service, while the kitchen turns out a fine repertoire of dishes in a modern British vein, as in a starter of breaded goats' cheese with a tangy plum and apple chutney, followed by chicken breast with button onions, mushrooms, bacon and red wine jus.

Chef Richard Birchall **Owner** Camanoe Estates Ltd **Times** 12-2/7-10 Closed 24-27 Dec **Prices** Fixed L 2 course £22.50, Fixed D 3 course £27.50, Starter £5.50-£9.25, Main £15-£22, Dessert £5.50-£7.95, Service included **Wines** 27 bottles over £20, 15 bottles under £20, 13 by glass **Notes** Sunday L, Vegetarian available, Civ Wed 300 **Seats** 70, Pr/dining room 300 **Children** Portions **Parking** 150

The Lough Pool Inn at Sellack

◉◉ British, International

Top-notch food in a charming, rustic pub setting

☎ 01989 730236
Sellack HR9 6LX
e-mail: enquiries@loughpool.co.uk
web: www.loughpool.co.uk
dir: 4m NW of Ross-on-Wye. 2m off A49 (Hereford road) follow signs for Sellack

This whitewashed and timbered inn in bosky Herefordshire ticks all the boxes for rustic charm: an ancient lough pool with weeping willows and quacking ducks outside, while indoors is all flagstones and beams,

open fires in inglenooks and wood-burners, hop bines and an array of real ales at the bar. Whether you eat in the bar or bistro-style restaurant, rare breed meat from local suppliers and home-grown herbs are married to great effect in skilfully cooked dishes with clearly-defined flavours. International influences add pizzazz to a menu of modern British cuisine. Seared scallops rub along nicely with clams and brown shrimps in garlic and coriander butter to start, then pork tenderloin comes with fondant potato, braised red cabbage and a creamy sauce of fortified wine and grain mustard. Finish with rum panna cotta with rhubarb compôte and pomegranate stew.

Times 12-2.30/6.30-9.30 Closed 25 Dec, Mon (Nov, Jan-mid Mar), D Sun (Nov, Jan-mid Mar)

Mulberry Restaurant

◉◉ Modern British, Mediterranean 🍃

Delightful riverside setting and modern cooking

☎ 01989 562569 🖷 01989 768460
Wilton Court Hotel, Wilton Ln HR9 6AQ
e-mail: info@wiltoncourthotel.com
dir: M50 junct 4 onto A40 towards Monmouth at 3rd rdbt turn left signed Ross-on-Wye then take 1st right, hotel on right

Elizabethan in origin, this small-scale country-house hotel has an idyllic location on the banks of the River Wye, just a short stroll from Ross-on-Wye centre. The Mulberry restaurant - named after the 300 year-old tree you can see in the garden - is a romantic spot, surprisingly light and airy in spite of its Tudor-era mullioned leaded windows and venerable oak beams. Straightforward, skilful modern British cooking uses the pick of locally-sourced ingredients to serve up fresh, well-defined flavours. Herefordshire beef fillet might appear as a carpaccio with pickled chicory to start, followed by slow-braised shoulder of mutton with seared loin, boulangère potatoes and white haricot beans. Finish with a dark chocolate mousse with mandarin caramel and spearmint ice cream.

Chef Michael Fowler **Owner** Roger and Helen Wynn **Times** 12-2.15/7-9 Closed L Mon-Sat, D Sun **Prices** Fixed L 2 course fr £13.95, Starter £5.75-£8.50, Main £13.95-£22, Dessert £5.95-£7.50, Service optional **Wines** 11 bottles over £20, 23 bottles under £20, 7 by glass **Notes** Sunday L, Vegetarian available, Dress restrictions, Smart casual preferred, Civ Wed 50 **Seats** 40, Pr/dining room 12 **Children** Portions, Menu **Parking** 25

ULLINGSWICK	Map 10 SO54

Three Crowns Inn

◉ British, French

Welcoming rural inn offering good British fare

☎ 01432 820279 📠 08700 515338
HR1 3JQ
e-mail: info@threecrownsinn.com
dir: Please telephone for directions

A charming village inn and gastro-pub which was originally a half-timbered 16th-century farmhouse and cider house. Cream washed walls, timber pillars and an eclectic mix of wooden furniture, including church pews, give its restaurant a relaxed, welcoming atmosphere. The simple, effective, no frills cooking is British in style with some French influences, and the kitchen sources the quality seasonal produce from local suppliers. Expect accomplished dishes such as a starter of little Hereford cheddar and spinach soufflé, and a main course of grilled megrim sole with capers, shrimps and herb butter.

Times 12-3/7-10 Closed 25 Dec, 1 Jan, Mon

HERTFORDSHIRE

BERKHAMSTED	Map 6 SP90

The Gatsby

◉ Modern European NEW

Modern dining in art-deco picture house

☎ 01442 870403
97 High St HP4 2DG
e-mail: nickpembroke@hotmail.co.uk
dir: M25 junct 20/A41 to Aylesbury in 3m take left turn to Berkhamsted following town signs. Restaurant on left on entering High St

What was once the Rex cinema - a wonderful 1930's art deco construction - is these days a bar and dining room with plenty of 21st-century appeal. The art-deco styling continues on the inside, too, with original wooden pillars and handcrafted cornices alongside a huge chandelier and black-and-white photos offering a nostalgic reminder of the golden age of cinema. A white baby grand piano recalls, perhaps, another era of restaurants. The refined modern cuisine is a crowd pleaser, with clean-cut dishes offering classics like Scottish dry-aged fillet steak served with a red wine sauce and dauphinoise to a contemporary favourite such as pan-roasted duck breast and confit leg, served with bubble-and-squeak and Savoy cabbage.

Chef Matthew Salt **Owner** Nick Pembroke
Times 12-3/5.30-10.30 Closed 25-26 Dec **Prices** Fixed L 2 course £12.95, Starter £6.75-£9.50, Main £13.95-£23.95, Dessert £6.75-£7.25, Groups min 6 service 12.5% **Wines** 25 bottles over £20, 15 bottles under £20, 20 by glass **Notes** Sunday L, Vegetarian available, Dress restrictions, Smart casual **Seats** 65 **Children** Portions **Parking** 10

BISHOP'S STORTFORD	Map 6 TL42

Ibbetson's Restaurant

◉◉ Modern British

Imposing Victorian hotel with accomplished modern cooking

☎ 01279 732100 & 01279 731441 📠 01279 730416
Down Hall Country House Hotel, Matching Rd, Hatfield Heath CM22 7AS
e-mail: info@downhall.co.uk
web: www.downhall.co.uk
dir: Take A414 towards Harlow. At 4th rdbt follow B183 towards Hatfield Heath, keep left, follow hotel sign

On the Hertfordshire and Essex border, this impressive Victorian country-house hotel stands in 100 acres of grounds. The Ibbetson's dining room is an intimate and relaxed place with discreet, professional service. It is matched by accomplished Modern British cooking, delivering contemporary dishes with well-defined flavours conjured from locally sourced ingredients, including vegetables and salad leaves from the hotel's own garden. Take a starter of smoked ham hock and foie gras terrine with piccalilli and brioche, followed, perhaps, by loin of venison with parsnip and honey purée, braised red cabbage and a juniper jus. Fig tart served with balsamic reduction and mascarpone sorbet is an appealing dessert.

Chef Mark Jones **Owner** Veladail Collection **Times** 7-9.45 Closed Xmas, New Year, Sun-Mon, L all week **Prices** Starter £8.50-£10.50, Main £16.50-£26.95, Dessert £7.75-£10.50, Service added but optional 10% **Wines** 55 bottles over £20, 12 by glass **Notes** Vegetarian available, Dress restrictions, Smart casual, Civ Wed 130, Air con **Seats** 30 **Parking** 100

DATCHWORTH	Map 6 TL21

The Tilbury

◉ Modern British NEW V 🌱

Superb British produce in rejuvenated pub

☎ 01483 815550 📠 01483 718340
1 Watton Rd SG3 6TB
e-mail: info@thetilbury.co.uk
dir: See website for details

Paul Bloxham is a man with something of a Midas touch when it comes to liberating old pubs alongside a burning passion for regional British produce and seasonality. This old village pub supports his philosophy and ethics, retaining original features like open fires, exposed brick walls and wooden floors, while customers sit at bare-wood tables and tuck into accomplished, seasonally-inspired dishes based around local produce. Kick off with warm walnut-crusted local goats' cheese with foraged greens and cherry tomatoes, then go for seared calves' liver and bacon with bubble-and-squeak and balsamic shallots. Daily specials are written-up on a blackboard.

Chef Paul Bloxham, Ben Crick **Owner** Paul Bloxham & Paul Andrews **Times** 12-3/6-late Closed 1 Jan, some BHs, D Sun **Prices** Fixed L 2 course £13.95, Fixed D 3 course £21.50, Starter £4-£11, Main £9-£22, Dessert £4-£8, Service optional, Groups min 6 service 10% **Wines** 16 bottles over £20, 16 bottles under £20, 12 by glass **Notes** Sunday L, Vegetarian menu **Seats** 70, Pr/dining room 14 **Children** Portions, Menu **Parking** 40

See advert on page 190

HARPENDEN	Map 6 TL11

The White Horse

◉ Modern British, French

Stylish gastro-pub in the heart of Herts

☎ 01582 713428 📠 01582 460148
Hatching Green AL5 2JP
dir: Telephone for directions

Originally known to the locals as The Grey Donkey, this smart country pub was given the gastro-treatment a few years back by celebrity chef Jean-Christophe Novelli. The Frenchman cut all ties with the place in 2009, but that's not to say standards have slipped. The bar has retained its pubby atmosphere, but foodies are drawn to the smart restaurant for the likes of pan-seared scallops with ham hock compresse and pea purée, or Cornish bream with

continued

HARPENDEN *continued*

English cockle and tarragon risotto, red pimento essence, hazelnut and parsley pesto. Dessert could be pineapple tarte Tatin with tonka bean and coconut ice cream.

Chef Daniel Brinklow **Owner** Sweet Medicine **Times** 12-3.30/6-9.30 Closed 1-7 Jan, Mon-Tue **Prices** Fixed L 2 course fr £14.95, Starter £4.95-£9, Main £9.95-£20, Dessert £5-£8, Service optional, Groups min 6 service 10% **Wines** 30 bottles over £20, 12 bottles under £20, 12 by glass **Notes** Sunday L, Vegetarian available **Seats** 55, Pr/dining room 12 **Children** Portions **Parking** 65

HATFIELD
Map 6 TL20

Kiplings at Bush Hall
@@ Modern British

Modern cooking in a delightfully historic setting

☎ 01707 271251 🖹 01707 272289 **Mill Green AL9 5NT** **e-mail:** enquiries@bush-hall.com **dir:** From A1 (M) follow signs for A414 (Hereford/Welwyn Garden City). Take slip road onto A1000 (signs for Hatfield Hse). Left at lights, immediately left into hotel drive

Dating back to 1574, the elegant Bush Hall hotel is surrounded by 120 acres of parkland with the River Lea meandering along the riverside terraces and lake garden. A wide ranging menu in the grand Kiplings restaurant may take in pan-seared smoked haddock set on warm potato curry topped with a free-range poached hen's egg, followed by an English pork collection - crisp belly, roasted loin and braised shoulder - served with caramelised apple and ginger and honey cream. Puddings include a trio of British favourites and 'afternoon tea' of burnt cream, Earl Grey sorbet and fruit cake biscuit. Outdoor enthusiasts will thrive on the range of activities on offer in the grounds, including clay pigeon shooting.

Chef Scott McKenzie **Owner** Kiplings **Times** 12-2/7-10 Closed D 25 Dec-early Jan, L Sat-Sun **Prices** Fixed L 2 course £21, Fixed D 3 course £25, Service added but optional 12.5% **Wines** 68 bottles over £20, 36 bottles under £20, 8 by glass **Notes** Vegetarian available, Dress restrictions, Smart casual, Civ Wed 150, Air con **Seats** 38, Pr/dining room 22 **Children** Portions **Parking** 100

Outsidein at Beales Hotel
@@ Modern British

Modern menu with modernist architectural backdrop

☎ 01707 288500 🖹 01707 256282 **Beales Hotel, Comet Way AL10 9NG** **e-mail:** outsidein@bealeshotels.co.uk **dir:** Please telephone for directions

The contemporary architecture of this branch of the Beales hotel group gives the place something of the appearance of a giant climbing-frame, with wood and glass used to striking effect. The same modernist approach distinguishes the interiors, where the wood-toned dining room is curtained off with a screen of hanging glass. Menus are written in the modern idiom, as shopping lists of ingredients, so that you might start with Sutton Hoo chicken terrine, pickled girolles, cured ham, and go on to Cornish monkfish, pancetta, leek, spinach, or braised blade of Sacombe Hill Farm beef, potato, parsnip, horseradish. It will be noted that, despite the terseness, local provenance is as enthusiastically celebrated as one hopes to see.

Chef Wayne Turner **Owner** Beales Ltd **Times** 10-2.30/6.30-10 **Prices** Food prices not confirmed for 2010. Please telephone for details. **Wines** 60 bottles over £20, 26 bottles under £20, 14 by glass **Notes** Vegetarian available, Civ Wed 300, Air con **Seats** 80, Pr/dining room 300 **Children** Portions, Menu **Parking** 126

HEMEL HEMPSTEAD
Map 6 TL00

The Bobsleigh Hotel
@ British NEW 🖑

British food in relaxed, well-run hotel

☎ 0844 879 9033 🖹 01442 832471 **Hempstead Rd, Bovingdon HP3 0DS** **e-mail:** bobsleigh@macdonald-hotels.co.uk **dir:** Please telephone for directions

Handy for the M25, this Macdonald hotel is a useful spot for lunch, dinner or even afternoon tea. It's possible to sit outside on the patio, but the dining room offers good views over the manicured garden from the safety of the conservatory if the weather isn't kind. The menu is refreshingly straightforward, but not unaccomplished. British favourites such as cream of broccoli soup or Loch Fyne smoked salmon are typical starters, and steak and kidney pudding, served with Savoy cabbage and a choice of potatoes, is the real deal. Service has a welcome degree of informality.

Chef Tracy White **Owner** Macdonald Hotels
Times 12-2.30/7-9.30 Closed L Sat, D Sun **Prices** Fixed L
2 course £12.95, Starter £3.95-£6.95, Main £11.95-
£18.95, Dessert £4.95-£6.95, Service optional **Wines** 28
bottles over £20, 6 bottles under £20, 14 by glass
Notes Sunday L, Vegetarian available, Civ Wed 100 **Seats**
Pr/dining room 16 **Children** Portions, Menu **Parking** 60

HITCHIN   Map 12 TL12

Redcoats Farmhouse Hotel

◉ Traditional European

- -

**Conservatory dining in a converted medieval
farmhouse**

☎ 01438 729500   ▤ 01438 723322
Redcoats Green SG4 7JR
e-mail: sales@redcoats.co.uk
dir: A602 to Wymondley. Turn left to Redcoats Green. At
top of hill straight over at junct

The original farmhouse dates back to the mid-15th
century, although it's been cunningly disguised since the
Victorian era with a redbrick façade. A spacious
conservatory extension with wicker chairs, together with a
pair of dining rooms, offer a range of settings for the
accomplished bistro-style cooking. You might embark
with Portobello mushrooms stuffed with pancetta, leeks
and gruyère in a mushroom velouté, before proceeding via
Scottish venison fillet on haggis, or baked whole bream
on spinach with a beurre blanc, to arrive at the end in the

enveloping embrace of a Kirsch-laced black cherry and
chocolate trifle with caramel cream.

Chef Scott Liversedge **Owner** Mr P Butterfield & Mrs J
Gainsford **Times** 12-6.30 Closed 1 wk after Xmas, BH
Mons, L Sat, D Sun **Prices** Fixed L 2 course fr £16.50,
Fixed D 3 course fr £26, Starter £5-£8, Main £22-£28,
Dessert £7.50-£8.50, Service optional, Groups min 8
service 10% **Wines** 114 bottles over £20, 45 bottles
under £20, 11 by glass **Notes** Sunday L, Vegetarian
available, Dress restrictions, Smart casual, No jeans or
T-shirts, Civ Wed 70 **Seats** 70, Pr/dining room 24
Children Portions **Parking** 30

POTTERS BAR   Map 6 TL20

Ponsbourne Park Hotel

◉◉ Modern International

- -

Fine dining in peaceful country setting

☎ 01707 876191 & 879277 ▤ 01707 875190
SG13 8QT
e-mail: reservations@ponsbournepark.co.uk
web: www.ponsbournepark.co.uk
dir: Telephone or see website for directions

This grand 17th-century manor sits in 200 acres of lovely
countryside on the Ponsbourne Park estate. The interior
uses contemporary colours and finishes alongside the
original features of the house, and appeals to both the
weddings and conferences markets. Two elegant rooms
make up the formal fine-dining Seymours restaurant

(named after Sir Thomas Seymour, one time owner who
married Catherine Parr, the widow of Henry VIII). The
extensive menu features modern European dishes firmly
rooted in the classics, with a few flavours from further
afield. Start with rabbit and lobster roulade with pigeon
and watercress salad and truffle dressing, before
mignons of pork with celeriac and sage rösti and apple
and Calvados hollandaise. Finish with iced blackcurrant
parfait with vanilla shortbread and crème anglaise. A
bistro complete with plasma TV screen offers an informal
alternative.

Ponsbourne Park Hotel

Owner Tesco **Times** 12-4/6.45-11 Closed 1 Jan, D Sun-
Wed **Prices** Food prices not confirmed for 2010. Please
telephone for details. **Wines** 10 bottles over £20, 20
bottles under £20, 3 by glass **Notes** Sunday L, Vegetarian
available, Dress restrictions, Smart casual, Civ Wed 86,
Air con **Seats** 60, Pr/dining room 90 **Children** Portions,
Menu **Parking** 80

Colette's at The Grove

Rosettes not confirmed at time of going to press

RICKMANSWORTH   Map 6 TQ09

Modern European

**Fine dining in smart, contemporary, relaxed setting of
'London's country estate'**

☎ 01923 296015 & 296010 ▤ 01923 221008
Chandler's Cross WD3 4TG
e-mail: restaurants@thegrove.co.uk
dir: M25 junct 19, follow signs to Watford. At 1st large
rdbt take 3rd exit. 5m, entrance on right

The 300 acre grounds of this seriously grand 18th-century
stately building offer a veil of protection from the real
world, including the M25 which isn't as far away as you
might think. There's a championship golf course,
luxurious spa, plus fine formal gardens and great views
over Charlotte's Vale. The imposing house has been
transformed into a world-class, contemporary hotel,

which successfully combines historic character with
cutting-edge modern design. Colette's is the fine dining,
evening-only option, with its own separate entrance and
stylish lounge and bar. Sit on smart cream leather chairs
at linen-clad tables, while the slick waiting staff keep
everything ticking along nicely (there is a relaxed and
unpretentious air about the place; no dress code, for
example). A new chef is at the helm. Dinner includes all
the extras from canapés in the bar through to pre-dessert
and petits fours, and the cooking is in the contemporary
European vein. Expect cumin-scented frog's legs to start,
with garlic mousse, parsley purée and shiso cress, then,
perhaps, poached Cornish skate with pig's cheek, carrots
flavoured with star anise, pak choi and finished with a
carrot foam.

Times 7-10 Closed Sun & Mon except BHs, L all week

RICKMANSWORTH Map 6 TQ09

Colette's at The Grove

— see page 191

ST ALBANS Map 6 TL10

Chez Mumtaj

◉ French, Asian NEW

Modern French and Asian cuisine in luxurious setting

☎ 01727 800033
136-142 London Rd AL1 1PQ
e-mail: info@chezmumtaj.com
web: www.chezmumtaj.com
dir: Please telephone for directions

This boutique-style restaurant aims to showcase a unique style of modern French-Asian cuisine. The restaurant has the opulent look of a gentlemen's club with its mahogany-panelled walls adorned with antique mirrors, and leather chairs and banquettes. The slightly open-plan aspect allows diners to view the kitchen while they eat. The menu offers an eclectic mix of classic French, Asian, Chinese and Thai cooking, creating diverse dishes such as foie gras with curried cauliflower purée or more traditional Asian lamb kebabs with crème fraîche. Try the dim sum with a light, well-flavoured mousse and a delightful broth of coriander, lime and chilli, followed by Barbary duck breast with spices, julienne of young vegetables, oriental rice and a rhubarb and apple compôte with five spice.

Chef Chad Rahman **Times** 12-2.30/6-11 Closed 25 Dec **Prices** Fixed L 2 course £14.95, Fixed D 3 course £26-£39, Starter £4.50-£12, Main £14.95-£19.95, Dessert £5.95-£6.95, Service added but optional 10% **Notes** Prix Fixe set menu, Sunday L, Vegetarian available, Dress restrictions, Smart casual, Air con **Seats** 100, Pr/dining room 14 **Parking** On street & car park nearby

St Michael's Manor

◉◉ Modern British

Modern British cooking in a beautiful English setting

☎ 01727 864444 🖷 01727 848909
Fishpool St AL3 4RY
e-mail: reservations@stmichaelsmanor.com
web: www.stmichaelsmanor.com
dir: At Tudor Tavern in High St into George St. After abbey & school on left, road continues onto Fishpool St. Hotel 1m on left

Set in 5 acres of landscaped gardens, this luxurious country-house hotel dates way back to 1585. As well as the high-ceilinged traditionally decorated restaurant, there's a conservatory and sun terrace with splendid views over the gardens and a lake. Service is attentive and very pro-active. The modern British cooking has plenty of European flavours. Start with a glazed fig tart served with rocket leaves and aged balsamic before a main-course lamb tourte with aubergine caviar, sweet carrots and lavender sauce. Finish with an iced winter fruit parfait and spiced plum compôte or chocolate fondant, Cassis ice cream and orange sauce. The candlelit dinner service makes this restaurant ideal for a romantic meal.

Chef Eric Moboti **Owner** David & Sheila Newling-Ward **Times** 12-2.30/7-9.30 Closed L 31 Dec, D 25 Dec **Prices** Fixed L 2 course fr £15.50, Fixed D 3 course fr £19.50, Starter £4.25-£8.50, Main £13.95-£19.95, Dessert £5.95-£8.50, Service added but optional 12.5% **Wines** 42 bottles over £20, 10 bottles under £20, 11 by glass **Notes** Sunday L, Vegetarian available, Dress restrictions, Smart casual, Civ Wed 90 **Seats** 95, Pr/dining room 24 **Children** Portions, Menu **Parking** 75

Sopwell House

◉ Modern British, European

Sophisticated dining in an elegant country-house hotel

☎ 01727 864477 🖷 01727 844741
Cottonmill Ln, Sopwell AL1 2HQ
e-mail: enquiries@sopwellhouse.co.uk
web: www.sopwellhouse.co.uk
dir: M25 junct 22, A1081 St Albans. At lights left into Mile House Ln, over mini-rdbt into Cottonmill Ln

This Georgian house was once the home of Lord Mountbatten and is these days a hotel, country club and spa. The latest addition to the dining options, alongside the bar-lounge and the restaurant, is a lively modern brasserie, an all-day affair serving classic dishes such as rib-eye steak and club sandwiches. The restaurant is a more refined space, but still contemporary in style, with linen-clad tables, black and white photos on the walls and lovely garden views. The modern British menu with European influences makes excellent use of seasonal local produce in dishes of ambition. Start with foie gras parfait with Chianti-poached pear and pain d'épice, moving onto sea bass with mussels marinière, black linguine and bitter lemon purée.

Times 12-3/7-10 Closed L Sat, Mon

Auberge du Lac

This Michelin Starred restaurant headed by Executive Chef, Phil Thompson, is set in a beautifully restored former 18th century hunting lodge which rests beside the tranquil Broadwater Lake,

overlooking the splendour of Brocket Hall, in Hertfordshire. The Estate, just 22 miles from London, also offers two Championship golf courses and the Faldo Golf Institute.

Auberge du Lac offers immaculate service and the finest seasonal Modern British cuisine.

Auberge du Lac

WELWYN   Map 6 TL21

French, European 🍴

Skilful cooking in peaceful, lakeside setting

☎ 01707 368888   📠 01707 368898
Brocket Hall Estate AL8 7XG
e-mail: auberge@brocket-hall.co.uk
web: www.brocket-hall.co.uk
dir: A1(M) junct 4, B653 to Wheathampstead. In Brocket Ln take 2nd gate entry to Brocket Hall

Set in a beautifully restored former 18th-century hunting lodge resting beside the tranquil Broadwater Lake, this formidable restaurant overlooks 543 acres of parkland and the stately splendour of Brocket Hall. It's an idyllic location and there is a timeless elegance to the airy restaurant with its large windows and many original features. Like the service, the kitchen's influence is

French, with a modern approach underpinned by classic techniques and skills. Flavours are well defined due to careful cooking and impeccable sourcing of top quality ingredients. A risotto of creamed garlic, Madeira braised snails, wild garlic leaf and parsley might be followed by poached Anjou pigeon rolled in pancetta, beetroot and reblochon gratin with foie gras pannacotta. Finish with a creative dessert such as poached pear with white chocolate, Roquefort mousse and olive oil, or go for the trolley piled high with French and British artisan cheeses. An impressive wine list should appeal to all palates and pockets.

Chef Phil Thompson **Owner** CCA International
Times 12-2/7-9.30 Closed Sun & Mon **Prices** Food prices not confirmed for 2010. Please telephone for details.
Wines 750 bottles over £20, 14 by glass **Notes** Tasting menu 6 course, Vegetarian available, Dress restrictions, Jackets required, no jeans or trainers, Civ Wed 60
Seats 70, Pr/dining room 24 **Children** Portions, Menu
Parking 50

TRING — Map 6 SP91

Pendley Manor

◉ Modern

Fine dining in an imposing manor house

☎ 01442 891891 📠 01442 890687
Cow Ln HP23 5QY
e-mail: sales@pendley-manor.co.uk
dir: M25 junct 20, A41 (Tring exit). At rdbt follow
Berkhamsted/London signs. 1st left signed Tring Station
& Pendley Manor

The Victorians rebuilt this ancient manor house in the
Tudor style after it burnt down in 1835, and the modern
world has grafted on a full package of leisure and spa
facilities that make it a popular place for weddings and
corporate bashes. Peacocks roam its 35 acres of wooded
parkland, and the grand public rooms offer period
grandeur in spades. The imposing Oak Room restaurant
stays true to style, with oak panelling, high ceilings, vast
bay windows and heavy drapes. The kitchen's roll call of
dishes is based around the modern English canon: first
up, seared king scallops come with champagne sauce,
Avruga caviar and pea purée, followed by pan-fried duck
breast with five spice scented orange sauce and sweet
potatoes.

Times 12.30-2.30/7-9.30

WARE — Map 6 TL31

Marriott Hanbury Manor Hotel

◉◉ French, European

Striking Jacobean country pile with voguish cooking

☎ 01920 487722 📠 01920 487692
SG12 0SD
e-mail: wendy.traynor@marriotthotels.com
dir: From M25 junct 25, take A10 towards Cambridge, for
12m. Leave A10 Wadesmill/Thundridge/Ware. Right at
rdbt, hotel on left

The Manor is an imposing Jacobean country pile set in
200 acres of Hertfordshire, with walled gardens and as
much interior panelling as you can handle. Its star
attraction, apart from the championship golf course, is
the stunning Zodiac restaurant, where ruched curtains,
portraits in oils and lavish floral adornments are adjuncts
to the astrological symbols painted on the ceiling. The
cooking strikes some voguish poses. Tracing a route
through the menu might take you from salmon tartare
with sauce gribiche to fillet of bream with pumpkin ravioli

and sauce antiboise, or slow-roast belly and cannon of
lamb with minted pea purée, to a grand finale of peach
tart with crystallised ginger and a cream cheese sorbet.

Chef Gopi Chandran **Owner** Marriott Hotels
Times 12-2/7.30-9.30 Closed Mon, L Sat, D Sun
Prices Fixed D 3 course £39.50-£49.50, Service optional
Wines 300 bottles over £20 **Notes** Sunday L, Vegetarian
available, Dress restrictions, Smart casual, jacket
preferred for men, Civ Wed 120 **Seats** 50, Pr/dining room
20 **Children** Portions **Parking** 200

WELWYN — Map 6 TL21

Auberge du Lac

◉◉◉ — see page 193

See advert on page 193

The Restaurant at Tewin Bury Farm

◉ British, French Ⓥ

Fine cuisine in an impressive converted barn setting

☎ 01438 717793 📠 01438 841495
Tewin Bury Farm Hotel, Hertford Rd AL6 0JB
e-mail: kim.correia@tewinbury.co.uk
web: www.tewinbury.co.uk
dir: A1M junct 6 (signposted Welwyn Garden City), 1st
exit A1000. 0.25m to B1000 Hertford Rd. Hotel on left

The enterprising Williams family diversified their dairy
farm business into the guest house and restaurant trade
over twenty years ago. The working farm sits in gorgeous
Hertfordshire countryside, and its 17th-century riverside
barn forms part of what has grown into a delightful
country-house hotel, while the chicken shed now houses
the smartly refurbished rustic-style restaurant. Scrubbed
wood floors, massive oak beams and solid oak furniture
set the scene for Mediterranean-tinged modern English
dishes made from great local ingredients. You could start
with a choice of meze, or home-made fishcakes with
minted pea purée, rocket and lemon oil. Roast rack of
lamb with bean cassoulet and rosemary jus, or the farm's
own trout served teriyaki style on stir-fried vegetables
might be among main courses.

Chef William Jordan **Owner** Vaughan Williams
Times 12-2.30/6.30-9.30 **Prices** Fixed L 2 course £10,
Fixed D 3 course £22, Starter £4.70-£7.25, Main £9.50-
£16.95, Dessert £4.50, Service optional **Wines** 18 bottles
over £20, 12 bottles under £20, 10 by glass **Notes** Tasting
menu available, Sunday L, Vegetarian menu, Civ Wed
150, Air con **Seats** 60, Pr/dining room 50
Children Portions, Menu **Parking** 400

WILLIAN — Map 12 TL23

The Fox

◉ Modern British ☕

Stylish country pub with sophisticated menu

☎ 01462 480233 📠 01462 676966
SG6 2AE
e-mail: info@foxatwillian.co.uk
dir: A1(M) junct 9 towards Letchworth, 1st left to Willian,
The Fox 0.5m on left

More than just a pub, the Fox lurks opposite the village
pond, waiting to take you by surprise. To one side is the
bar, while dining takes place on the other; choose from
the atrium-roofed dining-room or the sheltered terrace
with its bright parasols and exotic plants. Dishes are
carefully considered and based on sound ingredients,
such as the Norfolk oysters adorned only with a little
melted blue cheese and crisp pancetta lardons. Lamb
noisettes are cooked to appetising pink, and served with
rosemary-seasoned dauphinoise. Finish with well-made,
thin-crusted apricot and almond tart, served warm with
vanilla ice cream.

Chef Harry Kodagoda **Owner** Clifford Nye
Times 12-2/6.45-9.15 Closed D Sun **Prices** Starter £4.90-
£9.50, Main £10.95-£17.20, Dessert £5.25-£5.50, Service
added but optional 10% **Wines** 36 bottles over £20, 16
bottles under £20, 14 by glass **Notes** Sunday L,
Vegetarian available, Air con **Seats** 70 **Children** Portions
Parking 40

KENT

ASHFORD
Map 7 TR04

Eastwell Manor

◉◉ English, French

Creative, classical cooking in a grand manor house setting

☎ 01233 213000 📠 01233 635530
Eastwell Park, Boughton Lees TN25 4HR
e-mail: enquiries@eastwellmanor.co.uk
dir: From M20 junct 9 take 1st left (Trinity Rd). Through 4 rdbts to lights. Left onto A251 signed Faversham. 0.5m to sign for Boughton Aluph, 200yds to hotel

This splendid stately home hotel is the real deal: it dates from the Norman Conquest, and Richard Plantagenet lived here in the 16th century amid perfumed rose gardens in 62 acres of landscaped grounds. Magnificent plasterwork, carved oak panelling, walk-in fireplaces and antiques galore come as standard in its regal interior, and a state-of-the-art health spa and beauty treatment completes the upmarket package. It's no surprise, then, that service is on the formal side, given the baronial grandeur of the surroundings in the high-ceilinged restaurant, with its vast fireplace, contemporary artwork, and views of the gardens through leaded glass windows. There's no doubting the quality of the ingredients that go into the kitchen's output of creative French-accented modern English dishes. Lobster ravioli flavoured with ginger and tarragon starts on a luxurious note, followed by pan-fried John Dory with crushed potatoes, asparagus, morels and horseradish velouté. To finish, go for the palate-cleansing tang of a glazed lemon tart with crème fraîche.

Times 12-2.30/7-10

AYLESFORD
Map 6 TQ75

Hengist Restaurant

◉◉ Modern French Ⅴ

Contemporary design and modern French cooking

☎ 01622 719273 📠 01622 715027
7-9 High St ME20 7AX
e-mail: restaurant@thehengist.co.uk
dir: M20 junct 5 & 6, follow signs to Aylesford

Ancient Aylesford gets its name from 'Angle's Ford', where Hengist and his brother Horsa led invaders across the Medway in 449 AD and became the first kings of Kent. Interesting historic trivia, perhaps, but not much to do with this suave modern restaurant in a 16th-century timbered building. The striking contemporary interior is romantic in a sultry way, with decadent chocolate suede walls, smoked glass screens and sparkling chandeliers set against original oak beams and stonework. The kitchen brings modern twists to an essentially French menu, and has the technical finesse to coax intense flavours onto the plate. Pan-fried diver-caught scallops with crab and fennel risotto and crab bisque is a fine example, as is roasted fillet of brill with smoked Puy lentils, confit bacon, glazed salsify and creamed red wine fish sauce. Impeccably crafted desserts might include pear tarte Tatin with pain d'épice and hazelnut ice cream.

Chef R Phillips, Daniel Hatton **Owner** Richard Phillips, Paul Smith & Kevin James **Times** 12-3/6.30-11 Closed 26 Dec & 1 Jan, Mon, D Sun **Prices** Fixed L 2 course £10.95, Fixed D 3 course £19.95, Starter £7.25-£10.95, Main £16.95-£19.75, Dessert fr £7.95, Service added but optional 11% **Wines** 71 bottles over £20, 5 bottles under £20, 16 by glass **Notes** Fixed L Tue-Sun, Fixed D Tue-Thu, Sunday L, Vegetarian menu, Dress restrictions, Smart casual, Air con **Seats** 70, Pr/dining room 18 **Children** Portions **Parking** Free car park nearby

BEARSTED
Map 7 TQ85

Soufflé Restaurant

◉ Modern European

Understated, cosy and relaxed village setting

☎ 01622 737065
31 The Green ME14 4DN
dir: Please telephone for directions

The pretty 16th-century beamed cottage on the village green makes an excellent setting in which to sample some classic cookery with a modern twist. The front terrace is perfect for summer dining, while the interior is full of period character with exposed brickwork, low beams, timbers and an inglenook fireplace. Peruse the seasonal carte and choose, perhaps a starter of roast scallops with black puddings, olive oil hollandaise and parsley sauce, then follow with lamb rump with fondant potato, ratatouille and a basil and tomato sauce, and round off with hot passionfruit soufflé with white chocolate ice cream.

Chef Nick Evenden **Owner** Nick & Karen Evenden **Times** 12-2.30/7-10 Closed Mon, L Sat, D Sun **Prices** Fixed L 2 course fr £14, Fixed D 3 course £25, Starter £7-£9.50, Main £16-£21, Dessert £7-£7.50, Service added but optional 10% **Wines** 38 bottles over £20, 25 bottles under £20, 7 by glass **Notes** Sunday L, Vegetarian available **Seats** 40, Pr/dining room 25 **Children** Portions **Parking** 15

BIDDENDEN — Map 7 TQ83

The West House

◉◉◉ – see below

BOUGHTON MONCHELSEA — Map 7 TQ75

The Mulberry Tree

◉◉ Modern British NEW ✿

Serious cooking in Kent countryside setting

☎ 01622 749082 & 741058
Hermitage Ln ME17 4DA
e-mail: info@themulberrytreekent.co.uk
web: www.themulberrytreekent.co.uk
dir: B2163 turn into Wierton road straight over at crossroads, first left East Hall Hill

This former pub is now every bit the contemporary restaurant and bar, while its peaceful rural setting remains untouched by the passing of time. A blend of contemporary and traditional furniture gives the interior plenty of character and style: leather sofas in the bar, wooden floors throughout, and warm colours on the walls. The daily-changing menu displays proudly the list of suppliers from Kent and includes an appealing choice of modern British dishes. Feuillantine of wild rabbit with peas and pickled girolles is a well-conceived and superbly executed starter, pan-fried grey mullet comes with English asparagus, Jersey Royals and caper butter in an equally impressive main course, and crème brûlée with hazelnut shortbread is a notable finish. There are traditional bar snacks, too, including Welsh rarebit with sorrel cress, draught and bottled beers, and a good wine list.

Chef Alan Irwin **Owner** Karen Williams & Mark Jones **Times** 12-2/6.30-9.30 Closed 26 Dec, 1 Jan, Mon, D Sun **Prices** Fixed L 2 course £12.95, Fixed D 3 course £15.95, Starter £4.75-£8.25, Main £9.75-£18.50, Dessert £5.25, Service optional, Groups min 10 service 10% **Wines** 16 bottles over £20, 22 bottles under £20, 18 by glass **Notes** Sunday L, Vegetarian available **Seats** 70, Pr/dining room 12 **Children** Portions **Parking** 60

BRANDS HATCH — Map 6 TQ56

Brandshatch Place Hotel & Spa

◉◉ Modern British

Manor-house dining near the racing circuit

☎ 01474 875000 & 0845 072 7395 📠 01474 879652
Brands Hatch Rd, Fawkham DA3 8NQ
e-mail: brandshatchplace@handpicked.co.uk
dir: M25 junct 3/A20 West Kingsdown. Left at paddock entrance/Fawkham Green sign. 3rd left signed Fawkham Rd. Hotel 500mtrs on right

After a day spent in the petrol-head paradise of the Brands Hatch racing circuit, retire to the elegance of a red-brick Georgian manor house in 12 acres of rev-free gardens. Leisure and spa facilities complete the upmarket package for tranquil unwinding. The dining room has a smart classic style with plush fabrics and

---

The West House

BIDDENDEN — Map 7 TQ83

Modern European ✿

Self-assured cooking in a delightful setting

☎ 01580 291341
28 High St TN27 8AH
e-mail: thewesthouse@btconnect.com
dir: Junct of A262 & A274. 14m S of Maidstone

The fact that The West House occupies Grade II listed former weavers' cottages, dating from the 1500s, guarantees a certain charm. What works a treat is keeping the original features such as the heavy oak beams and adding well chosen contemporary furniture and striking artworks. Service is very relaxed and friendly. Chef-patron Graham Garrett is a passionate cook with an excellent pedigree (he's worked for Richard Corrigan and Nico Ladenis) and his dishes are extremely well

conceived. Great use of top-notch raw materials, many of which are local, and carefully balanced flavours combine with simple but effective presentation. Warm haddock carpaccio, for example, comes with bacon dressing, pickled rock samphire and pea shoots in an appealingly straightforward first course. Next up, perhaps, rabbit, the saddle roasted and the leg and shoulder served up in a cannelloni, with buttered hispi cabbage as an accompaniment. Deconstructed puddings might include 'cappuccino' of coffee pannacotta, liquorice ice cream, and tiramisù foam or 'carrot cake' of raisin purée, vanilla cream cheese and walnut ice cream.

Chef Graham Garrett **Owner** Jackie Hewitt & Graham Garrett **Times** 12-2/7-9.30 Closed 25 Dec-1 Jan, Mon, L Sat, D Sun **Prices** Food prices not confirmed for 2010. Please telephone for details. **Wines** 46 bottles over £20, 20 bottles under £20, 6 by glass **Notes** Sunday L **Seats** 32 **Children** Portions **Parking** 7

single flowers in tall specimen vases on linen-clothed tables. Menus change to showcase the seasons' best ingredients in dishes such as home-cured salmon blini with fromage blanc, or pan-fried fillet of black bream with red wine and clam and pancetta pearl barley.

Chef Stephen Redpath **Owner** Hand Picked Hotels **Times** 12-2/7-9.30 **Prices** Fixed D 3 course £35, Service optional **Wines** 103 bottles over £20, 2 bottles under £20, 18 by glass **Notes** Sunday L, Vegetarian available, Civ Wed 110, Air con **Seats** 60, Pr/dining room 110 **Children** Portions, Menu **Parking** 100

CANTERBURY
Map 7 TR15

The Dove Inn

French

Anglo-French cooking in deepest Kent

☎ 01227 751360
Plumpudding Ln, Dargate ME13 9HB
e-mail: nigel@thedoveinn.fsnet.co.uk
dir: 5m NW of Canterbury. Telephone for directions

Food is high on the agenda at the village of Dargate's only pub. Young chef-patron Phillip MacGregor combines French and British cooking techniques to provide a varied and appealing menu, based on top-notch ingredients. Starters might include foie gras and chicken liver parfait with Armagnac prunes, or Portland Bay crab with smoked salmon, crème fraîche and warm blinis. For the main

event try the Sussex lamb neck fillet with Puy lentils and pumpkin purée, and finish with a bitter chocolate tart with cardamom ice cream. The pub has an inviting country feel, with a log fire, oak beams and scrubbed pine floors and tables.

The Dove Inn

Times 12-2.30/7-9 Closed Mon, D Sun

The Goods Shed

British

Delicious, rustic food in converted Victorian railway shed

☎ 01227 459153
Station Road West CT2 8AN
dir: Please telephone for directions

The Goods Shed is a unique dining venue - a daily farmers' market with a vibrant restaurant serving rustic, unfussy British dishes using the pick of the crop from the downstairs food hall, all set within a quirky, beautifully renovated old railway shed. Expect original features like old beams, exposed brick and simple wooden furnishings, a relaxed, welcoming feel, and all the atmosphere of a bustling indoor market. Peruse the stalls, chat to the suppliers, then head upstairs to eat the quality (mostly organic) produce. The ingredients couldn't be fresher and the classic, British cooking with a Mediterranean twist shows skill and imagination. Take a crab and saffron tart with tarragon mayonnaise, crisp roast pork belly with apple and quince, hake with clams and salsa verde, and apple cake with apple sorbet. Booking is highly recommended.

Chef Rafael Lopez, Claire Brown **Owner** Susanna Sait **Times** 12-2.30/6-mdnt Closed 25 Dec, Mon, D Sun **Prices** Starter £5.50-£9, Main £11-£20, Dessert £6.50-£8.50, Service optional **Notes** Sunday L, Vegetarian available **Seats** 80 **Children** Portions **Parking** 40

Apicius

CRANBROOK
Map 7 TQ73

Modern European

Serious cuisine in a pretty Kentish town setting

☎ 01580 714666
23 Stone St TN17 3HF
dir: In town centre, opposite Barclays Bank, 50yds from church

Among the narrow streets of a well-heeled Kent town, a small restaurant goes quietly about its business in a way that should be enshrined as a template for superb food at sensible prices. Chef-proprietor Tim Johnson manages to put together his compact menus at prices that are nothing short of miraculous. With just a half-dozen or so tables in a low-beamed room fitted out with pale wooden floorboards and stylish high-backed chairs, dining doesn't come much more intimate. The menus read well

and let the ingredients do the talking, helped along by a chef with a confident mastery of combinations and top-level technical skills; Tim knows his business, having worked with the likes of Nico Ladenis. There's a lively modern creativity evident in classic combinations such as a starter of crab pannacotta with crab bouillon, tomato fondue and guacamole. Main courses aim equally high with poached and roast rump of lamb with French beans, roast garlic and sweet potato purée. Desserts feature the likes of glazed milk chocolate mousse with basil sorbet and mandarin cream. Service, led by Faith Hawkins, is personal, attentive and knowledgeable.

Chef Timothy Johnson **Owner** Timothy Johnson, Faith Hawkins **Times** 12-2/7-9 Closed 2 wks Xmas/New Year, Etr, 2 wks summer, Mon, L Tue, Sat, D Sun **Prices** Food prices not confirmed for 2010. Please telephone for details. **Wines** 26 bottles over £20, 5 bottles under £20, 7 by glass **Notes** Vegetarian available **Seats** 24 **Parking** Public car park at rear

CANTERBURY *continued*

Michael Caines ABode Canterbury

◉◉ Modern British

Sophisticated city centre dining

☎ 01227 766266 📠 01227 784874
High St CT1 2RX
e-mail: reservationscanterbury@abodehotels.co.uk
dir: M2 junct 7. Follow Canterbury signs onto ringroad. At
Wincheap rdbt turn into city. Left into Rosemary Ln, into
Stour St. Hotel at end

Although this hotel dates back to the 12th century, a total
makeover from the classy ABode boutique hotel chain has
brought it bang up-to-date. Start with aperitifs in the
Champagne Bar before moving into the Michael Caines
Restaurant, which follows the theme of the stylish hotel,
its tables clad in white linen and leather chairs coming in
cream or dark brown. The kitchen delivers some
accomplished modern food, impressing with its
presentation, balanced flavours and focus on high-quality
ingredients. Best end of Romney Marsh lamb, brochette
of saddle and kidney, spring vegetables, fondant potato
and a light lamb jus is a typical main course, and
perhaps peanut butter cheesecake with caramelised
banana and raspberry jelly to finish.

Chef Mark Rossi **Owner** Andrew Brownsword
Times 12-2.30/7-10 Closed D Sun **Prices** Fixed L 3 course

£9.95-£16, Fixed D 3 course £19.95-£25, Tasting menu
£55, Starter £10.95-£14.95, Main £19.95-£23.95, Dessert
£8.95-£11.50, Service added but optional 12%
Notes Sunday L, Vegetarian available, Dress restrictions,
Smart casual, Air con **Seats** 74, Pr/dining room 12
Children Portions **Parking** 15

CRANBROOK	Map 7 TQ73

Apicius

◉◉◉ — *see page 197*

DARTFORD	Map 6 TQ57

Rowhill Grange - Truffles

◉◉◉ — *see below*

DEAL	Map 7 TR35

Dunkerleys Hotel

◉◉ Modern British

Fresh seafood on the seafront

☎ 01304 375016 📠 01304 380187
19 Beach St CT14 7AH
e-mail: ddunkerley@btconnect.com
dir: Turn off A2 onto A258 to Deal - situated 100yds
before Deal Pier

Locally-landed fish cooked and served in traditional style
dominates the menu at this long-established, family-run
hotel restaurant, just a stone's throw from the beach and
pier. Pre-dinner drinks are served in the small bar where
you can relax on a comfy sofa before going through to
dinner in the bistro-style restaurant. Dishes like dressed
local crab, grilled Dover sole, sea bass with saffron

Rowhill Grange - Truffles

DARTFORD	Map 6 TQ57

Modern European **V**

Classy country setting for creative cooking

☎ 01322 615136 📠 01322 615137
Rowhill Grange Hotel & Spa DA2 7QH
e-mail: admin@rowhillgrange.com
dir: M25 junct 3, take B2173 towards Swanley, then B258
towards Hextable. Straight on at 3 rdbts. Hotel 1.5m on
left

The restaurant set in a 19th century country house has
lovely views of the grounds, which includes among its 9
acres a Victorian walled garden, mature woodland and a
lake. A Victorian conservatory is positioned to make the
very best of those views over the well-tended gardens,
with the terrace the place to head for if the weather
permits. Subtle, modern artwork blends seamlessly with

muted, neutral tones and tables are simply set with a
single gerbera adding a splash of colour. Service is
formal enough to impart a sense of occasion without
being intimidating. The cooking style gives a nod to
tradition but is executed in a modern, refreshing way
in-keeping with the chic, modern decor. The modern
European dishes contain several elements, using the best
in season, with the tried-and-tested flavour pairings
tending to be the most successful. Braised ox faggot,
pomme mousselline and red onion confit is a typical
starter, preceding, perhaps, slow-roasted Scottish halibut
with local oysters and watercress risotto. A deconstructed
tiramisù of zabaglione sabayon, Marsala jelly and
espresso ice cream is an inventive finish to a meal.

Chef Richard Cameron **Owner** Utopia Leisure
Times 12-2.30/7-9.30 Closed L Mon-Sat **Prices** Fixed D 3
course £42, Service added but optional 12.5% **Wines** 38
bottles over £20, 11 bottles under £20, 12 by glass
Notes Sunday L, Vegetarian menu, Dress restrictions, No

shorts, T-shirts, trainers, Civ Wed 150, Air con **Seats** 90,
Pr/dining room 160 **Children** Menu **Parking** 200

velouté, and pan-fried skate wing with Mediterranean vegetables and pesto will satisfy seafood lovers; some of the freshest produce around is given simple but skilful treatment. Meat is far from neglected, so steak and kidney pudding or confit duck leg are there if you need them. Finish with chocolate marquise with black cherry ice cream.

Chef Ian Dunkerley **Owner** Ian Dunkerley & Linda Dunkerley **Times** 12-2.30/7-9.30 Closed Mon, D Sun **Prices** Fixed L 2 course fr £11.95, Fixed D 3 course fr £26.50, Service optional **Wines** 29 bottles over £20, 47 bottles under £20, 11 by glass **Notes** Sunday L, Vegetarian available, Dress restrictions, Smart casual preferred, Air con **Seats** 50 **Children** Portions **Parking** Public car park

---

DOVER Map 7 TR34

The Bay Restaurant at The White Cliffs Hotel

◉ Modern British NEW ⬤

Fine local ingredients and creative cooking

☎ 01304 852229 & 852400 🖷 01304 851880
High St, St Margaret's-at-Cliffe CT15 6AT
e-mail: mail@thewhitecliffs.com
dir: From M2/M20 follow signs for Deal onto A258. 1st right for St Margaret's-at-Cliffe & after 2m take right at T-junct. Hotel in centre of village opposite church

A sister establishment to nearby Wallett's Court (see entry), this hotel and restaurant is in the centre of the village of St-Margaret's-at-Cliffe, close to the beach and not far from the famous cliffs. Its weather-boarded exterior gives a traditional feel, while the interior displays a mix of original features and contemporary good taste. The Bay restaurant uses plenty of local produce, much of it organic, in both traditional and modern influenced dishes such as a starter of pea and mint ice cream with baby broad bean salad, Ashmore cheese, pea shoots and croûtons, and a main course of Romney Marsh lamb with caramelised summer vegetables.

Chef Gavin Oakley **Owner** Gavin Oakley **Times** 12-2/7-9 Closed L Mon **Prices** Fixed L 2 course £15, Starter £4.50-£7.50, Main £14.50-£19, Dessert £5.50-£7.50, Service optional, Groups min 6 service 10% **Wines** 14 bottles over £20, 16 bottles under £20, 6 by glass **Notes** Sunday L, Vegetarian available **Seats** 50 **Children** Portions, Menu **Parking** 20

The Marquis at Alkham

◉◉ Modern British NEW ⬤

Boutique chic and modern British cooking in the Kent countryside

☎ 01304 873410 🖷 01304 873418
Alkham Valley Rd, Alkham CT15 7DF
e-mail: info@themarquisatalkham.co.uk
dir: M20 continue to A2. Take A260 exit & turn on to the Alkham Valley Rd

The village of Alkham on the Kent Downs is the sort of olde worlde haven that conjures images of leather on willow and warm beer on the green. But - sharp intake of breath - the old village pub was given a top-to-toe makeover in 2008 and is now a stylish boutique restaurant with rooms. And very chic rooms they are too, if you want to stay over and take full advantage of the modern British cuisine served in a sophisticated dining room with exposed red-brick and timber walls, unclothed dark wood tables and plush stripy fabrics. Head chef Charles Lakin learned his craft in a brace of the UK's best fine dining inns - the Star Inn at Harome among them (see entry) - and is now pulling in the foodies to sample his well-balanced menu of accurately-cooked, flavour-packed dishes made from the finest seasonal Kentish produce. A starter of lobster and salmon ravioli with lemongrass-infused lobster bisque has all the flavours singing in tune, while roast duck breast comes with a confit of duck hash, choucroute, turnips and thyme-scented liquor.

Chef Charles Lakin **Owner** Tony Marsden & Hugh Oxborough **Times** 12-2.30/6.30-9.30 Closed Mon, D Sun **Prices** Fixed L 2 course fr £15.50, Fixed D 3 course £22.95-£25.95, Starter £7.50-£11.50, Main £20-£27, Dessert £7.50-£10.50, Service optional **Wines** 60 bottles over £20, 28 bottles under £20, 13 by glass **Notes** Fixed ALC 2 course £27.95 3 course £34.95, Sunday L, Vegetarian available, Air con **Seats** 70, Pr/dining room 20 **Children** Portions **Parking** 17

Oakley & Harvey at Wallett's Court

◉◉ Modern British

Creative cooking in historic manor

☎ 01304 852424 🖷 01304 853430
Wallett's Court, West Cliffe, St Margarets-at-Cliffe CT15 6EW
e-mail: dine@wallettscourt.com
dir: M2/A2 or M20/A20, follow signs for Deal (A258), 1st right for St-Margaret's-at-Cliffe. Restaurant 1m on right

With a history documented back to the Domesday Book, this fine Jacobean manor house dates back to 1627 and is peacefully located in pretty gardens north of Dover. The restaurant is formally laid with white linen and high-backed chairs, set to a backdrop of oak beams, inglenook fireplaces and evening candlelight. But there's nothing remotely historic about the cooking. The accomplished modern British repertoire - driven by a commitment to quality local seasonal produce, including ingredients from the hotel's kitchen garden - comes fashionably

dotted with European influences. Expect interesting combinations, some exotic enhancements and well-balanced flavours and textures. Try foie gras terrine with peach chutney, baked lemon sole with grain mustard velouté, or rack of lamb with confit smoked garlic, and iced mascarpone parfait.

Chef Stephen Harvey **Owner** Gavin Oakley **Times** 12-2/7-9 Closed 25-26 Dec, L Mon-Sat **Prices** Fixed D 3 course £40, Service optional **Wines** 60 bottles over £20, 20 bottles under £20, 17 by glass **Notes** Sunday L, Vegetarian available **Seats** 60, Pr/dining room 40 **Children** Portions, Menu **Parking** 50

EDENBRIDGE Map 6 TQ44

Haxted Mill & Riverside Brasserie

◉ Modern British ⬤

Unfussy cooking using local produce in rustic, riverside setting

☎ 01732 862914
Haxted Rd TN8 6PU
e-mail: david@haxtedmill.co.uk
dir: M25 junct 6, A22 towards East Grinstead. Through Blindley Heath, after Texaco garage left at lights, in 1m 1st left after Red Barn PH. 2m to Haxted Mill

The name immediately conjures up the bucolic image of a working watermill, and that's exactly what you get here, plus the bonus of a homely, intimate, country-style restaurant in the mill's adjacent 500-year-old converted stables. The millstream races beneath the windows of the ground-floor bar and the beamed upstairs dining room features framed photographs, while an alfresco terrace overlooks the millpond. The accessible, modern brasserie-style cooking takes its cue from local, seasonal produce, with sympathetic handling and uncomplicated combinations allowing flavours centre stage; grilled whole sea bass is stuffed with herbs and lemon, and roast wood pigeon flamed in Armagnac.

Chef David Peek **Owner** David & Linda Peek **Times** 12-2/7-9 Closed 23 Dec-6 Jan, Mon, D Sun **Prices** Fixed L 2 course £14.95, Fixed D 3 course £18.95, Starter £5.95-£13.95, Main £10.95-£19.50, Dessert £6, Service added but optional 10% **Wines** 30 bottles over £20, 7 bottles under £20, 6 by glass **Notes** Sunday L, Vegetarian available, Dress restrictions, Smart casual **Seats** 52 **Parking** 100

FAVERSHAM — Map 7 TR06

Read's Restaurant

@@@ – *see below*

LENHAM — Map 7 TQ85

Chilston Park Hotel

@@ Modern British 🕙

Splendid Georgian mansion with elegant restaurant

☎ 01622 859803 📠 01622 858588
Sandway ME17 2BE
e-mail: chilstonpark@handpicked.co.uk
dir: M20 junct 8

Lost among tree-lined lanes in the Garden of England, Chilston Park is a top-drawer Georgian country-house hotel in 22 acres of serene landscaped gardens and parkland. It is a deeply traditional kind of place with enough period colours, antiques and paintings cramming the regal interior to qualify as a period drama film set. The sunken Venetian-style Culpeper's restaurant is a real one-off, with its ornate ceiling, grand fireplace and fancy crystal chandeliers. A modern British menu is clearly rooted in the French classics, but is not scared to offer some unusual and intriguing combinations. Try a luxuriant starter of poached skate and Parma ham with samphire, caviar and herb cream, followed by an assiette of pork with fresh peas and raisin jus. A serious wine cellar will grab the interest of oenophiles too.

Chef Gareth Brown **Owner** Hand Picked Hotels **Times** 12-2/7-9.30 Closed L Sat **Prices** Fixed L 2 course £10-£17.50, Fixed D 3 course £28.95, Starter £7.50-£8.50, Main £24.50-£29.50, Dessert £6.75-£8.50, Service added but optional **Wines** 90 bottles over £20, 1 bottles under £20, 18 by glass **Notes** Sunday L, Vegetarian available, Dress restrictions, Smart casual, Civ Wed 90 **Seats** 54, Pr/dining room 8 **Children** Portions, Menu **Parking** 100

ROCHESTER — Map 6 TQ76

Topes Restaurant

@@ Modern British 🕙

Modern British cooking in historic house

☎ 01634 845270
60 High St ME1 1JY
e-mail: julie.small@btconnect.com
dir: M2 junct 1, through Strood High Street over Medway Bridge, turn right at Northgate onto Rochester High Street

Close to the cathedral, this family-run restaurant is steeped in history. The house featured in Charles Dickens' novel *The Mystery of Edwin Drood* and parts of the building date back to the 15th century. The wooden beams and a narrow staircase leading to the kitchen and dining room are reminders of its history, but the style is contemporary. There is good use of local and regional produce on the modern British menu, which features daily specials, and suppliers are duly name-checked. A starter of potted shrimps on rye toast with horseradish potato salad might be followed by rump of English lamb, braised faggot, sage and onion sausage, black pudding and roast vegetable purée.

Topes Restaurant

Chef Chris Small **Owner** Chris and Julie Small **Times** 12-2.30/6.30-9 Closed 1 wk Jan, Mon-Tue, D Sun **Prices** Fixed L 2 course £15, Fixed D 3 course £18.50, Starter £6.50, Main £15.50, Dessert £6, Service optional **Wines** 15 bottles over £20, 25 bottles under £20, 6 by glass **Notes** Sunday L, Vegetarian available **Seats** 55, Pr/dining room 16 **Children** Portions, Menu **Parking** Public car park

---

Read's Restaurant

FAVERSHAM — Map 7 TR06

Modern British 🍴 🕙

Top-notch dining in an elegant Georgian manor

☎ 01795 535344 📠 01795 591200
Macknade Manor, Canterbury Rd ME13 8XE
e-mail: enquiries@reads.com
dir: From M2 junct 6 follow A251 towards Faversham. At T-junct with A2 (Canterbury road) turn right. Hotel 0.5m on right

David and Rona Pitchford's restaurant with rooms inhabits a classic Georgian manor set in 5 acres of mature Kent gardens. The walled kitchen garden earns its keep by providing 70 per cent of the vegetables and herbs (following the seasons, of course) and what doesn't come from the grounds is sourced from a network of local suppliers. Staff are professional but friendly enough, and contribute to the pleasantly relaxed atmosphere. David has a classical training and oversees his team with confidence delivering refined modern British dishes, and his sense of humour is revealed in the food- and drink-related quotations that accompany menu descriptions. Start with a hot soufflé of mature Montgomery cheddar cheese set on parmesan glazed smoked haddock in a creamed sauce ('when ordering lunch the big executives are just as indecisive as the rest of us' - William Feather). Main courses might bring pan-fried fillet of wild halibut on braised fennel and leaf spinach with cocotte potatoes and a sauce prepared from freshly peeled prawns ('how long does getting thin take? Pooh asked anxiously' - A.A Milne) and desserts a carpaccio of fresh pineapple with a coconut parfait and a home-made mango sorbet ('cuisine is when things taste like themselves' - Curnonsky).

Chef David Pitchford, Simon McNamara **Owner** David & Rona Pitchford **Times** 12-2.30/7-10 Closed BHs, Sun-Mon **Prices** Fixed L course £24, Fixed D 3 course £52, Tasting menu £52, Service optional **Wines** 250 bottles over £20, 12 bottles under £20, 6 by glass **Notes** Tasting menu 7 course, Vegetarian available, Dress restrictions, Smart casual, Civ Wed 60 **Seats** 40, Pr/dining room 30 **Children** Portions **Parking** 30

SEVENOAKS — Map 6 TQ55

Gavin Gregg Restaurant

◉◉ Modern British, European

Popular high street restaurant with hands-on owners

☎ 01732 456373
28-30 High St TN13 1HX
dir: 1m from Sevenoaks train station. 500yds from top of town centre towards Tonbridge on left

The building may be four centuries old, but the savvy owners are well in tune with the mood of 21st-century credit-crunch Britain. The smart interior retains all the character of a 16th-century listed building, but recent remodelling has created a two-tiered dining experience. A relaxed ground-floor brasserie serves classic modern dishes at prices that won't break the bank - perhaps roast breast of free-range chicken with thyme dauphinoise, aubergine caviar and Savoy cabbage - while the upstairs Oak Room opens evenings-only to deliver the full-on fine dining experience. Skilful cooking and creative presentation kick off with carpaccio of celeriac with spiced tuna, cucumber jelly and horseradish remoulade, then rump of Kentish lamb with Niçoise potatoes, aïoli and caramelised aubergine. Finish with an apple tarte fine with Calvados ice cream

Chef Andrew Wilson **Owner** Gavin & Lucinda Gregg
Times 12-2/6.30-9.30 Closed Mon, D Sun **Prices** Fixed L 2 course £14, Fixed D 3 course £22, Starter £5.50-£7.50, Main £12.50-£19, Dessert £6-£7.50, Service added 10% **Wines** 34 bottles over £20, 16 bottles under £20, 9 by glass **Notes** Sunday L, Vegetarian available, Air con **Seats** 80, Pr/dining room 32 **Children** Portions **Parking** Town centre

SISSINGHURST — Map 7 TQ73

Rankins

◉ Modern British

Bistro-style cuisine in rustic surroundings

☎ 01580 713964
The Street TN17 2JH
e-mail: rankins@btconnect.com
dir: Village centre, on A262

If seeing the exotic herbs at the world-famous Sissinghurst Gardens nearby has put you in the mood for food, head along the high street to Rankins. The classic weatherboarded Kentish house has a cottagey interior that is subtly-lit, cosy, but with well-spaced tables. A husband-and-wife-team have been in business here for 20 years, serving uncomplicated, soundly-cooked British bistro-style food. They know where to source the Garden of England's finest produce, snapping up fish from Rye and lamb from Romney Marsh, to form a concise menu of unpretentious, eclectic dishes. Rankins' smokie is a favourite starter, followed by crispy-crumbed Hastings cod fillet bites with caper and cornichon butter sauce. Finish with a golden syrup and apple sponge pudding with vanilla ice cream.

Chef Hugh Rankin **Owner** Hugh & Leonora Rankin
Times 12.30-2/7.30-9 Closed BHs, Mon, Tue, L Wed-Sat, D Sun **Prices** Fixed L 2 course £24.50, Fixed D 3 course £34.50, Service optional, Groups min 20 service 10% **Wines** 17 bottles over £20, 11 bottles under £20, 2 by glass **Notes** Sunday L, Vegetarian available, Dress restrictions, Smart casual **Seats** 25 **Children** Portions **Parking** On street

SITTINGBOURNE — Map 7 TQ96

Lakes Restaurant

◉ British, French

Refined cooking in a smart conservatory restaurant

☎ 01795 428020 🖹 01795 436362
Hempstead House, London Rd, Bapchild ME9 9PP
e-mail: lakes@hempsteadhouse.co.uk
dir: On A2 1.5m E of Sittingbourne

Now run by the Holdstocks, Hempstead House is nonetheless a testament to the Lake family who lived here in generations gone by, and one of whose scions built the place in the mid-19th century. The conservatory restaurant is a candlelit space, with well-upholstered chairs, properly dressed tables and a big chandelier, and the welcome is as warm as one would expect in a family-run place. The food aims for refinement in the form of a roast pigeon and rocket salad dressed in white truffle oil, topped off with a poached quail egg, with main courses such as tapenade-crusted cod with chorizo and tomato ragu, or beautifully tender, pink-cooked lamb with garlicky dauphinoise and green beans.

Chef John Cosgrove, Aaron Goldfinch **Owner** Mr & Mrs A J Holdstock **Times** 12-2.30/7-10 Closed D Sun to non residents **Prices** Fixed L 2 course £10-£15, Fixed D 3 course £24.50, Starter £5.50-£8.50, Main £12.50-£21.50, Dessert £6.50, Service optional **Wines** 30 bottles over £20, 25 bottles under £20, 4 by glass **Notes** Sunday L, Vegetarian available, Dress restrictions, Smart casual, Civ Wed 150 **Seats** 70, Pr/dining room 30 **Children** Portions, Menu **Parking** 100

TUNBRIDGE WELLS (ROYAL) — Map 6 TQ53

Hotel du Vin Tunbridge Wells

◉ British, French

Delightful bistro in elegant townhouse

☎ 01892 526455 🖹 01892 512044
Crescent Rd TN1 2LY
e-mail: reception.tunbridgewells@hotelduvin.com
dir: Please telephone for directions

The Kentish outpost of the highly regarded Hotel du Vin chain is in an imposing 18th-century building which has undergone the transformation into contemporary boutique hotel. Expect the company's stylish, comfortable accommodation and tastefully designed bar and bistro. The latter draws discerning diners with its inspired contemporary menu, which successfully balances modern dishes with simple classics, based around carefully selected local produce. You might begin with deep-fried frog's legs with aïoli, and then move on to grilled plaice with garlic butter and new potatoes. Finish with treacle tart with clotted cream, one of several classic puddings. The wine list, like at all HdVs, is excellent.

Times 12-2/7-10.30 Closed L 31 Dec

One Restaurant

◉ Modern British **NEW**

Chic design-led boutique hotel restaurant with contemporary cuisine to match

☎ 01892 520587 🖹 01892 617354
The Brew House Hotel, 1 Warwick Park TN2 5TA
e-mail: reception@brewhousehotel.com
web: www.thebrewhousehotel.net
dir: A267, 1st left onto Warwick Park, hotel immediately on left

A bijou boutique hotel in a made-over 18th-century building near the Pantiles in Tunbridge Wells, the Brew House has all the glossy looks needed to catch the eye in a style-conscious world. The all-white Number One restaurant looks like it might have beamed down from a futuristic moon base, with wavy walls, tubular

continued

TUNBRIDGE WELLS (ROYAL) *continued*

chandeliers and abstract art providing the occasional pool of colour. Cheery staff cut a contrast in smart black uniforms, and the kitchen deals in modern British cuisine on a well-balanced menu of beautifully-presented dishes. For starters there might be risotto with leeks, blue cheese and toasted pine nuts, followed by duck breast with creamed flageolet beans, Savoy cabbage and pancetta.

Chef Andrew Giles **Owner** Kevin Spencer **Times** 12-9.30 **Prices** Starter £4.50-£6, Main £14-£18.50, Dessert £4.50-£12, Service added but optional 12.5% **Wines** 28 bottles over £20, 8 bottles under £20, 18 by glass **Notes** 2-course meal for 2 with wine £27.95, Sunday L, Vegetarian available, Air con **Seats** 50, Pr/dining room 120 **Children** Portions, Menu **Parking** On street

The Spa Hotel

Modern, Traditional British

Country-house dining beneath crystal chandeliers

☎ 01892 520331 ▤ 01892 510575
Mount Ephraim TN4 8XJ
e-mail: info@spahotel.co.uk
dir: On A264 leaving Tunbridge Wells towards East Grinstead

An imposing Georgian house standing in 14 acres of carefully manicured grounds, the Spa might seem rather grandiose, but is actually run with a welcoming tone that puts guests at ease. They haven't called the dining room the Chandelier Restaurant for nothing, as you'll note when gazing up at its spangled magnificence. European and Asian influences play their several parts on menus that are solidly based on partnerships with local farmers and producers. Simplicity is the watchword, for main dishes such as herb-crusted Loch Duart salmon with clam chowder. On either side, consider veal sweetbreads with trompette mushrooms and creamy polenta, and an assiette of chocolate with peanut ice cream.

The Spa Hotel

Chef Steve Cole **Owner** Scragg Hotels Ltd **Times** 12.30-2/7-9.30 Closed L Sat **Prices** Fixed L 2 course £13-£15, Fixed D 3 course £32, Starter £4.95-£8, Main £14.50-£24, Dessert £5.50-£6.95, Service included **Wines** 69 bottles over £20, 29 bottles under £20, 8 by glass **Notes** Sunday L, Vegetarian available, Dress restrictions, Smart casual, No jeans or T-shirts, Civ Wed 200 **Seats** 80, Pr/dining room 200 **Children** Portions, Menu **Parking** 150

Thackeray's

⚜⚜⚜ – *see below*

WESTERHAM Map 6 TQ45

Rendezvous Café Brasserie

French, Mediterranean

Popular modern brasserie flying the tricolore

☎ 01959 561408 & 564245 ▤ 01959 561195
26 Market Square TN16 1AR
e-mail: info@rendezvous-brasserie.co.uk
web: www.rendezvous-brasserie.co.uk
dir: M25 junct 5 towards Westerham. M25 junct 6 onto A22, then A25 towards Oxted/Westerham

Kent may be the Garden of England, but, to paraphrase poet Rupert Brooke, there is a patch in Westerham that will be forever France. Bag a seat by the vast front

Thackeray's

TUNBRIDGE WELLS (ROYAL) Map 6 TQ53

Modern French V

Confident Anglo-European cooking at William Thackeray's place

☎ 01892 511921 ▤ 01892 527561
85 London Rd TN1 1EA
e-mail: reservations@thackeraysrestaurant.co.uk
dir: A21/A26, towards Tunbridge Wells. On left 500yds after the Kent & Sussex Hospital

The house was once owned by the Victorian novelist whose name it bears, although it predates him by some way, having been built in the mid-17th century. Set back from the road in the centre of Royal Tunbridge Wells, it has been tactfully restored so as to preserve much of its architectural character, but still looks the part as a modern restaurant and bar. There's a choice of 2 elegant dining rooms, with private dining and a lounge upstairs, and the place feels spacious and relaxing. Produce sourced from Kent and East Sussex informs the daily-changing menus, which work with the grain of established Anglo-European tradition. Start perhaps with sautéed cod cheeks, accompanied by root vegetables braised in port, cauliflower purée and a dressing of capers and raisins, and follow on with braised breast of Romney Marsh lamb, saddle of local venison, or perhaps fried mackerel served with marinated fennel, chorizo, dried plum tomato and butter beans, dressed in pesto. Desserts offer classic French modes, such as poached pear with matching sorbet and hazelnut parfait, but could equally well be as English as sticky toffee pudding.

Chef Richard Phillips, Christopher Bower **Owner** Richard Phillips **Times** 12-2.30/6.30-10.30 Closed Mon, D Sun **Prices** Fixed L 2 course fr £16.50, Fixed D 3 course fr £26.50, Tasting menu £88, Service added but optional 12.5% **Wines** 160 bottles over £20, 8 bottles under £20, 21 by glass **Notes** Sunday L, Vegetarian menu, Air con **Seats** 54, Pr/dining room 16 **Children** Portions **Parking** NCP, on street in evening

windows of this popular café-brasserie looking onto the high street, and you can people-watch just as you might across the other side of the Channel. The extensive menu offers flag-wavingly French cuisine; any ingredients that don't come from local suppliers or Billingsgate and Smithfields markets in London are imported from France. Starters don't come much more French than fish soup with rouille, croûtons and gruyère cheese, while confit of suckling pig stuffed with black pudding, comes with Puy lentils, Calvados sauce and apple Tatin.

Chef A Mourdi **Owner** A Mourdi **Times** 9.30am-10pm **Prices** Fixed L 2 course fr £11.95, Fixed D 3 course £14.95-£22.50, Starter £5.75-£8.75, Main £11.50-£19.75, Dessert £4.50-£5.50, Service added but optional 10% **Wines** 20 bottles over £20, 20 bottles under £20, 13 by glass **Notes** Sunday L, Vegetarian available, Dress restrictions, Smart casual, Air con **Seats** 65 **Children** Portions, Menu **Parking** 25, On-site parking available evenings & wknds

See advert below

The Swan

  British, European 🌱

A mix of modern and traditional cooking in a contemporary Kentish inn

☎ 01732 521910 ▤ 01732 522898
35 Swan St ME19 6JU
e-mail: info@theswanwestmalling.co.uk
dir: M20 junct 4 follow signs for West Malling

The core of the building may be a 15th-century coaching inn, but the Swan is very much a 21st-century bird. Brasserie dining, a brace of elegant modern bars and space for private functions are enhanced by modern paintings and artfully positioned mirrors. The service is relaxed and friendly, and the place supports local suppliers conscientiously (rare-breed meats, wild herbs and more). A listing of British classics such as fish pie or braised beef

and dumplings is the backbone of a menu that otherwise strays into more ambitious modern European modes. A tartlet of chicory and Oxford Blue comes with little heaps of Waldorf salad, while the pigeon breast main course (perhaps with authentic shot!) is well-served by puréed white beans, baby leeks and grapes in port.

Chef S Goss **Owner** Fishbone Ltd **Times** 12-2.45/6-10.45 Closed 26 Dec, 1 Jan, L 27 Dec, 2 Jan, D Sun **Prices** Starter £5-£10, Main £11-£22, Service added but optional 12.5% **Wines** 57 bottles over £20, 10 bottles under £20, 12 by glass **Notes** Sunday L, Vegetarian available, Dress restrictions, Smart casual, Civ Wed 100, Air con **Seats** 90, Pr/dining room 20 **Children** Portions, Menu **Parking** Long-stay car park

---

Crab & Winkle Seafood Restaurant

🌐 British Seafood 🌱

Popular harbour restaurant with great views and choice seafood

☎ 01227 779377 ▤ 01227 771249
South Quay, The Harbour CT5 1AB
e-mail: info@seafood-restaurant-uk.com
web: www.seafood-restaurant-uk.com
dir: Please telephone for directions

Located on the first floor of the fish warehouse overlooking Whitstable harbour, this modern restaurant sits on the

site of the railway built in 1830 to carry passengers and goods between Whitstable and Canterbury - known as the Crab and Winkle line. Local artists' paintings and drawings adorn the walls, complemented by light-wood tables and chairs. Grab a place on the decked balcony if you can. The owners of the fish market warehouse also own the restaurant so the head chef really does get the best catches of the day, straight from the boats and served simply cooked. Start with parsley and parsley-crusted oak-smoked salmon or grilled Whitstable rock oysters, then tuck into crispy skinned line-caught mackerel with warm salad of bacon, butternut squash, cauliflower purée and beetroot dressing.

Chef Beverley Ash, Brendon Ellis **Owner** Peter Bennett **Times** 11.30-9.30 Closed 25 Dec, D 26 Dec, 1 Jan **Prices** Fixed L 2 course £15, Starter £4.95-£8, Main £15-£25, Dessert £5-£7, Service added but optional 12.5%, Groups min 8 service 12.5% **Wines** 12 bottles over £20, 25 bottles under £20, 10 by glass **Notes** Vegetarian available, Air con **Seats** 72 **Children** Portions **Parking** Gorrel Tank Car Park

---

The Sportsman

 Modern British 🌱

Passionate cooking in unpretentious surroundings

☎ 01227 273370 ▤ 01227 262314
Faversham Rd, Seasalter CT5 4BP
e-mail: contact@thesportsmanseasalter.co.uk
dir: On coast road between Whitstable & Faversham, 3.5m W of Whitstable

The Sportsman is a foodie haven with all the right ingredients from land, estuary and sea on its doorstep. The Bohemian-chic interior of stripped pine floors, tables made from reclaimed oak, walnut and cherry and local art might create a relaxed, low-key vibe, but don't be fooled into thinking that this is any old gastro-pub. This is true 'cuisine de terroir', from an innovative chef who believes passionately in the integrity of produce, even

continued

WHITSTABLE *continued*

going as far as to make his own un-pasteurised butter, sea salt from the marshes near the pub and cure his own hams. The kitchen's inspiration and culinary standards come from eating at top restaurants, then aiming to match those flavours, minus the frills. Go for the eight-course tasting menu to put the kitchen through its paces and work through the likes of mussel and bacon chowder, braised brill fillet with smoked herring roe sauce, roast Monkshill Farm lamb, and pear ice lolly with ginger cake milk.

Chef Stephen Harris **Owner** Stephen & Philip Harris **Times** 12-2/7-9 Closed 25-26 Dec, Mon, D Sun **Prices** Starter £4.95-£9.95, Main £14.95-£21.95, Dessert £6.95, Service optional, Groups min 6 service 10% **Wines** 21 bottles over £20, 30 bottles under £20, 8 by glass **Notes** Pre-order tasting menu available Mon-Fri, 48 hrs notice req, Sunday L, Vegetarian available, Air con **Seats** 50 **Children** Portions **Parking** 20

LANCASHIRE

ACCRINGTON — Map 18 SD72

Mercure Dunkenhalgh Hotel & Spa

British, International **V**

Traditional hotel dining in splendid surroundings

☎ 01254 303400 📠 01254 872230 **Blackburn Rd, Clayton-le-Moors BB5 5JP** **e-mail:** H6617@accor.com **dir:** Telephone for directions

Castellated turrets, porticoes and wood-panelled rooms evoke memories of a bygone age at this 700-year-old manor house, which stands in beautifully maintained grounds close to the M65 (J7). In the attractively refurbished Cameo Restaurant you can savour some traditional British dishes from an extensive menu. Start with Goosnargh duck liver parfait with fig chutney, or smoked haddock and leek chowder, follow with monkfish wrapped in Parma ham with sun-dried tomato jus, or chargrilled rib-eye steak with all the trimmings, and finish with apple tart with cinnamon ice cream.

Chef Chris Nicholson **Owner** MREF Ltd **Times** 12-2/7-9.30 **Prices** Food prices not confirmed for 2010. Please telephone for details. **Notes** Vegetarian menu, Dress restrictions, Smart dress, Civ Wed 150, Air con **Seats** 80, Pr/dining room 40 **Parking** 300

BLACKBURN — Map 18 SD62

The Millstone at Mellor

Modern British

Classic fare in a traditional setting

☎ 01254 813333 📠 01254 812628 **Church Ln, Mellor BB2 7JR** **e-mail:** info@millstonehotel.co.uk **dir:** 4m from M6 junct 31 follow signs for Blackburn. Mellor is on right 1m after 1st set of lights

This stone-built former coaching inn makes an appealing base for a bit of peace and quiet in the Ribble Valley, or as a convenient out-of-town bolthole that is handy for doing business in major Lancashire towns. Although it has grown up into a hotel, it has kept plenty of quaint character in the traditional bar, where you can dine from a wide-ranging menu in a casual ambience. Otherwise, the smart beamed and wood-panelled restaurant is an elegant setting to take on classic dishes prepared without fussiness or affectation. The emphasis is firmly on locally-sourced seasonal Lancashire produce. You might start with king prawn and anchovy fritters on a bed of spiced parsnip purée, and move on to a succulent breast of sage-roasted chicken with creamed cabbage and smoked bacon and a good rich chicken gravy.

Chef Anson Bolton **Owner** Shire Hotels Ltd **Times** 12-2.15/6.30-9.30 **Prices** Fixed D 3 course £31.50-£33, Starter £3.95-£7.95, Main £15.95-£21.95, Dessert £4.95-£6.95 **Wines** 55 bottles over £20, 30 bottles under £20, 8 by glass **Notes** Sunday L, Vegetarian available, Dress restrictions, Smart casual, Civ Wed 60 **Seats** 62, Pr/dining room 20 **Children** Portions, Menu **Parking** 45, Also on street

BLACKPOOL — Map 18 SD33

Kwizeen Restaurant

Modern

Ambitious regional cooking within walking distance of the Tower

☎ 01253 290045 **47-49 Kings St FY1 3EJ** **e-mail:** info@kwizeen.co.uk **web:** www.kwizeenrestaurant.co.uk **dir:** From front of Blackpool Winter Gardens, 100yds to King St, and as road forks restaurant 30yds on left

The name won't win any spelling bees of course, but Kwizeen is a stylish modern venue situated a little way back from the Golden Mile in the Monte Carlo of Lancashire. The bright, white interior with marble bar and wood flooring sets the tone for the lively cooking, which is Lancashire through and through. Mrs Kirkham's cheese of that ilk makes a wonderfully fluffy souffléed pancake, while local lamb might turn up as roasted loin with

chorizo risotto. A roulade of suckling pig and bacon features quality meat and comes with excellent dauphinoise. Finish with banoffee crumble, accompanied by vanilla ice cream and toffee sauce.

Chef Marco Calle-Calatayud **Owner** Marco Calle-Calatayud, Antony Beswick **Times** 12-1.45/6-9 Closed 21 Feb-10 Mar, last wk Aug, Sun, L Sat **Prices** Starter £5.75-£7.95, Main £13-£15.95, Dessert £4.95-£12, Service included **Wines** 6 by glass **Notes** Dress restrictions, Smart casual **Seats** 40 **Parking** On street

GARSTANG — Map 18 SD44

Crofters Hotel & Tavern

British

Imaginative cooking in hotel brasserie

☎ 01995 604128 **New Rd, A6 Cabus PR3 1PH**

Crofters commands an impressive roadside position on the edge of the charming market town of Garstang and has up its sleeve, along with ample provision for business conferences and weddings, a popular brasserie. The relaxed, contemporary setting sees some confident cooking which includes some regional produce to give the menu a local flavour. Cauliflower and creamy Lancashire cheese soup is topped with chives in a first course, while roast loin of lamb comes with Bury black pudding among main courses. The menu does include some more far-flung flavours - finish, perhaps, with lemon tart with passionfruit sauce.

Times 12-9.30

LANCASTER — Map 18 SD46

Lancaster House Hotel

Traditional British

Modern country-house hotel flying the flag for Lancashire produce

☎ 01524 844822 📠 01524 844766 **Green Ln, Ellel LA1 4GJ** **e-mail:** lancaster@elhmail.co.uk **dir:** 3m from Lancaster city centre. From S M6 junct 33, head towards Lancaster. Continue through Galgate village, and turn left up Green Ln just before Lancaster University

The Foodworks restaurant in this modern country-house hotel sets out its stall with a simple concept: to showcase the best of Lancashire's brimming larder and down-to-earth hospitality. As a nod to the days of the region's hard-graft industrial heritage, cloth-capped workers look from a sketch mural into a muted interior palette of caramel, chocolate and ivory in a well-thought-out décor. The simple menu is all about the quality of the produce, with the local roots proudly on display all the way from a starter of field mushrooms stuffed with black pudding and goats' cheese, apple and cinnamon chutney, through to Fleetwood fish cakes with wilted watercress and Garstang blue cheese sauce and St Clements steamed sponge pudding with Lancashire clotted cream.

Chef Alistair Tasker **Owner** English Lakes Hotels **Times** 12.30-3/7-9.30 Closed L Sat **Prices** Fixed L 2 course £11-£24.90, Starter £4.50-£11.95, Main £13.50-£24.95, Dessert £4.75-£5.95, Service optional **Wines** 50 bottles over £20, 25 bottles under £20, 13 by glass **Notes** Sunday L, Vegetarian available, Dress restrictions, Smart casual, no jeans or sportswear, Civ Wed 100, Air con **Seats** 95, Pr/dining room 190 **Children** Portions, Menu **Parking** 140

LANGHO	Map 18 SD73

Northcote

◉◉◉ – see page 206

LONGRIDGE	Map 18 SD63

The Longridge Restaurant

◉◉◉ – see page 207

LYTHAM ST ANNES	Map 18 SD32

Chicory

◉ Modern International ✿

Eclectic cooking in a lively ambience

☎ 01253 737111 📠 01253 739115
5-7 Henry St FY8 5LE
e-mail: chicory@tiscali.co.uk
dir: In town centre, behind Clifton Arms Hotel

Since it opened its doors in 2002, this contemporary restaurant and cocktail bar has become a local landmark for its cosy and sophisticated interior, which boasts warm, bold colours, leather and suede furnishings and local artwork, and for its eclectic modern menu. Typical dishes include starters as diverse as duck and chicken skewers with satay sauce and braised pork belly with white onion purée and mustard cream. Main courses take in roast cod (from a local trawler) with chilli and

balsamic dressing, and rib-eye steak with béarnaise sauce. For pudding, try baked vanilla cheesecake with fruit compôte.

Chef F Santoni, Richard Martin **Owner** F Santoni & R Martin **Times** 12-2/6-9.30 Closed 25 Dec, 1 Jan, Mon **Prices** Fixed L 2 course £8.50-£10, Fixed D 3 course £10-£18.95, Starter £4.75-£7.75, Main £13.95-£17.95, Dessert £5.95-£7.95, Service optional **Wines** 27 bottles over £20, 11 bottles under £20, 17 by glass **Notes** Sunday L, Vegetarian available, Dress restrictions, Smart Casual, Air con **Seats** 70 **Children** Portions, Menu **Parking** On street

Greens Bistro

◉ Modern British ✿

Skilful modern cooking in charming atmosphere

☎ 01253 789990
3-9 St Andrews Road South, St Annes-on-Sea FY8 1SX
e-mail: info@greensbistro.co.uk
dir: Just off St Annes Sq

Husband-and-wife-team Paul and Anna Webster are dedicated to serving fresh seasonal produce and to creating a welcoming and friendly atmosphere in their restaurant. The cellar setting creates a sense of theatre, with tables discreetly hidden in nooks and crannies, and subtle lighting adding to the atmosphere. The modern British menu is full of local produce, such as sautéed Goosnargh chicken livers, served on toasted brioche and flavoured with grain mustard, or a grilled Bury black pudding with bubble-and-squeak, a soft-poached egg and crispy bacon. Baked egg custard with Yorkshire early rhubarb and orange shortbread is a typically seasonal finish.

Chef Paul Webster **Owner** Paul Webster **Times** 6-10 Closed 25 Dec, BHs, 2 wks Jan, 1 wk summer, Sun-Mon, L all week **Prices** Fixed D 3 course £15.95, Starter £4.50-£5.50, Main £13.50-£15.95, Dessert £4.50-£5, Service optional, Groups min 8 service 10% **Wines** 7 bottles over

£20, 15 bottles under £20, 7 by glass **Notes** Vegetarian available **Seats** 38 **Children** Portions **Parking** On street

The West Beach Restaurant

◉ Modern British ✿

Stylish hotel restaurant offering fine dining

☎ 01253 739898 📠 01253 730657
Clifton Arms Hotel, West Beach FY8 5QJ
e-mail: welcome@cliftonarms-lytham.com
dir: M55 junct 4, left onto A583 (Preston), take right hand lane. At lights right onto Peel Rd. Turn right at t-junct into Ballam Rd. Continue onto Lytham town centre. Turn right and then left into Queen St

The Clifton Arms Hotel has sat in its prime seafront position surveying the Ribble estuary for 300 years since its beginnings as a humble inn. The smart West Beach Restaurant is the focus of the hotel's culinary output, candlelit in the evening for atmospheric dining. An enticing menu relies on quality local ingredients to produce a repertoire of modern British cuisine, with starters such as tian of Lytham shrimps and Morecambe Bay crab with capers and basil oil, followed by, perhaps, grilled Lancashire lamb chops with mint pommes purée and red wine jus. Classic desserts include dark chocolate pudding with white chocolate ice cream and nougat glacé with hazelnut praline mousse and raspberry coulis.

Chef James Rodgers **Owner** Paul Caddy **Times** 12-2.30/6.30-9 **Prices** Fixed L 3 course £19.50-£25, Fixed D 3 course £25, Starter £5.95-£9.95, Main £12.95-£24.95, Dessert £6.95, Service optional **Wines** 55 bottles over £20, 19 bottles under £20, 10 by glass **Notes** Sunday L, Vegetarian available, Civ Wed 100 **Seats** 60, Pr/dining room 140 **Children** Portions **Parking** 50

Northcote

Modern British V 🍷 NOTABLE WINE LIST

A powerhouse of regional British gastronomy

☎ 01254 240555 📠 01254 246568
Northcote Rd BB6 8BE
e-mail: reservations@northcote.com
dir: M6 junct 31 take A59, follow signs for Clitheroe. Left at 1st traffic light, onto Skipton/Clitheroe Rd for 9m. Left into Northcote Rd, hotel on right

Back in the 1870s the owner of a textile mill built himself a house that displayed his wealth and power, and today his dream home is a hotel and foodie destination, renowned for celebrating the very best of regional produce. Nigel Haworth has been championing Lancastrian produce and promoting regional identity for a long time (he started as head chef here back in 1984) and these days can be seen doing the same on TV programmes such as *The Great British Menu*. But his food is far from stuck in the past. The restaurant leaves behind all thoughts of Victorian mill owners and brings us into the 21st century with a sophisticated and contemporary look, the walls punctuated with the work of renowned local man, Malcolm Fryer; the view through large bay windows of the organic kitchen garden and distant Ribble Valley hills is timeless. The cooking follows the seasons with evangelical zeal and is

intelligently uncomplicated, each dish well judged and perfectly balanced. Black pudding and buttered pink trout with mustard and nettle sauce is a red rose starter through and through, while lobster ravioli with organic garden leeks and roast chicory reveals some modern European sensibilities. There are plenty of menus to choose from, including the Gourmet which brings in co-owner Craig Bancroft's legendary skills at food and wine matching, plus vegetarian options and a flexible attitude towards children. Farmer Sharp's Herdwick slow-braised mutton with potato purée, Ascroft's yellow beetroot and dumplings is a main course firmly rooted in the terroir. Add a wine list of some 450 bins and service with a formal air of professionalism, and Northcote remains a foodie destination of national significance.

Chef Nigel Haworth, Lisa Allen
Owner Nigel Haworth, Craig Bancroft
Times 12-1.30/7-9.30 Closed 25 Dec
Prices Fixed L 3 course fr £24.50, Tasting menu fr £70, Starter £8-£14.50, Main £22.50-£30, Dessert £8.25-£10.80, Service optional **Wines** 300 bottles over £20, 9 bottles under £20, 6 by glass **Notes** Fixed D 5 course £50, Sunday L, Vegetarian menu, Dress restrictions, No jeans, Civ Wed 40
Seats 80, Pr/dining room 40
Children Portions, Menu **Parking** 60

The Longridge Restaurant

LONGRIDGE   Map 18 SD63

Modern British

Chic setting for first-rate British cuisine

☎ 01772 784969   📠 01772 785713
104-106 Higher Rd PR3 3SY
e-mail: longridge@heathcotes.co.uk
dir: Follow signs for Golf Club & Jeffrey Hill. Higher Rd is beside White Bull Pub in Longridge

Blink and you might miss Paul Heathcote's flagship restaurant on the outskirts of the village of Longridge. It's so tucked away in a row of three converted 19th century cottages that it would be easy just to drive on past - but what a shame if you did. A lounge - with pale grey walls, silver framed pictures and a glass cabinet displaying awards and cookbooks - leads the way to the interconnecting dining areas, decked out smartly in creams, greys and blacks, with a mixture of exposed brickwork, white-painted wood panelling and Julian McDonald wallpaper. Tall leather-backed chairs and well-spaced tables dressed in crisp linen with sparkling glassware complete the picture, while the service is polished but without any creaky formality. Discreet windows onto the kitchen let diners in on all the culinary action from head chef Chris Bell and his team. Its all about top-quality ingredients, mostly from Lancashire, handled with confident

simplicity. The seasonally-influenced, bistro-style carte of straightforward modern British dishes is complemented by daily specials. Start, perhaps, with a Paul Heathcote classic of ham hock and fois gras terrine with a tangy apple jelly. Perfectly timed corn-fed Goosnargh duck might follow, accompanied by caramelised plum and figs and superb cider fondant potatoes. For dessert iced apple parfait with honeycomb and crème fraîche comes with a garnish of cinder toffee and praline ice cream - a heavenly combination of flavours. Canapés, bread and petit fours are all equally impressive. If you really want to splash out, book the new 'chef's table' - a private dining room on the first floor seating 14, where a Longridge chef will prepare your meal before your very eyes. The chef's table is also now home to the Longridge Cookery School, with over 20 day courses available throughout the year, many of which are hosted by Paul Heathcote himself.

Chef Chris Bell **Owner** Paul Heathcote
Times 12-2.30/6-10 Closed 1 Jan, Mon-Tue, L Sat **Prices** Tasting menu £60, Starter £4.50-£11, Main £13-£25, Dessert £5-£8.50, Groups min 8 service 10% **Wines** 22 bottles under £20, 10 by glass **Notes** Sunday L **Seats** 70, Pr/dining room 14 **Children** Portions **Parking** 10, On street

PRESTON
Map 18 SD52

Pines Hotel

Traditional British

Traditional fare in comfortable surroundings

☎ 01772 338551   📄 01772 629002
570 Preston Rd, Clayton-Le-Woods PR6 7ED
e-mail: mail@thepineshotel.co.uk
web: www.thepineshotel.co.uk
dir: M6 junct 28/29 off A6 & S of B5256

Built in 1895 as the home of a cotton mill owner, The Pines stands within 4 acres of beautiful landscaped gardens and mature woodlands. Betty Duffin has been the owner and manager for nearly 50 years, and the place has a friendly, homely feel. The building has been extended over the years and the function suite is renowned for its busy programme of cabaret nights. The recently renamed Rosette Restaurant serves a menu of mostly classic English dishes. Try the marinated salmon gravad lax or the gruyère soufflé, following on with roast Goosnargh chicken breast or pan-fried fillets of sea bass, with orange and Grande Marnier tart to finish.

Chef Ryan Greene, Sarah Lowe, Paul Dugdale **Owner** Betty Duffin **Times** 12-2.30/6-9.30 Closed 28 Dec **Prices** Fixed L 2 course £12.50, Fixed D 3 course £15.50-£18.50, Service optional **Wines** 16 bottles over £20, 28 bottles under £20, 8 by glass **Notes** Fixed menu weekends £28.50 or ALC available, Sunday L, Vegetarian available, Dress restrictions, No jeans, T-shirts/trainers at certain times, Civ Wed 200 **Seats** 95, Pr/dining room 46 **Children** Portions **Parking** 150
See advert on page 205

THORNTON
Map 18 SD34

Twelve Restaurant and Lounge Bar

Modern British

Lively modern menu in a uniquely fashionable spot

☎ 01253 821212
Marsh Mill Village, Marsh Mill-in-Wyre FY5 4JZ
e-mail: info@twelve-restaurant.co.uk
web: www.twelve-restaurant.co.uk
dir: A585 follow signs for Marsh Mill Complex. Turn right into Victoria Rd East, entrance 0.5m on left

A touch of urban-chic and modern minimalism in a converted dance studio directly underneath one of the tallest working windmills in Europe, the beautifully restored 18th-century Marsh Mill. The funky lounge bar and restaurant is designed with exposed brickwork, steel girders and aluminium giving it a minimalist, industrial feel. Take pre-dinner drinks in the lounge bar, where the glazed roof and wall allow stunning views of the 60-foot windmill towering above it. The seasonally-changing menu offers traditional British cuisine given a modern twist, as you might expect, using as much locally-sourced food as possible. Try mackerel burger, squid rings and salsa verde to start, followed by haunch of Highland red deer with suet pudding and parsnip purée. Finish with cinnamon doughnut, raspberries and clotted cream ice cream.

Twelve Restaurant and Lounge Bar

Chef Paul Moss **Owner** Paul Moss & Caroline Upton **Times** 12-3/6.30-12 Closed 1st 2 wks Jan, Mon, L Tue-Sat **Prices** Fixed D 3 course £18.95-£26, Starter £5.95-£8.95, Main £14.95-£24, Dessert £5.50-£7.95, Service optional **Wines** 55 bottles over £20, 28 bottles under £20, 12 by glass **Notes** Sunday L, Vegetarian available, Air con **Seats** 90 **Children** Portions **Parking** 150

WHALLEY
Map 18 SD73

The Three Fishes at Mitton

Traditional British

Total commitment to local and seasonal produce

☎ 01254 826888   📄 01254 826026
Mitton Rd, Mitton BB7 9PQ
e-mail: enquiries@thethreefishes.com
dir: M6 junct 31, A59 to Clitheroe. Follow signs for Whalley, take B6246 and continue for 2m

A true English pub in the old-school, rugged northern style, established over 400 years ago, the Three Fishes is a relaxing place to dine. The range of features - from sun terrace to crackling log fires - caters for all weathers, and the cooking celebrates the best of Lancashire in a homely, familiar idiom. Leagram's organic Lancashire cheese is the foundation for a properly feather-light soufflé, and meats range from Ribble Valley beef cooked with kidney in a traditional rag pudding, to lamb reared on heather on the Bowland moors, served in - what else? - Lancashire hotpot. Morecambe Bay shrimps and battered haddock with chips cooked in dripping, together with robust puddings such as steamed chocolate and orange with clotted cream, complete the picture.

Chef Richard Upton **Owner** Craig Bancroft & Nigel Haworth **Times** 12-2/6-9 Closed 25 Dec **Prices** Starter £5.50-£7.50, Main £9.75-£19.60, Dessert £4.50-£5, Service optional **Wines** 22 bottles over £20, 24 bottles under £20, 13 by glass **Notes** Vegetarian available **Seats** 140 **Children** Portions, Menu **Parking** 70

WHITEWELL
Map 18 SD64

The Inn at Whitewell

Modern British

Confident cooking in historic inn with countryside views

☎ 01200 448222   📄 01200 448298
Forest of Bowland, Clitheroe BB7 3AT
e-mail: reception@innatwhitewell.com
dir: From S M6 junct 31 Longridge follow Whitewell signs. From N M6 junct 33 follow Trough of Bowland & Whitewell signs

Not the easiest place to find, but persevere because this ancient stone inn is a real one-off, beautifully situated by the River Hodder amid the wild beauty of the Forest of Bowland. Civilised and immensely charming, the rambling interior is filled with rustic furniture, antiques, books and mellow paintings, and owner Charles Bowman and his staff imbue the place with warmth, personality and pleasing quirkiness. A long-established culinary destination, expect simple modern British cooking using locally-sourced produce, including seasonal game and fresh fish. Typical dishes include rillettes of Gloucestershire Old Spot pork with home-made piccalilli, roast loin of venison with Cumberland sauce, and crème caramel. Don't miss the wine shop.

Chef Jamie Cadman **Owner** Charles Bowman/The Inn at Whitewell Ltd **Times** 12-2/7.30-9.30 **Prices** Starter £4.50-£9, Main £15-£25, Dessert £5, Service included **Wines** 120 bottles over £20, 60 bottles under £20, 20 by glass **Notes** Sunday L, Vegetarian available, Civ Wed 80 **Seats** 60, Pr/dining room 20 **Children** Portions **Parking** 70

WRIGHTINGTON
Map 15 SD51

The Mulberry Tree

Modern British

Lancashire village pub serving imaginative food

☎ 01257 451400
Wrightington Bar WN6 9SE
dir: 4m from Wigan. From M6 junct 27 towards Parbold, right after motorway exit, by BP garage into Mossy Lea Rd. On right after 2m

This relaxed and friendly modern gastro-pub and fine-dining restaurant is set in a tranquil Lancashire village, but within easy reach of the M6. Comfortably furnished throughout, it is popular with the locals who enjoy the accomplished dishes on the choice of menus. The bar menu offers a wide selection, while the restaurant delivers a more ambitious and elaborate repertoire. Expect generally modern British dishes with some French influences that make good use of local and seasonal ingredients. Try twice-baked Lancashire cheese soufflé with a spiced pear, rocket and walnut salad and a blue cheese salad to start. Follow with steamed chicken and ham hock pudding, hand-cut chips and parsley and chive cream sauce. The comprehensive wine list is worth a look

Times 12-2.30/6-9.30 Closed 26 Dec, 1 Jan

LEICESTERSHIRE

BELTON
Map 11 SK42

The Queen's Head
◎◎ Modern British ☺

Gastro-pub with modern attitude

☎ 01530 222359 📠 01530 224860
2 Long St LE12 9TP
e-mail: enquiries@thequeenshead.org
web: www.thequeenshead.org
dir: Located just off B5324 between Loughborough and
Ashby-de-la-Zouch

A modern, boutique-style pub with rooms, the Queen's
Head has a contemporary, minimalist feel throughout the
open-plan bar and two adjoining dining rooms. Polished
wood floors, leather sofas, modern art on cream walls,
chunky tables and chairs, and general overtones of
browns and beiges set the trendy scene for some
fashionable, modern British cooking. Chef David Ferguson
makes good use of quality, locally-sourced produce,
resulting in simple, well-balanced dishes with clear
flavours. Typically, start with moist and delicious scallops
served with crispy belly pork and black pudding, move on
to assiette of duck with smoked mash and Savoy
cabbage, then round off with a memorable coffee crème
brûlée served with fresh, light doughnuts. Service is
relaxed and friendly.

Chef David Ferguson **Owner** Henry & Ali Weldon
Times 12-2.30/6-9.30 Closed 25-26 Dec, D Sun
Prices Fixed L 2 course £13-£15.50, Fixed D 3 course
£15.50-£17.50, Starter £4.50-£9.50, Main £11-£21,
Dessert £4.50-£9.50, Service added but optional 10%
Wines 49 bottles over £20, 25 bottles under £20, 13 by
glass **Notes** Early bird menu available Fri-Sat, 3 course
£10, Sunday L, Vegetarian available, Civ Wed 60
Seats 70, Pr/dining room 40 **Children** Portions, Menu
Parking 20

CASTLE DONINGTON

**For restaurant details
see East Midlands Airport**

EAST MIDLANDS AIRPORT
Map 11 SK42

Best Western Premier Yew Lodge Hotel
◎ Modern British

Imaginative cooking in relaxed surroundings

☎ 01509 672518 📠 01509 674730
Packington Hill, Kegworth DE74 2DF
e-mail: info@yewlodgehotel.co.uk
dir: M1 junct 24, follow signs for Loughborough &
Kegworth on A6. At bottom of hill take 1st right onto
Packington Hill. Hotel 400yds on right

The combination of the peaceful setting and its proximity
to the motorway network and East Midlands Airport gives
family-owned Yew Lodge obvious appeal, not to mention
its spa and Orchard Restaurant. Take a drink in the
library bar before heading downstairs to the smartly
appointed dining room where large windows let in lots of
natural light, and diners sit at well-appointed tables. The
modern menu gives the provenance of many of the
ingredients, some of them regional. Start with celeriac
and pear soup with a stilton beignet, then pan-fried sea
bream with curly kale and champagne and mussel sauce.

Times 12-2.30/6.30-10 Closed L Sat

Donington Manor Hotel
◎ Modern British

Honest-to-goodness cooking in traditional comfort

☎ 01332 810253 📠 01332 850330
High St DE74 2PP
e-mail: enquiries@doningtonmanorhotel.co.uk
web: www.doningtonmanorhotel.co.uk
dir: Please telephone for directions

This former Georgian coaching inn was a popular pit stop
in the days of horse-drawn travel, but in the jet age it's
equally handy for East Midlands Airport, Chatsworth
House or Alton Towers. Beyond the classic Georgian
façade, the graceful Adam-style restaurant is appealing,
with its fancy plasterwork, grand fireplaces and crisp
linen. Contemporary dishes are kept simple and directed
at the comfort zone rather than any attempt at foam and
jelly wizardry. Take a good honest chicken liver pâté with
plum chutney and toasted ciabatta to start, then pan-
fried duck breast with black cherry Kirsch sauce and
fondant potato.

Chef Jeff Cadden **Owner** James Blick
Times 12-2.30/7-9.30 Closed Xmas & New Year, L Sat ex
by appointment **Prices** Fixed D 3 course £24.25-£25,
Service optional **Wines** 27 bottles over £20, 15 bottles
under £20, 9 by glass **Notes** Sunday L, Vegetarian
available, Civ Wed 120 **Parking** 40

The Priest House on the River
◎◎ Modern British V

Fine dining in historic house

☎ 01332 810649 📠 01332 811141
Kings Mills, Castle Donington DE74 2RR
e-mail: thepriesthouse@handpicked.co.uk
dir: Northbound: M1 junct 23A to airport. After 1.5m turn
right to Castle Donington. Left at 1st lights, 2m.
Southbound: M1 junct 24A onto A50. Take 1st sliproad
signed Long Eaton/Castle Donington. Turn right at lights
in Castle Donington

Nowadays a comfortable modern hotel with conference
rooms, a modern brasserie and a fine-dining restaurant,
this historic house perched on the banks of the River
Trent was mentioned in the Domesday Book. The cooking
style is contemporary, and the menus are both seasonal
and regional, focusing on local speciality ingredients and
dishes. Everything is home-made, including the olive oil
from the hotel's villa in Italy. Starters may include ceps
risotto with wild mushroom foam and baby tarragon,
followed by pan-fried Cornish mackerel with horseradish
croquettes and shellfish vinaigrette. Finish with autumn
fruit crumble and baked custard. A well-priced 'market
menu' also offers plenty of choice and the brasserie gives
a more informal experience.

Chef Will Abrahams **Owner** Hand Picked Hotels
Times 12-3/7-10 Closed L Sat, D Sun **Prices** Food prices
not confirmed for 2010. Please telephone for details.
Wines 75 bottles over £20, 2 bottles under £20, 8 by
glass **Notes** Sunday L, Vegetarian menu, Civ Wed 90
Seats 38, Pr/dining room 100 **Children** Portions, Menu
Parking 200

HINCKLEY
Map 11 SP49

Sketchley Grange Hotel
◎◎ British, European ☺

Elegant modern hotel with ambitious kitchen team

☎ 01455 251133 📠 01455 631384
Sketchley Ln, Burbage LE10 3HU
e-mail: reservations@sketchleygrange.co.uk
web: www.sketchleygrange.co.uk
dir: From M69 junct 1 take B4109 (Hinckley). Straight on
1st rdbt, left at 2nd rdbt & immediately right into
Sketchley Lane. Hotel at end of lane

Set in its own landscaped grounds in a rural setting only
minutes from the motorway, this elegant country-house

continued

HINCKLEY *continued*

hotel has been totally refurbished. It boasts a health and leisure complex and a choice of places to eat. The contemporary terrace bistro and bar has an informal Mediterranean-style menu, while in the spacious Willow Restaurant you'll find more ambitious stuff and panoramic views of the garden. The enthusiastic kitchen team deliver an imaginative modern menu of dishes using some locally-sourced ingredients. Start with warm mousseline of Arbroath smoked haddock, English mustard sauce and poached quail's egg, followed by lemon tea-smoked new season lamb with broad bean purée, stuffed lamb's kidneys and sweet sherry jus.

Chef Stewart Westwater **Owner** Nigel Downes **Times** 7-9.30 Closed Mon, L Tue-Sat, D Sun **Prices** Food prices not confirmed for 2010. Please telephone for details. **Wines** 32 bottles over £20, 36 bottles under £20, 4 by glass **Notes** Dress restrictions, Smart casual, Civ Wed 250, Air con **Seats** 80, Pr/dining room 40 **Children** Portions **Parking** 200

KEGWORTH

For restaurant details see East Midlands Airport

KNIPTON   Map 11 SK83

The Manners Arms

🍴 Modern British

Former hunting lodge with rooms and a serious kitchen

☎ 01476 879222 📠 01476 879228
Croxton Rd NG32 1RH
e-mail: info@mannersarms.com
web: www.mannersarms.com
dir: From Grantham take A607 (Melton road), after approx. 4m turn right at Croxton Kerrial

The Manners Arms is a handsome red-brick inn, built for the 6th Duke of Rutland in the 1880s as a hunting lodge, and part of the Rutland Estate. The current Duchess (the 11th) has redesigned the interior to create a very civilised and comfortable series of spaces, traditionally decorated with a country feel. The restaurant delivers contemporary

cooking with a classical grounding and features some produce from the estate. Seared scallops with crab risotto and porcini foam is a starter with modern European leanings, while fillet of Lincolnshire red beef comes with a braised faggot, creamed spinach and dauphinoise potatoes in a dish more rooted in the terroir.

Times 12.30-3/7-9 Closed D Sun (after 8pm), 25 Dec

LEICESTER   Map 11 SK50

Hotel Maiyango

🍴 Modern European **NEW** 🌑

Creative cooking in intimate Eastern-themed hotel restaurant

☎ 0116 251 8898 📠 0116 242 1339
13-21 St Nicholas Place LE1 4LD
e-mail: reservations@maiyango.com
dir: M1 junct 21, A5460 for 3.5m. Turn right onto A47 round St Nicholas Circle onto St Nicholas Place

A stylish, contemporary boutique hotel, Maiyango makes the most of its prime city centre location. The hotel's spectacular third floor roof-top terrace bar overlooks the city of Leicester and has gained a reputation for top-notch cocktails, which can be enjoyed before moving into the sophisticated, Eastern-themed restaurant. The kitchen is driven by the seasons and locally-sourced ingredients as much as it is by creativity and the result is an innovative style of cooking. Seared king scallops arrive with Thai-spiced mussels, cauliflower purée and herb salad, whilst a main course of chargrilled fillet of beef is accompanied by tempura king prawns, wasabi rösti and shallot jus.

Chef Phillip Sharpe **Owner** Aatin Anadkat **Times** 12-3/6.30-9.45 Closed 25 Dec, 1 Jan, L Sun **Prices** Fixed L 2 course £14.50-£16.50, Starter £5.50-£8.95, Main £13.50-£22.50, Dessert £4.95-£14.50, Service optional, Groups min 6 service 10% **Wines** 35 bottles over £20, 23 bottles under £20, 13 by glass **Notes** Tasting menu & pre-theatre menu available, Vegetarian available, Air con **Seats** 55, Pr/dining room 80 **Children** Portions **Parking** NCP

Watsons Restaurant & Bar

🍴🍴 Modern European, British **V** 🌑

Contemporary brasserie in former cotton mill

☎ 0116 255 1928 📠 0116 222 7771
5-9 Upper Brown St LE1 5TE
e-mail: watsons.restaurant@virgin.net
dir: City centre, next to Phoenix Arts Theatre

Set in an 18th-century former cotton mill, there's a contemporary feel to the stylish décor of this popular restaurant. Exposed brickwork, polished-wood floors and subtle halogen lighting combine with generously spaced tables, crisp linen and background jazz to create a relaxing atmosphere. Service is relaxed, friendly and professional. As for the food - classic French and Mediterranean influences run throughout the menu and there's a high level of skill and obvious attention to detail in the cooking, alongside the use of quality ingredients. You might start with smoked haddock, egg, crispy crumpet and new season asparagus, and follow with fillet of Aberdeen Angus with watercress and hotpot potatoes.

Chef Carmelo Percolla, Bradley Bickerton **Owner** Carmelo Percolla **Times** 12-2.30/6.30-10.30 Closed 2 wks Aug & BHs, Mon, L Sat, D Sun **Prices** Fixed L 2 course £15.95, Fixed D 3 course £18.95, Starter £4.95-£9.50, Main £14.95-£27.95, Dessert £6.50-£8.50, Service added but optional 10% **Wines** 12 bottles over £20, 18+ bottles under £20, 10 by glass **Notes** Fixed D available Tue-Fri, Sunday L, Vegetarian menu, Dress restrictions, No jeans, T-shirts or trainers, Air con **Seats** 80 **Children** Portions

MEDBOURNE   Map 11 SP89

The Horse & Trumpet

🍴🍴 Modern British

Culinary adventures in a sleepy village

☎ 01858 565000 📠 01858 565551
Old Green LE16 8DX
e-mail: enquiries@horseandtrumpet.com
dir: Between Market Harborough and Uppingham on B664

A former farmhouse and village inn, this solid stone-built thatched building behind the bowling green is these days a thriving restaurant with rooms. It's a smart and stylish place inside, easy on the eye, with original features such as old beams mixing with comfortable furniture and muted natural tones. Dine in one of three intimate rooms, or al-fresco if granted fine weather, and expect some seriously good modern British cooking. The food is refined, technically sound and balance of flavours is deftly handled throughout; a tasting menu shows justifiably the confidence this kitchen has in its abilities. Belly of pork comes with sweet potato, langoustine oil and five spice sauce in a creative first course, and wild sea bass, as a main, with lobster ravioli, beetroot and lemon shallot. The creativity continues at dessert stage: lemon curd with barley ice cream, basil meringue and raspberry syrup.

Chef G Magnani **Owner** Horse & Trumpet Ltd **Times** 12-1.45/7-9.30 Closed 1st week Jan, Mon, D Sun **Prices** Fixed L 2 course £16, Fixed D 3 course £27.50,

Starter £7.95-£11.25, Main £16.25-£20.25, Dessert £6.75-£10, Service optional, Groups min 16 service 10% **Wines** 40 bottles over £20, 6 bottles under £20, 8 by glass **Notes** Fixed D Tue-Thu only, Sunday L, Vegetarian available **Seats** 50, Pr/dining room 32 **Parking** On street parking

MELTON MOWBRAY — Map 11 SK71

Stapleford Park Country House Hotel

@@ Modern French V

Fine dining amid the splendour of 'Capability' Brown parkland

☎ 01572 787000 & 787019 🖹 01572 787001
Stapleford LE14 2EF
e-mail: reservations@stapleford.co.uk
dir: A1 to Colsterworth rdbt onto B676, signed Melton Mowbray. In approx 9m turn left to Stapleford

Surrounded by 500 acres of 'Capability' Brown-designed parkland, this 14th-century manor house makes a stunning country-house hotel that speaks of pampering and exclusivity. Named after the eponymous Victorian master woodcarver, whose superb Viennese Riding School-inspired artistry graces its walls, the Grinling Gibbons dining room is a suitably opulent setting for formal dining. But there's not a hint of stuffiness here - the staff's warmth sees to that. Luxury produce turns up in the dishes like debutantes at a ball, and there's plenty of more honest-to-goodness local ingredients too. An open lasagne of scallops with a light seafood foam and chervil sets the ball rolling, followed by a loin of veal with truffled artichoke purée and a foam of ceps.

Chef Steve Conway **Times** 12-2/7-9.30 Closed L Sat **Prices** Fixed L 2 course fr £18.50, Fixed D 3 course fr £46.50, Tasting menu fr £65, Starter £13.50-£21.50, Main £23.50-£31, Dessert £15-£17.50, Service added but optional 10% **Wines** 300 bottles over £20, 10 by glass **Notes** Tasting menu 7 course, Sunday L, Vegetarian menu, Dress restrictions, Collared shirt, no trainers, Civ Wed 150 **Seats** 60, Pr/dining room 160 **Children** Portions **Parking** 120

NORTH KILWORTH — Map 11 SP68

Kilworth House Hotel

@@ Modern British 🍴

Timeless elegance and good cooking techniques

☎ 01858 880058 🖹 01858 880349
Lutterworth Rd LE17 6JE
e-mail: info@kilworthhouse.co.uk
dir: Located on A4304, 4m E of M1 junct 20 towards Market Harborough

A country house with an enchanting blend of Victorian opulence, fine food and contemporary luxury, Kilworth House is set amid 38 acres of landscaped parkland in south Leicestershire. A grade II listed former family home, it has been sympathetically restored with period furnishings; the fine dining Wordsworth Restaurant has a domed ceiling, glittering chandeliers and double oak doors inlaid with delicate stained glass. One side of the restaurant has delightful views over the knot garden courtyard. The Wordsworth's menu has classical roots with an innovative twist here and there, with the simple dishes often the most successful. Think breast of wood pigeon, black truffle terrine and oyster mushrooms, followed by John Dory with stilton gnocchi, broccoli purée and caviar butter sauce. Finish with 'crunchy' banana pannacotta and white chocolate biscuit. The Orangery serves light lunches and snacks throughout the day.

Chef Carl Dovey **Owner** Mr & Mrs Mackay
Times 12-3/7-9.30 **Prices** Fixed D 3 course fr £40, Service optional **Notes** Sunday L, Dress restrictions, No jeans or trainers, Civ Wed 130 **Seats** 70, Pr/dining room 130 **Children** Portions, Menu **Parking** 140

STATHERN — Map 11 SK73

Red Lion Inn

@ Modern British

Reliable village inn in the Vale of Belvoir

☎ 01949 860868 🖹 01949 861579
2 Red Lion St LE14 4HS
e-mail: info@theredlioninn.co.uk
dir: From A1 take A52 towards Nottingham signed Belvoir Castle, take turn to Stathern on left

The whitewashed country inn with its asymmetrical roofline sits in a charming village not far from Melton Mowbray. It's a hive of activity, with a shop on the premises, as well as hand-pumped local ales and a decent wine list. International influences are at work in the menus, which take in local pigeon breast with Thai-spiced lentil salad to begin, with main-course options that range from textbook fish and chips to Vale of Belvoir partridge with pear, chestnut cabbage and bread sauce, or venison loin with butternut squash risotto. Blackberry and apple crumble with vanilla ice cream is an appealingly homely way to finish.

Times 12-2/7-9.30 Closed 1 Jan, Mon, D Sun

WOODHOUSE EAVES — Map 11 SK51

The Woodhouse

@@ Modern British V 🍴

Modish neighbourhood restaurant with sense of style

☎ 01509 890318
43 Maplewell Rd LE12 8RG
e-mail: info@thewoodhouse.co.uk
web: www.thewoodhouse.co.uk
dir: M1 junct 23 towards Loughborough, right into Nanpantan Rd, left into Beacon Rd, right in Main St & again into Maplewell Rd

The exuberant interior of this contemporary restaurant comes as quite a surprise after its unassuming whitewashed cottage façade. Take time to enjoy cocktails and canapés in the vampishly scarlet bar, before stepping down into the chic dining area, where dark blue high-backed chairs and crisply-set tables contrast with the vibrantly-hued walls. Service, too, hits the spot with a neat balance of confident relaxation and efficiency. The kitchen performs well, with a repertoire of contemporary flavours driven by prime local ingredients, sympathetically balanced and cleverly presented. So, Moroccan-spiced belly of pork is served with sand carrots (reputedly sweeter than the earth-grown type) and peanut milk, while lemon sole shares its plate with lemon carrots, girolles, leeks, chive potatoes and Noilly Prat sauce.

Chef Paul Leary **Owner** Paul Leary **Times** 12-3/6.30-12 Closed BHs, Mon, L Sat, D Sun **Prices** Fixed L 2 course fr £13.95, Fixed D 3 course fr £17.95, Service optional **Wines** 100 bottles over £20, 20 bottles under £20, 8 by glass **Notes** Fixed ALC 2/3 course £27.50-£33.50, Tasting menu available, Sunday L, Vegetarian menu **Seats** 50, Pr/dining room 40 **Children** Portions **Parking** 15

LINCOLNSHIRE

CLEETHORPES
Map 17 TA30

Kingsway Hotel

Traditional British V

Appealingly old-fashioned bonhomie on the Lincolnshire coast

☎ 01472 601122 📠 01472 601381
Kingsway DN35 0AE
e-mail: reception@kingsway-hotel.com
dir: At junction of A1098 and seafront

Run by four successive generations of the same family, the Kingsway looks out over the Humber estuary. It is a place where the traditional things are done well, from the first welcome to the professional service in the red-carpeted dining room with its smartly clothed tables. Classic dishes might be smoked salmon with capers and mustard mayonnaise, or strips of lamb's liver sautéed in Madeira to start, followed perhaps by breadcrumbed pork fillet topped with cranberry sauce and melted cheese, or grilled monkfish on celeriac mash with a lemon and parsley cream sauce.

Chef Guy Stevens **Owner** Mr J Harris
Times 12.30-1.45/7-9 Closed 26-27 Dec, D 25 Dec
Prices Fixed L 2 course fr £18, Fixed D 3 course fr £27.95, Starter £4.50-£8.95, Main £13.95-£24.95, Dessert £5.95, Service optional **Wines** 34 bottles over £20, 38 bottles under £20, 6 by glass **Notes** Vegetarian menu **Seats** 85, Pr/dining room 24 **Children** Portions **Parking** 50

GRANTHAM
Map 11 SK93

Harry's Place

❀❀❀ – see below

HORNCASTLE
Map 17 TF26

Magpies Restaurant

❀❀ British, European V

Creative cooking in small market town

☎ 01507 527004 📠 01507 525068
71-75 East St LN9 6AA
dir: 0.5m from town centre on A158 towards Skegness

Magpies is a small family-run restaurant that punches above its weight with an imaginative menu. Cuisine is mainly British, but with a nod to global influences; everything is driven by the seasons and - whenever possible - local produce. Inside the row of 200-year-old terraced cottages, you sink into a warm, cosseting ambience thanks to a honey and amber colour scheme, a wood-burning stove and silver candlesticks, fresh flowers and linen cloths on the tables. Dishes come impressively presented: take a pan-fried locally-smoked eel on toasted brioche with wild mushrooms and black truffle dressing to start, then roast turbot on Savoy cabbage and lobster mashed potato with broad beans and vanilla dressing. Puddings - for example, hot pineapple tarte Tatin with coconut ice cream and candied chilli - are no less inventive.

Chef Andrew Gilbert **Owner** Caroline Gilbert
Times 12-2/7-9.30 Closed 27-30 Dec, Mon-Tues, L Sat
Prices Fixed L 2 course £21, Fixed D 4 course £38, Tasting menu £42, Service optional **Wines** 62 bottles over £20, 50 bottles under £20, 4 by glass **Notes** Tasting menu available last Thu each month, Sunday L, Vegetarian menu, Dress restrictions, Smart casual, Air con **Seats** 34 **Children** Portions **Parking** On street

HOUGH-ON-THE-HILL
Map 11 SK94

The Brownlow Arms

❀ British

Popular village inn with locally-focused menu

☎ 01400 250234 📠 01400 251993
High Rd NG32 2AZ
e-mail: paulandlorraine@thebrownlowarms.com
dir: Please telephone for directions

Tucked away in a picturesque stone village, this magnificent 17th-century inn has the setting and atmosphere of an elegant country house, replete with oak beams, open fires, and tapestry-backed chairs in cosy panelled dining rooms. At polished wooden tables, topped with gleaming Riedel glassware, you can tuck into simply presented modern British dishes prepared from local ingredients, including game from surrounding estates. From broccoli and stilton soup, move on to venison loin with chestnut and celery mash and port jus, then round off with steamed treacle sponge with vanilla anglaise.

Harry's Place

GRANTHAM
Map 11 SK93

Modern French

Small restaurant, big heart

☎ 01476 561780
17 High St, Great Gonerby NG31 8JS
dir: 1.5m NW of Grantham on B1174

Harry's Place is a one-off experience. First of all, it must be one of the UK's smallest restaurants, serving 10 diners at 3 tables, usually in a 4-4-2 formation as favoured by many Premier League teams. And Harry and Caroline Hallam's set-up certainly comes into that category. What is more, they run it alone, in the charming domesticity of a listed Georgian building with the feel of a private house - after all, restaurants don't come much more intimate than this. The small-scale set up allows Harry to run a tight ship: there are no weak links in this

team of two. Just sit back and let Harry do his stuff in the kitchen while Caroline orchestrates service with sincere friendliness and a totally clued-up professionalism. You might need to be patient here and there because if chef isn't happy, the plates don't leave the kitchen. The hand-written menu is restricted to 2 choices at each course based on the best components they can get their hands on from a few trusted suppliers. What Harry excels at is the sort of cooking that lets the quality of the ingredients shine; French technique is at its foundations, boosted by outstanding technical skills and an unerring feel for flavour balance. Orkney scallops, lightly seared and served with hollandaise and reduced cooking juices kick the taste buds into life. Next up is loin of Gascony black pork with sautéed duck foie gras and Bramley apple in a sauce of Vouvray, sage and tarragon. To finish, how about prune and Armagnac ice cream with passionfruit?

Chef Harry Hallam **Owner** Harry & Caroline Hallam
Times 12.30-2.30/7-9 Closed 2 wks from 25 Dec, Sun-Mon **Prices** Starter £9.50-£19.50, Main £35-£38, Dessert

£7, Service optional **Wines** All bottles over £20, 4 by glass **Notes** Vegetarian available **Seats** 10 **Children** Portions **Parking** 4

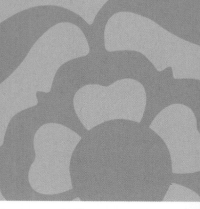

The landscaped terrace overlooks fields and is perfect for summer alfresco dining.

Chef Paul Vidic **Owner** Paul & Lorraine Willoughby **Times** 12-3/6.30-9.30 Closed 25-26 Dec, 1-23 Jan, 1 wk Sep, Mon, L Tues-Sat, D Sun **Prices** Food prices not confirmed for 2010. Please telephone for details. **Wines** 28 bottles over £20, 18 bottles under £20, 5 by glass **Notes** Sunday L, Vegetarian available, Air con **Seats** 80, Pr/dining room 26 **Parking** 26, On street

---

LINCOLN Map 17 SK97

Lakeside Restaurant

◉◉ Modern European V

Imposing Victorian setting for innovative modern food

☎ 01522 793305 📠 01522 790734
Branston Hall Hotel, Branston Park, Branston LN4 1PD
e-mail: jon@branstonhall.com
dir: On B1188, 3m S of Lincoln. In village, hotel drive opposite village hall

Beautifully situated in 88 acres of wooded parkland and lakes, this splendid country-house hotel was built in 1885. The Lakeside Restaurant retains plenty of original features and its elegant décor is in keeping with the building's character and era, with chandeliers, paintings and Italian-style chairs. Diners get beautiful views of the grounds. The impressive carte and fixed-price menus offer stylish modern dishes created with plenty of fine regional produce and cooked with imagination. Expect starters such as ricotta with purple figs, walnuts and wild rocket in a Cabernet Sauvignon dressing, or Cornish sprats with black olive toast and vine tomatoes, followed by fillet of Lincolnshire red beef with Scottish girolles, summer vegetables, glazed shallots and Madeira sauce.

Chef Miles Collins **Owner** Southsprings Ltd
Times 12-2/7-9.30 Closed 1 Jan **Prices** Fixed L 2 course £13.95, Fixed D 3 course £27.50, Starter £5.50-£9, Main £16.50-£22, Dessert £5.50-£8, Service optional **Wines** 17

bottles over £20, 36 bottles under £20, 14 by glass **Notes** Sunday L, Vegetarian menu, Dress restrictions, Smart casual, no jeans or T-shirts, Civ Wed 120 **Seats** 75, Pr/dining room 28 **Children** Portions **Parking** 75

The Old Bakery

◉◉ International ✆

Accomplished cooking in former bakery using quality local produce

☎ 01522 576057
26-28 Burton Rd LN1 3LB
e-mail: enquiries@theold-bakery.co.uk
web: www.theold-bakery.co.uk
dir: From A46 follow directions for Lincoln North then follow brown signs for The Historic Centre

It's easy to imagine the Victorian customers queuing for their penny buns outside the Old Bakery in Lincoln's historic Cathedral quarter. The original ovens and quarry-tiled floors still feature in the rustic interior of this charming restaurant with rooms, run by an Italian chef-patron who is passionate about food. Starting with basics, provenance of the top-class ingredients in his kitchen is a priority: 90% come from within twenty miles and suppliers are proudly highlighted on the menu. The cooking delivers sharp flavours and bears the clear stamp of the Mediterranean in dishes such as home-cured venison carpaccio with shaved parmesan, white truffle oil, marinated lentils and rocket, and mains of boneless saddle of rabbit wrapped in pancetta and spinach and served with Sardinian fregola (think couscous) and thyme-roasted tomato risotto.

Chef Ivano de Serio **Owner** Alan & Lynn Ritson, Tracey & Ivano de Serio **Times** 12-2.30/7-9.30 Closed Mon **Prices** Fixed L 2 course £13.50-£16.25, Tasting menu £60-£90, Starter £4.75-£9.95, Main £13.95-£20.50, Dessert £5.50, Service optional **Wines** 37 bottles over £20, 38 bottles under £20, 9 by glass **Notes** Tasting menu 9 course, Sunday L, Vegetarian available, Dress restrictions, Smart casual, Air con **Seats** 85, Pr/dining room 15 **Children** Portions **Parking** On street, public car park 20mtrs

Wedgwood Restaurant

◉ Modern British NEW

Attractive house in pretty gardens with traditional menu

☎ 01522 790340 📠 01522 792936
Washingborough Hall Hotel, Church Hill, Washingborough LN4 1BE
e-mail: enquiries@washingboroughhall.com
dir: From A46 south to A1434 to city centre, turn right at rdbt onto B1138 towards Branston. Turn left at lights to Washingborough. Turn right at mini rdbt onto Church Hill

Washingborough Hall is a Grade II listed Georgian manor in pretty grounds in a charming village just three miles from Lincoln. It's traditionally decorated in country-house style, including the restaurant with its typically high ceiling, large windows and lots of ornate plasterwork. Green is the theme in the room, with tables neatly laid for what is to come. And what comes is a range of traditional dishes including a salad of calves' liver with lardons and a honey-mustard dressing, followed by Lincolnshire Boston sausages with creamy mustard mash and a red wine and shallot sauce or the fish of the day, finishing with a sticky gingerbread pudding.

Chef Dan Wallis **Owner** Mr E & Mrs L Herring
Times 12-2/6.30-9 **Prices** Starter fr £4.95, Main £9.25-£22.95, Dessert £4.50, Service optional **Wines** 23 bottles over £20, 17 bottles under £20, 8 by glass **Notes** Vegetarian available, Civ Wed 50 **Seats** 40, Pr/dining room 36 **Children** Portions **Parking** 40

LOUTH Map 17 TF38

Brackenborough Hotel

◉ Modern European V ✆

Modern cooking in lively upmarket bistro setting

☎ 01507 609169 📠 01507 609413
Cordeaux Corner, Brackenborough LN11 0SZ
e-mail: reception@brackenborough.co.uk
web: www.oakridgehotels.co.uk
dir: Hotel located on main A16 Louth to Grimsby Rd

The popular bistro bar of this modern hotel just outside Louth makes good use of the region's produce, so fish comes from Grimsby, there's Cote Hill Farm cheese from Market Rasen, and Lincolnshire pork from Fulstow and Spilsby. It is a well designed space, with good natural light, and modish fixtures and fittings alongside exposed

continued

LOUTH *continued*

brickwork. The menu is full of contemporary ideas and combinations: confit pork is partnered with piccalilli and crab cakes with hand-cut fat chips and chilli mayonnaise. Desserts such as chocolate marquis with Malibu and treacle sponge with custard demonstrate the range of styles.

Chef Steven Bennett **Owner** Ashley Lidgard **Times** 11.30-9.45 **Prices** Fixed L 2 course £9.95-£19.95, Fixed D 3 course £24.95-£39.95, Starter £5-£8, Main £9.95-£22, Dessert £5-£6, Service optional **Wines** 42 bottles over £20, 32 bottles under £20, 12 by glass **Notes** Sunday L, Vegetarian menu, Civ Wed 70, Air con **Seats** 78, Pr/dining room 120 **Children** Portions, Menu **Parking** 80

SCUNTHORPE   Map 17 SE81

Forest Pines Golf and Country Club Hotel

◉ Modern, Traditional **NEW**

Fine-dining experience in elegant seafood restaurant

☎ 01652 650770 🖹 01652 650495
Ermine St, Broughton DN20 0AQ
e-mail: forestpines@qhotels.co.uk
dir: From M180 junct 4, travel towards Scunthorpe on A18. Continue straight over rdbt, hotel is situated on left

Grimsby's No. 1 fish dock opened in 1857 and the town became one of the largest fishing ports at that time. The restaurant Eighteen57 is part of Forest Pines Hotel, set in 190 acres of grounds. The freshest local fish is the star of the show, drawn from fully sustainable species and avoiding intensive fishing techniques. Imaginative dishes focus on simplicity and subtle flavours; some meat and vegetarian dishes are available, but seafood is the draw. Typical starters might include home-made Scarborough crabcakes served with lemon and chive mascarpone, followed by seared Orkney hand-dived king scallops with belly pork, white pudding and cauliflower purée, Savoy cabbage and cider butter sauce. For dessert, try vanilla crème brûlée served with home-made chocolate chip cookies.

Chef Paul Montgomery **Owner** Q Hotels **Times** 6.30-10 Closed Sun-Mon **Prices** Food prices not confirmed for 2010. Please telephone for details. **Notes** Vegetarian available

SLEAFORD   Map 12 TF04

The Bustard Inn & Restaurant

◉ Modern British, International **NEW**

Sensitively refurbished old inn in peaceful village

☎ 01529 488250
44 Main St, South Rauceby NG34 8QG
e-mail: info@thebustardinn.co.uk
dir: A17 from Newark, turn right after B6403 to Ancaster. A153 from Grantham, after Wilsford, turn left for S Rauceby

Legend has it that this pub acquired its name because the last great bustard in England was shot nearby. The beautiful Grade II listed stone building dates back to 1860, and has been sympathetically renovated to emphasise many of the striking features, including the courtyard, old brew house and stable which make up part of the dining area, as well as the ornate oriel window looking onto the beer garden. The restaurant has been beautifully restored to highlight the stone walls and original timbers. The décor is light and fresh, with tapestry chairs and hand-made solid ash tables. Food is locally sourced where possible and artistically presented. Expect tempura king prawns with sweet chilli dip, followed by fillet of halibut with creamed leeks, rösti potato and vermouth and chive sauce.

Chef Phil Lowe **Owner** Alan & Liz Hewitt **Times** 12-2.30/6-9.30 Closed 1 Jan, Mon, D Sun **Prices** Fixed L 2 course £10-£17, Starter £5.50-£12.50, Main £12-£28, Dessert £5.50-£8.50, Service optional **Wines** 34 bottles over £20, 16 bottles under £20, 9 by glass **Notes** Sunday L, Vegetarian available, Air con **Seats** 66, Pr/dining room 12 **Children** Portions **Parking** 18

STAMFORD   Map 11 TF00

The George of Stamford

◉ Traditional British ⚑ 🏴

Coaching inn popular for its old-fashioned charm and food

☎ 01780 750750 🖹 01780 750701
71 St Martins PE9 2LB
e-mail: reservations@georgehotelofstamford.com
dir: From A1(N of Peterborough) turn onto B1081 signed Stamford and Burghley House. Follow road to 1st set of lights, hotel on left

History seeps from the very stones of this venerable old Lincolnshire coaching inn. Its Cock Pit no longer provides poultry-based entertainment, but there's still a medieval crypt, pillars and archways to show for its long centuries spent as a hostelry on the Great North Road. A portrait of Daniel Lambert greets you in the entrance hall, a king-sized 53-stone customer who must have kept the kitchen busy in his day. Expect deeply traditional food to match the oak-panelled surroundings; locally sourced produce treated with care and skill, and old-style service from trolleys (dessert, cheese and carving). Typical dishes are warm salt-cod with bubble-and-squeak, fried quail's egg and mustard butter, or roast sirloin of beef carved off the bone at the table, with Yorkshire pudding and hot horseradish sauce.

Chef Chris Pitman, Paul Reseigh **Owner** Lawrence Hoskins **Times** 12.30-2.30/7.30-10.30 **Prices** Fixed L 2 course £19.55-£31.50, Starter £6.30-£15.35, Main £16.60-£35.70, Dessert £6.55, Service optional **Wines** 141 bottles over £20, 21 bottles under £20, 17 by glass **Notes** Sunday L, Vegetarian available, Dress restrictions, Jacket or tie, No jeans or sportswear, Civ Wed 50 **Seats** 90, Pr/dining room 40 **Children** Portions **Parking** 110

Jim's Yard

◉ French

Relaxed contemporary dining in attractive stone buildings

☎ 01780 756080
3 Ironmonger St PE9 1PL
e-mail: jim@jimsyard.biz
dir: Please telephone for directions

Jim's "yard" is an elegant courtyard, and this old stone building in historic Stamford has something of a French feel about it. Whether you're eating inside or out, there is a contemporary, rustic charm about the whole place, including the first-floor dining room with its lofty beamed ceiling. France figures on the menu, too, with the cooking rooted in classical tradition, plus some Italian and British preparations along the way; wild mushroom and tarragon risotto, for example, alongside moules marinière among starters. Main-course fillet of sea bass is served with fine beans and a butter sauce, and 9oz rib-eye comes with grilled field mushrooms and béarnaise sauce.

Chef James Ramsay **Owner** James & Sharon Trevor
Times 11.30-2.30/6.30-9.30 Closed 24 Dec 2 wks, last wk Jul-1st wk Aug, Sun-Mon **Prices** Fixed L 2 course £13.50, Starter £4.50-£8.25, Main £11.95-£17.50, Dessert £4.95-£6.50, Service optional **Wines** 56 bottles over £20, 28 bottles under £20, 13 by glass
Notes Vegetarian available, Air con **Seats** 55, Pr/dining room 14 **Children** Portions **Parking** Broad St

SUTTON ON SEA   Map 17 TF58

Grange & Links Hotel

◉ Traditional, International

A beautiful setting for freshly cooked fare

☎ 01507 441334   🖷 01507 443033
Sea Ln, Sandilands LN12 2RA
e-mail: grangeandlinkshotel@btconnect.com
dir: A1111 to Sutton-on-Sea, follow signs to Sandilands

With its own 18-hole golf course, this friendly, family-run hotel aims squarely at those who love 'a good walk, ruined', as Mark Twain put it. But with 5 acres of pleasant grounds close to a fine Lincolnshire beach, there are other attractions, not least the promise of flavoursome food, carefully prepared, including fish from Grimsby - lobster is a house speciality - or prime Lincolnshire Red beef. The wide-ranging European menu offers dishes such as chargrilled calves' liver with creamy mash, crispy bacon and sage jus to start, while main courses might be whole grilled Grimsby lemon sole with parsley and lemon.

Times 12-2/7-9

WINTERINGHAM   Map 17 SE92

Winteringham Fields

◉◉ Modern French, European ⚑NOTABLE WINE LIST 🕭

Luxurious restaurant with rooms

☎ 01724 733096   🖷 01724 733898
1 Silver St DN15 9PF
e-mail: wintfields@aol.com
web: www.winteringhamfields.com
dir: Village centre, off A1077, 4m S of Humber Bridge

You can see the iconic Humber Bridge from the pretty grounds of this luxurious restaurant with rooms. The 16th-century manor house may have a cellar that dates all the way back to the 1300s, but the present day sees a beautifully refurbished house full of contemporary comforts and traditional furnishings, with the addition of a new dining room. Owner Colin McGurran's restaurant is a lavish space dominated by rich colours, with a stained-glass dome in the ceiling, rich soft furnishings throughout, and smartly laid tables well spaced around the room. Sourcing of high quality produce is rightfully a priority here; much is grown on their own land, including the herb garden, and the modern European cooking aims for refinement and artful presentation. Roasted lobster risotto is a well timed version, topped with a lobster bisque, morels and parmesan, while main-course roasted breast of woodcock is paired with spätzle, amaretti and macadamia nuts, roasted shallots, parsnip purée and a grand veneur sauce.

Chef Colin McGurran **Owner** Colin McGurran
Times 12-1.30/7-9.30 Closed 2 wks Xmas, last 2 wks Aug, Sun-Mon **Prices** Fixed L 2 course fr £35, Fixed D 3 course fr £75, Service optional **Wines** 200 bottles over £20, 20 by glass **Notes** Menu surprise 7 course £79, Vegetarian available, Dress restrictions, Smart dress preferred **Seats** 60, Pr/dining room 12 **Children** Portions **Parking** 20

WOOLSTHORPE   Map 11 SK83

The Chequers Inn

◉ Modern British

Coaching inn turned gastro-pub

☎ 01476 870701   🖷 01476 870085
Main St NG32 1LU
e-mail: justinnabar@yahoo.co.uk
dir: From A1 exit A607 towards Melton Mowbray follow heritage signs for Belvoir Castle

Just a stone's throw from Belvoir's magnificent castle, this stylishly refurbished coaching inn successfully blends the traditional and contemporary, with bold colours, leather chairs, sturdy oak tables and a blazing log fire in the smart, beamed lounge, and a light and airy restaurant lined with modern artwork. Cooking is very much in the gastro-pub style, with both classic and simple, modern dishes prepared from local ingredients, including herbs from the garden and game from the Belvoir Estate. Start with confit duck terrine with orange and port syrup, then move on to pan-fried sea bass with braised fennel; pork belly, chorizo and white bean cassoulet; or gammon, egg, chips and battered pineapple, and finish with lemon possett.

Chef Mark Nesbit **Owner** Justin & Joanne Chad
Times 12-3/5.30-11 Closed D 25-26 Dec, 1 Jan
Prices Fixed L 2 course £11.50, Fixed D 3 course fr £16.50, Starter £4.95-£8.50, Main £9.50-£17.50, Dessert £5.50-£6.50, Service optional **Wines** 33 bottles over £20, 34 bottles under £20, 31 by glass **Notes** Sunday L, Vegetarian available **Seats** 70, Pr/dining room 14 **Children** Portions, Menu **Parking** 35

London

Index of London Restaurants

This index shows rosetted restaurants in London in alphabetical order, followed by their postcodes and map references. Page numbers precede each entry.

London Plan 1

London Plan 2

Maida Vale

0   220   440 yards
0 100 200 300 400 metres

PADDINGTON

Bayswater

Westbourne Green

West Kilburn

London Plan 4

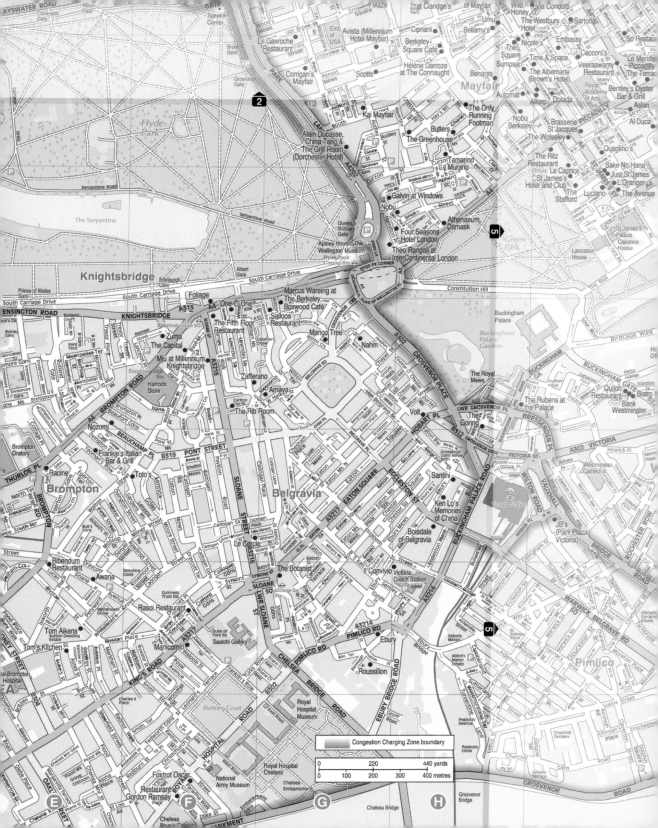

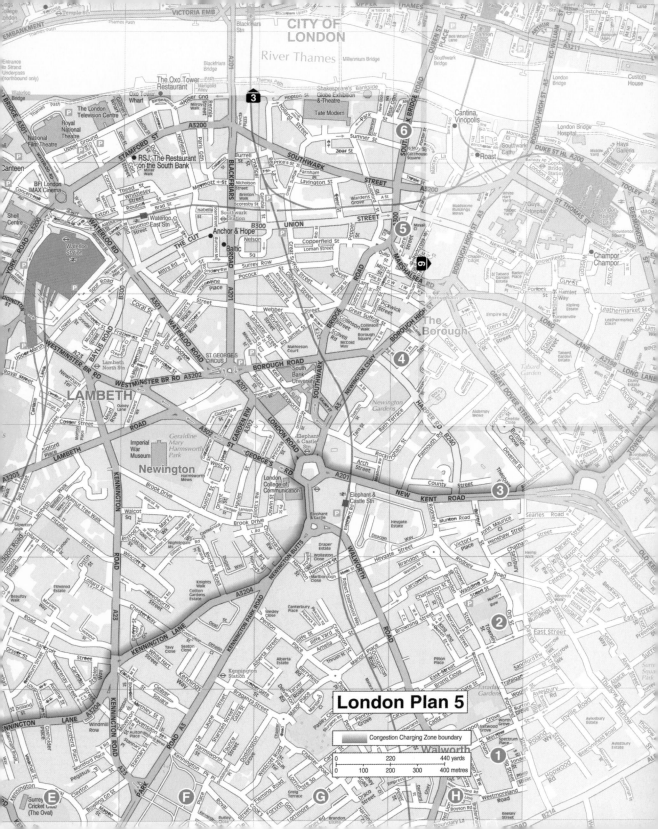

London Plan 5

Congestion Charging Zone boundary

| 0 | | 220 | | 440 yards |
| 0 | 100 | 200 | 300 | 400 metres |

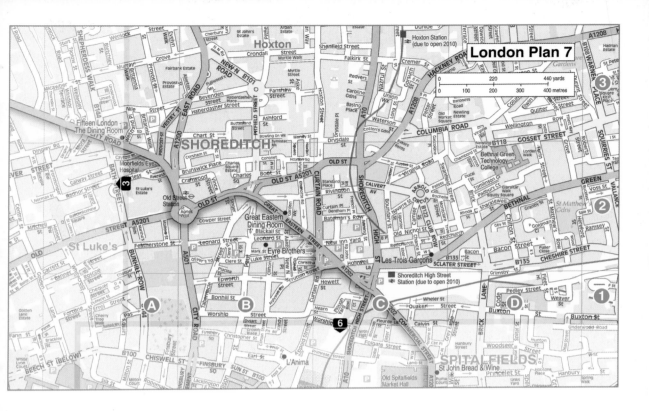

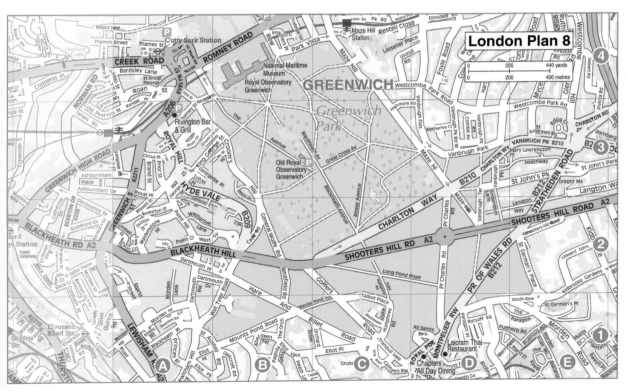

LONDON

Greater London Plans 1-9, pages 222-234. (Small scale maps 6 & 7 at back of Guide.) Restaurants are listed below in postal district order, commencing East, then North, South and West, with a brief indication of the area covered. Detailed plans 2-9 show the locations of restaurants with AA Rosette Awards within the Central London postal districts. If you do not know the postal district of the restaurant you want, please refer to the index preceding the street plans for the entry and map pages. The plan reference for each restaurant also appears within its directory entry.

LONDON E1

Café Spice Namasté

PLAN 1 F4

◉ Indian 🕭

Authentic pan-Indian dining in vibrant surroundings

☎ 020 7488 9242 ◼ 020 7488 9339
16 Prescot St E1 8AZ
e-mail: binay@cafespice.co.uk
dir: Nearest station: Tower Gateway (DLR), Aldgate, Tower Hill. Walking distance from Tower Hill

It may be set in a listed Victorian building that originally began life as a magistrate's court, but these days, Cyrus Todiwala's Whitechapel restaurant offers an altogether warmer welcome - 'Namasté' meaning 'gracious hello' in Hindi. Bright and vibrantly decorated in hot, spicy colours and swags of fabric, the high-ceilinged interior blends harmoniously with friendly service and a lengthy, equally eye-catching menu. Focusing on the regional foods of India, with the occasional influence from elsewhere in Asia thrown in, it is based on the very best British produce. Think fish from Cornwall driving a monkfish chettinad (served with a palate-tingling sauce and lime rice), or perhaps galinha xacutti (an intricate, full-flavoured chicken curry of more than 21 ingredients). There's also the alfresco Ginger Garden out back.

Chef Cyrus Todiwala, Angelo Collaco **Owner** Cyrus & Pervin Todiwala **Times** 12-3/6.15-10.30 Closed Xmas, BHs, Sun, L Sat **Prices** Food prices not confirmed for 2010. Please telephone for details. **Wines** 20 bottles over £20, 20 bottles under £20, 10 by glass **Notes** Tasting menu available, Dress restrictions, Smart casual, Air con **Seats** 120 **Children** Portions **Parking** On street; NCP

Marco Pierre White Steakhouse & Grill

PLAN 6 C5

◉◉ Modern European V

Quality City steakhouse in light, modern surroundings

☎ 020 7247 5050 ◼ 020 7247 8071
East India House, 109-117 Middlesex St E1 7JF
e-mail: info@mpwsteakhouseandgrill.com
dir: Nearest station: Liverpool Street. Please telephone for directions

From TV's *Hell's Kitchen* to the City of London. Marco's collaboration with James Robertson (founder of this former Lanes Restaurant & Bar) comes tucked away from Bishopsgate's bustle. The stylish, semi-basement room is a light, modern space, complete with mirrors, cream leather seating, white linen, crystal lights and clocks relaying times from Tokyo to Paris. A small lounge bar completes the picture, with the brasserie-style surroundings matching the MPW-influenced menu, which keeps things fresh, simple and quality driven, majoring on Aberdeen Angus steaks (rib-eye or fillet) with various adornments - perhaps béarnaise or porcini rubbed. Otherwise, daily comfort-style specials might deliver cottage pie (on Wednesday) or a treacle tart dessert (Thursday). Budget for side orders with main courses.

Owner James & Rachael Robertson **Times** 12-3/5.30-10 Closed BHs, 25 Dec, 1 Jan, Sun, L Sat **Prices** Starter £8.50-£15.50, Main £16.50-£30, Dessert £4-£9.50, Service added but optional 12.5% **Wines** 100 bottles over £20, 4 bottles under £20, 10 by glass **Notes** Vegetarian menu, Air con **Seats** 80, Pr/dining room 34 **Children** Portions **Parking** On street after 6.30 pm

St John Bread & Wine

PLAN 6 D6

◉ British

Unpretentious all-day restaurant, bakery and wine shop in Spitalfields

☎ 020 7251 0848 ◼ 020 7247 8924
94-96 Commercial St E1 6LZ
e-mail: reservations@stjohnbreadandwine.com
dir: Nearest station: Liverpool Street/Aldgate East

You'll find this ambitious bakery, wine shop and resoundingly British dining room tucked away behind old Spitalfields Market. It's the smaller, less formal eaterie to St John (see entry) and the robust, flavour-driven, 'nose to tail' cooking made famous at its big brother is replicated here. The trademark British food is unfussy, using quality seasonal produce and lesser-used ingredients, and food is boldly served and comes as described on the simple menu. Typically, tuck into salt beef and pickles, puffball and bacon, smoked sprats and horseradish, mallard and beetroot, and chocolate terrine. Whitewashed walls lined with clothes pegs, parquet flooring, simple wooden furniture and an open-to-view kitchen set a wonderfully utilitarian, buzzy, canteen-like tone. Service is friendly and well informed, while wines - like the great in-house breads - are on sale to take out.

Chef James Lowe **Owner** Trevor Gulliver & Fergus Henderson **Times** 9am-11pm Closed 25 Dec-1 Jan, BHs, **Prices** Starter £4.10-£7, Main £11.50-£14, Dessert £5.50-£6, Service optional, Groups min 6 service 12.5% **Wines** 31 bottles over £20, 15 bottles under £20, 25 by glass **Notes** Sunday L, Vegetarian available, Air con **Seats** 60 **Parking** on street

Les Trois Garçons

PLAN 7 C2

◉◉ French

A real one-off restaurant with authentic French cuisine

☎ 020 7613 1924 & 7613 5960 ◼ 020 7012 1236
1 Club Row E1 6JX
e-mail: info@lestroisgarcons.com
dir: Nearest station: Liverpool Street. From station, head along Bishop's Gate towards Shoreditch High St. Turn right after bridge onto Bethnal Green Rd. Restaurant on left

Where do you start in describing a former Victorian pub that has been stuffed to the gills with the contents of a Surrealist's mind? A hippo's head yawns a greeting, and, yes that's a full-size stuffed tiger over there; it's all a high camp Baroque fusion of Alice in Wonderland meets Victorian curio shop, with candlelight sparkling off Murano glass chandeliers and handbags hanging from the ceiling. But Les Trois Garçons is more than a fantasy interior: there is serious approach to cooking here. The chefs scour Borough Market for the very finest materials in a modern French repertoire that dabbles with flavours from a wider European context. A bilingual menu kicks off as it means to go on, with pedigree Gallic style in pan-seared foie gras with apples and foie gras caramel. Next up, duck from Dombes comes with a paupiette of Savoy cabbage and chorizo, lentils and cavolo nero purée. For dessert, you can't beat a Tahitian vanilla crème brûlée with blood orange cake.

Chef Jérôme Henry, Neill Vaughan **Owner** Stefan Karlson, Hussan Abdullah, Michel Lasserre **Times** 7-12 Closed Xmas & New Year, BH Mon, Sun, L all week **Prices** Fixed D 3 course £31, Tasting menu £72, Service added but optional 12.5% **Wines** 140 bottles over £20, 13 by glass **Notes** Fixed ALC £42.50-£49.50, Fixed D Mon-Wed, Vegetarian available, Dress restrictions, Smart casual, no shorts, Air con **Seats** 70, Pr/dining room 10 **Children** Portions **Parking** On street

LONDON E1 *continued*

Wapping Food PLAN 1 F4

◉ Modern International

Robust rustic cooking in unique urban setting

☎ 020 7680 2080
**Wapping Hydraulic, Power Station, Wapping Wall
E1W 3SG**
dir: Nearest station: Shadwell DLR Between Wapping Wall
& King Edward VII Memorial Park, parallel to the river

Part of the Wapping Project, this restaurant and art
gallery is housed in a former hydraulic pumping station
in London's East End. It's a chic, if urban, setting with
old machinery, tiles and girders from its industrial days
complemented by dangling chandeliers, designer
furniture and flickering candles. The food lives up to the
unique setting with a menu of seasonal European dishes
conjured from high-quality ingredients. Starters such as
chargrilled squid with chickpeas and morcilla precede
robust main courses like roast Middlewhite pork, Savoy
cabbage, mustard mash and spiced tomato relish.

Chef Cameron Emirali **Owner** Womens Playhouse Trust
Times 12-3/6.30-11 Closed 24 Dec-3 Jan, BHs, D Sun
Prices Fixed L 3 course £25-£47.50, Fixed D 3 course
£25-£47.50, Starter £6.50-£15, Main £12-£20, Dessert
£6.25-£8.50, Service added but optional 12.5%
Wines 132 bottles over £20, 8 bottles under £20, 34 by
glass **Notes** Brunch at wknds, Sunday L, Vegetarian
available **Seats** 150 **Children** Portions **Parking** 20

LONDON E2

The Thai Garden PLAN 1 F4

◉ Thai **V**

Authentic Thai cooking in Bethnal Green

☎ 020 8981 5748
249 Globe Rd, Bethnal Green E2 0JD
e-mail: thaigarden@hotmail.com
dir: Nearest station: Bethnal Green 2nd left off Roman Rd
(one-way street). Near London Buddhist Centre

To the casual passer-by, it may look like any old café
because of its simple shop frontage, but step inside and
this is the real deal when it comes to authentic Thai
cooking. The intimate dining room of this popular Bethnal
Green eatery only has twenty seats, which means booking
is advisable. The vegetarian and seafood-only cooking is
fragrant with plenty of heat coming from the abundant
use of chillies. The extensive menu is in Thai and English

and offers a wide choice of dishes, such as pahd ma-kua
(fried aubergines with chilli and basil leaves in black
bean sauce) and gra prou goong (fried prawns with
French beans, mushrooms, red chilli and basil leaves).

Chef Napathorn Duff **Owner** S & J Hufton
Times 12-2.30/6-11 Closed BHs, L Sat & Sun
Prices Starter £4.50-£5, Main £5.50-£7, Dessert £4-£5,
Service added but optional 10% **Notes** Vegetarian menu
Seats 32, Pr/dining room 12 **Children** Portions
Parking On street

LONDON E14

Four Seasons Hotel
Canary Wharf PLAN 9 A6

◉◉ Italian

**Authentic Italian cooking in sophisticated restaurant
with views**

☎ 020 7510 1999 📠 020 7510 1998
Westferry Circus, Canary Wharf E14 8RS
dir: Nearest station: Canary Wharf Just off Westbury
Circus rdbt

Located right on the River Thames at Westferry Circus,
this modern Docklands hotel offers spectacular views
over the London skyline. In the chic restaurant, you can
tuck into a versatile range of modern Italian dishes, or
some classic regional specialities, strong on fresh,
seasonal ingredients and packed with flavour. The food is
prepared with great accuracy in full view of diners in the
open-to-view theatre kitchen. Simple flavoursome
combinations might include a starter of beef carpaccio
with artichoke and parmesan shavings or one of several
pasta dishes, followed by an impressive main course of
roasted confit of duck leg with white polenta and pak
choi. The predominantly Italian staff are friendly and
enthusiastic.

Times 12-3/6-10.30

The Gun PLAN 9 D5

◉ British

**Smart Docklands gastro-pub serving modern British
food**

☎ 020 7515 5222 📠 020 7515 4407
27 Coldharbour, Docklands E14 9NS
e-mail: info@thegundocklands.com
dir: Nearest station: South Quay DLR, Canary Wharf. From
South Quay DLR, E down Marsh Wall to mini rdbt, turn
left, over bridge then take 1st right

This old London boozer originally used by dockers and
boatmen now caters to Canary Wharf executives in a
cracking spot with great views from the terrace across
the Thames to the Millennium Dome. The spit-and-
sawdust is gone, but the bar is still a splendid sight as
the centrepiece of a smart makeover that shows off dark
oak floors, Georgian fireplaces and historic gun artefacts
around crisp linen-clothed tables. The food aims high
with a mix of classics and modern British cooking that
lets the flavours do the talking. An exemplary foie gras

terrine with quince compôte and toasted sourdough is a
typically hearty starter. Fish fresh from Billingsgate
features in a main of roasted halibut with tagliatelle of
cockles, chervil and chives.

Times 12-3/6-10.30 Closed 25-26 Dec

The Narrow PLAN 1 G4

◉ Modern British

Ramsay gets the beers in by the river

☎ 020 7592 7950 📠 020 7592 1603
44 Narrow St E14 8DP
e-mail: reservations@gordonramsay.com
dir: Nearest station: Limehouse Please telephone for
directions

Gordon Ramsay's first foray into the burgeoning gastro-
pub market began a couple of years ago with this
renovated dock master's house with river views in
Limehouse. The Grade II listed building has been
sympathetically restored with half-wall panelling,
fireplaces and black and white vintage artwork. Ramsay
it might be but fine dining it ain't: informal, relaxed,
casual - in short, a proper pub. The menu boasts classic
British dishes with just the right degree of hearty appeal;
chicken livers on toast, perhaps, followed by braised
Gloucester pig cheeks with bashed neeps, finishing off
with lemon meringue pie. Alternatively, nurse a pint of
real ale in the bar and snack on a sausage roll and HP
sauce or fill up with a traditional ploughman's.

Chef John Collin, Mark Sargeant **Owner** Gordon Ramsay
Holdings Ltd **Times** 11.30-3/6-11 **Prices** Starter £5.50-
£6.75, Main £10.50-£16.50, Dessert £4.50-£5.50, Service
added but optional 12.5% **Wines** 24 bottles over £20, 12
bottles under £20, 10 by glass **Notes** Sunday L,
Vegetarian available, Air con **Seats** 80, Pr/dining room 14
Children Portions **Parking** 15

Plateau PLAN 9 B6

◉◉ Modern French

**Sophisticated, contemporary fine dining in futuristic
landscape**

☎ 020 7715 7100
Canada Place, Canada Square, Canary Wharf E14 5ER
e-mail: plateau@danddlondon.com
dir: Nearest station: Canary Wharf. Facing Canary Wharf
Tower and Canada Square Park

The light, modern rooftop restaurant is the epitome of
contemporary style and offers jaw-dropping views over

Canada Square and the high-rise skyline of Canary Wharf. The long, sleek, fourth-floor complex has a floor-to-ceiling glass frontage and two dining areas divided by a semi-open kitchen, each side with its own bar and outside terrace. The bustling Bar & Grill (offering a simpler menu) is up first, while the restaurant beyond is calmer, though both are high decibel. Their up-tempo Conran design mixes classic 1950s style with warm, restrained neutral colours and contemporary spin; think white 'tulip' swivel chairs, marble-topped tables, swirling banquettes and huge floor-standing arching lamps. But it's not all about interior design here: the kitchen's ambitious modern food turns on the style too, with highly accomplished dishes driven by prime ingredients and delivered dressed to thrill. Cod with Puy lentils, chorizo, artichoke and salsify, or perhaps Blackface lamb served with lasagne and pickled carrots. Service is equally slick and professional.

Times 12-3/6-10.30 Closed 25-26 Dec, 1 Jan, BHs, Sun, L Sat

Royal China
PLAN 9 A6

◉ Traditional Chinese **V**

Accomplished Chinese food with wonderful views of the river

☎ 020 7719 0888   📄 020 7719 0889
Canary Wharf Riverside, 30 Westferry Circus E14 8RR
e-mail: info@royalchinagroup.co.uk
dir: Nearest station: Canary Wharf Located near the Four Seasons Hotel & Canary Wharf Pier

The Royal China chain is defined by its glamorous exotic décor of imperial black and gold lacquered walls, flights of golden geese and mirrored ceilings. The river's edge at Canary Wharf is an impressive setting for this buzzy Chinese temple to Cantonese cuisine; its imposing glass frontage looks across the City skyline, with a splendid outdoor terrace for alfresco summer dining. Excellent dim sum have always been a big crowd-puller here, on a menu that takes in set meals and plenty of fish and seafood - perhaps steamed Icelandic cod with dried yellow bean paste, or steamed razor clams with garlic. Offerings such as stewed pork belly with preserved cabbage might catch the more adventurous diner's eye.

Chef Man Chau **Owner** Mr Peter Law **Times** Noon-11 Closed 23-25 Dec **Prices** Fixed L 2 course £15, Fixed D 4 course £30-£38, Starter £5.20-£42, Main £8.50-£55, Dessert £4.20-£6.50, Service included **Wines** 85 bottles over £20, 7 bottles under £20, 2 by glass **Notes** Vegetarian menu, Air con **Seats** 155, Pr/dining room 40 **Parking** 2 mins away

LONDON EC1

Ambassador
PLAN 3 F5

◉◉ European

Relaxed, super-friendly, all-day Clerkenwell dining

☎ 020 7837 0009
55 Exmouth Market EC1R 4QL
e-mail: clive@theambassadorcafe.co.uk
dir: Nearest station: Farringdon Take 1st right off Roseberry Av, heading N from Farringdon Rd junct. Turn right into Exmouth Market

The weather does not have to be all that warm in Exmouth Market for the crowds to fill up the outside tables of the Ambassador. Glass doors open onto the pavement to bring the outside in. The crowd-pleasing local restaurant-cum-cafe has broad appeal, opening for breakfast, brunch, lunch and dinner, while at the long bar, there's plenty of choice by the glass. The friendliest of service, good food and interesting wines - all at reasonable prices - help to make it an unpretentious, unassuming, local gem. Plainly decorated in magnolia, offset by the odd print, poster or mirror, the large, opened-up room comes decked out with dark green topped tables, simple café-style wooden chairs and crimson banquettes. The kitchen's pared-back modern approach suits the surroundings, is assured and accomplished, driven by quality ingredients on daily-changing menus; think fillet of sea bass with butternut squash purée, salsify and a red wine sauce, or perhaps roasted Middlewhite pork served with creamed Savoy cabbage, swede and thyme.

Times 8.30am-11pm (Sat 11am-11pm Sun 11-4/6-10.30) Closed 1 wk Xmas

The Bleeding Heart
PLAN 3 F4

◉ French 🍷

Discreet and romantic Hatton Garden favourite

☎ 020 7242 2056   📄 020 7831 1402
Bleeding Heart Yard, off Greville St EC1N 8SJ
e-mail: bookings@bleedingheart.co.uk
dir: Nearest station: Farringdon Turn right out of Farringdon Station onto Cowcross St, continue along Greville St for 50mtrs. Turn left into Bleeding Heart Yard

Set in a historic cobbled courtyard where society beauty Lady Elizabeth Hatton was found murdered in the 17th century, the Bleeding Heart also comprises a tavern and bistro as well as this popular and romantic cellar restaurant. Oozing atmosphere, with its wooden floors and low-beamed ceilings, wine-print lined walls, intimate lighting and smartly dressed tables, the restaurant buzzes with Gallic charm. Slick, friendly service is backed by uncomplicated modern French cooking driven by top-notch ingredients: red-wine braised halibut with bacon lardons, pommes mousseline and baby onions, and fillet of Scottish beef served with pommes Pont-Neuf and sauce béarnaise, alongside daily specials and a cracking wine list.

Chef Peter Reffell **Owner** Robert & Robyn Wilson **Times** 12-3/6-10.30 Closed Xmas & New Year (10 days),

Sat-Sun **Prices** Fixed L 3 course fr £29.95, Fixed D 3 course fr £29.95, Starter £7.95-£10.95, Main £12.95-£23.95, Dessert fr £6.45, Service added but optional 12.5% **Wines** 270 bottles over £20, 8 bottles under £20, 20 by glass **Notes** Vegetarian available, Dress restrictions, Smart casual, Air con **Seats** 110, Pr/dining room 40 **Parking** 20 evening only, NCP nearby

Le Café du Marché
PLAN 3 G4

◉ French

Provincial, rustic France in converted warehouse

☎ 020 7608 1609   📄 020 7336 7459
Charterhouse Mews, Charterhouse Square EC1M 6AH
dir: Nearest station: Barbican

The aptly named restaurant, secreted away in a quiet cobbled mews just a stone's throw from Smithfield Market, offers a truly welcoming slice of old France. Bare-brick walls, floorboards, exposed rafters, French posters and closely-set tables characterise the charmingly rustic interior, while attentive Gallic staff add to the colourful joie de vivre. Two dining rooms, Le Café on the ground floor and Le Grenier in the bright loft, share the same décor and set-price menu of provincial French bistro-style fare delivered from open kitchens. The competent cooking keeps things simple and fresh, driven on by quality ingredients; take grilled cod fillet served with a red pepper coulis, and perhaps an apricot and almond tart to finish. Do budget for the whopping 15% service charge. (Their separate lunchtime-only no-booking Le Rendezvous outlet - at the head of the mews - offers simpler fare.)

Chef Simon Cottard **Owner** Anna Graham-Wood **Times** 12-2.30/6-10 Closed Xmas, New Year, Etr, BHs, Sun, L Sat **Prices** Food prices not confirmed for 2010. Please telephone for details. **Notes** Air con **Seats** 120, Pr/dining room 65 **Children** Portions **Parking** Next door (small charge)

The Clerkenwell Dining Room & Bar
PLAN 3 G4

◉◉ Modern European

Relaxed fine dining in trendy Clerkenwell

☎ 020 7253 9000   📄 020 7253 3322
69-73 St. John St EC1 4AN
e-mail: restaurant@theclerkenwell.com
dir: Nearest station: Farringdon, Barbican. From Farringdon station, continue 60mtrs up Farringdon Rd, left into Cowcross St, left into Peters Ln, left into St John St

Regulars will notice The Clerkenwell's more upmarket black frontage, and, while the interior still delivers clean, light, contemporary lines, the white linen has gone and in has come less-formal polished-wood tables and chairs to ride alongside the cream or burgundy banquettes. One side of the dining area still has a more intimate feel, but both come with eye-catching modern artwork and attentive but unstuffy service. The kitchen's ambition

continued

LONDON EC1 *continued*

echoes the upbeat mood, its creatively presented, confident modern approach comes with a nod to the Med (perhaps a main course of steamed hake fillet served with a potage of squid and mussels, red pepper and pesto) as well as influences from far beyond (a starter of seared scallops accompanied by an aubergine pakora and curry spices). The short, fashionable wine list usefully comes by 375ml carafe as well as bottle. (Also see sister restaurant, The Chancery, EC4.)

Chef Andrew Thompson **Owner** Zak Jones & Andrew Thompson **Times** 12-3/6-11 Closed Xmas, BHs, Sun, L Sat **Prices** Starter £8-£12, Main £17-£22, Dessert £6-£9, Service added but optional 12.5% **Wines** 13 bottles over £20, 5 bottles under £20, 6 by glass **Notes** Vegetarian available, Dress restrictions, Smart casual, Air con **Seats** 100, Pr/dining room 40 **Children** Portions **Parking** On street (free after 6.30pm)

Club Gascon
PLAN 3 G3

◉◉◉ — *see below*

Le Comptoir Gascon
PLAN 3 F4

◉ Traditional French

Informal bistro/deli serving classic French dishes

☎ 020 7608 0851 📠 020 7608 0871
61-63 Charterhouse St EC1M 6HJ
e-mail: info@comptoirgascon.com
web: www.comptoirgascon.com
dir: Nearest station: Farringdon, Barbican, St Paul's, Chancery Ln Telephone for directions, or see website

Serving up traditional French food and wine - inspired by the South West of France - this is true cuisine terroir, where provenance is key; many items are sourced directly

from France. Part of the Club Gascon (see entry) family, this small, informal bistro-cum-deli opposite Smithfield Market comprises around a dozen tables, plus a few stools at the bar and a deli counter serving quality takeaway items from wine to foie gras and bread to patisserie. The décor's endearingly rustic-chic, with a sense of dining in a well-stocked foodstore, and there's bags of bonne vie. The compact core menu (bolstered by specials) thrives on prime ingredients and delivers clear flavours. The 'best of duck' section is something of a speciality, or there might be roast pollock with chorizo and wild mushrooms. Booking is advisable.

Chef Romuald Sanfourche **Owner** Vincent Labeyrie, Pascal Aussignac **Times** 12-2/7-11 Closed 25 Dec -1 Jan, Sun & Mon **Prices** Starter £4.50-£9.50, Main £8-£14, Dessert £3-£6.50, Service added but optional 12.5% **Wines** 15 bottles over £20, 3 bottles under £20, 6 by glass **Notes** Vegetarian available, Air con **Seats** 32

Hix Oyster & Chop House
PLAN 3 G4

◉◉ Traditional British NEW

First-class seasonal produce cooked without fuss

☎ 020 7017 1930
36-37 Greenhill Rents, Cowcross St EC1M 6BN
dir: Nearest station: Farringdon Turn left out of underground station (approx 12 min walk)

Once the man behind the Ivy's brand of British comfort food, Mark Hix is these days a respected food writer,

Club Gascon

LONDON EC1	**PLAN 3 G3**

Modern French ◉

Chic venue with classy cooking inspired by South West France

☎ 020 7796 0600 📠 020 7796 0601
57 West Smithfield EC1A 9DS
e-mail: info@clubgascon.com
dir: Nearest station: Barbican or Farringdon Please telephone for directions

The historic Lyons Teahouse building next to St Bartholomew's church and Smithfield meat market is a deceptive front for the sleekly-sophisticated modernity within; dazzling flower displays married with opulent veined marble walls, old oak floors and royal-blue banquettes. This is a legendary venue for long City lunches, so advance booking and reconfirmation are

essential, but once you're through the rigours of gaining entry, black-tied waiting staff deliver polished, unhurried service. While the restaurant has its roots in the garlic-and-goose-fat peasant cuisine of South West France, you can forget any notion of hearty cassoulets here: Club Gascon was in the vanguard of kitchens to dispense with the traditional three course format and serve dainty tapas-style 'tasting plates'. Menus break down into 'Le Marché' - a seasonal menu for the whole table, a three-course 'Déjeuner Club' lunch menu that offers good value for cooking at this level, or an array of 20 or so intriguingly inventive dishes, including a section devoted to riffs on a foie gras theme. Impeccable seasonal ingredients are painstakingly sourced from Gascony and turned into imaginative combinations that make you want to try them all. Mainstream dishes include a chaud-froid of black truffle and foie gras or suckling pig 'variation' with mustard ice cream and purslane, while more maverick pairings shoot off at a tangent with snail caviar fricassée, salsify sorbet and almonds. Champagne

granita, mango and pineapple cannelloni ends on a technically high note. The adventurous will find much to delight from lesser-known wine regions of South West France, as well as plenty of classics.

Chef Pascal Aussignac **Owner** P Aussignac & V Labeyrie **Times** 12-2/7-10 Closed Xmas, New Year, BHs, Sun, L Sat **Prices** Fixed L course £28, Starter £12.50-£19, Main £16.50-£25, Dessert £5.50-£14, Service added but optional 12.5% **Wines** 101 bottles over £20, 3 bottles under £20, 9 by glass **Notes** Fixed D 5 course £48, Vegetarian available, Air con **Seats** 45 **Children** Portions **Parking** NCP opposite restaurant

sometime TV star, director of food at Browns Hotel, and the man behind this eponymous Oyster & Chop House close to London's famous Smithfield meat market. The concept is rooted in the past, where seasonal produce takes the plaudits, with oysters (Colchester Rocks, perhaps) and top-rate meat (28-day aged Aberdeenshire beef) the stars of the show. The room fits the bill: original dark-wood panelling, tiles, and a long marble and wooden oyster bar, with white tablecloths and silver cutlery displaying just a touch of class. Salted ox cheek and green bean salad ably represents the style - simple, well-made food, based on excellent produce. There are non-meaty options (whole grilled brill), and even an own-brand beer. Hix Oyster & Fish House is a sister restaurant in Lyme Regis, Dorset.

Chef Stuart Tattersall **Owner** Mark Hix & Ratnesh Bagdai **Times** 12-3/6-11 Closed 25-26 Dec, 1 Jan, L Sat **Prices** Starter £6.50-£12, Main £14.50-£34.50, Dessert £1.90-£7.50, Service added but optional 12.5% **Wines** 55 bottles over £20, 5 bottles under £20, 16 by glass **Notes** Sunday L, Vegetarian available, Air con **Seats** 66 **Children** Portions **Parking** On street (meters)

Malmaison Charterhouse Square PLAN 3 G4

◉◉ Modern British, French ✿

Boutique hotel with buzzing, easy-going brasserie

☎ 020 7012 3700   📠 020 7012 3702
18-21 Charterhouse Square, Clerkenwell EC1M 6AH
e-mail: athwaites@malmaison.com
dir: Nearest station: Barbican

The Malmaison chain's London outpost sits in a cobbled courtyard just off Charterhouse Square - a great location whether you're up in town for a spot of pampering and retail therapy, or suited and booted for business in the Square Mile. If you're not familiar with the Malmaison ethos, expect a chic brasserie-style split-level restaurant with carefully-thought-out lighting to enhance nicely-contrasting textures of wood, silk, velvet and exposed brickwork in intimate alcoves. The menu sticks to classic brasserie-style fodder so French it should be wearing a beret and smoking a Gauloise, although the ingredients do come from named regional suppliers. Terrine of smoked ham hock, foie gras and black leg chicken, beef bourguignon with horseradish mash, and tarte fine aux pommes with thyme ice cream and caramel sauce show the style.

Chef John Woodward **Owner** Malmaison Hotels **Times** 12-2.30/6-10.30 Closed 23-28 Dec, L Sat **Prices** Fixed L 2 course £14.50-£16.50, Fixed D 3 course £17.50-£19.50, Starter £5-£9, Main £12-£25, Dessert £5, Service added but optional 12.5% **Wines** 200 bottles over £20, 6 bottles under £20, 21 by glass **Notes** Brunch style menu Sun, Vegetarian available, Air con **Seats** 70, Pr/dining room 12 **Children** Portions **Parking** Smithfield Market 200m

The Modern Pantry   PLAN 3 F4

◉◉ Global NEW

Creative cooking in Clerkenwell foodie destination

☎ 020 7553 9210
47-48 St John's Square EC1V 4JJ
e-mail: enquiries@themodernpantry.co.uk
web: www.themodernpantry.co.uk
dir: Nearest station: Farringdon, Barbican Please telephone for directions

Anna Hansen, a former business partner of the king of fusion Peter Gordon at Providores, has converted 2 Georgian buildings in Clerkenwell (one a former steel foundry, the other an old townhouse) into an exciting foodie destination with a range of enticing possibilities. There's a ground-floor Café - a modern and casual space serving lunch, breakfast and dinner 7 days a week for 40 people, a small bar, The Pantry (a modern traiteur serving an enticing range of delicatessen dishes such as sandwiches, pies and cakes to take away), and, finally, the first-floor dining room, which seats 60 in 2 rooms. The inventive, creative and appealing menu is imbued with a sense of adventure, which is not surprising given Anna's background. Start with hot-and-sour oxtail, snail, beetroot and wild garlic broth, then a confit rabbit leg with roast sweet potato mash, wild garlic and smoked chilli jam. Finish with roast peanut pannacotta with kalamansi lime, and wasabi jelly and a sesame honey wafer.

Chef Anna Hansen **Owner** Anna Hansen **Times** 9am-11pm **Prices** Fixed L 2 course £17.50, Starter £4.20-£8.20, Main £11.50-£18, Dessert £1-£8.50, Service added but optional 12.5% **Wines** 51 bottles over £20, 13 bottles under £20, 17 by glass **Notes** Pre-theatre D available, Sunday L, Vegetarian available, Air con **Seats** 110, Pr/dining room 60 **Children** Portions **Parking** On street (meter)

Moro   PLAN 3 F5

◉◉ Islamic, Mediterranean

Buzzy Clerkenwell hotspot with a neighbourhood vibe and Moorish food

☎ 020 7833 8336   📠 020 7833 9338
34/36 Exmouth Market EC1R 4QE
e-mail: info@moro.co.uk
dir: Nearest station: Farringdon or Angel 5 mins walk from Sadler's Wells theatre, between Farringdon Road and Rosebery Ave

Sam and Sam Clark's lively, ever-popular Exmouth Market restaurant continues to blaze a trail with its appealingly robust food driven by their collective passion for the flavours of Spain, North Africa and the Middle East. A third cookbook is out in 2009. The effortlessly cool, open-plan space of high ceilings, round coat-hook-lined pillars, closely-packed unclothed tables, café-style chairs and polished floorboards make for a relaxed, high-decibel atmosphere, complete with long zinc bar and an open kitchen at the back. Tapas is served all day at the bar, and the kitchen's unpretentious, generous approach - driven by quality ingredients - suits the surroundings, with food cooked on the charcoal grill or wood-burning oven. Hake is served with a hot paprika, garlic and sherry vinegar sauce, braised chard and potatoes, and to finish, perhaps a chocolate and apricot tart. The Iberian wine list adds further interest, and do check out the sherries.

Chef Samuel & Samantha Clark **Owner** Mr & Mrs S Clark & Mark Sainsbury **Times** 12.30-2.30/7-10.30 Closed Xmas, New Year, BHs, Sun **Prices** Fixed L 2 course £21-£27, Starter £6.50-£8.50, Main £14.50-£18.50, Dessert £5.50, Groups min 6 service 12.5% **Wines** 45 bottles over £20, 11 bottles under £20, 11 by glass **Notes** Tapas available 12.30-10.30pm, Vegetarian available, Air con **Seats** 90, Pr/dining room 14 **Children** Portions **Parking** NCP Farringdon Rd

LONDON EC1 *continued*

St John

PLAN 3 G4

◉◉ British

The best of British nose-to-tail eating

☎ 020 7251 0848   🖷 020 7251 4090
26 St John St EC1M 4AY
e-mail: reservations@stjohnrestaurant.com
dir: Nearest station: Farringdon 100yds from Smithfield Market, northside

Fergus Henderson's utilitarian-styled, former smokehouse continues to draw the crowds. Upstairs, accessed through the high-decibel, bustling bar and bakery with its even loftier ceiling and reached via wrought-iron staircase, the dining room is an equally pared-back affair of coat-hook-lined white walls, dove-grey painted floorboards, closely set, white-paper-clothed tables and wooden café-style chairs, set in serried ranks that echo the rows of industrial-style lights above. The kitchen is semi-open, staff are knowledgeable, friendly and relaxed (and clad in white), in tune with the no-frills surroundings and robust, honest, bold-flavoured British food that rightly prides itself on using the whole animal. Menus change twice daily and there's plenty of humble, lesser-used quality ingredients. Bone marrow's a bit of a signature dish, perhaps delivered roasted with a parsley salad, likewise, the Eccles cake and Lancashire cheese dessert, while, in between, perhaps braised rabbit with mustard and bacon. (There's a separate bar menu, and a Spitalfields spin-off, St John Food & Wine; see entry.)

Chef Christopher Gillard **Owner** T Gulliver & F Henderson **Times** 12-3/6-11 Closed Xmas, New Year, Etr BH, L Sat, D Sun **Prices** Food prices not confirmed for 2010. Please telephone for details. **Wines** 72 bottles over £20, 14 bottles under £20, 34 by glass **Notes** Vegetarian available, Air con **Seats** 100, Pr/dining room 18 **Parking** Meters in street

Smiths of Smithfield, Top Floor

PLAN 3 F4

◉◉ Modern British

Roof-top restaurant in warehouse conversion opposite Smithfield Meat Market

☎ 020 7251 7950   🖷 020 7236 5666
(Top Floor), 67-77 Charterhouse St EC1M 6HJ
e-mail: reservations@smithsofsmithfield.co.uk
dir: Nearest station: Farringdon, Barbican, Chancery Lane Opposite Smithfield Meat Market

Boasting views over the City skyline, the modern, window-lined Top Floor is the fine-dining restaurant at John Torode's SOS - a former warehouse complex now highly popular 4-floor drinking and eating emporium situated smack opposite Smithfield Meat Market. Original brick, reclaimed timber and steel all add to the fashionable industrial look on the lower floors, while the stylish Top Floor cranks up the ante and tones down the decibels. Polished-wood floors, leather chairs, white linen and a wall of windows offers everyone a view, while the alfresco decked terrace is a big hit in fair weather. Top-quality

produce and a kitchen passionate about provenance matches the informed, attentive service, with fine meats a signature; well-hung steaks from named rare breed, organic and additive-free stocks. Go for the 24-day-hung Longhorn sirloin, for example, served with béarnaise, parsley butter or creamed horseradish. However, the modern-focused menu offers lots more besides; think pan-fried halibut served with lobster mash and parsley sauce.

Chef Tony Moyse, Luke Rayment **Owner** John Torode **Times** 12-3.30/6.30-12 Closed 25-26 Dec, 1 Jan, L Sat, D Sun **Prices** Starter £6.50-£14, Main £15-£29.50, Dessert £7-£8.50, Service added but optional 12.5% **Wines** 150 bottles over £20, 4 bottles under £20, 29 by glass **Notes** Sunday L, Vegetarian available, Air con **Seats** 80, Pr/dining room 30 **Children** Portions **Parking** NCP: Snowhill

L' Anima

PLAN 6 C6

◉◉ Italian NEW

Classy regional Italian cooking in modish setting

☎ 020 7422 7000
1 Snowden St, Broadgate West EC2A 2DQ
dir: Nearest station: Liverpool Street

L'Anima is Italian for soul - something some might argue is a little lacking in the City of London - but Francesco Mazzei's restaurant has plenty to go around. He hails from Calabria - the toe of Italy's boot - and the menu is influenced by his home region as well as Puglia, Sicily and Sardinia; a crib sheet helps with some of the less well-known ingredients (paccheri, for example, a hard drum-shaped pasta). The room is decidedly cool and slick, split into bar and restaurant by a glass wall, both spaces dominated by limestone, marble and porphyry (an igneous rock); tables and chairs are brilliant white - the latter a cool combination of stainless steel and leather. The food is appealingly rustic but not unsophisticated. Tender octopus comes with cannellini beans and ricotta in a simple first course, then, if you've room squeeze in a pasta (butternut squash tortelli, perhaps) before slow-roasted belly of Black pig with N'Cantarata sauce (a piquant sauce of honey and paprika).

Times 11.45-3/5.30-10.30 Closed Sun

Boisdale of Bishopsgate

PLAN 7 C5

◉ Traditional British

A great taste of Scotland in the heart of the City

☎ 020 7283 1763
Swedeland Court, 202 Bishopsgate EC2M 4NR
e-mail: katie@boisdale-city.co.uk
dir: Nearest station: Liverpool Street Opposite Liverpool St station

Secreted away down a narrow alley that looks like a stage set from a TV Dickens adaptation, Boisdale, like its Belgravia sister venture (see entry), comes decked out in patriotic Scottish style with a buzzy, clubby atmosphere.

On the ground floor is a traditional champagne and oyster bar, while the restaurant and piano bar are in the cellar below. The Caledonian menu supports the theme, the accomplished kitchen's approach driven by traditional, prime north-of-the-border produce. Aberdeenshire dry-aged beef steaks are a signature, while roast Macsween haggis might be partnered by mash and bashed neeps. Whiskies, Cuban cigars and good wines please the deep-pocketed City lunchers, while live jazz in the evenings cranks up the decibels.

Chef Neil Churchill **Owner** Ranald Macdonald **Times** 11-3/6-9 Closed Xmas, 31 Dec, BHs, Sat & Sun **Prices** Fixed L 2 course £12.50-£18.70, Fixed D 3 course £27.50-£34.50, Starter £5.70-£8.50, Main £13-£42, Dessert £6.50-£8, Service added but optional 12.5% **Wines** 106 bottles over £20, 21 bottles under £20, 16 by glass **Notes** Vegetarian available, Air con **Seats** 100 **Parking** Middlesex St

Bonds

PLAN 6 B4

◉◉ Modern French

Grand setting for some slick modern cooking

☎ 020 7657 8088   & 7657 8090   🖷 020 7657 8100
Threadneedles, 5 Threadneedle St EC2R 8AY
e-mail: bonds@theetongroup.com
dir: Nearest station: Bank

Tucked away at the heart of the stylish Threadneedles hotel - a former Victorian banking hall turned boutique hotel - Bonds is a handsome dining room on a grand scale that successfully blends past and present, so soaring classical columns, high decorative ceiling and vast windows stand alongside contemporary wood-veneered panels, glass and potted greenery. City suits may appreciate a terrific-value lunch and early-evening 'Menu of the Day', while the succinctly scripted carte and tasting options come studded with luxury and show the aspiration of Barry Tonks's talented kitchen. The inventive cooking has a modern French and European-base, precise presentation and a light touch; take butter-roasted sea bass with borlotti bean, basil minestrone and mozzarella, and wild honey pannacotta to finish, served with macerated strawberries and Breton biscuits.

Chef Barry Tonks **Owner** The Eton Collection **Times** 12-2.30/6-10 Closed 2 wks Xmas, 4 days Etr & BHs, Sat, Sun **Prices** Fixed L course £17.50, Fixed D 3 course £17.50, Starter £7.95-£14.50, Main £14.50-£19.95, Dessert £4.95-£6.95, Service added but optional 12.5% **Wines** 137 bottles over £20, 11 bottles under £20, 18 by glass **Notes** Tasting menu available, Vegetarian available, Dress restrictions, Smart casual, Air con **Seats** 80, Pr/dining room 16 **Parking** London Wall NCP

Cinnamon Kitchen

PLAN 6 C5

◉◉ Modern Indian NEW

Imaginative Indian cooking in a former East India Company spice warehouse

☎ 020 7625 5000
9 Devonshire Square, LONDON EC2M 4YL
e-mail: info@cinnamon-kitchen.com
dir: Nearest station: Liverpool St. Off Bishopsgate Rd opposite Liverpool St Station

The new little sister to the Cinnamon Club in Westminster (see entry), the Cinnamon Kitchen occupies a former spice warehouse overlooking a smart covered square just a stone's throw from Liverpool Street station. More contemporary and informal than its sibling, the spacious restaurant has an industrial look, with high ceilings hung with ornate silver-plated brass globe lights, a colour palette of pale greys and greens, bare dark-wood tables and a pewter and black granite tandoor bar along one wall. The imaginative Indian cuisine is based on classic dishes but with a modern twist, as in a superb main course of wonderfully fresh grilled tandoori king prawns marinated with spices and coriander paste, served with a Bengali kedgeree with the added ingredients of a buttery yellow lentil dahl and tiny shrimps. The menu is less structured than at the Cinnamon Club, offering a selection of grills, appetisers, biryanis and side dishes designed for sharing.

Chef Vivek Singh, Abdul Yaseen **Times** 12-3.30/6-10.30 Closed 25-26 Dec, 1 Jan, some BHs, Sun, L Sat **Prices** Fixed L 2 course fr £15, Fixed D 3 course fr £24, Starter £5-£12, Main £14-£32, Dessert £5-£8, Service added but optional 12.5% **Wines** 30 bottles under £20 **Notes** Pre & post theatre menu available, Vegetarian available, Air con **Seats** 96, Pr/dining room 12 **Children** Portions **Parking** NCP Rodwell Hse on Bishopsgate

Eyre Brothers

PLAN 7 B2

◉◉ Spanish, Portuguese

Vivacious Spanish/Portuguese cooking from the brothers with the magic touch

☎ 020 7613 5346 🖷 020 7739 8199
70 Leonard St EC2A 4QX
e-mail: eyrebros@btconnect.com
dir: Nearest station: Old Street Exit 4

The brothers, David and Robert, grew up in Mozambique, and imbibed a love of the Portuguese cooking bequeathed to that country by its former colonial power. Thus it is that Iberian food ways come to be celebrated in their stylish, glass-fronted restaurant not far from Liverpool Street station. This is no mere tapas joint, though. Wood-roasted piquillo peppers stuffed with oxtail in red wine is one possible starter, and might be followed by grilled Ibérico pork marinated in smoked paprika, thyme and garlic, served with patatas pobres. Seafood might be presented in the Basque style, with sea bream and clams

cooked in white wine, and to finish, tarta di Santiago, an almond tart served with lime and orange confit, or perhaps El Suspiro, an unpasteurised goats' cheese from Toledo, with membrillo and walnut bread.

Chef Dave Eyre, Joao Cleto **Owner** Eyre Bros Restaurants Ltd **Times** 12-3/6.30-11 Closed Xmas-New Year, BHs, Sun, L Sat **Prices** Starter £6-£17.50, Main £10-£25, Dessert £6-£7, Service optional **Wines** 50 bottles over £20, 7 bottles under £20, 14 by glass **Notes** Vegetarian available, Air con **Seats** 100 **Parking** On street, 2 car parks on Leonard St

Great Eastern Dining Room

PLAN 7 B2

◉ Pan Asian

High-octane Asian-style eatery

☎ 020 7613 4545 🖷 020 7613 4137
54 Great Eastern St EC2A 3QR
e-mail: greateastern@rickerrestaurants.com
dir: Nearest station: Liverpool St, Old Street

The Great Eastern is as good-looking and design-conscious as the hip Hoxton crew that zeroes in on its buzzy vibe and sexily stark interior. All the boxes are ticked for style slaves by its black wood floors and walls, leather seating and funky chandeliers. It's not a place for a romantic tête-à-tête: diners and drinkers are elbow to elbow and sounds are pumped out at high decibels. When it comes to food, though, it stands apart from the other

continued

Rhodes Twenty Four

LONDON EC2 PLAN 6 C5

Modern British

Reinvented British food in the City sky

☎ 020 7877 7703 🖷 020 7877 7788
Level 24, Tower 42, 25 Old Broad St EC2N 1HQ
e-mail: reservation@rhodes24.co.uk
dir: Nearest station: Bank/Liverpool Street Telephone for directions, see website

Towers of banking became uncomfortably close to towers of Babel with the onset of the credit crunch, though nothing about that unfortunate development inhibits the pleasure of a visit to Gary Rhodes' restaurant in the City of London clouds. Ascend by express lift, and prepare for panoramic bedazzlement. That there is bedazzlement of the culinary kind in evidence too can only enhance the location, and that there certainly is. Officially, this is

traditional British cuisine in that the menu offers such manner of things as puddings (suet, rice or bread-and-butter), pies (both cottage and apple) and custard. That's only part of the story, as there's also crab raviolo - generously stuffed, bedded on baby leeks and sauced with frothy coral cream - lobster thermidor omelette, and buttered salmon with peas, white asparagus and chorizo (though the last is made in the Lake District). Where the traditional things are done traditionally, they are overwhelmingly successful, as in the gigantic mutton suet pudding with mashed swede, which comes with a gourmand's array of 3 sauce jugs - caper, mustard and mutton gravy. At dessert, a taste of lemon may encompass the Frenchified glazed tart and iced mousse, but also an exhilaratingly sour syllabub.

Chef Gary Rhodes, Adam Gray **Owner** Compass Group **Times** 12-2.30/6-9.15 Closed BHs, Xmas, New Year, Sat-Sun **Prices** Fixed L 2 course £40-£55, Starter £9.50-£17.90, Main £16.20-£32, Dessert £8.75-£11.50, Service added but optional 12.5% **Wines** 5 bottles under £20, 12 by glass **Notes** Vegetarian available, Dress restrictions, Smart casual, no shorts, Air con **Seats** 75, Pr/dining room 30 **Children** Portions **Parking** On street

LONDON EC2 *continued*

trendy hangouts in the area. Clued-up staff serve up a soundly-executed Pan-Asian menu built around an oriental tapas theme meant for grazing and sharing. Dishes take in the gamut of Asian cuisine, from dim sum to tempura, curries, barbecues, roasts or house specials; go for black cod with sweet miso, steamed sea bass with black bean or Argentinian beef sirloin with toban yaki.

Chef Ross Erickson **Owner** Will Ricker
Times 12-3/6-10.30 Closed Xmas & Etr, Sun, L Sat
Prices Starter £4-£6.50, Main £9.50-£21.50, Dessert £4-£4.75, Service added but optional 12.5% **Wines** 40 bottles over £20, 10 bottles under £20, 10 by glass
Notes Vegetarian available, Air con **Seats** 70

Mehek
PLAN 7 B5

◉ Indian

Modern Indian dining with innovative and classic dishes in stylish surroundings

☎ 020 7588 5043 & 7588 5044 📠 020 7588 5045
45 London Wall, Moorgate EC2M 5TE
e-mail: info@mehek.co.uk
dir: Nearest station: Moorgate/Liverpool St Close to junct of Moorgate and London Wall

Mehek - meaning 'fragrance' - is a slickly sophisticated Indian on historic London Wall. The lavish interior was designed by Vimlesh Lal, a famous Bollywood film-set designer, and unfolds Tardis-like into a series of chic eating areas, with a long bar guaranteed to pull in city slickers. Diligent staff do their bit to foster a relaxed ambience. The compendious menu takes in regional dishes from all over the sub-continent, crafted by a creative kitchen team that likes to put a modern spin on classics and old favourites. You'll find fish tikka and malai lamb chops marinated in yogurt, cream cheese and ginger grilled on charcoal in the tandoor oven, then seldom-seen treats such as venison cooked with flat beans, or Hyderabadi duck.

Chef A Matlib **Owner** Salim B Rashid
Times 11.30-3/5.30-11 Closed Xmas, New Year, BHs, Sat-Sun **Prices** Fixed L 3 course £14.90-£21.90, Starter £3.70-£10.90, Main £7.90-£16.90, Dessert £2.95-£3.50, Service added but optional 10% **Wines** 20 bottles over £20, 8 bottles under £20, 9 by glass **Notes** Vegetarian available, Dress restrictions, Smart casual, Air con **Seats** 120 **Parking** On street, NCP

Rhodes Twenty Four
PLAN 6 C5

◉◉◉ – *see page 241*

◉◉◉ – *see page 241*

LONDON EC3

Addendum
PLAN 6 C4

◉◉ Modern European

Skilled and concise cooking in slick, boutique hotel

☎ 020 7977 9500 & 7702 2020 📠 020 7702 2217
Apex City of London Hotel, 1 Seething Ln EC3N 4AX
e-mail: reservations@addendumrestaurant.co.uk
dir: Nearest station: Tower Hill, Fenchurch Street Follow Lower Thames St, left onto Trinity Square, left onto Muscovy St, right onto Seething Ln, opposite Seething Ln gardens

The Apex City of London Hotel's Addendum restaurant comes suited and booted with the understated design you'd expect in the corporate heart of the Square Mile. Butch leather seats, wooden floors, shades of dark chocolate and amber glow with subdued lighting and clever use of mirrors. Tables are clad in starched white to match the sharp shirts and ties of the clientele and the equally impeccably turned-out staff. The cooking, too, is businesslike and skilful, with plenty of guts in the ingredients. Menus offer seasonality and crisp, clear flavours, so a beetroot soup comes with confit of duck and crème fraîche, followed by a crab, chilli and coriander linguine coated with a velvet-rich fish bisque. At dessert, pumpkin pie is paired to great effect with a bitter chocolate sorbet.

Chef Darren Thomas **Owner** Norman Springford
Times 12-2.30/6-10 **Prices** Fixed D 3 course £19.50, Starter £5.50-£7.95, Main £10.50-£18.25, Dessert £5.75-£7.50, Service added but optional 12.5% **Wines** 100 bottles over £20, 11 bottles under £20, 16 by glass **Notes** Sunday L, Vegetarian available, Dress restrictions, Smart casual, Air con **Seats** 65, Pr/dining room 50 **Parking** Car park in Lower Thames St

Chamberlains Restaurant
PLAN 6 C4

◉◉ Modern British, Seafood

Fresh fish in the heart of the city

☎ 020 7648 8690 📠 020 7648 8691
23-25 Leadenhall Market EC3V 1LR
e-mail: info@chamberlains.org
dir: Nearest station: Bank and Monument Please telephone for directions

High octane City workers will find escape from the pressures of Mammon in this welcoming seafood restaurant. Outside, Leadenhall Market may bustle with lunchtime and early evening workers seeking refreshment away from their desks, but inside these walls you'll find a quiet oasis staffed by attentive, deferential waiters, and the reassuring sight of starched white linen and gleaming silver. The food easily meets expectations too, with fish and seafood as fresh as it gets away from the coast. Choose to have your fish simply cooked without frills, or served in a sauce that will bring out its natural

flavour (Dover sole, for example, in a crayfish broth). It's not all fish, with grilled steaks and other meats worth trying, too.

Chef Matthew Marshall **Owner** Chamberlain & Thelwell
Times 12-9.30 Closed Xmas, New Year & BHs, Sat-Sun
Prices Starter £6.50-£14.95, Main £18.95-£32, Dessert £6.50-£9.50, Service optional **Wines** 60 bottles over £20, 10 bottles under £20, 8 by glass **Notes** Vegetarian available, Air con **Seats** 150, Pr/dining room 65 **Children** Portions

Prism Restaurant and Bar
PLAN 6 C4

◉◉ Modern European

Confident cooking in popular City haunt

☎ 020 7256 3888 📠 0870 191 6025
147 Leadenhall St EC3V 4QT
e-mail: prismevents@harveynichols.com
web: www.harveynichols.com
dir: Nearest station: Bank and Monument Take exit 4 from Bank tube station, 5 mins walk

The grandly imposing former Bank of New York houses this popular City haunt, which is a lunch venue of choice for bankers and brokers. Built like a small cathedral from marble, alabaster and stone with tall columns and a striking ceiling, the restaurant has smartly laid tables that are well spaced to avoid any accidental eavesdropping on sensitive financial conversations. The food is attractively presented and the Modern British cooking is underpinned by classical techniques. Start with crispy ham hock with roasted garlic mayonnaise, quail's egg and a shot of parsley and ham soup and follow it with grilled fillets of lemon sole with fresh morels, courgettes and artichoke velouté. There's an excellent wine list too.

Chef Richard Robinson **Owner** Harvey Nichols
Times 11.30-2.30/6-10.30 Closed Xmas, BHs, Sat & Sun
Prices Fixed D 3 course £25, Starter £10.50-£15.50, Main £14.50-£39.50, Dessert £6.50-£75, Service added but optional 12.5% **Wines** 660 bottles over £20, 19 bottles under £20, 23 by glass **Notes** Vegetarian available, Air con **Seats** 120, Pr/dining room 40 **Children** Portions **Parking** On street & NCP

Restaurant Sauterelle

PLAN 6 B4

◎◎ French ♥

Unfussy French cuisine in landmark building

☎ 020 7618 2483 📠 020 7618 2490
The Royal Exchange EC3V 3LR
web: www.restaurantsauterelle.com
dir: Nearest station: Bank In heart of business centre.
Bank tube station exit 3

This small contemporary French restaurant on the first-floor mezzanine of the Royal Exchange overlooks an indoor courtyard surrounded by famous luxury boutiques and world-famous jewellers. The atmosphere in the restaurant is equally chic, while service is slick and professional. The food is simple, unfussy and dominated by the seasons and what's best at market on the day. Start with Scottish lobster and suckling pig belly with pickled vegetables and toasted cauliflower purée, before moving on to Anjou squab pigeon with baby turnips, haricot blanc and seared foie gras. Leave space for rhubarb and walnut crunch, vanilla and rhubarb ice cream. The set menu offers excellent value with 3 choices per course.

Chef Robin Gill **Owner** D & D London **Times** 12-2.30/6-10 Closed BHs, Sat-Sun **Prices** Fixed L 2 course £18, Fixed D 3 course £21, Starter £8.50-£14, Main £17-£21, Dessert £7-£8.50, Service added but optional 12.5% **Wines** 175 bottles over £20, 2 bottles under £20, 13 by glass **Notes** Vegetarian available, Air con **Seats** 66, Pr/dining room 20 **Children** Portions

LONDON EC4

The Chancery

PLAN 3 E3

◎◎ Modern British, French

Enjoyable brasserie-style dining in legal land

☎ 020 7831 4000 📠 020 7831 4002
9 Cursitor St EC4A 1LL
e-mail: reservations@thechancery.co.uk
dir: Nearest station: Chancery Lane Situated between High Holborn and Fleet St, just off Chancery Ln

Near to Lincoln's Inn and Chancery Lane, this chic, glass-fronted restaurant is tucked away among the side streets and venerable buildings of the law community. With just a dozen tables, it's a great venue for intimate dining à deux in a voguish monochrome setting - black leather chairs and white linen smartly partnered with polished mahogany floors, mirrors and modern abstract art on half-panelled black and white walls. Vibrant modern European cooking - light, unpretentious and with the

whiff of the Mediterranean about it - is the kitchen's stock-in-trade. Colourful dishes leap out against the neutral backdrop: lamb broth with crispy lamb and marjoram dumplings is a typical starter, followed by steamed hake fillet and potage of squid and mussels with red peppers and pesto. (Sibling to the Clerkenwell Dining Room, see entry.)

Times 12-2.30/6-10.30 Closed Xmas, Sat-Sun

Refettorio

PLAN 3 F2

◎◎ Traditional Italian

Refectory-style Italian dining

☎ 020 7438 8052 & 7438 8055 📠 020 7438 8088
Crowne Plaza London - The City, 19 New Bridge St EC4V 6DB
e-mail: loncy.refettorio@ihg.com
dir: Nearest station: Blackfriars, Temple, St Paul's Situated on New Bridge St, opposite Blackfriars underground (exit 8)

Giorgio Locatelli's convivial dining room in the Crowne Plaza Hotel offers a more sociable approach to eating than most, with the main feature being a long, refectory-style table in the middle of the room. (More conventional tables are also available.) The menu offers authentic Italian food in the classically structured fashion, with pasta and risotto options between the antipasti and the secondi. If you've an appetite, you might progress from scallops with celeriac purée and caper sauce, through a small portion of saffron risotto, to calves' liver with spinach in a balsamic reduction studded with pine nuts and raisins. Alternatively, there are light-bite dishes for sharing, at fixed prices, as well as deep-fried prawns and squid. Finish with a classic work-of-art Italian dessert, such as a chocolate pyramid in all three shades, served with orange sorbet.

Chef Mattia Camorani **Owner** Crowne Plaza **Times** 12-2.30/6-10.30 Closed Xmas & BHs, Sun, L Sat **Prices** Fixed D 3 course £23-£25, Starter £8-£10, Main £16.75-£22.75, Dessert £6.50-£7, Service added but optional 12.5% **Wines** 59 bottles over £20, 6 bottles under £20, 8 by glass **Notes** Pre-theatre D menu £20, Bi-monthly seasonal menu £35, Vegetarian available, Dress restrictions, Smart casual, Civ Wed 100, Air con **Seats** 85, Pr/dining room 33 **Children** Portions **Parking** NCP - Queen Victoria St

The White Swan Pub & Dining Room

PLAN 3 F3

◎ Modern, Traditional British

City gastro-pub with elegant first-floor dining room

☎ 020 7242 9696 📠 020 7404 2250
108 Fetter Ln EC4A 1ES
e-mail: info@thewhiteswanlondon.com
dir: Nearest station: Chancery Lane Tube Station Fetter Lane runs parallel with Chancery Lane in the City of London and it joins Fleet St with Holborn

This renovated pub near Chancery Lane tube station was once called the Mucky Duck, but is now tastefully reborn

as a handsome swan. Dark wood dominates the elegant interiors. The mezzanine level offers crow's-nest views of the goings-on, while the well-set-up restaurant on the first floor is where the main culinary action is. Crisp ox tongue with potato gribiche is a diverting opener, as is braised pig cheek with parsnip purée and thyme jus. Mains might offer poached monkfish with saffron potatoes and mussels in chilli and coriander broth, or twice-cooked guinea fowl with caramelised endive and game chips in sherry vinegar, before a finale of Cox's apple charlotte with cinnamon sauce.

Times 12-3/6-10 Closed 25 Dec, 1 Jan and BHs, Sat-Sun (except private parties)

LONDON N1

Almeida Restaurant

PLAN 1 F4

◎◎ French V

French-inspired dishes in suave setting

☎ 020 7354 4777 📠 020 7354 2777
30 Almeida St, Islington N1 1AD
e-mail: almeida-reservations@danddlondon.com
web: www.almeida-restaurants.co.uk
dir: Nearest station: Angel/Islington/Highbury Turn right from station, along Upper St, past church

If you're hankering after the sort of meal that usually requires a trip across the channel, Almeida provides an excursion into the traditional Gallic repertoire. The place is looking very Islington-suave after a recent makeover, a grown-up space of muted white and brown; a wine bar at the front lets you graze on nibbles and tapas-sized petits plats and slurp by the glass or pichet, while a smart main restaurant has an open kitchen and vast windows. The menu is rooted in France but lightens the touch by steaming, poaching and cutting out the cream. Modern riffs on French bourgeois classics include ballotine of duck foie gras with apple, walnuts, and toasted fig bread or East Anglian beef tartare with Poilâne melba, while mains take in roast and confit Barbary duck cassoulet.

Chef Alan Jones **Owner** D & D London **Times** 12-2.30/5.30-10.30 Closed 26 Dec, 1 Jan, L Mon, D Sun **Prices** Fixed L 2 course fr £14.50, Fixed D 3 course fr £17.50, Tasting menu £60, Starter £7-£8, Main £15-£18, Dessert £5-£6.50, Service added but optional 12.5% **Wines** 350 bottles over £20, 18 bottles under £20, 20 by glass **Notes** Tasting menu 7 course, Pre/post-theatre menu available, Sunday L, Vegetarian menu, Civ Wed 80, Air con **Seats** 100, Pr/dining room 18 **Children** Portions, Menu **Parking** Parking around building

LONDON N1 *continued*

Fifteen London – The Dining Room

PLAN 3 H6

Italian, Mediterranean V

Funky Italian-slanted cooking for a good cause

☎ 0871 330 1515 📠 020 7251 2749
15 Westland Place N1 7LP
dir: Nearest station: Old Street Exit 1 from Old St tube station, walk up City road, opposite Moorfields Eye Hospital

In a former sheet metal factory turned art gallery celebrity chef Jamie Oliver broke new ground 7 years ago with his not for profit charitable venture. A new influx of young apprentices are mentored here every year and the format has proved itself to be so much more than just a gimmick and has now been rolled out from Cornwall to Melbourne. Back in London, the style is retro with funky murals on the walls, while an open kitchen adds to the informal buzz. Descriptions of the modern Mediterranean dishes with an Italian influence (ingredients are carefully sourced from the UK and Italy) are Jamie-ed up so expect 'fantastic' salad of radicchio Trevisano, caramelised pears, gorgonzola dolce and fresh Sorrento walnuts, followed by main course 'wicked' Sicilian fisherman's stew. Confident and enthusiastic staff complete the experience.

Chef Andrew Parkinson **Owner** Fifteen Foundation
Times 12-2.45/6.30-9.30 Closed 25 Dec, 1 Jan
Prices Fixed L 2 course £22.50, Tasting menu £50-£60, Starter £8.50-£11, Main £17-£21, Dessert £6, Service added but optional 12.5% **Wines** 200+ bottles over £20, 12 by glass **Notes** Tasting menu min price for vegetarian option, Sunday L, Vegetarian menu, Dress restrictions, Smart casual, Air con **Seats** 68 **Children** Portions **Parking** On street & NCP

Frederick's Restaurant

PLAN 1 F4

Modern European

Imaginative cuisine in Islington antiques quarter

☎ 020 7359 2888 📠 020 7359 5173
Camden Passage, Islington N1 8EG
e-mail: eat@fredericks.co.uk
dir: Nearest station: Angel From underground 2 mins walk to Camden Passage. Restaurant among the antique shops

A family-run restaurant in the Camden Passage antiques quarter of Islington, diners in the airy Garden Room sit beneath a splendid vaulted glass roof, overlooking the patio and garden. In good weather you can eat outside. Modern art on the walls and clever lighting set the scene for stylish, skilful cooking that is imaginative but still retains its simplicity. Expect dishes with a distinct European accent, such as crispy duck confit, marinated cherries and watercress salad, or a main course of roast sea bass with shallot Tatin and blackcurrant hollandaise.

Finish with raspberry crème brûlée and biscotti. Set lunch and pre-theatre menus are also available.

Times 12-2.30/5.45-11.30 Closed Xmas, New Year, BHs, Sun (ex functions)

The Bull Pub & Dining Room

PLAN 1 E5

British, French

Lively modern gastro-pub offering confident cooking

☎ 0845 456 5033 📠 0845 456 5034
13 North Hill N6 4AB
e-mail: info@inthebull.biz
dir: Nearest station: Highgate 5 min walk from Highgate tube station

The Bull is an easy-going gastro-pub in a two-storey Victorian building popular with a young crowd who create a buzz in the central bar and smart dining area. It looks every inch the upmarket dining pub, with polished wood floors, leather banquettes and modern art inside, and a terrace out front for balmy days. Confident French-influenced modern British cooking is the kitchen's forté, delivered in a wide-ranging carte supplemented by blackboard specials. Seared scallops are paired with sweetcorn galette, pancetta and berry jus to start, with slow-roasted pork belly with black pudding mousseline, caramelised apple and cider jus to follow.

Times 12-3.30/6-10.30 Closed L Mon, D 25 Dec

Morgan M

PLAN 1 F5

Modern French V

Exemplary French cooking in relaxed, stylish setting

☎ 020 7609 3560 📠 020 8292 5699
489 Liverpool Rd, Islington N7 8NS
dir: Nearest station: Highbury & Islington Please telephone for directions

From the outside it could be mistaken for a rather smart Islington gastro-pub, but the large frosted glass windows and green-painted exterior conceal a very French affair. Chef-patron Morgan Meunier has created an intimate and personal restaurant with a style not dissimilar to that of a Gallic brasserie, where comfortable green arm chairs and oak floors combine with wood panels and a mix of floral wallpaper and rich burgundy colours to create a warm ambience in the room. The seasonal, modern

French menu combines the old and the new with well-defined flavours from luxury French ingredients and food is served by attentive, friendly staff. The chef is especially proud of his renowned six-course tasting menus and there is a high level of skill displayed in the kitchen. Pan-fried foie gras on toasted brioche served with apricot confit and curry and orange sauce is an innovative starter with perfect balance and contrasts, while main-course seared fillet of John Dory, butternut risotto, spinach, parsnip beignet and carrot juice is also a dish with harmonious flavour combinations. The wine list leans heavily towards France and amuse-bouche, breads and pre-dessert confirm the technical skills on display. A passionfruit soufflé and sorbet with crème anglaise rises to the occasion for dessert.

Chef M Meunier, S Soulard **Owner** Morgan Meunier
Times 12-2.30/7-10.30 Closed 24-30 Dec, Mon, L Tue, Sat, D Sun **Prices** Fixed L 2 course £22.50, Fixed D 3 course £39, Service added but optional 12.5% **Wines** 140 bottles over £20, 3 bottles under £20, 6 by glass

Notes Tasting menu £48 (vegetarian £43), Sunday L, Vegetarian menu, Dress restrictions, Smart casual, Air con **Seats** 48, Pr/dining room 12 **Children** Portions **Parking** On Liverpool Rd

LONDON N7

Morgan M
PLAN 1 F5

◉◉◉ – *see page 244*

LONDON N17

The Lock Restaurant
PLAN 1 F5

◉◉ Modern British

Chic eatery offering bold, modern food

☎ 020 8885 2829   📠 020 8885 1618
Heron House, Hale Wharf, Ferry Ln N17 9NF
e-mail: thelock09@googlemail.com
dir: Nearest station: Tottenham Hale, Black Horse Station
Telephone for directions

This go-ahead restaurant brought chic dining to an area of London not normally associated with gastronomic prowess. A short hop away from Tottenham Hale station, it has a light, open-plan warehouse feel, with classic urban loft styling - whitewashed walls with paintings by local artists, wooden floor, tiled tables and capacious sofas in the bar area - blended with hints of North Africa. The kitchen deals in modern British food cleverly tweaked with worldwide flavours - a pinch of Italy here, a sprinkle of Asia there - to keep your taste buds on their toes. The eclectic menu starts intriguingly: try sautéed foie gras with savoury bread-and-butter pudding and pickled beetroot; then stuffed saddle of rabbit with a fricassée of wild mushrooms, dates and baby onions. End with a hot chocolate fondant with caramel and cinnamon ice cream.

Chef Adebola Adeshina **Owner** The Forerib Ltd
Times 12-2/6.30-10 Closed Mon, L Sat (except match days), D Sun **Prices** Fixed L 2 course £10-£13, Fixed D 3 course £15-£18, Starter £3.95-£8, Main £8-£17, Dessert £3.95-£6, Service added but optional 10% **Wines** 10 bottles over £20, 15 bottles under £20, 12 by glass **Notes** Tasting menu available on request, Sunday L, Vegetarian available, Dress restrictions, Smart casual, no hats/caps, Air con **Seats** 60, Pr/dining room 18 **Children** Portions, Menu **Parking** 20

LONDON NW1

La Collina
PLAN 1 E4

◉ Italian

A taste of Italy in pretty Primrose Hill

☎ 020 7483 0192
17 Princess Rd, Chalk Farm NW1 8JR
dir: Nearest station: Chalk Farm/Camden Town. Please telephone for directions

If you're lucky enough to pitch up at La Collina on a fine, warm day, you can dine outside in the large rear garden and really feel like you're in Italy. Should the weather not be enough to transport you there, at least the authentic cooking will, helped along by the Italianesque décor of white-washed walls, linen-clothed tables, wooden chairs and stripped wooden floorboards. The menu - produced from an open kitchen - changes regularly but might offer the likes of home-made potato dumplings with braised rabbit and olives, roasted seafood in a tomato and wine sauce, and roasted quail with cherries. The home-made tiramisù is not to be missed.

Times 12-2.30/6-11 Closed Xmas wk, L Mon-Fri
Prices Food prices not confirmed for 2010. Please telephone for details

Dorset Square Hotel
PLAN 2 F4

◉ Modern British

Relaxed bar-restaurant with cricketing roots

☎ 020 7723 7874   📠 020 7724 3328
39-40 Dorset Square NW1 6QN
e-mail: info@dorsetsquare.co.uk
dir: Nearest station: Baker St/Marylebone Telephone for directions

Dorset Square is the site on which the original Lords cricket ground stood, and it now provides a welcome patch of green tree-filled space on the doorstep of this plush Regency townhouse hotel. As cricket is no longer on the cards, head down to the lower-ground floor, where the Potting Shed Restaurant and Bar offers a bucolic respite from central London's frenzy. Skylights ensure a warm, sunny ambience, while piles of terracotta pots, seed boxes and gardening what-nots add visual interest. The kitchen goes in for modern British cooking with a strong flavour of the Mediterranean, typically opening with a Dorset blue cheese and leek tart with grape chutney, then going on to rump of lamb with tapenade crust and courgette provençale.

Times 12-3/6-10.30 Closed 25 Dec, BHs, L Sat, D Sun

Gilgamesh
PLAN 1 E4

◉ Pan-Asian

Eclectic range of dishes in mega-lavish surroundings

☎ 020 7482 5757
Camden Stables Market, Chalk Farm Rd NW1 8AH
dir: Nearest station: Chalk Farm

When a restaurant and bar takes its inspiration from an ancient Mesopotamian epic you can expect something out of the ordinary. The kings of Babylon - or Las Vegas - would feel at home in this temple to decadent excess, and bohemian Camden is just the right spot for the unrestrained fantasy of Gilgamesh. Shoppers spill out of the market to mingle with local TV and film studio types based in a vast hall: imagine a huge bar of lapis stone, restlessly-shifting lighting, a vast retractable roof, and every surface embellished to the N-th degree with carved murals. Chef Ian Pengelley's Pan-Asian cuisine is served with panache by switched-on staff. The eclectic mix takes in sashimi and sushi - prepared by Japanese chefs - and the likes of tempura soft shell crab, or Gilgamesh signature dishes like roasted sea bass marinated in sweet plum miso sauce cooked in hoba leaf.

Times 12-2.30/6

Megaro
PLAN 3 C6

◉ British

Modern cooking in smart city hotel

☎ 020 7843 2221 & 7843 2222   📠 020 7843 2200
23 -27 Euston Rd, St Pancras NW1 2SD
e-mail: gm@hotelmegaro.co.uk
dir: Nearest station: King's Cross St Pancras

Situated opposite King's Cross and St Pancras stations, this stylish hotel may occupy a bustling central location but its Megaro Restaurant is a little oasis tucked away in a basement. Head down the staircase tiled with Italian granite and smooth Welsh slate into the smart, modern dining room with its red leather-style chairs and high quality beech-topped tables. Service is friendly and efficient and complemented by the kitchen team's modern cuisine and menu. The dishes are very much driven by quality ingredients and simple yet appealing presentation; take pan-fried sea bass with fennel purée, capers and red wine sauce, finishing with chocolate fondant with vanilla ice cream.

Chef Paul Ribbands **Owner** Antonio Megaro **Times** 5-10 Closed L all week **Prices** Starter £4-£7.50, Main £8.50-£14.50, Dessert £3.95-£6.50, Service added but optional **Notes** Sunday L, Vegetarian available, Air con **Seats** 36 **Children** Portions **Parking** NCP nearby

LONDON NW1 *continued*

Mirrors Restaurant

PLAN 3 C5

◉ Modern European

Sleek modern hotel restaurant with a wide-ranging carte

☎ 020 7666 9080 ▤ 020 7666 9100
Novotel London St Pancras, 100-110 Euston Rd NW1 2AJ
e-mail: h5309-fb@accor.com
dir: Nearest station: King's Cross/Euston/St Pancras International 3 min walk from St Pancras International. Hotel adjacent to the British Library

The stylishly contemporary restaurant in the busy Euston Road branch of the Novotel chain is handy for King's Cross, St Pancras and Euston railway stations and the British Library. Curvaceous mirrors greet you at the entrance of the bustling ground-floor bar and restaurant, where the action centres around a carvery and trendy open kitchen. The sharply-styled décor is a clean-cut space of glass and pale woods with bold modern maroon sofas and purple leather chairs injecting vibrant colours. Eclectic modern European dishes on the wide-ranging menu include Cornish crab and mackerel spring roll with plum compôte and wasabi mayonnaise, followed by roast Norwegian cod with pea and bacon risotto and roast garlic foam.

Chef Rees Smith **Owner** Accor UK Business & Leisure **Times** 12-2.30/6-10.30 Closed L Sat, Sun, BHs

Prices Fixed L 2 course fr £14, Fixed D 3 course £19-£23.50, Starter £6.95-£9.95, Main £14.95-£21.95, Dessert £5.50-£6.75, Service added but optional 10% **Wines** 15 bottles over £20, 14 bottles under £20, 18 by glass **Notes** Vegetarian available, Air con **Seats** 89, Pr/dining room 250 **Children** Portions, Menu **Parking** Ibis Euston

Odette's Restaurant & Bar

PLAN 1 E4

◉◉◉ – *see below*

St Pancras Grand

PLAN 3 C6

◉◉ British NEW

Great British menu at landmark railway station

☎ 020 7870 9900
St Pancras International NW1 9QP
dir: Nearest station: King's Cross St Pancras

Restaurant-wise, the pièce de résistance of the station's multi-million pound makeover, St Pancras Grand puts the romance of a bygone era back into station dining with its art deco design and traditional details such as an old railway clock and railway tickets in lieu of cloakroom tags. The large space, with room for 120 diners, also houses an oyster bar, and is open for breakfast, elevenses, lunch, afternoon tea and dinner. At the helm is Billy Reid, a man with experience in the MPW empire. For dinner, start off with potato and oyster soup or cold ox

tongue with parsley potatoes and move on to slow-roast belly of pork flavoured with marmalade and cloves. Puddings might include rice pudding with strawberry jam or custard tart served with butterscotch sauce and a Garibaldi biscuit. Service is quick and efficient, good news for those with a train to catch.

Chef Billy Reid **Times** 11-mdnt **Prices** Food prices not confirmed for 2010. Please telephone for details.

Sardo Canale

PLAN 1 E4

◉ Italian

Authentic Italian cuisine in a unique location

☎ 020 7722 2800 ▤ 020 7722 0802
42 Gloucester Av NW1 8JD
e-mail: info@sardocanale.com
dir: Nearest station: Chalk Farm/Camden Town Please telephone for directions

Located in a new building designed around an old tunnel and tower with links to the nearby Grand Union Canal, this modern Italian restaurant certainly occupies a unique position. Regional Italian cooking is the order of the day here, with the kitchen using fresh ingredients to create authentic Sardinian recipes. Service is formal, but the atmosphere is relaxed and friendly, so sit back with a glass of wine and choose from the extensive Italian menu, complete with English subtitles. Start with cream of potato soup flavoured with truffle oil and move on to fillet of plaice filled with ricotta and sun-dried tomatoes

Odette's Restaurant & Bar

LONDON NW1   PLAN 1 E4

Modern European V

Refined modern cooking in stylish Primrose Hill favourite

☎ 020 7586 8569 ▤ 020 7586 8362
130 Regent's Park Rd NW1 8XL
e-mail: info@primrosehill.com
dir: Nearest station: Chalk Farm. By Primrose Hill. Telephone for directions

Chef-patron Bryn Williams has been developing his TV career and at the same time building on his success at the Primrose Hill institution that is Odette's. There are some tables on the pavement, which fit in nicely with the village vibe of the area, and inside the designer has created spaces combining bold colours (bright yellow leather chairs), floral patterned wallpaper and plenty of

artistic touches. On the lower floor there is a small bar and conservatory. The kitchen delivers first-rate modern European food based around excellent produce, attractively presented, with a firm grasp on the balance of flavours in each dish. Chestnut broth, for example, comes with thyme dumplings, root vegetables and chestnut brioche, and hand-dived scallops with white crab meat, cucumber and vanilla and lime dressing. A splendid wintery main-course sees braised beef cheek partnered with ox tongue, parsnip purée and Swiss chard, and a summer dessert might be an artfully constructed strawberry cheesecake. There's an excellent value set lunch menu, two tasting menus (one is vegetarian), and meals include excellent breads, pre-starter and pre-dessert, and good coffee comes with petits fours.

Chef Bryn Williams **Owner** Bryn Williams **Times** 12-2.30/6.30-10.30 Closed 25 Dec -1 Jan, Mon (incl BH's), D Sun **Prices** Fixed L 2 course £12, Starter £8.95-£12.95, Main £14.95-£21.95, Dessert £8.95-£12.95, Service added but optional 12.5% **Wines** 134

bottles over £20, 3 bottles under £20, 20 by glass **Notes** Tasting menu 7 course, Sunday L, Vegetarian menu, Air con **Seats** 75, Pr/dining room 25 **Children** Portions **Parking** On street

served with white wine sauce and sautéed spinach, perhaps finishing with cardamom pannacotta.

Chef Claudio Covino **Owner** Romolo & Bianca Mudu **Times** 12-3/6-11 Closed 25-26 Dec, BHs, L Mon **Prices** Fixed L 3 course fr £13.50, Starter £6.90-£8.90, Main £9.90-£17.50, Dessert £5-£6.50, Service added but optional 12.5% **Wines** 75 bottles over £20, 10 bottles under £20, 19 by glass **Notes** Sunday L, Air con **Seats** 100, Pr/dining room 40 **Children** Portions **Parking** On street

The Winter Garden   PLAN 2 F4

◉◉ Modern British

Stunning atrium restaurant at Marylebone hotel

☎ 020 7631 8000   📠 020 7631 8088
The Landmark London, 222 Marylebone Rd NW1 6JQ
e-mail: restaurants.reservation@thelandmark.co.uk
dir: Nearest station: Marylebone. Exit M25 on to A40 and continue 16m following signs for West End. Continue along Marylebone Rd for 300 mtrs. Restaurant on left

One of the last great Victorian railway hotels built during the steam age, The Landmark, opposite Marylebone station, later became offices and headquarters of British Rail. Now a hotel again, The Winter Garden is its stunning open-plan restaurant situated at the base of a magnificent eight-storey atrium, complete with palm trees, in what was once the vast central courtyard. There's a real alfresco feeling during the day, while at

night, it's a more intimate affair, accompanied by a pianist. On the menu is modern British and international cuisine, with dishes like roasted baby beetroot with goats' cheese and pine nuts, or poached Scottish salmon with mousseline potato, samphire, tomato and herb butter sauce. The hotel is also home to the sophisticated Mirror Bar and the Cellars Bar and Restaurant, which offers a more informal menu.

Times 11.30-3/6-11.30

York & Albany   PLAN 1 E4

◉◉◉ – see below

LONDON NW3

Manna   PLAN 1 E4

◉ International Vegetarian V

Gourmet vegetarian and vegan dining

☎ 020 7722 8028   📠 020 7722 8028
4 Erskine Rd, Primrose Hill NW3 3AJ
e-mail: yourhost@manna-veg.com
dir: Nearest station: Chalk Farm Telephone for directions

An avant-garde crusader of the capital's veggie dining scene, founded back in the 1960s, Manna, in leafy Primrose Hill, doesn't stand still. The smart and stylish restaurant delivers top-quality organic ingredients in imaginative, accurately cooked dishes that take

inspiration from across the globe. Think tikka halloumi kebabs (skewers of mango, cherry tomato and halloumi cheese in a tikka marinade served with a raw beetroot and Puy lentil salad and tamarind and apricot chutney) to more homely organic bangers and mash, which is fennel and pumpkin seed sausages served with carrot, parsnip and dill mash, seasonal greens, a red wine, leek and thyme jus and onion rings.

Chef Marlin Janicki **Owner** S Hague, R Swallow, M Kay **Times** 12-3/6.30-11 Closed 25 Dec-1 Jan (open New Year's Eve), Etr Sun, L Mon **Prices** Starter £6-£7, Main £13, Dessert £6-£8, Service added but optional 12.5% **Wines** 10 bottles over £20, 20 bottles under £20, 4 by glass **Notes** Vegetarian menu, Air con **Seats** 50 **Children** Portions **Parking** On street

XO   PLAN 1 E5

◉ Pan Asian

Stylish Pan-Asian dining at trendy Belsize Park venue

☎ 020 7433 0888   📠 020 7794 3474
29 Belsize Ln NW3 5AS
e-mail: xo@rickerrestaurants.com
dir: Nearest station: Swiss Cottage/Belsize Park From Havistock Hill turn right into Ornan Road (Before BP garage), restaurant on right

XO is the fifth addition to the Will Ricker restaurant stable, similar in über-hip style to sibling establishments

continued

York & Albany

LONDON NW1   PLAN 1 E4

Modern British, European NEW
☎ 020 7388 3344   📠 020 7592 1603
127-129 Parkway NW1 7PS
e-mail: yorkandalbany@gordonramsay.com
dir: Nearest station: Camden Town. Please telephone for directions

Angela Hartnett, under the Gordon Ramsay umbrella, has brought some glamour to Regent's Park with the refurbishment of this John Nash building. It positively shines out among its Regency neighbours and is a valuable addition to the area. There's a lively bar, stylish restaurant, accommodation, and a delicatessen called Nonni's, which is housed in the former stables (yes...it's that kind of house) and packed full of Hartnett's favourite produce. Both the bar and restaurant are light and bright spaces with large windows and understatedly elegant

fixtures and fittings. Relax into the comfortable chairs and ponder the menu, which, although displaying plenty of the Italian influences Hartnett is famous for, is broadly modern European in outlook. The produce is given room to shine in dishes of refreshing clarity, and although presentation is sophisticated, the ideas are often simple and traditional. Salad of deep fried lamb's tongue with mâche lettuce makes a memorable starter, while a perfect piece of halibut comes with chorizo and white beans in a faultlessly balanced main course. Finish with chocolate parfait with hazelnut ice cream and a roasted William pear. Amuse-bouche, good sourdough bread and even a small box of salted popcorn served with coffee, confirm this as a confident restaurant delivering the goods.

Chef Angela Hartnett **Owner** Gordon Ramsay Holdings Ltd **Times** 12-3/6-11 **Prices** Fixed L 3 course fr £18, Starter £6-£9, Main £14-£18, Dessert £6-£8, Service added but optional 12.5% **Wines** 100 bottles over £20, 4 bottles under £20, 11 by glass **Notes** Vegetarian available, Dress

restrictions, Casual, no shorts or sportswear, denim ok, Civ Wed 40, Air con **Seats** Pr/dining room 70 **Parking** On street

LONDON NW3 *continued*

such as Notting Hill's E&O (see entry). Its fashionable location in well-heeled Belsize Park is certainly the right part of London for a trendy menu of pan-Asian fusion food. The buzzy low-lit cocktail bar aims squarely at the beautiful people, as does the high-gloss colonial-chic restaurant with white linen-clad tables, dark-wood floors, honeycomb trellis and grey leather banquette seating. The menu offers attractive grazing plates of fusion food, replacing the traditional starter/main course approach with categories such as dim sum, sashimi, tempura, curries and so forth; go for pad Thai, soft-shell crab tempura and black cod with sweet miso, finishing with a European pudding such as ginger cheesecake.

Chef Jon Higgonson **Owner** Will Ricker **Times** 12-3/6-11 Closed 25-26 Dec, **Prices** Fixed L 2 course 12, Fixed D 3 course £39, Starter £3.50-£10, Main £10.50-£23.50, Dessert £4-£4.75, Service added but optional 12.5% **Wines** 60 bottles over £20, 12 bottles under £20, 14 by glass **Notes** Sunday L, Vegetarian available, Air con **Seats** 92, Pr/dining room 22 **Children** Portions, Menu **Parking** On street

LONDON NW4

Fringe Restaurant
PLAN 1 D5

◉ British European

Dramatic setting for modern bistro cooking

☎ 020 8203 3341 & 020 8457 2502 ⬛ 020 8457 2502
Hendon Hall Hotel, Ashley Ln, Hendon NW4 1HF
dir: Nearest station: Hendon Central. M1 junct 2. A406. Right at lights onto Parson St. Next right into Ashley Lane, Hendon Hall is on right

Hendon Hall has its origins in the 16th century, and maintains a suitably historic ambience in its theatrical Gothic-inflected Fringe Restaurant. An opulent colour scheme of gunmetal and claret walls forms the backdrop for polished wooden tables and tangerine high-backed seating, and service from attentive staff is delightful. The kitchen delivers modern bistro-style dishes that are uncomplicated, uncluttered, and aim to pack punchy flavour combinations, as in a starter of warm smoked eel with celeriac, beetroot and horseradish remoulade salad. Continue with braised shoulder of pork, served with sage gnocchi, apple purée and black pudding, and end on a satisfying note with an espresso pannacotta, chocolate jelly and amaretti biscuits.

Chef Conrad Mitchell **Owner** Hand Picked Hotels **Times** 12-2.30/7-10 **Prices** Fixed L 2 course £17, Fixed D 3 course £30, Service included **Wines** 60 bottles over £20, 3 bottles under £20, 10 by glass **Notes** Sunday L, Dress restrictions, Smart casual, Civ Wed 100, Air con **Seats** 40, Pr/dining room 18 **Children** Portions, Menu **Parking** 150

LONDON NW6

Singapore Garden Restaurant
PLAN 1 E4

◉ Singaporean, Malaysian

Well-established oriental restaurant with authentic flavours

☎ 020 7328 5314 & 7624 8233 ⬛ 020 7624 0656
83 Fairfax Rd, West Hampstead NW6 4DY
dir: Nearest station: Swiss Cottage, Finchley Road Off Finchley Rd, on right before Belsize Rd rdbt

The Singapore Garden has been in business in an enclave of chic boutiques near Finchley Road tube station since 1984. The classy neighbourhood restaurant's winning formula is built on a slinky contemporary look in red, gold and beige, and of course its no-holds-barred authentic dishes inspired by the Malaysian, Singaporean and Chinese repertoire. Quality fresh ingredients are used, and the fiery spicing pulls no punches. Go for sour and spicy Singapore laksa soup, kuay pie tee (crispy pastry cups filled with shredded bamboo shoots, chicken and prawns), black pepper and butter crab, beef rendang and Assam curry Ikan (fish curry with okra and aubergines).

Chef Kok Sum Toh **Owner** Hibiscus Restaurants Ltd **Times** 12-2.45/6-10.45 Closed 4 days at Xmas, **Prices** Food prices not confirmed for 2010. Please telephone for details. **Wines** 39 bottles over £20, 4 bottles under £20, 6 by glass **Notes** Sunday L, Vegetarian available, Air con **Seats** 85 **Parking** Meters on street

LONDON SE1

The Anchor & Hope
PLAN 5 F5

◉◉ British

High octane gastro-pub with big-hearted cooking

☎ 020 7928 9898 ⬛ 020 7928 4595
36 The Cut SE1 8LP
e-mail: anchorandhope@btconnect.com
dir: Nearest station: Southwark/Waterloo Please telephone for directions

The A&H gets packed, often as soon as the doors open, and, as you can't book (except for Sunday lunch), it's a case of showing up and being prepared to wait your turn in the bar. Wooden floors and tables, dark aubergine walls and an open kitchen characterise the relaxed, pared-back hard-edged interior, with a heavy curtain separating the high-decibel bar from the dining area. Concisely scripted menus change every meal, driven on by well-sourced seasonal produce. There's no truck with three-course convention either, and some dishes, like tables, are set for sharing; perhaps a steak pie 'for two'. It's robust, gutsy, no-frills British food to warm the heart. Tuck into braised rabbit with cider and bacon, or skate, lentils and green sauce, with perhaps duck ham and quince to start. It's all delivered with informality and zeal by knowledgeable staff.

Chef Trish Hilferty, Warren Fleet **Owner** Robert Shaw, Mike Belben, Jonathon Jones, Harry Lester **Times** 12-2.30/6-10.30 Closed BHs, 25 Dec-1 Jan, L Mon,

D Sun **Prices** Starter £4-£9, Main £10.80-£22, Dessert £3.60-£5, Service optional **Wines** 25 bottles over £20, 26 bottles under £20, 13 by glass **Notes** Sunday L, Vegetarian available **Seats** 58 **Parking** On street

Baltic
PLAN 5 F5

◉ Eastern European

Authentic Eastern European cooking in stylish, modern surroundings

☎ 020 7928 1111 ⬛ 020 7928 8487
74 Blackfriars Rd SE1 8HA
e-mail: info@balticrestaurant.co.uk
dir: Nearest station: Southwark Opposite Southwark station, 5 mins walk from Waterloo

The cool, modern, minimalist Baltic comes with a long steely grey bar up front and airy restaurant behind with 40-foot-high wooden-trussed ceiling. There's a striking chandelier made of shards of amber and an exposed brick wall at the end of the bar, while light pours in through big dining-room skylights. Large contemporary artworks, plain white walls, grey seating and white linen continue the upbeat theme, while the menu encompasses the cooking of the Baltic to Adriatic, though with a suitably modern, clean-flavoured approach. Vodka cocktails, jazz and a decent bar menu add to the appeal, alongside dishes like pierogi (boiled dumplings) filled with spiced pork and bacon, or perhaps chargrilled rump of lamb with smoked aubergine and garlic yogurt.

Times 12-3/6-11 Closed Xmas, 1 Jan, BHs

Canteen
PLAN 5 E5

◉ British NEW

Traditional British cooking beneath the Royal Festival Hall

☎ 0845 686 1122
Royal Festival Hall, Southbank Centre, Belvedere Rd SE1 8XX
e-mail: rfh@canteen.co.uk
dir: Nearest station: Waterloo

Part of the Canteen family, with a sister restaurant in Baker Street (see entry), this place is all about traditional British food done well and served in a modern, comfortable environment. The environment in this case is the basement of the Royal Festival Hall, with the restaurant looking out onto a square where you can dine alfresco if the weather permits. You may not have tickets for a performance, but Canteen's open kitchen provides plenty of entertainment, while the food and the canteen-style furnishings will take you back to your schooldays. The all-day menu makes the most of top-notch British ingredients in classics like macaroni cheese and shepherd's pie, with steamed syrup sponge for pud.

Times 8am-11pm **Prices** Food prices not confirmed for 2010. Please telephone for details.

Cantina del Ponte

PLAN 6 D2

@ Italian

Informal Thames-side Italian with cracking views

☎ 020 7403 5403 📠 020 7940 1845

The Butlers Wharf Building, 36c Shad Thames SE1 2YE
e-mail: cantinareservations@danddlondon.co.uk
dir: Nearest station: Tower Hill, London Bridge. SE side of
Tower Bridge, on river front

Smack on the wharfside promenade, where, on warm
sunny days there's something of a Mediterranean air, the
Cantina's large alfresco terrace is a magnet with its
canopy, olive tree planters and superb views over Tower
Bridge. Inside, glass doors roll back, while clean lines,
fashionable furnishings, terracotta floor tiles and a huge
Italian market mural offer a modern take on the
traditional trattoria. The cooking plays safe, with a
straightforward, accomplished, accessible approach to
regional Italian cooking, with classics like spaghetti with
tomato, olives, capers, anchovy and chilli catching the
eye. Fish might appeal given the waterside location;
perhaps roast sea bass with a sunny fennel salad,
artichoke and walnuts. Italian wines complete the
picture.

Times 12-3/6-11 Closed 24-26 Dec

Cantina Vinopolis

PLAN 6 A3

@ Modern European 🍷

**Dining under the railway arches at London's wine
tasting attraction**

☎ 020 7940 8333 📠 020 7089 9339

1 Bank End SE1 9BU
e-mail: info@cantinavinopolis.com
dir: Nearest station: London Bridge 5 min walk from
London Bridge on Bankside between Southwark Cathedral
& Shakespeare's Globe Theatre

The arches of a Victorian railway viaduct are the setting
for London's wine tasting attraction, Vinopolis, and those
same arches form a stunning feature of the venue's main
restaurant. Cantina Vinopolis occupies a vast space with
high ceilings, exposed brickwork and displays of wine
bottles to remind diners of their whereabouts. The theatre
kitchen creates atmosphere, helped along by the subdued
lighting which also prevents the large room from feeling
cavernous. The menu is largely Mediterranean and each
dish comes with a wine recommendation. Try the freshly
made buffalo ricotta tortelloni with tomato pesto, and
finish with a well-made Valrhona chocolate fondant with
raspberry sorbet.

Chef Moges A Wolde **Owner** Claudio Pulze, Trevor Gulliver
Times 12-3/6-10.30 Closed BHs, D Sun **Prices** Food
prices not confirmed for 2010. Please telephone for
details. **Wines** 193 bottles over £20, 16 bottles under
£20, 50 by glass **Notes** Vegetarian available, Dress
restrictions, Smart casual, Air con **Seats** 200, Pr/dining
room 100 **Children** Portions

Champor Champor

PLAN 6 B2

@ Modern Malay-Asian

Subtle Malay-Asian cooking in magical setting

☎ 020 7403 4600

62-64 Weston St SE1 3QJ
e-mail: mail@champor-champor.com
dir: Nearest station: London Bridge, Joiner St exit. Left
onto Saint Thomas St & 1st right into Weston St,
restaurant 100yds on left

Just behind Guy's Hospital, a stone's throw from London
Bridge, is this charming little Malay restaurant. Step
through the door and you enter a perfumed world of Asian
treasures, with barely a space left uncovered by tribal
masks, Buddhist statues, brightly coloured wall paintings
and intricate carvings. Champor-Champor is a Malay
expression, which loosely translates as 'mix and match'
and the food reflects a mix of Asian cuisines grafted onto
distinctly Malay roots and given a creative twist. In line
with the quirky nature of the restaurant, the menu
eschews pork and veal in favour of more unusual options
including crocodile, soft-shell crab, ostrich, water buffalo
and eel, though there are more 'conventional' dishes as
well. Stir-fried frogs' legs with ginger might precede
roast fillet of ostrich, peanut and Szechuan peppercorn
sauce and compressed rice. To finish, try pandan sponge
and butter pudding with avocado and green tea ice
cream.

Chef Adu Amran Hassan **Owner** Champor-Champor Ltd
Times 6-10 Closed Xmas-New Year (7 days), Etr (5 days),
BHs, Sun, L by appointment only **Prices** Fixed D 3 course
fr £29.50, Tasting menu fr £42.50, Service added but
optional 15% **Wines** 19 bottles over £20, 22 bottles under
£20, 4 by glass **Notes** Tasting menu 7 course, Vegetarian
available, Air con **Seats** 38, Pr/dining room 8 **Parking** On
street, Snowsfields multi-storey

Chino Latino@ The
Riverbank Park Plaza

PLAN 5 D3

@ Modern Pan-Asian

Modern Pan-Asian food in a lively cosmopolitan setting

☎ 020 7769 2500 📠 020 7769 2400

The Riverbank Park Plaza, Albert Embankment SE1 7TJ
e-mail: yyucetepe@pphe.com
dir: Nearest station: Vauxhall Located on south side of
the River Thames at Vauxhall

Chino Latino is the main restaurant of the swish
Riverbank Park Plaza hotel on the South Bank of the River
Thames within easy strolling distance of the Houses of
Parliament. This is a big, buzzy style-conscious eaterie
with the lacquered look of the Orient, all Phillipe Starck-
esque dark wood tables, low-slung leather tub chairs,
back-lit glass panels and dramatic hues of black and
red. If the décor isn't a dead giveaway, the kitchen deals
in quality modern Pan-Asian fusion cooking, drawing on
influences and flavours from Japan, China and Thailand;
sushi and sashimi - available at a bar counter or served
at the table - to dim sum and tempura, and mains such
as black cod with spicy miso.

Chef Paul Thacker, Werner Seebash **Owner** Park Plaza
Hotels **Times** 12-2.30/6-10.30 Closed 25-27 Dec, 1 Jan, L
Sat-Sun **Prices** Fixed L 2 course £54-£74, Fixed D 2
course £54-£74, Starter £3.50-£10.50, Main £11-£26,
Dessert £6.50, Service added but optional 12.5%
Wines 45 bottles over £20, 9 bottles under £20, 8 by
glass **Notes** Vegetarian available, Dress restrictions, No
sportswear, Air con **Seats** 75 **Children** Portions
Parking 60

The County Hall Restaurant

PLAN 5 D5

@ British

**Stunning Thames-side dining in the heart of
Westminster**

☎ 020 7902 8000 & 020 7928 5200 📠 020 7928 5300
London Marriott Hotel, Westminster Bridge Rd SE1 7PB
e-mail: mhrs.lonch.fandb@marriott.com
dir: Nearest station: Waterloo/Westminster. Next to
Westminster Bridge on South Bank. Opposite side to
Houses of Parliament

For stunning views of the London Eye, the Thames and
the Westminster skyline, book a window table at this
riverside restaurant. The elegant crescent-shaped dining
room is located within the impressive Grade I listed
former County Hall and has original oak panelling and
high ceilings and attractively presented tables. The
heritage-style surroundings and the service may be
formal but the menus are bang up-to-date, offering a
good choice of contemporary British dishes prepared with
skill, although some dishes may lack depth of flavour.
Typically, try confit salmon with crab linguini and caviar,
guinea fowl with morel foam, and praline cheesecake
with pumpkin crisps.

Chef Christopher Basten **Owner** Marriott International
Times 12.30-3/5.30-10.30 Closed 26 Dec, **Prices** Fixed L
2 course fr £22, Fixed D 3 course fr £26, Starter £6-
£10.50, Main £17-£26, Dessert £6-£8, Service optional
Wines 95 bottles over £20, 14 by glass **Notes** Jazz menu
£25, Sunday L, Vegetarian available, Dress restrictions,
Smart casual, Civ Wed 100, Air con **Seats** 80, Pr/dining
room 60 **Children** Portions, Menu **Parking** 8, Valet
parking

LONDON SE1 *continued*

Magdalen
PLAN 6 C2

◉◉ British, French

Refined and robust cooking with first-class produce

☎ 020 7403 1342 & 077961 77219 📠 020 7403 9950
152 Tooley St SE1 2TU
e-mail: info@magdalenrestaurant.co.uk
web: www.magdalenrestaurant.co.uk
dir: Nearest station: London Bridge 5 min walk from
London Bridge end of Tooley Street. Restaurant opposite
Unicorn Theatre

Let your train from nearby London Bridge go without you
and eat here instead. The restaurant, covering two floors,
warmly decorated in burgundy and with tables dressed in
their best whites, delivers the kind of food it is worth
delaying a journey for. The fiercely seasonal daily-
changing menu contains produce that has sauntered over
from nearby Borough Market, and the kitchen keeps
things wonderfully simple, but certainly not boring. It's a
tad British, a little bit French, and deals in some of the
less commonly seen produce, cuts and combinations
(hurrah!). There's mutton hotpot with pickled red
cabbage, or how about potato and ogleshield pie? A fish
stew with gurnard, hake, mussels and aïoli is packed
with flavour, and roast grouse is perked up with celeriac,
caramelised apple and redcurrants. Service is charming,
while a notable, French-heavy wine list includes many by
the carafe and glass.

Chef James Faulks, Emma Faulks, David Abbott
Owner Roger Faulks & James Faulks
Times 12-2.30/6.30-10.30 Closed Xmas, BHs, 2wks Aug,
Sun, L Sat **Prices** Fixed L 2 course fr £15.50, Starter
£7.50-£11.50, Main £13.50-£22.50, Dessert £5-£6.50,
Service added but optional 12.5% **Wines** 56 bottles over
£20, 6 bottles under £20, 11 by glass **Notes** Vegetarian
available, Air con **Seats** 90 **Parking** On street

The Oxo Tower Restaurant
PLAN 3 F1

◉◉ Modern European V

Great Thames views and artistically presented food

☎ 020 7803 3888 📠 020 7803 3838
8th Floor, Oxo Tower Wharf, Barge House St SE1 9PH
e-mail: oxo.reservations@harveynichols.co.uk
web: www.harveynichols.com
dir: Nearest station: Blackfriars/Waterloo/Southwark
Between Blackfriars & Waterloo Bridge on the South Bank

Both wide-eyed tourists and blasé locals can't fail to be
impressed by the panoramic views of the river and across
to St Paul's cathedral from this large restaurant on the
8th floor of the Oxo Tower building. Floor-to-ceiling
windows and a terrace ensure everyone gets a good look.
Aping the design of a 1930s ocean liner, there is original
art on the walls, slate tables dressed in white linen
presided over by slick front-of-house staff. The food more
than passes muster. Dishes are essentially modern
British with European influences, so main courses might
include sea bream with razor clams, cockles and a spiced
red pepper sauce or suckling pig with fennel and lemon
verbena and coleslaw. The wine list is as extensive as the
space covering 26 countries over 26 pages.

Chef Jeremy Bloor **Owner** Harvey Nichols & Co Ltd
Times 12-2.30/6-11 Closed 25-26 Dec, D 24 Dec
Prices Fixed L 3 course £33, Starter £9-£16.50, Main
£17.50-£32, Dessert £7.50-£15, Service added but
optional 12.5% **Wines** 660 bottles over £20, 19 bottles
under £20, 23 by glass **Notes** Sunday L, Vegetarian menu,
Civ Wed 120, Air con **Seats** 250 **Children** Portions, Menu
Parking On street, NCP

Le Pont de la Tour
PLAN 6 D2

◉◉ Traditional French

**Stylish Thames-side destination dining with unbeatable
views**

☎ 020 7403 8403
The Butlers Wharf Building, 36d Shad Thames SE1 2YE
dir: Nearest station: Tower Hill, London Bridge SE of
Tower Bridge

With large windows to take in the superb views of Tower
Bridge and watch the world go by on the river and
wharfside promenade, Le Pont holds a winning hand, and
that's before you throw in the big front terrace. On sunny
days there's a real Riviera buzz, so the carte's luxury
items, like seafood platters or caviar capture the mood.
Fish has a strong say on the modern repertoire rooted in
French tradition, perhaps delivering John Dory meunière
with baby squid and an aromatic bouillon, while meat
figures in such dishes as an assiette of Pyrenean milk-
fed lamb with ragoût of haricots blanc and a rosemary
jus. The long dining room is a stylish white-linen zone,
decked out in pastel shades, while the impressive wine
list keeps expectation high. (The more informal Bar &
Grill adjoins.)

Times 12-3/6-11

Roast
PLAN 6 B3

◉ British 🍷

Well-sourced British produce above Borough Market

☎ 020 7940 1300 📠 020 7940 1301
The Floral Hall, Borough Market, Stoney St SE1 1TL
e-mail: info@roast-restaurant.com
dir: Nearest station: London Bridge Please telephone for
directions

Complementing the best views of the foodie haven that is
Borough Market, Roast offers up the best of British using
fantastically sourced produce to create simple,
flavoursome dishes. The split level room with plate glass
windows, partial wood panelling, a chocolate brown
carpet and upholstered brown leather chairs is a great
place to dive into potted Orkney kippers and savour slow-
roast goose leg with a spiced pear. Or pull up to the bar
for (Duchy of Cornwall) oysters and champagne or
perhaps the cocktail of the week which could be a Spring
Bird made with 'housemade' hibiscus vodka, Croft pink
port and sparkling wine. Roasts to share are available
with 24 hours notice.

Roast

Chef Lawrence Keogh **Owner** Iqbal Wahhab
Times 12-3/5.30-11 Closed D Sun **Prices** Starter £5.50-
£15, Main £12-£26, Dessert £5.50, Service added but
optional 12.5% **Wines** 100 bottles over £20, 6 bottles
under £20, 10 by glass **Notes** Sunday L, Vegetarian
available, Civ Wed 150, Air con **Seats** 110
Children Portions, Menu

RSJ, The Restaurant on the South Bank
PLAN 5 F6

◉ Modern

Long-standing restaurant on the South Bank

☎ 020 7928 4554 ▤ 020 7928 9768
33 Coin St SE1 9NR
e-mail: sally.webber@rsj.uk.com
dir: Nearest station: Waterloo Telephone for directions

This unpretentious little restaurant running parallel with
the Thames is ideal for pre- or post-concerts and plays in
the South Bank complex, and heaven sent when trains
are delayed at nearby Waterloo. It buzzes with lively
conversation when other restaurants are just thinking
about opening up, and the cosmopolitan menus can
render decision-making a deliciously slow process. The
menu is largely French with influences from neighbouring
countries, and the cooking is deft and confident, to match
the generous portions. Try something light like pan-fried
halibut and a Dutch tomato salad, or go for a filling slow-
roast shoulder of pork. Whatever your choice, the Loire-
dominated wine list will have something to complement
it.

Times 12-2/5.30-11 Closed Xmas, 1 Jan, Sun, L Sat

LONDON SE3

Chapters All Day Dining
PLAN 8 D1

◉ Modern British

Laid-back all-day dining in smart Blackheath

☎ 020 8333 2666 ▤ 020 8355 8399
43-45 Montpelier Vale, Blackheath Village SE3 0TJ
e-mail: chapters@chaptersrestaurants.co.uk
dir: Nearest station: Blackheath. 5 mins from station,
telephone for directions

The younger sibling of Chapter One (see entry, Bromley) is
these days an up-to-date all-day dining venue. In
Blackheath village (South East London's answer to
Hampstead), a short distance from the perimeter of the
heath itself, it offers breakfast, lunch, tea and dinner
from 8am eggs Benedict to Angus beef fillet cooked over
charcoal embers in the Josper oven. The ambience is
agreeably laid-back, the staff well-versed and chatty,
and the décor in keeping, with exposed brickwork,
undressed tables and outdoor dining too. Start with a
good, thick slab of ham hock, foie gras and celeriac
terrine with plum chutney and toasted sourdough and
end with warm treacle tart with Cornish clotted cream.

Chef Trevor Tobin **Owner** Selective Restaurants Group
Times 8am-11pm Closed 2-4 Jan, **Prices** Starter £3.95-
£6.95, Main £8.95-£22, Dessert £3.95-£6.95, Service
added but optional 12.5% **Wines** 40 bottles over £20, 11
bottles under £20, 15 by glass **Notes** Sunday L,
Vegetarian available, Air con **Seats** 100
Children Portions, Menu **Parking** Car park by station

Laicram Thai Restaurant
PLAN 8 D1

◉ Thai

Authentic Thai in a cosy setting

☎ 020 8852 4710
1 Blackheath Grove, Blackheath SE3 0DD
dir: Nearest station: Blackheath. Opposite station, near
library

The residents of Blackheath Village are lucky to have this
long-standing, authentic Thai restaurant on their
doorstep. It's easy on the wallet and has a homely feel,
decorated with traditional woodcarvings and prints of the
Thai Royal Family on the walls. The staff are friendly and
helpful, and the menu offers many familiar dishes such
as steamed dumplings, spare ribs, Thai salads, prawn
satay, green, yellow and red chicken and beef curries,
phad Thai noodles and pla neung (steamed sea bass with
lime sauce and fresh chilli).

Times 12-2.30/6-11 Closed Xmas & BHs, Mon

LONDON SE10

Rivington Bar & Grill - Greenwich
PLAN 8 A3

◉ British, European

Buzzy surroundings for simple British food

☎ 020 8293 9270 ▤ 020 3259 2082
178 Greenwich High Rd, Greenwich SE10 8NN
e-mail: greenwich@rivingtongrill.co.uk
dir: Nearest station: Greenwich (DLR)

Buzzy, informal brasserie located in a converted pub next
to the Greenwich Picture House. It delivers simple,
seasonal, modern British cooking using quality raw
materials, which shine through in dishes like deep-fried
lamb's sweetbreads with field mushrooms and gribiche
sauce, braised oxtail with parsnip mash, scallops with
squash and black pudding, and Wakefield rhubarb
syllabub. It's decked out in informal style, with dark
wooden floors, white-washed walls and white paper-
clothed tables, and there's a small alfresco terrace and a
mezzanine level above the ground floor.

Owner Caprice Holdings **Times** 12-4/6-11 Closed Mon, L
Tue-Wed **Prices** Starter £4.50-£7.50, Main £8.50-£21,
Dessert £4-£7, Service added but optional **Wines** 40
bottles over £20, 8 bottles under £20, 14 by glass
Notes Sunday L, Vegetarian available, Air con **Seats** 60
Children Portions **Parking** Car park

LONDON SE21

Beauberry House
PLAN 1 F2

◉◉ French, Japanese

**Contemporary French meets oriental fusion food in
Georgian splendour**

☎ 020 8299 9788 ▤ 020 8299 6793
Gallery Rd SE21 7AB
dir: Nearest station: West Dulwich. Telephone for
directions

Housed in a gorgeous snow-white Georgian mansion
(formerly Belair House) in leafy parkland near Dulwich
village, Beauberry is a chic French-meets-East Asian
fusion restaurant. The outdoor terraces have to be one of
south London's best spots for alfresco dining with views
over gardens and lawns, while the White Room with its
pearlescent shell chandeliers recalls images of John
Lennon singing *Imagine* in a pristine white room - even
the tables and chairs are all turned out in their best
whites on a glossy oak floor. The kitchen deals in hybrid
French cuisine with an oriental accent: take Wagyu beef
tartare to start, then caramelised black cod with miso
and black sesame sushi rice or chicken breast stuffed
with crab and mascarpone with chive mash and girolle
sauce.

Times 12-3/6-11 Closed Xmas, 1 Jan, Mon, D Sun

Franklins
PLAN 1 F2

◉ British

Hearty British cooking in Lordship Lane

☎ 020 8299 9598
157 Lordship Ln SE22 8HX
e-mail: info@franklinsrestaurant.com
dir: Nearest station: East Dulwich 0.5m S from station,
via Dog Kennel Hill and Lordship Ln

Looking from the outside like a traditional pub, and with
a small bar serving real ales, Franklins is more than
anything a neighbourhood restaurant. There's a farm
shop next door selling the same produce that appears on
the menu (fruit and vegetables from farms in Kent, for
example) and even some pre-prepared meals for eating
at home. You can watch the chefs at work through a wide
hatch into the kitchen and tuck into unfussy British food
with a real emphasis on old-fashioned cuts of meat and
classical cooking methods. The terse menu features
authentic, muscular dishes starting with Colchester rock
oysters or fillet of beef and piccalilli, and continuing into
mains along the lines of pork chop, duck egg and tomato
relish, with puddings such as treacle tart offering equally
full-on flavours. Go for the daily set lunch menu, offering
3 choices at each course, if you want top value for money.

Chef Ralf Witting **Owner** Tim Sheehan & Rodney Franklin
Times 12-12 Closed 25-26, 31 Dec, 1 Jan, **Prices** Food
prices not confirmed for 2010. Please telephone for
details. **Wines** 7 bottles over £20, 5 bottles under £20, 6
by glass **Notes** Sunday L, Vegetarian available, Air con
Seats 42, Pr/dining room 24 **Children** Portions
Parking Bawdale Road

The Palmerston
PLAN 1 F3

◉ Modern British

Relaxed pub serving good British food

☎ 020 8693 1629 📄 020 8693 9662
91 Lordship Ln, East Dulwich SE22 8EP
e-mail: info@thepalmerston.net
dir: Nearest station: East Dulwich. 10 min walk from
station

Lordship Lane may be full of pubs, bars and restaurants,
but The Palmerston's appeal is broad enough and distinct
enough to keep it throbbing with contented customers. It
is unashamedly 'gastro' in its intentions, although
drinkers help maintain the lively atmosphere. Fires blaze
in winter and, whatever the season, the panelled walls
and high ceiling give the space real character and charm.
The separate dining area has leather banquettes, wooden
chairs and tables, and delivers some impressive modern
British food with the emphasis firmly on good-quality
seasonal produce. Good, honest, but not unsophisticated
dishes include pan-fried foie gras, potato rösti, poached
duck egg yolk and red wine sauce, or peppered free-range
fillet steak with spinach and Cognac. There is also a good
value set lunch.

Chef Jamie Younger **Owner** Jamie Younger, Paul Rigby,
Remi Olajoyegbe **Times** 12-2.30/7-midnight Closed 25-26
Dec, 1 Jan, **Prices** Fixed L 2 course £11, Starter £5-£9,
Main £11.50-£19, Dessert £4.75-£6.50, Service added
but optional 10% **Wines** 34 bottles over £20, 22 bottles
under £20, 17 by glass **Notes** Sunday L, Vegetarian
available, Air con **Seats** 70 **Children** Portions **Parking** On
street

Babur
PLAN 1 G2

◉◉ Modern Indian

**Contemporary Indian cuisine in a stylish ethnic
brasserie**

☎ 020 8291 2400 & 8291 4881 📄 020 8291 4881
119 Brockley Rise, Forest Hill SE23 1JP
e-mail: mail@babur.info
web: www.babur.info
dir: Nearest station: Honor Oak Park 5 min walk from
station, where parking is available

The prowling Bengal tiger on the roof has become a local
landmark at this south London stalwart. Babur is a
stylish Indian brasserie that has been serving superior
cuisine since 1985 and is still going strong. The interior
is decked out with traditional Indian materials and eye-
catching artwork set against exposed Victorian brickwork,
industrial ducting and smart American walnut tables.
Inventive chefs blend traditional and new ideas with
panache and work with novelty ingredients such as
ostrich and buffalo - the latter in a vindaloo whose
tongue-frazzling properties are flagged up by two tiger
heads on the menu. Clove-smoked Yorkshire deer cutlet
with rock salt and fennel seeds might start the ball
rolling, followed by 'Dum-cooked rabbit' - pot-roasted
saddle filled with boneless leg and served with star anise
and ginger broth.

Chef Enam Rahman, Jiwan Lal **Owner** Babur 1998 Ltd
Times 12.30-2.30/6-11.30 Closed 25-26 Dec,
Prices Starter £5.95-£7.95, Main £10.25-£14.95, Dessert
£4.25-£5.50, Service optional **Wines** 9 bottles over £20,
32 bottles under £20, 11 by glass **Notes** Sunday L,
Vegetarian available, Air con **Seats** 72 **Parking** 15, On
street

Mela@ Herne Hill
PLAN 1 F2

◉ Indian V

Contemporary neighbourhood Indian restaurant

☎ 020 7738 5500 📄 020 7738 5505
136-140 Herne Hill SE24 9QH
e-mail: hernehillmela@gmail.com
dir: Nearest station: Herne Hill, Brixton Adjacent to Herne
Hill Station

Formerly known as 3 Monkeys, this upscale
neighbourhood Indian offers an intriguing spread of
pukka regional cuisine from around the sub-continent,
ranging from the Himalayas to the southern coconut
groves of Kerala. It has a smart modern look - no flock
wallpaper or paintings of the Taj Mahal here, thank you:
white walls are hung with modern artwork and furniture
is draped in white cotton. The aromas from the central
open bhatti grill set your taste buds dancing as soon as
you're through the door. Expect Lehsooni whitebait -
marinated in crushed garlic and caraway seeds - then a
Keralan fish Moilee that simmers fish and seafood in
saffron and coconut curry.

Chef Kuldeep Rathore **Owner** Kuldeep Singh
Times 12-2.30/5.30-11 Closed Xmas, **Prices** Fixed L 2
course £2.95-£6.95, Starter £2.25-£4.95, Main £4.95-
£8.95, Dessert £3.50-£3.95, Service added but optional
12.5% **Wines** 20% bottles over £20, 80% bottles under
£20, 9 by glass **Notes** Sunday L, Vegetarian menu, Air con
Seats 90 **Children** Portions, Menu **Parking** On street,
Carver Rd

Al Duca
PLAN 5 B6

◉ Italian

Classic Italian cooking at kindly prices

☎ 020 7839 3090 📄 020 7839 4050
4-5 Duke of York St SW1Y 6LA
e-mail: info@alduca-restaurant.co.uk
dir: Nearest station: Piccadilly 5 mins walk from station
towards Piccadilly. Right into St James's, left into Jermyn
St. Duke of York St halfway along on right

The aim to bring honest-to-goodness, relatively
affordable Italian cooking to central London - St James's,
no less - is a laudable one, and is what keeps Al Duca
buzzing with custom. The press of business can cause
unnerving signs of kitchen strain, and the tables are
tightly packed, but staff are adept and it's hard to argue
with dishes like chargrilled squid with beetroot in lemon
oil, roasted duck breast with braised endive and pine
nuts, and lime pannacotta with chocolate sauce. A range
of traditional pasta dishes and classics such as tiramisù
add to the appeal, as does a well-compiled, exclusively
Italian wine list.

Chef Michele Franzolin **Owner** Cuisine Collection, Claudio
Pulze **Times** 12-3/6-11 Closed Xmas, New Year, BHs, Sun
Prices Fixed L 2 course £22.50, Fixed D 3 course £27.50,

Service added but optional 12.5% **Wines** 118 bottles over £20, 5 bottles under £20, 20 by glass **Notes** Pre & post theatre menu 2-4 course £15-£18, Vegetarian available, Dress restrictions, Smart casual, Air con **Seats** 56 **Children** Portions **Parking** Jermyn St, Duke St

Amaya

PLAN 4 G4

Indian

Ultra chic Knightsbridge Indian

☎ 020 7823 1166 📠 020 7259 6464
Halkin Arcade, Motcomb St SW1X 8JT
e-mail: amaya@realindianfood.com
dir: Nearest station: Knightsbridge Please telephone for directions

By day the huge glazed atrium lets natural light spill into the main restaurant, showcasing the pink sandstone panels and shiny rosewood surfaces. At night the place is transformed into a darkened arena backlit by the dramatically bright open kitchen, where chefs working their tandoori ovens and sigris grills are caught in a theatrical spotlight. Bottles of infused oils add a colourful lustre to the chic cocktail bar. The menu takes its inspiration from all over India, with timeless flavours given a Western interpretation and a cutting-edge presentation. The food is for sharing, and comes in small or large sizes ranged by type with no obvious starters or mains. Try raan mussalam (leg of baby lamb, slow roasted with royal cumin and garam masala) or griddled stuffed baby peppers with goats' cheese and spinach.

Times 12-2.30/6-11.15 Closed 25 Dec

The Avenue

PLAN 5 B5

European

Buzzy, contemporary bar and restaurant

☎ 020 7321 2111 📠 020 7321 2500
7-9 St James's St SW1A 1EE
e-mail: avenue@egami.co.uk
dir: Nearest station: Green Park. Turn right past The Ritz, 2nd turning into St James's St.

The lively, modern Avenue occupies a vast space with a starkly minimalist design, yet it manages to feel intimate

rather than cavernous thanks to the recessed spotlights in the high ceiling, candles on tables and the sheer number of people who populate the bar for after work drinks, often followed by dinner. The lengthy brasserie-format menu offers a straightforward, modern approach, blending the more contemporary alongside classic European dishes. Plenty of seasonal, mostly British produce is in evidence, and in some cases ingredients are of the unfamiliar variety. For instance, an autumn meal may begin with seared diver-caught Poole scallops with Jerusalem artichoke purée, crosnes and red amaranth, followed by whole roast Red-legged partridge with bread sauce and game chips.

Times 12-3/5.45-11.30 Closed 25-26 Dec, 1 Jan, Sun, L Sat

Bank Westminster

PLAN 5 B4

Modern, International

Ultra-modern brasserie-style dining

☎ 020 7630 6644 & 7630 6630 📠 020 7630 5665
45 Buckingham Gate SW1E 6BS
e-mail: westminster.reservations@bankrestaurants.com
dir: Nearest station: St James's Park. Facing Buckingham Palace, left to Buckingham Gate, after 100mtrs hotel on right

A short walk from Buckingham Palace, attached to the elegant Crowne Plaze St James Hotel, sits the ultra-modern Bank Restaurant and its chic drinking partner, the stylish Zander cocktail bar, with its breathtaking long bar. The circular conservatory restaurant leads onto a Parisian-style terrace with a tranquil Victorian courtyard as a backdrop - perfect for summer alfresco dining. The cooking is modern and global, almost gastro pub-style with a mix of European and Asian dishes, such as chilli squid with Thai noodle salad, roast halibut with asparagus and shellfish dressing, and calves' liver with mash and onion rings.

Times 12-3/5.30-10.30 Closed 25 & 26 Dec, 1 Jan, BHs, Sun, L Sat

Boisdale of Belgravia

PLAN 4 H3

British

Scottish club-like restaurant in Belgravia

☎ 020 7730 6922 📠 020 7730 0548
15 Eccleston St SW1W 9LX
e-mail: info@boisdale.co.uk
dir: Nearest station: Victoria Turn left along Buckingham Palace Rd heading W, Eccleston St is 1st on right

The embassy of Highland hospitality south of the border, this Boisdale outpost is in an elegant Regency townhouse close to Buckingham Palace Road; it is named after a remote part in the Outer Hebrides, and is also home to The Boisdale Jazz and Cigar Club. The labyrinth of different dining areas include Auld Restaurant, the oldest part of the building, the elegant Jacobite Room, which is wood panelled and hung with paintings, ornate mirrors and chandeliers, and the informal back bar and courtyard garden. The patriotic menu showcases quality Scottish

produce. Start with pigeon, rabbit and pistachio terrine with Glenfarclas 10-year marinated prunes with melba toast, followed by seared fillet of organic Shetland sea trout with razor clams, wild garlic, purple sprouting broccoli, Jersey Royals and hollandaise sauce. There is a sister City venue at Bishopsgate (see entry).

Chef Colin Wint **Owner** Mr R Macdonald
Times 12-3/7-11.15 Closed Xmas, New Year, Etr, BHs, Sun, L Sat **Prices** Fixed L 2 course £18.70, Fixed D 3 course £18.70, Starter £5.70-£17.50, Main £13-£51.50, Dessert £6.50-£7.95, Service added but optional 12.5% **Wines** 150 bottles over £20, 8 bottles under £20, 30 by glass **Notes** Pre-theatre 3 course £18.70, Vegetarian available, Dress restrictions, Smart casual, Air con **Seats** 140, Pr/dining room 34 **Parking** On street, Belgrave Sq

The Botanist

PLAN 4 G2

British, French NEW

Lively and stylish Chelsea eatery

☎ 020 7730 0077 📠 020 7730 7177
7 Sloane Square SW1W 8EE
e-mail: info@thebotanistonsloanesquare.com
dir: Nearest station: Sloane Square Located in Sloane Square, to the right as you exit the tube station

The Botanist in mind is Sir Hans Sloane, a man who is worth Googling if you don't know his story already, not least for his part in the creation of milk chocolate. Ed and Tom Martin of the White Swan and Gun fame (see entries) have created a popular and stylish venue on a corner site in Sloane Square. Tables are tightly packed, windows open on to the street, there's a lively bar, and varying types of wood and earthy colours enhance the botanical theme. The menu has mostly modern British and French sensibilities. Start with globe artichoke, morel and spinach risotto with parmesan cream, followed by grilled 35-day aged rib-eye steak with hand-cut chips, rocket, red wine jus and béarnaise sauce.

Chef Shannon Wilson **Owner** Tom & Ed Martin
Times 12-3.30/6-10.30 **Prices** Starter £6.50-£11, Main £11.50-£19, Dessert £5-£9.50, Service added but optional 12.5% **Wines** 114 bottles over £20, 17 bottles under £20, 16 by glass **Notes** Pre-theatre D 2 course 5.30-6.30pm, Sunday L, Vegetarian available, Air con **Seats** 65 **Children** Portions **Parking** Metered parking available

LONDON SW1 *continued*

Boxwood Café

PLAN 4 G4

◉◉ British **V**

Slick brasserie in high-class hotel

☎ 020 7235 1010 ▤ 020 7235 1011
The Berkeley, Wilton Place, Knightsbridge SW1X 7RL
e-mail: boxwoodcafe@gordonramsay.com
dir: Nearest station: Knightsbridge Please telephone for directions or see website

The glitzy Knightsbridge location sets the tone for Gordon Ramsay's establishment in a basement beneath the Berkeley Hotel. This is a rather swish take on a New York-style café, all pastel leather, glossy surfaces and dark wood - shiny, metropolitan glamour, in short, and with a style-conscious clientele to match. Staff are young, cheery and well-briefed, in fact they add greatly to the ambience of this subterranean space. The cooking is modern British, jazzed-up brasserie fodder, with some inventive combinations among the classics. A lush starter of roast foie gras with poached spice, black fig, pickled ginger and hazelnuts hits the spot, then a vibrant fillet of halibut comes with garlic cream, Savoy cabbage and wild mushrooms.

Chef Stuart Gillies **Owner** Gordon Ramsay Holdings Ltd
Times 12-3/6-11 **Prices** Fixed L 2 course £21, Starter £7.50-£14.50, Main £12-£33, Dessert £7-£8, Service added but optional 12.5% **Wines** 100 bottles over £20, 12 by glass **Notes** Taste of Boxwood 6 course £55, Sunday L, Vegetarian menu, Air con **Seats** 140, Pr/dining room 16 **Children** Portions, Menu **Parking** On street

Brasserie Roux

PLAN 5 B6

◉ French

Simple French brasserie food on Pall Mall

☎ 020 7968 2900 ▤ 020 7389 7647
Sofitel St James London, 6 Waterloo Place SW1Y 4AN
e-mail: info@brasserieroux.com
dir: Nearest station: Piccadilly Circus. Please telephone for directions

The St James's branch of the Sofitel chain, on a corner of Pall Mall, is a suitably grand setting for the ground-floor brasserie, which has its own entrance. A rich yellow palette with furnishings in tones of red and green makes a refined environment for the Roux-influenced French cooking. Expect steamed leeks with a poached egg in sauce ravigote, omelette Arnold Bennett, and rack of lamb with roast garlic and ratatouille, while a crowd-pleasing option consists of a trio of mini-cheeseburgers, variously topped with Comté, goats' cheese and stilton. Finish classically with rum baba and pineapple.

Chef Paul Danabie **Owner** Accor UK **Times** 12-3/5.30-11 **Prices** Fixed L 3 course fr £19, Fixed D 3 course fr £19.50, Starter £7-£14, Main £14.50-£25, Dessert £7-£8.50, Service added but optional 12.5% **Wines** 12 by glass **Notes** Pre-theatre menu 5.30-6.30pm, Vegetarian available, Civ Wed 150, Air con **Seats** 100, Pr/dining room 130 **Children** Portions, Menu **Parking** NCP at Piccadilly

Brasserie Saint Jacques

PLAN 5 A6

◉◉ Traditional French **NEW**

Classic French brasserie in the heart of St James's

☎ 020 7930 7100
33 St James's St SW1A 1HD
e-mail: brasseriestjacques@btconnect.com
dir: Nearest station: Green Park Please telephone for directions

Occupying the original Petrus restaurant site in St James's, this bright, friendly French brasserie has yellow walls adorned with French framed posters. Polished wooden floors and tables plus red leather chairs and banquette seating in the booths add to the atmosphere. Pierre Koffmann, a chef of considerable reputation and experience, is acting as a consultant, putting together the menus and kitchen team. Expect a traditional brasserie-style service with a menu full of French classics, as well as daily specials with strong regional accents, beautifully cooked and full of flavour. Starters such as foie gras terrine with raisin brioche might precede cod cooked with shellfish in a saffron-flavoured broth. Finish with crème caramel or iced hazelnut nougat terrine for dessert. The extensive wine list is predominantly, but not exclusively, French.

Chef Pierre Koffmann, Rory Duncan **Owner** Claudio Pulze **Times** 12-2.30/6-11 Closed BHs, Sun **Prices** Starter £6-£9.50, Main £10-£18.50, Dessert £5.50-£6, Service added but optional 12.5% **Notes** Vegetarian available, Air con **Seats** 80, Pr/dining room 20 **Children** Portions

Le Caprice Restaurant

PLAN 5 A6

◉◉ Modern European **V**

Quality cooking in a restaurant that still brings out the stars

☎ 020 7629 2239 ▤ 020 7493 9040
Arlington House, Arlington St SW1A 1RJ
e-mail: reservation@le-caprice.co.uk
dir: Nearest station: Green Park Arlington St runs beside The Ritz. Restaurant is at end

Le Caprice has been a byword for timeless chic since it sashayed into the hearts of London diners over a quarter of a century ago. The décor exudes a certain 80s retro glamour, a clean-cut monochrome, smoky-glass Manhattan piano bar look that started here and became a template for many a metropolitan brasserie. Service is impeccably egalitarian, despite its ritzy St James's location, but you'll need to book well ahead to score a table. The high tally of celebs is bolstered by those framed in black-and-white David Bailey photographs. Perennials such as eggs Benedict, salmon fishcakes and deep-fried haddock and chips turn up on a medley of European brasserie comfort food, while a Thai-baked sea bass with fragrant rice flirts with exotica. Take top quality and seasonality of produce as read.

Chef Paul Brown **Owner** Caprice Holdings Ltd **Times** 12-3/5.30-12 Closed 25-26 Dec, 1 Jan, Aug BH, 24 Dec **Prices** Fixed D 3 course fr £25.50, Starter £6.50-£16.50, Main £14-£27.50, Dessert £5.75-£7.50, Service optional **Wines** 120 bottles over £20, 5 bottles under £20, 22 by glass **Notes** Sunday L, Vegetarian menu, Air con **Seats** 80 **Children** Portions **Parking** On street, NCP

Le Cercle

PLAN 4 F3

◉◉ Modern French

Discreet basement restaurant offering modern French grazing food

☎ 020 7901 9999 ▤ 020 7901 9111
1 Wilbraham Place SW1X 9AE
e-mail: info@lecercle.co.uk
web: www.clubgascon.com/lc_intro.php
dir: Nearest station: Sloane Square Just off Sloane St

If the name isn't a dead giveaway, Le Cercle is French through and through, with its roots in Gascony - it is, after all, an offshoot of Club Gascon (see entry). A whiff of discreet glamour suffuses this classy basement restaurant to suit its location just off Sloane Square. The menu is a Tour de France of regional dishes, divided into sections covering seafood, vegetables, 'the farm' and 'plaisirs', served in modishly small tapas-style portions. Food has a thoroughly Gallic pedigree, so dishes are not overworked and retain an excellent clarity of flavours. Knowledgeable staff deliver slick service and make confident recommendations from the menu. To start, foie gras Cercle is topped with a sweet Sauternes-type jelly and served with brioche, then translucent braised cod is served with chorizo on a bed of 'barleysotto'.

Chef Thierry Beyris, Pierre Sang Boyer **Owner** Vincent Labeyrie & Pascal Aussignac **Times** 12-3/6-11 Closed Xmas & New Year, Sun, Mon **Prices** Fixed L 3 course fr £15, Fixed D 3 course fr £17.50, Tasting menu fr £35, Starter £5-£8, Main £6.50-£35, Dessert £3-£6, Service added 12.5% **Wines** 216 bottles over £20, 15 by glass **Notes** Pre/post-theatre D 6-7pm & 10-11pm, Tasting menu 5 course, Vegetarian available, Air con **Seats** 60, Pr/dining room 12 **Children** Menu **Parking** Outside after 6pm, NCP in Cadogan Sq

The Cinnamon Club

PLAN 5 C4

◎◎ Modern Indian

Sophisticated Indian dining in former library

☎ 020 7222 2555 🖹 020 7222 1333
**The Old Westminster Library, 30-32 Great Smith St
SW1P 3BU**
e-mail: info@cinnamonclub.com
dir: Nearest station: Westminster Take exit 6, across
Parliament Sq, then pass Westminster Abbey on left. Take
1st left into Great Smith St

The impressive Grade II listed building - the old
Westminster Library - makes an unusual setting for a
contemporary Indian meal. Still with a gallery of books
lining walls above the spacious dining hall, its high
ceilings and skylights, parquet floors and dark wood
deliver a clubby, old-English colonial charm amidst the
aromas of Indian spices. High-backed banquettes and
chairs, crisp white linen on the tables and smartly
uniformed staff complete the elegant picture, while the
clean-cut, well-presented modern Indian cuisine comes
driven by fine ingredients and well-judged spicing.
Breakfast, lunch, fixed-price, carte and tasting menus
offer an appealing range; think chargrilled duck breast
served with sesame-tamarind sauce, and, from a decent
choice of desserts, perhaps date and semolina pudding
with caramelised walnut ice cream.

Chef Vivek Singh **Owner** Various Investors
Times 12-2.45/6-10.45 Closed BHs, Sun **Prices** Fixed L 2
course £19, Fixed D 3 course £25, Starter £7.50-£12,
Main £14-£35, Dessert £4-£12, Service added but
optional 12.5% **Notes** Vegetarian available, Dress
restrictions, Smart casual, Civ Wed 130, Air con
Seats 130, Pr/dining room 60 **Parking** Parliament Square

City Café

PLAN 5 C3

◎◎ Modern European NEW

**Contemporary dining at glossy art-themed city centre
hotel**

☎ 020 7932 4600 🖹 020 7233 7575
City Inn Westminster, 30 John Islip St SW1P 4DD
e-mail: westminster.citycafe@cityinn.com
dir: Nearest station: Pimlico/Westminster From Pimlico,
follow signs for Tate Britain, just beyond rear entrance.
From Westminster, head towards Millbank. Turn right at
Millbank Tower

The City Inn group's flagship hotel is a glossy modern
purpose-built chunk of glass on the riverside right by
Tate Britain. Art is quite a theme here - there's even an
in-house curator to ensure an ever-changing exhibition of
paintings for the walls. A floor-to-ceiling wall of glass
lets light flood in on the spacious, softly-textured neutral
tones of beige and cream in the City Café restaurant, or
the covered boulevard 'Art Street' terrace is great for
alfresco meals. A well-drilled, friendly team delivers
professional service and simple, modern European
cuisine with tried-and-tested flavour combinations.
Grilled mackerel with Lyonnaise potato cake and parsley
velouté is typical of starters, while main courses might
offer a rustic-style dish of braised salt beef with carrots,
cavolo nero and grain mustard broth.

Chef Peter Lloyd **Owner** City Inn Ltd **Times** 12-3/5.30-10.30
Prices Fixed L 2 course £9.95, Fixed D 3 course £16.50,
Starter £4.95-£6.95, Main £9.95-£19.95, Dessert £5.50-
£5.95, Service added but optional 10% **Wines** 44 bottles
over £20, 13 bottles under £20, 29 by glass **Notes** Sunday
L, Vegetarian available, Dress restrictions, Smart casual,
Civ Wed 130, Air con **Seats** 148, Pr/dining room 130
Children Portions, Menu **Parking** 35, Masterpark car park

David Britton at The Cavendish

PLAN 5 B6

◎ Modern British

**Prestigious St James's setting for traditional and
contemporary cuisine**

☎ 020 7930 2111 🖹 020 7839 2125
The Cavendish London, 81 Jermyn St SW1Y 6JF
e-mail: info@thecavendishlondon.com
web: www.thecavendishlondon.com
dir: Nearest station: Green Park, Piccadilly Situated
directly behind Fortnum & Mason department store

In a quiet location just minutes from Piccadilly Circus,
the stylish Cavendish Hotel is home to the popular David
Britton at The Cavendish Restaurant. It was once owned

and run by Rosa Lewis, 'the Duchess of Duke Street',
famous in London society for her hospitality and cooking.
The first-floor restaurant continues the tradition of
gracious hospitality with attentive staff and a relaxed
style with no dress code. Diners can watch the smart St
James's galleries and boutiques below through the large
plate-glass windows. The modern British food, with
European influences, is a blend of traditional favourites
and contemporary dishes, so expect starters such as
Scottish monkfish and tuna carpaccio with rocket salad
and lemon squash, followed by roasted Welsh lamb rump
with minted suet pudding, smoked bacon and carrot
purée.

Chef David Britton **Owner** Ellerman Investments Ltd
Times 12-2.30/5.30-10.30 Closed 25-26 Dec, 1 Jan, L
Sat-Sun & BH Mon **Prices** Fixed L 2 course £14.95, Fixed
D 3 course £19.95, Starter £6-£10.50, Main £14.50-
£19.50, Dessert £6.50, Service added but optional 12.5%
Wines 20 bottles over £20, 10 bottles under £20, 10 by
glass **Notes** Pre-theatre menu available 2 course £14.95,
Vegetarian available, Air con **Seats** 80, Pr/dining room 70
Children Portions, Menu **Parking** 60, secure on-site valet
parking

Ebury

PLAN 4 G2

◎ British, French

Fashionable, buzzy Pimlico bar-brasserie

☎ 020 7730 6784 🖹 020 7730 6149
11 Pimlico Rd SW1W 8NA
e-mail: info@theebury.co.uk
dir: Nearest station: Sloane Sq/Victoria. From Sloane Sq
tube, left into Holbein Place, then left at junct with
Pimlico Rd. The Ebury is on corner of Pimlico Rd &
Ranelagh Grove

With whopping arch-like windows, this easy-on-the-eye,
contemporary bar-brasserie makes a good first
impression. Inside it's a large, light, open space,
fashionably decked out with a stylish modern
arrangement of low-slung chocolate-brown leather
seating and low polished-wood tables, while the big
central bar has matching stools and high bar tables
(plus a separate bar menu). The kitchen's stock in trade
is simple, accessible, crowd-pleasing brasserie-style
food, so expect classics like calves' liver with traditional
bedfellows of bacon, onion marmalade and mash, or
perhaps a more modish offering of black bream served
with a warm salad of truffled artichokes. Desserts are the
comfort variety, maybe bread-and-butter pudding with
crème anglaise, though - as with all dishes here - light,
modern renditions.

continued

LONDON SW1 *continued*

Chef Christophe Clerget **Owner** First Restaurant
Times 12-3.30/6-10.30 Closed 24-30 Dec, **Prices** Fixed L
2 course £13.50, Starter £3.50-£9, Main £10-£16.50,
Dessert £5.50-£6.50, Service added but optional 12.5%
Wines 48 bottles over £20, 16 bottles under £20, 13 by
glass **Notes** Pre-theatre menu 2 course £13.50, 3 course
£16.50 6-7.30pm, Sunday L, Vegetarian available, Air con
Seats 60, Pr/dining room 50 **Children** Portions, Menu
Parking NCP

Fifth Floor Restaurant
PLAN 4 F4

◎◎ French, European

Fashionable dining at landmark London store

☎ 020 7235 5250 & 7235 5000 ▤ 0870 191 6019
Harvey Nichols, 109-125 Knightsbridge SW1X 7RJ
e-mail: reception@harveynichols.com
web: www.harveynichols.com
dir: Nearest station: Knightsbridge, Hyde Park Corner
Entrance on Sloane Street

Harvey Nick's Fifth Floor food hall is a perennial fixture on
the see and be seen list, as dear to the hearts of
Knightsbridge ladies-who-lunch as their Prada
handbags. The funky bar cranks up the decibels for a
drink before lunch or dinner with a bright new look
inspired by Russian 20th-century Constructivist art. The
clinically white space of the flagship restaurant brings to
mind retro 60s sci-fi, like a *Barbarella* film set with its
fibre optic lighting, glass-domed ceiling and leather and
chrome tubular chairs. As you'd expect, the kitchen's
modern-European brasserie dishes are easy on the eye,
but there's no lack of substance here: the menu is
focused, based on exemplary ingredients, and prepared
with sound skills, featured in beautifully-cooked roast
pollock with olive and pine nut salsa, and watercress and
parsley pesto. Tempting puddings might offer a bergamot
crème brûlée with passionfruit sorbet.

Chef Jonas Karlsson **Owner** Harvey Nichols Ltd
Times 12-3/6-11 Closed Xmas, Etr Sun, D Sun
Prices Fixed L 2 course £19.50, Fixed D 3 course £24.50,
Tasting menu £55, Starter £7.50-£14, Main £17.50-£26,
Dessert £7.50-£8.50, Service added but optional 12.5%
Wines 700 bottles over £20, 30 bottles under £20, 30 by
glass **Notes** Sunday L, Vegetarian available, Air con
Seats 120 **Children** Portions, Menu **Parking** On street,
NCP opposite

Foliage
PLAN 4 F4

◎◎◎◎ – *see opposite page*

The Goring
PLAN 4 H4

◎◎ Traditional British

Unapologetically nostalgic luxury with modern comforts

☎ 020 7396 9000 ▤ 020 7834 4393
Beeston Place SW1W 0JW
e-mail: reception@thegoring.com
web: www.thegoring.com
dir: Nearest station: Victoria From Victoria St turn left
into Grosvenor Gdns, cross Buckingham Palace Rd, 75yds
turn right into Beeston Place

This bastion of Britishness - presided over by 4th
generation Jeremy Goring - provides a nostalgic taste of
the past but with all the comforts of modern life. Just a
stroll from Buckingham Palace, the Victorian dining room
is as sumptuously decorated as you might expect from a
luxury hotel and also benefits from being light and airy.
Designer David Linley has brought the room into the 21st-
century and helped it to shake off any hint of stuffiness.
The staff are superbly friendly and service is exacting.
The menu is chock-full of British classics created using
the best of British produce. Start with deep-fried
whitebait or eggs Drumkilbo with brown bread and butter
before wing of Guernsey skate with black butter and
capers. Puddings and British cheeses are served from the
trolley. The garden bar and drawing room are popular for
more informal snacks, afternoon tea and cocktails.

Chef Derek Quelch **Owner** Goring Family
Times 12.30-2.30/6-10 Closed L Sat **Prices** Fixed L 3
course fr £35, Fixed D 3 course fr £47.50, Service added
but optional 12.5% **Wines** 400 bottles over £20, 10 by
glass **Notes** Pre-theatre D available, Sunday L,
Vegetarian available, Dress restrictions, Smart dress, Civ
Wed 50, Air con **Seats** 70, Pr/dining room 50
Children Portions, Menu **Parking** 7

Il Convivio
PLAN 4 H2

◎◎ Modern Italian

Stylish Italian dining in upmarket Belgravia

☎ 020 7730 4099 ▤ 020 7730 4103
143 Ebury St SW1W 9QN
e-mail: comments@etruscarestaurants.com
dir: Nearest station: Victoria 7 min walk from Victoria
Station - corner of Ebury St and Elizabeth St

The combination of the quiet residential street in smart
Belgravia and the handsomeness of the converted
Georgian house makes for an alluring and chic location.
The split-level premises has a few sought-after tables at
street level, with the main restaurant on the lower level. A
conservatory-style room has a sliding roof so the space
magically becomes alfresco when the weather allows.
Deep red walls hung with stone slabs inscribed with
quotes from Dante's *Il Convivio* are set off by modern
wooden-backed chairs and cream leather cushions. The
upmarket Italian cuisine includes a few unconventional
touches that show the kitchen has confidence. Wild
pollock carpaccio risotto comes with a fig and anchovy
pesto, and veal shank ravioli is served in a creamy wild
mushroom sauce. A wide-ranging choice is supplemented
by daily specials and an extensive wine list.

Chef Lukas Pfaff **Owner** Piero & Enzo Quaradeghini
Times 12-2.45/7-10.45 Closed Xmas, New Year, BHs, Sun
Prices Fixed L 2 course £14.50, Fixed D 2 course £17.50,
Starter £7.50-£14, Main £18-£26, Dessert £5.50-£10.50,
Service added but optional 12.5% **Wines** 156 bottles over
£20, 12 bottles under £20, 10 by glass **Notes** Vegetarian
available, Dress restrictions, Smart casual, Air con
Seats 65, Pr/dining room 14 **Parking** On street

Inn the Park
PLAN 5 C5

◎ British

**Relaxed all-day café and restaurant in city centre
Royal park**

☎ 020 7451 9999 ▤ 020 7451 9998
St James's Park SW1A 1AA
e-mail: info@innthepark.co.uk
dir: Nearest station: St James's Park, Charing Cross 200
metres down The Mall towards Buckingham Palace

Oliver Peyton's grass-roofed, Scandinavian-style
restaurant is, quite literally, a breath of fresh air when
fine weather lets you dine out on the decked terrace
overlooking the duck lake in St James's Park. Walls of
full-length glass mean you get the same lovely views
indoors, where there's an all-day café with a self-service
counter; in the evening it morphs into a relaxed, romantic
restaurant in one of the best spots in town. Expect
straightforward, full-flavoured, brasserie-style dishes
built on materials from artisan specialist producers. Start

continued on page 258

Foliage

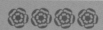

LONDON SW1 PLAN 4 F4

Modern European

Intricate cooking in one of the capital's most fashionable addresses

☎ 020 7235 2000 📠 020 7235 2001
Mandarin Oriental Hyde Park, 66 Knightsbridge SW1X 7LA
e-mail: molon-reservations@mohg.com
web: www.mandarinoriental.com/london
dir: Nearest station: Knightsbridge. With Harrods on right, hotel is 0.5m on left, opposite Harvey Nichols

The imposing Edwardian frontage with fluttering flags and liveried doormen on duty might give the impression of a five-star hotel from the old school. Think again. This imposingly luxurious Knightsbridge hotel, backing onto Hyde Park, is no dinosaur; from the cut of the staff's clothes to the no-expense-spared impact of the Foliage restaurant, this is a classy and contemporary destination. The park is the inspiration for the restaurant's name and look, but this is no theme park - striking flower displays, rosewood panelling and vast lit-glass panels filled with thousands of white silk leaves that change colour and mood, make for a calmly civilised and engaging space. The park itself can be seen through large picture windows. As we go to press, we hear that Chris Staines will be leaving during the life of this guidebook, and the exciting news that Foliage is the location where

Heston Blumenthal will be opening his new London restaurant in the autumn of 2010. Meanwhile, Foliage continues to offer a fixed-price carte, good value fixed-price lunch and tasting menu, all based on exceptional produce and delivering an array of wonderfully creative dishes. Presentation provides real impact, as in a stunning first-course foie gras terrine served with apricots (chutney and purée), hazelnuts, port jelly and a cep brioche. An intermediate course (part of both lunch and dinner menus) might be red mullet, partnered with squid 'bolognese', confit potato and parmesan foam, before main-course partridge with luscious truffle polenta, pistachios, mushroom purée and a shallot tarte Tatin. The technical proficiency of the kitchen and its dynamically modern European intentions can be seen in an apple tarte Tatin dessert, which is a superbly creative interpretation. Service is five-star and not without a personal touch.

Chef Chris Staines **Owner** Mandarin Oriental Hyde Park
Times 12-2.30/7-10.30 Closed 26 Dec, 1 Jan **Prices** Fixed D 4 course £60-£65, Service added but optional 12.5%
Wines 400 bottles over £20, 20 by glass
Notes Fixed L 4 course £29-£35, Sunday L, Vegetarian available, Dress restrictions, Smart casual, Civ Wed 250, Air con **Seats** 46 **Children** Menu
Parking Valet parking, NCP

LONDON SW1 *continued*

with smoked eel with bacon and dandelion followed by Shetland organic salmon and haddock fishcake with poached egg and herb butter sauce, and treacle tart with clotted cream for pudding.

Times 12-3/6-10.45 Closed D Sun-Mon (winter)

JB's Restaurant
PLAN 5 A3

◉ Modern French, Mediterranean

Modern hotel brasserie dining

☎ 020 7769 9772 & 020 7769 9999 🖹 020 7769 9998
Park Plaza Victoria, 239 Vauxhall Bridge Rd SW1V 1EQ
e-mail: gfernando@pphe.com
dir: Nearest station: 2 min walk from Apollo Victoria Theatre

Conveniently close to Victoria station, this smart modern hotel has airy, stylish public areas that include an elegant bar and restaurant as well as a popular coffee bar. The restaurant (JB's) follows the contemporary theme with its expansive windows and a lengthy, crowd-pleasing menu. It takes a something for everyone approach with its medley of modern and classic dishes; simple, good-looking, well-executed dishes, based on quality produce, include the likes of grilled sea bass with braised artichokes and saffron aïoli or chargrilled Bannockburn sirloin steak with Café de Paris butter and Madeira sauce. For dessert, perhaps a coconut cheesecake with spiced mango compôte.

Chef Jonathan Jones **Owner** Park Plaza Hotels **Times** 6-10 Closed BHs, Sun, L all week **Prices** Fixed D 2 course £18, Starter £5.50-£12.50, Main £9-£25, Dessert £5.95-£6.50, Service added but optional 12.5% **Wines** 27 bottles over £20, 11 bottles under £20, 12 by glass **Notes** Pre-theatre D available from 6-7pm 2 course £18, Dress restrictions, Smart casual, Air con **Seats** 90 **Children** Portions **Parking** 31

Just St James
PLAN 5 B5

◉ Modern British

Palatial bank building offering the best of British

☎ 020 7976 2222 🖹 020 7976 2020
12 St James's St SW1A 1ER
e-mail: bookings@juststjames.com
dir: Nearest station: Green Park Turn right on Piccadilly towards Piccadilly Circus, then right into St James's St. Restaurant on corner of St James's St & King St

The modern restaurant industry would be hard pressed without a steady supply of Victorian bank conversions to inhabit, and here is one of the more palatial. Formerly a Lloyd's, it boasts a marble-columned restaurant and lounge bar, among other spaces for eating and drinking. A menu of 'British provender' is offered, encompassing Colchester rock oysters in shallot vinegar, rump of spring lamb with minted sweetbread and pea ragout, a stuffed slow-roasted tomato and rosemary jus, or poached salmon with creamed potatoes in lemon and broad bean sauce. Desserts include banoffee pie and cherry

cheesecake, and there is also a listing of cheese-based savouries, such as Welsh rarebit made with Caerphilly.

Times 12-3/6-11 Closed 25-26 Dec, 1 Jan, Sun, L Sat

Ken Lo's Memories of China
PLAN 4 H3

◉ Chinese

Authentic Chinese cooking at legendary restaurant

☎ 020 7730 7734 🖹 020 7730 2992
65-69 Ebury St SW1W 0NZ
e-mail: memoriesofchina@btconnect.com
web: www.memories-of-china.co.uk
dir: Nearest station: Victoria. At junction of Ebury Street & Eccleston St

High quality, authentic Chinese cuisine is the order of the day at this long-established Pimlico restaurant. Quality extends to the stylish table settings, starched linen and chopsticks, as well as the contemporary, colourful Chinese décor and speedy and efficient service. A lengthy carte showcases the classic Chinese food, and there is also a set menu that offers excellent value for money from the same quality produce and delivering the same refined presentation; there's also a group menu for parties of 6 or more. Enjoy skilful, accurate cooking in dishes like crispy seaweed with almonds, three-spiced hot-fried salt-and-pepper pork choplettes, or quick fried 'three precious flavours' in black bean sauce (scallops, prawns and chicken).

Times 12-2.30/7-11 Closed BHs, L Sun

Luciano
PLAN 5 B5

◉◉ Italian

Glamorous 'Marco' Italian near Piccadilly

☎ 020 7408 1440 🖹 020 7493 6670
72-73 St James's St SW1A 1PH
e-mail: info@lucianorestaurant.co.uk
dir: Nearest station: Green Park Please telephone for directions

Madame Prunier's celebrated fish restaurant used to attract the rich and famous to this very spot until it closed a few decades ago. Now Luciano's has a similar cachet that matches the St James's Street setting. An impressively large bar, brightly lit and with a magnificent mosaic-tiled floor, encourages diners to linger over a dazzling menu of cocktails. Provocative photographs line the walls of the restaurant, where slate pillars run down both sides of the room, and mood lighting is subtly dimmed as the evening progresses. Well-trained staff are

attentive without being intrusive. Marco Pierre White has collaborated with Rocco Forte to create this glamorous venue, and the menus deliver classic Italian dishes made from first-class ingredients by top-notch chefs. Start with tuna tartare, following on with veal cutlet with porcini.

Chef Marco Corsica **Owner** Marco Pierre White **Times** 12-3/6-11 Closed Xmas, 1 Jan, Etr day, BHs, D 24 Dec **Prices** Fixed L 2 course fr £17.95, Starter £8.95-£13.95, Main £15.95-£25, Dessert £7-£7.50, Service added but optional 12.5% **Wines** 150 bottles over £20, 5 bottles under £20, 12 by glass **Notes** Vegetarian available, Air con **Seats** 130, Pr/dining room 22 **Children** Portions

Mango Tree
PLAN 4 G4

◉ Thai **V**

Fine-dining Thai restaurant in Belgravia

☎ 020 7823 1888 & 07786 626169 🖹 020 7245 9288
46 Grosvenor Place, Belgravia SW1X 7EQ
e-mail: reservations@mangotree.org.uk
dir: Nearest station: Victoria Please telephone for directions

The Mango Tree brings a taste of Thailand to Belgravia with authentic materials sourced directly from Thailand. The spacious interior is certainly reminiscent of the restaurants in the home country. The menu includes traditional Thai dishes from each of the four main culinary regions: rich and mild from the north, spicy from the east, mild dishes influenced by the Chinese cooking style from the central region, and hot and spicy dishes from the south. Typical dishes might include larb pla tuna (seared tuna salad with dry chilli and lemongrass), pla pow (grilled fillet of sea bass wrapped in banana leaves and served with spicy lime sauce), or gaeng kiew wan gai (corn-fed chicken and green curry). Festivals and events are held on a regular basis, with themed food and local music. Its sister restaurant Awana, is a Malaysian restaurant in Chelsea (see entry).

Chef Mark Read **Owner** Eddie Lim **Times** 12-3/6-11 Closed Xmas, New Year, **Prices** Fixed L 2 course £30-£35, Fixed D 3 course £25-£30, Starter £5.50-£7.50, Main £12.50-£18.50, Dessert £5.50-£6.50, Service added but optional 12.5% **Wines** 15 bottles over £20, 2 bottles under £20, 16 by glass **Notes** Tasting menu available, Sunday L, Vegetarian menu, Air con **Seats** 160 **Children** Portions, Menu **Parking** On Wilton St

Marcus Wareing at the Berkeley
PLAN 4 G4

◉◉◉◉◉ — *see opposite page*

Marcus Wareing at the Berkeley

LONDON SW1 PLAN 4 G4

Modern French V NOTABLE WINE LIST

A Knightsbridge cocoon with finely judged cooking from an immense talent

☎ 020 7235 1200 📄 020 7235 1266
The Berkeley, Wilton Place, Knightsbridge SW1X 7RL
e-mail: marcuswareing@the-berkeley.co.uk
dir: Nearest station: Knightsbridge, Hyde Park Corner Please telephone or check website for directions

To step into Marcus Wareing's restaurant at the five-star Berkeley is like slipping through a fault in the time-space continuum. Designed by the in-demand David Collins, presiding guru of the present era of British restaurant design, it is an unfashionably dark, enveloping cocoon, the deep wood panelling, claret seat upholstery and crepuscular lighting a welcome change after the monochromatics of so many other high-end eateries. They do things differently here. In a parallel world to Knightsbridge bustle, oceans of space separates the tables, the no-man's-land between them patrolled almost soundlessly by trolleys offering petits fours, cheeses, ancient brandies, whatever the heart desires. An astonishment of choice is offered on the menus too, not what we might expect at this rarefied level, when every dish is so

painstakingly wrought. Wareing is a Lancashire boy made good, who understands that what we want from top-drawer cooking primarily is sheer flavour, rather than fleeting delicacy. Thus we might begin with a large piece of seared foie gras, its refinement offset with basso profundo notes of gingerbread, chestnuts, Lapsang tea, rhubarb and quince, the whole coming together in remarkable harmony. Principal dishes such as sea bass with broccoli, Chantenay carrots and dauphinoise, the last superbly rendered as a purée, or Welsh suckling pig cooked round the clock and served with braised chicory and pommes mousseline, may sound more straightforward than the preceding, but lack for nothing in unanswerable impact. The salty caramel now so popular at dessert stage appears here wittily in the form of a jelly, alongside peanut parfait, with peanut and rice crispie brittle and a spume of raspberry. In among all this are a cavalcade of appetisers, amuses, pre-desserts and fantastic breads, a regimen that somehow stops short of the tipping-point to excess, because it is all so precisely, finely judged. This is, among other things, what five Rosettes are about.

Chef Marcus Wareing **Owner** Marcus Wareing Restaurants Ltd
Times 12-2.30/6-11 Closed 1 Jan, Sun, L Sat **Prices** Fixed L course £35, Fixed D 3 course £75, Tasting menu £90, Main £75, Service added but optional 12.5% **Wines** 900 bottles over £20, 4 bottles under £20, 10 by glass **Notes** ALC 3 course, Tasting menu 7 course, Vegetarian menu, Dress restrictions, Smart - jacket preferred, No jeans/trainers, Air con **Seats** 70, Pr/dining room 16 **Children** Portions **Parking** NCP and on street

LONDON SW1 *continued*

Mint Leaf

PLAN 5 C3

Modern Indian

Trendy, subterranean, nightclub-styled modern Indian

☎ 020 7930 9020 🖹 020 7930 6205
Suffolk Place, Haymarket SW1Y 4HX
e-mail: reservations@mintleafrestaurant.com
web: www.mintleafrestaurant.com
dir: Nearest station: Piccadilly/Charing Cross At end of
Haymarket, on corner of Pall Mall and Suffolk Place.
Opposite Her Majesty's Theatre, 100mtrs from Trafalgar
Square

Words like 'funky' and 'trendy' crop up when discussing
Mint Leaf and that's probably just what the owners
intended. The basement venue has a striking cocktail bar
and large dining area divided into intimate areas by
walnut louvres and designer wire mesh. Throw in a
central raised catwalk, dark-wood, modern seating, low
lighting and a backing track of contemporary music (plus
live DJs and musicians on Friday and Saturday evenings),
and you have nightclubby vibe. The kitchen fits the bill,
dealing in relatively straightforward but equally modern
Pan-Indian cooking. Many dishes are available in small
and large portions, such as turbot seared with chilli,
basil and lime, or baby lamb shanks roasted in the
tandoor.

Chef A Jay Chopra **Owner** Out of Africa Investments
Times 12-3/5.30-11 Closed 25-26 Dec, 1 Jan, L Sat, Sun
Prices Fixed L 2 course fr £15, Starter £5-£12, Main £12-
£24, Dessert £6-£7.50, Service added but optional 12.5%
Wines 130 bottles over £20, 8 bottles under £20, 12 by
glass **Notes** Pre-theatre menu 5-7pm 2 course £15,
Vegetarian available, Dress restrictions, Smart casual, no
scruffy jeans or trainers, Civ Wed 100, Air con **Seats** 144,
Pr/dining room 66 **Children** Portions **Parking** NCP, on
street

Mitsukoshi

PLAN 3 B1

Japanese

Friendly Japanese department store restaurant

☎ 020 7930 0317 🖹 020 7839 1167
Dorland House, 14-20 Lower Regent St SW1Y 4PH
e-mail: lonrest@mitsukoshi.co.jp
web: www.mitsukoshi-restaurant.co.uk
dir: Nearest station: Piccadilly Circus Telephone for
directions

Japanese tourists and expats love this department store
restaurant just a short stroll from Piccadilly, and it's
equally accessible to Westerners. A long sushi bar worked
by skilled chefs is ideal for those in a hurry, while the
main restaurant is a traditional Japanese eaterie with
patterned dividers to break up the large space, and plenty
of black lacquered furniture. The extensive menu includes
several set choices allowing the novice to experiment,
and there's a generous selection of carte dishes, sushi,
sashimi and side dishes. Try grilled black cod marinated
in sweet miso paste, or steamed tofu and eel with a
sticky soy dressing, served in a relaxed atmosphere.

Chef Yuya Kikuchi **Owner** Mitsukoshi (UK) Ltd
Times 12-2/6-10 Closed 25-26 Dec, 1 Jan, Etr,
Prices Fixed L 2 course £12-£27, Fixed D 2 course fr £22,
Fixed D 4 course £35-£60, Starter £4.50-£10, Main fr
£12, Dessert £2.50-£6, Service added 12.5% **Wines** 3
bottles over £20, 4 bottles under £20, 4 by glass
Notes Sunday L, Vegetarian available, Air con **Seats** 56,
Pr/dining room 20 **Children** Menu **Parking** NCP

MU at Millennium Knightsbridge

PLAN 4 F4

Asian

Asian-influenced 'tapas' in trendy Knightsbridge hotel

☎ 020 7201 6330 🖹 020 7201 6353
17 Sloane St, Knightsbridge SW1X 9NU
web: www.millenniumhotels.com/knightsbridge
dir: Nearest station: Knightsbridge/Victoria 200yds from
Knightsbridge Stn, near Harrods

The Millennium is a short flit from one of the entrances to
Knightsbridge underground station, although it's a fair
bet that not many of its patrons will arrive by tube train.
Designer opulence shrieks from its every crevice, and in
the sleekly elegant MU dining room, an unmistakably up-
to-the-minute catering operation offers dim sum-style
dishes that draw inspiration from east Asia. Chicken and
foie gras dumplings with truffle vinaigrette, ho fan
noodles with tofu, gai lan and hoisin sauce, and prawn

satay in shrimp mousse with oyster sauce are among the
possibilities. Wines by the glass and cocktails accompany
the food well.

Chef Paul Knight **Owner** Millennium & Copthorne Hotels
Times 5-10.30 Closed BH's, Sun-Mon, L all week
Prices Food prices not confirmed for 2010. Please
telephone for details, Service added but optional 12.5%
Wines 60 bottles over £20, 4 bottles under £20, 25 by
glass **Notes** Vegetarian available, Air con **Seats** 110, Pr/
dining room 50 **Children** Portions, Menu **Parking** 8, NCP
Pavilion Rd

Nahm

PLAN 4 G4

— *see opposite page*

One-O-One

PLAN 4 F4

— *see opposite page*

L'Oranger

PLAN 5 B5

Modern French

Classic French cuisine amid impeccable elegance

☎ 020 7839 3774 🖹 020 7839 4330
5 St James's St SW1A 1EF
e-mail: loranger@londonfinedininggroup.com
web: www.loranger.co.uk
dir: Nearest station: Green Park. Access by car via Pall
Mall

Often described as the most beautiful restaurant in
London, L'Oranger is the epitome of elegance and style.
Luxurious gold damask and silk drapes hang at the
windows, the richness picked up by the aged oak panels
lining the walls, and the pale gold banquette seating.
Huge flower displays add splashes of bright colour, and
natural light streams in through the glass atrium roof.
Modern art brings another dramatic dimension. The staff
offer a discreet and efficient presence. The cooking is
firmly based in classical French traditions, but given a
modern lift in the direction of Provence where much of its
inspiration is found. Fish is always heavily featured, and
game comes into its own too in season, with menus
changing to suit the markets. Expect beautifully
presented dishes brought from the kitchen with a flourish:
perhaps langoustine tempura with avocado and mango
curry parfait and lemongrass fragrances, and roast
pigeon with grapes, and a side dish of potato stew.

continued on page 262

Nahm

Thai

The very best Thai food in chic hotel

☎ 020 7333 1234   📠 020 7333 1100
The Halkin Hotel, Halkin St, Belgravia SW1X 7DJ
e-mail: res@nahm.como.bz
dir: Nearest station: Hyde Park Corner Halkin Street just
off Hyde Park Corner

Head for David Thompson's Nahm if you want to eat like a
King of Thailand. His passion for the cuisine of the
country and desire to bring back to life many recipes lost
in time, makes this restaurant in the heart of Georgian
Belgravia a must-visit destination for lovers of South-
East Asian cooking. The King of Thailand would certainly
feel at home in the Halkin Hotel, a luxurious bolthole
tucked away in a quiet street near Hyde Park Corner. The

bar is a place to see and be seen over a glass of
champagne or a cocktail before moving on to the
adjacent dining room, a minimalist space with large
columns, wooden screens and teak tables. The traditional
Nahm Arharn banquet style menu is perhaps the best way
to sample the food, with five dishes arriving at the same
time filling the table with aromas and colours, texture
and flavours; or you can have the freedom of the à la
carte menu. The freshness and quality of the produce
adds to the appeal. Start with the delicately spiced salted
chicken wafers with logans (rather like lychees) and Thai
basil before the arrival of the main dishes, perhaps a
crispy fish salad with sweet pork and mango (superb
flavours and textures) or a clear soup of minced pork
dumplings with shiitake mushrooms and cabbage.
Desserts such as Thai rice custard with 'ancestor'
smoked biscuits are well worth a try. It's not a cheap
experience.

Chef David Thompson, Matthew Albert **Owner** Halkin
Hotel Ltd **Times** 12-2.30/7-11 Closed 25 Dec & BHs, L

Sat-Sun **Prices** Fixed L 2 course £15-£30, Fixed D 3
course £35-£45, Starter £8-£14, Main £17-£25, Dessert
£8-£12, Service added but optional 12.5% **Wines** 190
bottles over £20, 12 by glass **Notes** Traditional Nahm
Arharn menu £55, Vegetarian available, Air con **Seats** 78,
Pr/dining room 36 **Children** Portions **Parking** On street

---

One-O-One

French, Seafood V

Inventive seafood cooking in the heart of Knightsbridge

☎ 020 7290 7101   📠 020 7201 7884
Sheraton Park Tower, 101 Knightsbridge SW1X 7RN
e-mail: darren.neilan@luxurycollection.com
dir: Nearest station: Knightsbridge. E from station, just
after Harvey Nichols

Superbly located in the heart of Knightsbridge, this
renowned fish and seafood restaurant has impressive
views over the city from its position in the Sheraton Park
Tower. The modern interior with a spacious oval-shaped
bar and elegantly dressed tables, uses subtle lighting,
contemporary tones and a central illuminated glass-
topped table to create a fashionable, modern look. Chef
Pascal Proyart cooks up a storm in the kitchen,

concentrating mainly on produce from the sea (although
there are plenty of alternatives if you must). The
presentation is refined while dishes show strong technical
skills and clever use of top-notch ingredients. Create your
own grazing menu of 'petits plats' or take the more
conventional three-course route. Start perhaps with
pan-roasted langoustine tournedos and duck foie gras,
Peking duck marmite and hoi sin froth before slow-cooked
skrei - Arctic cod from the Barents Sea - with Joselito
chorizo carpaccio and squid a la plancha. Finish with
coupe liégeoise of dark Manjari chocolate with coffee and
salt caramel ice cream.

Chef Pascal Proyart **Owner** Starwood Hotels & Resorts
Times 12-2.30/6.30-10 **Prices** Fixed L course £19, Fixed
D 3 course £38, Starter £14-£19, Main £23-£29, Dessert
£8, Service optional **Wines** 101 bottles over £20, 12 by
glass **Notes** Tasting menu 5 course, Sunday L, Vegetarian
menu, Dress restrictions, Smart casual preferred, Air con
Seats 50, Pr/dining room 10 **Children** Portions
Parking 60

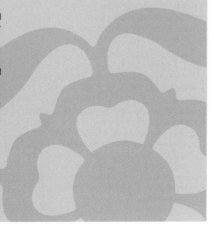

LONDON SW1 *continued*

Chef L Michel **Owner** A to Z Restaurants Ltd
Times 12-2.45/6.30-10.45 Closed Xmas, Etr, BHs, Sun, L
Sat **Prices** Fixed L 2 course £25-£29, Fixed D 2 course
£30-£60, Starter £12-£26, Main £22-£39, Dessert £8-£9,
Service added but optional 13.5% **Wines** 290 bottles over
£20, 4 bottles under £20, 12 by glass **Notes** Vegetarian
available, Dress restrictions, Smart casual, Air con
Seats 70, Pr/dining room 40 **Children** Portions
Parking On street or NCP

Osteria Dell'Angolo
PLAN 5 C3

◉ Italian **NEW**

Italian classics in the heart of Westminster

☎ 020 3268 1077 📄 020 3268 1073
47 Marsham St SW1P 3DR
e-mail: osteriadell_angolo@btconnect.com
dir: Nearest station: St James's Park/Westminster

Just a 5-minute walk from Westminster and the Houses of
Parliament, the 'corner tavern' brings Tuscan cuisine
from the Valdarnese Valley to the doorstep of lucky
Whitehall mandarins. Italophiles will be overjoyed that
this is the real deal, with impeccably fresh, carefully-
sourced ingredients and artisan produce combined with
passion and flair in gorgeous-looking dishes. Stretched
ravioli stuffed with burrata cheese is served with a
deliciously tender shredded duck stew; the flavours of
deep-fried squid on cauliflower 'carpaccio' with lemon
jam work astonishingly well; finish with a fun dessert of
semi-fredo di tiramisù with cocoa moondust that crackles
on the tongue. You're spoiled for choice with Italian wines
to suit all pockets.

Times 12-2.30/6.30-10.30 Closed Sun, L Sat

Quaglino's
PLAN 5 B6

◉ French Brasserie

Stunning restaurant offering classic brasserie food

☎ 020 7930 6767 📄 020 7930 2732
16 Bury St, St James's SW1Y 6AJ
e-mail: saschakn@danddlondon.com
dir: Nearest station: Green Park/Piccadilly Circus Bury St
is off Jermyn St

The still fashionably glamorous Quaglino's sits on the
site of the original Giovanni Quaglino society restaurant,
reinvented by Terence Conran in the 1990s (but no longer
connected to either of them). Its dramatic marble
staircase sweeps down from a mezzanine bar to a
cavernous dining room with high glass ceiling and serried
ranks of tables. Modern chairs and banquette seating,
mirrors and live music all add to the lively atmosphere.
Boasting a crustacea altar, there is a wonderful selection
of seafood, while the diverse, seasonal carte is inspired
by classic Parisian brasseries. Specialities include
plateau fruits de mer to start, followed by sirloin steak
with peppercorn sauce and pommes Pont-Neuf, and a
dessert of crème brûlée and orange shortbread.

Times 12-3/5.30-mdnt Closed 24-25 Dec, 1 Jan, L 31 Dec

The Quilon
PLAN 5 B4

◉◉ Indian

Haute-cuisine South Indian style

☎ 020 7821 1899 📄 020 7233 9597
41 Buckingham Gate SW1E 6AF
e-mail: info@quilonrestaurant.co.uk
web: www.quilon.co.uk
dir: Nearest station: St James's Park Next to Crowne Plaza
Hotel St James

It may rub shoulders with the best address in town - just
down the road from Buck Palace - but this sophisticated
Indian at the swanky Crowne Plaza hotel offers an
amazing-value lunch. Chef Sriram Aylur specialises in
South India's coastal cuisine, with its blend of authentic
and progressive dishes driven by tip-top produce and
focus on seafood and vegetarian options. Expect subtle
balance and refinement in attractively presented,
colourful dishes. At lunch, try the koondapur fish curry
(chunks of halibut simmered in coconut, chilli, onions
and tamarind gravy) with appams (bowl-shaped, soft-
centred, crisp-rimmed rice cakes) and finish with the
Goan-speciality dessert of bibinca and dodhol (soft-
textured baked cakes). Like the cuisine, the surroundings
are stylish and modern, with yellow banquettes, blond-
wood floor and sunny blue and yellow paintwork, though
carpets and big wall murals bring a slightly more dated
tone elsewhere.

Chef Sriram Aylur **Owner** Taj International Hotels Limited
Times 12-2.30/6-11 Closed 25-26 Dec, L Sat **Prices** Fixed
L course £20, Fixed D 3 course £37-£50, Starter £6-£8,
Main £15-£25, Dessert £5.50, Service added but optional
12.5% **Wines** 130 bottles over £20, 1 bottles under £20,
13 by glass **Notes** Sunday L, Vegetarian available, Dress
restrictions, Smart casual, Air con **Seats** 90
Children Portions **Parking** On street, NCP

Quirinale
PLAN 5 C3

◉◉ Italian

Modern Italian cooking in Westminster

☎ 020 7222 7080
North Court, 1 Great Peter St SW1P 3LL
e-mail: info@quirinale.co.uk
dir: Nearest station: Westminster From Parliament Sq to
Lambeth Bridge take 2nd left into Great Peter St,
restaurant on left

The restaurant is named after Rome's presidential
palace, fitting perhaps given the looming proximity of our
very own Mother of Parliaments. David Collins, restaurant

design wizard, has done a good job of turning a basement
dining room into a light, airy space, with cream leather
upholstery, limestone panels and a limed oak floor.
Modern Italian cooking revolves around fresh seafood
such as octopus in celery and apple salad, and fine pasta
making, put to good use in such dishes as Venetian-style
bigoli with duck ragu and porcini. Main dishes might see
Scottish beef cheek richly braised in Barolo, served with
polenta chips. Desserts are full of vivid flavours in the
Italian style, the tiramisù spiked with liquorice and
garnished with honey-glazed walnuts.

Times 12-3/6-12 Closed Xmas & New Year, 2 wks Aug,
Sat-Sun

The Rib Room
PLAN 4 F4

◉◉ British

Traditional beef restaurant in central Knightsbridge

☎ 020 7858 7250
**Jumeirah Carlton Tower Hotel, Cadogan Place
SW1X 9PY**
e-mail: JCTinfo@jumeirah.com
dir: Nearest station: Knightsbridge From major roads
follow signs for City Centre, towards Knightsbridge/Hyde
Park/Sloane Sq, then into Sloane St/Cadogan Place

Overlooking Cadogan Gardens, the traditionally styled
restaurant is located on the ground floor of the Carlton
Tower Hotel. Wooden panelled walls, effective use of
lighting and a large open-plan kitchen set the scene for
this old-school British beef restaurant. That said, there
are plenty of rarified dishes amid the classics, all of
which use good ingredients served with skill and care.
Start perhaps with a classic Rib Room Caesar salad with
anchovies and bacon or glazed onion soup with Guinness,
and for main course try the rib-eye steak with bone
marrow, shallots and port reduction or a fishy alternative
such as cumin-dusted monkfish loin with spiced
couscous.

Times 12.30-2.45/7-10.45

Roussillon
PLAN 4 G2

◉◉◉ – *see opposite page*

The Rubens at the Palace
PLAN 5 A4

◉ Modern British

**Quintessentially British hotel overlooking Buckingham
Palace**

☎ 020 7834 6600 📄 020 7828 5401
39 Buckingham Palace Rd SW1W 0PS
e-mail: bookrb@rchmail.com
dir: Nearest station: Victoria From station head towards
Buckingham Palace

This popular boutique hotel has seen some history since
it was built opposite Buckingham Palace mews to house
debutantes strutting their stuff at palace parties. In the
Second World War, it was HQ of the Polish Free State
army, and General de Gaulle stayed here too. The club-
style Library restaurant delivers classic cuisine, albeit

with some modern interpretations. West Coast Scottish scallops are served with potato rösti, spinach, fennel and chorizo to start, followed by Gressingham duck breast with celeriac dauphinoise, Savoy cabbage and spiced plum sauce. Classy formal service - fish filleted and smoked salmon carved at the table, for example - adds a romantic touch.

Chef Daniel Collins **Owner** Red Carnation Hotels **Times** 7.30-10.30 Closed Xmas week, L all week **Prices** Food prices not confirmed for 2010. Please telephone for details. **Wines** 4 bottles over £20, 8 bottles under £20, 12 by glass **Notes** Vegetarian available, Dress restrictions, No shorts, tracksuits or trainers, Air con **Seats** 30, Pr/dining room 50 **Children** Menu **Parking** NCP at Victoria Coach Station

St Alban
PLAN 5 B6

Modern Mediterranean

Celebrity hotspot serving Mediterranean food

☎ 020 7499 8558   📠 020 7499 6888
4-12 Lower Regent St SW1Y 4PE
dir: Nearest station: Piccadilly Circus. From Piccadilly Circus tube into Regent Street. Carlton Street 2nd left

The bright colours of the walls and seating can't help but lift the spirits at this buzzy restaurant, sister to The Wolseley (see entry), just down the road from Piccadilly Circus. Artwork by Damien Hirst joins the jazzy murals created by Michael Craig-Martin to make a unique

contemporary statement, matched only by the food for their vivid, vibrant palette. The kitchen's inspiration comes from the sun-drenched shores of Spain, Portugal and Italy whose rich Mediterranean flavours are authentically recreated. Look for Sardinian fish stew, braised rabbit with prunes and Spanish black pudding, and straight from the wood-burning stove, wood-roasted whole mackerel. Suited staff are on the ball.

Chef Dale Osborne **Owner** Chris Corbin & Jeremy King **Times** 12-3/5.30-11 Closed 25-26 Dec, 1 Jan, Aug BH, Sun, D 24 & 31 Dec **Prices** Fixed L 2 course £15.50, Starter £6.50-£16.50, Main £8.75-£60, Dessert £5.50-£8.50, Service added but optional 12.5% **Wines** 137 bottles over £20, 11 bottles under £20, 24 by glass **Notes** Fixed L Sat only, Pre/post-theatre D 2 or 3 course, Vegetarian available, Air con **Seats** 140

St James's Hotel and Club
PLAN 5 A5

International NEW

Sophisticated setting for modern Mediterranean cooking

☎ 020 7316 1600 & 7316 1614   📠 020 7316 1603
7-8 Park Place SW1A 1LP
e-mail: info@stjameshotelandclub.com
dir: Nearest station: Green Park Off St James's St, close to Piccadilly

Dating back to 1857, this elegant property with its distinctive neo-Gothic exterior is discreetly set in the

heart of St James's. Originally built as 'gentlemen's apartments', it was once a private members' club with many famous patrons. Extensive refurbishment has resulted in some impressive interior design and the small, intimate dining area exudes luxury and elegance. The restaurant is divided into two areas, one of which is separated from the kitchen by a glass screen, enabling diners to watch chefs in action. The Mediterranean cuisine has an Asian twist: lobster soup with coconut and chilli could be followed by rack of lamb with polenta, courgettes and aubergines. An all day menu is also served.

St James's Hotel and Club

Chef Philipp Vogel **Times** 12-2/7-10 Closed D Sun **Prices** Fixed L 2 course £35-£68, Fixed D 2 course £35-£68, Service added but optional 12.5% **Wines** 14 by glass **Notes** Vegetarian available, Air con **Seats** 30, Pr/dining room 40 **Parking** On street and NCP

Roussillon

LONDON SW1 PLAN 4 G2

Modern French V

Discreet French restaurant focused on the seasons

☎ 020 7730 5550   📠 020 7824 8617
16 St Barnabas St SW1W 8PE
e-mail: michael@roussillon.co.uk
dir: Nearest station: Sloane Square Telephone for directions

There is no doubting the serious aspirations of Alex Gauthier's Pimlico restaurant, which deserves wider recognition alongside its West End counterparts. Its large bow window catches the eye among the upmarket Georgian terraces just off the Pimlico Road, while a formal and professional French team - complete with sommelier - match its fine-dining aspirations and sophisticated ambience. Neutral tones are complemented

by brown banquette seating and chairs, colourful food-related artwork and prints, low lighting, flower displays and spacious tables donning their best whites. A great-value lunch menu (which includes a half-bottle of wine per person), plus carte and several specialist menus (including a dégustation and vegetarian menu) adopt a progressive take on a classical French theme and come driven by luxury seasonal ingredients. The cooking is accurate and highly imaginative, with flavours and presentation set to thrill. Take roasted John Dory and baby squid with coco bean and black truffle purée and fish reduction, and perhaps a classic apricot soufflé finish, served with compôte and sorbet. Peripherals like amuse-bouche, pre-desserts, breads and petits fours all hit form too, while the wine list is a cracker.

Chef A Gauthier, Gerard Virolle **Owner** J & A Palmer, A Gauthier **Times** 12-2.30/6.30-11 Closed 24 Dec-5 Jan, Sun, L Sat **Prices** Fixed L course £35, Fixed D 3 course £55, Tasting menu £65-£75, Service added but optional 12.5%, Groups min 10 service 15% **Wines** 560 bottles over £20, 20 bottles under £20, 20 by glass **Notes** Tasting menu & vegetarian tasting menu 8 course, Vegetarian menu, Dress restrictions, No shorts or flip flops, Air con **Seats** 50, Pr/dining room 28 **Children** Portions, Menu **Parking** NCP

LONDON SW1 *continued*

Sake No Hana
PLAN 5 B5

Traditional Japanese

Modern Japanese restaurant in the heart of St James's

☎ 020 7925 8988 📇 020 7925 8999
23 St James St SW1 1HA
e-mail: reservations@sakenohana.com
dir: Nearest station: Green Park, Piccadilly Circus From Green Park Station, head towards Piccadilly Circus, first right St James St & restaurant situated half way down on right hand side

This modern Japanese restaurant is located on the first floor, accessed via two narrow escalators. The restaurant is spacious and chic, decked out in a striking lattice of blond wood and bamboo, with traditional low tables flanking the picture windows. The menu is extensive and the army of staff are on hand to advise on choices, most of which are ideal for sharing. Japanese classics grouped under cooking methods feature alongside luxuries like Wagyu beef and white truffle rice. A starter of king crab with kanisu jelly might be followed by sea bass with ponzu sauce or Berkshire pork katsu with shiitake mushroom.

Chef Chi San **Owner** Evgeny Lebedev **Times** 12-2.30/6-11.30 Closed 24-25 Dec, D Sun **Prices** Fixed L 2 course £25, Fixed D 3 course £25-£70, Starter £5-£26.50, Main £8.50-£26.50, Dessert £5-£13.50, Service added but optional 13% **Wines** 31 bottles over £20, 7 by glass **Notes** Vegetarian available, Dress restrictions, Smart casual, Air con **Seats** 70, Pr/dining room 10 **Parking** NCP

Salloos Restaurant
PLAN 4 G4

Pakistani

Pakistani cooking in Knightsbridge mews

☎ 020 7235 4444
62-64 Kinnerton St SW1X 8ER
dir: Nearest station: Knightsbridge Kinnerton St is opposite Berkeley Hotel on Wilton Place

Salloos is a long-established, genuine family business with a good reputation for delivering consistently sound Pakistani cooking. The setting in a Knightsbridge mews sits well with the somewhat luxurious interior, with smartly set tables and lavish works of art. Meat for the tandoor is marinated 24-hours in advance (chicken tikka and tandoori chops among them) and the house specialities include pulao jahengiri (rice with chicken, tomatoes, roasted almonds and sautéed sultanas) and haleem akbari (shredded lamb with wheatgerm, lentils and spices). Curries range from murgh korma to gurda masala (kidneys with hot spices). The prices reflect the Knightsbridge location.

Chef Abdul Aziz **Owner** Mr & Mrs M Salahuddin **Times** 12-3/7-11.45 Closed Xmas, Sun **Prices** Starter £6.50-£11.95, Main £16.50-£19.50, Dessert £5.50, Service added but optional 12.5% **Wines** 40 bottles over £20, 3 bottles under £20, 2 by glass **Notes** Air con **Seats** 65 **Parking** Meters & car park Kinnerton St

Santini
PLAN 4 H3

Italian

Sophisticated, family-run Italian with large alfresco terrace

☎ 020 7730 4094 & 7730 8275 📇 020 7730 0544
29 Ebury St SW1W 0NZ
e-mail: info@santini-restaurant.com
dir: Nearest station: Victoria Take Lower Belgrave St off Buckingham Palace Rd. Restaurant on 1st corner on left

Established back in 1984, this refined Belgravia Italian has a glamorous reputation and a splendid alfresco terrace discreetly ringed by potted shrubs, glass screens and olive trees. Inside's all light pastel shades, with large etched-glass windows, marble floors, leather banquettes and low-slung tub-style chairs cutting a cool, sophisticated modern edge. The carte offers a typically lengthy repertoire of authentic regional Italian cooking with a Venetian accent and emphasis on simplicity and flavour, allowing the fresh, seasonal, quality ingredients to shine in well-presented dishes. The home-made pasta is a must; perhaps classic ricotta and spinach ravioli served with tomatoes, and to follow, poached sea bass with a mixed herb and balsamic dressing. While the prices are Belgravia, the attentive, professional service is as Latin as the short, all-Italian wine list.

Chef Luca Lamari **Owner** Mr G Santin **Times** 12-3/6-11 Closed Xmas, 1 Jan, Etr Sun & Mon, L Sat & Sun **Prices** Food prices not confirmed for 2010. Please telephone for details. **Wines** all bottles over £20, 7 by glass **Notes** Pre-theatre menu 3 course £25, Vegetarian available, Dress restrictions, Smart casual, Air con **Seats** 65, Pr/dining room 30 **Children** Portions **Parking** Meters (no charge after 6.30pm)

The Stafford Hotel
PLAN 5 A5

British

Luxurious hotel dining in exclusive location

☎ 020 7493 0111 📇 020 7493 7121
16-18 St James's Place SW1A 1NJ
e-mail: information@thestaffordhotel.co.uk
dir: Nearest station: Green Park

Discreetly situated in a quiet cul-de-sac in London's St James's, close to Green Park, the Stafford is a jewel among top-class luxury hotels, exuding an opulent country-house style. Enjoy an aperitif in the American bar, known for mixing a mean martini, which displays an eccentric collection of club ties, sporting mementoes and signed celebrity photographs. Split over two levels, the grand dining room is beautifully appointed with impeccably dressed tables. A serious approach to modern British cooking using top-quality ingredients is the hallmark of the kitchen. From the extensive carte order plump Orkney scallops with vegetable brunoise and a citrus and saffron broth, follow with roast wild mallard with caramelised pear and beetroot duck hash, and finish with a crisp banana and custard tart with pecan nuts in white chocolate. There is an excellent wine list.

Times 12.30-2.30/6-10.30 Closed L Sat

Volt
PLAN 4 H4

Italian

Trendy modern restaurant with Italian cooking

☎ 020 7235 9696 📇 020 7235 9599
17 Hobart Place SW1W 0HH
e-mail: info@voltlounge.com
dir: Nearest station: Victoria. Behind Buckingham Palace, off Eaton Square and Grosvenor Gardens

There's something of a nightclub-like vibe about this cool Belgravia lounge-bar-restaurant outfit. An elegantly curving dining room radiates around a funky bar area and velvet-clad central pillar decked out in vivid red. Eye-catching soft-purple neon tube lighting comes inset into Asian-style carved wood panelled walls framing the bar. Contemporary, low-slung chairs, leather banquettes and smartly set tables shout modern style too, while 3 equally trendy, intimate dining areas - fringing the main room - can be booked for private dining. The modern cooking suits the clubby surroundings; a classic Italian carte backed by a selection of innovative fixed-price meze menus driven by prime produce and clean-cut style and presentation. Think clams, garlic and tomato fettuccine, or almond sea bass fillet served with French bean and lemon risotto.

Chef Giovanni Andolfi **Owner** Bou Antoun **Times** 12-3/6-11 Closed Xmas, last 2 wks Aug, BHs, Sun, L Sat **Prices** Fixed L 2 course £8-£15, Fixed D 3 course £25-£30, Starter £4.50-£15, Main £8-£19, Dessert £5.50-£8.50, Service optional **Wines** 90 bottles over £20, 7 bottles under £20, 8 by glass **Notes** Pre-theatre menu £15, Vegetarian available, Dress restrictions, Smart casual, Air con **Seats** 120, Pr/dining room 45 **Children** Portions

Zafferano
PLAN 4 F4

– *see opposite page*

Zafferano

Italian 🏆NOTABLE WINE LIST

Pace-setting Italian, Knightsbridge-style

☎ 020 7235 5800   🖷 020 7235 1971
15 Lowndes St SW1X 9EY
e-mail: info@zafferanorestaurant.com
web: www.zafferanorestaurant.com
dir: Nearest station: Knightsbridge Located off Sloane St, behind Carlton Tower Hotel

Tucked discreetly away in the hinterland of Knightsbridge is an Italian gem, which has been impressing the denizens of this well-heeled part of town since 1995. If your culinary Italian is up to snuff, you won't be surprised to find the name echoed in the saffron-hued colour scheme of the frontage and seating. The place exudes class, from the attentive and impeccably turned-out staff to the Knightsbridge-rustic ambience, with its exposed brick walls. Expansion is afoot to cope with what has always been a steady press of business. The cooking is firmly in the mode of today's subtly updated Italian cuisine, with apposite combinations giving point to some immaculate raw materials. Burrata, fresh mozzarella with a creamy filling, makes a wickedly luxurious first course, garnished with sweet Sicilian-style caponata, or there may well be cuttlefish and green beans in a salad along with some of Liguria's fruity Taggiasca olives. Pasta options are more imaginative than most, perhaps taking in tagliolini with crab, courgettes and chilli, while the main courses achieve marvellous impact with such apparently simple materials as corn-fed chicken, roasted with lemon and capers. It would be odd indeed to come to a top-drawer Italian restaurant and not have a dessert, and the range encompasses hazelnut and vanilla cream served in a cocktail glass, and anointed at the table with espresso. A fine list of Italian wines, with plenty available by the glass, accompanies.

Chef Andrew Needham **Owner** A-Z Restaurants-London Fine Dining Group **Times** 12-2.30/7-11 Closed 1 wk Xmas & New Year, L Etr Mon **Prices** Fixed L 2 course £29.50, Fixed D 3 course £44.50, Service added 13.5% **Wines** 400 bottles over £20, 8 by glass **Notes** Seasonal truffle menu available, Vegetarian available, Dress restrictions, Smart casual, Air con **Seats** 85, Pr/dining room 20 **Children** Portions **Parking** NCP behind restaurant

Awana

PLAN 4 E2

🏵 Traditional Malaysian V

Authentic Malaysian restaurant and satay bar

☎ 020 7584 8880   🖷 020 7584 6188
85 Sloane Av SW3 3DX
e-mail: info@awana.co.uk
dir: Nearest station: South Kensington Left out of South Kensington station onto Pelham Rd. Continue past Fulham Rd and this will lead onto Sloane Av

The name means 'in the clouds' in Malay and Awana certainly aims high. The dining room's design is inspired by traditional Malaysian teak houses; think lush silk panels, delicate glass screens and burgundy leather seating to highlight the darkwood interior. There's a satay bar where you can watch the chefs at work (also relayed to TV monitors around the restaurant), perhaps making the not-to-be-missed roti (Malaysian-style flat bread). Modern style is given to authentic Malaysian cuisine too, the menu featuring satay (skewered dishes, perhaps corn-fed chicken or diver-caught scallops), starters, soups, curry, grills and stir-fries, and there's also a 10-course tasting option and chef's specials. Expect red snapper in a coconut curry with okra, tomato and aubergine, or perhaps a lamb and sesame stirfry with shiitaki mushrooms, pak choi and soy. (Sister venue to The Mango Tree in Belgravia.)

Chef Mark Read **Owner** Eddie Lim **Times** 12-3/6-11 Closed 25-26 Dec, 1 Jan, D 24 Dec **Prices** Fixed L 2 course fr £12.50, Fixed D 3 course £35-£40, Tasting menu £45, Starter £5.50-£18, Main £10.50-£25, Dessert £6-£8.50, Service added but optional 12.5% **Wines** All bottles over £20, 2 bottles under £20, 12 by glass **Notes** Sunday L, Vegetarian menu, Dress restrictions, Smart casual, Air con **Seats** 110 **Children** Portions, Menu **Parking** Car park

Bibendum

PLAN 4 E3

🏵🏵 European V 🏆NOTABLE WINE LIST

Modern classics at a landmark West London restaurant

☎ 020 7581 5817   🖷 020 7823 7925
Michelin House, 81 Fulham Rd SW3 6RD
e-mail: reservations@bibendum.co.uk
web: www.bibendum.co.uk
dir: Nearest station: South Kensington. Left out of South Kensington station onto Pelham Street. Walk to traffic lights, the Michelin building is opposite

Twenty-odd years down the line from its conversion to a style-led restaurant, the landmark Michelin building looks timelessly immune from the vagaries of fashion. The iconic wobble-bellied Michelin man, Bibendum, still looks down from his azure stained-glass windows in a building so manifestly French that it seems tailor-made as a setting for the strong Gallic overtones of the restaurant and oyster bar. But time has not stood still: modern cooking is no longer in thrall to M. Escoffier et al, so the menu of classic brasserie dishes is shot through with surprising flashes of contemporary verve. A beret-wearing starter of oeufs en meurette with saucisson Lyonnais and brioche sits next to sautéed lamb's tongue with braised sprout tops, crêpe Parmentier and sauce poivrade. Main courses such as grilled onglet with sweet potato purée and bordelaise sauce or roast cod with saffron potatoes and bouillabaisse sauce aim for the comfort zone.

Bibendum

Chef Matthew Harris **Owner** Sir Terence Conran, Simon Hopkinson, Michael Hamlyn **Times** 12-2.30/7-11.30 Closed 25 & 26 Dec, 1 Jan, D 24 Dec **Prices** Fixed L 2 course £25, Starter £8.50-£23.50, Main £17.50-£27, Dessert £7-£9.50, Service added but optional 12.5% **Wines** 530 bottles over £20, 20 bottles under £20, 10 by glass **Notes** Sunday supper menu also available 3 course £29.50, Sunday L, Vegetarian menu, Air con **Seats** 80 **Children** Portions **Parking** On street

The Capital

Modern French 🍷 NOTABLE WINE LIST

Inspired cooking and impeccable service at Knightsbridge landmark

☎ 020 7589 5171   📠 020 7225 0011
22 Basil St, Knightsbridge SW3 1AT
e-mail: reservations@capitalhotel.co.uk
web: www.capitalhotel.co.uk
dir: Nearest station: Knightsbridge Off Sloane St, beside Harrods

Eric Chavot is one of the top chefs working in Britain today, and the location of his restaurant, tucked discreetly away in a Knightsbridge side street, speaks volumes about his approach. Five-star, top-drawer, pure quality, but discreetly so, nothing flashy. M Chavot's CV twinkles with a stellar pedigree: he trained with the calibre of internationally-reputed chefs who are known to all by first name - Nico, Marco, Raymond, among others. The Capital Hotel itself is a haven of understated opulence, chic without crossing the line into ostentation, and Eric's domain in the restaurant is equally civilised - and surprisingly small. A dozen or so tables give it the feel of a private club but the soaring ceiling, big windows, blond-wood panelling and feminine chairs upholstered in swirly damask-patterned cerise inject the perfect amount of luxury. Irreproachably professional service hits the right notes of attentiveness and informed advice on

the finer points of the menu. The cooking is inspired by Eric's origins in the Gascon region of south-western France, and there's no question that you're in the hands of a French master - gutsy, deep flavours show classical technique of the first order, and dishes are assembled and presented with the same un-shouty classiness that defines every aspect of the Capital experience. It's not every day that you eat food at this level, so throw caution to the wind and go for the six-course Dégustation menu with matching wines; otherwise, the fixed-price lunch menu offers the budget-conscious gastronome phenomenal value - until you add wine. The biblical wine list is, at any rate, worth pushing out the boat for: phenomenal by anyone's standards, it is a who's who of France's blue-chip producers, and it even acknowledges the existence of the world beyond l'Hexagone. Well-established pairings appear in starters such as pan-fried foie gras with rhubarb or crab lasagne with langoustine cappuccino. Saddle of rabbit Provençale is paired with seared calamari and tomato risotto in a signature main course. Elegant desserts might feature vanilla pearls with roasted banana, rum pannacotta and mango sorbet.

Chef Eric Chavot **Owner** Mr D Levin **Times** 12-2.30/6.45-11 **Prices** Fixed L 2 course fr £27.50, Fixed D 3 course fr £63, Service added but optional 12.5% **Wines** All bottles over £20, 37 by glass **Notes** Dégustation menu 5 course £70, Sunday L, Vegetarian available, Dress restrictions, Smart casual, Air con **Seats** 35, Pr/dining room 24 **Parking** 10

LONDON SW3 *continued*

The Capital
PLAN 4 F4

◉◉◉◉ – *see opposite page*

Le Colombier
PLAN 4 D2

◉ French

Popular brasserie in Chelsea's heartland

☎ 020 7351 1155 ▤ 020 7351 5124
145 Dovehouse St SW3 6LB
e-mail: lecolombier1998@aol.com
dir: Nearest station: South Kensington Please telephone for directions

Elegance is personified at this smart neighbourhood restaurant in the heart of Chelsea, just a stone's throw from the Royal Marsden Hospital. Carefully groomed staff welcome diners with old-world courtesy, and the crisply set tables are snugly close together in a bright yellow and blue staging; a covered conservatory offers an alfresco-style experience minus the vagaries of the weather. A distinctly Parisian style of brasserie cooking sees classics like snails with garlic cream sauce and puff pastry, and leg of duck confit with curly endive salad, while a choice of oysters is a popular starter. Finish with crêpe Suzette or a selection of seasonal French cheeses.

Chef Philippe Tamet **Owner** Didier Garnier
Times 12-3/6.30-10.30 **Prices** Fixed L 2 course £18.50-£22, Starter £6.80-£13.20, Main £15.50-£25.80, Dessert £6.50-£7.50, Service added but optional 12.5%
Wines 200 bottles over £20, 12 bottles under £20, 10 by glass **Notes** Sunday L, Vegetarian available, Dress restrictions, Smart casual **Seats** 70, Pr/dining room 30 **Parking** Metered parking

Eight Over Eight
PLAN 1 E3

◉ Pan-Asian

Pan-Asian cooking in a chic Chelsea hangout

☎ 020 7349 9934 ▤ 020 7351 5157
392 King's Rd SW3 5UZ
e-mail: eightovereight@rickerrestaurants.com
dir: Nearest station: Sloane Sq, South Kensington Please telephone for directions

Eight is a Chinese lucky number, so double it up and life should work out a breeze. It certainly adds up to success here: the trendy King's Road hangout is a magnet for the beau monde who come to pose, people watch and graze on a pan-Asian menu. The setting is clean-cut minimal chic with elegant silk upturned-parasol-style lightshades and flower-shaped wrought iron screens as a nod to the oriental theme. But it's not just the social buzz that keeps Eight Over Eight bursting at the seams: the kitchen knows its stuff, serving up an enticing array of Asian cuisines ranging from dim sum to sashimi and sushi, tempura and roasts. Go for the house's take on black cod, served with sweet yuzu miso, or Madagascan black tiger prawns with ginger and lime.

Chef Clifton Muil **Owner** Will Ricker **Times** 12-3/6-11 Closed 24-29 Dec, Etr Sun, L Sun **Prices** Fixed L 2 course fr £15, Service added but optional 12.5% **Wines** 80 bottles over £20, 5 bottles under £20, 13 by glass **Notes** Vegetarian available, Air con **Seats** 95, Pr/dining room 14 **Children** Menu

Foxtrot Oscar
PLAN 4 F1

◉ Modern British

Gordon Ramsay's stylish neighbourhood bistro

☎ 020 7352 4448 ▤ 020 7592 1603
79 Royal Hospital Rd SW3 4HN
e-mail: foxtrotoscar@gordonramsay.com
dir: Nearest station: Sloane Square Please telephone for directions

Gordon Ramsay and his team were fond of filling up at Foxtrot Oscar after a busy evening's service at the nearby flagship restaurant - so fond, in fact, that he added this much-loved Chelsea bistro to his portfolio. The enterprise has all the hallmarks of Mr Ramsay: sound, unpretentious modern British bistro food, served in a bustling ambience. It has a dapper style with its chocolate leather chairs, wood tables and slate floor, and a comforting mix of classic and modern on the menu. You could start with Brixham crab on toast with lemon and chilli, or a fried duck egg with bubble-and-squeak. Main courses deliver full-on flavours in braised pig's cheeks and Foxtrot fishcakes. And who could resist ending with a retro knickerbocker glory?

Chef Emma Duggan **Owner** Gordon Ramsay Holdings Ltd **Times** 12-3/6-10.30 Closed 1 wk Xmas, Mon-Tue, L Wed-Thu **Prices** Starter £4.95-£7.50, Main £11.25-£15.95, Dessert £5.50, Service added but optional 12.5% **Wines** 20 bottles over £20, 6 bottles under £20, 10 by glass **Notes** Sunday L, Vegetarian available **Seats** 46, Pr/dining room 20 **Children** Portions **Parking** On street

Frankie's Italian Bar & Grill
PLAN 4 E3

◉ Italian

Glitzy basement restaurant serving simple Italian food

☎ 020 7590 9999 ▤ 020 7590 9900
3 Yeoman's Row, Brompton Rd SW3 2AL
e-mail: infofrankies@btconnect.com
dir: Nearest station: South Kensington/Knightsbridge Near The Oratory on Brompton Rd, close to Harrods

Marco Pierre White and jockey Frankie Dettori teamed up in 2005 to launch this ever-expanding mini-chain of family-friendly Italian restaurants. The original is secreted away in a quiet Knightsbridge side street, where you descend from ground floor level into an eye-popping basement that is a glitzy exercise in Marco-style bling, with mirror-lined walls and disco mirrorballs and a chequerboard mosaic floor. Given the razzamatazz of the surroundings, you might expect fancy-pants food, but you'd be wrong: on the menu is refreshingly fuss-free, simple Italian food, done well and served up to a 1950s backing track in a buzzy ambience. Choose from crowd-

pleasers such as bresaola with capers, rocket and pecorino, spaghetti with clams or a rib-eye steak with snails and garlic butter.

Times 12-3/6-11 Closed 26 Dec, D 25 Dec

Manicomio
PLAN 4 F2

◉ Italian

Buzzy, modern, informal Italian in stylish surroundings

☎ 020 7730 3366 ▤ 020 7730 3377
85 Duke of York Square, Chelsea SW3 4LY
e-mail: manicomio@btconnect.com
dir: Nearest station: Sloane Square. Duke of York Sq 100mtrs along King's Rd from Sloane Sq

Manicomio's large terrace in the fashionable Duke of York barracks development on Chelsea's King's Road is a perfect spot for people watching. A curving glass roof keeps off the worst of the weather and keeps the place bustling. Indoors, the stripped-out neutral chic of bare brickwork, bright modern artworks, blond-wood floors, oak tables and jazzy red leather banquettes takes over. The kitchen deals in straightforward contemporary Italian cuisine along the lines of oxtail ravioli with aged balsamic, sage and parmesan, or roast line-caught pollock with an olive crust and zucchini flower fritti. The deli/café next door does snacky things and excellent supplies to take home when you leave.

Chef Tom Salt **Owner** Ninai & Andrew Zarach **Times** noon-3/6.30-10.30 Closed Xmas & New Year, **Prices** Starter £7.85-£10, Main £12.75-£19.95, Dessert £4.50-£9, Service added but optional 12.5% **Wines** 64 bottles over £20, 9 bottles under £20, 20 by glass **Notes** Sunday L, Vegetarian available, Air con **Seats** 70, Pr/dining room 30 **Children** Portions **Parking** On street

Nozomi
PLAN 4 E4

◉◉ Japanese

Luxury Japanese cuisine in chic Knightsbridge

☎ 020 7838 1500 & 7838 0181
14 - 15 Beauchamp Place, Knightsbridge SW3 1NQ
e-mail: info@nozomi.co.uk
web: www.nozomi.co.uk
dir: Nearest station: Knightsbridge Telephone fo directions

Stay focused and make it beyond the glam of Nozomi's hyper-trendy bar, where brain-scrambling, cutting-edge cocktails could fatally blunt your taste buds, into the soothing décor of the dining rooms. Low-key lighting and softly-spoken waiters set a laid-back scene for top-flight Japanese cooking, although you may experience palpitations when the bill arrives. The extensive menu deals in neatly-delineated categories of sushi and sashimi, maki rolls, small dishes at big prices, then fish, tempura, meat and, ahem, Wagyu beef pitched at premiership diners. Go for marinated Chilean sea bass in spicy miso, baked on cedar wood or aka-miso lamb - grilled marinated cutlets served with erangi mushrooms, infused yuzu yogurt and chilli soy sauce.

Times 12-3/6.30-11.30

LONDON SW3 *continued*

Racine

PLAN 4 E3

French

Authentic neighbourhood French bistro

☎ 020 7584 4477   📠 020 7584 4900
239 Brompton Rd SW3 2EP
dir: Nearest station: Knightsbridge, South Kensington
Restaurant opposite Brompton Oratory

Metropolitan francophiles needing a fix of Gallic
authenticity should head for this Knightsbridge bistrot de
luxe where cross-Channel charm is guaranteed. A
curtained entrance opens into a smart setting featuring
brown leather banquettes, wooden floors and mirrored
walls, where waiters serve with verve and sound
knowledge. The menu is a consummate example of
classic cuisine bourgeoise - gutsy, rustic stuff such as
lamb's sweetbreads with a fricassée of morels and leeks
and beetroot purée to start. Quality produce sings through
in a slab of halibut with crushed peas, bacon lardons and
rosemary. Desserts are as French as, well, crème caramel,
or chocolate terrine with pistachio custard.

Chef Henry Harris, Mark Blatchford **Owner** Henry Harris,
James Lee, George Bennell **Times** 12-3/6-10.30 Closed 25
Dec, **Prices** Fixed L 2 course £17.50, Fixed D 3 course
£19.50, Starter £5.50-£12.50, Main £12.50-£26, Dessert
£5.50-£8, Service added but optional 14.5% **Wines** 55
bottles over £20, 10 bottles under £20, 19 by glass

Notes Fixed D up to 7.30pm only, Sunday L, Vegetarian
available, Air con **Seats** 75, Pr/dining room 18
Children Portions

Rasoi Restaurant

PLAN 4 F2

— *see below*

Restaurant Gordon Ramsay

PLAN 4 F1

— *see opposite page*

Sushinho

PLAN 4 D1

Japanese, Brazilian **NEW**

**Contemporary Chelsea Japanese with a Brazilian
flavour**

☎ 020 7349 7496
312-314 King's Rd, Chelsea SW3 5UH
e-mail: info@sushinho.com
dir: Nearest station: Sloane Sq On N side of King's Rd,
Between Old Church St & The Vale

The décor at Sushinho is thoroughly modern, with an
Oriental nightclub-like feel, and there's a sushi/cocktail
bar down one side. Neutral-tones, bamboo screens,
exposed brick, clever lighting and pale-wood tables come
set to an unexpected backing track of Latin-American
music. That's because Sushinho takes its inspiration
from Japanese-Brazilian culture (Brazil's Japanese
population being the largest outside Japan). The menu

(like the cocktail list, which includes saké alongside
batidas) delivers modern Japanese dishes (designed for
sharing) with some Brazilian touches. Take a feijoada
bean purée and chilli mango accompaniment to slow-
cooked pork belly, while more conventionally, halibut
might be teamed with sautéed oyster mushrooms, clams
and yuzu dressing. Classics like sushi, sashimi and
tempura feature, too.

Chef Michael Taylor **Owner** Oliver Girardet
Times 12-3/6-10.30 **Prices** Food prices not confirmed for
2010. Please telephone for details. **Seats** 80

Tom Aikens

PLAN 4 E2

— *see page 270*

Tom's Kitchen

PLAN 4 E2

British, French

**First-class brasserie food served in a buzzy Chelsea
diner**

☎ 020 7349 0202   📠 020 7823 3682
27 Cale St SW3 3QP
e-mail: info@tomskitchen.co.uk
dir: Nearest station: South Kensington. Cale St (Parallel
to Kings Rd), midway between Chelsea Green and St
Lukes Church

Around the corner from his five Rosette flagship
restaurant (see entry), Tom Aikens' version of a brasserie
continued on page 271

Rasoi Restaurant

LONDON SW3   PLAN 4 F2

Modern Indian Ⅴ

**Cutting-edge new Indian cuisine in lush Chelsea
surroundings**

☎ 020 7225 1881   📠 020 7581 0220
10 Lincoln St SW3 2TS
e-mail: info@rasoirestaurant.co.uk
dir: Nearest station: Sloane Square Near Peter Jones and
Duke of York Sq

If you haven't encountered the new Indian cuisine, you're
in for a big, and mightily pleasant, surprise. Vineet
Bhatia has been at the forefront of what he calls 'evolved
Indian' cooking in the capital for a number of years. It's
food that is steeped in classical tradition, but
reinterpreted with an innovative approach, a lighter touch
and a determination to aim for the 'wow' factor. An old

Chelsea townhouse off the King's Road, the place is
dripping with sub-continental style accoutrements, as
well as some more old-world touches such as elaborately
framed mirrors. A prawn platter combines a beautifully
spiced king prawn, tandoori-cooked prawns in a sticky
tomato dressing, and a kind of pannacotta flavoured with
coconut and chilli and topped with a brown shrimp
chutney. Meals might go on with grilled ginger and chilli
lobster, lamb shank chettinand with masala mash and a
coriander naan, or perfectly timed baked sea bass with
tandoori crushed potatoes and spicy crisped okra. A
separate vegetarian menu is offered. Finish with a
dessert platter that includes poached pear and baked
yoghurt, all luxuriously scented with saffron.

Chef Vineet Bhatia **Owner** Vineet & Rashima Bhatia
Times 12-2.30/6.30-10.30 Closed Xmas, New Year, BHs,
Sun, L Sat **Prices** Fixed L 2 course fr £19, Fixed D 3
course fr £55, Tasting menu £75, Service added but
optional 12.5% **Wines** 250 bottles over £20, 4 bottles
under £20, 10 by glass **Notes** Tasting menu 7 course,

Vegetarian menu, Dress restrictions, Smart casual, Air
con **Seats** 35, Pr/dining room 14 **Parking** On street

Restaurant Gordon Ramsay

French V NOTABLE WINE LIST

The mothership of the Gordon Ramsay empire

☎ 020 7352 4441 📄 020 7592 1213
68 Royal Hospital Rd SW3 4HP
dir: Nearest station: Sloane Square. At junct of Royal Hospital Road & Swan Walk

If you can't recall the name you must have been on the International Space Station... for the last 10 years. Gordon Ramsay's restaurant business includes ventures from Cape Town to New York, and his London outposts alone range from an East London pub to Heathrow's Terminal 5. Royal Hospital Road could be considered the flagship of the group, and it's where he struck out on his own for the very first time back in 1998. These days the kitchen is in the capable hands of executive chef Mark Askew, leading a brigade of 17 chefs in the recently refurbished and modernised kitchen. The frontage with its neatly trimmed shrubs, black paintwork on white walls and discreet awning is nicely understated, not at all showy and definitely not loud. Inside, it is not a large room - just 15 tables - which means it is a much more personal experience than a first-timer might imagine. Tones of cream and beige dominate the room, creating a refined and elegant space where the focus is on the food on the plate. Like the room, the menu does not deliver radical concepts or challenging innovations, rather it deals in impeccably produced French dishes of balance and refinement, put together with technical skill. Prices are high and the menus evolve at a slow pace. Lunch and dinner (choose from fixed-price lunch, carte or prestige menus) include all the extras you might imagine, from amuse-bouche to pre-dessert. Quail and wild mushroom pithivier with a confit of the leg and celeriac remoulade is a starter packed full of delicious flavours, while roasted fillet of line-caught turbot with langoustines, linguine and wild mushrooms is a beautifully presented main course based on superb produce. Poached white peaches with almond sable with raspberries, vanilla ice cream and champagne jelly is a well-balanced finale. Maître d' Jean-Claude Breton manages the front-of-house with charm and makes every customer feel as important as a Russian oligarch.

Chef Gordon Ramsay, Mark Askew
Owner Gordon Ramsay Holdings Ltd
Times 12-2.30/6.30-11 Closed 1 wk Xmas, Sat-Sun **Prices** Fixed L 3 course £45-£90, Fixed D 3 course £90, Tasting menu £120, Service added but optional 12.5% **Wines** 100+ bottles over £20, 2 bottles under £20, 13 by glass
Notes Tasting menu 7 course, Vegetarian menu, Dress restrictions, Smart dress, no jeans or trainers, Air con **Seats** 45 **Children** Portions

Tom Aikens

LONDON SW3   **PLAN 4 E2**

Modern French V  NOTABLE WINE LIST

Chelsea restaurant that tops the league

☎ 020 7584 2003   📄 020 7584 2001
43 Elystan St SW3 3NT
e-mail: info@tomaikens.co.uk
dir: Nearest station: South Kensington
Off Fulham Rd (Brompton Rd end)

Whether it was because of the credit crunch or financial downturn or something else, Tom Aikens got one hell of scare at the end of 2008 when his restaurant went into receivership. Luckily for him, and for us, his flagship restaurant did not close for a single day as financial backers were found. These backers clearly know a good thing when they see one, for this is surely one of the top restaurants in the UK, and Tom one of the country's most precocious talents. The restaurant on a quiet street in SW3 amid the urban piles of ordinary Chelsea folk is smartly understated and gives no inkling of what culinary stirrings are taking place within. The Anouska Hempel-designed interior is coolly minimalist with some natural materials (bamboo screens, dark-wood floors), black leather chairs and modern artwork giving a confident contemporary feel. Service gets the tone spot on, ensuring that, although everything is formal and professional, there is no trace of pomposity or stuffiness, while the wine list is astonishingly well put together. Tom's technical ability is second to none, his dishes crafted with considerable flair, and the menus - fixed-price lunch, carte and two tasting menus - are full of dishes that dazzle. Produce is uniformly outstanding, flavours hit the mark with relentless consistency, and everything from the bread (semolina, for example, or a glorious bacon and onion brioche) to the petits fours (a fabulous array including fruit-flavoured foams served on teaspoons) are made with phenomenal attention to detail. Langoustines of jaw-dropping freshness and flavour come both roasted and as a beignet, served with braised pig's cheek and a perfectly balanced ginger sauce. Main-course roast Ark chicken makes a star of this less glamorous of meats, partnered with a boudin, lemon macaroni, steamed egg yolk and a chicken jus that bursts with flavour. And for dessert a chocolate Dacuoise will send any lover of the cocoa bean into ecstasy - differing levels of intensity and varying flavours come from an array of mousses, creams and tuiles, with a milk ice cream to bring it all together. This is modern French cooking out of the top drawer.

Chef Tom Aikens **Owner** Tom Aikens
Times 12-2.30/6.45-11 Closed 2 wks Xmas & N Year, Etr, BHs & last 2 wks Aug, Sat & Sun **Prices** Fixed L from £29, Fixed D 3 course £65, Service added but optional 12.5% **Wines** 450 bottles over £20, 6 bottles under £20, 12 by glass **Notes** Vegetarian menu, Dress restrictions, Smart dress, no trainers/sportswear/T-shirts, Air con **Seats** 60, Pr/dining room 10 **Children** Portions **Parking** Parking meters outside

LONDON SW3 *continued*

combines an informal, lively ambience with traditional, seasonal food to create something for everyone. The large dining room is done out simply but with some style: oak is used for tables, chairs and flooring, there's a white marble-topped bar, and an open-to-view kitchen. There's also a cocktail bar and games room on the first floor, and a private dining room with its own lounge. The menu delivers British and French dishes of considerable flair, from breakfast and brunch (crispy bacon sandwich or brioche French toast), through lunch (Rhug Estate Cumberland sausages or macaroni cheese with black truffle) to dinner (Daylesford organic venison casserole with cranberries and root vegetable mash).

Chef Guy Bossom, Julien Maisonneuve **Owner** Tom Aikens **Times** 12-3/6-11.30 Closed 24-27 Dec, 1 Jan, L 28 Dec **Prices** Fixed L 2 course £16, Fixed D 3 course £19, Starter £5.50-£12, Main £12.50-£29, Dessert £6.50, Service added but optional 12.5% **Wines** 70 bottles over £20, 10 bottles under £20, 16 by glass **Notes** Fixed price menu not available all year round, Vegetarian available, Air con **Seats** 75, Pr/dining room 22 **Children** Portions **Parking** On street

Toto's
PLAN 4 F3

⊛ Traditional Italian

Relaxed Italian restaurant in elegant house

☎ 020 7589 2062 & 020 7589 0075   📠 020 7581 9668
Walton House, Walton St SW3 2JH
e-mail: totos.restaurant@btconnect.com
dir: Nearest station: Knightsbridge

This elegant white-painted house was once the home of Lady Clementine Spencer-Churchill, wife of Sir Winston. Tucked away just off Walton Street, with a discreet entrance shrouded by leafy potted shrubs, the corner property has a courtyard patio where you can lunch alfresco. Inside, a mezzanine overlooks the Mediterranean-style main dining room with its cheery sunflower yellow walls, porthole-shaped windows, leafy plants and impressive chandelier. Expect relaxed, attentive service and solid Italian cooking. The menu is lengthy and offers modern Italian cuisine underpinned with classic techniques. Expect carpaccio of milk-fed lamb with basil and white celery hearts, followed by roast monkfish with bacon and sage with crushed parsley potatoes and sun-dried tomato sauce.

Chef Paolo Simioni **Owner** Antonio Trapani **Times** 12.15-3/7-11 Closed 25-27 Dec, **Prices** Fixed L 2 course £23, Starter £9-£17, Main £12-£27, Dessert £7.50, Service added but optional 12.5% **Wines** 6 by glass **Notes** Sunday L, Vegetarian available, Dress restrictions, Smart casual, Air con **Seats** 90 **Children** Portions

LONDON SW4

Trinity Restaurant
PLAN 1 E3

⊛⊛⊛ – *see below*

Tsunami
PLAN 1 E3

⊛ Japanese

Japanese fusion food at affordable prices

☎ 020 7978 1610   📠 020 7978 1591
5-7 Voltaire Rd SW4 6DQ
dir: Nearest station: Clapham North Off Clapham High Street

Japanese-based fusion food has been one of the gastronomic stories of the past decade, but here in Clapham (there is also a branch in the West End), Tsunami offers the style at prices that are some way short of the eye-watering norm. Within the cool, minimalist surroundings with de rigueur open-plan kitchen, you can save the eye-watering for the wasabi-stuffed appetisers, such as salmon or yellowtail tuna tartare. Among the special dishes worth perusing are Sunkiss oysters dressed in chilli and coriander, roast duck and foie gras nigiri and, somewhat unexpectedly, a courgette flower filled with blue cheese, with miso for dipping. Most dishes work best for sharing, which doubles the fun.

continued

Trinity Restaurant

LONDON SW4   PLAN 1 E3

British, French

Creative, classy cooking in the heart of Clapham

☎ 020 7622 1199   📠 020 7622 1166
4 The Polygon, Clapham SW4 0JG
e-mail: dine@trinityrestaurant.co.uk
dir: Nearest station: Clapham Common Please telephone for directions

With its location in Clapham Old Town right next to the Common, Trinity is in the heart of the action, serving the local community, but the cooking of Adam Byatt has appeal well beyond the confines of SW4. Set well back from the road and with an open frontage, lunch can be an alfresco experience, while in the evening the room, done out in muted, natural colours, is somewhat sophisticated and always buzzing with the happy hum of contented customers. White-clothed tables, elegant cream and chocolate-coloured walls, comfortable cane-backed chairs and soft lighting, all provide a contemporary backdrop to the polished, modern cooking. There are also distant glimpses of the kitchen, plus a large private-dining 'kitchen table' that offers a closer window on all the action. Fixed-price lunch, à la carte and tasting menu reveal Byatt's highly inventive style, where creatively presented dishes based on classical French and modern European ideas combine with fine British produce and preparations. White onion and crayfish broth with seared crayfish, onion rings and rosemary is an imaginative first course, and Balmoral venison 'Wellington' comes with caramelised and creamed cauliflower, shaved Périgord truffles and juniper. Service gets the balance right, being both relaxed and professional.

Chef Adam Byatt **Owner** Angus Jones & Adam Byatt **Times** 12.30-2.30/6.30-10.30 Closed 24-26 Dec, L Mon, D Sun **Prices** Fixed L 2 course £15, Fixed D 3 course fr £20, Starter £7-£10, Main £16-£20, Dessert £6.50-£8, Service added but optional 12.5% **Wines** 80 bottles over £20, 9 bottles under £20, 10 by glass **Notes** Fixed D Mon-Thu, Tasting menu available, Sunday L, Vegetarian available, Air con **Seats** 63, Pr/dining room 12 **Children** Portions **Parking** On street

SW4 continued

Chef Ken Sam **Owner** Ken Sam **Times** 12.30-4/6-11 Closed 25 Dec-4 Jan, L Mon-Fri **Prices** Fixed L from £10.50, Fixed D 3 course £35-£45, Starter £4.90-£10.50, Main £7.70-£17.50, Dessert £3.95-£10.95, Service added but optional 12.5% **Wines** 37 bottles over £20, 11 bottles under £20, 10 by glass **Notes** Sunday L, Vegetarian available, Air con **Seats** 90 **Parking** On street

LONDON SW5

Cambio De Tercio
PLAN 4 C2

◉ Spanish

Contemporary Spanish cooking in buzzy atmosphere

☎ 020 7244 8970 📠 020 7373 2359
163 Old Brompton Rd SW5 0LJ
dir: Nearest station: Gloucester Road Close to junction with Drayton Gardens

The flamboyant interior of this small restaurant is as vibrant and lively as its friendly neighbourhood atmosphere. There's a black slate floor, bold paintwork (deep red, terracotta, pink and yellow) and equally audacious, eye-catching artwork, while white-clothed tables come with black undercloths and banquettes or round-backed chairs in black leather. You can follow three-course convention or, with all dishes also offered tapas style, go the grazing route instead. Expect quality ingredients, clear flavours and attractive modern presentation; perhaps a Basque-style monkfish in salsa verde with a stew of white asparagus and griddled oysters or slow-cooked rabbit with manzanilla sherry, thyme, broad beans and fig risotto.

Times 12-2.30/7-11.30 Closed 2 wks at Xmas, New Year

New Lotus Garden
PLAN 4 B2

◉ Chinese NEW

Snug neighbourhood Chinese handy for Earl's Court

☎ 020 7244 8984
15 Kenway Rd SW5 0RP
dir: Nearest station: Earl's Court

If you're looking for a cosy neighbourhood restaurant close to Earl's Court with a loyal local following, New Lotus Garden could be just the ticket. It's an unassuming, intimate place with just a dozen or so tables, but the food punches above its weight. The menu offers a tried-and-tested repertoire of Chinese classics, using fresh, well-prepared ingredients in crowd-pleasing dishes such as light and well-spiced pork dumplings, and crispy salt and pepper squid; mains offer exemplary versions of crispy duck or chicken with smoky black beans and green peppers. All accompanying dishes like fried rice and Singapore noodles are of an equally high standard.

Prices Food prices not confirmed for 2010. Please telephone for details.

LONDON SW6

Blue Elephant
PLAN 1 D3

◉ Traditional Thai V

Truly extravagant Fulham Thai

☎ 020 7385 6595 📠 020 7386 7665
3-6 Fulham Rd SW6 1AA
e-mail: london@blueelephant.com
dir: Nearest station: Fulham Broadway

From bustling Fulham Broadway, this extravagant, formidable-sized Thai restaurant (part of an international chain) instantly transports you to another world...the experience is almost like dining in a tropical rainforest. Imagine a stage-set canopy of lush verdant plants, trickling fountains, bridges spanning carp-filled ponds and a 12 metre gilded bar resembling a royal barge. Candles twinkle, while the scent of tropical flowers mingles with the heady aroma of exotic herbs and spices flown in fresh to service an equally flamboyant and lengthy menu. House favourites appear under a 'Suggestions' section, while the set 'Royal Thai Banquette' repertoire offers a tasting-style experience, otherwise main courses like green chicken curry, tamarind duck or ginger lobster might catch the eye.

Chef Somphang Sae-Jew **Owner** Blue Elephant International Group **Times** 12-2.30/7-12 Closed 25 Dec, 1 Jan, **Prices** Fixed L 2 course £12-£15, Fixed D 3 course £35-£39, Starter £6-£15, Main £12-£28, Dessert £8-£20, Service added but optional 12.5% **Wines** 80 bottles over £20, 9 bottles under £20, 14 by glass **Notes** Sunday L, Vegetarian menu, Dress restrictions, Smart casual, Air con **Seats** 350, Pr/dining room 14

Deep
PLAN 1 E3

◉◉ Seafood

Excellent seafood in restaurant with unbeatable waterside views

☎ 020 7736 3337 📠 020 7736 7578
8 The Boulevard, Imperial Wharf SW6 2UB
e-mail: info@deeplondon.co.uk
dir: Nearest station: Fulham Broadway From underground station take Harwood Rd then Imperial Rd

The stunning waterside location in London's Imperial Wharf is only part of the appeal of Deep - the luxurious dining room opens onto 2 terraces overlooking the water. The real draw is the Scandinavian-influenced contemporary cooking. From the open-plan kitchen comes carefully sourced seafood, plus some meaty options, with the high quality ingredients allowed to shine. Expect half a Devon crab with lemon and mayonnaise to start, while main courses might feature warm smoked trout with braised lentils and crispy leeks. A new 15-dish tasting menu showcases seafood from Sweden and there is a notable wine list tailored to match the fruits of the sea. With floor-to-ceiling windows and lots of stainless steel, backlit panels, pastel shades and suede seating, it's an appealingly modern venue.

Chef C Sandefeldt, F Bolin **Owner** Christian & Kerstin Sandefeldt **Times** 12-3/7-11 Closed Mon, L Sat, D Sun **Prices** Fixed L 2 course £21.50-£32.50, Fixed D 3 course £27.50-£35.50, Service added but optional 12.5% **Wines** 60 bottles over £20, 9 bottles under £20, 9 by glass **Notes** Tasting menu 7 course, Sunday L, Vegetarian available, Dress restrictions, Smart casual, Air con **Seats** 120 **Parking** Public car park, street parking after 5.30pm

The Harwood Arms
PLAN 1 D3

◉◉ British NEW

Fulham gastro-pub with creative, seasonal cooking

☎ 020 7386 1847
27 Walham Grove, Fulham SW6 1QR
dir: Nearest station: Fulham Broadway

From outside, this corner-sited pub doesn't stand out from the crowd, but looks can be deceptive. It has connections to the Ledbury in Notting Hill and the Pot Kiln in Berkshire (see entries), and that does make one sit up and take notice. Inside, there's a relaxed country-ish town-pub vibe, with contemporary huntin' and shootin' photos and a British menu fine-tuned to the seasons. Skilful simplicity, English produce and some lesser-seen combinations and thoughtful presentation drive chef Stephen Williams' highly creative repertoire. Game finds a strong hold, illustrated by a signature starter of game 'tea' with venison sausage roll, while the fish option might feature a crisp fillet of Wiltshire rainbow trout, perhaps served with smoked bacon, creamed spinach, semolina dumplings and sea purslane. Puds are comfort-style in the black treacle tart with clotted cream mould. With its smart, light, opened-up space inside, informed and unstuffy service, real ales and great food, is this the perfect gastro-pub?

Times 12-3/6.30-9.30

Marco
PLAN 1 D3

◉◉ Modern European

Stylish modern brasserie at Chelsea FC

☎ 020 7915 2929 📠 020 7565 1450
M&C Hotels At Chelsea FC, Stamford Bridge, Fulham Rd SW6 1HS
e-mail: reservations.chelsea@mill-cop.com
dir: Nearest station: Fulham Broadway

Blue is not the colour at Marco Pierre White's restaurant in the Chelsea Football Club complex at Stamford Bridge - expect sophisticated tones of black and brown and a striking golden pillar of Swarovski crystal. It's a collaboration between MPW and club owner Roman Abramovich, housed on the ground floor of the complex's Copthorne Hotel. It's a smartly cool venue, stylishly elegant with subtle black hues, low lighting, plush curved leather banquettes and white linen-clad tables - definitely a Premier League look. As you would expect from Marco the carte combines the refinement of French cuisine with modern British influences. The food avoids football clichés to deliver Morecambe Bay potted shrimps or a terrine of foie gras to start, followed by braised belly pork Marco Polo with buttered beans and braising juices. There's a fixed-price match day menu.

Times 12-2.30/6-10.30 Closed Sun, Mon

Memories of India on the River   PLAN 1 E3

Indian

Sophisticated Indian restaurant in luxury riverside development

☎ 020 7736 0077   ▤ 020 7731 5222
7 The Boulevard, Imperial Wharf, Townmead Rd, Chelsea SW6 2UB
dir: Nearest station: Fulham Broadway Close to Chelsea Harbour

Located in the scenic setting of the Imperial Wharf development beside the river in Chelsea, this restaurant offers a sophisticated gastronomic journey across the Indian subcontinent. The upmarket décor includes a centrepiece palm tree, polished-wood floors, tan leather banquettes and elegant chairs, white linen, wooden screens, interesting objets d'art, artworks and feature lighting. The lengthy menu features dishes that combine classic regional recipes with contemporary cooking trends, such as spicy, sweet and smoky flavoured chicken with traditional Indian spice, garnished with fresh lime, coriander and sesame seeds, or maybe lamb cooked in coconut milk tempered with mustard and curry leaf and served with coconut rice.

Chef Abdur Razzak **Owner** Mr Belal Ali & Mr Abdul Jalil **Times** 12-3/5.30-11.30 Closed 25 Dec **Prices** Food prices not confirmed for 2010. Please telephone for details. **Wines** 25 bottles over £20, 20 bottles under £20, 6 by glass **Notes** Sun brunch inc. 5 course menu, Vegetarian available, Air con **Seats** 100, Pr/dining room 30 **Children** Portions, Menu **Parking** 50

Saran Rom   PLAN 1 E3

Thai

Luxury Thames-side Thai specialising in authentic cuisine

☎ 020 7751 3111 & 7751 3110   ▤ 020 7751 3112
Imperial Wharf, The Boulevard, Townmead Rd SW6 2UB
e-mail: info@saranrom.com
dir: Nearest station: Fulham Broadway 1.5m from Stamford Bridge/Fulham Broadway tube station

The first reaction on entering this lavish Thai restaurant in a chic Chelsea riverside development is that the designers were let loose with a blank cheque. The sumptuous décor - an opulent Aladdin's cave of silk hangings, 19th-century antiques, teak carvings and ornate fretwork panels - owes more than a nod to Thailand's royal palaces. Add an outside terrace and river views from all levels, and you have a cracking setting for some interesting and skilfully-prepared cuisine. The mouth-searing potential of dishes is helpfully flagged up with red chilli symbols, so you might start with spicy

salmon tartare with subtle Thai herbs, and move on to main courses such as Massaman - a South Thailand slow-braised lamb curry with potatoes and cashews.

Chef Mr Tou **Owner** Blue Elephant Ltd **Times** 6-11 Closed 25 Dec, 1-4 Jan, L all week **Prices** Fixed L 2 course fr £15, Fixed D 2 course fr £35, Starter £7.50-£12, Main £15-£25, Dessert £6.50-£8.50, Service added but optional 12.5% **Wines** 40 bottles over £20, 9 bottles under £20, 22 by glass **Notes** Vegetarian available, Air con **Seats** 200, Pr/dining room 100 **Children** Portions **Parking** 100

Yi-Ban Chelsea   PLAN 1 E3

Chinese

Stylish modern oriental dining in Chelsea riverside development

☎ 020 7731 6606   ▤ 020 7731 7584
No 5 The Boulevard, Imperial Wharf, Imperial Rd SW6 2UB
e-mail: michael@yi-ban.co.uk
dir: Nearest station: Fulham Broadway Please telephone for directions

Yi Ban has a chic minimalist décor in keeping with its fashionable location in the swish riverside development at Imperial Wharf. If you make it past the glamorous cocktail bar with its cutting-edge concoctions, food is delivered in a dark, moodily-lit dining room with black-lacquered tables, where dark-wood fittings, shimmery voile curtains and dangling crimson lanterns put a contemporary spin on oriental décor. Youthful staff in long aprons provide slick, buzzy service, while the kitchen deals in contemporary, well-designed oriental cuisine to suit the surroundings. Chinese staples include black cod with yuzo miso or wok-fried monkfish with asparagus and cashew nuts.

Times 6-11 Closed 1 wk from 22 Dec, Sun, L all week

LONDON SW7

Ambassade de l'Ile   PLAN 4 C2

– see page 274

L'Etranger   PLAN 4 C4

French, Japanese

French food with a Japanese slant in a smart setting

☎ 020 7584 1118   ▤ 020 7584 8886
36 Gloucester Rd SW7 4QT
e-mail: axelle@circagroupltd.co.uk
dir: Nearest station: Gloucester Rd 5 mins walk from Gloucester Rd tube station at junct of Queens Gate Terrace and Gloucester Rd

East meets West at this elegant restaurant located at the Kensington Gardens end of Gloucester Road. The cooking style is an imaginative blend of classic French dishes with some Japanese flavours, resulting in a savvy menu that kicks away convention while respectfully

acknowledging it. Extravagantly beautiful dishes are deliberately eye-catching, and the competent cooking matched with top-notch ingredients ensures that satisfaction is more than merely visual. Opposites continue to attract with striking effect in the stylish table and wall decorations, where a blend of minimalism and luxury create a sophisticated calm. Choose from half a dozen caviars to start, or perhaps tartare de boeuf Charolais, followed by caramelised black cod with miso. The wine list is first-class too, and the dedicated sommelier heads a highly professional team.

Chef Jerome Tauvron **Owner** Ibi Issolah **Times** 12-3/6-11 Closed 25 Dec, 1 Jan, L Sat **Prices** Fixed L 2 course £16.50, Starter £8.50-£21.50, Main £15.50-£49, Dessert £8.50-£12.50, Service added but optional 12.5% **Wines** 1000+ bottles over £20, 9 bottles under £20, 14 by glass **Notes** Early Bird menu available Mon-Fri 6-6.45pm, Sun brunch 12-3, Sunday L, Vegetarian available, Dress restrictions, Smart casual, no T-shirts, Air con **Seats** 75, Pr/dining room 20 **Children** Portions **Parking** NCP

Madsen   PLAN 4 D3

European, Scandinavian NEW

Modern Scandinavian brasserie-style restaurant

☎ 020 7225 2772   ▤ 020 7225 2772
20 Old Brompton Rd, South Kensington SW7 3DL
e-mail: reservations@madsenrestaurant.com
web: www.madsenrestaurant.com
dir: Nearest station: South Kensington

Spearheading a Nordic cuisine renaissance, the glass-fronted Madsen stands out from the touristy eateries around South Ken tube station. It's a clean-lined, contemporary space, as you might expect, with pale woods, white walls and bright red bar stools and banquette seating; Poul Henningsen lighting is another Nordic style statement. The straightforward Scandinavian cooking is equally light and well presented (healthy too), blending tradition with modernity, using locally-sourced, seasonal ingredients. Expect skagen soup to open, and perhaps baked pollock teamed with pea purée, boiled potatoes and sauce vin blanc to follow on the evening carte, while lunch is exclusively smørrebrød (both cold and warm dishes). Big on eco-ethics, the little street-side terrace comes with blankets rather than patio heaters.

Chef René Madsen **Owner** Charlotte Kruse Madsen **Times** 12-4/6-10 Closed Xmas, **Prices** Starter £4.50-£8, Main £11.50-£18.50, Dessert £4.50-£7.50, Service optional, Groups min 5 service 12.5% **Wines** 31 bottles

continued

LONDON SW7 *continued*

over £20, 7 bottles under £20, 13 by glass **Notes** Sunday L, Vegetarian available, Air con **Seats** 50, Pr/dining room 14 **Children** Portions, Menu **Parking** On street

Zuma
PLAN 4 F4

◉◉ Modern Japanese

Glamorous setting for sophisticated Japanese cuisine

☎ 020 7584 1010 🖹 020 7584 5005
5 Raphael St SW7 1DL
e-mail: info@zumarestaurant.com
dir: Nearest station: Knightsbridge. Brompton Rd west, turn right into Lancelot Pl & follow road to right into Raphael St

Situated in the heart of Knightsbridge, Zuma offers an innovative twist on the traditional Japanese isakaya style of informal eating. The ultra modern restaurant is a positive temple to good design with stone, wood, glass, lighting and carefully placed plants combining to enhance the space. The menu relies on the freshest of produce and the elegantly presented dishes are served from the main kitchen, the sushi bar or the robata grill. Dishes are designed for sharing and are brought to the table continuously throughout the meal. Small dishes include hamachi usuzukuri pirikara ninniku gake (sliced yellowtail with green chilli relish, ponzu and pickled garlic) and from the robata grill there is hotate no ume

shiso yaki (grilled scallops with ume boshi, shiso and mentaiko), or rib-eye no daikon ponzu fuumi (steak with wafu sauce and garlic crisps).

Chef Ross Shonhan **Owner** Rainer Becker
Times 12-2.30/6-11 Closed 25-26 Dec, 1 Jan,
Prices Food prices not confirmed for 2010. Please telephone for details. **Wines** 2 bottles under £20, 13 by glass **Notes** Sunday L, Vegetarian available, Air con **Seats** 147, Pr/dining room 14 **Children** Portions **Parking** Street parking

LONDON SW8

Tom Ilic
PLAN 1 E3

◉◉ Modern European

Robust flavours from seasoned chef in Battersea

☎ 020 7622 0555
123 Queenstown Rd SW8 3RH
dir: Nearest station: Close to Clapham Junct & Battersea Power Station

Head to Queenstown Road for bold flavours and a relaxed and unpretentious atmosphere at Tom Ilic's eponymous restaurant. Everything from the unruffled confidence of the service through to the use of underrated cuts of meat on the menu, reflect the chef-patron's no-nonsense approach to modern European cooking. The room is simply decorated (wooden floors, terracotta and soft-pink colours on the walls) and does not distract - this place is

about good food and good company. Music adds to the buzz. There's a great value fixed-price lunch menu and an evening carte that is also unlikely to break the bank. Braised pig's cheeks and chorizo with garlic and parsley mash ably demonstrates the style of the food, following on, perhaps, with roast breast and confit leg of wild duck, served with creamed Savoy cabbage, parsnips and spiced pear. Dark chocolate fondant with pistachio ice cream is an indulgent end to a meal.

Chef Tom Ilic **Owner** Tom Ilic **Times** 12-2.30/6-10.30 Closed Last wk Aug, Xmas, Mon, L Tue & Sat, D Sun **Prices** Fixed L 2 course £14.50-£16.95, Starter £5.95-£8.50, Main £10.50-£15.50, Dessert fr £5.50, Service added but optional 12.5% **Wines** 8 by glass **Notes** Sunday L, Vegetarian available, Air con **Seats** 58 **Children** Portions **Parking** On street

---

Ambassade de l'Ile

LONDON SW7	PLAN 4 C2

Modern French **NEW**
☎ 020 7373 7774 🖹 020 7370 5102
117-119 Old Brompton Rd SW7 3RN
e-mail: direction@ambassadedelile.com
dir: Nearest station: Gloucester Rd/S Kensington

Jean-Christophe Ansanay-Alex is a man with both talent and hyphens in abundance. His restaurant on the l'Ile Barbe in Lyon (a small island in the River Saône which runs through the city) has been garlanded with praise and now he has a South Kensington outpost in an Edwardian building, once a library, on the Old Brompton Road. The dining room is far from Edwardian with white leather chairs and smartly set tables, and two plasma screens showing the action from the kitchen (there's a chef's table, seating four, for those who want to get up close and personal). The team of ten chefs use first-class

seasonal produce, including British meats and fish from the South Coast, and even the cheeseboard includes English cheeses among its number. The inspiration is the chef's home region. This is modern, refined cooking, all the way from the amuse-bouche (snail and mint polenta balls, for example) to a beautifully balanced soufflé of autumn apples with bourbon and vanilla syrup at dessert. In-between, scallops sit in a rich and creamy broth, and saddle of hare ballotine comes with pear and beetroot confit in a perfectly executed main course. There is a good value two- or three-course lunch menu, while à la carte and tasting menu prices are high. The French-focused wine list contains much of interest; prices start at £25.

Chef Jean-Christophe Ansanay-Alex **Owner** Jean-Christophe Ansanay-Alex **Times** 12-2/7-10 Closed Xmas, 3 wks Aug, Sun-Mon **Prices** Fixed L 2 course £20, Fixed D 3 course £45, Tasting menu £70, Starter £19-£24, Main £26-£30, Dessert £14, Service added but optional 12.5%, Groups min 8 service 15% **Wines** 450 bottles over £20, 8 by glass **Notes** Tasting menu 6 course, Vegetarian

available, Dress restrictions, Smart casual, Air con **Seats** 35, Pr/dining room 12 **Parking** On street

LONDON SW10

Aubergine
PLAN 4 C1

See below

Chutney Mary Restaurant
PLAN 1 E3

◎◎ Indian

Seductive, modern Indian offering refined cuisine

☎ 020 7351 3113   📄 020 7351 7694
535 King's Rd, Chelsea SW10 0SZ
e-mail: chutneymary@realindianfood.com
dir: Nearest station: Fulham Broadway On corner of King's Rd and Lots Rd; 2 mins from Chelsea Harbour

Chutney Mary has been in the business of wowing lovers of Indian cuisine with its revised, creative take on the sub-continent's delights since 1991. Moghul mirror-work murals lead to the classy split-level basement, moodily aglow with mirrors and antique Raj-era sketches, all romantically-lit with a forest of flickering candles. The kitchen brigade imports influences and expertise from their home regions, including the hottest trends from Mumbai, to keep their refined modern Indian cooking sharp and inventive without losing touch with pukka classical heritage. Take scallop Malabar, which bathes ultra-fresh seafood in coconut, ginger and saffron, and Kerala pepper-roast duck, served pink with cinnamon, coconut and black pepper sauce and sweet potato crumble. Wine and spicy food pairing is always tricky, so ask the knowledgeable staff for their input. (See entries for sister restaurants Veeraswamy and Amaya.)

Times 12.30–3/6.30–11.30 Closed L Mon-Fri, D 25 Dec

The Painted Heron
PLAN 1 E3

◎◎ Modern Indian

Stylish, upmarket and impressive modern Indian

☎ 020 7351 5232   📄 020 7351 5313
112 Cheyne Walk SW10 0DJ
e-mail: thepaintedheron@btinternet.com
dir: Nearest station: South Kensington Telephone for directions

On the embankment close to Battersea Bridge, a blue awning and glass frontage picks out this modern Chelsea Indian. Minimalist décor - black lacquered leather-upholstered chairs, dark slatted blinds and plain white walls adorned with striking modern art - deliver a stylish, contemporary edge to this deceptively roomy, split-level restaurant. There's just a hint of the nautical reflecting its Thames-side location, with blond-wood floors and black metal handrails lining steps, plus there's a small bar and alfresco courtyard. High-quality modern Indian cooking, with traditional dishes given contemporary spin and presentation, focuses on prime ingredients and balanced spicing. Cornish haddock, for example, in a Bengal mustard curry, or corn-fed chicken supreme stuffed with pickled chilli in a hot South Indian curry.

Times 12–3/6.30–11 Closed Xmas & Etr, L Sat

Vama
PLAN 1 E3

◎◎ Indian **V**

Authentic cooking in stylish modern Indian

☎ 020 7565 8500 & 7351 4118   📄 020 7565 8501
438 King's Rd SW10 0LJ
e-mail: manager@vama.co.uk
dir: Nearest station: Sloane Square, Earl's Court. About 20 mins walk down King's Rd

This stylish, contemporary Indian in World's End is elegantly decorated with rich ochre walls hung with oil paintings, hand-crafted teak chairs and hand-made crockery. Tables are dressed in white linen and the polite staff are smartly attired, all of which sets the scene for accomplished classical North-West Indian cuisine, mainly

continued

Aubergine

Rosettes not confirmed at time of going to press

LONDON SW10
PLAN 4 C1

Modern French

Rarefied French cuisine in well-heeled Chelsea

☎ 020 7352 3449   📄 020 7351 1770
11 Park Walk, Chelsea SW10 0AJ
e-mail: aubergine@londonfinediningroup.com
web: www.auberginerestaurant.co.uk
dir: Nearest station: South Kensington, Fulham Broadway W along Fulham Rd, close to Chelsea and Westminster Hospital

No matter that if this place were in the US, it would be called, less poetically, Eggplant, the aubergine is enthusiastically celebrated here - a trifle obsessively, you might think, as you push an aubergine-shaped door handle to get in. The dining room is a pastel-hued oasis of calm civility, with precise, formal service, and appointments that are as smart as the moneyed Chelsea location mandates. William Drabble, who took up the reins here in 1998, left as the guide went to press, with his former sous chef, Christophe Renou, stepping into his shoes (or should that be kitchen clogs?). The rarefied contemporary French cuisine keeps a weather eye on the seasons and it all comes at quite a price for a three-course menu. Carpaccio of monkfish shows the style, sharply supported by apple and fennel salad and lemon vinaigrette, while the appearance of pig's head galette with shallots and capers suggests a willingness to mine the more rustic seams of French cooking. Frogs and snails feature too, while main courses follow on with poached collar of bacon in foie gras, duck breast with figs in port, and roasted John Dory in rosemary butter. Desserts might include coffee soufflé with chocolate sauce and banana parfait with pistachios. An extensive wine list offers the produce of some of the world's best growers.

Chef Christophe Renou **Owner** London Fine Dining Group **Times** 12–2.30/7–11.30 Closed Xmas, Mon (except BHs), L Sat **Prices** Fixed L 3 course fr £35, Fixed D 3 course fr £55, Service added but optional 12.5% **Wines** 500 bottles over £20, 1 bottles under £20 **Notes** Menu gourmand 7 courses from £77, Vegetarian available, Dress restrictions, Smart casual preferred, Air con **Seats** 60 **Children** Portions **Parking** Local parking available

LONDON SW10 *continued*

Punjabi. There is a good use of marinades and spices with most of the dishes finished off in the clay oven to give the authentic taste of charcoal cooking. Typical dishes include marinated chicken fillet in a crispy chilli batter with crushed roasted cumin seeds and ginger, followed by prawn curry with coconut, mustard seeds and curry leaf sauce.

Chef Andy Varma **Owner** Andy Varma, Arjun Varma **Times** 12-4/6-11 Closed 25-26 Dec, 1 Jan, L Mon-Sat **Prices** Starter £5-£11.95, Main £6.25-£12.95, Dessert £6.95, Service added 12.5%, Groups min 6 service 12.5% **Wines** 12 bottles over £20, 1 bottles under £20, 3 by glass **Notes** Sunday L, Vegetarian menu, Dress restrictions, Smart casual, Air con **Seats** 120, Pr/dining room 35 **Parking** 25, Edith Grove, NCP

Wyndham Grand
London Chelsea Harbour
PLAN 1 E3

◎ International

Sophisticated waterside dining

☎ 020 7300 8443 📠 020 7351 6525
Chelsea Harbour SW10 0XG
dir: Nearest station: Fulham Broadway

Aquasia is a contemporary designed restaurant located on the first floor of the luxurious Wyndham Grand Hotel and enjoys stunning views over the Thames and Chelsea Harbour's small marina. Local gallery art adorns the walls, floors are wooden, tables are simply appointed, and there's a warm and intimate atmosphere in the evening. On warm summer days the restaurant's floor-to-ceiling glass panels open to allow guests a unique alfresco dining experience. Expect modern European cooking with an Asian twist and ambitious dishes that display an array of flavours and some unusual combinations; crab with grapefruit, chilli and avocado purée, pigeon with rosemary and balsamic sauce, and coconut and lemongrass crème brûlée.

Times All day

LONDON SW11

The Butcher & Grill
PLAN 1 E3

◎ Modern, Traditional

A carnivore's delight in warehouse-style surroundings

☎ 020 7924 3999 📠 020 7223 7977
39-41 Parkgate Rd, Battersea SW11 4NP
e-mail: info@thebutcherandgrill.com
dir: Nearest station: Clapham Junction, Battersea

The presence of a butcher's shop and delicatessen at the entrance to this grill firmly establishes its credentials as a serious restaurant. The menu is based around the first-rate meats on display in the shop, and the vast array of cheeses, cured meats, olives and peppers in the deli. Grills of all kinds dominate (you can choose your own cut from the display), though there's plenty for non-carnivores too. In the setting of this informal old

warehouse near Albert Bridge you can choose spinach and tomato dahl with feta samosa, and slow-roast paprika pork belly with clams and chorizo. Service fits the informal style of the place.

Chef Robert Arnott **Owner** Paul Grout, Dominic Ford, Simon Tindall **Times** 12-3.30/6-11 Closed 25-27 Dec, D Sun **Prices** Fixed L 2 course fr £12.50, Starter £4.95-£13.50, Main £7.50-£25, Dessert £5-£7.50, Service added but optional 12.5% **Wines** 52 bottles over £20, 16 bottles under £20, 13 by glass **Notes** Sunday L, Vegetarian available, Air con **Seats** 131 **Children** Portions, Menu **Parking** On street

Ransome's Dock
PLAN 1 E3

◎◎ Modern British 🍷

Seasonal, unpretentious cooking by the Thames

☎ 020 7223 1611 & 7924 2462 📠 020 7924 2614
35-37 Parkgate Rd, Battersea SW11 4NP
e-mail: chef@ransomesdock.co.uk
dir: Nearest station: Sloane Square/Clapham Junction Between Albert Bridge & Battersea Bridge

A mere stroll from one of London's prettiest river crossings, Albert Bridge, this easy-going restaurant occupies a former ice cream factory beside a disused wharf. The large brick building may look a bit austere on the outside, but inside is all relaxed charm and bistro-like décor. Cornflower blue walls are lined with photos and paintings, and generous wooden tables are given plenty of space. The kitchen demands absolute freshness from its produce, much of it organic, and it shows in the flavours and textures delivered by the menu. This is strictly food for enjoying rather than paying homage to, ably demonstrated by daily specials like devilled crab and medallions of monkfish in a mussel and saffron sauce. The award-winning wine list is worth a browse.

Chef Martin Lam, Vanessa Lam **Owner** Mr & Mrs M Lam **Times** 12-11 Closed Xmas, D Sun **Prices** Fixed L 2 course £15.50, Fixed D 2 course £15.50, Starter £5.50-£12.50, Main £10.50-£25, Dessert £5.50-£8, Service added but optional 12.5% **Wines** 360 bottles over £20, 22 bottles under £20, 10 by glass **Notes** Brunch menu Sat & Sun, Sunday L, Vegetarian available **Seats** 55 **Children** Portions **Parking** 20, Spaces in evenings & wknds only

LONDON SW12

Harrison's
PLAN 1 E2

◎ Modern British NEW

Friendly, modern, neighbourhood brasserie that puts Balham on the map

☎ 020 8675 6900 📠 020 8673 3965
15-19 Bedford Hill SW12 9EX
e-mail: info@harrisonsbalham.co.uk
dir: Nearest station: Balham Turn right from Balham High Rd opposite Waitrose, onto Bedford Hill. Restaurant on corner of Bedford Hill & Harberson Rd

The second venture from Sam Harrison (of Sam's Brasserie & Bar in Chiswick - see entry), this Balham

offshoot opened back in October 2007. It cuts a dash just off the bustling High Road, with its roll-back glass frontage, awnings and pavement tables, while inside a big, trendy, centrepiece metal-formed bar catches the eye, with its drinks counter and open kitchen. Large, low-slung lightshades, banquettes, simple modern chairs, unclothed tables and friendly, attentive service complete the relaxed, upbeat vibe. The cooking fits the bill; pared-back, straightforward, clean-cut brasserie dishes with a modern twist that come driven by quality ingredients. Take pan-fried hake with spinach and lemon risotto and caper butter, or rib-eye with fries and béarnaise sauce. There's also a bar menu.

Chef Dan Edwards **Owner** Sam Harrison **Times** 12-mdnt Closed 24-27 Dec, L 28 Dec **Prices** Fixed L 2 course fr £12, Fixed D 3 course fr £17, Starter £5-£7.50, Main £7.50-£14.50, Dessert £3.50-£7.50, Service added but optional 12.5% **Wines** 50 bottles over £20, 15 bottles under £20, 21 by glass **Notes** Sunday L, Vegetarian available, Air con **Seats** 80, Pr/dining room 40 **Children** Portions, Menu **Parking** On street

Lamberts
PLAN 1 E2

◎◎ Modern British

Seasonal British food in relaxed neighbourhood eatery

☎ 020 8675 2233
2 Station Pde, Balham High Rd SW12 9AZ
e-mail: bookings@lambertsrestaurant.com
dir: Nearest station: Balham Just S of Balham station on Balham High Rd

Still regarded by many as Balham's best restaurant, this fashionable, informal neighbourhood eatery has a large and loyal following. The muted colours and use of wood makes it a warm, relaxed space and the chilled out background music adds to its laidback ambience. The food is anything but laidback, with impeccable sourcing of ingredients from trusted suppliers. Some of the produce is organic, with most of the meat coming straight from the farms and fish arriving overnight from day boats. The menu is fiercely seasonal and staunchly British, with old favourites rubbing shoulders with contemporary interpretations of classics; think venison and apricot pie, wild rabbit hotpot with swede purée and treacle tart with vanilla ice cream.

Chef David Johnson **Owner** Mr Joe Lambert **Times** 12-5/7-10.30 Closed 25 Dec, 1 Jan, BH's (except Good Fri), Mon, L Mon-Fri, D Sun **Prices** Fixed L 2 course £17-£20, Fixed D 3 course fr £20, Starter £6-£7.50, Main £14-£19, Dessert £6-£8, Service added but optional 12.5% **Wines** 65 bottles over £20, 12 bottles under £20, 12 by glass **Notes** Sunday L, Vegetarian available, Air con **Seats** 50 **Children** Portions, Menu **Parking** On street

LONDON SW13

Sonny's Restaurant
PLAN 1 D3

◎◎ Modern European

Accomplished cooking in popular neighbourhood brasserie

☎ 020 8748 0393 📠 020 8748 2698
94 Church Rd, Barnes SW13 0DQ
e-mail: barnes@sonnys.co.uk
dir: Nearest station: Barnes/Hammersmith From Castelnau end of Church Rd on left by shops

A popular haunt for locals for almost a quarter of a century, Sonny's is in a parade of shops behind a glass frontage. This smart, recently refurbished neighbourhood restaurant is deceptively spacious (it goes back and back) and the interior is light and airy, with striking contemporary artwork, and an open fire set into a wall of opaque glass bricks at the far end. White tablecloths, a black floor and modern chairs hit the spot too, while the atmosphere is buzzy and upbeat and service on the money. The accomplished kitchen's modern European brasserie approach is skillfully executed and based around quality ingredients, clear flavours and colourful presentation; think gazpacho with a grilled scallop and tomato and basil sorbet followed by grilled fillet of veal with crisp potato, roasted marrow, girolles and sherry vinegar jus. Finish with white chocolate and pistachio parfait. Sonny's Food Shop and café is next door.

Times 12.30-2.30/7.30-11 Closed BHs, D Sun

LONDON SW14

The Depot Waterfront Brasserie PLAN 1 D3

◎ British, European

Popular, relaxed riverside brasserie

☎ 020 8878 9462 📠 020 8392 1361
125 Mortlake High St, Barnes SW14 8SN
e-mail: info@depotbrasserie.co.uk
dir: Nearest station: Barnes Bridge Between Barnes Bridge & Mortlake stations

With a waterfront location - situated in what used to be a stable block and courtyard - this Thames-side brasserie blends informality with contemporary decor. A stylish bar, banquette seating, simple bare tables, neutral shades and parquet flooring complement the unstuffy, upbeat atmosphere, while river-view window tables are sought after out back and the front courtyard terrace proves a fair-weather hit. The daily-changing menu delivers simply constructed, modern brasserie-style dishes driven by quality ingredients, such as roast cod partnered with grilled aubergines, cavolo nero and olive dressing.

Chef Gary Knowles **Owner** Tideway Restaurants Ltd
Times 12-3.30/6-11 **Prices** Fixed L 2 course fr £12.50, Starter £4.85-£6.80, Main £8.95-£17.95, Dessert £4.85-£7.50, Service added but optional 12.5% **Wines** 32 bottles over £20, 19 bottles under £20, 20 by glass **Notes** Sunday L, Vegetarian available **Seats** 120, Pr/dining room 60 **Children** Portions, Menu **Parking** Parking after 6.30pm and at weekends

LONDON SW15

Enoteca Turi
PLAN 1 D3

◎◎ Italian 🍷 NOTABLE WINE LIST

Seasonal, regional Italian cooking in Putney

☎ 020 8785 4449 📠 020 8780 5409
28 Putney High St SW15 1SQ
e-mail: enoteca@tiscali.co.uk
dir: Nearest station: Putney Bridge Opposite Odeon Cinema near bridge

Italophiles will find much to please if they make the journey to Giuseppe Turi's smart family-run set-up at the river end of Putney High Street. Polished blond-wood floors and warmly glowing ochre and terracotta shades speak of the Mediterranean in an interior that is contemporary without losing warmth. Giuseppe hails from Puglia, on the heel of Italy, so dishes from this region appear on the concise menu, together with traditional cuisine from the regions of Marche and Umbria. Yet dishes are not set in stone: the kitchen revels in reinterpreting old favourites without sacrificing their inherent character and bold flavours. Pasta dishes include a Puglian peasant favourite of orechiette ('little ears') with turnip tops, garlic and chilli, while main courses pack plenty of punch in roast and braised rabbit with olives and sun-dried tomatoes. A bin number alongside each dish suggests the perfect glass to go with it, otherwise there's an exciting 300-strong list covering every nook and cranny of Italy's wine regions.

Chef G Turi, M Tagliaferri **Owner** Mr G & Mrs P Turi
Times 12-2.30/7-11 Closed 25-26 Dec, 1 Jan, Sun, L BHs **Prices** Fixed L 3 course fr £15.50, Starter £7.50-£9.50, Main £10.50-£21.50, Dessert £5.75-£8.50, Service added but optional 12.5% **Wines** 300 bottles over £20, 16 bottles under £20, 11 by glass **Notes** Vegetarian available, Dress restrictions, Smart casual, Air con **Seats** 85, Pr/dining room 18 **Children** Portions **Parking** Putney Exchange car park, on street

Talad Thai Restaurant
PLAN 1 D3

◎ Thai

Authentic Thai cooking in Putney

☎ 020 8789 8084 📠 020 8789 8601
320 Upper Richmond Rd, Putney SW15 6TL
e-mail: info@taladthai.co.uk
dir: Nearest station: Putney/East Putney

Talad Thai started off as a small supermarket, selling a wide range of ingredients imported directly from Thailand. At the back of the store, Mrs Kriangsak held cooking demonstrations every Sunday as an attempt to spread the art of Thai cooking to her customers. It has now blossomed into an additional restaurant with a very homely air, its informal wooden tables packed closely together, and a relaxed and buzzing atmosphere. The traditional menu is fairly long and split into sections like starters, salads, soups, curries, stirfries and noodle dishes. Out front, the friendly waiting staff work hard to make you feel at home. Expect the likes of Thai beef salad, stir-fried basil with pork and garlic fried squid.

Chef Suthasinee Pramwew **Owner** Mr Sa-ard Kriangsak
Times 11.30-3/5.30-11 Closed 25-26 Dec, 1 Jan, Sat-Sun **Prices** Starter £4.55-£12, Main £5.50-£7.95, Dessert £3-£3.75, Service optional, Groups min 8 service 10% **Wines** 7 bottles under £20, 1 by glass **Notes** Vegetarian available, Air con **Seats** 40, Pr/dining room 40 **Parking** On street opposite

LONDON SW17

Chez Bruce
PLAN 1 E2

◎◎◎ – see page 278

Kastoori
PLAN 1 E2

◎ Indian V 🌶

Family-run Indian vegetarian

☎ 020 8767 7027 📠 020 8767 7027
188 Upper Tooting Rd SW17 7EJ
dir: Nearest station: Tooting Bec/Tooting Broadway. Situated between two stations.

Upper Tooting Road is full of Indian cafés, restaurants and shops selling saris, and among all this bustling life is the Thanki family's unpretentious and friendly vegetarian restaurant. It isn't dressed to thrill: closely-packed tables donned in vibrant yellow cloths and a dark blue carpet with lots of leafy fronds are not exactly cutting edge, but no matter. Kastoori is about well-executed, skilfully spiced Gujarati vegetarian dishes threaded with East African flavours, with many suitable for vegans. The hot-and-spicy tomato curry is a signature, or perhaps go for the chana bateta (chick pea and potato curry), and do ask about the chef's daily choices and Thanki family specials, like the matoki (a green banana curry).

Chef Manoj Thanki **Owner** Mr D Thanki
Times 12.30-2.30/6-10.30 Closed 25-26 Dec, L Mon & Tue **Prices** Food prices not confirmed for 2010. Please telephone for details. **Wines** 1 bottles over £20, 19 bottles under £20, 2 by glass **Notes** Sunday L, Vegetarian menu, Air con **Seats** 82 **Children** Portions **Parking** On street

LONDON SW19

Common
PLAN 1 D2

◉◉ Modern European 🌱

Vibrant food in country-house-style hotel

☎ 020 8879 1464 📠 020 8879 7338
Cannizaro House, West Side, Wimbledon Common SW19 4UE
e-mail: info@cannizarohouse.com
dir: Nearest station: Wimbledon From A3 (London Rd) Tibbets Corner, take A219 (Parkside) right into Cannizaro Rd, then right into West Side.

Named after the Sicilian Duke of Cannizaro and his Scottish wife, who lived here from 1817 until 1841, this elegant 18th century mansion has a long history of distinguished residents and guests, including the Duke of Wellington. Since 1987, it has been London's first self-styled country-house hotel and the popular Common dining room, with its comfortably upholstered chairs, fine art, murals and stunning fireplaces, is an added draw. Focusing on seasonal produce, classic French techniques underpin a menu of vibrant colours and contrasting textures. Dishes are simply presented, as in Falmouth Bay scallops with smoked potato purée, golden raisins and gingerbread, followed by corn-fed chicken breast, baby leek and salsify presse and roast chicken purée.

Chef Christian George **Owner** Bridgehouse Hotels **Times** 12-3/7-10 **Prices** Fixed L 2 course £19.50-£23.50, Fixed D 3 course £27-£30, Tasting menu £60, Starter £7-£14, Main £16-£24, Dessert £7-£10, Service optional **Wines** 110 bottles over £20, 20 bottles under £20, 14 by glass **Notes** Sunday L, Vegetarian available, Dress restrictions, No shorts, Civ Wed 100 **Seats** 46, Pr/dining room 120 **Children** Portions, Menu **Parking** 55

The Light House Restaurant
PLAN 1 D2

◉ Modern International

Simple modern cooking in upmarket suburbia

☎ 020 8944 6338 📠 020 8946 4440
75-77 Ridgway, Wimbledon SW19 4ST
e-mail: info@lighthousewimbledon.com
dir: Nearest station: Wimbledon From station turn right up Wimbledon Hill then left at mini-rdbt onto Ridgway, restaurant on left

With a deserved reputation as a friendly, popular and modern neighbourhood restaurant, the upbeat Light House stands out from the crowd in upmarket Wimbledon village. Contemporary good looks are apparent from the off, with two potted olive trees standing sentry like at the entrance and a big glass frontage. Inside follows the theme, all fashionable pale woods and light walls hung with modern art. It's a bright, breezy and relaxed open space, with cheery service and a long bar down one side with open kitchen towards the back. The cooking takes an equally appealing modern approach, delivering brasserie-style dishes with a nod to the Med, while keeping things simple and fresh. Think pan-fried bream served with Parmentier swede, fennel and a bouillabaisse sauce, and to finish, perhaps a vanilla pannacotta with poached apple and rhubarb.

Chef Chris Casey **Owner** Mr Finch & Mr Taylor **Times** 12-2.30/6-10.30 Closed 24-26 Dec, 1 Jan, D Sun **Prices** Fixed L 2 course £10-£14.50, Fixed D 3 course £18.50, Starter £5-£10.50, Main £12.50-£16.75, Dessert £5.50-£6.50, Service added but optional 12.5% **Wines** 56 bottles over £20, 17 bottles under £20, 12 by glass **Notes** Fixed D Mon-Thu order before 7.30pm, Sunday L, Vegetarian available, Air con **Seats** 80 **Children** Portions, Menu

Chez Bruce

LONDON SW17
PLAN 1 E2

Modern 🍷

Accomplished European cooking presented without undue fanfare

☎ 020 8672 0114 📠 020 8767 6648
2 Bellevue Rd, Wandsworth Common SW17 7EG
e-mail: enquiries@chezbruce.co.uk
dir: Nearest station: Wandsworth Common/Balham. Near Wandsworth Common station

The location in a quiet residential quarter of Wandsworth, overlooking the Common, has always given Bruce Poole's place the feel of a popular neighbourhood restaurant, and yet from its inception, it has punched way above that weight category, drawing custom from far afield. The plainly decorated interiors act as a neutral backdrop to accomplished cooking that draws on impeccable sources, and seeks its influences in the more domestic approach to European food articulated by such luminaries as Elizabeth David and Jane Grigson. Presentations can be appealingly rough-and-ready, which somehow emphasises rather than detracts from the quality of a dish. Grilled baby squid with chorizo are a case in point, each lump of sausage the base for a squid, with Gem lettuce underneath, a rouille sauce, and the final garnish a piece of crisply cooked hake. Main course might be a two-way serving of deeply flavoured coquelet (poussin), the breast herb-stuffed, the leg filled with leek, accompanied by creamy gnocchi, mushrooms and an assertively strong jus. Finish with tarte fine aux pommes, lightly glazed and presented with a serving of memorably rich Calvados and raisin ice cream.

Chef Bruce Poole, Matt Christmas **Owner** Bruce Poole, Nigel Platts-Martin **Times** 12-2/6.30-10 Closed 24-26 Dec, 1 Jan, L 27 & 31 Dec **Prices** Fixed L 2 course £19.50-£27.50, Fixed D 3 course fr £40, Service added but optional 12.5% **Wines** 700 bottles over £20, 5 bottles under £20, 15 by glass **Notes** Tasting menu available on request, Sunday L, Vegetarian available, Dress restrictions, Smart casual, Air con **Seats** 75, Pr/dining room 16 **Children** Portions, Menu **Parking** On street, station car park

LONDON W1

Alain Ducasse
PLAN 4 G6

@@@ — *see below*

The Albemarle
PLAN 3 A1

@@@ — *see page 280*

Alloro
PLAN 3 A1

@ Italian

Authentic modern Italian in the heart of Mayfair

☎ 020 7495 4768 📠 020 7629 5348
19-20 Dover St W1S 4LU
e-mail: alloro@hotmail.co.uk
web: www.londonfinedininggroup.com
dir: Nearest station: Green Park From Green Park station
continue towards Piccadilly, Dover St is 2nd on left

Italian for bay leaf, Alloro continues to be a popular venue
for well-heeled Mayfair residents and visitors in search of
a true taste of Italy. A smart, contemporary restaurant
and interconnecting bar with a blue awning and glass
frontage, the dining room is furnished with banquettes
and leather chairs, chessboard-like flooring, pastel tones
and smartly attired staff. The cooking delivers simplicity,
well sourced ingredients, clean flavours and a light touch.
Think thinly sliced roasted suckling pig with mixed leaves

salad, confit rabbit leg with fricassée of mushrooms,
bacon and sweet baby onions and perhaps a traditional
tiramisù with dark chocolate to finish, all accompanied
by an all-Italian wine list.

Alloro

Chef Daniele Camera **Owner** London Fine Dining Group
Times 12-2.30/7-10.30 Closed Xmas, 4 days Etr & BHs,
Sun, L Sat **Prices** Fixed L 2 course fr £27, Fixed D 3
course fr £35, Service added but optional 12.5%
Wines 200 bottles over £20, 2 bottles under £20, 16 by
glass **Notes** Vegetarian available, Dress restrictions, No
shorts or sandals, Air con **Seats** 60, Pr/dining room 16
Children Portions **Parking** On street

Arbutus Restaurant
PLAN 3 B2

@@@ — *see page 281*

Archipelago
PLAN 3 B3

@@ Modern, International

Unique, exotic and adventurous dining experience

☎ 020 7383 3346 📠 020 7383 7181
110 Whitfield St W1T 5ED
e-mail: info@archipelago-restaurant.co.uk
dir: Nearest station: Warren Street From underground
south along Tottenham Court Rd. 1st right into Grafton
Way. 1st left into Whitfield St

In a quiet Fitzrovia back street is one of the city's more
maverick eateries - a bijou Aladdin's cave filled with
more peacock feathers, golden Buddhas, exotic carvings,
bird cages and colourful objets than you'd find in a Bali
market. It all conjures a darkly romantic setting,
evocative of somewhere Marco Polo might have pitched
up on his travels. If you think the décor is a touch off the

continued

Alain Ducasse

LONDON W1   **PLAN 4 G6**

Modern French

Culinary legend meets famous hotel

☎ 020 7629 8866 & 7629 8888 📠 020 7629 8686
The Dorchester, 53 Park Ln W1K 1QA
e-mail: alainducasse@thedorchester.com
dir: Nearest station: Hyde Park Corner/Marble Arch

Alain Ducasse makes no bones about not being in the
kitchen here at The Dorchester, but his personality, style
and passion is firmly stamped on the restaurant that
bears his name. With his vast experience over 25 years-
plus he has learned a thing or two about putting together
top-class teams to deliver top-notch food, and here is no
exception. The large Patrick Jouin-designed dining room
within the legendary hotel is an arresting space,
somehow timeless and contemporary at the same time,

with a giant sparkling curtain of lights a shimmering
presence. Neutral shades predominate - creams, coffees,
those sorts of tones - while tables are generous and
immaculately laid. Service is up to the mark. Ducasse's
food is deeply rooted in the classics with modern
presentation and technique, and no shortage of luxury
ingredients. Simmered duck foie gras is cleverly
partnered with mango and a dolce forte sauce in a first-
class first course, while main courses might include
baked sea bass with razor clams and a parsley shellfish
jus. You may well be drawn to the rum baba dessert, with
the promise that it is 'like in Monte Carlo'. There's a
tasting menu, prices are perhaps not unsurprisingly on
the high side and the wine list is a heavyweight.

Times 12-2/6.30-9.45 Closed 26-30 Dec, 1-5 Jan, Etr,
Aug, Mon-Sun, L Sat

LONDON W1 *continued*

wall, wait until you see the menu: the food is a round-the-world tour of exotica that runs from gnu to kangaroo and chocolate covered scorpions for a pudding with a sting in the tail (not literally, of course). Despite the novelty element, the cooking is accomplished and service is clued-up, easy-going and amicable. Try crocodile fillet seared in vine leaves, then seared zebra with port and blackcurrant sauce and sour green mango soba noodles. Food miles? Don't even ask.

Chef Daniel Creedon **Owner** Bruce Alexander
Times 12-2.30/6-10.30 Closed Xmas, BHs, Sun, L Sat
Prices Food prices not confirmed for 2010. Please telephone for details. **Wines** 35 bottles over £20, 6 bottles under £20, 2 by glass **Notes** Vegetarian available, Air con
Seats 32 **Parking** NCP, on street

Artisan
PLAN 3 A2

◎◎ Modern European

Ambitious cooking in the heart of Mayfair

☎ 020 8382 5450 & 7629 7755 📄 020 7495 1163
The Westbury Hotel, Bond St W1S 2YF
e-mail: artisan@westburymayfair.com
dir: Nearest station: Oxford Circus, Piccadilly Circus, Green Park

A restaurant in its own right, Artisan's appeal goes far beyond the residents of the Westbury Hotel. With an enviable Mayfair location amidst some of London's most exclusive shopping streets, the airy restaurant is contemporary in style with clean lines, boldly-patterned velvet-covered seating contrasted with a light wooden floor, pale walls and striking flower displays. Ambitious cooking has its roots in the classics and appeals with oodles of high-quality luxury ingredients. Try a classic combination of breast of squab pigeon, morels, peas, broad beans and sherry vinegar dressing before a main course of oatmeal- and almond-crusted halibut with marinated fennel, baby spinach and Somerset cider velouté. Finish with a rich brioche bread-and-butter pudding with candied rhubarb, raisins and honeycomb ice cream.

Artisan

Chef Andrew Jones **Owner** Cola Holdings Ltd
Times 12-2.30/6.30-10.30 **Prices** Fixed L 2 course fr £19.50, Fixed D 3 course fr £25, Tasting menu £39-£99, Service added but optional 12.5% **Wines** 280 bottles over £20, 20 by glass **Notes** Fixed ALC 2 course £40, 3 course £45, Tasting menu 7 course, Sunday L, Vegetarian available, Dress restrictions, Smart casual, Civ Wed 20, Air con **Seats** 65, Pr/dining room 20 **Children** Portions **Parking** 20

The Athenaeum, Damask
PLAN 4 H5

◎ Modern British

Classic British cooking in sumptuous surroundings

☎ 020 7499 3464 📄 020 7493 1860
116 Piccadilly W1J 7BJ
e-mail: info@athenaeumhotel.com
web: www.athenaeumhotel.com
dir: Nearest station: Hyde Park Corner, Green Park

With its discreet Mayfair address, the Edwardian Athenaeum offers visitors an air of exclusivity, whilst being contemporary and informal at the same time. The Damask restaurant is a chic, relaxed space, with rich colours and glamorous soft furnishings. The kitchen goes

The Albemarle

◉◉◉

LONDON W1	**PLAN 3 A1**

Traditional British V 🅰 🖐

First-class British cooking in stylish landmark London hotel

☎ 020 7518 4004 📄 020 7493 9381
Brown's Hotel, Albemarle St W1S 4BP
e-mail: thealbemarle@roccofortecollection.com
dir: Nearest station: Green Park Off Piccadilly between Green Park tube station and Bond Street

Eleven Georgian townhouses make up Brown's, the first ever hotel to open in the capital way back in 1837, and indeed the first to open a restaurant. The record breaking days may be over, but the hotel and its restaurant, The Albemarle, go from strength to strength. The balance of traditional English grandeur and a keen eye on contemporary style make for appealing spaces, eminently civilised, classy without being stuffy, such as the restaurant with its elegantly laid tables, comfortable chairs and banquette seating, and oak-panelled walls hung with original artworks. Director of food Mark Hix and executive chef Lee Streeton have produced a menu rooted in British classics where the quality of the seasonal produce is second to none, flavours are allowed to shine, and the concept of simplicity is truly understood. Mussel soup, featuring Shetland Isles bivalves, is flavoured with fennel, while main-course (and seldom seen) Thornback ray is classically served with beurre noisette, and walnut tart is laced with whisky and served with clotted cream. There's always a roast on the carving trolley at lunchtime. Service is charmingly unfussy and the sommelier a real asset.

Chef Lee Streeton **Owner** The Rocco Forte Collection
Times 12-3/7-11 **Prices** Fixed L 2 course £25, Fixed D 3 course £30, Starter £7.25-£19.75, Main £14.50-£32.75, Dessert £6.25-£10.50, Service optional **Wines** 271 bottles over £20, 16 by glass **Notes** Pre-theatre D £25-£30 5.30-7.30pm, Sunday L, Vegetarian menu, Dress restrictions, Smart casual, Civ Wed 70, Air con **Seats** 80, Pr/dining room 70 **Children** Menu **Parking** Valet/ Burlington St

to great lengths to source high-quality seasonal ingredients, regional wherever possible. Classic and modern British dishes are mixed with some more individual items. Try a classic fishcake with caper butter sauce and mixed watercress, followed by chargrilled Scottish rib-eye steak with hand-cut chips and béarnaise sauce; finishing perhaps with sticky toffee pudding and vanilla ice cream.

Chef David Marshall **Owner** Ralph Trustees Ltd
Times 12.30-2.30/5.30-10.30 **Prices** Fixed L 2 course fr £19, Fixed D 3 course £28, Starter £9.50-£13, Main £20-£39, Dessert £8.50, Service optional **Wines** 44 bottles over £20, 15 by glass **Notes** All day dining menu 11am-11pm, Sunday L, Vegetarian available, Civ Wed 55, Air con **Seats** 46, Pr/dining room 44 **Children** Portions, Menu **Parking** Close car park

Automat
PLAN 3 A1

◉ American

American-style brasserie in Mayfair

☎ 020 7499 3033 📠 020 7499 2682
33 Dover St W1S 4NF
e-mail: info@automat-london.com
dir: Nearest station: Green Park Dover St is off Piccadilly

An American brasserie in the heart of Mayfair, Automat fuses the New York diner with the traditional English dining room. In the front half of the room there's wooden arched ceilings and walls and low-level booth seating,

while at the back there's a buzzier brasserie feel with banquette seating, white tiles, deep varnished wood and an open kitchen. The food is simple but well executed, with breakfast, lunch, dinner and brunch all done the New York way. Crab cake with guacamole, perhaps, following on with the signature burger or rib-eye steak and fries.

Chef Sujan Sarkar **Owner** Carlos Almada
Times 7-11/12-mdnt Closed Xmas, New Year,
Prices Starter £8-£14, Main £12-£48, Dessert £6, Service added but optional 12.5% **Wines** 78 bottles over £20, 15 by glass **Notes** Brunch available Sat-Sun, Brasserie menu available 11am-mdnt, Vegetarian available, Air con **Seats** 110 **Parking** On street

L'Autre Pied
PLAN 2 G3

◉◉◉ — *see page 282*

Avista
PLAN 2 G1

◉◉ Italian NEW

Classic Italian cooking in modern Mayfair restaurant

☎ 020 7629 9400 📠 020 7629 7736
Millennium Hotel Mayfair, Grosvenor Square W1K 2HP
e-mail: reservations@avistarestaurant.com
dir: Nearest station: Bond Street

After a long stint at Zafferano, one of London's top Italians, head chef Michele Granziera set up on his own

at a swish Mayfair address. The restaurant in the Millennium Hotel Mayfair has a separate entrance, and looks the part after a full refurb blending the earthy tones of bare brickwork, marble floors and taupe leather banquettes. After a glass of prosecco at the bar, diners can watch chefs putting the final touches to dishes at a granite-topped work station. What's on offer is a mix of modern Italian regional dishes and a fair sprinkling of classic crowd pleasers. A trio of starters sets out the stall with sea-fresh calamari in squid-ink batter, wafer-thin beef bresaola and oil-drizzled mozzarella, aubergine and peppers. Mains include slow-cooked pork cheeks with mashed potatoes, spinach and red wine sauce, and you might end with hot Valrhona chocolate foam with raspberries and ginger.

Times 12.30-2.30/6.30-10.30 Closed Sun

Barrafina
PLAN 3 B2

◉ Spanish

Barcelona-style tapas joint in the heart of Soho

☎ 020 7813 8016
54 Frith St W1D 4SL
e-mail: alice@barrafina.co.uk
dir: Nearest station: Tottenham Court Rd

As authentic and fun as it gets, this simple, relaxed, buzzy tapas bar brings a touch of Barcelona to the heart of Soho. With a no booking policy, arrive early or wait in

continued

Arbutus Restaurant

LONDON W1 | **PLAN 3 B2**

Modern French

Stunning but simple, affordable food and wine from Soho gem

☎ 020 7734 4545 📠 020 7287 8624
63-64 Frith St W1D 3JW
e-mail: info@arbutusrestaurant.co.uk
dir: Nearest station: Tottenham Court Road. Exit Tottenham Court Road tube station, turn left into Oxford St. Left onto Soho St, cross over or continue round Soho Sq, restaurant is on Frith St, 25mtrs on right

When Anthony Demetre and Will Smith's Soho restaurant opened its doors in 2006 it was straight away the talk of the town, with its mission to deliver hearty, top-level European comfort food at accessible prices. Four years down the line, the formula is still a winner: technically

superb cooking founded on humble seasonal ingredients, an informal vibe and a set lunch menu at prices that are hard to believe. And offering all wines in a two-glass carafe to encourage experimentation is an inspirational idea. You could easily pass by its stealthy gunmetal façade among the film and TV companies at the Soho Square end of Frith Street, and the interior is similarly understated - it goes for a neutral modern take on a French bistro in calming tones of cream and dark brown, buttoned black banquettes and dark wooden chairs. Will Smith still orchestrates out front, delivering well-oiled professional service; in the kitchen, Anthony Demetre's impeccable modern bistro cooking deliberately targets gutsy, unvarnished flavours, prepared with obvious pedigree technique in intelligently simple combinations. Squid and mackerel 'burger' is a signature starter, served with parsley emulsion, pea shoots, razor clams and finely sliced baby squid. Main courses bring saddle of rabbit - 3 generous pieces delivered with a separate pot of shoulder meat made into a cottage pie, and a rich reduced jus

with mustard seeds, or try 'pieds et paquets', a Provençal dish of lamb's tripe parcels and trotters with charlotte potatoes.

Chef Anthony Demetre **Owner** Anthony Demetre, Will Smith **Times** 12-2.30/5-11.30 Closed 25-26 Dec, 1 Jan, **Prices** Fixed L 3 course fr £15.50, Starter £6.95-£9.95, Main £13.95-£18.95, Dessert £5.95-£6.95, Service added but optional 12.5% **Wines** 40 bottles over £20, 10 bottles under £20, 50 by glass **Notes** Pre-theatre D 5-7pm 3 course £17.50, Sunday L, Vegetarian available, Air con **Seats** 75 **Children** Portions

LONDON W1 *continued*

the long, narrow room for one of the 23 high stools that run around the L-shaped, marble-topped bar counter in front of the open kitchen. The décor's modern - stainless steel, marble and glass - and the atmosphere's as upbeat as the quality, quick-turnover food. Sip on a glass of Spanish wine or sherry while you soak up the action and aromas and wait for plates of charcuterie, pimientos de padron, lamb cutlets, or tortilla like jambon and spinach, all driven by top-notch produce. There's bags of daily specials (including plenty of seafood) and staff are lively, informed and friendly.

Chef Nieves Barragan **Owner** Sam & Eddie Hart **Times** 12-3/5-11 **Prices** Starter £2-£4.75, Main £5.50-£12.50, Dessert £4-£6.90, Service added but optional 12.5% **Wines** 18 bottles over £20, 8 bottles under £20, 20 by glass **Notes** Sunday L, Vegetarian available, Air con **Seats** 23 **Children** Portions **Parking** On street

Bar Trattoria Semplice
PLAN 2 H2

◉ Italian NEW

Classic regional Italian food in a fun, relaxed setting

☎ 020 7491 8638
22 Woodstock St W1C 2AR
dir: Nearest station: Bond Street

Tucked away on a side street, Bar Trattoria Semplice is a stone's throw from its posher sibling, Ristorante Semplice (see entry). In a break from candles-in-Chianti-bottle tradition, the décor is all Scandinavian blond wood and clean lines with splashes of red to warm it up. On the bar counter, a fabulous old meat-slicing machine provides a focal point and reminds you of the business to hand. The food is classic regional Italian using pukka products - cheeses, prosciutto, salumi - imported from small producers. Presentation is simple, flavours are great - in short this is just like eating in a trattoria in Italy. Dishes run from hearty starters such as potato gnocchi with duck and Savoy cabbage ragù, to spatchcock baby chicken with spinach and potatoes roasted with rosemary. Explore the interesting list of Italian wines.

Prices Food prices not confirmed for 2010. Please telephone for details.

Bellamy's
PLAN 2 H2

◉ French

Classy French Mayfair brasserie and oyster bar

☎ 020 7491 2727 📠 020 7491 9990
18-18a Bruton Place W1J 6LY
e-mail: gavin@bellamysrestaurant.co.uk
dir: Nearest station: Green Park/Bond St Off Berkeley Sq, parallel with Bruton St

There's certainly a buzz at this popular French brasserie, tucked-away down a narrow mews-like lane just off Berkeley Square. The dark leather seating, closely-set linen-clad tables, professional service and deep-pocket pricing is resolutely Mayfair, while the pale-yellow walls lined with French prints, posters and mirrors conform to the brasserie signature. The dining room is accessed via the adjoining oyster bar and small food store. The carte's layout offers user-friendly simplicity alongside a bit of luxury (oysters, caviar or scrambled eggs with Périgord truffles for openers). Unashamedly classic French brasserie dishes include roasted turbot with hollandaise, or veal sweetbreads meunière. The wine list is patriotically French, too.

Bellamy's

Chef Stephane Pacoud **Owner** Gavin Rankin and Syndicate **Times** 12-3/7-10.30 Closed Xmas, New Year, BHs, Sun, L Sat **Prices** Fixed L 2 course £24, Fixed D 3 course £28.50, Starter £7-£15.50, Main £18.50-£28.50, Dessert £6.50, Service added but optional 12.5% **Wines** 54 bottles over £20, 20 by glass **Notes** Vegetarian available, Air con **Seats** 70 **Children** Portions **Parking** On street, NCP

L'Autre Pied

LONDON W1 PLAN 2 G3

Modern European **V**

Classy modern cooking and relaxed ambience in Marylebone village

☎ 020 7486 9696
5-7 Blandford St, Marylebone Village W1U 3DB
e-mail: info@lautrepied.co.uk
dir: Nearest station: Bond St Please telephone for directions

L'Autre Pied may be pitched at a less formal level than it's revered Fitzrovia sister, Pied à Terre, (see entry) but this classy act in Marylebone village is no Cinderella. At the helm is youthful head chef Marcus Eaves, who worked with Shane Osborn at the original Pied, and brings a full head of creativity and enthusiasm to the task in hand. With such a reputation to live up to and high expectations, the mood is set with a pleasant, unbuttoned formality: claret and chocolate leather banquettes combine with richly-grained dark-wood tables, hand-painted silk wallpapers, and backlit glass screens with curlicued images of flowers and spices casting an emerald sheen. The modern European cooking is highly polished - not that you'd know from the menu, whose tight-lipped descriptions hide the arsenal of techniques deployed in its purées, emulsions, nages and foams. It's all executed with a masterly touch: luxury ingredients slum it with peasant produce in harmonious dishes of full-on flavour. An open ravioli of peas, broad beans and baby gem lettuce is an exquisite starter, all flavours singing loud and clear. Next up, comes slow-cooked breast of lamb with glazed baby carrots, tarragon pommes purées and thyme jus - a rustic dish, maybe, but buffed up with refined presentation. Dessert is another hit: a tarte fine of mango, brought to table simply with mango sorbet and cream.

Chef Marcus Eaves **Owner** Marcus Eaves, Shane Osborn,

David Moore **Times** 12-2.45/6-10.45 Closed 4 days Xmas, 1 Jan **Prices** Fixed L 2 course £17.95, Fixed D 4 course £39.70, Tasting menu £52, Starter £9.45-£14.75, Main £16.20-£20.95, Dessert £7-£7.50, Service added but optional 12.5% **Wines** 10 by glass **Notes** Pre-theatre 2 course £17.95, 3 course £20.95, Sunday L, Vegetarian menu, Air con **Seats** 53, Pr/dining room 15

Benares

PLAN 2 H1

◎◎ Indian, British **V**

Striking design and cutting-edge Indian cooking

☎ 020 7629 8886 ▤ 020 7499 2430
12a Berkeley Square W1J 6BS
e-mail: reservations@benaresrestaurant.com
dir: Nearest station: Green Park E along Piccadilly
towards Regent St. Turn left into Berkeley St and continue
straight to Berkeley Square

A sophisticated and buzzy modern Indian restaurant from
highly acclaimed chef-patron Atul Kochhar, Benares is
discreetly located on the upstairs floor of a corporate-
looking building on Berkeley Square, in the heart of well-
heeled Mayfair. A wide staircase leads you from reception
to the stylish bar, with a series of water-filled ponds
decorated with brightly coloured floating flowers and
candles. The slick dining room is decked out with
limestone flooring, dark leather banquettes, black chairs
with beige upholstery, and formally-dressed tables waited
on by equally formally-dressed staff. The cooking is a
fusion of traditional Indian dishes with classic French
and English cuisine, as in terrine of confit duck leg with
pickling spices, and a main course of batter-fried John
Dory with crushed garden peas and Gorkha tomato
chutney. Save room for the five spiced chocolate pudding
with tarragon and blood orange, Kochhar's clever twist on
a hot chocolate fondant.

Chef Atul Kochhar **Owner** Atul Kochhar
Times 12-2.30/5.30-11 Closed 23-26 Dec, L 27-31 Dec,
Sat **Prices** Food prices not confirmed for 2010. Please
telephone for details. **Wines** All bottles over £20, 11 by
glass **Notes** Tasting menu available, Sunday L,
Vegetarian available, Vegetarian menu, Dress
restrictions, Smart casual, Air con

Bentley's Oyster Bar & Grill

PLAN 3 B1

◎◎ British, European

Classic seafood powerhouse

☎ 020 7734 4756 ▤ 020 7758 4140
11/15 Swallow St W1B 4DG
e-mail: reservations@bentleys.org
web: www.bentleysoysterbarandgrill.co.uk
dir: Nearest station: Piccadilly Circus 2nd right after
Piccadilly Circus

Just around the corner from Piccadilly Circus, this
Victorian building has been home to Bentley's since 1916,
and the current Richard Corrigan-run incarnation sees
much of the Arts and Crafts splendour of the original
remain. The place buzzes with life. The ground floor
houses the Oyster Bar, where you can sit at the bar or at
unclothed tables around it. The main restaurant - divided
into Grill room, Rib Room and Crustacea Room - is up on
the first floor, where beautiful Arts and Crafts interiors
display William Morris wall coverings, blue leather chairs
and original Bentley's fish prints. The menu, crammed
with seafood and some meat and game dishes, takes on
traditional preparations with a modern approach:
macaroni of lobster and basil might precede amazingly
fresh mullet with mussels, tomatoes and coriander.

Bentley's Oyster Bar & Grill

Chef Brendan Fyldes **Owner** Richard Corrigan
Times 12-11.30 Closed 25 Dec, 1 Jan **Prices** Fixed L 2
course fr £18.50, Starter £7-£18, Main £13.50-£38,
Dessert £6.50-£8.50, Service added but optional 12.5%
Wines 100 bottles over £20, 40 bottles under £20, 16 by
glass **Notes** Sunday L, Vegetarian available, Dress
restrictions, Smart casual, Air con **Seats** 90, Pr/dining
room 60 **Children** Portions **Parking** 10 yds away

Bocca di Lupo

PLAN 3 B2

◎◎ Italian NEW

**Delicious authentic regional Italian cuisine at sensible
prices in the heart of Soho**

☎ 020 7734 2223
12 Archer St W1D 7BB
web: www.boccadilupo.com
dir: Nearest station: Piccadilly Circus Turn left off
Shaftesbury Ave into Gt Windmill St, then right into Archer
St. Located behind the Lyric & Apollo theatres

With outstanding regional Italian food, amazing value for
money, a great Italian wine list, friendly attentive service
and stylish surroundings, Bocca di Lupo has hit on the
perfect recipe to ride out these credit crunch times.
Tucked away down a Soho side street, this restaurant hits
you with a great welcome. Try to bag one of the high
leather stools at the long marble bar to watch the chefs
doing their thing an arms length away. You can learn a
lot you didn't know about Italian cuisine just from reading
the menu, which notes the region of origin beside each
dish. The food is the real deal: simple, authentic, and
without flashy presentation - it's all about superb
flavours and top-notch ingredients. Go for fritto romano -

whole fried artichokes and veal sweetbreads - followed by
a superb bone marrow, Barolo and radicchio risotto.
Double torta Caprese is a moist lemon and chocolate
almond cake that melts in the mouth. The kitchen has
embraced the concept of large and small dishes so you
can try loads of new exciting flavours.

Chef Jacob Kenedy **Owner** Jacob Kenedy/Victor Hugo
Times 12.30-3/5.30-12 **Prices** Starter £4.50-£12, Main
£6.50-£24, Dessert £2-£7.50, Service added but optional
12.5% **Wines** 130 bottles over £20, 4 bottles under £20,
20 by glass **Notes** Vegetarian available, Air con **Seats** 60,
Pr/dining room 32 **Children** Portions **Parking** NCP Brewer
St

Butler's

PLAN 4 H6

◎ Traditional British

Traditional dining in the heart of Mayfair

☎ 020 7491 2622 ▤ 020 7491 4793
**Chesterfield Mayfair Hotel, 35 Charles St, Mayfair
W1J 5EB**
e-mail: meignex@rchmail.com
web: www.chesterfieldmayfair.com
dir: Nearest station: Green Park. From N side exit tube
station, turn left and then first left into Berkeley St.
Continue to Berkeley Sq and then left towards Charles St

Situated in the heart of Mayfair, this intimate hotel
resembles an exclusive gentleman's club. The Georgian
interior is furnished with high-quality antiques, leather
chairs and heavy fabrics, and the elegance continues into
Butler's restaurant, a bright, vibrant room with a strong
red and brown décor and a subtle African theme. Dine
here, or in the light and airy Conservatory, where the
traditional British cooking is far from stuck in the past,
and high-quality ingredients are used to good effect.
Starters might include mini beef Wellington with
horseradish mash, pan-fried foie gras and Madeira jus,
and for main course, perhaps, line-caught fillet of sea
bass with potato cake, roasted fennel and lobster foam.

Chef Ben Kelliher **Owner** Red Carnation Hotels
Times 12.30-2.30/5.30-10.30 **Prices** Fixed L 2 course fr
£17.50, Fixed D 3 course fr £25.50, Starter £7-£16.50,
Main £18-£37, Dessert £7-£8.50, Service added but
optional 12.5% **Wines** 84 bottles over £20, 20 by glass
Notes Pre-theatre menu available, Sunday L, Vegetarian
available, Civ Wed 100, Air con **Seats** 65, Pr/dining room
24 **Children** Portions, Menu **Parking** NCP (5 minutes
away)

LONDON W1 *continued*

Camerino
PLAN 3 B3

Modern Italian

Friendly Italian restaurant stamped with originality

☎ 020 7637 9900 ▤ 020 7637 9696
16 Percy St W1T 1DT
e-mail: info@camerinorestaurant.com
dir: Nearest station: Tottenham Court Rd, Goodge St
Please telephone for directions

It's refreshing to see a restaurant step away from the herd of neutral minimalism and leather banquettes. This smart Italian goes for a fun theatrical look that's quite a talking point with blocks of fuchsia pink drapes and swirling black patterns. Whatever its décor might say, the kitchen's Italian heart beats strongly. After a sincere Italian welcome you could just grab something simple for pre-theatre dining, but it would be a shame not to let the talented kitchen team show you what they are capable of. There's a lightness of touch and strong clear flavours in dishes that look as pretty as a picture. Try pan-fried baby squid with wild mushrooms and broad beans to get the taste buds in tune, then go for open ravioli with seafood and cannellini beans, or grilled calves' liver, seared pink and served with a herby hint of crispy sage and bacon.

Times 12-3/6-11 Closed 1 wk Xmas, 1st Jan, Etr Day, most BHs, Sun, L Sat

Canteen
PLAN 2 G3

British NEW

Classic British cooking showcasing the best of the nation's produce in a brasserie setting

☎ 0845 686 1122
55 Baker St W1U 8EW
e-mail: bakerstreet@canteen.co.uk
dir: Nearest station: Baker Street

From the owners of Canteen at the Royal Festival Hall (see entry) comes this casual all-day brasserie serving traditional British dishes made from high quality seasonal produce. Aptly, it has a canteen-like feel, with bare light oak tables with banquette seating and wooden chairs, and classic Bestlite lamps. Lone diners can sit up at the open kitchen and watch the chefs at work on such classics as potted duck with piccalilli, Lancashire hotpot, and nursery food desserts like rice pudding and gingerbread with pears. Breakfast is served all day, as well as bar snacks and cakes. A fourth Canteen was due to open at Canary Wharf at the time of going to press.

Times 8am-11pm

Cecconi's
PLAN 3 A1

Traditional Italian

Precise Italian cooking in smart surroundings near the Royal Academy

☎ 020 7434 1500 ▤ 020 7494 2440
5a Burlington Gardens W1X 1LE
dir: Nearest station: Piccadilly Circus/Oxford Circus Burlington Gdns between New Bond St and Savile Row

The smart interior décor of black-and-white striped floor, green seating and high barstools reflects the well-heeled location, a short hop from the art treasures of the Royal Academy. If nearly all cuisines turn out to have some version of tapas-style light bites, you may be less familiar with the Venetian cichetti, served all day here, and including items such as chicken liver crostini, breaded baby mozzarella, and Umbrian sausages with red pepper. The cooking is precise and full of freshness, with the traditional three-course format perhaps offering crab ravioli, followed by grilled swordfish with sprouting broccoli, tomato and olives. Get here early for the breakfast menu, and you could start the day as you mean to go on, with a plate of scrambled eggs and black truffle.

Times 7am-11.30pm (Sat 8am-11.30pm, Sun 8am-10.30pm) Closed Xmas, New Year

China Tang at The Dorchester
PLAN 4 G6

Classic Cantonese

Sophisticated Chinese restaurant in famously luxurious hotel

☎ 020 7629 9988 ▤ 020 7629 9595
Park Ln W1K 1QA
e-mail: reservations@chinatanglondon.co.uk
dir: Nearest station: Hyde Park Corner

Down in the basement of The Dorchester is a jewel of a Chinese restaurant, a scene of lavishly opulent art-deco styling, where mirrored pillars, stunning glass-fronted fish-themed artworks, tables with marble-insert tops laid with heavy silver chopsticks, hand-carved chairs and deep banquette seating create a scene reminiscent of colonial Shanghai or 1960s Hong Kong. It's unashamedly decadent with prices to match. There's a swish cocktail bar and a spacious dining room, where well-heeled diners tuck into classic Cantonese cooking made with first-rate produce, including dim sum and an extensive carte dotted with luxuries. Soft-shell crab cooked in egg yolk is bursting with flavour, the suckling pig mixed platter is a satisfying plate based around a top-quality animal, or try the salt and pepper lobster claw.

Owner Sir David Tang **Times** 11am-midnight Closed 25 Dec, **Prices** Fixed L 2 course fr £15, Starter fr £6, Main £12-£60, Dessert £9-£15, Service added but optional 12.5% **Wines** 512 bottles over £20, 5 bottles under £20, 12 by glass **Notes** Sunday L, Vegetarian available, Dress restrictions, Smart casual, Air con **Seats** 120, Pr/dining room 80 **Children** Portions

Cipriani
PLAN 2 H2

Italian

Venetian elegance in Mayfair

☎ 020 7399 0500 ▤ 020 7399 0501
25 Davies St W1E 3DE
dir: Nearest station: Bond Street Please telephone for directions

From the same people behind Harry's Bar in Venice, Cipriani remains the haunt of the fashionable, rich and famous. The modern glass-fronted exterior leads to a large, stylish dining room, where impeccable art-deco style meets beautiful Murano chandeliers, and white-jacketed staff offer slick, discreet service. Low, leather-upholstered seating and magnolia tablecloths provide added comfort, while the atmosphere fairly buzzes in line with its see-and-be-seen status. Classic, accurate, straightforward Italian cooking - with lots of Cipriani touches, authentic prime quality ingredients and unfussy presentation - hits the mark in dishes such as Dover sole with zucchini, or veal kidney with risotto alla Milanese, and do save room for the dessert selection of cakes.

Times 12-3/6-11.45 Closed 25 Dec

Cocoon
PLAN 3 B1

Pan-Asian

Dazzling design concept showcasing pan-Asian food

☎ 020 7494 7600 ▤ 020 7474 7607
65 Regent St W1B 4EA
e-mail: reservations@cocoon-restaurants.com
dir: Nearest station: Piccadilly Circus 1 min walk from Piccadilly Circus

Deliriously clashing reds and oranges set the tone for one of central London's more eye-catching venues, one with a champagne bar and a cocktail lounge manned by a DJ. Tables inlaid with rose-petals and a series of six interlocking rooms, including sushi counters, connected by a catwalk make the place an obvious lure for celebrity bookings, and the pan-Asian food is full of surprises, as well as tried-and-true classics. Crispy aromatic duck rolls with hoisin are well made, the ultra-trendy black cod appears with miso and mirin glaze, while the chicken green curry contains aubergine and pumpkin as well as coconut cream.

Chef Azman Said, Ricky Pang **Owner** Matt Hermer, Paul Deeming, Ignite Group **Times** 12-3/5.30-mdnt Closed 25-26 Dec, 1 Jan, Sun, L Sat **Prices** Fixed L 2 course fr £15, Fixed D 3 course £25-£50, Starter £6-£14, Main £12-£28.50, Dessert £7-£23, Service added but optional 12.5% **Wines** 100% bottles over £20, 14 by glass **Notes** Pre-theatre Bento Box offer £20, Vegetarian available, Dress restrictions, Smart casual, Air con **Seats** 180, Pr/dining room 14 **Parking** NCP Brewer St

Corrigan's Mayfair
PLAN 2 G1

— see opposite page

Dehesa

PLAN 3 A2

◉ Spanish, Italian

Stylish Carnaby Street joint serving tapas and charcuterie

☎ 020 7494 4170
25 Ganton St W1F 9BP
e-mail: info@dehesa.co.uk
dir: Nearest station: Oxford Circus Close to underground station, half way along Carnaby St on corner of Ganton & Kingly St

Looking like a rather cool New York diner with its stylish black awning, copper-fronted bar, high bench tables and tall, leather-cushioned stools, Dehesa, tucked away near Carnaby Street, offers an appealing blend of Spanish tapas and Italian charcuterie. Some of the tables are communal and sitting outside at street-side tables is ideal for people watching. Wherever you sit, you can expect to tuck into rustic dishes that rely on freshness and flavour rather than fussy presentation. Roast scallops with cauliflower purée is an appealingly contemporary choice, or there is the equally sophisticated roast guinea fowl with tarragon gnocchi and truffles; vegetarians might go for courgette flowers stuffed with Monte Enebro goats' cheese and drizzled with honey. No bookings are taken, so get there early in the evenings. Under the same ownership as Salt Yard; see entry.

Chef Lewis Hannaford **Owner** Simon Mullins, Sanja Morris **Times** 12-3/6-11 Closed D Sun **Prices** Starter £2-£13, Main £3.25-£10, Dessert £4.90-£8.50, Service added but optional 12.5% **Wines** 68 bottles over £20, 5 bottles under £20, 9 by glass **Notes** Sunday L, Vegetarian available, Air con **Seats** 40, Pr/dining room 12 **Parking** NCP

deVille

PLAN 2 G3

◉ Modern European NEW

Stylish hotel and restaurant in central location

☎ 020 7935 5599   🖷 020 7935 9588
The Mandeville Hotel, Mandeville Place W1U 2BE
e-mail: info@mandeville.co.uk
dir: Nearest station: Bond St & Baker St Located just off Wigmore St and at the end of Marylebone High St

The striking interior of this Marylebone townhouse confirms its credentials as a boutique hotel - stylish and flamboyant, The Mandeville blends the old and the new to create spaces that are both elegant and rather cool. The deVille restaurant has bold patterned floral wallpaper, Venetian mask wall lights and a bright pink wall at one end, and the food is as vibrant as the venue. Start with venison carpaccio with truffle and celeriac mayonnaise, before almond-crusted sea bass with braised endive and Jerusalem artichoke purée. The modern European vein continues with desserts such as chocolate fondant with strawberry, rhubarb and meringue ice cream. Service is professional and efficient.

deVille

Chef Gunter Geiger **Times** 12.30-3/7-11 Closed Sun **Prices** Fixed L 2 course fr £15.50, Fixed D 3 course £18.75-£40, Starter £7.50-£11.25, Main £15.50-£19.25, Dessert £7.50-£9.50, Service added but optional 12.5% **Wines** 80 bottles over £20, 6 bottles under £20, 20 by glass **Notes** Vegetarian available, Dress restrictions, Smart casual, Air con **Seats** 90, Pr/dining room 12 **Children** Portions **Parking** NCP nearby

Corrigan's Mayfair

LONDON RESTAURANT OF THE YEAR

LONDON W1   PLAN 2 G1

Modern British NEW

The best of British and Irish produce cooked with flair

☎ 020 7499 9943
28 Upper Grosvenor St W1K 7PF
e-mail: reservations@corrigansmayfair.com
web: www.corrigansmayfair.com
dir: Nearest station: Marble Arch

Richard Corrigan is a chef who puts the quality of the produce at the centre of everything he does and consequently his restaurants sparkle like the water in Galway Bay (see entry for Bentley's). There is a refreshing simplicity to his cooking, but it is not unrefined: who could resist grouse pie with ceps? His newest outpost is in the heart of Mayfair, the dining room displaying the same kind of pleasing and satisfying richness as the food - comfortable arctic blue leather banquettes and chairs, natural oak flooring, and white linen-clad tables. The menu brings us the best of Britain and Ireland, but it is a pragmatic selection, so Medjool dates partner beetroot and wild watercress and octopus carpaccio is invigorated with Clementine and almond. First-class langoustines make a fine starter with spiced chick pea purée, while main-course breast of pheasant is poached in butter and served with chestnuts, bacon and game toast. Desserts can be as comforting as rhubarb and custard or as modern as quince tart, golden raisins and Sauternes ice cream. Cheeses are 'From Our Islands' and the Irish soda bread is as good as you might expect.

Chef Richard Corrigan, Chris McGowan **Owner** Richard Corrigan Restaurants Ltd **Times** 12-2.30/6-11 Closed 23-27 Dec, L Sat **Prices** Fixed L 2 course £19.50, Starter £6-£15, Main £16.50-£25, Dessert £7.50, Service added but optional 12.5% **Wines** 400 bottles over £20, 4 bottles under £20, 12 by glass **Notes** Sunday L, Vegetarian available, Air con **Seats** 85, Pr/dining room 30 **Children** Portions **Parking** On street

LONDON W1 *continued*

Dinings

PLAN 2 E3

◎◎ Modern Japanese NEW

Contemporary Japanese food in unpretentious surroundings

☎ 020 7723 0666
22 Harcourt St W1H 4HH
dir: Nearest station: Edgware Rd

It may be hidden away in a Georgian townhouse in Marylebone's hinterland, but the capital's clued-up foodies beat a path here. Small wonder when you learn owner Tomonari Chiba is an ex-Nobu man. The interior is tiny and starkly utilitarian, with a six-seat ground-floor sushi bar and 32-seat basement dining room. Grey walls, concrete floors, bare tables and darkwood latticework are enlivened by cheery, helpful and informed service. The drawcard though is the contemporary Japanese cuisine (reasonably priced), with its repertoire of tapas-sized dishes brimful of inventiveness and flavour; steamed sea bass with a spicy black bean sauce, for example. Interesting sashimi and sushi (freshwater eel and foie gras sushi roll) find their place too, while successful East-meets-West desserts might feature jasmine tea pannacotta.

Chef Masaki Sugisaki **Owner** Tomonari Chiba
Times 12-2.30/6-10.30 Closed L Sat-Sun **Prices** Starter fr £4.50, Dessert fr £5.95 **Notes** Vegetarian available **Seats** 38

Dolada

PLAN 3 A1

◎◎ Italian

Upmarket, stylish and modern Mayfair Italian

☎ 020 7409 1011
13 Albermarle St W1S 4HJ
dir: Nearest station: Green Park

The low-key basement beneath the DKNY shop in Mayfair has been home to a series of ultra-posh Italians, the latest being Dolada in place of former incumbent Mosaico. New chef Riccardo de Pra, fresh from his family's upscale Ristorante Albergo Dolada in the Veneto, knows a thing or two about putting together top-end menus. The look is effortlessly chic - frieze-style mirrors for checking out the clientele, burgundy leather banquettes, cherry wood, polished limestone floors and jazzy Murano glass tumblers on the tables. An all-Italian team delivers slick, attentive service, while the food blends comfort and familiarity with flights of innovation. Ravioli filled with organic ricotta and dandelions might precede amazingly tender roasted baby monkfish, partnered with sweet artichokes and prosecco foam, and an exemplary vanilla pannacotta with pineapple salad and crisps holds form to the end.

Times 12-2.30/6.30-10.45 Closed Sun, L Sat, Sun, Xmas, Etr, BHs

Embassy London

PLAN 3 A1

◎◎ Modern European

Sophisticated cuisine at Mayfair restaurant and nightclub

☎ 020 7851 0956
29 Old Burlington St W1S 3AN
e-mail: embassy@embassylondon.com
dir: Nearest station: Green Park, Piccadilly Circus Just off Burlington Gardens (between Bond St & Regent St)

This contemporary Mayfair restaurant on two levels has a bright and airy atmosphere with its floor-to-ceiling windows providing plenty of natural daylight. The interior's subtle creams and browns, mirrored walls and modern artwork give it a somewhat sophisticated atmosphere. A small heated terrace stretches along the front of the restaurant for taking in the West End air. The menu offers modern British cuisine with a global reach. Expect accomplished cooking, clean-cut flavours and slick presentation in such dishes as a starter of Pacific tuna spring rolls with wasabi mayonnaise, and a main of Elwy Valley rump of lamb, pipérade and aubergine caviar with rosemary jus. Chocolate fondant with pistachio ice cream and brandy snap is an indulgent way to end the meal. Below the restaurant there is a private members' nightclub.

Chef David Landor **Owner** Mark Fuller
Times 12-3/6-11.30 Closed 25-26 Dec, 1 Jan, Good Fri, Sun-Mon, L Sat **Prices** Fixed L 2 course £8.95, Fixed D 3 course £27-£40, Starter £5.95-£10.95, Main £12.50-£27, Dessert £5.95, Service added but optional 12.5%, Groups min 10 service 15% **Wines** 63 bottles over £20, 2 bottles under £20, 6 by glass **Notes** Vegetarian available, Dress restrictions, Smart casual, no trainers, smart jeans only, Air con **Seats** 120 **Parking** NCP opposite restaurant

L'Escargot - The Ground Floor Restaurant

PLAN 3 C2

◎◎ French

Long-established West End favourite offering accomplished bistro cooking

☎ 020 7439 7474   📠 020 7437 0790
48 Greek St W1D 4EF
e-mail: sales@whitestarline.org.uk
web: www.lescargotrestaurant.co.uk
dir: Nearest station: Tottenham Court Rd, Leicester Square Telephone for directions

Very handy for the West End theatreland, L'Escargot is a long-running show in its own right. The atmosphere of an

elegantly appointed townhouse, complete with outsized mirrors and framed prints, makes for a pleasingly retro feel, and an enviable collection of original 20th-century artworks includes pieces by Miró, Chagall and Matisse. French service is well-schooled in the formalities, and the menus offer a refined spin on classical bistro cooking. Vibrantly flavoured ham hock and foie gras terrine wrapped in Parma ham with sauce gribiche is a winning way to start, and might be followed by roasted Scottish salmon with Puy lentils and samphire, or textbook daube of beef with puréed carrot. What could be more inimitably French than to conclude with dark chocolate fondant and marron glacé? The upstairs Picasso Room is now only open for private dining.

L'Escargot - The Ground Floor Restaurant

Chef Joseph Croan **Owner** Jimmy Lahoud
Times 12-2.30/6-11.30 Closed 25-26 Dec, 1 Jan, Sun, L Sat **Prices** Fixed L 2 course £15, Starter £9.50, Main £12.95-£15.95, Dessert £7.95, Service added but optional 12.5% **Wines** 275 bottles over £20, 6 bottles under £20, 8 by glass **Notes** Pre-theatre menu available, Vegetarian available, Air con **Seats** 70, Pr/dining room 60 **Children** Portions **Parking** NCP Chinatown, on street parking

Fino

PLAN 3 B3

◎◎ Spanish

Fashionable, classy tapas served up in style

☎ 020 7813 8010   📠 020 7813 8011
33 Charlotte St W1T 1RR
e-mail: info@finorestaurant.com
dir: Nearest station: Goodge St/Tottenham Court Rd Entrance on Rathbone St

The Hart brothers' upmarket, cool and lively modern Spanish restaurant comes hidden away in a surprisingly bright-and-airy basement off trendy, bustling Charlotte Street. High ceilings, pale-wood floor, red leather chairs, banquettes and an equally contemporary mezzanine bar set the stylish backdrop for sampling some skilfully cooked tapas. The daily menu lists both classic and contemporary dishes, and you can watch them being prepared from the counter seats in front of the semi-open kitchen. Expect some gutsy, clean-cut dishes and flavours driven by prime ingredients, such as chorizo Iberico, fresh baby squid served with Romesco sauce, calves' liver with celeriac purée and mint salad, or milk-fed lamb cutlets. There's also an Iberian wine list and slick, well-drilled service.

Chef Nieves Barragan Mohacho **Owner** Sam & Eddie Hart
Times 12-2.30/6-10.30 Closed Xmas & BH, Sun, L Sat
Prices Starter £5.70-£18.50, Main £6.20-£21.50, Dessert

£3.50-£7.50, Service added but optional 12.5% **Wines** 118 bottles over £20, 7 bottles under £20, 9 by glass **Notes** Vegetarian available, Air con **Seats** 90 **Children** Portions

Galvin at Windows
PLAN 4 G5

@@@ – see below

Galvin Bistrot de Luxe
PLAN 2 G3

@@ French

Authentic French food in classy bistro setting

☎ 020 7935 4007 📠 020 7486 1735
66 Baker St W1U 7DJ
e-mail: info@galvinrestaurants.com
dir: Nearest station: Baker Street

There is something timeless about the Galvin brothers' restaurant on Baker Street. Perhaps it's the Parisian-brasserie look of the place - chic yet informal - or the unfettered luxury of the food - classic, alluring and based on superb seasonal produce. Whatever the reason, this is a winning formula, delivering first-rate French dishes in a smart and comfortable space. Formal service and well-dressed tables provide a touch of class, while the carte can sort you out whether you're in the mood for something luxurious (lasagne of Dorset crab with chive beurre blanc) or a bit of French classicism (Challans duck breast and confit leg with salade Lyonnaise and Burgundy sauce). There's a very reasonably priced set lunch and early dinner menu. Portions are generous, technical proficiency is on display throughout, including in a tarte au citron dessert, and there's a smart bar - Le Bar - in the basement.

Chef Chris & Jeff Galvin, Sian Rees **Owner** Chris & Jeff Galvin **Times** 12-2.30/6-10.30 Closed 25-26 Dec, 1 Jan, D 24 Dec **Prices** Food prices not confirmed for 2010. Please telephone for details. **Wines** 110 bottles over £20, 7 bottles under £20, 22 by glass **Notes** Sunday L, Vegetarian available, Air con **Seats** 95, Pr/dining room 22 **Children** Portions **Parking** On street & NCP

Le Gavroche Restaurant
PLAN 2 G1

 – see page 288

Goodman
PLAN 3 A2

@ American NEW

Upmarket American-style steakhouse serving prime cuts

☎ 020 7499 3776
26 Maddox St W1S 1QH
dir: Nearest station: Oxford Circus

Goodman set up its (butcher's) shop in 2008, to 'bring the New York steakhouse to Mayfair'. This American-style temple to the T-bone certainly looks the part with its expanses of butch dark wood and liver-brown leather seats and banquettes, although it is actually part of a Russian chain. The steaks are presented in their red raw state at the table - and prime slabs of 28-day aged-in-house cow they are too, albeit at pretty beefy prices. Happily, after all the build up, the men at the grill can walk the walk: the cooking is accurate and flavours are head and shoulders above what is served at many so-called steakhouses. If you're man/woman enough to go for three courses, starters include mushroom 'unravioli' in a creamy truffled sauce with chive oil and parmesan and desserts run to caramelised apple tart with cinnamon ice cream.

Times noon-11 Closed Sun

Galvin at Windows

@@@

LONDON W1	**PLAN 4 G5**

Modern French

Majestic views and refined food

☎ 020 7208 4021 📠 020 7208 4144
London Hilton on Park Ln, 22 Park Ln W1K 1BE
e-mail: reservations@galvinatwindows.com
dir: Nearest station: Green Park, Hyde Park Corner. On Park Lane, opposite Hyde Park

'When a man is tired of London, he is tired of life', so said Samuel Johnson. Just about the whole of the city can be seen from the 28th-floor of the London Hilton on Park Lane, and although there may be a lot of life going on down below, the talents of chef-patron Chris Galvin, alongside head chef André Garrett, ensure that, for a few hours at least, their modern French cooking is all that matters. The room is captivating - reminiscent of the 1930s, glamorous and chic - with smartly set tables and comfortable leather chairs giving just the right amount of refinement. The staff glide between the tables, keeping their wits about them. This place is so 'with it' that they even have a Twitter menu (if you don't know, you probably don't want to know), plus a dégustation, pre-theatre, fixed-price carte backed up with market specials, set lunch, and even a bar express menu if you're in a hurry. The produce is first-rate, technical skill impressive, and presentation modern without being overblown. Warm Lincolnshire smoked eel with bordelaise sauce and celeriac remoulade is a refreshingly simple and accomplished first course, and main-course panaché of John Dory is a perfect piece of fish coming with curry-scented scallops, Roscoff onions and tarragon velouté.

Chef Chris Galvin, André Garrett **Owner** Hilton International **Times** 12-3/6-11 Closed Etr Mon, 26 Dec, L Sat, D Sun **Prices** Fixed L 3 course £29-£45, Fixed D 3 course £33-£58, Service added but optional 12.5% **Wines** 200 bottles over £20, 7 bottles under £20, 18 by glass **Notes** Fixed D 7 course £110 with wine, 3 course pre-theatre £19.50, Sunday L, Vegetarian available, Dress restrictions, Smart casual, Air con **Seats** 108, Pr/dining room 30 **Children** Menu **Parking** NCP

Le Gavroche Restaurant

LONDON W1 PLAN 2 G1

French

Mayfair's bastion of top-flight French tradition

☎ 020 7408 0881 & 7499 1826 📠 020 7491 4387
43 Upper Brook St W1K 7QR
e-mail: bookings@le-gavroche.com
dir: Nearest station: Marble Arch From Park Lane into
Upper Brook St, restaurant on right

The Roux brothers nurtured a mind-boggling roll call of
talented chefs who have flown the nest to make a huge
impact on the UK's gastronomic scene in their own right.
Today's Le Gavroche, under the direction of Michel Roux
Jnr, remains a bastion of exclusive luxury, refinement and
quality, delivering its timeless classical French cuisine in
a basement off Park Lane. Prices may be eye-watering,
but that's probably not a huge surprise. The house style
is opulent in a plush old-school French way - thick pile
carpets, sepulchral lighting, tables aglitter with crystal
and silver, and jackets for gentlemen, s'il vous plaît. And
then there's the Bentley-smooth service: Maître d' Silvano
Giraldin - a le Gavroche institution himself since 1971
- retired in 2008, handing over the baton to Emmanuel
Landré, who continues the correctly formal tone, that's to
say mind-reading waiters flourishing silver domes and
wheeling trolleys of pungently-perfect cheese and
aristocratic digestifs. The culinary director quite naturally
inherited his father's (and uncle's) ways and is true to
the values of the Larousse Gastronomique. While he has
little truck with the ephemeral winds of whim and fashion
that blow through London's restaurant scene, he is not
stuck in the past either. The bilingual menu still deals in
dishes that revel in richness - such as the perennial
cheese and double cream soufflé Suissesse - but a lighter
touch creeps in too. Tamworth pig's head on toast with
herb, apple and hazelnut salad starts on a surprisingly
rustic note, then returns to a more classical pan-roasted
sea bass with Puy lentil and bacon jus and Jerusalem
artichoke purée swiped artfully on the plate. Desserts
might offer pear roasted in Brittany butter with puff
pastry and coconut pannacotta.

Times 12-2/6.30-11 Closed Xmas, New Year, BHs, Sun, L
Sat

Gordon Ramsay at Claridge's

LONDON W1 PLAN 2 H2

Modern European V 🏵

Sophisticated dining in legendary hotel

☎ 020 7499 0099 📠 020 7499 3099
Brook St W1K 4HR
e-mail: reservations@gordonramsay.com
dir: Nearest station: Bond Street, Green Park

An internationally renowned hotel once much beloved of
royalty is these days under the guidance of that prince of
chefs, Gordon Ramsay. The restaurant remains one of
London's most celebrated dining rooms and its effortless
glamour thrills with 1930s-style sophistication, from its
magnificent three-tiered light shades to its delicate
etched-glass panels. It's a grand room with high ceilings
and a strong art deco theme which was brilliantly
restored by designer and architect Thierry Despont.
Service is efficient and well-oiled, with tables stylishly
appointed and well spaced. Head chef Mark Sargeant's
confident modern European cuisine focuses around top
class seasonal ingredients and features many signature
Ramsay dishes. There is a lightness of touch that allows
top drawer ingredients to speak for themselves and
flavours are clear and well defined. A starter of ravioli of
Scottish lobster and salmon with lemongrass and coconut
bisque might be followed by rump of Cumbrian lamb
stuffed with anchovies, carrot and cardamom sauce. A
stellar wine list matches the food.

Chef Mark Sargeant **Owner** Gordon Ramsay Holdings Ltd
Times 12-2.45/5.45-11 **Prices** Fixed L course £30, Fixed
D 3 course £70, Service added but optional 12.5%
Wines 800+ bottles over £20, 11 by glass **Notes** Prestige
menu 6 course £80, Sunday L, Vegetarian menu, Dress
restrictions, Smart, jacket preferred for gentlemen, Air
con **Seats** 100, Pr/dining room 100 **Children** Portions
Parking Mayfair NCP

LONDON W1 *continued*

Gordon Ramsay at Claridge's
PLAN 2 H2

@@@ – *see opposite page*

The Greenhouse
PLAN 4 H6

@@@@ – *see page 290*

The Grill (The Dorchester)
PLAN 4 G6

@@ Modern British V

Palatial grill room with Scottish theme and attentive service in an iconic hotel

☎ 020 7629 8888 ▤ 020 7629 8080
The Dorchester, Park Ln W1K 1QA
e-mail: restaurants@thedorchester.com
dir: Nearest station: Hyde Park Corner On Park Ln, overlooking Hyde Park

You might be forgiven for thinking you've wandered into a gathering of the clans in the Scottish-themed Grill at The Dorchester. Tartans swathe the chairs and carpet the floor, chandeliers sparkle and murals of kilted lairds survey the grand formal dining room from on high. Battalions of politely professional staff provide a five-star service in keeping with the classical tone, so if you're the casual type, remember that T-shirts and trainers just won't do in the iconic Dorchester. Expect straight-up grills and modern British classics; dishes - some as timeless as Angus beef with Yorkshire pudding and roast potatoes, or grilled Dover sole - are kept simple and based on peerless produce. An earthy starter sees saddle of wild rabbit stuffed with its own offal and served on toast with chanterelle mushrooms, and to finish, try a brandy soufflé with sage sorbet.

Chef Brian Hughson **Owner** The Dorchester Collection
Times 12.30-2.30/6.30-10.30 **Prices** Food prices not confirmed for 2010. Please telephone for details.
Wines 400 bottles over £20, 2 bottles under £20, 19 by glass **Notes** Tasting menu 7 course, Sunday L, Vegetarian menu, Dress restrictions, Smart casual, Air con **Seats** 75
Children Menu **Parking** 20

Hakkasan
PLAN 3 B3

@@ Modern Chinese

New-wave Chinese cooking in a see-and-be-seen basement setting

☎ 020 7927 7000 ▤ 020 7907 1889
8 Hanway Place W1T 1HD
e-mail: reservations@hakkasan.com
dir: Nearest station: Tottenham Court Rd From station take exit 2, then 1st left, 1st right, restaurant straight ahead

In case you were in any doubt that you were somewhere near Trend Central, note the trio of door staff, the hovering paparazzi and waiting chauffeurs outside, and the louche basement nightclub vibe to the place. With its black-lacquered design and marble flooring, it's a place

to see and be seen, although the crepuscular lighting levels might make the latter task more of a challenge. An extensive menu of new-wave Chinese dishes, along with some Cantonese classics, is offered, and you might be prepared to just stick in a few pins and see where they take you. A dim sum platter of scallop shumai, har gau and dumplings of Chinese chives and shimeji may be a good place to start. Hit main dishes are tender beef in a crispy noodle cage, flaked fish with spicy pineapple, and roasted mango duck with lemon sauce, while the real show-stoppers are specialities like Monk Jumps Over The Wall, a double-boiled soup with abalone, fish maw, dried scallops, sea cucumber and shiitakes, orderable 24 hours in advance. Get into the vibrant mood with one of the exotic cocktails as an aperitif.

Chef C Tong Chee Hwee **Owner** Alan Yau
Times 12-2.45/6-12.30 Closed 24-25 Dec, L 26 Dec, 1 Jan **Prices** Fixed L 3 course fr £40, Fixed D 3 course £55-£100, Starter £6.50-£16.50, Main £14-£58, Dessert £8-£13.50, Service added but optional 13% **Wines** 301 bottles over £20, 10 by glass **Notes** Wine flights available, Sunday L, Vegetarian available, Dress restrictions, No jeans, shorts, trainers, caps or vests, Air con **Seats** 225 **Parking** Valet parking (dinner only), NCP

Hélène Darroze at The Connaught
PLAN 2 H1

@@@@ – *see page 291*

Hibiscus
PLAN 3 A2

@@@@ – *see page 292*

Kai Mayfair
PLAN 4 G6

@ Chinese

Authentic Chinese cooking in opulent surroundings

☎ 020 7493 8988 ▤ 020 7493 1456
65 South Audley St W1K 2QU
e-mail: kai@kaimayfair.co.uk
dir: Nearest station: Marble Arch Please telephone for directions, or see website

Sheer luxury is the order of the day at this popular and exclusive Chinese restaurant in the heart of Mayfair. Expect sophistication and opulence in the two-tier restaurant with its abundance of rich reds, muted golds and silvers, complemented by mirrored pillars, granite flooring and modern lighting, while banquette seating, high-backed chairs and white linen accentuate the luxury

oriental feel. Service is appropriately professional, while the kitchen offers a wide-ranging menu of regional favourites and more innovative specialities. Expect wasabi prawns, lamb with Szechuan peppercorns and sea bass steamed with ginger and spring onions.

Chef Alex Chow **Owner** Bernard Yeoh
Times 12-2.15/6.30-11 Closed 25-26 Dec, 1 Jan,
Prices Fixed L 2 course fr £19, Starter £11-£21, Main £16-£53, Dessert £7-£10, Service added but optional 12.5% **Wines** 115 bottles over £20, 8 by glass
Notes Group set menu for 6 or more available on request, Sunday L, Vegetarian available, Air con **Seats** 110, Pr/dining room 12 **Parking** Directly outside

See advert on page 293

The Landau
PLAN 2 H4

@@@ – *see page 294*

Latium
PLAN 3 B3

@@ Italian

Authentic Italian cuisine offering a taste of Lazio

☎ 020 7323 9123 ▤ 020 7323 3205
21 Berners St W1T 3LP
e-mail: info@latiumrestaurant.com
dir: Nearest station: Goodge St or Oxford Circus

It's easy to imagine you are dining in Italy at this welcoming restaurant. Named after the Italian region of Lazio, home of chef-patron Maurizio Morelli, the intimate restaurant has a smart interior featuring dark leather banquettes, neutral walls with tumbled stone mosaics and colourful, abstract Italian photography. Maurizio Morelli cooks in a way that best represents the flavours and seasonal variations of his home country, sourcing fine Italian produce. The menu represents all regions of Italy but with particular emphasis on the cuisine of Lazio. Ravioli is a particular speciality, with starters, mains and desserts all featuring on the ravioli menu, including a selection of fish ravioli with sea bass bottarga. Main courses might include slow-cooked pork belly with Savoy cabbage, baby leeks and balsamic vinegar, and a sweet ravioli makes a fine finish.

Chef Maurizio Morelli **Owner** Maurizio Morelli, Claudio Pulze **Times** 12-3/6-10.30 Closed BHs, Sun, L Sat
Prices Food prices not confirmed for 2010. Please telephone for details. **Wines** 97 bottles over £20, 5 bottles under £20, 7 by glass **Notes** Air con **Seats** 50
Children Portions

The Greenhouse

LONDON W1 PLAN 4 H6

Modern European V NOTABLE WINE LIST

Modernist fine dining at a debonair Mayfair address

☎ 020 7499 3331 📄 020 7499 5368
27a Hay's Mews W1J 5NY
e-mail: reservations@
greenhouserestaurant.co.uk
dir: Nearest station: Green Park, Hyde Park, Bond St. Behind Dorchester Hotel just off Hill St

You enter this perennial bastion of sophisticated dining on a suitably botanical note, via a verdant urban garden tucked into a swish Mayfair mews. The suave interior sports a neutral beige and mushroom palette that doesn't upstage the sleek Philippe Hurel furniture. It's the very picture of Mayfair-minimal restraint and serenity, with an artistic arrangement of branches and twigs on a feature wall to break the neutrality with natural textures. Expert service is formal but far from frosty, delivering a smooth flow of immaculate appetisers, moreish bread and artful petits fours with barely a ripple between the courses. Lyonnais chef Antonin Bonnet came to The Greenhouse in 2006 with an impressive CV and has stamped his brand on the cooking. He clearly harbours a passion for Asian flavours, which add inventive fizz to his cerebral take on modern interpretations of French and

Mediterranean classics on menus that are full of surprise and intrigue. The highest quality produce is garnered from around Europe; this is not a kitchen that appears to wring its hands over food miles. An appetiser sets the tone, showing razor-sharp technique and entertaining flavour combinations from the off, in a carrot cigar filled with coconut cream and carrot juice with celery jelly. Simmental beef tartare with bone marrow, black truffle and purple Vienna kohlrabi is an excellent modern interpretation of a classic. Main courses such as slow-cooked Brittany monkfish with a delicate nora pepper crust, cauliflower and almond purées, and potato croquettes with chorizo, are equally refined. By the time dessert comes along, you have come to expect flair and top-level technique, so a Sicilian pistachio millefeuille with rubinette apple and yuzu lime marmalade is another triumph. The wine list is an impressive piece of work, but predictably, you need to be on good terms with the bank manager to explore its depths.

Chef Antonin Bonnet **Owner** Marlon Abela Restaurant Corporation
Times 12-2.30/6.45-11 Closed 23 Dec-5 Jan, Etr, Sun, L Sat **Prices** Fixed L 2 course fr £25, Tasting menu £65-£80, Service added but optional 12.5%
Wines 3131 bottles over £20, 19 bottles under £20, 23 by glass
Notes Vegetarian tasting menu also available, Vegetarian menu, Air con
Seats 65, Pr/dining room 10
Children Portions **Parking** NCP, Meter Parking

Hélène Darroze at The Connaught

LONDON W1 PLAN 2 H1

LONDON W1 PLAN 2 H1

Modern French NEW V

Mayfair opulence meets refined, contemporary cooking

☎ 020 3147 7200
Carlos Place W1K 2AL
e-mail: creservations@the-connaught.co.uk
dir: Nearest station: Bond Street/Green Park Please telephone for directions

The multi-million-pound refurbishment of The Connaught has not delivered too many surprises in the dining room, where dark-wood panelling and immaculately set tables are suitably luxurious. The service brigade is copious in number and mostly Gallic - very formal without being overbearing. The arrival of a new chef, though, has brought a spark of excitement to the place, and the fact that she runs an acclaimed restaurant on the Left Bank in Paris only adds to the expectation. The menu oozes high quality produce, including foie gras from the chef's native Landes and langoustines from Scotland, while a high degree of technical proficiency is on display from the very start with an amuse-bouche of foie gras crème brûlée with apple sorbet and peanut emulsion. There is the seemingly obligatory tasting menu - here called 'Signature' - a lunch menu and an à la carte, each of them appealing and dealing in strong yet deftly handled flavours. The main ingredient of each dish is written in French, thus les chipirons de ligne (baby squid - tender and delicious) is served with chorizo and confit tomatoes, black and creamy '2006 vintage' Carnaroli Acquarello rice and Reggiano parmesan foam as a starter. Main-course grouse (la grouse), a top quality bird, comes with a rustic mix of sprouts, reinette apples and chasselas de Moissac grapes, and, for dessert, les fruits exotiques is indeed exotic: a light lime jelly studded with small pieces of fruit and topped with coconut ice cream, a crisp piece of passionfruit paper and, finally, some delightful coconut marshmallows. The wine list is unsurprisingly focused on France, but does not ignore the rest of the world, while only a smattering of bottles can be found under £30.

Chef Hélène Darroze **Owner** Maybourne Hotel Group **Times** 12-2.30/6.30-10.30 Closed Sun-Mon **Prices** Fixed D 3 course £32, Tasting menu £85, Service added but optional 12.5% **Wines** 6 by glass **Notes** Fixed ALC L & D 3 course £75, Tasting menu 7 course, Vegetarian menu, Dress restrictions, Smart, no jeans or sportswear, Air con **Seats** 64, Pr/dining room 24

Hibiscus

LONDON W1   PLAN 3 A2

Modern French V

Bold experimentation French-style, just off Regent Street

☎ 020 7629 2999 📄 020 7514 9552
29 Maddox St W1S 2PA
e-mail: enquiries@hibiscusrestaurant.co.uk
dir: Nearest station: Oxford Circus

Claude Bosi's move from Shropshire to the bustling, intensely competitive centre of London a couple of years ago was a brave one, but the uprooting has paid dividends. The premises are a ground-floor venue in an office building a few yards off Regent Street, perfect for ladies (and anybody else, for that matter) who lunch. A cool, neutral palette in wood and slate tones creates a restful space and, while there is room between tables, the dimensions also feel human. Bosi's style has always been restlessly experimental in the French manner, and it is one that wins firm converts; multi-layered dishes make cumulative sense as you eat. Butter-roasted veal sweetbread is crusted with English mustard, dressed with wood sorrel and served with a fennel and truffle salad. A garnish of ultra-fine specks of pure lemon allows the diner to play with the different levels of acidity in the dish. Red mullet comes with a fricassée of Japanese artichokes, spätzle gnocchi, toast topped with bone marrow and gherkin, and a sauce that incorporates the mullet liver. The unfashionable bits of creatures are often served up in a manner reminiscent of French peasant cooking, as when tripe and a pig's ear find their way into a main course that also finds room for cuttlefish, the whole presented in its component parts for mixing and matching. The dessert menu features lentils, basil, Szechuan pepper and other savoury items, and even mushrooms as a silkily creamy tart topping, alongside macadamia sorbet and blood peach gel, in a stunning assemblage that reliably elicits the 'wow' response.

Chef Claude Bosi **Owner** Claude Bosi
Times 12-2.30/6.30-10 Closed 10 days Xmas/New Year, Sun-Mon, L Sat
Prices Fixed L 3 course fr £25, Fixed D 3 course fr £65, Service added but optional 12.5% **Notes** Fri-Sat dinner tasting menu only, Vegetarian menu, Air con **Seats** 45, Pr/dining room 18
Children Portions **Parking** On street

The Landau

LONDON W1 — PLAN 2 H4

Modern European V

Inspirational grand dining in an historic hotel

☎ 020 7965 0165 & 020 7636 1000 📠 020 7973 7560
The Langham London, Portland Place W1B 1JA
e-mail: reservations@thelandau.com
dir: Nearest station: Oxford Circus On N end of Regent St,
by Oxford Circus

The Langham Hotel sits on a little wiggle in the road at the top end of Regent Street, diagonally opposite the BBC, with which it shares almost as venerable a history. Discreet class is the first impression, as you pass through the separate restaurant entrance, and into the Artesian Bar, so named for its positioning, believe it or not, above just such a well (sadly no longer in use). A list of rum cocktails, the house specialities, might distract the attention here but, if you resist, pass through to the opulent, oval Landau dining room, with its equestrian sculptures, well-spaced tables, and staff who take a justifiable pride in the surroundings. The kitchen's stock-in-trade is highly skilled contemporary cooking based on interesting and (most importantly) successful combinations, presented in a way that highlights the quality of ingredients. Consider, for example, a starter called salade Isabelle, an assemblage of Orkney scallops, both types of artichoke and the perfectly judged bitterness of tamarind, the whole dish pungently redolent of truffle. Main course might be Barbary duck, the breast roasted, the leg confit fashioned into a torte, garnished with seared foie gras, and counterpointed with celeriac, orange and cardamom. This is inspirational grand dining. Browse for your wine choice in the dramatically lit vaulted wine corridor beforehand.

Chef Andrew Turner **Owner** Langham Hotels International
Times 12.30-2.30/5.30-10.30 Closed L Sat, D Sun
Prices Fixed L 2 course fr £19.95, Fixed D 3 course fr £26.50, Starter £7-£17.50, Main £19.50-£30, Dessert £7.50-£10, Service added but optional 12.5% **Wines** 135 bottles over £20, 20 by glass **Notes** Theatre menu 2-3 course, Grazing menu 5-8 course, Sunday L, Vegetarian menu, Dress restrictions, Smart casual, Civ Wed 220, Air con **Seats** 100, Pr/dining room 18 **Children** Portions, Menu **Parking** On street & NCP

Locanda Locatelli

LONDON W1 — PLAN 2 F2

Italian

Exemplary Italian cuisine in a stylish setting

☎ 020 7935 9088 📠 020 7935 1149
8 Seymour St W1H 7JZ
e-mail: info@locandalocatelli.com
dir: Nearest station: Marble Arch Opposite Marylebone police station

If it is top-end, sophisticated, authentic Italian food you are after, head for Giorgio Locatelli's West End gaff. It has a moneyed look but an atmosphere that is charmingly unaffected, helped by the engaging staff who combine the best of Italian passion with real knowledge of the menu. A safe distance from the craziness of Oxford Street, the restaurant, a separate business on the ground floor of a luxury hotel, has a sleek, contemporary design, with cream leather banquette seating or comfortable cream leather tub chairs and round tables with smart settings. It's stylish without being showy. The authentic Italian cooking combines the rusticity of peasant-style dishes with more refined techniques, and it's a winning combination. Oxtail ravioli is made with pasta that's as good as you might hope, while fillet of wild sea bass in a salt and herb crust is a main course of real impact (both in terms of presentation and superb flavours). For dessert, Savarin with coconut ice cream and pineapple carpaccio is simply and accurately made, and the excellent espresso is the natural conclusion. A large wine list focuses mainly on Italy with some good vintages at reasonable prices.

Chef Giorgio Locatelli **Owner** Plaxy & Giorgio Locatelli
Times 12-3/6.45-11 Closed Xmas, BHs **Prices** Food prices not confirmed for 2010. Please telephone for details. **Wines** 2 bottles under £20, 24 by glass **Notes** Sunday L, Vegetarian available, Air con **Seats** 70 **Children** Portions **Parking** NCP adjacent, parking meters

LONDON W1 *continued*

Levant
PLAN 2 G3

Lebanese, Middle Eastern

The scents and flavours of the Middle East

☎ 020 7224 1111 📄 020 7486 1216
Jason Court, 76 Wigmore St W1H 9DQ
e-mail: info@levant.co.uk
dir: Nearest station: Bond Street From Bond St station, walk through St Christopher's Place, reach Wigmore St, restaurant across road

Tucked away in a basement off Wigmore Street, Levant is accessed via a stone staircase dimly lit by lanterns. Inside it's like a scene from the *Arabian Nights*, with more lanterns and flickering candles, rich colours, sumptuous fabrics and an exotic atmosphere helped along by the nightly belly dancing. Try some traditional meze along with cocktails in the bar, dine à la carte or tuck into a set Middle Eastern 'feast'. The main dining room has banquette seating with individual tables, as well as some cosy private areas with floor cushions. Try the fatayer kreidis (baked pastries stuffed with prawns, shallots, dill and harissa), followed by the mixed fish platter, and check out the Moroccan and Lebanese wines.

Times 12-midnight Closed 25-26 Dec

Locanda Locatelli
PLAN 2 F2

— *see opposite page*

Maze
PLAN 2 G2

— *see page 296*

Maze Grill
PLAN 2 G2

Modern American

Classy grill room, part of the Ramsay stable

☎ 020 7495 2211 📄 020 7592 1603
London Marriott Hotel Grosvenor Square, 10-13 Grosvenor Square W1K 6JP
e-mail: mazegrill@gordonramsay.com
dir: Nearest station: Bond St

Modelled on the informal style New York grill restaurants, Jason Atherton's and Gordon Ramsay's second dining venue within this hotel (see entry for Maze) specialises in cooking outstanding quality steaks from different breeds of beef, some rare and expensive. This is modern fast food with a twist, with steaks quickly cooked on coals then under a unique grill at a high temperature. The impressive result is wonderfully full-flavoured steaks, say, a Hereford grass-fed rib-eye aged for 25 days, served on wooden boards with optional sauces, including a 'steak' sauce that's made at the table. Starters may take in Cornish crab and harissa soup, while non-meat-eaters will be content with lobster served with chips and ginger ketchup. The setting is a smart, modern, white linen-free zone; note the butcher's block table by the open kitchen that acts as a chef's table for 12.

Chef Jason Atherton **Owner** Gordon Ramsay Holdings Ltd
Times 12-2.30/5.45-11 **Prices** Fixed L 2 course £15, Starter £8.50-£14.50, Main £13.50-£28, Dessert £5-£8.50, Service added but optional 12.5% **Wines** 20 bottles over £20, 5 bottles under £20, 20 by glass **Notes** Sunday L, Dress restrictions, Smart casual, Air con **Seats** 80, Pr/dining room 12 **Children** Portions

Mews of Mayfair
PLAN 2 H2

Modern

Chic venue with cooking to match

☎ 020 7518 9388 & 7518 9395 📄 0207 7518 9389
10-11 Lancashire Court, New Bond St, Mayfair W1S 1EY
e-mail: info@mewsofmayfair.com
dir: Nearest station: Bond Street Between Brook St & New Bond St. Opposite Dolce & Gabbana

Tucked away in a pretty mews just off Bond Street, this chic restaurant occupies the 2nd floor of a 4-storey building, with a cocktail bar and terrace below, private dining above and a lounge-bar in the basement. Although small, the dining room is a bright and airy space, with white walls and furniture, stripped pale wood flooring, pristine white tablecloths and formally dressed waiting staff. The cooking shows French and British influences, as in a well-made ravioli with a paysanne filling and seared foie gras, and Gressingham duck with peppered lentils and Devils on Horseback.

Times 12-4/6-12 Closed 25-26 Dec, New Year, D Sun

Murano
PLAN 4 H6

— *see page 297*

Nicole's
PLAN 3 A1

Modern Mediterranean

Fashionable lunchtime retreat for the chic and well-heeled

☎ 020 7499 8408 📄 020 7409 0381
158 New Bond St W1S 2UB
e-mail: nicoles@nicolefarhi.com
dir: Nearest station: Green Park, Bond St Between Hermés & Asprey

When the Nicole in question is a certain Ms Farhi, and this stylish split-level restaurant lies below the exclusive Bond Street fashion outlet, you can expect a setting to match the designer label: an elegantly simple blend of classic oak floors, brown leather and white linen, somewhat in the fashion of a chic Parisian brasserie. The cooking takes a modern route, using simple top-quality materials with a distinct flavour of the Mediterranean; tuna ceviche with citrus fruits, chilli and coriander hits the mark as a starter, while mains are split into fish and meat sections, the latter offering ricotta and lemon thyme chicken with roasted artichokes and green olive relish. Summer fruit tart with crème fraîche ends without endangering svelte waistlines too much.

Times 12-3.30 Closed BHs, Sun, D all week

Nobu
PLAN 4 G5

Japanese

Super-cool Japanese overlooking Hyde Park

☎ 020 7447 4747 📄 020 7447 4749
The Metropolitan, 19 Old Park Ln W1K 1LB
e-mail: london@noburestaurants.com
dir: Nearest station: Hyde Park Corner/Green Park Located on 1st floor of Metropolitan Hotel

Nobu is a global brand, as well as being a person - Nobuyuki Matsuhisa - and this outpost of the group in The Metropolitan hotel (it has its own entrance) has been winning over the great and the good since 1997. Inside it is coolly minimalistic, with the closely-packed tables and muted tones relieved by some bold modern artworks and the happy hum of the trendy clientele. The first-floor room has great views over Park Lane and Hyde Park. The menu - designed for grazing and sharing - is predominantly Japanese with a few South American influences, but not everything is so obviously fusion as the yellowtail sashimi with jalapeno. Black cod with miso, rock shrimp tempura with ponzu, seafood udon and tenderloin of beef with teriyaki sauce are what to expect. Nobu Berkeley Street, also in W1, is another member of the family.

Chef Mark Edwards **Owner** Nobuyuki Matsuhisa
Times 12-2.15/6-10.15 **Prices** Food prices not confirmed for 2010. Please telephone for details. **Wines** 8 by glass **Notes** Vegetarian available, Dress restrictions, Smart casual, Air con **Seats** 160, Pr/dining room 40 **Parking** Car Park nearby

Nobu Berkeley Street
PLAN 5 A6

Japanese

Great Japanese food in the heart of Mayfair

☎ 020 7290 9222 📄 020 7290 9223
15 Berkeley St W1J 8DY
e-mail: berkeley@noburestaurants.com
dir: Nearest station: Green Park

The glam sister of the original Nobu restaurant off Park Lane (see entry) is something of a celeb magnet for watering, grazing and air kissing in one of the West End's most über-stylish venues. But don't let the self-conscious styling and the party-crowd bar distract you from the fact that the upstairs dinner-only restaurant is serious in its business of cooking remarkably good Japanese food. There's a sushi bar with an open kitchen, a wood-burning oven and a fun 12-seater hibachi table where you cook your own food with a little help from the chef, and the clued-up waiters are happy to talk you through the menu. Fish preparation skills are top-level in the house style of cutting-edge Japanese cuisine spiked with South American spicing, as typified by yellowtail sashimi with jalapeño. Crispy pork belly with spicy miso is a memorable main course and desserts such as Yuzu tart with Earl Grey ice cream come up trumps too.

Times 12-2.15/6-1am Closed 25 & 26 Dec, L Sat & Sun

Maze

LONDON W1 | **PLAN 2 G2**

French, Pacific Rim 🍷 NOTABLE WINE LIST

Pace-setting avant-garde cooking in the heart of London

☎ 020 7107 0000   📄 020 7107 0001
London Marriott Hotel Grosvenor Square, 10-13 Grosvenor Square W1K 6JP
e-mail: reservations@gordonramsay.com
dir: Nearest station: Bond Street

Maze can truly consider itself to be right at the heart of the restaurant action in the capital - in both senses. With an address on Grosvenor Square, within sight of the United States Embassy, it is well placed to serve the Mayfair moneyed classes, but it also has in Jason Atherton a chef with his finger on the pulse of gastronomic fashion, and one of the most extravagantly talented practitioners currently working in the Gordon Ramsay stable. The design of the place, by David Rockwell, is eye-catching indeed, creating a multi-level space that really is something of a maze for first-time visitors, with seating in dazzling yellow and a rosewood bar where a list of cocktails to shake and stir you is offered. The menu format centres on the lengthy list of tasting dishes, smaller (though by no means minuscule) compositions of arresting ingredients and seasonings. These are supplemented by four- or six-course lunch menus, and a seven-course chef's menu with a wealth of choice. Just deciding which of these routes to go down will be a formidable enough task. When you have chosen, what distinguishes the cooking is its high level of consistency. Dishes are inspired, creative and challenging, with execution flawless, and the tastes and textures both intense and subtly balanced. Among the tasting-menu successes are: slow-roast prawns with pumpkin purée, rye croutons, crab bisque and vanilla oil; pressed foie gras marinated with Pinot Noir caramel, smoked duck and fig jam; Loch Duart salmon with cavolo nero, bacon velouté and field mushroom purée; and a perfectly timed, pinkly tender honey- and soy-roasted quail with Landes foie gras and spiced pear chutney. Stellar reworkings of humdrum ideas reach their apogee in desserts such as Arctic roll and raspberry jelly, or rice pudding with raspberry and lemon thyme jam and mascarpone and pecan ice cream. A list of stunning pedigree wines accompanies, but expect to pay stunning pedigree prices.

Chef Jason Atherton **Owner** Gordon Ramsay Holdings Ltd
Times 12-2.30/6-10.30 **Prices** Starter £9-£10.50, Main £9.50-£12.50, Dessert £4-£7.50, Service added but optional 12.5% **Wines** 600+ bottles over £20, 27 by glass **Notes** Fixed L 4 & 6 course £28.50-£42.50, D 7 course £60.00, Sunday L, Vegetarian available, Dress restrictions, Casual, no shorts or sportswear, Air con **Seats** 100, Pr/dining room 40 **Parking** On Street

LONDON W1 *continued*

The Only Running Footman PLAN 4 H6

Modern British

Renovated Mayfair pub with informal all-day dining

☎ 020 7499 2988
5 Charles St, Mayfair W1J 5DF
e-mail: info@therunningfootman.biz
dir: Nearest station: Close to Berkeley Sq & Green Park tube station

A four-storeyed redbrick pub just off Berkeley Square, the Footman aims to offer 'true British grub'. There isn't much of that about in Mayfair, and it's a generously wide interpretation of the national heritage that takes in clam linguini with garlic, spiced halibut with fennel and orange compôte in coconut and coriander sauce, or chargrilled fillet steak in balsamic jus, but the performance is reliable enough not to get hung up on definitions. And anyway, there is Sussex pond pudding with lemon custard or apple pie with raspberry ripple ice cream to finish.

Chef Richard Robb **Owner** Barnaby Meredith
Times 12-2.30/6.30-10 Closed D 25 Dec, 1 Jan
Prices Starter £5.50-£7.50, Main £12.95-£25, Dessert £5.50, Service optional **Notes** Sunday L, Vegetarian available **Seats** 30, Pr/dining room 40 **Children** Portions

Orrery PLAN 2 G4

Modern European

Stylish and elegant restaurant above designer store

☎ 020 7616 8000 020 7616 8080
55-57 Marylebone High St W1U 5RB
e-mail: oliviere@conran-restaurants.co.uk
dir: Nearest station: Baker St, Regent's Park. At north end of Marylebone High St

First the science bit: an orrery is a heliocentric mechanical model of our solar system showing the relative movements of the planets and moons. With an impeccable address on Marylebone High Street and located above Terence Conran's fashionably expensive shop, the restaurant named after the model of our solar system is a classy affair, elegantly done-out in the unfussy Conran manner. Impressive arched windows look out over Marylebone Church Gardens opposite and give the room a real sense of style. Access is via a flight of stairs or lift and once through the door you're in the safe hands of the waiting staff. The cooking style and presentation is simple, with roots in the classics. Quality ingredients are handled with respect on the menu du jour, the à la carte and the seven-course menu gourmand. A starter of steamed shellfish and saffron risotto could be followed by roast cannon of lamb with olive crust, aubergine caviar, gratin dauphinoise and rosemary jus. Finish with Valrhona chocolate fondant and vanilla ice cream.

Times 12-2.30/6.30-10.30

Ozer PLAN 3 A3

Turkish, Middle Eastern

Authentic Turkish cuisine in the heart of London

☎ 020 7323 0505 020 7323 0111
5 Langham Place, Regent St W1B 3DG
e-mail: info@sofra.co.uk
dir: Nearest station: Oxford Circus. 2 min walk towards Upper Regent Street

Just north of Oxford Circus, Ozer is a bit of a Tardis - the lively bar at the front opens up into the expansive dining room. Sumptuously decorated with red walls, floaty white drapes, crisp white tablecloths and leather chairs, there is a contemporary edge to the place and the staff cope admirably with the numbers, always eager to please. The Turkish food is both authentic and well executed and Ozer remains deservedly busy. Start with good olives, pitta bread and their excellent houmous, then move on to the well made and sensibly-priced selection of hot and cold meze (falafel, grilled sardines or duck roll). Main courses can be as traditional as marinated lamb chargrilled on a skewer or as avante garde as black cod marinated in white miso. Finish with a traditional kunefe (pastry filled with cheese, pistachio and syrup).

Times Noon-mdnt

Murano

LONDON W1 PLAN 4 H6

Italian NEW V

☎ 020 7592 1222 020 7592 1213
20 Queen St W1J 5PP
e-mail: murano@gordonramsay.com
dir: Nearest station: Green Park Please telephone for directions or see website

Gordon Ramsay gave Angela Hartnett the platform to showcase her talents at The Connaught and now she's moved just a stone's throw away from the grand dame to their latest venture, the elegant and sophisticated Murano. The eponymous fine Italian glassware is used to good effect in modern light fittings, and the right degree of Mayfair chic is given to the room by the use of top-quality leather and marble. Colours are from a muted natural palette - tones of white, cream, grey - and it is all very calming and civilised. Hartnett's Italian heritage is at the heart of her cooking and here she blends a touch of simplicity with plenty of flair and imagination. The excellent breads (carta di musica, focaccia and Pugliese) arrive with wafer thin slices of first-class prosciutto before an inspired risotto with 2-year aged parmigiano Reggiano, rocket pesto and roasted pine nuts. The produce is second to none as in a superb piece of roasted turbot, which is served with smoked ham stock, pearl barley and autumn vegetables. A deft blending of traditional and modern ideas is evident throughout, from the impressive truffle arancini amuse-bouche to refined desserts such as chocolate and chestnut semi-fredo with popcorn ice cream and dulce di leche. The wine list majors on Italy but embraces the rest of the world, and there is a good selection by the glass.

Chef Angela Hartnett **Owner** Gordon Ramsay Holdings
Times 12-2.30/6-11 Closed 25-26 Dec, Sun **Prices** Fixed L fr £25, Fixed D 3 course £55, Tasting menu £70, Service added but optional 12.5% **Wines** 400 bottles over £20, 16 by glass **Notes** Tasting menu 7 course, Vegetarian menu, Dress restrictions, Smart, no shorts or sportswear (smart trainers and denim acceptable), Air con **Seats** 46, Pr/dining room 10

LONDON W1 *continued*

Passione

PLAN 3 B3

◉◉ Italian

Wonderful flavours from an intimate, lively Italian

☎ 020 7636 2833 ▤ 020 7636 2889
10 Charlotte St W1T 2LT
dir: Nearest station: Goodge Street 5 min walk from underground station

Its unassuming, pinkish-terracotta and glass frontage seem somewhat unremarkable for a widely esteemed Italian, though the name on the awning - sheltering a few fair-weather alfresco tables - perfectly sums up this small but big-hearted restaurant, epitomising chef-patron Gennaro Contaldo's love affair with great food. Pastel-green walls are hung with food photographs and mirrors, while blond-wood floors and chairs add a modern edge to close-set white-clothed tables and a lively, informal atmosphere. It's not difficult to see why Gennaro is a Jamie Oliver mentor, his regional Italian cooking may be pricey, but it's driven by the freshest prime produce and a simple, clean-flavoured style. Perhaps try ricotta cheese and lemon ravioli served in a butter and sage sauce, or grilled and pan-fried veal with asparagus and celeriac in thyme.

Times 12.30-2.15/7-10.15 Closed 1 wk Xmas, BHs, Sun, L Sat

Patterson's

PLAN 3 A2

◉◉ Modern European

Fine dining in family-run Mayfair restaurant

☎ 020 7499 1308 ▤ 020 7491 2122
4 Mill St, Mayfair W1S 2AX
e-mail: info@pattersonsrestaurant.co.uk
dir: Nearest station: Oxford Circus Located off Conduit St opposite Savile Row entrance

Combining the charm of a family-run restaurant with stylish, quality cuisine, Patterson's is tucked away in a tiny Mayfair street between Oxford Circus and New Bond Street. Wooden flooring, high-backed leather chairs and matching banquettes in the bar area and dining room make for an elegant setting, with colourful artwork and fish and lobster tanks providing interest if you're waiting for your guest to arrive. In the kitchen, father-and-son team Raymond and Tom aim for a classic modern European style but with a healthy, honest and creative approach. Good-quality seasonal ingredients, regional

and organic where possible, are sourced from farms and markets, while they remain true to their roots, sourcing langoustine, lobster and crabs from Scotland. Baked scallops with cabbage, glazed with a pancetta-flavoured fish sauce is a refined and intelligent first course, followed, perhaps, by rabbit and foie gras pie with a celery and parsley salad. Candied vanilla with ginger Puy lentils with white chocolate mousse is a creative finale.

Chef Raymond & Thomas Patterson **Owner** Raymond & Thomas Patterson **Times** 12-3/6-11 Closed 25-26 Dec, 1 Jan, Good Fri & Etr Mon, Sun, L Sat **Prices** Fixed L 2 course £15, Starter £15, Main £20, Dessert £10, Service added but optional 12.5% **Wines** 134 bottles over £20, 12 by glass **Notes** Vegetarian available, Air con **Seats** 70, Pr/dining room 20 **Children** Portions, Menu **Parking** Savile Row

La Petite Maison

PLAN 2 H2

◉◉ French, Mediterranean

A touch of the Côte d'Azur in Mayfair

☎ 020 7495 4774 ▤ 020 7629 8944
54 Brooks Mews W1K 4EG
e-mail: info@lpmlondon.co.uk
dir: Nearest station: Bond Street

La Petite Maison's original namesake in Nice is a hangout of international glitterati, who turn up for its light Mediterranean cuisine from Nice and Liguria, and to check out who's wearing what and who's eating with whom. The London version, ensconced in a quiet Mayfair mews behind Claridge's shares a similar raison d'être. The diamond-shaped open-plan room has a breezily Mediterranean laid-back vibe, and a jet-set Riviera-cool look with creamy walls, huge, discreetly-frosted windows and an open kitchen that lets you see the chefs' every move. Light and attractive dishes start with a pissaladière tart straight from the South of France, or warm prawns with olive oil. Main courses, with some Côte d'Azur price tags, are along the lines of whole roast black leg chicken, and grilled marinated lamb cutlets with aubergine caviar.

Chef Raphael Duntoye **Owner** Raphael Duntoye, Arjun Waney **Times** 12-3/6-11 Closed 25-26 Dec, **Prices** Food prices not confirmed for 2010. Please telephone for details. **Wines** 150 bottles over £20, 16 by glass **Notes** Sunday L, Vegetarian available, Air con **Seats** 85 **Parking** On street

Pied à Terre

PLAN 3 B3

◉◉◉◉ *– see opposite page*

The Providores

PLAN 2 G3

◉◉ International ▤

Globally-inspired fusion food in relaxed atmosphere

☎ 020 7935 6175 ▤ 020 7935 6877
109 Marylebone High St W1U 4RX
e-mail: anyone@theprovidores.co.uk
dir: Nearest station: Bond St, Baker St, Regent's Park From Bond St station cross Oxford St, down James St, into Thayer St then Marylebone High St

Peter Gordon's restaurant on fashionable Marylebone High Street, located in a rather handsome former Victorian pub, is a vibrant place delivering possibly the best fusion food in town. Peter was instrumental in bringing this style of cooking over from his native New Zealand in the 1990s, and his menus are packed with exciting combinations and exotic flavours. The ground-floor Tapa Room is a buzzy all-day affair and the upstairs dining room is a more formal space, though still lively, open for lunch and dinner. The fusion is globally-inspired, but much of it is West-meets-South East Asian, so roast Norwegian cod comes with ginger and wasabi arancini, pickled red cabbage, tomato chilli jam and miso beurre blanc. Produce is top-notch and the combinations intelligently innovative. Desserts maintain the standard: pear bavarois with satsuma and Cointreau jelly, poached pear, an Eccles cake and vanilla cream.

Chef Peter Gordon **Owner** P Gordon, M McGrath **Times** 12-2.30/6-10.30 Closed 24 Dec-3 Jan, Etr Mon, **Prices** Fixed D 3 course £42, Starter £8.80-£15, Main £18-£25, Dessert £9.20-£9.80, Service added but optional 12.5% **Wines** 81 bottles over £20, 2 bottles under £20, 23 by glass **Notes** Brunch menu on Sun, Vegetarian available, Air con **Seats** 38 **Children** Portions

Quo Vadis

PLAN 3 B2

◉◉ Grill

Soho dining landmark rejuvenated as a classic grill

☎ 020 7437 9585 ▤ 020 7734 7593
26-29 Dean St W1D 3LL
e-mail: info@quovadissoho.co.uk
dir: Nearest station: Tottenham Court Road/Leicester Square

A Soho stalwart since 1926, Quo Vadis was reinvented in 2008 by Sam and Eddie Hart, the pair behind Spanish restaurants Fino and Barrafina (see entries). Over the years it has been home to Karl Marx, and, more recently, part of the Marco Pierre White empire; it now trades as a classic grill restaurant. The look is not radically different - edgy Brit-art, leather banquettes and stained glass windows are still part of the vibe, but the kitchen now deals in straightforward modern British cooking driven by honest, well-sourced ingredients. Brasserie classics such as steak tartare, morels on toast, or for the dedicated carnivore, calves' brains appear among starters. Mains might be straight-up slabs of meat sizzling from the grill, including a 28-day aged rib of Hereford beef for two to share, or slow-braised ox cheeks, while puddings enter the well-trodden paths of treacle tart or chocolate fondant.

Times 12-2.30/5.30-11 Closed 24-25 Dec, 1 Jan, BHs, Sun

Pied à Terre

Modern French **V** NOTABLE WINE LIST

Refined and intelligent modern cooking in calm, contemporary surroundings

☎ 020 7636 1178 & 7419 9788
▤ 020 7916 1171
34 Charlotte St W1T 2NH
e-mail: info@pied-a-terre.co.uk
web: www.pied-a-terre.co.uk
dir: Nearest station: Goodge Street. S of BT Tower and Goodge St

The understated confidence of the exterior seems to sum up Pied à Terre in some way; it would be easy to walk past, imagining it to be a design studio or a gallery (not inconceivable on Charlotte Street), but that would be a mistake. This is not a restaurant that shouts its achievements from the rooftops; chef and co-owner Shane Osborn has published a cookbook or two, and front-of-house guru (and founding owner) David Moore does his stint on Raymond Blanc's TV show, The Restaurant, but still the restaurant remains their focus, their passion. Natural tones and colours, architectural glass, suede and rosewood furniture dominate over the three floors, which consist of two downstairs dining areas, a bar on the first floor and private dining room up top. It is a series of modern spaces, neither over-blown nor unmemorable. The service is as impeccable as everything else, well organised and pretty much seamless from the customers' perspective. Australian-born Shane's modern French cooking is both refined and classical, eschewing the extremes of radical experimentalism, while never standing still. The lunchtime Du Jour Menu is a bit of a steal at £24.50 (fantastic value, really), plus there's a theatre menu, a carte and the de rigeur tasting menu. Foie gras parfait with poppy seed crisps is an amuse-bouche displaying significant technical flair in the making and as for the scallops in a first-course with trompette de la mort, lemon oil, lemon thyme, Jerusalem artichokes and parmesan tuiles, they are as good as they get. Main-course saddle of rabbit is wrapped in winter truffle and parsnip and served with a boudin of confit leg, a smoked celery emulsion and roasted parsnips, and a star turn at dessert is bitter sweet chocolate tart - stunning pastry - with stout ice cream and macadamia nut cream. The wine list, too, will blow your socks off. See also entry for sibling restaurant, L'Autre Pied.

Chef Shane Osborn **Owner** David Moore & Shane Osborn **Times** 12-2.45/6.15-11 Closed 2 wks Xmas & New Year, Sun, L Sat **Prices** Fixed L 2 course fr £24.50, Fixed D 3 course fr £68, Tasting menu £85, Service added but optional 12.5% **Wines** 620 bottles over £20, 11 bottles under £20, 15 by glass **Notes** Tasting menu 10 course, Pre-post theatre D 3 course £39.50, Vegetarian menu, Air con **Seats** 40, Pr/dining room 12 **Parking** Cleveland St

LONDON W1 *continued*

Rasa Samudra
PLAN 3 B3

◉◉ Indian V

Bright, friendly and authentic Keralan restaurant

☎ 020 7637 0222 📄 020 7637 0224
5 Charlotte St W1T 1RE
e-mail: dasrasa@hotmail.com
dir: Nearest station: Tottenham Court Road, Goodge Street Telephone for directions

Flagship of the popular Rasa group of Indian eateries, Samudra's showy pink exterior certainly stands out from the crowd on bustling Charlotte Street's restaurant row. It's unabashedly not new-wave, and specialises in authentic Keralan cooking and is noted for its fish and seafood and vegetarian dishes. Inside is decorated in traditional style, with exotic Indian art, bright silks and traditional wood carvings. Courteous, attentive staff deliver an eye-catching array of crisp, poppadom-like snacks and home-made pickles to white-clothed tables. The lengthy roster includes soups, dosa and curries, including a selection of meat-based dishes too. But don't expect regular Indian food, instead enjoy the likes of a varutharacha meen curry (tilapia in a spicy sauce made from roasted coconut, red chillies, tomatoes and tamarind) that's just perfect with the fresh, tangy lemon rice (tossed with curry leaves and mustard seeds) and perhaps the speciality paratha bread to mop things up.

Chef Prasad Mahadevan Nair **Owner** Das Shreedharan **Times** 12-3/6-11 Closed 2 wks Dec, L Sun **Prices** Fixed D 4 course £22.50-£30, Starter £4.25-£7.50, Main £6.50-£12.95, Dessert £2.75-£3.50, Service added but optional 12.5% **Wines** 6 bottles over £20, 6 bottles under £20, 1 by glass **Notes** Fixed L 4 course £22.50-£30, Vegetarian menu, Air con **Seats** 100, Pr/dining room 70

The Red Fort
PLAN 3 B2

◉◉ Traditional Indian

Stylish contemporary Soho Indian

☎ 020 7437 2525 & 7437 2115 📄 020 7434 0721
77 Dean St W1D 3SH
e-mail: info@redfort.co.uk
dir: Nearest station: Leicester Square Walk N on Charing Cross Rd. At Cambridge Circus left into Shaftesbury Ave. Dean St 2nd right

This longstanding Indian - with red, carved-timbered exterior - might lead the uninitiated to believe it's lost in time, but its legion of savvy Soho admirers will tell you it's a stylish, contemporary, upmarket outfit that contradicts the old stereotypical viewpoint. The long ground-floor dining room comes in restful tones, with sandstone-coloured walls adorned with eye-catching Mughal arches inlaid with authentic artefacts, while at the back, there's a sleek water feature and open kitchen. Banquettes line the walls, tables are laid with white linen and staff come smartly attired, though, on occasions, can give the impression they're just going through the motions. The menu embodies the décor's theme, with the

primarily Mughal Court/North Western style dishes utilising tip-top ingredients such as the Herdwick lamb in Andhra gosht. The restaurant's buzzy bar, the Akbar, is in the basement.

Chef Mohammed Rais **Owner** Amin Ali
Times 12-2.15/5.45-11.15 Closed 25 Dec, L Sat & Sun **Prices** Fixed L 2 course £12, Fixed D 3 course £35-£45, Starter £6.50-£9.95, Main £15-£33, Dessert £7-£8, Service added but optional 12.5% **Wines** 70 bottles over £20, 15 bottles under £20, 7 by glass **Notes** Pre-theatre 3 course meal £16, Air con **Seats** 84

Rhodes W1 Brasserie and Bar
PLAN 2 F2

◉ Modern British

Accomplished British cooking in cool modern brasserie

☎ 020 7616 5930 📄 020 7479 3888
The Cumberland Hotel, Great Cumberland Place W1H 7DL
e-mail: brasserie@rhodesw1.com
web: www.rhodesw1.com
dir: Nearest station: Paddington, Marble Arch

Part of the Cumberland Hotel, this celebrity chef-driven restaurant occupies a prime spot in Marble Arch. The high-ceilinged restaurant is a chic, contemporary dining space, with unclothed wood tables, crimson upholstered chairs and banquette seating, and provides an impressive backdrop for some simply and well prepared modern and classic dishes, influenced by Gary Rhodes's distinctly British approach. The menu offers crowd-pleasing classics like smoked haddock with Welsh rarebit and tomato chive salad, followed by braised oxtails with soft mashed potatoes. Finish with a bit of British comfort food: jam roly-poly with hot jam sauce and vanilla custard.

Chef Gary Rhodes, Darrel Wilde **Owner** Gary Rhodes **Times** 12-2.30/6-10.15 **Prices** Fixed L 2 course £15.50-£19.95, Starter £6.65-£9.95, Main £13.95-£21.75, Dessert £6.50, Service added but optional 12.5%, Groups min 10 service 12.5% **Wines** 38 bottles over £20, 2 bottles under £20, 12 by glass **Notes** Pre-theatre bookings for groups on request, Sunday L, Vegetarian available, Air con **Seats** 140 **Children** Portions **Parking** NCP at Marble Arch

Rhodes W1 Restaurant
PLAN 2 F2

◉◉◉ *– see opposite page*

Ristorante Semplice
PLAN 2 H2

◉◉ Italian

Classy Italian with a passion for authenticity

☎ 020 7495 1509 📄 020 7493 7074
10 Blenheim St W1S 1LJ
dir: Nearest station: Bond Street

'Semplice' means 'simple' in Italian and that's certainly the kitchen's mantra at this chic, intimate Mayfair eatery, formerly 2 small restaurants. Highly polished ebony walls with gold carvings, leather seating in brown and cream, blond-wood floors and linen-clad tables, set the classy, upbeat tone. Exceptional ingredients form the foundation, either garnered from the best British producers, or flown in from home (mozzarella arrives daily) and are treated with due reverence. An appealing variety of regional Italian dishes are delivered with assured self confidence and emphasis on flavour. Free-range Italian meat also wows, perhaps roast milk-fed Piedmontese veal wrapped in Parma ham and served with sautéed spelt, asparagus and morel mushrooms, while fish options might see line-caught sea bass teamed with a chick pea sauce and sautéed spinach. Service is slick, well led and as Italian as the well-chosen wine list.

Times 12-2.30/7-10.30 Closed BHs, Sun

The Ritz London Restaurant
PLAN 5 A6

◉◉ British, French

Luxurious dining in legendary venue

☎ 020 7493 8181 & 7300 2370 📄 020 7493 2687
150 Piccadilly W1J 9BR
e-mail: enquire@theritzlondon.com
dir: Nearest station: Green Park 10-minute walk from Piccadilly Circus or Hyde Park Corner

Some hotels' names are immortalised in salads, but nowhere has the monopoly on, well, ritzy glamour, quite like this iconic hotel. Naturally, you can't just rock up in T-shirt and trainers, but top hat and tails aren't strictly necessary either, although you'll probably want to dress in tune with the palpable sense of occasion in the palatial interior. Entering the dining room, it's as if you have wandered into Versailles: Louis XVI furnishings, gilded garlands and gold chandeliers, a whole wall of panelled mirrors and tonnes of marble. Service is positively Jeevesian in its suave perfection, and the menu is not exactly short on luxury touches. That said, what comes out of the highly-skilled kitchen is not preserved in

continued on page 302

Rhodes W1 Restaurant

Modern European ▮ NOTABLE WINE LIST

Glamour, glitz and fine dining at The Cumberland Hotel

☎ 020 7616 5930 📄 020 7479 3888
The Cumberland Hotel, Great Cumberland Place W1H 7DL
e-mail: restaurant@rhodesw1.com
web: www.rhodesw1.com
dir: Nearest station: Paddington/Marble Arch Please telephone for directions or see website

Gary Rhodes' restaurant in The Cumberland Hotel at Marble Arch is an unapologetically high-toned venue, with two dozen dripping Swarovski chandeliers, ornate mirrors and rich velvet fabrics in tones of purple, black and taupe. This Kelly Hoppen designed room makes a diverting backdrop for the Rhodes cooking style, which matches European modes to a refined version of British demotic technique. Baked salmon, a beautifully timed portion, comes with a shellfish bisque and tortellini of smoked salmon and cucumber for one striking main course, while slow-cooked duck breast is partnered with home-style honey-glazed parsnips and a bay leaf-scented jus. Before that, you might have started with a meaty salad of roast lamb, glazed sweetbread, artichokes and a breadcrumbed quail's egg, while desserts aim to indulge with praline and

chocolate terrine, counter-pointed with kumquats and a light crème fraîche sorbet. The service style in the restaurant is suitably professional, and the hotel is also home to Rhodes W1 Brasserie, which deals in simpler dishes in slightly less grandiose surroundings (see entry).

Chef Gary Rhodes, Paul Welburn
Owner Gary Rhodes
Times 12-2.30/7-10.30 Closed Xmas, Sun-Mon, D Sat **Prices** Fixed L 2 course £19.95-£25.95, Fixed D 3 course £65-£85, Service added but optional 12.5%
Wines 250 bottles over £20, 13 by glass
Notes Tasting menu available, all dishes individually priced, Vegetarian available, Dress restrictions, Smart dress, no torn jeans, no trainers, Air con
Seats 46 **Parking** NCP at Marble Arch

LONDON W1 *continued*

aspic: contemporary presentations would not look out of place in London's trendiest venues. Take pig's head with potato and truffle terrine, served with sauce gribiche to start, then a crowd-pleasingly perfect steak and kidney pudding with silky pommes mousseline.

Chef John T Williams **Owner** The Ritz Hotel (London) Ltd **Times** 12.30-2.30/5.30-10 **Prices** Fixed L 3 course fr £36, Fixed D 3 course fr £45, Starter £18-£32, Main £29-£54, Dessert £15-£17, Service included **Wines** 400+ bottles over £20, 9 by glass **Notes** Pre-theatre D 3 course £45, Sunday L, Vegetarian available, Dress restrictions, Jacket & tie requested, No jeans or trainers, Civ Wed 60, Air con **Seats** 90, Pr/dining room 14 **Children** Portions, Menu **Parking** NCP on Arlington Street

Roka
PLAN 3 B3

⊛⊛⊛ – *see below*

Salt Yard
PLAN 3 B4

⊛ Italian, Spanish

Classy tapas just off Tottenham Court Road

☎ 020 7637 0657   020 7580 7435
54 Goodge St W1T 4NA
e-mail: info@saltyard.co.uk
dir: Nearest station: Goodge St Near Tottenham Court Rd

There's a dynamic buzz at this off-West End tapas bar which is a magnet for nearby office workers. Charming staff keep the atmosphere light and friendly, and the layout - lively and upbeat around the ground floor charcuterie bar, more formal downstairs in the basement - lends itself to any occasion. The tapas menu offers good, earthy cooking in a dazzling variety of guises; go for confit of Gloucestershire Old Spot pork belly with rosemary-scented cannellini beans; roasted chorizo with Moscatel vinegar; or maybe the smoked monkfish with gooseberry purée and pancetta. There are some sublime touches, including cold chocolate and espresso fondant with sea salt and almond caramel to finish.

Chef Benjamin Tish **Owner** Sanja Morris & Simon Mullins **Times** 12-3/6-11 Closed BHs, 25 Dec & 1 Jan, Sun, L Sat **Prices** Food prices not confirmed for 2010. Please telephone for details. **Wines** 43 bottles over £20, 6 bottles under £20, 15 by glass **Notes** Vegetarian available, Air con **Seats** 60 **Parking** NCP Cleveland St, meter parking Goodge Place

Sartoria
PLAN 3 A2

⊛ Italian

Modern Italian at the heart of Savile Row

☎ 020 7534 7000 & 7534 7030   020 7534 7070
20 Savile Row W1S 3PR
e-mail: sartoriareservations@danddlondon.com
dir: Nearest station: Oxford Circus/Green Park/Piccadilly Circus. Tube to Oxford Circus, take exit 3, turn left down Regent St towards Piccadilly Circus, take 5th right into New Burlington St, end of street on left

Rather like the suits made in its Savile Row neighbours' premises, there's an understated timeless elegance to this contemporary Mayfair Italian. The clean-cut dining room comes with a sleek metropolitan look - plain white walls and huge windows all down one side, mushroom carpeting and grey upholstered sofas and chairs. It's all as sleek and professional as the service, while the kitchen works with the seasons on its concise menus of classic Italian cooking. Luxury ingredients pepper the menu to keep the well-heeled clientele happy, but there are comfortingly gutsy peasant dishes too, as in a starter of pig's head sausage with fennel and apple sauce. The pasta section offers pheasant ravioli, while secondi include monkfish in Parma ham with potato cake and mushrooms.

Chef Alan Marchetti **Owner** D&D London **Times** 12-3/5.30-11 Closed 25-26 Dec, Sun (open for private parties only), L Sat **Prices** Fixed L 2 course

---

Roka

LONDON W1   PLAN 3 B3

Japanese

Superb contemporary Japanese food in Medialand

☎ 020 7580 6464   020 7580 0220
37 Charlotte St W1T 1RR
e-mail: info@rokarestaurant.com
dir: Nearest station: Goodge St/Tottenham Court Rd 5 min walk from Goodge St

With branches in Macau, Hong Kong and Arizona, Roka is on an international mission to bring contemporary Japanese food to the world. The London outpost - sister also to Zuma (see entry) - is in the area north of Oxford Street, where media folk come out to play. You can't miss the full-drop glass frontage. Centre-stage within is the robatayaki bar, where you can keep an eye on the barbecue chefs doing their stuff, but there are traditional restaurant tables too. The service is upbeat and helpful, so don't be afraid to show any uncertainty. As well as the robata dishes, there is a substantial menu of light bites, sushi, sashimi and salads, allowing for random-order nibbling, as well as some innovative desserts. Technical skills are superb, and timings of the cooked items are spot-on. Sea bream fillet cooked on the charcoal grill and dressed in miso and red onion is full of flavour and impact, the baby back ribs of pork come with a spicy glaze and cashews, while the assorted vegetable tempura are impeccably crisp. The zinging freshness of the maki rolls, the soft-shell crab and other shellfish are offset with piquant dressings of lime and soy, and gyoza dumplings of pork and scallop, flash-fried on one side, are nothing short of stunning.

Chef Nicholas Watt, Hamish Brown **Owner** Rainer Becker, Arjun Waney **Times** 12-3.30/5.30-11.30 Closed 25 Dec, 1 Jan **Prices** Food prices not confirmed for 2010. Please telephone for details, Service added but optional 13.5% **Wines** 9 by glass **Notes** Tasting menu £50, premier menu £75 pp, Vegetarian available, Air con **Seats** 90 **Children** Portions **Parking** On street, NCP in Brewers St

£17.50, Fixed D 3 course £19.50, Starter £7.50-£11, Main £10-£23, Dessert £5.50-£6.50, Service added but optional 12.5% **Wines** 340 bottles over £20, 10 bottles under £20, 12 by glass **Notes** Fixed D menu until 7.30pm, Vegetarian available, Dress restrictions, Smart casual preferred, Air con **Seats** 90, Pr/dining room 45 **Children** Portions **Parking** On street

Scott's Restaurant
PLAN 2 G2

◉◉ British

Fashionable, glamorous seafood restaurant and oyster bar in the heart of Mayfair

☎ 020 7495 7309 📄 020 7647 6326
20 Mount St W1K 2HE
dir: Nearest station: Bond Street Just off Grosvenor Sq, between Berkeley Sq & Park Ln

Reincarnated at the end of 2007 by Caprice Holdings (the people behind The Ivy, Le Caprice and J. Sheekey - see entries) this lively seafood restaurant is a Mayfair institution. Its oak-panelled interior has been given a glamorous makeover inspired by its 1960s heyday, with burgundy leather seating, oak flooring with a chartreuse-coloured marble mosaic, a stunning chandelier and specially commissioned modern art. A three-metre long onyx-topped crustacea bar in the style of a turn-of-the-century cruise liner forms a striking centrepiece. Top-notch ingredients are given the lightest of treatments in classic dishes such as Dover sole (grilled or meunière) and lobster (grilled or thermidor), while other options are slightly more adventurous, as in a main course of griddled shrimp burger with spicy mayonnaise. Meat eaters and vegetarians are not forgotten, while the service is super-slick and the people-watching is as prime as you'd expect from a sister restaurant to The Ivy.

Times 12-3/5.30-11 Closed Xmas, Jan 1, Aug BH

Shogun, Millennium Hotel Mayfair
PLAN 2 G1

◉◉ Japanese

Authentic Japanese food in the heart of Mayfair.

☎ 020 7629 9400 📄 020 7584 1877
Grosvenor Square W1A 3AN
dir: Nearest station: Bond Street/Green Park Grosvenor Square

This well-established dinner-only basement Japanese is located to the rear of Grosvenor Square's Millennium Hotel Mayfair. Although the subterranean room has a somewhat unfashionable wine-cellar atmosphere, authentic features like kyudo archery arrows (discreetly dividing tables), a large statue of a Samurai warrior and traditional prints, posters and lanterns all help bring the space to life. The discreet and friendly Japanese service is a testimony to the authenticity of the cooking, the lengthy roster including a selection of set house menus alongside the likes of hand-rolled sushi, sashimi, zenzai, tempura, or perhaps teriyaki such as grilled eel or Scotch sirloin. There's a small sushi bar at the front too.

Chef Hiromi Mitsuka **Owner** Hiromi Mitsuka **Times** 6-11 Closed Mon, L all week **Prices** Starter £4.50-£30, Main £19-£30, Dessert £3.50-£8.50, Service added but optional 12.5% **Wines** 30 bottles over £20, 3 bottles under £20, 2 by glass **Notes** Fixed D 6 course £49, Vegetarian available, Air con **Seats** 60 **Children** Portions

Sketch (Lecture Room & Library)
PLAN 3 A2

◉◉◉◉◉ – see page 304

So Restaurant
PLAN 3 B2

◉◉ Japanese

Modern Japanese with aspects of European cuisine

☎ 020 7292 0767 & 7292 0760
3-4 Warwick St W1B 5LS
e-mail: info@sorestaurant.com
dir: Nearest station: Piccadilly Circus Exit Piccadilly tube station via exit 1. Turn left along Glasshouse St. Restaurant next to The Warwick

Tucked away just off busy Glasshouse Street on the edge of Soho, this modern Japanese is easy to miss - but don't make that mistake. Spread across 2 floors, at ground level it has an almost café-like feel, with lacquered tables, high-backed chairs, lime green walls, a giant mirror which makes the space feel twice its size, and a sushi bar. Down in the basement the subdued lighting helps create a more intimate ambience, and there's an open-to-view kitchen. High quality, extremely fresh ingredients form the basis of the authentic Japanese cooking, with a European slant to some dishes. A starter of tempura soft-shell crab has a suitably light and crisp batter, while salmon and tuna sashimi are as fresh as can be, and the miso-marinated black cod is a good version.

Chef Kaoru Yamamoto **Owner** Tetsuro Hama
Times 12-3/5-10.30 Closed Xmas-New Year, Sun
Prices Fixed L 2 course £6.95-£20, Fixed D 3 course £28-£35, Starter £3.50-£8, Main £10-£40, Dessert £5.80-£7, Service added but optional 12.5% **Wines** 33 bottles over £20, 5 bottles under £20, 4 by glass **Notes** Pre-theatre meal 3 course £19.95. Tasting menu 3 course, Vegetarian available, Air con **Seats** 70, Pr/dining room 6 **Children** Portions **Parking** On street

The Square
PLAN 3 A1

◉◉◉◉ – see page 305

Sumosan Restaurant
PLAN 3 A1

◉ Japanese

Stylish Japanese in the heart of Mayfair

☎ 020 7495 5999 📄 020 7355 1247
26 Albermarle St, Mayfair W1S 4HY
e-mail: info@sumosan.com
dir: Nearest station: Green Park

Tucked away in the heart of fashionable Mayfair, this contemporary Japanese restaurant is as stylish as the majority of its affluent clientele. The interior is chic and business-like, with beige oak flooring, dark wooden tables and comfortable banquette seating. Despite the understated exterior, it's a busy place, particularly so at lunchtimes when the sushi and sashimi attract those with limited time, while those with plenty to discuss might go for teppan-yaki or the good value seven-course lunch selection. You might even begin with oysters poached with foie gras and sea urchin, before moving on to creamy spicy king crab or lamb chops furikaki.

Times 12-3/6-11.30 Closed Xmas, New Year, BHs, L Sat-Sun

Taman Gang
PLAN 2 F2

◉◉ South East Asian

Vivacious, upmarket basement venue with late opening and elegant cuisine

☎ 020 7518 3160 📄 020 7518 3161
141 Park Ln W1K 7AA
e-mail: info@tamangang.com
dir: Nearest station: Marble Arch

In a split second you're transported from the frenetic racetrack around Marble Arch into an exotic Balinese temple inside this chic pan-Asian bar and restaurant. A lengthy roll call of A-list celebs have hung out in its moodily candle-lit basement, surrounded by hand-sculpted limestone walls, carved buddhas, mahogany furniture, lanterns and low banquettes, so ditch the T-shirt and trainers and prepare for a cool, hyper-trendy, upmarket vibe. The kitchen takes you on a whistle-stop tour of south-east Asia, meandering through the cuisines of China, Japan, Thailand and Korea. The vogue for sharing and grazing is supported by a full cast of tempura, sushi and sashimi dishes, while mains take in chicken Thai red curry with roasted pumpkin and wild parsley, or beef bulgogi and kim chee aubergine.

Times 12-3.30/6-1 Closed L Mon-Sat

Sketch (Lecture Room & Library)

LONDON W1   **PLAN 3 A2**

Modern European V

A unique, dynamic and exciting dining experience

☎ 020 7659 4500   📄 020 7629 1683
9 Conduit St W1S 2XG
e-mail: info@sketch.uk.com
web: www.sketch.uk.com
dir: Nearest station: Oxford Circus. 4 mins walk from Oxford Circus tube station, take exit 3, down Regent St. Conduit St 4th on right

If you're a first timer, taking a look at the website might prepare you for what is to come; you'll find it quirky, charming (hopefully), wildly creative and just a little over the top (definitely). Do not think for a minute, though, that this individuality and playfulness means this is not a serious player in the London dining scene - it is, with knobs on. It all looks so 'normal' from the outside - a fine example of a London townhouse that could be an insurance brokers; the presence of a doorman might suggest a private club, and, indeed, membership certainly has its advantages. It was in fact once the London HQ of Christian Dior. Sketch is a collaboration between Algerian-born restaurateur Mourad Mazouz and French super-chef Pierre Gagnaire, describing itself as a 'destination place for food, art and music' and it is far from 'normal' on the inside. For a start, there is an abundance of options over the two floors, each space individually designed with flamboyance

and an eye for the iconic style statements of the last century. There's the Gallery brasserie (bursting with art deco style), the cool Parlour - tea room by day, hyper-trendy bar by night - while The Glade focuses on the healthy side of life. The fine-dining Lecture Room and Library upstairs - two parts of the same space - is elegantly decorated in shades of orange, with ivory walls of studded leather and ornately plastered high ceilings, while thick-piled, brightly coloured carpets and long dangling lampshades give it a somewhat Middle Eastern feel. Sit on feather-cushioned armchairs at well-spaced tables and marvel at the professional and informed service (they need to be, to help you through the menu). Head chef Pascal Sanchez successfully produces a menu that bears the hallmark of the creative flair of consultant Pierre Gagnaire, delivering a range of dishes that dazzle with their technical proficiency, hit the mark with their remarkable flavours and textures and delight with their eye-catching presentations. It is modern French cooking at its best. There's a Gourmet Rapide Lunch which constitutes pretty good value at this level, but, otherwise, the prices on the carte and tasting menu are high. That's H.I.G.H. The sheer complexity of the dishes is revealed in descriptions that last as long as some menus do, but what arrives from the kitchen delivers at every level. 'Seaweed' is a black pancake filled with top-notch seafood, served with an abundance of delights including a dulce and wakame spicy broth and a shellfish

custard with cuttlefish and nori seaweed. Follow that with 'Pig' - a rack of Baillet mountain pork roasted in sage with capucine capers, which comes with, amongst other things, a beetroot galette with maple syrup. An experience to be remembered for all the right reasons.

Chef Pierre Gagnaire, Pascal Sanchez **Owner** Mourad Mazouz
Times 12-2.30/6.30-11 Closed 18-29 Aug, 23-30 Dec, 1 Jan, BHs, Sun-Mon, L Sat
Prices Fixed L 2 course £30, Tasting menu £70-£90, Starter £20-£44, Main £28-£52, Dessert £11-£35, Service added but optional 12.5% **Wines** 637 bottles over £20, 13 bottles under £20, 34 by glass
Notes Tasting menu 8 course, Vegetarian tasting menu 7 course, Vegetarian menu, Civ Wed 50, Air con **Seats** 50, Pr/dining room 24 **Children** Portions **Parking** NCP Soho, Cavendish Sq

The Square

Modern French

A class culinary act in the heart of Mayfair

☎ 020 7495 7100   📄 020 7495 7150
6-10 Bruton St, Mayfair W1J 6PU
e-mail: info@squarerestaurant.com
web: www.squarerestaurant.com
dir: Nearest station: Bond Street, Green Park

Among the supercar showrooms and glossy designer sheen of the Mayfair streets you have to look the part, and The Square pulls off a classy act, pitching its refined style at just the right level without veering into self-absorption. A discreet frosted glass frontage shields its shiny diners from prying eyes and the dining room, with beige and burgundy walls splashed with vivid abstract art and designer mirrors, has tables spaced widely across a buffed parquet floor. Service is impeccable, hospitable and smoothly choreographed. Philip Howard's cooking has climbed a steady trajectory since 1991 when he set up shop with Nigel Platts-Martin after a thorough grounding in big-name kitchens. Founded on classical French technique, the food is bold, daring and exciting without ever losing the plot. Flavour and texture are pursued at all times in elaborately worked dishes that look deceptively effortless. An eight-course

tasting menu is the way to go on a big budget, or lunch menus offer staggering value if purse strings are tighter. Three courses at dinner weigh in at £75, but you do get an impressive procession of exquisitely-crafted add-ons - canapés, amuse-bouches, pre-dessert and exemplary breads - and all come with the same wow factor as the main events. An assiette of foie gras with elderflower and orange gives the three ingredients a virtuoso workout, balancing flavours and textures ranging from jelly to purée to terrine and a 1" square miniature club sandwich. A main course shows a solid grasp of what works with what by teaming roast turbot in a sourdough crust with a purée of new season's garlic, chopped morels and parsley velouté. Faultless standards and presentation are maintained through to a dessert of meltingly soft roasted pears served with caramelised wafers, salted caramel foam and dulce de leche ice cream. Those bitten by the Burgundy bug will find heaven in an astonishing wine list brimming with heavyweights from around the world, with a judicious sprinkling of sub-£50 bottles and a seriously expert sommelier to guide the way.

Chef Philip Howard **Owner** Mr N Platts-Martin & Philip Howard
Times 12-2.30/6.30-10.30 Closed 24-26 Dec,1 Jan, L Sat-Sun, BHs **Prices** Fixed L 2 course fr £30, Fixed D 3 course £75, Tasting menu £140, Service added but

optional 12.5% **Wines** 1400 bottles over £20, 3 bottles under £20, 14 by glass **Notes** Tasting menu includes wine, Vegetarian available, Dress restrictions, Smart casual, jacket & tie preferred, Air con **Seats** 75, Pr/dining room 18 **Children** Portions

LONDON W1 *continued*

Tamarind

PLAN 4 H6

◉◉ Traditional Indian

Contemporary, classy Mayfair Indian restaurant

☎ 020 7629 3561 ▤ 020 7499 5034
20 Queen St, Mayfair W1J 5PR
e-mail: manager@tamarindrestaurant.com
web: www.tamarindrestaurant.com
dir: Nearest station: Green Park. Towards Hyde Park, take
4th right into Half Moon St to end (Curzon St). Turn left,
1st right into Queen St

Indian food is sprinkled with a bit of fine dining magic in
this basement in the heart of Mayfair. It's a classy and
contemporary space with an uncluttered minimalist
approach; polished wood floor, stylish seating, low
lighting and cleverly placed mirrors. Colours are natural
(gold, white, brown) and the glass-fronted theatre kitchen
adds to the glamour of it all. The staff are knowledgeable
and charming. The cooking is derivative of traditional
Mogul cuisine, specifically focusing around the tandoor
oven where bread, fish, meat and game are cooked in the
authentic North-West Indian fashion. In addition to the
established favourites, new dishes are regularly devised
and the menu changes seasonally. Push the boat out and
try lobster karaikudi (chunks of lobster tossed with
cumin, red onions, curry leaves, tomatoes and spices), or
go for a kebab such as macchi zaffrani (monkfish
marinated in ginger, chilli, mustard and saffron).

Tamarind

Chef Alfred Prasad **Owner** Indian Cuisine Ltd
Times 12-2.45/5.30-11.15 Closed 25-26 Dec, 1 Jan, L
Sat, BHs **Prices** Fixed L 2 course fr £19.95, Fixed D 3
course fr £52, Starter £7.50-£12, Main £12.95-£28,
Dessert £7.50-£7.95, Service added but optional 12.5%
Wines 100 bottles over £20, 4 bottles under £20, 12 by
glass **Notes** Pre-theatre D £24 5.30-7pm, Sunday L,
Vegetarian available, Dress restrictions, No jeans or
shorts, Air con **Seats** 90 **Parking** NCP

Texture Restaurant

PLAN 2 F2

◉◉◉ – *see below*

Theo Randall@ InterContinental London

PLAN 4 G5

◉◉◉ – *see opposite page*

Time & Space

PLAN 3 A2

◉ Modern British **NEW**

Contemporary dining at the Royal Institution

☎ 020 7670 2956
**The Royal Institution of Great Britain, 21 Albemarle St
W1S 4BS**
dir: Nearest station: Green Park. 5 mins from Green Park.
Left out of station, Albermarle St is 3rd left.

A venerable Mayfair establishment housing a British
institution (home to scientific debate and Michael
Faraday) seems an unlikely venue to find a contemporary
restaurant, but a recent £12-million makeover delivers
just that. Occupying a handsome room, Time & Space
blends original features (high ceilings, antique books and
fireplaces) with modern styling (sleek black furniture and
carpet, purple drum-style lampshades and plate glass).
The cooking captures the mood; seasonal British but with
a modern take. So pan-fried cod is teamed with spinach,
new potatoes and an egg and parsley sauce and classics

Texture Restaurant

LONDON W1

PLAN 2 F2

Modern European V ▮NOTABLE
WINE LIST

Creativity and sophistication from a talented team

☎ 020 7224 0028
Best Western Mostyn Hotel, 34 Portman St W1H 7BY
e-mail: info@texture-restaurant.co.uk
dir: Nearest station: Marble Arch/Bond St.

You need plenty of self-confidence and ability to launch a
restaurant in the heart of Mayfair. Luckily Icelandic chef
Agnar Sverrisson and front-of-house manager and master
sommelier Xavier Rousset, came fresh from no less a
background than Raymond Blanc's Le Manoir aux Quat'
Saisons, after a long chain of top-flight kitchens. The
luxurious Georgian dining room delights with its stylishly
austere modern look, all understated ivory walls, caramel
leather chairs and blond-wood floors, flooded with light
from vast windows. A glass of something fizzy at the

centre-stage champagne bar is the obvious way to get in
the mood. Sverrisson's modern European cuisine is light
as air, delicate, creative and utterly contemporary. As the
name suggests, the kitchen's concept is to highlight
diverse textures, an ethos requiring top-level technical
skills. Scottish scallops with cauliflower textures shows
the style: intensely-flavoured scallops appear with
cauliflower as purée, foam and crisp. Main courses include
Lancashire suckling pig, slow-cooked for 12 hours and
partnered with squid and bonito sauce. Dessert keeps
those textures coming with Icelandic Skyr (a sort of Nordic
take on fromage blanc) and rhubarb, served poached, as
sorbet, granita and jus. The superb wine list is as long as
War and Peace, with as many aristocrats in its pages.

Chef Agnar Sverrisson **Owner** Xavier Rousset & Agnar
Sverrisson **Times** 12-2.30/6.30-11 Closed 2 wks Xmas, 2
wks Aug, Sun, L Sat **Prices** Fixed L 2 course £18.50,
Starter £9.50-£16.50, Main £19.50-£28.50, Dessert
£8.50, Service added but optional 12.5% **Wines** 110
bottles over £20, 12 by glass **Notes** Fixed D 5 course
£39.50, Vegetarian menu, Dress restrictions, Smart
casual **Seats** 55, Pr/dining room 16 **Parking** NCP
Bryanston St

like home-made steak and ale pie comes with bubble-and-squeak. The colour-coordinated contemporary bar offers some relatively friendly Mayfair prices.

Chef Julian Ward **Times** 12-2.30/6-9.30 Closed Sat (except during an event) and Sun **Prices** Food prices not confirmed for 2010. Please telephone for details. **Seats** 80

Trishna

PLAN 2 G3

◎◎ Modern Indian NEW V ✍

Indian coastal cuisine brought to Marylebone

☎ 020 7935 5624
15-17 Blandford St W1U 3DG
e-mail: info@trishnalondon.com
dir: Nearest station: Bond St/Baker St 5th right off Baker St, 1st left at number 1 Marylebone High St

Trishna's mission is to bring the coastal seafood cuisine of the South-West Indian state of Maharashtra to London. Style fans will find no fault with this slick operation's look: whitewashed bare brick walls and tasteful tawny smoky-oak floors come together in a minimalist Scandinavian chic. Head chef Ravi Deulkar (formerly of Rasoi Vineet Bhatia - see entry) has scoured the Indian coast to gather recipes and inspiration from fishermen's villages, and sources fine British piscine produce to make it all happen. The emphasis is on simple presentation and flavours, served as deep-fried pakora starters and main dishes hot from the charcoal sigri grill or clay tandoor oven. Signature dishes from the legendary

Bombay branch of Trishna appear, and each comes with a wine recommendation. Start with crunchy squid pakora in light spiced rice flour with lime zest and chilli, then market fish curry - perhaps super-fresh sea bass cooked simply in coastal spices and coconut masala.

Chef Ravi Deulkar **Owner** Karam Sethi
Times 12-2.45/6-10.45 Closed 24-29 Dec, 1 Jan,
Prices Fixed L 2 course £19.50-£25, Fixed D 3 course £19.50-£34.50, Tasting menu £34.50, Starter £5.50-£12.50, Main £12.50-£25, Dessert £6, Service added but optional 12.5% **Wines** 110 bottles over £20, 6 bottles under £20, 24 by glass **Notes** Early D 6-7pm £19.50-£21.50, Sunday L, Vegetarian menu, Air con **Seats** 60, Pr/dining room 12 **Parking** On street/NCP

La Trouvaille

PLAN 3 A2

◎◎ French

Modern approach to French bourgeois cooking in intimate surroundings

☎ 020 7287 8488 ▤ 020 7434 4170
12a Newburgh St W1F 7RR
e-mail: contact@latrouvaille.co.uk
web: www.latrouvaille.co.uk
dir: Nearest station: Oxford Circus Off Carnaby St by Liberty's

Tucked away in a cobbled pedestrianised road off Carnaby Street, La Trouvaille really is quite a find, offering a little piece of French refinement amid the hustle-and-bustle of

Soho. There's a chic ground-floor wine bar (open all day) serving simple stuff like good charcuterie and with a list of mainly organic/biodynamic French wines. The upstairs restaurant is charming (mirrors on the white walls, wood floor) with white linen-clothed tables adding a touch of formality and clear Perspex chairs hinting at the modern intentions of the place. Thoughtful but easygoing invention combines with well-sourced ingredients to produce the likes of broccoli and blue cheese tartlet with walnut sauce, or a daily-special such as fillet of pork with wild mushrooms and Banyuls sauce.

La Trouvaille

Chef Pierre Renaudeau **Owner** T Bouteloup
Times 12-3/6-11 Closed Xmas, BHs, Sun **Prices** Fixed L 2 course £16.50, Fixed D 3 course £35, Service added but optional 12.5% **Wines** 45 bottles over £20, 8 bottles under £20, 12 by glass **Notes** Pre-theatre menu 6-7pm 2 course £16.50, 3 course £20, Vegetarian available
Seats 45, Pr/dining room 30 **Children** Portions
Parking NCP (off Broadwick St)

Theo Randall@ InterContinental London

LONDON W1 PLAN 4 G5

Italian

Dedication to the best of Italy in five-star hotel surroundings

☎ 020 7318 8747 ▤ 020 7491 0926
1 Hamilton Place, Hyde Park Corner W1J 7QY
e-mail: reservations@theorandall.com
dir: Nearest station: Hyde Park Corner

There is a pleasing sense of contrast between the famously opulent environs of the InterContinental and the seasonally changing menus of demotic, even rustic, Italian cooking Theo Randall offers. Big tables dressed in fine linen, expertly drilled staff, paintings by Sir Peter Blake and oblique views of the quietly bustling kitchen are all part of the deal. Randall cooked for several years at the River Café, and imports the same style of suave,

but essentially dead-simple food, based on top-quality ingredients, here. Could anything be more straightforward than a starter of excellent buffalo mozzarella and marinated artichokes, with broad beans, rocket and caciotta? An intermediate pasta dish might be spaghetti with Dorset lobster, Italian tomatoes and chilli, a small but perfectly formed and piquantly seasoned dish. Main-dish preparations maintain the standard, for turbot wood-roasted on the bone with capers and Swiss chard, or chargrilled Limousin veal chop with Portobello and porcini mushrooms, spinach and salsa verde. Dip a toe into French waters with a dessert such as gariguette strawberry frangipane tart.

Chef Theo Randall **Owner** Intercontinental Hotels Ltd & Theo Randall **Times** 12-3/5.45-11.15 Closed Xmas, New Year, 1st wk Jan, BHs, Sun, L Sat **Prices** Fixed L 2 course £21, Fixed D 3 course £25-£45, Starter £8-£13, Main £20-£32, Dessert £6-£7, Service added but optional 12.5% **Wines** 250 bottles over £20, 3 bottles under £20, 11 by glass **Notes** Pre-theatre menu available, Vegetarian

available, Air con **Seats** 145, Pr/dining room 24
Children Portions **Parking** 100, Car park

Umu

LONDON W1   **PLAN 2 H2**

Japanese **NOTABLE WINE LIST**

Intricate Kyoto cuisine in the heart of Mayfair

☎ 020 7499 8881   📠 020 7016 5120
14-16 Bruton Place W1J 6LX
e-mail: reception@umurestaurant.com
dir: Nearest station: Green Park/Bond St
Off Bruton St & Berkeley Sq

Bona fide Japanese restaurants are not hard to find in the capital, but for something authentically different, with superb quality food and cool design, Umu hits the spot. Award-winning designer Tony Chi has recreated a modern Japanese environment in a slick and luxurious dining room complete with banquette seating and a chef's table. Service is professional and staff are equipped with the necessary knowledge to make sure you don't get lost in the menu of classic and modern interpretations of Kyoto cuisine. Intricate dishes may include sweet shrimp, sake jelly and caviar to start followed by monkfish tempura, veal jus and yuzu pepper with a Kyoto sundae of pumpkin and tofu ice cream with black sugar soy syrup and green tea cake to finish. Traditional and modern sashimi and sushi are also worth a look but for the full experience, choose from the wide variety of kaiseki or tasting menus comprised of beautifully crafted dishes influenced by Zen Buddhism. A huge sake list, though not to the detriment of the equally vast wine list, deserves exploration.

Chef Ichiro Kubota **Owner** Marlon Abela Restaurant Corporation
Times 12-2.30/6-11 Closed between Xmas & New Year, Etr & BHs, Sun, L Sat
Prices Fixed L 3 course £21-£49, Tasting menu £65-£135, Starter £6-£20, Main £10-£57, Dessert £5-£10, Service added but optional 12.5%
Wines 697 bottles over £20, 19 by glass
Notes Vegetarian available, Air con
Seats 60, Pr/dining room 12
Parking NCP Hanover Hill, On street

LONDON W1 *continued*

Umu
PLAN 2 H2

◎◎◎ – *see opposite page*

Vanilla Restaurant & Bar
PLAN 3 A4

◎◎ Modern European **NEW V**

Experimental cooking and cutting-edge design make for a dramatic dining experience

☎ 020 3008 7763 ▤ 020 3008 6652
131 Titchfield St W1W 5BB
e-mail: info@vanillalondon.com
dir: Nearest station: Great Portland St/Oxford Circus

This chic West End basement bar and restaurant's glam-dram design bathes a retina-frazzling white interior in mood-morphing LED lighting that fades in and out of shades of blue and pink. It's all very space-age ice-queen's boudoir in the cocktail lounge, while the restaurant goes for a more restrained mafia-chic look of black leather, swirling damask patterns and razor-edged linen. The cuisine - you may have seen this coming - is also out of the ordinary: the chef likes to experiment, so be prepared for minimal menu descriptions and adventurous combinations with theatrically successful results. Cod and chips comes with a deep-fried ball of brandade and sauce gribiche to start, and next up is chicken atop a round of dauphinoise potatoes with tortellini of chicken and mushroom mousse with a creamy lemon sauce and rocket. A deeply indulgent dessert of salted caramel, tonka bean, frozen cream and brownie is a memorable finale.

Chef Izu Ani **Owner** David Alberto **Times** 12-3/6.30-10.30 Closed Sun-Mon, L Sat **Prices** Fixed L 2 course £14.50, Fixed D 4 course £40, Service added but optional 12.5% **Wines** 142 bottles over £20, 8 bottles under £20, 11 by glass **Notes** Tasting menu available at D only, Vegetarian menu, Dress restrictions, Smart/elegant, no sportswear/trainers, Air con **Seats** 35 **Children** Portions

Vasco & Piero's Pavilion Restaurant
PLAN 3 B2

◎◎ Italian

Genuine taste of Umbria in intimate, family-run restaurant

☎ 020 7437 8774 ▤ 020 7437 0467
15 Poland St W1F 8QE
e-mail: eat@vascosfood.com
dir: Nearest station: Oxford Circus From Oxford Circus turn right towards Tottenham Court Rd, in 5min turn right into Poland St. Restaurant on corner of Great Marlborough St & Noel St

This ever-popular Italian Soho restaurant majors on authentic cooking from the Umbria region - a refreshingly earthy philosophy that calls for just two or three ingredients in each dish. It is everything a cosy, family-run restaurant should be: warmly hospitable, knowledgeable in its service and comfortingly reminiscent

of warmer climes in its glowing terracotta colours. Pukka ingredients are imported from Italian farms; pasta is, of course, hand-made and combined in rustic, home-style cooking. The menu changes after each serving. Clear flavours leap out from dishes such as tagliatelle with a rich beef and duck ragu, and a generous slab of seared tuna with cannellini beans and ginger dressing. Finish with a textbook classic tiramisù.

Chef Vasco Matteucci **Owner** Tony Lopez, Paul Matteucci & Vasco Matteucci **Times** 12-3/6-11 Closed BHs, Sun, L Sat **Prices** Fixed D 3 course £26-£31.50, Starter £5-£9.50, Main £12-£21, Dessert £6.95-£8.95, Service added but optional 12.5% **Wines** 40 bottles over £20, 6 bottles under £20, 4 by glass **Notes** Tasting menu if requested, Pre-theatre 2 course £19.50, Vegetarian available, Dress restrictions, No shorts, Air con **Seats** 50, Pr/dining room 36 **Children** Portions **Parking** NCP car park opposite

Veeraswamy Restaurant
PLAN 3 B1

◎ Indian

Sophisticated, stylish and popular Indian with refined, traditional cooking

☎ 020 7734 1401 ▤ 020 7439 8434
Mezzanine Floor, Victory House, 99 Regent St W1B 4RS
e-mail: veeraswamy@realindianfood.com
dir: Nearest station: Piccadilly Circus. Entrance near junct of Swallow St & Regent St, in Victory House

London's oldest Indian restaurant has been dramatically refurbished by the savvy owners (also behind Amaya and Chutney Mary - see entries) and restored to its glamorous former 1920s glory. Shimmering chandeliers and vibrant-coloured glass lanterns hang from ceilings, while plush Mogul-style carpets sit on dark-wood floors or gleaming black Indian granite speckled with gold to deliver a chic, exotic vibe to the first-floor room. Latticed silver screens, elegant seating and large tables provide comfort and luxury, backed by attentive service and views over Regent Street. Classic pan-Indian dishes ride alongside more contemporary things on the pricey menu, all authentically and freshly prepared using high-quality ingredients. Try begum bahar, a home-style Lucknow chicken korma with saffron, or perhaps sea bass pollichatu, a Kerala recipe where the fillets and red spices are cooked in a banana leaf.

Times 12-2.30/5.30-11.30 Closed D Xmas

Via Condotti
PLAN 3 A2

◎ Italian

Stylish Italian with classically-based menu

☎ 020 7493 7050 ▤ 020 7409 7985
23 Conduit St W1S 2XS
e-mail: info@viacondotti.co.uk
dir: Nearest station: Oxford Circus, Piccadilly Circus

Discreetly tucked away amongst the boutiques of fashionable Mayfair, this stylish Italian is picked out by its lilac frontage complete with smart awning and planters. The deceptively large interior is all lightwood floors, peach walls, striking framed posters, and dark red leather banquettes and chairs. Tables are quite closely packed, with pristine white tablecloths to match the immaculately dressed, and also very friendly, waiting staff. The restaurant has an intimate, and yet buzzy, feel and a pleasant ambience. The food is classic Italian, based around high quality ingredients treated with a lightness of touch and presented in a fine-dining style. Think squid ink tagliatelle with calamari, courgettes, carrots, garlic and extra virgin olive oil, or baked halibut with baked potatoes, Taggiasche olives and tomato sauce.

Chef Andrea Francescato **Owner** Claudio Pulze **Times** 12-3/6.30-11 Closed BHs, Sun **Prices** Fixed L 2 course fr £22.50, Fixed D 3 course fr £27.50, Service added but optional 12.5% **Wines** 70 bottles over £20, 8 bottles under £20, 15 by glass **Notes** Vegetarian available, Air con **Seats** 90, Pr/dining room 18 **Children** Portions

Villandry
PLAN 3 A4

◎ French, European

Vibrant restaurant, bar and quality foodstore

☎ 020 7631 3131 ▤ 020 7631 3030
170 Great Portland St W1W 5QB
e-mail: contactus@villandry.com
web: www.villandry.com
dir: Nearest station: Great Portland Street/Oxford Circus Entrance at 91 Bolsover St, between Great Portland St tube station & Oxford Circus

Make time to peruse the prime deli produce for sale in the shop before moving on through to the restaurant, a glass-fronted, high-ceilinged dining room with tables dressed in their best whites; there's also the choice of a table in the vibrant bar or at the charcuterie counter. The

continued

LONDON W1 *continued*

modern approach and accurate cooking makes the most of quality, seasonal produce via classic, brasserie-focused menus. Start with a Fenton farm egg en cocotte served with girolles, then try the cassoulet or salt and pepper squid with tartare sauce. The place has a child-friendly attitude and relaxed but professional service.

Chef David Rood **Owner** Jamie Barber
Times 12-3/6-10.30 Closed 25 Dec, D Sun & BHs
Prices Starter £5.50-£12.50, Main £13.50-£22.50, Dessert £5.75-£8.50 **Wines** 79 bottles over £20, 8 bottles under £20, 16 by glass **Notes** Sat & Sun brunch menu, Sunday L, Air con **Seats** 100, Pr/dining room 24 **Children** Portions, Menu

Wild Honey
PLAN 3 A2

◎◎ Modern European

Refined and intelligently straightforward food in Mayfair

☎ 020 7758 9160 ⓘ 020 7493 4549
12 Saint George St W1S 2FB
e-mail: info@wildhoneyrestaurant.co.uk
dir: Nearest station: Oxford Circus, Bond St

Wild Honey, the second venture from Anthony Demetre and Will Smith - the duo behind Arbutus (see entry) - is a class act. Applying the same winning formula here in Mayfair as in Soho, their take on the French bistrot de luxe theme sees the appealing combination of modestly priced food (cooked with flair and accuracy) and an approachable wine list (served by 250ml carafe as well as bottle) delivered in informal, friendly surroundings. Service is as unstuffy as it is informed. Set just off Conduit and Bond Streets, it oozes understated modernity; the high-ceilinged long room has warm oak panelling, banquettes, intimate booths alongside contemporary artworks, big lightshades and an onyx-topped front bar (with stools for bar dining). Daily-changing menus are driven by quality ingredients - the kitchen is not afraid to use lesser-seen cuts - and dishes are well balanced and attractively presented. Roast Norfolk hare is accompanied by caramelised endive and spätzle with pomegranate, and roasted Cornish skate with bacon, shrimps and capers. (The fixed-price lunch is astounding value in these parts.)

Chef Anthony Demetre **Owner** Anthony Demetre & Will Smith **Times** 12-2.30/6-11 Closed 25-26 Dec, 1 Jan, **Prices** Fixed L course £16.95, Starter £6.95-£10.95, Main £14.50-£21.95, Dessert £5.95-£6.95, Service added but optional 12.5% **Wines** 40 bottles over £20, 10 bottles under £20, 50 by glass **Notes** Pre-theatre D £18.95 (6-7pm), Sunday L, Vegetarian available, Air con **Seats** 65 **Children** Portions **Parking** On street

The Wolseley
PLAN 5 A6

◎ European

Bustling landmark brasserie offering stylish all-day dining

☎ 020 7499 6996 ⓘ 020 7499 6888
160 Piccadilly W1J 9EB
e-mail: reservations@thewolseley.com
dir: Nearest station: Green Park. 500mtrs from Green Park Underground station

This take on the grand-style European café-restaurant is still pulling in crowds who seemingly can't get enough of Messrs Corbin and King's glamorous and vibrant venue. Whether it's breakfast, lunch, afternoon tea or dinner, the setting in the former car showroom hums with life and fizzes with energy as diners marvel at the gilded splendour of it all and tuck into anything from eggs Benedict to roast Landaise chicken with Lyonnaise potatoes. In between the people watching, start with salt-cod brandade, follow on with whole-roasted sea bass with caponata, finishing with an apple strudel with Chantilly cream.

Chef Julian O'Neill **Owner** Chris Corbin & Jeremy King **Times** 7am-mdnt Closed 25 Dec, 1 Jan, Aug BH, D 24 Dec, 31 Dec **Prices** Starter £5.65-£22.50, Main £9.60-£28.75, Dessert £4.25-£7.50, Service added but optional 12.5% **Wines** 61 bottles over £20, 4 bottles under £20, 29 by glass **Notes** Sunday L, Vegetarian available, Air con **Seats** 150 **Children** Portions

Yauatcha
PLAN 3 B2

◎◎ Modern Chinese

Top-rate dim sum in seductive room

☎ 020 7494 8888 ⓘ 020 7494 8889
15 Broadwick St W1F 0DL
e-mail: reservations@yauatcha.com
dir: Nearest station: Tottenham Ct Rd, Piccadilly, Oxford Circus On corner of Broadwick St & Berwick St, Soho

A building designed by Sir Richard Rogers on the corner of a Soho street has been given a dose of glamour and downright sexiness by interior designer Christian Liagre. This is Yautacha. The ground floor is a rather tranquil tea house serving over 150 different varieties of the leaf and a selection of pastries, while the basement stairs descend to another place altogether: a seductively-lit space with tightly packed tables and low-level banquettes filled with the sounds of contented diners. Dim sum is the name of the game and here you'll get just about the best in town: the menu deals in traditional Cantonese favourites alongside more modern Pan-Asian influences including Wagyu beef from Japan. The classic stuff like char sui cheung fun, spare ribs and Shangai pork bun are superb versions, while the lengthy menu also has XO Australian lobster tail with asparagus. Service zips along at speed and the cocktails are worth exploring.

Chef Mr Soon Wah Cheong **Owner** Alan Yau **Times** 12-11.30 Closed 24-25 Dec, L 26 Dec, 1 Jan **Prices** Fixed L 3 course £40-£60, Fixed D 3 course £40-£60, Starter £3.50-

£15.50, Main £4.50-£38, Dessert £4.80-£13.50, Service added but optional 12.5% **Wines** 80 bottles over £20, 2 bottles under £20, 11 by glass **Notes** Sunday L, Air con **Seats** 109 **Parking** Poland Street - 100 yds

YMing
PLAN 3 C2

◎ Chinese **V**

Chinese regional specialities in theatreland

☎ 020 7734 2721 ⓘ 020 7437 0292
35-36 Greek St W1D 5DL
e-mail: cyming2000@blueyonder.co.uk
dir: Nearest station: Piccadilly Circus. From Piccadilly Circus tube station, head towards Palace Theatre along Shaftesbury Avenue

Separated by the buffer zone of Shaftesbury Avenue from the frenzy of Chinatown, Yming is a stylish Chinese with a healthy fan base of regulars built up over 20 years in business. Blue is the colour here: duck-egg walls with jade carvings in a series of small intimate rooms. Service is helpful in guiding the non-expert through the backwaters of an epic carte of Cantonese and regional dishes. The kitchen sticks to traditional cooking methods to produce full-on flavours but goes for fresh, healthy ingredients and light oils. Tibetan garlic lamb is an aromatic corker, or try a 'Treasure Case' of scallops, fish, squid and prawns steamed with fresh herbs in a lotus leaf.

Chef Aaron Wong **Owner** Christine Yau **Times** Noon-11.45 Closed 25-26 Dec, 1 Jan, Sun (ex Chinese New Year) **Prices** Fixed L 2 course fr £10, Fixed D 4 course £18-£25.50, Starter £4-£8.50, Main £7-£28, Dessert £2.80-£6.50, Service added 10% **Wines** 15 bottles over £20, 19 bottles under £20, 7 by glass **Notes** Pre-theatre 3 course + coffee £10, Vegetarian menu, Dress restrictions, Clean and presentable, Air con **Seats** 60, Pr/dining room 25 **Parking** Chinatown car park

Yumi Restaurant
PLAN 2 G3

◎ Japanese

Authentic Japanese cuisine, service and atmosphere

☎ 020 7935 8320 ⓘ 020 7224 0917
110 George St W1H 5RL
dir: Nearest station: Marble Arch

When a Japanese restaurant is full of Japanese diners, it's got to be a good sign, and so it is at Yumi. The authentic Japanese cooking is the obvious draw, while the feeling is more of a neighbourhood restaurant than a

WestEnder. The staff, dressed in traditional kimonos, enhance the atmosphere. There's a sushi counter and booth-style seating areas for more intimate dining. The menu is available in Japanese and English and has a broad choice, bolstered by chef's recommendations, set-price options and a separate sushi list. Try the home-made seafood dumplings, belly pork cooked in sake and soy, or king prawn tempura.

Times 5.30-10.30

LONDON W2

Angelus Restaurant
PLAN 2 D2

◎◎ Modern French 🌶️ 🌿

Classy Parisian-style neighbourhood brasserie close to Hyde Park

☎ 020 7402 0083 📠 020 7402 5383
4 Bathurst St W2 2SD
e-mail: info@angelusrestaurant.co.uk
dir: Nearest station: Lancaster Gate/Paddington Station Opposite Royal Lancaster Hotel

Next to the Hyde Park stables and minutes from the park, this chic, Parisian-style brasserie is full of art-deco touches: chandeliers and decorative mirrors vie with dark-wood panelling and studded red-leather banquettes to give a truly French feel. At the back there is a boudoir bar, downstairs a private dining room, and a chef's oak table for 6 diners is in the kitchen. Owner Thierry Tomasin (once general manager of Aubergine and head sommelier at Le Gavroche) is a hands-on host and the service is both professional and charming. The cooking is modern French: warm potato and crayfish salad with chives is a simple and well-flavoured start, or there is a luscious foie gras crème brûlée with caramelised almonds and toasted bread. Main-course pot-roasted pork belly and cheeks comes with Savoy cabbage, Chantenay carrots and fondant potatoes. As you'd expect, French wines dominate the extensive list of quality wines.

Chef Martin Nisbet **Owner** Thierry Tomasin **Times** 12-11 Closed 23 Dec-4 Jan, **Prices** Fixed L 3 course fr £36, Fixed D 3 course fr £38, Service added but optional 12.5% **Wines** 800 bottles over £20, 11 bottles under £20, 4 by glass **Notes** Vegetarian available, Air con **Seats** 40, Pr/dining room 20 **Children** Portions

Assaggi
PLAN 2 A2

◎◎ Italian

A touch of authentic Italy above a pub in W2

☎ 020 7792 5501 📠 020 7792 9033
39 Chepstow Place W2 4TS
e-mail: nipi@assaggi.demon.co.uk
dir: Nearest station: Notting Hill Gate

The unassuming entrance by the Chepstow pub doesn't give a lot away. But up the stairs is a jewel of an Italian restaurant; small, simply decorated with scrubbed pine furniture and wooden floors - Assaggi punches above its weight. Large floor-to-ceiling windows give the dining room character, while friendly staff give a warm welcome

and invaluable help with translating the menu. The Italian food leans towards regional Sardinian cooking and uses authentic ingredients in attractively presented dishes. Antipasti includes gamberoni with artichokes and burrata cheese with grilled aubergine, followed, perhaps, by lasagne bianca and then fegato di vitello (calves' liver). Finish with semi-fredo all'Amaretto or the excellent selection of Italian cheeses. Booking is most definitely advisable.

Chef Nino Sassu **Owner** Nino Sassu, Pietro Fraccari **Times** 12.30-2.30/7.30-11 Closed 2 wks Xmas, BHs, Sun **Prices** Food prices not confirmed for 2010. Please telephone for details. **Wines** All bottles over £20, 7 by glass **Notes** Vegetarian available, Air con **Seats** 35 **Children** Portions

Le Cafe Anglais
PLAN 2 B2

◎ French

Art deco beauty serving modern brasserie food

☎ 020 7221 1415 📠 020 7727 9604
8 Porchester Gardens W2 4DB
e-mail: info@lecafeanglais.co.uk
dir: Nearest station: Bayswater or Queensway

In part of the block that makes up Whiteley's shopping centre in Bayswater is this open-plan, tall-windowed, first-floor restaurant run by seasoned London chef Rowley Leigh. The art deco surroundings are something to behold, while views of the kitchen allow you to watch the rotisseries turning hypnotically. A menu of modern brasserie favourites takes in classic fish soup with rouille, smoked eel and bacon salad, Dover sole fillets and perhaps Middlewhite pork seasoned with fennel-seed and garlic from the rotisserie. A torrent of vegetable side-dishes is available, and desserts fit the bill with a roll-call of ice cream and sorbet flavours or custard tart with prunes.

Chef Rowley Leigh **Owner** Rowley Leigh & Charlie McVeigh **Times** 12-3.30/6.30-11.30 Closed 1 Jan, **Prices** Fixed L 2 course fr £16.50, Fixed D 3 course £25-£35, Starter £3.50-£12.50, Main £10-£24, Dessert £4.50-£7.50, Service added but optional 12.5% **Wines** 98 bottles over £20, 5 bottles under £20, 25 by glass **Notes** Sunday L, Vegetarian available, Air con **Seats** 170, Pr/dining room 26 **Children** Portions

Island Restaurant & Bar
PLAN 2 D2

◎ Modern British

Design-led hotel restaurant with seasonal cooking

☎ 020 7551 6070 📠 020 7551 6071
Royal Lancaster Hotel, Lancaster Ter W2 2TY
e-mail: eat@islandrestaurant.co.uk
web: www.islandrestaurant.co.uk
dir: Nearest station: Lancaster Gate

The large corner site of this hybrid lounge-bar-restaurant has its own entrance within the Royal Lancaster Hotel. If you want nothing more than to check out the glitterati over cool cocktails in the sleek bar, that's ok, but the open-plan kitchen in the split-level dining area knows its

onions too. Huge plate glass windows look over Hyde Park, while evening brings an extra touch of glamour, with black-clad staff swishing between dark-wood tables in a dramatically-lit setting. The cooking takes in modern British staples with European influences, using quality materials in an unaffected style. Beef carpaccio with wild rocket, truffle oil and parmesan is typical of starters, then do your bit for the planet with beer-battered sustainable pollock and hand-cut chips with tartare sauce.

Times 12-10.30 Closed Xmas, BHs, between Xmas and New Year

Jamuna Restaurant
PLAN 2 E3

◎◎ Indian

Quality modern Indian in a quiet Paddington neighbourhood

☎ 020 7723 5056 & 020 7723 5055 📠 020 7706 1870
38A Southwick St W2 1JQ
e-mail: info@jamuna.co.uk
web: www.jamuna.co.uk
dir: Nearest station: Paddington, Edgware Road

Both the décor and the food are refreshingly free of clichés at this modern Indian in a quiet Paddington neighbourhood. Clean-cut minimalism is the order of the day: an eclectic art exhibition on the brightly-painted walls is all for sale, floors are wooden and chairs are suede. The diverse menu has done away with chilli symbols grading the tongue-tingle factor of dishes, but chatty staff are more than happy to advise. Regional specialities from all over the continent showcase the kitchen's wide-ranging repertoire; sharply-defined flavours are a testament to the chefs' skills, and top-class ingredients - Kent salt-marsh lamb, and Highland venison, to name but two - are name-checked on the menu. A perennial crowd-pleasing chicken tikka uses French corn-fed chicken, tikka-ed up three ways with red, green and malai spices, followed by, perhaps, pan-fried halibut given simple treatment with fresh herbs and pilau rice.

Chef Shankar Jadhav **Times** 12-2.30/6-11 Closed 25 Dec-1 Jan, 2 weeks in Aug, L all week (unless prior notice given) **Prices** Food prices not confirmed for 2010. Please telephone for details. **Wines** 138 bottles over £20, 11 by glass **Notes** Reservation required for L, Vegetarian available, Dress restrictions, Smart dress, no jeans or T-shirts, Air con **Seats** 60

LONDON W2 *continued*

Nipa
PLAN 2 D2

🐾 Thai

Genuine Thai cuisine with Hyde Park views

☎ 020 7551 6039 📠 020 7551 6079
The Royal Lancaster Hotel, Lancaster Ter W2 2TY
e-mail: nipa@royallancaster.com
web: www.niparestaurant.co.uk
dir: Nearest station: Lancaster Gate Opposite Hyde Park
on Bayswater Rd. On 1st floor of hotel

Authenticity is taken seriously at this classy Thai
restaurant on the first floor of Bayswater's Royal
Lancaster Hotel. First off, the teak panelling, pukka Thai
artefacts and exuberant flower displays evoke the feel of
its namesake restaurant in Bangkok's Landmark Hotel,
although the views over Hyde Park bring you back to
London pretty sharpish. Then there's the food: the wide-
ranging carte and trio of set menus offer a good hit of the
intense flavours that are the hallmark of the kitchen's
regional specialities, peppered with herbs and
seasonings flown in from Thailand. Go for deep-fried soft-
shell crab in plum sauce, fried sole in green curry or stir-
fried marinated chicken wrapped in pandanus leaves.

Chef Nongyao Thoopchoi **Owner** Lancaster Landmark
Hotel Co Ltd **Times** 12-2/6.30-10.30 Closed week between
Xmas & New Year, BHs, Sun, L Sat **Prices** Fixed L 3
course £27-£32, Fixed D 3 course £27-£32, Starter £6-
£7.25, Main £9.50-£14.95, Dessert £6, Service added but
optional 12.5% **Wines** 9 by glass **Notes** Vegetarian
available, Dress restrictions, Smart casual, Air con
Seats 55 **Children** Portions **Parking** 50

Royal China
PLAN 2 B1

🐾 Chinese

Traditional Chinese cuisine in Queensway

☎ 020 7221 2535 📠 020 7221 2535
13 Queensway W2 4QJ
e-mail: royalchina@btconnect.com
dir: Nearest station: Bayswater, Queensway

Don't be fooled by the small shop front of this popular
restaurant just off the Bayswater Road; once inside it
opens into a spacious dining room that stretches a long
way back and is very popular with Chinese diners. Black-
and-gold lacquered walls, Chinese memorabilia, mirrors
and etched glass decorate the interior, and teak screens
divide it into cosy areas. The constantly evolving menu of
classic Chinese food reflects new trends and is prepared
with quality ingredients (especially seafood). The set
menu includes gourmet seafood, house dinner, and
vegetarian options, while the chef's favourite menu might
feature sautéed assorted seafood in a taro nest, or pan-
fried stuffed aubergine with minced shrimp in black bean
sauce. Dim sum is a favourite and is available daily.

Times 12-11 Closed 25-26 Dec

Urban Turban
PLAN 2 A2

🐾 Indian

Vibrant, buzzy modern Indian with dishes to share

☎ 020 7243 4200 📠 020 7243 4080
98 Westbourne Grove W2 5RU
e-mail: info@urbanturban.uk.com
dir: Nearest station: Bayswater & Notting Hill. 2nd exit at
Holland Park rdbt, at Notting Hill Gate traffic lights turn
left onto A4206, 3rd exit onto A4206, left onto Chepstow
Rd & right after Carluccios

The sub-continental wizardry of Vineet Bhatia (chef-
patron of Rasoi Restaurant SW3, see entry) has done
much to transform curry clichés. This trendy lounge-bar-
style eatery proposes snacky 'Indian tapas' - themed
dishes inspired by India's street cuisine. The busy ground
floor is a place where Notting Hill fashionistas perch on
high stools at the slinky central bar or sink into low-slung
chairs; for a less nightclubby vibe go for the more
intimate basement. Spicing and heat is somewhat polite
in the dinky 'desi tapas' dishes, perhaps masala crab
and sweetcorn cakes with spicy ketchup or Mumbai fish
fry with crushed garlic peas. If you're hungry, the
'volcanic rock grill platter' lets you cook meat and
seafood on a hot stone at the table, or there are grown-up
helpings of classic dishes you might see in your local Taj
Mahal - perhaps lamb biryani.

Chef Satish Shenoy **Owner** Mr Vineet & Mrs Rashima
Bhatia **Times** 12.30-4.30/6-11 Closed Xmas & New Year,
Prices Starter fr £6.50, Main £5-£12, Service added but
optional 12.5% **Wines** 34 bottles over £20, 3 bottles
under £20, 10 by glass **Notes** Sunday L, Vegetarian
available, Dress restrictions, Smart casual, Air con
Seats 150, Pr/dining room 32 **Children** Portions
Parking On street

The Devonshire
PLAN 1 D3

🐾 Traditional British

**Gordon Ramsay pub serving unpretentious classic
British food**

☎ 020 7592 7962 📠 020 7592 1603
126 Devonshire Rd, Chiswick W4 2JJ
e-mail: thedevonshire@gordonramsay.com
dir: Nearest station: Turnham Green 150yds from
Chiswick High Rd, opposite Turnham Green Terrace

The Gordon Ramsay brand extended its reach to this
Victorian corner pub in Chiswick a couple of years ago.
The modern gastro-pub look is all present and correct:
period grandeur, courtesy of high ceilings, wood
panelling, and light flooding through huge windows onto
modern chairs, bare wood tables, wooden floors, and
stark white walls hung with vintage monochrome photos.
You could just drop in for a casual pint and park in a
squashy sofa, but the Devonshire is really about food.
Retro-titled classic British dishes sound like a blast from
the past, but like the pub, have had a 21st-century
makeover. Modern fuss-free cooking serves up quality
seasonal produce, such as pork and veal pie with apple
and date chutney to start, then lamb and rosemary
sausages with champ and red onion gravy.

Chef Chris Arkadieff **Owner** Gordon Ramsay Holdings
Times 12-3/5-10.45 Closed Mon-Tue, L Wed-Thu
Prices Starter £6-£7.50, Main £11.50-£17.50, Dessert
£5.50-£7.50, Service added but optional 12.5% **Wines** 37
bottles over £20, 13 bottles under £20, 11 by glass
Notes Sunday L, Vegetarian available, Air con **Seats** 45
Children Portions **Parking** On street

High Road Brasserie
PLAN 1 D3

🐾 European

Cool, bustling west London brasserie

☎ 020 8742 7474
162 Chiswick High Rd W4 1PR
dir: Nearest station: Turnham Green

A fold-back glass frontage and awning-covered pavement
tables pick out this urban-chic brasserie from Nick Jones's
Soho House empire. Pillars and mirrors, darkwood or
pewter-topped tables, olive green leather banquettes, a
patchwork of colourful floor tiles and a big marble-topped
bar make this a stylish, good-looking modern venue with a
very New York air. The food - informal modern European
brasserie fare from a crowd-pleasing all-day menu - fits
the upbeat, buzzy surroundings, with service to match from
staff clad in black waistcoats and long white aprons. From
breakfast to late, enjoy dishes like sea bass served with
marinated fennel, or calves' liver and bacon. (There's also
a private members' club and boutique hotel rooms on site.)

Chef Jesse Dunford Wood **Owner** Soho House Group
Times 7am-mdnt **Prices** Fixed L 2 course fr £12, Starter
£5-£12, Main £9-£32, Dessert £6-£8, Service added but
optional 12.5% **Wines** 77 bottles over £20, 21 bottles
under £20, 14 by glass **Notes** Sunday L, Vegetarian
available, Air con **Seats** 120 **Children** Portions, Menu

Sam's Brasserie & Bar
PLAN 1 C3

◉◉ Modern European

Modern, informal brasserie with friendly service and quality food

☎ 020 8987 0555 🖷 020 8987 7389
11 Barley Mow Passage W4 4PH
e-mail: info@samsbrasserie.co.uk
dir: Nearest station: Chiswick Park/Turnham Green
Behind Chiswick High Rd, next to green, off Heathfield
Terrace

Set in a converted, one-time paper factory - secreted away on a narrow walkway just behind the Chiswick High Road - Sam's has something of a New York loft-style air. High ceilings, girders, pillars and exposed piping lend that industrial edge, while large oval lampshades, contemporary seating and blond-wood tables deliver lighter, relaxed modern lines to the vibrant space. There's a smaller mezzanine dining area at the front and a semi-open kitchen to the back, while, off to one side, the buzzy bar continues the theme. It's an open-all-day operation with daily-changing menus, the pared-back cooking delivering clean-cut dishes and flavours driven by quality ingredients that keep things simple and fresh. Take roast rump of lamb teamed with pea risotto and mint jus, or perhaps crisp sea bass served with crushed new potatoes and cherry tomatoes.

Chef Ian Leckie **Owner** Sam Harrison
Times 9am-10.30pm Closed 24-27 Dec, L 28 Dec
Prices Fixed L 2 course fr £12, Fixed D 3 course fr £17,
Starter £5-£8, Main £10.50-£17.50, Dessert £3.50-£7.50,
Service added but optional **Wines** 47 bottles over £20, 26
bottles under £20, 19 by glass **Notes** Sunday L,
Vegetarian available, Air con **Seats** 100
Children Portions, Menu **Parking** On street & car park

La Trompette
PLAN 1 C3

◉◉◉ — see below

Le Vacherin
PLAN 1 C3

◉ French

Smart bistro serving classic French cuisine

☎ 020 8742 2121 & 8742 0799 🖷 020 8742 0799
76-77 South Pde W4 5LF
e-mail: malcolm.john4@btinternet.com
dir: Nearest station: Chiswick Park From tube station turn
left, restaurant 400mtrs on left

This Parisian-style bistro is easy to spot by its smart
black awning and large windows overlooking Acton Green.

continued

La Trompette

LONDON W4 PLAN 1 C3

European

French-inspired cooking from respected team

☎ 020 8747 1836 🖷 020 8995 8097
5-7 Devonshire Rd, Chiswick W4 2EU
e-mail: reception@latrompette.co.uk
dir: Nearest station: Turnham Green From station follow
Turnham Green Tce to junct with Chiswick High Rd. Cross
road & bear right. Devonshire Rd 2nd left

The Chiswick outpost of the respected group of restaurants, which includes Chez Bruce in Wandsworth and The Glasshouse in Kew, has an immaculately trimmed hedge surrounding a few outside tables and a large awning providing protection from the sun's rays or light showers. Sliding glass doors open up the space when the weather allows. Inside, the restaurant matches the others in the group for understated, unpretentious style, with oak floors, leather banquette seating, muted tones of brown, and white linen-clad tables. Service is confident and knowledgeable and the atmosphere positively buzzes with conviviality. The accomplished cooking has its roots in France, and the South West of the country specifically, although there are broader influences at work. Foie gras and chicken liver parfait with toasted brioche is a classic starter, followed perhaps by breast of poulet noir with gratin daupinhoise, salsify and roasting juices, finishing off with an Italian interloper such as vanilla pannacotta with poached rhubarb and biscotti.

Chef James Bennington **Owner** Nigel Platts-Martin, Bruce
Poole **Times** 12-2.30/6.30-10.30 Closed 25-26 Dec, 1 Jan,
Prices Food prices not confirmed for 2010. Please
telephone for details. **Wines** 500 bottles over £20, 30
bottles under £20, 15 by glass **Notes** Sunday L,
Vegetarian available, Air con **Seats** 72 **Children** Portions
Parking On street

LONDON W4 continued

Gallic music, French themed posters and pictures decorating cream-coloured walls, mirrors, blond-wood floors, banquette seating and closely set tables and chairs in dark wood with white tablecloths set the scene for some classic French cooking. Try the twice-baked gruyère soufflé with endives and walnuts, followed by fillet of line caught sea bass with spinach and brown shrimps, and finish with an authentic tarte Tatin. The restaurant's namesake soft cow's milk cheese puts in an appearance in the likes of baked Vacherin with black truffle and almond crust, and in an ice cream as an unusual complement to a fig tart .

Chef Malcolm John **Owner** Malcolm & Donna John **Times** 12-3/6-11 Closed 25 Dec, BHs, L Mon **Prices** Fixed L 2 course £15.50-£25, Fixed D 3 course £28-£40, Starter £7-£12.50, Main £14-£22, Dessert £6.50-£8.50, Service added but optional 12.5% **Wines** 77 bottles over £20, 12 bottles under £20, 12 by glass **Notes** Sunday L, Vegetarian available, Air con **Seats** 72, Pr/dining room 36 **Children** Portions **Parking** On street (metered)

LONDON W6

Agni
PLAN 1 D3

◉ Traditional Indian

Regional Indian cuisine in comfortable surroundings

☎ 020 8846 9191 & 8748 6611
160 King St W6 0QU
e-mail: info@agnirestaurant.com
dir: Nearest station: Hammersmith Broadway, Ravenscourt Park

Renowned Indian chef Gowtham Karingi (formerly head chef at Zaika) and Neeraj Mittra's (ex manager at Chutney Mary) restaurant is in an unassuming spot opposite Hammersmith town hall. The colourful interior goes for an unfussy bistro style with wooden tables, cane-seated chairs and panelled walls. Watch the chefs at work in the glass-panelled kitchen turning out an eclectic mix of regional Indian dishes covering just about all the bases on the sub-continent, from a Goanese fish balchao, cooked with ginger, chilli, palm vinegar, shallots and dark rum, to traditional Hyderabadi biryani pots - lamb, prawn, chicken or veggies in rice perfumed with rose petals, saffron, vetiver and cardamom.

Times 5-11 Closed 25 Dec, L Mon-Sun

Anglesea Arms
PLAN 1 D3

◉ British, French

Bustling gastro-pub with appealingly robust cooking

☎ 020 8749 1291 📄 020 8749 1254
35 Wingate Rd W6 0UR
dir: Nearest station: Ravenscourt Park, Goldhawk Rd & Hammersmith From Ravenscourt Park tube, walk along Ravenscourt Rd, turn left onto Paddenswick then right onto Wellesley Rd

The Anglesea Arms is a South Ken institution with guaranteed hustle and bustle from a lively crowd of trendy locals and diners - in short, a thriving, fashionably shabby-chic, neighbourhood gastro-pub. There's a serious array of well-kept ales to fuel proceedings in the low-lit dark-panelled bar, while the dining area behind comes with a lived-in vibe and the theatre of an open kitchen. Blackboard menus change daily to offer modern British food that's a cut above the norm, with plenty of gutsy materials and full-on flavours. Duck on toast and pig's head salad rub along next to more delicate dishes such as steamed razor clams or simple Cornish crab with mayonnaise. Main courses might be smoked eel with mash and red wine sauce. There's a democratic no-bookings policy, so arrive early.

Chef Matt Cranston **Owner** Michael Mann, Jill O' Sullivan **Times** 12.30-2.45/7-10.30 Closed 25-27 Dec, **Prices** Starter £4.75-£8.95, Main £9.95-£16.95, Dessert £4.50-£5.20, Service optional, Groups min 6 service 12.5% **Wines** 86 bottles over £20, 14 bottles under £20, 20 by glass **Notes** Sunday L, Vegetarian available, Air con **Seats** 70 **Children** Portions **Parking** On street, pay & display (free at wknds)

The Brackenbury
PLAN 1 D3

◉ Modern European

West London neighbourhood restaurant offering a taste of Europe

☎ 020 8748 0107 📄 020 8748 6159
129-131 Brackenbury Rd W6 0BQ
e-mail: info@thebrackenbury.com
dir: Nearest station: Goldhawk Road, Hammersmith

The friendly neighbourhood Brackenbury is hidden away on a quiet residential street between Hammersmith and Shepherd's Bush. An attractive pavement terrace is perfect for good weather. The split-level interior is decorated in earthy colours with modern chairs or banquette seating, and service is suitably neighbourly. The sensibly-priced menu proffers good quality, seasonal British produce, sourced from small, independent suppliers, to create great-tasting, simple dishes with a modern European touch, and a particular connection to Italy. Try buffalo mozzarella with confit tomatoes and caponata to start, followed by red mullet with risotto nero and gremolata.

Times 12.30-2.45/7-10.45 Closed 24-26 Dec, 1 Jan, Etr Mon, Aug BH Mon, D Sun

The Gate
PLAN 1 D3

◉ Modern Vegetarian **V**

Inspirational vegetarian cooking

☎ 020 8748 6932
51 Queen Caroline St W6 9QL
e-mail: hammersmith@thegate.tv
dir: Nearest station: Hammersmith. From Hammersmith Apollo Theatre, continue down right side for approx 40 yds

Forget any clichéd notions of baked lentils and sandal-wearing diners: the Gate offers gourmet vegetarian food exploding with enough taste to convert the most rampant carnivore, and tempt high-profile celeb veggies out to the unusual converted church restaurant in a quiet corner of Hammersmith. It helps that the owners are inspired by an Indo-Iraqi Jewish heritage, and have pillaged the world's vegetable patch, with a special nod to Middle-Eastern cooking. The cooking is an inspiring alternative to lacklustre veggie fodder so, expect big flavours and inventive combinations, such as halloumi kibbi - chargrilled halloumi in a tikka marinade, skewered with red onions, peppers and courgettes, with pomegranate, herb and couscous salad, or a perfectly al dente risotto with roasted butternut squash, dolcelatte, walnuts and parmesan.

Chef Adrian Daniel, Mariusz Wegrodski **Owner** Adrian & Michael Daniel **Times** 12-3/6-11 Closed 23 Dec-3 Jan, Good Fri & Etr Mon, Sun, L Sat **Prices** Fixed L 2 course £18.75, Starter £5-£6.75, Main £12-£14.75, Dessert £5.50-£6, Service added but optional 12.5% **Wines** 35 bottles over £20, 9 bottles under £20, 12 by glass **Notes** Vegetarian menu, Air con **Seats** 60 **Children** Portions **Parking** On street

The River Café
PLAN 1 D3

◉◉◉ – see opposite page

Sagar
PLAN 1 D3

◉◉ Vegetarian, Indian **V**

Vegetarian Indian dining in the heart of Hammersmith

☎ 020 8741 8563
157 King St, Hammersmith W6 9JT
dir: Nearest station: Hammersmith 10min from Hammersmith Tube

South Indian vegetarian food is the specialty of this popular, lively restaurant in a row of shops in Hammersmith. The smooth blond-wood walls are dotted with elegant brass figurines attractively lit at night, and the tables are tightly packed, enhancing the bustling atmosphere. The extensive menu is focused on Udupi dishes from Karnataka, with highlights being the giant paper-thin dosas (rice and lentil pancakes with various fillings rolled up inside) and the uthappams (lentil pizzas). Starters include idli (puffy, spongy rice and lentil dumplings) with sambar and a fiery coconut chutney, and dahl potato puri with yogurt and tamarind sauce. For dessert, try the kulfi or the payasam - a hot, milky pudding made with fine vermicelli, cashew nuts and raisins. Expect low prices and if you're a little unsure what to order, the helpful staff will happily advise.

Times 12-2.45/5.30-10.45 Closed 25-26 Dec

LONDON W8

Babylon

PLAN 4 B4

⊛⊛ Modern British

Minimalist chic and extraordinary views

☎ 020 7368 3993 📠 020 7368 3995
The Roof Gardens, 99 Kensington High St W8 5SA
e-mail: babylon@roofgardens.virgin.com
web: www.roofgardens.virgin.com
dir: Nearest station: High Street Kensington From High St Kensington tube station, turn right, then right into Derry St. Restaurant on right

There's a fantasy world of exotic greenery and feathered wildlife up on the rooftops of Kensington, and Richard Branson's Babylon, sitting a level above the famous Roof Gardens, gets grandstand views. When the lift doors open on the 7th floor what greets you is not biblical decadence, but understated taste in a glammed-up vein: silky wood floors, muted colours enlivened by bright splashes of artwork, flowers afloat in glass bowls at tables in intimate booths. And of course there are those jaw-dropping views of the capital's skyline. Service is spot-on and the kitchen's modern approach is tailored to the slick setting. Top-quality British produce appears in a starter of seared Scottish diver-caught scallops with fennel purée, wild cress and winter truffle, followed by confit leg of Gressingham duck with braised Savoy cabbage, lentils and roast carrots.

Babylon

Chef Ian Howard **Owner** Sir Richard Branson
Times 12-2.30/7-10.30 Closed Xmas, D Sun **Prices** Fixed L 2 course £17.50-£20.50, Fixed D 3 course £24-£27, Starter £9-£15, Main £18-£28, Dessert £7-£16, Service added but optional 12.5% **Wines** 103 bottles over £20, 2 bottles under £20, 15 by glass **Notes** Sunday L, Vegetarian available, Dress restrictions, Smart casual, Civ Wed 500, Air con **Seats** 120, Pr/dining room 12 **Children** Portions, Menu **Parking** 10, NCP car park on Young St

The River Café

LONDON W6

PLAN 1 D3

Italian 🍷

The freshest food simply treated with reverence in Thames-side setting

☎ 020 7386 4200 📠 020 7386 4201
Thames Wharf, Rainville Rd W6 9HA
e-mail: info@rivercafe.co.uk
dir: Nearest station: Hammersmith Restaurant in converted warehouse. Entrance on S side of Rainville Rd at junct with Bowfell Rd

After a kitchen fire closed the River Café for 6 months in 2008 it reopened looking pretty well the way it always did. The fact is that Rose Gray and Ruth Rogers' Thames-side temple to authentic Italian cooking is a classic that needed no reinvention. It's still a cavernous white-painted room, just the right side of austere, showing off its steel and glass heritage from the original 18th-century warehouse, and flooded with light from a wall of plate-glass windows overlooking the wharf. Suitably industrial stainless-steel sheathes the open kitchen, and a wood oven, looking like a prop from Dr Who, takes centre stage. The vibe is buzzy and cosmopolitan, helped along by the casually-dressed but on-the-ball young staff. Menus change twice daily, and it's a good idea to eat early because popular dishes have usually sold out by the second sitting. The food is proper peasant stuff - mainly driven by the cuisine of Tuscany and Lombardy - so the reason you're paying an arm and a leg for it is that only the very best produce in optimum condition makes it onto the plate; many ingredients are hunted down specifically for their rarity, pedigree provenance and seasonality. Classic combinations are treated simply: scallops with anchovy dressing, borlotti beans and Treviso lettuce shows the trademark simplicity that lets the purity of the ingredients shine. Smoky notes from the wood-burning oven infuse roasted wood pigeon, stuffed with sage and thyme, and served with crunchy roast polenta and earthy cavolo nero. End with a sinful chocolate nemesis and a simple dollop of fresh cream.

Chef R Gray, R Rogers, Sian Owen **Owner** Rose Gray, Ruth Rogers **Times** 12.30-3/7-11 Closed 24 Dec-1 Jan, Easter, BHs, D Sun **Prices** Food prices not confirmed for 2010. Please telephone for details. **Wines** 155 bottles over £20, 6 bottles under £20, 18 by glass **Notes** Sunday L, Vegetarian available, Air con **Seats** 130 **Children** Portions **Parking** 29, Valet parking in evening

LONDON W8 *continued*

Belvedere

PLAN 1 D3

@@ French

Brasserie cooking in the middle of a famous London park

☎ 020 7602 1238 📠 020 7610 4382

Abbotsbury Rd, Holland House, Holland Park W8 6LU

e-mail: sales@whitestarline.org.uk

dir: Nearest station: Holland Park Off Abbotsbury Rd entrance to Holland Park

The former orangery in Holland Park is a delightful setting at all times, but perhaps most especially when the grounds are in full flower. It's as expansive as befits its erstwhile role as a ballroom, with film-set mirrors, scalloped light-fittings and only the crispest of napery. A brasserie menu offers more democratic eating than the venue might lead you to think, with the likes of creamy pea soup with ham, baked cod with crushed potatoes and Puy lentils, or beef rib-eye with big chips and garlic butter. For something more unusual, try the roast pigeon main, which comes with Morteau sausage, confit garlic and a grain mustard sauce. End on a light note with Prosecco jelly, served with raspberry coulis and vanilla ice cream, or go for broke with sticky toffee pudding and black treacle ice cream.

Chef Phillip Cooper **Owner** Jimmy Lahoud
Times 12-2.30/6-10.30 Closed 26 Dec, 1 Jan, D Sun
Prices Fixed L 2 course £15, Starter £6.50-£13.50, Main £12.95-£28.50, Dessert £7, Service added but optional 12.5%, Groups min 13 service 15% **Wines** 129 bottles over £20, 14 by glass **Notes** Sunday L, Vegetarian available, Dress restrictions, Smart casual, Air con **Seats** 90 **Parking** Council car park

Cheneston's Restaurant

PLAN 4 B4

@@ British

International cuisine in luxurious surroundings

☎ 020 7917 1000 📠 020 7917 1010

Milestone Hotel, 1 Kensington Court W8 5DL

e-mail: bookms@rchmail.com

dir: Nearest station: High St Kensington. M4/ Hammersmith flyover, take 2nd left into Gloucester Rd, left into High St Kensington, 500mtrs on left

The Milestone is a magnificent 19th-century architectural treasure that takes its name from an old cast iron milestone that stands beside it. Now a luxury hotel, it enjoys a prestigious location opposite Kensington Palace and Gardens. The luxuriously ornate, intimate Cheneston's Restaurant is splendidly furnished with mahogany furniture and during the day natural daylight pours in through leaded windows. The menu offers a broadly modern British menu with some international flavours and preparations, all based around organic and seasonal ingredients. Seared Orkney scallops with creamed leeks might precede hay-baked cannon and confit shoulder of Shetland lamb with aubergine caviar and natural pan juices, finishing up with a rich, warm dark chocolate tart with vanilla ice cream.

Chef Luke Davis **Owner** Red Carnation Hotels
Times 12-3/5.30-11 **Prices** Fixed L 2 course £21.50-£26.50, Fixed D 3 course £26.50-£30, Starter £8.50-£18.50, Main £14.50-£29.50, Dessert £8.50-£9.50, Service added but optional 12.5% **Wines** 250 bottles over £20, 12 by glass **Notes** Pre-theatre D £21.50, Tasting menu 7 course, Sunday L, Vegetarian available, Dress restrictions, Smart casual, Civ Wed 30, Air con **Seats** 30, Pr/dining room 8 **Children** Portions, Menu **Parking** NCP Young Street off Kensington High Street

Clarke's

PLAN 4 A5

@@ British, Mediterranean

Freshest seasonal food simply treated with flair and due respect

☎ 020 7221 9225 📠 020 7229 4564

124 Kensington Church St W8 4BH

e-mail: restaurant@sallyclarke.com

dir: Nearest station: Notting Hill Gate

Set among the antique shops of Kensington Church Street, you'll find this neat and understated shop-front restaurant adjoining Sally Clarke's famous bread (and more) shop and café. Dining takes place on two floors,

and though it first opened back in 1984, there's nothing retro about this operation; there's a bright, smaller ground floor and larger low-lit basement room with an open-plan kitchen. Décor is as light and uncluttered as the food, enhanced by fresh flowers, colourful artwork and white linen, while service is attentive yet endearingly unstuffy. Menus change daily, with impeccable, fresh, seasonal ingredients and a light modern touch, and it is this that continues to make the vibrant, clean-flavoured cooking so successful and enduring. There's a sunny nod to the Med too; take home-made gnocchi with Basque chorizo, parmesan, toasted pinenuts and wild rocket, or a fillet of Icelandic haddock roasted with a sauce of white wine, capers and home-grown marjoram served with spring vegetables.

Chef Sally Clarke, Raffaele Colturi **Owner** Sally Clarke
Times 12.30-2/7-10 Closed 8 days Xmas & New Year, Sun **Prices** Food prices not confirmed for 2010. Please telephone for details. **Wines** 86 bottles over £20, 10 bottles under £20, 8 by glass **Notes** Vegetarian available, Air con **Seats** 80, Pr/dining room 40 **Parking** On street

Eleven Abingdon Road

PLAN 4 A4

@@ European

Cool neighbourhood venue off High Street Kensington

☎ 020 7937 0120

11 Abingdon Rd, Kensington W8 6AH

e-mail: eleven@abingdonroad.co.uk

dir: Nearest station: Kensington High St

This light, modern, glass-fronted restaurant is tucked away in a little road just off High Street Ken and proves quite a find; it shares ownership with Sonny's in Barnes. The stylish, restrained, clean-lined split-level interior - with a small chic bar area up front decked out with glitzy leopard- and tiger-skin chairs - comes dominated by an eye-catching art collection set to a backcloth of sage-green walls, contemporary lighting, modern stainless-steel and tan leather director-style chairs and a friendly, upbeat vibe. Staff - dressed in long black aprons - deliver appealing, modern Mediterranean-accented dishes using quality seasonal ingredients that are as clean-cut as the décor. Think tagliolini with Scottish langoustine, girolles and tarragon, or perhaps roast rabbit served with soft polenta and wild mushrooms.

Times 12.30-2.30/6.30-11 Closed 25 Dec, BHs

Kensington Place

PLAN 4 A6

@ Modern British

Buzzing brasserie, popular with the Notting Hill set

☎ 020 7727 3184 📠 020 7792 8388

201-9 Kensington Church St W8 7LX

dir: Nearest station: Notting Hill Gate

A revolving door leads you inside this lively brasserie, which has been part of Notting Hill's dining scene since the late 80s. You can perch on a stool at the bar for a drink and a spot of people watching, before heading down the steps to one of the tightly packed tables in the *continued on page 318*

continued on page 318

Min Jiang

LONDON W8 **PLAN 4 B5**

Chinese **NEW** V

Imaginative modern cooking in a spacious room overlooking Kensington Gardens

☎ 020 7361 1988 📄 020 7361 1987
Royal Garden Hotel, 2-24 Kensington High St W8 4PT
e-mail: reservations@minjiang.co.uk
web: www.minjiang.co.uk
dir: Nearest station: Kensington High Street. Next to Kensington Palace & gardens on 10th floor of Royal Garden Hotel

The tenth floor of the Royal Garden Hotel has striking views over the tops of the trees in Kensington Gardens and Hyde Park with the London skyline beyond. The customers of Min Jiang can take in this inspiring vista while enjoying some truly impressive contemporary Chinese food. The setting is a modern, light and bright space, using natural colours (white, brown) softened with crisp linen tablecloths and displays of Chinese crockery. The menu deals mostly in the ingredients and flavours of Cantonese and Szechuan cooking, and from Beijing comes the famous duck - roasted over apple wood and served in a number of ways, including with garlic paste, radish and Tientsin cabbage, or in a salted vegetable soup with tofu. There is a dim sum menu - superb xiao long bao, delicious crispy Beijing duck rolls - and high quality is very much in evidence throughout. Pan-fried rib-eye with almonds in Yakiniku sauce and plump and succulent prawns in black bean sauce are fine main courses, while desserts are not given short shrift: chocolate tart with lychee ice cream shows good technical skill. The wine list includes some Chinese choices, while confident service further enhances the experience.

Chef Lan Chee Uooi **Owner** Goodwood Group **Times** 12-3/6-10.30 **Prices** Fixed L 2 course fr £19.50, Fixed D 2 course £48-£68, Starter £6-£12.80, Main £14-£48, Dessert £6-£7.50, Service optional, Groups min 8 service 10% **Wines** 149 bottles over £20, 15 by glass
Notes Sunday L, Vegetarian menu, Dress restrictions, Smart casual, Air con **Seats** 100, Pr/dining room 20 **Parking** 160

LONDON W8 *continued*

dining area, with their funky blue wooden chairs. Floor-to-ceiling glass provides a window on the world outside, while on the far wall is a striking, brightly-coloured mural of Kensington Gardens. It's a casual and relaxed setting in which to enjoy the kitchen's modern British cuisine, with a fairly heavy emphasis on fish (fish pie being a typical main course). Seasonal produce features prominently, too, as in a March starter of purple sprouting broccoli soup. Check out the restaurant's fish shop next door.

Chef Henry Vigar **Owner** D & D London
Times 12-3/6.30-10.30 **Prices** Fixed L 2 course fr £16.50, Fixed D 3 course fr £19.50, Service added but optional 12.5% **Wines** 123 bottles over £20, 12 bottles under £20, 15 by glass **Notes** Sunday L, Vegetarian available, Air con **Seats** 100, Pr/dining room 45 **Children** Portions, Menu **Parking** On street

Launceston Place Restaurant   PLAN 4 C4

◎◎ Modern British **V**

Stylish restaurant with thrilling modern food

☎ 020 7937 6912   ▤ 020 7938 2412
1a Launceston Place W8 5RL
e-mail: lpr@egami.co.uk
dir: Nearest station: Gloucester Road Just south of Kensington Palace

Tucked away in a quiet residential street in the heart of Kensington, this popular and sophisticated restaurant has been subject to something of a face-lift. The newly renovated, high-ceilinged rooms centre around a central bar and the rich brown walls are hung with vibrant modern art and fibre-optic chandeliers. Staff are impeccably dressed and deliver highly polished service. The British, fiercely seasonal menu combines traditional dishes with contemporary flair and just a touch of theatre. Take a starter of roast foie gras with rhubarb compôte and elderflower milk, followed perhaps by roast Herdwick lamb with Jerusalem artichokes and mint sauce. Brown bread parfait laced with rum and raisins rounds things off.

Chef Tristan Welch **Owner** D&D London
Times 12.30-2.30/6-10.30 Closed Xmas, New Year, Etr, L Mon **Prices** Fixed L 3 course £18-£24, Fixed D 3 course £42-£55, Service added but optional 12.5% **Wines** 87 bottles over £20, 5 bottles under £20, 13 by glass **Notes** Sunday L, Vegetarian menu, Dress restrictions, Smart casual, no T-shirts or caps, Air con **Seats** 60, Pr/dining room 10 **Children** Portions **Parking** Car park off Kensington High St

Min Jiang   PLAN 4 B5

◎◎◎ – *see page 317*

Park Terrace Restaurant   PLAN 4 B5

◎◎ Modern European

Elegant setting by Kensington Gardens offering inventive modern cuisine

☎ 020 7361 0602   ▤ 020 7361 1921
Royal Garden Hotel, 2-24 Kensington High St W8 4PT
e-mail: dining@royalgardenhotel.co.uk
web: www.royalgardenhotel.co.uk
dir: Nearest station: Kensington High Street Next to Kensington Palace, Royal Albert Hall, within Royal Garden Hotel

The Royal Garden Hotel overlooks most of what there is to see in this landmark-rich part of London, with Kensington Palace and its gardens, Hyde Park and the Royal Albert Hall all on the checklist. In the sumptuously appointed Park Terrace, on the ground floor, is a restaurant worthy of the surroundings, where a modern British menu draws on seasonal supplies from an Essex farming co-operative and Bristol Channel boats, among other sources. Fine, firm-textured halibut makes a regal main course, especially when accompanied by smoked garlic mash, a leek tart and mussel chowder, or there might be grilled organic beef sirloin with potato and cheese roulade. Preceding one of these, you might go for smoked Wye Valley salmon with prawn cocktail and lemon caponata, and round things off with lime curd tart served with marshmallow and mango sorbet.

Chef Steve Munkley **Owner** Goodwood Group
Times 12-3/6-10.30 **Prices** Fixed L 2 course fr £16.50, Fixed D 3 course fr £31, Service optional, Groups min 8 service 10% **Wines** 74 bottles over £20, 13 by glass **Notes** Sunday L, Vegetarian available, Dress restrictions, Smart casual, Air con **Seats** 90 **Children** Portions, Menu **Parking** 160

Timo   PLAN 1 D3

◎ Italian

Stylish, authentic Italian dining

☎ 020 7603 3888   ▤ 020 7603 8111
343 Kensington High St W8 6NW
e-mail: timorestaurant@fsmail.net
dir: Nearest station: Kensington High St 5 mins walk towards Hammersmith, after Odeon Cinema, on left of street

At the Olympia end of trendy Kensington High Street, this neighbourhood Italian offers a sincere friendly greeting and authentic regional cuisine that's a cut above the norm. Inside, it's a funky modern split-level place, long and thin in pastel hues and kitted out with high-backed suede chairs and banquettes on pale wooden floors. Pre-cinema and lunch menus offer good value for the credit crunch era, with the kitchen dealing in classic cooking and presentation, in dishes such as buffalo mozzarella with tomato, basil and aubergine purée, chestnut pasta with duck ragù or brill fillet with white wine, parsley sautéed French beans and olives.

Chef Franco Gatto **Owner** Piero Amodio
Times 12-2.30/7-11 Closed Xmas, New Year, BHs, D Sun

Prices Fixed L 2 course £13.90, Starter £6.90-£12.50, Main £14.90-£23.50, Dessert £5.50-£7.90, Service added but optional 12.5%, Groups min 10 service 15% **Wines** 3 bottles over £20, 3 bottles under £20, 8 by glass **Notes** Vegetarian available, Air con **Seats** 55, Pr/dining room 18 **Children** Portions **Parking** 3

Zaika   PLAN 4 B4

◎◎ Modern Indian

Modern Indian cuisine in heart of Kensington

☎ 020 7795 6533   ▤ 020 7937 8854
1 Kensington High St W8 5NP
e-mail: info@zaika-restaurant.co.uk
dir: Nearest station: Kensington High Street Opposite Kensington Palace

This is fine-dining, Indian-style, in a converted bank opposite Kensington Palace. Original features like carved high ceilings and double-height windows combine with contemporary chairs, banquettes in rich colours and Indian artefacts to create a feeling of opulence harking back to the colonial era. The highest quality British, seasonal produce is used to create a wide choice of updated classics and more innovative Indian dishes. Spicing is balanced and minimal oil is used in frying, thus food tastes light, healthy and fresh, while strong use of fresh herbs adds intense colour and flavour. Try the hand-dived Scottish scallops prepared three ways and served with chilli mash and spring onion naan, followed by the slow-cooked Herdwick lamb with coconut, mustard seeds and curry leaves, and finish with the chocolate samosas. Check out the extremely comprehensive wine list, offering 600 wines spanning 17 countries.

Chef Sanjay Dwivedi **Owner** Claudio Pulze, Sanjay Dwivedi **Times** 12-2.45/6-10.45 Closed BHs, Xmas, New Year, L Mon **Prices** Fixed L 2 course £16, Tasting menu £39, Starter £7.50-£12.50, Main £15-£21, Dessert £6-£12, Service added but optional 12.5% **Wines** 400+ bottles over £20, 8 bottles under £20, 17 by glass **Notes** Vegetarian available, Dress restrictions, Smart casual preferred, Air con **Seats** 84 **Children** Portions

LONDON W9

The Warrington   PLAN 2 C5

◎ Modern British

Posh pub food in historically ornate surroundings

☎ 020 7592 7960   ▤ 020 7592 1603
93 Warrington Crescent, Maida Vale W9 1EH
e-mail: warrington@gordonramsay.com
dir: Nearest station: Warwick Avenue, Maida Vale

The Warrington strikes a nice balance between gastro and pub since its assimilation into the Gordon Ramsay empire. This palatial slice of Victorian pomp has been lovingly buffed up to its former glory - take in the marble pillars, fireplaces, tobacco-hued wood panelling and glorious art nouveau stained glass over a lunchtime snack in the bustling main bar. Upstairs, the posh restaurant is pure 21st century in cream leather and beige amid fancy period plasterwork. Food is pubby in the modern British idiom, so expect Dorset snails with parsley butter or ham hock terrine with piccalilli, while shredded duck shepherd's pie gives an intense hit of ducky jus and cheesy mash. Desserts offer deep comfort in the shape of apple and blackberry crumble with stem ginger ice cream.

Chef Daniel Kent **Owner** Gordon Ramsay Holdings Ltd **Times** 12-2.30/6-10.30 Closed L Mon-Thu **Prices** Starter £6.95-£8, Main £8-£18.50, Dessert £5.50-£6.75, Service added but optional 12.5% **Wines** 60 bottles over £20, 18 bottles under £20, 13 by glass **Notes** Sunday L, Air con **Seats** 80, Pr/dining room 14 **Children** Portions **Parking** On Street

LONDON W11

E&O
PLAN 1 D4

◉ Pan Asian

Pan-Asian fusion cooking in super-chic oriental-style eatery and bar

☎ 020 7229 5454 📠 020 7229 5522
14 Blenheim Crescent, Notting Hill W11 1NN
e-mail: eando@rickerrestaurants.com
dir: Nearest station: Notting Hill Gate, from tube station turn right, at mini rdbt turn into Kensington Park Rd, restaurant 10min down hill

Über-trendy Notting Hill is the perfect location for this style-led pan-oriental restaurant. The sparsely decorated dining room lit by giant oval lampshades is all slatted walls, brown leather banquettes and black lacquered chairs on darkwood floors. It all goes down a treat with the hip young crew who come for the upbeat vibe and contemporary fusion menu that cherry picks its way through Asian cuisine. Tapas-sized dishes are designed for grazing and sharing and cover all the bases from dim sum to tempura, and sashimi to barbecues and roasts such as black cod with sweet miso, and specials along the lines of Korean-style lamb and kim chi.

Chef Simon Treadway **Owner** Will Ricker **Times** 12-3/6-11 Closed 25-26 Dec, 1 Jan, Aug BH, **Prices** Starter £3.50-£11, Main £9.50-£23.50, Dessert £4-£4.75, Service added but optional 12.5%, Groups min 10 service 15% **Wines** 6 bottles under £20, 59 by glass **Notes** Air con **Seats** 86, Pr/dining room 18 **Children** Portions, Menu **Parking** On street

Edera
PLAN 1 D4

◉◉ Modern Italian

Well-liked neighbourhood Italian in leafy Holland Park

☎ 020 7221 6090 📠 020 7313 9700
148 Holland Park Av W11 4UE
e-mail: edera@btconnect.com
dir: Nearest station: Holland Park

The upmarket neighbourhood Italian restaurant in Holland Park draws in passers-by with a handful of pavement tables, which look alluring in this leafy part of London. Light interiors with bare wood floor and simply dressed tables provide the setting for well-executed Italian cooking, which has a distinct fondness for that most fashionable of the regions, Sardinia. A bowl of summery minestrone makes an appealing, and often underrated, starter, replete with finely diced seasonal vegetables, or you might start with a hefty portion of fregola (Sardinian couscous-shaped pasta) with king prawns. Mains run from the show-stopping porceddu, a whole suckling pig cooked over embers, to baked sea bream with roasted potatoes on a sauce of Vernaccia white wine. Finish with fried puff-pastry shells filled with ricotta and honey, garnished with candied orange peel.

Times 12-2.30/6.30-11 Closed 25-26 & 31 Dec

The Ledbury
PLAN 1 D4

◉◉◉ – **see below**

The Ledbury

LONDON W11
PLAN 1 D4

Modern French V

Highly accomplished cooking in fashionable, residential Notting Hill

☎ 020 7792 9090 📠 020 7792 9191
127 Ledbury Rd W11 2AQ
e-mail: info@theledbury.com
dir: Nearest station: Westbourne Park, Notting Hill Gate. 5 min walk along Talbot Rd from Portobello Rd, on corner of Talbot and Ledbury Rd

Trust Notting Hill to have a neighbourhood restaurant of such class and calibre. It is a neighbourhood restaurant inasmuch as it provides the local community with an alternative to heading into the centre of town - there is no need to leave W11 when such refined, intelligent cooking is available on your doorstep - but, conversely, it is a destination restaurant, worth crossing town to visit. Nigel Platts-Martin and Philip Howard's (they also joint-own The Square in Mayfair, see entry) sophisticated venue is simply and stylishly done out, with large glass doors opening onto a small terrace, and the use of natural wood flooring and cream, brown and grey tones creating a modish but understated space. Tables are smartly dressed in white linen and the service is never less than professional without being stand-offish. Australian-born Brett Graham's cooking combines traditional French preparations with plenty of contemporary touches and eye-catching presentations, displaying excellent technical skills and based around first-rate seasonal produce. An amuse-bouche such as beetroot meringue with goats' cheese gets things off to a flying start before a starter of compôte of Berkshire hare, flavoured with juniper, pepper and orange, in a delightful partnership with pumpkin purée and chanterelles. Roast turbot with squid sautéed in sherry, cauliflower and tamarind is a well-balanced main course, and hot chocolate fondant a thrilling finish.

There's a good value set lunch, a tasting menu (including a vegetarian version), notable cheese trolley and superb wine list.

Chef Brett Graham **Owner** Nigel Platts-Martin, Brett Graham & Philip Howard **Times** 12-2.30/6.30-10.30 Closed 24-26 Dec, 1 Jan, Aug BH wknd **Prices** Fixed L 2 course fr £19.50, Tasting menu fr £70, Service added but optional 12.5% **Wines** 661 bottles over £20, 5 bottles under £20, 12 by glass **Notes** ALC 3 course £60, Tasting menu 8 course, Sunday L, Vegetarian menu, Air con **Seats** 62 **Parking** Talbot Rd (metered)

Notting Hill Brasserie

Modern Mediterranean

Fine food and unobtrusive service in chic west London environs

☎ 020 7229 4481　📄 020 7221 1246
92 Kensington Park Rd W11 2PN
e-mail: enquiries@nottinghillbrasserie.
com
dir: Nearest station: Notting Hill Gate. 3
mins walk from Notting Hill station

In a regency style building of 3 converted Edwardian houses, next to St Peter's church, the Notting Hill Brasserie is an elegantly understated and intimate series of dining spaces made up of 6 small rooms. Good-sized tables are dressed in white linen with high quality crockery, cutlery and glassware. Chef Karl Burdock has an impressive CV (The Square, Heston Blumenthal) and his pedigree shines through in good honest, modern cooking delivered in an unfussy manner. A well-balanced foie gras and chicken liver parfait with cherry compôte might lead onto a wonderfully fresh pan-fried fillet of halibut with potato purée, leeks and chive velouté, before a finale of chocolate fondant with just the right degree of runniness, served with brownie ice cream. The unobtrusive yet knowledgeable service gets the tone right, as does the separate bar area with its high leather-backed stools and small glass-topped occasional tables

with fake snakeskin-covered seating. This is just the kind of sophisticated and unpretentious place you would expect to find in an area like Notting Hill.

Chef Karl Burdock **Owner** Mitch Tillman **Times** 12-4/7-11 Closed Xmas, New Year **Prices** Fixed L 2 course fr £17.50, Starter £11-£14.50, Main £21-£28.50, Dessert £7-£8, Service added but optional 12.5% **Wines** 140 bottles over £20, 5 bottles under £20, 17 by glass **Notes** Sunday L, Vegetarian available, Air con **Seats** 110, Pr/dining room 44 **Children** Portions **Parking** On street

LONDON W11 *continued*

Lonsdale
PLAN 1 D4

British, European

Trendy lounge-style eatery

☎ 020 7727 4080 ▤ 020 7727 6030
48 Lonsdale Rd W11 2DE
e-mail: info@thelonsdale.co.uk
dir: Nearest station: Notting Hill/Ladbroke Grove One street parallel to Westbourne Grove. Between Portobello Rd & Ledbury Rd

Tucked away in a residential street and popular with young Notting Hill locals, this trendy evening-only venue has a fun and friendly atmosphere and youthful service. A lively cocktail bar at the front opens out into a small lounge-style eating area, with low-level dark wood tables, burgundy leather banquettes and large stools, mirror-lined walls and subdued lighting. The unfussy, modern British cooking perfectly matches the surroundings, with dishes like seared king scallops with peas and mint, St George's chicken bang bang, and caramelised vanilla rice pudding.

Times 6-12 Closed 25-26 Dec, 1 Jan, L all wk

Notting Hill Brasserie
PLAN 4 D4

⧉⧉⧉ – *see opposite page*

LONDON W14

Cibo
PLAN 1 D3

⧉⧉ Italian

Authentic Italian cooking to linger over

☎ 020 7371 2085 & 7371 6271 ▤ 020 7602 1371
3 Russell Gardens W14 8EZ
e-mail: ciborestaurant@aol.com
dir: Nearest station: Olympia, Shepherds Bush Central Line. Russell Gardens is a residential area off Holland Road, Kensington (Olympia) Shepherd's Bush

Italian proprietor; Italian staff; a fair proportion of Italian customers - it's fair to say that this relaxed Italian neighbourhood restaurant comes with solid credentials. Inside, creamy walls are hung with eye-catching Renaissance-style nude paintings, tables are draped with crisp linen and laid with boldly-coloured hand-made Italian Solimene crockery - in fact, when the sun shines and the full-length front windows fold back to open up the room to the street, you could almost imagine yourself

in Milan. Cooking is no-nonsense modern Italian fare that looks good on the plate. Top-notch ingredients are its backbone, and its strongest suits are fish, shellfish and excellent home-made filled pasta (black pasta filled with crab with a light tomato and clam sauce, for example), plus there's mussels and clams with wine, garlic and breadcrumbs, the juices mopped with a hunk of fresh olive bread.

Chef Alex Lombardi **Owner** Gino Taddei
Times 12.15-2.30/7-11 Closed Xmas, Etr BHs, L Sat, D Sun **Prices** Food prices not confirmed for 2010. Please telephone for details. **Wines** 41 bottles over £20, 5 bottles under £20, 4 by glass **Notes** Sunday L, Vegetarian available, Air con **Seats** 50, Pr/dining room 14 **Children** Portions **Parking** On street

LONDON WC1

Acorn House
PLAN 3 D5

Modern European

Eco-friendly cooking in King's Cross

☎ 020 7812 1842
69 Swinton St WC1X 9NT
dir: Nearest station: King's Cross St Pancras

Sustainability and impeccable green credentials are the cornerstones of this environmentally friendly restaurant which has its own urban vegetable garden, composting bins and sustainable energy. Located in a 1960s block, the long dining room is cool and contemporary with an open kitchen and a takeaway counter for the locals. Not surprisingly, seasonality and provenance are key to the menu with fish endorsed by the Marine Stewardship Council and an emphasis on regional produce. The modern European menu could start with smoked mackerel, heritage beetroots and pea shoots, with ravioli of Tuscan sausage, butternut squash and dolcelatte as a main course.

Times 12-3/6-10.30

Landseer British Kitchen
PLAN 3 C3

British ⧉

Elegant 1930s setting for relaxed dining

☎ 020 7347 1222 ▤ 020 7347 1001
The Bloomsbury hotel, 16-22 Great Russell St WC1B 3NN
e-mail: info@landseerbritishkitchen.com
dir: Nearest station: Tottenham Court Road

This impressive Neo-Georgian building - designed by renowned architect Sir Edwin Lutyens in the 1930s - retains bags of original features and is home to a smart, spacious and relaxed basement restaurant, the Landseer British Kitchen. Named after Lutyens (Landseer being his middle name) it has clean, traditional lines in keeping with the surroundings, as does the adjacent classic cocktail bar for aperitifs. The crowd-pleasing menu offers simply-prepared well-balanced dishes and flavours from fresh, quality home produce; take lobster bisque, 'Home Comforts' like braised Black Mountain Welsh Valley lamb

shank with mint bubble-and-squeak to 'Grills' like 28-day aged Perthshire steaks or a classic Bakewell tart finish.

Chef Paul O'Brien **Owner** The Doyle Collection **Times** 12-2.30/5-10.30 **Prices** Starter £6.50-£14, Main £13.50-£32, Dessert £6.50-£8 **Wines** 38 bottles over £20, 8 bottles under £20, 21 by glass **Notes** Pre-theatre menu, seasonal menu, Vegetarian available, Civ Wed 180, Air con **Seats** 120, Pr/dining room 30 **Children** Portions, Menu **Parking** NCP opposite the Hotel

Matsuri High Holborn
PLAN 3 E3

Japanese

Classic Japanese menu presented and served impeccably

☎ 020 7430 1970 ▤ 020 7430 1971
Mid City Place, 71 High Holborn WC1V 6EA
e-mail: eat@matsurihighholborn.co.uk
web: www.matsuri-restaurant.com
dir: Nearest station: Holborn On the corner of Red Lion St. Opposite the Renaissance Chancery Court Hotel

The matsuri in Japan are the seasonal festivals, and give their names to the various set menus at this high-end restaurant, which also has a branch in St James's. A high-tech teppan-yaki area, a dining room with standard open-to-view kitchen, and one of the longest sushi counters in the UK are the options at this Holborn corner site. Service is impeccably proper, and the menu is as weighty a tome as you would expect. Spanking-fresh nigiri and maki rolls, lunchboxes with miso soup, tempura-battered fish and vegetables, and teriyaki variations from chicken to foie gras and Wagyu beef: it's all exquisitely presented and overflowing with concentrated umami (savoury) flavour. Finish perhaps with green tea tiramisù and vanilla ice cream.

Chef H Sudoh, T Aso, S Mabalot **Owner** Matsuri Restaurant Group **Times** 12-2.30/6-10 Closed 25-26 Dec, 1 Jan, BHs, Sun **Prices** Food prices not confirmed for 2010. Please telephone for details. **Wines** 120 bottles over £20, 2 bottles under £20, 6 by glass **Notes** Fixed D 5 courses, Vegetarian available, Air con **Seats** 120, Pr/dining room 10 **Parking** On street (pay & display)

Pearl Restaurant & Bar

LONDON WC1   **PLAN 3 D3**

Modern French ☀ NOTABLE WINE LIST

Impressive cooking in opulent surroundings

☎ 020 7829 7000   📄 020 7829 9889
Renaissance Chancery Court, 252 High Holborn WC1V 7EN
e-mail: info@pearl-restaurant.com
web: www.pearl-restaurant.com
dir: Nearest station: Holborn 200 mtrs from Holborn tube station

The trails of hand-strung pearls making up the eye-catching chandeliers and the acres of walnut wood panels suggest this is somewhere a little different, somewhere opulent and glamorous. Housed in the former Pearl Assurance building, in what is now the Renaissance Chancery Court Hotel, the restaurant is as luxurious as they come. The sweeping staircases, archways and stately rooms of the building (dating from 1914) have been meticulously restored and the public areas are decorated from top to bottom in rare marble. Under Executive Chef Jun Tanaka, whom you might recognize from the TV, the modern French menu comes alive in seasonal dishes displaying great flavour combinations, skilful execution and yet more luxury. Kick things off with roast quail with a sausage roll and warm à la Greque vegetables, followed by brill with oyster tortellini, cockles, cucumber spaghetti

and seaweed and chervil velouté, and finish with dark chocolate pudding with banana bread-and-peanut butter ice cream. Classy signature cocktails and martinis, as well as an impressive 54 wines available by the glass, are served in the bar.

Chef Jun Tanaka **Owner** Hotel Property Investors **Times** 12-2.30/6-10 Closed Dec, BHs, 2 wks Aug, Sun, L Sat **Prices** Fixed L 2 course fr £26, Fixed D 3 course fr £55, Service added but optional 12.5% **Wines** 450 bottles over £20, 54 by glass **Notes** Fixed D 5 course £65, Tasting menu available, Vegetarian available, Dress restrictions, Smart casual, no trainers, Air con **Seats** 74, Pr/dining room 12 **Parking** NCP Drury Lane or on street after 6.30pm

LONDON WC1 *continued*

The Montague on the Gardens   PLAN 3 C4

Traditional British

Stylish hotel bistro with modern comfort classics

☎ 020 7637 1001   ▤ 020 7637 2516
15 Montague St, Bloomsbury WC1B 5BJ
e-mail: bookmt@rchmail.com
dir: Nearest station: Russell Square 10 minutes from Covent Garden, adjacent to the British Museum

A swish boutique hotel in the heart of Bloomsbury next to the British Museum, the Montague's Blue Door bistro offers an informal, modern bistro-style setting and menu to match. A light-and-airy space, it features mahogany panelling topped by a panoramic wall frieze of London circa 1849 and mirrored glass. Modern, accessible, comfort-dish classics are the order of the day; traditional beer-battered fish and chips, for example, with tartare sauce and mushy peas to more upmarket rack of lamb with a herb crust, dauphinoise and tomato and basil jus. Puddings follow the theme, from plum tart and clotted cream to rhubarb crumble with honeycomb ice cream.

Chef Martin Halls **Owner** Red Carnation Hotels
Times 12.30-2.30/5.30-10.30 **Prices** Fixed L 2 course fr £23.50, Fixed D 3 course fr £27.50, Starter £7-£12, Main £15-£29, Dessert £6-£10, Service added but optional 12.5% **Wines** 61 bottles over £20, 7 bottles under £20, 19 by glass **Notes** Pre-theatre, Business & Al fresco menu available, Sunday L, Vegetarian available, Civ Wed 90, Air con **Seats** 45, Pr/dining room 100 **Children** Portions, Menu **Parking** On street, Bloomsbury Square

Pearl Restaurant & Bar   PLAN 3 D3

— *see opposite page*

— *see opposite page*

LONDON WC2

L'Atelier de Joel Robuchon   PLAN 3 C2

— *see below*

Axis at One Aldwych   PLAN 3 D2

Modern British

Dramatic, contemporary dining in the heart of theatreland

☎ 020 7300 0300 & 7300 1000   ▤ 020 7300 0301
1 Aldwych WC2B 4RH
e-mail: axis@onealdwych.com
web: www.onealdwych.com/axis
dir: Nearest station: Covent Garden, Charing Cross At junct of Aldwych & The Strand opposite Waterloo Bridge. On corner of Aldwych & Wellington St, opposite Lyceum Theatre

One Aldwych is a fine, sophisticated hotel in the former home of the *Morning Post*, right opposite Waterloo Bridge and close to Covent Garden. Of two dining options, Axis is a dramatic double-height space, with a vast cityscape

continued

L'Atelier de Joel Robuchon

LONDON WC2   PLAN 3 C2

French

Slick, sexy sophistication from French super-chef

☎ 020 7010 8600   ▤ 020 7010 8601
13-15 West St WC2H 9HE
e-mail: info@joelrobuchon.co.uk
dir: Nearest station: Leicester Square/Covent Garden Left off Cambridge Circus & Shaftesbury Av

Some people can't just slip quietly into early retirement. After being crowned with every accolade under the gastronomic sun, legendary French über-chef Joël Robuchon returned with his 'Atelier' concept to take on the restaurant world again. By rolling out the Atelier stable in the glitz of Paris, Tokyo, New York and Monaco, M Robuchon clearly aims for high-profile glamour. And the London operation serves up self-conscious glamour in large portions; sleek staff clad in designer black like Bond-villain henchpersons lurk in a dimly-lit, futuristic crimson and black Yakuza-chic lair of lacquer, glass and black granite on the ground-floor. Here, the meaning of Atelier - 'workshop' - becomes apparent: high stools at the counter are ringside seats for watching the chefs at work in an open kitchen, turning out innovative miniature tasting dishes of intensely-flavoured, classically-prepared food. The first floor dining room, La Cuisine, is a brighter space sporting a monochrome chequerboard theme and is the place to eat if you're happier with the traditional three-course format (although you can do this on the ground floor too). Food here is deeply rooted in French classics, despite obvious inspiration drawn from Spain and Japan, so expect luxury ingredients, first-class produce, and combinations that veer from simple and classic to complex and innovative. Crabmeat and lobster jelly are served simply with shallots and flat parsley; a superbly-cooked veal sweetbread sits on a bed of Savoy cabbage, pine kernel, almond and pistachio. Don't skip dessert - a passionfruit soufflé with hazelnut ice cream and dried fruit hits another high note.

Chef Olivier Limousin **Owner** Bahia UK Ltd
Times 12-3/5.30-11 **Prices** Food prices not confirmed for 2010. Please telephone for details, Service added but optional 12.5% **Wines** 250 bottles over £20, 10 bottles under £20, 26 by glass **Notes** Tasting menu 9 course, Pre-theatre 2/3 course, Vegetarian available, Air con **Seats** 43 **Children** Portions **Parking** Valet parking service

LONDON WC2 *continued*

mural on one wall by the artist Richard Walker entitled 'Secret City'. It's an impressive contemporary dining space, replete with black leather upholstery and muted colours, a sweeping staircase entrance, and 92 slender birch trunks made of satin nickel, which create a striking backdrop. The modern British menu embraces quality seasonal ingredients from top-notch regional and organic suppliers, and dishes are prepared with imagination and simplicity. Take seared scallops with onion purée, glazed oxtail and braised lentils to start, with spiced monkfish tail with roast garlic, confit potato and curry velouté for main course, and treacle tart with clotted cream for pudding.

Chef Tony Fleming **Owner** Gordon Campbell Gray **Times** 12-2.30/5.30-10.45 Closed Xmas, New Year, Etr, Sun, L Sat **Prices** Fixed L 2 course £16.75, Fixed D 3 course £19.75, Service added but optional 12.5% **Wines** 126 bottles over £20, 1 bottles under £20, 12 by glass **Notes** Pre & post theatre D & Fixed price L menu available, Vegetarian available, Civ Wed 60, Air con **Seats** 120, Pr/dining room 40 **Children** Portions, Menu **Parking** NCP - Wellington St

Christopher's
PLAN 3 D2

◉ Contemporary American

Victorian grandeur meets contemporary American cooking

☎ 020 7240 4222   ▤ 020 7240 3357
18 Wellington St, Covent Garden WC2E 7DD
e-mail: coventgarden@christophersgrill.com
dir: Nearest station: Embankment/Covent Garden Just by Strand, overlooking Waterloo Bridge

This contemporary American restaurant occupies an elegant Victorian building which was once London's first licensed casino, in the heart of Covent Garden. Downstairs is a lively martini bar, while the large restaurant is accessed via a sweeping stone staircase. Period features like high ceilings and tall windows combine with a contemporary décor of bold colours and polished wood floors. The menu offers a selection of grilled steaks and fish, as well as more imaginative options. Start with Maryland crab cake or classic Caesar salad, and move onto surf 'n' turf or pan-fried fillet of sea bass, followed by New York cheesecake. Theatre menus and weekend brunch are popular.

Chef Francis Agyepong **Owner** Christopher Gilmour **Times** 12-3/5-11 Closed 24 Dec-2 Jan, 25-26 Dec, 1 Jan, D Sun **Prices** Fixed D 3 course £19.50, Starter £6-£14, Main £12.50-£36, Dessert £7.25-£7.50, Service added but optional 12.5% **Wines** 122 bottles over £20, 27 bottles under £20, 12 by glass **Notes** Sunday brunch available, Air con **Seats** 110, Pr/dining room 40 **Children** Portions, Menu

Clos Maggiore
PLAN 3 C2

◉◉◉ – *see opposite page*

Imperial China
PLAN 3 B2

◉ Chinese

Sophisticated Cantonese cooking meets contemporary décor in Chinatown

☎ 020 7734 3388
White Bear Yard, 25a Lisle St WC2H 7BA
e-mail: mail@imperial-china.co.uk
dir: Nearest station: Leicester Sq From station into Little Newport St, straight ahead into Lisle St, right into White Bear Yard

From bustling Lisle Street go through glass doors into a peaceful courtyard with a Chinese-style bridge over a pond of Koi carp, and on into the dining room with its modern wood panelling, lighting and artwork. Linen tablecloths, black chairs upholstered in gold fabric, and smartly dressed staff complete the sophisticated look. Skilfully prepared and attractively presented Cantonese cuisine, including an extensive range of dim sum, draws the crowds, including Chinese Londoners. From the similarly lengthy carte, expect lobster soup, braised abalone in oyster sauce, or roast duck Cantonese style.

Times 12-11.30 Closed 24-25 Dec

Incognico
PLAN 3 C2

◉ French, Italian

Franco-Italian food in the heart of theatreland

☎ 020 7836 8866   ▤ 020 7240 9525
117 Shaftesbury Av, Cambridge Circus WC2H 8AD
e-mail: incognicorestaurant@gmail.com
dir: Nearest station: Leicester Sq Off Cambridge Circus at crossing with Charing Cross Rd, opposite Palace Theatre

This charming French brasserie-style restaurant on Shaftesbury Avenue is popular for pre- and post-theatre dining. The very handsome interior is decked out with red leather chairs and banquettes, dark-wood panelling, globe lights, stripped wooden floors, mirrors, and a mixture of round and square tables laid with crisp white linen. The Franco-Italian cooking offers classic dishes such as rump of lamb with a spinach flan, diced tomato and tarragon jus, alongside others with a more modern slant like fillet of mackerel, beetroot, new potatoes and wasabi, and desserts extend to Amaretto crème brûlée.

Times 12-3/5.30-11 Closed 10 days Xmas, 4 days Etr, BHs, Sun

Indigo
PLAN 3 D2

◉ Modern European

Trendy mezzanine dining with a buzzy atmosphere

☎ 020 7300 0400 & 7300 1000   ▤ 020 7300 1001
One Aldwych WC2B 4RH
e-mail: indigo@onealdwych.com
web: www.onealdwych.com/indigo
dir: Nearest station: Covent Garden, Charing Cross Located where The Aldwych meets The Strand opposite Waterloo Bridge. On corner of Aldwych & Wellington St, opposite Lyceum Theatre

The mezzanine setting overlooking the Lobby Bar of the rather glamorous (and fantastically located) One Aldwych hotel makes Indigo the perfect place for people watching, but moreover it's a great spot for everything from breakfast to dinner, and especially handy for pre- and post-theatre dining. It's no slouch in the style stakes either: smart chairs, good use of lighting and a professional yet relaxed attitude from the staff give it a contemporary feel. The lively menu of modern European dishes, based on good produce, suits the informal atmosphere, so seared Scottish scallops come with crispy pork belly, sweetcorn purée and jus gras in a suitably fashionable starter, while pot-roasted monkfish cheeks, white beans, chorizo and piquillo pepper stew is a rustic main course.

Chef Tony Fleming **Owner** Gordon Campbell Gray **Times** 12-3/5.30-11.15 **Prices** Fixed D 3 course £19.75, Service added but optional 12.5% **Wines** 44 bottles over £20, 3 bottles under £20, 13 by glass **Notes** Sat & Sun brunch menu, Pre/post-theatre D available, Vegetarian available, Civ Wed 60, Air con **Seats** 62 **Children** Portions, Menu **Parking** Valet parking

Clos Maggiore

Modern French V NOTABLE WINE LIST

Romantic and classy Covent Garden restaurant

☎ 020 7379 9696   📠 020 7379 6767
33 King St, Covent Garden WC2E 8JD
e-mail: enquiries@closmaggiore.com
dir: Nearest station: Covent Garden 1 min walk from The Piazza & Royal Opera House

Right in the heart of Covent Garden, this classy, romantic restaurant in a Georgian townhouse, with its mulberry-coloured frontage, is, once you're inside, reminiscent of a stylish country inn in Provence or Tuscany. Warm colours abound in the intimate dining room with its smoked mirrors and wooden floors, plus, if you're after a bit of romance, there's a blossom-filled courtyard with flowers and box hedging (a fully opening glass roof slides back to reveal the stars). The Provençale décor complements the cooking from the talented Marcellin Marc, his appealing French cookery grounded in his classical training and based on top quality produce. Pan-fried duck foie gras and stuffed chicken wing is a good place to start, then perhaps slow-cooked fillet of Cornish cod glazed with ricotta cheese and chive. European artisan cheeses and lemon chiboust cream and pistachio feuillantine round things off nicely, while a stunning wine list offers something to suit every pocket.

Chef Marcellin Marc **Owner** Tyfoon Restaurants Ltd **Times** 12-2.30/5-11 Closed 24-26 Dec & 1 Jan, L Sat-Sun **Prices** Fixed L 2 course £19.50, Fixed D 3 course £19.50-£24.50, Tasting menu fr £55, Starter £6.50-£12.90, Main £16.50-£19.80, Dessert fr £5.90, Service added but optional 12.5% **Wines** 1900 bottles over £20, 50 bottles under £20, 15 by glass **Notes** Fixed 2 course L & D incl 1/2 bottle of wine, Vegetarian menu, Dress restrictions, Smart casual, Civ Wed 150, Air con **Seats** 70, Pr/dining room 26 **Children** Portions **Parking** NCP, on street

LONDON WC2 continued

The Ivy
PLAN 3 C2

British, International

Ever-popular Theatreland legend with brasserie-style menu

☎ 020 7836 4751   📄 020 7240 9333
1 West St, Covent Garden WC2H 9NQ
dir: Nearest station: Leicester Square

Thriving on its celeb-hangout status, getting a table here still isn't easy. Given the reputation, first-timers might find the room remarkably low key, with its club-like oak panelling, green leather seating, wooden floors and harlequin-like stained glass. However, there is a sense of occasion when eating at The Ivy, with non-celebs hoping the glamour will rub off on them. It can be a high-volume, bustling, sometimes hectic experience, but staff take it all in their stride and get the job done with dedicated efficiency. The lengthy, brasserie-style comfort menu pleases all comers, delivering simple but accomplished favourites (steak and kidney pie or kedgeree) alongside more challenging plates (perhaps rabbit and Parma ham served with Tuscan cavolo nero and polenta). Desserts are as homespun as treacle tart and baked Alaska.

Times 12-3/5.30-12 Closed 25-26 Dec, 1 Jan, Aug BH, L 27 Dec, D 24 Dec

J. Sheekey
PLAN 3 C2

Fish, Seafood

Renowned theatreland fish restaurant

☎ 020 7240 2565   📄 020 7497 0891
St Martin's Court WC2N 4AL
e-mail: reservations@j-sheekey.co.uk
dir: Nearest station: Leicester Square

The buzzing atmosphere and charmingly old-school service are reason enough to book a table at this legendary fish restaurant, which started life in 1896 as Josef Sheekey's oyster bar and is these days owned by Caprice Holdings (The Ivy, Scott's - see entries). It has expanded gradually over the decades into the neighbouring buildings and today there are four adjoining dining rooms, plus a seafood and oyster bar, all decked out in traditional style with wood panelling and tiled floors. As befits the location, and the restaurant's historic and (in many cases) current clientele, pictures of stars of the stage and screen decorate the walls. Fish and seafood, simply prepared, is the order of the day, although meat-eaters and vegetarians are well catered for. A classic crab bisque is full-flavoured, with just the right balance of cream and Cognac, while fried haddock is as fresh as can be, with a crisp, light batter.

Times 12-3/5.30-12 Closed 25-26 Dec, 1 Jan, Aug BH, D 24 Dec

Mon Plaisir
PLAN 3 C2

French

A Francophile's delight in theatreland

☎ 020 7836 7243   & 020 7240 3757   📄 020 7240 4774
19-21 Monmouth St WC2H 9DD
e-mail: monplaisirrestaurant@googlemail.com
dir: Nearest station: Covent Garden, Leicester Square Off Seven Dials

With its name and tricolour flag fluttering outside, this veteran of more than half a century is a haven of joie de vivre and about as French as it comes this side of the Channel. The entrance may be unassuming and the original front dining room little changed, but beyond there is a network of cosy rooms (including a mezzanine-style loft) decked out with a mix of French posters and artefacts, and modern abstracts and mirrors. The menu mixes the times too, offering classics such as cassolette d'escargots alongside the likes of roasted cod with butter beans and bacon. Closely-packed tables and resolutely French service create a lively atmosphere.

Chef Frank Raymond **Owner** Alain Lhermitte
Times 12-2.15/5.45-11.15 Closed Xmas, New Year, BHs, Sun, L Sat **Prices** Food prices not confirmed for 2010. Please telephone for details. **Wines** 70 bottles over £20, 19 bottles under £20, 13 by glass **Notes** Pre-theatre menu inc. glass of house wine/coffee, Vegetarian available, Dress restrictions, Smart casual, Air con **Seats** 100, Pr/dining room 28 **Children** Portions

Orso Restaurant
PLAN 3 D2

Modern Italian

Italian food in a buzzing basement

☎ 020 7240 5269   📄 020 7497 2148
27 Wellington St WC2E 7DA
e-mail: info@orsorestaurant.co.uk
dir: Nearest station: Covent Garden

The cavernous basement room was an orchid warehouse in a former life, but for nearly 25 years it's been home to Orso, and satisfying visitors to Covent Garden with its brand of vibrant Italian cooking. Discreet etched-glass

doors lead on to the stairway bedecked with black-and-white photos of stars of stage and screen. Open all day, the place reverberates with a buzz of conversation and the clinking of glasses. The crowd-pleasing menu showcases regional Italian cooking and offers bags of choice, from pizza (goats' cheese and roasted garlic, for example) and pasta (linguine with king prawns and hot peppers) to secondi piatti such as roast venison with cranberries and mashed celeriac. A pre-theatre menu and weekend brunch offer excellent value.

Chef Martin Wilson **Owner** Orso Restaurants Ltd
Times noon-midnight Closed 24-25 Dec, L Sat-Sun (Jul-Aug) **Prices** Fixed D 3 course £18, Starter £5.50-£11.50, Main £10.50-£19.50, Dessert £6, Service added but optional 12.5%, Groups min 8 service 12.5% **Wines** 46 bottles over £20, 10 by glass **Notes** Pre-theatre D available 2 or 3 course, Sunday L, Vegetarian available, Air con **Seats** 100 **Parking** On street

The Portrait Restaurant
PLAN 3 C1

Modern British

Sleek, contemporary, buzzy dining with rooftop views

☎ 020 7312 2490   📄 020 7925 0244
National Portrait Gallery, St Martins Place WC2H 0HE
e-mail: portrait.restaurant@searcys.co.uk
dir: Nearest station: Leicester Square, Charing Cross Just behind Trafalgar Square

Offering a jaw-dropping London landscape from the top of the national gallery of portraits, this sleek, light and contemporary restaurant certainly pulls in the crowds. A wall of windows means everyone gets an outlook, including Nelson's-eye views up Whitehall to Westminster, while an otherwise minimalist grey, cream and black colour scheme is interrupted only by the warmth of red leather high-back banquettes and a blond-wood floor. The modern bistro-style fare takes an equally light, simple, clean-lined approach, perhaps featuring fashionable cuts like Suffolk Middlewhite pork belly served with Savoy cabbage, parsnip and bacon, or maybe pollock, accompanied by monk's beard (a type of chicory), brown shrimps and lemon and horseradish butter. Be warned though, the hard surfaces and a bar up front ratchet up the decibels.

Times 11.45-2.45/5.30-8.30 Closed 24-26 Dec, 1 Jan, D Sat-Wed

The Strand
PLAN 3 C1

British, French

Contemporary cooking in landmark railway hotel

☎ 020 7747 8406   & 020 7747 8410   📄 020 7747 8431
Charing Cross Hotel, The Strand WC2N 5HX
e-mail: vidur.kapur@guoman.co.uk
dir: Nearest station: Charing Cross. Next to Charing Cross

The Charing Cross Hotel has been standing at the entrance to Charing Cross station since 1865. It's a grand building with ornate, high-ceilinged rooms with tall windows and inlaid floors, all harking back to the luxury of a bygone age. In recent years the grade II listed hotel has been completely refurbished to bring it fully into the 21st century, but without detriment to any of its magnificent period features. The elegant Strand boasts superb views across London, and is the setting for some contemporary European cuisine. Start with the duck and orange parfait, followed by a herb risotto, and hot apple and brandy crumble to finish.

Chef Franck Siblas **Times** 12-3/5-10 **Prices** Fixed L 2 course £25.95, Fixed D 3 course £29.95, Starter £7.50-£10.45, Main £16.50-£22.50, Dessert £6.50-£7.50, Service added but optional 12.5% **Wines** 15 by glass **Notes** Vegetarian available, Dress restrictions, Smart casual, Civ Wed 120, Air con **Seats** 30 **Children** Portions

Terroirs
PLAN 3 C1

Modern European NEW

Rustic French cooking in the heart of London

☎ 020 7036 0660
5 William IV St, Covent Garden WC2N 4DW
dir: Nearest station: Covent Garden, Embankment

With its rustic décor of prints and old signs, you could be forgiven for thinking you have entered a wine bar in a Paris back street, rather than just off The Strand in London's West End. Set across two levels with a bar taking up most of the lower part, this informal, lively bistro is the real deal when it comes to authentic French cooking. Start with slices of excellent terrine or saucisson from the charcuterie menu and then tuck into small plates of French classics like snails, bacon, garlic and parsley or even a whole Dorset crab. A concise plats du jour runs to bavette, shallots and red wine or pot-roasted quail, Italian artichokes, pancetta and gremolata. This is simple stuff, but produce is king and the flavours hit the mark. Desserts such as apricot and almond tart or pannacotta, blood orange and campari are no slouches and the wine list, with a focus on organic and biodynamic growers, is worth exploring.

Times 12-11 Closed Sun

32 Great Queen Street
PLAN 3 D3

British

The best of British at bustling Covent Garden gastro-pub

☎ 020 7242 0622 📠 020 7404 9582
32 Great Queen St WC2B 5AA
e-mail: greatqueenstreet@googlemail.com
dir: Nearest station: Covent Garden, Holborn

With connections to two of London's most iconic foodie boozers, The Eagle and the Anchor & Hope, 32 Great Queen Street has the same vibrant atmosphere and unpretentious style, and, more importantly, the same robust, straightforwardly appealing food. The pub-style room, done out in classic gastro-pub burgundy, thrums with conversation from the tightly packed tables (it can be noisy). Good quality produce shines out in everything from the refreshingly simple crab on toast to the Hereford

beef (rib or sirloin) to share. Brawn and ham hock terrine is great to see (and eat), Arbroath smokie is deliciously savoury, and buttermilk pudding with rhubarb a fine seasonal finish.

Chef Tom Norrington-Davies **Owner** R Shaw, T Norrington-Davies, J Jones, M Belben **Times** 12-2.30/6-10.30 Closed last working day in Dec-1st working day in Jan, BHs, L Mon, D Sun **Prices** Starter £4-£8, Main £10.80-£25, Dessert £2.80-£5, Service optional **Wines** 20 bottles over £20, 25 bottles under £20, 13 by glass **Notes** Sunday L, Vegetarian available **Seats** 70

12 Temple Place Restaurant
PLAN 3 E2

Modern British NEW

Innovative modern British cooking in individually styled hotel

☎ 020 7836 3555 & 7300 1700 📠 020 7379 4547
Swissotel The Howard, London, Temple Place WC2R 2PR
e-mail: 12templeplacerestaurant.london@swissotel.com
dir: Nearest station: Temple Opposite Temple tube station

12 Temple Place is the restaurant in the centrally-placed Swissôtel. The décor is a definite style statement, a cross-over between Regency splendour and contemporary designer flourishes. The walls are decorated in bold patterned wallpaper and the quirkiness extends to rag-cloth wrapped teapots used as vases on the tables. A 50-cover garden courtyard provides a wonderfully serene setting with waterfalls and lush with plant life. The tasting and à la carte menus are as bold and individual as the décor, with modern Britishness and top-quality produce at the heart of things. Crispy veal sweetbreads, for example, served with braised endive and mushroom salad, make for a good start, while roast Buccleuch beef fillet comes with an oxtail and bone marrow pie, shallot purée and pied-de-mouton. Earl Grey flavoured chocolate fondant with orange marmalade ice cream is an appealing combination at dessert. Flavoured beers and speciality British lagers are available to match the food.

Chef Brian Spark **Owner** New Ray Ltd
Times 12-2.30/5.45-10.30 Closed 1st wk Jan, BHs, Sun, L Sat **Prices** Fixed L 2 course £19.75, Fixed D 3 course fr £25, Starter £8-£12, Main £17.50-£24.50, Dessert £7.75, Service added but optional 12.5% **Wines** 120 bottles over £20, 10 by glass **Notes** Tasting menu 5 course, Vegetarian available, Dress restrictions, Smart, casual, Civ Wed 100, Air con **Seats** 56 **Parking** 30

GREATER LONDON

BARNET
Map 6 TQ29

Savoro

Modern European

Simply executed cooking in one of the district's oldest restaurants

☎ 020 8449 9888 📠 020 8449 7444
206 High St EN5 5SZ
e-mail: savoro@savoro.co.uk
web: www.savoro.co.uk
dir: M25 junct 23 to A1081, continue to St Albans Rd, at lights turn left to A1000

Over the years, these premises have fulfilled a number of diverse functions, having been an inn, boathouse, bakery, curiosity shop and traditional tea rooms. Now kitted out with contemporary design - glass screens, tiled floor, concealed lighting - they are the very image of a modern neighbourhood restaurant. 'Simple execution of good technique' is the kitchen's motto, demonstrable in dishes such as smoked venison carpaccio garnished with a quail egg, manchego and spiced red wine jelly, butterflied trout fillets with braised quinoa, roasted salsify and wild garlic purée, and perhaps a seasonal spin on knickerbocker glory to finish.

Chef Robert Brown **Owner** Jack Antoni **Times** 12-3/6-11 Closed 1 Jan, 1 wk New Year, D Sun **Prices** Starter £4.95, Main £14, Dessert £5, Service added but optional 10% **Wines** 20 bottles over £20, 12 bottles under £20, 12 by glass **Notes** Early eve menu Mon-Thu 2 course £10.50, Sunday L, Vegetarian available, Air con **Seats** 68 **Children** Portions **Parking** 9

Chapter One

Modern European — NOTABLE WINE LIST

Sumptuous contemporary design with food to match

☎ 01689 854848   📠 01689 858439
Farnborough Common, Locksbottom BR6 8NF
e-mail: info@chaptersrestaurants.com
dir: On A21, 3m from Bromley. From M25 junct 4 onto A21 for 5m

Housed in a Tudor-style building, Chapter One is nevertheless a cutting-edge contemporary restaurant in both its design and its culinary approach. A restaurant of one sort or another has been located here for around a century, but none can have looked quite so stylish as the vision that greets us today. The fine-dining room is a series of shimmering spaces created by the use of beaded curtains against a low-lit backdrop of deep, rich cherry, chocolate and cream tones, while the bar is constructed from German alabaster and volcanic rock. Foodie pictures remind us why we're here, and there is also a less formal brasserie area with bare tables and a simpler menu. Andrew McLeish's cooking tacks to the classical side of haute cuisine, but with a modern sensibility for quality ingredients and swish presentation. Roasted Scottish langoustines appear with crushed ratte potatoes mixed with some of the claw meat to create a visually stunning opener, set off with a parmesan tuile. Today's slow cooking is used to productive effect in dishes such as tenderly braised oxtail with pancetta, spinach and delightful puréed parsnip, or roasted pork belly with choucroute, baby leeks and caramelised onions. Fine technique is also evident in a thin-based lemon tart, from the evenly brittle glaze to the profundity of the lush filling, and crème fraîche sorbet makes a great accompaniment to it. Or try pear sablé with Poire William sauce and bitter chocolate ice cream. Home-made breads add to the sense of satisfaction.

Chef Andrew McLeish **Owner** Selective Restaurants Group
Times 12-2.30/6.30-10.30 Closed 1-4 Jan **Prices** Fixed L 3 course fr £18.50, Starter £4.50-£7, Main £14-£16, Dessert £4.50-£6, Service added but optional 12.5% **Wines** 133 bottles over £20, 17 bottles under £20, 10 by glass **Notes** Sunday L, Vegetarian available, Dress restrictions, No shorts, jeans or trainers, Air con **Seats** 120, Pr/dining room 55 **Children** Portions **Parking** 90

BECKENHAM

See LONDON SECTION plan 1-G1

Mello

◎◎ Modern European

Fashionable dining near suburban high street

☎ 020 8663 0994 📠 020 8663 3674
2 Southend Rd BR3 1SD
e-mail: info@mello.uk.com
web: www.mello.uk.com
dir: 0.5m from Beckenham town centre, directly opposite Beckenham train station

Beckenham is not where you normally go to look for imaginative, modern cuisine, but Mello is worth the detour into the 'burbs'. The Victorian listed building near the station looks good inside, with its high-backed leather and suede chairs and contemporary art on claret and honey-hued walls, and the kitchen clearly has the skill and self-assurance to work with top-class materials and produce clear-flavoured, elegantly-presented dishes. Classical roots underpin an appealing, broad-ranging modern European repertoire that might kick off with pan-seared scallops with smoked haddock cake and fig purée, then continue with pan-roasted fillet of English beef with braised and pressed oxtail, parsnip purée and crisps and Madeira jus. To finish, apple and cinnamon tarte Tatin with cinnamon ice cream gets the thumbs up.

Times 12-2.30/6-10 Closed D Sun

BROMLEY

See LONDON SECTION plan 1-G1

Chapter One

◎◎◎◎ – *see opposite page*

ENFIELD

Map 6 TQ39

Royal Chace Hotel

◎ Traditional British

Attractive hotel brasserie

☎ 020 8884 8181 📠 020 8884 8150
The Ridgeway EN2 8AR
e-mail: reservations@royalchacehotel.co.uk
dir: 3m from M25 junct 24, 1.5m to Enfield

Backing onto open fields in a peaceful north London location, the Royal Chace stands in 6 acres and is conveniently placed for the M25. The smart brasserie restaurant combines traditional furnishings with contemporary décor, while seasonal menus blend classic British dishes with new ideas, and presentation is imaginative, with thought given to colour and texture. Seared scallops on cauliflower purée with pancetta and watercress dressing, beef medallions on chive mash with parsley sauce, and vanilla pannacotta show the style. Less formal meals and snacks are served in the King's Bar and Lounge.

Chef Andy Stickings **Owner** B Nicholas **Times** 7-10 Closed Xmas, BH Mon, Mon, L Tue-Sat, D Sun **Prices** Starter £5-£7.95, Main £13.75-£19.95, Dessert £5.25, Service added but optional 10% **Wines** 14 bottles over £20, 24 bottles under £20, 6 by glass **Notes** Sunday L, Vegetarian available, Dress restrictions, No jeans or trainers, Civ Wed 220, Air con **Seats** 120, Pr/dining room 50 **Children** Portions, Menu **Parking** 220

HADLEY WOOD

Map 6 TQ29

The Mary Beale Restaurant

◎◎ Modern British 🍃

Solid British cooking in tranquil country-house hotel

☎ 020 8216 3900 📠 020 8216 3937
West Lodge Park Hotel, Cockfosters Rd EN4 0PY
e-mail: westlodgepark@bealeshotels.co.uk
dir: On A111, 1m S of M25 junct 24

Family-run, this charming country-house hotel may be a stone's throw from the M25, but it occupies a peaceful spot surrounded by 35 acres of fabulous parkland and gardens. It even has its own arboretum with 800 different species of trees from around the world. The newly refurbished Mary Beale Restaurant and Terrace Bar incorporates a contemporary feel with a reminder of the building's history in the form of original paintings, many by the painter Mary Beale herself. This mix of traditional and modern is echoed by the style of service and contemporary British cuisine. You might start with Cromer crab tian with avocado sorbet and gazpacho and move on to Gloucestershire Old Spot braised belly pork with roast fillet, sage mash and apple jelly.

Chef Wayne Turner **Owner** Beales Ltd **Times** 12.30-2.30/7-9.30 **Prices** Fixed L 2 course £15, Fixed D 3 course £25, Starter £7-£11, Main £14-£24, Dessert £7-£9, Service optional **Wines** 51 bottles over £20, 24 bottles under £20, 7 by glass **Notes** Sunday L, Vegetarian available, Dress restrictions, Smart casual, jacket & tie recommended, Civ Wed 72, Air con **Seats** 70, Pr/dining room 54 **Children** Portions **Parking** 75

HARROW ON THE HILL

See LONDON SECTION Plan 1-B5

Incanto Restaurant

◎ Modern Italian

Friendly Italian restaurant with a delicatessen

☎ 020 8426 6767 📠 020 8423 5087
41 High St HA1 3HT
e-mail: info@incanto.co.uk
web: www.incanto.co.uk

The 19th-century post office in historic Harrow on the Hill has been lovingly restored and converted to a modern Italian restaurant. Its stylish interior boasts a beautiful antique chandelier and full-length glass skylights, as well as wooden beams and floors and a spiral staircase. The authentic southern Italian cooking gives fresh seasonal British produce a contemporary Italian twist. Try slow-cooked British wild boar, red wine and chestnut raviolone with spicy nduja butter, or pan-fried wild black sea bass on a bed of spinach with potato and truffle dumplings, and red wine and wild mushroom sauce.

Chef Franco Montone **Owner** David Taylor & Catherine Chiu **Times** 12-2.30/6.30-11 Closed 25-26 Dec, 1 Jan, Etr Sun, Mon, D Sun **Prices** Fixed L 2 course £15.95, Fixed D 3 course £22.50, Starter £5.50-£7.95, Main £13.50-£18.95, Dessert £5.25-£6.95, Service added but optional 10% **Wines** 34 bottles over £20, 11 bottles under £20, 8 by glass **Notes** Tasting menu available, Sunday L, Vegetarian available, Air con **Seats** 64, Pr/dining room 30 **Children** Portions, Menu **Parking** On street

HARROW WEALD

See LONDON SECTION plan 1-B6

Grim's Dyke Hotel

◎◎ Modern British

Peaceful country-house conveniently close to London

☎ 020 8385 3100 📠 020 8954 4560
Old Redding HA3 6SH
e-mail: reservations@grimsdyke.com
dir: 3m from M1 between Harrow & Watford

The late 19th-century house is set within 40 acres of glorious gardens and parkland and Sir William Gilbert of Gilbert & Sullivan fame lived here for 20 years. The imposing Grade II listed mansion is now an elegant country-house hotel and is filled with memorabilia

continued

HARROW WEALD *continued*

associated with Gilbert's famous productions. The sumptuously decorated dining room overlooks the garden and boasts original features like ornate ceilings, traditional wallpapers and cathedral-like windows, and the traditional feel continues with gleaming cutlery and glasses on linen-dressed tables. Refined classic British cooking with a modern twist follows the seasons and is influenced by what is available from the hotel's kitchen garden. Typically, begin with chicken liver parfait with bacon and onion brioche, follow with seared salmon with Jerusalem artichoke risotto, and finish with chocolate tart with honey and parsnip ice cream.

Chef Daren Mason **Owner** Skerrits of Nottingham Holdings **Times** 12.30-2/7-9.30 Closed 24 Dec, 1 Jan, L Sat, D 25-26 Dec **Prices** Food prices not confirmed for 2010. Please telephone for details. **Wines** 70 bottles over £20, 10 bottles under £20, 10 by glass **Notes** Sunday L, Dress restrictions, No jeans or trainers (Fri-Sat), Civ Wed 88 **Seats** 60, Pr/dining room 88 **Children** Portions, Menu **Parking** 100

HEATHROW AIRPORT (LONDON)

See LONDON SECTION plan 1-A3

Sheraton Skyline Hotel

◉ Italian, International NEW

Modern Italian cooking in a stylish hotel restaurant

☎ 020 8564 3300 & 020 8759 2535 📄 020 8750 9154
Bath Rd, Hayes UB3 5BP
e-mail: jirayr.kececian@sheraton.com
dir: M4 junct 4 towards Terminals 1,2 & 3. Follow signs for A4 London entering Bath Rd, hotel 1m on left

Why jump on a flight all the way to Italy when you don't need to leave Heathrow for authentic Italian cooking in this upmarket hotel? The Sheraton is no looker from the outside, but inside, its Al Dente Ristorante is a different story. It is a wide-open airy space with a clean-cut contemporary look and warm lighting to soften the edges. Modern Italian cuisine is taken seriously here, so tables are laid with good quality olive oil and balsamic, Parma ham is carved on the bone and parmesan hewn from a huge wheel. The menu offers all the old favourites, with some clever new takes on classical dishes. To start, grilled Portobello mushrooms are served with a tasty and effective dressing of basil and olive oil, then a fine piece of oven-baked sea bass comes with a ragôut of mussels and prawns. For dessert, what else than a classic tiramisù, and they do serve a very fine example here.

Chef Marco di Tullio **Owner** Host Hotels & Resorts TRS UK Holdings Ltd **Times** 12-3/6-10.45 **Prices** Fixed L 2 course £18-£35, Fixed D 3 course £20-£45, Starter £6-£10, Main £15-£25, Dessert £5-£7 **Wines** 30+ bottles over £20, 15 by glass **Notes** Vegetarian available, Civ Wed 300, Air con **Seats** 80, Pr/dining room 10 **Children** Portions, Menu **Parking** 300

KEW

See LONDON SECTION plan 1-C3

The Glasshouse

◉◉◉ – see below

KINGSTON UPON THAMES

See LONDON SECTION plan 1-C1

Ayudhya Thai Restaurant

◉ Thai

Authentic, neighbourhood Thai in the heart of suburbia

☎ 020 8546 5878 & 020 8549 5984
14 Kingston Hill KT2 7NH
dir: 0.5m from Kingston town centre on A308; 2.5m from Robin Hood rdbt at junction of A3

Unassumingly set in a small parade of shops, this charmingly authentic, long-established Thai transports you to another continent with its pitched roof lines and traditional, dark-wood-panelled interior. Wood carvings, original artefacts, lantern-style lighting and Thai royal family pictures continue the illusion, complemented by oriental music and polite, authentic service. The mind-

The Glasshouse

KEW

Modern European 🍴 NOTABLE WINE LIST

Local favourite with confident, modern cooking

☎ 020 8940 6777 📄 020 8940 3833
14 Station Pde TW9 3PZ
e-mail: info@glasshouserestaurant.co.uk
dir: Please telephone for directions

Located next to Kew Gardens tube station, this busy neighbourhood restaurant is sister to acclaimed Wandsworth eatery Chez Bruce (see entry). A smart and elegant space with a bright and breezy contemporary décor, it draws a mix of loyal devotees. The precise, confident cooking is driven by seasonality and the imaginative dishes are unfussy and modern, flavours are well defined and the cooking displays a lightness of touch. Take a warm salad of wood pigeon with balsamic

vinegar and deep-fried truffled egg, or perhaps a ragout of smoked haddock, king prawn and mussels with vermicelli, crème fraîche and chives. To finish, home-made vanilla yogurt with rhubarb and raspberry and sherry trifle vie for attention. The appealing menus come at fixed prices (and includes a seven-course tasting option), while the wine list is top-notch, with a good choice available by the glass.

Chef Anthony Boyd **Owner** Larkbrace Ltd
Times 12-2.30/6.30-10.30 Closed Xmas, New Year,
Prices Fixed L 2 course £18.50-£24.50, Fixed D 3 course £37.50, Tasting menu £50, Service added but optional 12.5% **Wines** 376 bottles over £20, 5 bottles under £20, 13 by glass **Notes** Tasting menu Mon-Fri evening, Sunday L, Vegetarian available, Air con **Seats** 60 **Children** Portions, Menu **Parking** On street; metered

bogglingly long menu offers over 100 dishes including desserts, so be prepared to spend time making your choice. Perhaps try red chicken curry, steamed sea bass with lime and chilli, or pork with chilli and holy basil. Handy menu notes and a few set options aid the novice.

Times 12-2.30/6.30-11 Closed Xmas, BHs, L Mon

Frère Jacques

French

Popular Thames-side brasserie offering authentic French cooking and ambience

☎ 020 8546 1332 📠 020 8546 1956
10-12 Riverside Walk, Bishops Hall KT1 1QN
e-mail: john@frerejacques.co.uk
web: www.frerejacques.co.uk
dir: 50 mtrs S of Kingston side of Kingston Bridge, by the river

On a balmy summer's day, you couldn't ask for a better spot in Kingston than Frère Jacques' pitch on the riverside prom where boats see-saw at their moorings by the bridge. On less clement days, an awning and heaters keep out the chill, or move inside to the smart modern dining room, where red gingham tablecloths and a backing track of Gallic sounds combine with the accents of a mainly French team to make you think you've been whizzed across the channel. No surprise then, to find that the appealing fixed-price menu and carte mixes crowd-pleasing French brasserie staples with more modern offerings. Classic starters such as snails in garlic and parsley butter or moules marinière set the tone, before grilled sea bass with truffle mash, creamed leeks and spinach, tomato fondue and wine sauce.

Times 12-11 Closed 25-26 Dec, 1 Jan, D 24 Dec

See LONDON SECTION plan 1-B5

Friends Restaurant

Modern British

Modern dining in an ancient timbered house

☎ 020 8866 0286
11 High St HA5 5PJ
e-mail: info@friendsrestaurant.co.uk
dir: In centre of Pinner, 2 mins walk from underground station

The chocolate box black-and-white timbered façade of this 400-year-old cottage is well known to the faithful foodies of Pinner. The clean-cut interior sports a sharp monochrome style on both floors, neatly accessorised with linen-draped tables, high-backed leather seats and single flowers to inject a hint of colour. After a pedigree background at the Savoy and the Connaught, the chef-proprietor has been established here for 16 years, serving a modern repertoire of well-considered cuisine inspired by tried-and-tested classics. Zinging fresh ingredients and fuss-free presentation are evident in a well-textured terrine of salmon and halibut with tarragon dressing, and rump of lamb with roast parsnips and dauphinoise potatoes. End with an exemplary passionfruit crème brûlée.

Chef Terry Farr **Owner** Mr Farr **Times** 12-3/6.30-10.30 Closed 25 Dec, BHs, Mon in summer, D Sun **Prices** Fixed L 2 course fr £18.50, Fixed D 3 course fr £31.50, Service added but optional 10% **Wines** 16 bottles over £20, 10 bottles under £20, 14 by glass **Notes** Sunday L, Vegetarian available, Air con **Seats** 40 **Children** Portions **Parking** Nearby car parks x3

See LONDON SECTION plan 1-C2

Bingham

 – *see page 332*

La Buvette

French, Mediterranean

Charming French bistro serving up simple classics

☎ 020 8940 6264 📠 020 8940 6264
6 Church Walk TW9 1SN
e-mail: info@labuvette.co.uk
dir: 3 mins from train station, opposite St Mary Magdalene Church

Tucked away in a leafy square overlooking a church, La Buvette offers a genuine taste of France. Formerly the church refectory, the York stone building has a small walled courtyard for alfresco eating, while inside it's split into two intimate dining areas with closely packed tables, dark-wood beams, stripped wood flooring, neutral tones and big sash windows letting in plenty of light. Straightforward French bistro cooking is what keeps the locals returning. A faultless rustic fish soup comes with all the traditional trimmings (rouille, croûtons and gruyère), while a well-made ratatouille accompanies fillet of sea bream. The smartly turned out French staff are friendly and charming.

Chef Buck Carter **Owner** Bruce Duckett **Times** 12-3/6-10 Closed 25-26 Dec, 1 Jan, Good Fri **Prices** Fixed L 2 course £12.75, Fixed D 3 course £19.50, Service added but optional 12.5% **Wines** 19 bottles over £20, 6 bottles under £20, 16 by glass **Notes** Sunday L, Vegetarian available **Seats** 50 **Children** Portions, Menu **Parking** NCP - Paradise Road

Petersham Nurseries

Modern European, Italian

Rustic Italian dishes in a quirky upscale greenhouse café

☎ 020 8605 3627 📠 020 8605 3447
Off Petersham Rd TW10 7AG
e-mail: cafe@petershamnurseries.com
dir: Adjacent to Richmond Park & Petersham Meadows. Best accessed on foot or bicycle along the river

You know there's something special on the menu when flocks of foodies fork out top dollar to eat lunch in a ramshackle greenhouse at rickety old chairs and tables on a dirt floor. But this quirky café is in a leafy pocket of posh Richmond, and the celebrated chef Skye Gyngell is at the helm with her rustic Italian cooking. Daily changing menus offer just 4 or 5 choices per course, built on exemplary seasonal ingredients, including fruit, veg and fresh herbs from the walled kitchen garden of Petersham House. This is straightforward, no-nonsense cooking that coaxes distinctive flavours and vibrant colours onto each plate. Scallops come simply with rocket

continued

RICHMOND UPON THAMES *continued*

and chilli oil to start; among main courses is slow-cooked pork shoulder with borlotti beans and cime di rape (turnip greens). Finish with almond pannacotta with pomegranate. If the café's prices are a bit scary, go for afternoon tea in the tea house instead.

Chef Skye Gyngell **Owner** Francesco & Gael Boglione **Times** 12-2.45 Closed Etr Sun, 25 Dec, Mon-Tue, D all week **Prices** Food prices not confirmed for 2010. Please telephone for details. **Wines** 11 by glass **Notes** Vegetarian available **Parking** Town Centre, Paradise Road or The Quadrant

The Petersham Restaurant

❀❀ British, European

Elegant hotel with accomplished cooking

☎ 020 8940 1084 ☎ 8939 7471 🖹 020 8939 1098
The Petersham, Nightingale Ln TW10 6UZ
e-mail: restaurant@petershamhotel.co.uk
dir: From Richmond Bridge rdbt (A316) follow Ham & Petersham signs. Nightingale Lane off Petersham Rd, hotel on left

Managed by the same family for over twenty-five years, this attractive and elegant hotel is located on Richmond Hill overlooking water meadows and a sweep of the River Thames. The restaurant matches the classic-meets-contemporary style, with walnut panelling, mirrors and well-spaced tables, while the full-length windows make the best of those river views. In the kitchen, a contemporary British style is underpinned by classic French influences. The cooking is accomplished with well-defined flavours and some interesting combinations. Grilled quail and squid with tomato and mozzarella, aubergine caviar, orange and basil might precede confit of suckling pig and black pudding, braised onions and peanuts, Puy lentils and dressed mixed leaves.

Chef Alex Bentley **Owner** The Petersham Hotel Ltd **Times** 12.15-2.15/7-9.45 Closed 25-26 Dec, 1 Jan, D 24 Dec **Prices** Fixed L 2 course £18.50-£38, Fixed D 3 course £34-£46.50, Starter £7.50-£13, Main £19.50-£26.50, Dessert £7, Service added but optional 10% **Wines** 100 bottles over £20, 4 bottles under £20, 10 by glass **Notes** Degustation menu (6 course) £60, Sunday L, Vegetarian available, Civ Wed 40, Air con **Seats** 70, Pr/dining room 26 **Children** Portions, Menu **Parking** 60

See LONDON SECTION plan 1-A5

Hawtrey's Restaurant at the Barn Hotel

❀❀ Modern French

Imaginative, sophisticated cuisine in a smart hotel

☎ 01895 636057 ☎ 679999 🖹 01895 638379
The Barn Hotel, West End Rd HA4 6JB
e-mail: info@thebarnhotel.co.uk
dir: From M40/A40 exit at Polish War Memorial junct onto A4180 towards Ruislip. In 2m right at mini rdbt into hotel entrance

It's hard to imagine, but this smart hotel in 3 acres of gardens was once a farm, parts of which date from the 17th century. Hawtrey's restaurant pulls off a classy act,

Bingham

Modern British 🌱

Well-executed cuisine in stylish surroundings

☎ 020 8940 0902 🖹 020 8948 8737
61-63 Petersham Rd TW10 6UT
e-mail: info@thebingham.co.uk
web: www.thebingham.co.uk
dir: On A307

The Bingham has an enviable spot overlooking the Thames and, since the arrival of chef Shay Cooper, it has been making a splash in Richmond and beyond. The interior designer eschewed modernism for a rather opulent look: rich gold and green colours, mirrors on the walls, stylish chandeliers, and a long sideboard displaying an impressive range of Cognacs, ports and liqueurs. The menu takes quality British produce, pays due diligence to the seasons, and preparations are either home-grown or drawn from the European mainland. A starter of guinea fowl and foie gras terrine comes with earthy Scottish girolles and delicate sweetcorn purée, while a main course of line-caught sea bass is partnered by shredded squid (looking like linguine and full of wonderful flavour), pickled vegetables, orange, and squid ink vinaigrette. Presentation is simple yet refined and flavours intelligently balanced. Strawberry and almond tart with strawberry ice cream is a successful dessert and there is an excellent range of cheeses from small-scale producers. The high quality is maintained through coffee and petits fours, and service is efficient and knowledgeable, with each dish lovingly described by the waiter as it is delivered to table.

Chef Shay Cooper **Owner** Ruth & Samantha Trinder **Times** 12-2.30/7-10 Closed D Sun **Prices** Food prices not confirmed for 2010. Please telephone for details. **Wines** 178 bottles over £20, 5 bottles under £20, 14 by glass **Notes** Tasting menu 5 course, Sunday L, Vegetarian available, Civ Wed 90, Air con **Children** Portions, Menu **Parking** 8

conjuring the ambience of a Jacobean-style baronial hall with its coffered ceiling, glowing mahogany panels, and gilt-framed oil paintings. The kitchen team clearly have an impressive culinary pedigree with confident technical expertise underpinning the modern French menu. Go for the six-course prestige tasting menu to put them through their paces, and expect well-conceived dishes designed to showcase razor-sharp flavours, such as pea velouté, with pea pannacotta, seared diver-caught scallops, split peas and Parma ham salad, followed by a main course that serves roasted rack and confit shoulder of Welsh lamb with potato terrine, aubergine caviar, and Provençal vegetables.

Times 12-2.30/7-10.30 Closed L Sat, D Sun

SURBITON

See LONDON SECTION plan 1-C1

The French Table

◉◉ French, Mediterranean

Creative modern cuisine in ambitious neighbourhood restaurant

☎ 020 8399 2365 📠 020 8390 8589
85 Maple Rd KT6 4AW
e-mail: enquiries@thefrenchtable.co.uk
dir: 5 min walk from Surbiton station, 1m from Kingston

Eric and Sarah Guignard's pretty little restaurant in a small parade of shops and pubs in leafy suburbia is deservedly popular, suggesting the locals are aware they're on to a good thing. The interior is light, stylish and modern yet relaxed and unbuttoned, with plum-coloured banquette seating, simple blond-wood chairs and white linen, while a slate-tiled floor, rear atrium roof, modern art and friendly, attentive and informed service hit just the right note. The creative, clean-cut French/Mediterranean cooking certainly comes dressed to thrill, driven by quality fresh seasonal produce and flavour. Thus monkfish is wrapped in Parma ham and served with a summer vegetable terrine and garlic cream, organic Scottish lamb comes with a pastilla of dried fruits, and desserts include coconut flavoured pannacotta. It is the epitome of an understated yet classy neighbourhood restaurant.

Chef Eric Guignard **Owner** Eric & Sarah Guignard **Times** 12-2.30/7-10.30 Closed 25-26 Dec, 1-3 Jan, Mon, D Sun **Prices** Fixed L 2 course £15.50-£18.50, Dessert £5.95, Service added but optional 12.5% **Wines** 88 bottles over £20, 7 bottles under £20, 9 by glass

Notes Sunday L, Vegetarian available, Dress restrictions, Smart casual, Air con **Seats** 48 **Children** Portions **Parking** On street

TWICKENHAM

See LONDON SECTION plan 1-C2

A Cena

◉ Italian NEW

Simple, authentic cooking at elegant, family-run Italian

☎ 020 8288 0108
418 Richmond Rd TW1 2EB
dir: Please telephone for directions

A welcome change from the chain restaurants that dominate Richmond, this family-run Italian, just across Richmond Bridge, has an attractive black-painted frontage, with large windows looking out onto the street. The elegant interior is all stripped wooden floors, white-clothed tables - some with cosy banquette seating - and a striking wood-panelled bar decorated with lamps, bowls of fruit and flowers. Chef Nicola Parsons' honest Italian cooking is the main draw for the locals. Lemon and flat-leaf parsley cuts through the richness of a creamy soup with mussels and zucchini, while fresh John Dory fillets are pan-fried Sicilian style with a coating of egg and parsley, served on a bed of braised leeks and radicchio.

Chef Nicola Parsons **Owner** Camilla Healy **Times** 12-2.30/7-10.30 Closed L Mon, D Sun **Prices** Food prices not confirmed for 2010. Please telephone for details. **Seats** 55

WEST DRAYTON

For restaurant details see Heathrow Airport (London)

MERSEYSIDE

BIRKENHEAD Map 15 SJ38

Fraiche

◉◉◉ – see page 334

LIVERPOOL Map 15 SJ39

The London Carriage Works

◉◉ Modern International NEW 🌱

Modern restaurant with a focus on local and seasonal produce

☎ 0151 705 2222 & 0151 709 3000 📠 0151 709 2454
Hope Street Hotel, 40 Hope St L1 9DA
e-mail: eat@hopestreethotel.co.uk
dir: Follow Cathedral & University signs on entering city

Belonging to a classy boutique hotel, this stylish restaurant in a former 19th century carriage builders makes a fine figurehead for resurgent Liverpool. On a trendy street book-ended by the Anglican and Catholic cathedrals, the décor goes for lots of bare oak and exposed brickwork, dramatic modern art and glass sculptures. Paul Askew's cooking is modern international in style with a focus on local and organic materials, showcased in a 'miles better' fixed price menu using produce from within a 25 mile radius. To start, pan-roasted breast of wood pigeon comes with a well-executed wild mushroom and caramelised shallot risotto. Next, a main course pan-roast fillet of halibut teamed with brandade, leeks, baby spinach and saffron cream sauce hits the mark.

Chef Paul Askew **Owner** David Brewitt **Times** 12-3/5-10 Closed D 25 Dec **Prices** Fixed L 2 course £18.95-£23.95, Fixed D 3 course £26-£55.50, Starter £4.95-£14.50, Main £13.95-£28.50, Dessert £5.50-£11.50, Service optional, Groups min 8 service 10% **Wines** 164 bottles over £20, 10 bottles under £20, 14 by glass **Notes** Pre-theatre, tasting menu, wine-makers dinners, Sunday L, Vegetarian available, Dress restrictions, Smart casual, Civ Wed 60, Air con **Seats** 100, Pr/dining room 14, 30, 60 **Children** Portions **Parking** Street, nearby car parks

Malmaison Liverpool

◉ Modern British V 🌱

Contemporary brasserie cuisine in style-conscious surroundings on the Mersey waterfront

☎ 0151 229 5000 📠 0151 229 5025
7 William Jessop Way, Princes Dock L3 1QZ
e-mail: liverpool@malmaison.com
dir: Located on Princes Dock near the Liver Building

The Liverpool branch of this design-led chain of hotels has a prime location on the Mersey in the regenerated Princes Dock area within sight of the Liver Birds. This 'Mal' is the first purpose-built hotel in the stable, and has a sharp, edgy style with all the hallmarks of the brand: in-your-face colours, a dark, Manhattan-esque nightclub feel, glitzy champagne and cocktail bar; in case you need reminding that you're in the 'Pool', there's even a yellow submarine slung from the ceiling. The Brasserie menu takes in classic and contemporary dishes, ranging from good old moules marinière or mutton and barley broth starters, to mains such as braised venison faggots with Bury black pudding and mashed turnips, or straight-up grilled steaks.

Chef Daniel Leah **Owner** MWB **Times** 12-2.30/6.30-10.30 **Prices** Fixed L 2 course £13.50, Fixed D 3 course £15.50, Starter £4.50-£6.50, Main £9.95-£18.50, Dessert £4.95-£7.50, Service added but optional 10% **Wines** 70 bottles over £20, 40 bottles under £20, 12 by glass **Notes** Sunday L, Vegetarian menu, Air con **Seats** 87, Pr/dining room 10 **Children** Portions **Parking** Car park by hotel

LIVERPOOL *continued*

Simply Heathcotes

Modern British

Good British-based cooking in a glass restaurant

☎ 0151 236 3536   📠 0151 236 3534
Beetham Plaza, 25 The Strand L2 0XL
e-mail: liverpool@heathcotes.co.uk
dir: Opposite pier head, on The Strand near Princes Dock

The glass-fronted Liverpool arm of Paul Heathcote's mini-empire may be plumb in the middle of an office development, not far from the iconic Liver Building, but it behaves as though it's a country restaurant in that it has assiduously cultivated links with north-west farmers and growers for the food it serves. Scallops and bacon is a classic modern pairing, served here with 'smashed' peas, dressed in olive oil and raspberry vinegar, and might be followed by roast loin and braised leg of rabbit with pine nuts and raisins, or succulent herb-crusted cod with spinach and asparagus in hollandaise. At dessert, a glazed apple tart might be imaginatively served with goats' cheese and thyme ice cream.

Times 12-2.30/6-10 Closed Xmas, BHs (except Good Fri)

60 Hope Street Restaurant

Modern British V

Minimalist setting for smart modern dining

☎ 0151 707 6060   📠 0151 707 6016
60 Hope St L1 9BZ
e-mail: info@60hopestreet.com
web: www.60hopestreet.com
dir: From M62 follow city centre signs, then brown tourist signs for cathedral. Hope St near cathedral

Bracketed by Liverpool's two cathedrals, 60 Hope Street is ensconced in the city's creative quarter. A minimalist interior of white walls and pale wood greets you inside the Grade II listed Georgian townhouse, and the blend works rather well - particularly when the regularly changing art on the walls adds splashes of colour to relieve the neutral tone. Whether you dine in the main restaurant or the basement bistro, confident and accomplished cooking delivers punchy flavours. Take pan-fried scallops with pumpkin strudel and parmesan froth, for example, then braised daube of Cumbrian venison with potato cake, confit swede and venison jus. For pudding try a Bramley apple and pear tart with blackberry ice cream.

Chef Sarah Kershaw **Owner** Colin & Gary Manning **Times** 12-2.30/6-10.30 Closed BHs, Sun, L Sat **Prices** Fixed L 2 course fr £15.95, Starter £6.95-£12.95, Main £12.95-£28.95, Dessert £5.95-£8.95, Service optional, Groups min 8 service 10% **Wines** 70 bottles over £20, 18 bottles under £20, 6 by glass **Notes** Pre-theatre Mon-Sat 5-7pm, Vegetarian menu, Civ Wed 50, Air con **Seats** 90, Pr/dining room 40 **Children** Portions **Parking** On street

---

SOUTHPORT	Map 15 SD31

V-Café & Sushi Bar

Modern International NEW

Modern international dining in a chic designer hotel

☎ 01704 883800
Vincent Hotel, 98 Lord St PR8 1JR
e-mail: norbert@thevincenthotel.com
dir: M58 junct 3, follow signs to Ormskirk & Southport. Hotel on Lord St

Southport's hippest new hotel cuts a dash among all the traditional seaside resort's Victoriana. Its chic glass

---

Fraiche

BIRKENHEAD	Map 15 SJ38

Modern French V

Talented, hands-on chef cooking with real flair

☎ 0151 652 2914
11 Rose Mount CH43 5SG
e-mail: contact@restaurantfraiche.com
dir: M53 junct 3 towards Prenton. In 2m left towards Oxton. Fraiche on right

The Merseyside village of Oxton is very lucky. Very lucky indeed. Chef-patron Marc Wilkinson's intimate restaurant is a stellar little place delivering some seriously creative food. It's very civilised and understated on the inside, with colours and tones redolent of, as they describe it, "natural elements viewed from the shoreline" and some striking works of modern art on the walls. There is a small seating area at the front for an aperitif and a few outside tables on the rear patio for when the mercury is up. The food is notable for both its creativity and beautiful presentations, based around classical French ideas and contemporary innovations. The crisply-scripted menus include a fixed-price lunch and then a main menu consisting of three different options entitled 'elements' (three or four courses), 'signature' (six courses) or the 'bespoke', which is available only if pre-booked. Superb produce and the confidence to keep things simple makes for an impressive lunchtime light salad of fennel with smoked organic salmon, followed by slow-cooked pork belly with a purée of raisins and Earl Grey tea, braised fennel and fondant potato. On the 'signature' menu comes foie gras with pain d'épice and apple textures, while warm date cake with lime salt caramel is a dessert displaying excellent balance of flavours.

Chef Marc Wilkinson **Owner** Marc Wilkinson **Times** 12-1.30/7-9.30 Closed 25 Dec, 1 Jan, Mon-Tue, L Sun, Wed-Thu **Prices** Fixed L 2 course £20, Fixed D 3 course £40, Service optional **Wines** 232 bottles over £20, 24 bottles under £20, 6 by glass **Notes** Bespoke menu available £65, Vegetarian menu **Seats** 20, Pr/dining room 20 **Children** Portions **Parking** On street

frontage on Lord Street stands out from the neighbours, and the interior is all super-chic shiny marble, curvaceous creamy leather and polished herringbone parquet floors. When the weather's fine, the design-led cool of the trendy V-Café opens onto the street through floor-to-ceiling windows. The chefs work in a modish open kitchen, turning out a contemporary international repertoire including sushi prepared by a specialist Asian chef. Get off to a quirky start with mixed seafood served in cones on a stand alongside skinny fries and tartare sauce, and follow with Atlantic cod served on bubble-and-squeak with fab Southport shrimp and caper butter.

Chef Norbert Ruhdorfer **Owner** Paul Adams
Times 7-5/5-10 **Prices** Fixed D 2 course fr £12.95, Starter £3.95-£7.95, Main £9.95-£16.95, Dessert £4.95-£6.50, Service optional **Wines** 28 bottles over £20, 10 bottles under £20, 5 by glass **Notes** Wine & dine menu Sun-Thu dinner, Sunday L, Vegetarian available, Dress restrictions, Smart casual, Air con **Seats** 85, Pr/dining room 12 **Children** Portions **Parking** Valet parking

Warehouse Brasserie

◉◉ International

Cool warehouse conversion with international flavours

☎ 01704 544662 📠 01704 500074
30 West St PR8 1QN
e-mail: info@warehousebrasserie.co.uk
web: www.warehousebrasserie.co.uk
dir: Please telephone for directions

A regular haunt of Merseyside's great and good, the former warehouse is these days a distinctive restaurant, all glass and chrome, with a mix of contemporary and art deco styling. The place has a relaxed atmosphere and attracts a fashionable crowd, while the open-to-view kitchen adds to the vibe. Using locally grown produce, much of it from farms in the Merseyside and Lancashire region, the quality cooking manages to be both modern and classical, with dishes from around the world. So, crispy duck roll with cucumber and spring onions and oriental dressing is alongside herb-crusted rump of lamb with roast garlic cream. If you can't decide on a pud, go for the surprise platter for two. A private dining room for up to eighteen guests is available upstairs.

Chef Darren Smith **Owner** Paul Adams
Times 12-2.15/5.30-10.45 Closed 25-26 Dec, 1 Jan, Sun **Prices** Fixed L 2 course fr £13.95, Fixed D 3 course fr £17.95, Starter £4.50-£10.95, Main £10.95-£24.95, Dessert £4.95-£8.50, Service optional, Groups min 8 service 10% **Wines** 57 bottles over £20, 15 bottles under

£20, 5 by glass **Notes** Early D menu available Mon all night, Tue-Thu 5.30-7pm, Vegetarian available, Air con **Seats** 110, Pr/dining room 18 **Children** Portions **Parking** NCP - Promenade

---

THORNTON HOUGH Map 15 SJ38

The Lawns Restaurant

◉◉ Modern British

Modern fine dining meets historic country-house hotel

☎ 0151 336 3938 📠 0151 336 7864
Thornton Hall Hotel, Neston Rd CH63 1JF
e-mail: reservations@thorntonhallhotel.com
dir: M53 junct 4 onto B5151 & B5136, follow brown tourist signs (approx 2.5m) to Thornton Hall Hotel

The elegant Lawns Restaurant is the fine-dining option at Thornton Hall - a former Victorian manor turned country-house hotel. The recently refurbished restaurant was the hall's former billiard room and overlooks the stunning gardens. Expect slick modern British cooking driven by clear flavours and the freshest ingredients, sourced from local suppliers. Take a cannon of Welsh lamb with a soft herb crust, fresh mint and swede purée and fondant potato, or a warm liquid thyme chocolate tart with yogurt sorbet to finish. As we went to press the highly experienced Gordon Campbell joined the team here.

Chef Gordon Campbell **Owner** The Thompson Family
Times 12-2/7-9.30 Closed 1 Jan, L Sat **Prices** Fixed L 2 course £13.95, Starter £5.50-£9.25, Main £16.50-£21.50, Dessert £5.95-£8, Service included **Wines** 44 bottles over £20, 32 bottles under £20, 9 by glass **Notes** Sunday L, Vegetarian available, Dress restrictions, Smart casual, no T-shirts or jeans, Civ Wed 400 **Seats** 45, Pr/dining room 24 **Children** Portions **Parking** 250

NORFOLK

ALBURGH Map 13 TM28

The Dove Restaurant with Rooms

◉◉ French, European V

Family-run restaurant with a classic menu

☎ 01986 788315 📠 01986 788315
Holbrook IP20 0EP
e-mail: thedovenorfolk@freeola.com
dir: On South Norfolk border between Harleston & Bungay, by A143, at junct of B1062

The Oberhoffer family have run this erstwhile pub as a smart restaurant with rooms for nigh on thirty years, and husband-and-wife-team Robert and Conny are now at the culinary helm. The set-up models itself on the style of a French country inn, taking care in sourcing the pick of fresh local and home-grown materials for straightforward dishes cooked with sound technical skills. Starters take in home-made game and pistachio terrine with cranberry compôte, while mains might offer pan-fried Blythburgh pork tenderloin on sweet potato purée with grain mustard butter sauce. To finish, crêpes Suzette are flambéed at the table by the chef. In good weather there's an inviting

terrace for dining alfresco, and a cosy lounge fits the bill for aperitifs and digestifs whatever the climate throws at you.

Chef Robert Oberhoffer **Owner** Robert & Conny Oberhoffer **Times** 12-2/7-9 Closed Mon-Tue, L Wed-Sat, D Sun **Prices** Food prices not confirmed for 2010. Please telephone for details. **Wines** 6 bottles over £20, 25 bottles under £20 **Notes** Sunday L, Vegetarian menu, Dress restrictions, Smart casual **Seats** 50 **Children** Portions **Parking** 20

ATTLEBOROUGH Map 13 TM09

The Mulberry Tree

◉ Modern International

Trendy eatery with relaxed atmosphere and superb bedrooms

☎ 01953 452124
Station Rd NR17 2AS
e-mail: relax@the-mulberry-tree.co.uk
dir: Exit A11 to town centre. Continue on one-way system. Restaurant on corner of Station Rd

Transformed into a chic pub-restaurant with rooms by Philip and Victoria Milligan, the imposing red-brick Mulberry Tree has a buzzy, contemporary feel and plenty of original features. Big windows, fireplaces, stripped floors, leather chairs, and chunky wooden tables are the backdrop for some good modern cooking. Expect simple dishes with decent flavours; the short menu might kick off with white onion and chorizo soup, followed by roast pork belly with grain mustard mash and cider, apple and Calvados sauce, and vanilla and rhubarb crème brûlée to finish. Service is relaxed, friendly and professional.

Times 12-2/6.30-9 Closed 25-26 Dec, Sun

Sherbourne House Hotel

◉ British

Relaxed brasserie-style dining in friendly restaurant with rooms

☎ 01953 454363
8 Norwich Rd NR17 2JX
e-mail: stay@sherbourne-house.co.uk

Just a short stroll from the town centre, this imposing, red-brick Georgian hotel stands in well-tended mature grounds. Caring hosts offer a warm welcome and you'll find a cosy lounge, plus a bar and a tastefully decorated conservatory restaurant with a relaxed brasserie style and mood, and friendly, informal service. Daily-changing menus offer a traditional British note with a modern twist, and come driven by well-sourced produce (beef and shellfish from the local Norfolk larder) delivered with intelligent simplicity. Typical dishes include venison, pistachio and berry terrine with red onion marmalade, sea bass on sweet potato mash with Provençal sauce, and wild strawberry and pecan cranachan.

Times 12-2/6.30-9.30 Closed 25 Dec, Sun

BARNHAM BROOM — Map 13 TG00

Flints Restaurant

◉◉ Modern British, European

Country-club hotel with traditional-style restaurant and creative cooking

☎ 01603 759393 & 759522 · 📠 01603 758224
Barnham Broom Hotel, Golf & Country Club, Honingham Rd NR9 4DD
e-mail: enquiry@barnhambroomhotel.co.uk
dir: A47 towards Swaffham, turn left onto Honingham Rd, hotel 1m on left

Two championship golf courses and extensive leisure facilities are a prime draw at this hotel and country club set in 250 acres of lovely landscaped grounds. There's the Sports Bar and café for snacky food throughout the day, otherwise Flints is the main fine-dining restaurant. Efficient staff are as smartly turned out as the setting, which manages still to focus on the golf course action through a vast wall of windows. The kitchen makes fine use of excellent Norfolk materials in its confidently creative cooking, offered as a menu du jour or well-balanced carte. Spicy Cromer crab cakes are given an exotic twist with ginger, chilli, coriander, mooli salad and mango salsa to start, while a main course of pan-fried calves' liver comes with pickled shallot and sage mash, Savoy cabbage, capers and crispy bacon.

Chef John Batchelor **Owner** Barnham Broom Hotel
Times 7-9.30 **Prices** Food prices not confirmed for 2010. Please telephone for details. **Wines** 14 bottles over £20, 16 bottles under £20, 9 by glass **Notes** Sunday L, Vegetarian available, Dress restrictions, Smart casual, no jeans or trainers, Civ Wed 120 **Seats** 85, Pr/dining room 50 **Children** Portions, Menu **Parking** 500

BARTON BENDISH — Map 12 TL09

Spread Eagle Inn

◉ British, French

Charming village inn with modern pub menu

☎ 01366 347995 · 📠 0871 900 5576
Church Rd PE33 9GF
e-mail: info@spreadeaglenorfolk.co.uk
dir: From A1122 take Barton Bendish, turn 1st left onto Church Rd, continue past church on left, straight ahead into cul-de-sac, inn on left

In the 18th century, this traditional whitewashed village inn was an hour's ride from King's Lynn. It's less a stopover than a destination in its own right these days, with its exposed brickwork walls and low ceilings piling on the rustic appeal. The monthly-changing menus deal in superior modern pub food, with starters such as goats' cheese tart with onion marmalade, and mains like slow-roast belly pork on grain mustard mash in cider cream sauce, or tomato-stuffed chicken breast wrapped in smoked bacon. Regional cheeses are available, and there is a bar menu of staples and light snacks as well.

Chef John Horn **Owner** Martin & Lori Halpin
Times 12.30-2.30/6.30-11 Closed L Mon-Wed, D Sun
Prices Starter £5.50-£7.50, Main £9.95-£19.95, Dessert £5.50-£7.95, Service optional **Wines** 7 bottles over £20, 25 bottles under £20, 8 by glass **Notes** Sunday L, Vegetarian available **Seats** 46 **Children** Portions **Parking** 30

BLAKENEY — Map 13 TG04

The Blakeney Hotel

◉ Modern British

Panoramic North Norfolk coastal views

☎ 01263 740797 · 📠 01263 740795
The Quay NR25 7NE
e-mail: reception@blakeney-hotel.co.uk
dir: From A148 between Fakenham & Holt, take B1156 to Langham & Blakeney

You can't fail to be soothed by the views across pancake-flat salt marshes and the tidal estuary to Blakeney Point. On a good day, dining outdoors on the quayside terrace of this lovely flint-faced hotel is the perfect spot for taking it all in: vast Norfolk skies shelter a gentle landscape

---

Morston Hall

BLAKENEY — Map 13 TG04

Modern British, French V ◉

Accomplished modern British cooking in intimate country house

☎ 01263 741041 · 📠 01263 740419
Morston, Holt NR25 7AA
e-mail: reception@morstonhall.com
dir: On A149 (coast road)

The flint-built house dates back to Jacobean times, and is a country-house hotel on an intimate scale. An air of simple, light rural elegance prevails inside, and the tone is one of tender solicitude rather than overbearing formality. A day spent exploring the bird-rich north Norfolk coast hereabouts will set you up well for the accomplished, regionally based cooking, which is in the hands of a formidably experienced team. Daily-changing set menus deliver 4 well-balanced courses, with the choice of dessert or cheeses to conclude. A typical bill of fare might be ballotine of foie gras with roast pineapple and fennel mousse, ginger beer jelly and a brioche croûton, then poached cod, served with braised cabbage and a lemony beurre blanc, before the main business of saddle of local lamb in light Indian spicing, accompanied by celeriac Parmentier, ribbons of carrot and coriander mash in a white wine jus. Milk and honey ice cream is served with prune and Armagnac soufflé, its custard also laced with the brandy. Wines of the month form the headline attraction on a comprehensive, well-chosen list.

Chef Galton Blackiston **Owner** T & G Blackiston
Times 12.30-7.30 Closed 2 wks Jan, L Mon-Sat (ex party booking) **Prices** Fixed D 4 course fr £55, Service optional **Wines** 160 bottles over £20, 8 bottles under £20, 15 by glass **Notes** Sunday L, Vegetarian menu, Dress restrictions, Smart casual **Seats** 50, Pr/dining room 20 **Children** Portions, Menu **Parking** 40

echoing with the plaintive cries of wading birds. If the weather won't play ball, the restaurant is a subtly stylish place to put the inviting menu of modern British dishes through its paces. You might kick off with a nod to Provence in a local fish soup with saffron rouille, gruyère cheese and croûtons, and, given the availability of excellent local fish, go for a main course of pan-fried turbot on crushed sweet potatoes with a lightly-spiced mussel broth.

Chef Martin Sewell **Owner** Michael Stannard **Times** 12-2/6.30-8.45 Closed 24-27 Dec, D 31 Dec **Prices** Fixed L 2 course £13.90-£18.45, Fixed D 3 course £27.50-£42, Service optional **Wines** 31 bottles over £20, 34 bottles under £20, 11 by glass **Notes** Sunday L, Vegetarian available, Dress restrictions, Smart casual for D **Seats** 100, Pr/dining room 100 **Children** Portions **Parking** 60

The Moorings

◉ Modern British

Small, relaxed quayside bistro with a nice line in local fish and seafood

☎ 01263 740054 & 01328 878938
3-7 High St NR25 7NA
e-mail: reservations@blakeney-moorings.co.uk
dir: Off A149, at bottom of High St opposite White Horse Hotel

The Moorings suits Norfolk's luminous skies and wide-open marshy coastland to perfection. The quayside bistro is an easy-going place with the soft glow of the Mediterranean in its sunny yellow walls and oiled wooden floorboards; closely-packed tables add buzz to the casual atmosphere. With the sea on the doorstep, the kitchen majors in fish and seafood, bolstered by local meat, game and home-grown fruit and vegetables in season. Unpretentious modern British dishes are big on flavour, cooked accurately and without fuss. Go for local mussel and smoked haddock chowder with chives or spicy Norfolk crab cakes with lime mayonnaise to start, then look to fish again for mains - perhaps baked fillet of bream with fennel, herb crust and black olive dressing.

Chef Richard & Angela Long **Owner** Richard & Angela Long **Times** 10.30-5/6.30-9.30 Closed 2 wks Jan, Mon-Thu (Nov-Mar), D Sun **Prices** Starter £4.95-£7.95, Main £12-£18, Dessert £5.25-£6.25, Service optional **Wines** 8 bottles over £20, 18 bottles under £20, 8 by glass **Notes** Sunday L, Vegetarian available, Air con **Seats** 50 **Children** Portions, Menu **Parking** On street, car park 50mtrs

Morston Hall

◉◉◉ – see opposite page

BRANCASTER STAITHE Map 13 TF74

The White Horse

◉◉ Modern British, International ◔

Seafood and more beside the tidal marsh

☎ 01485 210262 ☷ 01485 210930
PE31 8BY
e-mail: reception@whitehorsebrancaster.co.uk
dir: On A149 (coast road) midway between Hunstanton & Wells-next-the-Sea

The view from the conservatory restaurant of the White Horse is North Norfolk to a tee: tidal marshes stretch across to the sand dunes with the open sea glistening in the distance. The décor is as fresh and welcoming as the view, with scrubbed pine tables, natural materials and seascape colours throughout, and the locally-sourced fish and shellfish on the menu is all part of the appeal. Brancaster Staithe oysters are not compulsory, but they should be: either served naturally or in tempura batter with wasabi mash, lemon syrup and tofu broth. The menu keeps pace with the changing seasons and the kitchen team deliver sound modern British food with balanced international touches. Baked Orford cod comes with pancetta, broad beans, peas and baby leeks, while slow-roasted belly of Norfolk pork and vegetarian options prove it's not only about the fruits of the sea.

Chef Rene Llupar **Owner** Clifford Nye **Times** 12-2/6.30-9 **Prices** Starter £5-£7.95, Main £10.95-£18.50, Dessert £4.95-£6.50, Service optional **Wines** 28 bottles over £20, 29 bottles under £20, 17 by glass **Notes** Sunday L, Vegetarian available **Seats** 100 **Children** Portions, Menu **Parking** 85

BRUNDALL Map 13 TG30

The Lavender House

◉◉ Modern British **V** ◔

Classy cooking in restored thatched cottage

☎ 01603 712215 ☷ 01603 712215
39 The Street NR13 5AA
e-mail: lavenderhouse39@aol.com
dir: A47 E, 4m from Norwich city centre

This Grade II-listed 16th-century thatched cottage may be one of the oldest buildings in the county but a sympathetic restoration has allowed the old oak beams to complement the fresh, modern interior. Now a restaurant and cookery school, there are comfortable sofas in the bar and high-backed wicker dining chairs and crisp white

---

table settings in the restaurant areas. The contemporary cooking makes the most of quality ingredients from artisan local suppliers. There is a tasting menu alongside the shorter fixed-price menu; start with pan-fried cod fillet, salt-cod brandade and lemon dressing before fillet and shin of local beef with smoked potato purée and roasted vegetables. A kitchen theatre table in the private dining room provides guests with a unique view of the chefs at work.

Chef Richard Hughes, Richard Knights **Owner** Richard Hughes **Times** 12-4/6.30-12 Closed 24-30 Dec, Mon, L Tue-Sat, D Sun **Prices** Fixed D 4 course £39.95, Service optional **Wines** 50 bottles over £20, 16 bottles under £20, 8 by glass **Notes** Fixed D 6 course, Tasting menu 8 course, Sunday L, Vegetarian menu **Seats** 50, Pr/dining room 36 **Children** Portions **Parking** 16

BURNHAM MARKET Map 13 TF84

Hoste Arms Hotel

◉◉ Modern British, Pacific Rim ◔

Charming inn to suit any occasion

☎ 01328 738777 ☷ 01328 730103
The Green PE31 8HD
e-mail: reception@hostearms.co.uk
dir: 2m from A149 between Burnham & Wells

The rather posh North Norfolk town of Burnham Market is full of art galleries, trendy boutiques and tempting delis - all in all, a perfect setting for this upmarket English pub. A classic pubby front bar greets you inside: bare red brick walls, beamed ceilings, crackling fires all present and correct; elsewhere, the décor blends antiquity with modern trappings in a handful of diverse eating areas, so you should be able to find somewhere that suits the mood, from casual to romantic to busy and bustling. The Indian and Moroccan-styled walled garden offers the bonus of year-round alfresco dining. The culinary style is modern-British-gone-global on an enticingly eclectic menu. Local man Lord Nelson was once a regular at the Hoste Arms, and he would surely have found no fault with a half dozen Brancaster oysters to start, followed by pan-fried saddle of Holkham venison with cauliflower purée, sautéed salsify and chocolate jus.

continued

BURNHAM MARKET *continued*

Chef Aaron Smith **Owner** Paul Whittome **Times** 12-2/7-9 Closed D 25 Dec **Prices** Starter £4.95-£6.95, Main £11.50-£20.25, Dessert £6.25-£6.95, Service optional **Wines** 153 bottles over £20, 14 bottles under £20, 21 by glass **Notes** Sunday L, Dress restrictions, Smart casual, Air con **Seats** 140, Pr/dining room 24 **Children** Menu **Parking** 45

CROMER — Map 13 TG24

See also **Sheringham**

Elderton Lodge Hotel & Langtry Restaurant

◉◉ Modern British ⓒ

Elegant country house serving first-class Norfolk produce

☎ 01263 833547 📠 01263 834673
Gunton Park, Thorpe Market NR11 8TZ
e-mail: enquiries@eldertonlodge.co.uk
dir: On A149 (Cromer/North Walsham road), 1m S of village of Thorpe Market

Less than five miles from the North Norfolk coastline, this charming country-house hotel stands in six acres of wooded grounds. Beautifully positioned overlooking 800 acres of deer park, this 200 year-old former shooting lodge was once frequented by Lillie Langtry, who lends her name to the elegant restaurant. Here, painted panel walls, clothed tables and crisp napkins set the scene for dishes majoring on fresh local produce. Start with Brancaster mussels cooked with shallots, oregano and cider cream sauce and follow on with local Gunton Park venison Wellington with horseradish and potato purée, glazed confit carrots and a fricassée of wild mushrooms. Finish with baked lemon and lime meringue pie with mango and passionfruit coulis.

Chef Daniel Savage **Owner** Rachel & Patrick Roofe **Times** 12-2.30/6.30-9 **Prices** Fixed L 2 course fr £13.50, Fixed D 3 course fr £17.50, Starter £5-£7, Main £12.50-£18.50, Dessert £5-£7.50, Service optional **Wines** 19 bottles over £20, 22 bottles under £20, 8 by glass **Notes** Sunday L, Vegetarian available, Dress restrictions, Smart casual, Civ Wed 55 **Seats** 50, Pr/dining room 25 **Children** Portions, Menu **Parking** 100

Frazers, Sea Marge Hotel

◉ Modern British

Sound cooking in elegant hotel with sea views

☎ 01263 579579 📠 01263 579524
16 High St, Overstrand NR27 0AB
e-mail: info@mackenziehotels.com
dir: A140 to Cromer, B1159 to Overstrand, 2nd left past Overstrand Church

This splendid Grade II listed former gentleman's residence stands in 5 acres of terraced gardens sweeping down to the clifftop. The Edwardian building has been lovingly restored and retains many period features, including a vaulted timber roof and minstrels' gallery in the Clement Scott Bar. Frazer's Restaurant comes with leather high-backed chairs and crisply-clothed tables. Local produce is the backbone of the menu and the cooking is unfussy. A starter of grilled fillet of red mullet with tarragon butter and braised gem lettuce might be followed by pan-roasted guinea fowl with creamed leeks and fondant potato.

Chef Darren Hill **Owner** Mr & Mrs Mackenzie **Times** 12-2/6.30-9.30 **Prices** Food prices not confirmed for 2010. Please telephone for details. **Wines** 10 bottles over £20, 21 bottles under £20, 6 by glass **Notes** Sunday L, Vegetarian available, Dress restrictions, Smart casual **Seats** 80, Pr/dining room 40 **Children** Portions, Menu **Parking** 50

White Horse

◉ Modern British NEW Ⓥ

Top-notch Norfolk produce cooked with passion and flair

☎ 01263 579237
34 High St, Overstrand NR27 0AB
e-mail: enquiries@whitehorseoverstrand.co.uk
dir: Please telephone for directions

You're just a couple of minutes from the beach in this family-run Victorian inn in the North Norfolk coastal village of Overstrand. The interior is looking swish after a recent refurbishment, and at the stoves is a young chef who is keen to put his kitchen on the map, starting with basics such as diligent sourcing of top-drawer Norfolk materials, and in-house preparation of all bread, pasta, ice cream, smoked fish and meats. The modern British menus read well, both in the bar where old favourites are given a modern twist, and in the restaurant, where unfussy dishes might deliver rabbit pie with cider gravy, ham hock terrine and date purée to start, followed by a Norfolk rib-eye steak with wild garlic butter, proper beef-dripping chips and a salad of local smoked Walsingham cheese. To end, try dark chocolate truffle cake with lavender-scented cream.

Chef Nathan Boon **Prices** Food prices not confirmed for 2010. Please telephone for details. **Notes** Sunday L, Vegetarian menu

GREAT BIRCHAM — Map 13 TF73

The Kings Head Hotel

◉ Modern British

Great food in stylish village hotel

☎ 01485 578265 📠 01485 578635
PE31 6RJ
e-mail: welcome@the-kings-head-bircham.co.uk
dir: Please telephone for directions

The Kings Head shows a traditional face to the world, but, inside, this 19th-century inn in a peaceful village close to Sandringham and the north Norfolk coastline reveals a real sense of contemporary style. The restaurant - no starchy tablecloths here - overlooks a sheltered courtyard which is just perfect for alfresco dining in summer. Lots of seasonal Norfolk produce helps give the simple menu of British and Mediterranean dishes a local flavour. Start with half a dozen Thornham oysters, or a moist and tender confit duck leg with a red onion marmalade. Main-course rib-eye steak is equally succulent, and comes with fat chips and a blue cheese sauce.

Times 12-2/7-9

GREAT YARMOUTH — Map 13 TG50

Café Cru Restaurant

◉ British ⓒ

Modern restaurant within imposing Victorian seafront hotel

☎ 01493 842000 📠 01493 852229
Imperial Hotel, North Dr NR30 1EQ
e-mail: reception@imperialhotel.co.uk
web: www.cafecru.co.uk
dir: follow signs to seafront, turn left. Hotel opposite tennis courts

Part of Great Yarmouth's grand old Imperial Hotel, this friendly, contemporary restaurant is decked out in neutral shades, with modern chandeliers and a choice of open-plan and booth seating. Have a drink in the upstairs Savoie Bar before tucking into the honest, unfussy, British food. Prime ingredients are cooked well and simply, and the seasonally-changing menu with daily specials includes scampi thermidor and roast breast of free-range chicken with dauphinoise potatoes, grilled pancetta and thyme gravy. Desserts include baked ginger and apple pudding with banana ice cream and warm butterscotch sauce.

Chef Simon Wainwright **Owner** Mr N L & Mrs A Mobbs **Times** 12-2/6.30-10 Closed 24-28 & 31 Dec, L Sat & Mon, D Sun **Prices** Fixed L 2 course £14.50, Starter £4.50-£9, Main £9.95-£22, Dessert £5.50-£8.50, Service optional **Wines** 25 bottles over £20, 68 bottles under £20, 10 by glass **Notes** Sunday L, Vegetarian available, Dress restrictions, Smart casual, No shorts or trainers, Civ Wed 140, Air con **Seats** 60, Pr/dining room 140 **Children** Portions **Parking** 45

The Lounge at Andover House

⚜ Modern European NEW ✿

Relaxed modern brasserie in contemporary restaurant with rooms

☎ 01493 843490 📠 01493 852546
28-30 Camperdown NR30 3JB
e-mail: info@andoverhouse.co.uk
web: www.andoverhouse.co.uk
dir: Follow signs for Great Yarmouth seafront. Continue along seafront until Wellington Pier. Turn right into Kimberley Terrace, follow road to right until Camperdown, hotel 75 yds on left

The Lounge is a fashionable bar and modern brasserie located within the recently refurbished Andover House, a boutique-style restaurant with rooms close to the town centre. Chunky wooden tables and high-backed leather chairs on a polished wood floor, and a chic black and cream décor set the contemporary scene for some competent modern European cooking with an Asian twist. Take a starter of sea bass on Thai asparagus with truffle oil dressing and lump fish caviar, and a main dish of pork belly slow-cooked in honey and five spices. Puddings include chocolate fondant served with home-made vanilla ice cream. On warm days dine alfresco on the terrace.

Chef Patrick Moore **Owner** Mr & Mrs Barry Armstrong **Times** 12-2/6-9.30 Closed Sun, D Mon **Prices** Fixed D 3 course £35, Starter £6.50-£8, Main £14-£42, Dessert £6-£9, Service optional **Wines** 40 bottles over £20, 8 bottles under £20, 12 by glass **Notes** Vegetarian available **Seats** 37, Pr/dining room 60 **Parking** On street

---

GRIMSTON · Map 12 TF72

Congham Hall Country House Hotel

⚜⚜ Modern British V

Imaginative, seasonal cooking in Georgian setting

☎ 01485 600250 📠 01485 601191
Lynn Rd PE32 1AH
e-mail: info@conghamhallhotel.co.uk
dir: 6m NE of King's Lynn on A148, turn right towards Grimston. Hotel 2.5m on left (do not go to Congham)

The grounds of this fine Georgian manor house cover 30 acres and include parkland, woodland, orchards, plus a kitchen garden which boasts around 700 varieties of herbs and supplies the Orangery restaurant. French windows open onto the terrace of the traditionally decorated, terracotta-painted dining room, where smartly set tables are adorned with fresh flowers. Seasonal, local produce is used to good effect in lively and modern dishes: monkfish tempura is served with hazelnuts, couscous and soused celery in a starter, while main-course Gressingham duck comes with fresh herb potato cake, confit cabbage, carrot Lyonnaise and port jus. Finish with cassis pannacotta with cinnamon and apple fritters, or British cheeses with celery and grapes.

Chef Jamie Murch **Owner** von Essen Hotels **Times** 12-2/7-9 **Prices** Fixed L 2 course £16.25, Fixed D 3 course £48, Starter £7, Main £35, Dessert £6, Service optional **Wines** 60 bottles over £20, 10 bottles under £20, 10 by glass **Notes** Gourmand menu L £35, D £65, Sunday L, Vegetarian menu, Dress restrictions, Smart casual, Civ Wed 100 **Seats** 50, Pr/dining room 18 **Children** Portions, Menu **Parking** 50

HETHERSETT · Map 13 TG10

Park Farm Hotel

⚜ British

Peacefully located hotel with appealing restaurant

☎ 01603 810264 📠 01603 812104
NR9 3DL
e-mail: enq@parkfarm-hotel.co.uk
dir: 6m S of Norwich on B1172

A few miles south of Norwich, Park Farm provides conference and leisure facilities amid 200 acres of grounds, and its smart orangery-style restaurant overlooks landscaped gardens. Tables are laid with crisp white linen and contemporary crockery and cutlery, while the set-price menu for lunch and dinner makes good use of seasonal local produce. Fresh local mussels come in a tomato, chilli and ginger sauce with toasted focaccia, while roast fillet of cod is topped with a walnut crust and served with creamed leeks and saffron potatoes. The lounge-bar has a menu of less formal bar snacks.

Times 12-2/7-9.30

HOLKHAM · Map 13 TF84

The Victoria at Holkham

⚜⚜ British, French

Norfolk hideaway with an interesting colonial feel

☎ 01328 711008 📠 01328 711009
Park Rd NR23 1RG
e-mail: victoria@holkham.co.uk
dir: 3m W of Wells-next-the-Sea on A149. 12m N of Fakenham

The Victoria is the Jewel in the Crown of the Holkham Estate, an inn built at the start of Queen Vic's reign to put up the entourages of aristos dropping in on the Earls of Leicester. Inside there's a relaxed shabby chic colonial vibe built around a collection of handsome Rajasthani furniture and hand-carved latticework doors. The seaside Holkham Estate provides venison, beef, game and eels for the kitchen while crabs come from Cromer and mussels from Brancaster. Unfussy modern British classics are the kitchen's stock in trade, served in a bohemian contemporary brasserie-style restaurant. Starters might be roast wood pigeon with crispy pork belly and carrot purée, while roast sea bass comes with braised chicory, carrots, sultanas and orange sauce among main courses.

Times 12-2.30/7-9.30

HOLT · Map 13 TG03

Butlers Restaurant

⚜ Modern European ✿

Accomplished cooking in bustling bistro

☎ 01263 710790
9 Appleyard NR25 6BN
e-mail: eat@butlersofholt.com
dir: Just off High Street, signed Appleyard

Situated in the popular market town of Holt, this family-run bistro has a bustling atmosphere. Relaxed and informal, with an open kitchen adding to the theatre, it is a light and airy space with a glass roof and large double doors opening onto the courtyard garden. Start with a drink at the large oak bar or relax in the garden beneath the 200-year-old copper beech tree. Everything here is made in the kitchen and local produce is a cornerstone of the unpretentious menu. Start with steamed Morston mussels in garlic, white wine, cream and parsley, then choose locally reared rib-eye steak with grilled field mushrooms with tarragon and wholegrain mustard butter, watercress salad and skinny chips.

Chef Sean Creasey **Owner** Sean & Ruth Creasey **Times** 12-3/6-9 Closed 25, 26 Dec, D Sun **Prices** Starter £5.95-£6.95, Main £8.95-£16.95, Dessert £4.95-£5.25, Service optional **Wines** 13 bottles over £20, 20 bottles under £20, 12 by glass **Notes** Monthly events with special menu, Sunday L, Vegetarian available, Air con **Seats** 50 **Children** Portions **Parking** On street (free after 6pm)

HOLT *continued*

The Lawns Wine Bar

◉ Modern European

Handsome townhouse with lively, modern menu

☎ 01263 713390
26 Station Rd NR25 6BS
e-mail: mail@lawnsatholt.co.uk
dir: Please telephone for directions

Major refurbishment in 2008 transformed this fine Georgian townhouse, situated in the heart of this bustling market town, into a stylish wine bar and restaurant with rooms, replete with an alfresco terrace and garden. A bar decked out with plush leather sofas draws local drinkers, while diners head for the smart dining room and conservatory for a simple, traditional, crowd-pleasing menu, and relaxed and unstuffy service. Using quality local and seasonal ingredients, dishes may include a rich game terrine with pickled pears, chicken breast stuffed with wild mushrooms and wrapped in pancetta, and stem ginger pudding with sticky ginger sauce.

Chef Leon Brookes, Jenner Hilton **Owner** Mr & Mrs Daniel Rees **Times** 12-2/6-9 **Prices** Starter £4.75-£6.95, Main £9.25-£13.75, Dessert £5-£6, Service optional **Wines** 6 bottles over £20, 29 bottles under £20, 9 by glass **Notes** Wine tasting D available, Sunday L, Vegetarian available **Seats** 24 **Children** Portions **Parking** 18

The Pigs

◉◉ British

Local pub with refreshingly unstuffy attitude and high standards

☎ 01263 587634
Edgefield NR24 2RL
e-mail: info@thepigs.org.uk

Let's start with what the Pigs is not: it is definitely not a pretentious gastro-pub, even though the fresh, Norfolk-sourced food served here would be the envy of many a place advertising itself with that moniker. The Pigs is first and foremost a pub. That means excellent ales from Peter Yetman's local micro-brewery range, to classics from Adnams and Woodforde's. Staff are nattily kitted out with black aprons and deliver with casual efficiency and down-to-earth friendliness. For starters, or just something snacky, 'Peckish' dishes include a plate of piggy pieces comprising sausage, black pudding, bacon, pig's ear, cheek and crackling - everything bar the oink - served with a shooter glass of apple sauce. Staying with a porcine theme, a main course of slow-cooked belly of pork comes with smoky bacon beans, black pudding and apple chutney.

The Pigs

Times 11-2.30/6-9 Closed Mon except BHs, D Sun

The Neptune Restaurant with Rooms

HUNTANTON Map 12 TF64

Modern British 🍃

A Georgian inn with a design and culinary makeover

☎ 01485 532122
85 Old Hunstanton Rd PE36 6HZ
e-mail: reservations@theneptune.co.uk
dir: Please telephone for directions

There may be many a converted Georgian coaching inn up and down the country, but this one has been renovated with some style. Old monochrome photographs of the nearby coastline, together with model boats on display, acknowledge the North Norfolk location, while the dining room has been treated to a coffee-hued minimalist design scheme. Kevin Mangeolles put the place firmly on the contemporary map when he moved here, importing a style of uncomplicated, but highly accomplished, modern British cooking. A stew of local mussels and smoked haddock makes a bracing opener, or there could be poached oysters with horseradish cream and (shades of the Fat Duck) passionfruit jelly. Mains raid the Norfolk larder for belly pork with veal sweetbreads and Savoy cabbage, while a more exotic note is sounded in the pickled coconut that garnishes a dish of red mullet with broccoli purée and a salad of crab and green beans. Desserts show a fondness for applying spices to traditional recipes, seasoning chocolate mousse with ras el hanout caramel or infusing the pannacotta with cardamom. Good breads, appetisers, pre-desserts and petits fours mean you won't feel neglected at any stage.

Chef Kevin Mangeolles **Owner** Kevin & Jacki Mangeolles **Times** 12-2/7-9 Closed 2 wks Nov & Jan, Mon (except BHs), L Tue-Sat (except by arrangement) **Prices** Fixed L 2 course fr £18.50, Starter £7.50-£9, Main £19.50-£22.50, Dessert £7.50-£8, Service optional **Wines** 45 bottles over £20, 17 bottles under £20, 10 by glass **Notes** Sunday L, Vegetarian available **Seats** 24 **Parking** 6, Street parking

HORNING
Map 13 TG31

Taps

◉ Modern British

Consistency and good value from an intimate local restaurant

☎ 01692 630219 📠 01692 631565
25 Lower St NR12 8AA
dir: From Norwich follow signs to The Broads on A1151. Through Wroxham, right to Horning & Ludham. After 3m right into Horning, Lower St 500yds on left

In the pretty Norfolk Broads village of Horning, Taps is an inviting neighbourhood eatery with a friendly laid-back ambience. A traditional, homely décor sets the tone for an eclectic modern British menu that draws its influences from far and wide and makes good use of fine East Anglian produce. Taps calls itself a steak house, but there's far more going on than simple slabs of protein - although if you're in the market for meat, these are fine cuts, properly aged on the bone for 28 days. Lunch menus offer phenomenal value, while house specials take in roast duck breast with butternut squash, pickled red cabbage and fondant potato and blackberry and ginger sauce, or fillet of sea bass with crayfish risotto and fresh herb sauce.

Times 12-2/7-9.30 Closed Mon, D Sun

HUNSTANTON
Map 12 TF64

The Neptune Restaurant with Rooms

◉◉◉ – *see opposite page*

ITTERINGHAM
Map 13 TG13

Walpole Arms

◉ Modern European NEW

Village gastro-pub serving modern cuisine

☎ 01263 587258 📠 01263 587074
NR11 7AR
e-mail: goodfood@thewalpolearms.co.uk
dir: Please telephone for directions

Located in picturesque countryside, this traditional 18th-century village pub is close to North Norfolk's beaches and the Broads. Its attractive restaurant delivers modern European cooking, featuring high-quality produce, much of it locally sourced, such as mussels from Morston or venison from nearby Gunton Hall. Expect dishes with lots of flavour and considered combinations of ingredients. Start with escabèche of red mullet with pine nuts, sultanas and butter beans, followed by confit duck leg with baby potatoes, salad of green beans, pickled peach and mixed leaves. The same menu is served in the oak-beamed bar.

Chef Jamie Guy **Owner** Alan & Cheryl Sayers
Times 12-2.30/7-9 Closed D Sun **Prices** Starter fr £6.75, Main £10.95-£18.95, Dessert fr £6.25 **Notes** Vegetarian available

KING'S LYNN
Map 12 TF62

Bank House Hotel

◉ British NEW

Local produce shines in Georgian former bank

☎ 01553 660492
King's Staithe Square PE30 1RD
e-mail: info@thebankhouse.co.uk
dir: Towards quay, follow to end, through floodgates, hotel on right

Right on the quayside in the heart of King's Lynn's business/historical quarter, Bank House is a true Georgian gem. The Grade II* listed building has had a colourful past - it was originally the home of a wine merchant before becoming Gurneys Bank in the 1780s (Gurneys eventually metamorphosed into Barclays Bank). These days it's a stylish boutique hotel decorated in contemporary style, with a relaxing bar and brasserie in the bank's old counting house. Head chef Ed Lewis, formerly of St John in London's Smithfield Market, works his magic on seasonal, local produce to create traditional English dishes with a few modern touches. Start with potted salmon with toast, and then, perhaps, tuck into a hearty steak and kidney pie with mash and greens for the main event.

NORTH WALSHAM
Map 13 TG23

Beechwood Hotel

◉◉ British, Mediterranean 🍴

Norfolk's best produce in popular hotel

☎ 01692 403231 📠 01692 407284
Cromer Rd NR28 0HD
e-mail: info@beechwood-hotel.co.uk
dir: From Norwich on B1150, 13m to N Walsham. Left at lights, next right. Hotel 150mtrs on left

The 18th-century property was frequented by Agatha Christie back in the day and there are letters from the writer to the family on display in the hallway. The restaurant is the real hub of the hotel, serving creative modern British dishes and displaying a true passion and commitment to the abundant Norfolk produce, including sourcing ingredients from within 10 miles of the hotel for the daily 'ten-mile dinner'. Cromer crab, Morston mussels, Thornham oysters and Sheringham lobster and local meat and vegetables are all served in season. For a great combination of flavours, try grilled halibut on crushed new potatoes with a vibrant herb crust with

spinach and a mussel, brown shrimp and tomato nage. Expect desserts such as vanilla pannacotta with tangy rhubarb compôte and brandy snap biscuit. Drinks can be taken in the garden or the clubby lounge bar.

Chef Steven Norgate **Owner** Don Birch & Lindsay Spalding **Times** 12-1.45/7-9 Closed L Mon-Sat **Prices** Fixed D 3 course £35, Service optional **Wines** 220 bottles over £20, 10 bottles under £20, 8 by glass **Notes** Sunday L, Vegetarian available, Dress restrictions, Smart casual **Seats** 60, Pr/dining room 20 **Children** Portions **Parking** 20

Divine Bar & Restaurant

◉ Modern, Traditional British NEW 🍴

Regionally based cooking in north Norfolk market town

☎ 01692 405590
4 Nicholas Court, Vicarage St NR28 9BY
dir: 200yds from centre of North Walsham, adjacent to St Nicholas Church

Hidden away in rural Norfolk, here is a smart, trendily designed restaurant offering modern British food based on locally sourced seasonal produce. The dark-wood tables, slate place mats and black granite floor aim for a rough-hewn look, with small modern artworks adding splashes of colour. Meats from a third-generation butcher in Aylsham, free-range poultry and locally shot game are strong suits, and the cooking is setting a cracking pace. Smoked haddock and crab fishcake is served with salad as a starter, wild boar loin with belly pork confit and garlic mash is a substantial main course, and go the whole hog with a dessert such as Belgian chocolate and Grand Marnier torte and clotted cream ice cream.

Chef Julian Falconer **Owner** Paul East **Times** 10-3/6-11 Closed Mon, D Sun **Prices** Fixed L 3 course fr £15, Fixed D 3 course £20, Starter £4-£6, Main £13-£18, Dessert £5 **Notes** Sunday L, Vegetarian available, Air con **Seats** 60, Pr/dining room 30 **Children** Portions **Parking** 5, Car park nearby

NORWICH
Map 13 TG20

Ah-So Japanese Restaurant

◉ Japanese

Authentic taste of the land of the rising sun

☎ 01603 618901 📠 01603 613527
16 Prince of Wales Rd NR1 1LB
e-mail: booking@ah-so.co.uk
dir: From station cross bridge, restaurant in 600yds on right, near Anglia TV

This smart, modern restaurant pulls in the crowds with its friendly, relaxed atmosphere and flamboyant culinary theatrics. Specialising in teppan-yaki, the chefs cook meals in front of you on large stainless steel griddles. The lengthy menu is authentically Japanese, assembling fresh, simple ingredients; kick off with vegetable tempura or sushi and sashimi, for example, then try something

continued

NORWICH *continued*

from the grill (salmon teryaki, yellowfin tuna, squid, sea bass or fillet steak). The set meals are an economical option, as well as offering the chance to sample a number of dishes at one sitting.

Times 12-9/6-12 Closed Mon, L Tue-Sat

Arlington Grill & Brasserie

◉ French ♨

Friendly family-run hotel serving classic brasserie-style dishes

☎ 01603 617841 📠 01603 663708
BW George Hotel, 10 Arlington Ln, Newmarket Rd NR2 2DA
e-mail: reservations@georgehotel.co.uk
web: www.arlingtonhotelgroup.co.uk
dir: Please telephone for directions

The George is a charming family-run hotel in a Victorian house in a tranquil conservation area just a short walk from Norwich city centre. The interior looks sprucely modern in the pubby bar and smart Arlington Brasserie, where polished pale wood floors, leather banquette seating and mirrored walls add up to a classic Gallic style. The menu too, has a classic French feel in its repertoire of tried and tested dishes - go for Brancaster mussels steamed with white wine, parsley, garlic and cream, and follow with a cassoulet of duck leg, pork belly, Toulouse sausage and haricot beans, or local pheasant breast with celeriac mash, root vegetables and red wine jus.

Chef Paul Branford **Owner** David Easter/Kingsley Place Hotels Ltd **Times** 12-2/6-10 **Prices** Food prices not confirmed for 2010. Please telephone for details. **Wines** 3 bottles over £20, 23 bottles under £20, 10 by glass **Notes** Sunday L, Vegetarian available, Air con **Seats** 44, Pr/dining room 80 **Children** Portions, Menu **Parking** 40

Best Western Annesley House Hotel

◉◉ British, European

Impressive cuisine overlooking tranquil water garden

☎ 01603 624553 📠 01603 621577
6 Newmarket Rd NR2 2LA
e-mail: annesleyhouse@bestwestern.co.uk
dir: On A11, close to city centre

Just a few minutes' walk from Norwich's historic city centre, this attractive Grade II listed Georgian property is located in a pretty tree-lined conservation area. It is set in 3 acres of landscaped gardens and grounds, including a peaceful water garden and waterfall, giving diners in the Mediterranean-style conservatory restaurant a great view. The cooking is simple and effective, with the menu offering a range of dishes, from traditional English to modern British with some European influences too. The high-quality ingredients shine through in starters like tuna Niçoise, or a main course of roast duck served with confit of turnip, dauphinoise potato and red wine jus. Finish with a classic, perfectly executed crème brûlée.

Chef Steven Watkin **Owner** Mr & Mrs D Reynolds **Times** 12-2/6-9 Closed Xmas & New Year, L Sun **Prices** Fixed L 2 course £12.50-£18.50, Fixed D 2 course £24, Fixed D 4 course £29.50, Service optional **Wines** 6 bottles over £20, 19 bottles under £20, 9 by glass **Notes** Pre-theatre menu available from 6pm by arrangement, Vegetarian available **Seats** 30, Pr/dining room 18 **Children** Portions **Parking** 25

Brummells Seafood Restaurant

◉◉ International, Seafood

Fresh fish in the historic heart of Norwich

☎ 01603 625555 📠 01603 766260
7 Magdalen St NR3 1LE
e-mail: brummell@brummells.co.uk
web: www.brummells.co.uk
dir: In city centre, 2 mins walk from Norwich Cathedral, 40yds from Colegate

With its blue-painted frontage, complete with bright blue awning, facing out onto historic Magdalen Street, Brummells - named after chef-patron Andrew Brummell - is hard to miss. The nautical theme continues inside the 17th-century building, with pictures of fish filling the walls. Exposed brickwork and beams lend the intimate little dining room charm and character, and at night it's a romantic space with candles on the neatly clothed tables. The freshest seafood, simply prepared, is the order of the day here. Start with some monkfish fritters with a crisp golden batter, served with a roast tomato relish and a wedge of lemon, and follow on with grilled halibut steak with a wild mushroom and basil compôte. Non fish fans are not forgotten, and desserts might include iced pear parfait with nutmeg mascarpone and

caramelised pear, or coconut custard brûlée with papaya jam and fine butter biscuit.

Chef A Brummell, J O'Sullivan **Owner** Mr A Brummell **Times** 12-2 (flexible)/6-9.30 (flexible) **Prices** Starter £6.50-£16, Main £17-£29.95, Dessert £6, Service optional, Groups min 7 service 10% **Wines** 56 bottles over £20, 27 bottles under £20, 3 by glass **Notes** Sunday L, Vegetarian available, Dress restrictions, Smart casual, Air con **Seats** 30 **Children** Portions **Parking** On street after 6.30pm & Sun, Car park nearby

De Vere Dunston Hall

◉ British, French

Accomplished cuisine in grand hotel

☎ 01508 470444 📠 01508 471499
Ipswich Rd NR14 8PQ
e-mail: dhreception@devere-hotels.com
dir: On A140 between Norwich & Ipswich

Built in the 19th-century by a wealthy Victorian family with a taste for Elizabethan style, Dunston Hall sits in 150 acres of wooded parkland with its own 18-hole golf course and a raft of leisure pursuits to help you work up an appetite. Stocking its larders from a network of producers and farmers' markets within a 30-mile radius, the La Fontaine restaurant deals in classic British and French dishes, and keeps a finger on the pulse of contemporary trends. Roast wild pigeon with langoustines, celeriac and ginger gratin, black pudding and beetroot might start you off, followed by roast rack and braised cheek of new season lamb with pea and mint purée and marrow chutney.

Chef Paul Murfitt, Gary Ellis **Owner** De Vere Hotels **Times** 7-10 Closed Sun, L Mon-Sat **Prices** Starter £5.95-£8.95, Main £13.50-£22.50 **Notes** Vegetarian available, Dress restrictions, Smart, No jeans, Air con **Seats** 45 **Children** Portions, Menu **Parking** 300

The Dining Room at the Old Rectory

◉◉ Modern British V ♨

Country-house style in a city location

☎ 01603 700772 📠 01603 300772
103 Yarmouth Rd, Thorpe St Andrew NR7 0HF
e-mail: enquiries@oldrectorynorwich.com
dir: From A47 take A1042 to Thorpe, then A1242. Hotel right after 1st lights

Set in well-maintained gardens full of mature trees, and enjoying commanding views over the Yare Valley, the Old Rectory was built in the mid-18th century. The Entwistles have been in residence since the 1990s, and run the place as a calm, relaxing country retreat, with a much more pastoral ambience than the city location might suggest. The modern British cooking strongly features local produce, including that for which chef James Perry has personally foraged. Good things include thin, crisp tart of Cromer crab, parmesan, spring onion and dill, and the slow-roasted Shropham pork fillet marinated in black treacle. Assured, polished technique is in evidence in the bitter chocolate fondant which, as the menu rightly assures us, 'takes 15 minutes but is well worth the wait'.

Chef James Perry Owner Chris & Sally Entwistle
Times 7-9 Closed Xmas & New Year, Sun-Mon, L all week
Prices Fixed D 3 course £27-£28, Service optional
Wines 14 bottles over £20, 8 bottles under £20, 5 by
glass Notes Vegetarian menu Seats 18, Pr/dining room
16 Children Portions Parking 16

Elm Hill Brasserie

🍴 French NEW

Relaxed brasserie in Norwich's historic heart

☎ 01603 624847
2 Elm Hill NR3 1HN
e-mail: reservations@elmhillbrasserie.co.uk

You can just see the tip of the cathedral spire towering
above the surrounding medieval buildings of Norwich
from this friendly, modern brasserie. Not that the
cathedral - or the castle for that matter - is far away, as
the Elm Hill Brasserie is right in the ancient heart of the
city. Chef-proprietor Simon Turner sources good quality,
seasonal, local produce to create a menu with a mainly
French slant. Norfolk crab with squid and saffron cream,
or pan-fried lamb's kidneys are typical starters. Main
course options might include fish cassoulet, or steak with
twice-cooked frites and confit garlic mayonnaise. Save
room for the moist chocolate brownie with blueberry ice
cream and blueberry compôte.

Times 12.30-2.30/7 Closed Sun-Mon

Marriott Sprowston Manor Hotel

🍴🍴 Modern British 🍷

Modern classics at a Norfolk country club

☎ 01603 410871 🖨 01603 423911
Sprowston Park, Wroxham Rd NR7 8RP
e-mail: mhrs.nwigs.frontdesk@marriotthotels.com
dir: From A47 take Postwick exit onto Norwich outer ring
road, then take A1151. Hotel approx 3m and signed

The house rises in step-gabled majesty at the end of a
tree-lined drive. It's a country club as well as a hotel, so
expect golf and a big lake, and the Manor itself
celebrated its 450th anniversary in 2009. In an
atmosphere of corporate luxe, a menu of modern classics
is served, taking in ham hock terrine with piccalilli, or
spinach and ricotta ravioli, to start, with main-course
options fielding roasted monkfish in Parma ham with
herbed risotto, or guinea-fowl supreme with a potato cake
and Puy lentils. At the finish, baked American-style
cheesecake with pistachio ice cream won't lack for
takers. Less formal eating may be had in the 1559 Bar
and the Zest Café-Bar and Grill.

Chef Mark Lutkin Owner Marriott International Inc
Times 12.30-3/6.30-10 Closed L Mon-Sat, D Sun
Prices Fixed D 3 course £25, Starter £6.50-£7.50, Main
£15.59-£29.50, Dessert £5.59-£7.50, Service optional
Wines 29 bottles over £20, 12 bottles under £20, 12 by
glass Notes Sunday L, Vegetarian available, Dress
restrictions, Smart casual, no shorts, Civ Wed 300, Air
con Seats 70, Pr/dining room 150 Children Portions,
Menu Parking 170

1 Up@ The Mad Moose

🍴🍴 Modern British

Intimate restaurant and modern food above trendy pub

☎ 01603 627687 🖨 01603 611933
The Mad Moose Arms & 1Up, 2 Warwick St NR2 3LD
e-mail: madmoose@animalinns.co.uk
web: www.themadmoose.co.uk
dir: A11 onto A140. Turn right at lights onto Unthank Rd,
then left onto Dover/Warwick St

Take the stairs to find the fine-dining part of the the Mad
Moose gastro-pub, which provides a bit of sophistication
for customers in the evening and for Sunday lunch.
Chandeliers, luxurious velvet curtains and striking
modern wall coverings are a chic blend of old and new.
Modern menus make much of high quality Norfolk
produce, and the dishes have good, clear flavours. Take
smoked eel with warm breast of pigeon, quince and
lemon aïoli, crème fraîche and watercress; and black
bream with crushed charlotte potatoes, wilted romaine,
sweet pickled cucumber, Parma ham and Pommery
mustard. Go for free-standing cinnamon crème brûlée
with grilled figs and plum ice cream for dessert. In
addition, a substantial bar menu is offered downstairs.

Chef Eden Derrick Owner Mr Henry Watt
Times 12-3/7-9.30 Closed 25-26 Dec, 1 Jan, L Mon-Sat, D
Sun Prices Fixed D 3 course £15-£18, Starter £5.50-
£8.50, Main £11-£17, Dessert £5.50-£6.50, Service
optional Wines 32 bottles over £20, 24 bottles under £20,
11 by glass Notes Sunday L, Vegetarian available
Seats 48 Children Portions Parking On street

St Benedicts Restaurant

🍴 Modern British

Confident cooking in cosy local restaurant

☎ 01603 765377 🖨 01603 624541
9 St Benedicts St NR2 4PE
e-mail: stbens@ukonline.co.uk
dir: Just off inner ring road. Turn right by Toys-R-Us, 2nd
right into St Benedicts St. Restaurant on left by
pedestrian crossing

Recently refurbished with calming green tones and
comfortable banquette seating, this popular local
restaurant in the heart of Norwich offers an intimate and
relaxed dining experience. The kitchen puts an emphasis
on bold flavours, using fresh, local, seasonal ingredients.
The signature starter of double-baked cheese soufflé
shows a lightness of touch, as does the roast sea bream
with fennel purée, local brown shrimps and baby salad
onions. Finish with one of the classic puddings, perhaps
iced praline parfait with toasted almonds, caramel sauce
and crème anglaise.

Chef Stuart Duffield, Nigel Raffles Owner Nigel & Jayne
Raffles Times 12-2/7-10 Closed 25-31 Dec, Sun-Mon
Prices Fixed L 2 course £8.95, Fixed D 3 course £16.95,
Starter £4.95-£6.50, Main £11.95-£14.95, Dessert £4.95,
Groups min 10 service 10% Wines 15 bottles over £20,
34 bottles under £20, 8 by glass Notes Vegetarian
available, Air con Seats 42, Pr/dining room 24
Children Portions Parking On street, Car parks nearby

St Giles Restaurant

🍴🍴 British 🍷

Grand city-centre hotel with classy restaurant

☎ 01603 275180 & 275182 🖨 0845 299 1905
St Giles House Hotel, 41-45 St Giles St NR2 1JR
e-mail: reception@stgileshousehotel.com
web: www.stgileshousehotel.com
dir: A11 into central Norwich. Left at rdbt signed
Chapelfield Shopping Centre. 3rd exit at next rdbt. Left
onto St Giles St. Hotel on left

Original wood panelling, ornamental plasterwork and
elegant marble floors have been complemented by a

continued

NORWICH *continued*

mixture of modern design and stunning chandeliers to give this stylish city-centre hotel, situated in an impressive Grade II listed building, a sense of sumptuous individuality. Enjoy a pre-prandial drink on the Parisian-style terrace on warm summer evenings before lingering over an intimate dinner in the art deco dining room. Classic dishes make sound use of locally sourced ingredients; take pan-fried scallops with green herb risotto, Gunton Park organic venison with sweet blackberry vinegar jus, and roasted plum and frangipane tart.

Chef Daniel Savage **Owner** Norfolk Hotels Ltd **Times** 11-10 **Prices** Fixed L 2 course £13.50, Fixed D 3 course £17.50, Starter £4.95-£7.50, Main £12.95-£21.50, Dessert £4.95-£7.50, Service optional **Wines** 38 bottles over £20, 25 bottles under £20, 9 by glass **Notes** Sunday L, Vegetarian available, Civ Wed 60, Air con **Seats** 50, Pr/dining room 48 **Children** Portions **Parking** 30

Shiki

◉ Modern Japanese

Sushi with style whether you want to eat in or takeaway

☎ 01603 619262 ▤ 01603 619110
6 Tombland NR3 1HE
e-mail: bookings@shikirestaurant.co.uk
dir: City centre. From Castle Meadow onto Upper Kings St, straight onto Tombland, restaurant on left

Just a stone's throw from the cathedral in an attractive Victorian building, this Japanese restaurant is tastefully done out in a minimalist style with stripped pine floors, dark-wood bench seating and white-painted walls. Freshly prepared sushi and the tapas-style menus are the main draw. Start with the mixed tempura of vegetables and prawns, or tuck into the Sushi Lover selection - a three-tiered platter of mixed sushi (including smoked eel, sea bass, salmon, squid, tuna and octopus) to share. Main courses include the likes of Japanese curries and chicken teriyaki. The staff are friendly and charming, and you can eat outside if the weather is fine.

Times 12-2.30/5.30-10.30 Closed Xmas, Sun

Stower Grange

◉ Traditional British, European

Attractive hotel with appealing modern menu

☎ 01603 860210 ▤ 01603 860464
School Rd, Drayton NR8 6EF
e-mail: enquiries@stowergrange.co.uk
dir: Norwich ring road N to Asda supermarket. Take A1067 (Fakenham road) at Drayton, right at lights into School Rd. Hotel 150yds on right

Dating from the 17th century, this pretty, ivy-clad hotel is popular for weddings and conferences as well as for its elegant restaurant. The grounds are a pleasant place for a stroll before lunch or dinner. The formal and traditional restaurant is dedicated to sourcing local produce with just about everything made on the premises. Ham hock terrine with home-made chutney and sun-dried tomato bread might kick things off, then, perhaps, home-tea-smoked wood pigeon with a peach and pear compôte, braised fennel and tarragon jus. There's a good choice for vegetarians.

Times 12-2.30/7-9.30 Closed 26-30 Dec, D Sun

The Sugar Hut

◉ Thai **V**

Relaxed Thai dining in smart city-centre restaurant

☎ 01603 766755 ▤ 01603 766755
4 Opie St NR1 3DN
e-mail: lhongmo@hotmail.co.uk
dir: City centre next to Castle Meadow & Castle Mall car park

This smartly relaxed Thai restaurant is housed in a characterful high-ceilinged building that was once a tailor's shop in the centre of Norwich. It's a fresh and fun place, decorated with a breezy blue and yellow colour scheme and interesting Thai artefacts. The kitchen serves up those authentically-perfumed oriental flavours using a mix of locally-sourced produce and imported exotica. Zinging freshness and clear flavours impress in dishes such as grilled giant king prawns with chilli oil, a classic green chicken curry, or deep-fried sea bass with sweet-and-sour chilli sauce. Smiling, uniformed staff are happy to advise on any of the dishes, and set menus available for 2 to 4 people are great value.

Chef Chartchai Fodsungnoen **Owner** Leelanooch Hongmo **Times** 12-2.30/6-10.30 Closed Sun **Prices** Fixed L 2 course £8.95-£15, Fixed D 4 course £26, Starter £4.50-

£6.50, Main £8.95-£15.95, Dessert £1.50-£4.50, Service optional, Groups min 7 service 10% **Wines** 6 bottles over £20, 24 bottles under £20, 7 by glass **Notes** Vegetarian menu, Air con **Seats** 40 **Children** Portions **Parking** Castle Mall

Tatlers

◉ Modern British ☺

Dependable neighbourhood restaurant by the Cathedral

☎ 01603 766670 ▤ 01603 766625
21 Tombland NR3 1RF
e-mail: info@tatlers.com
dir: In city centre in Tombland. Next to Erpingham Gate by Norwich Cathedral

Situated virtually at the gates of Norwich Cathedral, Tatlers is a converted Victorian townhouse. Dining is spread over a trio of individually decorated rooms, adorned with some fetching contemporary artworks, and the modern British cooking has made it a popular neighbourhood restaurant. Well-prepared local crab and avocado with herb mayonnaise and salad makes a crisply appetising starter, and could be followed by halibut linguini with mussels and brown shrimps, or casseroled venison with roasted parsnips, while steaks are as succulent as you could wish. Finish with glazed lemon tart and raspberry coulis. There's a decent selection of wines by the glass.

Chef Sean Creasey **Owner** Sean Creasey **Times** 12-2.30/6-10 Closed 25-26 Dec, Sun **Prices** Fixed L 2 course fr £12, Fixed D 3 course fr £20, Starter £4.95-£6.95, Main £9.95-£18.95, Dessert £5.25-£5.95, Service optional, Groups min 10 service 10% **Wines** 33 bottles over £20, 15 bottles under £20, 15 by glass **Notes** Vegetarian available **Seats** 75, Pr/dining room 33 **Children** Portions **Parking** Law courts, Elm Hill, Colegate, St Andrews

Thailand Restaurant

◉ Thai

Deservedly popular authentic Thai

☎ 01603 700444
9 Ring Rd, Thorpe St Andrew NR7 0XJ

You'd better book early to be sure of getting a table, because the Thailand Restaurant has quite a following amongst the residents of Norwich. Just off the ring road in a large detached, white-painted house, the restaurant looks smart and welcoming, with neatly clothed tables, dark bamboo-style chairs, and pictures of Thailand decorating the walls. Female staff are in traditional Thai dress, while their male counterparts wear black trousers and bow-ties. The service is attentive and friendly, and the food authentic. A typical main sees beef Musaman (beef slow braised in coconut cream with fresh chillies, cinnamon and shallots), while green curry is vibrant and flavoursome.

Times 12-3/6-9.30 Closed L Sun

RINGSTEAD
Map 12 TF74

The Gin Trap Inn

Modern British

Charming 17th-century inn turned gastro-pub

☎ 01485 525264 📠 01485 525321
6 High St PE36 5JU
e-mail: thegintrap@hotmail.co.uk
dir: A149 from King's Lynn towards Hunstanton. After
15m turn right at Heacham for Ringstead

Two miles inland from the beautiful north Norfolk coast,
this lively gastro-pub sits on the Peddars Way, the
footpath following the route of a Roman road. Built in
1667 as a coaching inn in a peaceful village on the
outskirts of Hunstanton, the rustic bar has a huge
fireplace with a wood-burning stove, exposed brickwork
and beams, and plain wooden tables. The restaurant is
more formal with linen tablecloths and candles. A
conservatory dining area is also available. Serving British
food, the kitchen sources good-quality produce, local
where possible, including organic meat, and mussels and
oysters from nearby Thornham. Well-flavoured dishes
include fresh beer-battered haddock, hand-cut chips, pea
purée and home-made tartare sauce, or Arthur Howell's
traditional pork sausages with mashed potato and red
onion gravy.

Chef Ethan Rodgers **Owner** Steve Knowles & Cindy Cook
Times 12-2/6-9 **Prices** Starter £5-£8.50, Main £8.50-
£15, Dessert £6-£7.50, Service optional **Wines** 8 bottles
over £20, 25 bottles under £20, 8 by glass **Notes** Sunday
L, Vegetarian available **Seats** 60, Pr/dining room 18
Children Portions, Menu **Parking** 20, On street

SHERINGHAM
Map 13 TG14

Marmalade's Bistro

British, International V

**Relaxed, rustic bistro serving quality, simply-cooked
produce**

☎ 01263 822830
5 Church St NR26 8QR
dir: A149 into town centre then left at clock tower

A venerable Tudor-beamed fishing cottage makes the
perfect setting for this rustic bistro run by a welcoming
husband-and-wife team. Country pine tables, fresh
cream paintwork and wood floors and chalkboards make
for a relaxed mood. It's reassuring to see that the kitchen
is driven by whatever seasonal, locally-sourced produce it
can get its hands on - including fish on a daily basis -
and when it's gone, it's gone, wiped from the chalkboards
ready for a new dish to appear. The cooking is intelligent
and without affectation and flavours are well-defined.
Local cider-pickled herrings with red onion, cucumber
and dill might precede a main course of roast pork loin
steak with caramelised pears in cider, honey and wild
garlic sauce.

Chef Ben Mutton **Owner** Mr & Mrs B Mutton
Times 12-2/6-9 Closed seasonal closures, Wed, L Mon, D

Sun **Prices** Starter £4.75-£6, Main £9.95-£15, Dessert fr
£5.95, Service optional **Wines** 3 bottles over £20, 17
bottles under £20, 6 by glass **Notes** Pre-theatre D
available, Sunday L, Vegetarian menu, Dress restrictions,
Smart casual, Air con **Seats** 30 **Children** Portions
Parking On street & town car parks

No. 10 Restaurant

Modern British

Seasonal dishes served in elegant surroundings

☎ 01263 824400
10 Augusta St NR26 8LA
e-mail: eat@no10sheringham.com
dir: Please telephone for directions

No 10 is an appealing place with its curving shop window
façade opening into an intimate interior with high
ceilings, artwork, gilt-framed mirrors and masses of
church candles flickering around the fireplace. Cheery
staff, smartly turned-out in black and white with long
aprons, deliver straightforward food with simple
combinations of wonderfully fresh local ingredients. Kick
off with dishes such as a French-style fish soup with
gruyère, then go for something like a sea bass fillet with
saffron risotto and red pepper dressing. To finish, an
orange and Cointreau crème brûlée is a winner.

Times 12-2/6.30-9 Closed Sun, Mon-Tue (Winter)

Upchers Restaurant

British, European

**Country-house dining in delightful parkland
surroundings**

☎ 01263 824555 📠 01263 822647
Dales Country House Hotel, Lodge Hill NR26 8TJ
e-mail: dales@mackenziehotels.com
dir: On B1157, 1m S of Sheringham. From A148 Cromer to
Holt road, take turn at entrance to Sheringham Park.
Restaurant 0.5m on left

The Dales is an impressive Grade II listed Victorian
country-house hotel set in its own 4 acres of gardens on
the edge of the National Trust grounds of Sheringham
Park. Its intimate Upchers Restaurant, with inglenook
fireplace, oak panelling and formal yet relaxed
atmosphere, fits seamlessly into its traditional but stylish
surroundings. The menu, which includes 'fresh fish board'
choices (perhaps roast halibut served with asparagus,
spring onion, confit tomatoes and sage oil), offers
accomplished dishes with clear flavours driven by
Norfolk's larder, including game from local estates. Other
choices might feature roast rump of lamb served with
Parmentier potatoes, herbs, shallots, sautéed courgettes
and a mint jus.

Times 12-2/7-9.30

STOKE HOLY CROSS
Map 13 TG20

The Wildebeest Arms

Modern British, European

Exotic take on a traditional pub with enticing menus

☎ 01508 492497 📠 01508 494946
82-86 Norwich Rd, Stoke Holy Cross NR14 8QJ
e-mail: wildebeest@animalinns.co.uk
dir: From A47 take A140, left to Dunston. At T-junct turn
left, Wildebeest Arms on right

Fusion cooking is a well-known theme, so how about an
Africa-meets-the-Fens fusion pub? A collection of masks,
musical instruments and sundry artefacts from the Dark
Continent transports this pub from the outskirts of
Norwich to the sub-Saharan savannah - an effect that
blends well with the bare floorboards, beams, panelling
and open fires of a traditional cosy pub. The
accomplished kitchen's style, on the other hand, fuses
Britain and France in set-price menus du jour and daily-
changing specials. Start with sautéed Dedham Vale lamb
fillet with truffled potato purée and King's Lynn brown
shrimps, then move on to roast cod served on a bed of
Parmentier potatoes with fresh samphire, broad beans
and smoked garlic purée. Friendly staff are helpfully
clued-up to offer advice on the locally-sourced produce.

Chef Daniel Smith **Owner** Henry Watt
Times 12-3.30/6-11.30 Closed 25-26 Dec, **Prices** Fixed L
2 course fr £13.95, Fixed D 3 course fr £19.95, Starter
£5.95-£7.50, Main £12.50-£18.95, Dessert £6.50-£6.95,
Service optional **Wines** 70 bottles over £20, 41 bottles
under £20, 13 by glass **Notes** Sunday L, Vegetarian
available, Air con **Seats** 75 **Children** Portions **Parking** 40

SWAFFHAM
Map 13 TF80

Best Western George Hotel

British, International V

**Enjoyable food in historic hotel overlooking market
square**

☎ 01760 721238 📠 01760 725333
Station Rd PE37 7LJ
e-mail: georgehotel@bestwestern.co.uk
web: www.arlingtonhotelgroup.co.uk
dir: Located on main X-roads in Swaffham

Situated in the ancient market town of Swaffham, this
Georgian hotel is a 300-year-old institution. The Green
Room restaurant is the setting for local and European

continued

SWAFFHAM *continued*

food prepared from quality produce. Here you can expect dark green seating and carver chairs, crisp napery, clothed tables and traditional-style crockery. The food is unfussy and uses good local ingredients. Potted Cromer crab with hot toast makes an enjoyable starter, followed perhaps by pan-fried medallions of pork fillet with roasted vine tomatoes and an English mustard and Madeira sauce.

Chef Pete Crundwell **Owner** David Easter
Times 12-2.30/6.30-9.30 Closed 25 Dec, **Prices** Starter £3.95-£6.95, Main £8.95-£21.95, Dessert £3.95-£6.95, Service optional **Wines** 5 bottles over £20, 20 bottles under £20, 7 by glass **Notes** Sunday L, Vegetarian menu **Seats** 40, Pr/dining room 18 **Children** Portions, Menu **Parking** 80

THETFORD — Map 13 TL88

Elveden Café Restaurant

Modern

Relaxed café-style dining on the Elveden Estate

☎ 01842 898068
London Rd, Elveden IP24 3TQ
e-mail: estate.shop@elveden.com
dir: On A11 between Newmarket & Thetford, 800 mtrs from junct with B1106

Stylishly converted old farm buildings on the Elveden Estate surround a glorious courtyard and house a host of upmarket shops (wine, clothes, arts and crafts) and this smart café. In summer, eat alfresco in the open-plan barbecue zone and dining area, or head indoors to a light and airy space with vaulted ceiling and beams, natural-wood floors, cream walls and black marble-topped tables partnered by modern-style wooden chairs. Eclectic menus range from restaurant-style meals and daily specials to lovely home-made sandwiches and cakes, all using local produce. Expect Brancaster mussels, beef and mushroom stew, toad-in-the-hole, and puddings like Cambridge burnt cream.

Chef Chris Allen **Owner** The Earl of Iveagh **Times** 9.30-5 Closed 25-26 Dec,1 Jan, D all week **Prices** Starter £4.95-£7.50, Main £5.95-£9.95, Dessert £5.50-£6.95, Service optional **Wines** 1 bottles over £20, 9 bottles under £20, 2 by glass **Notes** Vegetarian available, Air con **Seats** 60 **Children** Portions, Menu **Parking** 200

THORNHAM — Map 12 TF74

Lifeboat Inn

Traditional British ⌘

Beautifully situated historic North Norfolk inn

☎ 01485 512236   📠 01485 512323
Ship Ln PE36 6LT
e-mail: reception@lifeboatinn.co.uk
dir: A149 from Hunstanton for approx 6m. 1st left after Thornham sign

The Lifeboat Inn was a smugglers' alehouse in the 16th century: the customers have gone straight these days, and the food is decidedly more gastro, but the uplifting views across Norfolk marshes and dunes to Thornham Harbour are still timeless. Inside, it seems some previous incumbents had a nice line in architectural salvage: there's a splendid baronial fireplace, weathered oak beams, exposed brickwork and ancient oak beams for classic pub character, and a smart restaurant, with white-clothed, candlelit tables for romantic dinners. The daily specials board features 'what's been caught, shot, picked or dug locally each day'. Fish is high on the agenda, with starters such as Brancaster mussels steamed in Chardonnay with lemongrass, ginger and cream, then, to keep the carnivores happy, local partridge casserole with Guinness and mushrooms, bacon and herbs and creamy horseradish mash.

Chef Michael Sherman **Owner** Maypole Group plc **Times** 7-9.30 Closed L Mon-Sat **Prices** Food prices not confirmed for 2010. Please telephone for details. **Wines** 16 bottles over £20, 19 bottles under £20, 8 by glass **Notes** Sunday L **Seats** 70, Pr/dining room 18 **Children** Portions, Menu **Parking** 100

THURSFORD — Map 13 TF93

The Old Forge Seafood Restaurant

Seafood V ⌘

Locally caught seafood in a family-run restaurant with rooms

☎ 01328 878345
Seafood Restaurant, Fakenham Rd NR21 0BD
e-mail: sarah.goldspink@btconnect.com
dir: Located on A418

Pilgrims journeying to nearby Walsingham Abbey used to stop at this former coaching station with forge for food and rest. Fast-forward seven centuries and The Old Forge is still welcoming travellers who come for a peaceful break - and particularly for the excellent fresh seafood, cooked in an intelligently simple way by chef-patron Colin Bowett. The dining room is cosy and rustic, with York stone floors, beams, pine tables and chairs, and the original iron hooks for tying up horses still in the walls. Try the dressed Cromer crab, hot crayfish tails in garlic butter, roasted cod topped with melted potted shrimps, or go the whole hog with the mixed seafood platter.

Chef Colin Bowett **Owner** Colin Bowett
Times 12-2/6.30-9.30 Closed Mon **Prices** Fixed L 2 course £6-£8, Starter £3.50-£7.50, Main £12.50-£18.50, Dessert £3.50-£5.50, Service optional **Wines** 5 bottles over £20, 10 bottles under £20, 5 by glass **Notes** Vegetarian menu **Seats** 28 **Children** Portions **Parking** 12

TITCHWELL — Map 13 TF74

Titchwell Manor Hotel

Modern European ⌘

Global cuisine on the north Norfolk coast

☎ 01485 210221   📠 01485 210104
PE31 8BB
e-mail: margaret@titchwellmanor.com
dir: On A149 (coast road) between Brancaster & Thornham

You might not have expected to find a gentlemen's club on the wilds of the Norfolk coast, and yet here one once was. Titchwell Manor is now a charming country hotel, retaining many of its original indoor features and with a walled kitchen garden, from which vegetables and herbs flow. Choose between the bar, where good simpler dishes are on offer, or the green-framed conservatory dining-room, where the culinary stops are pulled out. A stylish way to start is with a pasta dish such as ravioli of sweet potato, sage and the local Binham Blue cheese. Go on perhaps to wild sea bass, richly partnered with braised Savoy cabbage and Alsace bacon, cream cheese rösti and a Jerusalem artichoke velouté, before a delectable Valrhona chocolate cake dessert. Incidentals are all top-notch, including the home-baked breads.

Chef Eric Snaith **Owner** Margaret and Ian Snaith **Times** 12-2.30/6-9.30 **Prices** Food prices not confirmed for 2010. Please telephone for details. **Wines** 27 bottles over £20, 25 bottles under £20, 9 by glass **Notes** Sunday L, Vegetarian available, Dress restrictions, Smart casual, Civ Wed 85, Air con **Seats** 80 **Children** Portions, Menu **Parking** 50

WYMONDHAM   Map 13 TG10

Number Twenty Four Restaurant

◎◎ Modern British

Skilled cooking in a relaxed and unpretentious ambience

☎ 01953 607750   ▤ 01953 607750
24 Middleton St NR18 0AD
dir: Town centre opposite war memorial

You could almost walk past the dainty row of listed 18th-century cottages without noticing that there's a rather good family-run restaurant within. There are no airs and graces here, just a pleasantly relaxed and friendly ambience perfect for enjoying a bottle of wine à deux with a nice line in internationally-accented modern British cuisine. The dining room's warm and sunny décor glows with the ochre hues of the Mediterranean, blending neatly with its period character. Ingredients come to the market in the town, giving the chef-proprietor the finest East Anglian produce on his doorstep. A typical starter might be a creamy leek and pea tart with goats' cheese and black pepper sauce, then seared loin of venison on piquant spiced red cabbage with parsnip mash and a garlic and Cognac jus.

Chef Jonathan Griffin **Owner** Jonathan Griffin **Times** 12-2/7-9 Closed 26 Dec, 1 Jan, Mon, L Tue, D Sun **Prices** Fixed L 2 course £14.50, Fixed D 3 course £24.95-£30 **Wines** 10 bottles over £20, 26 bottles under £20, 6 by glass **Notes** Sunday L, Vegetarian available, Dress restrictions, Smart casual, No shorts **Seats** 60, Pr/dining room 55 **Children** Portions **Parking** On street opposite. In town centre car park

NORTHAMPTONSHIRE

COLLYWESTON   Map 11 SK90

The Collyweston Slater

◎◎ Modern British Ⅴ ☺

Stylish village inn serving modern British food

☎ 01780 444288   ▤ 01780 444288
87-89 Main Rd PE9 3PQ
e-mail: info@thecollywestonslater.co.uk
web: www.thecollywestonslater.co.uk
dir: 4m S of Stamford, A43, 2m off A1

Named in honour of the local industry, this traditional inn has been sensitively refurbished. Elements of its 17th-century past, such as the oak beams and slate flooring, combine beautifully with the wooden tables, leather seating and contemporary lighting in the brasserie-style restaurant. The pub enjoys great views over the Wetland Valley and Fineshade Woods. The menu features modern British dishes given a twist here and there with some global ideas; the focus is on seasonal, good-quality local produce. Expect plenty of flavour - typical dishes might include 36-hour water-bath-cooked pork belly with lime pickle, roasted prawns and carrot purée, or pan-fried salmon with Vietnamese vegetables, peanut and coconut dressing, lime chutney and prawn mousse spring roll. Finish with a sliced and layered sticky toffee pudding with a toffee sauce and ice cream.

Chef Dameon Clarke **Owner** Dameon Clarke & Philip Robson **Times** 11.30-9.30 **Prices** Tasting menu £45, Starter £5.95-£8.95, Main £9.95-£16.95, Dessert £5.25-£6.25, Service optional **Notes** Sunday L, Vegetarian menu **Seats** 34, Pr/dining room 10 **Children** Portions, Menu **Parking** 32

DAVENTRY   Map 11 SP56

Equilibrium

◎◎◎ – *see page 348*

FOTHERINGHAY   Map 12 TL09

The Falcon Inn

◎ British, European ☺

Vibrant cooking in rural Northamptonshire

☎ 01832 226254   ▤ 01832 226046
Main St PE8 5HZ
e-mail: info@thefalcon-inn.co.uk
dir: From A605 at Warmington follow signs to Fotheringhay. Situated at centre of village

First the history lesson: it was in this sleepy Northamptonshire village that Richard III was born and Mary, Queen of Scots ended her days. The historic castle where it all happened is long gone so you're probably best heading for the pub. And anyone who likes a fine pint of real ale will be glad to find that the Falcon is a proper local with a smart restaurant attached. The modern British classics on offer here aim straight for the comfort zone, ranging from bar menu staples such as Grasmere Farm ale sausages and mash or omelette Arnold Bennett, to European-influenced dishes on the restaurant menu. These might be starters like corn-fed chicken and leek terrine with a rustic pumpkin chutney, followed by a perfectly-timed fillet of lemon sole and scallops with red wine risotto and pak choi.

Chef Danny Marshall **Owner** Harry Facer & Jim Jeffries **Times** 12-2.15/6.15-9.15 **Prices** Starter £4.50-£6.50, Main £7.50-£17.50, Dessert £4.50-£5.50, Service optional, Groups min 10 service 10% **Wines** 21 bottles over £20, 28 bottles under £20, 14 by glass **Notes** Pre-concert menu 3 course £15, Sunday L, Vegetarian available **Seats** 45, Pr/dining room 30 **Children** Portions, Menu **Parking** 50

KETTERING — Map 11 SP87

Langberrys Restaurant

◉ Modern British ◐

Impressive cuisine in a smart hotel restaurant

☎ 01536 416666   📠 01536 416171
Kettering Park Hotel, Kettering Parkway NN15 6XT
e-mail: kpark.reservations@shirehotels.com
dir: Off A14 junct 9

The welcoming Langberrys Restaurant is located on two levels in a modern hotel that successfully combines contemporary facilities with old-world charm. In Langberrys the decor is traditional, with subtle lighting, formal table service and a crackling fire in winter. In summer drinks or dinner can be taken on the terrace. Produce from local and regional suppliers features on the choice of à la carte, specials, bar and lounge and Sunday lunch menus. The cooking style is simple and straightforward, giving favourite combinations a modern flourish. Expect the likes of Bleikers oak-smoked trout croquettes with horseradish and citrus cream, while main courses might include country-style creamy chicken, pea and ham hock pie with thin fries.

Chef Stephen Robinson **Owner** Shire Hotels
Times 12-1.45/7-9.30 Closed Xmas & New Year (ex residents), L Mon-Sat **Prices** Starter £5.50-£9.95, Main £12.50-£22.50, Dessert £6.75, Service optional **Wines** 69 bottles over £20, 5 bottles under £20, 15 by glass

Notes Sunday L, Vegetarian available, Civ Wed 100 **Seats** 90, Pr/dining room 40 **Children** Portions, Menu **Parking** 200

Tresham Restaurant, Rushton Hall Hotel & Spa

◉ ◉   Modern European V

Highly accomplished cooking in magnificent surroundings

☎ 01536 713001   📠 01536 713010
Rushton NN14 1RR
e-mail: enquiries@rushtonhall.com
web: www.rushtonhall.com
dir: A14 junct 7. A43 to Corby, A6003 to Rushton, turn off after bridge

Having been put up in many a stately home on his travels around the country, Charles Dickens knew a good one when he saw it. The great writer was so taken with Rushton Hall that he immortalised it as Haversham Hall in *Great Expectations*. Rushton is everything you'd expect in a grand country-house hotel dating from 1438, and seriously overhauled with Victorian wealth. Walk-in stone fireplaces, delicate plasterwork and stained glass abound, and the tone continues into the magnificent oak linenfold-panelled dining room. In the kitchen, however, we're in a modern European realm: a talented new chef took over in March 2009, delivering classically-influenced cuisine of a high order. Noteworthy depth of flavour impresses, and simple menu descriptions belie the technical skill that has gone into dishes such as 'pressing of veal, sweetbread toastie, duck egg, anchovy'. The style is typified in a main course of Anjou pigeon, which is prepared in three styles - parfait, consommé and ballotine - and married with black pudding, baby turnips and jus spiced with cinnamon, star anise and stem ginger.

Chef Darren Curson **Owner** Tom & Valerie Hazelton
Times 12-2/7-9 **Prices** Tasting menu £35-£45, Starter £9-£13, Main £25-£29, Dessert £9.95, Service optional **Wines** 79 bottles over £20, 12 bottles under £20, 14 by glass **Notes** Tasting menu 3-5 course, Sunday L, Vegetarian menu, Dress restrictions, No jeans or trainers, Civ Wed 160 **Seats** 46, Pr/dining room 60 **Children** Menu **Parking** 140

Equilibrium

DAVENTRY — Map 11 SP56

Modern British V 🍷 ◐

High gastronomic ambition in stunning grand Tudor manor

☎ 01327 892000   📠 01327 892001
Fawsley Hall, Fawsley NN11 3BA
e-mail: info@fawsleyhall.com
web: www.fawsleyhall.com
dir: A361 (Daventry), follow for 12m. Turn right, signed Fawsley Hall

Fawsley Hall is a grandiose old pile that feels more like a full-blown stately home than a mere country-house hotel. There's plenty to keep amateur historians entertained, as the Georgians and Victorians added their efforts to the Tudor bit, 'Capability' Brown designed the gardens among its 2,000 acres of Northamptonshire countryside, and Queen Elizabeth I dropped in for a stay in 1575. Inside, expect a suitably baronial setting, notably during pre-dinner drinks in the Great Hall, where portraits of Tudor monarchs survey the scene beneath a vaulted oak ceiling. So it's a surprise to discover the muted contemporary tones in the Equilibrium Restaurant, where an accomplished kitchen team delivers innovative and technically interesting dishes. The whole arsenal of modern culinary wizardry is brought to bear on set dinner menus that might begin with roast pigeon and its own ice filtered tea - an involved riff that gives a workout of textures and flavour combinations featuring various parts of the bird presented as parfait, consommé, roast breast and confit leg with pickled pear, celeriac remoulade and hazelnuts. Daring pairings continue with fish in a main course of seared John Dory with smoked eel and horseradish croquette, red wine onions and Fourme d'Ambert cheese. Desserts continue to play with unusual bedfellows, teaming bitter chocolate soufflé with avocado ice cream and sea salt caramel.

Chef Nigel Godwin **Owner** Bahram Holdings **Times** 7-10 Closed Sun-Mon, L all week **Prices** Fixed D 3 course fr £59, Tasting menu £79-£119, Service added but optional 12.5% **Notes** Tasting menu 7 course, Vegetarian menu, Dress restrictions, Smart casual **Seats** 30, Pr/dining room 20 **Parking** 140

ROADE — Map 11 SP75

Roade House Restaurant

◉ Modern French

Popular village restaurant serving well-tuned modern British cuisine

☎ 01604 863372 🖷 01604 862421
16 High St NN7 2NW
e-mail: info@roadehousehotel.co.uk
dir: M1 junct 15 (A508 Milton Keynes) to Roade, left at mini rdbt, 500yds on left

Despite its nearness to the M1 and the high-octane world of Silverstone, this 18th-century restaurant with rooms is a rustic haven in a quiet Northamptonshire village. The summery hues of the oak-beamed dining room set a calming tone for Chris Kewley's seasonal menus. Fine produce from around the UK turns up in fuss-free, simply-conceived dishes with clear, hearty flavours. Starters typically offer rabbit terrine with prunes and brandy and walnut oil dressing, followed by roast breasts of wood pigeon with port and red wine sauce and pan-fried foie gras. Satisfying puddings continue the theme to finish with, perhaps, chocolate fondant with coffee and white chocolate ice cream.

Chef Chris Kewley **Owner** Mr & Mrs C M Kewley
Times 12-2/7-9.30 Closed 1 wk Xmas, L Sat, D Sun
Prices Fixed L 2 course fr £20, Fixed D 3 course fr £31, Service optional **Wines** 40 bottles over £20, 30 bottles under £20, 4 by glass **Notes** Sunday L, Vegetarian available, Dress restrictions, No shorts, Air con **Seats** 50 **Children** Portions **Parking** 20

TOWCESTER — Map 11 SP64

Vine House Hotel & Restaurant

◉◉ Modern, Traditional British

Rural setting for daily-changing menu of local produce

☎ 01327 811267 🖷 01327 811309
100 High St, Paulerspury NN12 7NA
e-mail: info@vinehousehotel.com
dir: 2m S of Towcester, just off A5

Two 300-year-old limestone cottages with creepers climbing the old walls is home to husband-and-wife team Marcus and Julie Springett's restaurant with rooms. The charming village setting enhances the relaxed and traditional tone of the place. Original features have been preserved throughout, and outside there is a carefully tended cottage garden and a romantic folly for an intimate lunch or dinner for two. A refreshingly concise three options are offered at each course from the fixed price menu, plus a slate of artisan British cheeses if you've room. The food is rustic and traditional, but not old fashioned: pâté of smoked mackerel comes with black pudding and curry oil, and a main-course corn-fed Goosnargh duck comes with triple-cooked chips and celeriac and pumpkin purée.

Chef Marcus Springett **Owner** Mr M & Mrs J Springett
Times 12-2/6-10 Closed Sun, L Mon **Prices** Fixed L 2

course fr £26.95, Fixed D 3 course fr £29.95, Service added 12.5% **Wines** 47 bottles over £20, 26 bottles under £20, 2 by glass **Seats** 26, Pr/dining room 10 **Parking** 20

WHITTLEBURY — Map 11 SP64

Murrays

◉◉ British, European

Fine-dining restaurant dedicated to Formula 1 commentator Murray Walker

☎ 01327 857857 & 0845 400 0001 🖷 01327 857867
Whittlebury Hall Hotel NN12 8QH
e-mail: sales@whittleburyhall.co.uk
web: www.whittleburyhall.co.uk
dir: A43/A413 to Whittlebury, through village, hotel at far end on right

The much-quoted Formula 1 commentator Murray Walker provides inspiration for this sophisticated restaurant in a purpose-built Georgian-style country-house hotel within walking distance of Silverstone. Mr Walker was prone to over-excitability in the heat of the moment, so there are plenty of anecdotes from his glory years, as well as F1 memorabilia to entertain diners. The kitchen deals in modern British cooking based on labour-intensive classical techniques. Pork belly, black pudding and seared scallops with caramelised cauliflower and pear chutney gets you off the grid, then accelerating down the straight with roasted cod fillet and shrimp potato cake, wilted spinach, caramelised baby onions, squash and garlic cream. Prune and Armagnac soufflé with Earl Grey ice cream takes you through the chequered flag.

Chef Craig Rose **Owner** Macepark (Whittlebury) Ltd
Times 7-10 Closed 24-26, 31 Dec, 1-7 Jan, Sun, Mon, L all week **Prices** Food prices not confirmed for 2010. Please telephone for details. **Notes** Vegetarian available, Dress restrictions, Smart casual, No jeans, trainers or shorts, Air con **Seats** 32, Pr/dining room 400 **Children** Portions, Menu **Parking** 300, On site

NORTHUMBERLAND

CORNHILL-ON-TWEED — Map 21 NT83

Tillmouth Park Country House Hotel

◉ Traditional British ❦

Splendid Northumbrian mansion with country-house cooking

☎ 01890 882255 🖷 01890 882540
TD12 4UU
e-mail: reception@tillmouthpark.force9.co.uk
dir: A698, 3m E from Cornhill-on-Tweed

The mansion is a glorious example of Victorian architectural pastiche, built in the 1880s to look at least a century older. It sits by the River Till in the tranquil border country, and if you're impressed by the outer view, just wait until you reach the galleried lounge and elegant dining room with its nourishing garden views. The cooking has the country-house idiom judged just right, with some neat inventive touches on an essentially traditional base. Smoked haddock risotto with a parmesan tuile is one way to start, with full-flavoured Barbary duck breast in orange syrup to follow. Finish indulgently with caramelised banana bavarois.

Chef Piotr Dziedzic **Owner** Tillmouth Park Partnership
Times 12-2/7-8.45 Closed 26-28 Dec, Jan-Mar, L Mon-Sat **Prices** Starter £4.95-£12, Main £11.50-£28, Dessert £5.95-£8, Service optional **Wines** 50 bottles over £20, 7 bottles under £20, 6 by glass **Notes** Sunday L, Vegetarian available, Dress restrictions, Smart casual, No jeans, Civ Wed 50 **Seats** 40, Pr/dining room 20 **Children** Portions **Parking** 50

HEXHAM — Map 21 NY96

Dukes Grill

◉ Modern British

Fine dining in an Edwardian mansion in expansive parkland

☎ 01434 673350 🖷 01434 673962
De Vere Slaley Hall, Slaley NE47 0BX
e-mail: slaley.hall@devere-hotels.com
dir: A1 from S to A68. Follow signs for Slaley Hall. From N A69 to Corbridge then take A68 S and follow signs to Slaley Hall

In the rugged hinterland of Newcastle-upon-Tyne, this grandiose Edwardian pile has an impressive 1,000-acre spread of parkland with a brace of golf courses, spa facilities and sweeping views over the Tyne Valley. Dukes Grill is the hotel's fine-dining option, a striking boldly-coloured setting that brings to mind an upmarket Parisian brasserie with deep purple chairs, elegant mirrors and chandeliers. Local seasonal produce drives menus of well-executed contemporary dishes, backed by prime slabs of protein blitzed on the Josper grill. Expect seared scallops with squid ink, celeriac and watercress as an opener, then follow with rump of lamb, potato and fennel Parmentier and aubergine confit.

continued

HEXHAM *continued*

Chef Paul Patterson **Owner** De Vere Hotels
Times 1-3/6.30-9.45 Closed Mon, **Prices** Fixed L 2 course
£21.50, Fixed D 3 course £24.95, Starter £6.50-£9.50,
Main £12.95-£58, Dessert £6-£9.50, Service added but
optional 10% **Notes** Sunday L, Vegetarian available,
Dress restrictions, Smart casual, Civ Wed 200, Air con
Seats 40, Pr/dining room 30 **Children** Portions
Parking 200

Josephine Restaurant

◎◎ Modern, European

14th-century castle dining with 21st-century menu

☎ 01434 688 888 🖨 01434 684 019
Langley Castle Hotel, Langley on Tyne NE47 5LU
e-mail: manager@langleycastle.com
web: www.langleycastle.com
dir: From A69 take A686 S, restaurant 2m on right

A 14th-century castle built during the reign of Edward III
sits in the South Tyne valley surrounded by 10 acres of
woodland. Retaining all its structural integrity, it is one
of the very few medieval fortified castle hotels in England.
The Josephine restaurant has a dining room to marvel at,
with its stained-glass windows, opulent fabrics and
blazing winter fires. There is nothing medieval about the
cooking, which may feature grilled lemon sole with
almonds, roast salsify and béarnaise to begin, succeeded
by lamb two ways - roast rump and confit shank - with
sweet potato and rosemary purée and balsamic onions.
Finish with an excellent dark chocolate fondant with milk
chocolate terrine and white chocolate parfait.

Chef Andy Smith **Owner** Dr S Madnick **Times** 12-2.30/7-9
Prices Fixed L 2 course £15-£18, Fixed D 3 course £35-
£40, Service optional **Wines** 19 bottles over £20, 20
bottles under £20, 7 by glass **Notes** Sunday L, Vegetarian
available, Dress restrictions, Smart casual, Civ Wed 120
Seats 48 **Children** Portions, Menu **Parking** 57

LONGHORSLEY   Map 21 NZ19

Dobson Restaurant

◎◎ Modern International

**Grade II listed country property set amid extensive
parkland**

☎ 01670 500000 🖨 01670 500001
Macdonald Linden Hall, Golf & Country Club NE65 8XF
e-mail: general.lindenhall@macdonald-hotels.co.uk
dir: 7m NW of Morpeth on A697 off A1

The Georgian mansion of Linden Hall sits in 450 acres of
park and woodland surrounded by beautiful countryside.
The hotel's fine-dining Dobson Restaurant comes suitably
decorated in plush reds and offers fine views, but, while
observing the civilised formalities of dress code, has a
friendly ambience. The kitchen takes a modern approach
- underpinned by classical themes - with accomplished
dishes driven by carefully-sourced produce. Take a duo of
Scottish lamb, for instance (short saddle and slow-
roasted shoulder), served with fondant potatoes,
butternut squash purée and rosemary jus, or wild sea
bass (from sustainable sources), pan-fried and
accompanied by saffron mashed potatoes and chorizo
sauce vierge. (The hotel's Linden Tree Pub offers a more
informal brasserie menu.)

Times 12-2.30/6.30-9.30 Closed L Mon-Sat

MATFEN   Map 21 NZ07

Matfen Hall

◎◎ Modern International

Elegant dining in a Victorian library

☎ 01661 886500 & 855708 🖨 01661 886055
NE20 0RH
e-mail: info@matfenhall.com
dir: A69 signed Hexham, leave at Heddon on the Wall.
Then B6318, through Rudchester & Harlow Hill. Follow
signs on right for Matfen

Ancestors of the Blackett family, who own Matfen, built
the Hall at the outset of the Victorian era. It is an
imposing, but supremely elegant edifice that makes a
grand base from which to roam the windswept
Northumberland coast, and is also a golfer's paradise,
with its 27-hole parkland course. Dining goes on amid
the book-lined ambience of the Library, and also on the
terrace, if you've a mind, when the sun comes out. The
emphasis of the menus is quality local ingredients cooked
in the imaginative modern idiom, with a parade of

---

incidentals (nibbles, canapés, a palate-cleansing sorbet)
adding interest and value. Start with a watercress
soufflé, followed up by roast leg of local lamb set in basil
mousseline, before coming to land with the must-have
chocolate brownie dessert.

Chef Phil Hall **Owner** Sir Hugh & Lady Blackett
Times 12.15-2.30/7-10 Closed L Mon-Sat **Prices** Starter
£5.95-£8.50, Main £16.50-£20.50, Dessert £5.50-£9.25,
Service optional **Wines** 56 bottles over £20, 37 bottles
under £20, 6 by glass **Notes** Sunday L, Vegetarian
available, Dress restrictions, Smart casual, Civ Wed 160
Seats 90, Pr/dining room 120 **Children** Portions
Parking 120

PONTELAND   Map 21 NZ17

Café Lowrey

◎ British, French

Relaxed bistro-style dining in a pleasant neighbourhood

☎ 01661 820357 🖨 01661 820357
33-35 The Broadway, Darras Hall NE20 9PW
web: www.cafelowrey.co.uk
dir: From A696, follow signs for Darras Hall. Left at mini
rdbt, restaurant in 200yds

Café Lowrey has an informal brasserie look that fits in
well with its location in a small shopping enclave in the
well-heeled residential area of Ponteland, near to
Newcastle airport. Peek through the huge double-fronted
windows: it's a warm and inviting place, kitted out simply
with quarry-tiled floors, clothed tables and old-style
wooden chairs, with cheery staff in long aprons doing
their bit to foster a relaxed ambience. Cracking local
ingredients are the basis of an enticing menu that offers
plenty of crowd-pleasers in a modern British and French
vein. Try a cheddar cheese and spinach soufflé to start,
then grilled sea bass with sauté potatoes, tapenade,
fennel salad and beurre blanc.

Chef Ian Lowrey **Owner** Ian Lowrey **Times** 12-2/5.30-10
Closed BHs, Mon, L Tue-Fri, D Sun **Prices** Fixed L 2 course
£13.50-£13.95, Fixed D 3 course fr £15.50, Starter £4.50-
£9.50, Main £10.50-£22.50, Dessert fr £5.50, Service
optional, Groups min 10 service 10% **Wines** 12 bottles
over £20, 18 bottles under £20, 6 by glass **Notes** Sunday
L, Vegetarian available, Dress restrictions, Smart casual,
Air con **Seats** 68 **Children** Portions **Parking** 15

NOTTINGHAMSHIRE

GUNTHORPE
Map 11 SK64

Tom Browns Brasserie

◉◉ Modern British ✪

Bustling riverside brasserie offering modern British food

☎ 0115 966 3642
The Old School House, Trentside NG14 7FB
e-mail: info@tombrowns.co.uk
dir: A6097, Gunthorpe Bridge

This popular brasserie mixes the original character of the Victorian period with a modern continental image in a converted Victorian schoolhouse setting. Named after the 19th-century novel *Tom Brown's Schooldays*, it has several dining areas and outside decking on the banks of the River Trent for warmer weather. Dark chocolate high-backed leather chairs, simply dressed, candle-lit tables and lively music create a trendy bar-brasserie atmosphere. The menu offers modern British food, with good-quality ingredients simply combined and well balanced to keep flavour to the fore. There is an early diners' evening menu as well as the main carte. Try cod and tarragon fishcakes with sweet red and yellow pepper relish, followed by fillet of Scotch beef, potato rösti, oxtail tortellini, roasted shallots, wilted spinach and port sauce.

Chef Peter Kirk **Owner** Adam & Robin Perkins **Times** 12-2.30/6-9.30 Closed D 25-26 Dec **Prices** Fixed L 2 course fr £13.95, Fixed D 3 course fr £15.95, Starter £4.50-£8.95, Main £11.95-£18.95, Dessert £5.75-£7.50, Service optional **Wines** 30 bottles over £20, 30 bottles under £20, 18 by glass **Notes** Fixed price menu is an early bird menu, Sunday L, Dress restrictions, Smart casual, Air con **Seats** 100, Pr/dining room 20 **Children** Portions **Parking** 9, On street

LANGAR
Map 11 SK73

Langar Hall

◉◉ Modern British ✪

Country-house hotel in an idyllic village setting

☎ 01949 860559   🖷 01949 861045
NG13 9HG
e-mail: imogen@langarhall.co.uk
web: www.langarhall.com
dir: Signed off A46 & A52 in Langar village centre (behind church)

Built in 1837, this delightful country-house hotel boasts a secluded rural location at the end of a long avenue of lime trees. Views of the 12th century church, medieval fishponds, gardens and parkland can all be enjoyed from the house, which is furnished in elegant style with antiques and works of art. In the romantic pillared dining room, fresh flowers and candles decorate the smart linen-clothed tables, while the service is friendly and not remotely stuffy. Seasonal, local ingredients - some sourced from the hotel's own grounds - are the mainstay of the modern British menu. Start with steamed English asparagus with a soft-boiled duck egg and brioche soldiers, followed by roast cutlet of Langar lamb with pea and mint and an olive oil mash, finishing up with bitter chocolate tart with black cherry sorbet.

Chef Gary Booth **Owner** Imogen Skirving **Times** 12-2/7-10 **Prices** Fixed L 2 course fr £12.50, Fixed D 3 course £25-£27.50, Service added but optional 10% **Wines** 20 bottles over £20, 30 bottles under £20, 4 by glass **Notes** Sunday L, Vegetarian available, Civ Wed 50 **Seats** 30, Pr/dining room 20 **Children** Portions **Parking** 40

MANSFIELD
Map 16 SK56

Lambs at the Market

◉ Modern British NEW ✪

Smart modern restaurant with a keen eye for local produce

☎ 01623 424880
Cattle Market Tavern, Nottingham Rd NG18 1BJ
e-mail: troylamb2003@yahoo.co.uk
dir: Please telephone for directions

Lambs at the Market could be said to have had a foodie connection since the 19th century, when it was the tavern joined to the cattle market. The handsome red-brick Victorian building beneath a pepperpot turret was resurrected in 2007 as a polished, family-run restaurant with a mission to source the best local produce from named suppliers. A thoroughly modern makeover certainly looks the part: exposed brick and aubergine-painted walls are married smartly with dark wood and creamy leather. The kitchen's stock-in-trade is very much British cuisine, but done with flair and style: posh fish fingers with pea purée and tartare dressing might start, then contrasts in flavour and texture abound in roast belly of Gotham pork with local black pudding, seared scallop and leek cream. Finish with a molten-centred chocolate pudding with vanilla ice cream.

Chef Troy Lamb **Owner** Ted & Brenda Dubowski, Alison & Troy Lamb **Times** 12-2.30/6.30-10 Closed 25 Dec & 1 Jan, Mon, D Sun **Prices** Fixed L 2 course fr £10.95, Fixed D 2 course fr £16.95, Starter £4.95-£6.25, Main £10.95-£16.50, Dessert £5.50-£6.95, Service optional **Wines** 28 bottles over £20, 25 bottles under £20, 8 by glass **Notes** Tasting menu available, Sunday L, Vegetarian available, Air con **Seats** 56 **Children** Portions **Parking** Public car parks adjacent or on street

NEWARK-ON-TRENT
Map 17 SK75

Cutlers at The Grange

◉ Modern British

Elegant Victorian setting for good, honest cooking

☎ 01636 703399   🖷 01636 702328
The Grange Hotel, 73 London Rd NG24 1RZ
e-mail: info@grangenewark.co.uk
dir: From A1 follow signs for Balderton, the hotel is opposite the Polish War Graves

The clue is in the name of the Cutlers restaurant at the friendly Grange Hotel: glass display cases of antique cutlery and themed prints decorate the walls in the elegant, red, gold and blue furnished Victorian room. The menu is flannel-free and reads enticingly - there is nothing fancy about the food here, no foams or savoury ice creams, just honest, natural flavours extracted from quality, seasonal ingredients. Unpretentious, well-balanced dishes are the kitchen's trademark, as in a starter of roast butternut squash risotto scented with sage and served with pine nuts and crisp Parma ham, followed, perhaps, by roast rack of lamb with courgettes, herb couscous and creamed ceps.

Chef Tamas Lauko **Owner** Tom & Sandra Carr **Times** 12-2/6.30-9.30 Closed 25 Dec-5 Jan, L Mon-Sat **Prices** Fixed L 2 course £12.95, Starter £4.95-£8.50, Main £10.95-£16.50, Dessert £5.50-£7.50, Service optional **Wines** 27 bottles over £20, 16 bottles under £20, 6 by glass **Notes** Sunday L, Vegetarian available **Seats** 40 **Children** Portions **Parking** 17

Cockliffe Country House

◉ Modern NEW

Elegant country house with modern European cooking

☎ 0115 968 0179　📠 0115 968 0623
Burntstump Country Park, Burntstump Hill, Arnold NG5 8PQ
e-mail: enquiries@cockliffehouse.co.uk
web: www.cockliffehouse.co.uk
dir: M1 junct 27, follow signs to Hucknall (A611), then B6011, right at T-junct, follow signs for Cockliffe House

This stone hotel sits in its own landscaped grounds with enviable countryside views. Some of the produce featured on the menu is grown in the grounds, while even more is sourced locally. There is a choice of two dining rooms, each formal and traditionally decorated. The menu is modern in its sensibilities, with Cornish diver-caught scallops, for example, partnered with slow-braised belly of pork and cauliflower purée in a decidedly à la mode first course. Follow on with a sorbet (forced rhubarb, perhaps, or basil and yogurt) before main-course lamb two ways, and rum and coconut rice pudding with tempura of banana.

Chef Richard Murray **Owner** Dane & Jane Clarke **Times** 12-2/6-9.30 Closed L Mon-Wed, D Sun **Prices** Fixed L 2 course £12.95, Fixed D 3 course £16.95, Starter £5.25-£10.95, Main £11.95-£23.95, Dessert £5.25-£8.95, Service optional, Groups min 8 service 10% **Wines** 25 bottles over £20, 14 bottles under £20, 11 by glass **Notes** Early evening menu Mon-Fri 6-7.30pm, Sunday L, Vegetarian available, Dress restrictions, Smart casual, Civ Wed 50 **Seats** 50, Pr/dining room 30 **Children** Portions **Parking** 50

Hart's Restaurant

◉◉ Modern British ⬧

Modern cooking in elegant city restaurant

☎ 0115 988 1900　📠 0115 947 7600
Hart's Hotel, Standard Court, Park Row NG1 6FN
e-mail: ask@hartsnottingham.co.uk
dir: M1 junct 24, follow A453 to city centre. Follow signs to the castle. Once on Maid Marion Way turn left at the Gala Casino, continue to top of the hill and turn left through black gates

Hart's is a chic modern boutique hotel and restaurant built on parts of the ramparts of the city's medieval

castle. Tim Hart is a man who has built his reputation over nearly thirty years at Hambleton Hall in Oakham (see entry) and here in Nottingham he has created a top-notch city restaurant. Across the car park from the hotel with its wonderful private gardens, is the busy and stylish restaurant, which delivers good quality ingredients, skilfully cooked in the modern British vein. The décor is warm and bright with banquette and booth seating and contemporary art on the walls. Start, perhaps, with roasted scallops, cauliflower, apple and oyster dressing, following on with loin of lamb with aubergine and goats' cheese and finished with a lamb jus. Dessert might be fennel pannacotta with confit pineapple and gingerbread ice cream.

Chef Gareth Ward **Owner** Tim Hart **Times** 12-2/6-10.30 Closed 26 Dec & 1 Jan, L 31 Dec, D 25 Dec **Prices** Fixed L 2 course fr £13.95, Fixed D 3 course fr £25, Starter £5.50-£12.95, Main £13.50-£22.50, Dessert £6.50-£9.50, Service added but optional 12% **Wines** 57 bottles over £20, 23 bottles under £20, 6 by glass **Notes** Pre-theatre menu 2 course £18, Sunday L, Vegetarian available, Civ Wed 100 **Seats** 80, Pr/dining room 100 **Children** Portions **Parking** 15

The Lobster Pot

◉ Seafood

Gem of an inland seafood restaurant

☎ 0115 947 0707
199 Mansfield Rd NG1 3FS
dir: From Nottingham city centre N on A60 for 0.5m, restaurant on left at the lights where Huntingdon St joins Mansfield Rd

Maybe not in the most fashionable part of town, but a blue exterior and dedicated approach picks this unpretentious, friendly and relaxed seafood restaurant out from the crowd. The simple, rustic décor features fish-themed objets d'art and Middle Eastern carvings alongside chunky wooden tables. The oyster, smoked salmon, mussel and shellfish selection prove particularly noteworthy, and there's also a daily specials board. Saucing is subtle and takes care not to dominate the quality core ingredient; sea-fresh lemon sole is grilled to perfection and simply served with a caper sauce, while starters like Thai fishcakes come with a balanced sweet chilli sauce.

Chef Mr & Mrs Pongsawang **Owner** Mr & Mrs Pongsawang **Times** 12-2/6-10.30 Closed BHs, Mon, L Sun **Prices** Starter £3.95-£6.95, Main £7.95-£35.95, Dessert £3, Service optional **Wines** 2 bottles over £20, 30 bottles under £20, 3 by glass **Notes** Air con **Seats** 40 **Children** Portions

Merchants Restaurant & Bar

◉◉ Modern British

Great brasserie menu in eye-catching surroundings

☎ 0115 958 9898　& 852 3232　📠 0115 852 3223
Lace Market Hotel, 29-31 High Pavement NG1 1HE
e-mail: restaurant@lacemarkethotel.co.uk
dir: Follow city centre signs for Galleries of Justice, entrance is opposite

The brasserie at this stylish boutique hotel was designed by the seemingly ubiquitous David Collins, and he has brought his trademark individualism to the task. Chainmail chandeliers and horsehair light fittings are among the head-turning aspects, and the frieze incorporating panels of lacework is a neat nod to the trade that once sustained this part of Nottingham. The cooking lives up to the surroundings, with an inspired contemporary approach that brings on a pairing of scallop and sea bream with butternut squash purée, chorizo and apple in one multi-faceted starter. Quality Loch Duart salmon gets teamed with gnocchi, pak choi and potato as a main course, or there might be rolled pork belly with its crackling, classically accompanied by apple and mash. Conclude with lemongrass crème brûlée and raspberry sorbet.

Chef Tom Earle **Owner** Finesse Hotels **Times** 6-10 Closed 26 Dec, 1 Jan, Sun-Mon **Prices** Fixed L 2 course fr £18.50, Starter £5.50-£12.50, Main £15.50-£22.50, Dessert £6.25-£8.25, Service added but optional 10% **Wines** 70+ bottles over £20, 5 bottles under £20, 12 by glass **Notes** Vegetarian available, Civ Wed 60, Air con **Seats** 50, Pr/dining room 20 **Children** Portions, Menu **Parking** On street. NCP adjacent

Restaurant Sat Bains with Rooms

◉◉◉◉ – see opposite page

World Service

◉◉ Modern British

Striking cuisine amid colonial-style grandeur

☎ 0115 847 5587　📠 0115 847 5584
Newdigate House, Castle Gate NG1 6AF
e-mail: enquiries@worldservicerestaurant.com
web: www.worldservicerestaurant.com
dir: 200mtrs from city centre, 50mtrs from Nottingham Castle

The 17th-century Newdigate House is the setting for an idiosyncratic restaurant that aims to pile on the style of

continued on page 354

Restaurant Sat Bains with Rooms

Modern British

A destination restaurant with rooms

☎ 0115 986 6566
Lenton Ln, Trentside NG7 2SA
e-mail: info@restaurantsatbains.net
dir: M1 junct 24, A453 for approx 8m. Through Clifton, road divides into 3 - take middle lane signed 'Lenton Lane Industrial Estate', then 1st left, left again. Follow brown Restaurant Sat Bains sign

There are seven bedrooms at Sat and Amanda Bains's restaurant, and staying over is the only way to extend the experience...an experience you're unlikely to want to end. You can lie in your own bed, of course, after the drive home, and recall the flavours and textures that you've just experienced, but, if you stay overnight, you can imagine with fevered expectation what breakfast might bring. For Sat is undoubtedly one of the top chefs in the UK. The proximity of the motorway and an industrial estate are of no importance once you've arrived at this converted farmhouse on the banks of the River Trent, with its small but attractive grounds, for all is quiet, relaxed and charming. Amanda oversees the service and, seated at comfortable high-backed leather chairs, everything is seamless from the diners' perspective; classical music plays

gently in the background and the two interconnecting dining rooms are chic and contemporary in an understated manner. Behind a frosted glass screen is a chef's table. The menu format is based around tasting menus - three of them, plus a bespoke version tailored to the customer's likes and dislikes - allowing the chef to take you on a 'journey of taste, texture and temperature', and what a ride it is! First and foremost the produce is absolute top quality and it's not all about luxury ingredients - more humble ingredients get a look-in, too. The cooking is innovative and capable of making the very best of new-fangled techniques without losing its way, and presentation is precise and visually arresting. A perfectly cooked scallop, for example, with chicory, apple, sultana and a sherry syrup, demonstrates a masterful control over the balance of flavours, while duck Royale is served in a jar, the lid lifted at the table to release the superb aroma, and comprises a layer of sublime duck parfait topped with velvety pumpkin, mandarin sorbet and top-notch aged parmesan. Cornish brill and braised chicken wings are brought together harmoniously with the help of a red wine jus flavoured with vanilla, and passionfruit tart is made with exquisite pastry and comes with textbook meringue and black sesame. It is a journey you don't want to end.

Chef Sat Bains **Owner** Sat Bains, Amanda Bains **Times** 7-9.30 Closed 2 wks Jan & 2 wks Aug, Sun, Mon, L all week **Prices** Tasting menu £55-£85, Service added 12.5% **Wines** 120 bottles over £20, 6 bottles under £20, 30 by glass **Notes** Chef's table £95, tasting menus 5, 7 & 10 course, Air con **Seats** 34, Pr/dining room 14 **Parking** 22

NOTTINGHAM *continued*

eras gone by. Step from the walled oriental garden into the plush lounge bar with its gilt armchairs, where the log fires will warm you almost as much as the bespoke cocktails do. Objets and artefacts from around the world provide visual distraction in the elegantly appointed trio of dining rooms, and the food makes its own striking impact. A classic modern partnering of scallops and black pudding on potato and apple purée is a tasty starter, and could be followed by Derbyshire beef fillet with curly kale and a rather free interpretation of sauce Diane, or poached salmon with gnocchi and sprouting broccoli in crayfish and saffron velouté. The gold star dessert is the white chocolate parfait with assertively spiced mandarins. Allow time for thorough perusal of a serious wine list.

Chef Preston Walker **Owner** Daniel Lindsay, Phillip Morgan, Ashley Walter, Chris Elson **Times** 12-2.15/7-10 Closed 25-26 Dec, 1-7 Jan **Prices** Fixed L 2 course £13, Starter £5-£13.50, Main £14-£19.75, Dessert £5-£8.50, Service added but optional 10% **Wines** 90 bottles over £20, 15 bottles under £20, 10 by glass **Notes** Sunday L, Vegetarian available, Civ Wed 50 **Seats** 80, Pr/dining room 34 **Children** Portions, Menu **Parking** NCP

OXFORDSHIRE

ARDINGTON   Map 5 SU48

The Boar's Head

Modern British 🍃

Peaceful village pub serving up good food

☎ 01235 833254   📠 01235 883254
Church St OX12 8QA
e-mail: info@boarsheadardington.co.uk
web: www.boarsheadardington.co.uk
dir: 2 m E of Wantage on A417, next to village church

The friendly, half-timbered Boar's Head pub and restaurant is situated in the beautiful Downland village of Ardington, tucked away beside the church. It has been providing a valuable service to locals and visitors for over 150 years, and never more so than in these times. Choose either the cosy village pub bar or the more formal restaurant and pick something off the regularly-changing menu, which makes full use of fresh, seasonal and locally-grown ingredients. Fish is a well-loved feature with daily deliveries from Cornwall, and everything is full of flavour and pleasing on the eye. Expect starters such as hot pheasant terrine with apple and Calvados chutney,

followed by Cornish sea bass with bacon and toasted ratatouille. Finish with chocolate and black cherry brownie, white chocolate mousse and raspberry ripple. The pub also has three well-appointed bedrooms.

The Boar's Head

Chef Bruce Buchan **Owner** Boar's Head (Ardington) Ltd **Times** 12-2/7-10 Closed 25 Dec, **Prices** Fixed L 2 course fr £15, Starter £6.45-£10.95, Main £16.50-£23.50, Dessert £7.50, Service optional **Wines** 70 bottles over £20, 30 bottles under £20, 12 by glass **Notes** Gastronomic menu 6 course £39.50, Sunday L, Vegetarian available **Seats** 40, Pr/dining room 24 **Children** Portions **Parking** 20

ASTON ROWANT   Map 5 SU79

Lambert Arms

Modern British NEW

Pub classics and modern British cuisine in a smart coaching inn

☎ 0845 459 3736   📠 01844 351893
London Rd OX49 5SB
e-mail: info@lambertarms.com
dir: M40 junct 6, at T-Junction take right turn towards Chinnor (B4009) back under the motorway. Shortly after take 1st left to Postcombe/Thame (A40)

The Lambert Arms is a historic black-timbered coaching inn at the foot of the Chiltern hills, classily made over with a 21st-century take on food and décor. The interior has retained the cosy familiarity of exposed brickwork and log fires, while injecting the modern style of dark wood tables and wooden floors into the clean-cut restaurant. Food ranges from bar snacks and pub classics done well, to straightforward modern British gastro-pub dishes, such as a starter of salmon tartare with avocado and ginger purée and coriander oil. Among robust main courses might be slow-cooked shoulder of lamb with gratin potato, roasted courgettes and rosemary jus.

Times 12-2.30/6.30-9

BANBURY   Map 11 SP44

Inglenook Restaurant

Modern British NEW

Original features and honest cooking in village setting

☎ 01295 730777   📠 01295 730800
Wroxton House Hotel, Silver St, Wroxton OX15 6QB
e-mail: reservations@wroxtonhousehotel.com
dir: From M40 junct 11 follow A422 (signed Banbury, then Wroxton). After 3m, hotel on 1st right bend

In the heart of the small village of Wroxton, the original parts of this semi-thatched hotel date from the 17th century. The cosy Inglenook Restaurant boasts the eponymous fireplace and plenty of original oak beams, and provides professional service in a relaxed atmosphere. The food is unfussy but not unrefined: fresh asparagus with soft-poached egg and hollandaise sauce is given a lift with the addition of chorizo, while main-course duo of lamb (roasted rump, braised shoulder) comes with celeriac purée, potato fondant and redcurrant jus. Finish with vanilla cheesecake with pineapple and black pepper syrup.

Chef Steve Mason-Tucker **Owner** John & Gill Smith **Times** 12-2/7-9 **Prices** Fixed L 2 course £12, Fixed D 3 course £27.50, Service optional **Wines** 9 bottles over £20, 17 bottles under £20, 5 by glass **Notes** Sunday L, Vegetarian available, Dress restrictions, Smart casual, Civ Wed 60 **Seats** 60, Pr/dining room 45 **Children** Portions, Menu **Parking** 70

BICESTER   Map 11 SP52

Bignell Park Hotel & Restaurant

Modern British

Creative cooking in a relaxed country setting

☎ 01869 326550 & 0870 042 1024   📠 01869 322729
Chesterton OX26 1UE
e-mail: enq@bignellparkhotel.co.uk
dir: M40 junct 9, follow A41 towards Bicester, turn off at Chesterton and hotel is signed at turning

Dating from 1740 and originally a farmhouse, Bignell Park is these days a small hotel in peaceful countryside near Bicester Shopping Village. In The Oaks restaurant, dine amid the oak beams of a converted barn; there's a minstrels' gallery, too, and at Sunday lunch a live jazz band adds to the atmosphere. The modern British menu is based on good produce and cooked with panache; start with Tay salmon fillet with cauliflower purée and confit lemon zest, following on with breast of Barbary duck, pak choi, spiced carrot purée and a star anise infusion.

Bignell Park Hotel & Restaurant

Times 12-2/7-9.30 Closed D Sun

BRITWELL SALOME
Map 5 SU69

The Goose

⊛⊛ Modern French, International

Serious cooking in former village pub

☎ 01491 612304 ≣ 01491 613945
OX49 5LG
e-mail: info@gooserestaurant.com
dir: M40 junct 6 take B4009 to Watlington, then towards Benson. Restaurant on left 1.5m

Surrounded by magnificent countryside below the Chiltern Hills, parts of this handsome brick-built restaurant date back to 1728. Original beams and fireplaces remain, but it is now a sophisticated, warm restaurant with modern décor, comfortable seating and a landscaped garden that makes a very attractive outside dining area. Service is attentive and friendly, from a young team who show great knowledge of the menu. Cooking skills are accomplished with the exciting menu including a starter of seared Oban scallops with veal sweetbreads and pumpkin and date chutney, followed by roasted Goosnargh duck breast with soya bean sprout risotto, potato chips and shiitake mushrooms. Roasted coconut crème brûlée with pineapple and rocket is one of several tempting desserts.

Chef Ryan Simpson **Owner** Paul Castle
Times 12-3/7-9.30 Closed Last wk Aug, 1st wk Sep, 5 days Xmas/New Year, 1st 2 wks Jan, Mon, D Sun
Prices Fixed L 2 course £14.95, Starter £7-£12.50, Main £13.50-£22, Dessert £6.95, Service optional **Wines** 35 bottles over £20, 3 bottles under £20, 8 by glass
Notes Tasting menu on request, Sunday L, Vegetarian available, Dress restrictions, Smart casual **Seats** 40
Children Portions **Parking** 35

BURFORD
Map 5 SP21

The Angel at Burford

⊛⊛ Modern European V

Restaurant with rooms serving modern brasserie cooking

☎ 01993 822714 ≣ 01993 822069
14 Witney St OX18 4SN
e-mail: paul@theangelatburford.co.uk
dir: From A40, turn off at Burford rdbt, down hill 1st right into Swan Lane, 1st left to Pytts Lane, left at end into Witney St

The Oxfordshire country town of Burford is known as the Gateway to the Cotswolds, and this 16th-century former coaching inn with a trio of rooms is what might be thought of as the quintessential Cotswold hostelry. A south-facing courtyard and tranquil walled garden are among the attractions of the place, and another is the brasserie-style modern cooking. Influences criss-cross creatively throughout, from Thai-style crab cakes with beetroot and apple chutney, to sea bass with fennel, pine nut and dill pasta stack, or venison medallions in gin-laced blackberry sauce, and desserts such as plum and amaretti bread-and-butter pudding with almond ice cream.

Chef David Latter **Owner** Paul Swain **Times** 12-2/7-9 Closed Early Jan-15 Jan, Mon, D Sun **Prices** Fixed L 2 course fr £10, Starter £4.95-£7.50, Main £14.50-£16.50, Dessert £5.50-£6.95, Service optional **Wines** 18 bottles over £20, 17 bottles under £20, 11 by glass
Notes Vegetarian menu, Dress restrictions, Smart casual **Seats** 34, Pr/dining room 18 **Children** Portions **Parking** On street

---

The Bay Tree Hotel

⊛ Modern British ℭ

Stylish Cotswold retreat with skilful kitchen

☎ 01993 822791 ≣ 01993 823008
Sheep St OX18 4LW
e-mail: info@baytreehotel.info
web: www.cotswold-inns-hotels.co.uk/baytree
dir: A40 or A361 to Burford. From High St turn into Sheep St, next to old market square. Hotel on right

The Cotswolds area does a nice line in classic English inns, and this mellow stone, wisteria-festooned 16th-century inn is a real corker. Heaven awaits in the form of a pint by the crackling log fire in the Woolsack bar, while the elegant restaurant's tapestry hangings, flagstone floor and leaded windows ring all the right bells for a romantic candlelit dinner. Fine local produce is treated without fuss in modern British dishes such as smoked haddock and salmon fishcakes with sweet chilli sauce and balsamic, seared fillet of sea bass with roasted couscous and spinach and prawn beurre blanc, and lush desserts like dark chocolate torte with mascarpone Chantilly.

Chef Brian Andrews **Owner** Cotswold Inns & Hotels
Times 12-2/7-9.30 **Prices** Fixed L 2 course fr £12.95, Fixed D 3 course fr £27.95, Service optional **Wines** 40 bottles over £20, 23 bottles under £20, 5 by glass
Notes Sunday L, Vegetarian available, Dress restrictions, No jeans or trainers, Civ Wed 80 **Seats** 70, Pr/dining room 24 **Children** Portions **Parking** 55

BURFORD continued

The Lamb Inn

⊚⊚ Traditional British 🍃

Traditional Cotswolds coaching inn with imaginative menu

☎ 01993 823155   🖨 01993 822228
Sheep St OX18 4LR
e-mail: info@lambinn-burford.co.uk
web: www.cotswold-inns-hotels.co.uk/lamb
dir: Exit A40 into Burford, downhill, take 1st left into Sheep St, hotel last on right

The 15th-century Lamb Inn was originally a row of weavers' cottages on the delightfully named Sheep Street. Inside its wisteria-clad Cotswold stone walls, an enchanting jumble of steps, corridors, flagstone floors, antiques, copper and brass and comfy sofas makes for a classic English country inn. In summer, the stone-walled courtyard is a buzzing place to be, but if it's a bit lively with alfresco diners, head into the cheerful restaurant, where cerise and cream walls, mullioned windows and frosted skylights combine in a bright and airy setting. The imaginative food is simply-conceived, cooked with skill and presented in an uncluttered eye-catching style. Home-smoked sirloin of local beef with truffled potato salad might turn up among starters, then perhaps roast pheasant with pheasant boudin, sweetcorn purée and fondant potato.

Chef Sean Ducie **Owner** Cotswold Inns & Hotels
Times 12-2.30/7-9.30 **Prices** Food prices not confirmed for 2010. Please telephone for details. **Wines** 37 bottles over £20, 17 bottles under £20, 9 by glass **Notes** Sunday L, Vegetarian available, Dress restrictions, Smart casual, no jeans or T-shirts **Seats** 55 **Children** Portions **Parking** Care of The Bay Tree Hotel

---

The Highwayman

⊚ British, International

Good food in traditional country inn

☎ 01491 682020
Exlade St RG8 0UA
dir: Exlade St signed off A4074 (Reading/Wallingford road), 0.4m

Located in the attractive village of Checkendon, The Highwayman dates back to the 17th century and sports the traditional country pub features - low beams, wooden floors and furniture, and a log-burning fireplace - combined with more modern fixtures and fittings. Tables are set between several intimate dining areas and the menu offers a choice of homely English and Continental dishes, prepared with good-quality, fresh local ingredients. Try king scallops with fennel and sesame crust, wild rocket and mango chilli salsa, followed by slow-roasted lamb shank with chive mash potato, braised baby vegetables and rosemary. You'll find the dessert blackboard hard to resist.

Chef Michael Keating **Owner** Mr Ken O'Shea
Times 12-2.30/6-10 Closed 26 Dec, 1 Jan, D Sun
Prices Food prices not confirmed for 2010. Please telephone for details. **Wines** 15 bottles over £20, 25 bottles under £20, 11 by glass **Notes** Sunday L, Vegetarian available, Dress restrictions, No work clothes or vests **Seats** 55, Pr/dining room 60 **Children** Portions, Menu **Parking** 30

Sir Charles Napier

⊚⊚ British, French 🍷

Pace-setting cookery in the upper reaches of the Chilterns

☎ 01494 483011   🖨 01494 485311
Sprigg's Alley OX39 4BX
e-mail: info@sircharlesnapier.co.uk
web: www.sircharlesnapier.co.uk
dir: M40 junct 6 to Chinnor. Turn right at rdbt, up hill for 2m to Sprigg's Alley

Perched high up in the Chilterns, the inn is surrounded by luxuriant beechwoods, where wild garlic, fennel, nettles and fungi are gathered at the appropriate seasons. A vine-shaded terrace allows for idyllic summer dining, while inside is as fully equipped with squashy sofas as the weary traveller could wish for. The dining room too feels exactly like being at home, other than that the formidably talented Sam Hughes is in charge. High-gloss cooking of great precision and fine raw materials is on offer from the handwritten menus that offer plenty of choice. A pressed terrine of seared foie gras and confit duck breast is a stunning starter, both visually and on the palate, and comes with delicately puréed sweetcorn and a walnut pancake. The rarefied tone thus set, meals might continue with Cornish cod alongside brandade, baby leeks and spinach in a nicely judged red wine sauce, and attention to detail is maintained all the way through to crème brûlée with a cranberry jelly layer.

Chef Sam Hughes **Owner** Julie Griffiths
Times 12-3.30/6.30-10 Closed 25-27 Dec, Mon, D Sun
Prices Fixed L 2 course £15.50, Fixed D 2 course £16.50, Starter £8.50-£15.50, Main £17.50-£26.50, Dessert £6.75, Service added but optional 12.5% **Wines** 200 bottles over £20, 23 bottles under £20, 9 by glass **Notes** Tasting menu available, Sunday L, Vegetarian available, Air con **Seats** 75, Pr/dining room 45 **Children** Portions, Menu **Parking** 60

The Sweet Olive

⊚ French

French restaurant in charming pub

☎ 01235 851272
Baker St OX11 9DD

The Entente Cordiale is alive and well at this quintessentially English pub which overflows with Gallic charm. Wine cases and bottles decorate the walls of the rustic interior, and the bar helps to enhance the traditional atmosphere. Honest French cooking from a mainly French team is what to expect, with daily specials bolstering the choice. One such special - smoked salmon fishcake with lime butter sauce - shows the confidence in the kitchen with good seasoning and well-considered flavours. Scottish scallops come with the roe intact on a well-made parmesan risotto, with a rocket salad and red wine vinegar reduction. Finish with a lemon cheesecake, raspberry coulis and passionfruit sorbet.

Times 12-2/7-9 Closed Feb, 1 wk Jul, Sun, Wed

DEDDINGTON
Map 11 SP43

Deddington Arms

Traditional British

Traditional but stylish coaching inn offering fine food

☎ 01869 338364   🖷 01869 337010
Horsefair OX15 0SH
e-mail: deddarms@oxfordshire-hotels.co.uk
web: www.deddington-arms-hotel.co.uk
dir: Please telephone for directions

In prime position just off the market square, this old, colour-washed one-time village coaching inn has been sympathetically converted and extended into a modern-day hostelry. While the bar retains original oak-beams, flagstones and cosy fireplace, the contemporary, air-conditioned restaurant comes with high-backed leather chairs and carved-wood panelling and archways. You'll find traditional British fare with an eye on quality local produce; duo of lamb (confit rump and roasted rack), for example, served with bubble-and-squeak cake and aubergine relish, or the more adventurous pan-fried red snapper fillet teamed with a pea croquette and tomato and chilli salsa on the dinner carte. The bar menu offers classic pub fare.

Chef Nick Porter **Owner** Oxfordshire Hotels Ltd
Times 12–2.30/6.30–9.45 **Prices** Fixed L 2 course fr £10, Fixed D 3 course fr £18.95, Starter £5.25–£7.25, Main £13.75–£16.25, Dessert £4–£7.50, Service added but optional 10%, Groups min 6 service 10% **Wines** 20 bottles over £20, 22 bottles under £20, 9 by glass **Notes** Sunday L, Vegetarian available, Air con **Seats** 60, Pr/dining room 30 **Children** Portions, Menu **Parking** 36

DORCHESTER (ON THAMES)
Map 5 SU59

White Hart Hotel

British, French

Simple but effective cooking in a star of the small screen

☎ 01865 340074   🖷 01865 341082
High St OX10 7HN
e-mail: whitehart@oxfordshire-hotels.co.uk
web: www.oxfordshire-hotels.co.uk
dir: Village centre. Just off A415/A4074. 3m from Wallingford, 6m from Abingdon

The Oxfordshire village in which the White Hart stands is telegenic enough to have starred many times in ITV's *Midsomer Murders* series, as has the centuries-old hotel itself. Its unexpectedly high-ceilinged restaurant is done out in homely style, with staff offering a warm welcome, and modern cooking that keeps things reasonably simple. Chicken liver parfait, monkfish in Parma ham with crushed peas and mustard cream, and grilled rib-eye with horseradish mash, are the kinds of dishes to expect. Sharply flavoured lemon posset would do better without its ice cream van-style topping of strawberry sauce, or you could try chocolate tart.

Times 12–2.30/6.30–9.30

FARINGDON
Map 5 SU29

The Folly Restaurant

British, International

Fine food in elegant Georgian house

☎ 01367 241272   🖷 01367 242346
BW Sudbury House Hotel & Conference Centre, London St SN7 8AA
e-mail: stay@sudburyhouse.co.uk
dir: Off A420, signed Folly Hill & Market Place

Historically famous for its stand in the Civil War against Oliver Cromwell's Roundhead army, the pretty market town of Faringdon can be traced back to Saxon times. With its fine buildings, the town remains an architectural delight and Sudbury House Hotel was itself once a Regency residence of note. Set in 9 acres of attractive grounds it has been extended in recent years and now blends modern facilities with traditional good looks. The graceful and comfortable Folly Restaurant offers a relaxed outlook over patio and gardens, while its menu is driven by seasonal produce, simplicity and well-defined flavours. Expect roast pigeon breast on sauté potatoes,

caramelised red onion and apple syrup, followed by loin of pork with a smoked garlic mash, green beans and a peppercorn sauce.

Chef Clifford Burt, J Massey, K Arlott, M Murray, J Sveta **Owner** Cranfield University **Times** 12.30–2/7–9.15 Closed 26–30 Dec, **Prices** Fixed L 2 course £19.50–£20, Fixed D 3 course £24.50–£25, Starter £5.25–£5.50, Main £14.50–£15, Dessert £4.75–£5, Service optional **Wines** 9 bottles over £20, 23 bottles under £20, 11 by glass **Notes** Early bird D Sun–Thu 5.30–7pm, Sunday L, Vegetarian available, Dress restrictions, Smart casual, Civ Wed 160, Air con **Seats** 100, Pr/dining room 40 **Children** Portions, Menu **Parking** 100

GORING
Map 5 SU68

The Leatherne Bottel

Modern European 🍷

Eat from a cosmopolitan menu while gazing at the river traffic

☎ 01491 872667   🖷 01491 875308
RG8 0HS
e-mail: leathernebottel@aol.com
dir: M4 junct 12 or M40 junct 6, signed from B4009 towards Wallingford

This country inn is set back sufficiently far from the road for tranquillity, and yet the location on the Thames and its passing river traffic means there is never a dull moment. A small conservatory extension and patio tables make the most of the summer weather, and you might even choose to arrive by boat. Gently formal, and properly attentive, service is in keeping with the tone, and the food displays inspired cosmopolitan leanings. Roast wild sea bass with crab and pea risotto and sweet chilli jam, or fricassée of lamb's kidneys with wholegrain mustard mash, bacon and red onion gravy, are possible main courses. Offal is well handled, as is the case in a starter of chicken livers with roasted pear and goats' cheese curd, while desserts such as dark chocolate truffle with a roasted peach will prove hard to resist.

Chef Julia Abbey **Owner** John Madejski
Times 12–2.30/7–9.30 Closed D Sun **Prices** Fixed L 2 course fr £19.50, Tasting menu £58–£95, Starter £8.50–£13.50, Main £17.50–£24.50, Dessert £7.50, Service added 10% **Wines** 175 bottles over £20, 1 bottles under £20, 15 by glass **Notes** Tasting menu available, Sunday L, Vegetarian available **Seats** 45 **Children** Portions **Parking** 40, extra parking available

GORING *continued*

The Miller of Mansfield

◉ Modern British NEW

Chiltern country inn with ultra-modern makeover

☎ 01491 872829
High St RG8 9AW
e-mail: reservations@millerofmansfield.com
web: www.millerofmansfield.com

A thoroughgoing contemporary makeover has been applied to this old Oxfordshire coaching inn, with a stunningly fresh design approach in both the restaurant and bar, not to mention the 10 guest rooms. A garden terrace provides for dining en plein air during the best months, and the menus faithfully list the local suppliers in today's approved fashion. The modern British idiom is mobilised effectively in dishes such as crab spring roll with dipping sauce, followed perhaps by parmesan-crusted cod with chorizo and smoked paprika, or there may be a more traditional French vein explored in generous chicken liver parfait with pungent onion chutney, and duck leg confit with braised lentils. To finish, there is hot cinnamon doughnuts for dipping in chocolate.

Prices Food prices not confirmed for 2010. Please telephone for details.

GREAT MILTON   Map 5 SP60

Le Manoir aux Quat' Saisons

◉◉◉◉◉ – *see opposite page*

HENLEY-ON-THAMES   Map 5 SU78

The Cherry Tree Inn

◉ Modern British, European

Popular inn with serious attitude to food

☎ 01491 680430   🖨 01491 682168
Stoke Row RG9 5QA
e-mail: info@thecherrytreeinn.com
dir: On A4155 from Henley-on-Thames exit B481 to Sonning Common. Follow Stoke Row signs, turn right for inn

At one of the highest points of the Chilterns, this 400-year-old inn in the hamlet of Stoke Row takes its name from the pretty cherry tree growing outside. It has a happy blend of original features and contemporary furnishings, while a nearby barn has been converted into

four chic bedrooms. The kitchen draws on good local produce and follows the seasons in a range of broadly European-inspired dishes. Start with a foie gras parfait, toasted brioche and a pear and beer chutney, moving on to grilled sea bass with roast vegetable couscous and a tomato and chilli dressing. Some dishes come with a recommended Belgian or English beer accompaniment.

Times 12-3/7-10 Closed 25-26 Dec

Hotel du Vin Henley-on-Thames

◉◉ Classic European

Converted riverside brewery turned classy boutique hotel

☎ 01491 848400   🖨 01491 848401
New St RG9 2BP
e-mail: info@henley.hotelduvin.com
dir: M4 junct 8/9 signed High Wycombe, take 2nd exit and onto A404 in 2m. A4130 into Henley, over bridge, through lights, up Hart St, right onto Bell St, right onto New St, hotel on right

Close to the riverside moorings, this stylish conversion of the former Brakspear Brewery retains the character and much of the Georgian architecture of the original building, while getting the full, vibrant HdV makeover. The boutique hotel chain's bistro-style restaurant is suitably relaxed and informal and the classic European cooking hits the spot. The kitchen team makes good use of top-notch local and regional produce to deliver simple classics that change seasonally. Starters might include soused herrings with beetroot carpaccio and celeriac remoulade, with mains such as roast Yorkshire grouse with fondant potato, crisp ham and orange jus. There's a small courtyard for alfresco dining with a new pavilion for smokers (the bar sells cigars and boasts a walk-in humidor).

Times 12-2.30/6-10

The White Hart Nettlebed

◉ Modern British

Historic inn with contemporary style serving modern British pub classics

☎ 01491 641245
28 High St, Nettlebed RG9 5DD
e-mail: info@whitehartnettlebed.com
dir: From Henley take A4130 towards Wallingford. Approx 5m

On the outside it looks like just another historic inn, but once through the door the spacious bistro is a thoroughly modern space, with inlaid spot lighting, clean lines and natural colours. The cooking fits the bill, keeping things simple, fresh and accessible, while making use of carefully-sourced produce. Straightforward classics, like calves' liver and bacon (with mash and red wine sauce), line up alongside more modern thinking, perhaps sea bass fillet served with a fennel and olive salad and parsley mash. Puddings follow the comfort chocolate-brownie route, but again, with sunnier options like lemon and thyme pannacotta teamed with red wine poached pear.

Times 12-2.30/6-9.30 Closed D Sun

KINGHAM   Map 10 SP22

Mill Brook Room at The Mill House Hotel

◉◉ British, French

Charming Cotswolds hotel with accomplished cooking

☎ 01608 658188   🖨 01608 658492
OX7 6UH
e-mail: stay@millhousehotel.co.uk
dir: Just off B4450, between Chipping Norton & Stow-on-the-Wold. On southern outskirts of village

This lovely country-house hideaway is a Cotswold-stone former mill house dating originally from Norman times, rebuilt in the 18th century and recently refurbished in 2008. It is the very image of the bucolic English idyll, set in 10 acres of lawned gardens with its own trout stream. An informal and relaxed mood prevails in the Mill Brook Room restaurant, where a skilled kitchen turns out classic French and modern British dishes based on locally-sourced, seasonal and largely organic ingredients. Starters range from roasted parsnip soup to terrine of foie gras with toasted brioche and Sauternes jelly, while mains might offer slow-roasted lamb shoulder with pea purée, field mushrooms and lamb jus. End with warm chocolate tart with vanilla and coffee sorbet or the fine selection of British and French cheeses.

Chef Martin White **Owner** John Parslow
Times 12-2/6.30-10 **Prices** Fixed L 2 course £10-£12.50, Fixed D 3 course £35, Starter £5, Main £15-£20, Dessert £5-£10, Service optional **Wines** 26 bottles over £20, 36 bottles under £20, 9 by glass **Notes** Sunday L, Vegetarian available, Dress restrictions, Smart casual, Civ Wed 80 **Seats** 70, Pr/dining room 50 **Children** Portions, Menu **Parking** 60

Le Manoir aux Quat' Saisons

Modern French V NOTABLE WINE LIST

Twenty-five years young

☎ 01844 278881 🖹 01844 278847
Church Rd OX44 7PD
e-mail: lemanoir@blanc.co.uk
dir: M40 junct 7 follow A329 towards Wallingford. After 1m turn right, signed Great Milton and Le Manoir aux Quat' Saisons

This guidebook has been going for 17 years and Raymond Blanc's mellow stone, 15th-century manor-house hotel has been in every edition. And in every edition it has had five rosettes. That in itself is a remarkable feat of consistency, commitment and dedication (from Raymond, not us). But, the truly remarkable thing is Le Manoir has not stood still, not for a second of its 25 year life, and in every edition of the guide there has been something new to describe, whether it's the opening of the cookery school (1991) or simply wonderful dishes that have thrilled inspectors (see below). Any visit would not be complete without a stroll around the gardens - think of it as an exploration of le terroir, for 90 types of vegetables and over 70 varieties of herbs for the kitchen are grown in the Oxfordshire soil, plus there are life-size bronze statues, sculptures, a Japanese garden, teahouse and organic potager. The hotel itself is elegantly imposing,

with mullioned windows and soaring chimneys, maintaining historic dignity without whilst embracing contemporary tastes within. The dining room is made up of a couple of interconnecting rooms, the main space being an expansive conservatory that has wonderful views during daylight hours and a charming glow in the evening. The service is a highlight of any visit, the staff well-drilled but not lacking personality. Gary Jones has been running the kitchen with Raymond since 1999 and, as always, the commitment is to modern French cooking, based around first-class, seasonal organic produce, with a light tone to many dishes. The rustic roots of Blanc's classical past are combined with contemporary ideas, bringing some perhaps unexpected flavours, but never over-working the dishes. Alongside the carte, fixed-price lunch and Les Classiques menus is the Découverte menu, a 10-course 'voyage of discovery' that brings on the newest dishes in the repertoire. A tartare of langoustine with a Japanese savoury custard is full of delightfully clear flavours, and confit of Landais duck liver sees a superb piece of foie gras, perfectly counter-pointed by pineapple and vanilla chutney and an artful stripe of bacon powder. Braised Cornish sole comes with a Falmouth Bay oyster, seaweed, cucumber and a sublime beurre blanc with a well-judged kick of wasabi. For dessert, Le Manoir tiramisù 'flavours' is a master-class in the balance of texture and flavours.

Bread is a heavenly basket brimming with French tradition, and the wine list has an awesome 1,000 bins and the sommeliers on hand to do it justice.

Chef Raymond Blanc, Gary Jones **Owner** Mr R Blanc **Times** 12-2.30/7-10 **Prices** Fixed L 3 course fr £49, Starter £32-£42, Main £41-£44, Dessert £21-£22, Service optional **Wines** 1100 bottles over £20, 15 by glass **Notes** Menu Découverte available daily, Menu Classiques 5 course, Vegetarian menu, Dress restrictions, No jeans, trainers or shorts, Civ Wed 50, Air con **Seats** 100, Pr/dining room 50 **Children** Portions, Menu **Parking** 70

MURCOTT
Map 11 SP51

The Nut Tree Inn

◉◉ Modern European

Confident cooking in a pretty village inn

☎ 01865 331253
Main St OX5 2RE
dir: M40 junct 9. A34 towards Oxford, take 2nd exit for Islip. At Red Lion pub turn left, then right towards Murcott

Overlooking the village pond and beside a paddock housing the owners' own pigs, this attractive 14th-century thatched inn has immediate picture postcard appeal. Local foodies have made the place their own since the chef-patron and his wife took over and the pub is well and truly on the gastro map. There are two intimate dining rooms with stripped oak beams and wood-burning stoves, as well as an airy conservatory decorated with modern art. Simple, unpretentious dishes show plenty of skill and an awareness of seasonality with good use made of local produce, including beef and rare-breed pork reared by the chef himself. Take a main course confit pork belly with potato purée and apple gravy, or maybe pan-fried Cornish pollock with herb sauce. Finish with Valrhona chocolate fondant with pistachio ice cream.

Chef Michael North **Owner** Michael North, Imogen Young **Times** 12-2.30/7-9 Closed D Sun (Winter) **Prices** Fixed L 2 course £15, Fixed D 3 course £18, Starter £6.50-£10, Main £15-£24, Dessert £6-£7.50, Service optional, Groups min 6 service 10% **Wines** 36 bottles over £20, 10 bottles under £20, 8 by glass **Notes** Tasting menu available Mon-Sat eve, Sunday L, Vegetarian available **Seats** 60, Pr/dining room 20 **Children** Portions **Parking** 30

OXFORD
Map 5 SP50

Arezzo Restaurant

◉ Modern Italian

Popular Italian-influenced food served in conservatory-style restaurant

☎ 01865 749988   📠 01865 748525
Hawkwell House Hotel, Church Way, Iffley Village OX4 4DZ
e-mail: info@hawkwellhouse.co.uk
dir: A34 follow signs to Cowley. At Littlemore rdbt take A4158 onto Iffley Rd. After lights turn left to Iffley

You can walk to the centre of Oxford along the Thames from the village of Iffley; note, though, that the city is about two miles away. The hotel is in a quintessentially English garden setting, but the restaurant, Arezzo, has its heart and soul in Italy. The décor has an understated Mediterranean feel, and Italian-style carefully prepared comfort food is the order of the day. Starters such as goats' cheese bruschetta or macaroni cheese might precede roast confit of duck with garlic mash and a cannellini and tomato stew. There are pizzas, too, and desserts include a strawberry version of tiramisù.

Times 12-2.30/7-9.30

Macdonald Randolph

◉◉ Traditional British

Classic Oxford dining experience

☎ 0844 879 9132   & 01865 256400   📠 01865 791678
Beaumont St OX1 2LN
e-mail: foodservice.randolph@macdonald-hotels.co.uk
web: www.macdonaldhotels.co.uk
dir: M40 junct 8, A40 towards Oxford, follow city centre signs, leads to St Giles, hotel on right

Built in 1864 in neo-Gothic style, the Randolph is named after Dr Francis Randolph, a benefactor of the Ashmolean Museum opposite. The grand, oak-panelled foyer with vaulted ceiling and sweeping staircase sets the tone for the day rooms, which include an elegant chandeliered lounge and the impressive, high-ceilinged restaurant, which is adorned with college shields from the university and boasts picture windows with grand views. Expect classic British cooking and consistently good food prepared by a skilful kitchen. Using top-notch ingredients dishes are simply prepared to allow key flavours to shine through, as seen in a well-executed confit of pork belly with black pudding, apple purée and braised red cabbage. This, preceded perhaps, by oxtail dumplings served with an intense carrot and swede purée, while a rich and light chocolate truffle, served with chocolate pudding and Baileys ice cream, makes for an impressive finale. Service is on the ball.

Chef Tom Birks **Owner** Macdonald Hotels
Times 12-2.30/5.30-10 **Prices** Food prices not confirmed for 2010. Please telephone for details. **Wines** 100 bottles over £20, 3 bottles under £20, 12 by glass **Notes** Sunday L, Vegetarian available, Dress restrictions, Smart casual, Civ Wed 300 **Seats** 90, Pr/dining room 30 **Children** Portions, Menu **Parking** 50 (chargeable - pre-booking essential)

Malmaison Oxford

◉ Modern

Contemporary brasserie dining in former prison

☎ 01865 268400   📠 01865 268402
3 Oxford Castle, New Rd OX1 1AY
e-mail: oxford@malmaison.com
dir: M40 junct 9 (signed Oxford/A34). Follow A34 S to Botley Interchange, then A420 to city centre

The popular, subterranean brasserie was formerly part of the city's prison and many of the rooms (including the hotel bedrooms) were the old cells, complete with original doors and bars. The décor is dark brown and aubergine, but seductively lit by candlelight. The menu offers eye-catching, modern brasserie-style fare, with a French flavour. Starters might include the wonderfully rich, fragrant, hand-carved Jabugo Iberico ham 'gran reserve' (from free range pigs that feed on fallen acorns), or roast tomato, goats' cheese and artichoke tart. Follow with spatchcock poussin and cassoulet of beans with a soft herb crust. There's also a Home-grown & Local menu featuring top-notch Oxfordshire produce.

Times 12-2.30/6-10.30

Mercure Eastgate Hotel

◉ French, British **NEW**

Lively, stylish brasserie close to the action

☎ 0870 400 8201   & 01865 248332   📠 01865 791681
73 High St OX1 4BE
e-mail: h6668-sb@accor.com
dir: A40 into Oxford. At Headington rdbt follow signs to city centre. Cross Magdalen Bridge & stay in the inside lane. Continue past lights then turn left into Merton St

The sights and sounds of Oxford are within easy walking distance of this hotel, built of Oxford stone, with an interior as contemporary as the outside is historic. The brasserie-style restaurant, The High Table, sees French and British classics steal the show. Seared Loch Fyne scallops - plump and succulent - sit on confit of leeks topped with Avruga caviar in a starter where the quality of the main ingredient does the talking, followed, perhaps, by Loch Duart salmon fishcakes with lemon mayonnaise and herb salad, finishing off with vanilla pannacotta with elderflower sorbet and honeycomb tuile. The setting is relaxed and unstuffy, service upbeat and casual.

Chef Pascal Ufferte **Owner** MREF Trade Co
Times 12-3/6-10 **Prices** Starter £3.95-£6.95, Main £9.50-£14.25, Dessert fr £4.50 **Notes** Vegetarian available

Old Parsonage Restaurant

◉ Modern British

Memorable Oxford setting for some ambitious British cooking

☎ 01865 292305 ☎ 310210 ▤ 01865 311262
The Old Parsonage Hotel, 1 Banbury Rd OX2 6NN
e-mail: restaurant@oldparsonage-hotel.co.uk
web: www.mogford.co.uk
dir: M40 junct 8, A40. Right onto ring road, 1st left into Banbury Rd. Hotel & restaurant on right just before St Giles Church

The roll call of famous scholars who have stayed at this wisteria-clad 17th-century Oxford institution between Keble and Somerville colleges includes Oscar Wilde, who said that 'the only way to get rid of a temptation is to yield to it'. Well, the Old Parsonage offers plenty of opportunity to follow Mr Wilde's advice. First off, there's the clubby warmth of a buzzy, all-day bar, while burnished oak tables and Russian red walls hung with Bloomsbury-era paintings catch the eye in the dining room. The kitchen's 'Best of British' philosophy offers a concise menu of modern interpretations of classic dishes - perhaps Jersey crab mayonnaise to start, then confit of duck with braised chicory, orange and juniper.

Chef Simon Cottrell **Owner** Jeremy Mogford **Times** 12-10.30 **Prices** Fixed L 2 course £12.95, Fixed D 3 course £29.50, Starter £6.50-£9.50, Main £12.50-£20.50, Dessert £6.95-£7.50, Service optional, Groups min 5 service 12.5% **Wines** 40 bottles over £20, 5 bottles under £20, 10 by glass **Notes** Sunday L, Vegetarian available, Civ Wed 20, Air con **Seats** 75, Pr/dining room 15 **Children** Portions, Menu **Parking** 16

Quod Brasserie & Bar

◉ Modern British, Mediterranean

Contemporary brasserie with impressive art collection

☎ 01865 202505 ▤ 01865 799597
Old Bank Hotel, 92-94 High St OX1 4BN
e-mail: quod@oldbank-hotel.co.uk
web: www.quod.co.uk
dir: Approach city centre via Headington. Over Magdalen Bridge into High St. Hotel 75yds on left

A former bank, this imposing building in the heart of Oxford is now a stylish hotel and restaurant with an impressive collection of contemporary British art. In the open-all-day brasserie expect the sort of modern seasonal food you might find on the Mediterranean coast or in a New York brasserie: great pizzas, burgers and pasta dishes alongside tempting specials such as hand-picked Jersey crab and fennel salad or duck confit with dauphinoise potatoes. Finish, perhaps, with treacle sponge and custard. The large outdoor terrace seating 100 on various levels is an added bonus.

Chef Michael Wright **Owner** Mr J Mogford **Times** 7am-11pm **Prices** Fixed L 2 course £9.95, Fixed D 3 course £23.50, Starter £5.95-£8.95, Main £6.95-£18.95, Dessert £5.50-£7.50, Service optional, Groups min 5 service 10% **Wines** 6 bottles over £20, 6 bottles under £20, 17 by glass **Notes** Sunday L, Vegetarian available, Air con **Seats** 164, Pr/dining room 24 **Children** Portions, Menu **Parking** 50

STADHAMPTON	Map 5 SU69

The Crazy Bear

◉◉ Modern British

Modern cooking in comfortable old coaching inn

☎ 01865 890714 ▤ 01865 400481
Bear Ln OX44 7UR
e-mail: enquiries@crazybear-oxford.co.uk
web: www.crazybeargroup.co.uk
dir: M40 junct 7, A329. In 4m left after petrol station, left into Bear Lane

The original features of a traditional 16th-century inn meet leather-bound tables, an abundance of mirrors and atmospheric lighting at this relaxing and popular place. Modern British dishes with lots of international influences are prepared using the best ingredients, and dishes are simply but effectively presented. A selection of crustacea delivered fresh from the boats every day makes for a fine start to a meal, although you could kick off with pressed duck foie gras with apple and vanilla chutney and

toasted brioche, before a main course of roasted saddle of Oxfordshire venison, caramelised baby beets and balsamic onions with parsnip crisps. Finish with bread-and-butter pudding with Madagascan vanilla custard.

The Crazy Bear

Times 12-10

Thai Thai at the Crazy Bear

◉◉ Modern Thai

Thai and Western cooking amid head-turning décor

☎ 01865 890714 ▤ 01865 400481
The Crazy Bear, Bear Ln OX44 7UR
e-mail: enquiries@crazybear-oxford.co.uk
web: www.crazybeargroup.co.uk
dir: M40 junct 7, A329. In 4m left after petrol station, left into Bear Lane

Thai cooking in Moroccan-themed décor at a country inn in Oxfordshire? But of course. If the head-turning decorative theming, with its quilted panelling and pink-upholstered chairs, gets too much, you can always bag a table in the garden. Whichever mode you choose, you have the option of some enlivening Thai cooking, taking in glass noodle salad with minced pork, chestnut mushrooms, onion and coriander, green tiger prawn curry with mini-aubergines and bamboo shoots cooked in coconut milk, and finishing perhaps with sweet sticky coconut rice with mango, or spicy Thai tea jelly with sweet milk. There is a western-style menu too, using ingredients from the group's farm shop, with main courses such as corn-fed chicken braised in fino sherry, with broad beans, diced potatoes and ham.

Times 12-3/6-12 Closed L Sun

SWERFORD
Map 11 SP33

The Mason's Arms

Modern British

Country gastro-pub with local flavour

☎ 01608 683212 📠 01608 683105
Banbury Rd OX7 4AP
e-mail: admin@masons-arms.com
dir: On A361 between Banbury & Chipping Norton

Set in beautiful Cotswold countryside, the Mason's Arms is a classic stone-built inn (a Masonic lodge in a former life) with a dining room extension and a pretty garden with lovely views. Food is placed high on the agenda, but this is still a place to sup a pint of real ale. It is light and airy on the inside, with wooden floors and tables, and pastel tones from the modern palette on the walls and woodwork. Service is as unpretentious as it is efficient. Good use is made of seasonal local produce (Oxford Down lamb, Gloucestershire Old Spot pork) with some Asian and European flavours added to the mix; start with timbale of crab with avocado parfait, followed by slow-cooked shoulder of lamb with dauphinoise potatoes and green beans.

Chef Bill Leadbeater **Owner** B & C Leadbeater, Tom Aldous **Times** 12-3/7-11 Closed 25-26 Dec, D 24 Dec, Sun **Prices** Fixed L 2 course £14.95, Fixed D 3 course £25.40, Starter £5.95-£8.95, Main £13.95-£18.95, Dessert £5.50, Service optional, Groups min 10 service 10% **Wines** 18 bottles over £20, 32 bottles under £20, 10 by glass **Notes** Sunday L, Vegetarian available **Seats** 75, Pr/dining room 40 **Children** Portions, Menu **Parking** 60

TOOT BALDON
Map 5 SP50

The Mole Inn

British, European NEW

Big flavours at a top-class dining pub

☎ 01865 340001 📠 01865 343011
OX44 9NG
e-mail: info@themoleinn.com
dir: Please telephone for directions

Since its recent refurbishment, the 300 year-old Mole Inn has weighed in as a serious contender on the Oxford area dining scene. The snoozy hamlet of Toot Baldon now draws diners the few miles out of the city centre to this top-class foodie pub. Textures are blended tastefully inside, from the wood and terracotta floors, to exposed stone and brickwork, and gnarled timbers. Chunky wooden tables, leather chairs and chocolate-coloured sofas complete the scene in the dining areas. Expect sound modern cooking using classic combinations and an emphasis on really good produce - 28-day hung Scottish beef, Cotswold free-range chicken and Cornish lamb for example. Seared scallops with crab risotto gets things off to a flying start, then good technical skills are evident in collar of Blythburgh pork with crushed potatoes and forest mushrooms, truffle essence and scrumpy cider sauce.

Chef Gary Witchalls **Owner** Gary Witchalls **Times** 12-2.30/7-9.30 Closed 25 Dec, 1 Jan, **Prices** Starter £4.95-£8.50, Main £12.50-£17.95, Dessert £5.95, Service optional **Notes** Sunday L, Vegetarian available **Seats** 70 **Children** Portions, Menu **Parking** 40

WALLINGFORD
Map 5 SU68

Lakeside Restaurant

Modern European V

Modern European cuisine in tranquil lakeside setting

☎ 01491 836687 & 0845 365 2697 📠 01491 836877
The Springs Hotel & Golf Club, Wallingford Rd, North Stoke OX10 6BE
e-mail: info@thespringshotel.com
dir: Edge of village of North Stoke

Outstanding scenery, well-maintained gardens and a wonderful view of the spring-fed lake give a peaceful atmosphere to the Springs Hotel, a place once frequented by Edward VIII. There's also the Springs golf course, set in beautiful parkland. Built in 1874, the hotel is mock-Tudor in style with plenty of period detail - exposed oak beams, blazing fires in open hearths - and comfortable lounges. The Lakeside Restaurant is in the glass-enclosed Winter Garden and offers attentive formal service and equal attention to detail in the cooking. Using quality, seasonal produce, the modern European menu offers plenty of choice in starters such as chicken, honey and tarragon terrine, followed by local rib-eye with cauliflower purée and shallot jus.

Chef Paul Franklin **Owner** Lakeside Restaurant **Times** 12-2/6.30-9.45 **Prices** Fixed L 2 course £15-£20, Fixed D 3 course £18-£25, Starter £6.50-£9.50, Main £15.50-£18.95, Dessert £6.50-£7.95 **Notes** Sunday L, Vegetarian menu, Dress restrictions, Civ Wed 90 **Seats** 60, Pr/dining room 30 **Children** Portions, Menu **Parking** 150

The Partridge

Modern French NEW

Top quality gastro-pub offering refined modern food

☎ 01491 825005 📠 01491 837153
32 St Mary's St OX10 0ET
e-mail: contact@partridge-inn.com
dir: Please telephone for directions

The Partridge is a slick operation that comes down firmly on the gastro side of the gastro-pub equation. A top-to-toe makeover has eradicated all traces of its days as a scruffy old boozer: flooring mixes textures of polished wood and cosier carpets, walls are bare brick or designer wallpaper. You can flop into a leather sofa for a pint in a bijou bar area, but the Partridge is really about food. Driving it all is a chef who has paid his dues in the kitchens of the Roux brothers, Raymond Blanc and Nico Ladenis - a pedigree that is reflected in classical techniques and simple yet refined presentation. Prime British produce leads the charge in dishes such as pan-fried scallops with cauliflower purée and crispy pancetta, or rump of English lamb with fondant potatoes and thyme jus. But when it comes to dessert, only Valrhona will do for a chocolate fondant with pistachio ice cream.

Chef Jose Cau **Owner** Jose Cau **Times** 12-2.30/6-9.30 Closed D Sun **Prices** Fixed L 2 course fr £13.95, Fixed D 3 course fr £16.95, Starter £5.20-£10.50, Main £12.50-£23, Dessert £6.50, Groups min 6 service 10% **Wines** 85 bottles over £20, 23 bottles under £20, 9 by glass **Notes** Sunday L, Vegetarian available, Dress restrictions, Smart casual, Air con **Seats** 50 **Children** Portions

WESTON-ON-THE-GREEN
Map 11 SP51

The Manor Restaurant

Modern British

Accomplished cooking in medieval manor-house hotel

☎ 01869 350621 📠 01869 350901
Weston Manor Hotel OX25 3QL
e-mail: reception@westonmanor.co.uk
dir: M40 junct 9, exit A34 to Oxford then 1st exit on left signed Weston-on-Green/Middleton Stony B4030. Right at mini rdbt, hotel 400yds on left

Dating back to the 11th century, this historic manor is now a luxurious country-house hotel that retains a wealth of original features. During World War II it was used as an officers' mess for American airmen, and the restaurant, in the oldest part of the building, was once the baronial hall. Spectacular linenfold oak panelling, a high-vaulted ceiling and minstrels' gallery, make it an impressive venue for weddings and functions. The well-balanced menu features appealing dishes using good produce from local suppliers. Start with home-smoked duck and pomegranate salad with hickory and honey dressing, followed by a main course of pan-fried halibut with beetroot and orange salad and new potatoes. Finish with a dessert of macadamia nut tart and pineapple salad with orange and cardamom reduction.

Times 12-2/7-9.30 Closed L Sat

WOODCOTE

Map 5 SU68

Woody Nook at Woodcote

British, International **V**

A touch of Oz in the Oxfordshire countryside

☎ 01491 680775 📄 01491 682943
Goring Rd RG8 0SD
e-mail: info@woodynookatwoodcote.co.uk
web: www.woodynookatwoodcote.co.uk
dir: Opposite village green

If you think that this relaxed restaurant sounds like an Aussie wine, you've hit the nail on the head. The name comes from its owners' award-winning Margaret River winery in Western Australia, so you can expect the wine list to be tailored accordingly. The wine may have its heart on the other side of the world, but the venue is pure English idyll, with the sound of leather on willow on the village green while you eat amid the rustic charm of low-beamed ceilings and leaded windows. Cooking is hearty, uncomplicated stuff peppered with international flavours, with a nod here and there to the Antipodes. Smooth chicken liver and Cognac parfait with Woody Nook port jelly might start things off, followed with breast of duck with roasted butternut squash and lavender and honey sauce.

Chef Stuart Shepherd **Owner** Jane & Peter Bailey
Times 12-2.30/7-9.30 Closed Mon & Tue, D Sun
Prices Fixed L 2 course £12.95, Fixed D 3 course £19.50, Starter £5.95-£9.95, Main £13.95-£19.95, Dessert £4.95-£6.95, Service optional, Groups min 6 service 10%
Wines 6 bottles over £20, 9 bottles under £20, 8 by glass
Notes Sunday L, Vegetarian menu **Seats** 50
Children Portions **Parking** 25

WOODSTOCK

Map 11 SP41

The Feathers

Modern British

Accomplished modern British cuisine at a sophisticated townhouse hotel

☎ 01993 812291 📄 01993 813158
Market St OX20 1SX
e-mail: enquiries@feathers.co.uk
web: www.feathers.co.uk
dir: from A44 (Oxford to Woodstock), 1st left after lights. Hotel on left

The Feathers, a 17th-century gem of a building close to the gates of Blenheim Palace, is an intimate and individual hotel. There's an understated elegance to match the decoration: original wood panelling, low-beamed ceilings, rich furnishings and antiques. The atmospheric restaurant has a quiet, sophisticated air. The kitchen draws on the local larder for seasonal produce, preparing dishes with classical origins and a modern twist. Look out for a starter of Cornish ling with cauliflower couscous, truffle, quail egg and watercress, then perhaps follow with Lighthorne lamb with aubergine and tomato purée with lamb jus, before rounding off with baked Cuban chocolate pudding with lime and chocolate chip sorbet. For grazing or a light meal you can eat in the bar or bistro.

Chef Russell Bateman **Owner** Empire Ventures Ltd
Times 12.30-2.30/7-9.30 Closed D Sun **Prices** Fixed L 3 course £19-£25, Fixed D 3 course £29-£50, Service added but optional 10% **Wines** 140 bottles over £20, 12 bottles under £20, 11 by glass **Notes** Sunday L, Dress restrictions, Smart casual, no trainers **Seats** 54, Pr/dining room 30 **Children** Portions, Menu **Parking** On street

Macdonald Bear Hotel

Modern British

Modern cooking in historic inn

☎ 0844 879 9143 📄 01993 813380
Park St OX20 1SZ
e-mail: bear@macdonald-hotels.co.uk
web: www.bearhotelwoodstock.co.uk
dir: M40 junct 9 follow signs for Oxford & Blenheim Palace. A44 to town centre, hotel on left

With Blenheim Palace practically on the doorstep, its no wonder that the Bear has seen a long procession of royalty and glitterati pass through in its 800 year history. The ivy-clad coaching inn is one of England's oldest, and looks the part from top to bottom. The restaurant is a treat, with gnarled oak beams, exposed stone walls and open fires, and good humoured staff keep things ticking over. The kitchen takes the modern British route with its unpretentious cooking, prepared skilfully from top-quality ingredients. The menu delivers seasonal dishes with well-balanced flavours, such as tortellini of wild mushrooms with truffle foam before pan-roasted pork fillet with Stornoway black pudding, mashed potato and Calvados sauce.

Chef Adrian Court **Owner** Macdonald Hotels
Times 12.30-2/7-9.30 **Prices** Food prices not confirmed for 2010. Please telephone for details. **Wines** 70 bottles over £20, 18 bottles under £20, 12 by glass **Notes** Sunday L **Seats** 80, Pr/dining room 30 **Children** Portions, Menu **Parking** 45

RUTLAND

CLIPSHAM — Map 11 SK91

The Olive Branch

◎◎ British, European **V** ◎

Rural pub with gastro credentials

☎ 01780 410355 🖥 01780 410000
Main St LE15 7SH
e-mail: rooms@theolivebranchpub.com
dir: 2m from A1 at Stretton junct, 5m N of Stamford

The unpretentious country pub with its well-kept, colourful gardens was once a trio of farm labourers' cottages, which came together as one in the late Victorian era. They are now joined in the business by Beech House, an elegant Georgian residence over the road where guest rooms are available. Farmhouse tables laid with chequered napkins set the tone in the Olive Branch, and while there are plenty of pub staples on the menus - prawn cocktail, game terrine, jam roly-poly with custard - there is also a more inventive streak that brings on tandoori halibut with lime and coriander rice or roast pork with sweet potato and black pudding Anna. Fine home-made breads are not to be missed, and lemon tart with short pastry and a brûlée top rounds things off in style.

Chef Sean Hope **Owner** Sean Hope, Ben Jones
Times 12-2/7-9.30 Closed 1 Jan, L 31 Dec, D 25-26 Dec
Prices Fixed L 2 course £16.50, Fixed D 3 course fr £25, Starter £4.95-£9.95, Main £13.95-£25, Dessert £4.75-£9.50, Service optional, Groups min 12 service 10%
Wines 20 bottles over £20, 25 bottles under £20, 8 by glass **Notes** Sat afternoon menu available 2.30-5.30, Sunday L, Vegetarian menu **Seats** 45, Pr/dining room 20 **Children** Portions, Menu **Parking** 15

OAKHAM — Map 11 SK80

Barnsdale Lodge Hotel

◎ Modern British

Sound cooking in converted farmhouse amid picturesque countryside

☎ 01572 724678 🖥 01572 724961
The Avenue, Rutland Water, North Shore LE15 8AH
e-mail: enquiries@barnsdalelodge.co.uk
dir: Turn off A1 at Stamford onto A606 to Oakham. Hotel 5m on right. (2m E of Oakham)

Located in the heart of unspoilt countryside in Rutland, Barnsdale Lodge Hotel has been in Thomas Noel's family since 1760 and formed part of the adjoining Exton Park, seat of the Earls of Gainsborough. Formerly a farmhouse, the building was converted by the owner in 1989 and it still retains its 17th-century bread ovens and stone floors, which blend well with the country-house style furnishings. Whether dining in the conservatory, the main dining room or alfresco in the courtyard, the service remains friendly and attentive. The style of cooking is modern British with seasonal, local ingredients coming to the fore in a starter of garden pea and pancetta risotto and a main course of Rutland water trout with colcannon mash, spring greens and lemon butter sauce.

Chef Richard Carruthers **Owner** The Hon Thomas Noel
Times 12-2.15/7-9.30 **Prices** Fixed L 2 course fr £12.95, Starter £3.50-£8.50, Main £11.95-£23.95, Dessert £4.95-£6.50, Service added but optional 10% **Wines** 45 bottles over £20, 33 bottles under £20, 10 by glass **Notes** Sunday L, Vegetarian available, Civ Wed 100 **Seats** 120, Pr/dining room 50 **Children** Portions, Menu **Parking** 250

Hambleton Hall Hotel

◎◎◎◎ *– see opposite page*

Nick's Restaurant at Lord Nelson's House

◎◎ Modern British **V**

Characterful setting for modern European cooking

☎ 01572 723199
11 Market Place LE15 6HR
e-mail: simon@nicksrestaurant
dir: Off A606 in town centre

Tucked away in the corner of Oakham's market square, this elegant restaurant with rooms offers fine dining in a quaint and cosy period dining room. A new head chef has taken the reins and he continues to deliver carefully crafted modern dishes utilising quality seasonal produce. Start with assiette of rabbit with a pea and ginger salad and olive dressing before moving onto herb-crusted loin of lamb with a fricassée of wild mushrooms and Swiss chard, lamb hotpot and a thyme jus. Finish with apple crumble crème brûlée with green apple tea sorbet. Incidentals such as canapés (smoked trout mousse, perhaps) add to the sense of occasion, while the small list of around 30 bins offers a good selection by the glass.

Chef David Lem **Owner** Simon McEnery
Times 12-2.30/6-9.30 Closed 25-26 Dec, Mon, D Sun
Prices Fixed L 2 course £15-£16, Fixed D 3 course £20-£25.75, Starter £8.95-£11.95, Main £17.50-£22.50, Dessert £6.75, Service optional **Wines** 22 bottles over £20, 13 bottles under £20, 9 by glass **Notes** Tasting menu available, Sunday L, Vegetarian menu **Seats** 45 **Children** Portions **Parking** 4

UPPINGHAM — Map 11 SP89

The Lake Isle

◎◎ British, French

Imaginative cooking in pretty market town

☎ 01572 822951 🖥 01572 824400
16 High Street East LE15 9PZ
e-mail: info@lakeisle.co.uk
web: www.lakeisle.co.uk
dir: From A47, turn left at 2nd lights, 100yds on right

This attractive townhouse was once a shop and the original mahogany fittings and panelled walls can still be seen. Now it is a delightful restaurant and small elegant bar, with a first-floor guest lounge and bedrooms, in the attractive market town of Uppingham. The cooking style is a mix of British and French and the menu changes regularly to make full use of quality ingredients, including local produce and seasonal fruit and vegetables. A typical starter might be butterflied Cornish sardines on caper and olive focaccia with a fresh tomato compôte and a salad of micro herbs. Follow with a main course of chargrilled beef steak with shiitake mushrooms and an oxtail and onion gravy, and finish with hot chocolate fondant pudding with peanut butter ice cream and brittle. The wine list is worth exploring.

Times 12-2.30/7-9 Closed L Mon, D Sun

Hambleton Hall Hotel

Modern British V NOTABLE WINE LIST

Romantic retreat serving the best of English country-house cuisine

☎ 01572 756991 📠 01572 724721
Hambleton LE15 8TH
e-mail: hotel@hambletonhall.com
web: www.hambletonhall.com
dir: 8m W of A1 Stamford junct (A606), 3m E of Oakham

Adrift on a peninsula tethered to Rutland Water, Hambleton Hall is a template for how to do the English country house experience properly. The many-gabled Victorian pile was built in 1881 by bon viveur Walter Marshall, as a base for blowing his brewing fortune on fox hunting, keeping an excellent table and fast living. Fast forward almost a century, and Tim and Stefa Hart are now weaving their magic in this sybaritic, sophisticated, rural retreat. Within it's all very grand and impeccably comfy in drawing rooms full of antiques, luxuriant sofas and log fires to boost the feelgood factor. Genteel staff are as well-dressed as the dining room, an intimate venue in warm hues with immaculate white linen, fulsome flower displays, lush brocades and oil paintings, all set to the scenic backdrop of the garden and lake. Chef Aaron Patterson's inspired cooking echoes that of his mentor, Raymond Blanc, in its pursuit of clarity of flavour and

insistence on sourcing seasonal produce that is second to none. And what better source than the hotel's own kitchen garden for fresh vegetables, herbs and salads - and local Rutland game is worth homing in on. The result is dishes that are carefully composed and immaculately presented in an array of fixed-price menus spiked with luxury materials - naturally, this sort of excellence comes at a price. The menu might start with cannelloni of squid and chorizo with piquant peppers, or if your luck is really in, a winter risotto of Périgord truffles. Main courses might propose a straightforward marriage of poached and roast Bresse pigeon with emulsified baked potato and Puy lentils, or a more speculative pairing of fallow venison loin with roast pineapple, gin and tonic jelly and cocoa-flavoured sauce. At dessert, hazelnut and chocolate fondant tart with Valrhona chocolate sorbet and an orange reduction should hit the spot, or you might go off-piste with more of those Périgord truffles, this time in ice cream form.

Chef Aaron Patterson **Owner** Mr T Hart **Times** 12-1.30/7-9.30 **Prices** Fixed L 2 course fr £20, Fixed D 3 course £37-£46, Starter £16-£25, Main £34-£39, Dessert £13-£16, Service added but optional 12.5% **Wines** 375 bottles over £20, 10 bottles under £20, 10 by glass **Notes** Tasting menu available, Sunday L, Vegetarian menu, Dress restrictions,

Smart dress, no jeans, T-shirts or trainers, Civ Wed 64 **Seats** 60, Pr/dining room 20 **Children** Portions, Menu **Parking** 36

WING

Map 11 SK80

Kings Arms Inn & Restaurant

Modern British

Traditional country inn with modern cooking

☎ 01572 737634 📠 01572 737255
13 Top St LE15 8SE
e-mail: info@thekingsarms-wing.co.uk
dir: 1m off A6003, between Oakham & Uppingham

Set in a peaceful, out-of-the-way village close to Rutland Water, this traditional village inn dates from 1649. Time-honoured charm can be found in the bar, with its stone floor, roaring log fires and head-cracking beams, while the refurbished dining room offers a more contemporary setting in which to sample a wide range of interesting dishes. There's something for everyone on the lengthy menu, from a simple home-made burger or the King's beer-battered cod with beef dripping chips to home-smoked charcuterie, venison saddle with fondant potato and berry glaze, brill with saffron and spinach risotto, and vanilla, lime and ginger pannacotta.

Chef James Goss **Owner** David, Gisa & James Goss **Times** 12-2.30/6.30-9 Closed Mon, D Sun **Prices** Fixed L 2 course £12, Starter £6-£8, Main £9-£22, Dessert £6-£7, Service optional, Groups min 7 service 10% **Wines** 20 bottles over £20, 28 bottles under £20, 20 by glass **Notes** Sunday L, Vegetarian available **Seats** 30, Pr/dining room 24 **Children** Portions **Parking** 30

SHROPSHIRE

BRIDGNORTH

Map 10 SO79

Old Vicarage Hotel and Restaurant

— *see below*

CHURCH STRETTON

Map 15 SO49

The Pound at Leebotwood

Modern British

Local produce cooked with flair in a popular country inn

☎ 01694 751477 📠 01694 751429
Leebotwood SY6 6ND
e-mail: info@thepound.org.uk
dir: On A49, 9m S of Shrewsbury

Drovers tend not to pass this way anymore, but no matter, for this 15th-century thatched inn (built for drovers taking their animals to market) appeals to the 21st-century customer who is after good fresh food in unpretentious, relaxed surroundings. Modern artwork and oak furniture are set against exposed beams, real fires, and woodblock and carpeted floors in an appealing blend of old and new. Outside, there is a screened area for alfresco dining. Perfectly seared king scallops with crispy bacon and fresh pea purée is typical of the modern British food, with the accuracy of the cooking confirmed

in main course Marshes pork chop with sharp apple and cider sauce. Knowledgeable and friendly service completes the picture.

The Pound at Leebotwood

Chef Wessel Van Yaarsveld **Owner** Paul & Barbara Brooks **Times** 12-2.30/6.30-9.30 Closed 25 & 26 Dec, **Prices** Starter £4.95-£6.95, Main £8.95-£16.95, Dessert £4.95-£5.95, Service optional **Wines** 15 bottles over £20, 26 bottles under £20, 9 by glass **Notes** Food served all day Sat & Sun, Sunday L, Vegetarian available **Seats** 60 **Children** Portions **Parking** 60

Old Vicarage Hotel and Restaurant

BRIDGNORTH

Map 10 SO79

Modern British

Fine local produce in a former vicarage

☎ 01746 716497 📠 01746 716552
Hallow, Worfield WV15 5JZ
e-mail: admin@the-old-vicarage.demon.co.uk
dir: Off A454, approx 3.5m NE of Bridgnorth, 5m S of Telford on A442, follow brown signs

Over twenty years the current owners have turned this red brick Edwardian house and former vicarage into a top-notch hotel and restaurant. They can't take credit for the tranquil Shropshire setting, within 2 acres of wooded farmland, but have added their stamp to the well-appointed lounge and attractive conservatory (perfect for a pre-prandial drink or afternoon tea). The Orangery Restaurant has fantastic views over the surrounding

countryside, while inside, fresh flowers and wooden floors and tables provide a modern, vibrant setting. A small team of knowledgeable staff are professional and thoughtful. Accomplished and accurate cooking features excellent local produce, which is given room to shine in unfussily presented modern British dishes. Vegetarians are well catered for, too, with a seasonally changing tasting menu. On the carte might be pressing of foie gras and mackerel with warm brioche and pickled apples, moving on to Scottish scallops with slow-roast chicken, parsley purée, baby leeks, Roman artichokes and truffle foam. Round things off with chocolate mousse, very lightly spiked with chilli, coconut and mango.

Chef Simon Diprose **Owner** Mr & Mrs D Blakstad **Times** 12-2.30/7-9.30 Closed L Mon Tue Sat (by reservation only), D 24-26 Dec **Prices** Fixed L 2 course £18.50, Fixed D 3 course £42, Service included **Wines** 50 bottles over £20, 25 bottles under £20, 10 by glass **Notes** Sunday L, Vegetarian available **Seats** 64, Pr/dining room 20 **Children** Portions, Menu **Parking** 30

The Studio

◉ British, French ✪

Confident modern cooking in former artist's studio

☎ 01694 722672
59 High St SY6 6BY
e-mail: info@thestudiorestaurant.net
dir: Off A49 to town, left at T-junct onto High St, 300yds on left

The original paint-palette sign over the door is the first reminder that this restaurant is housed in a former artist's studio. Inside, the owners' love of art is evident from the interesting collection of paintings and ceramics. Kick off with a drink in the intimate, welcoming bar or the charming patio garden with its view across the Shropshire hills. Modern, bistro-style food is the order of the day, and all dishes are created from carefully selected, local, seasonal produce, prepared with the classical and traditional skills of the husband-and-wife team. A starter of pan-fried scallops with smoked salmon and white wine velouté, flavoured with mustard and cheese, might be followed by haunch of Mortimer Forest venison steak with celeriac purée and red wine and cassis sauce.

Chef Tony Martland **Owner** Tony & Sheila Martland **Times** 7-9 Closed 2 wks Jan, 1 wk Apr, 1 wk Nov, Sun-Tue, L all week **Prices** Fixed D 3 course fr £26.50, Service optional **Wines** 13 bottles over £20, 27 bottles under £20, 6 by glass **Notes** Vegetarian available, Dress restrictions, Smart casual **Seats** 34 **Children** Portions **Parking** On street parking available

---

Saracens at Hadnall

◉ Modern British ✪

Skilful cooking at a elegant restaurant with rooms

☎ 01939 210877 📠 01939 210877
Shrewsbury Rd SY4 4AG
e-mail: reception@saracensathadnall.co.uk
dir: M54 onto A5, at junct of A5/A49 take A49 towards Whitchurch. Follow A49 to Hadnall, diagonally opposite church

The former Georgian farmhouse is these days a handsome restaurant with rooms. There are two dining rooms, the Georgian-style front room, with its polished-wood floor, panelled walls and stone fireplace, or the conservatory, which features a capped well. Local ingredients turn up in an appealing range of modern British dishes based on sound, classical principles. Rillette of Maynard's ham hock, celeriac remoulade and piccalilli is a starter full of complementary flavours, while main-course loin of local venison with braised red cabbage, caramelised cauliflower and a date and fig reduction is equally tempting.

Chef David Spencer **Owner** Ben & Allison M Christie **Times** 11.30-2.30/6.30-9.30 Closed Mon, L Tue, D Sun **Prices** Fixed L 2 course £11.95, Service optional **Wines** 11 bottles over £20, 20 bottles under £20, 6 by glass

---

Notes Early eve menu Tue-Fri before 7.30pm, Sunday L, Vegetarian available, Dress restrictions, Smart casual **Seats** 45 **Children** Menu **Parking** 20

Restaurant Severn

◉◉ British, French ✪

The best of local produce in historic Ironbridge

☎ 01952 432233 📠 01952 510086
33 High St TF8 7AG
web: www.restaurantsevern.co.uk
dir: Please telephone or check website for directions

The Grade II listed cottage is just a short hop from the famous Ironbridge and the River Severn which flows underneath. The hard working chef-patron Eric Bruce and wife Beb (who makes all the desserts and breads) are dedicated to using the very best local produce, which includes, from their own smallholding, the likes of asparagus, soft fruits, salads, herbs and root vegetables. Everything is sourced with care. The dining room has a pleasingly unfussy style, with high-backed leather chairs and dark-wood tables blending in well with the wealth of original features. Classical French technique is the bedrock of a menu that is far from stuck in the past and makes excellent use of the prime seasonal produce. Wild salmon and king scallop terrine with honey-dressed leaves might precede pot-roasted loin of pork with cider and Calvados sauce served with apple sauce and crispy crackling.

Chef Eric & Beb Bruce **Owner** Eric & Beb Bruce **Times** 12-2/6.30-9 Closed BHs, Mon-Tue, L Wed-Sat, D Sun **Prices** Fixed L 2 course £15.95, Fixed D 3 course £25.95-£27.95, Service optional, Groups min 8 service 5% **Wines** 15 bottles over £20, 25 bottles under £20, 5 by glass **Notes** Sunday L, Vegetarian available, Dress restrictions, Smart casual **Seats** 30 **Children** Portions **Parking** On street & car park opposite

---

The Waterdine

◉◉ Modern British

Relaxed dining in pretty, rural setting

☎ 01547 528214
LD7 1TU
e-mail: Info@waterdine.com
dir: From Knighton take B4355 toward Newtown, 4m to village of Lloyney. Turn right opposite Lloyney over river follow lane keeping left. Restaurant last property on left opposite church

Nestling in the picturesque upper Teme Valley in the hamlet of Llanfair Waterdine, this former drover's inn dates back over 400 years. Set in wonderful Shropshire countryside, and with the river flowing at the bottom of the garden, it's full of charm and character. The main restaurant has 2 different areas, The Garden Room and The Taproom - the oldest part of the building. Friendly, efficient hospitality from the owners puts you at your ease immediately. Here you'll find an experienced chef making great use of quality local produce, including fruit and vegetables from the inn's own garden. The menu is seasonal and changes regularly. Expect starters such as Cornish crab cannelloni on a bed of spinach with chive sauce, followed by rack of Shropshire lamb with couscous and Provençal vegetables. Finish with a lemon curd tart.

Times 12-1.45/7-9 Closed 1 wk spring, 1 wk autumn, Mon, L Sat, D Sun

---

La Bécasse

◉◉◉ – see page 368

The Clive Bar and Restaurant with Rooms

◉◉ Modern British ✪

Bright, modern restaurant in renovated Shropshire farmhouse

☎ 01584 856565 & 856665 📠 01584 856661
Bromfield SY8 2JR
e-mail: info@theclive.co.uk
web: www.theclive.co.uk
dir: 2m N of Ludlow on A49, near Ludlow Golf Club, racecourse & adjacent to Ludlow food centre

continued

LUDLOW *continued*

Ludlow has become a lodestone for foodie ventures out of all proportion to its modest country stature. One of the latest is this smart contemporary bar, bistro and restaurant with rooms in a red brick 18th-century farmhouse a couple of miles out of town; the Clive in question is Major-General Robert Clive of India. Style-wise, it's a clean-cut affair, all pale wood, scrubbed floors and exposed beams contrasting with dove grey and oxblood walls and stylish cutlery and glassware. There's a well-established network of local suppliers in Shropshire and the Welsh Marches to ensure fresh, seasonal goodies for the mainly Modern British dishes, although Mediterranean and exotic tinges sneak in here and there, as in a starter of cumin-dusted scallops, pan-fried with rocket, in a coconut and lime dressing. Pan-fried breast of guinea fowl with bubble-and-squeak and apple and cider sauce might follow.

Chef Martin Humphries **Owner** Paul & Barbara Brooks **Times** 12-3/6.30-10 Closed 25-26 Dec **Prices** Starter £4.95-£7.50, Main £8.95-£18.95, Dessert £4.50-£5.95, Service optional **Wines** 31 bottles over £20, 35 bottles under £20, 9 by glass **Notes** Sunday L, Vegetarian available **Seats** 90 **Children** Portions **Parking** 80

Dinham Hall Hotel

⊛ Traditional British, French NEW

Accomplished cooking in a smart country-house setting

☎ 01584 876464 ▤ 01584 876019
By the Castle SY8 1EJ
e-mail: info@dinhamhall.co.uk
dir: Town centre, off Market Place, opposite Ludlow Castle

The solid Georgian symmetry of Dinham Hall overlooks a rather grand, if somewhat ruined neighbour, in the magnificent shape of Ludlow Castle. Not to be outdone, the restaurant basks in Georgian elegance, with foot-wide oak floorboards, high ceilings, period pastel hues and a sweeping bay window over the densely wooded River Teme valley. With Ludlow's reputation, top-class seasonal ingredients are readily to hand for the kitchen to transform into skilfully prepared, intelligent dishes with a clear French leaning. Kick off with a twice-cooked parmesan soufflé with a salad of pears and chicory and Meaux mustard dressing, followed by moist free range chicken breast with a mousseline stuffing with creamy Savoy cabbage, dauphinoise potatoes and Madeira jus.

Times 12.30-1.45/7-8.45 Closed L 26 Dec, D 25 Dec

The Feathers Hotel

⊛ Modern British, French

Modern classic dishes in a magnificent timber-framed inn

☎ 01584 875261 ▤ 01584 876030
Bull Ring SY8 1AA
e-mail: enquiries@feathersatludlow.co.uk
web: www.feathersatludlow.co.uk
dir: from A49 follow town centre signs to centre. Hotel on left

The extravagantly timber-framed exterior is mentioned in Pevsner's architectural digest, while within, the tone is

La Bécasse

LUDLOW   **Map 10 SO57**

French V ✌

Experimental Anglo-French cooking of high ambition

☎ 01584 872325
17 Corve St SY8 1DA
e-mail: info@labecasse.co.uk
web: www.labecasse.co.uk
dir: In town centre opposite Feathers Hotel, at bottom of hill

Ludlow has long been a beacon of gastronomic excellence, and when the previous owners of this site headed off to London, it seemed only fitting that a new restaurant of comparable ambition should take their place. Step forward La Bécasse - named, like its sibling L'ortolan in Shinfield, Berkshire (see entry), after a French game bird. Settling in among the purveyors of fine wines,

fresh produce and decorative tiles, La Bécasse looks quite the part, and even more so inside, where a series of small interconnecting rooms is all about oak-panelled and stone-walled venerability overlaid with modern design touches. A modern British interpretation of the classic French repertoire best describes the culinary endeavours, mobilising innovative technique and unusual combinations to produce intense flavours and fascinating results. A first course of wood pigeon ballotine and sautéed foie gras, adorned with mango salsa, a port and sesame reduction and a streak of wasabi could so easily slide into incoherence in the wrong hands, but here achieves a sublime balance of flavour, texture and temperature contrasts. The same could be said of a main course of mallard, the breast poached, the leg confit presented cannelloni fashion, along with a root vegetable 'cassoulet' and a couple of little sausages, the whole covered in a truffled consommé. Dessert variations might juxtapose poached rhubarb with its own sorbet, as well as saffron rice pudding and ginger cake, and if you want

the chocolate tart, you'll have to finish up your parsnip ice cream too.

Chef Will Holland **Owner** Alan Murchison Restaurants Ltd **Times** 12-2/7-9.30 Closed Xmas, New Year, Mon, L Tue, D Sun **Prices** Fixed L 2 course fr £22, Tasting menu fr £60, Starter fr £15, Main fr £30, Dessert fr £10, Service added but optional 10% **Wines** 123 bottles over £20, 4 bottles under £20, 20 by glass **Notes** Tasting menu 7 course £60, surprise menu 10 course £85, Sunday L, Vegetarian menu **Seats** 40 **Children** Portions **Parking** 6

as friendly and welcoming as it gets, with rough-cast stone walls in the dining room and good table linen. A menu of tried-and-true modern dishes is served, starting perhaps with scallops and their now widely de rigueur accompaniments of cauliflower purée and pancetta, and going on with haunch of local venison, served with poached baby vegetables in an allspice jus, and finishing with summer pudding with more of its berries served as a compôte, alongside dark chocolate ice cream.

Chef Martin Jones **Owner** Ceney Developments **Times** 6.30-9.30 Closed L all week **Prices** Fixed D 3 course £36-£38, Service optional, Groups min 12 service 10% **Wines** 25 bottles over £20, 12 bottles under £20, 10 by glass **Notes** Vegetarian available, Dress restrictions, Smart casual, Civ Wed 80 **Seats** 60, Pr/dining room 30 **Children** Portions, Menu **Parking** 36

Fishmore Hall

◎◎ Modern European V ❀

Imaginative cooking in smartly renovated Georgian-house hotel

☎ 01584 875148   📠 01584 877907
Fishmore Rd SY8 3DP
e-mail: reception@fishmorehall.co.uk
dir: A49 from Shrewsbury, follow Ludlow & Bridgnorth signs. 1st left towards Bridgnorth, at next rdbt left onto Fishmore Rd. Hotel 0.5m on right after golf course

Until the end of 2007, this Georgian house was in a state of dereliction. With its Palladian-styling and superb location - sweeping views of the Clee Hills and Shropshire countryside, yet within easy reach of Ludlow's centre - its potential was clear, and it now has new life breathed into it. A classy modern minimalist interior sits comfortably with original period polished-wood floors and delicate plasterwork. In the kitchen, a clearly talented team delivers a flannel-free menu of imaginative, exciting modern cooking with clean-cut flavours and stylish presentation. Top-class Welsh Marches produce is sourced within a 30-mile radius. Expect dishes like roast wood pigeon with curried roast almonds and purées of cauliflower and apricot, then perfectly-timed John Dory with grelot onions, leek purée and razor clam.

Chef David Jaram **Owner** Laura Penman
Times 12-2.30/7-9.30 **Prices** Fixed L 2 course £20, Fixed D 3 course £46.50, Tasting menu £55, Starter £7-£13, Main £17-£23, Dessert £7-£9, Service optional, Groups min 9 service 10% **Wines** 100 bottles over £20, 8 bottles under £20, 11 by glass **Notes** Gourmand menu 10 course £65, Tasting menu 7 course, Sunday L, Vegetarian menu, Civ Wed 80, Air con **Seats** 80, Pr/dining room 20 **Children** Portions **Parking** 36

Mr Underhills

◎◎ Modern International

Individual and tasteful restaurant with rooms

☎ 01584 874431
Dinham Weir SY8 1EH
dir: From Castle Square: with castle in front, turn immediately left, proceed round castle, turn right before bridge, restaurant on left

It is hard to imagine a more English scene than the delightful aspect enjoyed by Mr Underhills. The River Teme flows seductively along at the end of the garden, the water breaking over the weir, while mature trees in the lush garden shield the house from the towers of Ludlow Castle beyond. Chris and Judy Bradley's idyllic restaurant with rooms has been a jewel in Ludlow's crown for 17 years. Chris's menu is individually tailored to suit the requirements of guests (likes and dislikes discussed when booking) and consists of seven courses with no choice until dessert. This allows Chris to focus on sourcing the very best market produce, with absolutely everything made in-house; the emphasis is firmly on seasonality and natural flavours. Start with a nage of lemon sole, sea bream and haddock before main-course roasted rack and slow-cooked shoulder of Mill Farm lamb, served with a mint and shallot salsa, olive and crushed new potato cake, creamy celeriac and red wine and thyme jus.

Times 7.30-8.30 Closed 1 wk Jan, 1 wk Jul, Mon-Tue, L all week

Overton Grange Country House & Restaurant

◎◎ Modern British, European

Modern food in charming Edwardian country house

☎ 01584 873500   ☎ 0845 476 1000   📠 01584 873524
Old Hereford Rd SY8 4AD
e-mail: info@overtongrangehotel.com
dir: M5 junct 5. On B4361 approx 1.5m from Ludlow towards Leominster

This country house hotel on the outskirts of Ludlow, a town synonymous with good eating, is surrounded by rolling countryside. The tone of the service is spot on: professional, unobtrusive and well informed. The dining room - split into two - captures the essence of Edwardian decorum while not looking dated, with tones of aubergine and cream, plenty of natural light and smartly-set tables creating a comfortable and contemporary environment. The daily-changing menu has its heart in France but makes excellent use of the best produce from this part of England. Pan-fried scallops with an avocado and pancetta beignet, Jerusalem artichoke purée and a warm beetroot and chorizo vinaigrette is a bold starter with a lot going on, while main-course Moreton Forest venison comes with confit ravioli, red cabbage, celeriac purée and blackberry jus. Good technical skills are evident through to desserts such as apple and plum Tatin, and amuse-bouche, pre-dessert, excellent breads and a well-chosen wine list complete the picture.

Chef Christophe Dechaux-Blanc **Owner** Metzo Hotels Ltd **Times** 12-2.30/7-10 **Prices** Fixed L course £32.50, Fixed D 3 course £42.50, Tasting menu £59.50, Service optional, Groups min 10 service 10% **Wines** 150 bottles over £20, 20 bottles under £20, 12 by glass **Notes** Pre-theatre meal available from 5.30pm, Sunday L, Vegetarian available, Dress restrictions, Smart casual, Civ Wed 50 **Seats** 40, Pr/dining room 24 **Parking** 50

The Roebuck Inn

◎◎ Modern

A French flavour in a peaceful English setting

☎ 01584 711230   📠 01584 711654
Brimfield SY8 4NE
e-mail: info@theroebuckludlow.co.uk
dir: Just off A49 between Ludlow & Leominster

Originally a coaching inn on the main Ludlow to Leominster road, providing accommodation and stabling for weary travellers, the 15th-century inn is these days a high class restaurant and bed and breakfast. The lounge bar retains many original features, including exposed beams, and is furnished in rustic style with polished-oak tables and tapestry-upholstered chairs. The separate dining room and bar have a more sophisticated feel, with a contemporary minimalist look (modern art and furnishings, crisp linen and subtle lighting). Chef-patron Olivier Bossut (ex Ludlow's Overton Grange) produces an imaginative repertoire of mostly French dishes using quality seasonal ingredients. Start with a classic French onion soup or gâteau of crab in a saffron beurre blanc, followed by venison lasagne with aged parmesan and truffle oil.

Times 12-2.30/7-9 Closed Xmas, D Sun

MARKET DRAYTON   Map 15 SJ63

The Cottage Restaurant at Ternhill Farm House

◎ Modern British ❀

Ambitious cooking in homely Georgian farmhouse

☎ 01630 638984   📠 01630 638752
Ternhill TF9 3PX
e-mail: info@ternhillfarm.co.uk
dir: On x-rds of A41 & A53, 3m W of Market Drayton

The 3-storey redbrick farmhouse dates from the Georgian era, and makes an attractive setting for the Cottage restaurant, a simply decorated space with oak beams, unclothed tables and a terracotta colour scheme. The modern British cooking is more ambitious than the surroundings might lead you to anticipate, but is founded on solid traditional principles. Game rillettes make a satisfying starter, served with red onion, cranberry and sloe gin chutney, and might be followed by accurately cooked beef fillet topped with stilton and sauced with Irish stout, or pancetta-wrapped haddock with warm pesto rice salad. A trio of little pots is an effective finale, comprising lemon posset, chocolate mousse and crème brûlée, served with shortbread.

continued

MARKET DRAYTON *continued*

Chef Michael Abraham **Owner** Michael & Joanne Abraham **Times** 6.30-mdnt Closed Sun & Mon, L all week **Prices** Starter £4.50-£6.25, Main £9.95-£17.95, Dessert £4.50-£6.25, Service optional **Wines** 4 bottles over £20, 20 bottles under £20, 6 by glass **Notes** Fixed D Tue-Thu, Vegetarian available, Dress restrictions, Smart casual **Seats** 20, Pr/dining room 12 **Parking** 16

Goldstone Hall

◉◉ Modern British ✆

Accomplished modern cooking amid period charm

☎ 01630 661202 📄 01630 661585
Goldstone Rd, Goldstone TF9 2NA
e-mail: enquiries@goldstonehall.com
dir: From A529, 4m S of Market Drayton, follow hotel signs

PG Wodehouse, sipping a Pimms beneath the acacia tree in Goldstone's garden, thought Shropshire's buxom hills were England's 'nearest approach to paradise'. And it must be said that a more quintessential image of gentle English peace is hard to imagine: a handsome Georgian country-house hotel in delightful gardens and woodland, complete with a snooker room and conservatory. Dinner in the oak-panelled dining room is a civilised affair, modern British in essence with clever use of seasonal produce, much of which comes from the walled kitchen garden. Choose from six well-balanced dishes at each course: seared hand-dived scallops served with crab, celeriac and apple salad delivers clean, clearly-defined flavours; beef bourguignon, strips of fillet marinated and cooked with red wine sauce and horseradish mash simply melts in the mouth, while a dessert of pear tart with rosemary ice cream leaves lingering memories.

Chef John Thompson **Owner** Mr J Cushing & Mrs H Ward **Times** 12-2.30/7.30-11 **Prices** Fixed L 2 course fr £18.10, Service included **Wines** 39 bottles over £20, 26 bottles under £20, 9 by glass **Notes** Sunday L, Vegetarian available, Dress restrictions, Smart casual, Civ Wed 100 **Seats** 40, Pr/dining room 20 **Children** Portions **Parking** 40

Raven Hotel

◉◉ British, Mediterranean

Modern cooking in old coaching inn

☎ 01952 727251 📄 01952 728416
30 Barrow St TF13 6EN
e-mail: enquiry@ravenhotel.com
dir: 10m SW from Telford on A4169, 12m SE from Shrewsbury. In town centre

The whitewashed exterior of this town-centre hotel gives nothing away - inside it retains many original features including exposed beams and open fires. The building incorporates several 15th-century almshouses and a medieval great hall, with a restored 17th-century coaching inn at its heart. The bright, attractive restaurant overlooks an inner courtyard where you can dine alfresco on warm summer evenings. The food is unfussy and uses plenty of local produce, with classic dishes given a modern twist. A starter of terrine of Shropshire pheasant and duck with pickled carrot, beetroot chutney and warm foccacia bread might be followed by lightly grilled skate wing with lemon caper and chive butter sauce. Finish with hot chocolate fondant pudding.

Times 12-2.30/6.45-9.30 Closed 25 Dec

Crown Country Inn

◉◉ Modern British ✆

Historic, charming inn with top-notch modern food

☎ 01584 841205
SY7 9ET
e-mail: info@crowncountryinn.co.uk
dir: On B4368 between Craven Arms & Much Wenlock

The Crown lies in deepest Shropshire near the rolling hills of Wenlock Edge and within striking distance of foodie-central Ludlow. Not that you'd need to head out that way, as this imposing, half-timbered Tudor inn has all you need in the way of rustic charm and gastronomic delights. Stone floors, exposed beams and logs crackling in inglenook fireplaces make the bar a cosy place to tuck in, choosing from daily updated menus that reflect what's available locally at the time. The Corvedale restaurant was once the courtroom of a 'Hundred House' where the infamous Judge Jeffries passed sentence. Nowadays, judgements passed on Master Chef Richard Arnold's modern English cooking are sure to be favourable, thanks to his well thought-out combinations and spot-on flavours. Start with crostini of black pudding and tomato fondue with local Wenlock Edge bacon and balsamic syrup, then go for Shropshire chicken breast oak-smoked in-house and served with Boston beans.

Chef Richard Arnold **Owner** Richard & Jane Arnold **Times** 12-2/6.45-9 Closed Xmas, Mon, D Sun **Prices** Fixed D 3 course £18, Starter £4.75-£7.50, Main £11.95-£16.95, Dessert £4.95, Service included **Wines** 13 bottles over £20, 29 bottles under £20, 5 by glass **Notes** Sunday L, Vegetarian available **Seats** 65, Pr/dining room 42 **Children** Portions **Parking** 20

Hundred House Hotel

◉◉ British, European ✆

Hands-on family hotel where quirky charm meets skilled modern cuisine

☎ 01952 580240 & 580265 📄 01952 580260
Bridgnorth Rd TF11 9EE
e-mail: reservation@hundredhouse.co.uk
web: www.hundredhouse.co.uk
dir: Midway between Telford & Bridgnorth on A442. In village centre

continued

Considering the stained glass panels on the front door announce that this Georgian coaching inn was once a 'Temperance Hall', the swings in the bedrooms (oh yes!) suggest that buttoned-up behaviour is no longer required. These days it's an unstuffy family-run hotel, full of original features, including exposed beams, rustic tiled floors, open fires and quirky objets which inject real character into the warren of rooms making up the bar, brasserie and main restaurant. An imaginative modern British menu is prepared with an impressive level of skill, delivering accurate cooking and great flavour combinations from the finest Shropshire produce, including a vast array of herbs from the kitchen garden. Griddled scallops with cauliflower purée, black pudding, crispy pancetta and cumin dressing is a winner to start, followed by duck breast and smoked local sausage with cracked black pepper and brandy sauce.

Chef Stuart Phillips **Owner** Mr H Phillips, Mrs S Phillips, Mr D Phillips, Mr SG Phillips **Times** 12-2.30/6-9.30 Closed D 26 Dec **Prices** Starter £4.95-£7.95, Main £10.95-£20.95, Dessert £5.95, Service optional, Groups min 7 service 10% **Wines** 30 bottles over £20, 15 bottles under £20, 10 by glass **Notes** Sunday L, Dress restrictions, Smart casual, Civ Wed 100 **Seats** 60, Pr/dining room 30 **Children** Portions, Menu **Parking** 30

Pen-y-Dyffryn Country Hotel

@@ Modern British 🏵

Confident cooking in a hillside hotel on the Welsh border

☎ 01691 653700
Rhydycroesau SY10 7JD
e-mail: stay@peny.co.uk
dir: 3m W of Oswestry on B4580

Perched on what is technically the last hill in Shropshire, a hundred-yard dash from the Welsh border, this handsome greystone house was once a rectory. The undulating landscape around makes a fine backdrop to tea on the terrace, and the rooms within are plentifully supplied with fresh flowers in the hot months and log fires in the cold. Making best use of local and organic produce, the kitchen delivers a confident version of modern Anglo-Welsh cooking, from king scallops with parsnip purée, apple and a curried butter sauce, to mains such as Wynnstay Estate duck breast with a confit leg in orange and cardamom sauce. Finish with damson liqueur parfait, garnished with poached plum and a brandy snap.

Chef David Morris **Owner** MJM & AA Hunter **Times** 6.45-11 Closed 20 Dec-21 Jan, L all week **Prices** Fixed D 3 course £30, Service optional **Wines** 30 bottles over £20, 40 bottles under £20, 3 by glass **Notes** Vegetarian available **Seats** 25 **Children** Portions, Menu **Parking** 18

Sebastian's Hotel & Restaurant

@@ French

Relaxed, personally-run outfit with accomplished French fare

☎ 01691 655444   📄 01691 653452
45 Willow St SY11 1AQ
e-mail: sebastians.rest@virgin.net
dir: Telephone for directions

This buzzy bistro-style restaurant in a 16th-century merchant's house bursting with period character is run with energetic hands-on charm by chef Mark Fisher (aka Sebastian). The interior is crammed with exposed oak beams, oak panelling and floors; fashionable high-backed leather chairs sit at linen-clothed tables, while walls are adorned with food- and French-themed artwork. The traditional cooking has a clear French bias too, as is evident from the two fixed-price menus in French with English sub-titles; the good-value, no-choice menu du marché changes weekly, and there's a monthly-changing five-course carte. There is considerable technical skill at work here, teasing rich, clear flavours from excellent local produce. Borlotti bean and vegetable soup starts things rolling, before cannelloni filled with duck and shiitake mushrooms with Madeira and black bean sauce. A sorbet then precedes a main course, such as medallions of monkfish with capers, celeriac, tomatoes and butter sauce.

Chef Mark Sebastian Fisher, Richard Jones **Owner** Mark & Michelle Fisher **Times** 6.30-9.30 Closed 25-26 Dec, 1 Jan, Sun-Mon, L all week **Prices** Fixed D 3 course £19.95-£37.50, Service optional **Wines** 16 bottles over £20, 38 bottles under £20, 6 by glass **Notes** Vegetarian available **Seats** 35 **Children** Portions **Parking** 25, Street parking

Wynnstay Hotel

@@ Modern European 🏵

Contemporary cooking in elegant Georgian building

☎ 01691 655261   📄 01691 670606
Church St SY11 2SZ
e-mail: info@wynnstayhotel.com
dir: In town centre, opposite church

Occupying a lovely spot overlooking a 200-year-old crown bowling green, this fine Georgian property was once a coaching inn and posting house. The hotel's elegant, traditionally decorated Four Seasons Restaurant offers a mixture of classic dishes with some modern interpretations, supported by a good use of locally

sourced produce - including salmon from the River Wye and ham from Carmarthen. Salmon and crab fishcake and sorrel sauce is a simply appealing starter, following on with main-course braised belly pork with pomme purée, red cabbage and apple jus. Finish with a baked cheesecake with Amaretto and vanilla served with sauce anglaise.

Owner Mr N Woodward **Times** 12-2/7-9.30 Closed 25 Dec, **Prices** Fixed L 2 course fr £14.50, Starter £4.95-£7.25, Main £12.50-£18.75, Dessert £4.95-£5.95, Service optional **Wines** 20 bottles over £20, 36 bottles under £20, 7 by glass **Notes** Early bird menu 3 course Mon-Fri 6-7.30pm, Sunday L, Vegetarian available, Dress restrictions, Smart casual, Civ Wed 90, Air con **Seats** 46, Pr/dining room 200 **Children** Portions, Menu **Parking** 80

Albright Hussey Manor Hotel & Restaurant

@ Modern British 🏵

Romantic Tudor manor with refined and contemporary cooking

☎ 01939 290571 & 290523   📄 01939 291143
Ellesmere Rd, Broad Oak SY4 3AF
e-mail: info@albrighthussey.co.uk
dir: 2.5m N of Shrewsbury on A528, follow signs for Ellesmere

Cross a stone bridge to reach this enchanting medieval timbered manor house, which dates from Tudor times and stands in glorious landscaped gardens. Hugely atmospheric within, with a wealth of oak panelling and beams, leaded windows and huge open fireplaces, the dining room overlooks the gardens and provides a romantic setting for savouring simply presented dishes prepared from top-notch Shropshire produce. From the well-balanced carte choose seared scallops, with celeriac, walnut purée and liquorice, braised pork belly with rhubarb relish and black pudding mash, and chocolate and peppermint soufflé.

Chef Michel Nijsten **Owner** Franco, Vera & Paul Subbiani **Times** 12-2.15/7-10 **Prices** Fixed L 2 course £12-£15, Fixed D 3 course fr £24.50, Starter £5.75-£12, Main £14-£25, Dessert £6.50-£6.95, Service optional, Groups min 6 service 10% **Wines** 53 bottles over £20, 43 bottles under £20, 5 by glass **Notes** Sunday L, Dress restrictions, No jeans, trainers or T-shirts, Civ Wed 200 **Seats** 80, Pr/dining room 40 **Children** Portions **Parking** 100

SHREWSBURY *continued*

Mercure Albrighton Hall

◉◉ International

Formal dining in the Shropshire countryside

☎ 0870 194 2129 🖷 01939 291123
Albrighton SY4 3AG
e-mail: H6629@accor.com
dir: From A49 take 2nd exit at next 3 rdbts & 4th at next.
Continue towards Wem on A528. Hotel 1m on left

Overlooking an ornamental lake in 15 acres of gardens,
this former ancestral home, dating back to 1630, is these
days an elegant country-house hotel. Recently
refurbished, it combines modern luxury with period
features such as oak panelling and log fires. The long
gallery-style dining room has well dressed, well spaced
tables creating a formal but not stuffy feel. The menu is
designed to have broad appeal, while placing strong
emphasis on the use of quality British produce. Gravad
lax with a sweet dill sauce, and Shropshire blue and
quince tart with rocket and chive salad are typical
starters. Main-course Cumberland sausage ring comes
with buttered mashed potatoes and roasted onion gravy,
and Arbroath smokies are complemented by parsley
sauce and seasonal vegetables. Dessert might be whole
William poached pear with dark Belgium chocolate sauce.

Times 7am-9.45pm

Mytton & Mermaid Hotel

◉◉ Modern British **V**

**Modern British food in historic setting by the River
Severn**

☎ 01743 761220 🖷 01743 761292
Atcham SY5 6QG
e-mail: admin@myttonandmermaid.co.uk
dir: Just outside Shrewsbury on B4380 (old A5). Opposite
Attingham Park

Standing on the banks of the River Severn, this stylish
Grade II listed hotel is within easy reach of Shrewsbury.
Dating back to the early 18th century, when it was a
coaching inn, it has retained many period features. The

smart restaurant is furnished with antique oak tables set
with candles and fresh flowers. Commitment to seasonal
local produce is unwavering and the hotel rightly enjoys a
reputation for good quality modern British food. Start
with scallops with peas and wilted baby gem, crispy
pancetta and girolle vinaigrette, followed by pan-roasted
rump of lamb with braised Savoy cabbage, celeriac purée,
borlotti beans, mint jelly and roast hazelnut and port jus.

Chef Adrian Badland **Owner** Mr & Mrs Ditella
Times 12-2.30/6.30-10 Closed 25 Dec, D 26 Dec, 1 Jan
Prices Starter £6.95-£7.50, Main £12.95-£16.95, Dessert
£6.25-£6.75, Service optional **Wines** 26 bottles over £20,
30 bottles under £20, 12 by glass **Notes** Sunday L,
Vegetarian menu, Civ Wed 90 **Seats** 100, Pr/dining room
12 **Children** Portions, Menu **Parking** 80

Rowton Castle Hotel

◉ Modern British

Accomplished cooking in restored 17th-century castle

☎ 01743 884044 🖷 01743 884949
Halfway House SY5 9EP
e-mail: post@rowtoncastle.com
dir: From Birmingham take M6 west. Then M54 & A5 to
Shrewsbury. Exit A5 at 6th rdbt. A458 to Welshpool. Hotel
4m on right

Standing in 17 acres on the site of a Roman fort, this
splendid 17th-century castle retains many of its original
features, including a handsome carved oak fireplace. Oak
panelling and velvet chairs add to the warm and intimate
ambience in the Cedar Restaurant, where a seasonal
menu that utilises fresh local produce is offered. Accurate
modern British cooking delivers pan-fried pigeon breast
served on a rocket salad with a balsamic reduction and a
baked olive oil croûte, and roasted rump of lamb, served
pink with black olives and fresh tomato sauce on basil
polenta. Finish with strawberry and champagne trifle with
crushed amaretti biscuit topped with crème anglaise.

Times 12-2/7-9.30

Park House Hotel

◉ Modern British **NEW**

**Modern English dining in a characterful Midlands
setting**

☎ 01952 460128 🖷 01952 461658
Park St TF11 9BA
dir: From M54 J4 take A464 through Shifnal; hotel 200yds
after railway bridge

Two 17th-century country houses as different as chalk
and cheese have been cleverly joined together in this
rambling Midlands hotel. The design team cleverly hung
on to many period features, so classic wood panelling
and plaster mouldings are grafted together with a boldly-
colourful modern look. Culinary endeavours focus on
Butler's Restaurant, which proposes a sensibly concise
menu, modern British in essence and with a keen eye for
seasonality and local produce. Start with pan-fried

Brixham scallops with chorizo and sauce vièrge, and
follow on with loin of lamb wrapped in pancetta with
dauphinoise potatoes, confit red cabbage and lamb and
port jus. Comfort zone desserts take in treacle sponge
pudding with butterscotch sauce and vanilla pod ice
cream.

Chef Paul Davies **Owner** Andrew Hughes **Times** 11-10
Prices Starter fr £6.45, Main fr £17.95, Dessert fr £5.95
Wines 33 bottles over £20, 31 bottles under £20, 6 by
glass **Notes** Vegetarian available, Dress restrictions,
Smart casual preferred, Civ Wed 150 **Seats** 50, Pr/dining
room 180 **Children** Portions, Menu **Parking** 80

Best Western Valley Hotel & Chez Maw Restaurant

◉◉ Modern British **V**

Imaginative menus in historic surroundings

☎ 01952 432247 🖷 01952 432308
TF8 7DW
e-mail: info@thevalleyhotel.co.uk
dir: M6/M54 from junct 6 take A5223 to Ironbridge for
4m. At mini island right, hotel 80yds on left

Modern Ironbridge echoes to the tinkle of teacups rather
than the bedlam of heavy industry, but even in its hellish
heyday, the factory owners lived in fine style. The Maws
family, manufacturers of ceramic tiles, once owned this
elegant Grade II listed Georgian building in gorgeous
parkland on the banks of the River Severn. The restaurant
named after them has a contemporary look with polished
wooden floors, toffee-hued décor with modern art on the
walls, and creamy high-backed chairs at well-spaced
tables. Daily-changing menus focus on local, seasonal
materials and combine them with thought and restraint
to avoid confusion on the plate. An eclectic array of
dishes with British and continental influences includes
king scallops with cauliflower purée, Parmentier potatoes
and curried cream, and braised shoulder of Shropshire
lamb with pommes Anna, root vegetable mash, aubergine
caviar and braising juices.

Chef Barry Workman **Owner** Philip & Leslie Casson
Times 12-2/7-9.30 Closed 26 Dec-2 Jan, L Sat & Sun
Prices Starter £4.95-£7.50, Main £12.95-£17.95, Dessert
£4.50-£6.50, Service optional **Wines** 2 bottles over £20,
27 bottles under £20, 7 by glass **Notes** Vegetarian menu,
Dress restrictions, Smart casual, Civ Wed 120, Air con
Seats 50, Pr/dining room 30 **Children** Portions, Menu
Parking 100

Hadley Park House

◉ Modern British

Modern cuisine in attractive conservatory restaurant

☎ 01952 677269   📠 01952 676938
TF1 6QJ
e-mail: info@hadleypark.co.uk
web: www.hadleypark.co.uk
dir: M54 junct 5, A5 (Rampart Way), at rdbt take A442 towards Hortonwood, over double rdbt, next rbdt take 2nd exit, hotel at end of lane

This elegant Georgian house, set in 3 acres of mature grounds, is an oasis of calm within the bustle of modern Telford. Built by Thomas Telford's chief engineer, the house has been sympathetically restored and the attractive conservatory restaurant has well-spaced, finely appointed tables, serviced by friendly, knowledgeable staff. The cooking is modern British with some French and Eastern influences, making full use of carefully sourced seasonal produce. Dishes comprise of no more than 4 core ingredients and cooking is accurate without over-embellishment. Start with Szechuan spiced scallops with sauté spring greens and fermented black bean dressing, followed by cumin-crusted lamb loin with smoked aubergine purée, spring vegetable ragout and pancetta.

Times 12-2/7-9.30 Closed L Sat (subject to availability), D Sun (subject to demand)

SOMERSET

BATH   **Map 4 ST76**

Bailbrook House Hotel

◉ Modern British

Modern cuisine in historic setting

☎ 01225 855100   📠 01225 855200
Eveleigh Av, London Road West BA1 7JD
e-mail: bailbrook@hilwoodresorts.com
web: www.bailbrookhouse.co.uk
dir: M4 junct 18, A46 towards Bath. In 8m take slip road signed Bath Centre, left onto A4, hotel 200mtrs on left

Bailbrook House Hotel is an 18th-century mansion set in 20 acres of gardens with its restaurant located in a contemporary building with a light and airy feel. The style of cooking is modern British showing obvious French classical influences, with fresh local produce delivered daily and turned into some memorable dishes. House favourites include rump of Somerset lamb with Puy lentils and red wine jus, or open ravioli of plaice and cod with vanilla sauce, while vegetarians (or anyone else for that matter) might plump for Provençale tian of courgette and aubergine topped with buffalo mozzarella and sun-dried tomato pesto.

Chef Ciaran Molloy **Owner** Hilwood Resorts & Hotels
Times 12.30-2.30/7-9.30 Closed 24-26 Dec **Prices** Fixed D 3 course £25-£30, Service optional **Wines** 17 bottles over £20, 22 bottles under £20, 4 by glass
Notes Vegetarian available, Civ Wed 160 **Seats** 80, Pr/dining room 25 **Children** Portions, Menu **Parking** 120

Barcelo Combe Grove Manor Hotel

◉◉ International

Confident cooking in peaceful Georgian house

☎ 01225 834644   📠 01225 834961
Brassknocker Hill, Monkton Combe BA2 7HS
e-mail: combegrovemanor@barcelo-hotels.co.uk
dir: Please telephone for directions

Located just outside of Bath, this charming Georgian mansion overlooking the Limpley Stoke valley is set in 80 acres of wonderful grounds. The elegant Georgian Room has a high ceiling and splendid countryside views, and delivers sound cooking with classical roots and modern presentation. The menu includes the likes of chicken, chorizo and pistachio ballotine with celeriac cream, followed by pot-roasted chicken, garlic and thyme

---

fondant, spinach and root vegetables. Granny Smith apple tart with apple purée and vanilla anglaise shows the form at dessert. The recently refurbished basement brasserie and bar has an adjoining terrace and gardens where eating outside is a summer treat.

Times 12-2/7-9.30

The Bath Priory Hotel, Restaurant & Spa

◉◉◉ – *see page 374*

Cavendish Restaurant

◉◉ Modern British ⓒ

Assured modern cooking in impressive Georgian town house hotel

☎ 01225 787960 & 787963   📠 01225 787961
Dukes Hotel, Great Pulteney St BA2 4DN
e-mail: info@dukesbath.co.uk
dir: M4 junct 18, A46 to Bath. At lights left towards A36, at next lights right, & right again into Gt Pulteney St

A few minutes' walk from the city's famous Pulteney Bridge, Dukes Hotel occupies a magnificent Grade I listed Palladian-style town house. The Cavendish Restaurant is on the lower-ground level but it is light, airy and understated, with access to an attractive secluded walled garden for alfresco eating on the patio. The cooking is contemporary, seasonal and defined by classical cooking underpinned by modern ideas and presentation. High quality produce, much of it organic and from the West Country, is used to good effect. Start with smoked quail, Scotch egg, celeriac, apple and hazelnuts, following on with fillet of wild sea bass, saffron and potato chowder and braised fennel, and ending with an apple, pear and sultana crumble with a rather bold star anise ice cream and cinnamon pannacotta.

Chef Fran Snell **Owner** Alan Brookes, Michael Bokenham
Times 12-2.30/6.30-10 Closed L Mon **Prices** Fixed L 2 course £12.95, Starter £8.95-£10.95, Main £17.95-£24.95, Dessert £7.95-£8.95, Service optional **Wines** 34 bottles over £20, 10 bottles under £20, 9 by glass
Notes Sunday L, Vegetarian available **Seats** 28, Pr/dining room 16 **Children** Portions **Parking** On street

BATH *continued*

The Dower House Restaurant

◉◉ Modern British **V** 🏆

Contemporary fine dining in Georgian splendour

☎ 01225 823333 📠 01225 339401
The Royal Crescent Hotel, 16 Royal Crescent BA1 2LS
e-mail: info@royalcrescent.co.uk
dir: Please telephone for directions

The splendid Georgian elegance of Bath's Royal Crescent provides one of the finest settings in the country for the eponymous luxury hotel's Dower House Restaurant. Tucked away behind the hotel in a secluded garden, where you can eat alfresco in summer, it is a luminous space, flooded with light from French windows framed by swathes of mink-hued silk. Abundant enthusiasm backed by sound technical skills is evident in the chef's style;

expect a repertoire of creative, elaborate dishes in a thoroughly modern British vein, shot through with Mediterranean and oriental flourishes. A roast wood pigeon tart with Puy lentils, creamed leeks and sweet pickled red cabbage comes topped with a quail's egg to start things off, then line-caught sea bass with sprout tops, glazed chestnuts and spiced parsnip purée.

Chef Gordon Jones **Owner** von Essen Hotels
Times 12.30-2/7-9.30 **Prices** Food prices not confirmed for 2010. Please telephone for details. **Wines** 270 bottles over £20, 8 by glass **Notes** Sunday L, Vegetarian menu, Dress restrictions, Smart casual, No denim, Civ Wed 60, Air con **Seats** 70, Pr/dining room 40 **Children** Portions, Menu **Parking** 17

Four Seasons Restaurant

◉ Traditional International

Accomplished cooking in traditional country-house setting

☎ 01225 723226 📠 01225 723871
Best Western The Cliffe Hotel, Cliffe Dr, Crowe Hill, Limpley Stoke BA2 7FY
e-mail: cliffe@bestwestern.co.uk
dir: A36 S from Bath for 4m. At lights left onto B3108 towards Bradford-on-Avon. Before rail bridge right into Limpley Stoke, hotel 0.5m on right

Once the billiard room of a private gentleman's residence, this traditional-styled restaurant overlooks the well-

tended gardens at The Cliffe Hotel just south of the city. It's an attractive country-house affair set in peaceful grounds with stunning views across the valley. Accomplished dishes come dotted with international influences on a seasonally-changing menu using fresh produce sourced locally. Think herb and mushroom ravioli teamed with a butter sauce, to pork loin steak accompanied by apple mash and an apple and Calvados sauce. Desserts follow the theme, perhaps tiramisù lining up alongside a fruit crumble or sticky toffee pudding.

Four Seasons Restaurant

Chef Martin Seccombe, Andrea Colla **Owner** Martin & Sheena Seccombe **Times** 12-2.30/7-9.30 **Prices** Fixed L 2 course £11.20-£14, Fixed D 3 course £24-£30, Starter £4.50-£9, Main £16-£24, Dessert £4.50-£7, Service optional **Wines** 30 bottles over £20, 10 bottles under £20, 6 by glass **Notes** Sunday L, Vegetarian available, Dress restrictions, Smart casual **Seats** 50, Pr/dining room 15 **Children** Portions, Menu **Parking** 30

The Bath Priory Hotel, Restaurant & Spa

BATH	**Map 4 ST76**

Modern European **V**

The best of West Country produce in the hands of a skilled kitchen team

☎ 01225 331922 📠 01225 448276
Weston Rd BA1 2XT
e-mail: mail@thebathpriory.co.uk
dir: Please telephone for directions or see website

The Bath Priory reopened in March 2009 following a refurbishment which heralded the arrival of Michael Caines as executive chef. Owners Andrew and Christina Brownsword also possess Gidleigh Park (see entry), where Michael has produced his style of creative modern European cooking since 1994, and as he himself puts it, "it is my intention to bring more synergy between Gidleigh Park and The Bath Priory, while retaining their unique

appeal". And the appeal of The Bath Priory is in part due to its splendid location in four acres of impeccably maintained gardens just a short walk from the centre of the historic city. The Gothic-style mansion built of Bath stone is a tranquil oasis with beautiful landscaped gardens and magical terraces. Inside, a fine collection of artworks adorns the walls and deep sofas and roaring winter fires maintain the comfort factor. The Priory restaurant is a light and elegant room, with deep damask banquette seating, feather cushions, contemporary lighting and mirrors and white linen-clad tables. Service is formal but refreshingly unstuffy. The due diligence taken to source top-class West Country produce at Gidleigh has indeed been transported to Bath, where name-checked regional ingredients appear on the menus (fixed-price lunch, carte, a brace of tasting menus and a grazing option). A meal includes inter-courses to set the pulses racing, starting, perhaps, with a boudin of langoustines on a fine ratatouille, topped with a langoustine foam. Confit of Creedy Carver duck, foie gras,

bitter leaves and a neat duck jelly containing orange segments is an auspicious, technically impressive first course, and roast fillet of mullet comes with braised belly pork, a raviolo of Brixham crab and lemongrass and ginger sauce in a refined and well-crafted main course. Dark chocolate millefeuille with praline and candied hazelnuts is a stellar finish to a meal.

Chef Michael Caines, James Sheridan **Owner** Mr A Brownsword **Times** 12-2.30/7-9.30 **Prices** Fixed L 2 course £24-£26, Fixed D 3 course £65, Tasting menu £90, Service optional, Groups min 10 service 12% **Wines** 466 bottles over £20, 20 bottles under £20, 14 by glass **Notes** Tasting menu 8 course, Early D menu 2 or 3 course, Sunday L, Vegetarian menu, Dress restrictions, No jeans, T-shirts or trainers, Civ Wed 64 **Seats** 64, Pr/dining room 64 **Children** Portions, Menu **Parking** 40

Jamie's Italian

◎ Italian NEW

Jamie's winning rustic Italian formula comes to Bath

☎ 01225 510051
10 Milsom Place BA1 1BZ
dir: Please telephone for directions

A beautiful Georgian building right in the heart of the city houses the Bath branch of Jamie Oliver's ever-growing chain of rustic Italian restaurants. And rustic it is, with wooden floors, half-stripped walls and a mixture of wooden and red metal chairs. Simple, authentic Italian dishes are based around top quality seasonal ingredients, including mozzarella and olive oil made exclusively for Jamie. The menu offers a tremendous choice and it's all reasonably priced, too. Excellent meat and vegetable antipasti are served on planks for sharing, pasta is all made in-house daily - and it shows - and classic desserts like tiramisù are near-faultless. The no-bookings policy can lead to long queues, but if you're prepared to stand and wait, there are drinks and tasting platters to keep your hunger at bay.

Times 12 noon-11pm **Prices** Food prices not confirmed for 2010. Please telephone for details.

Macdonald Bath Spa Hotel, Vellore Restaurant

◎◎ Traditional British, International V

Opulent setting for sound cooking

☎ 0844 879 9106 📠 01225 444006
Sydney Rd BA2 6JF
e-mail: sales.bathspa@macdonald-hotels.co.uk
dir: A4 and follow city-centre signs for 1m. At lights turn left towards A36. Turn right after pedestrian crossing then left into Sydney Place. Hotel 200yds on right

The elegant Georgian mansion, built in 1835 and previously a school and nurses' home, has been a hotel for the past 20 years. A short walk from the city centre, it is a grand building, set amid seven acres of peaceful formal gardens and boasts an abundance of facilities (contemporary spa, indoor pool and croquet lawn). It really is a luxurious affair, rich with neo-classical styling, from the imposing entrance to the murals that adorn the two restaurants: the conservatory-style Alfresco and the fine-dining venue, the Vellore. Once a ballroom, the latter delivers discreet, professional service and cooking based on sound technical skills; start with pressed Loch Fyne smoked salmon with all the traditional accompaniments, followed by main courses such as roast rump of Highland lamb with polenta croquettes and tomato chutney.

Chef Giles Stonehouse **Owner** Macdonald Hotels plc
Times 12-2/6.15-10 Closed L Mon-Sat **Prices** Fixed L 2 course fr £17.50, Fixed D 3 course £30.50-£51.50, Starter £6-£12.50, Main £17-£30, Dessert £7.50-£9, Service optional **Wines** 140 bottles over £20, 12 by glass **Notes** Sunday L, Vegetarian menu, Dress restrictions, No jeans preferred, Civ Wed 130 **Seats** 80, Pr/dining room 120 **Children** Portions, Menu **Parking** 160

The Olive Tree at the Queensberry Hotel

◎◎ Modern British 🍷 🖐

Confident modern cooking in stylish hotel restaurant

☎ 01225 447928 📠 01225 446065
4-7 Russel St BA1 2QF
e-mail: reservations@thequeensberry.co.uk
web: www.thequeensberry.co.uk
dir: 100mtrs from the Assembly Rooms

The Queensberry Hotel's restaurant is a stylish basement hideaway at the heart of honey-hued Georgian Bath. It's everything you'd hope for in a tasteful boutique hotel: leather banquettes, wooden tables and floor, soothing neutral colours, subtle lighting and cleverly-sited mirrors all blend with Georgian grace in an effortlessly polished setting. The kitchen's repertoire of skilled, unshowy dishes with flashes of innovative flair matches the mood perfectly. Seasonality and fully-traceable local ingredients are married in starters such as pan-fried scallops with celeriac purée and a perfectly-judged piece of pan-fried halibut with roasted fennel, crab ravioli and watercress salsa for mains. Rhubarb crumble tart with ginger beer ice cream is a typical dessert.

Chef Nick Brodie **Owner** Mr & Mrs Beere **Times** 12-2/7-10 Closed L Mon **Prices** Fixed L 2 course £16.50, Starter £6.75-£11.50, Main £16.95-£22.95, Dessert £7.75-£9.50, Service optional, Groups min 10 service 10% **Wines** 270 bottles over £20, 30 bottles under £20, 34 by glass **Notes** Sunday L, Vegetarian available, Air con **Seats** 60, Pr/dining room 30 **Children** Portions **Parking** On street pay/display

Woods Restaurant

◎ Modern British, French

Brasserie menu in Georgian townhouses

☎ 01225 314812 & 422493 📠 01225 443146
9-13 Alfred St BA1 2QX
e-mail: claude@woodsrestaurant.fsnet.co.uk
dir: Please telephone for directions

The expansive brasserie venue occupies the ground-floor of a row of townhouses, named after their architect, whose signature is all over Georgian Bath. Racing prints of the sport of kings adorn the walls, the ambience is briskly efficient, and the menus provide plenty of choice. Mainstays of the modern European repertoire include pork, black pudding and prune terrine with piccalilli; sea bass oriental-style with sweet soy seasoning; sirloin with

caramelised shallots in port; and desserts such as raspberry sorbet with cold vodka poured over it. A simpler bar-brasserie menu is served also, with the option of outdoor eating.

Chef Stuart Ash **Owner** David & Claude Price
Times 12-2.30/5.30-10 Closed 25-26 Dec, Sun (open for special request) **Prices** Fixed L 2 course £14.95, Fixed D 2 course £14.95, Starter £5.50-£8.50, Main £12-£21, Dessert £5.50, Service optional **Wines** 32 bottles over £20, 12 bottles under £20, 9 by glass **Notes** Pre-theatre D 5.30-7pm 2 course £14.95 Mon-Fri, Vegetarian available **Seats** 100, Pr/dining room 40 **Children** Portions, Menu **Parking** On street, car park nearby

---

BRIDGWATER Map 4 ST43

The Lemon Tree Restaurant

◎ Modern British

Cheerful hotel restaurant with touch of ambition

☎ 01278 662255 📠 01278 663946
Walnut Tree Hotel, Fore St, North Petherton TA6 6QA
e-mail: sales@walnuttreehotel.com
web: www.walnuttreehotel.com
dir: M5 junct 24, A38, hotel 1m on right opposite St Mary's Church

Opposite a magnificent 13th-century church, the Walnut Tree Hotel is a former coaching inn catering for conferences and weddings as well as the local community in its own restaurant, The Lemon Tree. The yellow and blue themed room is traditionally decorated in a homely kind of way, and service comes with genuine smiles. The kitchen delivers a modern British menu with a degree of ambition: hand-dived scallops with black pudding and tomato and pepper salsa is suitably à la mode, followed by confit shoulder of lamb with gâteau of vegetables and sweet potato rösti, and to finish a comforting apple and blackberry pie with proper, well-made custard.

Chef Mark Roy, Luke Nicholson, Debbie Palmer **Owner** Kristine & Stephen Williams
Times 12-2.30/6.30-9.30 **Prices** Fixed L 2 course £23, Fixed D 3 course £27.50, Starter £4.50-£8.50, Main £10-£22, Dessert £4.50-£6.50, Service optional **Wines** 14 bottles over £20, 21 bottles under £20, 12 by glass **Notes** Sunday L, Vegetarian available, Civ Wed 100, Air con **Seats** 40, Pr/dining room 100 **Children** Portions **Parking** 70

BRUTON · Map 4 ST63

Truffles

◉ British **V** ♨

Conscientious local cooking in a West Country cottage

☎ 01749 812255 📠 01749 812255
95 High St BA10 0AR
e-mail: mark@trufflesbruton.co.uk
dir: Near A303, in town centre, at start of one-way
system, on left

Not far off the A303, Truffles is located in a creeper-
covered cottage with original beams. It's a testament to
the conscientious efforts of the Chambers, refugees from
London who have built up a solid network of local
suppliers here. The monthly-changing menus offer the
likes of Devonshire beef hung for 28 days, served
irresistibly with triple-cooked chips, scallops from Lyme
Bay annointed with garlic butter, or sea bass with
anchovy dressing, purple sprouting broccoli and mash.
The warmly welcoming approach helps to maintain
popularity, and desserts such as chocolate and Grand
Marnier parfait or passionfruit tart probably have a hand
in that too.

Chef Mark Chambers **Owner** Mr & Mrs Chambers
Times 7-9.30 Closed Sun, Mon-Thu, L all week
Prices Fixed D 3 course fr £29.95, Service optional
Wines 13 bottles over £20, 23 bottles under £20, 3 by
glass **Notes** Vegetarian menu, Dress restrictions, Smart
casual preferred, Air con **Seats** 30, Pr/dining room 10
Children Portions **Parking** On street opposite

DULVERTON · Map 3 SS92

Tarr Farm Inn

◉ Modern British

Beautifully situated historic inn with focus on good food

☎ 01643 851507 📠 01643 851111
Tarr Steps, Exmoor National Park TA22 9PY
e-mail: enquiries@tarrfarm.co.uk
dir: From M5 junct 27 follow Tiverton signs. Then signs to
Dulverton. In Dulverton take B3223 signed Tarr Steps for
approx 6.5m

Tucked away in a wooded valley above the gurgling River
Barle and the famous Tarr Steps, one of Britain's finest
clapper bridges, this rambling inn dates back to
Elizabethan times. Eat by the fire in the rustic and cosy
bar or at candlelit tables in the more refined yet unstuffy
restaurant. A confident kitchen displays sound cooking
skills, a refreshing modern approach to cooking classic
dishes, and sources quality local produce, notably Exmoor
game and Devon Ruby Red beef. Typically, tuck into warm
salad of squid, chorizo and chick peas with spinach,
rocket and lemon oil, beef Wellington with foie gras,
caramelised baby shallots and red wine jus, and banana
pannacotta with mixed berry compôte.

Chef Paul Webber **Owner** Richard Benn & Judy Carless
Times 12-3/6.30-12 Closed 1-10 Feb **Prices** Starter £5-
£8.50, Main £13-£21, Dessert £4.50-£6.50, Service

optional **Wines** 53 bottles over £20, 40 bottles under £20,
8 by glass **Notes** Sunday L, Vegetarian available
Seats 50, Pr/dining room 20 **Children** Portions
Parking 40

Woods Bar & Dining Room

◉ British, French

Unpretentious and convivial venue for hearty cooking

☎ 01398 324007 📠 01398 323366
4 Banks Square TA22 9BU
dir: Telephone for directions

Woods does 'exactly what it says on the tin': at one end of
Dulverton's one-time bakery there's a welcoming wooden-
floored bar, complete with a warming log fire and owner
Paddy Groves leading the banter with wisecracking
locals; at the other, a rustic bistro restaurant with lots of
chunky wooden timbers and furniture. The word is out
that the place is run with a real passion for hearty food
and you can happily let the wine-loving owner guide you
to some great bottles on a cracking list. Cooking is
French-influenced, accurate, straightforward and built on
quality West Country materials, including lamb off the
surrounding hills. Kick off with Exmoor roe deer pâté with
pickled mushrooms, fried quail's egg and red onion jam,
and follow with rump of lamb with a fricassée of its liver
and sweetbreads.

Times 11-3/6-11.30 Closed 25 Dec

EXFORD · Map 3 SS83

Crown Hotel

◉◉ Modern British ♨

Comfortable stylish dining in country inn

☎ 01643 831554 📠 01643 831665
Park St TA24 7PP
e-mail: info@crownhotelexmoor.co.uk
web: www.crownhotelexmoor.co.uk
dir: From Taunton take A38 to A358. Turn left at B3224 &
follow signs to Exford

Situated at the bottom of a hill in this tranquil Exmoor
village, the Crown is a 17th-century coaching inn that
lays fair claim to being the region's oldest. Smartly
dressed tables and good pictures lift the tone of the
restaurant comfortably above the country-pub norm, and
the cooking makes ample use of quality seasonal
produce. Start with truffle-creamed Jerusalem artichoke
soup, or scallops with Serrano ham and apple. Multi-

layered main courses bring on monkfish with squid-ink
tagliatelle, shrimp beignets and baby fennel, in orange
and vermouth sauce, as well as a variety of roasted
dishes, from beef or venison to John Dory. Fruity desserts
such as plum tart or blackcurrant soufflé bring up the
rear, or go for West Country cheeses with charcoal wafers
and oatcakes.

Crown Hotel

Chef Darren Edwards **Owner** Mr C Kirkbride & S & D
Whittaker **Times** 7-9 Closed L all week **Prices** Starter
£4.50-£9.50, Main £8.50-£21.95, Dessert £4.50-£7.95,
Service optional, Groups min 8 service 10% **Wines** 25
bottles over £20, 16 bottles under £20, 19 by glass
Notes Sunday L, Vegetarian available, Dress restrictions,
Smart casual, No jeans, T-shirts, swimwear **Seats** 45, Pr/
dining room 20 **Children** Portions **Parking** 30

HINTON CHARTERHOUSE · Map 4 ST75

Homewood Park

◉◉ Modern British, European

Impressive cooking in elegant period house

☎ 01225 723731 📠 01225 723820
Abbey Ln BA2 7TB
e-mail: info@homewoodpark.co.uk
web: www.homewoodpark.co.uk
dir: 6m SE of Bath on A36, turn left at 2nd sign for
Freshford

Just a few miles from Bath, this charming period country-
house hotel sits in 10 acres of well-tended gardens. Its
smart restaurant makes the most of the pretty views and
has a classic, contemporary style, complete with high-

backed chairs, sparkling glassware and fine china. Food is the main focus of the operation and shows no shortage of ambition, the kitchen delivering plenty of flair and finesse. A typical starter of smoked salmon rillettes with a crayfish and samphire salad, dressed with lemon oil, might be followed by assiette of Aberdeen Angus beef with ox tongue, wild mushroom ragout and port jus. Finish with dark chocolate fondant served with caramel sauce and a toasted hazelnut parfait.

Times 12-1.45/6.30-9.30

HOLFORD   Map 4 ST14

Combe House Hotel

Modern British 🍃

Complex modern cuisine in a characterful Somerset hotel

☎ 01278 741382 📄 01278 741322
TA5 1RZ
e-mail: info@combehouse.co.uk
web: www.combehouse.co.uk
dir: Telephone for directions

Fashioned from an old tannery and adjacent workers' cottages, with a 26-foot waterwheel still on display, this hotel in the Quantocks also boasts 4 acres of lush gardens. The beamed restaurant is all period allure, with its stone fireplace and low ceilings. A mini market-garden furnishes many of the kitchen's needs, and the cooking is all about seasonality and well-conceived modern combinations. Start with a multifarious but effective assemblage of poached foie gras, confit duck and roasted pecans, with blood-orange jelly and artichoke purée, and follow up with sea bass, crayfish and spiced potato in cardamom and orange velouté. Dessert plates might be equally crowded with the likes of iced chocolate, sensational banana bavarois, a brownie, some fudge, a bitter toffee sauce and powdered caramel.

Chef Barrie Tucker **Owner** Gareth & Catherine Weed **Times** 12-2.30/7-9 **Prices** Fixed L 2 course £17.95-£19.95, Starter £5.50-£9.50, Main £15.50-£27.50, Dessert £4-£7.50, Service optional **Wines** 25 bottles over £20, 13 bottles under £20, 9 by glass **Notes** Tasting menu available, Sunday L, Vegetarian available, Civ Wed 120 **Seats** 80, Pr/dining room 8 **Children** Portions **Parking** 40

HUNSTRETE   Map 4 ST66

Hunstrete House Hotel

Modern British

Archetypal country house in idyllic setting with up-to-date cuisine

☎ 01761 490490 📄 01761 490732
BS39 4NS
e-mail: info@hunstretehouse.co.uk
dir: On A368 - 8m from Bath

Hunstrete House is the quintessential English country house hotel - an elegant Georgian mansion within 92 acres of rambling deer park on the edge of the beautiful Mendip hills. Inside, period detail comes in spades, with antiques and oil paintings liberally spread around. Popham's restaurant is its main dining room, with cooking that is modern English in style, thoughtful in conception but not over-fussy. In season much of the fresh produce comes from the hotel's own Victorian walled garden, bolstered by local suppliers and free-range meat from Wiltshire farms. Sharp technical skills are apparent in poached langoustine with dried cherry tomatoes and cauliflower pannacotta, followed by poached Devon lobster with pak choi and creamy mash lifted by a lemongrass and coriander sauce.

Times 12-2/7-9.30

LOWER VOBSTER   Map 4 ST74

The Vobster Inn

Modern Mediterranean, European

Lovely rural English setting and carefully sourced ingredients

☎ 01373 812920 📄 01373 812920
BA3 5RJ
e-mail: info@vobsterinn.co.uk
dir: 4m W of Frome, between Wells & Leigh upon Mendip

The old stone Vobster is a traditional 17th-century inn with a tastefully up-to-date décor. If the weather is up to it you can sit outside surrounded by four acres of grounds amid the beautiful Somerset countryside, while inside there's the choice of bar, lounge or restaurant. There are a few Spanish touches on the menu, reflecting the birthplace of the chef-proprietor. A great deal is made in-house, including ice creams, and everything else is sourced with due diligence; fish comes up daily from Cornwall and there's a strong emphasis on local West Country produce. Seared Cornish scallops with smoked paprika and tomato sauce, perhaps, before Vobster wild garlic and mushroom risotto.

Times 12-3/6.30-11 Closed 25 Dec, D Sun

MIDSOMER NORTON   Map 4 ST65

The Moody Goose At The Old Priory

Modern British

Historic setting for well-balanced modern cooking

☎ 01761 416784 & 410846 📄 01761 417851
Church Square BA3 2HX
e-mail: info@theoldpriory.co.uk
dir: Along High St, right at lights, right at rdbt in front of church

With all the character you'd expect from a 12th-century priory, the Moody Goose restaurant makes a memorable dining experience. It's one of the oldest buildings in Somerset, so expect flagstone floors, huge inglenooks and oak beams to greet you, giving way to a fresh modern look with watercolours on whitewashed walls, bold claret chairs and a 100-year-old cooking range in the restaurant. The kitchen aims high, with well-focused menus underpinned by sound technique that delivers clear flavours in considered combinations - as in a pan-fried fillet of Brixham red mullet with marinated fennel and beetroot. The kitchen garden sorts out the herbs, fruit and vegetables, while other materials are diligently sourced and kept local where possible: try a roast rump and braised shank of lamb with flageolet bean purée and rosemary pinach.

Times 12-1.30/7-9.30 Closed Xmas, New Year, BHs, Sun-Mon

PORLOCK   Map 3 SS84

The Oaks Hotel

Traditional British

Honest, homely cooking with fantastic sea views

☎ 01643 862265 📄 01643 863131
TA24 8ES
e-mail: info@oakshotel.co.uk
dir: At bottom of Dunstersteepe Road, on left on entering Porlock from Minehead

The Edwardian country-house hotel stands on a Somerset hillside, with seductive views towards the sea. It's run with consummate aplomb by the Rileys - he reigns out front, she cooks - and together they achieve a harmonious blend of skills. The mustard-coloured dining room, with its grandfather clock, has an appealing domestic feel, and the food lives up to the surroundings. A simple but effective starter might bring together chicken, avocado

continued

PORLOCK *continued*

and anchovy, and be succeeded by a main course of carefully timed venison cooked in mushrooms and red wine. An intermediate refresher course delivers a fine seafood tart. Meals might end with an excellent, gutsy chocolate soufflé, with a fondant-like molten centre.

Chef Anne Riley **Owner** Tim & Anne Riley **Times** 7-8 Closed Nov-Mar **Prices** Fixed D 4 course £32.50, Service included **Wines** 15 bottles over £20, 40 bottles under £20, 4 by glass **Seats** 22 **Children** Portions **Parking** 12

SHEPTON MALLET   Map 4 ST64

Charlton House

Traditional British 🖐

Chic conservatory-style restaurant, locally-farmed produce

☎ 01749 342008   📄 01749 346362
Charlton Rd BA4 4PR
e-mail: enquiries@charltonhouse.com
dir: on A361 towards Frome, 1m from town centre

The Sharpham Park restaurant is set in the informal splendour of the Charlton House Hotel close to Glastonbury Tor. The creators of the upmarket fashion label Mulberry own the hotel, and they have used their lavish fabrics and furnishings to create a stylish, contemporary country-house hotel and restaurant - comfortably luxurious, yet friendly and relaxed. Many of the ingredients for the imaginative menu come from their own organic and rare breed farm, including White Park cattle and Red deer. Sharpham Park spelt is used in their breads, pastries, risotto (known as speltotto) and the breakfast mueslis or granolas. Try White Park beef ragù with wet polenta and granolata, or a main course of marinated loin of Sharpham Park venison, potato and celeriac gratin with red cabbage and quince.

Chef Steve Horrell **Owner** Roger Saul
Times 12-2.30/7.30-9.30 **Prices** Fixed L 2 course fr £12.95, Tasting menu £60, Starter £6-£10.50, Main £10-£17, Dessert £6.50, Service optional, Groups min 8 service 10% **Wines** 130 bottles over £20, 10 bottles under £20, 8 by glass **Notes** Tasting menu 6 course, Sunday L, Vegetarian available, Civ Wed 120, Air con **Seats** 84, Pr/dining room 70 **Children** Portions, Menu **Parking** 70

Thatched Cottage

Modern British, European 🖐

Vibrant European cooking in stylish Somerset inn

☎ 01749 342058   📄 01749 343265
63-67 Charlton Rd BA4 5QF
e-mail: david@thatchedcottage.info
dir: 0.6m E of Shepton Mallet, at lights on A361

The Thatched Cottage is much more than a 370-year-old inn with a passion for local cider, although it is that, too. The exterior is all you might expect of an old-stone inn, and inside there are oak beams, log fires and panelled walls, but the overall feel is rather contemporary. The restaurant seeks inspiration from across Europe and the Mediterranean countries in particular, so spring mussel hotpot is flavoured with garlic, chorizo and a coriander cream sauce, while main-courses run to Somerset lamb cooked Moroccan-style and served with raisin and cranberry couscous, or Cornish pollock lightly poached with Pernod and dill.

Chef David Pledger, Callum O'Dywer **Owner** David Pledger **Times** 12-2.30/6.30-9.30 **Prices** Fixed L 2 course £10, Starter £4.95-£7.25, Main £9.95-£18.95, Dessert £4.50, Service optional, Groups min 8 service 9% **Wines** 7 bottles over £20, 27 bottles under £20, 23 by glass **Notes** Sunday L, Vegetarian available **Seats** 56, Pr/dining room 35 **Children** Portions **Parking** 35

The Three Horseshoes Inn

Modern, Traditional 🖐

Homely cooking amid the tranquillity of Somerset

☎ 01749 850359   📄 01749 850615
Batcombe BA4 6HE
dir: Signed from A359 Bruton/Frome

Set in the tranquil heart of Somerset, amid splashing streams and birdsong, this is a 17th-century coaching inn with a modern makeover. Eat in the bar with its vast inglenook fireplace, any of the dining rooms, or out in the garden if the sun's shining. A homely style of country inn cooking brings on scallops baked in the shell with tarragon and garlic butter, with mains such as baked salmon and minted new potatoes, or local lamb with roasted beetroot, confit shallots and red wine gravy. Hand-pumped ales and wines by the glass indicate a conscientious approach to drinking.

Chef Mike Jones, Bob Wood **Owner** Bob Wood & Shirley Greaves **Times** 12-2/7-9 Closed 25 Dec, Mon, D Sun **Prices** Starter £4.75-£7.50, Main £12.50-£17.25, Dessert £4.50-£5.50, Service optional, Groups min 10 service 10% **Wines** 8 bottles over £20, 28 bottles under £20, 8 by glass **Notes** Sunday L, Vegetarian available, Dress restrictions, Smart casual **Seats** 40, Pr/dining room 40 **Children** Portions **Parking** 30

SOMERTON   Map 4 ST42

The Devonshire Arms

Modern British 🍷

Hunting lodge turned stylish gastro-pub with modern brasserie-style cooking

☎ 01458 241271   📄 01458 241037
Long Sutton TA10 9LP
e-mail: mail@thedevonshirearms.com
dir: Off A303 onto A372 at Podimore rdbt. After 4m, left onto B3165, signed Martock and Long Sutton

Seen from the outside, the Devonshire Arms is a rather grand inn on an idyllic Somerset village green - but step inside and you'll see it has had a stylish makeover, but not to an extent that wipes out its soul. You could sink a pint at the bar without feeling the odd one out, but there's a clear focus on the gastro side of the equation too. Flagstones and wooden floors blend with chunky tables and leather chairs, and there are squashy sofas to sink into with a drink or coffee. The modern brasserie-style cuisine shows an understanding of basics and a clear sense of purpose in well-flavoured dishes: crab crème brûlée with rocket salad for starters, followed by breast and confit leg of Quantock duck with green vegetables and creamy mash.

Chef Sasha Matkevich **Owner** Philip & Sheila Mepham **Times** 12-2.30/7-9.30 Closed 25-26 Dec, 1 Jan, **Prices** Fixed L 2 course fr £11.50, Fixed D 3 course fr £20, Starter £4.50-£7.50, Main £12.95-£23.50, Dessert £4.95-£6.50, Service optional **Wines** 10 bottles over £20, 16 bottles under £20, 10 by glass **Notes** Sunday L, Vegetarian available **Seats** 40 **Children** Portions, Menu **Parking** 6, On street

STOKE SUB HAMDON   Map 4 ST41

The Priory House Restaurant

@@ Modern British 🖐

Homely ambience in lush rural setting

☎ 01935 822826   📠 01935 825822
High St TA14 6PP
e-mail: reservations@theprioryhouserestaurant.co.uk
dir: 0.5m from A303 in Stoke sub Hamdon centre

Not far from the arterial A303, Stoke sub Hamdon is a surprisingly bustling little West Country village, in which this building was once a guest-house serving the Priory. It has incorporated a restaurant for a good quarter-century, but Peter and Sonia Brooks have stamped their own personalities on it since 2003. Behind the shop-window frontage is an engaging, candlelit, supremely welcoming room run with unhurried charm and cheer. An ambitious style of country cooking encompasses seared Lyme Bay scallops with smoked bacon and lime dressing, and mains such as monkfish korma, loin of venison with sweet potato and confit garlic, or accurately cooked guinea-fowl with cep and onion risotto and a burnt orange jus. Finish with summer fruits set in a Merlot jelly accompanied by raspberry coulis.

Chef Peter Brooks **Owner** Peter & Sonia Brooks
Times 12-2/7-9.30 Closed 25 Dec, BHs, 2 wks May, 2wks Nov, Sun & Mon, L Tue-Fri **Prices** Fixed L 2 course fr £17, Starter £7-£10.50, Main £19-£21.50, Dessert £7.50, Service optional **Wines** 37 bottles over £20, 10 bottles under £20, 7 by glass **Notes** Vegetarian available **Seats** 25 **Parking** Free car park 200yds & street parking

STON EASTON   Map 4 ST65

Ston Easton Park

@@ Modern British V 🖐

New chef making an impression in glorious Palladian mansion

☎ 01761 241631   📠 01761 241377
BA3 4DF
e-mail: info@stoneaston.co.uk
dir: A39 from Bath for approx 8m. Onto A37 (Shepton Mallet). Hotel in next village

Humphry Repton is the man to thank for the magnificent grounds, the 18th century landscape gardener creating a sham castle here, a ruined grotto there, all set in 36 acres of beautiful parkland that leaves a lasting impression. The house is no slouch, either: a grand Palladian mansion built to impress. The estate provides many of the vegetables and herbs for the kitchen, which since early 2009 has been under the stewardship of a new chef, Matthew Butcher. The setting for his food is the Sorrel Restaurant, with its reassuringly country-house-style décor, elegantly laid tables and abundance of fine period features. The kitchen has a much more contemporary attitude, including a desire to make the restaurant as self-sustaining as possible using produce from the estate and local suppliers. The ambitious and innovative modern British food sees monkfish cheeks and

liver in a starter with rocket, roast baby courgettes and garden shoots, and main-course smoked venison loin partnered with prune and chestnut blinis and shallot and sprout purée. Service is skilled and free of starchiness.

Chef Matthew Butcher **Owner** von Essen Hotels
Times 12-2/7-9.30 **Prices** Fixed L 2 course fr £17.50, Starter £11.50-£17.50, Main £21-£31, Dessert £8.25-£10, Service added but optional 10% **Wines** 120 bottles over £20, 10 by glass **Notes** Sunday L, Vegetarian menu, Dress restrictions, Smart casual, Civ Wed 100 **Seats** 40, Pr/dining room 80 **Children** Portions, Menu **Parking** 100

TAUNTON   Map 4 ST22

Farthings Country House Hotel and Restaurant

@ Traditional British 🖐

Country-house hotel serving up local and regional ingredients

☎ 01823 480664 & 0785 668 8128   📠 01823 481118
Village Rd, Hatch Beauchamp TA3 6SG
e-mail: info@farthingshotel.co.uk
dir: M5 junct 25 towards Ilminster, Yeovil, Chard on A358

Farthings is a charming, small Georgian hotel secluded away in a historic village in deepest rural Somerset. It's a delightful country retreat with spacious gardens, an unhurried, timeless elegance, and staff who are genuinely attentive and considerate. Cooking is uncomplicated with top-notch local produce allowed to shine, and the dishes on the short menu are unpretentious and simply presented; a starter of scrambled duck egg with smoked eel, for example, followed by tender rump of Somerset lamb with roasted root vegetables and red wine jus. Comforting desserts include a classic crème brûlée.

Chef Simon Clewlow **Owner** John Seeger, Kevin Groves
Times 12-3/6.30-9.15 **Prices** Fixed L 2 course £27-£32, Fixed D 3 course fr £40, Starter £7-£11, Main £16-£25, Dessert £7-£11, Service optional **Wines** 48 bottles over £20, 3 bottles under £20, 4 by glass **Notes** Sunday L, Vegetarian available, Civ Wed 50 **Seats** 60, Pr/dining room 30 **Children** Portions **Parking** 25

The Mount Somerset Hotel

@@ British, French

Imposing Regency country mansion and assured, confident cooking

☎ 01823 442500   📠 01823 442900
Henlade TA3 5NB
e-mail: info@mountsomersethotel.co.uk
dir: M5 junct 25, A358 towards Chard/Ilminster; right in Henlade (Stoke St Mary), left at T-junct. Hotel 400yds on right

An elegant Regency country mansion enjoying splendid views over the Somerset landscape of the Quantocks and the Blackdown Hills, the original grandeur of the Italian-designed house can be seen in the high ceilings, large windows and sweeping, circular staircase. The restaurant is equally impressive, with a magnificent central

chandelier and two wonderful mirrors. Chairs are large and very comfortable and tables are smartly appointed with crisp linen, sparkling silver and contemporary crockery. The chef delivers highly focused dishes, with everything on the plate for a reason and assured technique very much in evidence. Cold pressed sea trout and potato with wasabi horseradish mayonnaise and green apple salad, for example, or a main course of boneless whole quail, chicken and herb stuffing, spring vegetable risotto and chervil jus. To finish, the thin apple tart with double vanilla ice cream melting over the top is well worth the 15-minute wait.

The Mount Somerset Hotel

Times 12-2/7-9.30

The Willow Tree Restaurant

@@ Modern British 🖐

First-class regional cooking in period surroundings

☎ 01823 352835
3 Tower Ln, Off Tower St TA1 4AR
e-mail: willowtreefood@aol.com
dir: 200yds from Taunton bus station

Tucked away in the winding back streets of Taunton, the Willow Tree is the sort of restaurant that you feel comfortable in as soon as you step over the threshold. Exposed beams, a huge inglenook fireplace, warm earthy tones and bright modern artwork make for a romantic setting inside the charming 17th-century townhouse, and, weather permitting, there's a rustic waterside patio for alfresco drinks and dining. The kitchen's razor-sharp technique draws clearly focused flavours from judiciously-sourced local produce. Unfussy three-course menus of French-based modern British food offer dishes such as a salad of sautéed lamb's sweetbreads with girolles and crispy bacon, followed by John Dory fillet with a 'lasagne' of celery, carrot and celeriac with samphire and mussel cream sauce. With cooking of this skill, dessert is a must: try baked gooseberry cheesecake on almond biscuit base with elderflower ice cream.

Chef Darren Sherlock **Owner** Darren Sherlock & Rita Rambellas **Times** 6.30-9.30 Closed Jan, Aug, Sun-Mon, L all week **Prices** Fixed L 2 course £17.50, Fixed D 3 course £22.50-£29.50, Service optional, Groups min 7 service 10% **Wines** 20 bottles over £20, 25 bottles under £20, 4 by glass **Notes** Vegetarian available, Dress restrictions, Smart casual **Seats** 25, Pr/dining room 15 **Parking** 20 yds, 300 spaces

TINTINHULL
Map 4 ST41

Crown & Victoria

British NEW

Handsome village pub serving good local produce

☎ 01935 823341 📠 01935 825786
14 Farm St BA22 8PZ
e-mail: info@thecrownandvictoria.co.uk
dir: W bound off A303 follow signs for Tintinhull

Situated in the heart of the village, the attractive gardens surrounding this Somerset-stone inn make eating outside a popular choice in the summer. The décor is comfortable and inviting, and the traditional pub food - unpretentious and entirely in keeping with the surroundings - is made using the best of local and regional organic produce. Start with potato, leek and watercress soup, followed by home-made chicken, mushroom and tarragon pie or Stembridge faggots in rich gravy, and finish with summer pudding stacks with clotted cream or Somerset cheeses with poached rose pear and biscuits.

Chef Steven Yates **Owner** Isabel Thomas/Mark Hillyard **Times** 12-2.30/6.30-9.30 **Prices** Starter £4.50-£5.50, Main £11.95-£16, Dessert £5-£5.50, Service optional **Wines** 13 bottles over £20, 18 bottles under £20, 10 by glass **Notes** Sunday L, Vegetarian available **Seats** 100, Pr/dining room 45 **Children** Portions, Menu

WELLS
Map 4 ST54

Best Western Swan Hotel

Modern British

Sound modern cooking in historic inn

☎ 01749 836300 📠 01749 836301
Sadler St BA5 2RX
e-mail: info@swanhotelwells.co.uk
dir: A39, A371, on entering Wells follow signs for Hotels & Deliveries. Hotel on right opposite Cathedral

This venerable former coaching inn has been at the historic heart of Wells for 5 centuries. Naturally, it oozes character, but is not preserved in aspic: recent years have seen extensive restoration and a stylish makeover that blends seamlessly with its period features. Intricately-carved linen-fold oak panelling and interesting antiques make for a real sense of occasion in the traditionally-styled dining room, and when the sun shines, you can move outside to the secluded walled garden and Garden Room. Careful preparation of top-class produce from Somerset suppliers conjures well-balanced daily-changing menus of thoughtful modern British dishes - perhaps linguine of River Exe mussels with Dijon mustard cream to start, and mains such as braised blade of Somerset beef with horseradish mash and sweet shallot jus.

Chef Paul Mingo-West **Owner** Kevin Newton **Times** 12-2/7-9.30 **Prices** Fixed L 2 course £14.25, Starter £4.95-£6.75, Main £12.50-£17.50, Dessert £5.75-£5.95, Service optional **Wines** 20 bottles over £20, 16 bottles under £20, 7 by glass **Notes** Sunday L, Vegetarian available, Civ Wed 70 **Seats** 60, Pr/dining room 100 **Children** Portions, Menu **Parking** 25

Goodfellows

European

Piscine pleasures in historic town

☎ 01749 673866
5 Sadler St BA5 2RR
e-mail: goodfellows@btconnect.com
dir: Town centre near Market Place

This fish restaurant, which eagle-eyed film buffs might recognise from the market place scenes in *Hot Fuzz*, is on 2 levels. Downstairs in the bustling restaurant the tables are arranged around an open plan kitchen while up a spiral staircase the more spacious room has low lighting, a glass atrium and skylight. The menu, using produce from the Brixham day boats, is Mediterranean influenced and heavily relies on light flavoured oils and vinaigrettes for added oomph, rather than heavier sauces. Confidently cooked with contemporary presentation, dishes might include black bream with a fennel consommé and beetroot jelly and orange scented oil or a selection of fish served with pak choi and shiitake, apple and vanilla compôte and a light curry sauce. An on site French patisserie means puddings and bread are superb.

Chef Adam Fellows **Owner** Adam & Martine Fellows **Times** 12-2/6.30-9.30 Closed 25-27 Dec, 1 Jan, Sun-Mon, D Tue **Prices** Fixed L 2 course £16.50, Fixed D 3 course £35, Starter £6.50-£13, Main £9.50-£23, Dessert £3.50-£8, Service optional **Wines** 45 bottles over £20, 12 bottles under £20, 13 by glass **Notes** Tasting menu 6 course, Vegetarian available, Air con **Seats** 30, Pr/dining room 20 **Children** Portions

The Old Spot

European

Contemporary restaurant with friendly, relaxed bistro vibe

☎ 01749 689099
12 Sadler St BA5 2SE
dir: On entering village, follow signs for Hotels & Deliveries. Sadler St leads into High St, Old Spot on left opposite Swan Hotel

Pale green walls, framed menus and wooden floorboards provide some fashionable touches to the high ceilinged space of this light and airy contemporary restaurant housed in a Georgian town house. Unclothed tables add to the relaxed, friendly atmosphere, and sought-after seats in the neat extension enjoy cathedral views. The kitchen takes an intelligently simple approach driven by local seasonal produce, with well-presented, clean-cut, bistro-style dishes. Take potted chicken livers with tarragon, roast pheasant with lentils, apples, bacon and cider, and poached pear with chocolate sauce. Service is both informal and professional.

Chef Ian Bates **Owner** Ian & Clare Bates **Times** 12.30-2.30/7-10.30 Closed 1 wk Xmas, Mon, L Tue, D Sun **Prices** Fixed L 2 course fr £12.50, Fixed D 3 course fr £27.50, Service optional, Groups min 6 service 10% **Wines** 49 bottles over £20, 15 bottles under £20, 12 by glass **Notes** Sunday L, Vegetarian available **Seats** 50 **Children** Portions **Parking** On street, Market Square

WEST CAMEL
Map 4 ST52

The Walnut Tree Hotel

British, French

Hearty food in friendly village hotel

☎ 01935 851292 📠 01935 852119
Fore St BA22 7QW
e-mail: info@thewalnuttreehotel.com
web: www.thewalnuttreehotel.com
dir: Just off A303 between Sparkford & The RNAS Yeovilton Air Base

The Walnut Tree has all the charm and convivial atmosphere you would expect of a small-scale family-run hotel in a quiet Somerset village. But time doesn't stand still, so the bar and fine dining Rosewood restaurant have been given a recent makeover with oak and flagstone floors, and smart cream and burgundy leather high-backed seats that sit comfortably with oak beams and exposed brickwork. Outstandingly friendly service still comes as standard, and the kitchen's sound skills continue to provide simple hearty cooking. The menu offers a wide choice, as well as daily-changing specials. Warm pigeon with black pudding and bacon salad is a typical starter, followed by a main course of pheasant Wellington - breast stuffed with livers and pâté in a crust of puff pastry.

Chef Peter Ball **Owner** Mr & Mrs Ball **Times** 12-2/6-8.45 Closed 25-26 Dec, 1 Jan, L Mon, D Sun **Prices** Fixed L 2 course £14.95, Starter £4.95-£7.95, Main £14.95-£22.95,

Dessert £4.95-£6.95 **Wines** 25 bottles over £20, 20 bottles under £20, 5 by glass **Notes** Sunday L, Vegetarian available, Dress restrictions, Smart casual **Seats** 40 **Children** Portions **Parking** 40

Holbrook House Hotel & Spa

◉◉ British, French ✿

Modern French modes amid English gentility

☎ 01963 824466 & 828844 📠 01963 32681
Holbrook BA9 8BS
e-mail: enquiries@holbrookhouse.co.uk
web: www.holbrookhouse.co.uk
dir: From A303 at Wincanton, turn left on A371 towards Castle Cary & Shepton Mallet

The ancestral history of the house can be traced back to the outset of the 13th century, although the building we see before us today is Georgian. Over 20 acres of Somerset surrounds it, and the tone in the Cedar restaurant is one of relaxed English gentility, with good pictures, swagged curtains and spotless table napery. The cooking is an impressive marriage of home-produced materials and modern Gallic manners, so expect herb-rolled chicken and foie gras ballotine, sauced with a fascinating coulis of sweetcorn and vanilla, and main courses such as accurately timed, earthy confit pork belly with gnocchi and petit pois. Desserts are headlined with their main ingredient, but 'Cherry' turns out to be nothing less than a deconstruction of Black Forest gâteau, in the separate forms of mousse and jelly, together with whole griottines. Fine breads and nibbles are not to be missed.

Chef Callum Keir **Owner** Mr & Mrs J McGinley
Times 12.30-2/7-9 Closed L Sat, D Sun **Prices** Fixed L 2 course £16.95-£19.95, Fixed D 2 course £29.50-£37.95, Starter £4.50-£10.50, Main £12.50-£18.50, Dessert £4.50-£10.50 **Wines** 86 bottles over £20, 20 bottles under £20, 10 by glass **Notes** Sunday L, Vegetarian available, Dress restrictions, Smart casual, Civ Wed 160 **Seats** 70, Pr/dining room 140 **Children** Portions **Parking** 100

Karslake House

◉ Modern British

Fresh local produce in charming country-house style

☎ 01643 851242 📠 01643 851242
Halse Ln TA24 7JE
e-mail: enquiries@karslakehouse.co.uk
dir: A396 to Winsford, then left up the hill

In the sylvan embrace of Exmoor's hills, this 15th-century malthouse offers a tranquil haven in an idyllic village. The hands-on owners have thoroughly restored and stamped their own character on the house, and created an inviting restaurant serving down-to-earth modern British food built from top-drawer Devon produce; the wine list, too, does its bit to keep it local, with bottles from Oakford winery on Exmoor. Fillets of Brixham red snapper on ratatouille with black olive dressing is a typical starter, followed by Somerset beef fillet with potato rösti and horseradish cream sauce. Desserts - such as Bakewell pudding with crème anglaise and fresh raspberries - are not to be missed.

Chef Juliette Mountford **Owner** Mr & Mrs F N G Mountford
Times 7.30-8.30 Closed Feb-Apr, Sun-Mon, D Tue-Thu (ex residents) **Prices** Fixed L 2 course £25.50, Service optional **Wines** 18 bottles over £20, 15 bottles under £20, 2 by glass **Notes** Vegetarian available, Dress restrictions, Smart casual **Seats** 18 **Parking** 12

Wookey Hole Inn

◉ Modern European

Vibrant cooking in quirky Somerset inn

☎ 01749 676677
BA5 1BP
e-mail: mail@wookeyholeinn.com

Proximity to the famous caves does not mean this large and imposing pub rests on its laurels. There is plenty to satisfy and entertain - how about eight Belgium beers on draught, the beautiful sculpture garden, plus a menu bursting with Mediterranean and British flavours? A relaxed, café atmosphere pervades behind the traditional pub exterior, with bright, warm colours, lots of objets d'art to catch the eye and Moroccan fabrics and cushions in the lounge area. The menu is based around good produce, much of it locally sourced. Expect a generous

platter of antipasti, or fishcakes with tartare sauce, and desserts such as vanilla cheesecake with blackberry and blackcurrant compôte.

Times 12-2.30/7-9.30 Closed L Sun

The Helyar Arms

◉ British

Unpretentious country cooking in a charming medieval inn

☎ 01935 862332 📠 01935 864129
Moor Ln, East Coker BA22 9JR
e-mail: info@helyar-arms.co.uk
dir: 3m from Yeovil. Take A37 or A30. Follow signs for East Coker. Helyar Arms 50mtrs from church

The traditional, low-beamed, 15th-century country inn really is the hub of village life in a Somerset hamlet immortalised by TS Eliot in the *Four Quartets*. Young, friendly staff ensure things run smoothly in the cosy dining room with its bare wood tables and plenty of pictures to ponder. The cooking is unpretentious rural fare, taking you from asparagus with Parma ham, a poached egg and parmesan, through a main course like slow-cooked belly pork with red cabbage and boulangère potatoes, to puddings such as apple crumble and custard, or warm lemon and ginger tart with clotted cream.

Times 12-2.30/6.30-9.30 Closed 25 Dec

Lanes

◉◉ Modern British

Crowd pleasing cooking in a fashionable space

☎ 01935 862555 📠 01935 864260
West Coker BA22 9AJ
e-mail: stay@laneshotel.net
dir: 2m W of Yeovil, on A30 towards Crewkerne

This Edwardian former rectory has been brought up-to-date with a vengeance to create a thoroughly contemporary venue of considerable style. None more so than the restaurant, which is located in a strikingly modern extension with glass plate floor-to-ceiling windows. Sleek, cream leather chairs and wooden tables dressed with linen napkins set the tone, where a chrome bar, plenty of mirrors and wooden floor complete the modern setting. The menu has something for everyone,

continued

YEOVIL *continued*

whether you're after the familiarity of a signature burger or fish and chips or something more unusual such as 'merlot sea salt' cured salmon, redcurrants and chestnuts. Or perhaps a main course of cod cheeks, palourde clams and artichokes, lemon and parsley, rounded off with elderflower pressé cheesecake and pink grapefruit sorbet. The wine list is helpfully divvied up by style of drinking so you can decide whether or not you're in the mood for a crisp, dry and fruity non-oaked white.

Chef Jason Eland **Owner** John & Alison Roehrig **Times** 12-2.30/7-9.30 Closed L Sat **Prices** Starter £4.25-£6.50, Main £8.50-£14.50, Dessert £4.95, Service optional **Wines** 27 bottles over £20, 21 bottles under £20, 10 by glass **Notes** Sunday L, Vegetarian available **Seats** 85, Pr/dining room 40 **Children** Portions **Parking** 65

Little Barwick House

◉◉◉ – *see below*

Yeovil Court Hotel & Restaurant

◉◉ Modern European

Family-run hotel with appealing menu

☎ 01935 863746   🖶 01935 863990
West Coker Rd BA20 2HE
e-mail: unwind@yeovilhotel.com
dir: On A30, 2.5m W of town centre

After a recent refurbishment, this welcoming, family-run hotel is looking very sharp. The restaurant has a spruce modern décor in a light and striking combination of

creams, brown and black against a crisp white backdrop. The kitchen too, goes for a modern style, with a menu of confident, understated dishes built on sound foundations of quality local produce. Classic British dishes such as game pie, braised lamb shanks and beer-battered hake are sure-fire crowd-pleasers, otherwise, a starter might be pan-seared scallops with crisp pancetta, chorizo oil and black pudding. Fresh market fish turns up in the form of seared bream with creamed potato, sautéed spinach and lemon butter; temptation rears its head as black cherry jelly with spiced mascarpone to finish.

Chef Simon Walford **Owner** Brian Devonport **Times** 12-1.45/7-9.30 Closed 26-30 Dec, L Sat **Prices** Fixed L 2 course fr £13, Starter £3.90-£8.90, Main £11-£19, Dessert £4.50-£6.50, Service optional **Wines** 12 bottles over £20, 27 bottles under £20, 5 by glass **Notes** Sunday L, Vegetarian available, Air con **Seats** 50, Pr/dining room 80 **Children** Portions **Parking** 65

Little Barwick House

YEOVIL	**Map 4 ST51**

Modern European 🏷️

Charming restaurant with rooms delivering first-class food

☎ 01935 423902   🖶 01935 420908
Barwick Village BA22 9TD
e-mail: reservations@barwick7.fsnet.co.uk
dir: Turn off A371 Yeovil to Dorchester opposite Red House rdbt, 0.25m on left

Situated in a quiet hamlet in just over 3 acres of grounds, this listed Georgian dower house is an ideal retreat for those in search of good food in restful surroundings. The small country-house style restaurant with rooms receives much hands-on tender love and care from chef-proprietor Tim Ford and his wife Emma, who leads an attentive front-of-house team. The table settings are formal and

there is a choice of two small lounges for pre- and post-prandial drinks. Tim is responsible for preparing the lion's share of the food which is simple but well thought out and carefully executed. Dinner is a leisurely affair with good use made of local ingredients; start, perhaps, with an individual pie of quail breast, quail dumplings and baby vegetables in a rich red wine sauce topped with puff pastry, following on with pan-fried medallion of Cornish sea bass with a white wine and chive sauce. Finish with a tasty fig and pear crumble to ensure the sweetest of dreams.

Chef Timothy Ford **Owner** Emma & Timothy Ford **Times** 12-2/7-9.30 Closed New Year, 2wks Jan, Mon, L Tues, D Sun **Prices** Food prices not confirmed for 2010. Please telephone for details, Service optional **Wines** 179 bottles over £20, 21 bottles under £20, 6 by glass **Notes** ALC L 2/3 course fr £20.95/fr £24.95, D 3 course £37.95, Sunday L, Vegetarian available, Air con **Seats** 40 **Children** Portions **Parking** 25

STAFFORDSHIRE

BURTON UPON TRENT — Map 10 SK22

The Grill Room

@ Traditional British 🕙

Victorian-themed hotel restaurant serving good, flavourful food

☎ 01283 523800 & 0845 230 1332 📠 01283 523823
Three Queens Hotel, 1 Bridge St DE14 1SY
e-mail: restaurant@threequeenshotel.co.uk
dir: On A511, at junct of High St & Bridge St

Set within the Three Queens, a comfortable town-centre hotel which dates back to 1531, the Grill Room is an intimate dining room, reminiscent of a Victorian gentlemen's dining club with its hardwood panelling and screens. Terracotta and cream walls blend with small tapestries and bold-coloured carpets, while high-backed dining chairs provide the comforts. The kitchen's suitably traditional style - delivered with modern, clean-cut presentation - focuses on fresh local produce, simplicity and flavour. Expect dishes like chicken and chorizo terrine with home-made piccalilli, loin of lamb with pea mash and redcurrant and rosemary jus, and sticky toffee pudding.

Chef Neil Hardy **Owner** Three Queens Hotel Ltd
Times 12-2.15/6.15-10 Closed L Sat-Mon **Prices** Fixed D 3 course £18, Starter £4.50-£7.50, Main £10.50-£20, Dessert £5-£6, Service optional **Wines** 17 bottles over £20, 18 bottles under £20, 8 by glass **Notes** Gourmet D £39.50, Vegetarian available, Air con **Seats** 36, Pr/dining room 60 **Parking** 40

LEEK — Map 16 SJ95

Peak Weavers Rooms & Restaurant

@ Modern British **NEW**

Fresh local ingredients from hands-on husband-and-wife-team

☎ 01538 383729 📠 01538 387475
21 King St ST13 5NW
e-mail: info@peakweavershotel.co.uk
dir: Please telephone for directions

Originally a local mill owner's house before moonlighting as a Catholic convent and latterly converted to today's guest house and intimate restaurant. Decked out in basic, traditional style, with tables laid with white napery and front windows overlooking a small garden. Husband Nick runs front of house, while wife Emma mans the stove, her freshly prepared dishes making the very best of the local larder and producers. The style is simple, homely and uncomplicated (no truck with flowery garnishes here), so expect Derbyshire rib-eye steak served with a marchand de vin sauce and home-made fries, or chocolate squidgy cake with home-made vanilla ice cream.

Chef Emma Bettany **Owner** Nick & Emma Bettany
Times 6.45-9 Closed Xmas & New Year, Sun-Wed
Prices Fixed L 2 course £16-£20, Fixed D 3 course £18-

£27, Starter £3.50-£6.95, Main £10.95-£18.95, Dessert £3.95-£5.95, Service optional, Groups min 10 service 7.5% **Wines** 15 bottles over £20, 30 bottles under £20, 4 by glass **Notes** Vegetarian available, Dress restrictions, Smart casual **Seats** 40 **Children** Portions **Parking** 18

Three Horseshoes Inn & Country Hotel

@ Modern British, Thai

Well cooked Thai and British cuisine in traditional inn

☎ 01538 300296 📠 01538 300320
Buxton Rd, Blackshaw Moor ST13 8TW
e-mail: enquiries@threeshoesinn.co.uk
dir: M6 junct 15 or 16 onto A500. Exit A53 towards Leek. Turn left onto A50 (Burslem)

Located in the Peak District National Park with stunning views of the Staffordshire Moorlands and Tittesworth reservoir, this family-run inn stands in immaculate grounds complete with a children's play area. Exposed beams, polished brass and rustic furniture set the scene and there's a choice of three eating options. The evening-only Brasserie offers a menu of hearty British and fragrant Thai specialities, with everything cooked before your eyes in the open, glassed kitchen. A starter of mussels cooked in coconut with lemongrass, galangal, lime leaf, coriander and basil could be followed by fillet of beef with daube of beef shin with creamed spinach, roasted garlic, sautéed wild mushrooms and Madeira sauce.

Chef Mark & Stephen Kirk **Owner** Bill, Jill, Mark & Stephen Kirk **Times** 6.30-9 (Fri-Sat 6.30-10)
Closed 26-30 Dec, L all wk **Prices** Starter £4.50-£8.50, Main £12.95-£16, Dessert £4.30-£6 **Wines** 30 bottles over £20, 50 bottles under £20, 10 by glass **Notes** Tasting menu available, Dress restrictions, Smart casual, Civ Wed 150 **Seats** 50, Pr/dining room 150 **Children** Portions, Menu **Parking** 100

LICHFIELD — Map 10 SK10

The Four Seasons Restaurant

@@ Modern British

Stunning mansion and impressive cuisine

☎ 01543 481494 📠 01543 480341
Swinfen Hall Hotel, Swinfen WS14 9RE
e-mail: info@swinfenhallhotel.co.uk
dir: 2m S of Lichfield on A38 between Weeford rdbt & Swinfen rdbt. Follow A38 to Lichfield, hotel 0.5m on right

Diners arriving at the Swinfen Hall Hotel may be wowed by the 100 acres of parkland and stunning entrance hall, but its sumptuous interior of carved ceilings and original oil paintings will impress still further. Dating back to 1757, the lavishly decorated mansion has been painstakingly restored to create today's exquisite country-house hotel. Its oak-panelled, high-ceiling Four Seasons Restaurant comes in luxurious rich reds and offers a three-course fixed-price fine-dining experience, showcasing the kitchen's contemporary approach on classical French themes. Top-quality ingredients drive dishes such as baked fillet of cod with white beans and chorizo, red pepper rouille and bouillabaisse, or tarte Tatin served with cider jelly and Calvados ice cream.

Times 12.30-2.30/7-9.30 Closed L Sat, D Sun

STAFFORD — Map 10 SJ92

Moat House

@@ British, French 🕙

Interesting modern menu in a canalside conservatory restaurant

☎ 01785 712217 📠 01785 715344
Lower Penkridge Rd, Acton Trussell ST17 0RJ
e-mail: info@thelewispartnership.co.uk
web: www.moathouse.co.uk
dir: M6 junct 13 towards Stafford, 1st right to Acton Trussell, hotel by church

The Moat House is a gem of a hotel in a 14th-century moated manor house on the canalside of a chocolate-box Staffordshire village. But things haven't stood still for these last 600 years: the half-timbered main building is all oak panelling and exposed beams, and there's an inviting brasserie-bar with an inglenook fireplace, but most people want a seat in the modern Conservatory Restaurant where the smart canopied dining area comes with a backdrop of barges to-ing and fro-ing on the Staffordshire and Worcester canal. The kitchen has a keen eye for top-class seasonal materials, and a flair for creative combinations that steer clear of cramming too many flavours onto one plate. Seared Scottish scallops appear with chicken wings, sultana purée, cauliflower fritters and curry oil, while main courses might offer cannon of lamb with black olive and honey, ratatouille, and celeriac dauphinoise. Lemon and green tea pannacotta with lemon ice cream makes a refreshing finish.

continued

STAFFORD *continued*

Chef Matthew Davies **Owner** The Lewis Partnership **Times** 12-2/6.30-9.30 Closed 25 Dec, **Prices** Fixed L 2 course fr £15.50, Fixed D 3 course £23.95-£30, Tasting menu fr £50, Starter £7-£11, Main £16-£25, Dessert £6-£9, Service optional **Wines** 94 bottles over £20, 41 bottles under £20, 16 by glass **Notes** Sunday L, Vegetarian available, Civ Wed 120, Air con **Seats** 120, Pr/dining room 150 **Children** Portions, Menu **Parking** 200

STOKE-ON-TRENT   Map 10 SJ84

The Elms, Passion of India

◉ Indian

Welcoming Indian restaurant serving healthy dishes

☎ 01782 266360 & 07774 119983   📠 01782 265172
Snowhill, Shelton ST1 4LY
dir: Please telephone for directions

The Elms, once the home of the potter John Ridgway, is a deservedly popular Indian restaurant, decorated in rich colours with murals of dancers adorning the walls and the original cornicing painted gold. Staff are smartly turned out and full of smiles. The regional Indian cooking takes a healthy approach, and spices are well handled. Prawn puri is a classic starter and main-course chicken tawa, served in a copper pot, is full of well-judged flavours. Sag paneer is a typical side dish and kulfi makes a satisfying finish if you've room.

Times 6-11.30 Closed 25 Dec, Sun, L Mon-Sat

The Manor at Hanchurch

◉◉ Modern British **NEW**

Creative flair from the kitchen in a grown-ups hotel

☎ 01782 643080 & 07703 744479   📠 01782 643714
Newcastle Rd, Hanchurch ST4 8SD
e-mail: info@hanchurchmanor.co.uk
dir: M6 junct 15, 3rd exit at rdbt & 3rd exit onto Clayton Rd A519, through lights. After driving under M6 mtrwy bridge, hotel is on right

Designed by Sir Charles Barry who worked on the Houses of Parliament, the elegant whitewashed Victorian manor house has Tudor-inspired flourishes and sits in the seclusion of wooded grounds. In the serene restaurant, light floods through leaded Tudor-style windows onto cool shades of honey and cream, and chairs and tables draped to the parquet floor in snowy linen; a 'jackets for gentlemen' dress code imposes a certain formality. The kitchen shows plenty of creative flair in its modern cuisine, working with the seasons to produce good flavours in artfully presented dishes. A playful hand is at work in a starter of seared hand-dived scallops and confit pork belly with a peppered toffee apple, peanut cookies and cream; mains might produce a warm pavé of liquorice salmon with frogs' legs, a soft-poached egg and cauliflower and peas.

Times 12-2.30/7-10

UTTOXETER   Map 10 SK03

Restaurant Gilmore at Strine's Farm

◉◉ Modern British ◉

Husband-and-wife-team in a charming converted farmhouse

☎ 01889 507100   📠 01889 507238
Beamhurst ST14 5DZ
e-mail: paul@restaurantgilmore.com
dir: 1.5m N of Uttoxeter on A522 to Cheadle. Set 400yds back from road along fenced farm track

A converted three-storey farmhouse in Staffordshire spa country, a little way out of Uttoxeter, this place is all charm. A kitchen garden supplies much of the fresh produce, and most of the rest is sourced locally. Menus change monthly, and the cooking style successfully blends British and southern European ways of doing things, dressing a salad of chicory, fennel and rocket with toasted pine nut oil, or using pesto as the medium for a fricassée of monkfish cheeks and peas. Main dishes can get quite elaborate, as when roasted quail appears with Jerusalem artichoke slaw, walnut terrine and Madeira gravy, while meals end with the likes of Valrhona chocolate and chipotle chilli soufflé and vanilla ice cream.

Chef Paul Gilmore **Owner** Paul & Dee Gilmore **Times** 12.30-2.30/7.30-9.30 Closed 1 wk Jan, 1 wk Etr, 1 wk Jul, 1 wk Oct, Mon-Tue, L Sat,Wed, D Sun **Prices** Fixed L 2 course £24, Fixed D 3 course £42.50, Service optional, Groups min 8 service 10% **Wines** 30 bottles over £20, 20 bottles under £20, 10 by glass **Notes** Sunday L, Vegetarian available, Dress restrictions, Smart casual **Seats** 24 **Children** Portions **Parking** 12

SUFFOLK

ALDEBURGH   Map 13 TM45

Best Western White Lion Hotel

◉ Modern British ◉

Elegant dining by the sea

☎ 01728 452720   📠 01728 452986
Market Cross Place IP15 5BJ
e-mail: info@whitelion.co.uk
dir: Please telephone for directions

Aldeburgh's oldest hotel dates back to 1563 and overlooks the shingle beach and sea. The current incarnation has been sympathetically refurbished and retains some original features, notably the intricately carved inglenook fireplace in the bar and the fine oak panelling in the restaurant. Traditional British cooking with modern twists uses fresh, seasonal and locally-sourced produce, in particular fish landed on the beach. Typical dishes include Gressingham duck confit, braised oxtail, pan-fried liver and bacon, devilled lambs' kidneys, and beer battered cod.

Chef Patrick Neal **Owner** Thorpeness & Aldeburgh Hotels Ltd **Times** 12-2.30/6.30-9.30 **Prices** Fixed L 2 course fr £12.95, Starter fr £4.50, Main fr £10.95, Dessert fr £5,

Service optional **Wines** 40 bottles over £20, 15 bottles under £20, 17 by glass **Notes** Sunday L, Vegetarian available, Civ Wed 80 **Seats** 60, Pr/dining room 80 **Children** Portions, Menu **Parking** 8

The Brudenell

◉◉ Modern European **V**

Mediterranean style on the Suffolk coast

☎ 01728 452071   📠 01728 454082
The Parade IP15 5BU
e-mail: info@brudenellhotel.co.uk
dir: Please telephone for directions

Only a pebble's throw from the sea, the hotel's restaurant, The Bru, has panoramic views of an unspoiled stretch of Suffolk coast. The split-level restaurant is modern and bright with wooden tables, colourful seating and Mediterranean shutters; go for a table on the terrace if the weather allows. The food is contemporary European, and a great deal of care is taken sourcing the freshest seasonal produce from local suppliers. These ingredients are used to good effect in uncomplicated dishes such as seared scallops with parsnip and apple purée, fondant potato and coriander-scented dressing, or pan-fried fillet of sea bream with pumpkin purée and roasted squash, and game dishes such as whole roast Suffolk partridge with game chips and redcurrant jelly.

Chef Justin Kett **Owner** Thorpeness & Aldeburgh Hotels Ltd **Times** 12-2.30/6.30-9.30 **Prices** Starter £4.50-£8.50, Main £10.50-£18.95, Dessert fr £5.50, Service optional **Wines** 62 bottles over £20, 16 bottles under £20, 37 by glass **Notes** Sunday L, Vegetarian menu, Dress restrictions, Smart casual **Seats** 100 **Children** Portions, Menu **Parking** 15

See advert on opposite page

152 Aldeburgh

◉ Modern British, European

Unpretentious food in friendly beachside brasserie

☎ 01728 454594
152 High St IP15 5AX
e-mail: info@152aldeburgh.co.uk
web: www.152aldeburgh.co.uk
dir: Please telephone for directions

This busy brasserie occupies a prominent corner position leading from the high street to the beach via one of Aldeburgh's attractive archways. Contemporary with clean lines, it's a bright and airy place with pine floors and furniture, fresh flowers and equally cheerful, friendly service. The short, seasonal menu makes a virtue of the local produce and might start with smoked haddock, cod and spring onion fishcake with soft poached egg and chive cream and follow with wild local sea bass with saffron risotto, roasted chicory and a white wine sauce.

Chef Mark Clements **Owner** Andrew Lister
Times 12-3/6-10 **Prices** Fixed L 2 course £12.95, Starter £4.95-£6.95, Main £9.50-£17.95, Dessert £5.25, Service optional **Wines** 13 bottles over £20, 24 bottles under £20, 7 by glass **Notes** Sunday L, Vegetarian available **Seats** 56 **Children** Portions, Menu **Parking** On street parking on High St & Kings St

Regatta Restaurant

◉ Modern British ◉

Buzzy bistro where local fish is the star

☎ 01728 452011 📠 01728 453324
171 High St IP15 5AN
e-mail: rob.mabey@btinternet.com
dir: Middle of High St, town centre

Regatta, a lively and contemporary bistro, has enjoyed a colourful past, including time as a toy shop and a centre for St John's Ambulance. These days, it's a popular eatery where locally-caught fish and seafood is one of the main draws. The catches of the day are marked up on a blackboard, while the printed menu lists a good choice of alternatives. Dishes are unfussy with defined flavours from well-sourced ingredients. Expect starters like tiger prawn tempura with dipping sauce, then perhaps crisp belly of pork with Thai spices, red onion chutney, sticky rice, red curry dressing and salad.

Chef Robert Mabey **Owner** Mr & Mrs R Mabey
Times 12-2/6-10 Closed 24-26 Dec, D Sun (Nov-Feb)
Prices Starter £4-£8, Main £9.50-£18, Dessert £4-£5.50 **Wines** 6 bottles over £20, 40 bottles under £20, 6 by glass **Notes** Sunday L, Vegetarian available, Air con **Seats** 90, Pr/dining room 30 **Children** Portions, Menu **Parking** On street

Wentworth Hotel

◉◉ Modern British

Great local seafood in a delightful seafront hotel

☎ 01728 452312 📠 01728 454343
Wentworth Rd IP15 5BD
e-mail: stay@wentworth-aldeburgh.co.uk
dir: From A12 take A1094 to Aldeburgh. In Aldeburgh straight on at mini rdbt, turn left at x-roads into Wentworth Rd. Hotel on right

Slap bang on the seafront, this traditional hotel looks out across the beach at the more tranquil end of town. Managed by a member of the same family since 1920, the hotel exudes a real sense of quality and retains the charm of a private residence. Three stylish lounges and a cocktail bar complement the dining room with its fabulous sea views. Decorated in rich reds with candlelit tables in the evenings, the food offers classic dishes with a modern flavour, with local and seasonal produce the driving force of the daily-changing menus. Start with local potted crab on toasted granary bread and move on to whole grilled Dover sole with beurre noisette, finishing with Bakewell tart and crème anglaise.

Chef Graham Reid **Owner** Wentworth Hotel Ltd/Michael Pritt **Times** 12-2/7-9 **Prices** Fixed L 2 course £10-£15, Fixed D 3 course £19.50-£22, Service optional **Wines** 35 bottles over £20, 25 bottles under £20, 10 by glass **Notes** Sunday L, Vegetarian available **Seats** 90, Pr/dining room 20 **Children** Portions, Menu **Parking** 33

The Bildeston Crown

Modern British ❦ NOTABLE WINE LIST

Classic culinary reinterpretations in an ancient timbered inn

☎ 01449 740510 📠 01449 714843
104 High St IP7 7EB
e-mail: hayley@
thebildestoncrown.co.uk
web: www.thebildestoncrown.co.uk
dir: A12 junct 31. B1070 to Hadleigh, B1115 to Bildeston

The endearing half-timbered building dates back to the 15th century, and retains much of its medieval character inside, with open fireplaces, low ceilings and beams. The bare wood floor and tables in the dining room do nothing to detract from the cosy ambience, and the place is decorated with fine antique touches from later eras, including some great landscape paintings. Organic and seasonal produce finds its way into the modern British dishes, which offer some interesting takes on traditional ideas. A starter salad might be a distant cousin of Caesar, with anchovy, bacon, tiny croûtons and parmesan, as well as a soft-poached quail's egg, but adorned with a generous portion of carefully cooked lobster. A version of osso bucco might wow you at main-course stage, the boned veal served with its marrow, white beans and braised lettuce, along with a splash of wild garlic purée for extra kick. Less frequently encountered ingredients are a commendable feature, as in the duck heart stew that accompanies breast and leg, and when it comes to dessert, old British memories are stirred with the likes of a trifle and 'Arctic Roll' of rhubarb, in which some of the fruit is poached with vanilla and cloves. A menu of fine British cheeses is a powerful temptation in itself.

Chef Chris Lee **Owner** Mrs G Buckle, Mr J K Buckle **Times** 12-7/3-10 Closed D 25-26 Dec, 1 Jan **Prices** Fixed L 3 course fr £18, Fixed D 3 course fr £18, Service optional, Groups min 10 service 12.5% **Wines** 118 bottles over £20, 18 bottles under £20, 17 by glass **Notes** Tasting menu available, Sunday L, Vegetarian available, Civ Wed 24 **Seats** 100, Pr/dining room 16 **Children** Portions **Parking** 36, Market Sq

BILDESTON
Map 13 TL94

The Bildeston Crown

@@@ – *see opposite page*

BUNGAY
Map 13 TM38

Earsham Street Café

@@ Modern British, Mediterranean

Anglo-Mediterranean cooking in an unpretentious café

☎ 01986 893103 📠 01986 894577
13 Earsham St NR35 1AE
e-mail: www.earshamstcafe@aol.com
dir: In village centre

The queues that often stretch to the door of this slate-coloured building tell their own tale. The Café is a proper café, not a designer interpretation of one. Book ahead to avoid missing out on the refreshingly straightforward cooking, which is essentially British but isn't afraid to mix in a few Italian influences in the form of pancetta and shaved parmesan with the seared scallops, or balsamic tomatoes with baked plaice. Meat dishes are good too, as is the case with properly crisp duck confit, served with gnocchi, wild mushrooms and wilted rocket. Come back to Blighty for puddings such as spotted dick, treacle tart or rice pudding with stewed rhubarb. Friendly service is unstuffy, but highly professional.

Chef Christopher Rice **Owner** Rebecca Mackenzie, Stephen David **Times** 9.30-4.30/7-9 Closed Xmas, New Year, BHs, D ex last Fri & Sat of month **Prices** Starter £4.50-£10, Main £10-£16, Dessert fr £5.50, Service optional **Wines** 27 bottles over £20, 22 bottles under £20, 16 by glass **Notes** Pre-concert lunches available, Sunday L, Vegetarian available **Seats** 55, Pr/dining room 16 **Children** Portions, Menu **Parking** Parking opposite

BURY ST EDMUNDS
Map 13 TL86

Angel Hotel - The Eaterie

@@ Modern British 🕏

Good use of local produce in grand former coaching inn

☎ 01284 714000 📠 01284 714001
Angel Hill IP33 1LT
e-mail: staying@theangel.co.uk
dir: Town centre, right from lights at Northgate St

A former coaching inn in the heart of Bury St Edmunds that once counted Charles Dickens among its guests; rumour has it he wrote part of *The Pickwick Papers* whilst in residence. In more recent times, the Georgian hotel and its two restaurants - The Eaterie and Vaults - have been sympathetically refurbished to create a stylish contemporary feel while retaining many impressive period features. The Eaterie and bar area are very modern in style with natural wooden tables, new artwork and light painted walls to create a relaxed vibe. There's an accessible lunch menu and things are kept simple in the evening with the likes of a sauté of lamb's kidneys and mushrooms on toast with a grain mustard velouté and breast of corn-fed chicken with a walnut and Gorgonzola tortellini and baby spinach. Around 80 per cent of ingredients are sourced locally, with Suffolk's Marybelle Dairy now supplying all dairy products.

Chef Simon Barker **Owner** Robert Gough **Times** 7am-10pm **Prices** Fixed L 2 course fr £12, Starter £4.95-£8, Main £12-£18.65, Dessert £4.50-£9, Service optional **Wines** 48 bottles over £20, 18 bottles under £20, 24 by glass **Notes** Sunday L, Vegetarian available, Dress restrictions, Smart casual/dress, Civ Wed 85 **Seats** 85, Pr/dining room 80 **Children** Portions, Menu **Parking** 30

Clarice House

@ Modern European

Upmarket health and beauty spa with modern menu

☎ 01284 705550 📠 01284 716120
Horringer Court, Horringer Rd IP29 5PH
e-mail: bury@claricehouse.co.uk
dir: From Bury St Edmunds on A143 towards Horringer and Haverhill, hotel 1m from town centre on right

This informal neo-Jacobean country house aims to attract the health-conscious to its spa and lovely landscaped gardens, but there's no self-control required when dining in its oak-panelled restaurant. The kitchen team produces modern European dishes which are served in a traditional setting with crisp white linen and well-spaced tables. Light options might include galia melon marinated in Earl Grey syrup with grapefruit, or marinated salmon with tempura oysters. If you prefer a more calorific spread, go for a warm tartlet of red onion and parmesan topped with a poached egg and chive hollandaise, then perhaps noisettes of spring lamb with ratatouille, grilled potatoes, red wine and basil sauce.

Chef Steve Winser **Owner** King Family **Times** 12-2/7-9 Closed 25-26 Dec, 1 Jan **Prices** Fixed L 2 course £17.95, Fixed D 3 course £25.95, Service optional **Wines** 20 bottles over £20, 12 bottles under £20, 11 by glass **Notes** Sunday L, Vegetarian available, Dress restrictions, Smart casual D, Air con **Seats** 40, Pr/dining room 20 **Parking** 82

The Leaping Hare Restaurant & Country Store

@ Modern British 🕏

Picturesque vineyard restaurant serving modern British dishes

☎ 01359 250287 📠 01359 252372
Wyken Vineyards, Stanton IP31 2DW
e-mail: info@wykenvineyards.co.uk
dir: 8m NE of Bury St Edmunds, 1m off A143. Follow brown signs at Ixworth to Wyken Vineyards

In beautiful Suffolk countryside at the heart of the Wyken Hall estate (mentioned in the Domesday Book), the restaurant is set in a 400-year-old barn. Used for cattle and barley until 1960, the building now houses the Country Store as well as the restaurant, which is adorned with paintings and tapestries of leaping hares. Wood-burning stoves heat the large, open space with its high ceilings, beams, wooden flooring and large windows overlooking fields and woods. On the menu is meat from local producers, and game, vegetables and herbs from the Wyken estate and garden. And, of course, you can drink the estate vineyard's award-winning wines. Start with pan-fried Wyken pigeon breast and bacon salad before main-course rack of Stowlangtoft lamb, winding up with steamed orange and syrup pudding with custard.

Chef Jon Ellis **Owner** Kenneth & Carla Carlisle **Times** 12-2.30/7-9 Closed 2 wks Xmas, D Sun-Thu **Prices** Fixed L 2 course £18.95, Starter £5.95-£7.95, Main £12.95-£17.95, Dessert £5.95, Service optional, Groups min 6 service 10% **Wines** 16 bottles over £20, 22 bottles under £20, 17 by glass **Notes** Sunday L, Vegetarian available **Seats** 55 **Children** Portions **Parking** 50

BURY ST EDMUNDS *continued*

Maison Bleue

◉◉ French

Upbeat modern French seafood brasserie

☎ 01284 760623 📠 01284 761611
30-31 Churchgate St IP33 1RG
e-mail: info@maisonbleue.co.uk
dir: Town centre, Churchgate St is opposite cathedral

This stylish modern French restaurant sports a sleek metropolitan style with ivory leather seating, white linen and walls a neutral shade of mushroom velouté. A metal sculpture of a John Dory gives a clue to where the kitchen's heart lies: fish and seafood are what Maison Bleue is all about, although the menus might list a couple of meat dishes - perhaps rack of lamb. At lunch, the 'plat du jour with coffee' is a super deal, and the plateau de fruits de mer are worth booking ahead for. Accurate cooking and clearly-defined flavours are key to high quality piscine cuisine: top-class freshness and flavour sings out from a salmon and brown shrimp terrine starter, then a main course of pan-fried halibut and braised endives is lifted by a zesty orange butter sauce.

Chef Pascal Canevet **Owner** Regis Crepy
Times 12-2.30/7-9.30 Closed Jan, 2 wks in summer, Sun-Mon **Prices** Food prices not confirmed for 2010. Please telephone for details. **Wines** 80 bottles over £20, 62 bottles under £20, 7 by glass **Notes** Vegetarian available, Dress restrictions, Smart casual preferred **Seats** 65, Pr/dining room 35 **Children** Portions **Parking** On street

Priory Hotel

◉◉ Modern European

Accomplished manor-house hotel dining

☎ 01284 766181 📠 01284 767604
Mildenhall Rd IP32 6EH
e-mail: reservations@prioryhotel.co.uk
dir: From A14 take Bury St Edmunds W slip road. Follow signs to Brandon. At mini-rdbt turn right. Hotel 0.5m on left

Built on the remains of a 13th-century priory - hence the name - this 18th-century listed property comes set in a pretty location on the edge of town. The hotel's aptly-named Garden Restaurant lies beyond the well-kept gardens, with modern artwork and a contemporary décor creating a comfortable ambience. Its well-executed cuisine offers a seamless blend of British and European influences driven by quality, locally-sourced ingredients and smart presentation on white crockery. So expect a duo of English lamb, perhaps served with a sweet potato fondant, pea purée and balsamic dressing, or grilled halibut with carrot and coriander pappardelle, baby turnips and wild garlic purée, while a glazed lemon tart (with vanilla mascarpone and raspberry coulis) might provide the finale.

Chef Graham Smith **Owner** Priory Hotel
Times 12.30-2/7-10 Closed L Sat **Prices** Fixed L 2 course

£15-£21, Fixed D 3 course £20-£27, Starter £5-£10, Main £12-£25, Dessert £5-£8, Service added but optional 10% **Wines** 20 bottles over £20, 12 bottles under £20, 6 by glass **Notes** Sunday L, Vegetarian available, Civ Wed 55 **Seats** 74, Pr/dining room 26 **Children** Portions **Parking** 60

Ravenwood Hall Hotel

◉◉ Traditional British

Tudor charm and traditional fare with a modern touch

☎ 01359 270345 📠 01359 270788
Rougham IP30 9JA
e-mail: enquiries@ravenwoodhall.co.uk
dir: 3m from Bury St Edmunds, just off A14 junct 45 signed Rougham

Dating back to the reign of Henry VIII, this hotel and restaurant retains its ornately carved oak structure and rare 16th-century paintings. Nestled within 7 acres of lawns and woodlands, the elegant restaurant, originally the main living hall, features carved timbers and a huge inglenook fireplace. In keeping with its heritage, the menu uses old English recipes alongside some more modern dishes, incorporating home-preserved fruits and vegetables and meat and fish smoked in-house. Try chicken liver parfait with truffle butter, sultanas soaked in jasmine tea and toasted brioche, followed by braised beef and Guinness suet pudding with parsnip purée served with its own rich gravy and, if you've still got room, finish with quince and fig tarte Tatin with vanilla ice cream.

Chef Saurav Kumar **Owner** Craig Jarvis
Times 12-2.30/7.30-9.30 **Prices** Food prices not confirmed for 2010. Please telephone for details. **Wines** 54 bottles over £20, 32 bottles under £20, 11 by glass **Notes** Vegetarian available, Civ Wed 120 **Seats** 50 **Children** Portions, Menu **Parking** 150

CHILLESFORD Map 13 TM35

The Froize Inn

◉ Traditional British **NEW** 🍴

Good British food in country pub setting

☎ 01394 450282
The Street IP12 3PU
e-mail: dine@froize.co.uk
dir: On B1084 between Woodbridge & Orford

The red brick Froize has a winning formula judging by the crowds who come to eat the food and soak up the atmosphere. The daily-changing menu takes inspiration from rustic British and French cooking, with local produce adding a regional flavour. There is an à la carte menu and a hot buffet; order a starter and then choose from the first-class produce on the buffet. Perhaps a steak and kidney pie - local beef, cooked slowly with lamb's kidneys and topped with superb pastry - or roast shoulder of Gloucestershire Old Spot pork with cracking crackling, proper gravy and home-made apple sauce.

Chef David Grimwood **Owner** David Grimwood
Times 12-2/7 Closed Mon (ex BHs) **Prices** Food prices not confirmed for 2010. Please telephone for details. **Wines** 6 bottles over £20, 14 bottles under £20, 14 by glass **Notes** Vegetarian available **Seats** 48 **Children** Portions

---

EYE Map 13 TM17

Lexington

◉ Modern British

Charming country-house dining

☎ 01379 870326
The Cornwallis Hotel, Rectory Rd, Brome IP23 8AJ
e-mail: reservations.cornwallis@ohiml.com
dir: Please telephone for directions

There's a traditional look to this small country-house hotel tucked away down a long, lime tree-lined drive - hardly surprising, really, as the venerable old house dates in parts from the 15th century, and sits in 23 acres of grounds with woodland and topiary. Ancient beams, open fireplaces and wood carvings all play their part indoors, while the refurbished Lexington restaurant is done out in a rich, romantic décor. Smart, black-clad staff serve up a repertoire of straightforward modern British dishes - perhaps king scallops with garlic butter and rocket to start, followed by pan-fried duck breast with creamy mash and morello cherry glaze.

Chef Alan Webber **Times** 12-3/6-9 Closed L Mon-Sat **Prices** Starter £5-£7.95, Main £11.95-£22, Dessert £5-£8.50, Service optional **Wines** 17 bottles over £20, 5 bottles under £20, 6 by glass **Notes** Sunday L, Vegetarian available, Dress restrictions, No jeans, Civ Wed 150 **Seats** 26, Pr/dining room 80 **Children** Portions **Parking** 60

FRESSINGFIELD Map 13 TM27

Fox & Goose Inn

◉◉ Modern British

Whitewashed village restaurant with plenty of history

☎ 01379 586247 📠 01379 586106
Church Rd IP21 5PB
e-mail: foxandgoose@uk2.net
dir: A140 & B1116 (Stradbroke) left after 6m - in village centre by church

When the place was built in the early 16th century, it was a guildhall dedicated to St Mary of Antioch. After a period as an extension of the local poorhouse, it was only in the late 1700s that it was reborn as an inn with its present name. It is, to be sure, more a restaurant than an inn these days, but the whitewashed front, beamed interiors and tranquil village setting next to the church are still very much in keeping with expectations. Whereas the food will undoubtedly exceed them, for creativity and polish. Seared scallops with puréed swede and a quenelle of parsley-laden mash could have come straight off a metropolitan menu, and the garlic-crusted chicken breast with gnocchi and roast celeriac likewise. Careful cooking of local ingredients achieves impressive results, right down to the tangy-sweet pairing of rhubarb and treacle in a crisp shortcrust tart.

Chef P Yaxley, M Wyatt **Owner** Paul Yaxley
Times 12-2/7-8.30 Closed 27-30 Dec, 2nd wk Jan for 2 weeks, Mon **Prices** Fixed L 2 course £12.50-£13.95, Tasting menu £38, Starter £4.50-£8.25, Main £11.95-£19.25, Dessert £4.95-£6.50, Service optional **Wines** 26 bottles over £20, 28 bottles under £20, 7 by glass **Notes** Sunday L, Vegetarian available **Seats** 48, Pr/dining room 25 **Children** Portions **Parking** 15

GREAT GLEMHAM   Map 13 TM36

The Crown Inn

◉ Traditional British, Mediterranean 🖐

Relaxed, classic country inn serving locally-sourced produce

☎ 01728 663693
The Street IP17 2DA
e-mail: crown-i.cottle@btconnect.com
dir: A12 (N) left at Marlesford signed Gt Glemham. In 3m, pub 250yds after church on left. A12 (S), right at Stratford St Andrew, follow Crown Inn signs

The 17th-century Crown Inn is just what a modern village pub should be. Dogs and wellies are welcome, Suffolk real ales are drawn from brass handpumps and you can sink into wooden pews and sofas in the snug warmth of open fires in inglenooks. Better still, the food is admirably put together from producers as local as the neighbouring Great Glemham estate. The kitchen steers an uncomplicated course, letting the food speak for itself and deliver clear, fresh flavours. Enjoy a crisp and golden smoked haddock and pea fishcake, served with lemon crème fraîche, then slow-roasted belly pork with crunchy crackling and dauphinoise potatoes. A good honest apple pie with clotted cream ice cream might tempt for dessert.

Chef Christopher Selby **Owner** D Cottle, R Ball
Times 11.30-2.30/6.30-9 Closed Mon (ex BHs)
Prices Starter £3.95-£6.25, Main £6.25-£12.95, Dessert £4.50, Service optional **Wines** 3 bottles over £20, 18 bottles under £20, 8 by glass **Notes** Sunday L, Vegetarian available **Seats** 55 **Children** Portions, Menu **Parking** 30

HINTLESHAM   Map 13 TM04

Hintlesham Hall

◉◉ Modern European

Classic cuisine in an Elizabethan manor

☎ 01473 652334   📠 01473 652463
IP8 3NS
e-mail: reservations@hintleshamhall.com
web: www.hintleshamhall.com
dir: 4m W of Ipswich on A1071

The imposing Grade I listed Elizabethan Manor, standing in 175 acres of grounds and landscaped gardens, delivers a high level of hospitality and service. Inside this country-house hotel, the oak staircase and plaster ceilings date back to Stuart times and add a real touch of grandeur. There are 3 dining rooms - most notably the elegant Salon restaurant with a high domed ceiling resplendent with gold leaf and ornate cornices. The formal setting in the restaurant is echoed in the style of service, with jackets required for dinner. The classic menu relies heavily on high class ingredients and encompasses fresh herbs from chef Alan Ford's garden. Start with smoked and then roasted haunch of venison with wild mushroom polenta and Madeira, and follow on with grilled garlic-infused fillet of sea bream with lemon and anchovy vinaigrette, finishing with an excellent hazelnut and chocolate parfait with almond crackling.

Times 12-2.30/7-10 Closed L Sat

HORRINGER   Map 13 TL86

The Ickworth Hotel

◉◉ Modern British V

Modern cooking in family-friendly hotel on a National Trust-owned estate

☎ 01284 735350   📠 01284 736300
IP29 5QE
e-mail: info@ickworthhotel.co.uk
dir: From A14 take 1st exit for Bury St Edmunds (junct 42). Follow signs for Westley & Ickworth Estate

This luxurious hotel occupies a wing of an amazing country pile with vast acreages of manicured 'Capability' Brown gardens and parkland that was gifted to the National Trust in 1956. The team behind Woolley Grange (see entry) have put together a child-friendly package with kids' play areas, horses and bikes to ride and a crèche. But it's not all about the children: inside, grown-ups who like a bit of style will note that country-house chintz has been ditched for a jazzy contemporary décor that gels perfectly with the Italianate period pomp. Frederick's is the adults-only dining room, where classic English cuisine comes with modern twists on a menu of clever ideas carried out with sound skills. Seared squid and Suffolk pork belly with roasted sweet potato gnocchi, toasted pine nuts and rocket starts things off, then perhaps rump of lamb with Puy lentils, aubergine pickle and salsa verde.

Chef Nick Claxton-Webb **Owner** von Essen
Times 12-2/6-9.30 **Prices** Fixed L 2 course £15, Fixed D 3 course £37.50, Starter £4.95-£6.95, Main £10.95-£19.95, Dessert £6-£7.50, Service optional **Wines** 24 bottles over £20, 7 by glass **Notes** Sunday L, Vegetarian menu, Dress restrictions, Smart casual, Civ Wed 40 **Seats** 40, Pr/dining room 40 **Children** Portions, Menu **Parking** 70

IPSWICH   Map 13 TM14

Best Western Claydon Country House Hotel

◉ Modern British

Small, friendly hotel dining

☎ 01473 830382   📠 01473 832476
16-18 Ipswich Rd, Claydon IP6 0AR
e-mail: enquiries@hotelsipswich.com
dir: A14, junct 52 Claydon turn off from rdbt, 300yds on left

This small, friendly hotel on the outskirts of town was originally fashioned from two old village houses. Its smart restaurant is a fairly traditional, classic affair with blue carpet, high-backed leather chairs at dark wood tables, smartly uniformed, professional staff and a relaxed atmosphere. The kitchen is driven by quality locally-sourced produce and intelligent simplicity; take mushroom bruschetta to start, followed by a light and crisply battered tempura cod served with hot tartare sauce, while to finish, try the chocolate fondant served with home-made vanilla ice cream.

Times 12-2/7-9.30

IPSWICH continued

Il Punto

◉ French V

Solid brasserie cooking on a vintage Belgian gunboat

☎ 01473 289748 📄 01473 288919
Neptune Quay IP4 1AX
e-mail: info@ilpunto.co.uk
dir: Please telephone for directions

It's all aboard for this floating French brasserie on a vintage vessel that started life as a Belgian gunboat and crossed the North Sea into retirement on Neptune Quay. The handsome interior is certainly shipshape, decked out with brass rails, polished mahogany, classy blue upholstery and white tablecloths, or eat alfresco on the deck. The rather misleading name is a leftover from its Italian restaurant days, but there's little prospect of pasta and pizza now, as the food is rooted firmly in the French brasserie style. Simple classics are cooked with well-executed precision; start on a suitably maritime note with a classic Mediterranean fish soup with rouille, croûtons and grated gruyère, moving on to rabbit hotpot with prune and white wine sauce.

Chef Frederic Lebrun **Owner** Mr R Crepy
Times 12-2.30/7-9.30 Closed Jan, Sun-Mon **Prices** Fixed L 2 course £12.95, Fixed D 3 course £24.95, Starter £4.95-£8.50, Main £12.95-£19.50, Dessert £5.95, Service optional **Wines** 72 bottles over £20, 78 bottles under £20, 6 by glass **Notes** Early D available from 6.30-7.30pm 2 course £15.95, Vegetarian menu **Seats** 80, Pr/dining room 30 **Children** Portions, Menu **Parking** NCP

Salthouse Harbour Hotel - Eaterie

◉◉ Modern European ✿

Marina-side dining with good use of local produce

☎ 01473 226789 📄 01473 226927
No 1 Neptune Quay IP4 1AX
e-mail: staying@salthouseharbour.co.uk
dir: A14 junct 53, A1156 to town centre & harbour, off Key St

Situated just a short walk from the town centre and overlooking Neptune Marina, this former 19th century warehouse is now a luxury 48 bedroom hotel with a busy contemporary ground-floor brasserie. From the same stable as The Angel Hotel in Bury St Edmunds (see entry), the Eaterie's kitchen uses seasonal local produce simply cooked to shine through, flavours to shine through. Think sautéed calamari and crispy pork belly salad with sweet chilli dressing, followed by monkfish medallions baked with an olive crust, and round off the meal with caramelised lemon tart with raspberries. The extensive wine list includes over 20 served by the glass.

Chef Simon Barker **Owner** Robert Gough **Times** 12-3/6-10 **Prices** Fixed L 2 course £12-£17, Starter £4.50-£8.50, Main £14-£24, Dessert £5-£7, Service optional **Wines** 35 bottles over £20, 18 bottles under £20, 24 by glass **Notes** Sunday L, Vegetarian available **Seats** 60 **Children** Portions, Menu **Parking** 30

IXWORTH Map 13 TL97

Theobalds Restaurant

◉ British

Village restaurant brimming with character and charm

☎ 01359 231707
68 High St IP31 2HJ
dir: 7m from Bury St Edmunds on A143 (Bury to Diss road)

The pretty village of Ixworth is home to Simon and Geraldine Theobald's restaurant, housed in a 16th-century timber-framed building on the main street. The interior is full of old oak beams and charming, traditional character. There's a large inglenook fireplace in the lounge area and a pretty patio garden for drinks when the weather allows. The menu changes with the seasons to use quality ingredients at their best. The classical cooking includes starters such as a terrine of chicken livers with redcurrant sauce and toasted brioche, following on, perhaps, with roast fillet of cod with mustard lentils and white wine sauce.

Chef Simon Theobald **Owner** Simon & Geraldine Theobald **Times** 12.15-1.30/7-9 Closed 10 days in Summer, Mon, L Tue, Thu, Sat, D Sun **Prices** Fixed L 2 course £23, Fixed D 3 course £29, Starter £6.75-£8.95, Main £14.95-£19.50, Dessert £6.75, Service optional **Wines** 44 bottles over £20, 16 bottles under £20, 6 by glass **Notes** Sunday L, Vegetarian available **Seats** 42, Pr/dining room 16 **Children** Portions **Parking** On street

---

KESGRAVE Map 13 TM24

Milsoms Kesgrave Hall

◉ Modern NEW ✿

Relaxed dining in a contemporary country bistro

☎ 01473 333741 📄 01473 617614
Hall Rd IP5 2PU
e-mail: reception@kesgravehall.com
web: www.kesgravehall.com
dir: A12 N of Ipswich/Woodbridge, rdbt onto B1214

This 18th-century Georgian mansion in gorgeous countryside is the latest addition to the enlightened East Anglian Milsom's portfolio. The buzzy bistro restaurant has modish oak floors, leather chairs and a soothing cream and sage colour scheme. Watch the chefs at work in the open-plan kitchen, while smart staff in long black aprons flit efficiently between the scrubbed pine tables. On fine days, you could move outdoors to the terrace overlooking a vast lawn. The extensive brasserie menu has a broad appeal, ranging from starters like fat and juicy spiced seared scallops with cauliflower purée, cumin velouté and Granny Smith apple, to a perfect 28-day-matured rib-eye steak with béarnaise sauce, skinny fries and watercress.

Chef Stuart Oliver **Owner** Paul Milsom **Times** 12-9.30 **Prices** Starter £4.75-£8.50, Main £8.50-£17.95, Dessert £5.75, Service optional **Wines** 33 bottles over £20, 18 bottles under £20, 15 by glass **Notes** Sunday L, Vegetarian available **Seats** 80, Pr/dining room 24 **Children** Portions, Menu **Parking** 150

LAVENHAM Map 13 TL94

The Angel

◉ Traditional English, Modern British ✿

Historic inn with appealing menu

☎ 01787 247388 📄 01787 248344
Market Place CO10 9QZ
e-mail: angel@maypolehotels.com
dir: Between Bury St Edmunds & Sudbury on A1141. In town centre, Market Place just off High St

This magnificent 15th century coaching inn was first licensed in 1420 and is believed to be Lavenham's oldest hostelry. It stands at the centre of one of England's finest medieval towns overlooking the market place and retains much of its Tudor character with lots of oak beams, a large inglenook fireplace with log fires and solid wooden tables and chairs. The cooking is rooted in traditional English dishes (soups, pies, casseroles and roasts) but it also takes in influences from further afield. Shellfish linguine with a chive, lemongrass and ginger cream sauce could be followed by slow-roasted belly pork with honey-roasted butternut squash and sherry sauce. End with tiramisù.

Chef Michael Pursell **Owner** Mr Alastair McEwen **Times** 12-2.15/6.45-9.15 **Prices** Starter £4.50-£6.25, Main £7.95-£15, Dessert £4.50-£5.75, Service optional, Groups min 10 service 10% **Wines** 15 bottles over £20, 26 bottles under £20, 10 by glass **Notes** Sunday L, Vegetarian available, Dress restrictions, Smart casual **Seats** 100, Pr/dining room 16 **Children** Portions **Parking** 5, Car park (40)

Lavenham Great House Restaurant with Rooms

◉◉ Modern French

Authentic Gallic charm in Tudor setting

☎ 01787 247431 📄 01787 248007
Market Place CO10 9QZ
e-mail: info@greathouse.co.uk
dir: In Market Place (turn onto Market Lane from High Street)

The Great House fits in seamlessly with the handsome Tudor houses and tipsy cottages of this peerless medieval town. While the burnished oak floors and walk-in inglenook of the beamed Tudor restaurant ooze Englishness - albeit with a recent contemporary makeover - the Great House is a bastion of Gallic authenticity, served by cheery French staff. Terse menu descriptions -

'piglet', or 'turbot', for example - belie the degree of skill and flair that the well-drilled kitchen team puts into turning top-drawer ingredients into dishes such as a duck foie gras starter from the Landes region of France, served warm in ravioli with Puy lentils, truffle oil and crispy pancetta, or roasted rack of lamb with rosemary sauce.

Chef Regis Crepy **Owner** Mr & Mrs Crepy
Times 12-2.30/7-9.30 Closed Jan & 2 wks summer, Mon, L Tue, D Sun **Prices** Fixed L 2 course £16.95, Fixed D 3 course £28.95, Starter £8.50-£12.50, Main £12.50-£23.50, Dessert £4.95-£6.95, Service optional, Groups min 10 service 10% **Wines** 65 bottles over £20, 75 bottles under £20, 10 by glass **Notes** Sunday L, Vegetarian available **Seats** 40, Pr/dining room 15 **Children** Portions **Parking** Market Place

The Swan Hotel

◉◉ British, European **V** ✍

Dine surrounded by medieval splendour

☎ 01787 247477 📠 01787 248286
High St CO10 9QA
e-mail: info@theswanatlavenham.co.uk
dir: From Bury St Edmunds take A134 (S) for 6m. Take A1141 to Lavenham

The timber-framed Swan Hotel has sat at the hub of Lavenham life for over 600 years. It played its part when the town grew rich on the wool trade - even the floor is

made of bricks used as ballast in wool ships - and hosted many a boozy night for Second World War airmen stationed at Lavenham airfield. Stepping indoors, you're greeted by the quintessential English inn, all venerable oak beams, panelled walls, head-grazing ceilings and cosy nooks and crannies. Go for pub food classics in the bar and lounges, or treat yourself to the fine dining option. The Gallery Restaurant in the faux-medieval great hall - an airy barn-like space, complete with a minstrels' gallery - makes a fine setting for skilfully-cooked, well-presented modern British and European dishes. Start with the likes of roasted scallops with pork belly and apples, followed by pan-fried cannon of lamb wrapped in chicken mousse with dauphinoise potatoes and thyme jus.

Chef David Ryan **Owner** Thorpeness & Aldeburgh Hotels Ltd **Times** 12-2.30/7-9.30 **Prices** Fixed L 2 course £10-£15, Fixed D 3 course £33.25-£43, Service optional **Wines** 80 bottles over £20, 20 bottles under £20, 14 by glass **Notes** Sunday L, Vegetarian menu, Dress restrictions, No jeans or trainers, Civ Wed 100, Air con **Seats** 90, Pr/dining room 32 **Children** Portions, Menu **Parking** 50

See advert below

LONG MELFORD Map 13 TL84

The Black Lion Hotel

◉ Traditional British

Honest cooking in Georgian hotel overlooking the village green

☎ 01787 312356 📠 01787 374557
Church Walk, The Green CO10 9DN
e-mail: enquiries@blacklionhotel.net
dir: From Bury St Edmunds take A134 to Sudbury. Right onto B1064 to Long Melford. Right onto A1092 towards Cavendish. Hotel on Long Melford village green

Once you've admired the Tudor turrets of Melford Hall and poked around the antique shops, it's time to settle in for

dinner at this elegant Georgian inn on Long Melford's village green. The more formal eating option sports summery primrose walls, antiques and oil paintings, and opens into a Victorian walled garden; otherwise, stay casual in the bar and you get views across the green to boot - the menu is the same whichever you go for. Expect wholesome, hearty and appealing British dishes with shades of France and the Mediterranean, such as confit chicken leg and foie gras terrine with poached rhubarb to start, then roast loin of Rougham Estate venison with potato and celeriac rösti and redcurrant and juniper jus.

Chef Annette Beasant **Owner** Craig Jarvis
Times 12-2/7-9.30 **Prices** Food prices not confirmed for 2010. Please telephone for details. **Wines** 53 bottles over £20, 31 bottles under £20, 10 by glass **Notes** Sunday L, Vegetarian available, Civ Wed 50 **Seats** 55, Pr/dining room 26 **Children** Portions, Menu **Parking** 10, and on street

Scutchers Restaurant

◉◉ Modern British

Confident cooking in bright and bustling bistro

☎ 01787 310200 📠 01787 375700
Westgate St CO10 9DP
e-mail: info@scutchers.com
dir: Approx 1m from Long Melford towards Clare

Dating from the 16th century, the former Scutchers Arms was once a haunt of hemp workers from a local linen

continued

LONG MELFORD *continued*

factory. The building has been made over from top to toe, but this welcoming bistro's spacious open-plan interior retains a tangle of gnarled beams that blends effortlessly with pine tables and cheery floral walls. Simple, unpretentious and approachable are words that apply equally to the atmosphere as well as the modern British style of cooking. A well-executed starter of sautéed foie gras on crunchy rösti with black pudding and Puy lentil gravy brings out nicely varied textures, following on, perhaps, with medallions of monkfish with a prawn risotto in a light curry sauce.

Chef Nicholas Barrett **Owner** Nicholas & Diane Barrett **Times** 12-2/7-9.30 Closed 25 Dec, 2 wks Mar, last wk Aug, Sun-Mon **Prices** Fixed L 2 course £18-£22, Fixed D 2 course £18-£22, Starter £8-£12, Main £12-£24, Dessert £6, Service optional **Wines** 90 bottles over £20, 7 bottles under £20, 17 by glass **Notes** Vegetarian available, Air con **Seats** 70 **Children** Portions **Parking** 12

LOWESTOFT   Map 13 TM59

The Crooked Barn

◉◉ Modern European 🍃

Characterful dining in a restful Broads setting

☎ 01502 501353   🖹 01502 501539
Ivy House Country Hotel, Ivy Ln, Oulton Broad NR33 8HY
e-mail: aa@ivyhousecountryhotel.co.uk
web: www.ivyhousecountryhotel.co.uk
dir: A146 into Ivy Lane

With views over beautiful gardens and ornamental lily ponds, this converted 18th-century thatched barn at the Ivy House Country Hotel is a popular dining venue. Local artists' work is displayed on the walls and tables are clad in pale green with crisp linen napkins, and there's a delightful courtyard for summer alfresco dining. Modern European dishes - made with fresh, predominantly local ingredients - stand out for their simplicity and freshness.

Try pan-fried pigeon breasts with black pudding, blackberry compôte and hazelnut pesto, followed by grilled sea bass with braised red cabbage and salsa verde, or baked venison saddle with thyme potato cake, roasted root vegetables and truffle jus. Round off with summer pudding served with home-made lavender ice cream.

The Crooked Barn

Chef Martin Whitelock **Owner** Caroline Coe **Times** 12-1.45/7-9.30 Closed 24 Dec-8 Jan **Prices** Fixed L 2 course £14.95-£16.95, Fixed D 3 course £27.50-£28.50, Starter £4.95-£10.95, Main £13.95-£26, Dessert £3.95-£9.75, Service optional **Wines** 20 bottles over £20, 17 bottles under £20, 4 by glass **Notes** Sunday L, Vegetarian available, Dress restrictions, Smart casual, No shorts, Civ Wed 80 **Seats** 45, Pr/dining room 24 **Children** Portions **Parking** 50

Hotel Victoria

◉ British NEW

Contemporary dining in clifftop Victorian hotel

☎ 01502 574433   🖹 01502 501529
Kirkley Cliff NR33 0BZ
e-mail: info@hotelvictoria.co.uk

This seaside classic is named after the monarch in whose reign it was built, and perches atop Kirkley Cliff, surveying the sweep of Blue Flag beaches below. Inside, a smart makeover has combined period features with up-

to-date style and comfort, and the Coast lounge bar and restaurant looks the part for contemporary dining with those great sea views. The kitchen team thinks local in sourcing daily-caught fish, cheeses and Dingley Dell pork for a well-designed menu of straightforward modern British dishes. Starters might include Brancaster mussels and clams in Aspall cider and leek cream sauce. Local wild rabbit with white bean and Toulouse sausage cassoulet is a typical main course, while chocolate tart comes with honey roasted fig and clotted cream to finish.

Chef Stuart Fisher **Times** 12-2/6.30-9 **Prices** Food prices not confirmed for 2010. Please telephone for details. **Notes** Sunday L

MILDENHALL   Map 12 TL77

The Olde Bull Inn

◉ Modern British NEW 🍃

A mix of old and new at charming coaching inn

☎ 01638 711001   🖹 01638 712003
The Street, Barton Mills IP28 6AA
e-mail: bookings@bullinn-bartonmills.com
dir: Off A11 between Newmarket & Mildenhall, signed Barton Mills. Hotel by Five Ways rdbt

Retaining much of the charm of the past with its stagecoach archway, picturesque courtyard, quaint gables and dormer windows, this delightful 16th-century coaching inn claims Elizabeth I as a past visitor. It has

been lovingly refurbished to create a choice of bars, lounge area and a smart brasserie-style restaurant, the Oak Room. Many ingredients come from small-scale local suppliers and are used to good effect in a mix of traditional and sometimes appealingly modern dishes. Fillet steak tower - best local beef covered in creamy pepper sauce layered with onions and resting on a parsnip and potato rösti - or Denham Estate pheasant served with bubble-and-squeak and a Guinness and cumin sauce.

Chef Cheryl Hickman, Matthew Cooke, Shaun Jennings **Owner** Cheryl Hickman, Wayne Starling **Times** 12-9 Closed 25 Dec **Prices** Starter £5-£7, Main £13-£20, Dessert £5-£7, Service optional **Wines** 15 bottles over £20, 15 bottles under £20, 8 by glass **Notes** Sunday L, Vegetarian available **Seats** 60, Pr/dining room 30 **Children** Portions, Menu **Parking** 60

See advert on opposite page

MONKS ELEIGH   Map 13 TL94

The Swan Inn

◉◉   Modern British

Serious dining experience in pretty Suffolk village

☎ 01449 741391
The Street IP7 7AU
e-mail: carol@monkseleigh.com
dir: On B1115 between Sudbury & Hadleigh

The traditionally thatched 16th-century inn stands in a pretty village in the heart of the Suffolk countryside and offers quality contemporary bistro-style cooking. Diners can choose the light modern bar area with its oak floors, beamed ceilings and an open fire, or go for one of the more formal dining rooms. The menu changes almost daily and is influenced by the fresh ingredients available from local suppliers, including a plentiful flow of game in the autumn and winter months. Expect starters such as pork, apricot and pistachio terrine served with home-made chutney, or spicy Thai pork appetiser served in lettuce cups finished with chilli and coriander. Follow with red snapper on a creamy coconut curry sauce with steamed rice, or chargrilled rib-eye steak with Roquefort cheese, tomatoes, onions and hand-cut chips.

Chef Nigel Ramsbottom **Owner** Nigel Ramsbottom **Times** 12-2/7-9.30 Closed 25-26 Dec, 1-2 Jan, Mon-Tue (except BHs) **Prices** Fixed L 2 course £12.15-£13.50, Fixed D 3 course £18-£34.50, Starter £4.50-£8, Main £9-£20, Dessert £4.50-£6.50, Service optional **Wines** 10 bottles over £20, 30 bottles under £20, 10 by glass **Notes** Sunday L, Vegetarian available **Seats** 30, Pr/dining room 24 **Children** Portions **Parking** 12

NEWMARKET   Map 12 TL66

Bedford Lodge Hotel

◉◉   Modern International ◉

Accomplished cooking in hotel close to Newmarket races

☎ 01638 663175   📠 01638 667391
Bury Rd CB8 7BX
e-mail: info@bedfordlodgehotel.co.uk
dir: From town centre take A1304 towards Bury St Edmunds, hotel 0.5m on left

Close to the gallops at Newmarket and popular with the racing fraternity, this imposing 18th-century Georgian hunting lodge combines period elegance and a pleasing informality. The Orangery restaurant, decorated in sympathy with the original property, offers an inventive and distinguished menu. An emphasis on seasonal and local produce is the cornerstone of the kitchen and well-executed dishes may take in salad of Irish black pudding and crisp Cumbrian ham, with poached egg and truffled hollandaise, followed by a marinated Norfolk duck breast with vanilla pomme purée, organic beetroot relish, honey and cracked pepper sauce for main course. To finish, try the Earl Grey tea bavarois with poached pear and bitter chocolate sauce.

Chef Paul Owens **Owner** Barnham Broom Golf Club **Times** 12-2/7-9.30 Closed L Sat **Prices** Fixed L 2 course fr £16.50, Fixed D 3 course £27.50, Service added but optional 10% **Wines** 158 bottles over £20, 8 bottles under £20, 12 by glass **Notes** Sunday L, Dress restrictions, No shorts, sandals, vests, Civ Wed 120, Air con **Seats** 47, Pr/dining room 150 **Children** Portions, Menu **Parking** 100

Carriages Restaurant at The Rutland Arms

◉   British, Mediterranean

Well-tuned food in former coaching inn

☎ 01638 664251   📠 01638 666298
The Rutland Arms Hotel, 33 High St CB8 8NB
e-mail: reservations.rutlandarms@ohiml.com
dir: In town centre at top of High St

Situated in the heart of the town, the popular Carriages Restaurant and wine bar has its own separate entrance at this former 16th-century coaching inn, now The Rutland Arms Hotel. Although the property is built around a cobbled courtyard and retains many of its original features, the style here is very much contemporary with light wood floors and coffee and cream colours. The well-priced modern British menu focuses on simple dishes done well, with starters including the likes of wild mushrooms on brioche toast. To follow, there might be slow-roasted Suffolk belly of pork with crushed herb potatoes and cider gravy.

Chef Shane White **Owner** Oxford Hotels & Inns **Times** 12-2.30/7-9.30 **Prices** Starter £3.95-£6.95, Main £8.95-£16, Dessert £4.25-£6.95, Service optional **Wines** 25 bottles over £20, 23 bottles under £20, 9 by glass **Notes** Sunday L, Vegetarian available **Seats** 50, Pr/dining room 20 **Children** Portions, Menu **Parking** 40

Tuddenham Mill

◉   Modern European

Relaxed, rustic-chic brasserie in former watermill

☎ 01638 713552
Tuddenham St Mary IP28 6SQ
e-mail: info@tuddenhammill.co.uk

This smart restaurant - set in idyllic rolling countryside - is a mix of rustic charm and modern-day sophistication. Laid out over 2 floors of a converted mill with its large illuminated wooden mill wheel dramatically covering one wall, huge exposed beams blend with contemporary prints, modern dark-lacquered tables and brown suede chairs, while staff don long black aprons. The cooking follows a modern European theme using the best of local seasonal produce; butter-poached halibut is served with slow-cooked sweet potato and confit oxtail and a chicken and mint velouté. Terraces are ideal for summer dining.

Times 12-2.30/6.30-10.30

ORFORD   Map 13 TM45

The Crown & Castle

◉◉   Modern V

The best of Suffolk produce handled with respect

☎ 01394 450205
IP12 2LJ
e-mail: info@crownandcastle.co.uk
dir: Off A12, on B1084, 9m E of Woodbridge

The Trinity is the name of the restaurant in David and Ruth Watson's red-brick Victorian hotel, next to the castle keep, in picture-postcard Orford. (There's been a hostelry on the site for 800 years, but it is the Victorian makeover that won the day.) Ruth is a food writer, cookbook author, and TV personality, and here her principles of taking first-rate produce (much of it local) prepared with a lack of fuss and great skill, are on display. The space itself is equally uncomplicated, so dark-wood tables and floors, and plush banquettes are the order of the day; well-trained and friendly staff help set the relaxed tone. The menu is split into sections: raw, cold, hot and desserts. Start with Carlingford Lough oysters, perhaps, or Buxlow Wonmil cheese (made a few miles away) in a salad with roasted butternut squash, red onion and pumpkin seeds, before main-course Gressingham duck breast with zippy Puy lentils and stir-fried pak choi.

Chef Ruth Watson, David Williams **Owner** David & Ruth Watson **Times** 12.15-2.15/7-9.30 Closed 4-7 Jan, L 31 Dec **Prices** Fixed L 2 course £17.95-£23.50, Starter £7.50-£11.50, Main £13.95-£19.50, Dessert £6.50, Service optional, Groups min 8 service 10% **Wines** 98 bottles over £20, 24 bottles under £20, 14 by glass **Notes** Fixed D Sat & BHs only, Sunday L, Vegetarian menu **Seats** 60, Pr/dining room 10 **Children** Menu **Parking** 19

The Crown

◉ Modern British ▪ 🏛️ 🖐️

Traditional British cooking at the Adnams nerve centre

☎ 01502 722275 📠 01502 727263
90 High St IP18 6DP
e-mail: crown.reception@adnams.co.uk
dir: A12 onto A1095 to Southwold. Hotel on left in High Street

The nerve centre of the Adnams operation combines a pub, wine bar, restaurant and hotel in one handy package, so whether you've come for a pint of the Suffolk brewer's best, a bottle from its wine merchant list, a deftly presented meal of modern British food, or a bed for the night, you're sorted. The ambience in the elegant Georgian inn is bright and airy, and the cooking hits the spot with the likes of ham hock terrine and chunky piccalilli, confit duck leg with braised red cabbage, or Lowestoft cod (MCS-approved) with caper mash, asparagus fritters and sauce vierge. Banoffee pudding with vanilla ice cream is a satisfying way to finish.

Chef Robert Mace **Owner** Adnams plc
Times 12-2/6.30-9.30 **Prices** Starter fr £6.50, Main fr £16, Dessert fr £6, Service optional **Wines** 144 bottles over £20, 73 bottles under £20, 14 by glass **Notes** Sunday L, Vegetarian available **Seats** 65, Pr/dining room 30 **Children** Portions, Menu **Parking** 15, Free car parks within 5 mins walking distance

The Randolph Hotel

◉ Modern, Traditional British

Chic gastro-pub close to Suffolk coast

☎ 01502 723603 📠 01502 722194
41 Wangford Rd, Reydon IP18 6PZ
e-mail: reception@randolph.co.uk
dir: 1m from Southwold

Situated just a fifteen minute stroll from the centre of picturesque Southwold, in the village of Reydon, this former pub is the perfect base for exploring the Suffolk Heritage Coast. It still has a traditional bar but contemporary

furnishings have been added, including high-backed leather chairs and comfortable sofas. Meals are served in the large dining area. The style of cooking is modern British, using locally-sourced ingredients to produce straightforward dishes. Steamed steak, ale and mushroom pudding, for example, served with mashed potato and roasted root vegetables, or pan-fried fillet of halibut wrapped in bacon with crushed Jerusalem artichokes, purple sprouting broccoli and a creamy fish sauce.

Chef Paul Buck **Owner** David Smith **Times** 12-2/6.30-9 Closed D 25 Dec **Prices** Food prices not confirmed for 2010. Please telephone for details. **Wines** 2 bottles over £20, 12 bottles under £20, 6 by glass **Notes** Vegetarian available **Seats** 65 **Children** Portions, Menu **Parking** 40

Sutherland House

◉◉ Modern British

Trendy dining in an ancient townhouse

☎ 01502 724544
56 High St IP18 6DN
e-mail: enquiries@sutherlandhouse.co.uk
dir: A1095 into Southwold, on High St on left after Victoria St

It's not often you eat under the same roof as a past King of England. This stylish townhouse was once home to James II, which explains the grandeur of its pargetted plasterwork ceilings, foot-wide elm floorboards and ancient beams that now blend with opulent modern fabrics and designer furniture. Its two classy dining areas, decked out with modish darkwood tables and plush purple chairs, are served by easy-going but efficient staff. Local produce is the bedrock of the kitchen's innovative modern output; food miles are taken seriously enough that they even appear on the menu. You could keep things as casual as a glass of wine and plate of Sussex tapas, or go for a starter of pan-fried scallops and confit potato with truffle and lemon vinaigrette, followed by slow-cooked Blythburgh pork belly with butternut squash purée, fondant potato and a pork reduction.

Chef Dan Jones **Owner** Peter & Anna Banks
Times 12-3/7-9.30 Closed 25 Dec, Mon-Tue (off season only) **Prices** Fixed L 2 course £9-£24, Starter £3.50-£6, Main £10.95-£21, Dessert £4-£7.50, Service optional **Wines** 35 bottles over £20, 15 bottles under £20, 10 by glass **Notes** Sunday L, Vegetarian available **Seats** 50, Pr/dining room 60 **Children** Portions, Menu **Parking** On street

Swan Hotel

◉◉ Modern British

Contemporary British cooking at the Adnams flagship

☎ 01502 722186 📠 01502 724800
Market Place IP18 6EG
e-mail: swan.hotel@adnams.co.uk
dir: A1095 to Southwold. Hotel in town centre. Parking via archway to left of building

Southwold being the centre of operations for the Adnams group, it plays host to not just The Crown hotel (see

entry), but this place too. It's another lovely old inn, a white-fronted, 17th-century building in the heart of town, with a lounge that faces the market square and rooms with views of the local lighthouse. The famous Adnams beer is brewed at the back of the Swan. A traditional dining room with smartly attired, supremely professional staff is the setting for some polished contemporary cooking, which might take the form of seared scallops with chorizo, finely sliced fennel and lemon oil, followed perhaps by the now classic presentation of two cuts of pork - fillet and belly - with cabbage and bacon and a serving of intensely aromatic rosemary mash. Populist dessert ideas take in peanut butter parfait and strawberry jelly.

Chef Rory Whelan **Owner** Adnams plc
Times 12-2.30/7-9.30 **Prices** Food prices not confirmed for 2010. Please telephone for details. **Wines** 60 bottles over £20, 75 bottles under £20, 8 by glass **Notes** Pre-theatre picnic hampers, Sunday L, Vegetarian available, Dress restrictions, Smart casual - no jeans, Civ Wed 40 **Seats** 65, Pr/dining room 36 **Children** Portions, Menu **Parking** 36

The Crown

◉◉ Modern British 🖐️

Boutique hotel and village inn in one

☎ 01206 262001 📠 01206 264026
CO6 4SE
e-mail: info@crowninn.net
dir: A12 junct 30, head towards Higham for 1m. At village green turn left & left again towards Stoke By Nayland. Hotel on right after approx 3m

A good base for exploring Constable country (aficionados will recognise the 120-foot tower of nearby St Mary's church from the Suffolk master's works), the white-fronted Crown is both boutique hotel and village inn. That latter role is still impressed on the place to the extent that food is ordered from the bar. Look to the blackboards for daily specials, not least the range of fish (perhaps lemon sole with cherry tomatoes and herb oil), which come from east coast boats, depending on the weather. Otherwise, go for crab cakes with home-made mayonnaise, steak and kidney pudding with horseradish mash, and maybe fig tart with clotted cream to finish. Cheeses, generally an Anglo-Irish array, are also taken seriously. Breakfasts, featuring fine local sausages and bacon, are served, too.

Chef Mark Blake **Owner** Richard Sunderland
Times 12-2.30/6-9.30 Closed 25-26 Dec **Prices** Starter £4.25-£7.50, Main £10.50-£19.95, Dessert £4.50-£5.95, Service optional **Wines** 160 bottles over £20, 41 bottles under £20, 29 by glass **Notes** Sunday L, Vegetarian available **Seats** 130, Pr/dining room 12 **Children** Portions, Menu **Parking** 47

STOWMARKET Map 13 TM05

The Shepherd and Dog

Modern British

Smart gastro-pub with confident cooking

☎ 01449 711361 & 710464
Forward Green IP14 5HN
e-mail: marybruce@btinternet.com
web: www.theshepherdanddog.com
dir: On A1120 between A14 & A140

This smart, recently extended Suffolk gastro-pub has a fresh, modern look with lightwood furniture, comfy leather chairs in cream and brown, and a racehorse theme. It is split into the bar and two restaurants, where ingredients are handled simply and transformed into interesting combinations. Kick off with cold duck breast with cucumber and spring onion salad and plum and hoi sin dressing, and then perhaps grilled fillet of salmon, sweet potato mash and ginger and spring onion dressing, followed by Bavarian bread pudding with apple, sultanas and rum, flaked almonds and ice cream.

Chef Christopher Bruce & Daniela Bruce **Owner** Christopher & Mary Bruce **Times** 12-2/7-11 Closed mid Jan, Mon, D Sun **Prices** Fixed L 2 course £17-£19.50, Fixed D 3 course £17.50-£20, Starter £5.25-£7.50, Main £13-£19.50, Dessert £5.75-£6.50, Service optional **Wines** 28 bottles over £20, 25 bottles under £20, 19 by glass **Notes** Sunday L, Vegetarian available **Seats** 50, Pr/dining room 24 **Children** Portions **Parking** 35

WALBERSWICK Map 13 TM47

The Anchor

Modern British

Gastro-pub serving modern and robust food

☎ 01502 722112 ᵈ 01502 724464
Main St IP18 6UA
e-mail: info@anchoratwalberswick.com
dir: On entering village The Anchor on right, immediately after MG garage

Sea air and Adnams ales go hand-in-hand at this 1920s Arts and Crafts-style pub, where you're close enough to the briny to hear waves tickling the pebbly beach. The Anchor strikes a neat balance between gastro and pub: an unpretentious place in a modern vein, with a bare bones interior of stripped pine tables and nautical grey-blue pastel-washed panelling. Beer is taken seriously enough to get equal billing with wines matched to dishes

on the menu. The lack of airs and graces extends to the kitchen, which raids the Suffolk larder for top-notch produce, including raw materials from the owners' allotments. Expect no-nonsense dishes with hearty, robust flavours such as seared scallops with cannellini beans and Anchor cured ham, followed by braised and glazed Blythburgh pork belly with mash, Savoy cabbage and cider jus.

Chef Sophie Dorber, Mike Keen **Owner** Sophie & Mark Dorber **Times** 11-4/6-11 Closed 25 Dec, Mon **Prices** Starter £4.75-£7.75, Main £10.75-£18.75, Dessert £3.50-£5.75, Service optional **Wines** 18 by glass **Notes** Vegetarian available **Seats** 55, Pr/dining room 26 **Children** Portions, Menu **Parking** 60

WESTLETON Map 13 TM46

The Westleton Crown

Modern British V 🍽

British hospitality in a 12th-century coaching inn

☎ 01728 648777 ᵈ 01728 648239
The Street IP17 3AD
e-mail: reception@westletoncrown.co.uk
dir: A12 N, turn right for Westleton just after Yoxford. Hotel opposite on entering Westleton

Dating back to the 12th century, this charming Suffolk coaching inn with 25 comfortable bedrooms offers a choice of places to eat from the elegant dining room, cosy parlour and large, stylish conservatory. The bustling bar has exposed beams and open fireplaces and enjoys the atmosphere of a welcoming local with real ales to match. Terraced gardens are an attractive place to enjoy a drink or eat alfresco in the warmer months. Menus are varied and make imaginative use of good quality local produce with plenty of hearty dishes and daily specials such as poached mussels in a white wine cream sauce and braised Blythburgh pork, celeriac risotto, curly kale and lime jus.

Chef Mark Brega **Owner** Agellus Hotels Ltd **Times** 12-2.30/7-9.30 Closed 25 Dec **Prices** Starter £4.50-£8.95, Main £9.50-£24.95, Dessert £4-£9, Service

optional **Wines** 29 bottles over £20, 22 bottles under £20, 9 by glass **Notes** Sunday L, Vegetarian menu **Seats** 85 **Children** Portions, Menu **Parking** 50

WOODBRIDGE Map 13 TM24

Crown Hotel

Modern International **NEW**

Refurbished town-centre hotel with relaxed dining

☎ 01394 384242
2 Thoroughfare IP12 1AD
e-mail: info@thecrownatwoodbridge.co.uk
dir: Please telephone for directions

A major refurbishment to the tune of three-quarters of a million pounds (by designer David Bentheim) has given this stylish hotel a new 85-seater restaurant and bar featuring a Windermere skiff (boat). The eccentric, modern inn in historic Woodbridge is the newest property from Thorpeness & Aldeburgh Hotels and offers relaxed, informal service and modern British cooking using seasonal and frequently locally-sourced ingredients. Great local breads are a good start to a meal, moving on to crispy grilled sprats with lemon, French beans and pine nut dressing, followed by twice-cooked pig's cheeks served with gnocchi dumplings, field mushrooms and wilted spinach. Finish with a light steamed chocolate pudding with a good home-made sauce anglaise.

Chef Stephen David **Owner** Thorpeness & Aldeburgh Hotels **Times** 12-2.30/6-9.30 **Prices** Starter £5-£10, Main £10-£20, Dessert £5-£7, Service optional **Wines** 40 bottles over £20, 10 bottles under £20, 10 by glass **Notes** Sunday L, Vegetarian available **Seats** 85, Pr/dining room 14 **Children** Portions, Menu **Parking** 30

Seckford Hall Hotel

Modern British 🍽

Sound cooking amid Elizabethan splendour

☎ 01394 385678 ᵈ 01394 380610
IP13 6NU
e-mail: reception@seckford.co.uk
dir: Hotel signed on A12 (Woodbridge bypass). Do not follow signs for town centre

The ancestral home of the Seckfords dates from the 16th century, and has been under the ownership of the Bunn family for over 50 years. Its imposing red-brick Tudor façade, soaring chimneys and huge carved oak front door never fail to impress modern visitors. The oak-panelled restaurant retains an ambience of stately elegance, with superb wall tapestries, wood carvings and exuberant flower displays combining in an intimate setting. Modern British cuisine is the kitchen's forté, founded on excellent local produce and sound technical ability. Pork rillettes with black pudding and apple compôte might precede a main course of confit leg of rabbit in a port reduction with dauphinoise potatoes and a tian of chargrilled vegetables. Rhubarb soufflé with ginger ice cream is the sort of dessert to expect.

Chef Mark Archer **Owner** Mr & Mrs Bunn **Times** 12.30-1.45/7.30-9.30 Closed 25 Dec, L Mon

continued

WOODBRIDGE continued

Prices Fixed L 2 course £13.95–£17.95, Starter £5.95–£9, Main £14.50–£25.95, Dessert £6.25–£8.95, Service included **Wines** 40 bottles over £20, 45 bottles under £20, 11 by glass **Notes** Sunday L, Vegetarian available, Dress restrictions, Smart casual, No jeans or trainers, Civ Wed 120, Air con **Seats** 70, Pr/dining room 100 **Children** Portions, Menu **Parking** 100

YAXLEY   Map 13 TM17

The Auberge

◎◎ International

Family-run restaurant with rooms

☎ 01379 783604   🖷 01379 788486
Ipswich Rd IP23 8BZ
e-mail: deestenhouse@fsmail.net
dir: 5m S of Diss on A140

The Auberge has grown from a simple North Suffolk country pub into a rather more sophisticated restaurant with rooms. Although extended, it has held on to its original character, pulling together the cosiness of a 16th-century inn – all gnarled oak beams and exposed brickwork – with solid modern cooking. The dining room is an intimate affair; tables are candlelit, laid with crisp napkins and bowls of limes, lemons and chillies for a splash of colour. Uncomplicated, gutsy fare bursts with flavour wrought from the pick of local produce. You might start with a classic, flavour-packed chicken liver parfait served with onion marmalade, then a main course of guinea fowl chasseur with shiitaki mushroom pilaf and caramelised red cabbage.

Chef John Stenhouse **Owner** John & Dee Stenhouse **Times** 12-2/7-9.30 Closed 1 Jan, Sun & Mon, L Sat **Prices** Fixed D 3 course £24.95–£29.70, Starter £4.75–£10.50, Main £12.50–£25, Dessert £4.50–£5.90, Service optional **Wines** 35 bottles over £20, 25 bottles under £20, 13 by glass **Notes** Air con **Seats** 60, Pr/dining room 20 **Children** Portions **Parking** 25

YOXFORD   Map 5 TM36

Satis House

◎◎ Modern British

Modern British cooking in grand house with literary connections

☎ 01728 668418   🖷 01728 668640
IP17 3EX
e-mail: enquiries@satishouse.co.uk
dir: off A12 between Ipswich & Lowestoft. 9m E Aldeburgh & Snape

Set in 3 acres of parkland in rural Suffolk, this splendid Georgian country house offers 18th-century character and 21st-century comforts. Charles Dickens, a family friend of the owners at that time, was a regular visitor and the property's name features in *Great Expectations*. The service in the restaurant is relaxed but formal. The cuisine is modern British with European and Pacific Rim influences, with local, seasonal ingredients used to create imaginative dishes that will please all tastes. Starters include red mullet with chorizo and fennel broth, while mains could be pheasant with buttered tagliatelle and horseradish cream sauce. Finish with rhubarb crumble with stem ginger ice cream.

Times 12-3/6.30-11 Closed L Mon, Tue, D Sun

See advert below

SURREY

ABINGER HAMMER   Map 6 TQ04

Drakes on the Pond

◎◎ Modern British

Skilful cooking in a classy village restaurant

☎ 01306 731174
Dorking Rd RH5 6SA
dir: On A25 between Dorking & Guildford

Beside the A25 on the edge of Abinger Hammer, this charming cottage looks out across its pond towards the Surrey Hills. Its enduring popularity among locals and visiting diners is down to the dedication of the friendly, hands-on owners, who run the restaurant with great attention to detail. Pale terracotta walls and chocolate brown furnishings create a comfortable and unpretentious setting in which to sample accomplished modern British cooking with a dash of French classical influences. Seasonal menus draw on fresh local produce, and dishes are well executed and simply presented. Start with pan-fried pigeon with red onion marmalade, followed by sea bass on crushed potatoes with Jerusalem artichoke purée and red wine jus, and round off with sticky toffee pudding with stem ginger ice cream. Set lunch menus are great value.

Chef John Morris **Owner** John Morris, Tracey Honeysett **Times** 12-2/7-10 Closed 2 wks Aug-Sep, Xmas, New Year, BHs, Sun (except Mothering Sun), Mon, L Sat **Prices** Fixed L 2 course fr £19.50, Starter £12–£16, Main £24–£27.50, Dessert £8, Service optional, Groups min 8 service 10% **Wines** 65 bottles over £20, 9 bottles under £20, 9 by glass **Notes** Vegetarian available, Dress restrictions, Smart casual, Air con **Seats** 32 **Parking** 20

The Latymer

BAGSHOT Map 6 SU96

Modern European

Innovative modern European cooking in smart setting

☎ 01276 471774 📄 01276 472317
Pennyhill Park Hotel & Spa, London Rd GU19 5EU
e-mail: enquiries@pennyhillpark.co.uk
dir: M3 junct 3, through Bagshot, left onto A30. 0.5m on right

Rolling Surrey countryside surrounds this fine Victorian house, which these days earns its crust as a hotel of considerable class. The 123-acre grounds include a nine-hole golf course and there is the obligatory spa to de-stress even the most tense of City bankers. The Latymer restaurant, and the craft of chef Michael Wignall, has created a dining destination which puts Pennyhill well and truly on the map. The restaurant is split into two sections, each elegantly decorated in warm tones, with pale green fabric on the chairs and banquettes and lots of original dark wood panelling - it's pleasingly contemporary yet in keeping with the grandeur of the building. Unobtrusive service is by an extremely knowledgeable and attentive team. The cooking is complex, but balance and clarity of flavours and textures is maintained, and great care is made to source first-rate ingredients, much of it from local suppliers. Bread, canapés and amuse-bouche display considerable technical proficiency right from the off, preceding a beautifully presented starter of pressing of marinated duck liver with slow-cooked shoulder of goat, liquorice-scented pear and liquorice espuma in brick paste. Braised neck end of milk-fed lamb with glazed sweetbreads and tongue, globe artichokes and parsley root purée is a perfectly executed main course and a joy to eat, as is a dessert of eucalyptus pannacotta with coconut jelly, plum sphère, vanilla pastry and cardamom ice cream. The menus are fairly priced by today's standards, including the tasting menu. There is an eight-seater chef's table, and the extensive wine list offers good choice by the glass.

Chef Michael Wignall **Owner** Exclusive Hotels **Times** 12-2/7-9.30 Closed 1-14 Jan, Mon & Sun, L Sat **Prices** Fixed L 3 course fr £32, Fixed D 3 course fr £58, Tasting menu fr £78, Service added but optional 12.5% **Wines** 220 bottles over £20, 20 by glass **Notes** Fixed L 8 course £58, Tasting menu 10 course, Vegetarian menu, Dress restrictions, Smart casual, Civ Wed 160, Air con **Seats** 50, Pr/dining room 12 **Parking** 500

BAGSHOT | Map 6 SU96

The Brasserie

◎◎ Modern British

Classy brasserie in five-star hotel setting

☎ 01276 471774 📠 01276 473217
Pennyhill Park Hotel & Spa, London Rd GU19 5EU
e-mail: enquiries@pennyhillpark.co.uk
dir: M3 junct 3, through Bagshot, left onto A30. 0.5m on right

The Latymer Restaurant with its four Rosettes (see entry) is undoubtedly the headline act at this classy country-house hotel, but The Brasserie is an admirable support act, offering a more informal alternative. It has its own head chef and is certainly no mere afterthought. A chic refurbishment keeps to the luxe tone of the hotel and the manicured garden makes for a charming backdrop. The menu follows the brasserie road and the kitchen, quite rightly, makes a big deal about the sourcing of local and regional produce. The crustacean plate for two is just about as 'brasserie' as you can get, and amongst the fine specimens delivered to the table is whole East Anglian cock crab. Marinated octopus with shaved fennel and liquorice is a classy first course, and you might follow that with something from the grill (a Barnsley chop) or roast sea trout with a fricassée of crayfish, wild mushrooms, asparagus and new season garlic.

Chef Iain Inman **Owner** Exclusive Hotels
Times 12-2.30/7-10.30 **Prices** Fixed D 3 course fr £25, Starter £6.50-£12.50, Main £16.50-£23, Dessert £6.50-£7.50, Service optional **Wines** 300+ bottles over £20, 20 by glass **Notes** Sunday L, Vegetarian available, Dress restrictions, Smart casual, Civ Wed 160, Air con **Seats** 120 **Children** Menu **Parking** 500

The Latymer

◎◎◎◎ — *see page 397*

BANSTEAD | Map 6 TQ25

Post

◎◎ Modern

First-class Post arrives in leafy Banstead

☎ 01737 373839
28 High St SM7 2LQ
e-mail: enquiries@postrestaurant.co.uk
web: www.postrestaurant.co.uk

The old Post Office on Banstead's High Street is the setting for celebrity chef Tony Tobin's cosmopolitan-style brasserie, restaurant and delicatessen, the sister restaurant to his Dining Room restaurant in Reigate (see entry). From the front deli step into the buzzy all-day brasserie, with its informal atmosphere and contemporary design, or head upstairs to the more intimate, fine-dining restaurant. Here, cream leather banquettes, funky swivel leather tub chairs and a small bar complete the upbeat, modern setting. A fixed-price repertoire includes a carte and tasting option to excite the palate and eye, using top

quality ingredients and bags of skill; spicy carrot soup with confit rabbit leg and coriander oil might precede roast sea bass with spring onion risotto, sweetcorn and thyme velouté.

Times 11am-10pm

CAMBERLEY | Map 6 SU86

Macdonald Frimley Hall Hotel & Spa

◎◎ Modern European

Smart country-house dining

☎ 0844 879 9110 📠 01276 691253
Lime Av GU15 2BG
e-mail: gm.frimleyhall@macdonald-hotels.co.uk
dir: M3 junct 3, A321 follow Bagshot signs. Through lights, left onto A30 signed Camberley & Basingstoke. To rdbt, 2nd exit onto A325, take 5th right

The epitome of English elegance, this dignified, ivy-clad Victorian manor comes set in beautiful grounds. The interior combines modernity with traditional features, and the fine-dining Linden Restaurant adopts the theme. With fresh contemporary styling and natural colours, it offers pretty views over a woodland garden from well-spaced tables, and looks elegant by candlelight in the evening. Quality seasonal ingredients are a feature of the modern European menu, where classical dishes are presented with modern twists. Braised chump of lamb, for instance, served with Moroccan spices and parsnip couscous, or maybe pan-fried line-caught sea bass teamed with sautéed squid and a hot-and-sour soup, while a classic glazed lemon tart with raspberry sorbet might head-up desserts.

Chef Marc Davies **Owner** Macdonald Hotels
Times 12.30-2/7-9.45 Closed L Sat **Prices** Fixed L 2 course £19-£21.50, Fixed D 3 course £29.50-£32, Starter £5.50-£7.50, Main £17.50-£22, Dessert £5.50-£7.50, Service added but optional 12.5% **Notes** Vegetarian available, Civ Wed 120, Air con **Seats** 70, Pr/dining room 200 **Children** Portions, Menu **Parking** 100

CHARLWOOD

For restaurant details see under Gatwick Airport (London), (Sussex, West)

DORKING | Map 6 TQ14

Emlyn Restaurant at the Mercure Burford Bridge Hotel

◎◎ Modern European ◎

Historic hotel offering contemporary design and accomplished dining

☎ 01306 884561 📠 01306 880386
Burford Bridge, Boxhill RH5 6BX
e-mail: H6635@accor.com
dir: M25 junct 9, A245 towards Dorking. Hotel within 5m on A24 at the Mickleham rdbt

Lord Nelson and Lady Hamilton reputedly met for the last time in this 16th-century hotel before the Battle of

Trafalgar. Fast forward 2 centuries, and it's a smart, contemporary hotel, with a classy restaurant. Low ceilings and candlelit tables overlooking the gardens make for a setting of understated elegance that Horatio and Emma would have enjoyed for their last meal together. There's a clear classical foundation to the modern cooking, which uses prime produce to craft a menu of sharply-flavoured, beautifully-presented dishes. Foie gras and pigeon ballotine with Amaretto jelly and bitter chocolate mousse is an eye-catching starter, followed by red mullet with a velvety cauliflower purée and langoustine. Warm treacle and honey tart with caramel syrup, caramelised hazelnuts and vanilla ice cream rounds things off.

Chef Nick Sinclair **Owner** MREF Ltd **Times** 12-2.30/7-9.30 Closed Mon, L Tue-Fri, D Sun **Prices** Fixed L 2 course £25, Fixed D 3 course £35, Service optional **Wines** 39 bottles over £20, 4 bottles under £20, 14 by glass **Notes** Sunday L, Vegetarian available, Civ Wed 200 **Seats** 70, Pr/dining room 16-200 **Children** Portions, Menu **Parking** 140

Two To Four

◎◎ Modern **V**

Stylish, lively restaurant in centre of town

☎ 01306 889923
2-4 West St RH4 1BL
e-mail: eliterestaurants@hotmail.com
web: www.twotofourrestaurant.com
dir: M25, exit at Leatherhead junct, follow signs to town centre

Originally 3 cottages, this charming Grade II listed building is now a restaurant on 3 floors. Located in an intriguing street full of lovely old properties and antique shops, the friendly restaurant is bright and modern, with ceramic-tiled floors and bare wooden tables. The service is as polished and professional as the food. The short carte and daily blackboard offer contemporary dishes with hints of Mediterranean influences. Expect starters such as tartare of fresh tuna with chilli, ginger, lime and soy, spring onion and coriander salad, and mains like cumin-roasted local rack of lamb with smoked aubergine purée, watercress salad and Madeira jus, or confit duck leg, green beans, caramelised onion potato cake with sweet-and-sour syrup.

Chef Rob Gathercole **Owner** Elite Restaurants
Times 12-2.30/6.30-10 Closed Xmas, Etr, BHs, 2 wks Aug, Sun **Prices** Food prices not confirmed for 2010. Please telephone for details. **Wines** 23 bottles over £20, 9 bottles under £20, 4 by glass **Notes** Vegetarian menu, Air con **Seats** 70, Pr/dining room 18 **Children** Portions **Parking** West St car park

EGHAM
Map 6 TQ07

The Oak Room at Great Fosters
Modern British V

Regal Elizabethan setting for highly accomplished cuisine

☎ 01784 433822 📄 01784 472455
Stroude Rd TW20 9UR
e-mail: enquiries@greatfosters.co.uk
dir: M25 junct 13

Steeped in history, this one-time royal hunting lodge, now a majestic Elizabethan manor hotel, comes complete with manicured formal gardens - including topiary, rose garden and Saxon moat. Dark-wood panelling, Jacobean fireplaces, decorative ceilings and deep sofas blend with other exquisite period features in its stately interior, while the Cocktail Bar and terrace overlooks the gardens. The elegant, fine-dining Oak Room restaurant cleverly blends modish design (bright contemporary tapestry and high-backed chairs) with traditional features (vaulted oak-beamed ceiling and mullioned windows). The kitchen's light touch is modern and clean-cut, underpinned by classical roots; thus duck is served with vanilla mash, sweet red cabbage and roasted beetroot, and a pistachio and olive oil tart comes with crème fraîche for dessert.

Chef Simon Bolsover **Owner** Great Fosters (1931) Ltd
Times 12.30-2.00/7.00-9.30 Closed L Sat **Prices** Fixed L 2 course £22, Fixed D 3 course £37.50, Starter £13, Main £26, Dessert £13, Service added but optional 10%
Wines 285 bottles over £20, 2 bottles under £20, 22 by glass **Notes** Sunday L, Vegetarian menu, Civ Wed 170 **Seats** 60, Pr/dining room 20 **Children** Portions, Menu **Parking** 200

EPSOM
Map 6 TQ26

Chalk Lane Hotel
British, French

Accomplished, modern cooking near Epsom racecourse

☎ 01372 721179 📄 01372 727878
Chalk Ln, Woodcote End KT18 7BB
e-mail: smcgregor@chalklanehotel.com
web: www.chalklanehotel.com
dir: M25 junct 9 onto A24 to Epsom. Right at lights by BP garage. Left into Avenue Rd, right into Worple Rd. Left at T-junct & hotel on right

If you're fond of a flutter on the horses, you can never be sure how the day will go, but this friendly hotel just a short canter from Epsom Racecourse is a safe bet. The Grade II listed building dates from 1805 and has plenty of period Georgian character, while the smartly-decorated restaurant has a relaxed, softly-lit ambience. Food here is a treat: ingredients are sourced with care, and the menu deals in imaginative dishes carried off with obvious technical skills. You could put the kitchen through its paces with a multi-course tasting menu, while choices from the regular carte might include roast loin of rabbit with piquillo pepper, baby chorizo, honey-glazed octopus and pea purée, followed by a trio of pork, presented as crispy belly with pickled cabbage, braised cheeks and black pudding mash, and a cassolette of spicy tripe. Finish with a bitter chocolate and basil fondant.

Chef Vincent Hiss **Owner** Steven McGregor
Times 12.30-2.30/7-10 Closed L Sat **Prices** Fixed L 2 course £12.50-£17.50, Starter £6-£12, Main £14-£26, Dessert £7-£9, Service added but optional 10% **Wines** 75 bottles over £20, 25 bottles under £20, 10 by glass **Notes** Sunday L, Vegetarian available, Dress restrictions, Smart casual **Seats** 40, Pr/dining room 20 **Children** Portions **Parking** 60

GODALMING
Map 6 SU94

La Luna
Modern Italian

Sophisticated modern Italian in the centre of town

☎ 01483 414155 📄 01483 418286
10 Wharf St GU7 1NN
e-mail: info@lalunarestaurant.co.uk
dir: In town centre, at junct of Wharf St & Flambard Way

This smart modern Italian in the heart of Godalming oozes style and sophistication. A recent redecoration has resulted in a change of colour, the décor now being warm caramel and chocolate, with solid oak tables. Service is provided by charming, knowledgeable staff, who are happy to help, especially when it comes to the extensive all-Italian wine list. When it comes to the food, the contemporary Italian cooking takes in Sicilian and Tuscan influences, the menus being seasonal and the dishes simple and well presented. Seafood risotto with rocket and Sicilian olive oil is full of flavour, while pork loin is rolled with smoked ham and fontina cheese. Finish with a lemon tart full of citrus freshness, served with mascarpone enlivened with orange zest and a blueberry coulis.

Chef Valentino Gentile **Owner** Daniele Drago, Orazio Primavera **Times** 12-2/7-10 Closed early Jan, 2 wks in Aug, Sun-Mon **Prices** Fixed D 4 course £40-£60, Starter £4.95-£7.95, Main £8.95-£17.95, Dessert £4.95-£5.95 **Wines** 136 bottles over £20, 9 bottles under £20, 6 by glass **Notes** Air con **Seats** 58, Pr/dining room 24 **Children** Portions **Parking** Public car park behind restaurant

The Restaurant at Lythe Hill

◉◉ Modern British

Unfussy food in charming small hotel

☎ 01428 651251 ▤ 01428 644131
Petworth Rd GU27 3BQ
e-mail: lythe@lythehill.co.uk
dir: 1m E of Haslemere on B2131

Thirty acres of parkland on the border of Hampshire and West Sussex surround this charming Elizabethan house, created from a small hamlet of old farm buildings, some of which date back to the 15th century. The oak-panelled restaurant is located in the timbered farmhouse and oozes historic charm. The menu is essentially modern British with classical French influences and dishes are unfussy and focused on flavour. Expect the likes of traditional brown onion, beef stock and real ale soup, followed by poached haddock fillet on creamed potatoes and curly kale with red wine butter sauce and roasted salsify. Finish with blackcurrant delice with caramelised apple and Calvados cream.

Chef David Doricott **Owner** Lythe Hill Hotel Ltd
Times 12.30-2.15/7.15-9.45 **Prices** Fixed L 2 course £16-£20, Fixed D 3 course £28-£32, Starter £6-£10, Main £11-£25, Dessert £8-£12, Service optional **Wines** 100 bottles over £20, 8 bottles under £20, 10 by glass
Notes Sunday L, Vegetarian available, Dress restrictions, Smart casual, Civ Wed 128 **Seats** 60, Pr/dining room 35 **Children** Portions, Menu **Parking** 150

HORLEY

For restaurant details see Gatwick Airport (London), (Sussex, West)

Alexander's at Limpsfield

◉◉ Modern

Sophisticated food with relaxed and friendly service

☎ 01883 714365
The Old Lodge, High St RH8 0DR
e-mail: info@alexanders-limpsfield.co.uk
dir: N of A25 on B269

Expect a modern, contemporary feel at this refurbished 16th-century building in the heart of this Surrey

commuter village. Next to the small bar and brasserie area serving its simple bistro fare, the fine-dining restaurant boasts a high vaulted ceiling, dark oak-panelled walls and candlelit tables. Cooking is assured and confident, with innovative combinations of ingredients, and presentation is simple and well thought out. With good use of local and seasonal ingredients, dishes may include rhubarb and foie gras ballotine with tempura vegetables, five spice pork belly with spinach, aubergine caviar, pomme purée and braised red onions, and dark chocolate fondant with Grand Marnier sauce and clotted cream ice cream.

Times 10-mdnt Closed Mon

Bryce's Seafood Restaurant & Country Pub

◉ Modern British, Seafood V

Fresh fish and seafood in charming country venue

☎ 01306 627430 ▤ 01306 628274
The Old School House RH5 5TH
e-mail: bryces.fish@virgin.net
dir: From M25 junct 9 take A24, then A29. 8m S of Dorking on A29

Fish fanatics beat a path to Bryce's thanks to its excellent reputation in Surrey and beyond for top-quality fish and seafood, much of it landed an hour away at Shoreham docks on the South Coast. It is a characterful country pub - actually the former gymnasium of a boys' boarding school dating from 1750 - whitewashed outside and beamed within. The specials board changes according to what the trawlers bring in - perhaps queen scallops on wilted spinach topped with a dollop of hollandaise, then herb-crusted fillet of pollock with minted pea purée and tomato sauce. End on a high note with citrus crème brûlée with pineapple salsa and white rum and pineapple sorbet.

Chef B Bryce, Ashley Sullivan **Owner** Mr B Bryce
Times 12-2.30/7-9.30 Closed 25-26 Dec, 1 Jan, D Sun (Nov & Jan-Feb) **Prices** Fixed L 2 course £10, Fixed D 3 course £15, Service optional, Groups min 8 service 10% **Wines** 15 bottles over £20, 29 bottles under £20, 15 by glass **Notes** ALC set menu 2 course £25, 3 course £31, Sunday L, Vegetarian menu **Seats** 50 **Children** Portions **Parking** 35

Nutfield Priory - Cloisters Restaurant

◉◉ Modern European

Stylish modern cooking in a Victorian Gothic setting

☎ 0845 0727486
Nutfield Rd RH1 4EL
e-mail: nutfieldpriory@handpicked.co.uk
dir: On A25, 1m E of Redhill, off M25 junct 8 or M25 junct 6, follow A25 through Godstone

Nutfield was built in the 1870s, as a piece of Victorian fantasy Gothic architecture, after the manner of Pugin's Houses of Parliament. It has never been a priory, though you might be fooled by the appointments of the Cloisters dining room into thinking it had. Seasonal menus take advantage of good Home Counties produce to furnish dishes such as beef carpaccio with goose liver and shaved parmesan, or look to the coast for crab and lobster tortellini in shellfish bisque. Multi-layered main dishes range from cod with chorizo, Puy lentils and dauphinoise, to free-range local pork belly with langoustines and sweet potato purée. Finish grandly with a hot orange soufflé, served with bitter chocolate ice cream.

Chef Neil Davison **Owner** Hand Picked Hotels
Times 12-2/7-9.30 Closed L Sat **Prices** Fixed L 2 course fr £20, Fixed D 3 course £36-£48, Starter £6-£12, Main £16-£28, Dessert £6-£10, Service optional **Wines** 90 bottles over £20, 2 bottles under £20, 18 by glass **Notes** Tasting menu available, Sunday L, Vegetarian available, Dress restrictions, No jeans or trainers, Civ Wed 80 **Seats** 60, Pr/dining room 100 **Children** Portions **Parking** 130

The Dining Room

◉◉ Modern British

Creative cooking from TV chef

☎ 01737 226650
59a High St RH2 9AE
dir: 1st floor restaurant on Reigate High St

Tony Tobin - as seen on TV - delivers a fine gastronomic experience in relaxed surroundings in this market town. The large, elegant dining room is classically decorated with rich curtains, artwork and mirrored walls. Tables are formally dressed with high quality linen and crockery. Tobin's brand of modern British cooking takes global influences in often unusual combinations, delivered via a carte, tasting and vegetarian menus (the latter offering much more than just the usual veggie stuff). Start with a salad of quail breast with a breaded quail's egg, potato blinis and lemon syrup, then move on to fillet of Charolais beef with a faggot, baby onions, baked potato jelly and Madeira jus. Desserts are equally as creative: pear arctic roll with avocado ice cream and Poire William syrup.

Times 12-2/7-10 Closed Xmas & BHs, L Sat, D Sun

Drake's Restaurant

RIPLEY Map 6 TQ05

Modern British **V**

Innovative, classy cooking in elegant house

☎ 01483 224777 📄 01483 222940
The Clock House, High St GU23 6AQ
web: www.drakesrestaurant.co.uk
dir: M25 junct 10, A3 towards Guildford.
Follow Ripley signs. Restaurant in village centre

Housed in a beautiful Georgian building, this eponymous, 2-roomed restaurant is home to chef-patron Steve Drake, who boasts a fine pedigree (he's worked for Nico Ladenis and Marco Pierre White). The refurbished dining room has been decorated in a simple, eclectic, boutique style giving the room a light, airy feel with spacious tables affording privacy, whilst local gallery art hangs on the walls. The restaurant also has a small lounge area where you can enjoy an aperitif or coffee, but in the warmer months, you will want to head outside to the attractive walled garden scented with herbs destined for the kitchen. Tables are formally laid, service is knowledgeable and attentive. Steve's cooking takes a light modern approach and displays great skill, flair and finesse, creating dishes presented with elegant simplicity and clean, well-defined flavours from the very best seasonal produce. Take ravioli of aromatic duck, smoked beetroot, duck

ham, langoustine and parmesan velouté, or perhaps poached and roasted saddle of venison, cocoa gnocchi, Jerusalem artichoke purée and venison burger. And do save room for desserts such as rhubarb fruit leather, bay leaf cream, ginger parfait and rhubarb consommé.

Chef Steve Drake **Owner** Steve & Serina Drake **Times** 12-1.30/7-9.30 Closed 2 wks Jan, 2 wks Aug, Sun-Mon, L Sat **Prices** Fixed L 2 course fr £21, Fixed D 3 course fr £46, Tasting menu £60, Service optional **Wines** 200 bottles over £20, 10 bottles under £20, 9 by glass **Notes** Tasting menu & vegetarian tasting menu available, Vegetarian menu **Seats** 34, Pr/dining room 14 **Children** Menu **Parking** 2

REIGATE continued

The Westerly

◉◉ Modern

First-class bistro with good food at fair prices

☎ 01737 222733
2-4 London Rd RH2 9AN
dir: Please telephone for directions

Chef-patron Jonathan Coomb, with his wife Cynthia at front-of-house, have created a modern bistro of considerable class that delivers high quality food at fair prices. It's a smart and relaxed place, with blond-wood floorboards, red banquettes or brown leather-seated chairs and modern artwork on the walls. The modern Mediterranean-inspired cooking is intelligently straightforward with the regularly-changing menu delivering an appealing blend of classical preparations and contemporary touches. Top-quality fresh seasonal produce is sourced from local suppliers and turns up in starters such as Catalan-style pork rillettes with green olive tapenade, or a main course bourride full of first-class fish and seafood (bream, monkfish, red mullet, mussels and clams). Finish with chocolate truffle cake with cherries in Kirsch and crème fraîche for dessert.

Times 12-2.30/7-10 Closed Sun, Mon, L Tue, Sat

RIPLEY Map 6 TQ05

Drake's Restaurant

◉◉◉ – see page 401

The Talbot Inn

◉ Modern British NEW

15th-century inn providing a thoroughly modern dining experience

☎ 0845 4591 492 📠 01483 211332
High St GU23 6BB
e-mail: info@thetalbotinn.com
dir: A3 exit for Ripley (just after the M25 exit). Follow Ripley signs. Inn on left of High Street

'Don't judge a book by its cover,' the saying goes, and this certainly applies to The Talbot, which looks every bit the traditional coaching inn from outside. It may retain its old-world beamed bar, but remodelling brings contemporary good looks to dining - a copper ceiling, glass conservatory extension, light-oak furniture and leather seating - while the modern British cooking comes driven by local and seasonal produce. Classics like liver and streaky bacon (with wilted gem lettuce, mash and onion gravy) please traditionalists, while more up-to-the-minute thinking might deliver a starter of pan-roasted Cornish scallops teamed with spiced pork belly, pak choi, and coriander and chilli dressing. Desserts have comfort-zone appeal, perhaps sticky toffee pudding.

Chef Ian Richards **Owner** Merchant Inns Ltd
Times 12-2.30/6.30-9.30 **Prices** Food prices not confirmed for 2010. Please telephone for details.

Notes Breakfast 7-9, weekends 8-10, available to non-residents, Sunday L **Seats** 80, Pr/dining room 130, 30 **Children** Menu

SHERE Map 6 TQ04

Kinghams

◉ Modern British

Local produce showcased in attractive cottage restaurant

☎ 01483 202168
Gomshall Ln GU5 9HE
e-mail: paul@kinghams-restaurant.co.uk
dir: M25 junct 10. On A25 between Guildford & Dorking

Shere is a picture-book English village and Kinghams, a charming 17th-century brick-and-timber cottage, awash with roses and with a colourful garden for alfresco dining, fits the setting perfectly. Low beams, cosy fires and elegant clothed tables with gleaming glassware lure discerning diners into the intimate dining room for classic British cooking with an imaginative twist. Seasonal menus are built around quality local ingredients and well-presented dishes may take in smoked haddock and leek tart with parmesan and basil crust, pan-fried calves' liver with pancetta, shallot tarte Tatin and peppercorn jus, and steamed lemon pudding with lemon mascarpone and raspberry compôte. Fish specials change daily depending on the catch of the day.

Chef Paul Baker **Owner** Paul Baker
Times 12.15-2.30/7-9.30 Closed 25 Dec-4 Jan, Mon, D Sun **Prices** Fixed L 2 course £16.50, Fixed D 3 course £22.45, Starter £5.95-£9.95, Main £12.95-£22.95, Dessert £5.95, Service optional, Groups min 8 service 10% **Wines** 12 bottles over £20, 26 bottles under £20, 6 by glass **Notes** Sunday L, Vegetarian available **Seats** 48, Pr/dining room 24 **Children** Portions **Parking** 16

STOKE D'ABERNON Map 6 TQ15

Oak Room@ Woodlands Park Hotel

◉ Modern British, French

Victorian grandeur with contemporary cuisine

☎ 01372 843933 📠 01372 842704
Woodlands Ln KT11 3QB
e-mail: woodlandspark@handpicked.co.uk
dir: A3 exit at Cobham. Through town centre & Stoke D'Abernon, left at garden centre into Woodlands Lane, hotel 0.5m on right

The Bryant family of safety match fame built this handsome red brick Victorian mansion in 10 acres of parkland in prime commuter-belt Surrey countryside. The grandiose features beloved of minted Victorian magnates are all present and correct - check out the grand hall with its splendid marble fireplace, the minstrels' gallery and carved oak staircase, antiques and chandeliers. The dark oak-panelled fine dining Oak Room goes in for tradition too: dishes are delivered on silver trays by clued-up, immaculately turned-out staff, and classically-rooted technique underpins the kitchen's imaginative cooking. Crab ravioli are served with seared scallops and shellfish bisque in a typical starter, followed by a classic teaming of roast rump of lamb with garlic and thyme potatoes and ratatouille-stuffed aubergines.

Chef Matthew Ashton **Owner** Hand Picked Hotels
Times 12-2.30/7-10 Closed Mon, L Tue-Sat, D Sun **Prices** Starter £6.50-£11.50, Main £21-£28.50, Dessert £6.50-£8.50, Service optional **Wines** 125 bottles over £20, 4 bottles under £20, 10 by glass **Notes** Sunday L, Vegetarian available, Dress restrictions, No jeans or trainers, Civ Wed 200 **Seats** 35, Pr/dining room 150 **Children** Portions, Menu **Parking** 150

SUSSEX, EAST

ALFRISTON Map 6 TQ50

Harcourts Restaurant

◉ Modern British 🌱

Accomplished cooking in elegant country house

☎ 01323 870248 📠 01323 870918
Deans Place Hotel, Seaford Rd BN26 5TW
e-mail: mail@deansplacehotel.co.uk
dir: off A27, signed Alfriston & Drusillas Zoo Park. Continue south through village

Under new ownership and management, this friendly hotel in the heart of the Sussex countryside is situated on the southern fringe of one of England's prettiest villages. Set in attractive gardens on what was originally a vast farming estate, Deans Place dates back 600 years. The elegant Harcourts Restaurant is traditional with a warm, intimate ambience, serving English cuisine with a French influence. Local produce is sourced wherever possible, particularly fish from the Sussex coast. Start with pan-fried local scallops, fennel and orange confit and purple basil cress, followed by rump of Ashmore Farm lamb with minted baby gem, roasted sweet potato, cumin and tomato ragout. The Friston Bar is a more informal alternative.

Chef Stuart Dunley **Times** 12-2.30/6.30-9.30 **Prices** Food prices not confirmed for 2010. Please telephone for details. **Wines** 50 bottles over £20, 30 bottles under £20, 11 by glass **Notes** Sunday L, Vegetarian available, Dress restrictions, Smart casual, Civ Wed 200 **Seats** 60, Pr/dining room 50 **Children** Portions, Menu **Parking** 100

BATTLE   Map 7 TQ71

Powder Mills Hotel

⊛ Modern British V

Modern menu in an attractive conservatory dining room

☎ 01424 775511   🖨 01424 774540

Powdermill Ln TN33 0SP

e-mail: powdc@aol.com

dir: M25 junct 5, A21 towards Hastings. At St Johns Cross take A2100 to Battle. Pass abbey on right, 1st right into Powdermill Ln. 1m, hotel on right

Giant plants, Italian statuary, marble floors, floor-to-ceiling windows and wicker chairs create a light and airy feel to the Orangery Restaurant at this elegant 18th-century mansion. Set in 150 acres of grounds, lakes and woodland, it was originally the site of a gunpowder works. With views across the terrace, swimming pool and garden, you can sample well-executed modern British dishes, prepared using quality ingredients from local suppliers. From the short, well-balanced menu start with pan-seared scallops with cauliflower purée and crisp pancetta, move on to beef medallions with red onion marmalade and port sauce, and finish with lemon posset or a plate of local cheeses.

Chef James Penn **Owner** Mr & Mrs D Cowpland **Times** 12-2/7-9 **Prices** Fixed L 2 course £30, Fixed D 2 course fr £42, Service added but optional 10%, Groups min 10 service 10% **Wines** 4 by glass **Notes** Sunday L, Vegetarian menu, Dress restrictions, Smart casual, no jeans, shorts or T-shirts, Civ Wed 100 **Seats** 90, Pr/dining room 16 **Children** Portions, Menu **Parking** 100

BRIGHTON & HOVE   Map 6 TQ30

Drakes

⊛⊛ British NEW

Fashionable boutique hotel with modern cooking and local flavour

☎ 01273 696934   🖨 01273 684805

43-44 Marine Pde BN2 1PE

dir: From A23 at Brighton Pier rdbt. Left into Marine Pde towards marina. Hotel on left before lights (ornate water feature at front)

Drakes is a fine Georgian townhouse, a double-fronted one with views out to sea and all that Brighton has to offer only a short stroll away. This grand old dame has had a makeover into a cool boutique hotel that fits nicely into the Brighton scene. Have a drink in the luxuriously stylish cocktail bar and soak up the sea view before heading down into the basement restaurant. It may be subterranean, but the dining room is brimming with character and elegant charm; tea lights flicker around a bold flower display, while cream leather banquettes, linen-clad tables and contemporary photographs show it to be serious without being stuffy, rather like the staff. The menu is modern British in spirit with local produce name-checked giving a sense of place. Pan-roasted Rye Bay scallops come in a successfully creative pairing with apple purée, cider sauce and caviar, while a main-course trio of South Downs lamb is made up of a herb-crusted cannon, crispy breast and sweetbreads.

Times 12.30-2/7-9.30 **Prices** Food prices not confirmed for 2010. Please telephone for details.

Due South

⊛ Modern British ❁

Seaside dining with genuine commitment to organic and local produce

☎ 01273 821218

139 Kings Road Arches BN1 2FN

e-mail: eat@duesouth.co.uk

web: www.duesouth.co.uk

dir: On seafront, beneath cinema

Due South stands out from the buzzing parade of beachfront cafés and bars in the Victorian arches beneath Brighton's prom by virtue of its quality approach. There's an alfresco terrace just a few steps from the pebbles, and inside, the decor is simple, contemporary and unfussy, with banquettes, polished pine tables and boarded floors. The kitchen is known for championing excellent Sussex produce and its sincere commitment to the environment - hence its maximum use of organic, free-range and seasonal produce in good combinations, as in a starter of smoked Brockwell's Farm wild venison ravioli with mushroom consommé. Fish is well represented - perhaps as a roast fillet of sea bass with carrot purée, hazelnut and pickled samphire. Wines are limited to English and European in order to cut down on food miles.

Chef Michael Bremner **Owner** Robert Shenton **Times** 12-3.30/6-9.45 Closed 25 Dec **Prices** Fixed L 2 course £22-£28, Fixed D 3 course £35-£40, Starter £5-£11, Main £9-£24, Dessert £5-£7.50, Service optional **Wines** 8 bottles over £20, 25 by glass **Notes** Sunday L, Vegetarian available, Civ Wed 55, Air con **Seats** 55, Pr/dining room 12 **Children** Portions, Menu **Parking** NCP behind Grand Hotel

The Gingerman Restaurant (Norfolk Square)

⊛⊛ Modern British ❁

Confident cooking in a Hove favourite

☎ 01273 326688

21A Norfolk Square BN1 2PD

e-mail: info@gingermanrestaurants.com

dir: A23 to Palace Pier rdbt. Turn right onto Kings Rd. At Art Deco style Embassy building turn right into Norfolk Sq

The endearingly small venue between the seafront and Brighton's main shopping street was where one of the city's more eye-catching culinary operations of recent years began - and continues. A low-ceilinged single room with beige walls and comfortable seating is ably staffed, and is the scene of some gastronomic displays that can verge on the pyrotechnical on a good day. Start with braised oxtail gnocchi in red wine with shaved Parmesan for a confident opener, and follow with roast haddock with garlic potato cakes, poached quail's eggs and dried tomatoes. Venison is accurately cooked, tender and pink, and served with creamed Savoy cabbage, juniper and thyme carrots and game sauce. Dessert soufflés are a good bet too, perhaps a raspberry version with white chocolate ice cream. The group includes a country cousin (see entry for the Ginger Fox) and a gastro-pub in Hove, the Ginger Pig.

Chef Ben McKellar, David Keates **Owner** Ben & Pamela McKellar **Times** 12.30-2/7-10 Closed 2 wks Xmas, Mon **Prices** Fixed L 2 course £16, Fixed D 3 course £30, Service optional, Groups min 6 service 12.5% **Wines** 12 bottles over £20, 7 bottles under £20, 8 by glass **Notes** Sunday L, Vegetarian available, Air con **Seats** 32 **Children** Portions

Graze Restaurant

⊛⊛ British, European V

Taster-sized dishes in opulent Hove venue

☎ 01273 823707

42 Western Rd BN3 1JD

e-mail: bookings@graze-restaurant.co.uk

dir: A23/A259 Brighton Pier. E for 1.5m onto Lansdowne Place. Restaurant on Western Rd on right

In the Brunswick Square area of Hove, this stylish and busy restaurant attracts a loyal following. The slide-back café-style doors at the front conceal an opulent interior inspired by its Regency surroundings and the famous Brighton Royal Pavilion. Graze's big idea is serving the food in starter-size portions, with the twenty choices split between seafood, meat and vegetarian. This makes for an opportunity to try lots of varying flavours as on the menu British dishes rub shoulders with ideas from Mediterranean cooking and even some Australian influences. Kick off with seared Rye Bay scallops with chorizo, apple and hazelnut salad and move on to crispy pork belly with fondant potato, black pudding, creamed celeriac and apple purée.

continued

BRIGHTON & HOVE *continued*

Chef Adrian Geddes **Owner** Kate Alleston, Adrian Geddes, Neil Mannifield **Times** 12-3/6-10 Closed 25-26 Dec, 1 Jan, Mon, D Sun **Prices** Fixed L 2 course £10.95, Fixed D 3 course £15, Tasting menu fr £32.95, Starter £4.95-£8.95, Main £9.50-£16.95, Dessert £5.95-£7.95, Service added but optional 12% **Wines** 34 bottles over £20, 18 bottles under £20, 11 by glass **Notes** Tasting menu 7 course & vegetarian tasting menu, Sunday L, Vegetarian menu **Seats** 50, Pr/dining room 24

Hotel du Vin Brighton

◉ French, European

Reliable brasserie dining just off the seafront

☎ 01273 718588 ▤ 01273 718599
Ship St BN1 1AD
e-mail: info@brighton.hotelduvin.com
dir: A23 to seafront, at rdbt right, then right onto Middle St, bear right into Ship St, hotel at sea end on right

The Brighton branch of this wine-oriented hotel chain is a few steps off the seafront in the centre of town. As well as a wine-bar that has a good buzz, there's a relaxing brasserie dining room where the group's trademark Anglo-French cooking is capably rendered. Start with smoked eel, served with potato salad and creamed horseradish, and follow on with seared sea bass on leek and herb risotto, or duck leg confit with dauphinoise in red wine jus. It's the kind of cooking that's easy to understand, and delivers big, positive flavours. Finish with honey-roast figs, mascarpone and toasted pine-nuts, or a selection of vibrantly flavoured, home-made ice creams.

Times 12-2/7-10 Closed D 31 Dec

The Meadow Restaurant

◉◉ British ©

Modern cooking with regional flavour

☎ 01273 721182
64 Western Rd BN3 2JQ
e-mail: info@themeadowrestaurant.co.uk
dir: Please telephone for directions

Chef-proprietor Will Murgatroyd flies the flag for the best local produce and his menu reveals that he is willing to leave no stone unturned in his quest to bring the region's bounty to the table, including raiding his own parents' garden. This first-rate produce is treated with due respect and attention to detail in modern British dishes with some European influences along the way; thus Sussex Red beef tartare is served in a starter with truffled polenta chips and rosemary salt, and main-course sea bass is pan-fried and served with fried oysters, crushed Morghew Park potatoes and spinach. Finish with rhubarb Eton mess with pink praline. The restaurant, in a light and airy former bank on the main high street through Hove, has a bright-and-breezy décor with blond-wood tables and chairs, and service that hits the right easy-going notes.

Chef Will Murgatroyd **Owner** Will Murgatroyd **Times** 12-2.30/6-9.30 Closed 25-26 Dec, BH's, Mon, D Sun **Prices** Fixed L 2 course fr £12, Fixed D 3 course fr £15, Starter £4.50-£7, Main £9.50-£16.50, Dessert £5.50-£7, Service added but optional 10% **Wines** 11 bottles over £20, 14 bottles under £20, 14 by glass **Notes** Fixed D only available before 7.30pm, Sunday L, Vegetarian available **Seats** 50 **Children** Portions, Menu **Parking** On street

Sevendials

◉◉ Modern European

Modern European brasserie cooking with sun terrace

☎ 01273 885555 ▤ 0870 9127408
1-3 Buckingham Place BN1 3TD
e-mail: info@sevendialsrestaurant.co.uk
dir: From Brighton station turn right 0.5m up hill, restaurant at Seven Dials rdbt

The redbrick former bank building is only a few minutes from Brighton station, on one side of the busy intersection after which it is named. As well as an expansive dining room with plenty of daylight, there is also a sun terrace for outdoor dining, so you can make a start on your tan before you even get to the beach. The modern European brasserie cooking scores many hits in dishes that can be quite substantial, as witnessed in a starter of potted local smoked salmon with creamed horseradish and beetroot, pickled carrot and toast. Mains deliver big, confident flavours too, in the form of confit pork belly with black pudding mash, caramelised apple and a cider jus, while desserts include dark chocolate tart with morello cherry compôte and mascarpone, as well as raspberry crème brûlée.

Times 12-3/6-10.30 Closed 25 Dec, 1 Jan, D Sun

Terre à Terre

◉◉ Modern Vegetarian V ©

Experimental vegetarian and vegan cooking from across the globe

☎ 01273 729051 ▤ 01273 327561
71 East St BN1 1HQ
e-mail: mail@terreaterre.co.uk
web: www.terreaterre.co.uk
dir: Town centre, close to Palace Pier & The Lanes

This vegetarian stalwart in a road leading down to the sea continues to draw the crowds, be it for a light lunch or the full works in the form of the tasting menu. It manages to melt the hearts of even the most fervent carnivores. Inside, luscious red-hued panels and upholstered seats contrast with the natural wood floors and light-wood undressed tables, while the food takes its influences from, well, just about everywhere. This is exciting and creative vegetarian cookery, with the descriptions of dishes highly detailed and frequently whimsical - anyone for elephant and rocket oil or perhaps rain vodka cherry chocolate churros for pudding? A timely munch crunch menu offers Gordon Brown's butter bruschetta followed by spaghetti spin and ed balls and

there's also a children's menu which brings on teeny weeny linguine.

Terre à Terre

Chef Dino Pavledis **Owner** Ms A Powley & Mr P Taylor **Times** 12-10.30 Closed 25-26 Dec, 1 Jan, Mon (open some BH's) **Prices** Fixed L 3 course £12-£25, Fixed D 3 course £15-£35, Starter £4.35-£8, Main £13-£14.60, Dessert £3.75-£7.70, Service optional, Groups min 6 service 10% **Wines** 45 bottles over £20, 15 bottles under £20, 25 by glass **Notes** Vegetarian menu, Air con **Seats** 110 **Children** Portions, Menu **Parking** NCP, on street

---

EASTBOURNE | Map 6 TV69

Conservatory at Langhams

◉ British NEW ▮NOTABLE WINE LIST

Good British cooking in seafront terrace restaurant

☎ 01323 731451 ▤ 01323 646623
Langham Hotel, 43-49 Royal Pde BN22 7AH
e-mail: neil@langhamhotel.co.uk
dir: A22 follow signs for seafront Sovereign Centre take 3rd exit onto Royal Pde. Hotel on corner Royal Pde and Cambridge Rd

With its huge windows, wooden floors and modern blinds, the feel is of a sunny conservatory at this fine dining restaurant within Langhams Hotel, which stands on Eastbourne's seafront and enjoys fabulous sea views. Well-executed dishes show imagination and good use of quality local produce, and emphasise the essentially British style of cooking. Start with chicken liver and wild mushroom parfait with roast garlic and thyme marmalade, move on to seared black bream with ginger, scallion and mussel broth or rack of South Downs lamb with redcurrant jus, and finish with peanut brittle pannacotta with lime parfait.

Times 12-2.30/6-9.30

Grand Hotel (Mirabelle)

◎◎ Modern, Classic

☎ 01323 412345 & 435066 ▤ 01323 412233
King Edward's Pde BN21 4EQ
e-mail: reservations@grandeastbourne.com
web: www.grandeastbourne.com
dir: Western end of seafront, 1m from Eastbourne station

One of the country's most magnificent Victorian hotels, The Grand Hotel is situated on the seafront at Eastbourne and dominates the shoreline; expect sea views in abundance. Built in 1875, it has welcomed many of the great and the good over the years including Winston Churchill, Charlie Chaplin and Elgar. The composer Debussy completed his symphony 'La Mer' here in 1905. Affectionately known as 'The White Palace', the Grand Hotel integrates late 19th-century charm and grandeur with modern comforts. Tastefully restored to its former glory, it's a suitably palatial venue that comes complete with spacious lounges, luxurious health club and a Grand Hall, where afternoon tea is served amid marble-columned splendour. The Mirabelle is the light-and-airy fine-dining restaurant and its decor and atmosphere follows the traditional theming, though the kitchen takes a more modern approach. Goats' cheese and onion marmalade tart, perhaps, followed by marinated spiced pork belly with apple compôte. Finish with Italian ice cream truffle with Amaretto crème anglaise.

Chef Keith Mitchell, Gerald Roser **Owner** Elite Hotels
Times 12.30-2/7-10 Closed 2-16 Jan, Sun-Mon
Prices Fixed L 2 course £18-£39.50, Fixed D 3 course £37-£59, Tasting menu £55, Service added but optional 10% **Wines** 390 bottles over £20, 39 bottles under £20, 15 by glass **Notes** Tasting menu 5 course, Vegetarian available, Dress restrictions, Jacket or tie for D, Civ Wed 200, Air con **Seats** 50 **Parking** 70

Anderida Restaurant

◎◎ British, European ⱽ

Grand hotel dining in a country-house setting

☎ 01342 824988 ▤ 01342 826206
Ashdown Park Hotel, Wych Cross RH18 5JR
e-mail: reservations@ashdownpark.com
dir: A264 to East Grinstead, then A22 to Eastbourne. 2m S of Forest Row at Wych Cross lights. Left to Hartfield, hotel on right 0.75m

The Anderida restaurant is the gastronomic heart of the upmarket Ashdown Park Hotel and Country Club, a swanky set-up that encompasses an 18-hole golf course, fitness and spa complex lost in 186 acres of landscaped gardens and parkland in the depths of the Ashdown Forest. Grandeur and formality reign in the restaurant, so expect unobtrusively friendly staff with shiny silver service skills. Modern twists jazz up the predominantly classical cooking, but there's nothing to scare the horses. A tasting of pork offers confit of belly pork, black pudding ravioli and pressed ham terrine with apple purée, English mustard dressing and a cider reduction; cannon of lamb comes with spätzle noodles and a pithivier of osso buco with Madeira sauce. Comforting puddings, such as blueberry cheesecake with yogurt sorbet, are simple and well executed.

Chef Roger Gadsden **Owner** Elite Hotels **Times** 12-2/7-10
Prices Fixed L 2 course £16.50-£20.75, Fixed D 3 course £37-£41.25, Main £49.50-£55.50, Service included **Wines** 334 bottles over £20, 14 bottles under £20, 16 by glass **Notes** ALC 3 course, Speciality menu from £47, Sunday L, Vegetarian menu, Dress restrictions, Jacket and tie for gentlemen after 7pm, Civ Wed 150 **Seats** 120, Pr/dining room 160 **Children** Portions, Menu **Parking** 120

Jali Restaurant at Chatsworth Hotel

◎ Traditional Indian **NEW**

Modern Indian cooking by the sea

☎ 01424 457300 & 720188 ▤ 01424 445865
7-11 Carlisle Pde TN34 1JG
e-mail: info@chatsworthhotel.com
dir: On Hastings seafront, near railway station

Jali is a trendy modern restaurant in a welcoming hotel on Hastings seafront. The smart contemporary bar and restaurant make the most of the views, as you mull over the wide-ranging menu, which extends beyond the old favourites such as kebabs, tandoori and Punjabi dishes. Expect some interesting combinations of herbs and spices, spot-on home-made breads - missi roti, for example - and full-on chutneys and pickles. Specialities from the south appear, such as a Goan macchli curry of local fish in coconut gravy and Goanese spices, or Bombay's famous bhel Puri; naturally, there's plenty for vegetarians too: try paneer lubaabdar (cheese in creamy tomato sauce with pungent notes of fennel and fenugreek). Best of all, the cuisine at Jali is light and modern.

Chef Ramesh Angre **Owner** Aristel Group of Hotels
Times 6.30-11 Closed L all week **Prices** Fixed D 3 course £16.50-£20, Starter £4.95-£6.95, Main £7.75-£9.95, Dessert £3.25-£4.25, Service added but optional 10% **Wines** 12 bottles over £20, 13 bottles under £20, 7 by glass **Notes** Fixed D 2 course, Vegetarian available, Dress restrictions, No shorts, Air con **Seats** 52, Pr/dining room 35 **Children** Portions **Parking** 8

Hungry Monk Restaurant

◎ British, French

Ancient flint building, the home of banoffee pie

☎ 01323 482178
BN26 5QF
web: www.hungrymonk.co.uk
dir: A22, turn towards Wannock at Polegate x-rds. Continue for 2.5m, restaurant on left

The venerable 14th-century flint building with its bright red sign was once a monk's retreat (hence the name), and presents a wealth of low-beamed, colourful interiors with more fireplaces than you can shake a log at. A series

continued on page 407

Newick Park Hotel & Country Estate

NEWICK   Map 6 TQ42

Modern European

Accomplished cooking in elegant country house

☎ 01825 723633   📄 01825 723969
BN8 4SB
e-mail: bookings@newickpark.co.uk
web: www.newickpark.co.uk
dir: Exit A272 at Newick Green, 1m, pass church & pub. Turn left, hotel 0.25m on right

Newick Park is the real essence of country-house eating. The 250-acres estate surrounding the secluded, lovingly restored Georgian house comprises peaceful parkland, two lakes, an organic walled garden, which supplies fruit and vegetables to the kitchen, and fabulous views towards the South Downs - so allow time to explore. Equally grand is the interior, filled with tasteful fabrics, fine antiques and cosy, winter log fires, with the elegant panelled dining room featuring lofty ceilings, splendid oil paintings, beautiful flower displays, and soothing views across the lake from floor-to-ceiling windows. The quality of the food is a match for the scenery, the well-balanced daily menus showcasing sound cooking skills and quality local, seasonal ingredients, including game from the estate. A modern approach sees Rye Bay scallops served with cauliflower purée, cumin velouté, spiced

caramel and apple, following on with venison loin with minced leg, beetroot purée, celeriac and venison, and finishing with peanut parfait with hot chocolate and peanut caramel. Service from professional and knowledgeable staff is formal and attentive. The wine list includes some bins of great character and individuality from smaller producers, plus a good selection by the glass.

Chef Chris Moore **Owner** Michael & Virginia Childs **Times** 12-2.30/7-9 Closed 31 Jan **Prices** Fixed L 2 course £20.50, Fixed D 3 course £42.50, Service optional **Wines** 85 bottles over £20, 25 bottles under £20, 9 by glass
Notes Sunday L, Vegetarian available, Civ Wed 120 **Seats** 40, Pr/dining room 74 **Children** Portions, Menu **Parking** 100

JEVINGTON *continued*

of cookery books expands the operation, and the food itself can be tried via a selection of fixed-price menus. A good starter might be a well-made creamy risotto of prawns, coconut and chilli, while a recommended main course is the generously served, crisp-skinned breast of Norfolk duckling, sauced with Calvados and spiced apples. The original banoffee pie was invented here, or there might be a surprisingly light three-layered chocolate tart with raspberry coulis.

Hungry Monk Restaurant

Chef Gary Fisher, Matt Comben **Owner** Mr & Mrs N Mackenzie **Times** 12-2/6.45-9.45 Closed 24-26 Dec, BHs, Mon, Tue (Jan-May) **Prices** Fixed D 3 course £33.95, Groups min 7 service 12.5% **Wines** 101 bottles over £20, 43 bottles under £20, 9 by glass **Notes** Sunday L, Vegetarian available, Air con **Seats** 38, Pr/dining room 16 **Children** Portions **Parking** 14

NEWICK   Map 6 TQ42

Newick Park Hotel & Country Estate

⑨⑨⑨ — *see opposite page*

Two Seven Two

⑨ Modern European

Skilful cooking in restful surroundings

☎ 01825 721272   🖷 01825 724698
20/22 High St BN8 4LQ
e-mail: twoseventwo@hotmail.co.uk
dir: On A272, 7m E of Haywards Heath & 7m N of Lewes

The cream-coloured restaurant is named after the A-road on which it stands. It's a light, breezy place with a pale beige decorative scheme, adorned with colourful prints. Attractively presented modern European dishes are good ambassadors for the kitchen's skills, bringing on warm smoked mackerel and leek tart with hollandaise, a neat combination, followed perhaps by crisp-skinned sea bass on mushroom risotto, accompanied by broad beans and pancetta, or calves' liver with beetroot and potato salad and onion rings. Smooth, delicately vanillary pannacotta is offset with black pepper shortbread, strawberries and a pistachio sauce.

Chef Neil Bennett **Owner** Simon Maltby
Times 12-2.30/7-9.30 Closed 25-26 Dec, 1-2 Jan, Mon, L Tue, D Sun **Prices** Fixed L 2 course £13.50, Fixed D 3 course £17.50, Starter £5.25-£8.50, Main £13.50-£28.50, Dessert £5.25-£8.50, Groups min 8 service 10%

Wines 52 bottles over £20, 35 bottles under £20, 6 by glass **Notes** Sunday L, Vegetarian available, Air con **Seats** 60 **Children** Portions **Parking** 10

RYE   Map 7 TQ92

The George in Rye

⑨ British, Mediterranean NEW

Mediterranean flavours in historic Sussex

☎ 01797 222114   🖷 01797 224065
98 High St TN31 7JT
e-mail: stay@thegeorgeinrye.com
dir: Please telephone for directions

Situated in the centre of historic Rye, the George dates from 1575 and has an original Georgian ballroom, which is used for weddings and banquets. Recent renovation has managed to comfortably blend old and new in its design, and includes both antique and modern furniture, natural materials and local art. The style of cooking shows Mediterranean influences, with food presented simply and with slavish respect for fresh, seasonal ingredients from local farms around Sussex and Kent. Much of the fish and seafood is sourced from the trawlers of Rye Bay. Typical dishes include seared Rye Bay scallops with quail's egg, chorizo and truffle oil, or chocolate-crusted rack of lamb with rösti potato, red cabbage and raisins. Go for a cocoa hit for dessert, with chocolate fondant with white chocolate ice cream.

Chef Rod Grossmann **Owner** Alex & Katie Clarke **Times** 12-3/6.30-9.30 **Prices** Fixed L 2 course £11.95-£16.95, Starter £5-£7.50, Main £13-£16.75, Dessert £5.25-£7.50, Service optional **Wines** 31 bottles over £20, 10 bottles under £20, 12 by glass **Notes** Sunday L, Vegetarian available, Civ Wed 100 **Seats** 30, Pr/dining room 100 **Children** Portions, Menu **Parking** On street

---

Mermaid Inn

⑨ English, French V ✋

Traditional and modern cooking in an ancient inn

☎ 01797 223065   & 223788   🖷 01797 225069
Mermaid St TN31 7EY
e-mail: info@mermaidinn.com
dir: A259, follow signs to town centre, then into Mermaid St

The Mermaid was rebuilt in 1420 on top of cellars that date from the mid-12th century, and such is its dignified old age that it has found itself starring in period dramas on the big and small screens, as indeed have the surrounding cobbled streets of Rye. Low beams hewn from ancient ships' timbers reinforce the tone, although the evidence of harmony between English and French traditions in the cooking might have surprised the original builders. Fixed-price menus offer glazed prawns with mango and rocket in black pepper vinaigrette, and chargrilled sirloin with straw potatoes, balsamic beetroot and horseradish froth, rounded off with something like summer pudding and mascarpone.

Mermaid Inn

Chef Roger Kellie, Matthew Hall **Owner** Mrs J Blincow & Mr R I Pinwill **Times** 12-2.30/7-9.30 **Prices** Fixed L 2 course £20-£21, Fixed D 3 course £34, Service added but optional 10% **Wines** 44 bottles over £20, 17 bottles under £20, 14 by glass **Notes** Sunday L, Vegetarian menu, Dress restrictions, Smart casual, no jeans or T-shirts **Seats** 64, Pr/dining room 14 **Children** Portions, Menu **Parking** 26

Webbes at The Fish Café

⑨ Modern British

Modern seafood restaurant with extensive menu of classics

☎ 01797 222226   & 222210   🖷 01797 229260
17 Tower St TN31 7AT
e-mail: info@thefishcafe.com
dir: 100mtrs before Landgate Arch

Look for the redbrick frontage with its semi-circular windows in the middle of picturesque Rye, and you will find a modern, accomplished fish restaurant that suits the mood of the times. An open-plan kitchen and staff who are fully au fait with the menus add to the appeal. A menu of tried-and-true favourites includes prawns in garlic butter, smoked mackerel pâté or pickled herrings with beetroot and potato salad to start, with mains such as succulently cooked sea bass accompanied by a fine creamy prawn and spring onion risotto. Finish on a high with sumptuous raspberry crème brûlée served with Drambuie ice cream. Under the same ownership as The Wild Mushroom in Westfield (see entry).

Chef Paul Webbe, Mathew Drinkwater **Owner** Paul & Rebecca Webbe **Times** 6-9.30 Closed 25-26 Dec, 2-11 Jan, Mon, L all week, D Sun **Prices** Starter £5.50-£9, Main £11-£22, Dessert £6-£6.50, Service optional **Wines** 52 bottles over £20, 16 bottles under £20, 9 by glass **Notes** Vegetarian available, Air con **Seats** 52, Pr/dining room 70 **Children** Portions, Menu **Parking** Cinque Port Street

TICEHURST — Map 6 TQ63

Dale Hill Hotel & Golf Club

Modern European

British cuisine in golfing hotel with views

☎ 01580 200112 ▤ 01580 201249
TN5 7DQ
e-mail: info@dalehill.co.uk
dir: M25 junct 5/A21. 5m after Lamberhurst turn right at lights onto B2087 to Flimwell. Hotel 1m on left

Located in beautiful, and historic countryside, this modern golfing hotel offers fabulous views across the ridges and valleys of the Kentish Weald, as well as two 18 hole golf courses and a swimming pool. There are two restaurants and a club house bar. The elegant Wealden Restaurant, country golf club in style and with views out to the course, delivers modern British cuisine with the emphasis on flavour. Good classic combinations might include halibut and scallop tartare served with crisp oyster tempura and lemongrass infusion, followed by rack of lamb with lamb's sweetbreads, butternut squash purée, roast baby turnips and thyme jus.

Times 12-2.30/6.30-9 Closed L Mon-Sat

UCKFIELD — Map 6 TQ42

The Dining Room

Modern, Traditional

Skilful cooking in elegant country-house hotel

☎ 01825 733333 ▤ 01825 732990
Buxted Park Hotel, Buxted Park, Buxted TN22 4AY
e-mail: buxtedpark@handpicked.co.uk
dir: Exit A22 Uckfield bypass (London-Eastbourne road), take A272 to Buxted. Cross lights, hotel entrance 1m on right

Built in 1722, Buxted Park's history is as colourful as it is long. Over the years, the house has played host to society's movers and shakers including William Wordsworth, Winston Churchill and Marlon Brando. It stands in 312 acres of private grounds and parkland, which includes 3 large lakes, a deer park and a walled garden. The restaurant, located in the original Victorian orangery, retains many original features but still feels modern and bright. It's a stylish and relaxing place in which to dine, with views over the gardens. Accomplished modern British and European cuisine blends classic and modern ideas and is based around top-quality

ingredients. Simply-presented dishes may include warm salad of pigeon with Jerusalem artichoke and vinaigrette jus, followed by grilled fillet of Sussex beef with an oxtail pithivier, chanterelles and winter vegetables.

Times 12-2/7-9.30

WESTFIELD — Map 7 TQ81

The Wild Mushroom Restaurant

Modern British

Impressive cuisine in a converted Victorian farmhouse

☎ 01424 751137 ▤ 01424 753405
Woodgate House, Westfield Ln TN35 4SB
e-mail: info@wildmushroom.co.uk
dir: From A21 towards Hastings, left onto A28 to Westfield. Restaurant 1.5m on left

In a quiet rural setting in 1066 country near Hastings, this red-brick Victorian farmhouse is quietly turning out some rather good food. The cosy L-shaped dining room has a respectably genteel ambience, with its starched white linen, low, cream-painted beams, muted earthy tones and high-backed chairs. You can settle in with an apéritif in the conservatory-style bar, or, weather permitting, in the lovely garden. Top-class raw materials are transformed into superbly-presented dishes by a kitchen that is clearly self-assured and technically skilful. Pan-fried salmon with beetroot risotto and horseradish foam might be followed by caramelised breast of Gressingham duckling with apple and Cassis sauce. Finish with panettone bread-and-butter pudding with Amaretto ice cream and orange peel. (Sister establishment to Webbes at The Fish Café, Rye - see entry).

Chef Paul Webbe **Owner** Mr & Mrs P Webbe
Times 12-2.30/7-10 Closed 25 Dec, 2 wks at New Year, Mon, L Sat, D Sun **Prices** Fixed L 2 course £15.95, Starter £5.50-£8, Main £11-£19, Dessert £6.50-£7.50, Service optional **Wines** 46 bottles over £20, 33 bottles under £20, 6 by glass **Notes** Tasting menu available 6 course, Sunday L, Vegetarian available, Dress restrictions, Smart casual **Seats** 40 **Children** Portions **Parking** 20

WILMINGTON — Map 6 TQ50

Crossways

Modern British

Fine food in relaxed and friendly country-house hotel

☎ 01323 482455 ▤ 01323 487811
Lewes Rd BN26 5SG
e-mail: stay@crosswayshotel.co.uk
dir: On A27, 2m W of Polegate

Run by the same owners for more than twenty years, this small Georgian country-house restaurant in the Cuckmere Valley is close to Glyndebourne, so popular with opera fans, but is also ideally situated to appreciate the beauty of the South Downs. Once home to Elizabeth David's parents, the current owners follow a philosophy that the influential food writer would doubtless fully appreciate:

food cooked simply using good, seasonal produce. Dishes are offered from a set monthly menu, including a daily home-made soup and fresh fish from the day's catch. Typically impressive dishes are seafood pancake or roast Gressingham duck with Puy lentils cooked with bacon, garlic and cream.

Chef David Stott **Owner** David Stott, Clive James
Times 7.30-8.30 Closed 24 Dec-24 Jan, Sun-Mon, L all week **Prices** Fixed D 4 course fr £36.95, Service optional **Wines** 18 bottles over £20, 25 bottles under £20, 10 by glass **Notes** Vegetarian available **Seats** 24 **Parking** 20

SUSSEX, WEST

ALBOURNE — Map 6 TQ21

The Ginger Fox

Modern European NEW

Classy country cousin of Brighton's Gingerman Restaurant

☎ 01273 857888
Henfield Rd BN6 9EA
dir: On A281 at the junction with B2117

Standing all alone on the outskirts of Albourne, the Ginger Fox has on its thatched roof one of the eponymous predators in hot pursuit of a pheasant. The pub has been smartly refurbished with the emphasis placed firmly on dining; it's owned by the chap who runs the Gingerman Restaurant in Brighton (Hove, actually; see entry). Customers turn up for the classy food - the same menu is served in the bar and dining area - which is decidedly above average in terms of the quality of the produce and the execution of the cooking. The three cheese ploughman's shows respect for traditional pub values, while chargrilled tuna loin with beetroot purée, beetroot vinaigrette and a soft herb salad reveals modern European leanings. Main-course pan-fried monkish with sweet pepper, butter beans, chorizo and grilled squid is full of Mediterranean flavours. There's a beer garden out front and local Harvey's on tap.

Times 12-2/6.30-10 **Prices** Food prices not confirmed for 2010. Please telephone for details.

AMBERLEY — Map 6 TQ01

Queens Room at Amberley Castle Hotel

— *see opposite page*

ARUNDEL   Map 6 TQ00

The Townhouse

◉ Modern Mediterranean

Elegant Regency townhouse offering assured modern cooking

☎ 01903 883847

65 High St BN18 9AJ

e-mail: enquiries@thetownhouse.co.uk

dir: Follow A27 to Arundel, onto High Street, establishment on left at top of hill

A listed Regency building opposite the castle features, among other things, a 16th-century gilded Florentine ceiling, beneath which some suitably civilised dining goes on. Some textbook modern combinations inform the cooking - scallops and belly pork, smoked haddock and leek in a risotto - but there are some less familiar ideas too, as in John Dory served with bubble-and-squeak and a red wine jus. Beef fillet is treated to the traditional trimmings, or there could be pork tenderloin with chorizo mash and a bean cassoulet. Dessert contrasts run from hot and cold (rhubarb gratin and vanilla ice cream) to creamy and sharp (pannacotta with blackcurrant compôte).

Chef Lee Williams **Owner** Lee & Kate Williams **Times** 12-2.30/7-9.30 Closed 2 wks Oct, Xmas, 2 wks Feb, Sun-Mon **Prices** Fixed L 2 course £14, Fixed D 3 course £27.50, Service optional **Wines** 29 bottles over £20, 15 bottles under £20, 6 by glass **Notes** Vegetarian available **Seats** 24 **Children** Portions **Parking** On street or nearby car park

BOSHAM   Map 5 SU80

Millstream Hotel and Restaurant

◉◉ Modern British ✿

Indulgent dining in a gorgeous village setting

☎ 01243 573234   🖷 01243 573459

Bosham Ln PO18 8HL

e-mail: info@millstream-hotel.co.uk

web: www.millstream-hotel.co.uk

dir: 4m W of Chichester on A259, left at Bosham rdbt. After 0.5m right at T-junct signed to church & quay. Hotel 0.5m on right

Part small manor house, part malthouse, the peaceful Millstream Hotel nestles in the curve of a stream in the historic, harbourside village of Bosham. The comfortable, traditionally-styled interior, with its friendly and relaxed bar and more formal restaurant is popular with the sailing fraternity and visitors looking for a quiet rural hotel close to Chichester. Food is innovative and successfully blends modern and traditional cooking styles. Dishes are freshly prepared by an ambitious kitchen and quality ingredients handled with care. Choices from the extensive dinner menu may include seared scallops with butternut squash foam and cauliflower and cumin purée for starters, followed by rack of Romney Marsh lamb with basil jus, and vanilla risotto rice pudding with roasted rhubarb and toasted almond crackling.

Chef James Fairchild-Dickson **Owner** The Wild family **Times** 12.30-2/6.45-9.15 **Prices** Fixed L 2 course fr £18, Fixed D 3 course fr £29, Service optional **Wines** 60 bottles over £20, 14 bottles under £20, 13 by glass **Notes** Sunday L, Vegetarian available, Dress restrictions, Smart casual, no jeans in the evenings, Civ Wed 92, Air con **Seats** 60, Pr/dining room 92 **Children** Portions, Menu **Parking** 40

Queens Room at Amberley Castle Hotel

AMBERLEY   Map 6 TQ01

Modern European V ✿

High-gloss modern European cooking in a medieval castle

☎ 01798 831992   🖷 01798 831998

BN18 9LT

e-mail: info@amberleycastle.co.uk

dir: Off B2139 between Storrington & Houghton

If you want grand, Amberley has the goods. From the moment the crenellated towers of the gatehouse heave into view above this winsome Sussex village, you know you're in for a treat. Inside, the 900-year-old castle is a world of Norman arches, lancet windows and vaulted stonework, where guests recline on four-poster beds and diners make a beeline for the 12th-century, barrel-vaulted, tapestried Queen's Room, which was done up comparatively recently to celebrate the Restoration. In this awe-inspiring setting, James Dugan's cooking completes the picture, rising to the occasion with a high-gloss version of modern European cuisine. A pavé of salmon served rare in a kind of minestrone complete with home-made pasta tubes is a fascinating starter, while the expected foie gras appears in a glazed terrine, complemented cleverly with smoked eel and apple. Local organic pork is served 2 ways, braised shoulder and a cutlet, along with colcannon and a sweet-pungent mix of turnip and plum, while inventiveness is maintained to the last, with finishers like spiced fig cake with matching ice cream, lemon jelly and a toasted almond-flavoured foam. A majestic wine list accompanies it all, and a dress code applies; leave your jeans at home.

Chef James Dugan **Owner** Amberley Castle Hotel Ltd **Times** 12-2/7-9.30 **Prices** Fixed L 2 course £25, Fixed D 3 course £60, Service optional, Groups min 10 service 10% **Wines** 155 bottles over £20, 4 bottles under £20, 14 by glass **Notes** Tasting menu 8 course, Sunday L, Vegetarian menu, Dress restrictions, Smart casual, jacket or tie, Civ Wed 55 **Seats** 70, Pr/dining room 40 **Children** Portions **Parking** 30

BURPHAM · Map 6 TQ00

George & Dragon

◉ British, French

Classic pub food in an idyllic spot on the South Downs

☎ 01903 883131 📠 01903 883341
BN18 9RR
dir: Off A27 1m E of Arundel, signed Burpham, 2.5m pub
on left

You couldn't ask for a more welcoming pub for refuelling
whilst exploring the beauty of the South Downs. The
George & Dragon is such a classic with its ancient
beams, stone floors and convivial atmosphere that it's
deservedly popular, particularly at weekends when
walkers are out in force, so book ahead for a good table.
Expect down-to-earth rustic pub grub from a kitchen that
doesn't faff about with the ingredients. Terrine of wild
boar and rabbit with home-made tomato chutney and
bacon and onion brioche might start things off, followed
by pan-roasted scallops with saffron cream and rice. The
concise carte is boosted by heaps of blackboard specials,
and a bonus lunchtime bar menu.

Times 12-2/7-9 Closed 25 Dec, D Sun

CHICHESTER · Map 5 SU80

Comme Ça

◉ French

Popular restaurant serving classical French cuisine

☎ 01243 788724 & 536307
67 Broyle Rd PO19 6BD
e-mail: comme.ca@commeca.co.uk
dir: On A286 near Festival Theatre

Comme Ça, a popular French restaurant just a short stroll
from the Chichester Festival, is situated in a Georgian inn
that has been lovingly restored, maintaining the original
oak beams and high ceilings. Decorated in bold colours,
with an interesting collection of prints and objets d'art, it
attracts a strong local following. There is also a bar-
lounge and garden room with French doors leading onto a
patio and sunken garden. The appealing bi-lingual menu
of classic French dishes includes twice-baked gruyère
soufflé garnished with their own sun-dried tomatoes,
following on with roasted fillet of Sussex venison served
with braised red cabbage and a juniper-flavoured red
wine sauce. Finish with a selection of French cheeses.

Chef Michael Navet, Mark Howard **Owner** Mr & Mrs Navet
Times 12-2/6-10.30 Closed Xmas wk & New Year wk,
BHs, Mon, L Tue, D Sun **Prices** Fixed L 2 course fr £21.95,
Fixed D 3 course fr £34.95, Service optional, Groups min 8
service 10% **Wines** 60 bottles over £20, 60 bottles under
£20, 7 by glass **Notes** Sunday L, Dress restrictions, Smart
casual **Seats** 100, Pr/dining room 14 **Children** Portions,
Menu **Parking** 46

Croucher's Country Hotel & Restaurant

◉◉ British, International

Sound cooking in smart former farmhouse

☎ 01243 784995 📠 01243 539797
Birdham Rd PO20 7EH
e-mail: crouchers@btconnect.com
dir: From A27 Chichester bypass onto A286 towards West
Wittering, 2m, hotel on left between Chichester Marina &
Dell Quay

Situated on the main road from Chichester to the
Witterings, this former farmhouse is a popular dining
venue with the locals. The recently refurbished restaurant
is very smart, with several windows overlooking the newly
landscaped gardens. A private dining room is also
available and there are alfresco terraces at the front and
rear of the building. The cooking is essentially British
with some modern touches and presentation is simple,
with an emphasis on local produce. A starter of seafood
ravioli with sautéed spinach and shellfish sauce could be
followed with grilled fillet of halibut with pesto crust,
crushed new potatoes and lemon and caper dressing.
Finish perhaps with the successfully paired flavours of an
Earl Grey pannacotta served with Baileys ice cream.

Chef G Wilson, N Markey **Owner** Mr L van Rooyen,
Mr G Wilson **Times** 12.30-2.30/7-11 Closed 26 Dec, 1 Jan,
Prices Fixed L 2 course £14.95, Fixed D 3 course £21.50,
Starter £4.50-£7.50, Main £6.50-£17.50, Dessert £5.50,
Service optional, Groups min 12 service 12.5% **Wines** 29
bottles over £20, 18 bottles under £20, 4 by glass
Notes Dress restrictions, Smart casual **Seats** 80, Pr/
dining room 20 **Children** Portions, Menu **Parking** 60

Earl of March

◉ Modern British NEW

Classy food in Downland pub

☎ 01243 533993
Lavant PO18 0BQ
e-mail: gt@theearlofmarch.com
dir: On A286, 2m N of Chichester towards Midhurst, on
the corner of Goodwood Estate

William Blake penned the rousing words to *Jerusalem*
during a stay in 1803 at this Sussex country pub on the
edge of the Goodwood estate. Inspirational South Downs
landscapes are all around, but in 2007 a former
executive head chef from the Ritz took over and ushered
in the 21st century with a stylish, country-chic makeover.
The bar retains the feel of a pub, with squashy sofas and
a crackling log fire, while the restaurant ratchets up the
style a notch or two with snazzy tables and brown high-
backed chairs. The culinary output is guided by a sure
hand. Blackboards showcase the best of local produce -
perhaps pan-seared diver-caught scallops with pea
purée, pancetta and truffle oil, or tender pink New Forest
venison served on buttery chive mash with roasted root
vegetables and a port wine jus.

Chef Giles Thompson **Owner** Giles Thompson
Times 12-2.30/6.30-9.30 Closed D Sun **Prices** Starter
£6.50-£8.95, Main £10.50-£15.95, Dessert £3.95-£5.95,

Service optional, Groups min 11 service 12.5% **Wines** 33
bottles over £20, 16 bottles under £20, 18 by glass
Notes Sunday L, Vegetarian available **Seats** 60, Pr/dining
room 12 **Children** Portions, Menu **Parking** 30

Hallidays

◉◉ Modern British 🍃

Intimate village restaurant serving modern cuisine

☎ 01243 575331
Watery Ln, Funtington PO18 9LF
e-mail: hallidaysdinners@aol.com
dir: Please telephone for directions

This charming row of flint and brick cottages dates from
the 13th century and for some 800 years has looked up to
the magnificent South Downs. The Grade II listed
building, clad with wisteria and roses and topped with a
traditional Sussex thatch, houses a beamed, two-room
restaurant, popular locally for its quiet charm and
impeccable service. The chef-proprietor cooks seasonally,
using produce sourced from local farmers and
smallholders and incorporating wild food - mushrooms,
nettles and berries - he has foraged for himself. The
menu changes every week, sometimes more, depending
on what catches chef's eye. Start with game terrine with
spiced oranges and griddled country bread, following on
with Racton Farm lamb three ways (cutlet, rump and
faggot), and Funtington raspberry millefeuille with
garden verbena ice cream to finish.

Chef Andrew Stephenson **Owner** Mr A & Mrs J Stephenson
Times 12-2.15/7-10.15 Closed 1 wk Mar, 2 wks Aug,
Mon-Tue, L Sat, D Sun **Prices** Fixed D 3 course £36,
Starter £5.25-£8.50, Main £12.50-£18.50, Dessert £5.25-
£7.50, Service optional **Wines** 65 bottles over £20, 25
bottles under £20, 5 by glass **Notes** Sunday L, Vegetarian
available, Dress restrictions, No shorts **Seats** 26
Children Portions **Parking** 12

Royal Oak Inn

◉ Modern British

**Traditional food and buzzy atmosphere with a
sophisticated twist**

☎ 01243 527434 📠 01243 775062
Pook Ln, East Lavant PO18 0AX
e-mail: info@royaloakeastlavant.co.uk
web: www.royaloakeastlavant.co.uk
dir: From Chichester take A286 towards Midhurst, 2m to
mini rdbt, turn right signed East Lavant. Inn on left

continued on page 412

West Stoke House

CHICHESTER Map 5 SU80

Modern British, French

Creative modern cuisine in a sophisticated but relaxed country restaurant with rooms

☎ 01243 575226 📠 01243 574655
Downs Rd, West Stoke PO18 9BN
e-mail: info@weststokehouse.co.uk
dir: 3m NW of Chichester. Off B286 to West Stoke, next to St Andrew's Church

West Stoke House is an effortlessly gorgeous Georgian mansion in wide-open South Downs countryside, but with the salty tang of yachty Chichester and the coast close to hand - the perfect basic ingredients, then, for a sophisticated country-house restaurant with rooms. Inside, you might have walked into the stylish English classicism of a Merchant Ivory film set, in a décor replete with French antiques, oak floors and unframed modern artwork by local Sussex artists. The elegant dining room in the old ballroom has huge sash windows opening onto views across primped lawns to the whaleback spine of the Downs. There's no standing on ceremony here: unlike the crisp table linen, staff are refreshingly un-starchy, but equally switched-on and clued up about the essential details of the menus. Plenty of thought goes into keeping fixed-price three-course menus focused on well-balanced combinations in a modern English key. The kitchen clearly has technical skills in abundance, balancing ambition and creativity with intelligence and simplicity, so expect eye-catching modern presentations with plenty of wow factor, built on solid classical French foundations. An intensely-flavoured starter partners seared breast of squab pigeon with a croustade of field mushroom duxelles, quail's egg and garlic purée, followed by mouthwatering pan-fried halibut fillet with cep risotto, artichokes, capers, pea shoots and morel sauce.

Chef Darren Brown **Owner** Rowland & Mary Leach
Times 12-2/7-9 Closed Xmas, 1 Jan, Mon-Tue
Prices Fixed L 2 course £19.50-£35, Fixed D 3 course £30-£45, Service optional, Groups min 8 service 12.5%
Wines 100 bottles over £20, 14 bottles under £20, 10 by glass **Notes** Sunday L, Vegetarian available, Civ Wed 60
Seats 50, Pr/dining room 26 **Children** Portions
Parking 20

CHICHESTER *continued*

A thriving and very stylish gastro-pub with rooms created from a tiny, 200-year-old inn, a Sussex barn and a flint cottage, and nicely tucked away in a sleepy downland village north of the city. Expect an open-plan bar and dining area, replete with wood and tiled floors, open log fires, leather sofas, fat church candles on scrubbed tables, and ales tapped from the cask. The modern British menu offers classy renditions of pub classics as seen in pork and rabbit terrine with fig chutney, wild halibut on Selsey crab and coriander cake with lime and coconut fish cream, and bread-and-butter pudding with vanilla custard.

Chef Simon Haynes **Owner** Charles Ullmann **Times** 10-3/6-10.30 **Prices** Starter £4.50-£8.50, Main £11-£21.50, Dessert £4.50-£6.50, Service optional **Wines** 45 bottles over £20, 12 bottles under £20, 20 by glass **Notes** Sunday L, Vegetarian available, Air con **Seats** 55 **Children** Portions, Menu **Parking** 25

See advert on page 411

West Stoke House

◎◎◎ — *see page 411*

CLIMPING
Map 6 SU90

Bailiffscourt Hotel & Spa

◎◎ Modern British

Fascinating architectural folly offering creative modern cooking

☎ 01903 723511   📠 01903 723107
BN17 5RW
e-mail: bailiffscourt@hshotels.co.uk
web: www.hshotels.co.uk
dir: From A27 (Arundel) take A284 towards Littlehampton. Take A259. Hotel signed towards Climping Beach

It is amazing what you can achieve with pockets as deep as Lord Moyne, aka Walter Guinness of the stout-brewing dynasty. At first sight, Bailiffscourt appears to be a medieval hamlet rooted into the Sussex coast. But it didn't exist before 1927, when the stonework and timbers were relocated from around England in a colossal project of architectural salvage. Since 1948, the faux-medieval manor house has been a sumptuous hotel packed with coffered ceilings, stone fireplaces and mullioned windows. The Tapestry restaurant, with its carved wooden ceiling, leaded windows in stone frames and tapestry-hung walls, continues the medieval charade. Happily, the kitchen is firmly rooted in the 21st century: precise, solidly-classical treatment is applied to upmarket ingredients to give sharp, well-judged flavour combinations. Dinner impresses at all stages: South

Coast crab ravioli with scallop velouté and tomato oil might precede roast rack of Sussex lamb in a grain mustard and peppercorn crust, with fondant potato, Provençal vegetables and rosemary jus.

Chef Russell Williams **Owner** Pontus & Miranda Carminger **Times** 12-1.30/7-9.30 **Prices** Fixed L 2 course £15.95, Fixed D 3 course fr £46, Service optional **Wines** 120 bottles over £20, 6 bottles under £20, 12 by glass **Notes** ALC 3 course £46, Sunday L, Vegetarian available, Dress restrictions, Smart casual, no jeans or T-shirts, Civ Wed 60 **Seats** 70, Pr/dining room 70 **Children** Portions, Menu **Parking** 80

COPTHORNE

For restaurant details see Gatwick Airport (London), (Sussex, West)

CRAWLEY

For restaurant details see Gatwick Airport (London), (Sussex, West)

CUCKFIELD
Map 6 TQ32

Ockenden Manor

◎◎◎ — *see below*

Ockenden Manor

CUCKFIELD
Map 6 TQ32

Modern French V 🏆

Creative cuisine in an elegant manor house

☎ 01444 416111   📠 01444 415549
Ockenden Ln RH17 5LD
e-mail: reservations@ockenden-manor.com
web: www.hshotels.co.uk
dir: Village centre

This delightful Elizabethan manor house is a slice of Sussex idyll to gladden the heart, tucked away down a tiny lane off the high street of postcard-pretty Cuckfield. Eight acres of grounds hold neatly-clipped topiary, a secluded walled garden, and a terrace with views across rolling fields to the South Downs. It is a cheerful summery place, considering its Tudor origins, bright and well-lit with a buttercup sheen to the décor that combines with

the warm welcome from smiling, professional staff to lift the spirits. The oak-panelled dining room is a fitting venue for seriously good French-oriented food. A rich seam of technical expertise and creativity runs through the set-price and seven-course tasting menus, all the way from an amuse-bouche of chilled gazpacho with white crab meat, via saddle and breast of new season lamb with confit fennel, courgette Provençale and a rosemary-skewered brochette of smoked bacon and kidney, to a textbook-perfect dessert of caramelised lemon tart with blackcurrant sorbet. The quality of the produce shines from start to finish, and there's an intelligent wine list brimming with pricey temptation.

Chef Steve Crane **Owner** The Goodman & Carminger Family **Times** 12-2/7-9 **Prices** Fixed L 2 course £14.95-£16.95, Fixed D 3 course £49.50, Service optional, Groups min 10 service 10% **Wines** 207 bottles over £20, 11 by glass **Notes** ALC fixed price, Sunday L, Vegetarian menu, Dress restrictions, No jeans, T-shirts, Civ Wed 74 **Seats** 40, Pr/dining room 75 **Parking** 45

EAST GRINSTEAD
Map 6 TQ33

Anise
◉◉ Modern British 🌿

Contemporary restaurant with creative cuisine to match

☎ 01342 337768 & 337700 📠 01342 337715
The Felbridge Hotel & Spa, London Rd RH19 2BH
e-mail: info@felbridgehotel.co.uk
web: www.felbridgehotel.co.uk
dir: A22 (southbound), 200mtrs beyond East Grinstead boundary sign

The Felbridge Hotel and Spa's restaurant offers a touch of metropolitan style after a modish makeover has injected understated hues of grey, cream and black to go with high-backed leather chairs, crisp white linen and gleaming silverware. The kitchen is well-placed to delve into the best produce from Sussex, Kent and Surrey for the foundations of its creative menus. Modern British cuisine with a clear French leaning is the order of the day, woven with a lively imagination that comes up with some engaging variations on tried-and-tested themes. South coast skate wing is poached in butter and served with pickled samphire, pancetta, golden raisin and chicory salad in a typical starter, then perhaps South Downs lamb as a poached fillet, kidney and tongue with pea, broad bean, mint, girolle and lamb broth flavours.

Chef Matthew Budden **Owner** New Century, East Grinstead Ltd **Times** 12-2/6.30-10 **Prices** Fixed L 3 course £25-£36.90, Fixed D 3 course £25-£36.90, Service added but optional 12.5% **Wines** 64 bottles over £20, 6 bottles under £20, 12 by glass **Notes** Sunday L, Vegetarian available, Civ Wed 200, Air con **Seats** 34, Pr/dining room 20 **Children** Portions, Menu **Parking** 200

See advert below

Gravetye Manor Hotel
◉◉◉ *— see page 414*

GATWICK AIRPORT (LONDON)
Map 6 TQ24

La Brasserie
◉ British, French NEW

Fine dining at a stylish airport hotel

☎ 01293 567070 & 555000 📠 01293 567739
Sofitel London Gatwick, North Terminal RH6 0PH
e-mail: h6204-re@accor.com
dir: M23 junct 9, North Terminal at Gatwick Airport

London Gatwick isn't exactly the first place that springs to mind on the list of culinary destinations, but the high standards of the Sofitel brand have sprinkled a bit of French magic here. Just off the soaring central atrium, the brasserie restaurant is styled in a clean-cut contemporary vein, featuring lots of wood, chrome and glass, but what stands out is the attentive staff whose friendly hospitality makes dining here a real pleasure. The kitchen uses high quality ingredients in accurately-cooked, well-thought-out dishes. Take rillettes of pork, duck and foie gras with Calvados jelly, crisp apple salad and onion toast to start, then free-range Rusper lamb (cutlets and sautéed sweetbreads) served with caramelised shallots, potato drop scone and port wine jus.

Chef David Woods **Owner** S Arora **Times** 6.30-10.30 Closed L all week **Prices** Fixed D 3 course fr £26, Starter £5.55-£10.75, Main £14.95-£23.95, Dessert £5.75-£7.50, Service added but optional 12.5% **Wines** 36 bottles over £20, 2 bottles under £20, 15 by glass **Notes** Vegetarian available, Dress restrictions, Smart casual, Air con **Seats** 85, Pr/dining room 40 **Children** Portions, Menu **Parking** 100

Langshott Manor
◉◉ Modern British V

Impressive cooking in elegant manor house

☎ 01293 786680 📠 01293 783905
Langshott Ln, Horley RH6 9LN
e-mail: admin@langshottmanor.com
dir: From A23 take Ladbroke Rd, off Chequers rdbt to Langshott, after 0.75m hotel on right

Despite being only 5 minutes from Gatwick Airport, this attractive timber-framed Elizabethan manor house has a rural feel. The Mulberry restaurant boasts original features that include leaded windows overlooking the landscaped gardens and pond. The elegant room, enhanced by contemporary artwork, discreet modern décor and smart linen-clad tables, is the backdrop for some serious and impressive cooking, with its roots firmly in the modern British camp and a keen eye on quality and seasonality, including some produce from the hotel's garden. Loin of venison comes with spiced pear and parsnip, and milk-poached turbot with leeks and potato purée, while desserts might include coconut rice pudding, poached pineapple and coconut sorbet.

continued

GATWICK AIRPORT (LONDON) *continued*

Chef Phil Dixon **Owner** Peter & Deborah Hinchcliffe
Times 12-2.30/7-9.30 **Prices** Fixed L 2 course fr £15,
Fixed D 3 course fr £42, Tasting menu £55, Service added
but optional 12.5% **Wines** 120 bottles over £20, 6 bottles
under £20, 11 by glass **Notes** Sunday L, Vegetarian menu,
Dress restrictions, Smart casual, no jeans or shorts, Civ
Wed 60 **Seats** 55, Pr/dining room 22 **Children** Portions
Parking 25

The Old House Restaurant

◉ Traditional

Sound cooking in charming old cottage

☎ 01342 712222 📄 01342 716493
Effingham Rd, Copthorne RH10 3JB
e-mail: info@oldhouserestaurant.co.uk
dir: M23 junct 10, A264 to East Grinstead. 1st left at 2nd
rdbt, left at x-rds, restaurant 0.75m on left

Set on the edge of the village of Copthorne, just a few
minutes' drive from Gatwick Airport and Crawley, this
delightful beamed 16th-century house oozes rustic charm
and features a collection of cosy lounges with intimate
lighting and comfortable seating. The sunny, elegant
dining room is suitably grand, in gold, cream and navy,
without being over-bearing. The emphasis is on good
quality ingredients, locally sourced wherever possible;
from the essentially traditional menu, begin with smoked

chicken and leek terrine with spiced tomato coulis and
move on to grilled pork loin, spiced apple purée and grain
mustard dressing. Round off with egg custard tart and
cinnamon ice cream.

The Old House Restaurant

Chef Alan Pierce **Owner** Mr & Mrs C Dormon
Times 12.15-2/6.30-9.30 Closed Xmas, New Year, Mon, L
Sat, D Sun **Prices** Fixed L 2 course £10, Fixed D 3 course
£26, Starter £6-£11, Main £18-£30, Dessert £6.50,
Service added but optional 10% **Wines** 112 bottles over
£20, 18 bottles under £20, 8 by glass **Notes** Sunday L,
Vegetarian available, Dress restrictions, Smart casual, no
jeans or trainers, Air con **Seats** 80, Pr/dining room 35
Parking 45

Restaurant 1881

◉◉ Modern French, Mediterranean

Good views and sound European cooking

☎ 01293 862166 📄 01293 862773
Stanhill Court Hotel, Stanhill Rd, Charlwood RH6 0EP
e-mail: enquiries@stanhillcourthotel.co.uk
dir: Please telephone for directions

Situated on Stan Hill in the medieval village of
Charlwood, the attractive Stanhill Court Hotel was built in
1881 as a family home for a Lloyds of London underwriter.
Built in Scottish baronial style, it has pitch pine panelling
with elaborate carvings, a minstrels' gallery and a barrel
roof with stained glass windows. Restaurant 1881,
formerly the main dining room of the house, has golden
wood panelling, elegantly set tables and a romantic
atmosphere aided by stunning views over the 35 acres of
gardens and ancient woodland. The menu deals in
European cooking, with simple, well-presented dishes
such as smoked salmon and crayfish salad with citrus
crème fraîche, followed by parmesan-glazed poached
smoked haddock with wholegrain mustard mash, wilted
spinach and petit pois.

Times 12-3/7-11 Closed L Sat

Gravetye Manor Hotel

| **EAST GRINSTEAD** | **Map 6 TQ33** |

Modern British 🍴

**Country-house cooking in oak-panelled splendour, with
gardens to match**

☎ 01342 810567 📄 01342 810080
Vowells Ln RH19 4LJ
e-mail: info@gravetyemanor.co.uk
dir: From M23 junct 10 take A264 towards East
Grinstead. After 2m take B2028. After Turners Hill, follow
signs

The Manor was built in Shakespeare's heyday by one
Richard Infield for his wife Katherine. In its time, the
house has been used as a store for smuggled goods, but
it was set firmly on the path of respectability by the
Victorian gardener William Robinson, who bought it in
1884, and designed the quintessential English gardens

that are still on view. The old-school tone extends to an
oak-panelled dining-room, where some skilful,
knowledgeable cooking is on display. The style mixes and
matches European modes, as when wood-pigeon and
seared foie gras are presented on a sheet of open
lasagna, and served with shredded cabbage and a
creamed celeriac sauce. Presentations might hark back
to an earlier era, so that a timbale of shellfish risotto is
wrapped in courgette strips to accompany sea bass, its
skin scored and browned from the frying. Classy desserts
include prune and Armagnac soufflé with matching ice
cream.

Chef Mark Raffan **Owner** A Russell & M Raffan
Times 12.30-2/7-9.30 Closed D 25 Dec **Prices** Fixed L 2
course £20, Fixed D 3 course £37, Starter £12, Main £29,
Dessert £11, Service added but optional 12.5%
Wines 500 bottles over £20, 15 bottles under £20, 25 by
glass **Notes** Vegetarian available, Dress restrictions,
Jacket & tie preferred, Civ Wed 45 **Seats** 50, Pr/dining
room 20 **Children** Portions **Parking** 45

GOODWOOD
Map 6 SU80

The Richmond Arms/The Goodwood Park Hotel

◉◉ Modern

Good food on the Goodwood Estate

☎ 01243 775537 📠 01243 520120
PO18 0QB
e-mail: reservations@thegoodwoodparkhotel.co.uk
dir: Just off A285, 3m NE of Chichester. Follow signs for Goodwood. In Goodwood Estate follow signs for hotel

Dating from 1786, this former coaching inn stands at the heart of the smart modern hotel and country club complex, noted for its excellent golf course and leisure facilities, set within the impressive 12,000 acre Goodwood Estate. Housed in the old stable block, with skylights, exposed rafters and a modern, contemporary feel, the barn-themed fine dining restaurant offers competent modern British cooking with adventurous flavours. Imaginative dishes make good use of top-notch local ingredients, as seen in a simple, well-executed starter of chicken, leek and prune terrine with pickled vegetables. A main dish of black bream served with a punchy, well-timed wild garlic risotto is equally impressive, and rich treacle tart with clotted cream rounds proceedings off nicely.

Chef Tim Powell **Owner** The Goodwood Estate Company Ltd **Times** 12-2.30/6-10.30 **Prices** Fixed L 2 course £18.50-£20, Fixed D 3 course £25-£30, Starter £6-£8.50, Main £16.50-£20, Dessert £6-£8, Service optional **Wines** 55 bottles over £20, 14 bottles under £20, 10 by glass **Notes** Sunday L, Vegetarian available, Civ Wed 120 **Seats** 80, Pr/dining room 120 **Children** Portions **Parking** 350

HAYWARDS HEATH
Map 6 TQ32

Jeremy's at Borde Hill

◉ Modern European

Modern European cooking in restaurant with attractive terrace

☎ 01444 441102 📠 01444 441355
Balcombe Rd RH16 1XP
e-mail: reservations@jeremysrestaurant.com
dir: 1.5m N of Haywards Heath. From M23 junct 10a take A23 through Balcombe

Located on the beautiful Borde Hill Estate, this converted stable block overlooks a Victorian walled garden and

boasts a fabulous south-facing terrace for when the Sussex sun is shining. The warmly coloured interior combines wooden floors and high-backed leather chairs with modern art on the walls. A menu of contemporary European cooking utilises the best seasonal produce, with dishes such as tortellini of pumpkin on radicchio and sage followed by saddle of rare Balcombe Estate venison with chestnut and truffled risotto and Madeira consommé. Finish with lemon posset with hazelnut meringue.

Chef J & V Ashpool, Richard Cook **Owner** Jeremy & Vera Ashpool **Times** 12-2.30/7-9.30 Closed 1st 2 wks Jan, Mon, D Sun **Prices** Tasting menu £32.50-£50, Starter £8-£10, Main £14.50-£23, Dessert £6-£8.50, Service optional, Groups min 8 service 10% **Wines** 70 bottles over £20, 18 bottles under £20, 10 by glass **Notes** Tasting menu Tue evening, Sunday L, Vegetarian available, Civ Wed 55 **Seats** 55 **Children** Portions **Parking** 20

HORSHAM
Map 6 TQ13

Restaurant Tristan

◉◉ Modern British, French

Adventurous modern cooking in a late-medieval hall

☎ 01403 255688
3 Stan's Way, East St RH12 1HU
e-mail: info@restauranttristan.co.uk
dir: Please telephone for directions

A heavily beamed building dating from the 1500s is the setting for a chef who trained with Marco Pierre White to show his paces. Tucked away just off Horsham's main street, it manages to be cosy and intimate, with neatly laid tables, at the same time as having bags of architectural character. Modern Anglo-French is the best way of describing cooking that might pair foie gras with camomile jelly, or rump and rack of lamb with a razor clam and black beans. That said, there are enjoyably rustic dishes too, like daube of beef with lardons and baby onions, and sea bream with herb salad. The richly oozy chocolate fondant does what is expected of it.

Chef Tristan Mason **Owner** Tristan Mason
Times 12-2.30/6.30-9.30 Closed Sun, Mon **Prices** Food prices not confirmed for 2010. Please telephone for details. **Wines** 44 bottles over £20, 6 bottles under £20, 7 by glass **Notes** Vegetarian available, Dress restrictions, Smart casual **Seats** 40

LOWER BEEDING
Map 6 TQ22

The Camellia Restaurant at South Lodge Hotel

◉◉◉ — see page 416

The Pass

◉◉◉ — see page 416

MANNINGS HEATH
Map 6 TQ22

Goldings Restaurant

◉ Modern British

Impressive cooking against a background of serious golf

☎ 01403 210228 📠 01403 270974
Mannings Heath Golf Club, Hammerpond Rd RH13 6PG
e-mail: enquiries@manningsheath.com
dir: From Horsham A281, for 2m. Approaching Mannings Heath, left at Dun Horse. To T-junct, left, then past village green. At T-junct, right, then right again

The restaurant arm of a Sussex golf club, Goldings is housed in a grand lodge full of rustic beams, and caters to golfers as well as a general local clientele. The simply written menus produce some impressive fare, from the pie and mash or minute steak and chips available in the lounge bar, to the full-dress Goldings deal. The latter takes in salmon tartare with herbed crème fraîche and citrus dressing, slow-roast belly of local pork on Puy lentils, with apple compôte and cider jus, and the delectable nougat glacé with raspberry sauce to finish.

Times 12-3/7-9 Closed D Sun-Wed

MIDHURST
Map 6 SU82

Spread Eagle Hotel and Spa

◉◉ Modern British 🌱

Accomplished classical cooking amidst Tudor character

☎ 01730 816911 📠 01730 815668
South St GU29 9NH
e-mail: reservations@spreadeagle-midhurst.com
dir: Town centre

Character is not in short supply at this ancient coaching inn, whose oldest parts date back to 1430. The venerable building creaks like a ship in a storm and is crammed with features - oak panelling and beams, Tudor bread ovens, Flemish stained glass, and a wig closet in the suite where, it is said, Elizabeth I stayed when she was in town. A vast copper-canopied stone fireplace separates the two adjoining rooms of the restaurant, where Christmas puddings dangling from the beams make a talking point for diners. Good technical skill and clear flavours are apparent in the cooking, typically smoked ham, pheasant and foie gras terrine with home-made piccalilli and toasted walnut and fig loaf, and steak and oyster pudding with mash, roasted root vegetables and red wine jus. Modern fun appears at dessert with a foam-topped chocolate and coffee cappuccino mousse.

Chef Gary Moreton-Jones **Owner** The Goodman family **Times** 12.30-2/7-9.30 **Prices** Fixed L 2 course £15.95, Fixed D 3 course £38.50, Service optional **Wines** 50 bottles over £20, 20 bottles under £20, 15 by glass **Notes** Sunday L, Vegetarian available, Dress restrictions, Smart casual, Civ Wed 80 **Seats** 50, Pr/dining room 12 **Children** Portions, Menu **Parking** 70

The Camellia Restaurant at South Lodge Hotel

LOWER BEEDING Map 6 TQ22

British, Mediterranean **V**

Technically impressive food with Downland views

☎ 01403 891711 📠 01403 891766
South Lodge Hotel, Brighton Rd RH13 6PS
e-mail: enquiries@southlodgehotel.co.uk
dir: On A23 left onto B2110. Turn right through Handcross to A281 junct. Turn left, hotel on right

If you're looking to forget about the realities of the real world for a while, then you can do a lot worse than visit South Lodge. The 19th-century lodge has wonderfully therapeutic views over the rolling South Downs and a sense of opulent luxury pervades throughout. Outside 90 acres of mature grounds are there to explore - note the 100-year old camellia wending its way up the wall that gave the restaurants its name - while afternoon tea in the lounge is a special treat. The candlelit restaurant maintains the special atmosphere with its wooden panels, oil paintings, chandeliers and ornate table lamps, crisp white linen, and views over the grounds. Service is professional without being over-the-top. The cooking balances excellent flavours and showcases a range of different cooking techniques. There's a good value lunch menu and the carte is split into classic and modern sections (you can cut and paste between the two). Start with a classic crayfish and Selsey prawn cocktail with saffron mayonnaise and broiled lemon and follow on with sea bass en papillote with new potatoes, fennel, smoked garlic and ginger. Impressively, every wine on the 200-odd list is available by the glass. The Pass (see entry) is the hotel's avante-garde take on the chef's table concept - an actual mini-restaurant in the kitchen.

Chef Lewis Hamblet **Owner** Exclusive Hotels **Times** 12-2.30/7-10 **Prices** Fixed L 2 course £15, Starter £9-£18, Main £19-£39, Dessert £9-£11, Service added but optional 10% **Wines** 250 bottles over £20, 4 bottles under £20, 250 by glass **Notes** Sunday L, Vegetarian menu, Civ Wed 130 **Seats** 75, Pr/dining room 140 **Children** Portions, Menu **Parking** 200

The Pass

LOWER BEEDING Map 6 TQ22

Modern European **NEW V**

☎ 01403 891711 📠 01403 891766
South Lodge Hotel, Brighton Rd RH13 6PS
e-mail: enquiries@southlodgehotel.co.uk
dir: From A23 turn left onto B2110 & then right through Handcross to A281

South Lodge has already made an impression as an elegant and luxurious hotel with a classy restaurant (Camellia, see entry), but it has now positioned itself at the cutting edge with the arrival of The Pass restaurant. For those not in the know, the pass is the area in the kitchen where dishes are given the once over by the head chef and then passed to the waiting staff. The chef's table concept is taking off around the country, but here at South Lodge there is a restaurant in the kitchen. It's all very modern, in keeping with the stainless steel of the kitchen, with lime green and cream leather seating and small plasma screens offering a view of the action to those with their backs to the pass. The tables run the length of the pass and there is a true sense of being at the heart of things. Choose from a selection of tasting menus of either four, seven or nine courses (there's a vegetarian option, too). Cooking is in the modern European vein with lively ideas, excellent presentation, and first-class ingredients. Terrine of confit rabbit, duck liver and pear with baby artichoke and liquorice syrup is an expertly crafted starter, and main-course fillet of bream is served with sautéed crosnes, fennel purée and lemongrass beurre blanc. A glazed lemon tart (excellent pastry) comes with yogurt sorbet and lime espuma. Service is formal and professional and being in the kitchen doesn't mean you miss out on amuse-bouche or petit four.

Chef Matt Gillan **Owner** Exclusive Hotels **Times** 12-2/7-9 Closed 1st 2 wks Jan, Mon-Tue **Prices** Food prices not confirmed for 2010. Please telephone for details, Service added but optional 10% **Wines** 200+ bottles over £20, 200+ by glass **Notes** Fixed L 4, 6 course £28 & £38, D 7, 9 course £68 & £78, Sunday L, Vegetarian menu, Air con **Seats** 22 **Children** Menu **Parking** 200

ROWHOOK
Map 6 TQ13

The Chequers Inn

⚜ Modern British

Good British cooking in rural pub

☎ 01403 790480
RH12 3PY
e-mail: thechequersrowhook@googlemail.com
dir: From Horsham A281 towards Guildford. At rdbt take
A29 signed London. In 200mtrs left, follow Rowhook signs

The inn in the hamlet of Rowhook dates from the 15th
century and is a classic rustic country bolthole with open
fires, oak beams, flagstone floors and wooden tables. It's
a warm and welcoming place with a laid-back
atmosphere and superb choice of well-kept real ales.
Top-notch Sussex produce appears in the bar menu, in
honest-to-goodness pub fodder, such as home-made
sausages with mash and onion gravy or bacon roly-poly
with home-made black pudding and free range duck egg.
The restaurant menu ups the culinary ante to offer well-
prepared modern British dishes with sound flavour
combinations, as in Scottish scallops with Jerusalem
artichoke purée, crispy pancetta and toasted celery seeds,
followed by roast chump of Sussex lamb with chorizo,
cannellini beans and Sarladaise potatoes.

Chef Tim Neal **Owner** Mr & Mrs Neal **Times** 12-2/7-9
Closed 25 Dec, D Sun **Prices** Starter £5.50-£9.75, Main
£13.50-£16.95, Dessert £5.50-£6.95, Service optional,
Groups min 8 service 10% **Wines** 22 bottles over £20, 29
bottles under £20, 8 by glass **Notes** Vegetarian available
Seats 40 **Children** Portions **Parking** 40

RUSPER
Map 6 TQ23

Ghyll Manor Hotel & Restaurant

⚜⚜ English, French

**Creative and accomplished cooking at peaceful
country-house hotel**

☎ 0845 345 3426 📠 01293 871419
High St RH12 4PX
e-mail: reception@ghyllmanor.co.uk
web: www.ghyllmanor.co.uk
dir: M23 junct 11, join A264 signed Horsham. Continue to
3rd rdbt, take 3rd exit towards Faygate and Rusper

A half-timbered 16th-century mansion in 45 acres of idyllic
grounds in the West Sussex village of Rusper, Ghyll Manor
has all the essentials of the classic English country house.
For aperitifs, there's a summery conservatory, or the terrace
overlooking the lake is a perfect spot on a balmy evening.
The oak-beamed Purus Restaurant is in the original part of
the house, so has heaps of period character and a relaxed,
cosy ambience. The kitchen goes in for a simple English
style with a strong French influence in its fixed-price dinner
menus - expect dishes such as smoked chicken and foie
gras terrine with ginger purée and brioche to start, while
mains might turn up a pork tenderloin with port wine
onions, creamed Puy lentils and roasted potatoes.

Chef Alec Mackins **Owner** Civil Service Motoring
Association **Times** 12-2/6.30-9.30 **Prices** Food prices not
confirmed for 2010. Please telephone for details.

Wines 76 bottles over £20, 16 bottles under £20, 8 by
glass **Notes** Sunday L, Vegetarian available, Dress
restrictions, Smart casual, Civ Wed 120 **Seats** 40, Pr/
dining room 30 **Children** Portions **Parking** 100

SIDLESHAM
Map 5 SZ89

The Crab & Lobster

⚜ British, Mediterranean

**Stylishly-renovated waterside hideaway with plenty of
seafood on the menu**

☎ 01243 641233
Mill Ln PO20 7NB
e-mail: enquiries@crab-lobster.co.uk
dir: A27 S onto B2145 towards Selsey. At Sidlesham turn
left onto Rookery Ln, continue for 0.75m

The Crab ticks all the right boxes if you're after a stylish
waterside bolthole that's strong on foodie pleasures.
Tucked away on the banks of Pagham Harbour Nature
Reserve, the 16th-century inn has been stylishly
transformed into a chic restaurant with rooms, blending
the textures of ancient flagstone floors and oak beams
with modern hues of damson and mushroom in a small
but perfectly-formed dining area. Naturally, locally-
caught fish and seafood is the main event, treated
without fuss, and given a Mediterranean or Asian accent
here and there. A crab and crayfish parcel is mixed with
crème fraîche cocktail sauce and wrapped in smoked

continued

SIDLESHAM *continued*

salmon to start, while sea trout comes with a rich creamy crab risotto as a main course.

Chef Sam Bakose **Owner** Sam & Janet Bakose **Times** 12-2.30/6-10 **Prices** Starter £5.25-£12.50, Main £13.50-£21.50, Dessert £4.95-£6.25, Service optional, Groups min 7 service 10% **Wines** 39 bottles over £20, 15 bottles under £20, 17 by glass **Notes** Sunday L, Vegetarian available **Seats** 54 **Children** Portions **Parking** 12

See advert on page 417

TURNERS HILL Map 6 TQ33

Alexander House Hotel & Utopia Spa

◎◎ Modern European

International cuisine in fine country-house hotel and spa

☎ 01342 714914 📠 01342 717328
East St RH10 4QD
e-mail: info@alexanderhouse.co.uk
web: www.alexanderhouse.co.uk
dir: On B2110 between Turners Hill & East Grinstead; 6m from M23 junct 10

Set on 170 acres of stunning private gardens and parkland in the heart of the Sussex countryside, Alexander House is both a boutique hotel and destination spa.This grand 17th-century country mansion has been sensitively restored and it combines understated luxury with original character. The restaurant is in the oldest part of the hotel and its opulent furnishings and impressive works of art are country-house grandeur to a tee. The cooking is based on classical French technique and brings in European and Asian flavours. Tortellini of lobster, for example, with langoustine risotto and shellfish foam to start, then perhaps Szechuan peppered beef fillet with black bean braised shin, plum and five spice purée and oriental sauce. Hot chocolate and blue cheese fondant with port sorbet and caramel tuile makes an interesting finale.

Times 12-3/7-10 Closed Mon, D Sun

Reflections at Alexander House

◎ Modern International **NEW**

Modern, relaxed hotel dining option

☎ 01342 714914 📠 01342 859759
East St RH10 4QD
e-mail: admin@alexanderhouse.co.uk
dir: From M23 junct 10 follow signs for East Grinstead. At 2nd rdbt take B2028 & follow signs for Turners Hill. Once in Turners Hill Village, turn left at the x-rds onto B2110 to East Grinstead. Hotel on left in approx 1.5m

The more casual and relaxed dining option at this boutique hotel and destination spa (see entry for Alexander House), Reflections is a sleek, contemporary space that overlooks the central courtyard and comes complete with its own champagne bar. The kitchen's straightforward brasserie-style output plays to the hotel's leisure market, offering something for everyone; from light bites (eggs Benedict) to salads (crispy duck) and veggie options (twice-baked cheese soufflé). Classics range from steak fillet burger to more adventurous pan-fried sea bass with beetroot purée, garlic pomme purée and cep mushroom foam, while daily-changing great British classics might deliver bangers and mash.

Chef Kirk Johnson **Owner** Peter & Deborah Hinchcliffe **Times** 12-3/6.30-10 **Prices** Food prices not confirmed for 2010. Please telephone for details. **Wines** 47 bottles over £20, 2 bottles under £20, 12 by glass **Notes** Vegetarian available, Air con **Seats** 70 **Children** Portions **Parking** 100

WORTHING Map 6 TQ10

Bryce's Seafood Brasserie

◎ British Seafood **NEW V**

Vibrantly fresh seafood on the Sussex coast

☎ 01903 214317 📠 01903 213842
The Steyne BN11 3DU
e-mail: info@seafoodbrasserie.co.uk
dir: On seafront at the corner of Steyne Gardens & Marine Parade

The elegant, white-fronted corner property in the centre of Worthing is home to a fine fish restaurant. A light, airy design approach is evident in stripped-wood floors, well-spaced tables and an open-plan kitchen, while in the summer months, there is seating on an outside decked area. Smartly dressed staff ensure things run smoothly. Locally sourced fish and shellfish find their way into dishes that are partly traditional combinations - scampi tails with tartare sauce, skate wing with lemon and caper butter - and partly stalwarts of the modern repertoire, such as seared scallops on cauliflower purée, teamed with herb-crusted black pudding. Ask about the chef's dish of the day, which could be something like vibrantly fresh plaice meunière served on the bone. (Same owner as Bryce's Restaurant & Country Pub in Ockley, Surrey; see entry).

Chef Richard Attkins **Owner** Bill & Elizabeth Bryce **Times** 12-3/6-10 Closed 25-26 Dec, 1 Jan, D Sun (Nov, Jan-Feb) **Prices** Fixed L 2 course £10, Fixed D 3 course £15, Starter £5.25-£6.95, Main £12.95-£15.50, Dessert £5.50, Service optional **Wines** 13 bottles over £20, 23 bottles under £20, 15 by glass **Notes** Sunday L, Vegetarian menu **Seats** 60 **Children** Portions

TYNE & WEAR

GATESHEAD Map 21 NZ26

Eslington Villa Hotel

◎ Modern British **V**

Relaxed and inviting dining in a charming setting

☎ 0191 487 6017 & 420 0666 📠 0191 420 0667
8 Station Rd, Low Fell NE9 6DR
e-mail: home@eslingtonvilla.co.uk
dir: off A1(M) exit for Team Valley Trading Estate. Right at 2nd rdbt along Eastern Av. Left at car showroom, hotel 100yds on left

There's such an air of relaxed calm about this substantial Victorian villa in 2 acres of lovely grounds, that it's hard to believe the industrial might of the Team Valley is close by. Eat in the stylish modern conservatory overlooking steeply-pitched gardens towards Newcastle city, or there's a more traditional dining room with the tartan-and-antlers character of a Victorian shooting lodge. The kitchen pulls off some highly satisfying results thanks to well-sourced seasonal ingredients that are left to speak for themselves. Pressed chicken and ham terrine with red onion jam is a typical starter, while mains might include seared salmon with vegetable and barley broth, truffle oil and herbs.

Chef Andy Moore **Owner** Mr & Mrs N Tulip **Times** 12-2/7-9.45 Closed 25-26 Dec, 1 Jan, BHs, L Sat, D Sun **Prices** Fixed L 2 course £16.50, Fixed D 3 course £22.50, Service optional **Wines** 17 bottles over £20, 24 bottles under £20, 8 by glass **Notes** Sunday L, Vegetarian menu **Seats** 80, Pr/dining room 30 **Children** Portions **Parking** 30

Blackfriars Restaurant

Traditional, Modern British

Modern dining in historical setting

☎ 0191 261 5945
Friars St NE1 4XN
e-mail: info@blackfriarsrestaurant.co.uk
web: www.blackfriarsrestaurant.co.uk
dir: Take only small cobbled road off Stowel St (China Town). Blackfriars 100yds on left

The former friar's eating hall in this early 13th-century monastery oozes medieval charm, the atmospheric, Gothic feel enhanced by massive stone walls, ancient beams, carved wooden chairs, huge inglenooks, and masses of chunky candles. In this unusual setting, expect to find a menu listing traditional and modern British dishes based on fresh local ingredients, with interesting flavours and simple, contemporary presentation. Try game terrine with pickled pears, haddock with grain mustard sauce, and chocolate tart with vanilla cream and raspberry coulis. There is also a peaceful courtyard for summer dining.

Chef Troy Terrington, Christopher Reygate **Owner** Andy & Sam Hook **Times** 12-2.30/6-12 Closed Good Fri & BHs, D Sun **Prices** Fixed L 2 course fr £12, Starter £5-£8, Main £9-£20, Dessert £5-£8, Service added but optional 10% **Wines** 26 bottles over £20, 17 bottles under £20, 8 by glass **Notes** Sunday L, Vegetarian available, Air con **Seats** 80, Pr/dining room 50 **Children** Portions, Menu **Parking** Car park next to restaurant

Brasserie Black Door

Modern British NEW

Brasserie dining in a commercial art gallery

☎ 0191 260 5411   📠 0191 260 5422
The Biscuit Factory, Shieldfield NE2 1AN
e-mail: info@blackdoorgroup.co.uk
dir: Please telephone for directions

The Biscuit Factory is Britain's largest commercial art gallery, an expansive, thriving space where works of art are displayed, auctioned and re-framed. The high warehouse ceilings and tall windows have been used to great effect in the conversion, and in the Black Door brasserie, the place boasts a fine eatery, the kind of place where you can dine in unhurried fashion from a menu of unpretentious modern dishes. Nods to older British tradition are also evident in the pease pudding that comes with a starter of seared chicken livers in sherry vinegar dressing, or the steamed mutton pudding main course with rosemary gravy. A piece of cod is nicely timed and well set off with roasted root veg and a dressing of olive oil and capers, while dessert might be pear financier with today's must-have salted caramel ice cream.

Chef David Kennedy **Owner** David Ladd, David Kennedy **Times** 12-3/7-10 Closed 25-26 Dec, D Sun **Prices** Fixed L 2 course fr £10, Fixed D 3 course fr £18.95, Starter £4.50-£7.95, Main £10-£20, Dessert £3.50-£6.50, Service added but optional 10% **Wines** 7 bottles over £20, 7 bottles under £20, 8 by glass **Notes** Sunday L, Vegetarian available, Air con **Seats** 70, Pr/dining room 24 **Children** Portions **Parking** 10, On street

Bridge Restaurant, Vermont Hotel

Modern British V

Elegant location for quayside dining

☎ 0191 233 1010   📠 0191 233 1234
Castle Garth NE1 1RQ
e-mail: info@vermont-hotel.co.uk
dir: City centre by high level bridge & castle keep

Next to the castle and overlooking the cathedral and the Tyne and Millennium bridges, the Vermont has a setting which is hard to beat. Built of Portland stone in 1910 and originally the County Hall, the Grade II listed building has the look of a Manhattan-style tower block about it. The aptly named Bridge Restaurant is on the 6th floor, looking directly out onto the Tyne Bridge. Smart leather chairs, banquette seating and white-clothed tables create a formal setting in which to enjoy a modern British menu. Begin with smoked mackerel fishcakes with horseradish crème fraîche, moving on to lamb rump with crushed potato and a tomato and basil jus, or butter-roasted pollock with cannellini beans, pancetta and pearl potatoes.

Chef Mark Percival **Owner** Lincoln Group
Times 12-2.30/6-11 **Prices** Fixed L 2 course fr £16, Fixed D 3 course fr £26 **Wines** 6 bottles over £20, 24 bottles under £20, 12 by glass **Notes** Couples menu Fri-Sun, Sunday L, Vegetarian menu, Civ Wed 150, Air con **Seats** 80, Pr/dining room 2-120 **Children** Portions **Parking** 80

Café 21 Newcastle

French, International V

Modern bistro eating by the revamped quayside

☎ 0191 222 0755   📠 0191 221 0761
Trinity Gardens, Quayside NE1 2HH
e-mail: bh@cafetwentyone.co.uk
dir: Please telephone for directions

A smart city-centre venue tucked away in a quiet street behind the law courts, near the redeveloped quayside, Café 21 is the image of a modern urban restaurant. With slate-grey walls, a dark wooden floor and cushioned banquettes, it's both understated and comfortable. The well-wrought bistro cooking answers to today's tastes too, with coarse-textured country pâté and cornichons, truffled chicken breast with grilled baby leeks and a poached egg, and crème brûlée to finish, constituting a highly satisfying lunch. Special prices for early evening diners tempt, as will dishes such as crab lasagne with langoustine cappuccino, or the 21-day-aged Northumbrian beef with béarnaise or roasted bone marrow.

Chef Christopher Dobson **Owner** Mr & Mrs T Laybourne **Times** 12-2.30/5.30-10.30 Closed 25-26 Dec, 1 Jan **Prices** Fixed L 2 course fr £15, Fixed D 3 course fr £18, Starter £7.50-£13.50, Main £14.50-£28.50, Dessert £5-£8.50, Service added but optional 10% **Wines** 98 bottles over £20, 11 bottles under £20, 21 by glass **Notes** Fixed price D Mon-Sat 5.30-7, Sunday L, Vegetarian menu, Air con **Seats** 129, Pr/dining room 40 **Children** Portions **Parking** NCP

NEWCASTLE UPON TYNE *continued*

Jesmond Dene House

◉◉◉ *– see below*

Malmaison Newcastle

◉ French

Good brasserie dining in trendy location

☎ 0191 245 5000 🖹 0191 245 4545
Quayside NE1 3DX
e-mail: newcastle@malmaison.com
dir: Telephone for directions

Malmaison's Newcastle branch is in the thick of the action in the upbeat revitalised quayside quarter overlooking the Millennium Bridge. The former warehouse has all the hallmarks of the 'Mal' brand: boudoir-chic shades of deep purple, crimson and plum, and textures of velvet, chrome, wood and leather. The moodily-lit bar has high stools and aubergine-coloured leather sofas and views of the River Tyne. After getting acquainted with the well-chosen wines that are a cornerstone of the Malmaison ethos, move into the brasserie, where the kitchen deals in classics with a modern spin - take corned beef terrine with warm piccalilli, or salmon and cod fishcake with spinach and beurre blanc. The 'Home Grown and Local' menu showcases produce from Tyneside and Northumbria.

Times 12-2.30/6-11

Sidney's Restaurant

◉ Modern British

Buzzing bistro in Tynemouth town centre

☎ 0191 257 8500 & 213 0284 🖹 0191 257 9800
3-5 Percy Park Rd NE30 4LZ
e-mail: bookings@sidneys.co.uk
dir: A1058 & follow signs for Tynemouth Village. Restaurant on corner of Front St & Percy Park Rd

Set back from Tynemouth's pretty seafront, this relaxed modern bistro is a local gem, with a vibrant, contemporary interior featuring local artwork, wooden floors, leather benches, and simple, unclothed tables. Diners beat a path to the door for daily menus that champion local produce, including quality, fresh fish landed at the quay, and hand-reared game and meat. Full-flavoured dishes are accurately cooked and everything is home-made, from a moist and creamy smoked chicken and spring onion risotto, and a beautifully tender pork fillet with cider fondant potato, black pudding and a rich meaty jus, to chocolate mousse with apricot sorbet for pudding. A great little bistro.

Times 12-2.30/6-12 Closed 24-26 Dec, BHs ex Good Friday, Sun

Best Western Salford Hall Hotel

◉ Modern British

Modern food in a historic setting

☎ 01386 871300 🖹 01386 871301
WR11 5UT
e-mail: reception@salfordhall.co.uk
dir: From A46 follow Salford Priors, Abbot's Salford & Harvington signs. Hotel 1.5m on left

Seventeenth-century Salford Hall has seen plenty of life in its long history: a bolthole for the bon viveur Abbot of Evesham Abbey, home to a Tudor family, and then a nunnery before becoming a hotel with spectacular views of the Severn Valley. Oak panelling, a huge walk-in fireplace, mullioned windows and chandeliers all add up to a memorable setting in the restaurant where straightforward modern British fare is the kitchen's forté. Curried mussels and clam broth flavoured with cinnamon, ginger and coriander, and marinated rump of lamb with thyme-roasted potatoes, mint, sweet pepper foam and aubergine caviar show the style.

Chef Andrew Robinson **Owner** Cube Hotels
Times 12.30-2/7-9.30 **Prices** Food prices not confirmed for 2010. Please telephone for details. **Wines** 15 bottles over £20, 22 bottles under £20, 7 by glass **Notes** Sunday

---

Jesmond Dene House

European V 🏴

Seriously good cooking in contemporarily styled grand house

☎ 0191 212 3000 🖹 0191 212 3001
Jesmond Dene Rd NE2 2EY
e-mail: info@jesmonddenehouse.co.uk
dir: From city centre follow A167 to junct with A184. Turn right towards Matthew Bank. Turn right into Jesmond Dene Rd

The sprawling Grade II listed building in the steep-sided wooded valley of Jesmond Dene was created by shipbuilding magnate Lord Armstrong in 1822 (the man was clearly doing rather well for himself). Despite being only five minutes from the town, it has a decidedly rural feel and there is an overwhelming sense of calm and

tranquillity about the place; make time for a gentle stroll in the gardens before lunch or dinner. Although many original features have been retained, the hotel is thoroughly contemporary in style. The restaurant is split into two attractive dining areas - the former music room and the light-and-airy Garden Room. The cooking is in the modern vein: European in focus, based around classical techniques, and hits the target when it comes to delivering clear and precise flavours. Black ink risotto with good bite comes with grilled baby squid and spring onions in a fine first course, and main-course roast collar of Berkshire pork is a beautifully cooked piece of meat, served with braised chicory, orange and ginger crisps. A thrilling finish is supplied by warm Maragda chocolate tart with mint ice cream.

Chef Pierre Rigothier **Owner** Terry Laybourne, Peter Candler **Times** 12-2.30/7-10.30 **Prices** Fixed L 2 course £21-£22, Fixed D 3 course £25-£35, Starter £9.50-£21.50, Main £12.50-£37, Dessert £4-£10.50, Service added but optional 10% **Wines** 217 bottles over £20, 14 bottles under £20, 17 by glass **Notes** Tasting menu & vegetarian tasting menu available, Sunday L, Vegetarian menu, Dress restrictions, Smart casual, Civ Wed 100 **Seats** 60, Pr/dining room 18 **Children** Portions, Menu **Parking** 64

L, Vegetarian available, Dress restrictions, No jeans or trainers, Civ Wed 100 **Seats** 50, Pr/dining room 50 **Children** Portions, Menu **Parking** 60

ALCESTER — Map 10 SP05

Essence

◉ Modern British NEW ✪

Modern restaurant and bar in one-time cottage

☎ 01789 762764 & 07900 210552
50 Birmingham Rd B49 5EP
e-mail: info@eatatessence.co.uk
dir: From town centre towards Birmingham & M42. Restaurant is opposite Alcester Grammar School

This small restaurant and bar set in a 17th-century cottage rather surprisingly turns out to be a modern good-looker. Combining old oak beams with simple cream-washed walls, modern art and leather chairs, while dark-wood tables and slate placemats continue the feel-good contemporary theme. The kitchen offers food to match, taking a distinctly modern approach conjured from fresh, seasonal and local produce. Take Ragley Estate venison and chestnut Wellington on a winter menu, perhaps teamed with fondant potato and sticky cherry essence, while to finish, a lemon curd soufflé with an iced lime soufflé might catch the eye.

Chef Chris Short **Owner** Chris Short **Times** 10-3/6.30-10 Closed Mon, D Sun **Prices** Starter £3.75-£9.50, Main £11.50-£19.95, Dessert £5.50-£7.95, Service optional **Wines** 20 bottles over £20, 10 bottles under £20, 6 by glass **Notes** Early D deal Tue-Fri 6.30-7.15pm, Sunday L, Vegetarian available, Air con **Seats** 42 **Children** Portions, Menu **Parking** 19

ALDERMINSTER — Map 10 SP24

Ettington Park Hotel

◉◉ British, French

Fine dining in Gothic splendour

☎ 01789 450123 📠 01789 450472
CV37 8BU
dir: M40 junct 15/A46 towards Stratford-upon-Avon, then A439 into town centre onto A3400 5m to Shipston. Hotel 0.5m on left

The dramatic Victorian-Gothic Ettington Park stands in 40-acres of tranquil formal gardens, woods and farmland in the Stour Valley, and is only 5 miles from the centre of Stratford-upon-Avon. The Oak Room Restaurant offers fine dining in magnificent surroundings, with crisp white linen, polished glassware and silver cutlery on the tables, and splendid views of the gardens and the Norman chapel. There's nothing old-world about the style of cooking: the comprehensive menu offers classic French cooking given a modern British interpretation, using top-quality produce. Expect perfectly executed dishes like pan-seared king scallops with cauliflower purée, black pudding and dill oil, or a main course of trio of Lightbourne lamb with mint hollandaise. The choice of desserts might include a dark chocolate tart with caramel and sea salt ice cream. There is also a six-course grazing menu.

Times 12-2/7-9.30 Closed L Mon-Fri

ATHERSTONE — Map 10 SP39

Chapel House Restaurant With Rooms

◉ British, French ✪

Elegant surroundings and imaginative cooking

☎ 01827 718949 📠 01827 717702
Friar's Gate CV9 1EY
e-mail: info@chapelhouse.eu
web: www.chapelhouse.eu
dir: Off Market Sq in Atherstone, behind High St

Florence Nightingale was a frequent visitor to this hidden gem, the one-time dower house to Atherstone Hall. Set within tranquil walled gardens in a corner of the historic market square, Chapel House was built in 1728 and, although extended over the years, many original features remain. The luxurious restaurant has garden views and smart white linen on the tables. The daily-changing menu offers classical French cuisine with a touch of contemporary style, and local produce is not overlooked. Expect fish dishes such as red drum baked with an almond and herb crust served with tomato and basil sauce garnished with king prawns, or chicken 'thatched cottage' - sliced breast of chicken with creamy stilton sauce, garnished with walnuts and roasted Mediterranean vegetables.

Chef Richard Henry Napper **Owner** Richard & Siobhan Napper **Times** 7-9 Closed 24 Dec-3 Jan, Etr wk, late Aug-early Sep, Sun, L all week **Prices** Food prices not confirmed for 2010. Please telephone for details. **Wines** 61 bottles over £20, 44 bottles under £20, 9 by glass **Notes** Vegetarian available, Dress restrictions,

Smart casual **Seats** 24, Pr/dining room 12 **Children** Portions **Parking** On street

KENILWORTH — Map 10 SP27

Petit Gourmand

◉ Modern British, French

Stylish bistro serving classically-based modern dishes

☎ 01926 864567 📠 01926 864510
101-103 Warwick Rd CV8 1HL
e-mail: info@petit-gourmand.co.uk
dir: A452. In main street in Kenilworth centre

New owners have installed Petit Gourmand in the premises formerly known as Simply Simpsons. After a top-to-bottom refurbishment, the interior of this laid-back contemporary brasserie is looking très chic with its bold fabrics, mellow tones of red and grey, mustard velours and crimson banquette seating. So, all change in the décor department, then, but head chef Iain Miller has stayed on in the kitchen, ensuring consistency and top quality in the contemporary Anglo-French output, which features fishcakes with petit ratatouille and pistou to start. Lamb en croûte with spinach and duxelles is served with crushed potatoes and green beans in a full-flavoured main course, and a textbook crème brûlée winds things up on a high note.

Chef Iain Miller **Owner** Midland Assured Leisure Ltd **Times** 12-2/6.15-9.45 Closed D Sun **Prices** Fixed L 2 course fr £12.95, Starter £3.95-£6.95, Main £9.95-£19.95, Dessert £5.50, Groups min 8 service 10% **Wines** 18 bottles over £20, 16 bottles under £20, 10 by glass **Notes** Sunday L, Vegetarian available, Air con **Seats** 70, Pr/dining room 54 **Children** Portions **Parking** 12

LEA MARSTON — Map 10 SP29

The Adderley Restaurant

◉ Modern British NEW V

Smart modern Midlands hotel with sound contemporary dining

☎ 01675 470468 📠 01675 470871
Lea Marston Hotel, Haunch Ln B76 0BY
e-mail: info@leamarstonhotel.co.uk
dir: From M42 junct 9/A4097 signed Kingsbury Hotel, 2nd turning right into Haunch Lane. Hotel 200yds on right

The smartly contemporary Lea Marston Hotel sits in 54 acres of grounds in pleasant Warwickshire countryside

continued on page 423

Mallory Court Hotel

Modern British **V**

Imaginative cooking in a grand country retreat

☎ 01926 330214 📄 01926 451714
Harbury Ln, Bishop's Tachbrook CV33 9QB
e-mail: reception@mallory.co.uk
dir: M40 junct 13 N'bound. Left, left again towards Bishop's Tachbrook. 0.5m, right into Harbury Ln. M40 junct 14 S'bound, A452 for Leamington. At 2nd rdbt left into Harbury Ln

Mallory Court is every inch the grand country retreat. Covered neatly in creepers, it stands amid 10 acres of immaculate gardens, with all the accoutrements a modern top-end hotel is expected to provide, from tennis courts to a pool. The Brasserie is listed separately (see entry), but the oak-panelled restaurant is where the most opulent eating takes place. On fine days, a terrace provides outdoor dining with views of the Warwickshire countryside. To a background of discreet classical music, a well-judged style of country-house cuisine is built around top-drawer ingredients on menus that change from day to day. Successful dishes include the salmon mi-cuit with pickled beetroot and horseradish mayonnaise, a starter to awaken the taste buds, and the main-course duo of veal (fillet and braised shin) that is given an extra punch of richness with a foie gras bonbon and truffle-oiled mash. Desserts take in poached rhubarb topped with crème brûlée, served with advocaat and ginger ice cream. A magisterial list of fine wines accompanies.

Chef Simon Haigh **Owner** Sir Peter Rigby **Times** 12-1.45/6.30-8.45 Closed L Sat **Prices** Fixed L 2 course £23.50, Fixed D 3 course £39.50-£55, Service optional **Wines** 2 bottles under £20, 7 by glass **Notes** Sunday L, Vegetarian menu, Dress restrictions, No jeans or sportswear, Civ Wed 160 **Seats** 56, Pr/dining room 14 **Children** Portions, Menu **Parking** 100

LEA MARSTON *continued*

close by the main Midlands motorway arteries. Not surprisingly, the venue is big on conferences and events, but that's not to the detriment of individual travellers, who will also find a friendly atmosphere and plenty of opportunity to work up a good appetite in the leisure complex and around the 9-hole golf course. Dining here is a relaxed affair, with modern British food prepared by a team that sticks to the basic culinary rules of sourcing fresh local ingredients and cooking them accurately to create clear, well-balanced flavours. A tartlet of goats' cheese and roasted vegetables with mixed leaves and pesto might precede a flavour-packed slow-roasted blade of beef served simply with squash purée, truffle mash and a shallot and tarragon jus.

Chef Richard Marshall **Owner** Blake Family
Times 7.00-9.30 **Prices** Fixed D 3 course £24.50, Starter £4.50-£11, Main £12.95-£23, Dessert £4.50-£8.95, Service optional **Wines** 26 bottles over £20, 11 bottles under £20, 6 by glass **Notes** Sunday L, Vegetarian menu, Dress restrictions, Smart dress, Civ Wed 100, Air con **Seats** 100, Pr/dining room 30 **Children** Portions, Menu **Parking** 200

LEAMINGTON SPA (ROYAL)   Map 10 SP36

The Brasserie at Mallory Court

⚯ Modern British **V**

The simpler dining option in opulent Mallory Court

☎ 01926 453939
Harbury Ln, Bishop's Tachbrook CV33 9QB
e-mail: thebrasserie@mallory.co.uk
web: www.mallory.co.uk
dir: Please telephone for details

The secondary eating option in the luxurious Mallory Court Hotel (see separate entry) is done in muted black and cream, with nods to art-deco styling. A garden for outdoor dining and a very chic cocktail bar come as part of the package too. The menu of straightforward brasserie classics is cooked with confidence, and takes in rich chicken parfait with tomato chutney and brioche, pink-cooked beef rump with truffle-oiled mash and red wine sauce, and beer-battered fish and chips. Desserts to write home about include glazed lemon tart with fine short pastry and a soft, piquant filling, served with raspberry sorbet.

Chef Simon Haigh **Owner** Sir Peter Rigby
Times 12-2.30/6.30-9.30 Closed D Sun **Prices** Fixed L 2 course fr £9.50, Fixed D 3 course fr £25, Starter fr £4, Main fr £11.50, Dessert fr £5.50, Service optional **Wines** 30 bottles over £20, 2 bottles under £20, 6 by glass **Notes** Sunday L, Vegetarian menu, Civ Wed 160, Air con **Seats** 80, Pr/dining room 24 **Children** Portions, Menu **Parking** 100

Mallory Court Hotel

⚯⚯⚯ – *see opposite page*

Restaurant 23

⚯⚯ Modern European

Modern comfort and contemporary cooking

☎ 01926 422422   📄 01926 422246
23 Dormer Place CV32 5AA
e-mail: info@restaurant23.co.uk
dir: M40 junct 13 onto A452 towards Leamington Spa. Follow signs for town centre

Occupying a Regency-style building typical of the town, the inside of this relaxed restaurant is comfortably modern and stylish. The open-plan kitchen is the main focal point of the deceptively spacious dining room, and diners can watch the chefs produce an interesting mix of classical and modern European dishes. Ingredients are well sourced and as local as possible, and flavours are clear and intelligently paired. Diver-caught scallops, for example, in a starter with cauliflower, caper and golden raisin dressing, or main-course rump of Finnebrogue venison served with fondant potato, roasted butternut squash, braised red cabbage and spiced jus. Finish with banana in the form of a sponge, mousse and 'consommé' with candied pecans and maple syrup.

Chef Peter Knibb **Owner** Peter & Antje Knibb
Times 12.15-2.30/6.15-9.45 Closed 25 Dec, 2 wks Jan, 2 wks Aug, Sun-Mon **Prices** Fixed L 2 course £14-£15, Fixed D 3 course £36-£37, Service optional, Groups min 7 service 10% **Wines** 50 bottles over £20, 14 bottles under £20, 7 by glass **Notes** Pre-theatre 2 or 3 course menu available, Vegetarian available, Air con **Seats** 24 **Parking** On street opposite

STRATFORD-UPON-AVON   Map 10 SP25

The Legacy Falcon Hotel

⚯ British **NEW**

Atmospheric hotel with ambitious cooking

☎ 0870 832 9905   📄 0870 832 9906
Chapel St CV37 6HA
e-mail: res-falcon@legacy-hotels.co.uk
dir: M40 junct 15, follow town centre signs towards Barclays Bank on rdbt. Turn into High Street, between Austin Reed & WH Smiths. Turn 2nd right into Scholars Lane & right again into hotel

The black-and-white façade of the Falcon is as every American tourist would hope it to be - picture book Stratford. Inside it is a successful blend of quite bold modernism and traditional features. Will's Place restaurant (there's a bistro, too) delivers English food with a twist or two along the way: red mullet comes with sweet potato, wilted spinach and paw paw coulis - bold flavours working well together - and main-course sea bass is served with a seared scallop, Niçoise salad, sauté potatoes, plum tomatoes and herb oil. Finish with coffee crème brûlée with coffee ice cream and shortbread.

Chef Charles Anderson **Owner** Legacy Hotels
Times 12.30-2/6-9 **Prices** Starter £4.95-£9.95, Main £10.50-£11.95, Dessert £5.50-£7.95 **Notes** Vegetarian available

Macdonald Alveston Manor

⚯ Modern British

Modern dining in an Elizabethan manor

☎ 01789 205478   📄 01789 414095
Clopton Bridge CV37 7HP
e-mail: events.alvestonmanor@macdonald-hotels.co.uk
dir: 6m from M40 junct 15, (on edge of town) across Clopton Bridge towards Banbury

Local lore has it that *A Midsummer Night's Dream* was first performed beneath a venerable cedar in the primped grounds of this eye-catching red-brick, half-timbered hotel. The old Tudor manor house hasn't lost much of its Elizabethan charm since it became a hotel; leaded windows and magnificent oak panelling and beams are still present and correct in the restaurant, although unclothed tables add a modern twist. Expect unfussy modern British dishes, as in scallops with cauliflower purée and caper vinaigrette to start, followed by breast and confit leg of mallard with potato pie and pumpkin. End with firm favourites like sticky toffee pudding or a more refined apple and brandy parfait.

Chef Jason Buck **Owner** Macdonald Hotels plc
Times 12-2.30/6-9.30 Closed L Mon-Sat **Prices** Food prices not confirmed for 2010. Please telephone for details. **Wines** 69 bottles over £20, 14 bottles under £20, 15 by glass **Notes** Pre-theatre menu available, Sunday L, Vegetarian available, Civ Wed 120, Air con **Seats** 110, Pr/dining room 40 **Children** Portions, Menu **Parking** 120

Menzies Welcombe Hotel Spa and Golf Course

⚯⚯ Modern, Traditional **V**

Traditional manor house serving seasonal food

☎ 01789 295252   📄 01789 414666
Warwick Rd CV37 0NR
e-mail: welcombe@menzieshotels.co.uk
dir: M40 junct 15, A46 to Stratford-upon-Avon. 1st rdbt left onto A439, hotel 3m on right

This Jacobean-style manor house hotel is set within 157 acres of landscaped parkland, and its Trevelyan restaurant - traditional in style with French glass chandeliers - benefits from superb views over the Italian gardens, golf course and water features. The frequently changing menu of English and European dishes utilises high quality produce with an eye on seasonality. For starters you could expect the likes of pan-fried red mullet

continued

STRATFORD-UPON-AVON *continued*

with herb linguini and shellfish broth, with main courses such as roast stuffed saddle of rabbit with spring vegetables, diced potato and tarragon cream. Save room for a dessert like rhubarb and vanilla pannacotta with blackcurrant sorbet or the platter of British and continental cheeses.

Chef Robin Smith **Owner** Menzies Hotels **Times** 12.30-2/7-9.30 Closed L Sat **Prices** Fixed L 2 course £19, Fixed D 3 course fr £35, Service optional **Wines** 125 bottles over £20, 5 bottles under £20, 16 by glass **Notes** Pre-theatre D menu available, Sunday L, Vegetarian menu, Dress restrictions, Smart casual, shirt with collar, Civ Wed 180 **Seats** 70, Pr/dining room 150 **Children** Portions, Menu **Parking** 150

Mercure Shakespeare

@ Traditional British

Contemporary cuisine in historic old building

☎ 01789 294997 📄 01789 415411
Chapel St CV37 6ER
e-mail: h6630@accor.com
dir: Follow signs to town centre. Round one-way system, into Bridge St. At rdbt turn left. Hotel 200yds on left

Situated in the centre of Stratford-upon-Avon and looking every inch the historic landmark with its traditional black-and-white timbered façade dating back to the 17th-century, this is one of the oldest hotels in the town. Inside it overflows with original beams, log fires and rich furnishings. There are two restaurants, although the David Garrick is temporarily closed as we go to press, leaving the newly-refurbished Othello's bar brasserie to fly the flag with some lively modern British cooking. It's a contemporary looking space, relaxed and casual, and delivers a menu ranging from tapas and sandwiches to pork belly with pancetta mash, wilted spinach and red wine jus, or ale-battered cod, chunky chips, pea purée and tartare sauce.

Chef Paul Harris **Owner** Mercure Hotels **Times** 12-10 **Prices** Fixed D 3 course £16.95-£25, Starter £3-£5.95, Main £8.50-£15.95, Dessert fr £4.95, Service included **Wines** 20 bottles over £20, 25 bottles under £20, 12 by glass **Notes** Pre-theatre menu available, Sunday L, Vegetarian available, Civ Wed 100 **Seats** 80, Pr/dining room 90 **Children** Portions, Menu **Parking** 35

The Stratford

@ Modern European

Comforting classics in modern hotel

☎ 01789 271000 📄 01789 271001
Arden St CV37 6QQ
e-mail: thestratfordreservations@qhotels.co.uk
web: www.qhotels.co.uk
dir: A439 into Stratford. In town follow A3400/Birmingham, at lights left into Arden Street, hotel 150yds on right

A former Victorian workhouse and hospital, this contemporary hotel is a short stroll from the town centre. The spacious restaurant comes with exposed beams and ornately carved furniture, and the cooking is an honest, straightforward mix of old and new. The crowd-pleasing range of dishes might include as a starter pan-seared chicken livers with buttered leeks, smoked bacon, black pudding and red wine jus, with main courses taking in chicken supreme stuffed with St Oswald cheese, sun-dried tomatoes, wilted greens or seared calves' liver with crisp smoked bacon and olive truffle mash.

Chef Mark Grigg **Owner** QHotels **Times** 12.30-2/6-9.45 **Prices** Fixed D 3 course £20-£30, Starter £4.50-£8.50, Main £11.50-£16.50, Dessert £5-£7, Service included **Wines** 43 bottles over £20, 12 bottles under £20, 15 by glass **Notes** Pre-theatre 2 course £19.99, 3 course £24.99, Sunday L, Vegetarian available, Civ Wed 160, Air con **Seats** 90, Pr/dining room 120 **Children** Portions, Menu **Parking** 102

Stuart Restaurant

@@ Modern, Traditional British

Modern cooking in historic manor house

☎ 01789 279955 & 767103 📄 01789 764145
Barcelo Billesley Manor Hotel, Billesley, Alcester B49 6NF
e-mail: billesleymanor@barcelo-hotels.co.uk
dir: M40 junct 15, A46 S towards Stratford/Worcester. E over three rdbts. 2m then right for Billesley

Away from the tourist bustle of Stratford, the centuries-old manor house stands in 11 acres of typically English gardens, 3 miles from Shakespeare's birthplace. Within, its public rooms are impressive, with oak panelling, leather chairs, chandeliers, old tapestries, and log fires in huge stone fireplaces, and fine garden views through stone-mullioned windows in the restaurant take in some splendid yew topiary. Well-sourced local ingredients are carefully handled, the short, modern British carte taking in such starters as seared pigeon with beetroot confit and

sage gnocchi and red wine, and chicken liver parfait with thyme butter and apple jelly. Main courses may include braised ox cheek and shallot suet pudding with thyme jus, and seared cod with mussels, saffron and spring herb nage. For pudding, try the dark chocolate and praline tart with spearmint ice cream.

Chef Ian Buckle **Owner** Barcelo Hotels **Times** 12.30-2/7-9.30 **Prices** Fixed L 3 course fr £24.95, Fixed D 3 course fr £37.50, Service optional **Wines** 46 bottles over £20, 4 by glass **Notes** Sunday L, Vegetarian available, Dress restrictions, Smart Casual, Civ Wed 100 **Seats** 42, Pr/dining room 100 **Children** Portions, Menu **Parking** 100

THURLASTON   Map 11 SP47

Draycote Hotel

@ Modern British NEW

Hotel and golf club with modern cuisine

☎ 01788 521800 📄 01788 521 695
London Rd CV23 9LF
e-mail: mail@draycotehotel.co.uk
dir: M1 junct 17 onto M45/A45. Hotel 500mtrs on left

Set in pretty Warwickshire countryside with easy access to the Midlands motorway arteries, the Draycote Hotel is handily placed for exploring the Shakespeare trail or fitting in a round of golf at its own club. The light modern structure makes the most of its voluminous design, with soaring beams above and a great sense of space in the public areas. Slurp a cocktail to the tinkling tones of a grand piano in the smart bar, before moving into the sleek contemporary style of the Papaveri restaurant. Sound cooking in a modern English vein runs from the likes of crab ravioli with parsnip purée and a creamy hazelnut sauce, to lamb three ways (chump, belly and breast, since you ask), and to finish vanilla brûlée with lovely crumbly almond shortbread.

Chef Glyn Jacklin **Owner** John Mason **Times** 12-3/7-10 Closed D 25 Dec **Prices** Fixed D 3 course £24.95, Starter £3.95-£8.95, Main £9.45-£17.50, Dessert £4.95-£6.95, Service optional **Wines** 11 bottles over £20, 21 bottles under £20, 12 by glass **Notes** Sunday L, Vegetarian available, Civ Wed 250, Air con **Seats** 100, Pr/dining room 150 **Children** Portions, Menu **Parking** 200

WARWICK
Map 10 SP26

The Lodge Restaurant at Ardencote Manor Hotel

◉ British, International

Waterside restaurant with ambitious modern menu

☎ 01926 843111 & 843939 📠 01926 842646
The Cumsey, Lye Green Rd CV35 8LT
e-mail: hotel@ardencote.com
dir: Off A4189. In Claverdon follow signs for Shrewley & brown tourist signs for Ardencote Manor, approx 1.5m

A short stroll away from the main hotel building, on the lake shore, stands the Lodge. Patio doors open on to a waterside terrace, and inside the decorative scheme is built around dark brown leather partitions. Wine-themed pictures adorn the room, while the list itself features plenty of New World treats. The Old World is very much the idiom of the menu, at least insofar as its Latin titles go. The dishes themselves are bang up-to-date, with complex combinations such as black pearl scallops with pig cheek and beetroot spring roll, truffled Belle de Fontenay potato purée and vanilla butter - and that's just for starters. With so many ingredients, balance can get out of kilter, as when cannon of well-timed lamb is overpowered by its Cashel Blue crust. There are grilled dishes from La Plancha, too.

Chef Luciano Catalinotto **Owner** TSB Developments Ltd
Times 12-3/6-11 **Prices** Fixed L 2 course fr £12.95, Starter £6-£8.95, Main £15.95-£22.50, Dessert £5.75-£7.50, Service included **Wines** 65 bottles over £20, 43 bottles under £20, 10 by glass **Notes** Sunday L, Vegetarian available, Civ Wed 180 **Seats** 75, Pr/dining room 40 **Children** Portions, Menu **Parking** 350

WELLESBOURNE
Map 10 SP25

Barcelo Walton Hall

◉◉ British NEW

Interpretations of traditional dishes in an elegant Queen Anne house

☎ 01789 842424 📠 01789 470418
Walton CV35 9HU
e-mail: waltonhall.mande@barcelo-hotels.co.uk
dir: Please telephone for directions

This member of the quality Barcelo international hotel group is a thoroughly elegant Queen Anne house, set within 65 acres of sumptuous grounds. The Moncreiffe restaurant is its flagship dining room, a handsomely attired space with boldly coloured wallpaper, dramatic chandeliers and views over the manicured lawns. Taking inspiration from classic British dishes, the cooking is well-executed, allowing for maximum flavour impact and showing formidable technical ability. You might start with a crab and prawn cocktail, elevated above the humdrum with freshest seafood, and textural contrasts of avocado purée and Bloody Mary jelly. Follow on with loin of lamb, partnered with the sautéed sweetbreads, alongside caramelised cauliflower purée, and a jus full of confit garlic, a precision performance that lives in the memory. Dessert could be as simple as lemon pannacotta with crunchy biscotti and a garnish of whole raspberries.

Chef Darren Long **Owner** Barcelo Hotels & Resorts
Prices Food prices not confirmed for 2010. Please telephone for details. **Wines** 52 bottles over £20, 13 bottles under £20, 8 by glass **Notes** Vegetarian available, Air con **Seats** 60, Pr/dining room 22 **Children** Portions, Menu **Parking** 240

WEST MIDLANDS

BALSALL COMMON
Map 10 SP27

Oak Room

◉ Modern

Delightful cooking in an attractive country house

☎ 024 7646 6174 📠 024 7647 0720
Nailcote Hall, Nailcote Ln, Berkswell CV7 7DE
e-mail: info@nailcotehall.co.uk
dir: On B4101 towards Tile Hill/Coventry, 10 mins from NEC/Birmingham Airport

A 17th-century building that was damaged by Cromwell's army during the English Civil War, Nailcote Hall stands in 15 acres of grounds with its own 9-hole championship golf course. The Oak Room restaurant with its dark beams is spacious and comfortable and the food is both ambitious and accomplished. Try the seared duck breast with a honey and black pepper glaze, spiced plums and ginger dressing for starters, or roulade of chicken for main course, served with Spanish chorizo, sweet potato rösti and roasted pepper sauce. Round off with lemon cheesecake crumble and fresh berries.

Chef Daniel Topa **Owner** Richard Cressman
Times 12-2.30/7-9.30 Closed L Sat, D Sun **Prices** Fixed L

2 course £14, Fixed D 3 course £27.50, Starter £5.25-£8.95, Main £15-£28, Dessert £5.95-£15, Service optional **Wines** 80 bottles over £20, 6 bottles under £20, 8 by glass **Notes** Sunday L, Vegetarian available, Dress restrictions, Smart casual, no jeans, trainers or T-shirts, Civ Wed 90 **Seats** 50, Pr/dining room 120 **Children** Portions, Menu **Parking** 150

BARSTON
Map 10 SP27

The Malt Shovel at Barston

◉ Traditional British

Popular local foodie pub in a rural setting

☎ 01675 443223 📠 01675 443223
Barston Ln B92 0JP
web: www.themaltshovelatbarston.com
dir: M42 junct 5, take turn towards Knowle. 1st left on Jacobean Ln, right at T-junct (Hampton Ln). Sharp left into Barston Ln. Restaurant 0.5m

This popular country pub lies in the well-heeled countryside fringing Birmingham. The freshly-styled rustic-chic interior has floors of terracotta and stripped wood, cosy open fires and distressed beams hinting at southern climes, and there's also a delightful garden. Blackboard specials from the fine-dining restaurant - which is situated in a smartly converted barn - bolster the bar menu. This is good gastro-pub fodder: soundly-cooked, uncomplicated dishes that come in generous portions. To start, a trio of juicy king scallops comes on a base of butternut squash with coriander shoots and sun-dried cherry tomatoes, followed by plaice fillets with roast parsnips, crisp diced chorizo and béarnaise sauce. A nicely wobbly vanilla pannacotta with lemon sorbet and
continued

BARSTON *continued*

pineapple compôte brings matters to a satisfying conclusion.

Chef Max Murphy **Owner** Caroline Furby & Chris Benbrook **Times** 12-2.30/6-9.30 Closed D Sun **Prices** Fixed L 2 course £21.50-£22.50, Fixed D 3 course £25.50-£30.50, Starter £3.95-£7.95, Main £10.95-£22.95, Dessert £5.50-£6.95, Service optional, Groups min 6 service 10% **Wines** 12 bottles over £20, 14 bottles under £20, 6 by glass **Notes** Sunday L, Vegetarian available, Air con **Seats** 40 **Children** Portions **Parking** 30

BIRMINGHAM   Map 10 SP08

Birmingham Marriott

◉ Modern British, French

Modern brasserie in elegant city-centre hotel

☎ 0121 452 1144 📄 0121 456 3442
12 Hagley Rd, Five Ways B16 8SJ
dir: Leebank Middleway to Five Ways rdbt, 1st left then right. Follow signs for hotel

The large, comfortable Edwardian hotel occupies a prominent position on the edge of the city centre. The smart public areas include the relaxed West 12 restaurant, which is popular with both business travellers and leisure guests. Service is typically professional and friendly and the extensive brasserie-style menu comprises traditional dishes with some modern influences. Start

with the Maryland crabcakes, lemon and tartare sauce before grilled fillet of sea bass with crushed new potatoes and basil jus or pan-fried calves' liver with soft polenta, mushrooms and pancetta. Finish with classic baked New York cheesecake and poached orange.

Chef James Carrol **Owner** Marriott International Ltd **Times** 12-2.30/6-10 Closed L Sat **Prices** Fixed L 2 course £14.95, Fixed D 3 course £20.95-£29.95, Starter £4.95-£10.95, Main £11.95-£23.95, Dessert £4.25-£7.25, Service optional **Wines** 20 bottles over £20, 10 bottles under £20, 10 by glass **Notes** Sunday L, Vegetarian available, Civ Wed 80, Air con **Seats** 60, Pr/dining room 60 **Children** Portions, Menu **Parking** 60

City Café

◉ Modern European NEW 🦮

Modern British food in contemporary restaurant

☎ 0121 643 1003 📄 0121 643 1005
City Inn Birmingham, 1 Brunswick Square, Brindley Place B1 2HW
e-mail: birmingham.citycafe@cityinn.com
dir: M6 junct 6, A38M, follow signs for A456, right into Sheepcote St, hotel straight ahead

In the city centre, close to all the shops and cultural attractions, this hotel is also only 20 minutes' drive from the NEC. The restaurant's blend of neutral tones of white, grey and beige give it a comfortable, relaxed feel, and there are views out over Brindley Place, plus a terrace for

alfresco eating in warm weather. The style of cooking is modern British, using well-sourced and seasonal produce; velouté of leek and potato with smoked haddock beignet, for example, followed by pan-fried sea bass served with a warm Mediterranean salad and pepper dressing. Finish with a light raspberry and white chocolate soufflé with white chocolate ice cream.

Chef Neil Peers **Owner** City Inn Ltd **Times** 12-2.30/6-10.30 **Prices** Food prices not confirmed for 2010. Please telephone for details. **Wines** 36 bottles over £20, 12 bottles under £20, 29 by glass **Notes** Sunday L, Vegetarian available, Dress restrictions, Smart casual, Civ Wed 100, Air con **Seats** 110, Pr/dining room 50 **Children** Portions, Menu **Parking** 24, NCP behind hotel

Hotel du Vin Birmingham

◉ Mediterranean, French 🦮

Chic hotel with a winning bistro menu

☎ 0121 200 0600 📄 0121 236 0889
25 Church St B3 2NR
e-mail: info@birmingham.hotelduvin.com
dir: M6 junct 6/A38(M) to city centre, over flyover. Keep left & exit at St Chads Circus signed Jewellery Quarter. At lights & rdbt take 1st exit, follow signs for Colmore Row, opposite cathedral. Right into Church St, across Barwick St. Hotel on right

Elegant and trendy, with a swish champagne bar, a wine boutique, health club and luxuriously appointed, wine-

---

Purnell's

RESTAURANT OF THE YEAR ENGLAND

BIRMINGHAM   Map 10 SP08

Modern European

Stellar cooking with bags of local pride

☎ 0121 212 9799
55 Cornwall St B3 2DH
e-mail: info@purnellsrestaurant.co.uk

Glynn Purnell's cooking could surely unite the fans of both Villa and City in a chorus of uniform approval. In one of Brum's conservation areas, this red-brick and terracotta former warehouse is the setting for some compellingly modern, lovingly and skilfully prepared food. The space inside is cool, contemporary and uncluttered, with enigmatic photographs of Birmingham landscapes

further enhancing the local flavour. The fixed-price carte and seven-course tasting menu is based on first-rate produce, local wherever possible, and lunch and dinner include excellent breads, amuse-bouche and petits fours (peanut cream lollipop, perhaps). Presentation is superb, and technical dexterity evident in a starter of chicken liver parfait with home-cured beef, confit of pineapple, jelly of the same fruit, and a port reduction. Main-course brill cooked in coconut milk with Indian lentils and cumin and toffee carrots reflects the multi-cultural heritage of the city. The finale is no less impressive: dark chocolate torte with warm chocolate mousse and passionfruit sorbet.

Chef Glynn Purnell **Owner** Glynn Purnell **Times** 12-2/7-9.30 Closed Xmas, New Year, 1 wk Etr, 2 wks end Jul-beginning Aug, Sun-Mon, L Sat **Prices** Fixed L 2 course fr £17, Tasting menu £65, Service added but optional **Wines** 248 bottles over £20, 6 bottles under £20, 18 by glass **Notes** Fixed 3 course £40, 5 course £55, Tasting menu 7 course, Vegetarian available, Dress

restrictions, Smart casual **Seats** 45, Pr/dining room 15 **Parking** On street, car park nearby

themed rooms, this former Eye Hospital is home to Birmingham's part of the HdV chain. The early Victorian building retains many original features including stylish, high-ceilinged rooms and a grand sweeping staircase. The informal bistro-style restaurant is a shrine to all things wine-related and the daily-changing menu lists classic French dishes, cooked simply using quality ingredients. Take crayfish and haddock fishcakes with chilli jam for starters, a main dish of calves' liver with caramelised shallots and sauce diable, then round off with warm Valrhona chocolate cake with white chocolate ice cream. The global wine list is formidable.

Chef Nick Turner **Owner** MWB **Times** 12-2/6-10 **Prices** Fixed L 2 course fr £15, Starter £5-£8, Main £12-£20, Dessert £5-£7, Service added but optional 10% **Wines** 600 bottles over £20, 40 bottles under £20, 16 by glass **Notes** Sunday L, Vegetarian available, Civ Wed 84 **Seats** 85, Pr/dining room 120 **Children** Portions, Menu **Parking** 20, NCP Livery St

Opus Restaurant

◉◉ Modern British **V**

Stylish contemporary design showcasing quality produce

☎ 0121 200 2323 ▤ 0121 200 2090
54 Cornwall St B3 2DE
e-mail: restaurant@opusrestaurant.co.uk

The understated modern design of Opus, by Suzanne Barnes, has won an award for its un-showy elegance. On the ground floor of one of the city's busiest financial buildings, this is a contemporary urban restaurant of the most stylish kind, now also boasting a chef's table for those who like to see their dinner coming together. Free-range meats, fresh fish and Irish oysters are all part of the draw. Starters could be as traditional as moules marinière or as invigorating as lobster and mango salad, while mains fashionably pair fish and meat such as belly pork and scallops with spring onion pomme purée, or Devon cod with Alsace bacon and winter greens. Finish with delicate pannacotta served on poached rhubarb, with a firmly textured sorbet of the same on a disc of shortbread.

Chef David Colcombe **Owner** Ann Tonks, Irene Allan, David Colcombe **Times** 12-2.30/6-10 Closed between Xmas and New Year, Sun, L Sat **Prices** Fixed L 2 course £16.50-£18.50, Fixed D 3 course £16.50-£18.50, Starter £7.50-£12.50, Main £13-£24.50, Dessert £6-£8.50, Service added but optional 10% **Wines** 80 bottles over £20, 8 bottles under £20, 18 by glass **Notes** Tasting menu for chef's table 6 course, Vegetarian menu, Air con **Seats** 85, Pr/dining room 64 **Children** Portions, Menu **Parking** On street

Pascal's

◉◉ Modern French

Fabulous dining experience in a leafy Birmingham suburb

☎ 0121 455 0999 ▤ 0121 455 0999
1 Montague Rd, Edgbaston B16 9HN
e-mail: info@pascalsrestaurant.co.uk

Located on the outskirts of Birmingham's busy centre, Pascal's offers city dining with a distinctly country ambience. Set in the stunning grounds of Asquith House, the restaurant enjoys splendid views over the garden and the conservatory-style restaurant is the setting for professional service and contemporary French food cooked with skill and imagination. Expect starters such as home smoked Gressingham duck with broccoli risotto and apple jelly, followed by fillet of bream with spiced lentils, sautéed lettuce and onions. Leave room for passionfruit pannacotta with fruit coulis and ice cream.

Times 12-2/7-10 Closed 1 wk Xmas, 1 wk Etr, last 2 wks Jul, Sun-Mon, L Sat

Purnell's

◉◉◉ – *see page 426*

Simpsons

◉◉◉ – *see below*

Simpsons

BIRMINGHAM Map 10 SP08

Modern French **V**

Exemplary cooking in stylish Georgian villa

☎ 0121 454 3434 ▤ 0121 454 3399
20 Highfield Rd, Edgbaston B15 3DU
e-mail: info@simpsonsrestaurant.co.uk
dir: 1m from city centre, opposite St Georges Church, Edgbaston

An elegant Grade II listed Georgian villa in leafy Edgbaston, Simpsons remains a Midlands culinary powerhouse. The four individually designed rooms are sophisticated and stylish and the sense of occasion is heightened by discreetly attentive staff, who are well informed on the menu and wine list. The modern menu focuses on quality seasonal ingredients of the highest provenance (Severn and Wye smoked salmon, Scottish scallops, Finnebrogue venison, Cornish lamb etc.) and these top-notch ingredients are cooked with precision and beautifully presented on the plate. The array of first-class breads is a joy to behold and both lunch and dinner include all the bells and whistles from inventive canapés to creative petits fours. Start with fillet of gilt head bream with a potato crust, baby spinach and Avruga caviar, and move on to pavé of Aberdeenshire beef with slow-cooked ox cheek, root vegetables, celeriac purée and grain mustard. Agonise over your choice for dessert - toffee soufflé with banana and lime ice cream, perhaps, or chilled rhubarb rice pudding with poached rhubarb and ginger nut ice cream? There are vegetarian and children's menus, a choice of tasting menus, and a serious wine list.

Chef Luke Tipping **Owner** Andreas & Alison Antona **Times** 12-2.30/7-9.30 Closed BHs, D Sun **Prices** Fixed L 3 course £30, Fixed D 3 course £32.50, Tasting menu fr £70, Starter £9.50-£14, Main £20-£27.50, Dessert £8.50-£11.50, Service added but optional 12.5% **Wines** 600 bottles over £20, 130 by glass **Notes** Chef's table tasting menu with wine, 6-8 people £150.00 p.p, Sunday L, Vegetarian menu, Dress restrictions, Smart casual, Air con **Seats** 70, Pr/dining room 22 **Children** Portions, Menu **Parking** 12, On Street

BIRMINGHAM *continued*

Thai Edge Restaurant

◉ Thai

Vibrant Thai cuisine in an elegant modern setting

☎ 0121 643 3993 ▤ 0121 643 3994
Brindley Place B1 2HS
e-mail: birmingham@thaiedge.co.uk
dir: Brindley Place just off Broad St (approx 0.5m from B'ham New Street station)

With branches in Leeds and Cardiff too, Thai Edge is all about bringing one of southeast Asia's best-loved cuisines right up-to-date. Authentic Thai artefacts adorn a space that is divided up by wood and glass screens, with smartly attired staff on hand to offer guidance to the uninitiated. Fixed-price set menus supplement the lengthy carte, which draws influences from the various regions in cooking that is vibrant with chilli heat, fish sauce and curry pastes. Green chicken curry served in a coconut shell, red-hot tom yum goong soup, marinated sea bass wrapped in a banana leaf, and choo chee roast duck are among the firm favourites, along with the expected noodle salads and satays. Thai beers supplement the well-chosen wines.

Times 12-2.30/5.30-11 Closed 25-26 Dec, 1 Jan

Turners

◉ Modern French NEW

Ambitious cooking in smart, intimate restaurant

☎ 0121 426 4440
69 High St, Harborne B17 9NS
e-mail: info@turnersofharborne.com
dir: Please telephone for directions

Harborne, a suburb of Birmingham some 3 miles from the centre of the city, has a class act its midst in the form of Turners restaurant. Striking dark blue mirrors line the walls of this intimate place and the quarry tiles on the floor add a bit of original character. The small kitchen team produces an ambitious menu which is based on French classicism and delivers plenty of modern, sometimes innovative, ideas. Start, perhaps, with tartare of scallops with pickled beetroot and avocado and move on to a pavé of wild sea bass, textures of parsnip, garlic, spinach and red wine sauce. Round things off with vanilla pannacotta, poached clementines and orange ice cream.

Times 12-2/6.30-9.30 Closed Mon

DORRIDGE Map 10 SP17

The Forest

◉◉ Modern European

Impressive cooking in modern, boutique surroundings

☎ 01564 772120 ▤ 01564 732680
Station Approach B93 8JA
e-mail: info@forest-hotel.com
dir: M42 junct 5, through Knowle right to Dorridge, left before bridge

A sophisticated boutique-style hotel set within a red-brick, late Victorian building smack opposite the railway station in Dorridge town centre, The Forest has an easy-on-the-eye modern look within, with cool, urbane styling in the handsome airy bar and the trendy, brasserie-style restaurant. The crowd-pleasing, broadly European style of cooking suits the contemporary surroundings. Well-conceived dishes are prepared from quality seasonal ingredients, and cooking is precise, simple and intelligent. Start with braised mutton with root vegetable broth, move on to grilled red bream with baked fennel, mussels and saffron, or confit pork belly with roast loin and ham savelov, and finish with poached pink rhubarb with white chocolate and vanilla mousse. Competitive pricing and informal, professional service hit just the right note, too.

Chef Dean Grubb **Owner** Gary & Tracy Perkins
Times 12-2.30/6.30-10 Closed 25 Dec, D Sun
Prices Fixed L 2 course £13, Fixed D 3 course £15.50, Starter £4.50-£6.75, Main £7.50-£19.50, Dessert £4.90-£6.50, Service added but optional 10% **Wines** 12 bottles over £20, 30 bottles under £20, 9 by glass **Notes** Fixed L & D Mon-Fri only, Sunday L, Vegetarian available, Civ Wed 100, Air con **Seats** 70, Pr/dining room 150 **Children** Portions, Menu **Parking** 40

HOCKLEY HEATH Map 10 SP17

Nuthurst Grange Country House Hotel

◉◉ British, French

Fine dining with bags of imagination and country-house style

☎ 01564 783972 ▤ 01564 783919
Nuthurst Grange Ln B94 5NL
e-mail: info@nuthurst-grange.com
web: www.nuthurst-grange.com
dir: Off A3400, 0.5 mile S of Hockley Heath, turn at sign into Nuthurst Grange Ln

---

Nuthurst Grange is a creeper-clad country house in 7 acres of landscaped gardens and woodland in the leafy fringes of Birmingham. The grand tree-lined drive certainly makes an impression when you turn up, and the upmarket mood continues through to the light and airy dining room, where candlelight twinkles off classy crystal, and roses from the garden complete the romantic setting. The kitchen brigade turns out a repertoire of imaginative modern French and British cuisine ranging from classics to more inventive ideas. Ceviche of scallops with pickled beetroot and wasabi ice cream shows a light touch, while a blanquette of veal, sweetbreads, glazed root vegetables and mustard sauce makes a refined main course. To finish, how about a perfectly-balanced caramel soufflé with banana pannacotta and gingerbread ice cream?

Times 12-2/7-9.30 Closed 25-26 Dec, L Sat

MERIDEN Map 10 SP28

Manor Hotel

◉ Modern British, French

Fine dining in Georgian manor house

☎ 01676 522735 ▤ 01676 522186
Main Rd CV7 7NH
e-mail: reservations@manorhotelmeriden.co.uk
dir: M42 junct 6 take A45 towards Coventry then A452, signed Leamington. At rdbt join B4102, signed Meriden, hotel 0.5m on left

The elegant Georgian Manor Hotel is located in the quiet village of Meriden, said to be the exact centre of England. It has a picturesque country setting, yet is only minutes away from the National Exhibition Centre. The formal Regency Restaurant specialises in classical dishes given a light, modern touch and attractively presented. Typical main course dishes might include tenderloin and confit of belly pork, black pudding and cabbage with apple poached potato, or roast fillet of pollock, served with cassoulet of beans, mussel tempura and chorizo foam. There is also the Triumph Buttery, which serves informal lunches and snacks.

Chef Darion Smethurst **Owner** Bracebridge Holdings
Times 12-2/7-9.45 Closed 27-30 Dec, L Sat
Prices Starter £3.95-£8.50, Main £12.95-£17.95, Dessert £4.95-£5.50, Service optional **Wines** 25 bottles over £20, 19 bottles under £20, 6 by glass **Notes** Sunday L, Vegetarian available, Civ Wed 120, Air con **Seats** 150, Pr/dining room 220 **Children** Portions, Menu **Parking** 180

SUTTON COLDFIELD — Map 10 SP19

New Hall

◉◉ Modern British

A modern take on classic dishes in reputedly the oldest inhabited moated house in England

☎ 0121 378 2442 ▤ 0121 378 4637
Walmley Rd B76 1QX
e-mail: sales@newhall.co.uk
dir: On B4148, E of Sutton Coldfield, close to M6 & M42

A stunning moat house dating back 800 years, New Hall delivers on old-fashioned grandeur, featuring flagstone floors, open fires and exposed beams. Set within 26 acres, the sympathetic renovation has brought the facilities into the present while retaining much of the property's medieval charm and character. In the small intimate dining room service is attentive and unhurried and is delivered by a young friendly team. Carefully sourced ingredients are used in the likes of pan-fried scallops with slow-roasted pork belly, Jerusalem artichokes and parsley purée, or pan-fried sea bream with gnocchi, langoustines and a shellfish consommé. An impressively creative lemon chiffon crumble with orange tuile, caramelised compressed pineapple and gingerbread ice makes for a fine finish to a meal.

Chef Wayne Thomson **Owner** Hand Picked Hotels **Times** 12-2/7-9.30 Closed L Sat, D Sun & Mon **Prices** Starter £8.50-£14, Main £16.50-£28, Dessert £6.50-£9, Service optional **Wines** 65 bottles over £20, 14 bottles under £20, 10 by glass **Notes** Sunday L, Vegetarian available, Civ Wed 150 **Seats** 30, Pr/dining room 50 **Children** Portions, Menu **Parking** 60

WALSALL — Map 10 SP09

Fairlawns Hotel and Spa

◉◉ Modern British

Smart hotel with sound modern cooking

☎ 01922 455122 ▤ 01922 743148
178 Little Aston Rd, Aldridge WS9 0NU
e-mail: reception@fairlawns.co.uk
web: www.fairlawns.co.uk
dir: Outskirts of Aldridge, 400yds from junction of A452 (Chester Rd) & A454

Just 5 miles from the M5 and M6, this popular family-run hotel is set in 9 acres of landscaped gardens, located in an extended Victorian building complete with fitness centre and spa. The restaurant's contemporary elegance sets the scene for some accomplished cooking. International influences are evident on the essentially British menu, which makes the most of fresh, seasonal ingredients from local producers where possible. Simply prepared yet imaginative and well-presented dishes feature on the two- and three-course dinner menus, and on the wide-ranging brasserie-style lunch menu available Monday to Friday. Start with seared hand-dived Orkney Island scallops on vanilla mash and follow with slow-cooked collar of local free-range pork served with apple jelly, garlic confit potato, Savoy cabbage and bacon.

Chef Neil Atkins **Owner** John Pette **Times** 12-2/7-10 Closed 25-26 Dec, 1 Jan, Good Fri, Etr Mon, May Day, BH Mon, L Sat **Prices** Fixed L 2 course fr £16, Fixed D 3 course fr £28.50, Starter £5.50-£12.50, Main £10.95-£29.95, Dessert £5.50-£7.50, Service optional **Wines** 36 bottles over £20, 30 bottles under £20, 12 by glass **Notes** Sunday L, Vegetarian available, Dress restrictions, No jeans, trainers, sports clothing, Civ Wed 100, Air con **Seats** 80, Pr/dining room 100 **Children** Portions, Menu **Parking** 120

WOLVERHAMPTON — Map 10 SO99

Bilash

◉ Bangladeshi NEW

Family-run south Asian restaurant achieving remarkable standards

☎ 01902 427762 ▤ 01902 311991
2 Cheapside WV1 1TU
e-mail: m@thebilash.co.uk
dir: Opposite Civic Hall & St Peter's Church

Owned by the same family for a quarter of a century, Bilash moves with the gastronomic times; it has been refined into one of the best South Asian eateries in the Midlands, an area hardly short of competition. A stone's throw from the Civic Hall in the heart of the city, the discreet beige frontage hides a vibrant, minimalist interior adorned with quality artworks and subtle lighting, where two dining-rooms are furnished with well-spaced tables and staffed by smartly uniformed waiters. The regulation massive menu of Bangladeshi/Indian restaurants is eschewed in favour of a shorter, well-composed listing that aims to recreate the atmosphere of Asian home cooking with style and panache. Tangri chicken kebabs coated in spices and cooked in the tandoor explode with flavour, and, similarly, monkfish jhalfry presents accurately cooked fish in an abundantly spiced stir-fry of red peppers, red onion and shallots.

Chef Sitas Khan **Owner** Sitas Khan **Times** 12-2.30/5.30-10.30 Closed 25-26 Dec, Sun **Prices** Fixed L 2 course £10.90-£14.90, Fixed D 3 course £21.90-£26.90, Tasting menu fr £39.90, Starter £5.90-£12.90, Main £10.90-£28.90, Dessert £5.90-£8.90 **Notes** Pre-theatre D, tasting menu with wine, Vegetarian available, Dress restrictions, No tracksuits & trainers, Air con **Seats** 48, Pr/dining room 40 **Children** Portions, Menu **Parking** 15, Civic car park

WIGHT, ISLE OF

FRESHWATER — Map 5 SZ38

Farringford

◉ Modern British ⓥ

Country-house dining in Tennyson's old home

☎ 01983 752500 ▤ 01983 756515
Bedbury Ln PO40 9PE
e-mail: enquiries@farringford.co.uk
dir: A3054, left to Norton Green down Pixlie Hill. Left to Freshwater Bay. At bay turn right into Bedbury Lane, hotel on left

The poet Alfred, Lord Tennyson moved to Farringford in 1853. He wrote many of his famous works there, including *The Charge of the Light Brigade* and *Maud*, and it's easy to see why he loved the place so much. The grand Georgian house is these days a charming hotel in 33 acres of grounds. Ruskins Restaurant, with its large picture windows, overlooks the meticulously maintained gardens. The cooking is modern British with a few unusual flavour combinations, as in peppered prime Isle of Wight beef fillet with chargrilled vegetables, champ and a coffee barbecued onion sauce. Local seafood turns up in a terrine served with caviar and a chive vinaigrette, and rhubarb from the garden comes with shortbread and lemon cream.

Chef Mr P Reddy **Owner** Martin Beisly & R Fitzgerald **Times** 12-2.30/6.30-9 Closed Nov-Mar, L Mon-Sat **Prices** Fixed L 3 course £16.50, Fixed D 4 course £32, Starter £7-£12, Main £12.50-£17.50, Dessert £5-£7.50 **Wines** 50 bottles over £20, 25 bottles under £20, 6 by glass **Notes** Sunday L, Vegetarian menu, Dress restrictions, No sports clothes or denim, Civ Wed 150 **Seats** 100, Pr/dining room 20 **Children** Portions, Menu **Parking** 50

RYDE — Map 5 SZ59

The St Helens

◉◉ Modern British ⓒ

Unfussy food using the best Isle of Wight produce

☎ 01983 872303 & 0771 7175 444
Lower Green Rd, St Helens PO33 1TS
e-mail: chefmarkyoung@live.co.uk
dir: Follow B3330 to St Helens

The nautically designed décor has a New England feel about it, with its blue and white colour scheme, wooden floor and tables and seaside artwork, but outside stands one of England's largest village greens to confirm you're still in the old country. Outside tables make the best of the setting when the southern sun allows. The kitchen uses the best Isle of Wight produce and is mindful of the seasons when it creates its simple, rustic dishes. Start perhaps with a signature dish of crab brulee with a parmesan and brioche crust and an Arreton leaf salad. Move on to Italian braised chicken with pancetta and figs and finish with a bit of British comfort in the form of apple and sultana crumble with vanilla ice cream.

continued

RYDE *continued*

Chef Mark Young, Jason West **Owner** Mark Young, Lian Beadell **Times** 12-2.30/6.30-9.30 Closed 25-26 Dec, Mon (Nov-Mar), L Mon-Sat **Prices** Starter £4.50-£7.95, Main £12.50-£30, Dessert £4.50-£7.50, Service optional, Groups min 8 service 10% **Wines** 9 bottles over £20, 13 bottles under £20, 4 by glass **Notes** Sunday L, Vegetarian available, Dress restrictions, Shirt & shoes must be worn **Seats** 40 **Children** Portions, Menu **Parking** On street, car park 100yds

---

SEAVIEW | Map 5 SZ69

Priory Bay Hotel

◉ Modern

Peaceful hotel with wonderful views and food to match

☎ 01983 613146   📠 01983 616539
Priory Dr PO34 5BU
e-mail: enquiries@priorybay.co.uk
dir: B3330 towards Seaview, through Nettlestone. (Do not follow Seaview turn, but continue 0.5m to hotel sign)

Between Bembridge and Seaview, 2 of the Isle of Wight's premier sailing resorts, this 14th-century priory turned holiday haven once played home to a community of monks, who no doubt made the most of its peaceful location. Offering remarkable views of the Solent and Spithead, the house is still a good place to get away from it all, although these days tranquillity comes with an array of temptations that include a private beach, 6-hole golf course and outdoor swimming pool. The Regency-styled, candlelit Island Room is a romantic evening setting for some flavourful food: local blue crab velouté with wild garlic and crustacean tortellini, for example, followed by best end of Dunsbury Farm lamb with lemon thyme, fennel and tomato gratin and wild garlic jus.

Times 12.30-2.15/7-9.30

The Restaurant at The Seaview

◉◉ Modern British ✿

Bright and lively hotel with a choice of restaurants

☎ 01983 612711   📠 01983 613729
High St PO34 5EX
e-mail: reception@seaviewhotel.co.uk
dir: Take B3330 from Ryde to Seaview, left into Puckpool Hill, follow signs for hotel

The Seaview is just a short stroll from the seafront, and the Solent can be spied from selected vantage points within this elegant and nautically themed hotel. There is the lively Pump Bar at the heart of the hotel, and the popular restaurant serving the same menu in two dining rooms: choose between the small Victorian dining room, or the more spacious brasserie-style Sunshine Restaurant with its own conservatory and bright-and-breezy blue colour scheme and seafaring pictures on the walls. The fixed-price menus focus on good local produce, with plenty of stunning seafood, and there's also a five-course Menu Surprise. The modern British repertoire runs to wild mushroom soup with truffle jelly, followed by pan-fried pollock with beetroot mash, spinach and lemon balm, finishing with a selection of island cheeses.

Chef Graham Walker **Owner** Techaid Facilities Ltd **Times** 12-2/6.30-9.30 Closed 21-26 Dec, Mon, L weekdays during winter, D Sun **Prices** Fixed D 3 course £26.50, Service optional, Groups min 8 service 12.5% **Wines** 22 bottles over £20, 14 bottles under £20, 4 by glass **Notes** Menu surprise £32, Sunday L, Vegetarian available, Air con **Seats** 80 **Children** Portions, Menu **Parking** 15

VENTNOR | Map 5 SZ57

The Leconfield

◉ Traditional British NEW V ✿

Wonderfully situated hotel with traditional menu

☎ 01983 852196   📠 01983 856525
85 Leeson Rd, Upper Bonchurch PO38 1PU
e-mail: enquiries@leconfieldhotel.com
web: www.leconfieldhotel.com
dir: Situated Upper Bonchurch on A3055, 1m from Ventnor, 2m from Shanklin opposite turning, Bonchurch Shute

The Leconfield has a wonderful position up on St Boniface Down above the village of Bonchurch, giving superb views across the English Channel. The Seascape dining room, with its picture windows framing those amazing views, offers a fine dining menu that makes good use of the island's produce. The glass-topped tables and comfortable wicker chairs are smart and rather stylish and a pleasant change from the ubiquitous white linen cloths and leather seats going on elsewhere. Start with crayfish tail and cucumber salad with a sweet chilli dressing, then a sorbet (kiwi fruit, perhaps) before main-course baked salmon with asparagus and béarnaise sauce.

Chef Jason Lefley **Owner** Paul & Cheryl Judge **Times** 6.30-8.30 Closed 24-26 Dec, 3 wks Jan, L all week (except by prior arrangement) **Prices** Fixed D 3 course £21.40-£27.95, Starter £3.50-£4.95, Main £13.95-£17.50, Dessert £3.95-£5.50, Service optional **Wines** 8 bottles over £20, 20 bottles under £20, 14 by glass **Notes** Vegetarian menu, Dress restrictions, Smart casual **Seats** 28 **Parking** 14

The Pond Café

◉ Mediterranean

Confident cooking and tranquil island views

☎ 01983 855666
Bonchurch Village Rd, Bonchurch PO38 1RG
e-mail: info@thepondcafe.com
dir: Please telephone for directions

Located in a pleasant Isle of Wight village, a stone's throw from the eponymous pond, the Café (sister restaurant to Robert Thompson The Hambrough - see entry) offers simplicity at its best. Bare tables with crisp napkins indicate the homely approach, and the cheerful front-of-house staff reinforce it. The food is broadly modern European with more Italian leanings than anything else, offering bresaola, followed by rabbit gnocchi or calves' liver with cavolo nero, castelluccio lentils and pancetta, but there might also be fine chicken liver and foie gras parfait, and roasted lamb rump with fondant potato and crushed peas. Fish-lovers may opt for sea bass with shrimp and artichoke linguini, and desserts run to baked lemon tart with blackcurrant sorbet.

Chef Andrew Beaumont **Owner** Robert Thompson **Times** 12-2.30/6.30-9.30 Closed 2 wks in Jan, Tue-Wed **Prices** Food prices not confirmed for 2010. Please telephone for details. **Wines** 27 bottles over £20, 8 bottles under £20, 6 by glass **Notes** Sunday L, Vegetarian available **Seats** 26 **Children** Portions **Parking** On street

Robert Thompson The Hambrough

◉◉◉ *– see opposite page*

Robert Thompson The Hambrough

Modern French V

Confident modern cooking in stylish hotel

☎ 01983 856333 📄 01983 857260
Hambrough Rd PO38 1SQ
e-mail: info@thehambrough.com
web: www.thehambrough.com
dir: Please telephone for directions

The arrival of chef Robert Thompson in the summer of 2008 at this elegant Victorian villa with splendid views over the bay has confirmed its place as the dining destination on the island, and indeed a significant player on the South Coast. It's a beautiful spot, perched on a green, lush hillside high above the harbour, and the un-showy refinement of the building is reflected in the muted tones and stylish simplicity of the rooms, including the dining room with its large bay windows revealing the moods of both sea and sky. Tables are smartly laid with white linen and service hits the right note. Thompson has a serious pedigree and it shows in the craft and refinement of his modern European cooking, and pleasingly the fixed-price carte, tasting menu and set lunch all represent good value by today's standards. Squid ink in the breadsticks and an amuse-bouche of perfectly balanced lobster bisque display the chef's credentials right from the off, while a starter of pan-roasted

veal sweetbreads is beautifully cooked and comes with Chantenay carrots and coriander shoots. Deft handling of flavours is to the fore in main-course salmon and fennel confit with lemon and pink peppercorn saffron pasta and a dark chocolate fondant dessert, paired with quince compôte and cinnamon ice cream.

Chef Robert Thompson **Owner** Robert Thompson **Times** 12-1.30/7-9.30 Closed 2 wks New Year & Jan, April & Nov, Sun-Mon **Prices** Fixed L 2 course fr £20, Fixed D 3 course fr £45, Tasting menu £59-£80, Service optional **Wines** 67 bottles over £20, 9 bottles under £20, 9 by glass **Notes** Tasting menu 7 course, Vegetarian menu, Dress restrictions, Smart casual, No sportswear, Air con **Seats** 45, Pr/dining room 22 **Children** Portions **Parking** On street

VENTNOR *continued*

The Royal Hotel

◉◉ Modern British **V**

Sophisticated cuisine in a timelessly elegant setting

☎ 01983 852186 🖹 01983 855395
Belgrave Rd PO38 1JJ
e-mail: enquiries@royalhoteliow.co.uk
dir: On A3055 (coast road) into Ventnor. Follow one-way
system, left at lights into Church St. At top of hill left into
Belgrave Rd, hotel on right

The Isle of Wight is something of a step back in time, and
this refined old hotel built in 1832 in gorgeous gardens
looking onto the sea still values the Victorian way of
doing things properly. A timeless air of sophistication
hangs over the grand old dame of a restaurant with its
high ceilings and crystal chandeliers, hues of apricot and
deep blue, heavily swagged curtains and oil paintings.
The cooking, however, is firmly rooted in the modern
British style: down-to-earth dishes built on seasonal,
local produce, underpinned by good technical skills. Pan-
fried Ventnor crab cakes come with pickled winter
vegetables, and a roast fillet of cod is married with garlic
and chive creamed potatoes, smoked bacon, chanterelles
and fish jus. An exotic take on tarte Tatin - pineapple and
mango, infused with star anise and vanilla - might round
things off.

Chef Alan Staley **Owner** William Bailey
Times 12-1.45/6.45-9 Closed 2 wks Jan or 2 wks Dec, L
Mon-Sat **Prices** Fixed L 2 course £18.50-£26, Fixed D 3
course £36-£51, Service optional **Wines** 57 bottles over
£20, 18 bottles under £20, 6 by glass **Notes** Sunday L,
Vegetarian menu, Dress restrictions, Smart casual, no
shorts or trainers, Civ Wed 150 **Seats** 100, Pr/dining room
40 **Children** Portions **Parking** 50

Brasserie at The George Hotel

◉◉ British, Mediterranean 🍃

A taste of the Mediterranean on the Solent

☎ 01983 760331 🖹 01983 760425
The George Hotel, Quay St PO41 0PE
e-mail: jeremy@thegeorge.co.uk
web: www.thegeorge.co.uk
dir: Between castle & pier

A short stroll from the ferry terminal, the 17th-century
colour-washed George stands in a great location between
Yarmouth's pier and the old castle walls in peaceful
shoreline grounds. Refurbished with style and panache,
the bright, contemporary and sunny brasserie enjoys
stunning Solent views and offers an up-beat
Mediterranean-inspired menu. Seasonally changing,
using top-notch local ingredients, expect simple, unfussy
dishes cooked well to allow the freshness and flavours to
shine through. From fishy starters like tempura salt and
pepper squid with rocket and harissa, or spider crab with
spaghettini and chilli, the menu extends to braised
pheasant with red wine and root vegetables, and roast
gurnard with horseradish and beetroot salsa. Desserts
may include chocolate tart with pistachio ice cream.

Chef Jose Graziosi **Owner** John Illsley, Jeremy Willcock
Times 12-3/7-10 **Prices** Fixed L 2 course £27.95-£29.95,
Fixed D 3 course £35.95-£44.95, Starter £7.25-£12.50,
Main £14.50-£27.50, Dessert £6.75-£7.95, Service
optional **Wines** 40 bottles over £20, 20 bottles under £20,
10 by glass **Notes** Sunday L, Vegetarian available, Dress
restrictions, Smart casual, Air con **Seats** 60, Pr/dining
room 20 **Children** Portions, Menu **Parking** The Square

The Tollgate Inn

◉◉ Modern British 🍃

Solid cooking in a quintessential village pub

☎ 01225 782326 🖹 01225 782805
Ham Green BA14 6PX
e-mail: alison@tollgateholt.co.uk
web: www.tollgateholt.co.uk
dir: M4 junct 18, A46 follow Bradford-on-Avon signs, take
A363, left onto B3105. In Holt left onto B3107 towards
Melksham. Inn 100yds on right

This charming English village pub offers a choice of
several dining areas but it has retained its pubby
atmosphere. Downstairs, there's a cosy room furnished
with pews and cushions and a wood-burning stove, while
upstairs, the larger first-floor restaurant occupies what
was originally a Baptist chapel for the weavers who
worked in the shed below. The fine modern British cuisine
is underpinned by produce carefully sourced from the
local area including fish delivered daily from Brixham.
Corned beef hash and fish pie make an appearance at
lunchtime, but there's also more complex fare: pan-fried
haddock on smoked haddock fish cake with champagne
crayfish sauce, for example, or chargrilled calves' liver on
creamed mustard mash with a rich onion sauce.

Chef Alexander Venables **Owner** Alexander Venables,
Alison Ward-Baptiste **Times** 11-2.30/5.30-11
Closed 25-26 Dec, Mon, D Sun **Prices** Fixed L 2 course
£12.50-£25.30, Fixed D 3 course £18.75-£31.25, Starter
£5-£8.50, Main £12.50-£18.80, Dessert £4.50-£6.50,
Service optional, Groups min 6 service 10% **Wines** 12
bottles over £20, 23 bottles under £20, 9 by glass
Notes Sunday L, Vegetarian available, Air con **Seats** 60,
Pr/dining room 38 **Parking** 40

Widbrook Grange

◎ Modern British, European ✱

Sound cooking in peaceful country-house hotel

☎ 01225 864750 📄 01225 862890
Trowbridge Rd, Widbrook BA15 1UH
e-mail: stay@widbrookgrange.com
dir: 1m S of Bradford-on-Avon on A363

An elegant 250-year-old Georgian country-house hotel, Widbrook Grange is peacefully located amid 11 acres of grounds on the outskirts of the ancient town of Bradford-on-Avon, close to the Kennet and Avon Canal. The hotel has an intimate relaxing atmosphere and informality with cosy lounges and a log fire burning on cold winter nights. A more casual style of dining is offered in the Bee Bole Conservatory, while the fine dining Medlar Tree Restaurant offers British classics with some modern flourishes. Cornish crab thermidor tartlet, for example, with pan-fried Looe Bay scallops, comes with a tarragon and saffron butter sauce; follow on with braised lamb shank with roasted root vegetables in a mint and redcurrant jus.

Chef Phil Carroll **Owner** Peter & Jane Wragg
Times 11.30-2.30/7-11 Closed 24-30 Dec, L Sun
Prices Starter £5.50-£6, Main £15.50-£16, Dessert £6-£6.50, Service included **Wines** 16 bottles over £20, 11 bottles under £20, 6 by glass **Notes** Vegetarian available, Dress restrictions, Smart casual, Civ Wed 50 **Seats** 45, Pr/dining room 12 **Children** Portions, Menu **Parking** 50

Woolley Grange

◎◎ Modern British V

Child-friendly atmosphere and excellent dining in Jacobean manor

☎ 01225 864705 📄 01225 864059
Woolley Grange Hotel, Woolley Green BA15 1TX
e-mail: info@woolleygrangehotel.co.uk
dir: Please telephone for directions

The philosophy behind this upmarket Jacobean manor house hotel is that life doesn't have to stop when you start a family. Children and stylish accommodation with excellent cuisine are not mutually exclusive here. There is always plenty to keep the children occupied, plus the services of a trained nanny on duty, too, while the grown-ups can find a haven at the end of the day in the restaurant. As well as sourcing fine local materials, the kitchen at Woolley Grange grows its own Soil Association-certified organic vegetables, fruits and herbs in a lovely walled garden, neatly assuring seasonality in one fell swoop. Beautifully presented dinners kick off with the likes of sautéed quail with braised lentils and sherry jus, followed by roast rump of lamb with roasted winter vegetables and cumin cream sauce.

Chef Mark Bradbury **Owner** Luxury Family Hotels & von Essen Hotels **Times** 12-2/7-9.30 **Prices** Fixed D 3 course fr £37.50, Starter £8, Main £22.50, Dessert £7, Service optional **Wines** 72 bottles over £20, 10 bottles under £20, 8 by glass **Notes** Sunday L, Vegetarian menu, Dress restrictions, Smart casual, Civ Wed 50 **Seats** 40, Pr/dining room 22 **Children** Portions, Menu **Parking** 25

CASTLE COMBE Map 4 ST87

The Bybrook at the Manor

◎◎◎ – see below

COLERNE Map 4 ST87

Park Restaurant Lucknam Park

◎◎◎ – see page 434

The Bybrook at the Manor

CASTLE COMBE Map 4 ST87

Modern British V

Country-house cooking of rare distinctiveness

☎ 01249 782206 📄 01249 782159
Manor House Hotel SN14 7HR
e-mail: enquiries@manorhouse.co.uk
dir: M4 junct 17, follow signs for Castle Combe via Chippenham

There's nothing quite like a long, sweeping drive through 365 acres of grounds, with a championship golf course somewhere off in the distance, to pique expectations. The Manor House doesn't disappoint. From a 14th-century original, it has been progressively embellished into the textbook country-house hotel we see before us. Ravishing views over the Italian gardens are afforded by the tall windows in the Bybrook restaurant, staff are punctiliously helpful and professional, and the cooking from Richard Davies is memorable for its high shine and its dynamic approach. Take a duck egg, cook it slowly but so that it retains a runny centre, and team it with razor-thin pancetta, delicately timed foie gras and a truffled celeriac emulsion sauce, and you have many people's idea of a luxurious opening course. Timing is all, as in a main course of turbot that comes poached in red wine with a purée of parsnip and a big, belting sauce of olives and anchovies, offset by the gentling effect of some baby gem lettuce. Slow cooking might also be applied to fillet of beef, with its accoutrements of wild mushroom ravioli and cauliflower soubise. Thin, crisp, buttery pastry distinguishes a tarte fine of apple with matching caramel ice cream and sauce.

Chef Richard Davies **Owner** Exclusive Hotels
Times 12.30-2/7-10 Closed L Sat **Prices** Fixed L 2 course £17-£46, Fixed D 3 course £30-£52, Tasting menu £65, Service optional **Wines** 305 bottles over £20, 12 by glass **Notes** Tasting menu 7 course, Sunday L, Vegetarian menu, Dress restrictions, Smart casual, Civ Wed 90 **Seats** 60, Pr/dining room 90 **Children** Portions, Menu **Parking** 100

Park Restaurant Lucknam Park

Map 4 ST87

Modern British V ✋

Fantastic food in an archetypal country house

☎ 01225 742777 📄 01225 743536
SN14 8AZ
e-mail:
reservations@lucknampark.co.uk
dir: M4 junct 17, A350 to Chippenham, then A420 towards Bristol for 3m. At Ford left towards Colerne. In 4m right into Doncombe Ln, then 300yds on right

Down a sweeping, tree-lined drive lies this 17th-century country-house hotel set in 500 acres of well-kept gardens and parkland. Opulence reigns here with an interior bedecked with oil paintings and luxurious furnishings. The drawing room, ideal for a pre-prandial drink, boasts chandeliers and comfy sofas, while service in the impressive dining room, with its sky mural in the mansion's former ballroom, is highly polished. Plenty of local supplier name-checking goes on in the delightfully crafted gourmet and à la carte menus (including a veggie version). Hywel Jones showcases his talents with accomplished cooking, which draws on his classical background and displays plenty of contemporary ideas. Luxurious starters might include slow-cooked Burford Brown egg with truffled baby artichokes and leeks, parmesan and Richard Vine's shoots, or roast Scottish

diver scallops with brandade fritters, tomato and cumin vinaigrette and éscabeche of carrots. For main course fillet of wild turbot with braised oxtail, broccoli and Lyonnaise potatoes shows the style, and passionfruit cream with lemongrass and palm sugar sorbet, delivered with a mango shot, is a classy finish.

Chef Hywel Jones **Owner** Lucknam Park Hotels Ltd **Times** 12-2.30/6.30-10 Closed Mon, L Tue-Sat, D Sun
Prices Fixed D 3 course fr £65, Service optional **Wines** 450 bottles over £20, 10 by glass **Notes** Sunday L, Vegetarian menu, Dress restrictions, Jacket & tie preferred, no jeans or trainers, Civ Wed 110 **Seats** 80, Pr/dining room 30
Children Portions, Menu **Parking** 80

HIGHWORTH
Map 5 SU29

Jesmonds of Highworth

🏵🏵 Modern European

Inventive modern European cuisine in stylish restaurant with rooms

☎ 01793 762364 📠 01793 861201
Jesmond House SN6 7HJ
e-mail: info@jesmondsofhighworth.com
dir: Please telephone for directions

Situated on the edge of the Cotswolds, this Grade II listed restaurant with rooms is an elegant mix of traditional Georgian and contemporary styles. There's a fine dining restaurant, a brasserie and the option to eat alfresco in the Italian-style courtyard. The restaurant, refreshingly uncluttered, with high-backed leather chairs and wooden tables, is the setting for some seriously good modern European cuisine. The freshest fish, game, meat and seasonal produce, locally sourced wherever possible, is prepared with great attention to detail, creating dishes with a fine combination of textures and flavours. Start with parsnip and thyme mousse, parsnip foam and walnut emulsion, following on with pavé of Cornish brill served with white onion and cinnamon and brown shrimp tortellini. Desserts are equally as creative, such as a treatise on rhubarb featuring apple mousse, poached and jelly served with ginger biscuit ice cream.

Chef William Guthrie **Owner** Andrew Crankshaw & Sven Saint-Calbre **Times** 12-2.30/7-9.15 **Prices** Fixed D 3 course £37.50, Starter £5.50-£6.50, Main £9.50-£16, Dessert £5-£6, Service optional **Wines** 20 bottles over £20, 40 bottles under £20, 12 by glass **Notes** Sunday L, Vegetarian available, Air con **Seats** 60, Pr/dining room 10 **Children** Portions

HINDON
Map 4 ST93

The Lamb at Hindon

🏵 Traditional British NEW ☺

Fine food, wine and ales in a historic country inn

☎ 01747 820573 📠 01747 820605
High St SP3 6DP
e-mail: info@lambathindon.co.uk
dir: From M3 take junct 8 onto A303. Turn off towards Hindon 4m after Salisbury exit & follow signs to Hindon

This 12th-century inn deep in Wiltshire's huntin', shootin' and fishin' country overflows with character; think inglenook fireplaces, heavy beams, flagged floors and rich red walls. Wooden tables and old settles line up alongside good ales and extensive wine and whisky lists. The Boisdale group (see London SW1 and EC2) are the proprietors, so there's a good scattering of Scottish produce and influences, from Macsween haggis to South Uist king scallops, amongst the local bounty. Grilled Stourhead Barnsley lamb chop with Swiss chard and dauphinoise, for example, plus daily fish deliveries, game and offal dishes, and West Country or Aberdeenshire beef.

Chef Andrzej Piechocki, Christopher Kendall **Owner** Ranald Macdonald (Boisdale Plc) **Times** 12-2.30/6.30-9.30 **Prices** Starter £4.75-£9.50, Main £7.50-£20.95, Dessert £5.45-£6.50, Service added but optional 10% **Wines** 68 bottles over £20, 21 bottles under £20, 9 by glass **Notes** Sunday L, Vegetarian available, Civ Wed 70 **Seats** 52, Pr/dining room 32 **Children** Portions, Menu **Parking** 16

HORNINGSHAM
Map 4 ST84

The Bath Arms at Longleat

🏵 Modern, Traditional British

Home-grown food on the historic Longleat Estate

☎ 01985 844308 & 07770 268359 📠 01985 845187
Longleat Estate BA12 7LY
e-mail: enquiries@batharms.co.uk
dir: Please telephone for directions

The unspoilt village of Horningsham forms part of the Longleat Estate. The historic stone-built country inn has been transformed into a stylish boutique hotel and among its many features is an opulent main dining room complete with dramatic chandeliers, French-style wallpaper, wooden tables and floor, and huge candlesticks. The menu focuses on simple and perfectly cooked modern British food, home grown where possible (including the pigs), or sourced from within a 50-mile radius of Longleat. Expect ravioli of salmon and prawns

continued

The Harrow Inn at Little Bedwyn

LITTLE BEDWYN
Map 5 SU26

Modern British Ⓥ

Accomplished cooking in stylish restaurant with notable wine list

☎ 01672 870871
SN8 3JP
e-mail: reservations@harrowinn.co.uk
web: www.theharrowatlittlebedwyn.co.uk
dir: Between Marlborough & Hungerford, well signed

Tucked away down winding country lanes in the depths of Wiltshire, what was once the village pub is now a smart country restaurant with a formidable reputation. The dining room - split into 2 sections - is bright and contemporary, featuring dark leather high-backed chairs and neatly dressed tables laid with Riedel glasses and colourful Villeroy & Boch crockery. Service, led by Sue Jones, is friendly and relaxed, and husband Roger mans the stove. There's also a small garden at the rear for summer alfresco dining and aperitifs. Roger's approach in the kitchen puts great emphasis on the freshness and sourcing of quality ingredients; fish from day boats landed at Brixham, while meat and game is from specialist farmers and butchers, and salads and herbs are specifically grown in North Devon. The cooking style is straightforward and intelligent, with ingredients allowed to shine and delivering clear flavours. Seared diver-caught scallops, for example, with pea purée and chorizo, followed by a platter of young new season Welsh mountain lamb with autumn vegetables, chilli and mint. The stunning wine list displays plenty of passion and high quality.

Chef Roger Jones, John Brown **Owner** Roger & Sue Jones **Times** 12-3/7-11 Closed Xmas & New Year, 2 wks Aug, Mon-Tue, D Sun **Prices** Fixed L 3 course £30, Fixed D 4 course fr £40, Tasting menu £70-£150, Starter £12-£15, Main £24-£28, Dessert £9-£12, Service optional **Wines** 900 bottles over £20, 20 by glass **Notes** Vegetarian menu, Dress restrictions, Smart casual **Seats** 34 **Children** Menu **Parking** On street

HORNINGSHAM *continued*

with lemongrass and tarragon nage, followed by West Country rib-eye steak, blue cheese potato croquettes, kidneys and red onions, and a summer fruit pudding and clotted cream for dessert.

Chef Frank Bailey **Owner** Hillbrooke Hotels **Times** 12-2.30/7-9 **Prices** Food prices not confirmed for 2010. Please telephone for details. **Wines** 21 bottles over £20, 10 bottles under £20, 8 by glass **Notes** Vegetarian available **Seats** 45, Pr/dining room 60 **Children** Portions, Menu **Parking** 8, On street

---

LITTLE BEDWYN   Map 5 SU26

The Harrow Inn at Little Bedwyn

⊛⊛⊛ – *see page 435*

LOWER CHICKSGROVE   Map 4 ST92

Compasses Inn

⊛ Modern British

Quality produce in charming country inn

☎ 01722 714318
SP3 6NB
e-mail: thecompasses@aol.com
dir: Off A30 signed Lower Chicksgrove, 1st left onto Lagpond Ln, single-track lane to village

There's a timeless feel to this attractive 14th-century thatched inn, lost down lanes deep in rolling Wiltshire countryside. An old cobbled path leads to the low latch door and the charmingly unspoilt bar, which oozes character and atmosphere, with worn flagstones, low old beams, soft candlelight and intimate booth seating. Cooking is bang up-to-date, the simple, modern approach championing local, seasonal produce such as Dorset lamb and Wiltshire rare breed pork. Look to the chalkboard for game terrine with pickled red cabbage, roast lamb

shoulder with red wine and redcurrant jus, and pear tarte Tatin with home-made cinnamon ice cream.

Chef Dave Cousin, Damian Trevett **Owner** Alan & Susie Stoneham **Times** 12-3/6-11 Closed 25-26 Dec, **Prices** Starter £5-£8.50, Main £9-£22, Dessert £5.50-£6.50, Service optional **Wines** 18 bottles over £20, 16 bottles under £20, 8 by glass **Notes** Sunday L, Vegetarian available **Seats** 50, Pr/dining room 14 **Children** Portions, Menu **Parking** 35

MALMESBURY   Map 4 ST98

Best Western Mayfield House Hotel

⊛ British

Modern cuisine based on local produce in Cotswold country-house hotel

☎ 01666 577409   📠 01666 577977
Crudwell SN16 9EW
e-mail: reception@mayfieldhousehotel.co.uk
dir: M4 junct 17, A429 to Cirencester. 3m N of Malmesbury on right in Crudwell

This Cotswold country-house hotel has a convivial bar with snug, a comfortable lounge and traditional restaurant, as well as a spacious walled garden. Situated in a small village, it is an ideal location for exploring a wide range of nearby Wiltshire and Cotswold attractions. The seasonal menu uses the freshest locally-sourced ingredients and herbs from the hotel's own gardens. Starters might include home-smoked Bibury trout on potato and spring onion salad, while slow-cooked local game casserole with horseradish dumplings and parsnip crisps is a typical main course. Finish with honeycomb cheesecake served with poached rhubarb.

Chef Nick Batstone **Owner** David Beeson & Frank Segrave-Daly **Times** 12-2/6.15-9 **Prices** Fixed L 2 course fr £14, Fixed D 3 course fr £19, Starter £4.50-£7, Main £12.50-£21, Dessert £5-£6, Service optional **Wines** 25 bottles over £20, 16 bottles under £20, 10 by glass **Notes** Sunday L, Vegetarian available, Dress restrictions, Smart casual **Seats** 50, Pr/dining room 30 **Children** Portions **Parking** 40

Old Bell Hotel

⊛⊛ Modern British, French

Venerable setting for a modern British menu

☎ 01666 822344   📠 01666 825145
Abbey Row SN16 0BW
e-mail: info@oldbellhotel.com
dir: M4 junct 17, follow A429 north. Left at 1st rdbt. Left at T-junct. Hotel next to Abbey

Parts of the building date back to the early 13th century, and with what remains of Malmesbury Abbey for a neighbour, there is no doubt this is historic England at its proudest. The décor in the main dining room is Edwardian, which in the setting counts as positively avant-garde, while the welcome and warmth of the staff bring the place right up-to-date in the best way. Modern British cooking that steers clear of outlandish

combinations is the order of the day. A slice of pork belly with ceps and pumpkin purée are the shrewd accompaniments for a serving of seared Scottish scallops, and cannon and shoulder of lamb with spiced aubergine, fondant potato and a rosemary jus makes a satisfying main course. Variations on chocolate and orange, in the shapes of a slice of tart, mini-fondant and sorbet, is the show-stopping dessert.

Chef Tom Rains **Owner** The Old Bell Hotel Ltd **Times** 12.15-2/7-9.30 **Prices** Starter £7.95-£8.95, Main £18.50-£24.50, Dessert £6.75-£8.50, Service optional **Wines** 109 bottles over £20, 8 bottles under £20, 9 by glass **Notes** Tasting menu 7 course available, Sunday L, Vegetarian available, Dress restrictions, Smart dress preferred, Civ Wed 80 **Seats** 60, Pr/dining room 48 **Children** Portions, Menu **Parking** 35

Whatley Manor

⊛⊛⊛⊛ – *see opposite page*

MELKSHAM   Map 4 ST96

Beechfield House Hotel & Restaurant

⊛ Modern British NEW

Relaxed country-house dining in elegant surroundings

☎ 01225 703700   📠 01225 790118
Beanacre SN12 7PU
e-mail: reception@beechfieldhouse.co.uk
web: www.beechfieldhouse.co.uk
dir: M4 junct 17, take A350 by-passing Chippenham. Hotel on left leaving Beanacre

A delightful late-Victorian country-house hotel built of Bath stone in the eye-catching Venetian style makes a grand setting for dining. Relax in the elegant restaurant with its open fire, crystal chandelier and pleasant views over the formal grounds, and enjoy locally sourced, seasonal ingredients from a kitchen with an eye for detail; roasted Wiltshire venison loin, perhaps, served with braised red cabbage, dauphine potato and sprouts and a peppercorn sauce. Many of the vegetables and herbs are from the hotel's potager, while items like ice creams are home-made (vanilla, perhaps, to accompany a sticky date pudding and toffee sauce dessert).

Chef Tony Thurlby **Owner** Chris Whyte **Times** 7-9 Closed D Sun **Prices** Fixed D 3 course £28.50, Service optional **Wines** 27 bottles over £20, 14 bottles under £20, 7 by glass **Notes** Sunday L bar menu only L Mon-Sat, Vegetarian available, Dress restrictions, Smart casual, Civ Wed 70 **Seats** 22, Pr/dining room 20 **Children** Portions, Menu **Parking** 100

Whatley Manor

MALMESBURY Map 4 ST98

Modern French NOTABLE WINE LIST

Technically brilliant contemporary French food in a luxury spa hotel

☎ 01666 822888 📄 01666 826120
Easton Grey SN16 0RB
e-mail:
reservations@whatleymanor.com
web: www.whatleymanor.com
dir: Please telephone for directions

Whatley Manor is an old manor house built to impress and it is probably making more of an impression in the 21st century than at any time in its history. Handsomely built of Cotswold stone, its 12 acres of idyllic surroundings certainly help to bring down the blood pressure, and, if exploring the meadows and woodland doesn't do the trick, there's always the spa. Diners can be reassured of the provenance of much of the food by glancing over to the kitchen garden from whence it came. The Dining Room offers dinner only in an elegant contemporary fine dining setting devoid of stuffiness. It seats only 40 but it seats them extremely comfortably. The Swiss-owned hotel also houses the more informal (and larger) brasserie, Le Mazot, which is open for lunch and dinner and has a splendid alfresco patio. The standard of cooking at both is consistently high from the team headed up by chef Martin Burge, delivering

classical French food with a modern interpretation. At the Dining Room, whether you choose from the à la carte or seven-course tasting menu, you are guaranteed combinations of flavours that really deliver without unnecessary over-embellishment. Presentation is a strong suit, from the selection of canapés to pre-desserts and petits fours. Start with an intense and perfectly balanced roasted celeriac ravioli layered with truffle mushroom reduction, iced porcini and celeriac apple gel, moving onto a stunningly presented roasted venison loin dressed with smoked shallot purée, lightly pickled red cabbage and white balsamic. Desserts are no less technically thrilling: treacle tart with iced custard, pineapple sherbet and topped with coconut foam, for example. An impressive wine list features a fine global selection.

Chef Martin Burge **Owner** Christian Landolt & Alix Landolt **Times** 7-10 Closed Mon-Tues, L all week
Prices Tasting menu fr £85, Service added but optional 10% **Wines** 362 bottles over £20, 12 bottles under £20, 15 by glass **Notes** ALC menu £68, Vegetarian available, Civ Wed 120
Seats 40, Pr/dining room 30
Children Portions **Parking** 120

OAKSEY — Map 4 ST99

The Wheatsheaf Inn

◎◎ Modern British

Confident cooking in relaxed village gastro-pub

☎ 01666 577348
Wheatsheaf Ln SN16 9TB
e-mail: info@thecompletechef.co.uk
dir: Off A429 towards Cirencester, near Kemble

Close to Malmesbury and Cirencester on the edge of the Cotswolds, The Wheatsheaf enjoys a beautiful location. A traditional Cotswold stone pub dating back to the 14th century, the original inglenook fireplace, flagstones and beams of the bar are complemented by the light and airy contemporary restaurant area with its sisal carpet, wooden tables and shelves filled with wine bottles and jars of preserves. Modern British pub food is the order of the day, with a keen eye on seasonality and local produce. Enjoy a pint of local ale or choose from the varied wine list as you order dishes such as fish pie, braised pork belly with cabbage and mustard mash, finishing with chocolate fondant, vanilla ice cream and rum-soaked sultanas.

Chef Tony Robson-Burrell **Owner** Tony & Holly Robson-Burrell **Times** 12-2/6.30-9.30 Closed Mon, D Sun **Prices** Starter £4-£7, Main £5-£15, Dessert £4.95-£7, Service optional **Wines** 12 bottles over £20, 16 bottles under £20, 9 by glass **Notes** Sunday L, Vegetarian available **Seats** 44, Pr/dining room 8 **Children** Portions, Menu **Parking** 15

PURTON — Map 5 SU08

The Pear Tree at Purton

◎◎ Modern British

Former vicarage with ambitious, carefully-sourced food

☎ 01793 772100 📠 01793 772369
Church End SN5 4ED
e-mail: stay@peartreepurton.co.uk
dir: From M4 junct 16, follow signs to Purton. Turn right at Spa shop, hotel 0.25m on right

The airy conservatory restaurant at this charming 15th-century former vicarage (made of Cotswold stone and sitting amid extensive landscaped gardens in a peaceful location in the Vale of the White Horse) is committed to using local and fairtrade produce. Justly proud of its green credentials, the carefully-sourced produce is put to good use in accurately cooked dishes, with a penchant for interesting flavours. Take, for example, a starter of corn-fed chicken and pistachio roulade scented with truffle and served with white onion marmalade. Main courses might include seared plaice fillets with shredded carrots, ginger, teriyaki and coriander dressing, and wind up with an orange and caramel jelly cheesecake.

Times 12-2/7-9.15 Closed 26-30 Dec, L Sat

ROWDE — Map 4 ST96

The George & Dragon

◎◎ Modern British, Italian V ◑

Charming old inn with a relaxed gastro-pub atmosphere

☎ 01380 723053
High St SN10 2PN
e-mail: thegandd@tiscali.co.uk
dir: On A342, 1m from Devizes towards Chippenham

If you're into fish and gorgeous, convivial old village inns, make a beeline for the George & Dragon. The venerable old house dates from the 16th century and has dark wooden beams throughout, a well-used log fire to keep the cold at bay in the cosy bar, while the restaurant has a clean-cut gastro-pub look with wooden furniture and simple unclothed tables. Excellent supplies come daily from St Mawes in Cornwall and appear in simple specials such as whole grilled crab or lobster served with garlic butter or lemon mayonnaise. Expect starters like creamy crab risotto spiked with chilli and rocket, or if you're in the mood for something meaty, go for braised oxtail with creamy mash and black truffle oil. Puddings follow the same straightforward, flavour-driven lines with excellent home-made ice creams or apple and raspberry crumble with Jersey cream.

Chef Christopher Day **Owner** Christopher Day, Philip & Michelle Hale **Times** 12-3/7-11 Closed D Sun **Prices** Fixed L 2 course fr £14.50, Starter £7.50-£10.50, Main £9.50-£25, Dessert fr £6, Service optional **Wines** 35 bottles over £20, 13 bottles under £20, 9 by glass **Notes** Sunday L, Vegetarian menu **Seats** 35 **Children** Portions, Menu **Parking** 14

SALISBURY — Map 5 SU12

Best Western Red Lion Hotel

◎ Modern European

Imaginative cooking in historic surroundings

☎ 01722 323334 📠 01722 325756
Milford St SP1 2AN
e-mail: reception@the-redlion.co.uk
dir: Please telephone for directions

The Red Lion feels rooted into the very fabric of Salisbury - perhaps because it has been there since it was purpose-built in the 13th century to house draughtsmen working on the magnificent cathedral. What's more, the same family has owned this historic gem for a hundred years. In the Vine Restaurant, named after the 300 year-old Virginia creeper in the courtyard, there are plenty of intriguing objets to catch the eye - unusual clocks, pottery and antiques - not to mention a medieval wattle-and-daub wall. On offer is imaginative cooking in a mix of modern and traditional European-influenced dishes: pan-fried local pigeon with beetroot rösti, parsnip purée and thyme jus, followed by roast pheasant with braised Savoy cabbage and red wine and berry sauce.

Times 12.30-2/7-9.30 Closed L Mon-Sat

Salisbury Seafood & Steakhouse

◎ Modern

Re-styled brasserie focusing on seafood and steaks

☎ 01722 417411 & 424111 📠 01722 419444
Milford Hall Hotel, 206 Castle St SP1 3TE
e-mail: simonhughes@milfordhallhotel.com
dir: From A36 at rdbt on Salisbury ring road, right onto Churchill Way East. At St Marks rdbt left onto Churchill Way North to next rdbt, left in Castle St

Formerly the 206 Brasserie, a makeover has resulted in a change of name and a smart new look, which extends to extensive use of fashionable tones of brown and cream, leather chairs on wooden floors, one wall filled with wine racks and another padded with leather. A bar area has also been added, and in warm weather the opening of large sliding glass doors brings the outside in, or is it the other way around? Friendly staff are smartly turned-out. The new menu deals in seafood and steaks as promised (plus a few vegetarian interlopers), starting with prawn cocktail '70s style' or a modern dish like pan-fried scallops with Parma ham and celeriac mash, before rib-eye steak (good quality) served with an excellent house salad and a disappointingly bought-in béarnaise.

Chef Chris Gilbert **Owner** Simon Hughes **Times** 12-2/6.30-10 Closed 26 Dec, **Prices** Starter £4.50-£9, Main £9-£24 Dessert £4.50-£6.50, Service optional **Wines** 6 bottles over £20, 27 bottles under £20, 6 by glass **Notes** Sunday L, Civ Wed 50 **Seats** 55, Pr/dining room 20 **Children** Portions, Menu **Parking** 50

STANTON ST QUINTIN   Map 4 ST97

Stanton Manor Hotel

Modern European

Contemporary cooking in country-house hotel

☎ 01666 837552 & 0870 890 02880   📠 01666 837022
SN14 6DQ
dir: M4 junct 17 onto A429 Malmesbury/Cirencester, within 200yds turn 1st left signed Stanton St Quintin, entrance to hotel on left just after church

The charming manor house - mentioned in the Domesday Book - is a mellow stone classic in 5 acres of delightful gardens with its own golf course just off the M4. The refurbished restaurant sports apricot-washed walls, pale wood floor and original artworks by young Asian artists. The kitchen aims to serve imaginative European cuisine based on good use of local produce treated without fuss. There's a good value lunch menu, and interesting wine list to back up the carte, which offers the likes of rillettes of shredded duck with mango and coriander, followed, perhaps by slow-braised shank of Wiltshire lamb with rosemary and redcurrant fumet. Round things off with white chocolate bread and butter pudding.

Times 12-2.30/7-9.30

SWINDON   Map 5 SU18

The Brasserie at Menzies Swindon

Modern British

Newly refurbished brasserie in centrally-located hotel

☎ 01793 528282   📠 01793 541283
Fleming Way SN1 1TN
e-mail: swindon@menzieshotels.co.uk
dir: Just off Whalbridge rdbt next to Debenhams

Right in the centre of Swindon, the Menzies hotel is popular with business travellers, who undoubtedly appreciate not only the location but the appealing Brasserie restaurant. It's a modern hotel, styled in the contemporary manner, and The Brasserie fits the bill perfectly with its dark wood and muted tones of white, yellow and brown, and its relaxed atmosphere. There's a small bar area or you can head straight to the table and tuck into the likes of potted game terrine or twice-baked goats' cheese and butternut squash soufflé. The brasserie-style cooking continues into main courses such as herb-crusted bream or chicken breast stuffed with smoked cheese and bacon.

Chef Marcus Bradley **Owner** Menzies Hotels **Times** 7-9.30 Closed Sun, L all week **Prices** Food prices not confirmed for 2010. Please telephone for details. **Notes** Vegetarian available, Civ Wed 100, Air con **Seats** 90, Pr/dining room 50 **Children** Portions, Menu **Parking** NCP car park

Chiseldon House Hotel

Modern International

Creative cooking in Regency manor house

☎ 01793 741010 & 07770 853883   📠 01793 741059
New Rd, Chiseldon SN4 0NE
e-mail: info@chiseldonhousehotel.co.uk
web: www.chiseldonhousehotel.co.uk
dir: M4, junct 15, A346 signed Marlborough. After 0.5m turn right onto B4500 for 0.25m, hotel on right

A charming Regency manor house surrounded by lawned gardens, Chiseldon has been tastefully converted into a comfortable hotel and is equally convenient for both the town centre and the M4. The location is quiet and the atmosphere is friendly and relaxed throughout the well-decorated public areas and the small, intimate restaurant, which overlooks the garden. The young kitchen brigade put great emphasis on carefully prepared seasonal produce, resulting in well-balanced and well-matched flavours. An excellent ham hock terrine is served with a red onion tart and mustard-dressing leaves, a full-flavoured lamb rump comes with garlic and herb mash and a rich jus, and finish with a filo pastry tart filled with pears, flavoured with cinnamon and partnered with lemon curd ice cream.

Times 12-5.30/7-9.30

WARMINSTER   Map 4 ST84

Bishopstrow House Hotel

Modern British

Conservatory dining in the heart of Wiltshire

☎ 01985 212312   📠 01985 216769
BA12 9HH
e-mail: info@bishopstrow.co.uk
dir: From Warminster take B3414 (Salisbury). Hotel signed

A peaceful country-house retreat dating back to Georgian times, Bishopstrow offers vibrant modern British cooking which favours good seasonal and organic produce. The grounds are something to behold with 27 acres of Wiltshire countryside complete with a river garden (trout fishing available), summerhouses, a ha-ha, orchards and a frequently plundered vegetable garden. A recent refurbishment aims to make the most of the stunning surroundings with an outdoor terrace and conservatory restaurant opening up the view to diners. The menu brings on cream of cauliflower soup with glazed raspberry and thyme sabayon to start, then tenderloin of pork on a white bean cassoulet with young beets, mustard and rosemary sauce, and perhaps iced banana and pistachio parfait on banana loaf with lemon sauce and glazed bananas to finish.

Times 12-2.30/7-9.30

WHITLEY   Map 4 ST86

The Pear Tree Inn

Modern British

Attractive inn serving well-cooked local produce

☎ 01225 709131   📠 01225 702276
Top Ln SN12 8QX
e-mail: peartreeinn@maypolehotels.com
dir: Please telephone for directions

An ancient wisteria-clad stone farmhouse is certainly a sound starting point from which to fashion a characterful country inn. Kit out the interior with a neatly contemporary look featuring exposed stone walls, roaring log fires, old agricultural implements and simple stripped-wooden tables, and you have the delightful Pear Tree. The country-chic restaurant looks through walls of windows into a lovely garden, and 8 classy bedrooms mean you can stay over and put the menu and wine list through their paces. The draw here is European-influenced modern British cuisine made from as much local produce as the kitchen can lay its hands on. The well-thought-out menu offers an appealing choice of good hearty dishes such as seared scallops on a fricassée of chopped chorizo, mushrooms and butternut squash, followed by another good mix of flavours in herb-crusted fillet of halibut with creamed Savoy cabbage and smoked salmon, braised baby onions and lemon butter sauce.

Chef Karl Penny **Owner** Maypole Group plc
Times 12-2.30/6.30-9.30 **Prices** Fixed L 2 course £12.50-£16, Starter £4.95-£6.75, Main £11.25-£19.95, Dessert £5.95-£6.95, Service optional, Groups min 10 service 10% **Wines** 34 bottles over £20, 22 bottles under £20, 15 by glass **Notes** Sunday L, Vegetarian available **Seats** 80 **Children** Portions, Menu **Parking** 60

WORCESTERSHIRE

ABBERLEY — Map 10 SO76

The Elms Hotel & Restaurant

◉◉ Modern, Traditional British

English country elegance and fine dining in family-friendly hotel

☎ 01299 896666 📠 01299 896804
Stockton Rd WR6 6AT
e-mail: info@theelmshotel.co.uk
web: www.theelmshotel.co.uk
dir: On A443 near Abberley, 11m NW of Worcester

The imposing Queen Anne Elms - built in 1710 by a pupil of Sir Christopher Wren - has recently been brought up-to-date with the addition of a luxurious health spa and a family-friendly approach. Overlooking beautiful grounds, the lavish interiors complement the grandiose exteriors, with ornate ceilings, carved fireplaces, antique furnishings and stained-glass windows. In the intimate Brooke Restaurant the technically adept kitchen creates accomplished, classically inspired, clean-cut modern British dishes with imaginative use of first-class ingredients. Roasted fillet and braised blade of rare-breed Herefordshire beef, for example, teamed with roasted shallots, truffled cauliflower and spring greens, or perhaps grilled fillet of brill served with an escabèche of fennel, orange and lacquered shiitake and sesame. (The all-day Pear Tree Brasserie is a more informal choice.)

Times 12-2.30/7-9.30

BEWDLEY — Map 10 SO77

The Mug House Inn

◉ Modern British

Modern classics in a sympathetically restored inn on the Severn

☎ 01299 402543 📠 08701 236417
12 Severnside North DY12 2EE
e-mail: drew@mughousebewdley.co.uk
dir: B4190 to Bewdley. On river, just over bridge on right

The present inn dates from the early 19th century, its name referring back to earlier times (a mughouse was somewhere one could buy mugs of ale). It sits on a bank of the Severn in a pretty Georgian town. The restaurant's name - The Angry Chef - may sound unnerving, but don't worry, there are no expletive-strewn histrionics here. Instead, subtle lighting, crisp napery and attentive, friendly staff have a collectively soothing effect, and the cooking is in the best gastro-pub idiom. The modern classic of seared scallops on cauliflower purée, garnished with crisped pancetta, is well handled. Even better is a main-course duo of seared breast and confit leg of duck, sweetly sauced with honey and orange, on a crunchy root vegetable rösti.

Chef Drew Clifford, Martin Warner **Owner** Drew Clifford **Times** 12-2.30/6.30-9 Closed D Sun **Prices** Fixed L 2 course £12.95-£15.95, Fixed D 3 course £15.95-£17.95, Starter £3.95-£5.95, Main £10.95-£26, Dessert £4.95-£5.95, Service optional **Wines** 6 bottles over £20, 23 bottles under £20, 9 by glass **Notes** Sunday L, Vegetarian available, Dress restrictions, Smart casual **Seats** 26, Pr/dining room 16 **Parking** Car park 100mtrs along river

---

BROADWAY — Map 10 SP03

Barcelo The Lygon Arms

◉◉ Modern European 🍷

Light Anglo-French cooking in grandiose setting

☎ 01386 852255 & 854400 📠 01386 854470
High St WR12 7DU
e-mail: info@thelygonarms.co.uk
dir: A44 to Broadway

A mere inn back in the early 16th century, the Lygon has grown grander with the passing years until what confronts us today is a full-scale manor house. Its owners remained neutral while the Civil War raged, accommodating both Charles I and, during the Commonwealth, Oliver Cromwell. The Great Hall boasts a barrel-vaulted ceiling and minstrels' gallery, but also appealing modern cooking. The Anglo-French idiom brings on casserole of pheasant with choux farci and pomme fondant, or spiced salmon with curried new potatoes and peas, bookended perhaps by seared scallops with puréed apple and chive oil, and pear Tatin with strikingly flavoured, smooth vanilla ice cream. A brasserie called Goblets, next door to the Lygon Arms, offers lighter dining.

Chef Peter Manner **Owner** Barceló Hotels & Resorts **Times** 12-2/7-9.30 **Prices** Fixed L 2 course £19-£25, Fixed D 3 course £37.50, Starter £8.50-£12.50, Main £29.50-£32.95, Dessert £8.50-£12.50, Service optional **Wines** 145 bottles over £20, 18 by glass **Notes** Gourmet 7 course with wine £75 on request, Sunday L, Vegetarian available, Dress restrictions, Smart casual, no jeans, T-shirts or trainers, Civ Wed 80, Air con **Seats** 80, Pr/dining room 110 **Children** Portions, Menu **Parking** 150

Dormy House Hotel

◉◉ British, French

Imaginative flavours at this luxurious Cotswold retreat

☎ 01386 852711   📠 01386 858636
Willersey Hill WR12 7LF
e-mail: reservations@dormyhouse.co.uk
dir: 2m E off A44, top of Fish Hill, turn for Saintbury/
Picnic area. After 0.5m left, hotel on left

Well-heeled residents plus competition for the tourist
dollar keep culinary standards high in the Cotswolds
honey-pot of Broadway. Dormy House is a small-scale
honey-stone 17th-century farmhouse, tastefully converted
to keep up to speed with 21st-century guests'
expectations. Modern country house pampering is
assured, with classy rooms and thoughtful staff
delivering polished, friendly service. Whether you go for
pub food in the recently-revamped Barn Owl bar, or put
on the glad rags for the classier ambience of the Dining
Room, judiciously-sourced produce will be on the plate.
The menus are essentially European affairs with fine
individual flavours from a kitchen with sound skills and a
flair for spot-on combinations, as in a starter of
Blythburgh pork belly and poached lobster with apple and
vanilla purée, quail eggs and red chard. Slow-cooked sea
bream comes with crushed new potatoes, red cabbage,
spinach and crispy chicken wing with chicken jus.

Chef Andrew Troughton **Owner** Mrs I Philip-Sorensen
Times 12-2/7-9.30 Closed 24-27 Dec, L Mon-Sat
Prices Food prices not confirmed for 2010. Please
telephone for details. **Wines** 70 bottles over £20, 10
bottles under £20, 10 by glass **Notes** Sunday L,
Vegetarian available, Dress restrictions, No jeans, Civ
Wed 150, Air con **Seats** 80, Pr/dining room 170
Children Portions, Menu **Parking** 80

Russell's

◉◉ Modern British

Fine dining in a chic restaurant with rooms

☎ 01386 853555
20 High St WR12 7DT
e-mail: info@russellsofbroadway.com
dir: A44 follow signs to Broadway, restaurant on High St
opposite village green

Named after Gordon Russell, the celebrated furniture
designer, who once had his headquarters at this mellow
16th-century Cotswold-stone house, the self-styled
restaurant with rooms stands on the high street in
postcard-perfect Broadway. Beautifully restored, the
restaurant successfully blends period features - note the
grand stone fireplace that showcases the fine wines -
with a muted modern décor and contemporary art. Simply
prepared, Mediterranean-inspired, modern British dishes
make good use of quality local ingredients. The accurate
cooking and friendly service draw loyal locals and tourists
in for roast tomato and goats' cheese tart with rocket and
balsamic syrup, grilled mackerel with potato and spinach
curry and mint yogurt relish, and a crunchy iced
caramelised peanut parfait. Set lunch menus are a steal

and best enjoyed in the secluded courtyard on sunny
summer days.

Chef Matthew Laughton **Owner** Andrew Riley, Barry
Hancox **Times** 12-2.30/6-9.30 Closed D Sun & BH Mon
Prices Fixed L 2 course £12, Fixed D 3 course £15-
£22.95, Starter £8-£12, Main £12-£28, Dessert £6-£8,
Service optional **Wines** 38 bottles over £20, 12 bottles
under £20, 12 by glass **Notes** Sunday L, Vegetarian
available, Air con **Seats** 55, Pr/dining room 14
Children Portions **Parking** 16

BROMSGROVE   Map 10 SO97

Grafton Manor Restaurant

◉ Modern British, Indian V

**Period setting for modern food spiced up with some
Indian dishes**

☎ 01527 579007   📠 01527 575221
Grafton Ln B61 7HA
e-mail: stephen@graftonmanorhotel.co.uk
dir: Off B4091, 1.5m SW of Bromsgrove

The Gunpowder Plot conspirators met at this 16th-century
manor in 1605 before failing to blow up Parliament.
Today, the baronial atmosphere of the red brick manor
means it will never be short of wedding trade, and makes
a suitably grand setting for inventive modern menus,
spiked with exotica such as Sali Goa chicken caffrael
with Indian vegetables, or a sweet gulab jamun with lime
custard. The Indian influence comes from Simon Morris's
travels in India, but his more orthodox offerings are based
on classic French foundations, as in ham hock terrine
with a caper and cornichon dressing, pork belly with
carrot purée, roast potatoes, kale and Madeira sauce.
Finish boozily with Lord of Grafton's whisky steamed
pudding with whisky cream.

Chef Adam Harrison, Tim Waldon **Owner** The Morris family
Times 12.30-1.30/7-9.30 Closed New Year, BHs, L Sat, D
Sun **Prices** Fixed L course £22.50, Fixed D 3 course
£28.95, Service optional **Wines** 46 bottles over £20, 24
bottles under £20, 3 by glass **Notes** Sunday L, Vegetarian
menu, Dress restrictions, Smart casual, Civ Wed 120
Seats 60, Pr/dining room 60 **Children** Portions
Parking 60

CHADDESLEY CORBETT   Map 10 SO87

Brockencote Hall Country House Hotel

◉◉ Modern French V 🐾

Divine French cooking at an elegant manor house

☎ 01562 777876   📠 01562 777872
DY10 4PY
e-mail: info@brockencotehall.com
dir: On A448 just outside village, between Kidderminster
& Bromsgrove

Built in the style of a French château, this impressive
Victorian mansion stands in 70 acres of landscaped
grounds, with its own lake, dovecote and gatehouse. The
country-house style is reinforced by the interior design,

and the cool elegance of the intimate dining room -
elegant drapes, chandeliers, pastel shades - provides the
perfect backdrop for the accomplished modern French
cuisine of Didier Philipot. With passion, skill and
imagination he successfully adds a contemporary touch
to classic French dishes. Using top-notch seasonal
produce, accurately cooked dishes deliver good flavour
clarity and balance of textures without being over
embellished, as experienced with succulent seared
scallops with a delicious saffron and butter sauce; tender
and pink roast lamb rump with confit tomato, home-
grown wild garlic and basil and olive oil jus; and a
perfect crème brûlée. Still one to watch.

Chef Didier Philipot **Owner** Mr & Mrs Petitjean
Times 12-1.30/7-9.30 **Prices** Fixed L 2 course £15, Fixed
D 3 course £34.30, Starter £14.50, Main £23.50-£27.50,
Dessert £9-£12.50, Service included **Wines** 160 bottles
over £20, 26 bottles under £20, 13 by glass
Notes Dégustation menu 6 course £55, Sunday L,
Vegetarian menu, Dress restrictions, Smart casual, no
jeans, Civ Wed 80 **Seats** 60, Pr/dining room 30
Children Portions, Menu **Parking** 45

DROITWICH   Map 10 SO86

The Hadley Bowling Green Inn

◉◉ Modern European NEW 🐾

Considered cooking in a historic inn

☎ 01905 620294   📠 01905 620771
Hadley Heath WR9 0AR
e-mail: info@hadleybowlinggreen.com
dir: Telephone for directions

So named for its location next to the country's oldest
bowling green, the inn has a claim to fame all of its own.
One Guido (better known as Guy) Fawkes is known to have
been a guest in the summer of 1604, and may well have
embarked on the initial planning here for history's most
famous failed bomb plot. Dining is split in the traditional
manner between a simpler bar menu, and the fine dining
Hadley restaurant, where crisply dressed tables with
fresh flowers await. The cooking is good, full of
considered attention to detail, as in the trio of beetroot
preparations - pickled, puréed and pan-fried - that comes
with a starter of Ragstone goats' cheese mousse and
watercress. Free-range pork, served as confit belly, is
well-trimmed but packed with flavour, and is supported
by black pudding and a piece of the crackling in a
tomato-based nage with apple and sage. Excellent
breads give further notice that this is a kitchen that
means business.

Chef Martin Lovell **Owner** Malcolm Carle
Times 12-2.30/6-9.30 **Prices** Fixed L 2 course £9.95-
£11.95, Fixed D 3 course fr £23.95, Starter £5.95-£6.95,
Main £11.95-£19.95, Dessert £5.50-£7.95, Groups min 8
service 10% **Notes** Sunday L, Civ Wed 120 **Seats** 70, Pr/
dining room 24 **Children** Portions, Menu **Parking** 120

EVESHAM | Map 10 SP04

The Evesham Hotel

International

Relaxed Georgian style and appealing menu

☎ 01386 765566 📠 01386 765443
Coopers Ln, Off Waterside WR11 1DA
e-mail: reception@eveshamhotel.com
dir: Coopers Lane is off road by River Avon

Georgian in appearance, this grand old hotel actually
dates back to 1540 when it was a Tudor farmhouse. Set
in secluded grounds and run in their own jolly style by the
Jenkinson family for over 30 years, it contains a wealth of
quirky memorabilia. The Cedar Restaurant is an elegant
Georgian room, providing a comfortable and relaxed
venue for some simple honest cooking using quality fresh
ingredients. From a lengthy, crowd-pleasing menu begin
with smoked haddock risotto, follow with braised lamb
shank with rosemary jus, and round off with lemon
parfait with raspberry coulis.

Chef Adam Talbot **Owner** John Jenkinson
Times 12.30-2/7-9.30 Closed 25-26 Dec **Prices** Starter
£3.50-£8, Main £12.50-£17, Dessert £3.60-£5.20, Service
included **Wines** 391 bottles over £20, 303 bottles under
£20, 5 by glass **Notes** Buffet L available £9.50, Sunday L,
Air con **Seats** 55, Pr/dining room 12 **Children** Portions,
Menu **Parking** 45

Northwick Hotel

Traditional British

Traditional dining in welcoming hotel

☎ 01386 40322 📠 01386 41070
Waterside WR11 1BT
e-mail: enquiries@northwickhotel.co.uk
dir: M5 junct 9, A46 Evesham, follow town centre signs.
At River Bridge lights turn left, hotel 50yds on left

Located a short walk from the town centre, this
modernised hotel benefits from its position overlooking
the River Avon and its adjacent park. The aptly named
contemporary-style fine-dining Courtyard Restaurant has
an airy garden feel, overlooking the courtyard, raised
beds and pond. The straightforward carte delivers simple,
well-presented traditional dishes of real flavour, based on
home-made and local ingredients. Fishcakes with sweet
chilli sauce to start, perhaps, followed by pork medallions
with garlic potato rösti and a roasted apple and cider
sauce, and white and dark chocolate parfait with fruit
coulis for dessert.

Chef Kevin Attwood **Owner** Mrs Start **Times** 12-2/7-9.30
Closed Xmas **Prices** Food prices not confirmed for 2010.
Please telephone for details. **Wines** 32 bottles over £20,
16 bottles under £20, 10 by glass **Notes** Sunday L,
Vegetarian available, Civ Wed 70 **Seats** 50, Pr/dining
room 30 **Children** Portions, Menu **Parking** 120

KIDDERMINSTER | Map 10 SO87

The Granary Hotel & Restaurant

Modern European

Modern food in contemporary comfort

☎ 01562 777535 📠 01562 777722
Heath Ln, Shenstone DY10 4BS
e-mail: info@granary-hotel.co.uk
web: www.granary-hotel.co.uk
dir: On A450 between Worcester & Stourbridge. 2m from
Kidderminster

This modern hotel has a tranquil rural setting that gives
handy access to the business arteries of the Heart of
England. Decorated in an uncluttered contemporary style
with muted tones and plenty of space between the tables,
the restaurant's forte is clean-cut modern dishes, each
built around a handful of core ingredients, accurately
cooked without fuss or over-embellishment. Excellent
local produce is the mainstay of the menu, and the hotel
is currently developing its own 2-acre market garden to
reinforce further its credentials. A typical starter might be
pan-fried sea bass with crab risotto and vanilla beurre
blanc, before a duo of Worcestershire lamb, comprising
pink pan-fried slices and a miniature shepherd's pie, and
traditional bread-and-butter pudding with crème fraîche
to finish. For simpler weekday lunches, a carvery serves
daily-changing roasts.

Chef Tom Court **Owner** Richard Fletcher
Times 12-2.30/7-11 Closed 25 Dec, L Mon & Sat, D Sun
Prices Fixed L 2 course £9.50-£11.95, Fixed D 3 course
£15-£18.50, Starter £4.95-£7.95, Main £12.50-£19.50,
Dessert £4.50-£5.25, Service optional **Wines** 14 bottles
over £20, 29 bottles under £20, 11 by glass **Notes** Sunday
L, Vegetarian available, Civ Wed 200, Air con **Seats** 60,
Pr/dining room 40 **Children** Portions **Parking** 95

MALVERN | Map 10 SO74

L'Amuse Bouche

Traditional French

**French-style cooking in a quintessentially English
setting**

☎ 01684 572427 📠 01684 572952
The Cotford Hotel, 51 Graham Rd WR14 2HU
e-mail: reservations@cotfordhotel.co.uk
dir: Please telephone for directions

The family-run Cotford Hotel is a Gothic-style Victorian
mansion originally built for the Bishop of Worcester.
Tucked beneath the buxom Malvern Hills in landscaped
grounds with glorious views, its L'Amuse Bouche
restaurant deals in French-style cooking in an elegant
setting that blends period charm with contemporary
design. Service likes to maintain a certain gravitas in
keeping with the surroundings, and menus are changed
daily in order to take the pick of local suppliers' produce -
all quality stuff with a strong organic presence. A double-
baked goats' cheese soufflé served on a macadamia
nut-dressed salad shows the style, while main courses
might offer pan-fried chicken breast and asparagus
served with wild mushrooms, pine nuts and spinach.

Chef Christopher Morgan **Owner** Christopher & Barbara
Morgan **Times** 12-1.30/6-8 **Prices** Fixed L 2 course
£22.50, Fixed D 3 course £27.50, Service optional
Wines 11 bottles over £20, 14 bottles under £20, 8 by
glass **Notes** Pre-theatre menu available, Sunday L,
Vegetarian available, Dress restrictions, Smart casual
Seats 36, Pr/dining room 12 **Parking** 15

Holdfast Cottage Hotel

Traditional, Modern British

Charming cottage setting and confident cooking

☎ 01684 310288 & 311481 📠 01684 311117
Marlbank Rd, Welland WR13 6NA
e-mail: enquiries@holdfast-cottage.co.uk
dir: On A4104 midway between Welland & Little Malvern

Magnificent views of the Malvern Hills and 2 acres of
gardens and woodland to explore are part of the appeal of
this 17th-century property, which was extended in Victorian
times. The oak-beamed hall retains the original cast iron
range, while the cosy Victorian-style bar opens onto the
wisteria-covered terrace. The attractive dining room with
its oak tables, fresh flowers and simple cutlery and
glassware overlooks the garden. The cuisine is ostensibly
traditional but is not adverse to some contemporary
flourishes, and makes good use of seasonal produce. So,
grilled goats' cheese comes on toasted brioche with a
beetroot glaze, served with dressed leaves, and main-
course loin of pork steak comes with colcannon and black
pudding with a light mustard sauce and crisp leeks.

Chef Adam Cambridge **Owner** Guy & Annie Dixon
Times 12.30-2.30/7-8.30 **Prices** Fixed L 2 course £19.95,
Fixed D 3 course £27.50, Service optional **Wines** 11
bottles over £20, 24 bottles under £20, 2 by glass
Notes Sunday L, Vegetarian available **Seats** 30
Children Portions **Parking** 15

Outlook Restaurant

British, European

Ambitious cooking in charming hotel with stunning views

☎ 01684 588860 📄 01684 560662
**The Cottage in the Wood Hotel, Holywell Rd, Malvern
Wells WR14 4LG**
e-mail: reception@cottageinthewood.co.uk
dir: 3M S of Great Malvern off A449, 500yds N of B4209, on opposite side of road

With panoramic views of the Severn Valley, this delightful family-run hotel is perched on the side of the Malvern Hills. The restaurant is located in the heart of the elegant Georgian dower house and the floor-to-ceiling windows offer diners a stunning aspect. The ambitious cooking takes its lead from modern British cuisine and focuses on quality local, seasonal produce and bold flavours. Take escabèche of wood pigeon with marinated vegetables and pickled chicory, or perhaps roast crusted monkfish with basil polenta, roasted cherry tomatoes, lobster tortellini and crab and lobster bisque. The large wine list is packed with interest, enthusiasm and a refreshing lack of pretension, with a good selection of half bottles.

Chef Dominic Pattin **Owner** The Pattin family
Times 12.30-2/7-9.30 **Prices** Fixed L 2 course £18.50, Starter £5.50-£14, Main £12.50-£24, Dessert £7.50-£15, Service optional **Wines** 348 bottles over £20, 72 bottles under £20, 10 by glass **Notes** Pre-theatre D available from 6pm, Sunday L, Vegetarian available, Air con
Seats 70, Pr/dining room 20 **Children** Portions
Parking 40

Seasons Restaurant at Colwall Park Hotel

Modern British

Elegant hotel with plenty of culinary ambition

☎ 01684 540000 📄 01684 540847
Walwyn Rd, Colwall WR13 6QG
e-mail: hotel@colwall.com
dir: On B4218, off A449 from Malvern to Ledbury

An independently owned country house hotel at the foot of the Malvern Hills, Colwall Park is a handsome building of black-and-white timbered and red brick construction, and inside it is grand without ever being overbearing. There are splendid views from the garden. The Lantern Bar is a good option for a light meal or a pint of local ale, while the Seasons Restaurant, with its light oak panelling and well spaced, elegantly set tables, is where to head for some ambitious modern British cooking. Start with hand-dived scallops with carpaccio of tuna, cauliflower, bacon and a quail's egg in a well executed starter, followed by chargrilled fillet of Scottish beef with fondant potato, crisp pancetta, baby onions and a well-made red wine sauce. Pineapple and black pepper tarte Tatin with coconut ice cream has excellent pastry and a successful balance of flavours.

Chef James Garth **Owner** Mr & Mrs I Nesbitt
Times 12-2/7-9 Closed L all week (ex by arrangement)
Prices Fixed L 2 course fr £16.95, Starter £6.95-£7.95, Main £18.95-£21.95, Dessert £6.95-£7.95, Service included **Wines** 32 bottles over £20, 40 bottles under £20, 9 by glass **Notes** Sunday L, Vegetarian available, Air con **Seats** 40, Pr/dining room 100 **Children** Portions, Menu **Parking** 40

OMBERSLEY Map 10 SO86

The Venture In Restaurant

British, French

Accurate cooking of local produce in a medieval draper's house

☎ 01905 620552 📄 01905 620552
Main Rd WR9 0EW
dir: From Worcester N towards Kidderminster on A449 (approx 5m). Left at Ombersley turn. Restaurant 0.75m on right

Dating from 1430, the black-and-white Venture In is on the main street and positively overflows with charm and character. Fresh flowers and gentle colours enhance the comfortable, beamed interior, which is furnished with bare wooden tables and high-backed leather chairs. The log fire is just the ticket in chilly weather. The chef-proprietor cooks in an Anglo-French style using the best locally sourced ingredients and dishes are simply presented on white plates. Highlights include warm home-made bread rolls to start, and a creamy vanilla pannacotta, perfectly complemented by a slightly sharp rhubarb coulis, to finish. For a memorable main course try roast loin of new season lamb with pan-fried sweetbread, sweet pickled red cabbage and boulangère potatoes.

Chef Toby Fletcher **Owner** Toby Fletcher
Times 12-2/7-9.30 Closed 25 Dec-1 Jan, 2 wks summer & 2 wks winter, Mon, D Sun **Prices** Fixed L 2 course £22, Fixed D 3 course £36, Service optional **Wines** 40 bottles over £20, 20 bottles under £20, 6 by glass **Notes** Sunday L, Vegetarian available, Dress restrictions, Smart casual, Air con **Seats** 32, Pr/dining room 32 **Parking** 15, on street

TENBURY WELLS Map 10 SO56

Cadmore Lodge

Modern British

Contemporary cooking in idyllic location

☎ 01584 810044
Berrington Green, St Michaels WR15 8TQ
e-mail: reception.cadmore@cadmorelodge.com
dir: Off A4112 from Tenbury Wells to Leominster. 2m from Tenbury Wells, turn right opposite St Michael's Church

On the banks of a lake in a 70-acre private estate and nature reserve, this family-run hotel was once a fishing lodge, and still has fishing facilities as well as a 9-hole golf course. The country-style restaurant's warm colour scheme and log fire make for a relaxing atmosphere, and diners can enjoy lovely views of the surrounding countryside. The daily-changing dinner menu offers contemporary dishes carefully presented, such as baked field mushroom topped with Parma ham and mozzarella to start, with a typical main course of pan-fried salmon, cracked black pepper and lemon crushed potatoes and salsa verde. For dessert, you might try white chocolate truffle cake.

Chef Mark Griffiths, Chris Bushell **Owner** Mr & Mrs J Weston **Times** 12-2/7-9.15 Closed 25 Dec, L Mon **Prices** Fixed L 2 course £11.50, Fixed D 3 course £23.50 **Wines** 3 bottles over £20, 13 bottles under £20, 6 by glass **Notes** Sunday L, Civ Wed 100, Air con **Seats** 50, Pr/dining room 50 **Children** Portions, Menu **Parking** 100

TENBURY WELLS *continued*

Whites@ the Clockhouse

◉◉ Modern British

Accomplished modern bistro incorporating tapas and wine options

☎ 01584 811336 📠 01584 811895
14 Market St WR15 8BQ
e-mail: whites@theclockhouse.net
dir: A456/A4112 into Tenbury Wells. Over bridge, along main street. Restaurant on right adjacent to The Royal Oak

The striking white-fronted building on the high street, with its clock (of course) and full-length windows, is hard to miss. A tapas joint and wine bar throughout the day, it also offers a full lunch and dinner carte. Climb the spiral staircase to the beamed main restaurant, where an atmosphere of civility reigns, complete with quality table settings and classical music. A brasserie-type menu of tried-and-true modern dishes offers the likes of open ravioli of smoked chicken and leek, based on fine home-made pasta, followed perhaps by perfectly timed steamed brill with broad beans, crushed potatoes and sorrel sauce. Good pastry work distinguishes pear and amaretti frangipane tart, served with creamy caramel ice cream, or there might be summery strawberry and elderflower syllabub with ginger-snaps.

Times 10.30am-11pm Closed 2 wks mid Jan, Mon, L Tue-Wed, D Sun

UPTON UPON SEVERN   Map 10 SO84

White Lion Hotel

◉ Modern British

Historic hotel with contemporary feel and flavour

☎ 01684 592551 📠 01684 593333
21 High St WR8 0HJ
e-mail: info@whitelionhotel.biz
dir: From A422 take A38 towards Tewkesbury. After 8m take B4104 for 1m, after bridge turn left to hotel

The 16th-century White Lion has an engaging history, mentioned in Henry Fielding's novel *Tom Jones*, and involved in the last days of the Civil War when boozy Royalist troops let in the opposition after a drinking session in the inn. In the Pepperpot Brasserie, named after the town's landmark church spire, its venerable beams now rub shoulders with an updated interior design with fresh flowers on chunky oak tables. The kitchen's modern British output focuses on seasonal, local produce to deliver sound, accurate cooking with clearly-defined flavours. Monkfish, for example, is tea-smoked in-house and served on black noodles with soya dressing, while collops of rare venison sit atop braised red cabbage with creamy mash and juniper jus.

Chef Jon Lear, Richard Thompson **Owner** Mr & Mrs Lear **Times** 12-2/7-9.15 Closed 31 Dec-1 Jan, L few days between Xmas & New Year **Prices** Fixed L 2 course £9.50, Starter £5-£7, Main £13-£18, Dessert £6-£7, Service

optional **Wines** 5 bottles over £20, 26 bottles under £20, 4 by glass **Notes** Sunday L, Vegetarian available **Seats** 45 **Children** Portions **Parking** 16

WORCESTER   Map 10 SO85

Brown's Restaurant

◉◉ Modern International

Skilful modern cooking in stylishly converted corn mill

☎ 01905 26263 📠 01905 25768
The Old Cornmill, 24 Quay St, South Quay WR1 2JJ
e-mail: enquiries@brownsrestaurant.co.uk
dir: From M5 junct 7 to city centre, at lights turn into Copenhagen St

There are fabulous views over the River Severn and the swan sanctuary - very romantic by night - from this Victorian former corn mill, magnificently restored since the floods of 2007/8. Enter through two huge glass doors, opening into a massive high ceilinged space of metal rafters and lighting suspended on several single wires, before settling into the stylish and comfortable mezzanine-level lounge. Black diamond-patterned carpeted stairs lead down into the restaurant with its well-spaced, smartly-set tables. Quality seasonal ingredients are used to good effect in well-judged, uncluttered dishes such as smoked haddock rarebit, followed by an accurately cooked, very fresh sea bream in tomato pot-au-feu, set on crushed new potatoes, finishing with rhubarb tart with ginger custard.

Chef Ian Courage **Owner** Mr & Mrs R Everton **Times** 12-2.30/6-9.30 Closed 25-26 Dec, New Year, D Sun **Prices** Fixed L 2 course £9.95-£11.95, Fixed D 3 course £20-£25, Starter £5.95-£7.95, Main £13.95-£38.95, Dessert £5.95-£9.95, Service optional **Wines** 93 bottles over £20, 30 bottles under £20, 7 by glass **Notes** Sunday L, Vegetarian available, Dress restrictions, Smart casual preferred **Seats** 110 **Children** Portions **Parking** 6, Large car park adjacent to the restaurant

The Glasshouse

◉◉ Modern British ✋

Bustling town-centre brasserie with cathedral views

☎ 01905 611120
55 Sidbury WR1 2HU
e-mail: eat@theglasshouse.co.uk
dir: M5 junct 7 towards Worcester. Continue straight over 2 rdbts, through 2 sets of lights. At 3rd lights left into car park, restaurant opposite

After a decade in the acclaimed Merchant House in Ludlow, chef Shaun Hill (see also entry for The Walnut Tree, Abergavenny) set up shop in lucky old Worcester. The designers were let loose behind the vast plate-glass windows of a landmark town-centre building, kitting out the brasserie with grey slate floors, stripy banquettes and leather chairs. It's a lively place, humming with conversation that filters upwards to an upstairs dining room with views of the cathedral. With Shaun Hill overseeing the kitchen, this is more than straightforward brasserie fodder - rest assured that the finest raw

materials will be cooked and presented without fuss or pomposity. High-quality starters include a warm chicken liver tart with walnut salad, and mains might be Cornish rack of lamb served with a tender crumbed breast, dauphinoise potatoes and baby carrots.

Chef Tom Duffill **Owner** Shaun Hill **Times** 12-2.30/5.30-10 Closed 26 Dec, 1 Jan & BHs, Sun **Prices** Fixed L 2 course £10, Fixed D 3 course £21.95, Starter £6-£9, Main £15-£20, Dessert £7.50-£15, Service added but optional, Groups min 8 service 10% **Wines** 18 bottles over £20, 5 bottles under £20, 25 by glass **Notes** Pre-theatre menu available, Vegetarian available, Air con **Seats** 100, Pr/dining room 16 **Children** Portions, Menu **Parking** Pay & display 100yds

YORKSHIRE, EAST RIDING OF

BEVERLEY   Map 17 TA03

The Pipe and Glass Inn

◉ Modern British V ✋

Charming countryside inn with hearty food

☎ 01430 810246
West End, South Dalton HU17 7PN
e-mail: email@pipeandglass.co.uk
dir: Just off B1248

The rambling 17th-century building stands in an elegant Wolds estate village and is the perfect example of a charming country inn run with modern style and great attention to detail. Bag a seat by the fire in the traditional beamed snug bar or a bespoke wooden table in the stylish dining areas and peruse the monthly-changing menu, which bristles with locally-sourced produce. James Mackenzie's exciting modern British repertoire includes some interesting combinations; take crispy wild rabbit rissoles with cockles, capers and sorrel for starters, a main dish of squid with ham hock, white bean and grain mustard cassoulet, and Barnsley lamb chop with nettle and mint sauce.

Chef James Mackenzie **Owner** James & Kate Mackenzie **Times** 12-2/6.30-9.30 Closed 25 Dec, 1 wk Jan, Mon, D Sun **Prices** Starter £6.95-£8.95, Main £8.95-£19.95, Dessert £4.95-£8.95, Service optional **Wines** 71 bottles over £20, 26 bottles under £20, 10 by glass **Notes** Sunday L, Vegetarian menu, Air con **Seats** 70, Pr/dining room 26 **Children** Portions, Menu **Parking** 60

Tickton Grange Hotel

◉◉ Modern British ✋

Period charm and local cuisine in well-maintained Georgian country house

☎ 01964 543666 📠 01964 542556
Tickton HU17 9SH
e-mail: info@ticktongrange.co.uk
dir: From Beverley take A1035 towards Bridlington. After 3m hotel on left, just past Tickton

Three miles east of Beverley, this bright white Georgian hotel is all about period style. Take aperitifs in the library lounge, before progressing to the 1920s-fashioned dining room, where crisply clothed tables and candlelight set the scene. Attractively presented modern British dishes are the order of the day, with local supply-lines in heartening evidence on the menus. Start with smoked breast of Hornsea chicken with crab-apple chutney, or dressed Bridlington crab, and go on with grilled rainbow trout with dauphinoise, pink grapefruit and capers, or flavourful Rosedale Farm duck breast with parsnips and elderberries in a reduction of port. The star dessert may well be baked chocolate cheesecake, served with clearly defined ginger and mint sorbet, but there are also regional cheeses to consider.

Chef David Nowell, John MacDonald **Owner** Mr & Mrs Whymant **Times** 12-2/7-9.30 Closed 26 Dec **Prices** Food prices not confirmed for 2010. Please telephone for details. **Wines** 33 bottles over £20, 32 bottles under £20, 8 by glass **Notes** Sunday L, Vegetarian available, Civ Wed 150 **Seats** 45, Pr/dining room 20 **Children** Portions, Menu **Parking** 75

KINGSTON UPON HULL   Map 17 TA02

Boars Nest

◎ Modern British ✪

Accomplished cooking in an Edwardian butcher's shop

☎ 01482 445577
22 Princes Av HU5 3QA
e-mail: boarsnest@boarsnest.karoo.co.uk
dir: 1m from Hull city centre. From Ferensway onto Spring Bank, turn right onto Princes Ave

In Hull's trendy rejuvenated Princes Avenue area, the Boars Nest fits in well among the bijou boutiques, delis and buzzy eateries. Its shabby-chic style blends the glorious ceramic wall-and-floor tiles of the original Edwardian butcher's shop with buttoned leather banquettes and an eclectic mishmash of chairs, tasselled light shades, the odd chandelier and boudoir hues of crimson. The kitchen goes in for forthright, no-frills British cooking with full-on flavours in dishes such as potted smoked salmon with melba toast, Whitby-landed halibut with pea purée, buttered peas and morels and red wine jus, and sticky toffee pudding with black treacle ripple ice cream and caramelised quince for afters.

Chef Simon Rogers, M Bulamore, H Pepper, D Cutsforth **Owner** Simon Rogers, Dina Hanchett **Times** 12-2/6.30-10 Closed 26 Dec, 1 Jan **Prices** Fixed L 2 course £8, Fixed D 3 course £20, Starter £4.50-£8, Main £15-£22, Dessert £5-£7.50, Service added but optional 10% **Wines** 22 bottles over £20, 19 bottles under £20, 13 by glass

Notes Pre-theatre menu available, Sunday L, Vegetarian available **Seats** 62, Pr/dining room 24 **Children** Portions

---

Cerutti's

◎ Traditional, Seafood

Simple seafood cookery by the Humber estuary

☎ 01482 328501   📠 01482 587597
10 Nelson St HU1 1XE
e-mail: ceruttis@ceruttisltd.karoo.co.uk
dir: Please telephone for directions

A charming seafood restaurant close to the docks, Cerutti's has long been a main player on the Hull scene. Step upstairs to the first-floor dining room, which is done in shell pink, with pictures of seascapes and ships. No-nonsense fish and shellfish cookery is what it's about, with king prawns in garlic butter, chargrilled scallops on gorgeously velvety crayfish sauce, or moules marinière, to start, followed by something like fillets of sea bass with crisp-fried seaweed and more garlic butter. If you're not a fish person, you might opt for a fillet steak with a choice of sauces. Pumpkin tart with cinnamon ice cream makes an unexpectedly sumptuous dessert.

Chef Tim Bell **Owner** Anthony Cerutti **Times** 12-2/7-9.30 Closed 1 wk Xmas & New Year, Sun, L Sat **Prices** Fixed L 2 course fr £16.50, Fixed D 3 course fr £19.50, Starter £4.75-£11.95, Main £12.95-£23, Dessert £5.75-£6.95, Service optional **Wines** 18 bottles over £20, 28 bottles under £20, 8 by glass **Notes** Vegetarian available, Dress restrictions, Smart casual **Seats** 40 **Children** Portions **Parking** 6

WILLERBY   Map 17 TA03

Best Western Willerby Manor Hotel

◎◎ Modern European ✪

Peaceful setting for high-quality cuisine

☎ 01482 652616   📠 01482 653901
Well Ln HU10 6ER
e-mail: willerbymanor@bestwestern.co.uk
dir: M62/A63, follow signs for Humber Bridge, then signs for Beverley until Willerby Shopping Park. Hotel signed from rdbt next to McDonald's

Situated in 3 acres of attractive landscaped garden, this family-run hotel is 4 miles from Hull. Once the home of a wealthy shipping merchant, it has been renovated and refurbished to provide the fine-dining Icon Restaurant and the contemporary Figs Brasserie, which boasts a luxury outdoor area complete with heating and lighting. In the restaurant, typical starters might include Yorkshire pea soup topped with sliced foie gras, or carpaccio of tuna Niçoise, with mains of sautéed cod with cod cake, pickled clams and parsley, or guinea fowl with polenta cake, Provençal vegetables and garlic crisps. A few dishes are available as either starters or mains.

Chef David Roberts, Ben Olley **Owner** Alexandra Townend **Times** 12.30-2.30/7-9.30 Closed 1st wk Jan, last 2 wks Aug, BHs, L Mon-Sat, D Sun **Prices** Fixed D 3 course fr £25, Starter £5.20-£6.20, Main £14.75-£17, Dessert

£5.20-£5.40, Service optional **Wines** 7 bottles over £20, 23 bottles under £20, 4 by glass **Notes** Sunday L, Vegetarian available, Civ Wed 300, Air con **Seats** 40, Pr/dining room 40 **Children** Portions **Parking** 200

YORKSHIRE, NORTH

ASENBY   Map 19 SE37

Crab and Lobster Restaurant

◎◎ British, European

Brimming with quirky charm and a seafood-focused menu

☎ 01845 577286   📠 01845 577109
Dishforth Rd YO7 3QL
e-mail: enquiries@crabandlobster.co.uk
web: www.crabandlobster.co.uk
dir: From A19/A168 take A167. Through Topcliffe, follow signs for A1. Restaurant on left 8m from Northallerton

Approaching the Crab and Lobster one gets an idea of what lies within - the thatched restaurant is festooned with old advertising signs, flags raised up high poles and a myriad of potted plants and climbers. Once inside, the riot of memorabilia covers nearly every inch of the walls and ceiling, from the intimate bar to the main dining room and bright pavilion conservatory. While the atmosphere is relaxed and unpretentious, food and service are rightly taken very seriously. Fresh local seafood served in generous portions dominates the menus - the fish and chips would satisfy the heartiest appetite - alongside a choice of traditional English dishes. Presentation is modern and carnivores might go for crisp leg of Barbary duck leg, presented as a main course with black pudding mash and rich sage gravy. There are outside areas for drinking and eating.

Chef Steve Dean **Owner** Vimac Leisure **Times** 12-2.30/7-9.30 **Prices** Fixed L 2 course £13, Service optional **Wines** 8 bottles over £20, 8 bottles under £20, 8 by glass **Notes** Sunday L, Vegetarian available, Civ Wed 75 **Seats** 85, Pr/dining room 24 **Children** Portions **Parking** 80

AUSTWICK
Map 18 SD76

The Austwick Traddock

Modern British V

Georgian country-house hotel and exclusively organic produce

☎ 015242 51224 📠 015242 51796
Settle LA2 8BY
e-mail: info@austwicktraddock.co.uk
dir: From Skipton take A65 towards Kendal, 3m after Settle turn right signed Austwick, cross hump back bridge, hotel 100yds on left

Built as a gentleman's residence in the 1700s, this intimate Georgian country house is the perfect base for exploring the Yorkshire Dales National Park. Follow a walk through the glorious surrounding countryside with a drink by one of the roaring log fires in the comfortable, antique-furnished lounges, and savour local wild and organic food in the cosy, candlelit restaurant, an elegant, well-appointed room that was once the library. Follow seared scallops with fennel purée and bacon jus, with roast rack of Mansergh Hall lamb with port jus, and a dark chocolate torte with caramel sauce. Expect relaxed, professional service from smartly dressed staff.

Chef John Pratt **Owner** Bruce & Jane Reynolds **Times** 12-3/6.45-11 **Prices** Fixed L 2 course fr £12.95, Starter £4.95-£6.50, Main £15.50-£19.25, Dessert £5.95-£7.95, Service optional **Wines** 18 bottles over £20, 21 bottles under £20, 8 by glass **Notes** Sunday L, Vegetarian menu **Seats** 36, Pr/dining room 16 **Children** Portions, Menu **Parking** 20

AYSGARTH
Map 19 SE08

The George & Dragon Inn

British NEW

Traditional inn with bags of character

☎ 01969 663358 📠 01969 663773
DL8 3AD
e-mail: info@georgeanddragonaysgarth.co.uk
web: www.georgeanddragonaysgarth.co.uk

This 17th-century, white-painted inn, bedecked with hanging baskets, is ideally located for exploring the Yorkshire Dales National Park. It offers comfortable accommodation and good, honest cooking. The dining room is full of character (and furniture and memorabilia) with a real fire and beams on the ceiling. Blackboard specials are listed in the bar or there is the printed menu, both featuring straightforward British food with some international touches; start with black pudding and streaky bacon with a poached egg, before pan-fried duck breast with dauphinoise potatoes, served with fine beans and carrots in a mini copper pan.

The George & Dragon Inn

Chef Gavin Smith **Times** 12-2/5.30-8.30 (9 wknds) **Prices** Food prices not confirmed for 2010. Please telephone for details.

BOLTON ABBEY
Map 19 SE05

The Burlington Restaurant

 – *see below*

The Burlington Restaurant

BOLTON ABBEY
Map 19 SE05

Modern French V

Top-flight cooking on a beautiful Yorkshire estate

☎ 01756 718111 & 710441 📠 01756 710564
The Devonshire Arms Country House Hotel & Spa BD23 6AJ
e-mail: res@devonshirehotels.co.uk
dir: On B6160 to Bolton Abbey, 250 yds N of junct with A59 rdbt

There's plenty of space for walking off gastronomic over-indulgence amid the Yorkshire Dales beauty of the Duke and Duchess of Devonshire's 30,000-acre Bolton Abbey Estate. The Devonshire Arms started life as a 17th-century coaching inn, and has morphed into a consummate country mansion hotel with open fires, amazing flower displays, antiques and oil paintings from the Devonshires' Chatsworth House collection in its opulent lounges. Burnished antique tables, the glint of silver and crystal, and articulate, good-humoured service from a polished team set the correct tone in the fine-dining Burlington Restaurant. There has been a distinct buzz here since the arrival of Head Chef Steve Smith lit a fire under the young and enthusiastic kitchen team in Spring 2008, and they are all on board with his new concept of culinary fireworks. The kitchen gardens and Bolton Abbey estate come up with much of the produce, backed by a fair peppering of top-notch, luxury ingredients. Steve Smith's cooking is characterised by outstanding technical skills conjuring complex dishes that blow you away with intense flavours and exciting, playful presentation. The menu eschews florid prose, so 'foie gras' appears in ballotine form with duck textures, fig fluid gel, red wine jelly and toasted brioche all singing in harmony. A signature dish of lamb comprises slow-cooked loin, confit, sweetbreads and boudin of tongue with vibrant red pepper purée and olive gnocchi. Phenomenal technique pulls off a masterly deconstruction of tiramisù delivered as mascarpone parfait, coffee, amaretti biscuits and liquorice ice cream. The premier-league wine list is a sight to behold, reading as a who's who of top-class producers.

Chef Stephen Smith **Owner** Duke & Duchess of Devonshire **Times** 12.30-2.30/7-10 Closed Mon, L Tue-Sat **Prices** Fixed L 3 course fr £35, Fixed D 3 course fr £58, Tasting menu £65, Service added but optional 12.5% **Wines** 2300 bottles over £20, 30 bottles under £20, 12 by glass **Notes** Tasting menu 8 course, Prestige menu 10 course £70, Sunday L, Vegetarian menu, Dress restrictions, Smart dress, no jeans or T-shirts, Civ Wed 90 **Seats** 70, Pr/dining room 90 **Children** Menu **Parking** 100

BOROUGHBRIDGE
Map 19 SE36

The Dining Room

◉◉ British, French

Assured cooking in comfortable local restaurant

☎ 01423 326426
20 St James Square YO51 9AR
e-mail: chris@thediningrooms.co.uk
dir: A1(M) Boroughbridge junct, follow signs to town.
Opposite fountain in town square

Situated in the market town of Boroughbridge, this popular neighbourhood restaurant is housed in a Grade II listed Queen Anne building that was once an inn. It's now run by chef Christopher Astley with his wife Lisa heading the front-of-house team. The Dining Room is light, airy and modern with wooden beams, high-backed chairs and crisp linen. The enclosed terrace is perfect for relaxed alfresco dining or pre-dinner drinks. Intelligently short menus (supplemented by specials) deliver seasonal, well-balanced dishes that let the well-sourced local ingredients speak for themselves. Typical starters might include Cajun spiced king prawns with cucumber and mint dressing, with confit of duck with a wild mushroom sauce and local black pudding to follow, rounded off with iced praline parfait with Amaretto sauce.

Chef Christopher Astley **Owner** Mr & Mrs C Astley
Times 12-2/7-9.30 Closed 26-28 Dec, 1 Jan, BHs, Mon, L Tue-Sat, D Sun **Prices** Fixed L 2 course £19.50, Fixed D 3 course £28, Starter £6.50-£9.50, Main £13.95-£22.95, Dessert £6.50-£8.50, Service optional **Wines** 81 bottles over £20, 20 bottles under £20, 9 by glass **Notes** Sunday L, Vegetarian available, Dress restrictions, Smart casual, no T-shirts **Seats** 32 **Children** Portions **Parking** On street/ Private on request

BURNSALL
Map 19 SE06

Red Lion Hotel & Manor House

◉ Modern British

Riverside inn serving comforting classics

☎ 01756 720204 ◈ 01756 720292
By the Bridge BD23 6BU
e-mail: info@redlion.co.uk
dir: 10m from Skipton on B6160

Originally a 16th century Ferryman's inn, the Red Lion is set beside a 5-arch bridge over the River Wharfe. This Dales village inn has avoided the trend to modernise, and retains real charm and character. Expect flagstone floors, hand-pump ales, roaring winter fires, low ceilings and exposed beams. Dine in the elegant restaurant, or more casually in the oak-panelled bar. The cooking is straightforward and bold from a committed kitchen. Using fresh, local ingredients, Thai-style fish fritters with aubergine yogurt and confit duck leg with smoked sausage and pancetta, white bean and tomato cassoulet are fine examples of the style.

Times 12-2.30/6-9.30

BYLAND ABBEY
Map 19 SE57

The Abbey Inn

◉ British NEW ♨

Hearty food in fabulously situated romantic inn

☎ 01347 868204 ◈ 01347 868678
YO61 4BD
e-mail: paul.tatham@english-heritage.org.uk
dir: Please telephone for directions

Located on the edge of the North Yorkshire Moors, this charming inn is owned by English Heritage, which also owns the abbey ruin opposite. The pub has been fully refurbished but has retained its character with exposed stone walls, flagstone floors and rugs adding to the ambience. There are 3 interconnecting dining areas, including the Piggery, which did indeed used to be a courtyard for keeping pigs. These days, rare breed pigs feature more on the menu, the backbone of which is local produce from named farms and suppliers. Expect generous portions of rustic British cooking: pressed terrine of Saddleback brawn with home-made piccalilli and leaves, followed by slow-braised wild rabbit in red wine with creamed mash, wilted curly kale, wild mushrooms and deep-fried garden thyme.

Chef Wayne Rodgers, Andrew Ball **Owner** English Heritage
Times 12-2.30/6-8.30 Closed Xmas, New Year, BHs, Mon-Tue **Prices** Starter £3.50-£6.95, Main £10-£18, Dessert £4.50-£6.50, Service optional **Wines** 8 by glass **Notes** Sunday L, Vegetarian available **Seats** 60, Pr/dining room 8 **Children** Portions

CRATHORNE
Map 19 NZ40

Crathorne Hall Hotel

◉◉ British ♨

Edwardian country house with impressive contemporary cuisine

☎ 01642 700398 ◈ 01642 700814
TS15 0AR
e-mail: crathornehall@handpicked.co.uk
dir: Off A19, 2m E of Yarm. Access to A19 via A66 or A1, Thirsk

Views of the Leven Valley and the Cleveland Hills form the backdrop wherever you are in this splendid Edwardian property, including the Leven Restaurant, where oak panelling, intricate gilt coffered ceilings, gold-framed oil paintings and a carved stone fireplace offer period grandeur in spades. Expect service to be formal and professional but not at all stuffy. Classical roots underpin the kitchen's modern British output, with menus offering a repertoire of thoughtful combinations, kept simple and not over-worked so as to emphasise the pedigree produce. Pan-roasted Lyme Bay scallops with celeriac purée, tomato fondue and truffle dressing shows the style; next up, Yorkshire beef fillet is teamed with braised ox cheek, snails and parsley risotto. Modern puddings might include iced pistachio parfait with parmesan ice cream, basil jelly and Kalamata olive tuile.

Chef Michael Bell **Owner** Hand Picked Hotels
Times 12.30-2.30/7-9.30 **Prices** Fixed L 2 course £27-£37, Fixed D 3 course £35-£45, Starter £6-£12, Main £14-£25, Dessert £5-£8, Service optional **Wines** 98 bottles over £20, 1 bottles under £20, 18 by glass **Notes** Sunday L, Vegetarian available, Civ Wed 90 **Seats** 45, Pr/dining room 26 **Children** Portions, Menu **Parking** 80

EASINGTON
Map 19 NZ71

The Grinkle Park Hotel

◉ Modern British NEW

Country estate setting, modern British cuisine

☎ 01287 640515 ◈ 01287 641278
TS13 4UB
e-mail: info.grinklepark@classiclodges.co.uk
dir: 9 miles from Guisborough, signed off A171 Guisborough-Whitby road.

The 3,000-acre estate is renowned for its moorland, with opportunities for shooting and other activities, plus there are lots of beautiful grounds for pre or post-dinner strolls. The Baronial-style Victorian country house is traditionally decorated in keeping with the grandeur of the building. Conyers Restaurant, with views over expansive lawns, delivers modern British cooking with, when available, game from the estate, plus a few global touches. Start with roast quail with wild mushroom risotto and truffle oil, before wild sea bass with langoustine tempura, green olive tapenade, Provençal couscous and roast tomato and pimento dressing, finishing with cinnamon pannacotta with caramelised apples and caramel sauce.

Times 12.15-7.15

ESCRICK Map 16 SE64

The Parsonage Country House Hotel

◉ Modern British V

Good service and hearty cooking in delightful country house

☎ 01904 728111 📄 01904 728151
York Rd YO19 6LF
e-mail: sales@parsonagehotel.co.uk
dir: From A64 take A19 Selby. Follow to Escrick. Hotel on right of St Helens Church

Handy for visits to York, this Victorian parsonage sits in 6 acres of smartly-tended grounds and woodland on the Escrick Estate. The fine-dining Lascelles restaurant got a new modern look in 2008, with high-backed leather chairs in eye-catching crimson and white clothed tables against a backdrop of creamy mustard walls. Satisfyingly hearty portions of classic country-house cooking with flashes of modern flair are prepared using prime Yorkshire ingredients. Starters might include sautéed king scallops with confit pork belly and cauliflower purée, followed by roast crown of pigeon with creamed baby leeks and black pudding tortellini.

Chef Neal Birtwell **Owner** P Smith **Times** 12-2/6.30-9 Closed L Sat **Prices** Fixed L 2 course fr £10, Fixed D 3 course £19.95-£25, Starter £5.25-£8, Main £14.95-£21, Dessert £5.95-£8, Service included **Wines** 20 bottles over £20, 26 bottles under £20, 10 by glass **Notes** Early D 6-7pm Mon-Thu 3 course £17.95, Sunday L, Vegetarian menu, Dress restrictions, No jeans, Civ Wed 120 **Seats** 70, Pr/dining room 40 **Children** Portions, Menu **Parking** 100

GUISBOROUGH Map 19 NZ61

Macdonald Gisborough Hall

◉ Modern British

Fine dining at an elegant country-house hotel

☎ 0844 879 9149 📄 01287 610844
Whitby Ln TS14 6PT
e-mail: general.gisboroughhall@macdonald-hotels.co.uk
dir: A171, follow signs for Whitby to Waterfall rdbt then 3rd exit into Whitby Lane, hotel 500yds on right

Gisborough Hall sits in beautiful landscaped grounds on the edge of the North Yorkshire Moors, and is full of period charm. The hotel's Tockett's restaurant was originally the Edwardian billiards room and is traditionally decorated with large windows looking out over the gardens. On a chilly evening, begin your meal with an aperitif by the roaring log fire in the hall, before moving through to the candlelit dining room. The cooking is classically-based with a modern slant. Take pressed ham hock terrine with home-made pease pudding, followed by steamed cod with warm samphire and green bean salad with a lemon butter sauce. Make room for desserts such as crème brûlée with shortbread.

Chef Dave Sotheran **Owner** Lord & Lady Gisborough **Times** 12.30-2.30/6.30-9.30 **Prices** Food prices not confirmed for 2010. Please telephone for details.

Wines 20+ bottles over £20, 1 bottles under £20, 20 by glass **Notes** Sunday L, Vegetarian available, Dress restrictions, Smart casual, no trainers or sportswear, Civ Wed 300 **Seats** 90, Pr/dining room 24 **Children** Portions, Menu **Parking** 100

HAROME Map 19 SE68

The Star Inn

◉◉ Traditional British V ▮ ◔

Creative cuisine at a popular village inn

☎ 01439 770397 📄 01439 771833
YO62 5JE
e-mail: jpern@thestarinnatharome.co.uk
dir: From Helmsley take A170 towards Kirkbymoorside, after 0.5m turn right towards Harome. After 1.5m, inn 1st building on right

The Star is a 14th-century thatched inn in the rolling foothills of the North York moors, where the Pern family have carved a niche for their brand of cheery hospitality and award-winning cooking. The tightrope between gastro and pub is a hard balancing act to pull off, but it works here: the perfume of wood smoke and bees wax pervades the low-beamed bar, where the local community rub along with visiting foodies in a convivial ambience. Menus are chalked on blackboards as well as printed, and offer the same dishes in both bar and restaurant. Chef-proprietor Andrew Pern's book, *Black Pudding and Foie Gras*, says it all: luxury and humble ingredients sit happily together in his creative cooking, and his raw materials are a celebration of Yorkshire's finest produce. So, black pudding and pan-fried foie gras with Pickering watercress, apple and vanilla chutney and a scrumpy reduction is a signature starter, followed by John Dory fillet with broad bean and lovage risotto, summer truffle juices and garlic roast snails. If you want a repeat performance at home, the Corner Shop deli opposite the pub sells dishes from the restaurant.

Chef Andrew Pern **Owner** A & J Pern
Times 11.30-3/6.30-11 Closed 25 Dec, L Mon, D Sun **Prices** Starter £5-£14, Main £14-£25, Dessert £5-£11, Service optional **Wines** 10 by glass **Notes** Chef's table for 6-8 people, 6-8 course, Sunday L, Vegetarian menu, Civ Wed 50 **Seats** 70, Pr/dining room 10 **Children** Portions **Parking** 30

HARROGATE Map 19 SE35

The Boar's Head Hotel

◉◉ Modern British ◔

Charming old coaching inn with creative kitchen team

☎ 01423 771888 📄 01423 771509
Ripley Castle Estate HG3 3AY
e-mail: reservations@boarsheadripley.co.uk
dir: On A61 (Harrogate/Ripley road). In village centre

Sir Thomas and Lady Ingilby are the current custodians of Ripley Castle; they're the 26th generation of the family to reside in the beautiful building. The Boar's Head is the old coaching inn of the village, the whole of which is privately owned by the Ingilbys. The hotel is smart and traditional in a hunting-shooting-fishing kind of way, with old oil paintings of Ingilbys gone by, comfortable lounges with real fires, and a choice of two dining areas (restaurant and bistro). The bistro offers more straightforward dishes (Caesar salad, perhaps), while the formal restaurant serves up refined but not over-blown modern British dishes such as seared king scallops with peas and bacon to start, and main-course roast breast of Gressingham duck with Sarladaise potatoes and confit of shallots. Menus, based on good local produce, change with the seasons.

Chef Oliver Stuart **Owner** Sir Thomas Ingilby & Lady Ingilby **Times** 12-2/7-9 **Prices** Fixed L 2 course fr £16.95, Starter £6-£9, Main £12-£20, Dessert £7, Service optional **Wines** 50 bottles over £20, 20 bottles under £20 **Notes** Sunday L, Dress restrictions, Smart casual, Civ Wed 150 **Seats** 40, Pr/dining room 40 **Children** Portions, Menu **Parking** 45

Clocktower

⊚⊚ Modern British ✍

Yorkshire Food Heroes celebrated in style

☎ 01423 871350 📠 01423 872286
Rudding Park Hotel & Golf, Follifoot HG3 1JH
e-mail: reservations@ruddingpark.com
web: www.ruddingpark.co.uk
dir: A61 at rdbt with A658 follow signs 'Rudding Park'

An integral part of the Rudding Park hotel and golf set-up, the Clocktower has become one of North Yorkshire's destination eateries. Both the vibrant bar with its long counter and the ostentatiously chandliered dining room have a multi-hued but soothing colour scheme. A Yorkshire Food Heroes menu celebrates the best suppliers within an area bounded by Whitby, York and Harrogate, and offers the likes of crab and crayfish cocktail, or game pie with watercress and grape compôte. On the main menu, expect sea bass crusted in pine nuts with herb risotto to start, followed perhaps by Nidderdale lamb three ways, or roast partridge from the North York Moors. Another three-way format might see apple materialising as brûlée, tart and sorbet. Wine suggestions paired with each dish, by the glass or bottle, represent a forward-thinking approach.

Chef Stephanie Moon **Owner** Simon Mackaness
Times 12-2.30/7-9.30 **Prices** Fixed L 2 course £22.50, Fixed D 3 course £29.50, Starter £7.50-£12.50, Main £19.50-£27, Dessert £8-£17.50, Service optional **Wines** 60 bottles over £20, 15 bottles under £20, 14 by glass **Notes** Sunday L, Vegetarian available, Civ Wed 180, Air con **Seats** 170, Pr/dining room 240 **Children** Portions, Menu **Parking** 250

Hotel du Vin Harrogate

⊚⊚ British, Mediterranean

Fine food and wine in famous spa town

☎ 01423 856800 📠 01423 856801
Prospect Place HG1 1LB
e-mail: info.harrogate@hotelduvin.com
dir: A1(M) junct 47, A59 to Harrogate, follow town centre signs to Prince of Wales rdbt, 3rd exit, remain in right lane. Right at lights into Albert St, right into Prospect Place

Near the centre of town, this luxurious hotel was created from a row of eight Georgian town houses. It overlooks the 200-acre common, The Stray, which contains many of the town's famous mineral springs. HdV's philosophy is to focus on the importance of both food and wine, and this one is no different. Local ingredients are used to deliver classic dishes, cooked simply. The bistro menu changes daily and is available throughout the day; start with local game terrine with fig chutney and hazelnut and raisin bread, then pan-fried turbot with braised oxtail and cockles to follow. In summer you can dine outside in the courtyard.

Times 12-2/6.30-10

Orchid Restaurant

⊚ Pacific Rim

Authentic Pacific Rim cuisine in stylish setting

☎ 01423 560425 📠 01423 530967
Studley Hotel, 28 Swan Rd HG1 2SE
e-mail: info@orchidrestaurant.co.uk
dir: Opposite Mercer Art Gallery

Give your taste buds a complete tour of Asia at this dynamic restaurant. Located within the Studley Hotel, its slick, contemporary décor includes elegant lacquered tables, rattan bamboo steamers and Asian clay pots. High-quality traditional and unusual ingredients (imported where necessary) are used to good effect in well-flavoured dishes. A typical starter might be Malaysian satay of marinated strips of chicken (or beef) served with a lightly spiced warm peanut sauce, or a main course of fried sea bass fillets covered with a richly spiced curry made from Thai herbs, shredded lime leaves and coconut cream. Sushi and sashimi are served on Tuesdays, and there's a good-value buffet lunch on Sundays.

Chef Kenneth Poon **Owner** Bokmun Chan
Times 12-2/6.30-10 **Prices** Fixed L 2 course £10.95, Fixed D 3 course £19.95-£27.95, Starter £4.50-£8, Main £6.50-£18, Dessert £4.50-£6, Service added but optional 10% **Wines** 13 bottles over £20, 15 bottles under £20, 8 by glass **Notes** Tue D sushi & sashimi, Sunday L, Vegetarian available, Air con **Seats** 72, Pr/dining room 18 **Parking** 18

Van Zeller

⊚⊚ Modern British NEW

Home-coming chef makes a Harrogate splash

☎ 01423 508762
8 Montpellier St HG1 2TQ
dir: Please telephone for directions

The few minutes' walk from the hurly-burly of Harrogate's town centre turns out to be well worth the effort to find Tom van Zeller's restaurant. A classy, up-to-date interior, with dark wooden floors and cream walls with ornate cornicing, is adorned with good abstract paintings and neutral-toned furnishings. Friendly, attentive staff have the front-of-house tone just right. Van Zeller has globe-trotted from London to Sydney and New York in a glittering trajectory so far, but returns now to his native Harrogate, where he once (yes, really) worked at Betty's Tea Rooms. The menu is admirably understated in its presentation, with a 5-course tasting menu supplementing the main carte. How about a perfectly straightforward spring starter of buttered asparagus with broad beans and pink grapefruit? Timings are pitch-perfect, as in the case of sea bream that is lightly pan-seared, and served with fennel in a tomato and saffron broth. Finish with Yorkshire rhubarb and lime cheesecake. The wine list features an excellent by-the-glass listing.

Chef Tom van Zeller **Owner** Tom van Zeller
Times 12-2.30/6-10 Closed Mon, D Sun **Prices** Fixed L 2 course £14.95, Tasting menu £35-£53, Starter £4.95-£12.50, Main £13.50-£19.50, Dessert £4.95-£8.95, Service optional **Wines** 58 bottles over £20, 8 bottles under £20, 9 by glass **Notes** Pre-theatre menu £14.95, Sunday L, Vegetarian available, Air con **Seats** 34 **Children** Portions **Parking** Montpellier Hill St

---

HELMSLEY   Map 19 SE68

Black Swan Hotel

See page 450

Feversham Arms Hotel & Verbena Spa

⊚⊚ Modern British V

High achiever in rugged North Yorkshire

☎ 01439 770766 📠 01439 770346
1-8 High St YO62 5AG
e-mail: info@fevershamarmshotel.com
dir: A1 junct 29 follow A170 to Helmsley, at mini-rdbt turn left then right twice

Built of Yorkshire stone, the hotel stands on the site of an old country inn, remodelled in the mid-19th century by the Earl of Feversham. Its latest feature is the Verbena Spa, where luxurious treatments await to rejuvenate you, as indeed might Simon Kelly's cooking, which is deeply rooted in the surrounding landscape and served in a relaxing, elegant, red-walled dining room. Lightly poached mackerel with pea shoots, diced beetroot and horseradish cream is a fine, vibrant opener. Accurate timing also distinguishes a main course of breast and confit leg of mallard, served with celeriac purée and kale in a top-notch, richly gamey jus. Dessert could be caramelised pineapple tart, accompanied by a flavour-packed coconut sorbet. Good canapés and petits fours add to the sense of professionalism.

Chef Simon Kelly **Owner** Simon Rhatigan
Times 12-2/7-9.30 **Prices** Fixed D 3 course £33, Starter £7.50-£11.50, Main £18-£25, Dessert £7.50-£8.95, Service optional **Wines** 215 bottles over £20, 5 bottles under £20, 11 by glass **Notes** Tasting menu available, Sunday L, Vegetarian menu, Dress restrictions, Smart casual, Civ Wed 35 **Seats** 55, Pr/dining room 35 **Children** Portions, Menu **Parking** 35

Black Swan Hotel

Rosettes not confirmed at time of going to press

Modern British

Charming hotel with first-class food

☎ 01439 770466
Market Place YO62 5BJ
e-mail: enquiries@blackswan-helmsley.co.uk
dir: A170 towards Scarborough, on entering Helmsley hotel at end of Market Place, just off mini-rdbt

Head for the North York Moors National Park if you want some breathtaking scenery to explore and, if you pop into Helmsley, the Black Swan, right at the heart of things in the market square, can sort you out for just about everything else you might desire. There's a spa to relax tired muscles, comfortable bedrooms to sleep in, a tearoom and patisserie to set you up for the afternoon, and you can even get married here (assuming you've planned it in advance!). And there is a first-class restaurant with a new chef at the helm. The old creeper-clad hotel originally dates from the 14th century so it is no slouch when it comes to original features, but it has not been preserved in aspic and is decorated with a bit of contemporary style without ever losing its dignity. A series of lounges offer a bit of old-school comfort and the restaurant overlooks the pretty walled garden. The new chef's daily-changing menu might start with a salad of east coast mackerel and dressed crab coated in a creamy truffle dressing, then perhaps slow-roasted pork belly with parsnip purée and a sage and onion jus. Finish with classic Yorkshire curd tart with liquorice ice cream. (The Black Swan is sister to the town's Feversham Arms Hotel & Verbena Spa - see entry.)

Chef Paul Peters **Owner** Simon Rhatigan
Times 12.30-2.30/7-9.15 Closed L Mon-Sat **Prices** Fixed D 3 course fr £30, Starter £8.50-£15, Main £15-£30, Dessert £6.50-£10 **Wines** 169 bottles over £20, 9 bottles under £20, 19 by glass **Notes** Tasting menu 7 course, Sunday L, Vegetarian available, Dress restrictions, Smart casual, Civ Wed 100 **Seats** 85, Pr/dining room 30 **Children** Portions, Menu **Parking** 40

General Tarleton Inn

◉◉ Modern British

Former coaching inn providing the best of Yorkshire produce

☎ 01423 340284 📠 01423 340288
Boroughbridge Rd, Ferrensby HG5 0PZ
e-mail: gti@generaltarleton.co.uk
dir: A1(M) junct 48 at Boroughbridge, take A6055 to Knaresborough. 4m on right

Originally a coaching inn, this restaurant on the outskirts of Harrogate has been sympathetically restored and modernised and is now a well-regarded foodie destination. The original beamed ceilings and rustic walls are set off by black and white still-life pictures and tables are set minimally. Upholstered high-backed chairs and good lighting helps make for an inviting and intimate atmosphere. The menu comes under the heading of 'food with Yorkshire roots' and local produce is certainly highlighted on the menu and frequently changing specials board. Portions are substantial and service unobtrusive with staff showing good knowledge of the menu. Start with Nidderdale oak-roast smoked salmon with potato blini, Pickering watercress and chive crème fraîche, then, perhaps, crisp slow-braised Yorkshire belly pork with crushed root vegetables and red onion marmalade.

Chef John Topham **Owner** John & Claire Topham
Times 12-1.45/6-9.15 Closed L Mon-Sat, D Sun
Prices Fixed L 2 course £10, Fixed D 3 course £18, Starter £4.95-£7.95, Main £9.95-£18.95, Dessert £4.50-£6, Service optional, Groups min 6 service 10% **Wines** 70 bottles over £20, 20 bottles under £20, 9 by glass **Notes** Sunday L, Vegetarian available, Dress restrictions, Smart casual **Seats** 64, Pr/dining room 36 **Children** Portions, Menu **Parking** 40

Burythorpe House Hotel

◉ Modern European NEW

Smart boutique hotel with appealing menu

☎ 01653 658200 📠 01653 658204
Burythorpe YO17 9LB
e-mail: burythorpe.house@realyorkshirepubs.co.uk
dir: 4m S of Malton & 4m from A64 (York to Scarborough road)

The creeper-covered hotel has been refurbished to a high standard and has spa facilities and stylishly appointed public rooms. The Priory Restaurant is an oak-panelled room with stripped floors, and the walls adorned with modern artworks (there's a second room if needed). Service is formal - canapés are taken in the lounge - and the menu has seasonality as a top priority. Warm salad of Mr Spillman's asparagus, baby leeks, Périgord truffle and perfectly cooked deep-fried hen's egg (from the village) is an appealing starter, followed by braised neck fillet of Burdass lamb with poached spring vegetables and sweet cicely velouté. Desserts include hazelnut frangipane with chocolate ice cream.

Chef Daniel Farrall **Owner** Real Yorkshire Pubs Ltd
Times 7-9.30 Closed L all week **Prices** Fixed D 3 course fr £28, Service optional **Wines** 12 bottles over £20, 46 bottles under £20, 5 by glass **Notes** Vegetarian available, Dress restrictions, Smart casual, Air con **Seats** 40, Pr/dining room 20 **Children** Portions, Menu **Parking** 30

MASHAM   Map 19 SE28

Samuel's at Swinton Park

◉◉◉ — *see below*

Vennell's

◉◉   Modern British

Confident cooking in cosy village restaurant

☎ 01765 689000
7 Silver St HG4 4DX
e-mail: info@vennellsrestaurant.co.uk
dir: 8m from A1 Masham exit

The unassuming frontage of this Grade II listed restaurant conceals a sophisticated décor of muted shades of beige with plenty of artwork on the walls. Laura runs front-of-house with relaxed informality while chef-patron (and husband) Jon is at the stove. There's a cosy lounge downstairs to sup a pre-meal drink and scan the short, intelligent menu, which majors on local ingredients and relies on good technical skills to produce well defined, unfussy dishes. Start with ham hock terrine with onion marmalade, truffle oil and brioche, followed by confit duck leg, shallot tarte Tatin, creamed potato and braised cabbage. Finish with chocolate and Grand Marnier bavarois with roasted pistachios and palmiers.

Chef Jon Vennell **Owner** Jon & Laura Vennell
Times 12-2/7.15-mdnt Closed 26-29 Dec, 1-14 Jan, 1 wk Sep, BHs, Mon, L Tue-Sat, D Sun **Prices** Fixed L course £19.95, Fixed D 3 course fr £27.50, Service optional **Wines** 54 bottles over £20, 18 bottles under £20, 8 by glass **Notes** Sunday L, Vegetarian available **Seats** 30 **Children** Portions **Parking** On street and in Market Sq

NORTHALLERTON   Map 19 SE39

The Monks Table

◉   British NEW

Ambitious cooking in country inn with objets d'art sold alongside

☎ 01609 882464
Welbury DL6 2SG

The sheer singularity of this place is driven by the forceful personalities of its owners, who acquired it in 2007 and set about creating a highly idiosyncratic enterprise. In the village of Welbury, 6 miles out of Northallerton, it is at once a country pub, a retail outlet for designer furnishings and objets d'art, and an informal but seriously ambitious restaurant. The monthly-changing menu features well-conceived seasonal dishes such as truffle-oiled asparagus soup, escorted to table with a parcel of warm goats' cheese dressed in red pepper pesto, or lusciously tender braised veal cheek with spring greens, morels and hazelnut butter. Dessert could be utterly simple but effective Yorkshire curd tart with rosewater ice cream. One to watch.

Owner Mike Oldroyd **Times** 12-3/5-9 Closed D Sun-Thu **Prices** Food prices not confirmed for 2010. Please telephone for details. **Notes** Vegetarian available

---

Samuel's at Swinton Park

MASHAM   Map 19 SE28

British, French ✍

Grandiose castle offers classic dining

☎ 01765 680900   🖷 01765 680901
Swinton HG4 4JH
e-mail: enquiries@swintonpark.com
dir: A1 take B6267, from Masham follow brown signs for Swinton Park

This grand old castle, complete with the requisite turret and gatehouse, has been a family home since the 1800s and it's now a spectacular place to go for a classy fine dining experience. The artwork, flooring and furnishings have all been lovingly restored (the original part of the castle dates back to the 17th century). The dining room was built by the current owner's great-great-great-grandfather and is opulence itself with its gold leaf decorated ceiling, crisp white linen and views over the grounds. Smooth, attentive service adds to the sense of occasion. After lunch or before a summer's dinner, perhaps, take a stroll around the 200 acres of parkland attached to the hotel. The food itself is classic French with British influences, with much of the produce sourced from the estate in which it sits. Start with sea trout with beetroot, cauliflower and caviar, following on with estate venison with walled garden vegetables and grand veneur sauce, and finish with a treatise on pineapple: sorbet, upside down cake and Piña Colada. The predominantly French wine list has a very good selection by the glass.

Chef Simon Crannage **Owner** Mr and Mrs Cunliffe-Lister **Times** 12.30-2/7-9.30 Closed L Mon-Tue except BHs **Prices** Fixed L 2 course £22.50, Fixed D 4 course £45, Tasting menu £52, Service optional **Wines** 121 bottles over £20, 18 bottles under £20, 14 by glass **Notes** Sunday L, Vegetarian available, Civ Wed 100 **Seats** 60, Pr/dining room 20 **Children** Portions, Menu **Parking** 80

OLDSTEAD
Map 19 SE57

The Black Swan at Oldstead

◎◎ Modern British V 🖐

Impressive cooking in lovely country inn

☎ 01347 868387
YO61 4BL
e-mail: enquiries@blackswanoldstead.co.uk
web: www.blackswanoldstead.co.uk
dir: A1 junct 49, A168, A19 S (or from York A19 N), then
Coxwold, Byland Abbey, Oldstead

Owned by the Banks family who have lived in the small
village of Oldstead for generations, this 16th-century inn
is surrounded by rolling National Park countryside with
views of the North York Moors. The bar has an open fire,
stone flagged floor and oak furnishings, while the airy
upstairs restaurant sports a Persian rug-strewn oak floor
and antique tables and chairs. There is a good use of
local, seasonal produce, and the precise, confident
cooking offers beautifully crafted modern British dishes.
Celeriac velouté with roast king scallops, grilled
pancetta, capers and shallots might be followed by a
roast Aberdeen Angus rump steak and braised beef hash
with fricassée of shiitake mushrooms. Leave room for the
dark chocolate truffle cake and hazelnut mousse and
bitter caramel.

Chef Adam Jackson **Owner** The Banks family
Times 12-2/6-9 **Prices** Starter £5.25-£6.95, Main

£11.50-£17.50, Dessert £5.50-£6.95, Service optional
Wines 30 bottles over £20, 22 bottles under £20, 19 by
glass **Notes** Sunday L, Vegetarian menu, Air con
Seats 30, Pr/dining room 20 **Children** Portions, Menu
Parking 25

PICKERING
Map 19 SE78

Fox & Hounds Country Inn

◎ Modern British

**Country-inn dining on the edge of the North York
Moors**

☎ 01751 431577 📠 01751 432791
Main St, Sinnington YO62 6SQ
e-mail: foxhoundsinn@easynet.co.uk
web: www.thefoxandhoundsinn.co.uk
dir: In Sinnington centre, 3m W of Pickering, off A170

A stone-built inn in the unruffled village of Sinnington,
the Fox & Hounds is smartly maintained and has a
pleasingly informal air, with unclothed tables and a light,
contemporary feel in the dining room. Starters may all be
upgraded to main-course portions as in coriander crab
cakes with spiced vegetable and cashew salad and sweet
chilli dipping sauce, or go for a duo of lamb - tender
noisettes alongside a rich mini-shepherd's pie with
smooth, lightly gratinated mash. Lemon tart is deliciously
tangy, and served with top-notch clotted cream and
raspberry coulis.

Chef Mark Caffrey **Owner** Mr & Mrs A Stephens
Times 12-2/6.30-9 Closed 25-26 Dec **Prices** Starter
£4.75-£7.95, Main £9.95-£16.95, Dessert £4.75-£6.25,
Service optional **Wines** 10 bottles over £20, 26 bottles
under £20, 7 by glass **Notes** Sunday L, Vegetarian
available, Dress restrictions, Smart casual, No shorts
Seats 40, Pr/dining room 12 **Children** Menu **Parking** 35

The White Swan Inn

◎ British 🖐

Traditional market-town inn with intelligent menu

☎ 01751 472288 📠 01751 475554
Market Place YO18 7AA
e-mail: welcome@white-swan.co.uk
dir: Just beyond junct of A169/A170 in Pickering, turn
right off A170 into Market Place

A couple of miles' hike from the edge of the North York
Moors, the White Swan is to be found in a charming
market town. The red-painted walls, flagged floors and
unclothed tables may look traditional enough, but there is
a well-honed modern culinary intelligence at work in the
menus. These feature the likes of well-seasoned pigeon
and pea tart to start, followed perhaps by grilled bream
with aïoli and rocket, or slow-roast Tamworth belly and
fillet of pork with wine-braised cabbage and mustard
mash. Sticky toffee pudding with vanilla ice cream is a
simple way to finish. The children's menu is apparently
handwritten (though presumably not cooked) by a
youngster.

Chef Darren Clemmit **Owner** The Buchanan family
Times 12-2/6.45-9 **Prices** Starter £4.95-£10.95, Main
£9.95-£19, Dessert £3.50-£11.95, Service optional
Wines 55 bottles over £20, 21 bottles under £20, 9 by
glass **Notes** Sunday L, Vegetarian available, Civ Wed 50
Seats 50, Pr/dining room 18 **Children** Portions, Menu
Parking 35

PICKHILL
Map 19 SE38

Nags Head Country Inn

◉ Modern British V 🕭

Charming countryside inn with great food, fine wines and real ales

☎ 01845 567391 & 567570 📠 01845 567212
YO7 4JG
e-mail: reservations@nagsheadpickhill.co.uk
dir: 1m E of A1, 4m N of A1/A6 junct

The Boynton family have been welcoming visitors to their extended, former 17th-century coaching inn, conveniently situated in a peaceful village just off the A1, for over 30 years. Expect Yorkshire hospitality at its best, a beamed and comfortably furnished Library Restaurant, a tie-adorned main bar serving tip-top ales and top-notch wines, and some imaginative and often adventurous cooking. Using local game and seafood, dishes are hearty and full flavoured, perhaps including duck liver parfait with rhubarb compôte; fish pie; roast belly of rare breed Berkshire pork with sauerkraut, apple and beetroot; excellent Sunday roast lunches; and sticky toffee pudding with butterscotch sauce. Smartly uniformed staff are attentive and friendly.

Owner Edward & Janet Boynton **Times** 12-2/6-9.30 Closed 25 Dec **Prices** Starter £3.95-£7.50, Main £5.95-£19.95, Dessert £3.95-£5.95, Service optional **Wines** 30 bottles under £20, 8 by glass **Notes** Sunday L, Vegetarian menu **Seats** 40, Pr/dining room 24 **Children** Portions **Parking** 50

RICHMOND
Map 19 NZ10

Frenchgate Restaurant & Hotel

◉ Modern British

Cosy dining room in a Georgian hotel amid cobbled streets

☎ 01748 822087
59-61 Frenchgate DL10 7AE
e-mail: info@thefrenchgate.co.uk
web: www.thefrenchgate.co.uk
dir: From A1 Scotch Corner take A6108 to Richmond. After schools on left, straight over rdbt, past petrol station on left, through lights & 1st left into Lile Close

The hotel is a sensitive Georgian conversion on 3 storeys amid the cobbled streets of old Richmond. A nice balance of contemporary elegance and period allure is struck in the dining room, with its street views and displays of the work of local artists. The seasonally driven menu is constructed from good Yorkshire produce, which might appear in the form of venison served 2 ways as a starter, the haunch shredded up for rillettes, the loin smoked, accompanied by celeriac purée and a blackcurrant vinaigrette. The multi-faceted approach might then see Whitby cod served 3 ways for main - pan-roasted fillet, salt-cod brandade and deep-fried in Yorkshire beer batter - along with creamed wild mushrooms for that earthy kick.

Chef Ross Hadley **Owner** David & Luiza Todd **Times** 12-2.30/7-9.30 **Prices** Fixed L 2 course £10.95, Fixed D 3 course £29-£34, Service optional, Groups min 8 service 10% **Wines** 80 bottles over £20, 20 bottles under £20, 9 by glass **Notes** Sunday L, Vegetarian available, Civ Wed 100 **Seats** 24, Pr/dining room 24 **Children** Portions **Parking** 12

See advert on opposite page

SCARBOROUGH
Map 17 TA08

Best Western Ox Pasture Hall Country Hotel

◉ Modern French

Imaginative cuisine in traditional country-house hotel

☎ 01723 365295 📠 01723 355156
Lady Edith's Dr, Raincliffe Woods YO12 5TD
e-mail: oxpasture.hall@btconnect.com
web: www.oxpasturehall.com
dir: A171, left onto Lady Edith's Drive, 1.5m, hotel on right

Nestling amongst the fields and woodland of the North York Moors National Park, this attractive hotel sits in 17 acres of landscaped gardens and grounds, just 2 miles from the popular seaside resort of Scarborough. The Courtyard Restaurant, which overlooks a pretty courtyard,

continued

SCARBOROUGH *continued*

offers the relaxing atmosphere of a traditional country-house hotel, serving interesting dishes created from seasonal and local produce. Fine seafood features in dishes like smoked salmon and halibut terrine with potato and truffle salad. Expect main courses like rare breed Yorkshire pork with grain mustard and sage pappardelle and parsnips. In summer you can eat on the terrace with views over the gardens. The brasserie, with its traditional bar, offers a less formal dining alternative.

Times 12-2.45/6.30-10.15 Closed Sun-Mon

See advert on page 453

SCAWTON   Map 19 SE58

The Hare Inn

Modern British NEW

Rievaulx Valley inn serving good and hearty British food

☎ 01845 597769
YO7 2HG
e-mail: info@thehareinn.co.uk
dir: From A170 Sutton Bank take 1st left signed Rievaulx Abbey. Restaurant in 1.5m along road

The Hare is everything you'd expect of a traditional 13th-century rural village inn. In the Rievaulx Valley, close to the famous abbey, the pub has all the regulation low ceilings and doorways, log fires and real ales, plus, thanks to the hands-on proprietors, some good, hearty British food. The restaurant - done out with William Morris wallpaper, pine tables and church candles - is open-plan to the cosy bar, while the honest and uncomplicated cooking ticks all the right boxes for local and seasonal produce. A light-lunch option is a traditional affair (steak and kidney pie), while the carte cranks up the ante (roast rack of Masham Lamb with fresh tarragon); puds are comfort style, perhaps hazelnut and raspberry Pavlova.

Chef Geoff Smith **Owner** Geoff & Jan Smith
Times 12-2/6-9.30 Closed 4 days Feb, Mon, D Sun
Prices Starter £5.95-£8.50, Main £13.50-£18.50, Dessert fr £5.95, Service optional **Wines** 15 bottles over £20, 10 bottles under £20, 10 by glass **Notes** Sunday L, Vegetarian available **Seats** 70, Pr/dining room 16 **Children** Portions **Parking** 12

SUTTON-ON-THE-FOREST   Map 19 SE56

The Blackwell Ox Inn

British

Gastro-pub using the best Yorkshire produce

☎ 01347 810328 & 690758 📠 01347 812738
Huby Rd YO61 1DT
e-mail: enquiries@blackwelloxinn.co.uk
dir: Off A1237, onto B1363 to Sutton-on-the-Forest. Left at T-junct, 50yds on right

Built in the 1820s, this charming inn set in the picturesque village of Sutton-on-the-Forest is named after a famous Shorthorn Teeswater ox - undoubtedly one of very few celebrity oxen seen in England - which stood six foot tall and was butchered in 1779. Completely modernised and refurbished, there's a traditional bar and smart, country-style restaurant. The kitchen displays a passion for Yorkshire produce, including a wide range of local cheeses, and the daily-changing menu offers good, hearty cooking with plenty of rustic flavours, the suppliers duly name-checked. Start with scallops with squash purée and truffle, then, perhaps, sea bass infused with lemon and parsley and served with fresh horseradish potato salad.

Chef Thomas Kingston **Owner** Blackwell Ox Inns (York) Ltd **Times** 12-2/6-9.30 Closed 25 Dec, 1 Jan, D Sun **Prices** Fixed L 2 course £10.95, Fixed D 3 course £13.95, Starter £4-£7.95, Main £9.95-£18.95, Dessert £4.95-£7.95, Service optional **Wines** 36 bottles over £20, 32 bottles under £20, 20 by glass **Notes** Early bird menu before 7pm, Sunday L, Vegetarian available **Seats** 36, Pr/dining room 20 **Children** Portions, Menu **Parking** 19

Rose & Crown

Modern British

Relaxed, country-dining pub

☎ 01347 811333 📠 01347 811444
Main St YO61 1DP
e-mail: ben@rosecrown.co.uk
web: www.rosecrown.co.uk
dir: 8m N of York towards Helmsley on B1363

This smartly presented dining pub is focused on delivering good, fresh (quite often local) food with professional yet unfussy service. Old world charm has been retained inside and out - hanging baskets and neatly kept borders outside and an uncluttered, beamed interior with wooden floors and open fires within. There's

a bright conservatory as well as a large decked 'tropical gazebo' (as they put it), where food can be enjoyed under African-inspired thatched parasols. Daily specials bolster the carte, which deals in dishes such as ham hock and foie gras terrine with piccalilli and honey and mustard dressing; and roast duck breast with fondant potato, wild mushrooms and a rosemary and beetroot jus. Portions are generous, including a well-proportioned lemon tart served with a raspberry sorbet.

Chef Danny Jackson **Owner** Ben & Lucy Williams
Times 12-2/6-9.30 Closed 1st wk Jan, Mon, D Sun
Prices Fixed L 2 course fr £15.95, Fixed D 3 course fr £19.95, Starter £4.50-£8.95, Main £10.50-£19.50, Dessert £4.50-£8.95, Service optional **Wines** 50 bottles over £20, 20 bottles under £20, 12 by glass **Notes** Sunday L, Vegetarian available, Civ Wed 80 **Seats** 80 **Children** Portions **Parking** 12

WEST WITTON   Map 19 SE08

The Wensleydale Heifer

International V

Top-notch seafood in the heart of the Yorkshire Dales

☎ 01969 622322 📠 01969 624183
Main St DL8 4LS
e-mail: info@wensleydaleheifer.co.uk
dir: On A684 (3m W of Leyburn)

The 'heifer' theme runs throughout the quirky rooms and restaurant in this 17th-century former coaching inn. The elegant seafood restaurant is spacious enough to have 3 different dining areas, all with their own ambience and character, while the fish bar, with its seagrass flooring, wooden tables and rattan chairs, is less formal. Using the finest seafood and superb local meat and vegetables, the kitchen team produces modern British cooking with influences from Asia, particularly Thailand, and the emphasis on seafood. The à la carte menu has many dishes that are such firm favourites with regulars that the chef dare not change them, so lots of additional menus are run throughout the year to keep things varied. Try tian of Whitby crab and lobster, shallot and potato salad with citrus fruit dressing, and a main of sweet chilli roast sea bass, Thai salad and buttered rice. Finish with sticky toffee pudding, fresh cream and butterscotch sauce for dessert.

Chef David Moss **Owner** David & Lewis Moss
Times 12-2.30/6-9.30 **Prices** Food prices not confirmed for 2010. Please telephone for details. **Wines** 43 bottles over £20, 35 bottles under £20, 14 by glass **Notes** Sunday L, Vegetarian menu **Seats** 70 **Children** Portions, Menu **Parking** 30

WHITBY   Map 19 NZ81

Dunsley Hall

Modern, Traditional **V**

Enticing cooking on the Yorkshire coast

☎ 01947 893437   📠 01947 893505
Dunsley YO21 3TL
e-mail: reception@dunsleyhall.com
dir: 3.5m from Whitby off A171(Teeside road)

A family-run hotel on the North Yorkshire coast (prime walking country), Dunsley is a handsome Victorian country mansion. Despite the imposing dimensions, including a vast dining room, the place benefits from the human touch, from the fresh floral displays on tables to the sympathetic approach of the front-of-house staff. Good Yorkshire fare, from locally reared beef to the famous Whitby cod, forms the backbone of the enticing menus. That beef might appear as a piece of immaculate fillet, chargrilled and served with dauphinoise, wild mushrooms, roasted shallots, kale and a garlic jus. To start, scallops hailing from a little further afield (Shetland) might be partnered with crushed minted peas, pancetta and a quail egg. The curtain comes down with the likes of raspberry sablé with matching ice cream and a scoop of creamy mascarpone.

Chef Philip Harper **Owner** Mr & Mrs W Ward
Times 12-2/7.30-9.30 **Prices** Fixed L 2 course £10.95-£17.95, Starter £6.25-£8.25, Main £16.95-£19.95, Dessert £5.50-£6.95, Service optional **Wines** 10 bottles over £20, 10 bottles under £20, 10 by glass **Notes** Sunday L, Vegetarian menu, Dress restrictions, Smart casual, no jeans or shorts, Civ Wed 100 **Seats** 85, Pr/dining room 30 **Children** Portions, Menu **Parking** 30

Estbek House

Modern British **NOTABLE WINE LIST**

Immaculately fresh seafood in a Yorkshire coastal village

☎ 01947 893424   📠 01947 893625
East Row, Sandsend YO21 3SU
e-mail: info@estbekhouse.co.uk
web: www.estbekhouse.co.uk
dir: From Whitby follow A174 towards Sandsend. Estbek House just before bridge

In the winsome coastal village of Sandsend, the stone building dates from the mid-18th century, and was once an office for local mining operations. Inside has a modern look and feel, with bare wood floor, chunky tables, stylish leather chairs and subdued lighting from ceiling spots. As seems only fitting for the location, fish and seafood predominate, and the quality and freshness of raw materials is outstanding. That is evident in a fabulous main course of halibut, the fish sea-fresh and perfectly timed, well served by accompaniments of duchess potatoes, purple broccoli and anchovy butter. To start, there could be upstandingly flavoured pressed pork belly with spiced apple sauce and herb salad, or lobster and brown shrimp ravioli topped with a scallop, and to finish, a lustrously textured crème brûlée with a compôte of wild berries.

Times 6-9

See advert below

The White Horse & Griffin

Modern, Traditional European

Brasserie menu in historic Whitby inn

☎ 01947 825026 & 604857
Church St YO22 4BH
e-mail: info@whitehorseandgriffin.co.uk

First opening for business during the reign of Charles II, the inn catered to a world where drunken sailors were press-ganged into the fleet after collapsing in Whitby's cobbled alleys. It's all rather more civilised now, with highly polished, bare wooden tables the setting for a brasserie menu of modern fare. Ham hock and pea terrine with beetroot relish is an earthy starter, and could be the prelude to curried mussel chowder, or herb-crusted lamb noisettes with onion farçi. A range of steak options with crisp-battered onion rings proves popular, and meals might conclude with baked egg custard, served with chocolate crunch and red berries.

Times 12-3/5-9 Closed D 25 Dec

YARM   Map 19 NZ41

Judges Country House Hotel

— *see page 456*

Judges Country House Hotel

YARM   Map 19 NZ41

Modern British, French

Ambitious classical cooking in elegant rural retreat

☎ 01642 789000   📠 01642 782878
Kirklevington TS15 9LW
e-mail: enquiries@judgeshotel.co.uk
dir: 1.5m from junct W A19, take A67 towards
Kirklevington, hotel 1.5m on left

The tranquillity and restful atmosphere of this rural retreat with 42 acres of landscaped grounds was once the preserve of the circuit judges who lodged here. Built in 1881 as a private residence for a prominent local family, the grand old hall was turned into accommodation for QCs as recently as 1980 but it is now a luxurious country-house hotel, privately owned and managed by the Downs family, who offer a warm welcome with a high

level of service. Traditionally and elegantly furnished, the house is the setting for some ambitious cooking in the conservatory restaurant, which boasts views of the gardens. The fixed-price carte (with supplements) is based around classical French cooking but demonstrates an eye for innovation and presentation. Cured Gressingham duck breast comes with marinated figs and melon in a starter, while main-course roast halibut is partnered with veal, ceps, salsify and bordelaise sauce. Finish with macadamia nut parfait, pears, prunes and Earl Grey.

Chef John Schwarz **Owner** Mr M Downs
Times 12-2/7-9.30 **Prices** Fixed L 2 course £14.95, Fixed D 3 course £27.50, Starter £8.50-£14, Main £27-£35, Dessert £8.50, Service optional **Wines** 117 bottles over £20, 45 bottles under £20, 12 by glass **Notes** Sunday L, Vegetarian available, Dress restrictions, Jacket & tie preferred, No jeans or trainers, Civ Wed 200 **Seats** 60, Pr/ dining room 50 **Children** Portions, Menu **Parking** 110

YORK   Map 16 SE65

Blue Bicycle

◉ Modern European

Sound cooking in busy city centre bistro

☎ 01904 673990   📠 01904 658147
34 Fossgate YO1 9TA
e-mail: info@thebluebicycle.com
web: www.thebluebicycle.com
dir: In city centre, just off Parliament St

At the turn of the 20th century the cellar of this city-centre eatery was a brothel of some repute; reflect on this restaurant's colourful history as you enjoy a pre-dinner drink overlooking the River Foss. The dining area exudes warmth and a busy atmosphere, with deep colours, subtle lighting and secluded corners setting the scene in the two-floored restaurant. The kitchen brings creative

touches to popular dishes, delivering a wide-ranging modern European menu with an emphasis on local ingredients. Start with seared scallops and pressed pork belly with apple and sage purée, and then move on to pan-fried halibut with spinach, brown shrimp and caper butter.

Chef Simon Hirst **Owner** Lawrence Anthony Stephenson
Times 12-2.30/6-9.30 Closed 24-27 Dec, 1-10 Jan, L Mon-Wed & 28 Dec, 31 Dec, 11 Jan **Prices** Starter £4.50-£11.50, Main £15-£24, Dessert £6.25-£11, Service added but optional 10% **Wines** 53 bottles over £20, 28 bottles under £20, 14 by glass **Notes** Fixed D for parties over 20 £40-£50 per head, Vegetarian available **Seats** 83 **Parking** On street & NCP

D.C.H at the Dean Court Hotel

◉◉ Modern British ✿

Fabulous York Minster views and fine food

☎ 01904 625082   📠 01904 620305
Duncombe Place YO1 7EF
e-mail: sales@deancourt-york.co.uk
web: www.deancourt-york.co.uk
dir: City centre, directly opposite York Minster

The hotel's stunning location overlooking York Minster is second to none in the city, and some tables in the restaurant have views over the historic building. Built to house the clergy, the elegantly refurbished hotel now has a contemporary style and offers a choice for diners - the popular D.C.H. restaurant for fine dining and the informal café-bistro, The Court, for lighter dishes. The restaurant menu delivers modern British/European favourites, skilfully cooked, using high-quality ingredients. There are also modern takes on classic dishes like pre-dessert mini baked Alaska. Typical starters might include ham hock and apricot terrine with toasted home-made loaf and spiced apple compôte, and main courses such as pan-fried guinea fowl breast with creamed potato and pancetta lardons.

D.C.H. at the Dean Court Hotel

Chef Valerie Storer **Owner** Mr B A Cleminson **Times** 12.30-2/7-9.30 Closed L 31 Dec, D 25 Dec **Prices** Fixed L 2 course £14.50, Starter £6.10-£9.50, Main £14.95-£19.95, Dessert £6.25-£7.75 **Wines** 79 bottles over £20, 22 bottles under £20, 19 by glass **Notes** Sunday L, Vegetarian available, Civ Wed 50, Air con **Seats** 60, Pr/dining room 40 **Children** Portions, Menu **Parking** Car park nearby (pay & display)

Hotel du Vin York

◉ European, French

Luxury bistro with exciting food and wine to match

☎ 01904 557350 ▤ 01904 557351
89 The Mount YO24 1AX
e-mail: reception.york@hotelduvin.com
dir: Please telephone for directions

The Hotel du Vin chain has hit on a winning formula, taking characterful old buildings and kitting them out with quirkily opulent rooms, and bar and bistro areas that tick all the right boxes with style-conscious customers. True to form, the York branch is a dynamic place with a vibrant contemporary bistro - all bare wood, chocolate leather chairs, French-style prints and wine memorabilia. Clued-up staff are happy to recommend from an outstanding wine list, and a menu of simple classic dishes delivers the likes of salt cod brandade with paprika and herb crostini to start, then perhaps braised ox cheeks with fresh buttered tagliatelle, finishing with an apple and cinnamon tarte fine with vanilla ice cream.

Chef Nico Cecchella **Owner** MWB **Times** 12-2.30/6.30-10.30 **Prices** Fixed L 2 course fr £17.95, Fixed D 3 course £35, Starter £4.95-£8.95, Main £10.95-£18.95, Dessert £6.95-£8.50, Service added but optional 10% **Wines** 21 bottles over £20, 18 by glass **Notes** Sunday L, Vegetarian available, Air con **Seats** 80, Pr/dining room 24 **Children** Portions, Menu **Parking** 18

Ivy Brasserie

◉◉ Brasserie classics

Brasserie dining a short hop from the Minster

☎ 01904 644744 ▤ 01904 612453
The Grange Hotel, 1 Clifton YO30 6AA
e-mail: info@grangehotel.co.uk
dir: A19 (York/Thirsk road), approx 400yds from city centre

The Grange Hotel is a short stroll from York Minster, and is a handsome porticoed edifice built in the 1830s for a wealthy local clergyman. Its main eating draw is the Ivy Brasserie, where traditional and modern décor mingle to productive and eye-catching effect. Careful, clean presentations of contemporary metropolitan food are the norm here, bringing on stuffed saddle of lamb with fondant potato or seared monkfish in crab sauce, perhaps preceded by ham hock terrine with tangy piccalilli. Fish and meat combinations work well, as in halibut with chorizo or plaice and smoked bacon, and crystal-clear flavours distinguish a dessert like mango and coconut parfait with pineapple and ginger salsa.

Chef James Brown **Owner** Jeremy & Vivien Cassel **Times** 12-2/6-10.30 Closed L Mon-Sat, D Sun **Prices** Fixed L 2 course £12.95, Starter £5.50-£6.75, Main £12.50-£19.95, Dessert £5.50-£7.75, Service optional **Wines** 23 bottles over £20, 20 bottles under £20, 8 by glass **Notes** Sunday L, Vegetarian available, Civ Wed 60 **Seats** 60, Pr/dining room 60 **Children** Portions **Parking** 26

Melton's

◉ British ♥

Bustling bistro with wide-ranging menu

☎ 01904 634341 ▤ 01904 635115
7 Scarcroft Rd YO23 1ND
e-mail: greatfood@meltonsrestaurant.co.uk
dir: South from centre across Skeldergate Bridge, restaurant opposite Bishopthorpe Road car park

Run by the same owners for the past 20 years, this charming restaurant continues to be a big hit with the locals. Behind the Victorian terraced frontage, there is a light and airy dining room with a bustling ambience. The walls are covered with mirrors and large murals depicting the chef and his customers to a backdrop of city scenes. Tables are unclothed, floors are polished wood and service is friendly and relaxed. The cooking is contemporary and shows an international influence: smoked haddock carpaccio and caponata could be followed by confit pork belly, glazed apples, spring greens and pease pudding.

Chef Michael Hjort **Owner** Michael & Lucy Hjort **Times** 12-2/5.30-10 Closed 23 Dec-9 Jan, Sun-Mon **Prices** Food prices not confirmed for 2010. Please telephone for details. **Wines** 62 bottles over £20, 21 bottles under £20, 6 by glass **Notes** Pre-theatre D, early evening 2/3 courses £18.50-£21, Vegetarian available, Air con **Seats** 30, Pr/dining room 16 **Children** Portions **Parking** Car park opposite

YORK continued

Middlethorpe Hall & Spa

◉◉ Modern British ⟨icon⟩

Classical cooking in elegant country house

☎ 01904 641241 📠 01904 620176
Bishopthorpe Rd, Middlethorpe YO23 2GB
e-mail: info@middlethorpe.com
dir: A64 exit York West. Follow signs Middlethorpe & racecourse

Now part of the National Trust, Middlethorpe Hall is a splendid William III country house set in 20 acres of garden and parkland that includes a walled garden and small lake. Close to the city and conveniently located adjacent to York racecourse, this grand house also offers a luxury health and fitness spa. The elegant, candlelit, oak-panelled dining room, with its long sash windows overlooking the gardens, offers an accomplished menu of classical and regional cuisine, using well-sourced ingredients. Choose from starters such as Whitby smoked salmon, brown shrimps and lemon crème fraîche, perhaps followed by slow-cooked Yorkshire beef fillet, cottage pie and Savoy cabbage. Finish with apple and blackberry soufflé with apple crumble and apple sorbet.

Chef Nicholas Evans **Owner** The National Trust
Times 12.30–2/7–9.45 **Prices** Fixed L 2 course £17, Starter £9.50–£15.50, Main £18.50–£27.50, Dessert £7.50–£11.50, Service included **Wines** 221 bottles over £20, 17 bottles under £20, 9 by glass **Notes** ALC price D only, Gourmet 6 course menu £65, Sunday L, Vegetarian available, Dress restrictions, Smart, no trainers, tracksuits or shorts, Civ Wed 56 **Seats** 60, Pr/dining room 56 **Children** Portions **Parking** 70

One 19 The Mount

◉ British

Elegant dining in a popular hotel

☎ 01904 619444 📠 01904 631444
Mount Royale, The Mount YO24 1GU
dir: W on B1036, towards racecourse

Situated in 2 delightful William IV houses that are now the Mount Royale Hotel, this bright modern restaurant is off the beaten track, yet still close to the centre of York. It is a popular place with both locals and tourists, and diners can enjoy views of the delightful gardens. The imaginative menu combines Mediterranean cuisine with the best British ingredients, cooked simply with the

emphasis on flavour. Try crab and king prawn cake with a sweet chilli dressing, served on a bed of winter salad to start. Follow with pork fillet flamed in Calvados with caramelised apples and crème fraîche.

Times 12–2.30/6–9.30 Closed 1–6 Jan, Sun

The Piano Restaurant

◉ Modern British NEW

Mansion house hotel with creative kitchen team

☎ 01904 644456
The Churchill Hotel, 65 Bootham YO30 7DQ
e-mail: info@churchillhotel.com
web: www.churchillhotel.com
dir: Along Bootham from York Minster, hotel on right

This centrally placed hotel dates from 1827 and is brimming with original features, including an impressive central staircase. The Piano Bar is the place for a pre-dinner drink before taking a seat in the dining room, with its high ceiling and huge windows giving views over the garden. The modern British menu pays good attention to the seasons and uses plenty of local produce, so spiced rump of Yorkshire lamb is accompanied by a samosa of the shoulder meat, aubergine and sweet potato, yogurt and home-made chutney. Starters include John Dory fillet with oxtail cannelloni and sweet potato purée, and Granny Smith tarte Tatin is a typical dessert.

Chef Glenn Morrill **Owner** Dennis Deursnap
Times 11–2.30/6–9.30 **Prices** Food prices not confirmed for 2010. Please telephone for details. **Wines** 23 bottles over £20, 15 bottles under £20, 6 by glass **Notes** Sunday L, Vegetarian available, Civ Wed 70 **Seats** 30, Pr/dining room 30 **Children** Portions **Parking** 35

YORKSHIRE, SOUTH

CHAPELTOWN Map 16 SK39

Greenhead House

◉ European

Exciting food of consistent quality in country-style restaurant

☎ 0114 246 9004
84 Burncross Rd S35 1SF
dir: 1m from M1 junct 35

With its own pretty walled garden, this homely little restaurant set within a fine Georgian building has a cosy, country feel in an otherwise built-up area north of Sheffield. It retains its period charm with oak beams, open log fires and traditional, country-style furnishings. The cooking is equally accurate, stylish and refined, with Mediterranean flair and skill evident throughout the set monthly-changing menu. Fancy presentation is eschewed; this is good, tasty food prepared from quality local produce. Expect a starter of white fish mousse, followed by hare casserole topped with a chestnut and sage crumble and served with redcurrant jelly and port with chocolate and prune truffle gâteau to finish.

Chef Neil Allen **Owner** Mr & Mrs N Allen **Times** 12–1/7–9 Closed Xmas-New Year, 2wks Etr, 2wks Aug, Sun-Tue, L Wed, Thu & Sat **Prices** Fixed D 4 course £39.95–£44.50, Service included **Wines** 30 bottles over £20, 13 bottles under £20, 20 by glass **Notes** Vegetarian available **Seats** 32 **Children** Portions **Parking** 10

ROSSINGTON Map 16 SK69

Best Western Premier Mount Pleasant Hotel

◉ Modern British

Refined atmosphere in a country hotel

☎ 01302 868696 & 868219 📠 01302 865130
Great North Rd, Rossington DN11 0HW
e-mail: reception@mountpleasant.co.uk
dir: S of Doncaster, adjacent to Robin Hood Airport, on A638 between Bawtry & Doncaster

Five miles outside Doncaster, the Mount Pleasant is a soothing retreat, surrounded as it is by 100 acres of sumptuous woodland. The interiors are maintained to a very high order, with a refined dining room offering the full-dress country hotel ambience in the form of crisply starched linen, comfortable chairs with armrests and fresh flowers. The cooking keeps things relatively simple for such dishes as Yorkshire cheese soufflé (with optional flaked haddock), roast venison with bone marrow mash and thyme jus, or crab and ginger fishcakes with chilli jam. Conclude in style with Granny Smith trifle, served with cinnamon doughnuts and cider granita.

Chef Dave Booker **Owner** Richard McIlroy
Times 12–2/6.45–9.30 Closed 25 Dec **Prices** Starter £4.95–£8.95, Main £12.95–£24.95, Dessert £6.50–£7.95, Service optional **Wines** 38 bottles over £20, 15 bottles

under £20, 7 by glass **Notes** Sunday L, Vegetarian available, Dress restrictions, Smart casual preferred, Civ Wed 150, Air con **Seats** 72, Pr/dining room 200 **Children** Portions, Menu **Parking** 140

SHEFFIELD Map 16 SK38

Nonna's Ristorante Bar and Cucina

Modern Italian V

Friendly, relaxed trattoria with a passion for Italian cooking

☎ 0114 268 6166
535-41 Ecclesall Rd S11 8PR
e-mail: info@nonnas.co.uk
dir: Large red building on Ecclesall Rd

This trattoria-style Sheffield institution is a bustling haunt of the city's Italophiles, who drop by for a daily shot of espresso and authentic Italian vibes at one of the high bar stools in the front window. Naturally, the cooking is the real McCoy - passionately Italian, put together from ingredients sourced direct from Italy and fresh produce from the 'seven hills of Sheffield'. Classic elbows-on-the-table dishes, such as a rustic Puglian conchiglie pasta with turnip-top greens, chilli, garlic and olive oil, showcase the regions, while local pork is chargrilled and served with black pudding, roast apple and sage polenta. The owners are clearly wine mad, so dive into the wide-ranging choice, and visit the deli before you leave.

Chef Jamie Taylor **Owner** Gian Bohian, Maurizio Mori **Times** 12-3.30/6-9.45 Closed 25 Dec, 1 Jan **Prices** Fixed L 2 course £12, Fixed D 3 course £18, Starter £2.50-£7.95, Main £9.50-£18.50, Dessert £3-£5.50, Service optional, Groups min 6 service 10% **Wines** 90 bottles over £20, 18 bottles under £20, 17 by glass **Notes** Pre-theatre menu available, Sunday L, Vegetarian menu, Air con **Seats** 75, Pr/dining room 32 **Children** Portions, Menu **Parking** On street

Rafters Restaurant

Modern European

Brasserie cooking off the beaten city track

☎ 0114 230 4819
220 Oakbrook Rd, Nethergreen S11 7ED
dir: 5 mins from Ecclesall road, Hunters Bar rdbt

The building dates back to the time of the Battle of Waterloo, as attested by the exposed oak beams that give the restaurant its name. It's situated above a row of shops in a quiet suburb of Sheffield, and eschews razzmatazz in favour of an understated, rustic decorative scheme. Attentive service is both knowledgeable and courteous. The cooking mixes international styles on a menu that changes every couple of months. Expect sliced roast duck in Thai-style noodle salad dressed in black sesame, honey and soy, or a bowl of butternut squash soup with crisp-roasted belly pork, to start. Sea bass with prawn tempura, ratatouille and chive butter sauce offers a harmonious mix of traditions, while desserts such as cherry crumble with roast pear ice cream are the alternative to well-kept northern cheeses.

Chef Marcus Lane **Owner** Marcus Lane **Times** 7-10 Closed 25-26 Dec, 1wk Jan, 2 wks Aug, Sun, Tue, L all week **Prices** Fixed D 3 course £36, Service optional, Groups min 8 service 10% **Wines** 20 bottles over £20, 25 bottles under £20, 7 by glass **Notes** Vegetarian available, Dress restrictions, Smart casual, No jeans, Air con **Seats** 38 **Children** Portions **Parking** 15

Sheffield Park Hotel

Modern, Traditional NEW

Accessible, modern hotel dining

☎ 0114 282 9988   📠 0114 237 8140
Chesterfield Road South S8 8BW
e-mail: info.sheffield@pedersenhotels.com
dir: From N: M1 junct 33, A630 Sheffield. A61 Chesterfield. After Graves Tennis Centre follow A6/Chesterfield/M1 South signs. Hotel 200yds on left

The Restaurant - Sheffield Park's bustling, contemporary hotel dining room - has a modern, brasserie-style look and a lengthy crowd-pleasing menu. Comfort and classic options (Chesterfield pork sausages with mash and onion gravy) mix with more adventurous choices (roast red mullet wrapped in prosciutto and served with pesto-scented plum tomatoes), but with the emphasis on freshness, quality and simplicity. Desserts follow suit, with traditional Bakewell pudding and sauce anglaise

lining up alongside lemongrass fool with white chocolate shavings. The modern Lounge Bar or alfresco patio is the place for aperitifs.

Chef Paul Thompson **Owner** Park Hotel (Sheffield) Ltd **Times** 12.30-2/6.30-9.45 Closed L Sat **Prices** Starter £4.50-£6.75, Main £9.50-£19.60, Dessert £4.95, Service included **Wines** 19 bottles over £20, 27 bottles under £20, 14 by glass **Notes** Sunday L, Vegetarian available, Civ Wed 475, Air con **Seats** 140, Pr/dining room 280 **Children** Portions, Menu **Parking** 260

Staindrop Lodge Hotel

British, European

Art deco-style brasserie in a smart hotel

☎ 0114 284 3111   📠 0114 284 3110
Lane End, Chapeltown S35 3UH
e-mail: info@staindroplodge.co.uk
dir: M1 junct 35, take A629 for 1m, straight over 1st rdbt, right at 2nd rdbt, hotel approx 0.5m on right

Handy for the M1, this much extended and refurbished early 19th-century building stands in mature gardens and offers smart, modern public areas and accommodation. The split-level brasserie is in art deco style with lots of glass and overlooks the courtyard garden. The modern menu draws on fresh local ingredients and reflects influences from around the globe, with dishes such as butternut squash, Ribblesdale cheese and rocket risotto, blade of beef with thyme and horseradish dumpling and crushed celeriac, roast duck with stir-fried vegetables and plum sauce, and Bramley apple pie and custard. A similar menu is also available in the bar.

Chef Andrew Roebuck **Owner** David Slade, John Wigfield **Times** 12-9.30 **Prices** Food prices not confirmed for 2010. Please telephone for details. **Wines** 6 bottles over £20, 33 bottles under £20, 7 by glass **Notes** Vegetarian available, Civ Wed 80, Air con **Seats** 100, Pr/dining room 20 **Children** Portions, Menu **Parking** 60

Whitley Hall Hotel

Modern British

Seasonal local produce in a 16th-century country house

☎ 0114 245 4444   📠 0114 245 5414
Elliott Ln, Grenoside S35 8NR
e-mail: reservations@whitleyhall.com
dir: Please telephone for directions

Standing in 20 acres of landscaped grounds with lakes and immaculate gardens, this 16th-century ivy-clad country house continues to delight. Relax in the comfortable oak-panelled restaurant and enjoy a menu of traditional and contemporary dishes utilising the best of local produce from South Yorkshire, all thoroughly in tune with the seasons. The enthusiastic young kitchen team create imaginative and flavoursome food (Sunday lunch is particularly popular). From the à la carte, potted brisket of beef with pickled turnip is a well-rounded

continued

SHEFFIELD *continued*

starter, while charred pork chop with Bramley apple mash is tender and beautifully cooked. A chocolate brownie with toffee cream is a good way to bring a meal to a close.

Chef Ian Spivey **Owner** Mr D Broadbent
Times 12-2/7-9.30 Closed D 25-26 Dec,1 Jan
Prices Fixed L 2 course £15-£16.95, Fixed D 3 course £25-£31.95, Service optional **Wines** 50 bottles over £20, 30 bottles under £20, 14 by glass **Notes** Sunday L, Vegetarian available, Dress restrictions, Smart Casual, Civ Wed 100 **Seats** 80, Pr/dining room 16 **Children** Portions **Parking** 80

WORTLEY   Map 16 SK39

Montagu's at the Wortley Arms

◉◉ Modern British

Intimate restaurant serving imaginative modern fare

☎ 0114 288 8749 📄 0114 288 5218
Halifax Rd S35 7DB
e-mail: thewortleyarms@aol.com
dir: M1 junct 36. Follow Sheffield North signs, right at Tankersley garage, 1m on right

Montagu's is the fine-dining venue at this spruced-up traditional village pub on the Wharncliffe Estate. With just 40 covers in the formally-set, upmarket-looking upstairs dining room, it is pretty much essential to book a table. The skilful kitchen's modern approach shows flair and innovation, and takes its cue from prime local produce on a fixed-price, three-course menu that includes canapés, amuse-bouche, coffee and petits fours. So, expect stylishly presented dishes such as poached salmon with liquorice and fennel velouté to start, perhaps followed by beef fillet with fondant potato and Madeira jus, with banana bread with caramelised bananas and Baileys ice cream to finish. Local cask ales and carefully prepared, informal meals are served in the beamed bar downstairs.

Times 7-9 Closed Mon, L Tue-Sat, D Sun

YORKSHIRE, WEST

CLIFTON   Map 16 SE12

Black Horse Inn Restaurant with Rooms

◉ British, Mediterranean

Welcoming Yorkshire coastal inn with enjoyable dining

☎ 01484 713862 📄 01484 400582
Westgate, Brighouse HD6 4HJ
e-mail: mail@blackhorseclifton.co.uk
dir: M62 junct 25, Brighouse, follow signs

This traditional village inn has a cheerful pub atmosphere and good coastal views. The white linen tablecloths and brown leather chairs, mixing easily with oak beams and open fires, don't seem out of place in this former Luddite meeting house. The cooking takes a traditional line but with the occasional Mediterranean flourish; think homely beef and Black Sheep Ale pie (with horseradish mash and broccoli hollandaise) to the more sunny gilt head sea bream served with sun-blushed tomato, crushed new potatoes, mussels, fèves and smoked vanilla foam. Desserts follow suit, with the ubiquitous sticky toffee pudding lining up alongside crème brûlée.

Times 12-3/5.30-9.30 Closed 25-26 Dec

DEWSBURY   Map 16 SE22

Healds Hall Hotel

◉ Modern British

Charming 18th-century family-run hotel with bistro and restaurant

☎ 01924 409112 📄 01924 401895
Leeds Rd, Liversedge WF15 6JA
e-mail: enquire@healdshall.co.uk
dir: M1 junct 40, A638. From Dewsbury take A652 signed Bradford. Left at A62. Hotel 50yds on right

This 18th-century mill owner's residence, built in ivy-clad mellow stone has the look of a setting for a period drama, and does indeed have links with the Brontë family. Inside, however, we're firmly in the present tense in a stylish buzzy bistro kitted out with pale woods, curvy leather seats and floaty voile drapes, or there's the fine-dining Harringtons Restaurant if you want to see what the kitchen is capable of. A solid network of local producers supplies the materials for unfussy dishes ranging from

---

crispy local pork belly, braised pig's cheeks with bubble-and-squeak and a cider reduction, to seared king scallops with roast artichokes, wild mushrooms and red wine and thyme sauce.

Chef Phillip McVeagh, David Winter **Owner** Mr N B & Mrs T Harrington **Times** 12-2/6-10 Closed 1 Jan, BHs, L Sat, D Sun (ex residents) **Prices** Fixed L 2 course £8.50, Fixed D 3 course £16.95-£22.95, Starter £4.50-£8, Main £8.50-£21.50, Dessert £4.75-£5.50, Service optional **Wines** 21 bottles over £20, 31 bottles under £20, 8 by glass **Notes** Sunday L, Vegetarian available, Civ Wed 100, Air con **Seats** 46, Pr/dining room 30 **Children** Portions **Parking** 90

HALIFAX   Map 19 SE02

Holdsworth House Hotel

◉◉ Modern British ◉

Grand Yorkshire manor house with extensive menu

☎ 01422 240024 📄 01422 245174
Holdsworth HX2 9TG
e-mail: info@holdsworthhouse.co.uk
dir: From Halifax take A629 (Keighley road), in 2m right at garage to Holmfield, hotel 1.5m on right

The grand manor house was built during the reign of Charles I, and stands in lush, secluded gardens a short drive north of Halifax. Inside, it retains many of the original features, with low, beamed ceilings, and in the oak-panelled restaurant has a dining room worthy of its context. A large menu card offers plenty of seasonal choice, as well as a tasting menu of five courses plus coffee, matched if you will to selected wines. Otherwise, the range takes in king prawn tempura with curried carrots and spinach to begin, followed by cannon of beef with braised ox cheek and roast tongue served bourguignon fashion. A good, mainly English cheese menu supplements dessert temptations such as rhubarb délice with ginger ice cream.

Chef Lee Canning **Owner** Gail Moss, Kim Wynn
Times 12-2/7-9.30 Closed Xmas (open 25-26 Dec L only) **Prices** Fixed L 2 course fr £15.95, Fixed D 3 course fr £19.95, Tasting menu £45, Starter £5-£7.50, Main £14.95-£19.95, Dessert £6, Service optional, Groups min 10 service 10% **Wines** 40 bottles over £20, 32 bottles under £20, 13 by glass **Notes** Tasting menu 5 course, Sunday L, Vegetarian available, Dress restrictions, Smart casual, No shorts, Civ Wed 120 **Seats** 45, Pr/dining room 120 **Children** Portions **Parking** 60

The Old Bore at Rishworth

@ Modern British 🕮

Quality cuisine in one-time coaching inn

☎ 01422 822291
Oldham Rd, Rishworth HX6 4QU
e-mail: chefhessel@aol.com
dir: M62 junct 22/A672 towards Halifax, 3m on left after reservoir

Located in the striking West Yorkshire countryside, this 200-year-old coaching inn has been converted into a popular dining pub. The walls are filled with pictures and curios (including a stags head), floors are flagged, and the formal restaurant brings to mind a posh shooting lodge with its oak floors and beams, antique or high-backed leather chairs, white linen-clad tables and candlelit dinners. The cooking style is modern British and the quality seasonal ingredients are sourced from a strong network of local suppliers. Typically, tuck into fillet of black bream, Moroccan chick pea and chorizo stew, spinach and crispy squid, or steak and Bore bitter pie with a mustard suet crust, thick chips and crunchy vegetables.

Chef Scott Hessel **Owner** Scott Hessel
Times 12-2.15/6-9.30 Closed 2 wks in Jan, Mon-Tue
Prices Fixed L 2 course £15, Fixed D 2 course £15, Starter £4.95-£9.95, Main £11.95-£21.95, Dessert £3.95-£5.50, Service optional **Wines** 30 bottles over £20, 15 bottles under £20, 9 by glass **Notes** Sunday L, Vegetarian available **Seats** 80, Pr/dining room 20 **Children** Portions **Parking** 20

Weavers Restaurant with Rooms

@ Modern, Traditional British **V** 🕮

Robust northern cooking in Brontë country

☎ 01535 643822 📠 01535 644832
15 West Ln BD22 8DU
e-mail: weaversltd@btconnect.com
web: www.weaverssmallhotel.co.uk
dir: From A629 take B6142 towards Haworth, follow signs for Brontë Parsonage Museum, use museum car park

Plumb in the heart of Brontë country, a mere cobblestone's throw from the Parsonage Museum, Weavers is so named because it was fashioned from what was once a group of hand-loom weavers' cottages. The ambience is as cosy as can be, with subdued lighting in the evenings and the walls crowded with diverting pictures. Regional produce finds its way into robust, well-wrought dishes such as seared scallops with split-pea purée, crisp-fried pancetta and a balsamic reduction, chicken breast with sweetcorn potato cake, banana fritter and fruit chutney, and a filo basket filled with apple and Wensleydale, served with fruitcake ice cream. The lunchtime menu is supplemented by inexpensive snack dishes.

Chef Colin & Jane Rushworth **Owner** Colin & Jane Rushworth and family **Times** 11.30-2.30/6.30-9.30 Closed 10 days Xmas/New Year, Mon & Sun, L Tue & Sat **Prices** Fixed L 2 course £15.50, Fixed D 3 course £17.50, Starter £5-£7.50, Main £11.50-£22.50, Dessert £4.50-£6.50, Service optional, Groups min 6 service 10% **Wines** 10 bottles over £20, 54 bottles under £20, 8 by glass **Notes** Vegetarian menu, Dress restrictions, Smart casual, Air con **Seats** 65, Pr/dining room 14 **Children** Portions **Parking** Brontë Museum car park (free 6pm-8am)

Moyles

@ Modern European **NEW** 🕮

Confident cooking in stylish restaurant with rooms

☎ 01422 845727 📠 01422 847663
6-10 New Rd HX7 8AD
e-mail: enquire@moyles.com
dir: M62 junct 24. A646 Halifax to Burnley through Hebden Bridge. Located in the centre of town opposite marina

Once a rundown guest house, this old Victorian building in the heart of Hebden Bridge has been transformed into a chic, contemporary hotel. The light and airy restaurant is informal and relaxed with muted duck-egg blue colours, a stone floor and an abundance of wood and natural materials. The seasonal menu is based around modern European cooking with a few Asian flourishes. A starter of carpaccio of Dexter beef fillet arrives with a crisp oriental salad and a fragrant soy and chilli dressing and might be followed with slow-roasted crispy Tamworth pork with butternut squash and ginger purée, purple sprouting broccoli and a liquorice-scented jus.

Chef Nicholas Wilson **Owner** Simon Moyle
Times 12-3/6-10 **Prices** Fixed L 2 course £12.45, Fixed D 3 course £15.95, Tasting menu £49.95, Starter £4.95-£7.50, Main £12.95-£26.50, Dessert £5.95-£7.50, Service optional **Wines** 10 by glass **Notes** Early bird menu 2 course £12.45, tasting menu 7 course, Sunday L, Vegetarian available **Seats** 70 **Children** Portions **Parking** NCP opposite

---

The Weavers Shed Restaurant with Rooms

@@ Modern British 🍷 🕮

Inventive local cooking in a former woollen mill

☎ 01484 654284 📠 01484 650980
86-88 Knowl Rd, Golcar HD7 4AN
e-mail: info@weaversshed.co.uk
dir: 3m W of Huddersfield off A62. Please telephone for further directions

The venue is a converted 18th-century woollen mill in a Pennine village not far from Huddersfield. Five guest rooms in the former mill-owner's residence allow you to lord it in some style, or else just come for the locally sourced modern British food, where 'locally' includes the kitchen garden at nearby Holywell Green. The mixing and matching of culinary modes might see crab ravioli presented with choi sum, coconut and coriander to begin, while mains offer calves' liver and bacon with red onion mash and cavolo nero, or sea bass with crushed new potatoes and creamed peas and lettuce. Imaginative desserts take in a vanilla ice cream lollie for dipping into hazelnut praline, toasted muscovado and bitter chocolate, or there's blackcurrant croustade with milk ice cream.

Chef S Jackson, I McGunnigle, C Sill **Owner** Stephen & Tracy Jackson **Times** 12-2/7-9 Closed 25 Dec-7 Jan, Sun-Mon, L Sat **Prices** Fixed L 2 course £14.95, Service optional **Wines** 63 bottles over £20, 14 bottles under £20, 8 by glass **Notes** Vegetarian available **Seats** 24, Pr/dining room 16 **Parking** 20

Best Western Rombalds Hotel & Restaurant

@ Modern European, International

Relaxed hotel restaurant serving imaginative food

☎ 01943 603201 📠 01943 816586
11 West View, Wells Rd LS29 9JG
e-mail: reception@rombalds.demon.co.uk
dir: From Leeds take A65 to Ilkley. At 3rd main lights turn left & follow signs for Ilkley Moor. At junct take right onto Wells Rd, by bank. Hotel 600yds on left

Located in a smart terrace between the town and Ilkley Moor, this elegant Georgian townhouse began its life as a

continued

ILKLEY continued

rooming house back in the early 19th century. Nowadays it offers weary travellers (or plain old tourists) comfortable rooms and a traditional restaurant with a relaxed atmosphere. Local produce is used to create ambitious modern European dishes with occasional influences from further afield. A starter of rabbit and prune terrine with tea syrup and walnut salad, followed by rump of lamb, spring onion and bacon mash with redcurrant jus, might end with rich chocolate brûlée with coconut tuile.

Chef Paul Laidlaw **Owner** Colin & Jo Clarkson **Times** 12-2/6.30-9 Closed 28 Dec-2 Jan **Prices** Starter £4.95-£6.95, Main £11.95-£19.95, Dessert £5.25-£5.75, Service optional **Wines** 46 bottles over £20, 58 bottles under £20, 6 by glass **Notes** Sunday L, Vegetarian available, Civ Wed 70 **Seats** 34, Pr/dining room 50 **Children** Portions **Parking** 22

Box Tree

🏵🏵🏵 – see below

The Harlequin Restaurant

🏵 Modern British

Eclectic cooking in friendly Yorkshire village restaurant

☎ 01535 633277   📠 01535 633927
139 Keighley Rd, Cowling BD22 0AH
e-mail: enquiry@theharlequin.org.uk
dir: On A6068 in Cowling, between Crosshills & Colne. 6m from M65

In the village of Cowling, on the edge of the Yorkshire Dales, this double-fronted restaurant in a stone-built terrace is an oasis of friendly civility. Smart table linen and comfortable banquette seating make for relaxation, and there is some good Yorkshire-based eclectic cooking to contemplate. King scallops with tapenade and beurre blanc is one way to embark, the journey continuing with sea bass on creamed shallots and broad beans with pesto dressing, or rack of lamb on roasted Mediterranean vegetables, sauced with Madeira, apricots and rosemary. Vegetarians might opt for crisp vegetable spring rolls on red pepper noodles with sweet chilli dressing.

Times 12-3/5.30-11 Closed 4 days at Xmas, BHs, Mon-Tue

Anthony's Restaurant

🏵🏵🏵 – see opposite page

The Calverley Grill

🏵🏵 British 🖐

Delightful hotel offering traditional British cuisine

☎ 0113 282 1000   📠 0113 282 8066
De Vere Oulton Hall, Rothwell Ln, Oulton LS26 8HN
e-mail: oulton.hall@devere-hotels.com
dir: 2m from M62 junct 30, follow Rothwell signs, then 'Oulton 1m' sign. 1st exit at next 2 rdbts. Hotel on left. Or 1m from M1 junct 44, follow Castleford & Pontefract signs on A639

Just 15 minutes from the city, this impressive Grade II listed mansion is surrounded by the Yorkshire Dales. As well as well maintained gardens there's an adjacent 27-hole golf course, whilst the house itself combines the traditional with the modern. The newly refurbished restaurant is a striking and elegant room in black and crimson, with rich fabrics, leather banquettes and an abundance of dark wood. It's a traditional grill room with classic British dishes the order of the day, including fifteen different cuts of beef to choose from, or maybe go for the roast chicken for two or the classic mixed grill. Service is friendly and attentive, with some dishes prepared at the table.

Box Tree

ILKLEY   Map 19 SE14

Modern British, French 🍴

Yorkshire institution that has kept pace with the times

☎ 01943 608484   📠 01943 607186
37 Church St LS29 9DR
e-mail: info@theboxtree.co.uk
dir: On A65 from Leeds through Ilkley, main lights approx 200yds on left

The Box Tree was part of the culinary revolution that took off in England in the early 1960s, when post-war austerity was finally only a memory, and we all began to eat a little more adventurously, which was to say, continentally. Over the years, it has seen gastro-fashions come and go, and where once haute cuisine Française was the name of the game, today it's all rather more eclectic. Neatly trimmed box topiary greets you on arrival, and inside the place is a haven of civility, with high-backed chairs, quality tableware and proper fires in winter. The Mediterranean larder is raided for starters such as finely sliced Jabugo ham, served with pickled vegetables, shaved fennel, olives and pea shoots, or there might be vichyssoise, presented hot with a garnish of smoked salmon mousse. Main-course fillet of local grass-fed beef makes a regal dish with celeriac mash, a cocotte of spring vegetables with lardons and bone marrow, and tomatoey sauce Choron. Nor do desserts let invention flag, when treacly-rich muscovado sponge cake comes with medjool date purée, crème patissière and orange sorbet. Prices are high, but the cooking is highly reliable.

Chef Mr S Gueller **Owner** Mrs R Gueller **Times** 12-2/7-9.30 Closed 27-31 Dec & 1-5 Jan, Mon, L Tue-Thu, D Sun **Prices** Fixed L 2 course £20, Fixed D 3 course £30, Starter £8-£16.50, Main £27-£32, Dessert £9.50-£10, Groups min 8 service 10% **Wines** 256 bottles over £20, 8 bottles under £20, 7 by glass **Notes** Sunday L, Vegetarian available, Dress restrictions, Smart casual, Air con **Seats** 50, Pr/dining room 16 **Parking** NCP

Chef Dean Rodgers **Owner** De Vere Hotels
Times 12.30-2/7-10 **Prices** Fixed L 2 course fr £19.95, Fixed D 3 course fr £30, Starter £6-£12.95, Main £14-£48.95, Dessert £6.25-£9.95, Service added but optional 10% **Wines** 250 bottles over £20, 10 bottles under £20, 13 by glass **Notes** Sunday L, Vegetarian available, Dress restrictions, Smart casual, no T-shirts, shorts or trainers, Civ Wed 250, Air con **Seats** 130, Pr/dining room 60 **Children** Portions, Menu **Parking** 200

Malmaison Leeds

British, French

Accomplished French cooking in stylish hotel brasserie

☎ 0113 398 1000 & 398 1001 ☐ 0113 398 1002
1 Swinegate LS1 4AG
e-mail: leeds@malmaison.com
dir: City centre. 5 mins walk from Leeds railway station. On junct 16 of loop road, Sovereign St & Swinegate

A one-time bus and tram company office, the Leeds offshoot of this stylish modern hotel chain is located 5 minutes from the city's fashion boutiques and department stores. The brasserie has bags of elegant style, with an impressive vaulted ceiling, leather booths and a contemporary glass fireplace. Choose between the carte or the admirable 'home grown and local' set menus. Simple French cooking is given a modern twist to produce vibrant dishes with well defined flavours; crab ravioli with butternut velouté, followed by Yorkshire lamb rump with

dauphinoise potatoes, lamb's sweetbreads and truffle jus, and strawberry and champagne terrine or a plate of excellent cheese to finish.

Chef James Key **Owner** Malmaison
Times 12-2.30/6.30-9.30 Closed L 26 Dec, D 25 Dec **Prices** Fixed L 2 course fr £14.50, Fixed D 3 course fr £16.50, Starter £4.50-£7.95, Main £10.95-£19, Dessert fr £4.95, Service added but optional 10% **Wines** 90% bottles over £20, 10% bottles under £20, 25 by glass **Notes** Sunday L, Vegetarian available, Air con **Seats** 95, Pr/dining room 40 **Children** Portions, Menu **Parking** Criterion Place car park

Thorpe Park Hotel & Spa

Modern British

Chic modern dining showcasing local produce

☎ 0113 264 1000 ☐ 0113 264 1010
Century Way, Thorpe Park LS15 8ZB
e-mail: thorpepark@shirehotels.com
dir: M1 junct 46, follow signs off rdbt for Thorpe Park

A spot of pampering in the classy state-of-the-art spa is high on the agenda for many of the guests at this modern honey-stone hotel. There's all-day snacky grazing to be had, too, in the terrace and courtyard as well as a slick contemporary open-plan restaurant, done out with pale wood, black leather and abstract art. The kitchen favours a modern British approach, built on seasonal materials

from Yorkshire suppliers. Starters might be Bleiker's oak-smoked salmon with horseradish cream and lemon, while mains range from grilled breast of chicken with basil and broad bean gnocchi and formaggio sauce to hearty local pork and leek sausages with mash and rich onion gravy.

Times 12-2/6.45-9.30 Closed L Sat & Sun

MARSDEN Map 16 SE01

The Olive Branch Restaurant with Rooms

Modern French

Popular roadside inn with ambitious kitchen output

☎ 01484 844487
Manchester Rd HD7 6LU
e-mail: mail@olivebranch.uk.com
dir: On A62 between Slaithwaite & Marsden

An old roadside pub on the edge of Marsden Moor, transformed into a comfortable restaurant with rooms. In a warren of intimate, snug rooms you can relax by the open fire with a glass of wine, or on fine days sip champagne on the sun deck and admire the far-reaching moorland views. The modern French-inspired menu reflects the seasons with good use of local produce, all prepared with flair and imagination. Take a smooth chicken liver parfait, a moist, deliciously flavoured pork belly with mustard mash and a wine and garlic sauce,

continued

Anthony's Restaurant

LEEDS Map 19 SE23

Modern European

A shining star of the north

☎ 0113 245 5922
19 Boar Ln LS1 6EA
e-mail: anthonys@anthonysrestaurant.co.uk
dir: 500 yds from Leeds Central Station towards The Corn Exchange

Boar Lane is a rather ordinary urban high street, however, once across the threshold of Anthony's, the realities of life are left behind: this is a restaurant that fizzes with excitement and delivers creative cooking with a bit of northern charm. The ground-floor bar is the starting point, before descending into the chic, minimalist dining room, which feels remarkably light and open for a basement. Immaculately set laid tables are well spaced,

modern artworks hang on the walls, and the service is slick and professional without being stand-offish. The crisply-scripted menus (carte, tasting and set lunch) are full of bold and intriguing combinations based around top-notch ingredients, and attention to detail is evident from the three butters (salted, olive and parmesan) that come with the bread. Cod cheek and tuna consommé amuse-bouche precedes a first-course deep-fried duck egg - perfectly cooked - with a piece of roast hake and asparagus, followed by fillet of lamb and braised shoulder served with lychees and broad beans. The inventiveness and assured control over the balance of flavours continue into desserts, where mango rice pudding comes with gingerbread and coconut ice cream. Anthony's presence in the city includes a patisserie, a restaurant in a clothing store (Flannels), and the latest venture, Piazza by Anthony, a stunning brasserie in the old Corn Exchange.

Chef Anthony Flinn **Owner** Anthony Flinn
Times 12-2/7-9.30 Closed Xmas-New Year, Sun, Mon **Prices** Fixed L 2 course £19.95-£34, Fixed D 3 course fr £42, Tasting menu £60, Service optional **Wines** 100 bottles over £20, 8 bottles under £20, 6 by glass **Notes** Vegetarian available, Air con **Seats** 40 **Children** Portions **Parking** NCP 20 yds

MARSDEN *continued*

and a simple, well-executed sticky toffee pudding with vanilla ice cream.

Chef Paul Kewley **Owner** Paul Kewley & John Lister **Times** 6.30-9.30 Closed 26 Dec, 1st 2 wks Jan, L Mon-Sat **Prices** Fixed L 2 course fr £13.95, Fixed D 3 course fr £18.95, Starter £5.50-£9.95, Main £13.95-£23.50, Dessert £5.95-£7.50, Service optional **Wines** 100 bottles over £20, 30 bottles under £20, 16 by glass **Notes** Sunday L, Vegetarian available **Seats** 65, Pr/dining room 40 **Children** Portions **Parking** 20

OTLEY
Map 19 SE24

Lakeside Restaurant

◉ Modern British, European

Lakeside restaurant with accomplished cooking

☎ 01943 467818 🖷 01943 850335
Chevin Country Park Hotel, Yorkgate LS21 3NU
e-mail: chevin@crerarhotels.com
dir: A658 towards Harrogate. Left at 1st turn towards Carlton, 2nd left towards Yorkgate

There is something undeniably Scandinavian about this hotel and spa situated in attractive woodland by a lake. Log-built and Finnish in style, it is conveniently located for both major road links and the airport. The recently extended and refurbished Lakeside Restaurant makes a feature out of the log cabin walls, which adds a warmth to the room. The menu is extensive and European in style; start with roasted wild duck, honey parsnip fritter, potato gnocchi and plum sauce, and move on to venison Wellington with pumpkin rösti, baby spinach and roasted chestnut sauce. Pear and apple sponge pudding is one of several comforting desserts.

Chef Debbie Rhodes **Owner** Crerar Hotels **Times** 12-2/6.30-9.15 Closed L Sat **Prices** Fixed L 2 course £12.95-£15.95, Fixed D 3 course £29.95-£32.95, Starter £5.95-£9.95, Main £15.95-£19.95, Dessert £6.95-£8.95, Service included **Wines** 19 bottles over £20, 36 bottles under £20, 10 by glass **Notes** Sunday L, Vegetarian available, Dress restrictions, Smart casual, Civ Wed 120 **Seats** 70, Pr/dining room 30 **Children** Portions, Menu **Parking** 100

PONTEFRACT
Map 16 SE42

Wentbridge House Hotel

◎◎ Modern British V 🖐

Classical cuisine in elegant country-house hotel

☎ 01977 620444 🖷 01977 620148
The Great North Rd, Wentbridge WF8 3JJ
e-mail: info@wentbridgehouse.co.uk
dir: 4m S of M62/A1 junct, 0.5m off A1

Dating from 1700, this long-established country house hotel was once the home of the Bowes-Lyon family and the Leathans (founders of Barclays bank). Set in magnificent grounds and just a short drive from the A1 in the picturesque Went Valley, dinner is served in either the contemporary brasserie or elegant Fleur de Lys restaurant, a traditional, candlelit room where some dishes are cooked at the table. The modern British and French dishes are created from first-class produce and might include a starter of seared king scallops with fondant potato and truffle foam, followed by loin of lamb, beetroot, damson and port jelly. Banana fritters, yogurt sorbet and Yorkshire blossom honey is one of the tempting desserts.

Chef Steve Turner **Owner** Mr G Page **Times** 7.15-9.30 Closed 25 Dec eve, L Mon-Sat, D Sun **Prices** Starter £8-£12, Main £18.50-£29.95, Dessert £6.95-£9.95, Service optional **Wines** 100 bottles over £20, 30 bottles under £20, 10 by glass **Notes** Sunday L, Vegetarian menu, Civ Wed 130 **Seats** 60, Pr/dining room 24 **Children** Portions **Parking** 100

SHIPLEY
Map 19 SE13

Marriott Hollins Hall Hotel & Country Club

◉ Traditional British

Victorian country-club hotel with unpretentious dining and lovely views

☎ 01274 530053 🖷 01274 534187
Hollins Hill BD17 7QW
e-mail: mhrs.lbags.frontdesk@marriotthotels.com
dir: From A650 follow signs to Salt Mill. At lights in Shipley take A6038. Hotel 3m on left

Close to Leeds and Bradford, Hollins Hall was built by the Victorians in 1858 in the Elizabethan style. The setting, in 200 acres of grounds with glorious views over the Pennines, is ideal for a smart country club hotel with extensive conference and events facilities. Heathcliff's Restaurant occupies the original drawing room, where

cheery and helpful staff play their part in setting a relaxed mood. The kitchen deals in a mix of traditional and modern dishes with uncomplicated flavour combinations; expect the likes of home-made black pudding with spiced Granny Smith apples and grain mustard dressing, and slow-roasted belly pork with caramelised onion mash, crackling and Savoy cabbage.

Chef Mark Brankin **Owner** Marriott International **Times** 12-2/6.30-9.30 Closed L Sat, D BHs **Prices** Fixed L 2 course fr £13.95, Fixed D 3 course fr £27.50, Starter fr £5, Main fr £17.50, Dessert fr £5, Service optional **Wines** 33 bottles over £20, 31 bottles under £20, 15 by glass **Notes** Sunday L, Vegetarian available, Dress restrictions, Smart casual, Civ Wed 120, Air con **Seats** 120, Pr/dining room 30 **Children** Portions, Menu **Parking** 250

WETHERBY
Map 16 SE44

Wood Hall Hotel

◎◎ Modern International

Contemporary cuisine in classic country house

☎ 01937 587271 🖷 01937 584353
Trip Ln, Linton LS22 4JA
dir: From Wetherby take A661 (Harrogate road) N for 0.5m. Left to Sicklinghall/Linton. Cross bridge, left to Linton/Woodhall, right opp Windmill Inn, 1.25m to hotel (follow brown signs)

The glorious sweeping drive leading to this beautiful Georgian manor provides a wow factor before you've even arrived. Set on a hillside in 100 acres of lush parkland and woodland, it's a classic country house on the outside, but the interior is more contemporary. The cooking style is also modern, mainly western European but with influences coming from far and wide. Top-quality British produce is used, much of it seasonal and local. The impressive menu might include beautifully crafted and presented dishes like Orkney-dived scallops, veal belly, ceps marmalade and summer truffle to start, followed by butter-poached lobster and Bresse chicken linguine with Yorkshire asparagus and morels. For dessert, try strawberry tart with vanilla cream and Pimms sorbet. Staff are wonderfully attentive, adding to the overall experience.

Times 12-2.30/6.30-9.30 Closed L Mon-Sat

CHANNEL ISLANDS
GUERNSEY

CASTEL
Map 24

Cobo Bay Restaurant

◉◉ British, European

Good seafood cookery on the Guernsey seafront

☎ 01481 257102 ▤ 01481 254542
Cobo Bay Hotel, Cobo Bay GY5 7HB
e-mail: reservations@cobobayhotel.com
web: www.cobobayhotel.com
dir: From St Peter Port follow Castel/Cobo/West Coast
signs. At coast road turn right, hotel 100mtrs on right

Standing proud of the lush golden beach by about 25 yards, Cobo Bay is a holiday destination and then some. As you would expect, the dining room makes the most of that location, with panoramic sea views from the trimly dressed tables. Seafood from the bay is naturally a strong point, offering scallops wrapped in pancetta on roasted sweet potato mash with onion and garlic velouté to baked brill with asparagus and roasted cherry tomatoes, sauced with hollandaise. If you're not a fish-lover, try chargrilled beef fillet on wild mushrooms with stilton croûtons in red wine jus. A bowl of strawberries served with the local cream is going to be the must-have dessert for summer holiday makers.

Chef John Chapman **Owner** Mr D Nussbaumer
Times 12-2/6.30-9.30 Closed Jan & Feb, L Mon-Sat
Prices Fixed L 2 course £12.95-£22.95, Fixed D 3 course
£25-£35 **Wines** 21 bottles over £20, 24 bottles under
£20, 6 by glass **Notes** Sunday L, Vegetarian available,
Dress restrictions, Smart casual, Air con **Seats** 110
Children Portions, Menu **Parking** 50

La Grande Mare Hotel Golf & Country Club

◉ Modern

Welcoming resort hotel restaurant serving accomplished cuisine

☎ 01481 256576 ▤ 01481 256532
The Coast Rd, Vazon Bay GY5 7LL
e-mail: simon@lagrandemare.com
dir: From airport turn right. 5 mins to reach Coast Rd.
Turn right again. Hotel 5 min drive

Occupying a splendid setting next to the sandy beach of Vazon Bay, La Grande Mare is a family-owned and run resort hotel. It is set in 120 acres of private grounds, which includes an 18-hole golf course and a health suite. The friendly restaurant boasts oak floors, granite fireplaces and several arches. Dishes are based on the wealth of fabulous local produce available, from organic vegetables and Guernsey cheese to freshly caught seafood. Specialities of the house include flambé and rotisserie dishes. Start with home-cured citrus salmon gravad lax with caviar dressing, follow on with pan-fried duck breast with pickled red cabbage, thyme fondant and honey and orange sauce.

Times 12-2/7-9.30

ST MARTIN
Map 24

The Auberge

◉◉ Modern European

Seasonal cooking with jaw-dropping marine views

☎ 01481 238485 ▤ 01481 230967
Jerbourg Rd GY4 6BH
e-mail: dine@theauberge.gg
web: www.theauberge.gg
dir: End of Jerbourg Rd at Jerbourg Point

The Auberge occupies a stunning location near St Peter Port on one of Guernsey's highest clifftops. Extremely courteous, knowledgeable staff ensure that the place runs smoothly, and the ambience of unclothed tables is appealingly unfussy, with huge windows affording luscious panoramic sea views. A mix of cooking styles is brought to bear on spanking-fresh seasonal produce, which might translate as local scallops with scallion mash, smoked bacon and pesto, or a main course of wonderfully presented sea bream with roast cherry tomatoes, tapenade, saffron risotto and shellfish sauce, offering a colour and taste sensation. It isn't all seafood -

meat-lovers may go for Provençal-style roast lamb rump - while desserts impress with traditional combinations spun in new ways, such as pineapple tarte Tatin with coconut ice cream.

Chef Daniel Green **Owner** Lapwing Trading Ltd
Times 12-2/7-9.30 Closed 25-26 Dec, Mon (Winter), D
Sun (Winter) **Prices** Fixed L 2 course £12.95-£18.95,
Starter £6.95-£7.95, Main £13.95-£21.95, Dessert £6.95-
£7.50, Service optional **Wines** 19 bottles over £20, 16
bottles under £20, 12 by glass **Notes** Vegetarian
available **Seats** 70 **Children** Portions, Menu **Parking** 25

La Barbarie Hotel

◉ British, French

Tranquil Guernsey hotel with a strong local reputation

☎ 01481 235217 ▤ 01481 235208
Saints Rd GY4 6ES
e-mail: reservations@labarbariehotel.com
dir: At lights in St Martin take road to Saints Bay. Hotel
on right at end of Saints Rd

Things have quietened down in St Martin since Barbary Coast pirates kidnapped the owner of this old stone priory in the 17th century, and serendipitously gave it a name. Excitement nowadays tends to come in a culinary form, unless you count the sedate pleasures of exploring the quiet lanes and superb beaches nearby. Guernsey's coasts and meadows supply a cornucopia of fresh fish, seafood, meat, cream and butter for La Barbarie's kitchen team, whose French influences are obvious in the simply cooked and presented dishes. Typical dishes are roast rack of spring lamb with Provençal vegetables, fondant potato and thyme jus, or for a special taste of Guernsey, try a pan-fried escalope of local Meadow Court Farm veal with mushrooms and Rocquette cider, Guernsey cream, spinach and local new potatoes.

Chef Colin Pearson **Owner** La Barbarie Ltd
Times 12-1.45/6-9.30 Closed 2 Nov-13 Mar **Prices** Fixed
D 4 course £21.50, Starter £5.25-£7.55, Main £10.95-
£16.95, Dessert £4.95-£5.80, Service optional **Wines** 6
bottles over £20, 16 bottles under £20, 6 by glass
Notes Early D £6.95, Sunday L, Vegetarian available
Seats 70 **Children** Portions, Menu **Parking** 60

ST PETER PORT — Map 24

The Absolute End

Mediterranean, International

Fresh seafood in a harbourside cottage

☎ 01481 723822 📠 01481 729129
St Georges Esplanade GY1 2BG
e-mail: absoluteendrestaurant@hotmail.com
dir: Less than 1m from town centre. N on seafront road towards St Sampson

The bright white restaurant overlooks the harbour, as befits a former fisherman's cottage. It's an airy, uplifting space with a mix of rough plaster walls and panelling and some diverting artwork. Fish and seafood are the strong suits, naturally, although meat eaters are by no means neglected. Start with Cajun scallops in a subtly spiced dressing, continue with crisp-skinned sea bass on crab and prawn risotto, and finish with a classic, properly zingy lemon tart. If meat's your bag, try veal saltimbocca, or beef medallions on rösti. Attentive, knowledgeable service keeps things running smoothly.

Chef Guiseppe Cerciello Rega **Owner** Guiseppe Cerciello Rega **Times** 12-2.30/7-10.30 Closed Jan, Mon, D Sun **Prices** Fixed L course £15, Fixed D 3 course £20, Starter £4.95-£7.90, Main £10.50-£16, Dessert £4.50 **Wines** 17 bottles over £20, 35 bottles under £20, 3 by glass **Notes** Sunday L, Civ Wed 50, Air con **Seats** 55, Pr/dining room 22 **Children** Portions **Parking** On street

Christophe

Modern French

A dining room with a view

☎ 01481 230725 📠 01481 230726
Fort Rd GY1 1ZP

If the sun is shining over this smart hotel restaurant in a beautiful setting, with stunning views out over Fermain Bay towards Jersey, try and bag a place on the terrace. Cream walls, tiled flooring and leather upright chairs complement sumptuous brown leather sofas in the open-plan restaurant. The food is modern French with an English twist or two along the way, seasoning is spot on, and the simply presented dishes deliver excellent flavours. The understated, simply written menu might feature lobster, slow-cooked in citrus butter and served on a vanilla risotto, followed by seared duckling breast with mint and liquorice jus and brown butter mash. Finish with red fruit stew set in Montbazillac jelly with shortbread, yogurt and pepper sorbet.

Times 12-2/7-10 Closed 2 wks Nov, 2 wks Feb, BHs, Mon, D Sun

Governor's

Traditional French

Intimate dining in restaurant with stunning sea views

☎ 01481 738623 📠 01481 724429
Old Government House Hotel, St Ann's Place GY1 2NU
e-mail: governors@theoghhotel.com
dir: At junct of St Julian's Ave & College St

Arguably the most historical hotel in the Channel Islands, the Old Government House dates back to 1858 and was formerly the official residence of the Governor, the Queen's representative to the Bailiwick of Guernsey. The location is superb, overlooking the harbour and town, and the Governor's fine-dining restaurant is a beautifully decorated, traditionally themed room full of memorabilia and photographs of former island governors. Shaped seating, rich fabrics and patterned wallpaper recollect the glorious décor of the early 19th century. The classic cooking fits the bill, influenced by the French chef, who offers a seven-course 'degustation surprise' menu in addition to carte and lunch. Local produce features strongly in dishes such as steamed scallops with Asiatic herbs, a light curry sauce and apple croustillante, followed by boneless roast Dover sole with wilted spinach and prawn bisque.

Times 12-2/7.30-10 Closed L Sat, Sun, D Mon

Mora Restaurant & Grill

◉ Traditional European

Contemporary eatery in 18th-century wine cellars overlooking the harbour

☎ 01481 715053 📠 01481 715453
The Quay GY1 2LE
e-mail: eat@mora.gg
dir: Facing Victoria Marina

An 18th-century vaulted wine cellar on the historic seafront is home to Mora. Occupying two storeys, there's a brasserie on the ground floor (Little Mora), while upstairs is a formal restaurant with a curved ceiling, coffee and cream décor, and large windows overlooking the port. Soft lighting, black-and-white photographs of local fishermen and an open kitchen add to the ambience. Straightforward cooking of local produce is offered on a long menu delivering crab salad, fish and chips and grilled lobster, alongside haunch of venison with red wine and chocolate sauce.

Chef Jose Lopez **Owner** Nello Ciotti
Times 12-2.15/6.30-10 **Prices** Fixed L 2 course fr £12.50, Fixed D 3 course fr £23.50, Starter £4.15-£9.95, Main £13.95-£19.50, Dessert fr £5.80, Service optional **Wines** 31 bottles over £20, 29 bottles under £20, 12 by glass **Notes** Sunday L, Vegetarian available, Air con **Seats** 90 **Children** Portions **Parking** On pier

ST SAVIOUR — Map 24

The Farmhouse Hotel

◉ Modern International NEW

Creative cooking in stylishly refurbished hotel

☎ 01481 264181 📠 01481 266272
Route Des Bas Courtils GY7 9YF
e-mail: admin@thefarmhouse.gg
web: www.thefarmhouse.gg
dir: From airport, left to 1st traffic lights, left then left again. After 1m turn left at x-rds. Hotel 100mtrs on right

Originally a 15th-century working farm, this property has been a hotel for over 40 years but has recently been completely refurbished, and very smart and sophisticated it looks, too. Very pleasant staff help set a professional and friendly tone. There are 5 individual restaurant areas under one roof, plus dining by the pool, on the terrace or in one of the gazebos in the extensive gardens in the summer. Creative dishes make good use of high-quality local Guernsey produce, with the emphasis on fresh fish

and Asian flavours. Take farmhouse salad tossed with shredded duck, fresh greens, spring onion and roasted cashew nuts, followed by Guernsey crispy sea bass with wok-fried rice and crunchy Kenya beans. A choice of local ice creams is a good choice for dessert.

Chef Ankur Biswas **Owner** David & Julie Nussbaumer **Times** 12-2/6.30-9.30 **Prices** Starter £5-£8.80, Main £9.50-£24, Dessert £5-£7, Service optional **Wines** 50 bottles over £20, 20 bottles under £20, 8 by glass **Notes** Sunday L, Vegetarian available, Dress restrictions, Smart casual, Air con **Seats** 100, Pr/dining room 25 **Parking** 70

See advert opposite

HERM

HERM — Map 24

White House Hotel

◉ Modern, Mediterranean

Escape to a timeless hotel with simple fresh food

☎ 01481 722159 📠 01481 710066
GY1 3HR
e-mail: hotel@herm-island.com
dir: Close to harbour. Access by regular 20 min boat trip from St Peter Port, Guernsey

A visit to the tiny car-free island of Herm is always a bit special, and the tranquil White House takes the de-stressing factor that extra step by banishing phones, televisions and clocks. Every table in the bright and airy restaurant has a sea view, but the laid-back ethos stops short of letting men off the requirement to wear a jacket and tie for dinner. The kitchen team keeps things simple on its concise menu, with daily specials to take advantage of what has just been landed. Table d'hôte menus might kick off with a creamy chicken liver and foie gras parfait with red onion chutney, then follow with sea bass with crushed potatoes and chorizo. Check out one of the best wine lists in the Channel Islands.

Times 12.30-1.30/7-9 Closed Oct-Apr

JERSEY

GOREY — Map 24

Suma's

◉◉ Modern Mediterranean

Fine fish-based cookery with seductive maritime views

☎ 01534 853291 📠 01534 851913
Gorey Hill JE3 6ET
e-mail: info@sumasrestaurant.com
dir: From St Helier take A3 E for 5m to Gorey. Before castle take sharp left. Restaurant 100yds up hill on left (look for blue & white blind)

A 15-minute drive from St Helier, Suma is the younger sibling of Longueville Manor (see entry). Overlooking the harbour, the restaurant also boasts views of Mont Orgueil castle and has some diverting local artwork on the walls. Lightness and freshness are the watchwords of the modern cooking, which makes resourceful use of southern European techniques in dishes such as Niçoise salad with roast calamari, or brill fillet with a fricassée of escargots, pancetta and mushrooms, served with saffron potatoes and béarnaise. Seafood is the main draw, a main course of strongly flavoured lobster tail on crab and prawn risotto amply demonstrating why. Finish with a pear poached to softness in Sauternes, and offset with a coconut sorbet.

Chef Daniel Ward **Owner** Mrs Butts & Mr M Lewis
Times 12-2.30/6.15-10 Closed late Dec-mid Jan (approx), D Sun **Prices** Fixed L 2 course £16.50, Starter £5.50-£13.25, Main £12.50-£23.75, Dessert £5.75-£13.50, Service included **Wines** 42 bottles over £20, 20 bottles under £20, 12 by glass **Notes** Early supper Mon-Sat 6.15-8pm, Sunday L, Vegetarian available, Dress restrictions, Smart casual, Air con **Seats** 40 **Children** Portions, Menu **Parking** On street

GOREY *continued*

The Village Bistro

◉ Modern British, Mediterranean **V** ✋

Farmhouse atmosphere in a Jersey village

☎ 01534 853429
Gorey Village JE3 9EP
e-mail: thevillagebistro@yahoo.co.uk
dir: Take A3 E from St Helier to Gorey. Restaurant in village centre

A welcoming, rustic bistro in a converted church in sleepy Gorey offers outdoor patio dining when the sun shines on Jersey, and a farmhouse ambience of wooden tables, beams and old farm implements indoors. The cooking reaches a little beyond the bucolic surroundings, though, with pan-roasted squid to start, accompanied by chorizo, tomatoes and rocket, followed perhaps by sea bass on pommes Anna with fennel, or crisp-skinned chicken breast on lemon and thyme risotto with pak choi. Finish with home-made ice creams and sorbets (the mango is a winner), or cherry and almond tart.

Chef Sarah Copp **Owner** Sean & Sarah Copp **Times** 12-2.30/7-10.30 Closed Mon, D Sun **Prices** Fixed L 2 course £13.50, Fixed D 3 course £18.50, Starter £7.15-£8.50, Main £14.25-£17.50, Dessert £4.25-£5.75, Service optional, Groups min 8 service 10% **Wines** 14 bottles over £20, 20 bottles under £20, 4 by glass **Notes** Sunday L, Vegetarian menu, Dress restrictions, Smart casual **Seats** 40 **Children** Portions **Parking** On street and public car park

ROZEL   Map 24

Château La Chaire

◉◉ Traditional British, French

Victorian country retreat offering imaginative cuisine

☎ 01534 863354 📠 01534 865137
Rozel Bay JE3 6AJ
e-mail: res@chateau-la-chaire.co.uk
dir: From St Helier NE towards Five Oaks, Maufant, then St Martin's Church & Rozel; 1st left in village, hotel 100mtrs

Victorian gentlemen always had an eye for beautiful locations when they built their swanky residences. This splendid château is hidden in a tranquil wooded valley, with paths leading to clifftop walks and meandering down to the colourful fishing harbour of Rozel. Choose from two dining venues: an airy conservatory and terrace for balmy summertime, or an oak-panelled dining room where the Victorian ancestors would still feel at home - even the table legs are decorously clothed. The Anglo-French menu does not always steer a traditional course, so salad of king prawns tempura with spicy dressing to start, precedes roast monkfish wrapped in Parma ham with red wine risotto, and be sure to leave room for a blackcurrant trifle to finish.

Chef Simon Walker **Owner** The Hiscox family **Times** 12-3/7-10 **Prices** Food prices not confirmed for 2010. Please telephone for details. **Wines** 51 bottles over £20, 18 bottles under £20, 12 by glass **Notes** Sunday L, Vegetarian available, Dress restrictions, No jeans or trainers, Civ Wed 60 **Seats** 60, Pr/dining room 28 **Children** Portions **Parking** 30

ST AUBIN   Map 24

The Boat House

◉ Modern European ✋

Harbourside restaurant specialising in local seafood

☎ 01534 744226 & 747141 📠 01534 499993
One North Quay JE3 8BS
e-mail: enquiries@jerseyboathouse.com
dir: Please telephone for directions

Built on the site of an old boat repair yard, this popular venue overlooks the harbour with fabulous views across the Bay of St Aubin. Downstairs, the bar and brasserie menu offers a more casual style, while the serious dining is upstairs. Wood and glass is the theme, with large windows making much of the natural light. In the glass-enclosed kitchen, the cooking is modern European with an emphasis on local seafood cooked simply, allowing the freshness of the ingredients to speak for themselves, whether it's fresh oysters, steamed mussels, local scallops or shellfish soup with rouille and fresh crab. Main courses include pan-fried gilt head bream with Puy lentil jus, creamed garlic mash and caramelised shallots.

Chef Adrian Goldsborough, David Cameron **Owner** Mill Holdings (St Brelade) Ltd **Times** 12-2/6-9.30 Closed 25 Dec & 1-31 Jan, Mon-Tue (Winter), L Wed-Thu & Sat (Winter), D Sun (Winter) **Prices** Fixed L 2 course £15-£25, Fixed D 3 course £20-£35, Starter £7.50-£9, Main £14.50-£18, Dessert £5.50-£6, Service optional, Groups min 8 service 10% **Notes** Early bird menu available 6-7pm, Sunday L, Vegetarian available, Civ Wed 120 **Seats** 120 **Children** Portions, Menu **Parking** On street, public car park

The Salty Dog Bar & Bistro

◉ Modern International **V** ✋

Lively bistro with global reach

☎ 01534 742760 📠 01534 742932
Le Boulevard, St Aubins Village JE3 8AB
e-mail: info@saltydogbistro.com
web: www.saltydogbistro.com
dir: Walking from centre of St Aubin Village along harbour, approx halfway along, slightly set back

The Salty Dog sits in a courtyard on St Aubin's scenic harbour, a great place for chilled-out sunny day dining. Harbours conjure images of setting sail around the world, and the eclectic décor here evokes a global beachcomber chic, hinting at Morocco, South-East Asia and the Caribbean. The wide-ranging menu similarly takes its influences from the global basket to produce fun fusion cuisine from a melting pot of international flavours, with super-fresh Jersey produce to the fore. Seafood dishes are made for pan-Asian treatment, so king prawns Pana - fat tiger prawns with a spicy black bean sauce served in a sizzling skillet - is a popular starter. Mains include Creole tuna with fresh basil, sweet chilli and jasmine rice.

The Salty Dog Bar & Bistro

Chef Damon James Duffy **Owner** Damon & Natalie Duffy **Times** 12.30-6/6-1.30am Closed 2 wks Xmas, Mon (Jan-Feb), L Tue-Fri (Jan-Mar) **Prices** Fixed L course £22.50, Fixed D 3 course £22.50-£29.95, Starter £6.90-£9.50, Main £11.95-£27, Dessert £4.50-£5.95, Service added but optional 9.71% **Wines** 24 bottles over £20, 23 bottles under £20, 7 by glass **Notes** Sunday L, Vegetarian menu **Seats** 60 **Children** Portions, Menu **Parking** Car parks & on street parking nearby

Somerville Hotel

◉◉ International ✋

A romantic setting for local seafood

☎ 01534 741226 📠 01534 746621
Mont du Boulevard JE3 8AD
e-mail: somerville@dolanhotels.com
dir: From village follow harbour, then take Mont du Boulevard

Enjoying spectacular views of St Aubin's Bay, the Tides Restaurant is popular with locals as well as residents for its superbly fresh local fish and seafood. The views help, too, making for a romantic setting. Tables are simply laid with runner cloth and modern oil lamps, with luxuries appearing on the plate - perhaps local lobster, oysters and prawns - and some quality produce from across the water in France. Start with foie gras two ways, served with roast apple and rhubarb chutney, celeriac remoulade and toasted brioche, followed by grilled fillets of lemon sole with wood sorrel, risotto of summer peas, grilled gambas and velouté of watercress.

Chef Wayne Pegler **Owner** Mr W Dolan **Times** 12.30-2/7-9 **Prices** Fixed L 2 course fr £12.50, Fixed D 3 course fr £29.50, Starter £8.95-£9.50, Main £18.50-£21.50, Dessert £7.95, Service optional **Wines** 42 bottles over £20, 23 bottles under £20, 6 by glass **Notes** Sunday L, Vegetarian available, Dress restrictions, Smart casual at D, Civ Wed 40 **Seats** 120, Pr/dining room 40 **Children** Portions **Parking** 30

ST BRELADE — Map 24

L'Horizon Hotel and Spa

◉◉ British, French

Superb views and range of dining options

☎ 01534 743101 📠 01534 746269
Route de la Baie JE3 8EF
e-mail: lhorizon@handpicked.co.uk
dir: 2m from Jersey Airport, 5m from St Helier

The golden sands of St Brelade's Bay provide a wonderful setting for this relaxed and luxurious hotel with excellent facilities including a spa and leisure club. Built in 1850 by a Colonel in the Bengal army, it has a light and spacious interior and a variety of dining options. The Grill restaurant, Brasserie, Lounge & Bar and elegant Crystal Room restaurant mean there's something to suit all occasions (there's a large beach-facing terrace, too). Food is light and modern in the main and leans towards the classical. The Grill menu is focused heavily on local seafood with the likes of seared hand-diver caught scallops with roasted beetroot and Granny Smith foam, and fillet of brill pan-fried with Jersey spider crab ravioli with ginger and lemongrass and, to finish, passionfruit sushi with coconut and lime.

Times 7-9.45 Closed Xmas, Sun-Mon, L all wk

Hotel La Place

◉ Modern British

Sound cooking in converted farmhouse

☎ 01534 744261 📠 01534 745164
Route Du Coin, La Haule JE3 8BT
e-mail: hotlaplace@aol.com
dir: Please telephone for directions

Located in the heart of the countryside, only a short walk from the picturesque St Aubin's Harbour and St Brelade's Bay, this hotel is a conversion of a 17th-century farmhouse. Enjoy a drink in the cocktail bar overlooking the pool in fine weather, or by the log fire in the lounge, and then head through to the beamed Retreat Restaurant. The menu suits the setting and makes good use of local produce in dishes like flash-fried Jersey scallops with chilli mange-tout and chorizo, followed by fried beef fillet medallions with shallot, ceps, potato purée and a red wine jus.

Times 12-2/7-9

Ocean Restaurant at the Atlantic Hotel

◉◉◉ — see page 470

ST CLEMENT — Map 24

Green Island Restaurant

◉ Mediterranean

Great local seafood in bustling beach café

☎ 01534 857787
Green Island JE2 6LS
e-mail: greenislandrestaurant@jerseymail.co.uk
dir: Please telephone for directions

This popular beach café and restaurant occupies a delightful spot on the edge of the sea. It's a relaxed place with half the tables outside when the weather is fine and it's advisable to book. The views out over Green Island are well worth savouring, as is the stylish modern Mediterranean cooking with much emphasis on fresh fish dishes. Expect fresh grilled sardines, crab and lobster to be on the menu when available. Saffron mascarpone risotto with fresh crevettes and scallops might be followed by an accurately cooked roasted monkfish tail served on an oriental vegetable stir-fry with fragrant rice and red Thai curry sauce.

Times 12-3/7-10 Closed 21 Dec-Mar, Mon, D Sun

ST HELIER — Map 24

Bohemia Restaurant

◉◉◉◉ — see page 471

Grand, Jersey

◉◉◉ — see page 472

Hotel Savoy

◉ Modern British NEW

Imaginative cuisine in former manor house

☎ 01534 727521
37 Rouge Bouillon JE2 3ZA
e-mail: info@thesavoy.biz
dir: Please telephone for directions

This 19th-century manor house is now a family-run hotel set in tranquil grounds a short walk from the main shopping area of St Helier. The stylish Montana Restaurant, a lovely dramatic room overlooking the front garden, is decorated in gold and maroon and furnished with round tables and high-backed black leather chairs. The menu offers modern British/European cooking with classical roots, focusing on good local produce. Try crispy shredded chicken or duck with carrot, coriander, red onions, salad leaves and spicy salad dressing to start, and follow with a main course of pan-fried sea bream with roasted shallot pomme purée and lemon thyme white wine sauce.

Chef Daniel Bracewell **Owner** Mr J Lora **Times** 6.30-9 Closed L ex by prior arrangement **Prices** Fixed D 3 course fr £17 **Notes** Vegetarian available

La Petite Pomme

◉◉ Modern European

Local seafood in famous hotel with views

☎ 01534 880110 📠 01534 737781
Pomme d'Or Hotel, Liberation Square JE1 3UF
e-mail: enquiries@pommedorhotel.com
dir: 5m from airport, 0.5m from ferry terminal

The Pomme d'Or is one of Jersey's most famous hotels and has been a focal point of the island's hospitality for more than 175 years. Located in the centre of the island, overlooking Liberation Square, it was the German naval headquarters during the World War II occupation, and is the scene of the annual liberation celebrations (May 9th). La Petite Pomme, the hotel's fine dining area, occupies the first floor overlooking the square and St Helier harbour. The restaurant is sumptuously decorated with well-spaced tables and the innovative dishes are contemporary and skilfully prepared from the freshest local produce. Recommendations include Jersey scallops served with a native oyster beignet and a warm vichyssoise sauce, and seared local plaice in a dill purée with braised baby fennel and a red wine jus.

Chef James Waters, Chris Morris **Owner** Seymour Hotels **Times** 7-10 Closed 26-30 Dec, Sun, L all week **Prices** Starter £6.15-£8.20, Main £13.35-£19.95, Dessert £5.50-£7.50, Service optional **Wines** 34 bottles over £20, 41 bottles under £20, 12 by glass **Notes** Vegetarian available, Dress restrictions, Smart casual, Air con **Seats** 50, Pr/dining room 50 **Children** Portions, Menu **Parking** 100 yds from hotel

Restaurant Sirocco@ The Royal Yacht

◉◉ Modern British

Serious modern cooking overlooking the harbour

☎ 01534 720511 & 615403 📠 01534 767729
The Weighbridge JE2 3NF
e-mail: reception@theroyalyacht.com
dir: Adjacent to Weighbridge Park overlooking Jersey Harbour

Thought to be the oldest established hotel in St Helier, the stylishly refurbished Royal Yacht enjoys views across the bustling marina and steam dock from the contemporary-styled Sirocco Restaurant - the fine dining option among a good range of eateries. With a passion for using the finest seasonal and organic ingredients on the island, the confident and ambitious kitchen produces some impressive, full-flavoured modern British dishes

continued

Ocean Restaurant at the Atlantic Hotel

ST BRELADE Map 24

Modern British V NOTABLE WINE LIST

Scintillating cooking with gorgeous bay views

☎ 01534 744101 📄 01534 744102
Le Mont de la Pulente JE3 8HE
e-mail: info@theatlantichotel.com
web: www.theatlantichotel.com
dir: A13 to Petit Port, turn right into Rue de la Sergente & right again, hotel signed

The Atlantic occupies a prime spot on the Jersey coast, overlooking St Ouen's Bay, its low-slung white frontage evoking the seaside architecture of the 1930s. Inside, the place is decorated in cool, neutral tones, with nothing to jar the senses. White shutters frame the outward view from the Ocean Restaurant, with the sun going down behind the sub-tropical gardens. It all makes a fitting context for the scintillating cooking of Mark Jordan, who has turned this place into a real Channel Islands destination. Ideas and techniques are full of imagination, and dishes look stunning. Consider a first course of dry-roasted duck foie gras, accompanied by salted caramel nougatine, charentais melon sorbet and passionfruit foam, in which the components combine to form thought-provoking flavours, or another of seared langoustines with globe artichoke purée, asparagus and crisped pork belly. Mains

are divided equally between fish and meat, and the former might proffer halibut served in the manner of lamb, with crushed minted peas and baby turnips. Desserts come headlined with their main ingredient, and display quite as much culinary firepower as the foregoing courses. 'Raspberry' brings on marinated berries, along with their sorbet, but also crunchy nougatine and spears of caramel. The six-course tasting menu with accompanying wines is probably the best way to explore the range, for those in the mood to splash out.

Chef Mark Jordan **Owner** Patrick Burke
Times 12.30-2.30/7-10 Closed Jan
Prices Fixed L 2 course £20, Fixed D 3 course £50, Tasting menu £70, Service included **Wines** 385 bottles over £20, 15 bottles under £20, 11 by glass
Notes Fixed ALC 2 course £50, 3 course £60, Sunday L, Vegetarian menu, Dress restrictions, Smart dress, Civ Wed 80
Seats 60, Pr/dining room 20
Children Portions, Menu **Parking** 60

Bohemia Restaurant

Modern British, French V

Pace-setting contemporary cooking in a smart spa hotel

☎ 01534 880588 & 876500
🖷 01534 875054
The Club Hotel & Spa, Green St JE2 4UH
e-mail: bohemia@huggler.com
dir: In town centre. 5 mins walk from main shopping centre

Opening in the summer of 2005, the Club Hotel and Spa immediately laid claim to being St Helier's hottest property. Set a little apart from the town-centre bustle, it has nonetheless become a focal point and magnet for Jersey's smart set. 'Chic' is a word that crops up reliably in any description of the Bohemia Restaurant, where the Jane Goff design is oriented towards a laid-back, international feel, with dark brown tones, leather seating and quality tableware predominant. Shaun Rankin's menus aim to make the most of what he calls the 'natural kitchen garden that is Jersey'. Menu formats range from a top-value fixed-price lunch to the all-singing, all-dancing Taste and Combination Menu, where nine dishes plus extras are productively teamed with pre-selected wines. The culinary style is modern Anglo-French, as befits the location, with novel ideas that refresh and redefine the traditional repertoire. Variations on Jersey crab start off a

meal in fine style, offering perfectly fresh crabmeat in a salad, along with ravioli of crab, avocado and tomato, a crab beignet and a sweetly fruity olive oil sorbet. Meat and fish partnerships are all the rage, and turn up here in the shape of veal and turbot, the former as braised shin and a portion of glazed sweetbread, the latter roasted, and matched with chopped kumquats and dill-seasoned baby carrots. Desserts are no less finely detailed, rhubarb crumble soufflé appearing with white chocolate fudge cannelloni, or Amaretto parfait with salted caramel, barley ice cream and lemon curd. Incidentals (breads, canapés, petits fours) are fully up to the mark. This is without doubt a destination restaurant.

Chef Shaun Rankin **Owner** Lawrence Huggler **Times** 12-2.30/6.30-10 Closed Sun, L BH Mon **Prices** Fixed L 2 course £18.50-£42.50, Fixed D 3 course fr £49.50, Starter £17.50-£20.50, Main £27.50-£35, Dessert £8.50, Service added but optional 10% **Wines** 3 bottles over £20, 3 bottles under £20, 16 by glass **Notes** Tasting menu 11 course, Vegetarian menu, Dress restrictions, Smart casual, Civ Wed 60, Air con **Seats** 60, Pr/dining room 20 **Children** Portions **Parking** 20, Opposite

ST HELIER *continued*

with interesting combinations. From an innovative menu choose, perhaps, warm spider crab cannelloni with juicy seared scallops and oyster butter, then duo of Woodside lamb (moist loin and braised breast) with rosemary gnocchi, celeriac soubise and crushed broad beans, finishing with chilled vanilla rice pudding, cherry soup and pistachio ice cream.

Chef Fred Tobin **Owner** Lodestar Group **Times** 12-2/7-10 Closed D Sun **Prices** Fixed L 2 course £21-£25, Fixed D 3 course £25-£32, Tasting menu £75-£98, Starter £8-£12, Main £15-£32, Dessert £8-£10, Service optional **Wines** 175 bottles over £20, 23 bottles under £20, 16 by glass **Notes** £98 tasting menu includes wines, Sunday L, Vegetarian available, Dress restrictions, Smart casual, Civ Wed 300, Air con **Seats** 65, Pr/dining room 20 **Children** Portions **Parking** Car park

Seasons

◎ British, International ✍

Popular hotel with local produce-driven menu

☎ 01534 726521 📄 01534 768804
Best Western Royal Hotel, 26 Davids Place JE2 4TD
e-mail: manager@royalhoteljersey.com
dir: Please telephone for directions

This long-established hotel is located in the centre of town, close to the business district and shops. The

Seasons restaurant is contemporary with wooden floorboards, well-spaced white-clothed tables and a relaxed, friendly atmosphere. The menu is centred around local produce, and modern British dishes are underpinned with classical techniques. Salad of artichoke and Jersey asparagus with parmesan and a poached egg might be followed by local line-caught sea bass, pan-fried and set on risotto nero with roasted calamari and buttered asparagus. Chocolate bread-and-butter pudding with Jersey black butter ice cream shows the form at dessert.

Chef Alun Williams **Owner** Morvan Hotels
Times 12-2/6.30-9 Closed L Mon-Sat (unless by prior arrangement) **Prices** Fixed D 3 course £18.50-£22, Starter £5-£8, Main £12-£18, Dessert £5-£8, Service optional **Wines** 6 bottles over £20, 39 bottles under £20, 5 by glass **Notes** Vegetarian available, Dress restrictions, Smart casual, Civ Wed 35, Air con **Seats** 100, Pr/dining room 50 **Children** Portions, Menu **Parking** 14

The Waterfront Brasserie & Terrace

◎ Modern European

Contemporary waterfront brasserie dining in the heart of St Helier's marina

☎ 01534 671100 📄 01534 671101
Radisson Blu Waterfront Hotel, The Waterfront, La Rue de L'Etau JE2 4HE
e-mail: info.jersey@radissonsas.com
dir: Head towards Elizabeth Harbour turn right at rdbt, hotel at end of road

You couldn't ask for a better setting than this sleek modern hotel's spot at the heart of the marina in St Helier, with the promenade, waterfront and town's chic boutiques on the doorstep. Sipping a sundowner cocktail while watching exotic fish in the Martello Bar's vast floor-to-ceiling aquarium should set the mood nicely for dinner in the neutral modern minimalism of the brasserie-style restaurant. The menu plays to the crowd with fresh, honest and simple dishes with plenty of nods to the nearby continent: how about crab and leek bake with herb crust for starters, and pan-fried lamb cutlets with black pudding mash, ratatouille and confit garlic, or a classic rib-eye steak with dauphinoise potatoes to follow?

Chef Robert Cauchi **Owner** T Clucas **Times** 12.30-4/7-10 Closed L Nov-Mar **Prices** Fixed L 2 course fr £22, Fixed D 3 course fr £32, Starter £7.50-£12.50, Main £13-£19.50, Dessert £6.50-£9, Service optional **Wines** 27 bottles over £20, 4 bottles under £20, 4 by glass **Notes** Sunday L, Vegetarian available, Civ Wed 200, Air con **Seats** 100, Pr/dining room 80 **Children** Portions, Menu **Parking** 85

Grand, Jersey

ST HELIER Map 24

Modern European

Stylish décor and innovative cooking at landmark hotel

☎ 01534 722301 📄 01534 737815
The Esplanade JE4 8WD
e-mail: reception@hilwoodresorts.com
dir: Located on St Helier Seafront

The Grand Hotel has earned its status over the years as a local landmark but a recent multi-million pound refurbishment means it is also bang up-to-date in terms of contemporary swagger. Set on The Esplanade, with views across St Aubin's Bay to the front and the buzzy St Helier streets at the back, the hotel has a modern Brasserie, Victoria's, and a Champagne Bar offering over 100 vintages, plus the fine-dining Tassili restaurant. Here, the black and pink colour scheme works to great

effect with black chairs and tables set against pink-hued curtains. Only open Thursday to Saturday evenings, Tassili is headed up by Richard Allen, who cooks with the best local Jersey produce with an emphasis on fish and seafood. Sesame-scented tuna tartar with aromatic braised octopus, watermelon vinaigrette and oyster tempura is a creative first course, followed by poached then roasted breast of black leg chicken, jambonette of the leg, confit potato and sunflower seed purée. Finish off with a coffee sundae of coffee brownie, white coffee ice cream, latte mousse and amaretti crumbs.

Chef Richard Allen **Owner** Hilwood Resorts & Hotels **Times** 7-9.30 Closed L all week, D Sun-Wed **Prices** Fixed D 3 course fr £47, Tasting menu £65, Service optional **Wines** 200 bottles over £20, 6 bottles under £20, 15 by glass **Notes** Tasting menu 7 course, Vegetarian available, Dress restrictions, Smart casual, Civ Wed 200, Air con **Seats** 32 **Parking** 32, NCP

Longueville Manor

Modern British NOTABLE WINE LIST

Relaxed country-house dining in Jersey

☎ 01534 725501 📄 01534 731613
JE2 7WF
e-mail: info@longuevillemanor.com
web: www.longuevillemanor.com
dir: From St Helier take A3 to Gorey, hotel 0.75m on left

Set in 15 acres of woodland with a lake, which is home to black swans, this 14th-century Norman manor house is full of charm and character. Comfortable country-house furnishings just beg you to settle down for some afternoon tea in the drawing room, but be sure to take in the magnificent grounds replete with its own rose garden. Inside, there are 2 dining rooms - the 13th-century oak-panelled room and the English manor-style garden room (more suitable for lunchtime dining). There are also 3 private dining rooms. Much of the fruit, vegetables and herbs come from the walled kitchen gardens and Victorian glasshouses. The elaborate, carefully constructed dishes deal in balanced flavours; grilled hand-dived scallops, for example, with girolles, slow-roast belly pork, honey and five spices, following on with loin of lamb with braised shoulder, flageolet beans, baby vegetables and thyme jus. Finish with chocolate Pandora with praline, banana and warm vanilla cream.

Chef Andrew Baird **Owner** Malcolm Lewis **Times** 12.30-2/7-10 **Prices** Fixed L 2 course fr £17, Fixed D 3 course £55-£68.75, Service included **Wines** 300+ bottles over £20, 20 bottles under £20, 23 by glass **Notes** 5-course Taste of Jersey menu & 7-course Prestige menu available, Sunday L, Vegetarian available, Dress restrictions, Smart casual, jacket required, Civ Wed 40 **Seats** 65, Pr/dining room 22 **Children** Portions, Menu **Parking** 45

ST LAWRENCE — Map 24

Indigos

◉ Modern ⌣

Eclectic cooking coupled with breathtaking views

☎ 01534 758024 📠 01534 758028
Hotel Cristina, Mont Felard JE3 1JA
e-mail: cristina@dolanhotels.com
dir: A10 to Mont Feland Exit, hotel on left

Superb beaches as well as some of Jersey's unique heritage sites are on the doorstep of this lovely hotel and restaurant, perched in beautiful gardens on a hillside with sweeping views over St Aubin's Bay. On a balmy evening, unwind on the seaview terrace or in the bistro-style restaurant, where a smart contemporary look with a warm terracotta glow sets the scene for uncomplicated dishes influenced by the cuisine of the Mediterranean. Well-sourced, good-quality produce turns up in a starter of steamed Jersey mussels with pancetta, saffron and grain mustard; main courses might include herb-crusted rack of lamb with a cassoulet of summer beans, chorizo and rosemary.

Chef Mark Rowan **Owner** W G Dolan
Times 12-2/6.30-8.30 Closed Nov-Mar **Prices** Fixed D 3 course fr £24, Starter £5.50-£7.95, Main £13.95-£16.95, Dessert £6.95-£9.95, Service optional **Wines** 7 bottles over £20, 24 bottles under £20, 10 by glass **Notes** Vegetarian available, Dress restrictions, Smart casual, Civ Wed 60 **Seats** 120 **Children** Portions **Parking** 60

ST PETER — Map 24

Greenhills Country Hotel

◉ Traditional, European

Fine dining in peaceful period surroundings

☎ 01534 481042 📠 01534 485322
Mont de L'Ecole JE3 7EL
e-mail: reserve@greenhillshotel.com
dir: A1 signed St Peters Valley (A11). 4m, turn right onto E112

The Bromley family have run this heavenly 17th-century country-house hotel with hands-on enthusiasm for half a century. You can see why they want to stay put: the sylvan peace of St Peter's valley enfolds their own award-winning gardens, which explode into exuberant colour through the summer. The small-scale intimate ambience is at its most soothing in the traditional restaurant, where you can expect European-influenced cuisine, with the emphasis on fresh local produce and seafood in some quite complex flavour combinations. Try herb and lemongrass-marinated gambas with saffron crème fraîche and bell pepper coulis to start, followed by Jersey line-caught sea bass with braised matchstick potatoes, tomatoes and shallots and parsley sauce.

Chef Ronny Friedrich **Owner** Peter Bromley
Times 12.30-2/7-9.30 Closed 20 Dec-6 Feb **Prices** Fixed L 2 course £10, Fixed D 4 course £25.50-£28, Starter

£5.95-£12.95, Main £18.95-£28, Dessert £5.95-£8 **Wines** 37 bottles over £20, 37 bottles under £20, 4 by glass **Notes** Sunday L, Vegetarian available, Dress restrictions, Smart casual, Civ Wed 40, Air con **Seats** 90, Pr/dining room 40 **Children** Portions, Menu **Parking** 45

ST SAVIOUR — Map 24

Longueville Manor

◉◉◉ — **see page 473**

TRINITY — Map 24

Water's Edge Hotel

◉◉ Modern British

Stunning coastal setting for enjoyable cuisine

☎ 01534 862777 📠 01534 863645
Bouley Bay JE3 5AS
e-mail: mail@watersedgehotel.co.je
dir: 10-15 mins from St Helier, A9 N onto A8 onto B31, follow signs to Bouley Bay

What this art-deco-style hotel's name promises it certainly delivers - nestling in tranquil Bouley Bay it comes with wonderful views over the water and across to the distant French coastline. The split-level Waterside Restaurant makes the most of those views, complemented by a dining terrace. Modern British cuisine is offered on the restaurant's carte or fixed-price market menu, with fresh local fish and seafood not surprisingly the order of the day. Take a starter of seared Jersey scallops and langoustine, for instance, perhaps served with Jerusalem artichoke purée in a crispy millefeuille, pea shoot salad and balsamic reduction, while Dover sole served meunière with green vegetables and Jersey Royals might catch the eye at mains. Formal service and crisp table linen complete the traditional experience.

Times 7-9.15 Closed Nov-Mar, L all week

SARK

SARK — Map 24

La Sablonnerie

◉◉ Modern, Traditional International

Creative cuisine in an idyllic setting

☎ 01481 832061 📠 01481 832408
GY9 0SD
e-mail: lasablonnerie@cwgsy.net
web: www.lasablonnerie.com
dir: On southern part of island. Horse & carriage transport to hotel

No cars are allowed on the tiny island of Sark, so the sheer quirkiness of arriving at this hidden time-warp restaurant in the hotel's own horse and carriage takes some beating. Summery curtains of flowers festoon the walls of the whitewashed stone cottage, and, once inside, low ceilings with four hundred-year-old oak-beams make for an intimate dining room. English and French influences shape a menu of modern international dishes, thus a starter of plump Sark lobster is seasoned with a lime and ginger glaze, then roast Barbary duck comes with parsnip and potato purée and a black pepper jus. Produce could hardly be sourced more locally: the hotel has its own herb garden and dairy herd of Guernsey cows.

Chef Martin Cross **Owner** Elizabeth Perrée
Times 12-2.30/7-9.30 Closed mid Oct-Etr **Prices** Fixed L 2 course £16.80-£22.30, Fixed D 3 course £23.60-£30.10, Starter £5.80-£7.80, Main £11-£14.50, Dessert £5.80-£6.80, Service added 10% **Wines** 9 bottles over £20, 41 bottles under £20, 6 by glass **Notes** Sunday L, Vegetarian available **Seats** 39 **Children** Portions, Menu

ISLE OF MAN

DOUGLAS
Map 24 SC37

Sefton Hotel

@@ Modern European

Fine dining beside the sea

☎ 01624 645500 📄 01624 676004
Harris Promenade IM1 2RW
e-mail: info@seftonhotel.co.im
dir: From sea terminal, hotel 1m along Promenade

It maybe a Victorian seafront hotel, but it comes with a contemporary fine-dining restaurant (aptly called the Gallery), decorated with bright artwork and enjoying superb views out to sea. Imaginative modern cooking is the order of the day, driven by fine ingredients in a mix of European-style and classic-French dishes, with a touch of flambé (aka, crêpe Suzette) or carving at the table (chateaubriand for 2) thrown in for that sense of occasion. Otherwise, expect turbot fillet, pork belly, langoustines and braised oxtail served with dill gnocchi, curly kale and a red wine jus, while a classic caramelised lemon tart (with ginger beer granité, fresh strawberries and mint sugar) might provide the finale.

Times 12-2/6-10 Closed L Sun

Scotland

Urquhart Castle, Loch Ness

SCOTLAND
CITY OF ABERDEEN
ABERDEEN   Map 23 NJ90

Atlantis at the Mariner Hotel

◎ Modern British, Seafood V

Family-run hotel dining with focus on local seafood and meats

☎ 01224 588901 📠 01224 571621
349 Great Western Rd AB10 6NW
e-mail: info@themarinerhotel.co.uk
web: www.themarinerhotel.co.uk
dir: From S, 400yds right off A90 at Great Western Rd lights

Fresh local seafood is the mainstay of the extensive menu at this popular restaurant set within the Mariner Hotel, a well-maintained, family-run hotel situated west of the city centre. Expect a maritime feel to the split-level restaurant, with its wood floors, panelled walls and conservatory extension. In addition to oysters, Cove lobsters and the cold seafood platter (for two), you can sample mussels with herb and chilli crust, teriyaki seafood brochette, and baked calamari. Carnivores are not forgotten - try the excellent Aberdeen Angus steaks or roast venison with redcurrant jus - and finish with sticky toffee pudding.

Chef George Bennett **Times** 12-2.30/6-10 Closed 26 Dec, 1-2 Jan, L Sat **Prices** Fixed L 2 course £17, Fixed D 3 course £21, Starter £4-£8.50, Main £11.50-£28, Dessert £4.50-£5.50, Service optional **Wines** 31 bottles over £20, 12 bottles under £20, 9 by glass **Notes** Sunday L, Vegetarian menu **Seats** 50 **Children** Portions, Menu **Parking** 50

Malmaison Aberdeen

◎◎ Modern British NEW 🍴

Stylish brasserie with theatre kitchen serving modern Scottish cuisine

☎ 01224 327370 📠 01224 327371
49-53 Queens Rd AB15 4YP
e-mail: info.aberdeen@malmaison.com
dir: Please telephone for directions

The Aberdeen outpost of the Malmaison chain has taken the old Queen's Hotel, where Balmoral staff once lived, and given it a major revamp. A cast-iron art nouveau entrance canopy opens into a modish décor that will

strike a chord with fans of the Mal brand: touchy-feely textures and the sort of bold statement colours that look the business in a grand old building like this. A glass tunnel leading to the Brasserie restaurant houses the wine cellar - look down and there's more beneath a glass floor. Sexy modern tartans clothe the seating, or you could grab a bar stool at the grill next to the chefs toiling over the coals of the centrepiece Josper oven. Modern Scottish cuisine founded on cracking materials is the order of the day - say hand-dived Orkney scallops with cauliflower purée, lime segments and crispy pancetta to start, followed by seared loin of venison with dauphinoise potato, sautéed foie gras and raspberry tea syrup.

Chef Mark Pollock **Owner** Malmaison **Times** 12-2.30/5.30-10.30 Closed D 25 Dec **Prices** Fixed L 2 course £14.50, Fixed D 3 course £17.50, Starter £4.95-£11.50, Main £10.50-£35, Dessert £4.95-£8.50, Service added but optional 10% **Wines** 161 bottles over £20, 7 bottles under £20, 13 by glass **Notes** Sunday L, Vegetarian available, Air con **Seats** 90, Pr/dining room 12 **Children** Portions, Menu **Parking** 50

Maryculter House Hotel

◎ Scottish NEW

Historic old mansion with modern Scottish cooking

☎ 01224 732124 📠 01224 733510
AB12 5GB
e-mail: info@maryculterhousehotel.com
dir: Off A90 to S of Aberdeen and onto B9077. Hotel is located 8m on right, 0.5m beyond Lower Deeside Caravan Park

The Knights Templar once trained on this spot in the 13th century, but modern guests can leave the hairshirts at home and indulge in a homely stay at this Scottish mansion on the River Dee. The comfortingly traditional Priory restaurant is in the oldest part of the building, where exposed stone walls, an open fire and candlelight work together in a romantic setting. The kitchen thinks local with its sourcing and turns out good honest cooking in a classic Scottish style with some modern flourishes. You're never far from fantastic fresh fish and seafood here, so start with brandade of smoked haddock and watercress with cauliflower cream, and move on to the likes of pan-roasted Scottish hake with trompette de mort mushrooms, olive crushed potatoes, baby fennel and vanilla broth.

Chef David Bell **Owner** James Gilbert **Times** 7-9 Closed L all week **Prices** Starter £5.95-£7.95, Main £16.95-£25.95, Dessert £5.95-£7.95, Service optional **Wines** 23 bottles over £20, 18 bottles under £20, 2 by glass **Notes** 8 course gourmet menu available Fri & Sat, Vegetarian available, Dress restrictions, Smart casual, no jeans or T-shirts, Civ Wed 120 **Seats** 40, Pr/dining room 18 **Children** Portions **Parking** 150

Norwood Hall

◎ British, European

Fine dining in a grand Victorian mansion

☎ 01224 868951 📠 01224 869868
Garthdee Rd, Cults AB15 9FX
e-mail: info@norwood-hall.co.uk
dir: From S, exit A90 at 1st rdbt, cross bridge, left at rdbt into Garthdee Rd, hotel in 5m

Seven acres of secluded woodland surround this imposing Victorian mansion with carved ceilings, ornate fireplaces, sweeping staircases and stained glass windows. As you settle in to dinner in the opulent oak-panelled Tapestry restaurant, it becomes clear where the restaurant gets its name, as the walls are indeed clad with lovely tapestries framing widely-spaced candlelit tables laid with classy crockery and glassware. Top-class seasonal Scottish produce, with an emphasis on game and seafood, drives the kitchen's repertoire of classic and more inventive dishes. Simple, well-balanced flavours are what it's all about here, and a starter of pan-fried wood pigeon with wild mushrooms and creamed cabbage sums up the style. Mains could be straight-up grills of beef, lamb or trout.

Owner Monument Leisure **Times** 12-2.30/6.30-9.45 Closed L Mon-Fri **Prices** Food prices not confirmed for 2010. Please telephone for details. **Wines** 43 bottles over £20, 23 bottles under £20, 9 by glass **Notes** Vegetarian available, Dress restrictions, Smart casual, Civ Wed 180 **Seats** 28, Pr/dining room 180 **Children** Portions, Menu **Parking** 100

The Silver Darling

◎◎ French, Seafood

Locally landed seafood prepared with a French touch

☎ 01224 576229 📠 01224 588119
Pocra Quay, North Pier AB11 5DQ
dir: At Aberdeen Harbour entrance

The one-time customs house turned conservatory restaurant is located at the entrance to Aberdeen harbour, meaning diners can enjoy stunning views of passing ships and, if you're lucky, dolphins. Tables all have panoramic views with linen tablecloths and sparkling glasses and service from the experienced front-of-house team is attentive without being cloying. The intimate setting makes for romantic dining with lunch trade particularly busy. The name - silver darling - is a reference to a colloquial term for herring and the focus of the French influenced menu is firmly on the locally landed fruits de mer. Lunch dishes may include perfectly cooked seared king scallops served with Parma ham, an aubergine and new potato caviar and a Parma ham and chervil cappuccino; or an excellent steamed halibut with caramelised fennel and baby vine tomatoes, tapenade, frisée salad and Riviera sauce.

Times 12-1.45/6.30-9.30 Closed Xmas-New Year, Sun, L Sat

ABERDEENSHIRE

BALLATER Map 23 NO39

The Auld Kirk

Modern Scottish NEW

Fine Scottish cuisine in former church

☎ 01339 755762 & 07918 698000 📄 0700 603 7559
Breamar Rd AB35 5RQ
e-mail: info@theauldkirk.com
dir: From Braemar on A93, on the right before entering village

You'll find the place easily enough - look for the soaring church spire. Sensitively converted, this former Victorian Scottish Free church is now a restaurant with rooms. Its Spirit Restaurant has the expected high-vaulted ceilings and ecclesiastic windows, while wood-panelled walls, chandeliers and centrepiece Spirit Statue catch the eye, too. Canvas-style artwork and white leather seating give the space a contemporary feel, while the accomplished Scottish cooking takes its cue from fresh, prime local produce and proudly advertises its suppliers. Generous portions, accuracy and seasonality prevail in dishes like fillet of pork with a potato, apple and haggis pie with apple and cider jus, or warm tart of plums and hazelnut frangipane served with wild blackberry ice cream.

Chef Tony Fuell **Owner** Tony Fuell, Peter Graydon
Times 6.30-9 Closed Xmas, 1st 2 wks Jan, Tue & Wed

(winter), D Sun (summer) **Prices** Fixed D 3 course £33.50-£35.50, Service optional **Wines** 15 bottles over £20, 22 bottles under £20, 4 by glass **Notes** Vegetarian available **Seats** 26, Pr/dining room 20 **Children** Portions **Parking** 6

Darroch Learg Hotel

– see below

The Green Inn

Modern British V

Intimate, family-run conservatory-style restaurant

☎ 013397 55701
9 Victoria Rd AB35 5QQ
e-mail: info@green-inn.com
dir: In village centre

The O'Halloran family run their restaurant with rooms in an erstwhile temperance hotel with well-oiled efficiency

and real flair. The addition of a conservatory has boosted seating capacity, but dinners are still an intimate affair, and everything unfolds at a relaxed pace. Chef Chris O'Halloran - ably assisted by mum, Evelyn - directs the action at the stoves, while dad Trevor takes care of front-of-house duties. Chris trained with Raymond Blanc, so expect modern cooking founded on solid French classical technique. His eye-catching dishes are based on top-drawer local produce, home-grown when available. Roasted local wood pigeon wrapped in Parma ham with creamed wild mushrooms and date sauce shows the style, then perhaps navarin of Scottish lamb with confit shoulder served with buttered vegetables, pesto, turnip purée and thyme jus.

Chef Chris & Evelyn O'Halloran **Owner** Trevor & Evelyn O'Halloran **Times** 7-9 Closed 2 wks Nov, 2 wks Jan, Sun, Mon, L all week **Prices** Fixed D 3 course £32.50, Service optional **Wines** 59 bottles over £20, 5 bottles under £20, 7 by glass **Notes** Vegetarian menu, Dress restrictions, Smart casual **Seats** 30, Pr/dining room 24 **Parking** On street & car park nearby

---

Darroch Learg Hotel

BALLATER Map 23 NO39

Modern Scottish

Country-house splendour in the Highlands

☎ 013397 55443 📄 013397 55252
56 Braemar Rd AB35 5UX
e-mail: enquiries@darrochlearg.co.uk
web: www.darrochlearg.co.uk
dir: On A93 at the W end of village

'The oakwood on the sunny hillside' is a reasonably accurate translation of the name, for those whose knowledge of old Gaelic isn't up to snuff. A Victorian country residence in the heart of Royal Deeside, it is indeed perched on a lushly wooded hill, and has been in the Franks family for the past forty years or so. Inside is as plush as can be, with a flawlessly smart dining room that extends into a refreshing conservatory space. A fairly

traditional culinary philosophy nonetheless draws on some modern technique and makes the most of the provender of north-east Scotland, from the legendary Arbroath smokies to incomparable Highland raspberries in the season. Dinner might begin with wood pigeon en croûte, dressed with spiced pear chutney, or perhaps smoked haddock in a raviolo with its own velouté. Aberdeen Angus beef fillet is treated with fitting dignity as one main course, with accompaniments of ox tongue, potato gratin and a relish of beetroot and horseradish. The finale may be sticky toffee pudding with caramel sauce, banana, and rum and raisin ice cream. A six-course tasting menu offers the option of avoiding having to make choices.

Chef David Mutter **Owner** The Franks family
Times 12.30-2/7-9 Closed Xmas, last 3wks Jan, L Mon-Sat **Prices** Fixed L course £25, Fixed D 3 course £45-£52, Tasting menu £56, Service included **Wines** 186 bottles over £20, 4 by glass **Notes** Sunday L, Vegetarian

available, Dress restrictions, Smart casual **Seats** 48 **Children** Portions, Menu **Parking** 15

BALLATER *continued*

Loch Kinord Hotel

⊛ Modern British

Victorian hotel with imaginative cooking

☎ 013398 85229 📄 013398 87007
Ballater Rd, Dinnet AB34 5JY
e-mail: stay@lochkinord.com
dir: From Aberdeen take A93 W towards Braemar, hotel on A93 between Aboyne & Ballater

A handsome, stone-built hotel in Royal Deeside, Loch Kinord was built in the late Victorian era, but is furnished these days with luxuries our forebears couldn't have conceived of, including plasma TVs, and a regionally based menu of imaginative Scottish food. Spring pea soup with dry-cured bacon and crème fraîche is a straightforward enough opener, and could be followed by a beautifully timed piece of sea-fresh cod on crushed potatoes, with wild garlic purée and aubergine caviar. To finish, a lustrously smooth crème brûlée is revved up with the flavour of espresso coffee.

Times 6.30-9 Closed L all week

BALMEDIE	Map 23 NJ91

Cock & Bull

⊛ Modern Scottish **NEW**

Atmospheric inn with local flavour

☎ 01358 743249 📄 01358 742466
Ellon Rd, Blairton AB23 8XY
e-mail: info@thecockandbull.co.uk
dir: 6m N of Aberdeen on A90

Located north of Aberdeen, close to the famous sand dunes of Balmedie, this former coaching inn has broad appeal, whether you're looking for a light lunch in the bar or dinner in the atmospheric restaurant with its bare-stone walls, beams and smart table settings (there's a more informal conservatory, too). The work of local artists is displayed throughout, adding a bit of local flavour. The modern Scottish cooking sees squash soup enlivened with a touch of chilli, and crisp, golden crab cakes are also given the chilli treatment (a sweet, spicy sauce), while dark chocolate cheesecake is a delightful ending.

Chef Ryan Paterson **Owner** Rodger Morrison
Times 12-5.30/5.30-late Closed 25-26 Dec, 1-2 Jan
Prices Starter £3.95-£6.25, Main £9.75-£22.95, Dessert £5.25-£6.95, Service optional **Wines** 13 bottles over £20, 15 bottles under £20, 7 by glass **Notes** Sunday L, Vegetarian available **Seats** 80 **Children** Portions, Menu

---

BANCHORY	Map 23 NO69

Banchory Lodge Hotel

⊛ Traditional Scottish **NEW** 🍽

Great Scottish produce in a tranquil setting

☎ 01330 822625 & 822681 📄 01330 825019
AB31 5HS
e-mail: enquiries@banchorylodge.co.uk
dir: Off A93 18m W of Aberdeen

Game, salmon and Aberdeen Angus beef regularly feature on the dinner menu at this former 16th-century coaching inn, set in a tranquil location beside the River Dee. The traditional, Victorian-style dining room makes the most of the river view and the classic Scottish menu uses local seasonal produce to great effect. Well-executed dishes display a passion for traditional Scottish flavours as seen in oak-smoked haddock with Cullen skink, roast venison with bacon and winter cabbage and red wine jus, and creamed rice with pears poached in mulled wine.

Chef Jeff Purvis **Owner** Mrs M Jaffray
Times 12-2.30/6.30-9 **Prices** Food prices not confirmed for 2010. Please telephone for details. **Wines** 43 bottles over £20, 31 bottles under £20, 10 by glass
Notes Vegetarian available, Dress restrictions, Smart casual, Civ Wed 50 **Seats** 90, Pr/dining room 20
Children Portions, Menu **Parking** 50

CRATHES
Map 23 NO79

The Milton Restaurant

🍴 Modern Scottish NEW

Contemporary Scottish dining at the gateway to Royal Deeside

☎ 01330 844566   📠 01330 844474
Banchory AB31 5QH
web: www.themilton.co.uk
dir: Please telephone for directions

With the gateway to Royal Deeside and the Whisky and Castle Trails starting at its doorstep, the Milton is in a top spot for exploring this special part of Scotland. You could lose yourself for hours browsing the art galleries and craft shops clustered all around, and when hunger strikes, the restaurant makes a smart rustic venue, with yet more artworks on its whitewashed walls, or there's an airy, light-flooded conservatory extension. The kitchen serves up a thoughtful menu of modern international cuisine utilising great Scottish ingredients, as in a terrine of free-range duck, chicken and wild rabbit with pickled wild mushrooms and morello cherry chutney to start. Halibut with a macadamia nut crust is served with pak choi and a lemongrass and coconut emulsion among main courses.

Chef David Littlewood **Owner** Neil Rae **Times** 9.30am-9.30pm **Prices** Starter £3.95-£6.45, Main £9.95-£23, Dessert £5.50 **Notes** Early D available 5-6.30pm 2/3 course £13.25-£17.50, Vegetarian available

See advert on opposite page

OLDMELDRUM
Map 23 NJ82

Meldrum House Hotel Golf & Country Estate

🍴 Modern Scottish

Elegant dining in a splendid country mansion

☎ 01651 872294   📠 01651 872464
AB51 0AE
e-mail: enquiries@meldrumhouse.co.uk
dir: 11m N of Aberdeen (from Aberdeen to Dyce), A947 towards Banff, through Newmachen along outskirts of Oldmeldrum, main entrance large white archway

Meldrum House has been a fixture in the local landscape since the 13th century. It stands foursquare, baronial turrets to attention, amid 350 acres of wooded parkland and the golf course that is firmly on the agenda for many guests. The kitchen thinks local with its approach to sourcing produce for its European-accented Scottish country-house cooking. Tortellini of smoked haddock with lemon and chive sauce might serve as a curtain raiser to a main course of roast loin of venison with braised red cabbage, roasted root vegetables, gratin potato and sage sauce. To finish, there's the likes of blood orange bavarois with sablé biscuits, aniseed sauce and chocolate ice cream.

Times 12-2.30/6.30-9

PETERHEAD
Map 23 NK14

The Grill Room at Buchan Braes Hotel

🍴 Modern British NEW 🍷

Stylish modern hotel serving seriously good food

☎ 01779 871471   📠 01779 871472
Boddam AB42 3AR
e-mail: info@buchanbraes.co.uk
dir: From Aberdeen take A90, follow Fraserburgh/Peterhead signs. Right at Toll of Birness. 1st right in Stirling signed Boddam. 50mtrs, 1st right

It seems that this low-slung modern building in the village near Peterhead was destined from the off to be in the business of feeding people well. Originally the officers' mess building at RAF Buchan, it has been smartly made over in a bold modern style with jazzy colours in the open-plan lounge and grill room, where an open kitchen lets diners watch the chefs at the stoves. Local produce is showcased with pride on a broad-based modern Scottish menu that reads enticingly. Ravioli of Amity langoustine with fennel and cucumber relish might start, then garlic-scented roast best end of lamb with herb crust comes with dauphinoise potatoes and rosemary jus. Finish with the intense flavours of hot chocolate fondant with lemon curd ice cream and kumquat compôte.

Chef Gary Christie, Paul McLean **Owner** Kenneth Watt **Times** 11.45-2.30/6-9.30 **Prices** Food prices not confirmed for 2010. Please telephone for details. **Wines** 16 bottles over £20, 16 bottles under £20, 7 by glass **Notes** Sunday L, Vegetarian available, Civ Wed 250, Air con **Seats** 70 **Children** Portions, Menu

---

STONEHAVEN
Map 23 NO88

Carron Art Deco Restaurant

🍴 Modern British

Eye-catching temple of art deco with modern cooking

☎ 01569 760460
20 Cameron St AB39 2HS
e-mail: jacki@cleaverhotels.eclipse.co.uk
dir: From Aberdeen, right at town centre lights, 2nd left onto Ann St, right at road end, 3rd building on right

Lovers of the eponymous design movement will relish the place. Accessed via a sunken garden, and boasting a nine-foot mirror adorned with a naked female form in Picasso style, the restaurant first opened in the 1930s. Brilliantly renovated, it now offers a menu in tune with the times that moves from the signature crab soup, deepened with sherry and cream, or deep-fried battered beetroot in chilli mango mayonnaise, to parmesan-crusted sea bass served on sweetly rich bean cassoulet. To finish, there may be pears poached in mulled wine, or well-made raspberry crème brûlée with a shortbread biscuit.

Chef Robert Cleaver **Owner** Robert Cleaver
Times 12-2/6-9.30 Closed 24 Dec-10 Jan, Sun-Mon **Prices** Starter £3.45-£5.95, Main £11.50-£16.95, Dessert £5.10-£6.25, Service optional **Wines** 12 bottles over £20, 15 bottles under £20, 5 by glass **Notes** Vegetarian available **Seats** 80, Pr/dining room 30 **Children** Portions, Menu **Parking** Town Square

---

Tolbooth Restaurant

🍴 Modern British, Seafood 🍷

Quayside restaurant serving seafood straight off the boats

☎ 01569 762287
Old Pier, Stonehaven Harbour AB39 2JU
e-mail: enquiries@tolbooth-restaurant.co.uk
dir: 15m S of Aberdeen on A90, located in Stonehaven harbour

The aim of this restaurant is to transfer the freshest local fish and seafood from the quayside onto the plate in the shortest possible time. And it is in the right spot to pull it off: Stonehaven's oldest building - four centuries and counting - is right on the quayside. Steady legs are a help for the steep stairs ascending to the upstairs restaurant - a fresh, well-lit place with whitewashed and panelled walls, wooden floors and classy table settings. Light aromatic sauces and dressings complement the piscine produce without bullying it into submission, in offerings such as crab and lobster cakes with red pepper and ginger coulis, and turbot poached in red wine with mussel risotto, asparagus spears and vanilla sauce.

Chef Craig Somers **Owner** J Edward Abbott
Times 12-4/6-12 Closed 2 wks Xmas & Jan, Sun (Oct-Apr) & Mon **Prices** Fixed L 2 course £12.95, Starter £3.95-£7.25, Main £13.95-£19.95, Dessert £5.95-£6.95, Service optional, Groups min 10 service 10% **Wines** 24 bottles over £20, 8 bottles under £20, 3 by glass **Notes** Vegetarian available **Seats** 46 **Children** Portions **Parking** Public car park, 100 spaces

ANGUS

CARNOUSTIE — Map 21 NO53

Dalhousie Restaurant

Modern Scottish

Fine dining in a championship location

☎ 01241 411999 📠 01241 411998
Carnoustie Golf Hotel, The Links DD7 7JE
e-mail: reservations.carnoustie@ohiml.com
dir: From A92 exit at Upper Victoria junct, follow signs for town centre, then signs for golf course

With windows looking out onto the magnificent Carnoustie Golf Course - home of the 2007 British Open - the Dalhousie Restaurant is certainly a prime spot for golf buffs. Part of the modern Carnoustie Golf Hotel, the restaurant is bright and airy, contemporary but elegant, and has well appointed tables set off with quality silver and sparkling glassware. Service is attentive and friendly, and the cooking style is modern Scottish with an emphasis on seasonal ingredients. A typical starter might be oak-roasted smoked salmon with potato salad, Arran mustard and dill crème fraîche. Main-course roasted loin of venison with Savoy cabbage, game and thyme jus could precede a dessert of raspberry shortcake with fresh whipped cream.

Times 7-9.30 Closed L all week

GLAMIS — Map 21 NO34

Castleton House Hotel

Modern & Traditional British

Victorian country house with culinary flair

☎ 01307 840340 📠 01307 840506
Castleton of Eassie DD8 1SJ
e-mail: hotel@castletonglamis.co.uk
dir: On A94 midway between Forfar & Coupar Angus, 3m W of Glamis

The impressive, moated Victorian country-house hotel provides a genuine sense of seclusion and tranquillity. Beautiful grounds include a croquet lawn and a menagerie of ducks, chickens and pigs. Vases of seasonal flowers adorn the conservatory dining room, overlooking the garden that also supplies the kitchen with fresh vegetables and herbs. Prime-quality ingredients drive the menu, and there is a strong emphasis on local, seasonal produce from the abundant Scottish larder. Take seared hand-dived scallops from Orkney served on cauliflower purée with a fennel and apple salad, and to follow, perhaps a loin of Glen Prosen venison, delivered with pearl barley risotto, port-braised shallots and parsnip crisps.

Times 12-2/6.30-9 Closed 25 Dec, New Year

INVERKEILOR — Map 23 NO64

Gordon's

Modern British

Creative Scottish cooking from a friendly family team

☎ 01241 830364
Main St DD11 5RN
e-mail: gordonsrest@aol.com
dir: From A92 exit at signs for Inverkeilor (between Arbroath & Montrose)

It's well worth a detour into the tiny village of Inverkeilor to this welcoming family-run restaurant with rooms. Inside, there's a real sense of Scotland in the cosy dining room with its beams, huge open fire and rugs on wooden floors. Mum Maria is the front-of-house star, while the eponymous Gordon and his son Garry make a talented team in the kitchen, turning out sharp modern cooking with a definite wow factor. A sound grasp of classical technique and what works with what, and why, underpins the tersely-worded menus. Quail boudin with black pudding, spinach, apple and Puy lentils may start off proceedings, before an intermediate course - perhaps an artichoke velouté with scallop brunoise, pancetta and truffle crème fraîche. Scotch beef might appear as a main course, as slow-cooked featherblade and seared fillet cassoulet with confit shallot, vanilla parsnip and Pinot Noir jus. If there's room left, try pear soufflé with marzipan ice cream, tonka bean anglaise and pear tuile.

Chef Gordon & Garry Watson **Owner** Gordon & Maria Watson **Times** 12-1.45/7-9 Closed 1st 2 wks Jan, Mon, L Sat, D Sun (in Winter) **Prices** Fixed L course £27, Fixed D 4 course £44, Service optional **Wines** 19 bottles over £20, 25 bottles under £20, 3 by glass **Notes** Sunday L, Vegetarian available, Dress restrictions, Smart casual **Seats** 24, Pr/dining room 8 **Parking** 6

ARGYLL & BUTE

ARDUAINE — Map 20 NM71

Loch Melfort Hotel

Modern British

Great local seafood in restaurant with stunning views

☎ 01852 200233 📠 01852 200214
PA34 4XG
e-mail: reception@lochmelfort.co.uk
dir: On A816, midway between Oban & Lochgilphead

Spectacularly located on the west coast of Scotland, this family-run hotel is a quiet hideaway with views across Asknish Bay towards the islands of Jura, Scarba and Shuna. Set against a breathtaking backdrop of woodlands and the magnificent mountains of Argyll, it is a glorious spot. The setting is the perfect complement to the wonderful local fish and seafood on offer in the attractive dining room with its stunning views. Skilful cooking makes excellent use of an abundance of local produce. Start with langoustines from Luing served in the shell with mayonnaise or hot garlic butter and follow with roast rack of Barbreck lamb, creamed Savoy cabbage and

cranberry sauce. Finish with a selection of Scottish cheeses.

Chef Matt Mitchell **Owner** Calum & Rachel Ross **Times** 7-9 Closed L all week **Prices** Fixed D 4 course £31, Starter £4.95-£9.95, Main £8.95-£18.95, Dessert £4.95-£7.95, Service optional **Wines** 25 bottles over £20, 40 bottles under £20, 8 by glass **Notes** Vegetarian available, Dress restrictions, Smart casual, no jeans, Civ Wed 100 **Seats** 75, Pr/dining room 14 **Children** Portions, Menu **Parking** 65

CARRADALE — Map 20 NR83

Dunvalanree

Modern British V

Superb seafood (and more) in stunning coastal location

☎ 01583 431226 📠 01583 431339
Port Righ PA28 6SE
e-mail: stay@dunvalanree.com
web: www.dunvalanree.com
dir: On B879. In Carradale turn right at x-rds, restaurant at end of road

Robert the Bruce landed here in 1306 while he was fleeing the English army. Enjoying outstanding views across the Kilbrannon Sound to the hills of Arran, it's an ideal place to explore the Mull of Kintyre. This is a genuine family-run operation with mum in the kitchen and father and daughter welcoming guests in the traditional restaurant. There is one sitting, which adds to the dinner party feel. Skilful Scottish cuisine is conjured from the very best local ingredients in a daily-changing menu that might include Kilbrannon scallops with coriander and lime, followed by Kintyre venison with celeriac mash and red wine jus.

Chef Alyson Milstead **Owner** Alan & Alyson Milstead **Times** 7pm Closed Jan-Feb, L all week **Prices** Fixed D 3 course £26, Service optional **Wines** 12 bottles under £20, 4 by glass **Notes** Vegetarian menu **Seats** 20 **Children** Portions **Parking** 8

ERISKA — Map 20 NM94

Isle of Eriska

— *see opposite page*

KILCHRENAN · Map 20 NN02

The Ardanaiseig Hotel

☺☺ Modern Scottish V

Excellent food in peaceful hotel with stunning views

☎ 01866 833333 · 🖶 01866 833222
PA35 1HE
e-mail: info@ardanaiseig.com
dir: From A85 at Taynuilt onto B845 to Kilchrenan. Left in front of pub (road very narrow) signed 'Ardanaiseig Hotel' & 'No Through Road'. Continue for 3m

Set amid lovely gardens and breathtaking scenery where the slopes of Ben Cruachan fall into the clear waters of Loch Awe, this tranquil country-house hotel was built in a Scottish baronial style in 1834. Accessed via a long and winding single-track road, the interiors are very much in keeping with the early Victorian period, with gorgeous antiques and fine art, all very understated and uncluttered. The kitchen produces innovative food, skilfully and faultlessly cooked with good use made of local produce. Dinner is a complete five-course experience, with dishes such as seared scallops with Chantenay carrots and Sauternes sauce and fillet of line-caught sea bass with ratatouille, sautéed langoustines, tortellini of clam and shellfish essence.

The Ardanaiseig Hotel

Chef Gary Goldie **Owner** Bennie Gray **Times** 12-2/7-9 Closed 2 Jan-10 Feb **Prices** Fixed D 4 course £48, Service optional **Wines** 94 bottles over £20, 4 bottles under £20, 16 by glass **Notes** Vegetarian menu, Dress restrictions, Smart casual, no jeans or trainers, Civ Wed 50 **Seats** 36 **Children** Portions, Menu **Parking** 20

Taychreggan Hotel

☺☺ Traditional British V

Highland hospitality by the shores of the loch

☎ 01866 833211 & 833366 · 🖶 01866 833244
PA35 1HQ
e-mail: info@taychreggan.co.uk
dir: W from Crianlarich on A85 to Taynuilt, S for 7m on B845 (single track) to Kilchrenan

Originally a 17th-century drovers' inn, this country-house hotel stands in splendid isolation on a small peninsula that juts out into Loch Awe. It's set in 40 acres of gardens and woodland with spectacular Highland scenery on all sides, and the beautiful views can be taken in from the arched windows of the stylish dining room. The imaginative menus make full use of fine Scottish produce to create a range of British dishes that are both rustic and contemporary. A starter partridge sits on celeriac and potato rösti and is surrounded by a Puy lentil and chanterelle broth, and main-course herb-crusted halibut comes with a warm potato and fine bean salad and an egg, onion and parsley sauce.

Chef Alan Hunter **Owner** North American Country Inns **Times** 7.30-8.45 Closed 24-26 Dec **Prices** Food prices not confirmed for 2010. Please telephone for details, Service added but optional 10% **Wines** 23 bottles over £20, 16 bottles under £20, 2 by glass **Notes** Fixed D 5 course £44, Vegetarian menu, Dress restrictions, Smart casual, Civ Wed 60 **Seats** 45, Pr/dining room 18 **Children** Portions, Menu **Parking** 40

Isle of Eriska

ERISKA · Map 20 NM94

Traditional British 🏆 🌹

Luxurious island retreat with first-class team in the kitchen

☎ 01631 720371 · 🖶 01631 720531
Benderloch, By Oban PA37 1SD
e-mail: office@eriska-hotel.co.uk
dir: Exit A85 at Connel, onto A828, follow for 4m, then follow hotel signs from N of Benderloch

You may dream of owning your own private island one day and, while you're working on achieving that goal, a stay at the Isle of Eriska Hotel will whet your appetite still further. Once you've crossed from the mainland over the iron bridge you are on the 300-acre island estate, with the Victorian baronial-style house (doing a fine impression of a castle) at its heart. If that isn't impressive enough, the hotel is luxuriously and elegantly appointed, with a spa to ease away what stress remains and a newly refurbished restaurant headed up by the talented Robert MacPherson. The new-look dining areas - now open to non-residents, too - make the best of the proportions of the rooms and their period details, with wood-panelling and ornate plasterwork alongside modishly lit shelves, richly coloured fabrics and tables traditionally set with crisp linen cloths. It looks Scottish but with no hint of a cliché. The kitchen's daily-changing dinner menu is based around top-notch Scottish produce - some from the hotel's garden - and offers refined, intelligently constructed dishes which are based on classical techniques and seek to maximise flavour. Pithivier of ham hough with a quince purée, pickled shiitake and mustard velouté is an impressive first course; next up, perhaps local Dover sole filled with a scallop and dill mousseline and served with a surf clam essence and Swiss chard. The creativity and attention to detail continues with desserts such as orange chiboust with a black olive cake and citrus sorbet. The wine list does justice to the excellent food.

Chef Robert MacPherson **Owner** Mr Buchanan-Smith **Times** 8-9 Closed Jan **Prices** Fixed D 4 course £40, Service optional **Wines** 236 bottles over £20, 43 bottles under £20, 10 by glass **Notes** Vegetarian available, Civ Wed 110, Air con **Seats** 50, Pr/dining room 20 **Children** Portions, Menu **Parking** 50

LOCHGILPHEAD Map 20 NR88

Cairnbaan

◉ British, European

Traditional fish cookery by the canal

☎ 01546 603668 📄 01546 606045
Crinan Canal, Cairnbaan PA31 8SJ
e-mail: info@cairnbaan.com
dir: From Lochgilphead 2m N to Cairnbaan on A83, hotel 1st on left

Next to the Crinan canal, with alfresco dining in the sunshine, this hotel restaurant is a split-level space with fine watery views. Colourful artworks abound, and the tone is one of unforced informality. A menu of simple classics majors on fish, with satisfying langoustine chowder to begin, then maybe Parma-wrapped monkfish to follow, or the traditional house fish pie. Meat-eaters might go for a chargrilled rib-eye steak with chips and a choice of sauces. Poppyseed cheesecake with blueberry coulis is an unusual and enjoyable dessert, or there is a range of Mövenpick ice creams.

Times 12-2.30/6-9.30

LUSS Map 20 NS39

Colquhoun's

◉◉ Modern British 🌱

Idyllic Loch Lomond location for fine dining

☎ 01436 860201 📄 01436 860203
The Lodge on Loch Lomond G83 8PA
e-mail: res@loch-lomond.co.uk
dir: N of Glasgow on A82

It's all in the name - The Lodge on Loch Lomond hotel boasts a fantastic location with magnificent, uninterrupted views across the water. The fine-dining Colquhoun's restaurant makes the most of the vista with its large windows and a decked terrace where you can

dine alfresco as the water laps the shore below. The split-level restaurant - with a lounge bar on the upper level - blends traditional Scottish décor with Scandinavian-style touches of pinewood walls and pillars. Tables are glass-topped and well-appointed, and you can watch the chefs in the open kitchen once it's too dark to enjoy the view. The brasserie-style modern menu has strong Scottish flair and features good quality, locally-sourced produce, while service is friendly and efficient. To start, try Isle of Mull Old Smokehouse fish tian with cucumber and dill salad, lemon and baby caper dressing, followed by oven-roasted loin of Blairatholl Estate venison with fondant potato, spiced red cabbage, maple-glazed butternut squash, redcurrant and bramble jus.

Colquhoun's

Chef Donn Eadie **Owner** Niall Colquhoun
Times 12-5/6-9.45 **Prices** Fixed L 2 course £7.90-£16.90, Fixed D 3 course £29.95, Starter £6.50, Main £16.95, Dessert £6.50, Service optional **Wines** 29 bottles over £20, 20 bottles under £20, 7 by glass **Notes** ALC 3 course, Sunday L, Vegetarian available, Civ Wed 100 **Seats** 100, Pr/dining room 40 **Children** Portions, Menu **Parking** 70

OBAN Map 20 NM82

Coast

◉◉ Modern

Contemporary design and fabulously fresh local seafood

☎ 01631 569900
104 George St PA34 5NT
e-mail: coastoban@yahoo.co.uk
web: www.coastoban.co.uk
dir: On main street in town centre

Within the granite façade of a former bank, this impeccably-styled Oban restaurant has created a soothing interior of trendy cream and cocoa hues, pale wood, classy fabrics, metal and modern art. It's all rather a quantum leap from the neighbouring chippies, as is the food: the kitchen takes a modern Scottish line to deliver imaginative but uncomplicated dishes that rely on the zinging fresh quality of local raw materials - wriggling-fresh fish and seafood, for example, only has to cross the road after it is landed on Oban's quayside. Among starters, might be crab with crème fraîche, avocado, tomato mousse and pesto, followed by pan-seared scallops with chive gnocchi, buttered leeks and roast Stornoway black pudding; round it off with chocolate mousse with peanut brittle and tonka bean ice cream.

Coast

Chef Richard Fowler **Owner** Richard & Nicola Fowler
Times 12-2/5.30-9.30 Closed 25 Dec, Sun (Nov-Mar), L Sun **Prices** Fixed L 2 course £12, Starter £4.50-£8.95, Main £12.50-£22.50, Dessert £5.95, Service optional, Groups min 8 service 10% **Wines** 19 bottles over £20, 22 bottles under £20, 6 by glass **Notes** Early eve menu 2-3 course £12-£15, Vegetarian available **Seats** 46 **Parking** On street

Manor House Hotel

◉ Traditional European

Elegant Georgian dower house with quality local produce

☎ 01631 562087 📄 01631 563053
Gallanach Rd PA34 4LS
e-mail: info@manorhouseoban.com
web: www.manorhouseoban.com
dir: follow MacBrayne Ferries signs, pass ferry entrance for hotel on right

The Duke of Argyll chose his spot well when he built this lovely Georgian manor house overlooking Oban Bay with views to the nearby Isle of Kerrera and the distant peaks of Mull. The hotel has been spared a modern makeover and revels in its authentic Georgian elegance. Watch the Calmac ferries come and go from the harbour below over pre-dinner drinks in the bar and classy drawing room, then settle in to the traditional dining room, with its deep green walls, tartan carpet and white linen. Five-course dinners work around a repertoire of European-influenced cuisine; kick off with a twice-baked goats' cheese soufflé with poached pear and walnuts, and progress via soup and sorbet to grilled fillet of turbot with Oban Bay prawns, scallop and asparagus tagliatelle.

Chef Patrick Freytag, Shaun Squire **Owner** Mr P L Crane **Times** 12-2.30/6.45-8.45 Closed 25-26 Dec **Prices** Starter £3-£8, Main £15-£25, Dessert £7, Service optional **Wines** 27 bottles over £20, 24 bottles under £20, 7 by glass **Notes** Fixed D 5 course £36, Vegetarian available, Dress restrictions, Smart casual, Civ Wed 30 **Seats** 34 **Children** Portions **Parking** 18

PORT APPIN   Map 20 NM94

Airds Hotel and Restaurant

◉◉◉ – *see below*

STRACHUR   Map 20 NN00

Creggans Inn

◉ Modern British ☺

Fine food in breathtaking location

☎ 01369 860279   ▤ 01369 860637
PA27 8BX
e-mail: info@creggans-inn.co.uk
dir: A82 from Glasgow, at Tarbet take A83 towards Cairndow, left onto A815 to Strachur Or by ferry from Gourock to Dunoon onto A815

This charming, family-run country hotel occupies a stunning spot overlooking Loch Fyne, set against a breathtaking backdrop of rugged, unspoilt countryside. Sit with a glass of whisky from a large selection and take in the fabulous vista as you peruse the menus in the elegant, terracotta-painted restaurant. Five picture windows overlook the hotel garden and loch beyond. In summertime, posies of home-grown flowers decorate the tables. In winter, the real log fire and candlelit tables create an intimate atmosphere, and the baby grand piano stands open, inviting guests to play. Scottish dishes star on a menu that makes the most of local produce; sautéed salmon fillet on a fine vegetable and vermouth sauce could be followed by seared loin of Balagowan venison with celeriac purée, Lyonnaise potatoes, red onion and thyme jus.

Chef Gordon Smilie **Owner** The MacLellan family **Times** 7-9 Closed 25-26 Dec, L all week **Prices** Fixed D 4 course fr £37, Service optional **Wines** 32 bottles over £20, 33 bottles under £20, 6 by glass **Notes** Vegetarian available, Dress restrictions, Smart casual, Civ Wed 80 **Seats** 35 **Children** Portions, Menu **Parking** 25

TARBERT LOCH FYNE   Map 20 NR86

Stonefield Castle Hotel

◉ Modern British

Plenty of local flavours in an old baronial keep

☎ 01880 820836   ▤ 01880 820929
PA29 6YJ
e-mail: reservations.stonefieldcastle@ohiml.com
dir: From Arrochar follow signs for A83 through Inveraray & Lochgilphead, hotel on left 2m before Tarbert

A fine example of Scottish baronial architecture, this impressive castle was built in 1837 and stands in 60 acres of woodland gardens high on the Kintyre peninsula. The restaurant is rich in baronial elegance and picture windows command stunning views over Loch Fyne. Food offers a good balance of classical and modern cooking, with an emphasis on quality produce, including seafood landed at Tarbert and local estate game, accurate cooking and good flavours. Take crisp, well-balanced lobster and halibut fishcakes to start, treacle-glazed pork belly with black pudding, white bean and apple mash for main course, and a light, fluffy orange syrup sponge with cardamom syrup for pudding.

Chef Oscar Sinjorgo **Owner** Oxford Hotels & Inns **Times** 12-9 **Prices** Starter £5-£15, Main £9-£30, Dessert £5-£15, Service optional **Wines** 23 bottles over £20, 38 bottles under £20, 6 by glass **Notes** Sunday L, Vegetarian available, Dress restrictions, Smart casual, Civ Wed 120 **Seats** 120, Pr/ dining room 40 **Children** Portions, Menu **Parking** 65

Airds Hotel and Restaurant

◉◉◉

PORT APPIN   Map 20 NM94

Modern British V

Memorable surroundings and high-quality seasonal food

☎ 01631 730236   ▤ 01631 730535
PA38 4DF
e-mail: airds@airds-hotel.com
web: www.airds-hotel.com
dir: On A828 (Oban to Fort William road) follow signs for Port Appin. 2.5m, hotel on left

Formerly an 18th-century ferry inn for farmers and livestock going to market, this small but sophisticated country-house style hotel benefits from superlative views of Loch Linnhe and is located on the edge of the Sound of Lismore. Low ceilings, rich fabrics and candlelit tables coupled with large windows to drink in the surroundings make for a relaxed and romantic atmosphere. The very short menu is modern British with Scottish and French influences. Fish and seafood comes fresh from the Oban fishing boats and the small kitchen team sets great store by seasonality. Combinations are uncomplicated allowing the clean, clear flavours of the superior local ingredients to shine through. Hand-dived local scallops with Stornoway black pudding and grape chutney might start, followed by local turbot and salmon wrapped in pastry with mushroom, served with a beurre blanc, while desserts include marbled chocolate cake with orange sauce. Service is formal but not stuffy, and the wine list has something for the most erudite of wine drinkers.

Chef J Paul Burns **Owner** Mr & Mrs S McKivragan **Times** 12-1.45/7.30-9.30 **Prices** Fixed L 2 course fr £21.95, Fixed D 4 course £49.50, Service optional **Wines** 151 bottles over £20, 13 bottles under £20, 6 by glass **Notes** Sunday L, Vegetarian menu, Dress restrictions, Smart casual at D, no jeans/trainers/T-shirts, Civ Wed 40 **Seats** 32, Pr/dining room 8 **Children** Portions, Menu **Parking** 20

TIGHNABRUAICH
Map 20 NR97

An Lochan

◉◉ Modern Scottish ☺

Complex modern cooking with wonderful sea views

☎ 01700 811239 📠 01700 811300
Shore Rd PA21 2BE
e-mail: info@anlochan.co.uk
dir: From Strachur, on A886, right onto A8003 to
Tighnabruaich. Hotel on right at bottom of hill. From
Dunoon ferry terminal left onto B8000

The whitewashed, three-storeyed hotel rises majestically
above the loch shore, with views towards the wild
seascape of the Kyles of Bute, and is run with appreciable
bonhomie by the McKie family. A choice of dining options
is available, either the wood-floored Deck, or the more
formal Crustacean room, with its enclosed terrace making
the most of those marine views. The modern Scottish
cooking features some vibrant ideas, as in a pairing of
pork cheek and foie gras in a terrine, accompanied by red
onion jam and a 'sour apple explosion'. Mains introduce a
gentler note in the form of infusions and foams, in multi-
faceted dishes such as venison loin cooked sous-vide,
with braised red cabbage, blackcurrant jelly, roast
parsnip and a potato infusion. Even desserts keep things
interesting, with combinations such as carrot and orange
fondant, with beetroot tartare and lavender ice cream.

Chef Paul Scott **Owner** The McKie family
Times 12-2.30/6.30-9 Closed Xmas **Prices** Starter £7-
£10, Main £11-£25, Dessert £5-£8, Service optional
Wines 50 bottles over £20, 14 bottles under £20, 6 by
glass **Notes** Tasting menu available, Sunday L,
Vegetarian available, Civ Wed 50 **Seats** 35, Pr/dining
room 20 **Children** Portions **Parking** 20

AYRSHIRE, EAST

SORN
Map 20 NS52

The Sorn Inn

◉◉ Modern British ☺

**Contemporary-styled coaching inn with modern
cuisine**

☎ 01290 551305 📠 01290 553470
35 Main St KA5 6HU
e-mail: craig@sorninn.com
dir: From A77 take A76 to Mauchline. Take B743,
4m to Sorn

The Sorn Inn sets out its manifesto clearly as a 'gastro-
pub with rooms'. And it does exactly what it says on the
tin with great flair. Inside, the whitewashed 18th-century
coaching inn puts on modern clothes in a glowing, rustic-
posh décor, and the restaurant has restyled its menu to
offer a medley of fine dining and brasserie-style dishes,
whether you choose to eat in the cosier pub-style Chop
House or the rather more chic fine-dining restaurant.
Well-established favourites from the modern British
arsenal are raised to a higher level by judicious tweaks
and twists on a wide-ranging, seasonally-changing

menu. Kick off with a salad of smoked wild mallard
breast with pickled walnut vinaigrette, before chump of
lamb with chorizo crushed potatoes, balsamic braised
shallots, sun-dried tomatoes and rosemary jus.

Chef Craig Grant **Owner** The Grant Partnership
Times 12-2.30/6-9 Closed 2 wks Jan, Mon, D Sun
Prices Fixed L 2 course £14.95-£15.95, Fixed D 3 course
£23.95-£24.95, Starter £4-£5.50, Main £9-£23.50,
Dessert £4.50-£5.50, Service optional, Groups min 8
service 10% **Wines** 42 bottles over £20, 17 bottles under
£20, 13 by glass **Notes** Sunday L, Vegetarian available
Seats 42 **Children** Portions, Menu **Parking** 9

AYRSHIRE, NORTH

DALRY
Map 20 NS24

Braidwoods

◉◉ Modern Scottish

Creative flair from a talented husband-and-wife-team

☎ 01294 833544 📠 01294 833553
Drumastle Mill Cottage KA24 4LN
e-mail: keithbraidwood@btconnect.com
dir: 1m from Dalry on Saltcoats road

With two very talented and passionate chef-patrons in
the kitchen, Braidwoods delivers a level of culinary
expertise way beyond what you might expect from its
rustic whitewashed cottage exterior. The two dining areas
within are a natty mix of dark beams and exposed stone
with a modern décor of jaunty stripes, hues of blue and
white and stylish high-backed metal chairs. Husband-
and-wife-team Keith and Nicola Braidwood both have
impressive CVs, and know that any good kitchen has to
start by getting the basics right, so their approach to
local sourcing is of the highest order. This painstaking
preparation pays off in delivering top-quality modern
Scottish dishes of intense flavour and clarity. Four course
dinners might start with seared hand-dived Wester Ross
scallops, perfectly timed and served on a bed of
cardamom, coriander and lentil dhal, then procede via a
creamy soup of local carrots and cumin to honey-glazed
breast of Gressingham duck with a wee cottage pie of
duck confit.

Times 12-1.45/7-9 Closed 25-26 Dec, 1st 3 wks Jan, 1st
2 wks Sep, Mon, L Tue (Sun Etr-Sep), D Sun

AYRSHIRE, SOUTH

AYR
Map 20 NS32

Enterkine Country House

◉◉ Traditional **V**

**The best of Scottish produce in an art deco country
house**

☎ 01292 520580 📠 01292 521582
Annbank KA6 5AL
e-mail: mail@enterkine.com
dir: 5m E of Ayr on B743

An impressive 350-acre estate encompassing meadows,
woodland and lovely views over the Ayr valley surrounds
this stylish art deco country-house hideaway. Inside,
there's something of the feel of an Agatha Christie novel
set in a posh private house, with food served in an
expansive restaurant with low ceilings, a log fire in winter
and Shaker-style panelling. The kitchen deals in French-
influenced Scottish country house-style cooking using
materials such as the estate's own pork, local berries and
Buccleuch organic beef. Straightforward, modern-style
dishes might include Arbroath smokie and goats' cheese
soufflé with spinach, red pepper and Meaux mustard,
followed by Blackface Castle Douglas lamb three ways -
roast loin, caramelised sweetbreads and seared kidneys.
Meals end with lush desserts such as dark Valrhona
chocolate fondant with chocolate ice cream and griottine
cherries.

Chef Paul Moffat **Owner** Mr Browne **Times** 12-2/7-9
Prices Fixed L 3 course £18.50-£25, Fixed D 4 course
£30-£45, Service optional **Wines** 36 bottles over £20, 14
bottles under £20, 4 by glass **Notes** Tasting menu
available, Sunday L, Vegetarian menu, Dress restrictions,
Jackets required, Civ Wed 70 **Seats** 40, Pr/dining room 14
Children Portions, Menu **Parking** 20

Fairfield House Hotel

◉◉ Traditional British

Modern Scottish cooking in hotel with sea views

☎ 01292 267461 📠 01292 261456
12 Fairfield Rd KA7 2AS
e-mail: reservations@fairfieldhotel.co.uk
dir: From A77 to Ayr South. Follow signs for town centre.
Left into Miller Rd. At lights turn left, then right into
Fairfield Rd

Situated in a leafy cul-de-sac close to the esplanade, this
magnificent Victorian mansion enjoys stunning views of

the Isle of Arran and the Ayrshire coastline. Once the home of a Glasgow tea merchant, the seafront hotel is full of original features with the Martin's Bar and Grill boasting Grecian-style pillars as well as feature plants and original artwork. An outside terrace makes the most of the views and is spot-on for pre-meal drinks. The cooking is unpretentious and simple with a focus on local ingredients in the Scottish dishes. Try roast loin of Scotch venison with braised red cabbage, fondant potatoes, honey-roast root vegetables and berry vinegar reduction, finishing with pineapple tarte Tatin and vanilla ice cream. There is a wide selection of fine wines, plus a good collection of single malts.

Owner G Martin **Times** 11am-9.30pm **Prices** Food prices not confirmed for 2010. Please telephone for details. **Wines** 34 bottles over £20, 16 bottles under £20, 6 by glass **Notes** Civ Wed 150, Air con **Seats** 80, Pr/dining room 12 **Children** Portions, Menu **Parking** 50

See advert below

Fouters

◎◎ French, Scottish

Intimate basement restaurant with ambitious cooking

☎ 01292 261391 📠 01292 619323
2A Academy St KA7 1HS
e-mail: chef@fouters.co.uk
dir: Town centre, opposite Town Hall

An old bank vault, dating from 1772, provides the setting for this small basement restaurant, located down a narrow, cobbled lane in the seaside town of Ayr. The vaulted ceiling and flagstone floor provide atmosphere, while linen-clothed tables and modern artworks add a touch of warmth and comfort. The imaginative menus are based on great ingredients, including plenty of local seafood and game. Main-course duck, pink and tender, is set on a bed of red cabbage and sultanas with chocolate and Grand Marnier sauce - a fine combination. Choux beignets, covered in cinnamon, filled with Chantilly cream

and served with apple purée and Calvados ice cream is an indulgent end to proceedings.

Chef Adele Wylie, Victoria Semple **Owner** Barry Rooney **Times** 12-2/6-9 Closed 2 wks Feb, 2 wks Nov, 1 Jan, Sun-Mon **Prices** Starter £3.95-£6.50, Main £12.95-£24.95, Dessert £3.95-£6.50, Service optional **Wines** 22 bottles over £20, 10 bottles under £20, 3 by glass **Notes** Pre-theatre D Tue-Sat 6-7pm 2/3 course £14.95-16.95, Vegetarian available, Air con **Seats** 36, Pr/dining room 22 **Children** Portions **Parking** On street

The Western House Hotel

◎◎ Traditional British

Modern and traditional cuisine within sight of the racing at Ayr

☎ 0870 055 5510 📠 0870 055 5515
2 Craigie Rd KA8 0HA
e-mail: msimpson@ayr-racecourse.co.uk
dir: From Glasgow M77 then A77 towards Ayr. At Whitletts rdbt take A719 towards town centre

Close by Ayr racecourse, the hotel logically enough chooses an equestrian theme for the Jockey Club restaurant, which is adorned with old monochrome racing photos against a relaxing cappuccino-hued decorative scheme. A mix of modern and traditional Scottish cooking is on offer, running from well-timed langoustine risotto, followed by herb-crusted rack of lamb with sugar snaps and onion confit, to more complex dishes such as lemon sole fillets filled with crab and salmon mousseline, with fennel and leek 'spaghetti' and lemon butter. Super-rich Scots tablet might be the basis for an ice cream to accompany textbook tarte Tatin, or there could be ginger-based lemon and champagne cheesecake with citrus syrup. Home-made breads are of real quality.

Times 12-2/7-9.30

BALLANTRAE Map 20 NX08

Glenapp Castle

◎◎◎ *– see page 488*

TROON Map 20 NS33

Lochgreen House Hotel

◎◎◎ *– see page 488*

MacCallums of Troon

◎ British, European

Simple seafood cookery by the harbour

☎ 01292 319339
The Harbour KA10 6DH
dir: Please telephone for directions

Wander down Memory Lane via the Americas Cup yachting depicted in sketches and paraphernalia on the walls of this harbourside restaurant. It was once the hydraulic pump station, and still commands views of trawlers landing their catch. Informal, friendly service provides a welcome for the European-influenced seafood cookery. Lobster and langoustine cocktail is fresh and flavourful, or there may be gravad lax or oysters to start. Mains keep things reasonably simple, with the likes of a parmesan-glazed seafood crêpe bursting with goodies, served with wild mushrooms and a rocket salad, and finish with strawberry Pavlova, served with top-notch white chocolate and Amaretto ice cream.

Chef Philip Burgess, Neil Marriot **Owner** John & James MacCallums **Times** 12-2.30/6.30-9.30 Closed Xmas, New Year, Mon, D Sun **Prices** Starter £4.95-£8.95, Main £9.50-£27.50, Dessert £4.85-£5.85, Service optional, Groups min 12 service 10% **Wines** 9 bottles over £20, 17 bottles under £20, 4 by glass **Notes** Sunday L **Seats** 43 **Children** Portions **Parking** 12

Glenapp Castle

BALLANTRAE	Map 20 NX08

Modern British **V**

Elegant castle hideaway with accomplished, innovative cuisine

☎ 01465 831212 📄 01465 831000
KA26 0NZ
e-mail: info@glenappcastle.com
dir: S through Ballantrae, cross bridge over River Stinchar, 1st right, hotel in 1m

This luxury retreat near the village of Ballantrae surveys the wild Ayrshire coast with views to the Isle of Arran and the granite crag of Ailsa Craig. Glenapp Castle is a romantic Victorian confection of towers and turrets in 36 acres of heavenly grounds that are an oasis of mature woodland and exotic colour amid the native bracken and gorse. The stately interior is all opulence - endless expanses of oak panels, chandeliers, antiques, oil paintings - and the kitchen team rises to the occasion. Dishes here are designed to wow at every stage; cooking is sharp, innovative, accurate and, when necessary, highly technical. The very finest from Scotland's larder, including fruit, veg and herbs from the castle's gardens, underpins the menus, which run from three courses at lunch, to well-balanced six-course dinner menus. An amuse-bouche of carrot and vanilla velouté with liquorice cream precedes a terrine of rabbit and Morteau sausage with home-made piccalilli and hazelnuts. The pace continues with a fish course - pan-fried red mullet with langoustine and minestrone consommé, then a choice appears at the main course - perhaps roasted grey leg partridge with salsify, red cabbage and a cannelloni of confit leg. Perfectly-ripened Scottish cheeses come before dessert: Scottish cranachan soufflé with raspberries and raspberry sorbet. Formal service is correct without being intimidating.

Chef Adam Stokes **Owner** Graham & Fay Cowan **Times** 12.30-2/7-10 Closed 2 Jan-14 Mar, Xmas **Prices** Fixed L 3 course fr £35, Service optional **Wines** 200 bottles over £20, 8 by glass **Notes** Fixed D 6 course £55, Sunday L, Vegetarian menu, Civ Wed 40 **Seats** 34, Pr/dining room 20 **Children** Portions, Menu **Parking** 20

Lochgreen House Hotel

TROON	Map 20 NS33

Modern British

Grand restaurant in grand golf hotel

☎ 01292 313343 📄 01292 318661
Monktonhill Rd, Southwood KA10 7EN
e-mail: lochgreen@costleyhotels.co.uk
dir: From A77 follow Prestwick Airport signs, take B749 to Troon. Hotel on left, 1m from junct

Set in 30 acres of immaculately maintained grounds and woodland, Lochgreen House is a beautifully presented country house and golf hotel, which has been sympathetically restored and gracefully extended. The Ayrshire surroundings deliver genuine wow factor, with views out to the sea and across the golf links. The Tapestry restaurant is the culinary draw with its large, grand atrium-style room, chandeliers cascading from the vaulted ceiling, high-backed chairs and well-spaced tables. Head chef Andrew Costley takes great pride in his Scottish heritage and it shows through on the menu with the use of high quality, seasonal ingredients. Highly original canapés kick things off with aplomb while the excellent texture and strong flavours in a terrine of Ayrshire ham hough and foie gras with sauce gribiche and a herb salad hit the mark. Main course wild sea bass with hand-dived scallops, langoustines, Provençale vegetable tart and langoustine vinaigrette might precede rhubarb crème brûlée with ginger parfait and pain d'épice. Formal service comes from an impeccably presented team.

Chef Andrew Costley **Owner** Mr W Costley **Times** 12-2/7-9 **Prices** Fixed L 2 course £19.95 **Wines** 82 bottles over £20, 27 bottles under £20, 9 by glass **Notes** Fixed D 5 course £42.50, Dress restrictions, Smart casual, Civ Wed 100, Air con **Seats** 80, Pr/dining room 30 **Children** Portions, Menu **Parking** 60

TURNBERRY
Map 20 NS20

Malin Court

Scottish

Bistro cooking in a golfing hotel with great coastal views

☎ 01655 331457 📄 01655 331072
KA26 9PB
e-mail: info@malincourt.co.uk
dir: on A74 to Ayr, take A719 to Turnberry & Maidens

Overlooking the famous championship course and a prime slice of Ayrshire coastline, the hotel is a highly refined bolt-hole for golf-mad travellers. The tone in Cotters restaurant is fairly formal, though staff are friendly, and the menu offers a balance of traditional and modern bistro dishes. Smoked duck with pineapple and peppery chutney is one way to begin, or you might opt for textbook prawn cocktail. Salmon rolled in couscous, served on buttered cabbage with (faintly) cumin-spiked crème fraîche, is a neat idea, while meat dishes might include mushroom-stuffed pork fillet with toasted cashews in white wine sauce.

Times 12.30-2/7-9

Turnberry Resort

Traditional

Fine dining with coastal views across famous golf courses

☎ 01655 331000 📄 01655 331706
KA26 9LT
e-mail: turnberry@westin.com
dir: from Glasgow take A77/M77 S towards Stranraer, 2m past Kirkoswald, follow signs for A719/Turnberry. Hotel 500mtrs on right

The location – nestled on the rugged Ayrshire coastline – could hardly be more beautiful, and now the Turnberry Resort has been taken to new heights of luxury following a massive refurbishment. Bedrooms, public rooms and the spa have all been given – or are about to be given – a new look, and that includes dramatic changes to the hotel's dining options. The main restaurant has been renamed 1906 after the year Turnberry opened, and it makes the most of those sweeping views over the golf links to the Ailsa Craig through its picture windows. The menu hadn't been finalised as we went to print, but expect classic dishes inspired by the surrounding landscape and using the best local ingredients. The hotel's Grand Tea Lounge has been resurrected as part of the revamp, plus there are two new bars and a more informal restaurant – the Tappie Toorie – within the golf clubhouse.

Times 7-10 Closed Xmas, L Mon-Sun

DUMFRIES & GALLOWAY

AUCHENCAIRN
Map 21 NX75

Balcary Bay Hotel

Modern French V

Top-notch food on the glorious Solway coastline

☎ 01556 640217 & 640311 📄 01556 640272
Shore Rd DG7 1QZ
e-mail: reservations@balcary-bay-hotel.co.uk
dir: on A711 between Dalbeattie & Kirkcudbright. In Auchencairn follow signs to Balcary along shore road for 2m

It's water, water everywhere at this whitewashed 17th-century country house on the shores of Balcary Bay. The day starts and finishes with the sound of waves lapping the sandy beach, and superb views soar beyond the Solway coast to the peaks of Cumbria. It's the perfect location to work up a healthy appetite on a beachcombing ramble, or visiting the art galleries of nearby Kircudbright. And it's an equally ideal spot for the hotel's kitchen to source seasonal local produce - Galloway beef, lamb, seafood and Balcary Bay salmon. Sound technical skills are evident here, establishing a refined but unpretentious tone with clever combinations and sharp, clear flavours. Seared king scallops with pea and lettuce purée, crisp pancetta and shiitake vinaigrette might start, followed by poached saddle of rabbit, Jerusalem artichoke risotto, wild mushrooms and liquorice foam. And if it's a hard call between desserts and exciting Scottish cheeses - Mull cheddar, Dunsyre Blue and ewe's milk Cairnsmore, or an iced Glayva parfait with rhubarb compôte - why not do both?

Chef Stuart Mathieson **Owner** Graeme A Lamb & family
Times 12-2/7-8.30 Closed early Dec-early Feb, L prior booking only Mon-Sat **Prices** Fixed L course £19.75, Fixed D 4 course £36.75, Starter £5.25-£9.95, Main £11.95-£23.95, Dessert £7.95-£8.25, Service optional **Wines** 60 bottles over £20, 25 bottles under £20, 12 by glass **Notes** Sunday L, Vegetarian menu, Dress restrictions, Smart casual **Seats** 55 **Children** Portions, Menu **Parking** 45

GATEHOUSE OF FLEET
Map 20 NX55

Cally Palace Hotel

Traditional V

Scottish cooking in a stately setting

☎ 01557 814341 📄 01557 814522
DG7 2DL
e-mail: info@callypalace.co.uk
dir: From A74(M) take A75, at Gatehouse take B727. Hotel on left

Situated in 150 acres of grounds on the Solway coast, the Cally Palace is an opulent country mansion with the ambience of a bygone age. Built in 1763 in a superb setting overlooking the Galloway hills and bordered by the Fleet Oak Woods, the hotel has its own 18-hole golf course sculpted into the natural contours of the parkland. The elegant dining room is in keeping with its grand past; a pianist plays most evenings and a jacket and tie are obligatory for men. The chef and his team use the local Galloway produce, including wild Solway salmon, for their Scottish menu. Expect pan-fried Galloway venison with parsnip purée, fondant potato, green beans and rosemary jus, or steamed sea bass, wilted greens, moules marinière and saffron potatoes.

Chef Jamie Muirhead **Owner** McMillan Hotels
Times 12-1/6.45-9 Closed 3 Jan-early Feb **Prices** Fixed D 4 course £29.50-£39.50, Starter £2.90-£4.25, Main £12.95-£15, Dessert £3.75-£4.75, Service optional **Wines** 34 bottles over £20, 48 bottles under £20, 11 by glass **Notes** Sunday L, Vegetarian menu, Dress restrictions, Jacket and tie, Air con **Seats** 110 **Children** Portions, Menu **Parking** 70

GRETNA — Map 21 NY36

Smiths at Gretna Green

Modern Scottish, International

Contemporary hotel with modern, globally-inspired food

☎ 01461 337007 ▤ 01461 336000
Gretna Green DG16 5EA
e-mail: info@smithsgretnagreen.com
web: www.smithsgretnagreen.com

Smiths injects a note of contemporary gloss to the capital of runaway weddings, so any couples getting hitched here nowadays can expect modishly minimal décor with modern art, sumptuous fabrics and tastefully muted colours. Suitably polished service in the open-plan bar and brasserie-style dining room sets the right tone for a menu of well-balanced dishes. Scottish produce from the nearby coast and farmland is pepped up with international global influences. Chicken liver parfait comes with baked plums, toasted brioche and kumquat compôte, while a main course of roast Goosnargh duck breast is served with sweet potato gratin, spiced pear and Madeira jus. Try a Valrhona dark chocolate mousse with light coconut cream and rosé champagne sorbet to finish.

Times 12 noon-9.30

KIRKBEAN — Map 21 NX95

Cavens

British, French 🖐

Sound cooking in peaceful country house

☎ 01387 880234 ▤ 01387 880467
DG2 8AA
e-mail: enquiries@cavens.com
dir: From Kirkbean, follow signs for Cavens

Situated on the Solway coast, close to the stunning Galloway Forest Park, Britain's largest forest park, Cavens is one of the most popular country-house hotels in Dumfries & Galloway. Set in 6 acres of peaceful, beautifully landscaped gardens, it was once a private family manor house and is now owned by the Fordyce family who provide warm hospitality and welcome guests like old friends. The intimate dining room has a limited number of well-spaced tables, and a daily set menu at dinner offers a choice of two dishes at each course, plus alternatives on request. Main courses could be sea bass

on a bed of leeks with lemon butter sauce or rack of Galloway lamb with thyme crust and roasted baby tomato sauce.

Chef A Fordyce **Owner** A Fordyce **Times** 7-8.30 Closed Dec-1 Mar, L all week **Prices** Fixed D 3 course £35, Service included **Wines** 20 bottles over £20, 7 bottles under £20, 2 by glass **Notes** Vegetarian available, Dress restrictions, Smart casual, Civ Wed 100 **Seats** 16, Pr/dining room 20 **Parking** 20

MOFFAT — Map 21 NT00

Hartfell House & The Limetree Restaurant

Modern British 🖐

Modern cooking in Victorian house with views

☎ 01683 220153
Hartfell Crescent DG10 9AL
e-mail: enquiries@hartfellhouse.co.uk
web: www.hartfellhouse.co.uk
dir: Off High St at war memorial onto Well St & Old Well Rd. Hartfell Crescent on right

The Limetree Restaurant was previously in the high street but has moved into Hartfell House, an imposing Victorian house situated in a peaceful terrace high above the town. The traditionally-styled dining room has an ornate ceiling with crystal chandeliers and local art on the walls. There is a simple, intuitive approach to the traditional and modern cooking here, big on taste and flavour with great combinations. Fillets of sea bream is pan-fried with fennel seeds, smoked paprika and lemon, and comes with fresh herb risotto and dressed baby spinach leaves; finish with steamed ginger pudding and orange curd ice cream.

Chef Matt Seddon **Owner** Robert & Mhairi Ash **Times** 12.30-2.30/6.30-9 Closed Xmas, Mon, L Tue-Sat, D Sun **Prices** Fixed L 2 course £18, Fixed D 3 course £26.50, Service optional, Groups min 6 service 10% **Wines** 8 bottles over £20, 16 bottles under £20, 4 by glass **Notes** Sunday L **Seats** 26 **Children** Portions **Parking** 6

Well View

Traditional V

Fine food and views in a homely setting

☎ 01683 220184
Ballplay Rd DG10 9JU
e-mail: johnwellview@aol.com
dir: M74 junct 15, into Moffat. Exit Moffat on A708 for 0.5m, left into Ballplay Rd. Restaurant 300yds on right

Sitting in pretty gardens high up above the town, this small hotel enjoys fine views across historic Moffat to the hills beyond, and over the wild open fells. The house is traditionally decorated, and proprietors Janet and John Schuckardt pride themselves on their personal service and attention to detail. Janet is in charge of the kitchen and her cooking follows a classical route, making the most of top quality local produce. A set six-course menu is served at dinner, with wines personally chosen by wine buff John. Canapés kick things off, next up, perhaps, Mull of Kintyre cheese and chive soufflé, followed by seared duck breast on a julienne of seasonal vegetables with pak choi in a red wine jus. A selection of cheeses precedes dessert - think chocolate chip steamed pudding with a vanilla crème anglaise, or Eton mess.

Chef Janet & Lina Schuckardt **Owner** Janet & John Schuckardt **Times** 12.30-7.30 Closed L Mon-Sat **Prices** Fixed L 3 course £19-£22, Fixed D 4 course £40, Service included **Notes** Sunday L, Vegetarian menu, Dress restrictions, Smart dress **Seats** 10, Pr/dining room 10 **Parking** 4

NEWTON STEWART — Map 20 NX46

Kirroughtree House

Modern British

Formal dining in Scottish mansion

☎ 01671 402141 ▤ 01671 402425
Minnigaff DG8 6AN
e-mail: info@kirroughtreehouse.co.uk
dir: From A75 take A712, entrance to hotel 300yds on left

Built in 1719 on the edge of Galloway Forest Park, Kirroughtree is a handsome country house in the Scottish baronial style, with various add-ons courtesy of a Victorian Major Armitage. The mansion's rich history has seen visits by poet Robert Burns, who sat on the grand staircase to recite his poetry. Dinner, amid the opulent formality of the dining room, is a refined affair with professional, attentive service at tables set with good-quality china, linen and glassware. The chef makes good use of Galloway's bountiful larder, using local lobster, salmon, Kirroughtree venison and Cairnsmore cheeses in his modern British output. Expect starters such as breast of quail on barley, pancetta and celery risotto to precede supreme of guinea fowl filled with truffle mousse, served with carrot and potato rösti, Jerusalem artichoke and Madeira sauce.

Chef Rolf Mueller **Owner** Mr D McMillan
Times 12-1.30/7-9 Closed 2 Jan-mid Feb **Prices** Fixed D 3 course £35, Starter £3.50-£6.50, Main £12.75-£18.75, Dessert £3.50-£5.50, Service optional **Wines** 73 bottles over £20, 21 bottles under £20, 5 by glass **Notes** ALC available L only, Sunday L, Vegetarian available, Dress restrictions, Jacket must be worn after 6.30pm **Seats** 45 **Parking** 50

PORTPATRICK   Map 20 NW95

Knockinaam Lodge

@@@ – *see below*

DUNBARTONSHIRE, WEST

BALLOCH   Map 20 NS38

The Cameron Grill

@ British

Scottish through and through on the shores of Loch Lomond

☎ 01389 755565   📄 01389 759522
Cameron House on Loch Lomond G83 8QZ
e-mail: reservations@cameronhouse.co.uk
dir: M8 (W) junct 30 for Erskine Bridge. A82 for Crainlarich. 14m, at rdbt signed Luss, hotel on right

Cameron House is a Scottish big-hitter on the shores of Loch Lomond which has recently undergone a refurbishment and seen the arrival of a star chef - see entry for Martin Wishart at Loch Lomond. The Cameron Grill offers something a little different. It's a fabulous space full of dark wood and leather chairs and banquettes, and a large mural depicting a raucous looking banquet being enjoyed by traditionally attired gents. The lively menu is full of Scottish favourites, brasserie classics and steaks. Start with cream of broccoli soup, moving on to roasted rack of lamb served with a mini shepherd's pie, and finish with Granny Smith tarte fine with vanilla ice cream.

Owner De Vere Hotels **Times** 5.30-9.30 Closed L all week
Prices Food prices not confirmed for 2010. Please telephone for details. **Children** Menu

---

Martin Wishart at Loch Lomond

@@@ – *see page 492*

CLYDEBANK   Map 20 NS47

Arcoona at the Beardmore

@ Modern 🍷

Fine dining in a modern setting

☎ 0141 951 6000   📄 0141 951 6018
Beardmore Hotel, Beardmore St G81 4SA
e-mail: info@beardmore.scot.nhs.uk
web: www.thebeardmore.com
dir: M8 junct 19, follow signs for Clydeside Expressway to Glasgow road, then A814 (Dumbarton road), then follow Clydebank Business Park signs. Hotel on left

continued

Knockinaam Lodge

PORTPATRICK   Map 20 NW95

Modern Scottish V 🍷

Classical Scottish cooking in an unbeatable coastal location

☎ 01776 810471   📄 01776 810435
DG9 9AD
e-mail: reservations@knockinaamlodge.com
dir: From A75, follow signs to Portpatrick, follow tourist signs to Knockinaam Lodge

When the Knockinaam brochure mentions 'rock and roll' as one of the hotel's attractions, rest assured that musical evenings with AC/DC are not on the agenda. The reference is to the rolling of the surf against the rocks of the Galloway coastline beneath the lodge. The location is tranquillity at its purest. There are 30 acres of gardens and woodland, a private strip of shore from which to gaze over towards Ireland, and a dining room done in restful pastels of orange and peach. So secluded is it that Sir Winston Churchill met General Eisenhower here in the dark days of war. When it comes to dinner, you won't even be subjected to the rigour of choosing (other than between cheese or dessert), as the drill is a daily-changing set menu. Tony Pierce has perfected an understated style of classical Scottish cooking, with one or two modern flourishes along the way. It's the kind of approach that knows when to leave well alone, so you might begin with a simply grilled fillet of salmon, served with nothing other than a relish of coriander pesto. A soup follows, perhaps butterbean and parsley with a topping of white truffle oil, and then the main meaty business, where stops are pulled out. Roast cannon of local lamb might appear with pomme purée, root veg and a little 'bonbon' of haggis, richly sauced with port and rosemary. If you're not in the market for the excellent British and French cheeses with walnut and sultana bread, the sweet alternative could be pear and almond tart with praline ice cream, Amaretto sabayon and vanilla custard.

Chef Antony Pierce **Owner** David & Sian Ibbotson
Times 12.30-2/7-9 **Prices** Food prices not confirmed for 2010. Please telephone for details, Service optional **Wines** 335 bottles over £20, 18 bottles under £20, 10 by glass **Notes** Fixed L 4 course £37.50, Fixed D 5 course £50, Sunday L, Vegetarian menu, Dress restrictions, No jeans, Civ Wed 40 **Seats** 32, Pr/dining room 18 **Children** Menu **Parking** 20

CLYDEBANK *continued*

Times change. This smart modern hotel and conference centre stands on the riverside site of the William Beardmore shipyards where great battleships and liners were once built and launched into the Clyde. The Arcoona restaurant takes its name from a passenger ship that was built here, and still runs a pretty shipshape operation with a smart contemporary look and professional, friendly service. The kitchen's focus is modern British cooking with elements of classical French inspiration. Start, perhaps, with seared scallops, boudin noir, smoked pancetta, potato scone and sauce à la Russe, and wave the Scottish flag for loin of Blair Atholl venison, potato and parsnip crumble, buttered kale and forestière sauce.

Chef Iain Ramsay **Owner** Scottish Executive **Times** 7-10 Closed Festive period, L all week **Prices** Fixed D 3 course fr £21.50, Starter £5.25-£6.95, Main £9.95-£23.25, Dessert £5.35-£6.30, Service optional **Wines** 39 bottles over £20, 30 bottles under £20, 12 by glass **Notes** Fixed D 2-3 course served Mon-Thu, Vegetarian available, Civ Wed 174, Air con **Seats** 60, Pr/dining room 16 **Children** Portions, Menu **Parking** 400

CITY OF DUNDEE

DUNDEE   Map 21 N043

Alchemy Restaurant

@@ French, Scottish V

Enterprising cooking in a modern riverside hotel

☎ 0845 365 0002 & 01382 202902   📄 01382 201401
Apex City Quay Hotel & Spa, 1 West Victoria Dock Rd DD1 3JP
e-mail: alchemy@apexhotels.co.uk
dir: From A90 Perth, A85 to Dundee. Cross 2 rdbts, follow signs to City Quay

A modern hotel building in the regenerated Dundee quayside area, the Apex City Quay offers a wealth of facilities, including those all-important spa treatments, in a refreshing location overlooking the river. Among the various eating options, Alchemy is where the fine dining goes on, with a thoroughly contemporary menu of enterprising Scottish cooking. Dishes are headlined by their main ingredient, so if 'Asparagus' catches your eye on a spring menu, expect a velouté of the spears with smoked salmon foam and brown bread ice cream. Among mains, 'Trout' turns out to involve a crisp-skinned fillet, with dill gnocchi and a mussel emulsion infused with saffron, while 'Lamb' delivers the rack pinkly roasted, with spiced aubergine, baby spinach and a Niçoise jus.

Chef Michael Robinson, Nigel Liston **Owner** Mr Norman Springford **Times** 7-9 Closed Various dates throughout

the year, Sun-Wed, L all week **Prices** Fixed D 3 course fr £34, Tasting menu £34-£38, Service optional **Wines** 12 bottles over £20, 8 bottles under £20, 2 by glass **Notes** Tasting menu 5 course, Vegetarian available, Vegetarian menu, Dress restrictions, Smart dress, Civ Wed 250, Air con **Seats** 30, Pr/dining room 10 **Parking** 150

CITY OF EDINBURGH

EDINBURGH   Map 21 NT27

Agua

@ Modern

Stylish restaurant offering quality seafood

☎ 0845 365 0002 & 0131 243 3456   📄 0131 225 6346
Apex City Hotel, 61 Grassmarket EH1 2JF
e-mail: agua@apexhotels.co.uk
dir: into Lothian Rd at west end of Princes St, 1st left into King Stables Rd. Leads into Grassmarket

Located in a fashionable square in the shadow of Edinburgh Castle, this stylish restaurant and bar is housed within the Apex City Hotel. Two of the restaurant walls are adorned with modern art while a third has floor-to-ceiling dark wood concealing doors to the kitchen. The restaurant focuses on quality ingredients and boasts a chic crustacea bar full of fresh seafood. Order your own mix of seafood from the bar or choose from the à la carte or fixed-price menu. Meat and vegetarian dishes are also

Martin Wishart at Loch Lomond

BALLOCH   Map 20 NS38

Modern French NEW V

Top chef's new venture in old baronial mansion hotel

☎ 01389 722504
Cameron House on Loch Lomond G83 8QZ
e-mail: info@mwlochlomond.co.uk
dir: From A82, follow signs for Loch Lomond. Restaurant 1m after Stoneymullan rdbt on right

Martin Wishart's Leith restaurant (see entry) has been flying the cross of St Andrew for Scottish fine dining since 1999 and it is only now that he has ventured to open a satellite restaurant. He's chosen Cameron House (where he once worked) and moved over some of his team from Leith, headed-up by Stewart Boyles, creating in so doing another key address on Scotland's culinary tour. The room, decorated in natural tones of browns and creams

and designed around high quality fixtures and fittings, is in keeping with the refined and classy French-influenced Scottish cuisine. The fixed-price menus (set lunch, evening carte and tasting menus) are based on first-class produce, while individual flavours never seem to get lost in the mix. Presse of foie gras and confit Gressingham duck is a superb dish, with pickled beetroot and white radish salad, duck bonbon and praline toast providing well-judged and perfectly balanced flavours. Main-course braised shin of Ross-shire beef is allowed to take centre stage and a dessert of lemon mousseline has just the right amount of sharpness. The charming and professional service fits the bill.

Chef Stewart Boyles **Owner** Martin Wishart **Times** 12-2.30/6.30-10 Closed Mon-Tue, L Wed-Sat **Prices** Tasting menu £50, Service optional, Groups min 6 service 10% **Wines** 190 bottles over £20, 12 by glass **Notes** Fixed L £25, Fixed D ALC £45, Tasting menu 5 course, Sunday L, Vegetarian menu, Dress restrictions, Smart casual, Air con **Seats** 40 **Children** Portions **Parking** 150 available. Expect starters such as Agua shellfish and fish bouillabaisse, followed by black bream, pancetta and pea and mint broth, or braised belly of pork and prawn tail with Madeira and shallot reduction.

Times 12-4.30/5-10 Closed 20-28 Dec

Apex International Hotel

@@ Modern Scottish

Accomplished cooking and magnificent castle views

☎ 0845 365 0002 & 0131 300 3456 📄 0131 220 5345
31-35 Grassmarket EH1 2HS
e-mail: heights@apexhotels.co.uk
dir: Into Lothian Rd at west end of Princes St, then 1st left into King Stables Rd, leads into Grassmarket

Standing in the shadows of Edinburgh Castle, the dramatic and appropriately-named Heights Restaurant boasts stunning views of the city. Occupying the 5th floor of this contemporary, stylish boutique hotel, the modern décor combines floor-to-ceiling windows with glass and chrome, wood and marble and subdued minimalist lighting. The menu is short but to the point, with a focus on the best seasonal Scottish ingredients, with plentiful seafood and game. Expect well-tuned, intelligent and defined flavours in dishes like carpaccio of venison, roasted pear, sloe gin tartare and roasted walnuts. A main course of fillet of sea bream, saffron potato, pancetta and mint pea broth could be followed by espresso sabayon and lemon biscotti.

Chef John Newton **Owner** Norman Springford
Times 7-9.30 Closed Sun-Wed, L all week **Prices** Fixed D 3 course £23.50-£25, Starter £5.50-£8.95, Main £14-£17.95, Dessert £5.50-£9.95, Service optional **Wines** 11 bottles over £20, 9 bottles under £20, 6 by glass **Notes** Vegetarian available, Civ Wed 100 **Seats** 85, Pr/dining room 120 **Parking** 65, On street, NCP

The Atholl at The Howard

@ Modern Scottish 🕓

Stylish Georgian townhouse with intimate dining room

☎ 0131 557 3500 📄 0131 557 6515
34 Great King St EH3 6QH
e-mail: reception@thehoward.com
dir: E on Queen St, 2nd left, Dundas St. Through 3 lights, right, hotel on left

The five-star Howard is made up of three grand Georgian townhouses in the heart of the city, just a short walk from Princes Street. Sip a cocktail in the elegant drawing room with its ornate chandeliers, lavish drapes and views of the wide cobbled streets, before moving onto the Georgian splendour of The Atholl, the small dining room with smartly laid tables and hand-painted murals on the walls dating back to the 1820s. The menu deals in classical dishes with flashes of innovation and plenty of Scottish touches; langoustine ravioli comes with pieces of lobster and a sharp citrus emulsion, followed by highland venison - pink and tender - with spiced red cabbage and roasted garlic and parsley mash.

Chef William Poncelet **Owner** Peter Taylor
Times 12-2/6-9.30 **Prices** Starter £6-£11, Main £14-£28, Dessert £7-£9, Service optional **Wines** 40 bottles over £20, 6 bottles under £20, 10 by glass **Notes** Pre-theatre menu available, Sunday L, Vegetarian available, Civ Wed 40 **Seats** 18, Pr/dining room 40 **Children** Portions **Parking** 10

Atrium

@@ Modern Scottish 🕓

Good, clear flavours from the best of Scottish produce

☎ 0131 228 8882 📄 0131 228 8808
10 Cambridge St EH1 2ED
e-mail: eat@atriumrestaurant.co.uk
web: www.atriumrestaurant.co.uk
dir: Restaurant to left of Usher Hall. Shares entrance with Blue Bar Café & Traverse Theatre

In the heart of the financial district, flanked on each side by period buildings, Atrium serves a daily-changing menu featuring the best of local Scottish produce simply prepared and presented. The modern, clean lines in the restaurant - an abundance of copper and rustic furnishings, dark-wood tables and soft lighting - make for a cool and stylish setting. Local artisan producers, growers and breeders take pride of place on a menu which delivers clear flavours by using 4 or less core ingredients per dish. Start with pigeon carpaccio with pickled vegetables and wild herbs, move on to pan-fried wild sea bass with clam and potato vinaigrette and wild garlic, and round things off with warm apricot and sultana bread-and-butter pudding.

Chef Neil Forbes **Owner** Andrew & Lisa Radford
Times 12-2/6-10 Closed 25-26 Dec, 1-2 Jan, Sun (apart from Aug), L Sat (apart from Aug & international rugby matches) **Prices** Fixed L 2 course £14, Fixed D 3 course £20-£44, Starter £5.50-£12.50, Main £15.50-£23.50, Dessert £6-£9, Service optional, Groups min 5 service 10% **Wines** 250+ bottles over £20, 10 bottles under £20, 250 by glass **Notes** Tasting menu 6 courses, Vegetarian available, Civ Wed 100, Air con **Seats** 80, Pr/dining room 20 **Children** Portions **Parking** Castle Terrace Car Park and on Cambridge St

Channings Bar and Restaurant

@ Modern British 🕓

Well-judged modern food in a bright basement

☎ 0131 315 2225 📄 0131 332 9631
Channings Hotel, 12-15 South Learmonth Gardens EH4 1EZ
e-mail: restaurant@channings.co.uk
dir: From Princes St follow signs for Forth Bridge (A90), cross Dean Bridge, 4th right into South Learmonth Ave. Follow to bottom of hill

Channings comes from the same boutique townhouse stable as the stylish Bonham (see entry for The Restaurant at The Bonham), so you can expect a polished experience on all fronts. One of the houses in this quintet of converted Edwardian properties was once home to the Antarctic explorer Sir Ernest Shackleton. The hotel's modern basement restaurant now provides a fuss-free foodie bolt-hole in the trendy urban village of Stockbridge. The kitchen has an intelligent approach and turns out a well-crafted repertoire of exciting modern dishes with clear focus on seasonality and top-quality organic produce. Pan-fried wood pigeon is teamed with pearl barley risotto, vegetable rösti and pigeon jus; next up, a pan-fried fillet of sea bream sits well with plum tomato and parmesan tart and sautéed potatoes.

Chef Karen MacKay **Owner** Mr P Taylor
Times 12-2.30/6-10 **Prices** Fixed L 2 course £13, Starter £5.50-£8, Main £15-£25, Dessert £6-£7, Service optional, Groups min 10 service 10% **Wines** 26 bottles over £20, 16 bottles under £20, 6 by glass **Notes** Sunday L, Vegetarian available **Seats** 40, Pr/dining room 30 **Children** Portions **Parking** On street

Dungeon Restaurant

@@ Modern European

Creative cuisine in a truly unique setting

☎ 01875 820153 📄 01875 821936
Dalhousie Castle & Aqueous Spa, Bonnyrigg EH19 3JB
e-mail: info@dalhousiecastle.co.uk
dir: From A720 (Edinburgh bypass) take A7 south, turn right onto B704. Castle 0.5m on right

It's not often you have the chance to eat in a vaulted dungeon beneath a medieval castle in acres of wooded parkland on the banks of the River Esk. Naturally, such a unique setting is big with those about to tie the knot, but

continued

EDINBURGH *continued*

it's not all about weddings: the swish hydro-spa offers decadent pampering on a Roman scale. Descend to the Dungeon restaurant, and you're in an arsenal of medieval weaponry and armour hung from stone walls beneath vaulted ceilings, all candlelit for romance. With so much to bring in the customers, some kitchens might rest on their laurels. Not so here: there's a vibrant creativity going on in the French-influenced menus, giving modern twists to classic dishes; take smoked duck with a thyme and bitter chocolate mousse, dandelion salad and nettle coulis, followed by lamb loin and casserole with lavender jus, pea purée, cocotte potatoes and smoked aubergine.

Chef Francois Graud **Owner** von Essen Hotels **Times** 7-10 Closed L all week **Prices** Starter £5.10-£7.75, Main £13-£19.10, Dessert £6.30-£6.90, Service optional **Wines** 100 bottles over £20, 23 bottles under £20, 15 by glass **Notes** Fixed D 5 course £47, Sunday L, Civ Wed 100 **Seats** 45, Pr/dining room 100 **Children** Portions **Parking** 150

La Garrigue

◉◉ Traditional French

Classic regional French cuisine in the heart of the city

☎ 0131 557 3032
31 Jeffrey St EH1 1DH
e-mail: lagarrigue@btconnect.com
web: www.lagarrigue.co.uk
dir: Halfway down Royal Mile towards Holyrood Palace, turn left at lights into Jeffrey St

This French neighbourhood restaurant, with its wooden floors and cool blue walls, brings a taste of Languedoc to Edinburgh. The woodcarver and artist Tim Stead made the chunky wooden tables and chairs, and the restaurant showcases the work of Scottish painter Andrew Walker. The authentic regional cooking style delivers homely rustic dishes with a great balance of flavours, using fine local produce as well as specialist ingredients sourced by the chef. To start there's traditional fish soup, or snails in walnut and parsley sauce with smoked bacon, followed by a classic cassoulet, which is a textbook version, and finish with the likes of lavender crème brûlée with almond tuile.

Chef Jean Michel Gauffre **Owner** Jean Michel Gauffre **Times** 12-3/6.30-10.30 Closed 25-26 Dec, 1-2 Jan, Sun **Prices** Fixed L 2 course £13.50, Fixed D 3 course £28, Service added but optional 10% **Wines** 24 bottles over

£20, 10 bottles under £20, 11 by glass **Notes** Vegetarian available, Air con **Seats** 48, Pr/dining room 11 **Children** Portions **Parking** On street, NCP

Hadrian's

◉ Modern European NEW

Buzzy, stylish brasserie with a cosmopolitan menu

☎ 0131 557 5000 & 556 2414   📠 0131 557 3747
The Balmoral Hotel, 1 Princes St EH2 2EQ
e-mail: hadrians@roccofortehotels.com
dir: Follow city centre signs. Hotel at E end of Princes St, adjacent to Waverley Station

Edinburgh locations don't come much better than the landmark Balmoral Hotel's pitch on Princes Street. The fashionable Hadrian's is every inch the slick contemporary brasserie, from its staff in black waistcoats and long white aprons to the art deco-influenced interior, with walnut floors and walls in hues of lime and violet. The menu takes quality Scottish ingredients on a soothing roam around Europe's classics. Comforting familiarity appears in a warm tart of Dunsyre blue cheese and creamed leeks, main courses like roast saddle of venison with braised cabbage and fondant potato or, sizzling from the grill, a fillet of Shetland salmon with spiced couscous and lemon butter. Old favourites such as tarte Tatin, or lemon tart with thyme ice cream round things off nicely.

Chef Jeff Bland **Owner** Rocco Forte Hotels **Times** 12-2.30/6.30-10.30 **Prices** Fixed L 2 course £14-£20, Fixed D 3 course £19-£25, Starter £7.50-£9.50, Main £10-£24, Dessert £5, Service optional, Groups min 8 service 10% **Wines** 42 bottles over £20, 8 by glass **Notes** Sunday L, Vegetarian available, Dress restrictions, Smart casual, Civ Wed 60, Air con **Seats** 100, Pr/dining room 26 **Children** Portions, Menu **Parking** 40

Haldanes

◉◉ Modern

Clubby basement restaurant beneath an Edinburgh hotel

☎ 0131 556 8407   📠 0131 653 2240
The Albany, 39a Albany St EH1 3QY
e-mail: dinehaldanes@aol.com
web: www.haldanesrestaurant.com
dir: Please telephone for directions

After a brief sojourn in other premises, the restaurant has returned to its original home in a basement room beneath The Albany. Dark wood and leather chairs help to create a relaxed, clubby ambience, while the place is still a shrine to the work of Scotland's modern maestro, Jack Vettriano. A menu of modern European dishes, drawing quite heavily on French technique, furnishes the likes of green pea velouté with contrasting garnishes of coconut foam and mint oil, or haggis bonbons with turnip purée and whisky sauce, to start, succeeded by a fine pairing of baked halibut with pork cheek ravioli in tomato butter, where the counterpoints of flavour and texture are a triumph.

Dessert may be chocolate fondant with candied oranges, or lemon tart with raspberry coulis and orange sorbet.

Times 12-2/5.30-9 Closed L Sat-Sun

Hotel du Vin Edinburgh

◉ European NEW

Modern Scottish brasserie cooking in a fashionable hotel

☎ 0131 247 4900   📠 0131 247 4901
11 Bistro Place EH1 1EZ
dir: Please telephone for directions

In its Edinburgh outpost, the Hotel du Vin brand has sprinkled its magic on a former lunatic asylum in a prime location in the Old Town. The interior goes for a timeless clubby look - there are scuffed leather armchairs and tartans to suit a Highland laird in the whisky snug, while a bustling mezzanine bar overlooks the brasserie with the chain's trademark wooden floors, unclothed tables and wine-related memorabilia on its walls. Waiting staff know their stuff, and the kitchen injects a sense of place into its Scottish-inflected brasserie menus, kicking off with an Isle of Mull cheddar soufflé and moving on to pan-seared salmon with lentils and chorizo. As with all branches of HdV, you can be sure of a cracking wine list.

Times 12-2.30/5.30-10.30 **Prices** Food prices not confirmed for 2010. Please telephone for details.

Iggs

◉ Spanish

Convivial and welcoming taste of Spain near the Royal Mile

☎ 0131 557 8184   📠 0131 652 3774
15 Jeffrey St EH1 1DR
e-mail: info@iggs.co.uk
dir: In heart of Old Town, 0.5m from castle, just off Royal Mile

Situated just a stone's throw from the Royal Mile, this modern, glass-fronted restaurant brings a touch of the Mediterranean to the city, with a truly Spanish theme to the décor, through warm shades of terracotta complemented by large cast-iron candlesticks and antique dressers, and oils and mirrors adorning the walls. The cooking also speaks with a Spanish accent, creating simple, well-constructed modern dishes that mirror the vibrancy of the atmosphere and deliver quality ingredients and good flavours. Try a hearty seafood stew with squid, clams and mussels and aïoli to start, with paprika-spiced monkfish with beans and mussels, or caramelised pork belly with celeriac purée for main course. Spanish wine-lovers will find plenty to excite them on the list.

Iggs

Times 12-2.30/6-10.30 Closed Sun

The Indian Cavalry Club

☺ Indian

Quality Indian restaurant in West End of Edinburgh

☎ 0131 220 0138 & 343 1712   ▤ 0131 220 0145
22 Coates Crescent EH3 7AF
e-mail: shahid@indiancavalryclub.co.uk
dir: 3 mins walk from Haymarket Railway Stn on west end of Princes St

Well and truly settled into its elegant new surroundings, this Edinburgh Indian restaurant continues to offer a fine-dining experience. It's all very understated inside with neutral décor and elegant table settings, including ICC branded vases. Well-sourced ingredients and spices are cooked in the traditional styles of both North and South India, the extensive menu featuring recommended side dishes and wine suggestions for each main course; various banquet options are also available. Start with South Indian baby dosa, or green herb pakora, before a main-course methi (flavoured with fenugreek leaves and ginger) and its recommended accompaniment, pineapple sambhar.

Chef Muktar Miah, Firoz Hossain **Owner** Shahid Choudhury **Times** 12-4/5.30-11.30 **Prices** Fixed L course £10, Fixed D 3 course £26.90-£33.90, Starter £4.85-£10.85, Main £13.95-£24.50, Dessert £3.85-£6.50, Service added but optional 10% **Wines** 15 bottles over £20, 16 bottles under £20, 2 by glass **Notes** Vegetarian available **Seats** 120, Pr/dining room 50 **Parking** On street

The Kitchin

☺☺☺ *– see below*

Macdonald Holyrood Hotel

☺ Modern Scottish

Relaxed dining in the shadow of Holyrood Palace

☎ 0131 550 4500   ▤ 0131 550 4545
Holyrood Rd EH8 6AU
e-mail: holyrood@macdonald-hotels.co.uk
dir: Holyrood area parallel to the Royal Mile

You'd be pushed to find a better base for exploring Edinburgh than this sizeable modern hotel in the heart of the Old Town, and a short stroll from the Scottish Parliament. The Opus 504 restaurant fits the surroundings neatly with its clean-cut contemporary décor and unfussy modern Scottish cuisine with cosmopolitan twists. This is just the spot to show off Scotland's superb produce, thus a starter pairs pan-seared Loch Fyne scallops with caper and cauliflower purée, and a whole Arbroath smokie comes with creamed mash and spinach in a simple, hearty main course. Finish with a luscious chocolate and hazelnut terrine with strawberry coulis.

Times 12-2/6.30-10 Closed D 25 Dec

The Kitchin

EDINBURGH   **Map 21 NT27**

Scottish, French ▮

Nature-to-plate cooking of a very high order in fashionable Leith

☎ 0131 555 1755   ▤ 0131 553 0608
78 Commercial Quay, Leith EH6 6LX
e-mail: info@thekitchin.com
dir: In Leith opposite Scottish Executive building

Part of the buzzy Leith waterfront scene, The Kitchin is an old whisky distillery fronting on to the piazza. The outer view may be serene enough, but inside is even more restful, a gently subdued atmosphere with soft lights and blinds, the better to coax your attention in the direction of the kitchen window, where you can see the team calmly working hard. Tom Kitchin lends his readily punning name to the place, and his culinary philosophy - 'From

nature to plate' - is inscribed all over the menus. French-oriented technique of a very high order is applied to the best the Scots larder has to offer, with many out-of-the-ordinary ingredients showing up. Arisaig razorfish with chorizo and lemon confit is one starter, or there could be a duo of boned and rolled pig's cheek with roasted Anstruther langoustines, alongside a galette made from the crisply shredded pig's ear. The daily market menu is always worth a look, and might offer rump of Dornoch lamb with a brochette of the kidneys, served with peas à la française, braised lettuce hearts and tapenade. Memorable desserts include pear and Earl Grey crumble with Poire William ice cream.

Chef Tom Kitchin **Owner** Tom & Michaela Kitchin **Times** 12.30-1.45/6.45-10 Closed Xmas, New Year, 1st wk Jul, Sun, Mon **Prices** Fixed L course £24.50, Tasting menu £60-£100, Starter £12.50-£17, Main £24-£67, Dessert £8.50-£9.50, Service optional, Groups min 8 service 10% **Wines** 116 bottles over £20, 15 bottles under £20, 28 by glass **Notes** Tasting menu 7 course, Vegetarian available **Seats** 45 **Children** Portions **Parking** On site parking eve. Parking nearby daytime

EDINBURGH *continued*

Malmaison Edinburgh

◉◉ British, French ✱

Unpretentious, well cooked food in brasserie with waterfront views

☎ 0131 468 5000 📠 0131 468 5002
One Tower Place, Leith EH6 7DB
e-mail: edinburgh@malmaison.com
dir: A900 from city centre towards Leith, at end of Leith Walk, through 3 lights, left into Tower St. Hotel on right at end of road

Perched on the banks of the Forth in Leith, and only minutes from the hubbub of the city centre, the Edinburgh hotel in this chic chain was originally built as a seaman's mission. The hotel has a castle-like appearance and inside there's a decidedly French vibe. The brasserie has recently been restored to its original atmospheric glory, and is dressed with leather banquettes and an abundance of candlelight and wrought ironwork. Look out across the cobbled concourse to the quayside as you enjoy unfussy, classic dishes using plenty of local produce (there is a separate 'Homegrown and Local' menu). Try Scotch egg with curried mayonnaise and move on to confit pork belly, rösti potato, apple and prune compôte. Finish with Bakewell tart and pear sorbet.

Chef Colin Manson **Owner** Malmaison Hotels Ltd **Times** 12-2/6-10.30 Closed D 25 Dec **Prices** Fixed L 2 course £13.50, Fixed D 3 course £15.50, Starter £4.50-£7.95, Main £12.50-£18.50, Dessert £4.95, Service added but optional 10% **Wines** 146 bottles over £20, 14 bottles under £20, 12 by glass **Notes** Sun brunch menu available, Sunday L, Vegetarian available, Civ Wed 70, Air con **Seats** 62, Pr/dining room 60 **Children** Portions **Parking** 48

Marriott Dalmahoy Hotel & Country Club

◉◉ Modern, Traditional

Stylish Scots cooking in Georgian splendour

☎ 0131 333 1845 📠 0131 333 1433
Kirknewton EH27 8EB
e-mail: mhrs.edigs.frontdesk@marriotthotels.com
dir: Edinburgh city bypass (A720) turn onto A71 towards Livingston, hotel on left in 2m

The handsome Georgian mansion was built in the 1720s to a design by William Adam; the modern history of the place began in 1976, when it became a country club. Sheltered at the foot of the Pentland hills, it sits in 1,000 acres of wooded parkland, but is not so distant from Edinburgh that you can't see the castle. Fine Scottish produce is shown off to great effect in the main dining room, with smoked salmon, oatmeal-crumbed haggis and Arbroath smokies turning up among the starters alone.

Main courses might offer slow-cooked pork belly with red cabbage and creamed haricots, but see also the catch of the day. Then finish with regional cheeses and oatcakes, or perhaps rum savarin with poached sultanas and cream.

Chef Alan Matthew **Owner** Marriott Hotels Ltd **Times** 7-10 Closed L all week **Prices** Starter £5.50-£8.50, Main £16.50-£24, Dessert £5.50-£6.50, Service optional **Wines** 18 bottles over £20, 8 bottles under £20, 8 by glass **Notes** Vegetarian available, Dress restrictions, Smart casual, Civ Wed 300, Air con **Seats** 120, Pr/dining room 16 **Children** Portions, Menu **Parking** 350

North Bridge Brasserie

◉ Modern British, Scottish **NEW**

Stylish setting for relaxed, modern fine dining

☎ 0131 622 2900 & 556 5565 📠 0131 652 3652
The Scotsman, 20 North Bridge EH1 1YT
e-mail: northbridge@tshg.co.uk
dir: Town centre, next to railway station, 1 min from Royal Mile & 2 mins to Princes St

Once the head office of The Scotsman newspaper, this stunning Victorian building, now an opulent hotel, combines the best of the grand original features with cutting-edge design. The classical elegance of the bustling brasserie and the intimate, fine-dining Vermillion Restaurant, complete with marble staircase

---

Norton House Hotel

| **EDINBURGH** | **Map 21 NT27** |

Modern British, French

Sophisticated fine-dining restaurant in elegant hotel

☎ 0131 333 1275 📠 0131 333 5305
Ingliston EH28 8LX
e-mail: nortonhouse@handpicked.co.uk
dir: M8 junct 2, off A8, 0.5m past Edinburgh Airport

Norton House was always intended as a refuge from the hurly-burly of Edinburgh; the Usher family of Scottish brewing wealth once tucked themselves away here amid 55 acres of parkland and woods. Now we can all indulge in the luxuries of the plush country-house hotel, get pampered in the top-drawer spa and tuck into seriously good food. The designers have been at work inside, grafting on a tasteful contemporary edge to its period grandeur. A chic new black leather and dark-wood

brasserie offers a relaxed way in to sample the kitchen's talents, but if you really want to see what the team is capable of, Ushers is the sophisticated fine-dining option. It's a soothingly stylish, low-lit space rather like stepping into an upmarket Parisian chocolatier with its luscious colours of café crème, caramel and milk chocolate brown. With just 8 well-spaced tables to care for, the staff deliver impeccable service, always attentive, arriving with first-class breads and clever canapés. The kitchen takes a modern tack with classic French cuisine; as with all top-level cooking, prime ingredients are the key here, impeccably sourced and put into the talented hands of a team that has the technical skills and confidence to let the materials talk for themselves. Dishes are composed with deceptive simplicity and precise, balanced flavours, as with torchon of duck foie gras married with a tangy rhubarb chutney and toasted gingerbread preceding pan-fried sea bass fillet with olive gnocchi and a cassoulet-style confection of butterbeans, tomato fondant, chorizo and caper berries. Unmissable desserts

include a textbook prune and Armagnac soufflé with white chocolate cappuccino and bitter chocolate spring roll.

Chef Graeme Shaw, Glen Bilins **Owner** Hand Picked Hotels **Times** 7-9.30 Closed 26 Dec, 1 Jan, Sun-Mon, L all week **Prices** Starter £8.50-£12.95, Main £23.95-£26.95, Dessert £8.50-£8.95, Service optional **Wines** 168 bottles over £20, 12 by glass **Notes** Vegetarian available, Civ Wed 140, Air con **Seats** 22, Pr/dining room 40 **Children** Portions **Parking** 100

and pillars and baronial wood panelling, blends seamlessly with the contemporary bedrooms. Housed in former offices, the brasserie offers technically accomplished and creative dishes, which make good use of quality Scottish produce, on sensibly compact menus. Take sea bream with smoked salmon risotto and braised onions, haunch of venison with braised red cabbage, and warm chocolate pudding.

Chef Spencer Wilson **Owner** The Eton Collection/The Scotsman Hotel Group **Times** 12-2.30/6-10.30 **Prices** Fixed L 2 course fr £12, Starter £5.50-£9.50, Main £9-£18.50, Dessert £5.50-£6, Service added but optional 10% **Wines** 80 bottles over £20, 12 bottles under £20, 14 by glass **Notes** Sunday L, Vegetarian available, Dress restrictions, Smart casual, Civ Wed 80, Air con **Seats** 80, Pr/dining room 80 **Children** Portions, Menu **Parking** Station car park

Norton House Hotel

🌸🌸🌸 — *see opposite page*

Number One, The Balmoral Hotel

🌸🌸🌸 — *see below*

Plumed Horse

🌸🌸🌸 — *see page 498*

The Restaurant at the Bonham

🌸🌸 Modern Scottish ⌘

Stylish urban setting for lively, modern cooking

☎ 0131 274 7444 📠 0131 226 6080
35 Drumsheugh Gardens EH3 7RN
e-mail: restaurant@thebonham.com
dir: At W end of Princes St

Instead of buying glossy magazines for interior décor inspiration, come for dinner in the swish restaurant of this modish West End boutique hotel. The Bonham ticks all the boxes: oodles of period charm - wooden floors, oak panelling and intricate plasterwork in abundance - blended with a permanent modern art exhibition to form a palette of exuberantly tasteful colour. The restaurant set-up oozes class with its dark-wood tables set with fine glassware, cutlery, linen napkins and candles, and the slick service and imaginative cuisine both rise to the challenge. The French chef marries classical influences with modern Scottish flair and faultless raw materials in his well-judged dishes. A starter of roasted hand-dived scallops with gutsy pig's trotter croquettes and langoustine ravioli sets the bar high, and the momentum is kept up through roast loin of venison with gnocchi, braised red cabbage cracker and bitter chocolate sauce.

Chef Michel Bouyer **Owner** Peter Taylor, The Town House Company **Times** 12-2.30/6.30-10 **Prices** Fixed L 2 course £13.50, Starter £6-£12, Main £15-£23, Dessert £6-£8.50, Service added but optional 10%, Groups min 6 service 10% **Wines** 22 bottles over £20, 12 bottles under £20 **Notes** Sunday L, Vegetarian available **Seats** 60, Pr/dining room 26 **Children** Portions **Parking** 16, NCP

Restaurant Martin Wishart

🌸🌸🌸🌸 — *see page 499*

Number One, The Balmoral Hotel

Modern Scottish, French

First-class fine dining at prestigious Edinburgh hotel

☎ 0131 557 6727 📠 0131 557 8740
1 Princes St EH2 2EQ
e-mail: numberone@roccofortecollection.com
dir: follow city centre signs. Hotel at E end of Princes St, adjacent to Waverley Station

With a prestigious address at the top of Princes Street, and fine views over the city and castle, this elegant hotel presides grandly over the heart of the city. Fine-dining restaurant Number One is set on the lower-ground floor, but is none the worse for that; designed by Olga Polizzi, the space is opulent, luxurious and multi-textured. Walls are rich, dark-red lacquered and adorned with modern artworks, the carpet is a deep pile job, tables are well-spaced and the service is suitably formal; jackets are expected for gentlemen and other traditional touches such as the cheese, bread and liqueur trolleys all add to the sense of occasion. Classical preparations meet modern interpretations in dishes based on excellent Scottish produce and showing high technical skills. Start, perhaps, with crab millefeuille with brown crab pannacotta and wasabi mayo, then maybe a main course of fillet of Borders beef with oxtail ravioli, squash purée and braised leeks. Finish with a chocolate chiboust with blood oranges and Manjari chocolate sorbet. For less formal dining, there's the hotel's Hadrian's brasserie (see entry).

Chef Jeff Bland, Craig Sandle **Owner** Rocco Forte Hotels **Times** 6.30-10 Closed 1st 2 wks Jan, L all week **Prices** Fixed D 3 course £57.50, Tasting menu £65-£110, Service optional, Groups min 6 service 12.5% **Wines** 350 bottles over £20, 8 by glass **Notes** Tasting menu 6 course, Vegetarian available, Dress restrictions, Smart casual preferred, Civ Wed 60, Air con **Seats** 50, Pr/dining room 50 **Children** Portions **Parking** NCP: Greenside/St James Centre

Plumed Horse

RESTAURANT OF THE YEAR

EDINBURGH   Map 21 NT27

Modern European

Imaginative cuisine served in Georgian grandeur

☎ 0131 554 5556 & 05601 123266
50-54 Henderson St, Leith EH6 6DE
e-mail: plumedhorse@aol.com
web: www.plumedhorse.co.uk
dir: From city centre N on Leith Walk, left into Great Junction St & 1st right into Henderson St. Restaurant 200mtrs on right

The brainchild of chef-proprietor Tony Borthwick, the Plumed Horse makes the most of its relocation from Castle Douglas to Leith by using locally landed fish and seafood. With its rather sedate exterior, the Georgian building sits in the middle of a mainly residential area. Once inside though, the grandeur of its heritage comes to the fore with many features being sympathetically retained and formal table settings with matching chair covers and crisp linen adding to the grand atmosphere. Service is formal but delivered with genuine friendliness by a small team. Imaginative cooking is perfectly executed and plenty of local ingredients appear on the menus alongside that fine seafood. Start perhaps with a twice-baked parmesan and truffle soufflé with tomato and cucumber salad and move onto a fillet

of monkfish roasted with curry spices, gratin of Jerusalem artichokes, green beans and orange and vermouth sauce before pushing the boat out with fudge and ginger parfait, ginger beer, vanilla, lime and 'Sailor Jerry' sorbet.

Chef Tony Borthwick **Owner** The Company of The Plumed Horse Ltd **Times** 12-3.30/7-11.30 Closed Xmas, New Year, 2 wks Summer, 1 wk Nov, Sun-Mon **Prices** Fixed L 2 course £23-£25, Fixed D 3 course £43, Service optional **Wines** 165 bottles over £20, 24 bottles under £20, 10 by glass **Notes** Air con **Seats** 36, Pr/dining room 10 **Parking** On street

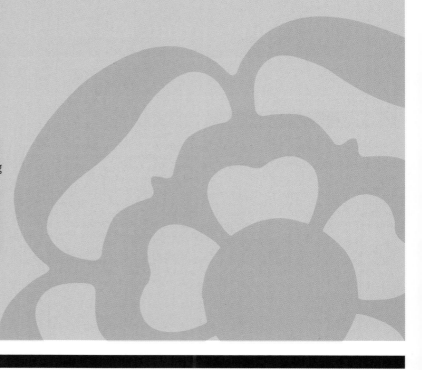

Restaurant Martin Wishart

Modern French **V** **NOTABLE WINE LIST**

Imaginative, memorable French cooking in intimate, fashionable waterfront venue

☎ 0131 553 3557   🖨 0131 467 7091
54 The Shore, Leith EH6 6RA
e-mail: info@martin-wishart.co.uk
web: www.martin-wishart.co.uk
dir: Please telephone for directions/map on website

During his 10 years in Leith, Martin Wishart has created a restaurant with a reputation that spreads far beyond the city limits, county boundaries, and the national border. There is now a cookery school bearing his name just five minutes from the restaurant, and a new outpost - Martin Wishart at Loch Lomond - has opened in Cameron House on Loch Lomond, in West Dunbartonshire (see entry). But fear not, Mr Wishart is not spreading himself too thinly. His flagship restaurant remains a bastion of elegant simplicity, where classical French traditions and a lightness of touch, plus exciting combinations and first-class Scottish produce, equals a stunning dining experience. The room is chic and elegant, based around natural tones of brown and cream, with stylish fixtures-and-fittings, contemporary artworks and well-spaced, well-dressed tables. The fixed-price menus (set-lunch, carte, tasting, plus a bespoke

vegetarian version) are full of excitingly creative combinations and it is clear from the canapés (gougére and many others) and excellent bread that you are in safe hands. Langoustine ravioli with endive braised with orange and a langoustine and olive oil jus displays well-judged flavours, while main-course grilled lemon sole with sautéed veal kidneys is a delicate and highly successful partnership, with caramelised cauliflower, capers and endive. Assiette of rhubarb and yogurt, ginger beer sorbet and lemongrass sauce come together in a divine dessert. Service is suitably slick and avoids pomposity, and the sommelier is on hand to guide the way through the seriously impressive wine list.

Chef Martin Wishart **Owner** Martin Wishart **Times** 12-2/6.30-10 Closed 25-26 Dec, 1 Jan, 2 wks Jan, Sun-Mon **Prices** Fixed L 3 course £24.50-£60, Fixed D 3 course fr £60, Tasting menu £65, Service optional, Groups min 6 service 10% **Wines** 200+ bottles over £20, 2 bottles under £20, 12 by glass **Notes** Tasting menu 6 course, Vegetarian menu, Dress restrictions, Smart casual **Seats** 50, Pr/dining room 10 **Children** Portions **Parking** On street

EDINBURGH *continued*

Rhubarb - the Restaurant at Prestonfield

◉◉ Modern European ▲NOTABLE WINE LIST

Opulent setting for impressive food

☎ 0131 225 1333 📠 0131 220 4392
Prestonfield House, Priestfield Rd EH16 5UT
e-mail: reservations@prestonfield.com
web: www.rhubarb-restaurant.com
dir: Exit city centre on Nicholson St, onto Dalkeith Rd. At lights turn left into Priestfield Rd. Prestonfield on left

Rhubarb occupies two richly appointed oval rooms within the unapologetically opulent and decadent Prestonfield Hotel, a stunning, lavishly restored and richly refurbished Regency house hidden away in 20 acres of parkland on the outskirts of the city. Portraits of former owners, one, Sir Alexander Dick, who first introduced rhubarb to Scotland, adorn the walls of the hotel's luxurious dining venue, which enjoys fine views from crisp, linen-clothed tables. Top-notch seasonal Scottish produce is handled with care, with the ambitious, modern European menu listing classic dishes like lamb cutlets with mint hollandaise or beef sirloin with peppercorn jus, alongside turbot with confit lemon, razor clams and caper butter, or braised haunch and roast loin of venison with smoked garlic cream. Desserts are a strength, such as bitter chocolate tart with lime ice cream, mango and Thai basil.

Chef John McMahon **Owner** James Thomson OBE
Times 12-2/6-11 **Prices** Fixed L 2 course £16.95, Fixed D 3 course £30, Starter £7.50-£14, Main £10-£28, Dessert £6.95-£8.95, Service optional, Groups min 8 service 10% **Wines** 500+ bottles over £20, 12 by glass **Notes** Theatre D 2 course £16.95, Afternoon tea £16.95, Sunday L, Vegetarian available, Civ Wed 500 **Seats** 90, Pr/dining room 500 **Children** Portions **Parking** 200

The Royal Terrace Hotel

◉ Modern British **NEW**

Creative brasserie food in handsome Georgian Edinburgh

☎ 0131 557 3222 📠 0131 557 5334
18 Royal Ter EH7 5AQ
dir: A8 to city centre, follow one-way system, left into Charlotte Sq. At end right into Queens St. Left at rdbt. At next island right into London Rd, right into Blenheim Place leading to Royal Terrace

Part of an immaculately restored Georgian terrace not far from the city centre, the hotel is in as handsome a location as Edinburgh affords. High ceilings and lovely cornices inside set the tone for the ground-floor restaurant, which extends into a conservatory area that overlooks the impeccably maintained sloping gardens. Danish chef Morten Rengtved is something of an old Scottish hand by now, and brings a modern brasserie sensibility to conscientiously sourced materials. It all looks good too, as witnessed in a croquette of smoked haddock bedded on vivid pea purée, with mustard-dressed leaves, on a slate slab. Continue to finely judged pork, served two ways in the modern style: Parma ham-wrapped fillet and slow-cooked belly.

Chef Morten Rengtved **Owner** Prima Hotel Group
Times 5-9.30 Closed L all week **Prices** Food prices not confirmed for 2010. Please telephone for details.

Stac Polly

◉ Modern Scottish

Scottish cuisine in city centre

☎ 0131 229 5405 & 558 3083 📠 0131 557 9779
8-10 Grindlay St EH3 9AS
e-mail: bookings@stacpolly.com
dir: In city centre beneath castle, near Lyceum Theatre

Situated in the lee of the castle and a few minutes' walk from the Princes Street shops, this popular restaurant is one of three in the city; the others are in Dublin Street (see next entry) and St Mary's Street. Lurking behind a plain exterior is a colourful basement restaurant of softly lit rooms, furnished with tartan chairs and curtains, and prints on the walls. The menu delivers Scottish food with some well-judged international flavours and preparations, so filo pastry parcels of haggis are served with red wine and sweet plum sauce, and main-course roast rack of lamb with cocotte potatoes, Stornoway black pudding and a game and Madeira reduction.

Chef Steven Harvey **Owner** Roger Coulthard
Times 12-2/6-10 Closed Xmas, New Year, Sun, L Sat

Prices Fixed L 2 course £12.95-£15.95, Starter £6.95-£8.25, Main £17.95-£19.95, Dessert £6.65-£8.55, Service added but optional 10% **Wines** 50 bottles over £20, 6 bottles under £20, 6 by glass **Notes** Pre-theatre menu 6-7pm, 2 course £15.95, 3 course £19.95 **Seats** 98, Pr/dining room 50 **Children** Portions **Parking** NCP - Castle Terrace

Stac Polly

◉ Modern Scottish

Modern Scottish cuisine in atmospheric surroundings

☎ 0131 556 2231
29-33 Dublin St EH3 6NL
e-mail: enquiry@stacpolly.com
dir: On corner of Albany St & Dublin St

The Dublin Street branch of the three Stac Polly restaurants in Edinburgh is located in the basement labyrinth of rough stone-walled cellars of a 200-year-old building. Named after Stac Pollaidh, a mountain on the North-West coast of Scotland, the restaurants serve modern Scottish cuisine with a flourish, putting a bit of zest into traditional fare while showing off the Scottish larder to best advantage. The cosily rustic restaurant serves up warm salad of honey-glazed duck breast and Puy lentils with a raspberry vinegar and ginger dressing, followed by baked fillet of halibut with prawn risotto, broccoli and sun-blush tomatoes and basil oil.

Chef Stan Andre **Owner** Roger Coulthard
Times 12-2/6-10 Closed 25-26 Dec, 1 Jan, Sun, L Sat
Prices Fixed L 2 course fr £12.95, Fixed D 3 course fr £20, Starter £6.95-£8.25, Main £17.95-£19.95, Dessert £6.65-£8.25, Service added but optional 10% **Wines** 40+ bottles over £20, 7 bottles under £20, 8 by glass **Seats** 100, Pr/dining room 54 **Children** Portions **Parking** On street - after 6.30pm

The Stockbridge Restaurant

◉ Modern European

Dramatic basement restaurant focusing on well-sourced produce

☎ 0131 2266766
54 St Stephen St EH3 5AL
e-mail: jane@thestockbridgerestaurant.com
web: www.thestockbridgerestaurant.com
dir: From A90 towards city centre, left Craigleith Rd B900, 2nd exit at rdbt B900, straight on to Kerr St, turn left onto St Stephen St

Follow the fairy light trail down the steps into this charmingly quirky theatrical grotto in the heart of bohemian Stockbridge. You can't fail to fall under the spell of the decadent boudoir setting: Gothic black walls, gold satin drapes and bold Scottish colourist prints, all candlelit for maximum opulence and romance. Not to be upstaged, the kitchen's output also has oodles of flair and flourishes, wrought from a sound foundation of well-sourced produce and solid technique. Modern European dishes are conceived with imagination and kept sensibly uncomplicated. To start, there might be smoked haddock risotto with roasted butternut squash and parmesan crisp, then perhaps seared bream with ratatouille, parmesan crackling, sautéed ratte potatoes and pesto.

Chef Jason Gallagher **Owner** Jason Gallagher & Jane Walker **Times** 12.30-2.30/7-9.30 Closed 1st 2 wks Jan after New Year, Mon, L Tue-Fri **Prices** Fixed L 2 course £12.95-£13.95, Fixed D 3 course £22.95-£24.95, Starter £4.95-£12.95, Main £16.95-£22.95, Dessert £3.95-£6.95, Service optional, Groups min 6 service 10% **Wines** 34 bottles over £20, 19 bottles under £20, 5 by glass **Notes** Pre-theatre menu available in Aug, Sunday L, Vegetarian available **Seats** 40 **Parking** On street

Tower Restaurant & Terrace

Modern British

Inventive cooking with fantastic rooftop city views

☎ 0131 225 3003 📄 0131 220 4392
National Museum of Scotland, Chambers St EH1 1JF
e-mail: reservations@tower-restaurant.com
web: www.tower-restaurant.com
dir: Above Museum of Scotland building at corner of George IV Bridge & Chambers St, on level 5

The smartly uniformed doorman guides you to the express lift that takes you to the rooftop restaurant of the Museum of Scotland. The views from the terrace towards the castle and cathedral are not to be missed. Contemporary design has produced a chic, colourful

interior with velvet hangings and sexily curvaceous tweed banquettes. Lighting is agreeably low, and the food offers an eclectic mix of styles, based on choice Scots produce. Start with soused red mullet with marinated endive and beetroot purée, before a good, thick, chunky fillet of cod with lentil 'kedgeree' and coriander gremolata, then ginger cake with confit apples and Granny Smith ice-cream.

Chef Gavin Elden **Owner** James Thomson OBE **Times** 12-11.30 Closed 25-26 Dec **Prices** Fixed L 2 course £12.95, Fixed D 3 course £30, Starter £6.50-£9, Main £14-£26, Dessert £6.50-£9, Service optional, Groups min 8 service 10% **Wines** 150 bottles over £20, 30 bottles under £20, 14 by glass **Notes** Theatre supper £12.95, Sunday L, Vegetarian available, Air con **Seats** 96, Pr/dining room 90 **Parking** On street

The Vintners Rooms

French

Candlelit restaurant with vintage charm

☎ 0131 554 6767 📄 0131 555 5653
The Vaults, 87 Giles St, Leith EH6 6BZ
e-mail: enquiries@thevintnersrooms.com
dir: At end of Leith Walk, left into Great Junction St, right into Henderson St. Restaurant in old warehouse on right

Leith can stake a claim as the restaurant capital of Scotland and the Vintners Rooms has been helping put the area on the map for a long time now. The restaurant, lit only by flickering candles, is housed in the old wine merchants' auction room of a 16th-century former warehouse, set over the historic vaults, and is full of charm and character. The food is refined and imaginative, with modern French dishes created from quality Scottish produce, and the wine list runs to 200 bins. Perfectly cooked, sea-fresh scallops are set on sautéed girolles and gremolata, while main-course lamb (pink and tender) is full of flavour, with a herb crust and rosemary jus.

Chef Patrice Ginestière **Owner** Patrice Ginestière **Times** 12-7-10 Closed 1-16 Jan, Sun-Mon **Prices** Starter £6.50-£13.50, Main £14.50-£30, Dessert £6-£7.50, Service added but optional 10%, Groups min 5 service 10% **Wines** 160 bottles over £20, 12 bottles under £20, 6 by glass **Notes** Vegetarian available **Seats** 64, Pr/dining room 34 **Children** Portions **Parking** 4

The Witchery by the Castle

Traditional Scottish

A one-off destination restaurant in historic location

☎ 0131 225 5613 📄 0131 220 4392
Castlehill, The Royal Mile EH1 2NF
e-mail: mail@thewitchery.com
web: www.thewitchery.com
dir: Top of Royal Mile at gates of Edinburgh Castle

The theatrical romance of the Witchery has made it almost as famous as the castle by whose gates it has stood since 1595 - and it's something of a celeb-magnet to boot. It takes its name from the benighted period of history when hundreds of people were burnt at the stake as witches on Castlehill. The décor in the dining rooms is darkly opulent: tapestry-hung walls, 17th-century oak panelling, flagged floors and magnificent candelabra conjure a moody setting in the Witchery, while the Secret Garden, reached via a stone staircase from the courtyard has lovely painted ceiling panels. Well-sourced Scottish materials provide a rock-solid base for a menu of straightforward contemporary classics. Fish bisque comes with garlic croûtons, gruyère and rouille, while braised rump, seared liver and grilled cutlet of Borders lamb is served with broad bean purée and aubergine relish.

Chef Douglas Roberts **Owner** James Thomson OBE **Times** 12-4/5-11.30 Closed 25-26 Dec **Prices** Fixed L 2 course £12.95, Fixed D 3 course £30, Starter £6.95-£12.95, Main £14.95-£30, Dessert £6.95-£7.50, Service optional, Groups min 8 service 10% **Wines** 700+ bottles over £20, 20 bottles under £20, 14 by glass **Notes** Theatre supper 2 course £12.95, Sunday L, Vegetarian available, Air con **Seats** 120, Pr/dining room 70

FALKIRK

BANKNOCK — Map 21 NS77

Glenskirlie House Restaurant

@@ Modern British

Fashionable Scottish castle with terrific food

☎ 01324 840201 📠 01324 841054
Glenskirlie House & Castle, Kilsyth Rd FK4 1UF
e-mail: macaloneys@glenskirliehouse.com
dir: From Glasgow take A80 towards Stirling. Continue past Cumbernauld, at junct 4 take A803 signed Kilsyth/Bonnybridge. At T-junct turn right. Hotel 1m on right

Forget the tartan-and-antlers school of Scottish castles: Glenskirlie gives a 21st-century kick in the pants to the old genre with boutique-style boudoirs to pamper yourself in and the food follows through with a genuine wow factor. The made-over Edwardian country house sits bang in the centre of Scotland in tranquil parkland. Every aspect of the restaurant is finely tuned: knowledgeable staff deliver slick service, a sumptuous décor boosts the feel-good factor and the kitchen team deals in meticulously prepared food with razor-sharp technical execution. Modern takes on classic Scottish dishes might kick off with honey-roast pork belly with seared foie gras, Puy lentils and cider jus; hot-carved venison arrives with skirlie - a stuffing of oatmeal and onion - caramelised apple, red onion marmalade and a nicely gamey port and thyme jus. Desserts appear on the showpiece trolley.

Chef David Jordan **Owner** John Macaloney, Colin Macaloney **Times** 12-2/6-9.30 Closed 26-27 Dec, 1-3 Jan, D Mon **Prices** Fixed L 2 course fr £18.75, Starter fr £6.25, Main fr £19.50, Dessert fr £8.25, Service optional **Wines** 40 bottles over £20, 20 bottles under £20, 8 by glass **Notes** Sunday L, Vegetarian available, Civ Wed 150, Air con **Seats** 54, Pr/dining room 150 **Children** Portions, Menu **Parking** 100

FIFE

ANSTRUTHER — Map 21 NO50

The Cellar

@@@ — *see opposite page*

CUPAR — Map 21 NO31

Ostlers Close Restaurant

@@ Modern British V 🕙

Modern, elegant restaurant making good use of excellent local ingredients

☎ 01334 655574
Bonnygate KY15 4BU
dir: In small lane off main street, A91

This restaurant in a 17th-century dwelling and erstwhile temperance hotel is tucked up a skinny alley off Cupar main street and is easy to miss if you don't know where to look. The owners are so committed to sourcing fresh, local ingredients, that they have taken things into their own hands: their kitchen garden ensures fruit, veg and herbs appear in the kitchen half-an-hour after being picked. Wild mushrooms, picked from local woodland are a particular passion, too. Handwritten menus see classic dishes brought up-to-date with clear unfussy flavours, and saucing driven more by punchy stocks and reductions than dairy produce. A roast fillet of Pittenweem hake with smoked haddock mash, parsley velouté and crispy Serrano ham makes a robust starter. Moving on, meaty main courses offer roast saddle of venison with wild mushrooms, roast root vegetables and red wine sauce. Desserts are a match for intensity with chocolate mocha tart with white chocolate ice cream and espresso sauce.

Chef James Graham **Owner** James & Amanda Graham **Times** 12.15-1.30/7-9.30 Closed 25-26 Dec, 1-2 Jan, 2 wks Oct, 2 wks Apr, Sun-Mon, L Tue-Fri **Prices** Starter £5.95-£12.50, Main £12.50-£21.50, Dessert £6.25-£7.25, Service optional **Wines** 60 bottles over £20, 31 bottles under £20, 6 by glass **Notes** Vegetarian menu **Seats** 26 **Children** Portions **Parking** On street, public car park

DUNFERMLINE — Map 21 NT08

Cardoon

@ Modern, Traditional

Contemporary cooking in relaxed conservatory restaurant

☎ 01383 736258 📠 01383 621600
BW Keavil House Hotel, Crossford KY12 8QW
e-mail: gm@keavilhouse.co.uk
dir: M90 junct 3, 7m from Forth Road Bridge, take A985, turning right after bridge. From Dunfermline, 2m W on A994

Expect modern, brasserie-style cooking in the stylish conservatory restaurant overlooking the gardens of this 16th-century former manor house. Rich colours and a bright, airy, relaxed atmosphere set the tone, while the crowd-pleasing menu focuses on quality produce and some unusual combinations. Dishes are well balanced and accurately cooked, as witnessed in a full-flavoured smoked ham hock terrine with balsamic mayonnaise, perfectly-cooked scallops with cauliflower risotto, and a rich and visually pleasing chocolate parfait served with a griottine cherry jelly. Extras include an array of quality flavoured breads.

Chef Phil Yates **Owner** Queensferry Hotels Ltd **Times** 12-2/6.30-9.30 **Prices** Food prices not confirmed for 2010. Please telephone for details. **Wines** 12 bottles over £20, 22 bottles under £20, 9 by glass **Notes** Sunday L, Vegetarian available, Dress restrictions, No football colours, Civ Wed 200 **Seats** 80, Pr/dining room 22 **Children** Portions, Menu **Parking** 175

The Cellar

Seafood

Excellent fish and seafood cooking in a former smokery

☎ 01333 310378 📄 01333 312544
24 East Green KY10 3AA
web: www.cellaranstruther.co.uk
dir: Behind Scottish Fisheries Museum

Hiding behind the Scottish Fisheries Museum, a little way from Anstruther's harbour front, is this little gem of a restaurant. Housed in a 17th-century listed building, it has a charming cobbled courtyard, and original beams inside. On winter evenings, the fire crackles welcomingly, candles flicker on the tables, and the cooking is never less than a delight. Susan Jukes is a good advocate for husband Peter's food, knows her wines, and is full of useful advice when needed. The premises were once a cooperage and smokery in Scotland's herring industry, and something of that past is honoured in the starter of marinated herring with gravad lax that has been a tradition here for over a quarter of a century. Alternative, equally memorable dishes include crayfish bisque glazed with gruyère and cream, or an omelette stuffed with Finnan haddock. Mains continue to celebrate the harvest of the sea, perhaps with pesto-crusted cod with pak choi, basil mash and balsamic, or grilled halibut with smoked bacon, pine nuts and hollandaise. Meat-eaters might consider a piece of prime Scots beef, served with wild mushrooms, caramelised onions and stovies, in a grain mustard sauce. An interesting dessert idea is a version of Pavlova, filled with lemon curd ice cream, on rhubarb coulis.

Chef Peter Jukes **Owner** Peter Jukes
Times 12.30-1.30/6.30-9.30
Closed Xmas, Sun (Sun & Mon Winter), L Mon-Tue **Prices** Fixed L course £23.50, Fixed D 3 course fr £37.50, Service optional **Wines** 5 by glass **Seats** 38
Children Portions **Parking** On street

| **ELIE** | Map 21 NO40 |

Sangsters

◉◉ Modern British

Good Scottish cooking in relaxed surroundings

☎ 01333 331001
51 High St KY9 1BZ
e-mail: bruce@sangsters.co.uk
dir: From St Andrews on A917 take B9131 to Anstruther, right at rdbt onto A917 to Elie (11m from St Andrews)

A small seaside village restaurant it may be, with a relaxed and peaceful atmosphere and comfortable lounge, yet the place has pedigree. Chef-patron Bruce Sangster's cooking is skilful, precise and accomplished, his modern approach driven by fresh, quality seasonal ingredients from the abundant Scottish larder. Take a twice-baked cheese soufflé starter using Isle of Mull Tobermory cheddar, or to follow, Scotch beef fillet accompanied by a red cabbage compôte, onion marmalade and gratin potatoes. Heading-up desserts, a caramelised apple pastry with Calvados custard, caramel sauce and apple sorbet might catch the eye. The dining room comes in bright, clean and simple lines, the walls hung with local prints and watercolours.

Times 12.30-1.30/7-9.30 Closed 25-26 Dec, early Jan, mid Feb/Oct, mid Nov, Mon, L Tue & Sat, D Sun

| **MARKINCH** | Map 21 NO20 |

Balbirnie House

◉◉ Classic

Accomplished Scottish cuisine in imposing Georgian mansion

☎ 01592 610066   ▤ 01592 610529
Balbirnie Park KY7 6NE
e-mail: info@balbirnie.co.uk
dir: M90 junct 13 follow signs for Glenrothes & Tay Bridge, right onto B9130 to Markinch & Balbirnie Park

Dating back to 1777, Balbirnie House is one of Scotland's foremost listed buildings. The impressive Georgian mansion, set in 400 acres of stunning landscaped parkland, is now a luxurious country-house hotel. The refurbished restaurant, The Orangery, is sumptuously decorated in shades of silver, copper and chocolate with floor-to-ceiling lunette windows and a glass roof. The menu features beautifully presented classical cuisine, using the very best from Scotland's rich larder, much of it locally sourced. Expect impressive dishes such as Cullen skink or Isle of Lewis lamb shoulder pie served with the loin - pink and tender - on a bed of curly kale with potato Anna. Finish with banana parfait and peanut butter ice cream, and note the more informal Balbirnie bistro is also worth a punt.

Times 12-1.30/7-9 Closed Mon-Tue

| **PEAT INN** | Map 21 NO40 |

The Peat Inn

◉◉◉ – **see below**

The Peat Inn

| **PEAT INN** | Map 21 NO40 |

Modern British ▲ 🍴

Classy cooking using first-class local produce

☎ 01334 840206   ▤ 01334 840530
KY15 5LH
e-mail: stay@thepeatinn.co.uk
dir: At junction of B940/B941, 6m SW of St Andrews

There's been no resting on their laurels for owners Geoffrey and Katherine Smeddle since they took over this 300-year-old coaching inn with a recent history as one of Scotland's top dining destinations. Pleasingly the restaurant with rooms continues to go from strength to strength. A comfortable lounge, decorated in an elegant country style, is dominated by a large log fire and leads through to 3 intimate dining rooms. Reflecting the natural setting, the rooms are painted in muted colours with fresh flowers adorning the linen-clad tables. Produce comes from small local suppliers wherever possible and, with Geoffrey at the helm in the kitchen, ingredients are imaginatively paired and balanced to bring out the maximum depth and flavour. The visual impact of the food is stunning, as in a mosaic of rabbit, sweetbreads and confit duck perfectly pointed by accompanying pickled mushrooms and spiced walnuts. Perfect timing and high quality produce is evident in a John Dory main course, with fricassée of shellfish and white beans, potato gnocchi and mushroom purée. An accurately cooked mango soufflé with yogurt sorbet provides a confident close.

Chef Geoffrey Smeddle **Owner** Geoffrey & Katherine Smeddle **Times** 12.30-2/7-9.30 Closed 25-26 Dec, 1-14 Jan, Sun-Mon **Prices** Fixed L 3 course £16-£18, Fixed D 3 course fr £32, Tasting menu £50-£54, Starter £9-£15, Main £17-£25, Dessert £9-£11, Service optional **Wines** 250 bottles over £20, 9 by glass **Notes** Tasting menu 6 course, Vegetarian available **Seats** 40, Pr/dining room 14 **Parking** 24

ST ANDREWS   Map 21 NO51

Inn at Lathones

◉◉ Modern European

Creative combinations in a charming coaching inn

☎ 01334 840494 📠 01334 840694
Largoward KY9 1JE
e-mail: lathones@theinn.co.uk
dir: 5m SW of St Andrews on A915. In 0.5m before Largoward on left, just after hidden dip

This lovely old coaching inn, parts of which are 400 years old, houses a cosy restaurant serving modern Scottish and European food; and it's close enough to St Andrew's for a spot of golf, too. Although tables are formally laid, the friendly staff and colourful interior give it a relaxed vibe, enough, hopefully, to allay any fears about meeting the resident ghost. Imaginative flavour combinations utilise top-notch local ingredients in dishes such as fillet of hare and fresh scallops on a salad of rocket dressed with a blackcurrant and thyme vinaigrette. Main-course roasted gigot of lamb comes with mutton stovies, a garlic cream and succulent red cabbage, and end on a sweet note with orange blossom crème brûlée with a local fruit compôte and yogurt ice cream.

Inn at Lathones

Chef Richard Brackenbury **Owner** Mr N White **Times** 12-2.30/6-9.30 Closed 26 Dec, 1st 2 wks Jan **Prices** Fixed L 2 course £15.50, Starter £3.95-£7.50, Main £16.50-£22, Dessert £5.95-£7.50, Service optional **Wines** 89 bottles over £20, 13 bottles under £20, 5 by glass **Notes** Sunday L, Vegetarian available, Dress restrictions, Smart casual, Civ Wed 40 **Seats** 40, Pr/dining room 40 **Children** Menu **Parking** 35

Macdonald Rusacks Hotel - Old Course Restaurant

◉◉ Scottish, International

Fine food in world famous golf hotel

☎ 0844 879 9136 📠 01334 477896
Pilmour Links KY16 9JQ
e-mail: general.rusacks@macdonald-hotels.co.uk
dir: M90 junct 8, A91 to St Andrews. Hotel on left on entering town

The Macdonald Rusacks Hotel in St Andrews is one of the most famous golfing hotels on the planet. The long-established hotel enjoys an unrivalled location close to the 18th hole with superb views across the world-renowned course. Take your eyes off the green and you'll find the food up to par, served in the smart restaurant with huge windows to take in those views. The traditional

continued

The Road Hole Restaurant

ST ANDREWS   Map 21 NO51

British V 🍷 NOTABLE WINE LIST

Golfing views and Scottish produce

☎ 01334 474371 📠 01334 477668
Old Course Hotel, Golf Resort & Spa KY16 9SP
e-mail: reservations@oldcoursehotel.co.uk
dir: M90 junct 8 then A91 to St Andrews

A haven for golfers, the internationally renowned Old Course Hotel stands adjacent to the 17th hole of the championship course. There are various places to eat in the elegant and modern hotel, and for something a bit special go for The Road Hole Restaurant. First though, have a drink in the Road Hole Bar, which offers a selection of over 200 whiskies. In the restaurant, complete with chandeliers, oak-panelled floors and crisply laid tables, the floor-to-ceiling windows offer dramatic views over the old course and sweeping coastal vista. The Road Hole Table in the corner is positioned directly over the 17th road hole of the course for those die-hard fans. For those who can take their eyes off the view, the open kitchen provides a sense of theatre indoors. There are 3 menu options available - the à la carte, eight-course tasting and vegetarian tasting menu - and each makes good use of Scottish, and often organic, ingredients. Try Severn Valley smoked eel with a crispy herb risotto, white asparagus, samphire and cockle vinaigrette, followed by cranberry and bitter chocolate granola crusted wild boar loin with haunch cottage pie, black pudding, mustard swede and Swiss pie, and leave room for rhubarb and custard jelly, sorbet and biscuit.

Chef Paul Hart **Owner** Kohler Company **Times** 7-10 Closed Sun-Mon, L all week **Prices** Food prices not confirmed for 2010. Please telephone for details. **Wines** 400 bottles over £20, 11 by glass **Notes** Tasting menu & vegetarian tasting menu available, Vegetarian menu, Dress restrictions, Smart, no jeans/trainers, collared shirt required, Civ Wed 200 **Seats** 70, Pr/dining room 20 **Children** Portions, Menu **Parking** 100

ST ANDREWS *continued*

Scottish and international cuisine offers a tempting range of sophisticated, contemporary, weekly-changing dishes, including the likes of foie gras terrine with Madeira jelly as a starter, or mains such as fillet of wild halibut with braised oxtail, horseradish blini, parsnip purée and port wine reduction. For those with a sweet tooth, the warm chocolate fondant with vanilla ice cream and pistachio anglaise will definitely appeal.

Chef Cameron Roberson **Owner** Macdonald Hotels **Times** 12-2.30/6.30-9 **Prices** Food prices not confirmed for 2010. Please telephone for details. **Wines** 35 bottles over £20, 15 bottles under £20, 13 by glass **Notes** Vegetarian available, Dress restrictions, Smart casual, Civ Wed 60 **Seats** 70 **Children** Portions, Menu **Parking** 23

The Road Hole Restaurant

◉◉◉ – *see page 505*

Rufflets Country House & Terrace Restaurant

◉◉ Modern Scottish

Scottish cuisine in friendly country-house hotel

☎ 01334 472594 ▤ 01334 478703
Strathkinness Low Rd KY16 9TX
e-mail: reservations@rufflets.co.uk
dir: 1.5m W of St Andrews on B939

This turreted mansion a few minutes' drive from the town centre was originally built in 1924 as a private home for the widow of a prominent Dundee jute baron. Located one mile west of St Andrews, the charming Edwardian country house with splendid formal gardens and woodland has been in the same family ownership since 1952. The restaurant features a simple and stylish traditional décor with lots of colourful artwork. Service is particularly friendly and attentive making the diner feel really at ease. Cooking style is Scottish with Mediterranean influences, using fresh local produce. Typical dishes include a starter of malt whisky cured organic Scottish salmon with caper crème fraîche, followed by a main of braised Fife lamb shank with pearl barley risotto and port wine jus.

Chef Mark Nixon **Owner** Ann Murray-Smith **Times** 12.30-2.30/7-9 Closed L Mon-Sat **Prices** Fixed L 2 course £10.95-£20, Starter £4.75-£8.50, Main £14.95-£29.75, Dessert £6.50-£9, Service optional, Groups min 20 service 10% **Wines** 88 bottles over £20, 18 bottles under £20, 9 by glass **Notes** Sunday L, Vegetarian available, Dress restrictions, No shorts, Civ Wed 130 **Seats** 80, Pr/dining room 130 **Children** Portions, Menu **Parking** 50

The Seafood Restaurant

ST ANDREWS   Map 21 NO51

Modern Seafood

Superb seafood in a stunning glass building above the waves

☎ 01334 479475 ▤ 01334 479476
The Scores KY16 9AS
e-mail: reservations@theseafoodrestaurant.com

The glass cube perched on the sea wall above the waves certainly makes a style statement in the tweedy golfing Mecca of St Andrews. It is an elemental setting for a restaurant dealing in the ocean's bounty: look out of the floor-to-ceiling windows - that is where your food is coming from. In fact, the connection with the sea is so direct that the staff could dangle a line outside and haul fish straight from waves to pan. Inside, too, is a modishly minimalist and sleek tableau of glinting glass, metal and wood. The kitchen team have nowhere to hide in the gleaming steel theatre of their open-plan kitchen; perhaps this is why they go about their business with quiet, effortless professionalism. No tantrums or drama here, just unbeatably fresh fish and shellfish treated simply and married thoughtfully with clear, modern flavours, as in a starter of sesame seed and cumin-crusted cod served with butternut squash and pancetta velouté and sage oil. Next up, pan-seared halibut is given robust treatment with Parmentier potatoes, shiitake mushrooms, oxtail, garlic purée and red wine reduction. All that light and healthy seafood means there's no need to skip dessert: try a warm chocolate fondant with toasted marshmallow and pistachio ice cream.

Chef Craig Millar, Scott Swift **Owner** Craig Millar, Tim Butler **Times** 12-2.30/6.30-10 Closed 25-26 Dec, Jan 1 **Prices** Food prices not confirmed for 2010. Please telephone for details. **Wines** 180 bottles over £20, 5 bottles under £20, 8 by glass **Notes** Sunday L, Vegetarian available, Air con **Seats** 60 **Children** Portions **Parking** 50mtrs away

Russell Hotel

Scottish, International

Imaginative cooking in an intimate setting

☎ 01334 473447   📄 01334 478279
26 The Scores KY16 9AS
e-mail: russellhotel@talk21.com
dir: From A91 left at 2nd rdbt into Golf Place, right in 200yds into The Scores, hotel in 300yds on left

This friendly, family-run hotel on The Scores overlooking St Andrews Bay has lovely sea views. The restaurant is cosy and candlelit by night, creating an intimate atmosphere in which to enjoy some imaginative Scottish cooking. Take a drink in the welcoming Victorian Lounge Bar with its roaring log fire before dinner. High-quality local ingredients appear in dishes like steamed Loch Fyne mussels in white wine and coconut milk with lime, chilli and coriander, and trio of Aberdeen Angus beef (medallion fillet, braised oxtail and tongue). Baked lemon tart with champagne sorbet and a raspberry coulis makes a fitting finale.

Times 12-2/6.30-9.30 Closed Xmas

St Andrews Golf Hotel

Scottish

Timeless dining with a modern Scottish accent

☎ 01334 472611   📄 01334 472188
40 The Scores KY16 9AS
e-mail: reception@standrews-golf.co.uk
dir: follow 'Golf Course' signs into Golf Place, 200yds turn right into The Scores

The superb location and spectacular views at the family-run St Andrews Golf Hotel gives it broad appeal well beyond the golfing fraternity, although the name is a bit of a giveaway. The elegant Number Forty Restaurant is decked out in muted tones of brown and cream, making for a bright modern space. Scottish ingredients are used

to good effect by a kitchen which has a definite eye for presentation. Think salted-cod brandade with paprika and herb crostini, followed by braised ox cheeks with fresh buttered pasta. Desserts are quite traditional and might feature pear crumble with pouring cream or a selection of home-made sorbets such as lemon, mulled wine or orange.

Times 12.30-2/7-9.30 Closed 26-28 Dec

Sands Restaurant

International

Stylish restaurant within upmarket golf-resort hotel complex

☎ 01334 474371 & 468228   📄 01334 477668
The Old Course Hotel, Golf Resort & Spa KY16 9SP
e-mail: reservations@oldcoursehotel.co.uk
dir: M90 junct 8 then A91 to St Andrews

The Old Course Hotel overlooks the 17th fairway of the golf links that are a Mecca for golf fans worldwide who come to visit the cradle of the game here in St Andrews. The Sands Restaurant is the more informal of the hotel's dining options. It has a butch, rather clubby feel with black leather and dark wood - a classy look, but one that is scheduled for refurbishment in early 2010. The cooking is accurate and unfussy in style: top-drawer Scottish produce is used with a clear inclination towards brasserie-style dishes infused with a hint of the Mediterranean. Kyle of Tongue oysters with lemon, shallot and Cabernet Sauvignon vinaigrette gets things of to a classic start, then roast organic Shetland cod with chorizo, mussels and borlotti beans might follow.

Chef Simon Whitely **Owner** Kohler Company
Times 12-6/6-10 **Prices** Food prices not confirmed for 2010. Please telephone for details. **Wines** 70 bottles over £20, 11 by glass **Notes** Vegetarian available, Dress restrictions, Smart casual, Civ Wed 200 **Seats** 80, Pr/dining room 40 **Children** Portions, Menu **Parking** 100

The Seafood Restaurant

— *see opposite page*

— *see opposite page*

ST MONANS Map 21 NO50

The Seafood Restaurant

Modern Scottish, Seafood

Impeccably fresh seafood by the harbour

☎ 01333 730327   📄 01333 730508
16 West End KY10 2BX
e-mail: info@theseafoodrestaurant.com
dir: Take A959 from St Andrews to Anstruther, then W on A917 through Pittenweem. In St Monans to harbour then right

There is nothing that accompanies great seafood better than a great view, and this smart restaurant offers both in spades. The elder sibling of the restaurant of the same name at St Andrews (see entry) looks across the Firth of Forth towards Edinburgh from a sophisticated setting

featuring light beech wood and Rennie Mackintosh-style chairs - originally an old fisherman's cottage with an 800-year-old freshwater well with mystical healing powers. What else could you ask for? Ah yes, slithery fresh fish and seafood, prepared with simplicity and a light touch. A half-dozen Kilbrandon oysters might precede sea-fresh collops of monkfish with crispy smoked haddock and leek risotto cake and cauliflower and truffle purée. Rich, grown-up puddings, such as bitter dark chocolate tart with fennel ice cream, round things off. Unrelenting carnivores are appeased by a token meat dish.

Chef Craig Millar, Roy Brown **Owner** Craig Millar, Tim Butler **Times** 12-2.30/6-9.30 Closed 25-26 Dec, 1-2 Jan, Mon-Tue (Sep-Jun) **Prices** Fixed L 2 course fr £20, Fixed D 3 course fr £37, Service optional **Wines** 40 bottles over £20, 18 bottles under £20, 6 by glass **Notes** Oct-1 Apr fixed D menu 3 course £19.95 Wed-Fri, Sunday L, Vegetarian available **Seats** 44 **Children** Portions **Parking** 10

CITY OF GLASGOW

GLASGOW Map 20 NS56

An Lochan

Scottish, seafood

Simple café style in a trendy residential area, serving Scottish produce

☎ 0141 338 6606   📄 01700 811300
340 Crow Rd, Broomhill G11 7HT
e-mail: glasgow@anlochan.co.uk
dir: Please telephone for directions

Named after one of its restaurants that is situated by a loch, the Glasgow outpost of this select group is housed in a former bank. Step through the original door to find a lively restaurant with a cheery bistro-style décor, with blue walls adorned with local art, white leather chairs and white tablecloths. The restaurant serves modern Scottish food, simply cooked to make the most of fresh local produce. Light snacks, a blackboard tapas menu and pre-theatre dinners feature alongside the evening carte. Majoring on seafood, a sample evening menu might include smoked haddock chowder, followed by fish stew with crusty bread, or sea bass with lemon dressing, with winter berry soufflé or a plate of Scottish cheeses to finish.

Chef Claire McKie, Andrew Moss **Owner** The McKie family **Times** 12-3/6-11.30 Closed 24-26 Dec, 1-3 Jan, Mon, D Sun **Prices** Fixed L 2 course £8.95-£30, Fixed D 3 course £15.95-£55.95, Starter £4.95-£8.95, Main £10.95-£26.95, Dessert £4.95-£8.95, Service added but optional, Groups min 6 service 10% **Wines** 17 bottles over £20, 8 bottles under £20, 5 by glass **Notes** Early evening menu available Fri-Sat 5.30-7 pm, Sunday L, Vegetarian available, Air con **Seats** 40 **Children** Portions **Parking** On street

GLASGOW *continued*

La Bonne Auberge

◎ French, Mediterranean

Classic French cuisine in a modern hotel

☎ 0141 352 8310 🖨 0141 332 7447
Holiday Inn Theatreland, 161 West Nile St G1 2RL
e-mail: info@higlasgow.com
dir: Please telephone for directions

In the heart of the city's fashionable theatreland district and handy for the shops, this popular and relaxed French brasserie-style restaurant is found in the contemporary Holiday Inn. The crowd-pleasing repertoire necessarily plays to the crowds, with a wide range of accomplished, honest, French- and Mediterranean-inspired dishes. Menus take in a fixed-price pre-theatre option, while lunch might deliver simple classics like French onion soup, chargrilled rib-eye with green peppercorn sauce and French fries, or specialities like croque-monsieur, while dinner cranks up the ante with slow-cooked belly and pan-roasted pork loin served with parsnip purée and pork jus.

Chef Gerry Sharkey **Owner** Chardon Leisure Ltd
Times 12-2.15/5-10 **Prices** Food prices not confirmed for 2010. Please telephone for details. **Wines** 26 bottles over £20, 23 bottles under £20, 8 by glass **Notes** Air con **Seats** 90, Pr/dining room 100 **Children** Portions, Menu **Parking** NCP opposite

Brian Maule at Chardon d'Or

◎ French V 🍷 NOTABLE WINE LIST

Confident cooking in a classy city-centre venue

☎ 0141 248 3801 🖨 0141 248 3901
176 West Regent St G2 4RL
e-mail: info@brianmaule.com
dir: 10 minute walk from Glasgow central station

A Victorian townhouse in the heart of the city provides the setting for this elegant restaurant. Inside it is every inch the contemporary dining space - smart but understated, with suede and leather banquette seating, high-backed chairs and white-clothed tables set against wooden floors, cream walls and glass panels. There is a bar upstairs and an extended area downstairs with three private dining rooms. The cooking is classical French with Scottish produce to the fore: lamb (pan-fried fillet with creamed potatoes) is full of flavour, and scallops with chorizo and aubergine caviar is a well-judged starter.

Chef Brian Maule **Owner** Brian Maule at Chardon d'Or
Times 12-2/6-10 Closed 25-26 Dec, 1-2 Jan, 2 wks Jan, 2 wks Aug, BHs, Sun, L Sat **Prices** Fixed L 2 course £16.50, Fixed D 3 course £19.50, Tasting menu £55, Starter £7.20-£12, Main £21-£26.50, Dessert £8.20-£11.75, Service optional, Groups min 8 service 10% **Wines** 280 bottles over £20, 6 by glass **Notes** Tasting menu 6 course, Pre-theatre 6-6.45pm, Vegetarian menu, Dress restrictions, Smart casual, Air con **Seats** 90, Pr/dining room 60 **Children** Portions **Parking** Metered parking on street

City Café

◎ Modern European NEW 🍷

Modern cuisine beside the Clyde

☎ 0141 227 1010 & 240 1002 🖨 0141 248 2754
City Inn Glasgow, Finnieston Quay G3 8HN
e-mail: glasgow.citycafe@cityinn.com
dir: M8 junct 19 follow signs for SECC. Hotel on left 200yds before entrance to SECC

On the banks of the River Clyde, this restaurant has wonderful panoramic views of the surrounding area. Its relaxed and informal bistro style works well, with vibrant artwork on the walls and a cosy mixture of chairs and bench-style seating. You can also eat alfresco on the riverside terrace in good weather. The well-balanced menu uses quality ingredients to good effect, producing modern cuisine that ranges from informal comfort foods to fine dining dishes, including smooth chicken liver parfait with red onion marmalade and toasted brioche, followed by Shetland cod fillet and fine French beans with hollandaise sauce.

Chef Scott MacDonald, Charles Hilton **Owner** City Inn Limited **Times** 12-2.30/6.30-10.30 **Prices** Fixed L 2 course £9.95, Fixed D 3 course £16.50, Starter £4.95-£6.95, Main £9.95-£19.95, Dessert £5.50-£5.95, Service optional **Wines** 36 bottles over £20, 12 bottles under £20, 29 by glass **Notes** Sunday L, Vegetarian available, Dress restrictions, Smart casual, Civ Wed 50, Air con **Seats** 80, Pr/dining room 22 **Children** Portions, Menu **Parking** 120

Hotel du Vin Bistro at One Devonshire Gardens

GLASGOW	**Map 20 NS56**

Modern European

Fine dining in sophisticated townhouse hotel

☎ 0141 339 2001 🖨 0141 337 1663
1 Devonshire Gardens G12 0UX
e-mail: bistro.odg@hotelduvin.com
dir: M8 junct 17, follow signs for A82 after 1.5m turn left into Hyndland Rd

Arguably the jewel in the Hotel du Vin crown, One Devonshire Gardens has been a destination hotel in the heart of Glasgow's West End for many a year. The fashionable hotel chain has remodelled the building, situated on a tree-lined Victorian terrace, into its own image, which is entirely in-keeping. The boutique styling makes the best of the grand original features of the building, while adding all the expected modern comforts.

Sink into a deep sofa in the bar-lounge to sip an aperitif, or head straight into one of the quartet of oak-panelled rooms that make up the bistro. The crisp linen tablecloths give a clue to the fact that this HdV leans more towards fine dining than its siblings. The kitchen's output of modern and classic dishes supports the group's philosophy - quality food cooked simply with the freshest local ingredients. But again, here they've cranked up the ante with all the extra trappings such as amuse-bouche and petits fours and some ambitious cooking supporting the classics. Dishes are constructed to deliver visual impact, as with a foie gras and guinea fowl terrine served with pain d'épice and an avante-garde sweetcorn pannacotta and sweet-and-sour reduction. Main-course butter-roasted monkfish tail with ratte potatoes and curried mussel jus might precede a perfectly risen soufflé (coffee coulant with Tokaji lollipop and crème vierge). The HdV wine list is well worth exploring and the sommelier is on hand with some good advice.

Chef Paul Tamburrini **Owner** MWB/Hotel du Vin
Times 12-2.30/6-10.30 Closed L Sat **Prices** Fixed L 2 course fr £14.50, Starter £6.50-£12, Main £14-£32, Dessert £6.75-£15, Service added but optional 10% **Wines** 600 bottles over £20, 12 bottles under £20, 12 by glass **Notes** Tasting menu 6 course, Sunday L, Vegetarian available, Civ Wed 70 **Seats** 78, Pr/dining room 70 **Children** Portions, Menu **Parking** Nearby

Gamba

◉◉ Scottish, Seafood ✿

Well-regarded seafood restaurant in the West End

☎ 0141 572 0899 🖷 0141 572 0896
225a West George St G2 2ND
e-mail: info@gamba.co.uk
dir: Please telephone for directions

A basement restaurant in the heart of the fashionable West End of Glasgow, Gamba has been serving consistently good food for over 10 years, earning it a well deserved reputation in the city as the place to go for all things fishy. Decidedly Mediterranean in feel, the décor of warm terracotta colours along with some booth seating helps create an appealing, intimate setting. Gamba is the Spanish for king prawn and paintings of seafood with their Latin names points up the food to come. There are both Mediterranean and Asian influences in dishes such as the favourite Gamba soup (still delicious), and the use of top quality ingredients, served in generous portions, means the standards remain high in the likes of mussel and onion stew with sundried tomato, basil and aged balsamic or roast monkfish with stewed red cabbage, redcurrant and rosemary.

Chef Derek Marshall **Owner** Mr A C Tomkins & Mr D Marshall **Times** 12-2.30/5-10.30 Closed 25-26 Dec, 1-2 Jan, BHs, L Sun **Prices** Fixed L 2 course fr £15.95, Starter £8-£12, Main £12-£30, Dessert £6-£9, Service optional, Groups min 6 service 10% **Wines** 60 bottles over £20, 8 bottles under £20, 8 by glass **Notes** Pre-theatre £15 inc wine 5-6pm, Vegetarian available, Air con **Seats** 66 **Parking** On street

Hotel du Vin Bistro at One Devonshire Gardens

◉◉◉ — *see opposite page*

Killermont Polo Club

◉ Traditional Indian

Creative Indian cooking in a setting fit for a maharaja

☎ 0141 946 5412 🖷 0141 946 0812
2002 Maryhill Rd, Maryhill Park G20 0AB
dir: Please telephone for directions or visit website

No, this is not some snooty country house hotel with starched waiters, nor is it your everyday Indian curry house either. The subcontinent's age-old fascination with polo provides the inspiration for the interior, while Dum

Pukht is the culinary speciality - an esoteric cuisine that tickled the taste buds of Indian Moghul emperors. Subtle spices are blended with others brought from the Silk Road city of Samarkand in Uzbekistan to create a new style of slow-cooked dishes. The kitchen delivers a compendious list of dishes, taking in old favourites from the tandoor oven to Dum Pukht offerings such as murgh Wajid Ali - chicken breast stuffed with fresh pomegranate, mint, cheese and onions and braised in orange and saffron juices.

Times 12-2.30/5-11.30

the left bank

◉ Traditional International

Great value global food in vibrant urban setting

☎ 0141 339 5969
33-35 Gibson St, Hillhead G12 8NU
e-mail: contact@theleftbank.co.uk
dir: M8 junct 17, A82. After Kelvinbridge turn left onto Otago St, left onto Gibson St. Restaurant on right

This funky modern eatery in Glasgow's vibrant West End will sort you out with just about any meal for any time of day. Its eclectic menu ricochets around a global whirl of diverse flavours from satay skewers to Aberdeen Angus rib-eye steak, and from moules marinière to garlic masala fried fish on Goan seafood curry with Malabar garlic pickle and tomato rice - wherever the eye lands, South Asian influences are never far away. The vibe is casual, with split-level nooks and crannies to tuck yourself away from the madding crowd and admire the maverick style of local artists: the Timorous Beasties did the wallpaper and light fittings, and sculptor Chris Bannerman created the unique concrete bar.

Chef Liz McGougan **Owner** Catherine Hardy, Jacqueline Fennessy, George Swanson **Times** 9am-mdnt Closed 25 Dec, 1 Jan **Prices** Fixed L 2 course £10.95, Fixed D 3 course £12.95, Starter £3.50-£5.95, Main £7.25-£24.95, Dessert £2.95-£4.75, Service optional, Groups min 6 service 10% **Wines** 5 bottles over £20, 17 bottles under £20, 15 by glass **Notes** Fixed D served until 7pm, Vegetarian available **Seats** 75 **Children** Portions

The Living Room

◉ Traditional, International

Laid-back piano bar and restaurant that aims to please

☎ 0141 229 0607 🖷 0141 221 7148
150 St Vincent St G2 5NE
e-mail: glasgow@thelivingroom.co.uk
dir: In city centre between Hope St & Wellington St

In the heart of Glasgow's bustling office area, this laid-back bar and restaurant brings a touch of Manhattan chic to the city. The richly furnished dining room sports mood lighting, secluded booths and alcoves and acres of leather, and the extensive menu offers comfort food and fine dining dishes to suit all tastes and pockets. Share small plates of lamb meatballs in tomato sauce, and marinated Italian olives, then tuck into classic dishes like pork belly with grain mustard mash and caramelised

parsnips, or something like pan-fried sea bass with Tuscan vegetable and chorizo cassoulet, and round off with warm chocolate fudge cake.

Chef Chris Gibson **Owner** Premium Bars & Restaurants **Times** 11-5/5-10 Closed 25-26 Dec, 1-2 Jan **Prices** Food prices not confirmed for 2010. Please telephone for details. **Wines** 40 bottles over £20, 14 bottles under £20, 11 by glass **Notes** Pre-theatre menu 2 course £15.95 incl glass wine or beer, Sunday L, Vegetarian available, Dress restrictions, Smart casual, no sportswear, Air con **Seats** 140, Pr/dining room 12 **Children** Portions, Menu **Parking** On street

Malmaison Glasgow

◉ Modern French, Scottish

Fine-dining brasserie using locally-sourced produce

☎ 0141 572 1001 🖷 0141 572 1002
278 West George St G2 4LL
e-mail: glasgow@malmaison.com
dir: From George Square take St Vincent Street to Pitt Street. Hotel on corner with West George St

Far removed from its origins as a 19th-century Greek Orthodox church, this member of the boutique hotel chain is full of atmosphere and opulent décor. The stylish restaurant is housed in the vaulted crypt and furnished with smart leather banquettes and chairs and subtle lighting that makes for an intimate setting. First-class regional produce is used to create the traditional Scottish and French dishes on the seasonally-changing à la carte menu and the daily-changing 'home-grown and local' menu. Typical dishes include steamed Fassfern mussels with garlic and black pepper bacon, or slow-roasted shin of beef with winter vegetable cassoulet and horseradish dumplings, and smoked Finnan haddock gratin with boulangère potatoes and mustard sauce.

Chef Graham Digweed **Owner** Malmaison Hotels Ltd **Times** 12-2.30/5.30-10.30 **Prices** Fixed L 2 course £13.50, Fixed D 3 course £15.50, Starter £4.50-£5.75, Main £9.95-£18.50, Dessert £4.95-£8.50, Service added but optional 10%, Groups min 10 service 10% **Wines** 160 bottles over £20, 20 bottles under £20, 20 by glass **Notes** Sunday L, Vegetarian available **Seats** 85, Pr/dining room 22 **Children** Portions, Menu **Parking** Q Park Waterloo St

Michael Caines Restaurant

◉◉ Modern European

High-impact cooking in former prime minister's home

☎ 0141 221 6789 🖷 0141 221 6777
ABode Hotel Glasgow, 129 Bath St G2 2SZ
e-mail: restaurantmanagerglasgow@michaelcaines.com
dir: Please telephone for directions

The ABode group's expansion has done Michael Caines proud, proving that a proliferating hotel chain under a star chef's imprimatur needn't become a recipe for dull standardisation. The Glasgow branch of operations is housed within a hotel that used to be the home of the

continued

GLASGOW *continued*

Edwardian prime minister Sir Henry Campbell-Bannerman. Understated décor in the main, wood-floored dining room includes a glass-fronted wine store. There is nothing understated about the cooking, which aims for big flavour impact and achieves it in dishes such as crab cannelloni with langoustine mayonnaise, poached wild sea bass with scallop and truffle mousse, and Mey beef sirloin with prune purée and wild mushrooms in Madeira.

Chef Craig Dunn **Owner** ABode Hotels
Times 12-2.30/6-10 Closed 1st 2 wks Jan, 14-28 Jul, Sun-Mon **Prices** Fixed L course £12.95, Fixed D 3 course £19.95, Tasting menu £55, Starter £10.50-£12.95, Main £19.50-£23.95, Dessert £7.50, Service added but optional 11% **Wines** 100 bottles over £20, 8 by glass
Notes Tasting menu 7 course, Vegetarian available, Air con **Seats** 40, Pr/dining room 40 **Children** Portions

La Parmigiana

◎◎ Italian, Mediterranean NEW

A taste of classical Italy in cosmopolitan Glasgow

☎ 0141 334 0686 📠 0141 357 5595
447 Great Western Rd G12 8HH
e-mail: sgiovanazzi@btclick.com
dir: Please telephone for directions

This family-run restaurant is located on the vibrant and busy Great Western Road, close to the river. It's an intimate space decked out with dark-wood panelling and deep red paint on the walls. The wonderfully friendly service is in keeping with the traditional style of the operation. The food is classical Italian, prepared with care and attention to detail. Cuttlefish pasta with shellfish, olive oil, parsley and chilli has generous amounts of seafood, while medallions of venison with porcini and Italian sausage, served on chargrilled polenta, is a hearty main course. The wine list is predominantly Italian with some interesting bottles from the less well known wine producing areas.

Chef Peppino Camilli **Owner** Sandro & Stefano Giovanazzi
Times 12-2.30/5.30-10.30 Closed 25-26 Dec, 1 Jan, Sun **Prices** Fixed D 3 course £14.40, Starter £4.20-£10.50, Main £15.30-£24, Dessert £4.95-£7.90, Service optional
Wines 50 bottles over £20, 7 bottles under £20
Notes Pre-theatre 2 courses £15.70, 3 courses £17.80 5.30-7.30pm, Vegetarian available, Air con **Seats** 50 **Children** Portions

Rococo

◎◎ Modern European

Quality cooking in stylish city centre restaurant

☎ 0141 221 5004 📠 0141 221 5006
48 West Regent St G2 2RA
e-mail: res@rococoglasgow.co.uk
dir: City centre

Located in the heart of Glasgow's city centre, Rococo offers modern European food with a firm emphasis on top-notch seasonal, local produce. Terrine of oxtail, potato and watercress with langoustine tartare and horseradish emulsion might feature as a starter on the dinner menu, with perhaps spiced Barbary duck breast with honey-glazed shallots, salsify, minted peas and Madeira jus as a main course. Round things off with a dessert of chocolate parfait with passionfruit and sesame wafers. The more simple lunch and pre-theatre menu is excellent value for money.

Times 12-3/5-10.30 Closed 26 Dec, 1 Jan

Shish Mahal

◎ Modern Indian

Smart Indian restaurant with universal appeal

☎ 0141 339 8256 & 334 7899 📠 0141 572 0800
60-68 Park Rd G4 9JF
e-mail: reservations@shishmahal.co.uk
dir: From M8/A8 take exit towards Dumbarton. On Great Western Rd 1st left into Park Rd

Located in Kelvinbridge, a mainly residential quarter of Glasgow, Shish Mahal remains deservedly popular. Service is from a team in formal black and white, with long, brasserie-style aprons, and the inspired modern Indian food draws influences from many regions. Generously sized dishes include prawn zahrani, in a sweet-and-sour sauce with coconut, lime and fresh chillies, citrussy butter chicken finished with fresh apricot, and tender lamb cooked in fenugreek. Finish with phirnee, a Punjabi pudding of clotted cream, crushed rice and cinnamon, garnished with hazelnuts. Incidentals like naan breads and rice are all up to the mark.

Chef Mr I Humayun **Owner** Ali A Aslam, Nasim Ahmed
Times 12-2/5-11 Closed 25 Dec, L Sun **Prices** Fixed L 3 course £5.50-£7.25, Starter £2.95-£7.50, Main £6.50-£15.95, Dessert £2.50-£3.95, Service optional, Groups min 5 service 10% **Wines** 3 bottles over £20, 13 bottles under £20, 1 by glass **Notes** Fixed L 4 course, Vegetarian

available, Air con **Seats** 95, Pr/dining room 14 **Children** Portions **Parking** Side street, Underground station car park

Stravaigin

◎◎ Modern International

The global larder comes to Glasgow

☎ 0141 334 2665 📠 0141 334 4099
28 Gibson St, Kelvinbridge G12 8NX
e-mail: stravaigin@btinternet.com
web: www.stravaigin.com
dir: Next to Glasgow University. 200yds from Kelvinbridge underground

'Not a tablecloth in sight,' proclaim the owners of this three-storey Glasgow tenement restaurant that combines an informal approach with chic décor. Eat in the bar or the restaurant - or even out on the street in clement weather - and note the same high standards apply throughout. World cuisine is the name of the game, with Far Eastern spices and seasonings especially notable. A fragrant sweet chilli and lemongrass sauce is the medium, therefore, for plump, fresh mussels and chunky bread. Continue the voyage of exploration with a main course of tamari-glazed duck breast with sesame-roast yams, kimchi (Korean preserved veg) and anise gravy, while Belgian chocolate délice with blueberry jelly will wow the chocoholics.

Chef Daniel Blencowe **Owner** Colin Clydesdale
Times 12-3.30/5-11 Closed 25-26 Dec, 1 Jan, L Mon-Thu **Prices** Starter £5.95-£11.95, Main £12.95-£21.95, Dessert £5.95-£7.95, Service optional **Wines** 39 bottles over £20, 17 bottles under £20, 9 by glass **Notes** Sun brunch menus available, Vegetarian available, Air con **Seats** 76 **Children** Portions, Menu **Parking** On street, car park 100yds

Ubiquitous Chip

◎◎ Traditional Scottish

Reliable Scottish cuisine in a unique setting

☎ 0141 334 5007 📠 0141 337 6417
12 Ashton Ln G12 8SJ
e-mail: mail@ubiquitouschip.co.uk
dir: In West End, off Byres Rd. Adjacent to Hillhead
underground station

You might be forgiven for thinking you have taken a
wrong turn and pitched up in the Glasgow Botanic
Gardens on arriving at this constant of the West End
dining scene. The Ubiquitous Chip has been going for
nigh on forty years and the owner's drive to showcase the
very finest Scottish produce remains undimmed. A glass
canopy shelters a cobbled courtyard with a jungly tangle
of greenery beneath a mezzanine gallery, plus there's a
skylit dining room, brasserie and a trio of pubby venues.
The kitchen takes a no-nonsense, fiercely Scottish line
with its output and likes to throw in off-the-wall
combinations - gingerbread and strawberries with
sautéed duck livers - alongside Seil Island crab with salt
and pepper tuiles, saffron and fennel with pastis sauce,
or a game suet pudding with deep-fried cabbage and
sweet potatoes.

Times 12-2.30/5.30-11 Closed 25 Dec, 1 Jan

Urban Bar and Brasserie

◎ Modern French

Contemporary bar-brasserie with food to match

☎ 0141 248 5636 📠 0141 248 5720
23/25 St Vincent Place G1 2DT
e-mail: info@urbanbrasserie.co.uk
dir: In city centre between George Sq & Buchanan St

As banks around the UK have slashed branches, many of
their grandiose buildings have been recycled as
characterful restaurants for lucky diners. Urban Bar and
Brasserie was once a biggie: the erstwhile Scottish HQ of
the Bank of England, no less, is now a stylish modern
restaurant and champagne bar. Beneath soaring ceilings
and a glass skylight, an imposing décor blends
traditional plasterwork and wood panelling with
burnished blond-wood floors, tobacco-brown banquettes
and vibrant modern art on white walls. Not to be outshone
by its surroundings, the kitchen team rises to the
challenge with skilled cooking that delivers clearly-
defined flavours from quality Scottish produce - fish soup
with crabmeat, stem ginger and prawn dumplings for
example, or fillet of sea bass on plum tomato, feta,
prawns and basil.

Chef Derek Marshall, John Gillespie **Owner** Alan Tomkins,
Derek Marshall **Times** 12-5/5-10 Closed 25-26 Dec, 1-2
Jan **Prices** Fixed L 2 course £15.95, Fixed D 3 course
£18.95, Starter £6-£10, Main £12-£22, Dessert £5.95-
£7.50, Groups min 6 service 10% **Wines** 40 bottles over
£20, 20 bottles under £20, 10 by glass **Notes** Pre-theatre
menu 5-6pm £15, Sunday L, Vegetarian available, Air con
Seats 110, Pr/dining room 20 **Children** Portions
Parking NCP West Nile St

HIGHLAND

ABRIACHAN Map 23 NH53

Loch Ness Lodge

◎◎ French, Scottish NEW

Stylish restaurant with stunning Loch Ness views

☎ 01456 459469 📠 01456 459439
Brachia, Loch Ness-Side IV3 8LA
e-mail: escape@lodgeatlochness.com
dir: From S on A9 to 1st rdbt. Follow signs to A82 Fort
William/Loch Ness Rd. On right hand side after Clansman
Hotel. From Airport take A96 to Inverness. At Raigmore
Interchange join A9 north to 1st rdbt. follow signs Fort
William/Loch Ness

This beautifully designed, purpose-built restaurant with
rooms enjoys spectacular views over Loch Ness from its
prominent loch-side position. Money has been lavished on
the interior, with bold colours and a contemporary look,
yet the feel and atmosphere is more country house than
designer-chic. Original artwork, discreet music and
gleaming glassware on immaculate, linen-dressed tables
set the relaxed mood in the modern restaurant. Bag a
window seat if you can and take in the stunning loch
views over a well-executed five-course dinner prepared
from quality seasonal ingredients. The kitchen displays
originality, flair and good technical skills resulting in
imaginative, full-flavoured dishes. Take a delicious brown
crab velouté, which packs a punch with great flavours
and accurate seasoning, a gamey warm salad of wood
pigeon, and an impressive main course of moist and
tender loin and leg of wild hare with garlic crisps and
truffle oil. Dessert, perhaps a rich dark chocolate tart
with prune and Armagnac parfait, follows a plate of
Scottish cheeses.

Chef Ross Fraser **Owner** Scott & Iona Sutherland
Times 7-11.30 Closed 2-31 Jan, L all week (except by
arrangement) **Prices** Food prices not confirmed for 2010.
Please telephone for details, Service optional **Wines** 43
bottles over £20, 2 bottles under £20, 6 by glass
Notes Fixed D 5 course £45, Dress restrictions, Smart
casual, Civ Wed 24 **Seats** 14 **Children** Portions
Parking 10

ACHILTIBUIE Map 22 NC00

The Summer Isles Hotel

◎◎ Modern British

Top-drawer Scottish produce with gorgeous sea views

☎ 01854 622282 📠 01854 622251
IV26 2YG
e-mail: info@summerisleshotel.co.uk
dir: 10m N of Ullapool. Left off A835 onto single track
road. 15m to Achiltibuie. Hotel 100yds after post office on
left

Terry and Irina Mackay purchased the hotel in 2008 from
a family who had run it for over 40 years. They wisely left
well alone when it came to the style and tone of the
place, and the white-fronted house remains a haven of
tranquillity with drop-dead gorgeous sea views. Smart
table settings in the cream-coloured dining room
establish a mood of quiet refinement, and the menus deal
in the top-drawer Scots produce for which Summer Isles
has always been renowned. Dinner might begin with a filo
parcel of monkfish, served with tamarind sauce, and go
on to a pairing of langoustines and spiny lobster, served
whole in the shell with hollandaise. The meat main course
could be roast rib of Aberdeen Angus with wild
mushrooms and red onions, sauced with red wine. Choose
desserts from a trolley, and leave room for the excellent
cheeses.

Times 12.30-2/8 Closed mid Oct-Etr

BOAT OF GARTEN Map 23 NH91

Boat Hotel - The Capercaille

◎◎ Modern Scottish

**Scottish cuisine with a modern twist amid beautiful
Cairngorms scenery**

☎ 01479 831258 📠 01479 831414
Deshar Rd PH24 3BH
e-mail: info@boathotel.co.uk
dir: Turn off A9 N of Aviemore onto A95. Follow signs to
Boat of Garten

You could arrive in period style by steam train on the
Strathspey Railway from Aviemore at this smartly
modernised restaurant in a Victorian station hotel at the
heart of the Cairngorms. As you're in Speyside, a wee
dram from the bar's array of over 80 single malts
wouldn't go amiss before dining in the intimate,
restaurant, where a real fire and dark blue walls hung
with striking modern artwork make for a stylish setting.
The kitchen's line in Scottish cuisine takes the pick of
local produce and prepares it with imagination and
contemporary flair. Well-balanced combinations might
begin with marinated Scottish salmon with poached West
Coast oysters and basil aïoli, followed by an assiette of
Spey Valley pork with buttered spinach, baby turnips and
Madeira jus.

Chef John Dale **Owner** Mr J Erasmus & Mr R Drummond
Times 7-9.30 Closed Dec-Feb (bookings only), L all week
Prices Fixed D 2 course £27-£35, Service optional
Wines 40 bottles over £20, 6 bottles under £20, 4 by
glass **Notes** Tasting menu 7 course, Sunday L, Vegetarian
available, Dress restrictions, No jeans **Seats** 30, Pr/dining
room 40 **Parking** 36

BRORA
Map 23 NC90

Royal Marine Hotel

◎ Modern Scottish

Traditional Highland hotel with reliable cooking

☎ 01408 621252 ▤ 01408 621181
Golf Rd KW9 6QS
e-mail: info@highlandescape.com
dir: off A9 in village towards beach & golf course

With the lovely Highland village of Brora, a renowned golf course and glorious beaches on its doorstep, it's not hard to see what keeps guests coming to this Edwardian country house. It is looking sharp after a smart refurbishment, and you have a choice of 3 dining venues: a café-bar overlooking the pool, a buzzy modern bistro and the formal Lorimer Dining Room, which serves up good wholesome cooking with clear flavours in the modern Scottish idiom. Kick off with an old favourite like Cullen skink, then move on to breast of chicken wrapped in Parma ham with wild mushrooms and asparagus, and end with blueberry and raspberry pannacotta.

Times 12-2/6.30-8.45 Closed L (pre booking only)

CONTIN
Map 23 NH45

Achilty Hotel

◎ Traditional, Mediterranean

Scottish and Mediterranean flavours in former drovers' inn

☎ 01997 421355 ▤ 01997 421923
IV14 9EG
e-mail: info@achiltyhotel.co.uk
dir: A9 N of Inverness onto A835 to Contin. Hotel 0.5m W of village

Surrounded by the stunning Scottish countryside of the north Highlands, this former drovers' inn is a warm and welcoming hotel. Dating back to the 1700s, the attractive open-plan restaurant features high ceilings and stone walls, as well as well-appointed tables and efficient, friendly service. Expect traditional Scottish dishes combined with a Mediterranean influence. So, Cullen skink joins chicken bruschetta among starters, and main courses range from saddle of venison with a rich port and cranberry sauce to monkfish tail poached in white wine and served with spicy tomato sauce and saffron rice.

Times 12-2/5-8.30 Closed L Mon-Tue

Coul House Hotel

◎ Modern Scottish V

Georgian country-house hotel with superb views and ambitious fine dining

☎ 01997 421487 ▤ 01997 421945
IV14 9ES
e-mail: stay@coulhousehotel.com
dir: A835 signed Ullapool, 12m Contin. Hotel drive 100yds on right after petrol station

You can't fail to be impressed by the surroundings when you dine at this classic Georgian country house. The dramatic Octagonal Restaurant is the magnificent centrepiece, while extensive grounds give outstanding views of distant mountains. The lengthy menu offers contemporary Scottish cuisine with classic French overtones, backed up by a biblical wine list. Kick off with dishes such as hickory smoked rabbit saddle, served tender and lightly cooked, with pan-fried gnocchi, before main-course pan-seared sea bass - a fine piece of fish - with a rather complex mêlée of contrasting flavours comprising three pimento mousse, lemon and spinach risotto, tomato and balsamic cappuccino and an artichoke salad with spring onion and chorizo oil.

Chef G Kenley **Owner** Stuart MacPherson
Times 12-2.30/6.30-9 Closed 24-26 Dec **Prices** Starter £4-£10.50, Main £14-£25, Dessert £4-£5.95, Service optional **Wines** 77 bottles over £20, 20 bottles under £20, 9 by glass **Notes** Sunday L, Vegetarian menu, Civ Wed 120 **Seats** 70, Pr/dining room 40 **Children** Portions, Menu **Parking** 60

DORNOCH
Map 23 NH78

Dornoch Castle Hotel

◎ Scottish, Fusion

Modern Scottish brasserie food in a stylishly renovated 15th-century castle

☎ 01862 810216 ▤ 01862 810981
Castle St IV25 3SD
e-mail: enquiries@dornochcastlehotel.com
dir: 2m N of Dornoch Bridge on A9, turn right to Dornoch. Hotel in village centre

Built originally as the bishop's palace for the nearby 12th-century cathedral, Dornoch Castle has been restored over the last decade in a characterful blend of ancient stone walls and classy modern style. The walled castle gardens make a charming backdrop for dining in the purpose-built Garden Restaurant, or the same menu is on offer in the Bishop's kitchen bar, where a roaring log fire in a huge fireplace and exposed 15th-century stone walls give a bit of ye aulde Scotland. The daily menus, however, take a modern Scottish route, offering brasserie-style dishes such as duck confit with chestnut ravioli and warm plum sauce, followed by braised oxtail with parsnip and vanilla purée, roasted shallots and wild mushrooms.

Times 12-3/6-9.30 Closed 25-26 Dec

2 Quail Restaurant & Rooms

◎◎ International

Classic cooking in tiny Highland restaurant

☎ 01862 811811
Inistore House, Castle St IV25 3SN
e-mail: theaa@2quail.com
dir: On main street, 200yds from cathedral

Small is certainly beautiful at this homely restaurant with rooms in the Royal Burgh of Dornoch on the Highland coast. With just three rooms and 12 covers in the restaurant, booking ahead is a wise move, and well worth it for the civilised ambience and accomplished cuisine. Kerensa Carr - one half of the husband-and-wife-team who run 2 Quail with hands-on hospitality - delivers efficient, cheery service in the book-lined dining room, while chef Michael makes everything in-house from the best available locally-sourced ingredients. Three-course dinners might open with Maryland-style crab cake with a pink peppercorn beurre blanc, followed by roast best-end of Dornoch lamb with dauphinoise potatoes, Provençal vegetables and thyme jus. And for dessert, dark chocolate marquise with griottines. There's a serious approach to wine too, with a thoughtful array served by the glass or bottle.

Chef Michael Carr **Owner** Michael and Kerensa Carr
Times 7.30-9.30 Closed Xmas, 2 wks Feb-Mar, Sun-Mon, L all week **Prices** Fixed D 3 course £38, Service optional **Wines** 44 bottles over £20, 2 bottles under £20, 8 by glass **Notes** Vegetarian available, Dress restrictions, Smart casual **Seats** 14 **Parking** On street

FORT AUGUSTUS
Map 23 NH30

The Lovat

◎ Modern Scottish ✿

Intimate bistro-style dining with fine Highland produce and views

☎ 0845 450 1100 & 01456 459250 ▤ 01320 366677
Loch Ness PH32 4DU
e-mail: info@lovatarms-hotel.com
dir: A82 between Fort William & Inverness

The Lovat Arms has much to recommend it: the friendly, family-run Victorian hotel sits above the lochside village of Fort Augustus at the southern point of Loch Ness, where the Caledonian Canal joins at a daunting five-lock 'staircase' amid moody mountain scenery. But this is not a hotel that dwells in Victoriana: while there's plenty of original period charm, the contemporary bistro-style restaurant is revamped with 21st-century style in the form of oak floors, shiny tubular chrome seating, bold colours and low-key lighting. The kitchen chooses carefully from the Highlands' legendary produce - including über-fresh fish and seafood from Mallaig - and its modern Scottish repertoire includes citrus-cured Scottish salmon with ginger and coriander yogurt, followed with roast haunch of venison with braised red cabbage, herb mash and port redcurrant jus.

Chef Colin Clark **Owner** David, Geraldine & Caroline Gregory **Times** 7-9 Closed Hogmany (Jan) - guests only,

Nov-Mar, D Sun-Mon **Prices** Fixed L 3 course £15-£25, Fixed D 3 course £30-£45, Starter £4.25-£7.95, Main £9.95-£22.50, Dessert £5.50-£7.25, Service optional, Groups min 8 service 10% **Wines** 20 bottles over £20, 20 bottles under £20, 10 by glass **Notes** Sunday L, Vegetarian available **Seats** 27, Pr/dining room 50 **Children** Portions, Menu **Parking** 30

FORT WILLIAM   Map 22 NN17

Inverlochy Castle Hotel

◉◉◉ – see below

Lime Tree Hotel & Restaurant

◉ Modern European

Stylish small hotel with art gallery and modern menu

☎ 01397 701806
Lime Tree Studio, Achintore Rd PH33 6RQ
e-mail: info@limetreefortwilliam.co.uk
web: www.limetreefortwilliam.co.uk
dir: Please telephone for directions

This stylish family-owned boutique hotel, restaurant and art gallery has fantastic views of Loch Linnhe and the hills beyond. An old stone manse, it is now fresh and contemporary thanks to the original artwork on display and the chic décor, but real fires and the clever use of natural materials remain as touchstones to the past. The menu is a blend of local ingredients and modern European ideas: Highland lamb 'osso bucco' is made using a gigot of Lochaber lamb leg, slow cooked with orange and bay leaf, served with a creamy parmesan risotto and seasonal vegetables, while local loch mussels are cooked in white wine, fresh herbs, cream and salted kale. Finish with passionfruit soufflé served with lavender ice cream.

Lime Tree Hotel & Restaurant

Chef Ross Sutherland **Owner** David Wilson & Charlotte Wright **Times** 12-2.30/6.30-9 Closed Nov **Prices** Starter £3.95-£5.50, Main £12.50-£30, Dessert £3.95-£5.50, Service optional **Wines** 14 bottles over £20, 17 bottles under £20, 5 by glass **Notes** Sunday L, Vegetarian available, Civ Wed 50 **Seats** 30 **Children** Portions **Parking** 10

Moorings Hotel

◉ Modern, Traditional

Popular Highland hotel with contemporary cooking

☎ 01397 772797 ▤ 01397 772441
Banavie PH33 7LY
e-mail: reservations@moorings-fortwilliam.co.uk
web: www.moorings-fortwilliam.co.uk
dir: From A82 take A830 W for 1m. 1st right over Caledonian Canal on B8004, signed Banavie

The Moorings Hotel has a plum location right on the Caledonian Canal next to the daunting flight of locks known as Neptune's Staircase, with the hump of Ben Nevis as a backdrop. Catch the right time of day and you'll see the Jacobite steam train go past on the way to the fishing port of Mallaig. And at the end of a day's Highland activities, you can settle into the beamed

continued

Inverlochy Castle Hotel

FORT WILLIAM   Map 22 NN17

Modern British V ▤

Fine dining in opulent and historic Scottish building

☎ 01397 702177 ▤ 01397 702953
Torlundy PH33 6SN
e-mail: info@inverlochy.co.uk
dir: 3m N of Fort William on A82, just past Golf Club, N towards Inverness

Built in 1863 by the first Lord Abinger, near the site of the original 13th-century fortress, Inverlochy Castle sits in the foothills of Ben Nevis amidst some of Scotland's finest scenery. Lavishly appointed in classic country-house style, it makes a truly impressive setting for fine dining - aperitifs are taken in the sumptuous lounge or on the terrace on warm sunny days, while dinner is an experience to savour in any of the 3 dining rooms, each with elaborate period furniture and stunning mountain views. Genuine comfort and luxury abound, while service is highly professional but with a relaxed and friendly tone. The kitchen's accomplished modern approach - underpinned by a classical theme - suits the surroundings and makes fine use of the abundant Highland larder, as well as produce from the estate's walled garden, on its repertoire of daily-changing five-course dinner and tasting menus. Expect high-level technical skill and clear flavours in dishes like caramelised scallops with morel tortellini and sweetcorn velouté, followed by cannon of lamb with a chicory and goats' cheese Tatin. There's an excellent wine list, too, with an extensive range of half-bottles to enjoy. Pack your jacket and tie gentlemen, as they are required.

Chef Matthew Gray **Owner** Inverlochy Hotel Ltd **Times** 12.30-1.45/6.30-10 **Prices** Food prices not confirmed for 2010. Please telephone for details. **Wines** 283 bottles over £20, 8 by glass **Notes** Fixed D 4 course, Vegetarian menu, Dress restrictions, Jacket & tie for D, Civ Wed 80 **Seats** 40, Pr/dining room 20 **Children** Portions, Menu **Parking** 20

FORT WILLIAM *continued*

Jacobean Restaurant with a menu of soundly-prepared British and European cuisine built on West Coast seafood and game. Start, perhaps, with West Coast hot-smoked salmon on potato and mustard salad, followed by pan-fried scallops and mallard duck in an orange and grain mustard dressing.

Chef Paul Smith **Owner** Mr S Leitch **Times** 7-9.30 Closed 24-26 Dec, L all week **Prices** Starter £5.10-£8.95, Main £12.95-£21.95, Dessert £5.10-£8.95, Service optional **Wines** 17 bottles over £20, 28 bottles under £20, 4 by glass **Notes** Vegetarian available, Dress restrictions, Smart casual, Civ Wed 120 **Seats** 60, Pr/dining room 120 **Children** Portions **Parking** 50

FOYERS — Map 23 NH42

Craigdarroch House

◉◉ Modern Scottish **NEW V**

Fine dining in idyllically placed country house

☎ 01456 486400 📠 01456 486444
IV2 6XU
e-mail: info@hotel-loch-ness.co.uk
dir: Take B862 from either end of the Loch, then B852 signed Foyers

The house looks across Loch Ness - and the view across the water to the surrounding hills is breathtaking. Inside, the house has plenty of character, with high ceilings, wood-panelling, real fires and a bar stocking around 130 malt whiskies. Dinner is served at 8 with the tables by the windows much in demand, although all of them are handsomely dressed in white linen. The daily-changing fixed-price menu makes good use of the local larder in modern Scottish dishes of some refinement. West Coast scallops (bursting with flavour) and Stornoway black pudding is given an exotic touch with the addition of a mango salsa, while a fine piece of halibut is a star main course. Bread and petits fours are home-made, and vanilla rice pudding with caramelised figs is a memorable dessert.

Chef Martin Donnelly **Owner** Martin & Elinor Donnelly **Times** 8pm **Prices** Food prices not confirmed for 2010. Please telephone for details. **Wines** 51 bottles over £20, 18 bottles under £20, 8 by glass **Notes** Fixed D 5 course £35, Vegetarian menu, Civ Wed 30 **Seats** 18 **Parking** 24

GLENFINNAN — Map 22 NM88

The Prince's House

◉◉ Modern British 🍽

Welcoming old coaching inn with fine Scottish produce

☎ 01397 722246 📠 01397 722323
PH37 4LT
e-mail: princeshouse@glenfinnan.co.uk
dir: From Fort William N on A82 for 2m. Turn left on to A830 Mallaig Rd for 15m to hotel

This charming 17th-century coaching inn sits on the 'Road to the Isles' between Fort William and Mallaig in exactly the sort of romantic mountain and forest Highland landscape that tourists come here for. It is a perfect location, also, for sourcing the very finest fresh fish and seafood, game from surrounding estates and excellent beef and lamb. The kitchen keeps things simple, leaving the quality of the produce to talk for itself. A three-course dinner might feature a pan-seared breast of Highland wood pigeon with baked Portobello mushrooms, port reduction and truffle oil, then baked turbot fillet and Arisaig scallops with braised fennel and West Coast prawn broth. The icing on the cake is the renowned welcome and service in this superbly friendly family-run hotel.

Chef Kieron Kelly **Owner** Kieron & Ina Kelly **Times** 7-9 Closed Xmas, Jan-Feb, Low season - booking only, L all week **Prices** Fixed D 3 course £35-£38, Service included **Wines** 50 bottles over £20, 15 bottles under £20, 8 by glass **Notes** Vegetarian available **Seats** 30 **Children** Portions **Parking** 18

GRANTOWN-ON-SPEY — Map 23 NJ02

The Glass House Restaurant

◉◉ Modern British **V** 🍽

Modern British cooking in conservatory setting

☎ 01479 872980
Grant Rd PH26 3LD
e-mail: info@theglasshouse-grantown.co.uk
dir: Turn off High St between the bank and Co-op into Caravan Park Rd. First left onto Grant Rd, restaurant on left

Tucked away down a quiet back street, this unique glass conservatory restaurant occupies a lovely setting overlooking landscaped gardens. The conservatory is attached to the side of a stone cottage and the light and airy space has a relaxed, informal feel with solid oak tables and chairs, wooden floors and an open fire. The modern British food is dictated by the seasons and local produce, with 4 choices per course. Start with slow-braised gammon, potato and pea terrine wrapped in Parma ham with hawthorn jelly and warm toast and follow it with peppered Highland beef with sautéed king oyster mushrooms, pak choi and new potatoes in soy sauce.

Chef Stephen Robertson **Owner** Stephen and Karen Robertson **Times** 12-1.45/7-9 Closed 2 wks Nov, 1 wk Jan, 25-26 Dec, 1-2 Jan, Mon, L Tue, D Sun **Prices** Fixed L 2 course £15, Starter £3.95-£8.50, Main £17.95-£20.75, Dessert £6.50-£8.50, Service optional **Wines** 14 bottles over £20, 15 bottles under £20, 5 by glass **Notes** Sunday L, Vegetarian menu **Seats** 30 **Children** Portions **Parking** 10

INVERGARRY — Map 22 NH30

Glengarry Castle

◉ Scottish, International

Country-house hotel with traditional cooking in a majestic setting

☎ 01809 501254 📠 01809 501207
PH35 4HW
e-mail: castle@glengarry.net
dir: 1m S of Invergarry on A82

At the heart of the Great Glen in the Highlands, by the side of one of a chain of beautiful lochs, stands the ruined Invergarry Castle, erstwhile family seat of the MacDonell clan. Just a stone's throw from the ruins, the Glengarry Castle Hotel is a mid-Victorian building, owned and run with great care and attention by the MacCallum family. The hotel boasts breath-taking views of Loch Oich, and the cooking is as proudly Scottish as the setting. Start with a richly textured Highland game terrine with port sauce, pause for a soup (perhaps green bean and almond), and then prepare for the main business. Corn-fed chicken suprême with brandy peppercorn sauce is packed with flavour.

Chef John McDonald **Owner** Mr & Mrs MacCallum **Times** 12-1.45/7-8.30 Closed mid Nov to mid Mar, L Mon-Sun **Prices** Food prices not confirmed for 2010. Please telephone for details. **Wines** 32 bottles over £20, 20 bottles under £20, 9 by glass **Notes** Vegetarian available **Seats** 40 **Children** Portions, Menu **Parking** 30

INVERGORDON — Map 23 NH76

Kincraig House Hotel

◉ Modern Scottish

Fine dining in a lovingly restored period house

☎ 01349 852587 📠 01349 852193
IV18 0LF
e-mail: info@kincraig-house-hotel.co.uk
web: www.kincraig-house-hotel.co.uk
dir: Off A9, past Alness towards Tain. Hotel is 0.25m on left past church

Set in its own landscaped grounds with glorious views over the Cromarty Firth and Black Isle, this charming country-house hotel was once the seat of the MacKenzie clan. It retains period features and the fine dining restaurant brims with character, featuring a lovely stone fireplace, deep red walls, immaculately dressed linen-clothed tables and superb views. Modern Scottish cooking is accurate and honest with good use of quality local produce evident in such dishes as steamed mussels and surf clams in a spicy tomato and chorizo sauce, Black Isle lamb on Puy lentils with rosemary jus, and chocolate mocha cups with Chantilly cream. Informal meals are served in the bar.

Chef Mikael Helies **Owner** Kevin Wickman
Times 12.30-2/6.45-9 **Prices** Fixed D 3 course £29.50, Service optional **Wines** 29 bottles over £20, 23 bottles under £20, 4 by glass **Notes** Sunday L, Dress restrictions, Smart casual, Civ Wed 50 **Seats** 30, Pr/dining room 40 **Children** Portions, Menu **Parking** 40

INVERNESS	Map 23 NH64

Abstract Restaurant & Bar

◉◉◉ – *see below*

Bunchrew House Hotel

◉◉ Modern, Traditional

Scottish and European cooking in beautiful setting

☎ 01463 234917   📠 01463 710620
Bunchrew IV3 8TA
e-mail: welcome@bunchrew-inverness.co.uk
dir: 3m W of Inverness on A862 towards Beauly

On the shores of the Beauly Firth, this imposing 17th-century Scottish baronial mansion sits in 20 acres of woodland and landscaped gardens. The carefully restored and upgraded house is steeped in history and has a timeless atmosphere. Its wood-panelled restaurant has magnificent views over the water to the mountains beyond - book ahead for a window table and the chance to see a stunning summer sunset. The cooking is a fusion of Scottish and European styles, using the best the Highland larder can offer, distinguished by accomplished technique. Typical dishes may include pink breast of woodland pigeon, spiced couscous with a Madeira sauce to start, with prime roast fillet of finest Scottish beef, pomme fondant, asparagus, sweet potato ribbons and wild mushroom gratin to follow.

Chef Walter Walker **Owner** Terry & Irina Mackay
Times 12-1.45/7-9 Closed 23-26 Dec **Prices** Fixed L 2 course £25.50, Fixed D 2 course £41.50, Service optional **Wines** 4 by glass **Notes** Sunday L, Vegetarian available, Civ Wed 92 **Seats** 32, Pr/dining room 14 **Children** Portions, Menu **Parking** 40

Culloden House Hotel

◉◉ Modern Scottish

Serious Scottish cuisine in historic setting

☎ 01463 790461   📠 01463 792181
Culloden IV2 7BZ
e-mail: info@cullodenhouse.co.uk
dir: From A96 left turn at junction of Balloch, Culloden, Smithton. 2m, hotel on right

This grand Palladian mansion of brick and stone exudes a genuine sense of occasion and history. It was, after all, where Bonnie Prince Charlie spent the night before his hopes and ambitions were definitively crushed at the battle of Culloden in 1746. Despite the palatial grandeur of its crystal chandeliers and soaring ceilings, Adam fireplaces and fancy plasterwork, amicable staff make Culloden House an inviting place. Scottish produce takes centre stage in four-course dinners amid the awe-inspiring grandeur of the Adam dining room. Classic dishes strewn with luxury produce kick off with lobster ravioli with truffle cream and chervil oil; an intermediate course of chilled asparagus soup with black truffle oil and parmesan crisp is slotted in before mains weigh in with tournedos of Scottish beef fillet, with shin and barley croquette and braising jus. Dessert ends with a thoroughly Scottish Drambuie parfait, shortbread wafer and raspberry sorbet.

continued

Abstract Restaurant & Bar

INVERNESS	Map 23 NH64

Modern French V ◉

Refined French dining in elegant townhouse hotel

☎ 01463 223777   📠 01463 712378
Glenmoriston Town House Hotel, 20 Ness Bank IV2 4SF
e-mail: reception@glenmoristontownhouse.com
web: www.glenmoristontownhouse.com
dir: 2 mins from city centre, on river opposite theatre

Abstract occupies the ground floor of the stylish Glenmoriston Town House Hotel on the banks of the River Ness. A slick piano bar with a mind-bending array of malts sets the tone for the smooth contemporary look of the dining room, where moody lighting falls on textures of wood and leather amid a scene of chic minimal elegance. The food is inventive stuff, driven by sharp classical technique; the finest, freshest Scottish materials get cutting-edge modern French treatment. Unusual flavour pairings are a hallmark of the kitchen's creative flair, but there's nothing outlandish here - just clever, well-balanced dishes. Served only at the chef's table, the eight-course tasting menu delivers Black Isle roe deer, served as a spring roll of shoulder and smoked fillet with butternut squash mousse and orange caramel. The carte might start with seared squid and pig's head terrine with parsley froth and smoked herring caviar, followed by halibut cooked in olive oil with parsnip and vanilla purée and razor clams. Desserts are complex collages such as a riff on coffee comprising coffee bean bavarois, Kahlua jelly and cappuccino foam, and black coffee ice cream. France is foremost on an impressive wine list and the less formal 'Contrast' is the hotel's bistro-style alternative.

Chef Geoffrey Malmedy **Owner** Larsen & Ross South
Times 6-10 Closed 26-28 Dec, Sun-Mon, L all week **Prices** Tasting menu £50, Starter £10-£14.50, Main £16-£25, Dessert £8-£10, Service optional, Groups min 6 service 12.5% **Wines** 90% bottles over £20, 10% bottles under £20, 11 by glass **Notes** Tasting menu 8 course (served at 6-seater chef's table), Vegetarian menu, Civ Wed 100 **Seats** 50, Pr/dining room 15 **Children** Portions, Menu **Parking** 50

INVERNESS *continued*

Chef Michael Simpson **Owner** Culloden House Ltd
Times 12.30-2/7-9 Closed 25-26 Dec **Prices** Fixed D 3
course £40, Starter £7.50-£13.50, Main £17.50-£28.50,
Dessert £7.80-£8.50, Service optional **Wines** 76 bottles
over £20, 8 by glass **Notes** Sunday L, Vegetarian
available, Dress restrictions, Smart casual, Civ Wed 65
Seats 50, Pr/dining room 17 **Children** Portions
Parking 50

The Drumossie Hotel

◎◎ Modern Scottish

**Art deco country-house hotel producing high-quality
food**

☎ 01463 236451 ▤ 01463 712858
Old Perth Rd IV2 5BE
e-mail: stay@drumossiehotel.co.uk
dir: Please telephone for directions

Overlooking the Moray Firth from a hillside just south of
Inverness, this shipshape art deco building has a classy
country-house feel blending old-style clubby refinement
with modern design. The elegant Grill Room restaurant is
as well turned out as its dinner-suited maître d' and
black-aproned staff, who serve with an edge of formality
that suits the setting. The kitchen has a serious approach
to its work, starting with meticulous sourcing of Scottish
materials and excellent attention to detail in its modern
Scottish repertoire. Orkney scallops with Arbroath smokie
potato cake is a fine way to begin, then perhaps free
range chicken with sun-blushed tomato and Stornoway
black pudding or, from the grill, rib-eye steak.

Chef Lynsey Horne **Owner** Ness Valley Leisure
Times 12.30-2/7-9.30 **Prices** Food prices not confirmed
for 2010. Please telephone for details. **Wines** 10 by glass
Notes Vegetarian available, Civ Wed 400, Air con
Seats 90, Pr/dining room 500 **Children** Portions, Menu
Parking 200

Riverhouse

◎ British

Informal dining on banks of the River Ness

☎ 01463 222033
1 Greig St IV3 5PT
e-mail: riverhouse.restaurant@unicombox.co.uk
dir: On corner of Huntly St & Greig St

Close to the city centre and the main shopping district,
this intimate bistro-style restaurant occupies a lovely
spot on the banks of the River Ness. The wood-panelled
interior has an intimate atmosphere, and from here you
can watch the chefs at work in the open kitchen. Classic
dishes are simply prepared using quality produce. A
starter of Orkney crab cakes with watercress salad and a
lemon, dill and natural yogurt dressing might be followed
by pan-seared fillet of line caught sea bass with potato,
garlic and saffron broth. Finish with a classic bread-and-
butter pudding.

Times 12-2.15/5.30-10 Closed Mon, L Sun

Rocpool

◎◎ Modern European

Sleek design and eclectic, stylish cooking

☎ 01463 717274
1 Ness Walk IV3 5NE
e-mail: info@rocpoolrestaurant.com
web: www.rocpoolrestaurant.com
dir: Please telephone for details

Since it opened in 2002, Rocpool has brought stylish
modern eating to the tranquil Highland city of Inverness.
Sitting on a corner site on the west bank of the Ness, the
restaurant boasts sleek, smart décor and the kind of buzz
that draws in an appreciative, quality-conscious crowd.
Modern European cooking blends influences from all over,
perhaps serving emperor prawns and calamari with pak
choi, chorizo and chilli jam, or scallops with duck confit
and pineapple carpaccio, to start. Presentations aren't
always so involved - a main course of simply grilled
turbot is a delight - but when they are, they nonetheless
work well. Treat yourself at dessert stage to something

like the sensuous dark chocolate tart with prune and
Armagnac sorbet.

Chef Steven Devlin **Owner** Mr Devlin
Times 12-2.30/5.45-10 Closed 25-26 Dec, 1-2 Jan, Sun
Oct-Mar, L Sun Apr-Sep **Prices** Fixed L 2 course fr £10.95,
Starter £3.95-£8.95, Main £8.95-£19.95, Dessert £4.95-
£5.95, Service optional **Wines** 25 bottles over £20, 17
bottles under £20, 11 by glass **Notes** Early D
5.45-6.45pm 2 course £12.95, Vegetarian available, Air
con **Seats** 55 **Children** Portions **Parking** On street

KINGUSSIE   Map 23 NH70

The Cross at Kingussie

◎◎◎ – *see opposite page*

KYLE OF LOCHALSH   Map 22 NG72

The Waterside Seafood Restaurant

◎ Modern, Traditional Seafood ◔

Quirky setting for fresh seafood and stunning views

☎ 01599 534813 & 577230
Railway Station Buildings, Station Rd IV40 8AE
e-mail: seafoodrestaurant@btinternet.com
dir: Off A87

The view from your table is reason enough to visit the
MacRae family's restaurant at the end of the pier. Housed
in a former railway building, it looks out towards the Skye
Bridge in one direction and up Loch Duich in the other.
The interior is simply furnished and the menu follows the
same, uncomplicated theme. It's all about the fruits of
the local waters, cooked at their freshest and thus
without the need for much in the way of embellishment.
Kick off with a plate of Skye oysters or the baked crab,
followed by Stromeferry queen scallops or Isle of Skye
salmon fillet with a red pepper crust.

Chef Jann MacRae **Owner** Jann MacRae
Times 11-3/5-9.30 Closed end Oct-beginning Mar, Sun
(please phone to confirm opening hrs) **Prices** Food prices
not confirmed for 2010. Please telephone for details.
Wines 2 bottles over £20, 15 bottles under £20, 2 by
glass **Notes** Vegetarian available **Seats** 35
Children Portions **Parking** 5

The Cross at Kingussie

KINGUSSIE Map 23 NH70

Modern Scottish

Top-notch restaurant with rooms in an idyllic setting

☎ 01540 661166 📄 01540 661080
**Tweed Mill Brae, Ardbroilach Rd
PH21 1LB**
e-mail: relax@thecross.co.uk
dir: From lights in Kingussie centre along Ardbroilach Rd, 300yds left onto Tweed Mill Brae

The Cross at Kingussie was once a textile mill, but there's nothing tweedy about David and Katie Young's classy restaurant with rooms. Four idyllic acres of grounds and woodland are home to red squirrels, abundant birds and wild flowers, and the Gynack Burn bubbles by an alfresco terrace that is the perfect place to de-stress with a glass of bubbly before dinner. It is hard to fault the Cross: the stone building has been beautifully restored and manages to be tasteful, relaxed and utterly without pretension. Rough stone walls and heavy beams blend seamlessly with modern artworks and natural wood tables with quality glassware in the spacious dining room. The food is both fabulous and unfussy in keeping with its surroundings. Wild mushrooms are foraged locally and Scotland's finest materials are showcased in compact daily-changing menus of modern Scottish dishes. A terrine of organic Highland chicken with prosciutto and fig chutney shows the kitchen's well-balanced, uncluttered approach to flavour combinations. Main courses might offer a baked whole Scrabster lemon sole with wild mushrooms, marsh samphire, spring truffle and purple eye potato cake. Dark chocolate and pear tart with liquorice ice cream makes an exemplary finale. The wine list balances serious quality with fair pricing, and the service and hospitality are a template for how things should be done.

Chef Becca Henderson, David Young
Owner David & Katie Young
Times 7-8.30 Closed Xmas & Jan (excl New Year), Sun-Mon, L all week
Prices Fixed D 4 course £50-£55, Service included, Groups min 6 service 10% **Wines** 200 bottles over £20, 20 bottles under £20, 4 by glass
Notes Vegetarian available **Seats** 20
Parking 12

The Boath House

Modern French, Traditional Scottish

Stunning food and effortless service in small country-house hotel

☎ 01667 454896 📄 01667 455469
Auldearn IV12 5TE
e-mail: wendy@boath-house.com
dir: 2m E of Nairn on A96 (Inverness to Aberdeen road)

There's a real sense of occasion when you dine at this magnificent Regency house. A crunchy gravel drive leads to one of Scotland's most special small hotels, a lovingly restored mansion in 20 acres of mature woodlands with an ornamental lake stocked with brown and rainbow trout - you can even have a mini safari in the grounds spotting badgers and roe deer. Owners Don and Wendy Matheson break the ice quickly with their chatty, hands-on enthusiasm and they have packed their elegant lounges and dining room with colourful ceramics, sculpture and vibrant paintings - in fact Boath is designated an art gallery and showcases works by many contemporary Highland artists. In the stylish, candlelit dining room, comfy high-backed chairs look through expansive French windows over the gardens and lake - you may even see trout jumping as you settle in for a six-course dinner. After all, interior splendour aside, one of the main attractions here is chef Charles

Lockley's inspired cooking. 'Let the ingredients do the talking' is the kitchen's ethos, but top-level technical skills founded on classics, backed by lively imagination and a virtuoso grasp of what works with what, and why, doesn't go amiss either. Ingredients are sourced from the finest Scottish producers, and the walled garden does its bit in contributing organic fruit, herbs, vegetables and honey from the hotel's own hives. Curt menu descriptions do little justice to what arrives on the plate. Cured scallops might turn up with truffles and salsify; pork belly is teamed with chorizo and apple, and John Dory is accompanied by rice, crab and crosne (Japanese artichoke). Scottish artisanal cheeses arrive the French way before pudding, which might be white chocolate and tonka mousse with madeleines. If you want to really go to town, stay over in one of the six tasteful bedrooms and pamper yourself with a spa treatment.

Chef Charles Lockley **Owner** Mr & Mrs D Matheson **Times** 12.30-1.45/7-7.30 Closed Xmas, L Mon-Wed **Prices** Fixed L 2 course £21, Service included **Wines** 153 bottles over £20, 5 bottles under £20, 7 by glass **Notes** Fixed D 6 course £65, Sunday L, Dress restrictions, Smart casual, no shorts/T-shirts/jeans, Civ Wed 30 **Seats** 28, Pr/dining room 8 **Children** Portions **Parking** 25

LOCHINVER
Map 22 NC02

Inver Lodge

@@ Modern British

Relaxed, imaginative fine dining in wonderful location

☎ 01571 844496 · 01571 844395
IV27 4LU
e-mail: stay@inverlodge.com
dir: A835 to Lochinver, left at village hall, private road for 0.5m

Secreted away in a far corner of the Highlands, this quality modern hotel's restaurant has spectacular views over a small harbour and the ocean beyond, and, on a clear day, even the Western Isles can be seen through its big picture windows. The accomplished kitchen makes full use of the abundant local larder, including freshly landed fish, and, from the land, perhaps Highland lamb, maybe appearing on the daily-changing menu as a roast rump, served with horseradish mash, wild mushrooms and a port wine glaze. Sea bass might feature as the offering from the sea, perhaps pan-fried and teamed with courgette spaghetti and a shellfish bisque.

Chef Peter Cullen **Owner** Robin Vestey **Times** 7-9 Closed Nov-Mar, L Mon-Sun **Prices** Fixed D 2 course £30, Fixed D 4 course £50, Service included **Wines** 23 bottles over £20, 41 bottles under £20, 5 by glass **Notes** Vegetarian available, Dress restrictions, No jeans, shorts, tracksuit trousers, Civ Wed 60 **Seats** 50 **Children** Portions **Parking** 30

MUIR OF ORD
Map 23 NH55

Ord House Hotel

@ Traditional British, French

Country-house comforts and fresh local produce

☎ 01463 870492 · 01463 870297
IV6 7UH
e-mail: admin@ord-house.co.uk
dir: off A9 at Tore rdbt onto A832. 5m, through Muir of Ord. Left towards Ullapool (A832). Hotel 0.5m on left

The 17th-century seat of the Lairds of the Clan McKenzie has been well-established as a comfortable country-house hotel for 40 years. The estate stretches to 60 acres of gardens and woodlands - plenty of room to supply the kitchen with fresh vegetables, herbs and fruit. Husband-and-wife-team John and Eliza Allen have taken the traditional route with their elegant hotel, and the kitchen stays in step, with simple country-house classics prepared from fresh, local, seasonal produce. Pan-seared scallops with ginger, basil and lime or West Coast oysters are typical starters, while local salmon in whisky and mushroom sauce to follow. Comforting desserts include sticky gingerbread pudding with ginger wine and brandy sauce.

Chef Eliza Allen **Owner** Eliza & John Allen **Times** 7-9 Closed Nov-end Feb **Prices** Fixed D 3 course £28, Starter £7-£12, Main £15-£24, Dessert £4.50-£8, Service included **Wines** 14 bottles over £20, 18 bottles under £20, 4 by glass **Notes** Vegetarian available **Seats** 26 **Children** Portions **Parking** 24

NAIRN
Map 23 NH85

The Boath House

@@@@ – *see opposite page*

Golf View Hotel & Leisure Club

@ Modern NEW V

Fine dining in hotel with sea views

☎ 01667 452301 · 01667 455267
Seabank Rd IV12 4HD
e-mail: golfview@crerarhotels.com
dir: Off A96 into Seabank Rd & continue to end

Located on the coast overlooking the Moray Firth, the Golf View will not only satisfy lovers of the game - strolling along the sandy beaches and enjoying the stunning views across to the Black Isle has universal appeal. The hotel has plenty of period detail, as does the comfortable restaurant, making a charming setting for some serious fine dining. Attentive staff help set the formal tone. The modern Scottish cooking is underpinned by traditional French influences but local produce is the cornerstone of the kitchen; start with pressed Roxburghshire rabbit terrine and beetroot chutney and move on to roasted saddle of Highland venison with parsnip purée, braised root vegetable hotpot and juniper sauce.

Chef Lee Pattie **Owner** Crerar Hotels **Times** 6.45-9 Closed L Mon-Sat **Prices** Fixed D 3 course £29-£34.50, Service optional **Wines** 22 bottles over £20, 23 bottles under £20, 8 by glass **Notes** Sunday L, Vegetarian menu, Dress restrictions, Smart casual, Air con **Seats** 50 **Children** Portions, Menu **Parking** 30, & next to hotel on street

Newton Hotel

@ Traditional European

Enjoyable food in hotel with famous former guests

☎ 01667 453144 · 01667 454026
Inverness Rd IV12 4RX
e-mail: salesnewton@ohiml.com
dir: A96 from Inverness to Nairn. In Nairn hotel signed on left

Once a house and farm, the Newton Hotel dates from 1640 and past guests include Harold Macmillan and Charlie Chaplin who used to take over the entire second floor with his family and staff for three-week holidays. Today's visitor can choose from the traditional restaurant or the more contemporary bistro. The cooking style is traditional, as reflected in starters like black pudding and haggis croquettes or smoked haddock and potato soup, while main courses feature a selection of steaks from the grill, plus something like pan-fried venison and beef fillet on potato rösti with wild berry red wine jus.

Times 12-2.30/6-9

NETHY BRIDGE
Map 23 NJ02

The Restaurant at The Mountview Hotel

@@ Modern British ♨

Highland retreat with scenery as appetising as the cooking

☎ 01479 821248 · 01479 821515
Grantown Rd PH25 3EB
e-mail: info@mountviewhotel.co.uk
dir: From Aviemore follow signs for Nethy Bridge, through Boat-of-Garten. In Nethy Bridge over humpback bridge & follow hotel signs

Set amid the ravishing scenery of the Cairngorms, alongside a forest of Caledonian pines, a little to the south of the whisky town of Grantown-on-Spey, the Mountview makes the most of its location. Views are dramatic, and the interiors have bags of character. A cosy lounge has a real fire to ward off the Highland chill, and the dining room has quality table settings and a menu of fine contemporary Scottish cuisine. A twice-baked soufflé of Isle of Mull cheddar is garnished with spinach as a starter, and main-course rack of new season's lamb is pinkly roasted and bursting with flavour, served with duchess potatoes, baby carrots and garlic confit. Finish with textbook chocolate fondant, its molten centre deep and rich, alongside impressive vanilla ice cream.

Chef Lee Beale **Owner** Kevin & Caryl Shaw **Times** 12-2/6-11 Closed 25-26 Dec, Mon-Tue, L Mon-Sat **Prices** Starter £4.50-£7.50, Main £12.50-£21, Dessert £5.25-£7.50, Service optional **Wines** 4 bottles over £20, 14 bottles under £20, 4 by glass **Notes** Sunday L, Vegetarian available **Seats** 24 **Children** Portions, Menu **Parking** 20

ONICH
Map 22 NN06

The Restaurant at The Onich Hotel

@ Traditional Scottish

Fine Scottish food and stunning loch views

☎ 01855 821214 · 01855 821484
PH33 6RY
e-mail: enquiries@onich-fortwilliam.co.uk
dir: Beside A82, 2m N of Ballachulish Bridge

On the shores of Loch Linnhe, this friendly hotel offers wonderful views across its beautifully landscaped gardens to the water and mountains beyond. The cocktail bar, sun lounge and restaurant all enjoy panoramic views of the loch. The kitchen's style displays a lightness of touch, using local Scottish produce and herbs and salad from the hotel's own garden to good effect. West Coast seafood and Highland game regularly feature on the restaurant menu. Expect the likes of carpaccio of peppered Lochaber venison served on a bed of rocket leaves dressed with balsamic vinegar and crème fraîche, followed by poached smoked West Coast haddock fillet with chive mash, seasonal roasted vegetables and a tomato velouté.

continued

ONICH *continued*

Chef Graeme Kennedy **Owner** Mr S Leitch **Times** 7-9 Closed Xmas, L all week **Prices** Fixed D 3 course £25-£28, Starter £3.75-£6.95, Main £11.95-£17.95, Dessert £4.25-£6.95 **Notes** Vegetarian available, Civ Wed 150 **Seats** 50, Pr/dining room 120 **Children** Portions, Menu **Parking** 50

SHIEL BRIDGE Map 22 NG91

Grants at Craigellachie

Modern Scottish NEW

Beautiful setting for bold Scottish flavours

☎ 01599 511331
Craigellachie, Ratagan IV40 8HP
e-mail: info@housebytheloch.co.uk
dir: A87 to Glenelg, 1st right to Ratagan opposite the Youth Hostel sign

The sound of birdsong or a bit of background jazz is all you will hear out in the rural splendour of Craigellachie, while views over Loch Duich and the Five Sisters mountains are a feast for the eyes. The dining room is in the conservatory at the back of this white-painted house and, although a small space, tables are smartly and rather elegantly appointed. The magnificent local larder is well used in bold, modern Scottish dishes: cannelloni is filled with shredded goose, and knuckle of veal comes with a sweet, vine-ripened tomato sauce, while hogget (year-old sheep), full of flavour, is served with fondant potato and ratatouille. Finish with crumble and full-cream custard.

Chef Tony Taylor **Owner** Tony & Liz Taylor **Times** 7-11 Closed mid Nov-mid Feb, L all week **Prices** Fixed D 4 course fr £38.50, Starter £6-£10, Main £13-£28, Dessert £6-£10, Service optional **Wines** 42 bottles over £20, 16 bottles under £20, 5 by glass **Notes** Restaurant open only by reservation, Vegetarian available **Seats** 14 **Children** Portions

---

SHIELDAIG Map 22 NG85

Tigh an Eilean Hotel Restaurant

Modern Scottish

Innovative cooking in a lochside inn

☎ 01520 755251   📠 01520 755321
IV54 8XN
e-mail: tighaneilean@keme.co.uk
dir: From A896 follow signs for Shieldaig. Hotel in village centre on water's edge

The vista alone is worth the journey to Chris and Cathryn Field's small white-painted hotel in the fishing village of Shieldaig. Sitting on the edge of Loch Torridon, the hotel, which was built around 1800, has stunning views across the water from its light and airy dining room. Chris's modern Scottish cuisine with French and Spanish influences offers exciting, accurately prepared dishes where nothing is more important than flavour. Daily-changing dinner menus rely on local produce, including seafood delivered directly from the village jetty to the

kitchen door. Start with Shieldaig spiny lobsters with a rose de mai sauce and home-made melon sorbet, following on, perhaps, with medallion of fillet of Highland beef with ceps, olive and manchego butter sauce and Pedro Ximenez. Fresh apricot tart served warm with a chilled crème anglaise makes a fitting finale. Slightly more straightforward dishes are served in the refurbished bar, now renamed the Shieldaig Bar and Coastal Kitchen.

Times 7-9 Closed end Oct-mid Mar (except private booking), L all week

---

SPEAN BRIDGE Map 22 NN28

Russell's at Smiddy House

Modern Scottish

Good cooking in friendly Highland hotel

☎ 01397 712335   📠 01397 712043
Roy Bridge Rd PH34 4EU
e-mail: enquiry@smiddyhouse.co.uk
dir: In village centre, 9m N of Fort William, on A82 towards Inverness

Spean Bridge in the Great Glen occupies pole position for taking on Ben Nevis and generally testing yourself against terrain where World War Two commandos once trained. All that fresh-air exertion should sharpen the appetite for the accomplished cuisine on offer in this convivial restaurant in the 'Smiddyhouse' - once the village blacksmith's. It's an intimate spot when candlelight twinkles off the glasses, fine china and silver cutlery, and the kitchen makes sure that local ingredients are to the fore on a regularly-changing menu. Start with local peat-smoked salmon and potato pancake with lemon and chive crème fraîche dressing, then pan-fried venison with haggis, turnip and grain mustard sauce. Don't miss plum and ginger pudding with warm toffee sauce to finish.

Chef Glen Russell **Owner** Glen Russell, Robert Bryson **Times** 6-9 Closed 2 days a week (Nov-Apr), L all week **Prices** Fixed D 3 course £29.95-£36.95, Service optional **Wines** 21 bottles over £20, 11 bottles under £20, 5 by glass **Notes** Vegetarian available, Dress restrictions, Smart casual **Seats** 38 **Children** Portions, Menu **Parking** 15

STRONTIAN Map 22 NM86

Kilcamb Lodge Hotel & Restaurant

Modern European V

Creative cooking in peaceful lochside setting

☎ 01967 402257   📠 01967 402041
PH36 4HY
e-mail: enquiries@kilcamblodge.co.uk
dir: Take Corran ferry off A82. Follow A861 to Strontian. 1st left over bridge after village

Whilst strolling in the peaceful 22 acres of meadow and woodland on the shores of Loch Sunart, it's sobering to think that this tranquil retreat was a military barracks around the time of the Jacobite uprising. Thought to be one of the oldest stone houses in Scotland, Kilcamb Lodge is now a luxurious country-house hotel. The intimate restaurant in warm shades of pink and red offers a mix of modern European dishes, with great attention shown to clarity of flavours and constructions erring on the side of intelligent simplicity. Fresh local produce, in particular fish and shellfish caught at the bottom of the garden, is cooked with flair and imagination. A four-course dinner might start with ham hough terrine with apple compôte and rosemary brioche, before goats' cheese petits fours with beetroot carpaccio, and then the main course, perhaps roasted fillet of beef and braised oxtail with pickled onions and carrots, and some farmhouse cheeses as an alternative to dessert.

Chef Tammo Siemers **Owner** Sally & David Fox **Times** 12-1.30/7.30-9.30 Closed 1 Jan-1 Feb **Prices** Fixed L course £14.75, Fixed D 4 course £48, Service optional, Groups min 10 service 10% **Wines** 45 bottles over £20, 20 bottles under £20, 10 by glass **Notes** Chef's tasting menu available Fri & Sat, Sunday L, Vegetarian menu, Dress restrictions, Smart casual, no jeans, T-shirts or trainers, Civ Wed 60 **Seats** 26 **Parking** 28

Glenmorangie Highland Home at Cadboll

◎◎ French, International

House party-style dining in Highland hideaway

☎ 01862 871671 📠 01862 871625
Cadboll, Fearn IV20 1XP
e-mail: relax@glenmorangie.co.uk
dir: N on A9, at Nigg Rdbt turn right onto B9175 (before Tain) & follow signs for hotel

Overlooking the unspoilt shores of the Dornoch Firth, this remote Highland home is owned by the Glenmorangie whisky company. Formed from a 17th-century farmhouse and an 18th-century castle, this splendid hideaway has its own beach, plus walled orchards and gardens which provide produce for the house. Expect to dine house-party style, at one long table, after introductions in the drawing room over drinks. Impressive cuisine capitalises on wonderful local produce, including fresh seafood and venison from neighbouring estates. Dinner is a six-course meal (with just one choice at an interim course), produced by classically trained chefs. Expect the likes of lightly-spiced local scallops with herb potato pancake, whisky marinated smoked salmon and pimento sauce, followed by seared breast of duck with dauphinoise potatoes, wilted spinach, poached pear, confit of vegetables and port wine sauce.

Chef David Graham **Owner** Glenmorangie Ltd **Times** 8pm Closed 23-26 Dec, 4-27 Jan, L all week (except by prior arrangement) **Prices** Food prices not confirmed for 2010. Please telephone for details, Service added but optional **Wines** 38 bottles over £20, 5 bottles under £20, 15 by glass **Notes** Fixed D 5 course £50, Sunday L, Dress restrictions, Smart casual, no jeans or T-shirts, Civ Wed 60 **Seats** 30, Pr/dining room 12 **Children** Portions **Parking** 60

Forss House Hotel & Restaurant

◎ Modern Scottish 🌱

Elegant dining in spectacular Highland surroundings

☎ 01847 861201 📠 01847 861301
Forss KW14 7XY
e-mail: anne@forsshousehotel.co.uk
dir: On A836, 5m outside Thurso

Fans of the great outdoors will find no fault with this 200 year-old shooting lodge, hidden away in a wooded glen below a waterfall. Smartly refurbished in a plush country-house style, Forss House Hotel is the ideal base for fishing, hunting, hiking and golfing. When the day's exertions are done, the romantic dining room comes complete with an elegant Adams fireplace and idyllic view of the winding River Forss. Straightforward modern Scottish dishes use top-class ingredients from the rivers, coastline and estates all around. Try the Orkney scallops with braised pork cheek, radish and apple salad and curried vinaigrette, followed by roast loin of Berriedale venison with root vegetables, fig compôte and dauphinoise potatoes.

Chef Kevin Dalgleish, Gary Leishman **Owner** Ian & Sabine Richards **Times** 7-9 Closed 23 Dec-4 Jan, L All week **Prices** Food prices not confirmed for 2010. Please telephone for details. **Wines** 26 bottles over £20, 9 bottles under £20, 4 by glass **Notes** Vegetarian available **Seats** 26, Pr/dining room 14 **Children** Portions **Parking** 14

See advert below

Ben Loyal Hotel

◎ Modern, Traditional

Sound Scottish cooking in magnificent location

☎ 01847 611216 📠 01847 611212
Main St IV27 4XE
e-mail: benloyalhotel@btinternet.com
dir: In village centre at junction of A836 & A838

Located in the centre of Tongue, this hotel enjoys outstanding views over the unspoiled Sutherland landscape and is the perfect place from which to explore the northern Highlands. The relaxed restaurant has picture windows that overlook the Kyle of Tongue, Ben Loyal, Ben Hope and the ruin of Castle Varrich that sits on the hill line opposite. Alongside informal, friendly service, quality, simply prepared and presented food is offered with an emphasis on local Scottish produce, particularly seafood. A traditional starter of haggis, neeps and tatties with whisky cream sauce might be followed by pan-seared wild Alaskan salmon fillet, crushed new potatoes, thyme-infused peas and caper beurre blanc. Finish with cranachan trifle.

Chef Neil Keevil **Owner** Mr & Mrs P Lewis **Times** 12-2.15/6-8.15 Closed 30 Nov-1 Mar **Prices** Starter £3.50-£11.50, Main £8.50-£16.50, Dessert £5.50, Service optional **Wines** All bottles under £20, 4 by glass **Notes** Vegetarian available **Seats** 50 **Children** Portions, Menu **Parking** 20, plus opposite hotel & on main street

TONGUE *continued*

Borgie Lodge Hotel

Modern British

Seasonal cooking in secluded Highland hotel

☎ 01641 521332 📠 01641 521889
Skerray KW14 7TH
e-mail: info@borgielodgehotel.co.uk
web: www.borgielodgehotel.co.uk
dir: 0.5m off A836 6m from Tongue

Located in a quiet, secluded Highland glen on the banks of the beautiful River Borgie in North Sutherland, this Victorian sporting lodge continues to provide a welcome retreat for today's sportsmen, particularly anglers. There's a relaxed and friendly atmosphere in the cosy lounge and bar, where you can settle down by the fire and listen to tales about 'the one that got away'. A skilful kitchen makes good use of local produce in modern British and Scottish dishes. The concise menu changes daily depending on what's in season, but might include pickled herring with dressed leaves and herb oil, followed by fillet of Caithness beef with rösti potato, sautéed pak choi and field mushrooms, with warm apricot and almond tart to finish.

Times 12-2/7-8.30 Closed 25 Dec

TORRIDON   Map 22 NG95

The Torridon Restaurant

Modern British

Impressive lochside location and fantastic home-grown produce

☎ 01445 791242 📠 01445 712253
IV22 2EY
e-mail: info@thetorridon.com
dir: From Inverness take A9 N, follow signs to Ullapool (A835). At Garve take A832 to Kinlochewe; take A896 to Torridon. Do not turn off to Torridon Village. Hotel on right after Annat

The sympathetically restored elegant Victorian shooting lodge surely has one of the most idyllic locations on the West Coast of Scotland - 58 acres of parkland at the head of a magnificent sea loch. Two interconnecting dining rooms feature wood panelling, wood detail on the ceiling and high backed chairs, heavy drapes, oil paintings and a lovely fireplace; it's all very luxurious. The two-choice, five-course British menu with French

influences uses lots of ingredients from the 2 acres of fruit and vegetable gardens, and scours the local Highland larder for most of the rest. You can even request a tour with head gardener Les Bates. Dishes might include home-tea-smoked organic salmon tartare with cress, then grilled fresh wild halibut with basil jus, and island cheeses with oat snaps and chutneys, or warm yellow polenta and chocolate soufflé with very vanilla ice cream to finish. The bar serves an impressive selection of over 320 different malt whiskies.

Times 12-2/7-9 Closed 2 Jan for 3 wks, L bar only

INVERCLYDE

KILMACOLM   Map 20 NS37

Windyhill Restaurant

Modern British V

Contemporary British cuisine in a relaxed setting

☎ 01505 872613
4 St James Ter, Lochwinnoch Rd PA13 4HB
e-mail: matthewscobey@hotmail.co.uk
dir: From Glasgow Airport, A737 take Bridge of Weir exit. Onto A761 to Kilmacolm. Left into High Street

Dynamic owners are constantly fine tuning the décor and menu of this smart contemporary restaurant. Inspired by the great architect Charles Rennie Mackintosh's house, Windyhill, the black shop-front façade opens into a classily casual setting with moody lighting, dark-wood furniture and modern artwork to inject splashes of colour to pristine white walls. The cooking is founded on top-drawer, locally-sourced produce, put to good use in uncomplicated but effective dishes with some interesting flavour combinations. Monthly menus offer a half-dozen choices at each stage; smoked Finnan haddock and leek risotto with lemon oil, followed by rump of lamb with sweet potato champ and roast root vegetables. Don't dodge puddings such as steamed black treacle and date pudding with walnut ice cream.

Chef Matthew Scobey **Owner** Matthew Scobey & Careen McLean **Times** 12-3/6-10 Closed Xmas-New Year, last wk Jul, 1st wk Aug, Sun-Mon, L Tue-Thu & Sat **Prices** Fixed L 2 course £15-£20, Fixed D 3 course £20-£30, Starter £3.95-£6.95, Main £9.95-£18.95, Dessert £4.95-£6.50 **Wines** 5 bottles over £20, 18 bottles under £20, 6 by glass **Notes** Vegetarian menu **Seats** 45 **Children** Portions, Menu **Parking** On street, car park opposite

LANARKSHIRE, SOUTH

BIGGAR   Map 21 NT03

Chancellors' at Shieldhill Castle

Modern British, International

Accomplished cooking in imposing old mansion

☎ 01899 220035 📠 01899 221092
Quothquan ML12 6NA
e-mail: enquiries@shieldhill.co.uk
dir: A702 onto B7016 (Biggar to Carnwath road), after 2m left into Shieldhill Road. Hotel 1.5m on right

Dating back almost 800 years, this fortified country mansion is surrounded by beautiful woodland and landscaped parkland and even has its own cricket pitch. Public rooms are atmospheric and packed with original features, from the oak-panelled lounge to the high-ceilinged Chancellors' restaurant. The kitchen delivers imaginative modern dishes with a focus on well-defined flavours conjured from local seasonal produce - including the estate game. All dishes are available as starter or main course and might include a classic fisherman's bouillabaisse or steamed steak and ale pudding with honey-roasted parsnips and spiced red cabbage. Finish with fig and ginger tart with ginger and honey ice cream. The wine list is well worth exploring.

Chef Christina Lamb **Owner** Mr & Mrs R Lamb **Times** 12-1.45/7-8.45 **Prices** Fixed L 2 course fr £15.95, Fixed D 3 course fr £19.95, Starter £6.15-£10.95, Main £9.95-£12.95, Dessert £7.45-£8.95, Service optional, Groups min 10 service 5% **Wines** 17 bottles under £20, 30 by glass **Notes** Sunday L, Vegetarian available, Civ Wed 150 **Seats** 32, Pr/dining room 30 **Children** Portions **Parking** 60

EAST KILBRIDE   Map 20 NS65

Macdonald Crutherland House

Scottish, International

Polished cooking in surroundings of great elegance

☎ 01355 577000 📠 01355 577047
Strathaven Rd G75 0QZ
e-mail: general.crutherland@macdonald-hotels.co.uk
dir: Follow A726 signed Strathaven, straight over Torrance rdbt, hotel on left after 250yds

Built at the beginning of the 18th century as a dower house, the white-fronted hotel is set in 37 acres of mature parkland. It now offers itself as a wedding venue and health spa, with a supremely elegant panelled dining room, where restful lighting and comfortable leather chairs set the tone. The menu has an up-market bistro feel to it, with special dishes appearing on designated days of the week (Tuesday is beef stroganoff day), and good Scottish produce in evidence throughout. Start with Cullen skink, or Stornoway black pudding and egg in a salad, before proceeding to Atholl Estate venison loin with dauphinoise and roasted celeriac, or hake in a cockle and saffron broth. Dark chocolate tart with vanilla ice cream is a crowd-pleasing finale.

Chef Kevin Hay **Owner** Macdonald Hotels **Times** 6.30-9.30 Closed L all week **Prices** Starter £5-£10, Main £14-£25, Dessert £5-£9, Service optional **Wines** 62 bottles over £20, 14 bottles under £20, 14 by glass **Notes** Vegetarian available, Dress restrictions, Smart dress, Civ Wed 300, Air con **Seats** 80, Pr/dining room 300 **Children** Portions, Menu **Parking** 200

STRATHAVEN   Map 20 NS74

Rissons at Springvale

@ Modern Scottish ❂

Relaxed restaurant with modern Scottish cuisine

☎ 01357 520234 & 521131
18 Lethame Rd ML10 6AD
e-mail: rissons@msn.com
dir: M74 junct 8, A71, through Stonehouse to Strathaven

Husband-and-wife-team Anne and Scott Baxter have refurbished their small and friendly restaurant with rooms in a clean-cut contemporary style. The Victorian merchant's house overlooks the local park, making for a relaxed setting in the light and airy restaurant and adjoining conservatory. It's an easy-going place with clued-up service, and the kitchen likes to keep things simple with a modern-bistro repertoire to match the mood. Dishes are kept unfussy and put together with attention to detail and sharp, well-balanced flavours. A starter of haggis balls with clapshot and Drambuie cream has Scotland stamped all over it, while mains might follow up with haunch of venison with sweet red cabbage and parsnip purée.

Chef Scott Baxter, Leonard Allen, Stephen Conway **Owner** Scott & Anne Baxter **Times** 12-2.30/6-9.30 Closed New Year, 1 wk Jan, 1st wk July, Mon-Tue, L Sat **Prices** Fixed L 2 course £13.95, Starter £4-£8, Main £10-£16, Dessert £4.75-£6.50, Service optional **Wines** 13 bottles over £20, 23 bottles under £20, 6 by glass **Notes** Sunday L, Vegetarian available **Seats** 40 **Children** Portions, Menu **Parking** 10

LOTHIAN, EAST

DIRLETON   Map 21 NT58

The Open Arms Hotel

@ Modern Scottish

Relaxed country hotel with local produce on the menu

☎ 01620 850241   📄 01620 850570
EH39 5EG
e-mail: openarmshotel@clara.co.uk
dir: from A1, follow signs for North Berwick, through Gullane, 2m on left

Occupying a lovely spot overlooking the village green and 13th-century Dirleton Castle, this long-established hotel boasts inviting public areas including a choice of lounges and a cosy bar. You can eat in either Deveau's Brasserie or the fine-dining Library Restaurant. The latter has soft lighting, clothed tables and formal settings. Staff are

helpful and friendly, and the menu offers a variety of carefully prepared dishes. Local flavours are apparent in breast of pheasant with a pork and redcurrant stuffing and red onion jus and grilled fillet of sea bass with lemon cream sauce.

Times 12-2/7-9 Closed D Sun

GULLANE   Map 21 NT48

La Potinière

@@ Modern British ❂

Ambitious cooking in cottage-style restaurant

☎ 01620 843214
Main St EH31 2AA
dir: 20m SE of Edinburgh. 3m from North Berwick on A198

Keith Marley and Mary Runciman carry off their chef-proprietor double act with unfailing charm and serious skills: both are at work in the kitchen, while Keith juggles front-of-house and wine waiter duties to boot. The small cottagey dining room hardly lends itself to grand style statements, but its elegant, traditional charm and crisply-presented tables make a fine foil to the leisurely four-course dinners (three courses at lunch). Local, seasonal produce drives the cooking - suppliers are proudly named on the day's menu - in a repertoire of artfully presented modern British dishes, with two choices at each stage. Royale of foie gras with sweetcorn cream and apricot salad precedes superbly fragrant Thai coconut soup with poached scallops, then braised halibut with crushed new potatoes in champagne and marjoram sauce. Round things off with passionfruit mousse or chocolate pudding.

Chef Mary Runciman, Keith Marley **Owner** Mary Runciman **Times** 12.30-1.30/7-8.30 Closed Xmas, Jan, Mon-Tue, D Sun (Oct-May) **Prices** Fixed L 2 course fr £18.50, Fixed D 4 course fr £40, Service optional **Wines** 28 bottles over £20, 8 bottles under £20, 5 by glass **Notes** Sunday L, Vegetarian available, Dress restrictions, Smart casual **Seats** 30 **Children** Portions **Parking** 10

NORTH BERWICK   Map 21 NT58

Macdonald Marine Hotel & Spa

@@ European

Grand setting for fine dining

☎ 0870 400 8129   📄 01620 894480
Cromwell Rd EH39 4LZ
e-mail: sales.marine@macdonald-hotels.co.uk
dir: from A198 turn into Hamilton Rd at lights then 2nd right

Returned to its former grandeur after extensive refurbishment, this majestic Grade II listed Victorian property is located on East Lothian's famous championship golf course overlooking the Firth of Forth. The recently decorated Craigleith Restaurant sports rich red walls, deep red, gold and brown striped curtains and

lighting that is a mix of spotlights and chandeliers. There are great views of the golf course and the coastline. The menu features classic European cooking with some modern elements, made using top-notch local and seasonal ingredients. Expect simply-presented starters such as terrine of ham hock with olive oil and plum chutney, followed by loin of venison served with sauté potatoes, buttered greens, sticky red cabbage, parsnip purée and redcurrant sauce. Finish with caramelised banana bavarois and banana sorbet.

Times 12.30-2.30/6.30-9.30

LOTHIAN, WEST

LINLITHGOW   Map 21 NS97

Champany Inn

@@ Traditional British ⬥NOTABLE WINE LIST

Properly hung Angus beef is the star of the show

☎ 01506 834532 & 834388   📄 01506 834302
Champany Corner EH49 7LU
e-mail: reception@champany.com
dir: 2m NE of Linlithgow. From M9 (N) junct 3, at top of slip road turn right. Champany 500yds on right

A short trip out from Edinburgh, the Champany has long been a beacon for prime Scots beef. Partly dating back to the days of Mary, Queen of Scots, the rambling buildings centre on an octagonal dining room that has become a temple to the king of meats. You might start with giant prawns in piri-piri seasoning, or Loch Gruinart oysters, and finish with perfectly executed crème brûlée with rhubarb and ginger compôte, but the chances are that what you're mainly here for are the minimally garnished cuts of 3-week-hung Aberdeen Angus, such as charcoal-grilled half-sirloin or sauced entrecote. Other meats might include double loin chops of lamb, or breast and leg of corn-fed chicken with chorizo mousseline. Formal but friendly service gets the balance right.

Chef C Davidson, D Gibson, Liam Ginname **Owner** Mr & Mrs C Davidson **Times** 12.30-2/7-10 Closed 25-26 Dec, 1-2 Jan, Sun, L Sat **Prices** Food prices not confirmed for 2010. Please telephone for details. **Wines** 650 bottles over £20, 8 bottles under £20, 8 by glass **Notes** Vegetarian available, Dress restrictions, No jeans or T-shirts **Seats** 50, Pr/dining room 30 **Parking** 50

LINLITHGOW *continued*

Livingston's Restaurant

◉◉ Modern Scottish

Traditional Scottish cooking in a charming family-run restaurant

☎ 01506 846565
52 High St EH49 7AE
e-mail: contact@livingstons-restaurant.co.uk
web: www.livingstons-restaurant.co.uk
dir: Opposite post office

Set in the shadows of Linlithgow Palace, this charming restaurant is reached through a vennel off the main street. Once the stables for Linlithgow Palace during the reign of Mary, Queen of Scots, family-run Livingston's provides an authentic Scottish experience. Set partly in a conservatory looking on to the garden with a glimpse of the loch through the trees, ruby red fabrics, tartan carpets and soft candlelight unite to create a relaxed, Caledonian atmosphere. The modern Scottish menu showcases local ingredients in dishes such as whisky and orange cured salmon with rocket, orange and shallot vinaigrette. This could be followed by roast rack of Border Blackface lamb, slow-cooked shoulder fritter, spring greens, heritage potatoes and new season garlic.

Times 12-2.30/6-9.30 Closed 1 wk Jun, 1 wk Oct, 2wks Jan, Sun-Mon (except Mothering Sun)

Ship 2 Shore 24

◉ Modern Scottish **NEW** ◐

The best of Scottish seafood

☎ 01506 840123
57 High St EH49 7ED
dir: On the High St, across road from the Palace

Located in the heart of historic Linlithgow, this is a restaurant that has a clear focus: presenting the freshest fish to the customer. The menus list the names of the skippers who landed the fish, and their wares are also on display - and available to buy - at a wet fish counter. The dining room is decorated with vibrant Scottish artworks and, at weekends, tablecloths appear to create a more intimate ambience. Service is informal, the daily specials revealed with enthusiasm. The freshness and quality of the produce is the draw here, such as the smoked haddock in a Cullen skink starter, and main-course fillet of halibut with fennel, Parisienne potatoes and mussel and Pernod sauce.

Chef Douglas Elliman **Times** 12-2.15/5.30-10 Closed 25 Dec, 1 Jan **Prices** Fixed D 3 course fr £30.50, Starter £3.50-£6.50, Main £4.95-£20, Dessert £4.90-£5.85, Service optional **Wines** 46 bottles over £20, 30 bottles under £20, 9 by glass **Notes** Early dining menu Tue-Fri 5.30-7.30, Vegetarian available, Air con **Seats** 50

The Tower

◉ Traditional British

Confident cooking in historic house

☎ 0844 879 9043 📠 01506 854220
Macdonald Houstoun House EH52 6JS
e-mail: houstoun@macdonald-hotels.co.uk
dir: M8 junct 3 follow Broxburn signs, straight over rdbt then at mini-rdbt turn right towards Uphall, hotel 1m on right

Built in the 1600s and counting Mary, Queen of Scots amongst its previous guests, Houstoun House is steeped in history. These days it's a peaceful hotel, part of the Macdonald group, nestled in several acres of private grounds and landscaped gardens. There's a choice of dining options, including a vaulted cocktail bar and the elegant fine-dining restaurant, The Tower, with garden views. The accomplished cooking is underpinned by classical techniques and quality Scottish ingredients are used. A starter of Ugie smokehouse smoked salmon, lettuce and capers might be followed by loin of Atholl estate venison, dauphinoise potatoes and roasted celeriac.

Chef David Murray **Owner** Macdonald Hotels **Times** 6.30-9.30 Closed L all week **Prices** Food prices not confirmed for 2010. Please telephone for details. **Wines** 74 bottles over £20, 16 bottles under £20, 13 by glass **Notes** Vegetarian available, Dress restrictions, Smart casual, no jeans or trainers, Civ Wed 200 **Seats** 65, Pr/dining room 30 **Children** Portions, Menu **Parking** 200

Archiestown Hotel

◉ Modern British, International

International cuisine in small Victorian country-house hotel

☎ 01340 810218 📠 01340 810239
AB38 7QL
e-mail: jah@archiestownhotel.co.uk
dir: Turn off A95 onto B9102 at Craigellachie

Set in the heart of a Speyside village, this small hotel is popular with visiting anglers while its restaurant is also much appreciated by the locals. A Victorian country house in the heart of whisky and salmon fishing country, it also has its own charming walled garden. The intimate bistro-style restaurant offers a seasonally-changing menu of dishes with an international influence. Home-smoked chicken and spicy vegetable spring rolls on herb leaf with a sweet chilli and ginger dipping sauce makes an impressive starter, followed by pan-fried breast of duck, compôte of Cognac-marinated prunes, potato rösti and red wine jus.

Times 12-2/7-9 Closed Xmas, 3 Jan-10 Feb

Craigellachie Hotel

◉ Traditional Scottish

Scottish cuisine in the heart of whisky country

☎ 01340 881204 📠 01340 881253
AB38 9SR
e-mail: info@craigellachie.com
dir: 12m S of Elgin, in village centre

Set in a village in the heart of Speyside, Scotland's malt whisky distilling area, it will come as no surprise that this imposing Victorian hotel features almost 700 malts in its bar. Speyside and the North East of Scotland is also renowned for its local produce, and the Ben Aigan Restaurant makes full use of the prime Aberdeen Angus beef, Cabrach lamb and Moray Firth fish and seafood. Expect dishes such as Craigellachie smoked salmon served with a millefeuille of wholemeal bread and herb butter, and pan-fried rib of Aberdeen Angus beef with a leek and potato terrine.

Times 12-2/6-10

CULLEN   Map 23 NJ56

Cullen Bay Hotel

◎ Traditional Scottish ♥

Restaurant with glorious sea views and traditional Scottish fare

☎ 01542 840432   📠 01524 840900
AB56 4XA
e-mail: stay@cullenbayhotel.com
dir: On A98, 0.25m W of Cullen

The Moray Firth is one of the UK's wildlife hotspots for sighting dolphins, porpoises and minke whales, and this small family-run hotel perched above Cullen Bay's beach gets grandstand views of their playground. You can make the most of the splendid views through full-length picture windows while tucking into traditional Scottish cooking with modern European twists in the relaxed restaurant. Local boats provide seafood, while the verdant hills of the hinterland cater for meat, game and cheese. While you're in the homeland of Cullen skink, that seems the obvious way to start, followed by grilled red mullet fillets with orange-glazed fennel and a pesto dressing.

Chef Gail Meikle, Graham Kirby, David Allan **Owner** Mr & Mrs Tucker & Sons **Times** 12-2/6.30-9 Closed From 2 Jan for 10 days **Prices** Food prices not confirmed for 2010. Please telephone for details. **Wines** 6 bottles over £20, 42 bottles under £20, 8 by glass **Notes** Sunday L, Vegetarian available, Civ Wed 150 **Seats** 60, Pr/dining room 40 **Children** Portions, Menu **Parking** 100

PERTH & KINROSS

AUCHTERARDER   Map 21 NN91

Andrew Fairlie @ Gleneagles

◎◎◎◎ *– see page 526*

The Strathearn

◎◎ Classic

Memorable food and service in ballroom-style setting

☎ 01764 694270   📠 01764 662134
The Gleneagles Hotel PH3 1NF
e-mail: resort.sales@gleneagles.com
web: www.gleneagles.com
dir: Off A9 at exit for A823, follow signs for Gleneagles Hotel

Set in a breathtaking 850-acre estate in the Scottish glens, the world-renowned Gleneagles resort offers a choice of dining options, including The Strathearn Restaurant, a truly classic dining room. The elegant ballroom-style room is huge, with high ceilings and pillars, and a pianist adds to the traditional atmosphere. Classical dishes are given a modern slant on the seasonal menu, while a whole brigade of staff provides formal but by no means stuffy service. Flambés and carving trolleys, along with the top-notch wine list, help make the occasion memorable. Expect a choice of hot or cold starters such as seared Loch Fyne scallops with roast cauliflower and spiced lentils, or Gleneagles-style dressed crab. Main courses might include loin and shoulder of Scotch lamb, sweetbreads and bubble-and-squeak.

Chef Paul Devonshire **Owner** Diageo plc
Times 12.30-2.30/7-10 Closed L Mon-Sat **Prices** Fixed L course £40, Fixed D 3 course £55, Service optional **Wines** 100% bottles over £20, 15 by glass **Notes** Sunday L, Vegetarian available, Dress restrictions, Smart casual, Civ Wed 250 **Seats** 322 **Children** Portions, Menu **Parking** 1000

COMRIE   Map 21 NN72

Royal Hotel

◎ Traditional British

Traditional food in an elegant environment

☎ 01764 679200   📠 01764 679219
Melville Square PH6 2DN
e-mail: reception@royalhotel.co.uk
web: www.royalhotel.co.uk
dir: In main square, 7m from Crieff, on A85

Comrie's central square sits at the junction where the rolling lowlands climb towards the Perthshire Highlands, a great location for this well-established 18th-century coaching inn. Inside, it's an elegantly stylish small hotel, all polished-wood floors, classy fabrics, cosy log fires and antiques. There's a choice of the clubby lounge bar, conservatory-style brasserie, and classic formal dining room when it comes to eating, as the lovely walled garden in the warmer months. Traditional British dishes have their roots in local materials - fillet of sea bass with potato rösti and butter sauce, or roast rack of lamb with root vegetables and dauphinoise potatoes are typical of the style.

Chef David Milsom **Owner** The Milsom family
Times 12-2/6.30-9 Closed Xmas **Prices** Fixed L 2 course £13.25-£26, Fixed D 3 course £27.75-£33.65, Starter £4.75-£7.25, Main £7.45-£19.95, Dessert £5.75, Service optional **Wines** 46 bottles over £20, 47 bottles under £20, 7 by glass **Notes** Sunday L, Vegetarian available **Seats** 60 **Children** Portions **Parking** 25

DUNKELD   Map 21 NO04

Kinnaird

◎◎◎ *– see page 527*

FORTINGALL   Map 20 NN74

Fortingall Hotel

◎◎ Modern Scottish ♥

Imaginative cooking in luxurious small hotel

☎ 01887 830367 & 830368
PH15 2NQ
e-mail: hotel@fortingallhotel.com
web: www.fortingallhotel.com
dir: B846 from Aberfeldy for 6m, left signed Fortingall for 3m. Hotel in village centre

The Arts and Crafts village of Fortingall is in Glen Lyon, Scotland's longest glen, and the impressively refurbished hotel has a prime position with views over wooded slopes and towering peaks. The main dining room follows the Arts and Crafts theme with its furniture and tweed curtains, and a second slightly more informal room, the Yew dining room, has views over the garden. The daily-changing menu makes good use of regional produce in a range of modern Scottish dishes with European influences: start with sweetbread and chicken terrine with mint jelly, followed by chargrilled lamb - excellent quality - with Arran mustard rösti, root vegetables and wild mushroom sauce. Friendly service comes from a young team.

Chef Darin Campbell **Owner** Iain & Janet Wotherspoon **Times** 12-2/6.30-9 **Prices** Starter £3.95-£6.95, Main £13.95-£21.95, Dessert £5.50-£7.95, Service optional **Wines** 42 bottles over £20, 30 bottles under £20, 4 by glass **Notes** Sunday L, Vegetarian available **Seats** 30, Pr/dining room 30 **Children** Portions, Menu **Parking** 20

Andrew Fairlie @ Gleneagles

AUCHTERARDER	Map 21 NN91

Modern French

Dramatic setting, inspired food

☎ 01764 694267 📠 01764 694163
PH3 1NF
e-mail: andrew.fairlie@gleneagles.com
web: www.andrewfairlie.com
dir: From A9 take Gleneagles exit, hotel in 1m

Gleneagles is a name that has long been synonymous with golf, but these days, thanks to Andrew Fairlie, it is also associated with world-class dining. Operating as an independent business on the ground floor of this imposing, classy hotel, the restaurant, open only for dinner, produces refined, intelligent and intricate cooking. As the first ever Roux Scholarship winner, and having trained under the legendary Michel Guérard, it is perhaps not surprising that Fairlie's inspiration is the South West of France, and, of course, the superb produce of his native Scotland. The elegant dark-panelled walls, floor-to-ceiling silk drapes and banquettes sumptuously covered in rich fabrics with a stylish leaf motif, and bespoke artworks by Archie Frost, create a smart and stylish space. Service is highly polished, the welcome warm and genuine. Menus du marché and dégustation are available if all on a table are agreed, otherwise the à la carte offers a choice of five at each

course and brings plenty of pleasures along the way. Amuse-bouche such as pumpkin and hazelnut velouté with sherry and mushroom espuma reveals the sheer technical skill and deftly handled flavours that await. First-course foie gras ballotine is perfectly partnered with an almond jelly, fig purée and divinely light brioche, and main-course fillet of wild venison comes with a wintery mix of roots and fruits, including beetroot, pumpkin, salsify, apples and pears. Presentation is stunning throughout, not least at dessert, where no holds are barred in the making of a dish of caramelised banana with peanut butter mousse, with the addition of space dust bringing a tingle to the tongue. The wine list, and sommelier, do justice to the food.

Chef Andrew Fairlie **Owner** Andrew Fairlie **Times** 6.30-10 Closed 24-25 Dec, 3 wks Jan, Sun, L all week **Prices** Starter £25-£35, Main £36, Dessert £14, Service optional **Wines** 300 bottles over £20, 12 by glass **Notes** Degustation 6 course £95, Du Marché 6 course £85, Dress restrictions, Smart casual, Air con **Seats** 54 **Parking** 300

GLENDEVON
Map 21 NN90

An Lochan Tormaukin

◎ Modern Scottish

High quality local produce in relaxed, rustic surroundings

☎ 01259 781252
FK14 7JY
e-mail: tormaukin@anlochan.co.uk
dir: From A9 take A823 towards Dollar

The third addition to the McKie family's mini empire has taken a charming 17th-century country inn lost among the rolling Ochil hills close to Gleneagles and treated it to a tasteful modern makeover. Crackling log fires, bare-stone walls and unclothed wooden tables contrasting with vibrant artwork set the tone in the snug and dining room, or there's a bright and airy conservatory. As in the other An Lochan properties in Glasgow and Tighnabruaich (see entries), modern Scottish menus are constructed from locally-sourced materials - Highland beef, Perthshire lamb, venison, game and seafood. Typical offerings include wild boar terrine with fig chutney and toasted brioche and roast rump of Highland beef in a herb shallot crust with dauphinoise potatoes and black cabbage.

Chef Gary Noble **Owner** Roger & Bea McKie
Times 12-3/5.30-9.30 **Prices** Fixed L 2 course fr £10.95, Fixed D 3 course fr £19.95, Starter £3.95-£9.50, Main £7.25-£23.95, Dessert £4.25-£5.50, Service optional **Wines** 25 bottles over £20, 6 bottles under £20, 4 by glass **Notes** Early evening menu available 5.30-6.30pm, Sunday L, Vegetarian available **Seats** 40, Pr/dining room 25 **Children** Portions, Menu **Parking** 30

GLENFARG
Map 21 NO11

The Famous Bein Inn

◎ Scottish, French **NEW**

Traditional inn offering good Scottish food

☎ 01577 830216 📠 01577 830211
PH2 9PY
e-mail: enquiries@beininn.com
web: www.beininn.com
dir: 2m N of Glenfarg, on the intersection of A912 & B996

Located in a wooded valley south of Perth, the immodest Bein Inn has a lively bar and a restaurant which delivers some sound Scottish cuisine. The dining room is comfortable in a traditional kind of way and the kitchen uses good Scottish produce to deliver the likes of Cullen skink and Highland rabbit and foie gras terrine among starters, and fish of the day - John Dory, perhaps - alongside rump of Perthshire Blackface lamb served with sesame potatoes, cauliflower purée with broad beans, minted peas and a natural jus as main courses. Finish with dark chocolate and rosemary fondant with home-made white chocolate and heather honey ice cream.

The Famous Bein Inn

Chef Ian Simpson **Owner** John & Allan MacGregor **Times** 12-9 Closed 25 Dec **Prices** Fixed L 2 course £15-£18, Fixed D 3 course £21.95-£26, Starter £4-£7, Main £10-£21, Dessert £4.50-£7, Service optional **Wines** 10 bottles over £20, 13 bottles under £20, 5 by glass **Notes** Sunday L, Vegetarian available **Seats** 30, Pr/dining room 30 **Children** Portions, Menu **Parking** 26

Kinnaird

◎◎◎

DUNKELD
Map 21 NO04

Modern European

Exquisite country house in glorious setting serving innovative food

☎ 01796 482440 📠 01796 482289
Kinnaird Estate PH8 0LB
e-mail: enquiry@kinnairdestate.com
dir: From A9 N take B898 for 4.5m. Hotel on right

Kinnaird is all you might imagine a Scottish country estate to be, from the rugged elegance of the house's Georgian façade, to the 7,000 acres of prime Perthshire countryside. Everything about this imposing baronial mansion is built on a grand scale and its position overlooking the wooded valley of the River Tay is breathtaking. This is hunting-shooting-fishing country but the hotel provides a bit of luxurious cosseting however you choose to spend your time. The public rooms are traditionally furnished with considerable elegance, so fine antiques and an impressive collection of art fill inviting lounges which are warmed by roaring log fires. The dining room is an elegantly refined space, with ornate Italian frescoed walls, marble fireplace, a central chandelier and views out onto the garden through the huge bay windows. Jacket and tie are required at dinner, but given the formal silver service and grand scale of the place, that doesn't seem unreasonable. The food is focused on seasonal local produce and classically-based ideas meet modern sensibilities on fixed-price lunch, dinner and tasting menus (there's afternoon tea as well). Langoustines with an oyster tempura and oyster velouté is a luxuriant start, followed by lamb shank and loin with Puy lentils, kohlrabi and thyme jus, and finishing with hot passionfruit soufflé with chocolate sorbet.

Chef Jean-Baptiste Bady **Owner** Mrs C Ward
Times 12.30-1.45/7-9.30 **Prices** Food prices not confirmed for 2010. Please telephone for details.

Wines 158 bottles over £20, 2 bottles under £20, 7 by glass **Notes** Tasting menu 6 course & vegetarian tasting menu, Sunday L, Vegetarian available, Dress restrictions, Smart dress, jackets at D, Civ Wed 45 **Seats** 35, Pr/dining room 40 **Children** Portions **Parking** 15

KENMORE — Map 21 NN74

Taymouth Restaurant

◉ Traditional Scottish

Historic inn with Tay views and quality Scottish cooking

☎ 01887 830205 📠 01887 830262
The Kenmore Hotel, The Square PH15 2NU
e-mail: reception@kenmorehotel.co.uk
web: www.kenmorehotel.co.uk
dir: off A9 at Ballinluig onto A827, through Aberfeldy to Kenmore, hotel in village centre

Built in 1572, Scotland's oldest inn, the historic Kenmore Hotel, sits on the beautiful banks of the Tay. The poet Rabbie Burns himself was so taken with the area that he composed a poem to it, written in pencil on the chimney breast of the cosy Poets' bar. But life's not all stuck in the 16th-century here: the restaurant is a modern, light-and-airy conservatory-style affair with glorious views of the river and woodland. The kitchen takes the season's fresh local produce to deliver a menu of good, honest Scottish fare. Take sage and garlic-scented terrine of wild boar with toasted brioche and sloe berry jelly to start, followed by seared collops of Highland venison with Savoy cabbage, crispy pomegranate seeds and game jus.

Chef Duncan Shearer **Owner** Kenmore Estates Ltd
Times 12-6/6-9.30 **Prices** Fixed L 2 course £13.50-£18, Fixed D 3 course £22-£26.50, Starter £3.35-£5.65, Main £10.50-£22.50, Dessert £3.85-£5.25, Service optional

Wines 14 bottles over £20, 35 bottles under £20, 11 by glass **Notes** Taste of Scotland menu £29.50, Sunday L, Vegetarian available, Civ Wed 140, Air con **Seats** 140, Pr/dining room 140 **Children** Portions, Menu **Parking** 40

See advert below

KILLIECRANKIE — Map 23 NN96

Killiecrankie House Hotel

◉◉ Modern Scottish

Modern cooking in a delightful small country-house hotel

☎ 01796 473220 📠 01796 472451
PH16 5LG
e-mail: enquiries@killiecrankiehotel.co.uk
dir: From A9 take B8079 N of Killiecrankie, hotel is 3m on right, just past village signpost

Killiecrankie is a Victorian former dower house overlooking the River Garry at the gateway to the Pass of Killiecrankie, now turned into an easy-going, small-scale country hotel. Work up an appetite with a leg-stretcher around the lovely landscaped gardens, then take your seat for some impressive modern Scottish cooking. Fresh local ingredients including herbs and vegetables from the kitchen garden drive the four-course dinner menus, starting with the well-matched flavours of sautéed wild mushrooms, Parma ham and garlic served in puff pastry with parsley cream sauce. Main course might be pan-fried fillet of venison and wood pigeon breast with braised Savoy cabbage, chive mash and redcurrant game jus. Each dish comes matched with a wine from an excellent list, and there's an expertly-chosen array of malts to round things off.

Times 6.30-8.30 Closed Jan- Feb, L all week

KINCLAVEN — Map 21 NO13

Ballathie House Hotel

◉◉ Modern Scottish V

Grand country-house by the river Tay

☎ 01250 883268 📠 01250 883396
PH1 4QN
e-mail: email@ballathiehousehotel.com
dir: From A9, 2m N of Perth, take B9099 through Stanley & follow signs, or from A93 at Beech Hedge follow signs for Ballathie, 2.5m

Ballathie was once a railway halt on the route from Glasgow to Aberdeen, the overgrown track now half-concealing the remains of an old Episcopalian chapel. It would all be a sleepy backwater, were it not for the majestic Ballathie House, which rises in conical turrets above the surrounding green. Overlooking the River Tay, it's a popular retreat for anglers, and a perfect backdrop to a spot of high living, with its overstuffed chairs, open fires and opulently attired dining room. This last is the setting for some ambitious country-house cooking, which ranges from classic comforts such as chicken liver parfait with port-soaked plums and toasted brioche to startling (and successful) ideas like the salad of shredded rabbit with Puy lentils and a prune fritter. Sorbet or a soup, such as earthy mushroom and Madeira, come next on the prix-fixe menu, and are followed by multi-layered mains like roast Gressingham duck breast with creamed Savoy cabbage, fondant potato, chanterelles, parsnip, carrots and sauce moscovite. A little less complexity might sometimes help the food to even greater impact.

Chef Andrew Wilkie **Owner** Ballathie House Hotel Ltd
Times 12.30-2/7-9 **Prices** Fixed L 2 course £18.50, Fixed D 3 course £41.50, Service optional **Wines** 220 bottles over £20, 4 bottles under £20, 6 by glass **Notes** Sunday L, Vegetarian menu, Dress restrictions, Jacket & tie preferred, No jeans/T-shirts, Civ Wed 75 **Seats** 70, Pr/dining room 32 **Children** Portions **Parking** 100

KINLOCH RANNOCH Map 23 NN65

Dunalastair Hotel

◉ Modern British

Traditional Highland hotel with confidently prepared food

☎ 01882 632323 & 632218 📄 01882 632371
PH16 5PW
e-mail: info@dunalastair.co.uk
dir: From Pitlochry N, take B8019 to Tummel Bridge then B846 to Kinloch Rannoch

Dunalastair is a solidly traditional Highland house dating from 1770, and in its long history has served as a staging post and barracks for Jacobite troops. There's certainly no forgetting that you're north of the border amid the baronial oak panelling, antler chandeliers and tartan carpets in the restaurant. The kitchen takes traditional country-house cuisine built on excellent Scottish produce and gives it a modern spin, delivering accurately cooked, uncomplicated dishes with beautifully balanced flavours. Go for confit duck leg with red onion compôte and an orange reduction, and move on to chargrilled beef fillet with butternut squash purée, glazed shallots and Madeira jus.

Times 12-2.30/6.30-9

KINROSS Map 21 NO10

The Green Hotel

◉ Modern International

Contemporary restaurant with classic-based modern cuisine

☎ 01577 863467 📄 01577 863180
2 The Muirs KY13 8AS
e-mail: reservations@green-hotel.com
dir: M90 junct 6 follow Kinross signs, onto A922 for hotel

Nothing to do with eco-friendly philosophy, the Green in this hotel's name is the type that golf balls are whacked along. It has its origins as an 18th-century staging post on the road north from Edinburgh, but the two golf courses and prospect of trout fishing on Loch Leven are just two of the pursuits that bring travellers to a halt these days. Colourful artwork and exuberant flower displays make Basil's restaurant a cheery place for tucking into the kitchen's modern interpretations of classic dishes. Look out for terrine of monkfish with foie gras, wild mushrooms and Madeira jus for starters, followed by grilled sea bass with mussel and cider broth.

Times 7-9.30

PERTH Map 21 NO12

Acanthus Restaurant

◉◉ Modern British

Imaginative, accomplished cuisine in a Victorian setting

☎ 01738 622451 📄 01738 622046
Parklands Hotel, St Leonards Bank PH2 8EB
e-mail: info@acanthusrestaurant.com
dir: Adjacent to Perth station, overlooking South Inch Park

The former residence of the Lord Provost enjoys an impressive location with stunning views over the South Inch, yet is within easy reach of the town centre. Public areas at the Parklands Hotel include a choice of restaurants, with the stylish Victorian Acanthus Restaurant providing the fine-dining option. Service here is formal and a menu of creative, well-prepared dishes features top-notch local and seasonal ingredients. Tuck into starters such as rabbit and white bean terrine with onion toast and pickled walnuts, perhaps followed by pan-roasted halibut with clam and squid ink spaghetti and vermouth sauce. For a stylish finale, perhaps warm hazelnut tart with honeycomb and clotted cream.

Chef Graeme Pallister **Owner** Scott & Penny Edwards
Times 7-9 Closed 26 Dec-7 Jan, Sun-Tue, L Wed-Sat
Prices Fixed D 3 course £29.95, Service optional, Groups min 8 service 10% **Wines** 33 bottles over £20, 55 bottles under £20, 6 by glass **Notes** Vegetarian available, Dress restrictions, Smart casual, no shorts or jeans, Civ Wed 30 **Seats** 36, Pr/dining room 22 **Children** Portions, Menu **Parking** 25

Best Western Huntingtower Hotel

◉ Traditional British

Traditional Britsh cuisine in secluded setting

☎ 01738 583771 📄 01738 583777
Crieff Rd PH1 3JT
e-mail: reservations@huntingtowerhotel.co.uk
dir: 3m W off A85

This country-house hotel on the outskirts of Perth dates back to 1892 when it was the home of a mill owner. Situated in 6 acres of secluded landscaped gardens and grounds, it mixes period features and modern facilities. Lunch is served in the conservatory, while the charming oak-panelled dining room sets the scene for more formal, intimate dining. The traditional menu features British cuisine with European influences, making good use of local produce, and might include starters such as pan-fried scallops with pesto and parmesan salad, followed by roast loin of Perthshire lamb, dauphinoise potatoes, roast root vegetables and rosemary gravy.

Times 12-2/6-9.30

Deans @Let's Eat

◉◉ Modern Scottish

Modern and imaginative Scottish cooking

☎ 01738 643377 📄 01738 621464
77-79 Kinnoull St PH1 5EZ
e-mail: deans@letseatperth.co.uk
web: www.letseatperth.co.uk
dir: On corner of Kinnoull St & Atholl St, close to North Inch

The Deans' lively and welcoming corner restaurant, close to the centre of town, is housed in a converted 19th-century theatre. These days there are no dramas or tragedies being played out, simply confident, contemporary Scottish cooking. There's a cosy bar for pre-dinner drinks and a dining room decorated in warm tones with tables immaculately laid and perfectly appointed. Service is friendly and attentive. The modern Scottish cooking is strong on the nation's best produce, notably prime Scotch beef and seafood. Accurately cooked fillet of halibut is grilled in lemongrass oil and comes with cumin rice, basil purée and warm lentil dressing, and chilled orange soufflé is a perfectly executed dessert.

Chef Willie Deans, Simon Lannon **Owner** Mr & Mrs W Deans **Times** 12-2.30/6.30-10 Closed Sun-Mon
Prices Fixed L 2 course fr £13.95, Fixed D 3 course fr £25, Starter £3.95-£8.95, Main £11.95-£17.95, Dessert £5.75-£6, Service optional **Wines** 40 bottles over £20, 23 bottles under £20, 8 by glass **Notes** Early eve supper Tue-Thu from 6pm, Vegetarian available, Dress restrictions, Smart casual **Seats** 70 **Children** Portions **Parking** Multi-storey car park (100 yds)

PERTH *continued*

Old Masters, Murrayshall House Hotel

@@ Modern British V ✋

Fine Scottish cuisine with stunning views

☎ 01738 551171 📄 01738 552595
New Scone PH2 7PH
e-mail: info@murrayshall.co.uk
dir: From Perth A94 (Coupar Angus) turn right signed
Murrayshall before New Scone

Two golf courses are a major draw at this fine old
mansion set in 350 acres of the Grampian Hills. All that
fresh air out on the links should help sharpen the
appetite for a session in the Old Masters restaurant,
where it's a good idea to try to bag a window seat with
those magnificent views. Professional, friendly staff help
foster a relaxed ambience for meals built on Scotland's
bounty. Classic combinations are cooked with
imagination and flair. Take rabbit served in a pastry case
with Madeira jus and chanterelles to start, then Isle of
Skye scallops with pig's cheeks and chorizo foam, and
finish with a textbook chocolate fondant that releases its
molten interior to perfection.

Chef Jonathan Greer **Owner** Old Scone Ltd
Times 12-2.30/7-9.45 Closed 26 Dec, L Sat **Prices** Fixed
L 2 course £12.50, Fixed D 3 course £30, Starter £6-
£8.50, Main £8-£11.50, Dessert £6-£8.50, Service
optional **Wines** 30 bottles over £20, 20 bottles under £20,
8 by glass **Notes** Sunday L, Vegetarian menu, Civ Wed
100, Air con **Seats** 55, Pr/dining room 40
Children Portions, Menu **Parking** 90

Opus One

@@ Modern British NEW

**Exciting culinary developments in city-centre boutique
hotel**

☎ 01738 823355 📄 01738 628969
The New County Hotel, 11-20 County Place PH2 8EE
e-mail: enquiries@newcountyhotel.com
web: www.newcountyhotel.com
dir: A9 junct 11, Perth. Follow signs for town centre. Hotel
on right after library

At the heart of the garden city of Perth, this white-fronted
boutique hotel is situated next to the Bell Library.
Catering for a business clientele as well as the Perthshire
smart set, the emphasis is on sleek, modern design with
the minimum of flounce. Café 22 and a bar-bistro offer
simpler food, but the main gastronomic draw is the Opus
One restaurant, where wooden floors, simply appointed
bare tables, cream walls and low lighting create a restful,
and supremely cool, ambience. Service is professionally
polished but versed in the civilities too, and Ryan Young's
modern British cooking is making waves. Constructively
resisting the temptation to over complicate, dishes
achieve great resonance, as in seared king scallops
bedded on truffled mash in a foamy seafood sauce - a
starter of notable intensity. Go on perhaps to tender
venison loin with duck liver ravioli and rosemary-scented
celeriac purée, sauced lightly and fragrantly with

Marsala, before finishing with something like iced
hazelnut parfait with pineapple carpaccio in a subtle
syrup. This is definitely one to watch.

Chef Ryan Young, David Cochrane **Owner** Mr Owen Boyle,
Mrs Sarah Boyle **Times** 12-2/6.30-9 Closed Sun-Mon
Prices Fixed L 2 course £15.95-£17.95, Fixed D 3 course
£27.95-£36.45, Service optional **Wines** 18 bottles over
£20, 11 bottles under £20 **Notes** Vegetarian available
Seats 48 **Children** Portions **Parking** 10, plus opposite &
on street

63 Tay Street

@@ Modern Scottish V

Modern Scottish cooking in Perth

☎ 01738 441451 📄 01738 441461
63 Tay St PH2 8NN
e-mail: info@63taystreet.com
dir: In town centre, on river

In a city centre location, this stylish modern restaurant,
housed in a large period building, serves imaginative
dishes with a strong emphasis on fresh local produce.
Views of the River Tay make it a popular lunch venue and
in the evening it's more of a formal dining atmosphere,
aided by skilled waiting staff. The modern Scottish
cooking might take in well-executed hand-dived scallops
with Jerusalem artichoke, truffle and hazelnut dressing,
or a main course of tasting of pork, comprising a
pudding, beetroot-glazed cheek, confit with liver and
crumbed belly, accompanied by garlic potato and apple
sauce. Rhubarb and almond tart with rhubarb fool and
root ginger ice cream confirms the kitchen's deft handling
of flavours.

Chef Graeme Pallister **Owner** Scott & Penny Edwards,
Graeme Pallister **Times** 12-2/6.30-9 Closed Xmas, New
Year, 1st wk Jul, Sun-Mon **Prices** Fixed L 2 course
£13.95-£14.95, Fixed D 3 course £32.50-£37.95, Service
optional, Groups min 6 service 10% **Wines** 65 bottles
over £20, 26 bottles under £20, 9 by glass
Notes Vegetarian menu **Seats** 35 **Children** Portions

PITLOCHRY **Map 23 NN95**

Green Park Hotel

@ Modern, Traditional Scottish ✋

Fine cuisine in a lochside country-house hotel

☎ 01796 473248 📄 01796 473520
Clunie Bridge Rd PH16 5JY
e-mail: bookings@thegreenpark.co.uk
dir: Turn off A9 at Pitlochry, follow signs for 0.25m
through town

The sylvan shores of Loch Faskally make a superb setting
for this family-run country-house hotel. The traditional
dining room in soothing shades of plum and honey looks
over well-kept gardens towards the loch, providing a
delightful backdrop to the classic Scottish cuisine. The
kitchen works with a splendid array of Perthshire produce
- seafood and game feature strongly, as well as seasonal
herbs and salads from the kitchen garden - in dishes

such as a baked filo parcel of chicken with oven-dried
tomatoes and lovage mousse. Main courses might take in
roast loin of pork with herbs and oats, poached apples,
watercress and cider sauce, or roast pheasant breast
filled with haggis in whisky cream sauce.

Chef Chris Tamblin **Owner** Green Park Ltd
Times 12-2/6.30-8.30 Closed L all week (ex residents)
Prices Fixed D 3 course £21, Service optional **Wines** 10
bottles over £20, 65 bottles under £20, 8 by glass
Notes Sunday L, Vegetarian available, Dress restrictions,
smart casual **Seats** 100 **Children** Portions, Menu
Parking 52

The Old Armoury Restaurant

@ Modern British NEW

Modern British cooking in a historic old house

☎ 01796 474281
Armoury Rd PH16 5AP
e-mail: info@theoldarmouryrestaurant.com
dir: Turn off main street onto Rieachan Rd & follow signs
for Fishladder. Restaurant on left

The Old Armoury is a charming old stone-built house just
off Pitlochry's main street, yet surrounded by woodlands
near to Loch Faskally; the name derives from its
associations with the Black Watch regiment. Inside,
several connecting dining rooms have a light and airy
ambience with wooden floors, heaps of artwork on
tongue-and-groove panelled walls, and large French
doors opening onto a delightful garden. The cooking is
modern British fare that picks the best of Perthshire
produce in a menu of traditional favourites with some
innovative flourishes. Start with a simply-grilled young
goats' cheese crottin with apple chutney, followed by
grilled organic salmon with steamed asparagus, creamy
mash and chive and caper butter. And who could turn
down a steamed marmalade pudding with brown bread
ice cream to finish?

Chef Angus McNab **Owner** Angus McNab
Times 12-2.30/5.30-8.30 Closed Xmas, Jan-Feb, Mon-
Wed (Nov-Dec), D Sun (Nov-Dec) **Prices** Starter £3.25-
£6.60, Main £10.15-£17.65, Dessert £5.65, Service
optional **Wines** 3 by glass **Notes** Pre-theatre menu
available, Sunday L, Vegetarian available **Seats** 54, Pr/
dining room 22 **Children** Portions **Parking** 8, or on street

ST FILLANS **Map 20 NN62**

Achray House Hotel

@ Traditional British

Family-run hotel, loch views and traditional cooking

☎ 01764 685231 📄 01764 685320
PH6 2NF
e-mail: info@achray-house.co.uk
dir: Please telephone for directions

Achray House sits in lovely gardens in a serene spot on
the shores of Loch Earn at the gateway to the Highlands
in the Loch Lomond and Trossachs National Park. It's a
welcoming and friendly, family-run place with a homely

feel you can slide into like a comfy pair of shoes. You get glorious views over the loch to go with aperitifs in the conservatory-style bar, before moving into the restaurant for confidently-cooked, straightforward dishes that showcase splendid Scottish ingredients. Daily-changing menus might start with mallard duck terrine with plum chutney before salmon fillet with an oatmeal, herb and lemon crust and Arran mustard cream. End with the comfort of an apple and cinnamon crumble.

Chef Andrew J Scott **Owner** Andrew J Scott **Times** 12-2.30/6-8.30 Closed 3-31 Jan **Prices** Fixed L 2 course fr £15.95, Starter £3.95-£6.95, Main £9.95-£17.95, Dessert £3.95-£4.95, Service optional **Wines** 11 bottles over £20, 24 bottles under £20, 9 by glass **Notes** Sunday L, Vegetarian available **Seats** 70, Pr/dining room 30 **Children** Portions, Menu **Parking** 20

The Four Seasons Hotel

◉◉ Modern British **V**

Breathtaking lochside scenery and bold cuisine

☎ 01764 685333 🖹 01764 685444
Lochside PH6 2NF
e-mail: info@thefourseasonshotel.co.uk
dir: From Perth take A85 W, through Crieff & Comrie. Hotel at west end of village

Originally built in the early 19th century for the manager of the local limekilns, this lochside lodge served as a schoolmaster's house before becoming a romantic small hotel. Take the dog if you like - pets are welcome - since its location, tucked beneath steep forested hillsides on the edge of Loch Earn, is perfect for striding into the great outdoors of Perthshire. Sublime views come as standard amid the contemporary style of the waterside Meall Reamhar fine-dining restaurant. Cracking Scottish produce is used to great effect in modern British dishes with well-layered flavours and creative pairings. Pan-seared hand-dived Scrabster scallops with Aberdeenshire black pudding and asparagus cream start things off, then roast rack of Perthshire lamb with dauphinoise potatoes and braised red cabbage.

Chef Peter Woods **Owner** Andrew Low **Times** 12-2.30/6-9.30 Closed Jan-Feb & some wkdays Mar, Nov & Dec **Prices** Fixed L 2 course fr £9.99, Fixed D 4 course £35, Service optional **Wines** 71 bottles over £20, 29 bottles under £20, 416 by glass **Notes** Sunday L, Vegetarian menu, Civ Wed 100 **Seats** 60, Pr/dining room 20 **Children** Portions, Menu **Parking** 30

SPITTAL OF GLENSHEE   Map 23 NO17

Dalmunzie Castle Hotel

◉◉ Traditional British 🍴NOTABLE WINE LIST

Cooking fit for a laird

☎ 01250 885224 🖹 01250 885225
PH10 7QG
e-mail: reservations@dalmunzie.com
dir: On A93 at Spittal of Glenshee, follow signs to hotel

Fresh Highland air and action-packed outdoor pursuits are on the doorstep of this turreted Scots baronial pile tucked away in a secretive glen. You're not going to bump into your fellow guests too often on the 6,500-acre estate, but if you're after company, the pistes of Glenshee are within easy reach for a day's skiing. Inside, it is the archetypal Laird's retreat, with antiques and log fires in comfy lounges, and an elegant blue and cream dining room, softly-lit at dinner. Top-notch seasonal Scottish bounty forms the backbone of French-tinged British dishes on a daily-changing menu featuring the likes of roasted pork tenderloin with Tuscan bean stew, parsnip purée and redcurrant jus, followed by seared Scottish venison with celeriac pommes dauphinoise, clapshot (that's potato and swede mash to non-Scots), caramelised spiced pear and red wine sauce.

Chef Katie Cleary **Owner** Scott & Brianna Poole **Times** 12-2.30/7-9 Closed 1-28 Dec **Prices** Fixed D 4 course fr £42, Service included **Wines** 45 bottles over £20, 17 bottles under £20, 4 by glass **Notes** Fixed D 4 course, Vegetarian available, Dress restrictions, Smart casual, Jacket & tie preferred, Civ Wed 70 **Seats** 40, Pr/dining room 18 **Children** Portions **Parking** 40

RENFREWSHIRE

HOWWOOD   Map 20 NS36

Country Club Restaurant

◉ Modern British

Converted mill serving seasonal Scottish cuisine

☎ 01505 705225 🖹 01505 705230
Bowfield Hotel & Country Club PA9 1DZ
e-mail: enquiries@bowfieldhotel.co.uk
dir: From M8 take A737 (Irvine Rd), exit at Howwood, take 2nd right up country lane, turn right at top of hill

Surrounded by farmland and the rolling hills of Renfrewshire, this hotel is a convenient stopover for travellers using Glasgow Airport. Located in a converted 17th-century bleaching mill, it combines the traditional character of beamed ceilings, brick and white-painted walls and open fires with modern leisure club facilities. Seasonal Scottish produce, especially fish, shellfish and game, is cooked with skill and well presented. Expect the likes of West Coast scallops with Ayrshire bacon and crushed new potatoes, followed by medallion of Aberdeen Angus beef fillet with cabbage and celeriac, potato cake and onion confit and jus. Finish with cranachan mousse with raspberry sorbet and oatmeal praline.

Chef Ronnie McAdam **Owner** Bowfield Hotel & Country Club Ltd **Times** 6.30-9 Closed L all week **Prices** Food prices not confirmed for 2010. Please telephone for details. **Wines** 8 bottles over £20, 21 bottles under £20, 7 by glass **Notes** Sunday L, Vegetarian available, Dress restrictions, Smart casual, Civ Wed 120 **Seats** 40, Pr/dining room 20 **Children** Portions, Menu **Parking** 100

RENFREWSHIRE, EAST

UPLAWMOOR   Map 10 NS45

Uplawmoor Hotel

◉◉ Modern Scottish

Good Scottish cuisine in former smugglers' haunt

☎ 01505 850565 🖹 01505 850689
Neilston Rd G78 4AF
e-mail: info@uplawmoor.co.uk
web: www.uplawmoor.co.uk
dir: M77 junct 2, A736 signed Barrhead & Irvine. Hotel 4m beyond Barrhead

Tucked away in a tranquil village only minutes from Glasgow, this one-time coaching inn used to be frequented by smugglers travelling between Glasgow and the coast. Extensive renovation in the 1950s by architect James Gray added the Charles Rennie Mackintosh-inspired exterior. The beamed restaurant, formerly the barn, now has rich furnishings and subtle lighting; there's a cocktail bar, too, with a large copper canopied fireplace and displays of modern art. A choice of menus offers a good range of Scottish dishes, including prime beef from 5 local farms. Expect starters such as seared West Coast king scallops, Stornoway black pudding, crispy bacon and balsamic dressing, and a main course of peppered fillet, flamed in brandy and finished with cream.

Chef Barry Liversidge **Owner** Stuart & Emma Peacock **Times** 12-3/6-9.30 Closed 26 Dec, 1 Jan, L Mon-Sat **Prices** Fixed L 2 course £15-£18, Fixed D 3 course £25-£27.50, Starter £5-£9.50, Main £13-£23, Dessert £4.50-£6.50, Service optional **Wines** 7 bottles over £20, 19 bottles under £20, 9 by glass **Notes** Early evening menu available 5.30-7 Sun-Fri, Sunday L, Vegetarian available, Dress restrictions, Smart casual **Seats** 30 **Children** Portions, Menu **Parking** 40

The Horseshoe Inn

EDDLESTON Map 21 NT24

Modern French

Refined French cuisine on the Scottish borders

☎ 01721 730225 📄 01721 730268
EH45 8QP
e-mail:
reservations@horseshoeinn.co.uk
web: www.horseshoeinn.co.uk
dir: On A703, 5m N of Peebles

Once the home of the village blacksmith, hence the name, the inn enjoys a tranquil location not far from Peebles in the majestic Scottish border country. The classically elegant pillared dining room has high-backed chairs, smart table settings and gilt-framed mirrors - the perfect backdrop to Patrick Bardoulet's accomplished cooking. Bardoulet brings the modern culinary techniques of his native France to bear on quality Scots produce, resulting in such creative but utterly winning dishes as dill-cured salmon with horseradish ice cream and toasted brioche, monkfish tail with leeks and butternut fondant in shallot and champagne sauce, and braised oxtail with Jerusalem artichoke and pied blue mushrooms. Bardoulet has clearly taken some inspiration from his new home, too, as evidenced by a serving of loin of lamb with its tongue, liver and haggis, alongside turnip purée (his own interpretation of the traditional Scottish mashed neeps) and pearl

barley. Excellent cheeses - served with Scottish oatcakes, not bread in the French style - are the alternative to sweet things such as pear parfait with liquorice cream and honey syrup.

Chef Patrick Bardoulet **Owner** Border Steelwork Structures Ltd
Times 12-2.30/7-9 Closed 25 Dec, early Jan, mid Oct, Mon, D Sun **Prices** Fixed L course £19.50, Tasting menu fr £60, Starter £9-£14, Main £15-£25, Dessert £7-£9, Service optional **Wines** 71 bottles over £20, 31 bottles under £20
Notes Sunday L, Vegetarian available, Dress restrictions, Smart casual, Jackets for men preferred **Seats** 40
Parking 20

SCOTTISH BORDERS

EDDLESTON Map 21 NT24

The Horseshoe Inn

◉◉◉ — *see opposite page*

KELSO Map 21 NT73

The Roxburghe Hotel & Golf Course

◉ Modern, Traditional ✋

Scottish country-house sporting destination with fine dining

☎ 01573 450331 🖨 01573 450611
TD5 8JZ
e-mail: hotel@roxburghe.net
dir: From A68, 1m N of Jedburgh, take A698 for 5m to Heiton

The Duke of Roxburghe certainly has plenty of space on his 54,000 acre estate, where this grand Jacobean country-house hotel is secreted among woodlands in vast grounds encompassing a championship golf course. Make no mistake, this is a seriously upmarket stately home of a hotel, with a dining experience to match. The Scottish Borders are prime huntin' shootin' fishin' territory, renowned for top-notch fish, meat and game which the kitchen puts to good use, together with wild mushrooms from the estate and herbs from the garden, in menus of French-influenced modern country-house cuisine. Expect starters like pressed ham hock and foie gras with fig and apple chutney to precede roast breast and confit leg of duck with fondant potato and smoked butternut squash. The Duke's cellar is a treasure trove of bottles for all occasions.

Chef Alasdair Stewart **Owner** Duke of Roxburghe
Times 12-2/7.30-9.45 **Prices** Fixed L 2 course fr £15, Fixed D 3 course fr £39.95, Service optional **Wines** 80 bottles over £20, 8 bottles under £20, 10 by glass **Notes** Sunday L, Vegetarian available, Dress restrictions, No jeans, trainers or T-shirts, Civ Wed 50 **Seats** 40, Pr/dining room 18 **Children** Portions, Menu **Parking** 150

MELROSE Map 21 NT53

Burt's Hotel

◉◉ Modern Scottish 🔸 ✋

Friendly, family-run Borders hotel with modern Scottish menu

☎ 01896 822285 🖨 01896 822870
The Square TD6 9PL
e-mail: enquiries@burtshotel.co.uk
web: www.burtshotel.co.uk
dir: A6091, 2m from A68, 3m S of Earlston. Hotel in market square

The Henderson family have run this smart townhouse hotel for the best part of 4 decades. Built on the market square in 1722, it is rooted into the heart of life in the quiet Borders town of Melrose. It's run well by cheery, nattily-uniformed staff and, for dining, there's a choice of a traditional clubby restaurant, with green Regency-striped walls, sporting prints and high-backed chairs, or a more pubby-feeling bistro bar. Seasonally-driven menus revolve around modern Scottish dishes built on quality local produce. An assiette of Eyemouth crab comes as crab cake, tian, and spring roll with chilli and lime crème fraîche to start; you might follow with pan-fried Highland venison, fondant potato, Scottish winter chanterelles and truffle jus, and end on a thoroughly Scottish note with a duo of cranachan - mousse and brûlée - with honey and Drambuie ice cream.

Chef Trevor Williams **Owner** The Henderson family
Times 12-2/7-9 Closed 26 Dec, 2-3 Jan **Prices** Fixed L 2 course £22-£29.50, Fixed D 3 course £35-£39, Service optional **Wines** 40 bottles over £20, 20 bottles under £20, 7 by glass **Notes** Sunday L, Vegetarian available, Dress restrictions, Jacket & tie preferred **Seats** 50, Pr/dining room 25 **Children** Portions **Parking** 40

PEEBLES Map 21 NT24

Cringletie House

◉◉ Modern British

Imaginative modern British cooking in a magisterial Victorian house

☎ 01721 725750 🖨 01721 725751
Edinburgh Rd EH45 8PL
e-mail: enquiries@cringletie.com
dir: 2.5m N of Peebles on A703

The house rises above the 28 acres of gardens and woodland that surround it, a masterpiece of Victorian Scots baronial architecture. Interiors are as elegant as is expected, easy on the eye, with an effective trompe l'oeil ceiling in the dining room, offset with contemporary fabrics and furniture. Much of the kitchen's fresh produce is grown in the grounds, and the up-to-date cooking style draws on a bedrock of established national tradition. Seared scallops are served with Jersey Royals in season, decorated with foam and a vivid, smooth watercress purée. Proceed, perhaps, to corn-fed chicken breast, intelligently teamed with crayfish cannelloni and an array of colourful seasonal vegetables, while dessert might bring a set of strawberry variations, including a terrine and ice cream.

Times 7-9 Closed L Mon-Sat

Renwicks

◉ British

Accomplished cooking with stunning views

☎ 0844 879 9024 & 01896 833600 🖨 01896 831166
Macdonald Cardrona Hotel, Golf & Country Club, Cardrona Mains EH45 6LZ
e-mail: general.cardrona@macdonald-hotels.co.uk
dir: From Edinburgh on A701 signed Penicuik/Peebles. Then A703, at 1st rdbt beside garage turn left onto A72, hotel 3m on right

Golf is firmly on the agenda at this smart modern hotel on the banks of the River Tweed, but you don't have to swing a niblick to fit in here. After a day's mountain biking or hiking in the Borders hills, the classy spa facilities or a dip in the huge pool will probably hit the spot. Then, there's the food which comes with glorious views from vast picture windows in the second-floor Renwicks restaurant. The kitchen's set-price menus aim to offer quality seasonal Scottish produce such as fresh seafood and well-hung game in unaffected, well-balanced dishes, with delightful service from a strong, professional team. Meals might start with sun-blushed tomato and basil pannacotta with chargrilled artichoke and feta cheese salad, then move on to a seared Highland venison steak with braised red cabbage, plum compôte and juniper berry jus.

Chef Ivor Clark **Owner** Macdonald Hotels
Times 12-2.30/6.30-9.45 **Prices** Fixed L 2 course £27.50-£32.50, Service included **Wines** 70 bottles over £20, 12 bottles under £20, 18 by glass **Notes** Sunday L, Vegetarian available, Dress restrictions, Smart casual, Civ Wed 150, Air con **Seats** 70, Pr/dining room 200 **Children** Portions, Menu **Parking** 100

ST BOSWELLS
Map 21 NT53

The Tweed Restaurant

Scottish **NEW**

Impressive modern Scottish cuisine in a grand Victorian country house

☎ 01835 822261 🖹 01835 823945
Dryburgh Abbey Hotel TD6 0RQ
e-mail: enquiries@dryburgh.co.uk
dir: B6356 signed Scott's View & Earlston. Through Clintmains, 1.8m to hotel

Dryburgh Abbey Hotel is a baronial red-brick Victorian mansion next to the romantically-ruined abbey in acres of sprawling grounds on the banks of the River Tweed. The classic interior sports the high ceilings and fancy plasterwork you expect in such a grandiose pile, while the first-floor Tweed Restaurant lives up to its name, with sweeping views over the river and glorious Borders scenery. Done out in elegant hues of claret and cream, it is a smart traditional setting for accomplished Scottish cuisine that shows a skilled hand at work in the kitchen, turning out well-balanced flavours with obvious technical flair. Ballotine of partridge with smoked mushrooms, hot mulled wine jelly and carrot and star anise purée shows a splendid array of flavours at work; a main course of monkfish wrapped in Parma ham with parsnip purée, tempura clams, haricot blanc cassoulet and mustard foam has real visual impact and an arsenal of textures.

Chef Mark Greenaway **Owner** John Wallis **Times** 7.30-9 Closed L all week **Prices** Food prices not confirmed for 2010. Please telephone for details, Service included **Wines** 52 bottles over £20, 28 bottles under £20, 11 by glass **Notes** Fixed menu 8 courses £35, Vegetarian available, Dress restrictions, No jeans or sportswear, Civ Wed 110 **Seats** 78, Pr/dining room 40 **Children** Portions, Menu **Parking** 50

SWINTON
Map 21 NT84

The Wheatsheaf at Swinton

Modern British **V** 🍷

Confident cooking in the heart of the Borders

☎ 01890 860257 🖹 01890 860688
Main St TD11 3JJ
e-mail: reception@wheatsheaf-swinton.co.uk
dir: A697/A1 onto B6461

In the heart of the Scottish Borders, in the sleepy village of Swinton, The Wheatsheaf is very much the hub of the community. A stone-built country inn with rooms, it has developed a formidable local reputation for its food, enjoyed in the bright and airy pine-clad conservatory, the more traditional dining room or the cosy bar lounge with its open fire. Local produce is the cornerstone of the appealing menus, with seafood landed at Eyemouth harbour, just twelve miles away, and all meat coming from local butchers. Wild salmon, venison and game dominate the menu in their seasons and such fine provenance is clear in dishes like breast of wood pigeon and black pudding on celeriac with orange and

redcurrant sauce, and main-course chargrilled sirloin of Scotch beef with a three peppercorn and brandy sauce.

Owner Mr & Mrs Chris Winson **Times** 12-2/6-9 Closed 25-27 Dec **Prices** Starter £4.25-£6.95, Main £14.95-£19.95, Dessert £5.45-£7.95, Service optional, Groups min 12 service 10% **Wines** 84 bottles over £20, 34 bottles under £20, 12 by glass **Notes** Sunday L, Vegetarian menu, Civ Wed 50 **Seats** 45, Pr/dining room 29 **Children** Portions, Menu **Parking** 6, On street

STIRLING

CALLANDER
Map 20 NN60

Callander Meadows

Modern British 🍷

Restaurant with rooms in historic town

☎ 01877 330181
24 Main St FK17 8BB
e-mail: mail@callandermeadows.co.uk
web: www.callandermeadows.co.uk
dir: M9 junct 10, A8 for 15m, restaurant 1m in village on left past lights

This Georgian restaurant with rooms in the centre of the town is run with a hands-on approach by a husband-and-wife-team - he does the starters and main courses, she makes the desserts and the bread. The house is impeccably maintained, with plenty of original features, and the service is refreshingly relaxed and informal. Local produce is sourced with care and attention to detail is evident throughout. Chicken liver paté is served with plum chutney and slices of toasted walnut bread as a starter, while main-course coley comes with a cheese crust, julienne of vegetables and parsley sauce. Good value lunches include the likes of shepherd's pie.

Chef Nick & Susannah Parkes **Owner** Nick & Susannah Parkes **Times** 12-2.30/6-9 Closed 25-26 Dec, Tue-Wed **Prices** Fixed L 2 course £7.95-£10.95, Fixed D 4 course fr £25, Starter £4.50-£7.50, Main £11.95-£24.95, Dessert £4.50-£7.50 **Wines** 15 bottles over £20, 17 bottles under £20, 8 by glass **Notes** Sunday L, Vegetarian available **Seats** 40, Pr/dining room 16 **Children** Portions **Parking** 6, 80 yds council parking

Roman Camp Country House Hotel

– *see opposite page*

STRATHYRE
Map 20 NN51

Creagan House

French, Scottish

17th-century Trossachs farmhouse with warm hospitality and good food

☎ 01877 384638 🖹 01877 384319
FK18 8ND
e-mail: eatandstay@creaganhouse.co.uk
dir: 0.25m N of village, off A84

The husband-and-wife-team who run this immaculately-restored 17th-century farmhouse put heart and soul into the place. The journey alone is a real treat, and when the sun has set on the jaw-dropping Highland scenery, a baronial dining room with a grandiose stone fireplace and burnished refectory tables awaits. The kitchen delivers classical French treatment with strong Scottish flavours in accurately-cooked dishes; sticklers for food of local provenance should be reassured to know that local small-holdings grow produce specifically for Creagan House, and meat is all reared on Perthshire farms. Among starters might be truffled langoustine mousseline with hand-dived Orkney scallops in Chartreuse-scented cream sauce, followed by collops of venison with red onion marmalade and baked fig in gin and juniper berry sauce. Should the weather confine you to the house, a 100-bin wine list and 50-odd malts should keep you entertained.

Chef Gordon Gunn **Owner** Gordon & Cherry Gunn **Times** 7.30-8.30 Closed 4-19 Nov, Xmas, 21 Jan-5 Mar, Wed-Thu, L all week (ex parties) **Prices** Fixed D 3 course fr £29.50, Service optional **Wines** 43 bottles over £20, 24 bottles under £20, 8 by glass **Notes** Dress restrictions, Smart casual **Seats** 15, Pr/dining room 6 **Children** Portions **Parking** 25

Roman Camp Country House Hotel

CALLANDER   Map 20 NN60

Modern French V

Innovative French-influenced cooking in luxurious manor house

☎ 01877 330003   📄 01877 331533
FK17 8BG
e-mail: mail@romancamphotel.co.uk
dir: N on A84 through Callander. From Main St turn left at East End into drive

So named, at the outbreak of the Second World War, for its proximity to one of the Romans' more northerly encampments, the hotel has been lavishly appointed. The interiors, indeed, are a sight for sore eyes, with their positively rococo colour schemes, fabrics and tapestries. The expansive, elliptical dining room is softly candlelit, the tables decorated with ornamental flower features that nearly reach the low ceiling. The strongly Francophile cooking revolves around thrilling combinations, with prime seasonal Scottish produce underpinning it. Curry-dusted scallops are a well-judged opener, served with puréed celeriac and raw apple, and then comes an intermediate soup course, perhaps white bean infused with Périgord black truffle. Roe deer is a majestic main course, the loin wrapped in pancetta, sweetly set off with honey-roasted parsnips, puréed beetroot and a 'cigarette' of dates. Only an overwhelming coffee foam upsets the balance of the dish. An ingenious

dessert is the dark chocolate délice, which oozes forth pistachio cream, fondant-fashion, and comes with nicely contrasting mascarpone ice cream. With breads, canapés and extras all up to the mark, this is without doubt a destination restaurant.

Chef Ian McNaught **Owner** Eric Brown
Times 12-2/7-9 **Prices** Fixed L 3 course £25-£30, Fixed D 4 course £45-£55, Starter £9.75-£19.75, Main £24.50-£35.50, Dessert £9.75-£12.75, Service optional **Wines** 185 bottles over £20, 15 bottles under £20, 16 by glass
Notes Sunday L, Vegetarian menu, Dress restrictions, Smart casual, Civ Wed 120 **Seats** 120, Pr/dining room 36
Children Portions **Parking** 80

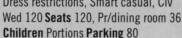

SCOTTISH ISLANDS
ARRAN, ISLE OF

BRODICK — Map 20 NS03

Kilmichael County House Hotel

◉◉ Modern British ✊

Fine Scottish fare in historic country house

☎ 01770 302219 📄 01770 302068
Glen Cloy KA27 8BY
e-mail: enquiries@kilmichael.com
dir: Turn right on leaving ferry terminal, through Brodick & left at golf club. Follow brown sign. Continue past church & onto private drive

This elegant, white-painted house, believed to be the oldest on the island and listed as a building of historic and architectural interest, has been lovingly restored to create a very stylish country-house hotel. Sitting in 4 acres of gardens in a peaceful glen, it has been furnished with a mix of antiques, interesting artworks and fabulous china. In the comfortable restaurant, the menu features first-class produce, including eggs from their own chickens and ducks, and fruit and vegetables and herbs from their own garden or the estate. Expect canapés, followed by a starter such as locally smoked salmon and prawn cheesecake (a rich mascarpone cream on an Arran oatcake and coriander base). After a sorbet follow with a main course of fillet of Scottish lamb baked with cinnamon-scented basmati rice and a rich Persian sauce.

Chef Antony Butterworth **Owner** G Botterill & A Butterworth **Times** 7-8.30 Closed Nov-Mar, Tue, L all week **Prices** Fixed D 4 course £42, Service optional **Wines** 32 bottles over £20, 23 bottles under £20, 3 by glass **Notes** Vegetarian available, Dress restrictions, Smart casual, no T-shirts or bare feet **Seats** 18 **Parking** 12

HARRIS, ISLE OF

SCARISTA — Map 22 NG09

Scarista House

◉◉ Modern Scottish

Remote country house with great views and island produce

☎ 01859 550238 📄 01859 550277
HS3 3HX
e-mail: timandpatricia@scaristahouse.com
web: www.scaristahouse.com
dir: On A859 15m S of Tarbert

Picture a Georgian manse looking over 3 miles of shell sand beach and the wild Atlantic coast of the Isle of Harris, heather-carpeted mountains all around: that's Scarista House. What's more, all this natural beauty comes with great food at the end of a day's exploration, taken in an elegant traditional dining room. Silver cutlery and candlesticks gleam on oak tables, original art hangs on the walls, and open fires cast a cosy glow. The kitchen takes fish and seafood, fruit and vegetables, fresh game and meat from the islands, going for organic whenever possible, and transforms it all into dishes such as velouté of Jerusalem artichokes and Puy lentils with Uist peat-smoked scallops, followed by Harris Minch langoustines served simply with garlic mayonnaise, crushed olive potatoes and salad from the garden. Exquisite desserts include Cointreau baba with caramelised blood oranges.

Chef Tim Martin **Owner** Tim & Patricia Martin **Times** L Mon-Sat 7.30-8 Closed 25 Dec, Jan-Feb **Prices** Fixed D 3 course £39.50, Service optional **Wines** 25 bottles over £20, 25 bottles under £20, 2 by glass **Notes** Sunday L, Vegetarian available, Civ Wed 40 **Seats** 20, Pr/dining room 14 **Children** Portions, Menu **Parking** 10

ISLAY, ISLE OF

BOWMORE — Map 20 NR35

The Harbour Inn

◉ Scottish, International

Wonderful views and fresh island produce

☎ 01496 810330 📄 01496 810990
The Square PA43 7JR
e-mail: info@harbour-inn.com
dir: Bowmore approx 8m from both ports (Port Ellen & Port Askaig)

The name sums up the location; a modest-looking whitewashed inn set in an idyllic fishing village offering wonderful views over the harbour to the loch beyond. Inside there's a surprisingly sizeable modern restaurant awash with the colours of the ocean. Its menu relies on premium produce from the island larder, with dishes keeping things very simple and fresh. World-class seafood and fish from local boats might turn up as fillet of monkfish wrapped in oak-smoked salmon and simply served with a mushroom risotto and citrus and honey vierge, or, from the land, a loin of Islay lamb with minted pea purée and aubergine and a port and rosemary reduction.

Times 12-2.30/6-9.30

MULL, ISLE OF

TOBERMORY — Map 22 NM55

Highland Cottage

◉◉ Modern Scottish, International ✊

Traditional Mull hotel with appealing menu jam-packed with local produce

☎ 01688 302030
24 Breadalbane St PA75 6PD
e-mail: davidandjo@highlandcottage.co.uk
web: www.highlandcottage.co.uk
dir: Opposite fire station. Main St up Back Brae, turn at top by White House. Follow road to right, left at next junct into Breadalbane St

If you believe in reducing food miles to a minimum, the restaurant of this family-run Hebridean hotel keeps the tally impressively low. Fish and seafood are landed either round the corner on Tobermory's pier or sourced from the waters around Mull and the mainland. The cottage dining room has a homely, welcoming atmosphere, and the food fits the bill to a tee: unfussy, skilful home cooking from a chef with the self-assurance to let the unbeatably fresh produce do the talking. Expect modern Scottish dishes with flashes of international flair, and of course, plenty of that local seafood, such as smoked Inverlussa mussels with mango mayonnaise to start, followed by seared diver-caught scallops with Argyll ham, sautéed potatoes and herb and garlic butter.

Chef Josephine Currie **Owner** David & Josephine Currie **Times** 7-9 Closed Nov-Feb, L all week **Prices** Fixed D 4 course £45, Service included **Wines** 33 bottles over £20, 21 bottles under £20, 11 by glass **Notes** Vegetarian available, Dress restrictions, Smart casual **Seats** 24 **Children** Portions **Parking** On street in front of establishment

Tobermory Hotel

◉ Modern Scottish ✊

Modern Scottish cooking in a harbourside setting

☎ 01688 302091 📄 01688 302254
53 Main St PA75 6NT
e-mail: tobhotel@tinyworld.co.uk
dir: On Main St opposite harbour

The hotel is an amalgam of fishermen's cottages fronting on to the Bay, where yachting folk and working fishing boats animate the scene. The Water's Edge restaurant capitalises on the setting with both local seafood and island produce such as game and cheeses informing the menus. Begin with smoked trout seasoned with chilli and lime on sesame toasts with a salad of pickled cucumber and spring onions and, after an intervening soup or sorbet, follow on with a pairing of Glengorm beef and Ulva Bay langoustines, dressed in tequila, lime and coriander butter. A selection of steamed mini-puddings served with ice creams makes for an original finale.

Chef Helen Swinbanks **Owner** Mr & Mrs I Stevens **Times** 6-9 Closed Xmas, Jan, L all week **Prices** Fixed D 3 course £31.50, Service optional **Wines** 18 bottles over £20, 24 bottles under £20, 5 by glass **Notes** Vegetarian available **Seats** 30 **Children** Portions, Menu **Parking** On street

ORKNEY ISLANDS

ST MARGARET'S HOPE   Map 24 ND49

Creel Restaurant

◉◉   Modern, Seafood ◐

Deserved reputation for making best of first-class Orkney produce

☎ 01856 831311
The Creel, Front Rd KW17 2SL
e-mail: alan@thecreel.freeserve.co.uk
dir: 13m S of Kirkwall on A961, on seafront in village

Situated a 20-minute drive south from Kirkwall, across the famous Churchill Barriers, the Creel restaurant and rooms occupies a stunning seafront spot in the picturesque village of St Margaret's Hope. This charming restaurant specialises in local produce, served in a relaxed dining room with local artwork on the walls and sea views. The freshest of fish is always on the menu, including unusual species such as wolf-fish, megrim, torsk and sea-witch. Hand-dived scallops, mackerel caught in a nearby bay, mussels and lobster from local creels feature when in season, as does Glenarm salmon, prime Orkney beef and seaweed-fed lamb from North Ronaldsay. All these are accompanied by locally grown vegetables, ales from the island's award-winning brewery, and malt whiskies from the Highland Park and Scapa distilleries. Chunky fish soup is brimful with cod cheeks, haddock belly and ling roe, while seared North Sea hake comes as a main course with Orkney scallops and crushed garden peas.

Chef Alan Craigie **Owner** Alan & Joyce Craigie **Times** 7-9 Closed Jan-Mar, Nov, Mon & Tue (Apr, May, Sep, Oct), L all week, D Mon **Prices** Fixed D 3 course £35-£40, Service optional **Wines** 10 bottles over £20, 18 bottles under £20, 4 by glass **Notes** Vegetarian available **Seats** 34, Pr/dining room 14 **Children** Portions **Parking** 12

SKYE, ISLE OF

COLBOST   Map 22 NG24

The Three Chimneys

◉◉◉ – *see page 538*

ISLEORNSAY   Map 22 NG71

Hotel Eilean Iarmain

◉◉   Traditional Scottish

Accomplished cooking on Skye

☎ 01471 833332   ▤ 01471 833275
IV43 8QR
e-mail: hotel@eileaniarmain.co.uk
dir: Mallaig & cross by ferry to Armadale, 8m to hotel or via Kyle of Lochalsh

Occupying an idyllic setting with spectacular views, this 19th-century former inn retains its old world charm and gives guests a truly genuine Highland experience. The hotel is situated on a sheltered bay in the south of Skye, with expansive views over the Sound of Sleat to the hills of Knoydart on the mainland. Take pre-dinner drinks in front of a roaring fire in the cosy lounge before moving into the elegant panelled restaurant with its view of Ornsay Lighthouse. Scottish fare prepared from high quality local ingredients is offered from a daily menu,

continued on page 539

The Three Chimneys

Modern Scottish NOTABLE WINE LIST

Immaculate local cooking in a wild remote location

☎ 01470 511258 📄 01470 511358
IV55 8ZT
e-mail:
eatandstay@threechimneys.co.uk
web: www.threechimneys.co.uk
dir: 5m W of Dunvegan take B884
signed Glendale. On left beside loch

In a location to restore the soul, Three Chimneys is housed in an original stone crofthouse on the shore of Loch Dunvegan, one of Skye's many almost mystical landscapes. In the little low-ceilinged dining room, simplicity is all, the bare stone walls, sturdy beamed fireplaces and polished wood tables all contributing an air of homely intimacy, while peek-a-boo views of the loch through the small windows are a delight at sunset. The produce that turns up on the fixed-price menus is never less than superb, with dishes changing daily in celebration of it, in a style that takes as its bedrock finely tuned traditional Scottish cooking, but with a modern approach. The result is skilful combinations with clear, crisply etched flavours. Seared breast of Perthshire wood pigeon comes with accompaniments of Ayrshire bacon, pearl barley, turnip, kale and game jus to make a perfectly composed first

course that delivers more straightforwardly than its rollcall of ingredients might suggest. Don't miss the seafood cookery, though, on show in a brilliant main course of grilled Mallaig halibut crusted with pine nuts, teamed with flawlessly timed Sconser scallops, layered roots and a dramatically rich claret velouté. Dishes may change daily around it, but the famous hot marmalade pudding with Drambuie custard has earned its place as a long stayer, or there may be Skye whisky and lemon parfait with grapefruit, poppyseed tuiles and aniseed brittle - a complex but arresting array. When the amuse-bouche alone might be a serving of brandy-laced Skye lobster bisque, you know you're going to get looked after.

Chef Michael Smith **Owner** Eddie & Shirley Spear **Times** 12.30-2.30/6.30-10 Closed 7-28 Jan, L Nov-Mar **Prices** Fixed L 2 course £25-£35, Fixed D 3 course £55-£61, Tasting menu £70, Service optional, Groups min 8 service 10% **Notes** Tasting menu 7 course, Vegetarian tasting menu, Dress restrictions, Smart casual preferred **Seats** 38, Pr/dining room 10 **Children** Portions

ISLEORNSAY *continued*

including venison from their own estate. Specialities include pan-seared local hand-dived scallops and Loch Bracadale crab mayonnaise with guacamole and beetroot dressing, followed by roast rump of West Highland hill-reared lamb with olive oil mash, rosemary and redcurrant jus.

Times 12-2.30/6.30-8.45

Iona Restaurant

◎◎ Modern Scottish **V** ♨

Stylish haven of peace serving Skye's wonderful produce

☎ 0845 055 1117 & 01471 833231 📄 01471 833231
Toravaig House Hotel, Knock Bay IV44 8RE
e-mail: info@skyehotel.co.uk
web: www.skyehotel.co.uk
dir: Cross Skye Bridge, turn left at Broadford onto A851, hotel 11m on left. Ferry to Armadale, take A851, hotel 4m on right

A visit to the Isle of Skye is food for the soul, so make sure you feed your inner gourmet at the same time. Toravaig House is a luxurious boutique hotel in a jaw-dropping location overlooking the Sound of Sleat towards the Knoydart Hills on the wild mainland. A day's sailing on the hotel's own yacht should sharpen the appetite for dinner in the classy Iona restaurant, where white-clothed

tables and high-backed leather chairs set a smart tone. The island's ample larder provides peerless fish, game or lamb for daily-changing menus, thoughtfully put together by a kitchen confident enough not to mess about with produce of this class. Start with duck breast - smoked in-house over oak from Talisker casks - with brioche croûton, liver pâté and red onion marmalade, then try oven-baked pork tenderloin, sticky braised belly, parsnip purée, baby turnips and pan juices.

Iona Restaurant

Chef Andrew Lipp **Owner** Anne Gracie & Ken Gunn
Times 12.30-2/6.30-9.30 **Prices** Fixed D 2 course £20-£30, Fixed D 4 course £25-£45, Starter £6-£9.95, Main £15-£29.95, Dessert £4.50-£9.95, Service optional **Wines** 20 bottles over £20, 20 bottles under £20, 6 by glass **Notes** Sunday L, Vegetarian menu, Dress restrictions, Smart casual, Civ Wed 18 **Seats** 30 **Parking** 20

See advert on page 537

Kinloch Lodge

◎◎◎ *– see below*

Restaurant at the Duisdale

◎ Modern European **NEW** ♨

Boutique-style country-house hotel dining with stunning views

☎ 01471 833202 📄 01471 833404
Duisdale Country House Hotel IV43 8QW
e-mail: info@duisdale.com
dir: 7m N of Armadale ferry & 12m S of Skye Bridge on A851

Duisdale House looks every inch the grand Victorian lodge from the outside, but inside it's clear that the old girl has had a top-to-toe chic boutique makeover. Classy contemporary fabrics in dramatic black and gold blend with neutral mushroom shades and period features in a décor worthy of a trendy city hotel, but relocated in the wilds of the Isle of Skye. Sitting in the atmospheric candlelit restaurant with sublime views across landscaped gardens to the Sound of Sleat, you realise that the beach is just a few hundred yards away. The cooking lets top-grade local produce - seafood in particular - do the talking, with simple treatment and clean-cut presentation. Local hand-dived scallops with orange and basil beurre blanc might turn up among

continued

Kinloch Lodge

ISLEORNSAY Map 22 NG71

French **NEW V** ♨

The best of the Skye larder in Baronial splendour

☎ 01471 833214 & 833333 📄 01471 833277
Sleat IV43 8QY
e-mail: reservations@kinloch-lodge.co.uk
web: www.kinloch-lodge.co.uk
dir: 1m off main road, 6m S of Broadford on A851, 10m N of Armadale

This is the home of food and cookery writer Claire Macdonald, AKA Lady Claire Macdonald, and Kinloch is the Highland pile she shares with her husband, the High Chief of Clan Donald. This seat of the clan dates from the 16th century and is idyllically situated with views over the rugged scenery of Sleat and the water of Na Dal sea loch. Portraits of Macdonalds through the centuries adorn

the walls of the formal dining room, where crisp white linen-clad tables are laid with good quality crockery and vintage silver cutlery. Given Claire's devotion to regional and seasonal produce, the kitchen, under the command of Marcello Tully, uses first-class ingredients to good effect in well-balanced and imaginative modern Scottish dishes. Things start with a soup (parsnip and Pernod, perhaps), following on with an impressive construction of roast shredded duck with Stornoway black pudding, then perhaps a superb piece of halibut, and finishing with pleasingly bitter dark chocolate torte.

Chef Marcello Tully **Owner** Lord & Lady Macdonald
Times 12-2.30/6.30-9 Closed 1 wk Xmas, **Prices** Fixed D 4 course £52, Service optional **Notes** Fixed L 4/5 course £24.95-£27.95, Fixed D 5/6 course £55-£60, Sunday L, Vegetarian menu **Seats** 40, Pr/dining room 20 **Children** Portions **Parking** 20

ISLEORNSAY *continued*

starters, while fillet of lamb with truffle risotto and wild thyme and whisky jus is typical of main courses.

Chef Graham Campbell **Owner** K Gunn & A Gracie **Times** 12-2/6.30-9.30 **Prices** Fixed L 2 course £9.50-£23, Fixed D 3 course £15-£40.50, Starter £4.50-£9.50, Main £9.50-£27.50, Dessert £4.50-£7.50, Service optional **Wines** 39 bottles over £20, 11 bottles under £20, 9 by glass **Notes** Tasting menu available, Sunday L, Vegetarian available, Civ Wed 58 **Seats** 50 **Children** Portions **Parking** 30

PORTREE
Map 22 NG44

Bosville Hotel

@@ Modern British ✋

Superb cooking of truly local produce with great harbour views

☎ 01478 612846 📠 01478 613434 **9-11 Bosville Ter IV51 9DG** **e-mail:** bosville@macleodhotels.co.uk **web:** www.bosvillehotel.co.uk **dir:** A87 signed Portree, then A855 into town. Cross over pedestrian crossing, follow road to left

Set high up in the picture-postcard fishing village of Portree, with glorious views over the harbour, the Bosville is an extended fisherman's cottage with a popular bistro, a smart bar (formerly the village bank), and the Chandlery Restaurant. Themed around a ships' chandlery, the restaurant is stylish and modern with innovative monthly menus built around the fantastic produce to be found on Skye. Chef John Kelly's cooking is creative and focused on flavour, as seen in a starter of langoustine tails served with slow-braised belly pork, pear and ginger purée, and a light soya and star anise jus. For main course, try guinea fowl on roast butternut squash and a light jus with chanterelles, then finish, perhaps, with a

crumble rhubarb tart with Glendale mint and rhubarb salad and cardamom ice cream.

Chef John Kelly **Owner** Donald W Macleod **Times** 6.30-9.30 Closed L all week **Prices** Food prices not confirmed for 2010. Please telephone for details. **Wines** 20 bottles over £20, 20 bottles under £20, 12 by glass **Notes** Vegetarian available **Seats** 30 **Children** Portions **Parking** 10, On street

---

Cuillin Hills Hotel

@@ Modern British

West coast ingredients in a classic country-house setting

☎ 01478 612003 📠 01478 613092 **IV51 9QU** **e-mail:** info@cuillinhills-hotel-skye.co.uk **dir:** 0.25m N of Portree on A855

This former hunting lodge, built for the Isle of Skye's Lord MacDonald, turned country-house hotel has fantastic views overlooking Portree Bay and the Cuillin Hills. Chic table settings in the convivial split-level restaurant, presided over by relaxed and friendly service, complement the traditional décor. West coast ingredients are used in dishes which allow them to shine. The cuisine has a distinctly Scottish influence, with Cullen skink served as an extra course, but there are also plenty of European, particularly French, influences. Start perhaps with home-cured salmon in treacle and whisky with lemon and capers and baby flowers, move on to Isle of Skye lobster with Jack Daniels and parmesan cream sauce and fancy leaf salad. Sautéed strawberries in Drambuie cream provide a boozy finish.

Chef Robert Macaskill **Owner** Wickman Hotels Ltd **Times** 12-2/6.30-9 Closed L Mon-Sat **Prices** Fixed D 3 course £35-£40, Service optional **Wines** 41 bottles over £20, 21 bottles under £20, 4 by glass **Notes** Sunday L, Vegetarian available, Civ Wed 70 **Seats** 48 **Children** Portions, Menu **Parking** 56

Rosedale Hotel

@ Traditional Scottish

Welcoming waterfront hotel with seafood a speciality

☎ 01478 613131 📠 01478 612531 **Beaumont Crescent IV51 9DB** **e-mail:** rosedalehotelsky@aol.com **dir:** On harbour front

Once a group of fishermen's cottages, this delightful, family-run waterfront hotel offers a wonderfully warm, intimate atmosphere. Inside, a labyrinth of corridors and stairs connects the lounges, bar and restaurant which are set on different levels. A window seat is a must in the charming first-floor restaurant with fine views overlooking the bay and Portree's busy harbour. You can expect plenty of local produce, including a good smattering of seafood, prepared with panache. As the guide went to press we heard there had been a change of chef here, please see theAA.com for the latest information.

Times 7-8.30 Closed 1 Nov-1 Mar, L all week

STAFFIN
Map 22 NG46

Flodigarry Country House Hotel

@ Modern Scottish NEW V

Glorious views and superb fish and seafood at intimate country house

☎ 01470 552203 📠 01470 552301 **IV51 9HZ** **e-mail:** info@flodigarry.co.uk **dir:** Flodigarry is situated on the NE coast of the island, just off the A855, approx 20m from Portree

History and romance come in spades at this enchanting country house on the Isle of Skye, and its setting beneath the dramatic Trotternish Ridge with views across the sea to the mainland Torridon mountains truly deserves the over-used 'jaw-dropping' epithet. The intimate stone-walled house and neighbouring cottage were once home to Scottish heroine Flora MacDonald, and loving restoration has produced a relaxed haven of modern luxury, with great food to boot. Those glorious views form a backdrop to the kitchen's modern Scottish cuisine, conjured from superb local fish, shellfish and game. Pan-fried scallops play the starring role in a beautiful starter, with honey and mustard sauce used sparingly, followed by seared line-caught sea bass with spinach and potato cake and lemon butter sauce.

Chef Joseph Miko **Owner** Robin Collins **Times** 12-2.30/7-9.30 Closed Nov & Jan **Prices** Starter £6.95-£16.75, Main £18-£32, Dessert £5.95-£8, Service included **Wines** 4 by glass **Notes** Sunday L, Vegetarian menu, Civ Wed 80 **Seats** 30, Pr/dining room 24 **Children** Portions, Menu **Parking** 30

The Glenview

◉ British, French NEW ◔

Accomplished cooking in a friendly restaurant with rooms

☎ 01470 562248
Culnacnoc IV51 9JH
e-mail: enquiries@glenviewskye.co.uk
dir: 12m N of Portree on A855, 4m S of Staffin

This small restaurant with rooms has a to-die-for location on the Isle of Skye's superbly-scenic Trotternish Peninsula. Youthful owners run this charming small hotel in an old whitewashed croft house with genuine friendliness, and a further bonus is the top-class cooking on offer. The key here is fresh, top-notch local produce that is proudly name-checked - take Orbost heather-grazed beef, for example - on the concise three-course dinner menus offering two choices at each stage. A starter of brown crab with watercress soup delivers intense flavours, then local Iron Age pork is served with Skye kale, polenta cake and turnips with apple sauce. To finish, a freshly-baked brioche with warm plum compôte and home-made ice cream makes a well-thought-out dessert.

Chef Simon Wallwork **Owner** Kirsty Faulds **Times** 7-8.30 Closed Jan, Mon, L all week **Prices** Fixed D 3 course £27.50, Service optional **Wines** 4 bottles over £20, 15 bottles under £20, 4 by glass **Notes** Vegetarian available **Seats** 22 **Children** Portions, Menu **Parking** 12

STEIN   **Map 22 NG25**

Loch Bay Seafood Restaurant

◉ British Seafood ◔

Welcoming approach in a lochside fish restaurant

☎ 01470 592235   ▤ 01470 592235
IV55 8GA
e-mail: david@lochbay-seafood-restaurant.co.uk
dir: 4m off A850 by B886

The location, at the end of a dead-end road next to the loch on Skye, is as out-of-the-way as they come, the restaurant being a conversion of little fishermen's cottages. Expect the freshest fish and seafood from menus chalked up on boards, and a thoroughly welcoming, homely approach. Grilled razor clams in parsley butter, or a bowl of Cullen skink, might set the ball rolling, and then be followed by anything from halibut to hake, John Dory to monkfish tail, all cooked with the minimum of intervention to allow their flavours and freshness to shine forth. Finish with apple and apricot crumble.

Chef David Wilkinson **Owner** David & Alison Wilkinson **Times** 12-2/6-9 Closed Nov-Etr (excl. 1wk over Hogmanay), Sun-Mon **Prices** Fixed L 2 course £12.95, Starter £3.60-£9, Main £12.50-£20.70, Dessert £4.50-£5.20, Service optional **Wines** 15 bottles over £20, 17 bottles under £20, 5 by glass **Notes** Extensive blackboard choices **Seats** 26 **Children** Portions **Parking** 6

STRUAN   **Map 22 NG33**

Ullinish Country Lodge

◉◉◉ *– see page 542*

Ullinish Country Lodge

STRUAN Map 22 NG33

French **V**

Culinary paradise for foodies in an idyllic Skye setting

☎ 01470 572214 📄 01470 572341
IV56 8FD
e-mail: ullinish@theisleofskye.co.uk
web: www.theisleofskye.co.uk
dir: 9m S of Dunvegan on A863

Hidden away at the end of one of Skye's less-trodden tracks, Ullinish Lodge is a tranquil bolthole with some of Scotland's most uplifting scenery on the doorstep. Bracketed by lochs on three sides and with jaw-dropping views of the Black Cuillins and MacLeod's Tables, it's no wonder literary companions Samuel Johnson and James Boswell chose to tarry a while. The interior has survived the wave of makeovers sweeping country houses, remaining comfortingly traditional with calmly genteel service in the dining room, where wood-panels and a tartan carpet are a reminder of where you are - if any were needed, given the rugged romance visible through the windows. Johnson and Boswell noted in 1773 that 'there is a plentiful garden in Ullinish' - in that respect, 21st-century guests will be pleased to note that little has changed: the local larder still provides most of what turns up in the kitchen's imaginative modern output. Chef Bruce Morrison's passion for food comes

through loud and clear in creative pairings, his masterful classical technique extracting big flavours and pulling off intriguing combinations and striking presentation with panache. All the stops are pulled out at dinner, starting with roasted local hand-dived scallops teamed with creamy purslane, caper and raisin purée, crispy quail's eggs and garlic foam, before a riff on a pig theme delivers braised cheek, crispy belly and croquette of trotter with cucumber relish, horseradish marshmallow and a razor clam and fennel salad. An intermediate parmesan sorbet and sweetcorn jelly fits in before a finale of rum and raisin soufflé, crème brûlée ice cream and sea buckthorn 'caviar'. And all the bits and treats from canapés, to breads, amuse-bouche, pre-desserts and petits fours are winners, made with the same precision and attention to detail as the main events.

Chef Bruce Morrison **Owner** Brian & Pam Howard **Times** 12-2.30/7.30-8.30 Closed Jan, 1 wk Nov, **Prices** Fixed L 2 course £20, Fixed D 4 course £49.50, Service optional **Wines** 45 bottles over £20, 10 bottles under £20 **Notes** Sunday L, Vegetarian menu, Dress restrictions, Smart casual, No T-shirts **Seats** 22 **Parking** 10

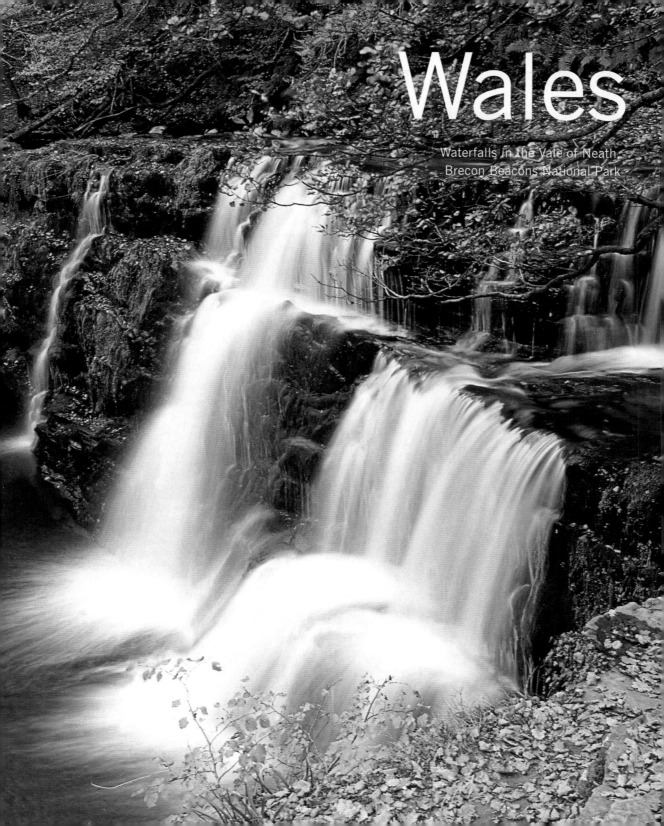

Wales

Waterfalls in the Vale of Neath
Brecon Beacons National Park

BEAUMARIS Map 14 SH67

Bishopsgate House Hotel

🌐 Traditional Welsh V

Green-fronted hotel overlooking the Menai Strait

☎ 01248 810302 📠 01248 810166
54 Castle St LL58 8BB
e-mail: hazel@bishopsgatehotel.co.uk
dir: from Menai Bridge onto A545 to Beaumaris. Hotel on left in main street

Set in a Georgian terrace a short hop from the Menai waterfront, the hotel has a green pastel-shaded façade that helps it stand out. Inside, a low-ceilinged dining-room with green walls and a large fireplace is full of character, and is the scene for accomplished cooking that doesn't aim to make an undue show of itself. Smoked salmon mousse has the right ethereally light texture, while beef braised in red wine with shallots, bacon, mushrooms, herbs and garlic might put many a boeuf bourguignon to shame. Lemon tart has a sharply flavoured, creamy filling.

Chef H Johnson Ollier, I Sankey **Owner** Hazel Johnson Ollier **Times** 12.30-2.30/7-9.30 Closed L Mon-Sat **Prices** Food prices not confirmed for 2010. Please telephone for details. **Wines** 15 bottles over £20, 17 bottles under £20, 3 by glass **Notes** Sunday L, Vegetarian menu, Dress restrictions, Smart dress **Seats** 40 **Children** Portions **Parking** 10

Ye Olde Bulls Head Inn

◎◎ Modern British

Historic inn serving top-notch Anglesey produce

☎ 01248 810329 📠 01248 811294
Castle St LL58 8AP
e-mail: info@bullsheadinn.co.uk
dir: Town centre, main street

Charles Dickens and Dr Samuel Johnson are just 2 of the famous guests to have visited this historic 14th-century coaching inn, a staging post on the route to Ireland. Now the décor is striking and contemporary, but the antique weaponry on view is a sign of its colourful past. The elegant Restaurant is up in the eaves, the oldest part of the pub, still with the original exposed beams. The daily-changing menu uses top-notch Anglesey produce, including Welsh Black beef and salt marsh lamb, to create imaginative modern British dishes such as home-cured gravad lax of organic salmon with an oyster fritter, confit tomato presse and herb salad, followed by saddle of wild venison, tomato farci, celeriac lasagne, roasted garlic and chocolate sauce. The lively Brasserie is an informal alternative.

Times 7-9.30 Closed 25-26 Dec, 1 Jan, Sun, L Mon-Sat

LLANGEFNI Map 14 SH67

Tre-Ysgawen Hall Country House Hotel & Spa

🌐 Modern European NEW

Atmospheric country-house hotel with local flavour

☎ 01248 750750 📠 01248 750035
Capel Coch LL77 7UR
e-mail: enquiries@treysgawen-hall.co.uk
web: www.treysgawen-hall.co.uk
dir: A55 junct 6, enter town & follow signs for B5111

As soon as you cross the Menai Straits to the Isle of Anglesey you feel you have taken a step back from life's bustle. And this Victorian country house is a step further into seclusion, with its acres of landscaped gardens and woodland between you and the world outside. So after a hard day's unwinding and de-stressing, head for Noëlle's Restaurant, where classic country-house cooking rubs shoulders with some more inventive modern British dishes. Expect excellent local, seasonal produce in starters such as a warm salad of scallops pointed up with truffle, apple and celeriac, followed by breast of Guinea fowl with bubble-and-squeak and wild mushroom boudin; finish with dark chocolate and orange fondant with Florentine ice cream.

Chef Stephen Duffy **Owner** Mr & Mrs Neil Rowlands **Times** 12-2/7-9.30 **Prices** Fixed L 3 course £19.50, Fixed D 3 course £29.50, Starter £7.25-£8.95, Main £17.25-£24.95, Dessert £6.25-£8.75, Service optional **Wines** 50 bottles over £20, 22 bottles under £20, 6 by glass **Notes** Sunday L, Vegetarian available, Civ Wed 150 **Seats** 60, Pr/dining room 18 **Children** Portions, Menu **Parking** 70

BRIDGEND Map 9 SS97

The Great House & Restaurant

◎◎ Modern British NEW

Modern cuisine in historic building

☎ 01656 657644
High St, Laleston CF32 0HP
e-mail: enquiries@great-house-laleston.co.uk
dir: On A473 300yds from junct with A48

A fine stone building dating back to the 16th century, this relaxed hotel is set in attractive gardens in a tranquil village setting. The smart Leicesters Restaurant boasts a feature inglenook fireplace and an old stove set into a side wall, but the décor is modern with discreet lighting and warm colours creating an appealing ambience. Staff are friendly and efficient, showing good knowledge of the modern British menu which is produce-driven and backed by good technical skills. A starter of leek and Carmarthenshire ham linguini with poached duck egg might be followed by Gressingham duck breast marinated in rhubarb and ginger, rosemary polenta, spring greens and game jus. The tempting desserts include butterscotch and vanilla pannacotta with chocolate and Baileys sorbet.

Chef Nick Collins **Owner** Stephen & Norma Bond **Times** 12-2/6-9.30 Closed Xmas, BH Mon, D Sun **Prices** Fixed L 2 course £8.95-£14.95, Fixed D 3 course fr £19.95, Starter £3.50-£9.95, Main £7.50-£22.95, Dessert £4.95-£5.95, Service optional, Groups min 10 service 10% **Wines** 4 by glass **Notes** Early bird menu 2/3 course £14.95-£19.95, Sunday L, Vegetarian available, Civ Wed 50, Air con **Seats** 45, Pr/dining room 40 **Children** Portions **Parking** 33

CARDIFF

CARDIFF   Map 9 ST17

Cardiff Marriott Hotel

◉ British, French NEW

Relaxed city-centre brasserie

☎ 029 2078 5872 & 0870 4007290 🖹 029 2039 5578
Mill Ln CF10 1EZ
dir: M4 junct 29/A48M E follow signs city centre & Cardiff
Bay. Continue on Newport Rd for 3m then turn right onto
Mill Lane

A contemporary interpretation of a classic French
brasserie, Centrale is in the modern, city-centre Cardiff
Marriott Hotel. A two-tier, easy-on-the-eye modern space,
Centrale comes decked out with contemporary wood
tables, ceramic tiled or wooden flooring and mood
lighting. The cooking hits the right note, too, mostly with
a French flavour, plus some British influences, and all
driven by well-sourced local produce. The menu plays to
the gallery with something for everyone, from classics like
coq au vin, moules or escargots, to British grass-fed beef
steaks with choice of sauces (perhaps béarnaise), while
Gallic desserts (apple tarte Tatin) can include a Brit twist
as in croissant-and-butter pudding.

Chef Tino Pardon **Owner** Marriott International
Times 12-2.30/5.30-10.30 **Prices** Food prices not
confirmed for 2010. Please telephone for details. **Wines** 9
bottles over £20, 15 bottles under £20, 7 by glass
Notes Sunday L, Vegetarian available, Civ Wed 350, Air
con **Seats** 120 **Children** Portions, Menu **Parking** 140

First Floor Restaurant

◉◉ Modern British

British cooking in a stylish, modern setting

☎ 0870 122 0020 🖹 029 2048 8894
Mercure Holland House, 24-26 Newport Rd CF24 0DD
e-mail: H6622-am@accor.com
dir: Newport Rd 300mtrs from Queen St. Adjacent to
Institute for the Blind & Cardiff University buildings

If you like to people-watch, this modern hotel restaurant
with its floor-to-ceiling windows should be just the job.
It's right in the hub of things, and like the city outside it
has an upbeat vibe, helped along by an open kitchen,
friendly staff and jazzy music. Those big windows let in
plenty of natural light by day, while coloured lighting at
night casts a rather funky glow on the contemporary
bistro-style seating and unclothed tables. The menu is
full of British favourites with some international
diversions. Start, for instance, with twice baked Cheddar
cheese soufflé with red onion marmalade, or Parma ham
and fresh figs with a balsamic reduction, followed by
buttered chicken balti with basmati rice and garlic and
coriander nan, or braised lamb shank with minted gravy
and dauphinoise potatoes.

Times 12-2/6-10 Closed L 1 Jan, D 25 Dec

Le Gallois-Y-Cymro

◉◉ Modern European

Creative cooking in Cardiff's Canton district

☎ 029 2034 1264 🖹 029 2023 7911
6-10 Romilly Crescent CF11 9NR
e-mail: info@legallois-ycymro.com
dir: From town centre, follow Cowbridge Rd East. Turn
right to Wyndham Crescent, then to Romilly Crescent.
Restaurant on right

Not far from the centre of town, and the castle and
Millennium Stadium, Le Gallois has a new chef with a
globe trotting CV, which includes stints in such
glamorous locations as Beverly Hills and Hong Kong. In
Cardiff, large picture windows and a minimalist décor
make for a stylish location for some innovative modern
European cooking; the food is less overtly Gallic than
under previous chefs. Staff help set a relaxed and
unpretentious tone. Canapés get the ball rolling in style -
an appealing combination of parsnip and game crisps
and bacon crackling with a crème fraîche dip, perhaps.
Celeriac and salsa verde soup is an attractively presented
first course displaying excellent balance of flavours, and
main-course sea bream, with lemon-crushed potatoes
and spinach butter sauce, is an excellent piece of fish,
accurately cooked. Dark chocolate parfait with poached
pear and crème anglaise is a star among desserts.

Chef Grady Atkins **Owner** The Dupuy Family
Times 12-2.30/6-9.30 Closed Xmas, New Year, Mon, D
Sun **Prices** Fixed L 2 course fr £15.95, Starter £8.90-
£12.90, Main £13.95-£19.95, Dessert £6.50-£7.95,
Service added but optional 10% **Wines** 76 bottles over
£20, 16 bottles under £20, 10 by glass **Notes** Tasting
menu available, Sunday L, Vegetarian available, Air con
Seats 60 **Children** Portions **Parking** 7

The Laguna Kitchen & Bar

◉ Traditional European

Good Welsh produce in contemporary hotel restaurant

☎ 029 2011 1103 🖹 029 2011 1102
Park Plaza Cardiff, Greyfriars Rd CF10 3AL
e-mail: ppcres@parkplazahotels.co.uk
dir: City centre, next to New Theatre

Cardiff Park Plaza Hotel's Laguna Kitchen and Bar is far
from a bland identikit hotel restaurant. The clean-cut
contemporary décor strikes the right chords with dark wood
floors, a palette of cream and chocolate browns, and
textures of leather and glass, while a thirst-inducing wall
of wine separates the brasserie-style restaurant from the
lively bar. An open-plan kitchen provides a bit of culinary
theatre, and Welsh suppliers cater for the lion's share of
produce for a wide-ranging menu. Expect clear, full-on
flavours, whether you keep it simple with classic grills of
fish and meat, or go for something more involved, such as
pan-fried sea bass paired with crispy fried confit of belly
pork, baby beetroot and fennel salad with a citrus dressing.

Chef Mark Freeman **Owner** Martin Morris
Times 12-2.30/5.30-10.30 **Prices** Fixed L 2 course £12,
Starter £4-£10, Main £8-£22.50, Dessert £4.65-£6.50,

Service added but optional 10% **Wines** 44 bottles over
£20, 36 bottles under £20, 12 by glass **Notes** Sunday L,
Vegetarian available, Civ Wed 140, Air con **Seats** 110, Pr/
dining room 150 **Children** Portions, Menu **Parking** NCP

Manor Parc Country Hotel & Restaurant

◉ Modern European

Welcoming hotel serving fresh local fare

☎ 029 2069 3723 🖹 029 2061 4624
Thornhill Rd, Thornhill CF14 9UA
e-mail: enquiry@manorparc.com
dir: M4 junct 32. Turn left at lights, pass Den Inn. Take
next left, left at lights on A469

This welcoming, family-run hotel is set in open
countryside on the northern edge of Cardiff. The grand,
orangery-style restaurant overlooks the terrace and
grounds. There's a choice of menus, using local
ingredients as far as possible. Typical dishes from the à
la carte menu might include savoury pancakes filled with
Welsh leek and blue cheese ragu to start, followed by
pan-fried tenderloin of pork with a cider cream sauce
served on celeriac mash, or breast of chicken stuffed with
wild mushrooms and served with a white wine and
wholegrain mustard cream. To finish, choose from the
daily-changing dessert trolley.

Chef Mr D Holland, Alun Thomas **Owner** Mr S Salimeni &
Mrs E A Salimeni **Times** 12-2/6-9 Closed 26 Dec-2 Jan, D
Sun **Prices** Fixed L 3 course £21.50-£23.50, Fixed D 3
course £21.50-£23.50, Starter £4.75-£8, Main £14.50-
£16.50, Dessert £4.50, Service optional, Groups min 6
service 10% **Notes** Sunday L, Vegetarian available, Civ
Wed 100 **Seats** 70, Pr/dining room 100 **Children** Portions
Parking 85

The Old Post Office Restaurant

◉ British, European

Contemporary restaurant in former post office

☎ 029 2056 5400 🖹 029 2056 3400
Greenwood Ln, St Fagans CF5 6EL
e-mail: info@theoldpostofficerestaurant.co.uk
dir: A48 E through Cardiff to St Fagans sign. Right at
lights, 1.4m, in village turn right into Croft-y-Genau Rd,
right into Greenwood Lane

In the pretty village of St Fagans, this contemporary
restaurant is housed in the old post office and police
station. The conservatory dining room is based on a New
England style with clean modern lines, high-backed chairs
and dark unclothed tables, but you can expect a
traditionally warm welcome. The menu also offers a mix of
old and new, delivering traditional dishes given a bit of a
contemporary dimension with some modern European
ideas. A typical starter might be soused fillets of red mullet
on bruschetta with a rocket and lemon dressing, followed
by braised shin of Brecon beef in a dark rich sauce with
mash, braised celery and roasted carrots. Expect desserts
such as baked figs in red wine with mascarpone cream.

Times 12-3/7-9.30 Closed Xmas, 1st 2 wks Jan, Mon, D
Sun

CARDIFF *continued*

Raglans Restaurant

◎◎ Modern European

Inventive cooking in a lakeside setting

☎ 029 2059 9100 📄 029 2059 9648
**Copthorne Hotel Cardiff, Copthorne Way, Culverhouse
Cross CF5 6DH**
e-mail: sales.cardiff@millenniumhotels.co.uk
dir: M4 junct 33 take A4232 (Culverhouse Cross), 4th exit
at rdbt (A48), 1st left

In the heart of a business and shopping park on the
outskirts of Cardiff is the modern Copthorne Hotel and its
popular Raglans Restaurant. Large windows look out over
the hotel's own lake, where copious birdlife has taken up
residence amongst the reeds. The interior of Raglans is
all wood panelling, well-spaced tables with comfortable
seating, and subtle lighting which sets the mood at
night. Service is attentive and friendly, and the modern
European cooking ambitious but accomplished, and
based around mostly local produce. Kick off with the pan-
seared gambas with fine beans, affila cress and
Japonaise dressing, moving on to braised collar of pork
and crackling stick with fondant potato, prune and Earl
Grey tea compôte. Dessert might be gooseberry mousse
with gooseberry compôte and fennel ice cream, or pan-
fried bara brith with green apple sorbet, cinnamon tuile
and mulled wine syrup.

Times 12.30-2/6.30-9.45 Closed 25 Dec

The Thai House Restaurant

◎ Thai V

First-rate Thai cooking in Cardiff

☎ 029 2038 7404 📄 029 2064 0810
3-5 Guildford Crescent, Churchill Way CF10 2HJ
e-mail: info@thaihouse.biz
dir: At junct of Newport Rd & Queen St turn left past
Queen St station, before lights turn left into Guildford
Crescent

Thai House introduced Wales to the fragrant delights of
its national cuisine in 1985, and stays firmly in the
premier league of the country's Thai eateries. Ingredients
that can't be found among excellent local Welsh produce
are flown in from Bangkok, and nasty E-numbers have no
place here. What you can expect is pukka cooking from a
chef who learnt her trade as an apprentice to her mother
on a small market stall back home. A vast choice of
exotica is on offer: Thai-style mussels steamed with
basil, lemongrass and kaffir lime leaves; crispy fried duck
with tamarind sauce; grilled Welsh lamb marinated in
soy, honey and mint and served with a lime, honey and
chilli dressing.

Chef Sujan Klingson **Owner** Noi & Arlene Ramasut
Times 12-2.30/6-11 Closed Xmas, 1 Jan, Sun
Prices Fixed L 2 course fr £8.95, Fixed D 3 course £25,
Starter £4.95-£11.95, Main £8.50-£17.95, Dessert £4.50-
£6.95, Service optional, Groups min 8 service 10%
Wines 34 bottles over £20, 23 bottles under £20, 16 by

glass **Notes** Vegetarian menu, Dress restrictions, Smart
casual **Seats** 130, Pr/dining room 20 **Children** Portions
Parking On street & NCP opposite

Woods Brasserie

◎ Modern European

Modern brasserie in fashionable Cardiff Bay

☎ 029 2049 2400 📄 029 2048 1998
Pilotage Building, Stuart St, Cardiff Bay CF10 5BW
e-mail: serge@woods-brasserie.com
dir: In heart of Cardiff Bay. From M4 junct 33 towards
Cardiff Bay, large stone building on right

The old customs house building overlooks Cardiff Bay,
and large windows make the best of the views over the
water; a table on the patio is a good bet when the sun
shines. The open-plan kitchen and bare-wood tables
confirm its brasserie credentials, as does the menu,
where fine Welsh produce is put to good use in British
and European preparations: pressed ham hock and free-
range chicken terrine with spiced grape chutney to start,
followed by smoked haddock and leek risotto with
parmesan shavings and leek crisps, and maybe a
selection of Welsh and continental cheeses to finish.

Chef Wesley Hammond **Owner** Choice Produce
Times 12-2/5.30-10 Closed 25-26 Dec & 1 Jan, D Sun
(Sep-May) **Prices** Fixed L 2 course £13.50, Starter £4.95-
£9.95, Main £10.45-£21.45, Dessert £5.50-£6.95, Service
optional, Groups min 6 service 10% **Wines** 35 bottles
over £20, 25 bottles under £20, 20 by glass **Notes** Pre-
theatre meals available, Sunday L, Vegetarian available,
Air con **Seats** 90, Pr/dining room 40 **Children** Portions,
Menu **Parking** Multi-storey car park opposite

LAUGHARNE	Map 8 SN31

The Cors Restaurant

◎◎ Modern Welsh

Great Welsh food in Bohemian splendour

☎ 01994 427219
Newbridge Rd SA33 4SH
e-mail: nickpriestland@hotmail.com
web: www.the-cors.co.uk
dir: A40 from Carmarthen, left at St Clears & 4m to
Laugharne

In a former Victorian vicarage in the village of Laugharne,
made famous by Dylan Thomas, the grounds were once a
bog ('cors' in Welsh), but these days the glorious aspect
is of trees, shrubs, ponds and sculptures. Secluded areas
of seating screen the house from the main street, and, on
the inside, there's an air of Bohemian splendour about
the place. Modernist paintings and old antiques are side
by side, and the owners have no truck with credit cards or
printed menus. The chef-proprietor uses first-class
regional produce, including organic Welsh Black beef,
lamb from the salt marshes of Laugharne and fish from
Carmarthen market, to create fine traditional Welsh
cuisine combined with some contemporary ideas. Expect

roasted butternut squash with Carmarthen ham,
parmesan shavings and balsamic dressing to start, and
mains such as roasted rack of Welsh Preseli new season
spring lamb with a rosemary garlic crust and caramelised
onion gravy.

Times 7-9.30 Closed 25 Dec, Sun-Wed

LLANDEILO	Map 8 SN62

The Angel Salem

◎◎ Modern

Good cooking in rural village

☎ 01558 823394
Salem SA19 7LY
e-mail: eat@angelsalem.co.uk
dir: Please telephone for directions

Set in a quiet rural village in the Carmarthenshire
countryside, this family-run inn serves food that could
hold its own anywhere in the country. The attractively
beamed dining and bar areas are simply and
unpretentiously decorated, and wooden chairs have
upholstered seats to assure a touch of comfort. Fresh
local produce is the focus of the seasonally-changing
menu (bolstered with lunchtime blackboard specials),
and everything from the bread to the ice cream is made
on the premises. Ravioli of pheasant on sautéed strips of
peppered cabbage served with apricot sauce is a well-
made starter, and roast breast of Gressingham duck with
apple boudin, sage forcemeat and parsnip purée an
impressive main course. The Angel Inn assiette of (6)
mini desserts solves any dessert dilemmas.

Chef Rod Peterson **Owner** Rod Peterson & Liz Smith
Times 12-3/7-9 Closed 2 wks in Jan, Mon (ex BHs), L Tue,
D Sun **Prices** Starter £4.25-£7.50, Main £9.95-£17.95,
Dessert £4.95-£7.95, Service optional **Wines** 18 bottles
over £20, 21 bottles under £20, 5 by glass **Notes** Sunday
L, Vegetarian available **Seats** 70 **Children** Portions
Parking 25

The Plough Inn

Modern Welsh, International

Varied menu in friendly roadside hotel

☎ 01558 823431 📠 01558 823969
Rhosmaen SA19 6NP
e-mail: info@ploughrhosmaen.com
dir: On the A40 1m north of Llandeilo travelling towards Llandovery. From M4 via A483 at Pont Abraham

This roadside hotel and restaurant overlooks the Towy Valley on the edge of the Brecon Beacons National Park. Eat in the bar or the smart dining room, and choose from a menu that truly covers all the bases. A range of traditional dishes (fish and chips, curries, lasagne) sit alongside more ambitious modern Welsh cooking with some international touches: coarse farmhouse paté with shallot and apple chutney and toasted rustic breads, followed by roasted duck with braised red cabbage, pears poached in red wine, potato cake with confit duck and pomegranate jus. Local ice creams, Welsh cheeses or desserts such as warm apple and frangipane slice finish things off.

Chef Andrew Roberts, Abi Kumar **Owner** Andrew Roberts **Times** 11.30-3.30/5.30-9.30 Closed 31 Jan **Prices** Fixed L 2 course £9.95, Fixed D 3 course £14.95, Starter £4-£8.95, Main £6.95-£18.95, Dessert £4.50-£5.50, Service optional **Wines** 15 bottles over £20, 28 bottles under £20, 7 by glass **Notes** Sunday L, Vegetarian available, Civ Wed 100, Air con **Seats** 190, Pr/dining room 35 **Children** Portions, Menu **Parking** 70

NANTGAREDIG Map 8 SN42

RESTAURANT OF THE YEAR FOR WALES

Y Polyn

Modern British

Well-sourced food served in farmhouse surroundings

☎ 01267 290000
SA32 7LH
e-mail: ypolyn@hotmail.com
dir: Follow brown tourist signs to National Botanic Gardens, Y Polyn signed from rdbt in front of gardens

A black-beamed, whitewashed building in the Towy Valley, Y Polyn was once a tollhouse (its name, meaning 'The Pole', probably referred to the barrier that once stretched across the road). It's now a friendly, attractively rustic bar-restaurant with farmhouse furniture and a quarry-tiled floor. The daily-changing menus offer heart-warming, homely food of the likes of crispy pig's ear salad with capers and red onion, or smooth chicken liver parfait with a plum and apple chutney of good bite, to start. Carefully timed John Dory on local samphire with hollandaise is a well-judged main dish, while Welsh lamb daube caters for heartier appetites. Good pastry distinguishes a nectarine frangipane tart, served warm, with rich vanilla ice-cream. Don't miss the excellent home-made breads.

Chef Susan Manson, Maryann Wright **Owner** Mark & Susan Manson, Simon & Maryann Wright **Times** 12-2/7-9 Closed Mon, D Sun **Prices** Fixed L 2 course fr £10, Fixed D

3 course £28.50-£32.50, Starter £4-£7.50, Main £8.50-£15.50, Dessert £5.50, Service included **Wines** 20 bottles over £20, 31 bottles under £20, 7 by glass **Notes** ALC prices for L only, Sunday L, Vegetarian available **Seats** 40 **Children** Portions **Parking** 25

CEREDIGION

ABERAERON Map 8 SN46

Harbourmaster Aberaeron

Modern Welsh

Quayside restaurant offering the best local produce

☎ 01545 570755
Pen Cei SA46 0BA
e-mail: info@harbour-master.com
dir: A487 (coast road). In town follow signs for Tourist Information Centre. Restaurant next door on harbourside

Originally the harbourmaster's residence, perhaps unsurprisingly the Grade II listed building occupies a dramatic quayside location. It has been sympathetically updated and the adjacent grain warehouse has recently been converted into a spacious bar overlooking the harbour. Eat in the bar or in the bright, airy brasserie with its ships' chandlery décor and impressive spiral staircase. Relaxed, bilingual service delivers modern Welsh dishes based on the best local produce. Start with the pan-fried diver caught scallops, black pudding and quince and pear chutney before a main course of Welsh Black beef fillet au poivre with dauphinoise potatoes and spinach.

Chef Rhiannon Jenkins **Owner** Glyn & Menna Hevlyn **Times** 12-2.30/6-9 Closed 25 Dec **Prices** Fixed L 2 course fr £12.50, Starter £4.50-£8.50, Main £14.50-£22.50, Dessert £5.50, Service optional, Groups min 8 service 10% **Wines** 30 bottles over £20, 30 bottles under £20, 15 by glass **Notes** Sunday L, Vegetarian available, Air con **Seats** 50 **Children** Portions **Parking** 8, On street

Ty Mawr Mansion

Modern British, Welsh

Tranquil country-house with plenty of local flavour

☎ 01570 470033
Cilcennin SA48 8DB
e-mail: info@tymawrmansion.co.uk
dir: 4m from Aberaeron on A482 to Lampeter road

You can expect the finest produce from the superb Welsh larder at this grey-stone and slate Georgian mansion above the Aeron Valley. And if you're counting food miles, rest assured that they are minimal: 90% of the

ingredients that turn up on your plate come from within a 10-mile radius. Ty Mawr sits in 12 acres of grounds - a space large enough for the owners to breed their own pigs - and is a smart set-up, sumptuously refurbished, graciously proportioned and full of light. There's no hint of stuffiness in the service, while the kitchen team shine at their task - technically skilful modern dishes with a Welsh theme deliver zinging flavours to the table. A textbook terrine of salmon and local trout in a herb pancake with crème fraîche dressing starts things off, followed by medallions of Welsh Black beef with red wine and thyme sauce and rösti potatoes.

Chef Jeremy Hywell Jones **Owner** Martin & Catherine McAlpine **Times** 7-9 Closed 26 Dec-7 Jan, Sun, L all week **Prices** Fixed D 3 course £24.95-£26.95, Starter £6.95-£9.95, Main £17.95-£24.95, Dessert £5.95-£9.95, Service optional **Wines** 23 bottles over £20, 13 bottles under £20, 6 by glass **Notes** Vegetarian available, Dress restrictions, Smart casual **Seats** 35, Pr/dining room 12 **Parking** 20

ABERYSTWYTH Map 8 SN58

Conrah Hotel

Modern Welsh

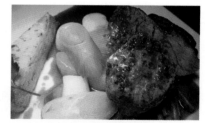

Proud Welsh cooking in beautiful setting

☎ 01970 617941 📠 01970 624546
Ffosrhydygaled, Chancery SY23 4DF
e-mail: enquiries@conrah.co.uk
web: www.conrah.co.uk
dir: On A487, 3m S of Aberystwyth, between Llanfarian & Blaenpluf

A sparkling white façade and views down the Ystwyth valley distinguish the Conrah. There are sumptuous landscaped gardens and, should you succumb to wanderlust, a path that leads out from the grounds down to the heritage coastline of Cardigan Bay. The graceful interior décor makes a good setting for some finely crafted, modern Welsh cooking. Grilled sardines are marinated in rosemary, and served with herbed roast potatoes and sage butter to make a starter of intriguing contrasts, while mains include duck breast with carrot purée and stir-fried vegetables; vegetarians may choose wild mushroom risotto with Welsh rarebit gratin and sweet shallot sauce.

Chef Meredith Rendell **Owner** Dilwyn Robers **Times** 12-2/7-9 Closed 26-28 Dec, D 25 Dec **Prices** Food prices not confirmed for 2010. Please telephone for details. **Wines** 15 bottles over £20, 29 bottles under £20, 4 by glass **Notes** Sunday L, Vegetarian available, Civ Wed 70 **Seats** 35, Pr/dining room 40 **Children** Portions, Menu **Parking** 50

DEVIL'S BRIDGE   Map 9 SN77

The Hafod Hotel

⚙ Modern Welsh

Local produce cooked with flair in former hunting lodge

☎ 01970 890232 🖷 01970 890394
SY23 3JL
e-mail: hafodhotel@btconnect.com

Originally built as a hunting lodge in the 1700s, this family-run hotel occupies an enviable position beside the Devil's Bridge beauty spot and overlooking the spectacular wooded gorges of the Mynach and Rheidol rivers. There are 6 acres of pretty grounds and 16 traditionally furnished rooms. Local, seasonal produce forms the backbone of the menu in the dining room, where a typical meal might begin with a chicken and asparagus terrine, followed by pan-fried duck breast with honey, lemon and black pepper sauce, apple purée and braised red cabbage, finishing with chocolate mousse with chocolate ice cream and walnut biscotti.

Times 7-8.30 Closed Sun-Mon, L all week

EGLWYS FACH   Map 14 SN69

Ynyshir Hall

⚙⚙⚙ — *see below*

LAMPETER   Map 8 SN54

Valley Restaurant at the Falcondale Mansion

⚙⚙ Modern British V ✍

Grand mansion showcasing inspired modern cookery

☎ 01570 422910 🖷 01570 423559
Best Western Falcondale Mansion, Falcondale Dr
SA48 7RX
e-mail: info@falcondalehotel.com
dir: 1m from Lampeter take A482 to Cardigan, turn right at petrol station, follow for 0.75m

A Victorian mansion set in 14 acres of manicured grounds, Falcondale is particularly famed for its dazzling springtime shows of rhododendrons and azaleas. Built for a banking family, the place combines plutocratic grandeur with a homelier approach these days. Modern spins on classical dishes are the kitchen's stock-in-trade, with the pick of Ceredigion and Carmarthenshire produce stars of the show. A regally risen soufflé of Gorwydd Caerphilly has fine, featherlight texture and is well-served by accompaniments of braised shallots and asparagus. Loin of Welsh lamb comes with a mini-shepherd's pie, braised red cabbage and a textbook redcurrant and rosemary jus, while the dessert to aim for seems to be the melting chocolate fondant with deeply flavoured peanut-butter ice cream. Canapés, home-made breads and the plentiful petits fours are all up to the mark.

Chef Michael Green **Owner** Chris & Lisa Hutton
Times 12-2/6.30-9 **Prices** Fixed L 2 course fr £10, Fixed D 4 course fr £35, Tasting menu £50, Starter £5-£9.50, Main £12.50-£19.50, Dessert £5.50-£7.50, Service optional, Groups min 10 service 10% **Wines** 22 bottles over £20, 26 bottles under £20, 14 by glass **Notes** Tasting menu 8 course (pre-booked), Sunday L, Vegetarian menu, Dress restrictions, Smart casual, no shorts, Civ Wed 80 **Seats** 36, Pr/dining room 20 **Children** Portions **Parking** 60

Ynyshir Hall

EGLWYS FACH   Map 14 SN69

Modern British ⬥

Adventurous and stunning country-house cuisine

☎ 01654 781209 🖷 01654 781366
SY20 8TA
e-mail: ynyshir@relaischateaux.com
dir: On A487, 6m S of Machynlleth

Queen Victoria once kept this white-painted Georgian longhouse as a hideaway for shooting parties and would surely be content that it is in the hands of owners who have lavished so much love and care on it. Make no mistake: Ynyshir Hall offers one of the UK's truly top-drawer culinary and country-house experiences. First off, there's the setting: 14 acres of superb gardens on the splendid Dovey estuary. After nature's grandeur, the small-scale of this intimate retreat is a delightful surprise - with just 9 rooms, guests are hardly falling over one another. Inside, the colour sense of a painter is apparent in a bold, modern colour scheme and walls hung with bright canvasses. The restaurant is a quintessentially country-house affair, where head chef Shane Hughes marries first-rate seasonal Welsh produce with wild herbs and vegetables from Ynyshir's walled garden. Clear flavours leap from the plate in dishes like confit pork and langoustine with peas and quail's egg, then braised duck leg with parsnip and sherry purée and potato galette. Flavours come thick and fast in a finale of warm treacle tart with walnuts, banana, clotted cream and Grand Marnier foam.

Chef Shane Hughes **Owner** von Essen Hotels, Rob & Joan Reen **Times** 12.30-1.30/7-8.45 **Prices** Fixed L 2 course fr £25, Fixed D 4 course fr £65, Tasting menu £80, Service optional **Wines** 250 bottles over £20, 5 bottles under £20, 25 by glass **Notes** Sunday L, Vegetarian available, Dress restrictions, No jeans, beachwear or shorts, Civ Wed 40 **Seats** 30, Pr/dining room 16 **Parking** 15

CONWY

ABERGELE
Map 14 SH97

The Kinmel Arms

◎◎ Modern Welsh

Local produce and sound cooking in popular restaurant with rooms

☎ 01745 832207 📄 01745 822044
The Village, St George LL22 9BP
e-mail: info@thekinmelarms.co.uk

Ideally situated close to Llandudno and Chester on the North Wales coastline, The Kinmel Arms is also a golfer's paradise with 3 championship courses within fifteen minutes' drive. A 17th-century inn in the Elwy Valley, the pub boasts oak floors, a conservatory with marble tables and a central slate-topped bar with a stained glass header. The food is uncomplicated and well presented, with dishes based on local ingredients and offered alongside a good wine selection and well-kept real ales. With daily fish specials, recommendations include smoked haddock and organic salmon fishcake with chicory and watercress salad and a dill and mixed citrus yogurt, or pan-fried Welsh rib-eye steak with béarnaise sauce, sautéed onions, mixed leaf salad and home-made chips.

Times 12-2/6.30-9.30 Closed 25 Dec, 1-2 Jan, Mon, Sun, D Sun

BETWS-Y-COED
Map 14 SH75

Craig-y-Dderwen Riverside Hotel & Restaurant

◎ Traditional, International 🍴

Relaxing country-house dining in picturesque Snowdonian surroundings

☎ 01690 710293 📄 01690 710362
LL24 0AS
e-mail: info@snowdoniahotel.com
dir: On A5 near Waterloo Bridge

Tucked away at the end of a tree-lined drive beneath dramatic wooded slopes in 16 acres of gloriously tranquil grounds, this Victorian country-house hotel is worth seeking out for its River Conwy views and its relaxing atmosphere. The formal restaurant provides well prepared dishes with an emphasis on seasonal local ingredients, including produce from their own kitchen garden. To start, try mussel chowder served in a home-made bread pot, follow with roast Conwy Valley mutton with garlic cream potatoes, or sea bass with caper sauce, and finish with summer pudding with mixed berry compôte. There is also a substantial wine list with helpful tasting notes.

Chef Paul Goosey **Owner** Martin Carpenter
Times 12-2.30/6.30-9.30 Closed 25 Dec, 2 Jan-1 Feb, L Mon-Fri **Prices** Starter £4.50-£6.95, Main £9.95-£16.25, Dessert £4.75-£5.95, Service optional **Wines** 52 bottles over £20, 40 bottles under £20, 3 by glass **Notes** Sunday

L, Vegetarian available, Dress restrictions, Smart casual, Civ Wed 125 **Seats** 82, Pr/dining room 40
Children Portions, Menu **Parking** 50

Llugwy Restaurant

◎ Modern British, Welsh 🍴

Former coaching inn with quality Welsh cuisine

☎ 01690 710219 📄 01690 710603
Royal Oak Hotel, Holyhead Rd LL24 0AY
e-mail: royaloakmail@btopenworld.com
web: www.royaloakhotel.net
dir: on A5 in town centre, next to St Mary's church

The peaks of Snowdonia looming nearby draw in mountain hikers eager to fuel their exertions in this former coaching inn at the centre of postcard-pretty Betws-y-Coed. The Royal Oak Hotel contains the modern

continued

Tan-y-Foel Country House

BETWS-Y-COED
Map 14 SH75

Modern British 🍴

Fine food in Snowdonia

☎ 01690 710507 📄 01690 710681
Capel Garmon LL26 0RE
e-mail: enquiries@tyfhotel.co.uk
dir: A5 onto A470; 2m N towards Llanrwst, then turning for Capel Garmon. Country House on left 1m before village

Situated high above the Conwy valley and set in 6 acres of woodland with attractive gardens and country walks leading from the grounds, this delightful 17th-century country house has superb views in all directions. Set above the attractive village of Betws-y-Coed, this family-run hotel may look unassuming from the outside, but it conceals a chic and sophisticated interior which blends country-house comfort with minimalist modern design in

a series of individual rooms, including an intimate restaurant which seats only a dozen diners at a time. Local and organic produce is allowed to speak for itself in accomplished, well presented and executed dishes. The short, fixed-price dinner menu changes daily and features a choice of two dishes at each course, with wine recommendations accompanying main courses. Start with carpaccio of Welsh Black beef with crisp nutty celeriac, walnut oil and stilton mustard dressing, perhaps followed by pan-seared breast of Gressingham duck, with chorizo and smoked paprika risotto, fennel and basil cream dressing.

Chef Janet Pitman **Owner** Mr & Mrs P Pitman
Times 7.30-8 Closed Dec-Jan, Mon, L all week
Prices Fixed D 3 course £45, Service optional **Wines** 81 bottles over £20, 7 by glass **Notes** Dress restrictions, No jeans, trainers, tracksuits, walking boots **Seats** 12 **Parking** 14

BETWS-Y-COED *continued*

Grill Bistro, the popular Stables Bar (much-favoured by the locals) and the more formal Llugwy Restaurant. Modern Welsh cuisine with inventive global influences is the order of the day in the restaurant. A starter such as céviche of hand-dived scallops with lime sabayon and peppered frisée leaves might be followed by tenderloin of Gloucestershire Old Spot pork with Savoy cabbage, Puy lentil and smoked bacon sauce and carrot dauphinoise, and to finish, perhaps a tartly-sharp summer berry pudding with natural yogurt.

Llugwy Restaurant

Chef Dylan Edwards **Owner** Royal Oak Hotel Ltd **Times** 12-3/6.30-9 Closed 25-26 Dec, Mon-Tue, L Wed-Sat, D Sun **Prices** Fixed L 2 course £10.95-£12.95, Fixed D 3 course £20-£31, Starter £4.95-£9.85, Main £12.95-£22.50, Dessert £5.25-£6.75, Service optional **Wines** 16 bottles over £20, 40 bottles under £20, 11 by glass **Notes** Welsh tasting menu available 4-5 course, Sunday L, Vegetarian available, Dress restrictions, Smart casual, no jeans, shorts or T-shirts, Civ Wed 85 **Seats** 60, Pr/dining room 20 **Children** Portions, Menu **Parking** 100

Tan-y-Foel Country House

@@@ *– see page 549*

Dawsons@ The Castle Hotel Conwy

@@ Modern British

Local produce drives the menu in this landmark hotel

☎ 01492 582800 📄 01492 582300
High St LL32 8DB
e-mail: mail@castlewales.co.uk
dir: A55 junct 18, follow town centre signs, cross estuary (castle on left). Right then left at mini-rdbts onto one-way system. Right at Town Wall Gate, right onto Berry St then High St

Standing on the site of a Cistercian abbey, there has been a hotel here since the 14th century. The family-run coaching inn is one of the town's most celebrated buildings with past visitors including Telford and Wordsworth. A modern bar offers light meals, but the Dawsons restaurant is the main event, a fine-dining restaurant that takes its name from the distinguished Victorian artist and illustrator John Dawson-Watson, who designed the impressive frontage of the hotel. Local Welsh produce drives the modern British cooking with the suppliers listed proudly on the menu. Expect the likes of Snowdonia cheddar cheese and roasted onion tart followed by roasted rump of Conwy Valley lamb topped with a mint and pistachio nut crust, creamed pearl barley risotto and root vegetable gratin.

Chef Graham Tinsley **Owner** Lavin Family & Graham Tinsley **Times** 12-10 Closed D 26 Dec **Prices** Fixed L 2 course £15.95, Fixed D 3 course £23.95, Starter £4.95-£6.75, Main £10.50-£18.95, Dessert £4.50-£5.95, Service added but optional 10% **Wines** 16 bottles over £20, 20 bottles under £20, 15 by glass **Notes** Sunday L, Vegetarian available **Seats** 70 **Children** Portions, Menu **Parking** 36

The Groes Inn

@ Traditional British

Honest, wholesome food in a characterful inn

☎ 01492 650545 📄 01492 650855
Tyn-y-Groes LL32 8TN
e-mail: reception@groesinn.com
dir: On B5106, 3m from Conwy

As pubs go, you'd be pushed to find a more attractive package than the Groes Inn. If it feels rooted into the fabric of the Conwy Valley, that may be because it has been in business since 1573, when it was the first house in Wales to be granted a licence. Inside, a tangle of cosy nooks and crannies makes for an oasis of civilised libation, and hands-on owners ensure a genuine welcome and take pride in the creative effort taking place in the kitchen. Salt marsh lamb and game are local, as are fish and seafood, so to start perhaps a platter with smoked salmon and trout and an excellent Marie Rose sauce. Next, a roast rack of local lamb is served succulently pink with a sharp cranberry jus and a crisp, brightly-hued array of vegetables.

Chef Mark Williams **Owner** Dawn & Justin Humphreys **Times** 12-2.15/6.30-9 Closed 25 Dec **Prices** Food prices not confirmed for 2010. Please telephone for details. **Wines** 12 bottles over £20, 27 bottles under £20, 16 by glass **Notes** Sunday L, Vegetarian available, Dress restrictions, Smart casual **Seats** 54, Pr/dining room 20 **Children** Portions **Parking** 100

Sychnant Pass House

@ Modern British

Modern British cuisine in Snowdonia National Park

☎ 01492 596868 📄 01824 790441
Sychnant Pass Rd LL32 8BJ
e-mail: info@sychnant-pass-house.co.uk
dir: Pass Visitors Centre in Conwy, take 2nd left into Uppergate St. Up hill for 2m, restaurant on right

This peaceful country-house hotel is surrounded by 3 acres of lawns, trees and a wild garden with ponds and a stream running through it. And all that within the foothills of the Snowdonia National Park. Built in 1890, it is family-run and its modern facilities include a smart swimming pool, gym, hot tub and fire pits. The restaurant has a relaxed and informal feel with wooden tables and slate place mats. The fixed-price menu offers a good choice of modern British food. Expect the likes of hot-smoked mackerel with young leaves and horseradish sauce as a starter, followed by sorbet and then a main course of rib-eye of beef pan-fried with a tomato and garlic coulis.

Chef Daniel Wilkinson **Owner** Graham & Bre Carrington-Sykes **Times** 12.30-2.30/7-9 Closed Xmas & Jan, L Mon-Sat **Prices** Food prices not confirmed for 2010. Please telephone for details, Service optional **Wines** 22 bottles over £20, 38 bottles under £20, 6 by glass **Notes** Fixed D 5 course £32.50, Sunday L, Vegetarian available, Dress restrictions, Smart casual, Civ Wed 100 **Seats** 40, Pr/dining room 14 **Children** Portions **Parking** 30

DEGANWY | Map 14 SH77

Vue

@@ Modern British

Panoramic views, contemporary surrounds and innovative food

☎ 01492 564100 📠 01492 564115
Quay Hotel & Spa, Deganwy Quay LL31 9DJ
e-mail: info@quayhotel.com
dir: From S, M6 junct 20 signed North Wales/Chester. From N, M56 onto A5117 then A494. Continue on A55 to junct 18 (Conwy). Straight over 2 rdbts, at lights left over rail crossing, right at mini rdbt, hotel on right

This sophisticated boutique-style hotel enjoys a fabulous waterside location with stunning views over the beautiful Conwy estuary to the castle and rolling hills beyond. Clean-cut styling epitomises the hotel's cool, chic design and the first-floor restaurant and cocktail bar - aptly called The Vue - continues the contemporary approach, its 2 dining areas separated by cleverly lit glass partitions that bring the nautical theme indoors. Expect an informal, brasserie-style experience, backed by relaxed and friendly service. The cooking is suitably modern too, focusing on quality local produce; take beef carpaccio with celeriac remoulade, braised leg of lamb with roast garlic and basil-crushed potatoes, crayfish and smoked bacon tagliatelle, and hot chocolate soufflé with marshmallow and chocolate truffle.

Times 12-2/6.30-9.30

LLANDUDNO | Map 14 SH78

Bodysgallen Hall and Spa

@@@ – see below

Empire Hotel

@ British

Family-run hotel restaurant offering traditional cuisine

☎ 01492 860555 📠 01492 860791
Church Walks LL30 2HE
e-mail: reservations@empirehotel.co.uk
web: www.empirehotel.co.uk
dir: From Chester, A55 junct 19 for Llandudno. Follow signs to Promenade, turn right at war memorial & left at rdbt. Hotel 100yds on right

This grand Victorian hotel is a bastion of unchanging civility, run by the Maddocks family for over 60 years, and ably-assisted by an experienced team of long-serving staff. Naturally, the cooking follows the same time-honoured lines with resolutely traditional, tried-and-tested flavour combinations and crowd-pleasing old favourites such as cod in batter with mushy peas and tartare sauce, or classic roasts. Starters might include home-made salmon and smoked haddock fishcake with crispy Savoy cabbage, while mains range from pot-roasted Welsh lamb shank with crushed parsnip, swede and minted jus, to pan-seared salmon on a creamy compôte of leeks and baby prawns.

Empire Hotel

Chef Michael Waddy, Larry Mutisyo **Owner** Len & Elizabeth Maddocks **Times** 12.30-2/6.45-9.30 Closed 19-30 Dec, L Mon-Sat **Prices** Fixed D 4 course £19.95-£21.50, Service optional **Wines** 39 bottles over £20, 47 bottles under £20, 7 by glass **Notes** Sunday L, Vegetarian available, Dress restrictions, Smart casual, Air con **Seats** 110, Pr/dining room 18 **Children** Portions, Menu **Parking** 44, On street

Bodysgallen Hall and Spa

LLANDUDNO | Map 14 SH78

Modern V 🏆NATIONAL WINE LIST

Sumptuous dining in classic country-house setting

☎ 01492 584466 📠 01492 582519
LL30 1RS
e-mail: info@bodysgallen.com
dir: From A55 junct 19 follow A470 towards Llandudno. Hotel 2m on right

Majestic Bodysgallen Hall may have started out with humble beginnings as a 13th-century lookout post for Conwy Castle, but it now lords it over the whole area. Turn a circle, and your gaze scans from Conwy Castle and the estuary to Snowdonia, then the Isle of Anglesey, Victorian Llandudno and the Great Orme. Most of the National Trust-owned mansion that you see now grew up in the 17th century, including over 200 acres of parkland, parterres and rose gardens. Inside is all antiques, oil paintings, oak panels and open fires. Traditional, then, and as reassuring as the genteel, well-oiled service that runs like a Swiss watch. But while Bodysgallen respects the past, it doesn't turn its back on the present when it comes to dining: the cooking grafts sound French techniques onto top-drawer Welsh produce in fixed-price menus of modern British dishes. Starters might bring lightly-smoked quail breast with cider and green apple jelly, pickled mushrooms and soft-boiled egg, while a main course of herb-poached fillet of Welsh beef, sticky ox cheek, celery salt mash, roasted shallots, carrot and thyme ought to push all the comfort buttons. Desserts are not to be passed on either - try warm chocolate fondant with Amaretto ice cream, sugared banana and coffee sabayon. The wine list is a joy too, with plenty to mull over from France before setting off around the world.

Chef Gareth Jones **Owner** The National Trust **Times** 12.30-1.45/7-9.30 Closed Mon (winter), D Sun (winter) **Prices** Food prices not confirmed for 2010. Please telephone for details. **Wines** 100 bottles over £20, 30 bottles under £20, 8 by glass **Notes** Pre-theatre D available, Sunday L, Vegetarian menu, Dress restrictions, Smart casual, no trainers/T-shirts/tracksuits, Civ Wed 55, Air con **Seats** 60, Pr/dining room 40 **Children** Portions **Parking** 40

LLANDUDNO *continued*

Imperial Hotel

◉ Modern, Traditional British

Contemporary cooking on the seafront

☎ 01492 877466 📠 01492 878043
The Promenade LL30 1AP
e-mail: reception@theimperial.co.uk
dir: A470 into town. Hotel is on the Promenade

A traditional seaside hotel right on the promenade, the Imperial has magnificent views across Llandudno Bay. With its impressive, grandiose façade, the hotel dominates the Victorian seafront. The interior, in contrast, is more unassuming and modern in style. The elegant Chantrey's Restaurant features contemporary British cooking on its seasonally-changing menu and offers a varied choice of dishes to suit just about all tastes. Start with Pantysgawn goats' cheese, roasted shallot and leek pâté with roasted red pepper jelly and tomato salsa, followed by pan-fried fillet of sea bass, brown shrimp, linguine, sautéed pak choi and laverbread foam.

Times 12.30-3/6.30-9.30

Osborne House

◉ Modern British

Opulent seaside hotel with bistro-style food

☎ 01492 860330 📠 01492 860791
17 North Pde LL30 2LP
e-mail: sales@osbornehouse.com
web: www.osbornehouse.co.uk
dir: A55 at junct 19, follow signs for Llandudno then Promenade, at War Memorial turn right, Osborne House on left opposite entrance to pier

The magnificent Victorian townhouse occupies a splendid spot overlooking the seafront at Llandudno. Luxuriously decorated with opulent drapes, dazzling chandeliers, Roman-style pillars, gilt-edge mirrors and original art, the elegant, high-ceilinged dining room has a Palladian feel. Despite the grand surroundings, service is friendly and informal and the extensive bistro-style menu is based on comfortingly contemporary ideas, using plenty of local ingredients. Typically, order warm goats' cheese and bacon tart with beetroot chutney and Conwy Valley lamb shank with mashed potatoes and rosemary jus.

Chef Michael Waddy **Owner** Len & Elizabeth Maddocks **Times** 12-3/5-10 Closed 19-30 Dec **Prices** Fixed L 2 course £9.95, Fixed D 3 course £17.60, Starter £3.90-£8.35, Main £7.35-£17.15, Dessert £3.50-£4.45, Service optional, Groups min 12 service 10% **Wines** 17 bottles over £20, 24 bottles under £20, 6 by glass **Notes** Pre-theatre menu 5pm, Sunday L, Vegetarian available, Dress restrictions, Smart casual, Air con **Seats** 70, Pr/dining room 18 **Children** Portions **Parking** 6, On street

St Tudno Hotel and Restaurant

◉◉ Modern British

Accomplished cuisine in elegant surroundings on the seafront promenade

☎ 01492 874411 📠 01492 860407
The Promenade LL30 2LP
e-mail: sttudnohotel@btinternet.com
dir: In town centre, on Promenade, opposite pier entrance (near Great Orme)

In pole position on the seafront opposite the Victorian pier and gardens, this genteel traditional hotel is a refuge from identikit modern minimalism. Maybe the moody Welsh weather is to blame, but the interior designers had their heads in balmy Italian climes in the elegant Terrace restaurant, where a mural of Lake Como forms a dreamy backdrop to Italian chandeliers suspended from a tented ceiling and a gently trickling lion's head fountain. The kitchen here brings sound French classical technique to bear on classy, well-sourced Welsh ingredients, put together in some inventive modern combinations. Expect starters like Gorau Glas cheese crème brûlée with crab apple jelly and beetroot glaze, followed by Welsh spring lamb with rosemary boulangère and roast garlic jus. Creative desserts might include a tonka bean brûlée with vanilla salt, passionfruit parfait and plum financier.

Chef Ian Watson **Owner** Mr Bland **Times** 12.30-2/7-9.30 **Prices** Fixed L 2 course £18, Starter £5.95-£7.50, Main £16.50-£22.50, Dessert £5.95-£7.95, Service optional **Wines** 154 bottles over £20, 18 bottles under £20, 12 by glass **Notes** Pre-theatre meals available, Sunday L, Vegetarian available, Dress restrictions, Smart casual, no shorts, tracksuits or jeans, Civ Wed 70, Air con **Seats** 60 **Children** Portions, Menu **Parking** 9

Terrace Restaurant, St George's Hotel

◉ Modern, Traditional ◉

Imaginative regional food in a plum spot overlooking Llandudno Bay

☎ 01492 877544 & 862184 ▤ 01492 877788
The Promenade LL30 2LG
e-mail: info@stgeorgeswales.co.uk
web: www.stgeorgeswales.co.uk
dir: A55, exit at Glan Conwy for Llandudno. A470 follow signs for seafront (distinctive tower identifies hotel)

The elegant façade of this Victorian hotel dominates the promenade overlooking Llandudno Bay. The contemporary and sophisticated Terrace Restaurant enjoys spectacular views of the bay and deals in local and regional produce, duly following the seasons. The imaginative and well-balanced menu might include crab with a coriander risotto cake, soft poached hen's egg and saffron aïoli, followed by a main course of pan-fried fillet of sea bass with sweet potato fondant and a watercress and caper dressing. Round off a meal with a vanilla bean parfait and bitter dark chocolate sorbet served with fresh strawberries, blueberries and raspberries.

Chef Grant Dicker **Owner** Anderbury Ltd
Times 12–2.30/6.30–9.30 **Prices** Fixed L 2 course £12–£26, Fixed D 3 course £20–£32, Starter £4–£9, Main £10–£20, Dessert £5–£8, Service optional **Wines** 18 bottles over £20, 32 bottles under £20, 10 by glass **Notes** Pre-theatre menu available, Sunday L, Vegetarian available, Dress restrictions, Smart casual, Civ Wed 150, Air con **Seats** 110, Pr/dining room 12 **Children** Portions, Menu **Parking** 36

DENBIGHSHIRE

LLANDEGLA　　　　　　　　　Map 15 SJ15

Bodidris Hall

◉ Modern British **NEW** ◉

Modern cooking in a historic country-hotel setting

☎ 01978 790434 ▤ 01978 790335
LL11 3AL
e-mail: reception@bodidrishall.com
dir: A483/A525 (Wrexham-Ruthin). Turn right onto A5104. Hotel signed 1m on left

Standing in extensive grounds teeming with wildlife, this elegant and impressive 15th-century country-house hotel - reached by a mile-long drive - oozes history from every mullion window and oak beam. The interior comes brimful of original features, highlighted by quality art and furnishings, and this extends to the baronial-style restaurant. The daily-changing fixed-price British repertoire comes driven by fresh local produce, with game from adjacent estates a feature in season. Expect accurate cooking and clear flavours from slow-roast Welsh lamb Henry, served with beetroot mash and ruby port reduction, or classic crème brûlée with candied raspberries and bourbon vanilla.

Chef Brian Eccles, Gary Turnbull **Owner** Stephanie & David Booth **Times** 12–2/7–9 **Prices** Food prices not confirmed for 2010. Please telephone for details. **Wines** 24 bottles over £20, 11 bottles under £20, 6 by glass **Notes** Dress restrictions, Smart casual, Civ Wed 90 **Seats** 40, Pr/dining room 25 **Children** Portions **Parking** 50

RHYL　　　　　　　　　Map 14 SJ08

Barratt's at Ty'n Rhyl

◉◉ British, French

Historic house serving imaginative food

☎ 01745 344138 & 0773 095 4994 ▤ 01745 344138
Ty'n Rhyl, 167 Vale Rd LL18 2PH
e-mail: EBarratt@aol.com
dir: From A55 take Rhyl exit onto A525. Continue past Rhuddlan Castle, supermarket, petrol station, 0.25m on right

The poet Angharad Llwyd once lived in this stone-built 16th-century house - the oldest in Rhyl. Now it's a charming family-run hotel in an acre of tranquil mature gardens, with a plush interior of oak panelling, squashy sofas and a choice of 2 eating venues. In the Georgian part of the house, the pretty primrose-coloured dining room has a smart country-house feel with lovely oak floors and well-spaced linen-clad tables, or you could go for a table in the spacious conservatory. Menus change daily to make the most of what's local and in season, and offer well-balanced dishes with classic sauces. The kitchen's output typically runs to breast of wood pigeon in blackberry sauce, and mains such as roasted fillets of sea bream and sea bass on fluffy mash with creamy dill sauce.

Times 12–2.30/7.30–9 Closed 26 Dec, 1 wk for holiday

RUTHIN　　　　　　　　　Map 15 SJ15

Bertie's @ Ruthin Castle

◉◉ Modern European

Classy intimate restaurant in a rebuilt Welsh castle

☎ 01824 702664 ▤ 01824 705978
Castle St LL15 2NU
e-mail: reservations@ruthincastle.co.uk
dir: From town square take road towards Corwen for 100yds

Ruthin (the 'red fort') is a 13th-century castle that was flogged off by Charles I, and extensively rebuilt in the 1820s. Medieval theme evenings are a thrill, with costumed groups invited to tour the ancient torture facilities, but the more pacifically-minded might settle for dinner in the supremely comfortable Bertie's restaurant, with its quality linen and glittering chandeliers. Plotting a course through the modern European menu might take you from langoustine consommé with cauliflower and salmon tartare, through poussin with pancetta, baby turnips and a basil jus, to classic lemon tart.

Chef Phillip Ashe, Darren Shenton-Morris **Owner** Mr & Mrs Saint Claire **Times** 12.30–2/7–9.30 **Prices** Starter fr £5.95, Main fr £19.95, Dessert fr £6.95, Service optional **Wines** 60 bottles over £20, 30 bottles under £20, 12 by glass **Notes** Sunday L, Vegetarian available, Dress restrictions, Smart casual, Civ Wed 120 **Seats** 60, Pr/dining room 26 **Children** Portions, Menu **Parking** 120

RUTHIN *continued*

The Wynnstay Arms

◉◉ Traditional, International

Popular town-centre brasserie in former coaching inn

☎ 01824 703147 📠 01824 705428
Well St LL15 1AN
e-mail: reservations@wynnstayarms.com
dir: Please telephone for directions

This town centre inn, established in 1549, was once a coaching inn and a secret Jacobite meeting place. These days, extensive renovation has transformed it into a smart restaurant with rooms, offering quality accommodation, plus an attractive café-bar and contemporary Fusions Brasserie. Here service is friendly and informal, but always professional. The menu fuses contemporary-style tapas dishes with modern British gastro-pub dishes, with an emphasis on local seasonal ingredients, including Welsh lamb and Black beef. Good examples are tapas nibbles of meat balls in tomato, garlic and herb sauce and king prawns pan-fried with olive oil, garlic and white wine, and main dishes like pork tenderloin with bacon mash, apple and herb gravy, and pan-fried bream with lemon and saffron sauce.

Chef Jason Jones **Owner** Jason & Eirian Jones, Kelvin & Gaye Clayton **Times** 12-2/6-9.30 Closed Mon **Prices** Starter £2-£5.95, Main £11.50-£15.50, Dessert £3.95-£5.50, Service optional **Wines** 6 bottles over £20, 31 bottles under £20, 6 by glass **Notes** Sunday L, Vegetarian available **Seats** 40, Pr/dining room 40 **Children** Portions **Parking** 12

ST ASAPH · Map 15 SJ07

The Oriel

◉ Modern British

Imaginative cooking in idyllic location

☎ 01745 582716 📠 01745 585208
Upper Denbigh Rd LL17 0LW
e-mail: reservations@orielhousehotel.com
dir: Please telephone for directions

Just a short stroll from the village of St Asaph in the attractive North Wales countryside, The Oriel was originally built as a gentleman's residence. In the 1760s, it became a boys' school which closed its doors in the 1970s when it was converted into a hotel. Since 1998, the hotel has been given a new lease of life under the current owners and the stylish Terrace Restaurant adjoins a sunny terrace for a spot of alfresco dining. Imaginative food is served, with clear flavours in dishes like pan-fried whole tiger prawns in a garlic and chilli butter, followed by seared duck breast with a Cointreau and orange glaze. For dessert, try dark bara brith-and-butter pudding with vanilla custard.

Chef Ray Williams **Owner** Gary Seddon **Times** 12-6/6-9.30 **Prices** Food prices not confirmed for 2010. Please telephone for details. **Wines** 37 bottles over £20, 17 bottles under £20, 6 by glass **Notes** Sunday L, Vegetarian

available, Dress restrictions, Smart casual, Civ Wed 220 **Seats** 30, Pr/dining room 240 **Children** Portions **Parking** 100

GWYNEDD

ABERSOCH · Map 14 SH32

Neigwl Hotel

◉ British, European

Sound cooking in family-run hotel with sea views

☎ 01758 712363 📠 01758 712544
Lon Sarn Bach LL53 7DY
e-mail: relax@neigwl.com
dir: on A499, through Abersoch, hotel on left

Situated on the edge of the village, close to the harbour and beach, this privately-owned and run hotel has unrivalled views of Cardigan Bay and St Tudwalls islands from both its attractive restaurant and comfortable lounge. Good use is made of local produce in the imaginative modern British dishes with European influences. Try local Aberdaron crab mornay with green salad, followed by roast rack of new season Welsh lamb on leek mash and port wine sauce, or sirloin of Welsh Black beef with café de Paris butter. Book ahead for a window table.

Chef Nigel Higginbottom **Owner** Mark Gauci & Susan Turner **Times** 7-9 Closed Jan, L all week **Prices** Food prices not confirmed for 2010. Please telephone for details. **Wines** 7 bottles over £20, 16 bottles under £20, 5 by glass **Notes** Dress restrictions, Smart casual **Seats** 40 **Children** Portions, Menu **Parking** 30

Porth Tocyn Hotel

◉◉ Modern, Traditional 🍷NOTABLE WINE LIST

Accomplished cooking in friendly hotel with great views

☎ 01758 713303 📠 01758 713538
Bwlch Tocyn LL53 7BU
e-mail: bookings@porthtocyn.fsnet.co.uk
web: www.porth-tocyn-hotel.co.uk
dir: 2m S of Abersoch, through Sarn Bach & Bwlch Tocyn. Follow brown signs

Run by the same family since 1948, Porth Tocyn occupies a stunning position overlooking Cardigan Bay and the mountains of Snowdonia. Originally converted from a row of lead miners' cottages, the friendly hotel is an ideal base for touring the area, but it has a long tradition of

being a destination for good food. Marine watercolours adorn the walls of the dining room, with large picture windows providing impressive views across the bay. The menu changes daily and is governed by the produce and the seasons. Dishes are unfussy and let the main ingredient take centre stage. A starter of honey-roast belly pork with mushy peas, caramelised garlic and thyme jus could be followed by pan-fried sea bass with caramelised onion mash, sautéed leeks, Welsh farmhouse cheese beignet and a mustard sauce. The wine list is well worth a browse.

Chef L Fletcher-Brewer, J Bell **Owner** The Fletcher-Brewer Family **Times** 12.15-2/7.30-9 Closed mid Nov, 2 wks before Etr, L Mon-Sat **Prices** Fixed D 3 course £39, Service included **Wines** 63 bottles over £20, 37 bottles under £20, 4 by glass **Notes** Sunday L, Vegetarian available, Dress restrictions, Smart casual preferred **Seats** 50 **Children** Portions

---

BARMOUTH · Map 14 SH61

Bae Abermaw

◉ Modern British

Contemporary cooking in hotel with sea views

☎ 01341 280550 📠 01341 280346
Panorama Rd LL42 1DQ
e-mail: enquiries@baeabermaw.com
dir: From Barmouth centre towards Dolgellau on A496, 0.5m past garage turn left into Panorama Rd, restaurant 100yds

An impressive Victorian house in an elevated position overlooking Cardigan Bay, this boutique coastal hotel may have a dark stone façade, but step inside and it's a bright and contemporary place. Set in landscaped grounds, with French doors that open on to the garden, the wooden floors, fresh white walls, exposed brickwork, marble and slate fireplaces and modern art prints help to create a vibrant and warm ambience. The modern British cooking is underpinned by classic French influences in dishes like confit of local duck leg with mango and ginger salsa and dressed leaves, followed by grilled fillet of Barmouth sea bass on creamy mash and citrus butter.

Times 7-9 Closed 2 wks Jan, Mon, L all week (ex parties of 10+ pre booked)

CAERNARFON — Map 14 SH46

Rhiwafallen Restaurant with Rooms

◎◎ Modern British NEW ☺

Husband-and-wife-team's charming rural retreat with good food

☎ 01286 830172
Rhiwafallen, LLandwrog LL54 5SW
e-mail: robandkate@rhiwafallen.co.uk
dir: A487 from Caernarfon, A499 restaurant 1m on left

This attractive old farmhouse, perfectly positioned to explore Snowdonia National Park and the Llyn Peninsula, has been stylishly and sympathetically restored, with bedrooms enticingly named after foods such as Chocolate and Damson. The conservatory dining room has contemporary art on the walls and rich upholstered chairs at pale wooden tables, and the friendly and professional tone of the service sets the mood. Local, seasonal foods feature on the sensibly concise set-price menu, where a choice of four appealingly modern dishes is available at each course (plus a slate of Welsh cheeses). Monkfish, king prawns and baby squid are covered in a beautifully light batter for a tempura starter (served with wasabi remoulade and yakitori dressing), and breast of duck is marinated in five spice in a well balanced main course.

Chef Rob John **Owner** Kate & Rob John **Times** 12.30-7 Closed 25-26 Dec, 1-2 Jan, Mon, L Tue-Sat, D Sun **Prices** Fixed L 3 course £19.50-£22, Fixed D 3 course £35-£37.50, Service optional **Wines** 16 bottles over £20, 18 bottles under £20, 6 by glass **Notes** Sunday L, Vegetarian available, Air con **Seats** 20 **Parking** 12

Seiont Manor Hotel

◎◎ Modern British V ⚫NOTABLE WINE LIST

Culinary hideaway in Snowdonia

☎ 01286 673366 ▤ 01286 672840
Llanrug LL55 2AQ
e-mail: seiontmanor@handpicked.co.uk
dir: From Bangor follow signs for Caernarfon. Leave Caernarfon on A4086. Hotel 3m on left

A sympathetic conversion of a farmstead and its adjoining manor house combine to create this peaceful, friendly country hotel, stunningly situated in 150 acres of parkland a short drive from Snowdon. Public areas boast original features like ancient stone floors, exposed brick and wood panelling, alongside an upmarket, contemporary feel with modern fabrics and mellow colours. In the beamed restaurant, well appointed with fresh flowers, crisp linen and gleaming tableware, local ingredients and classical cooking techniques are used to create modern dishes. Typically, start with sautéed pigeon breast with celeriac purée and game jus, move on to sea bass on herb risotto with mussels and basil pesto, or rack of lamb with redcurrant reduction, and finish with caramelised lemon tart.

Chef Martyn Williams **Owner** Hand Picked Hotels **Times** 12-2/7-9.30 **Prices** Fixed L 2 course £12.50-£15,

Fixed D 3 course £29.50-£37, Starter £5-£7.95, Main £17-£25, Dessert £5-£7, Service optional **Wines** 98 bottles over £20, 3 bottles under £20, 19 by glass **Notes** Sunday L, Vegetarian menu, Dress restrictions, Smart casual, Civ Wed 100 **Seats** 55, Pr/dining room 20 **Children** Portions, Menu **Parking** 40

CRICCIETH — Map 14 SH53

Bron Eifion Country House Hotel

◎ Modern British

Modern British food in conservatory restaurant

☎ 01766 522385 ▤ 01766 523796
LL52 0SA
e-mail: enquiries@broneifion.co.uk
dir: A497, between Porthmadog & Pwllheli

With a backdrop of the Welsh coastline and close to the rugged beauty of Snowdonia National Park, this elegant Grade II listed country house enjoys beautiful views of formal gardens and the sea. The Great Hall with its minstrels' gallery and timbered roof is an imposing spot for pre-dinner drinks, or choose the cocktail bar, before dining in the Orangery Restaurant, a conservatory with panoramic views of the gardens by day, candlelit at night. Local suppliers bring fish and shellfish from Pwllheli, beef and lamb from Caernarfon and fresh produce from Anglesey. Modern British cooking (with some foreign accents) sees Llanloffan Welsh buck rarebit with fried egg and ham hock terrine as a starter alongside main-course pan-fried breast of duck with fresh beetroot purée and fondant potato, glazed figs and duck jus.

Chef Aiden McGuckin, Martin Morrall **Owner** John & Mary Heenan **Times** 12-2/6.30-9 **Prices** Fixed L 2 course £18.95, Fixed D 3 course £30, Service included **Notes** Gourmand menu 8 course £55, Sunday L, Vegetarian available, Dress restrictions, No jeans, T-shirts, Civ Wed 50, Air con **Seats** 50, Pr/dining room 16 **Children** Portions, Menu **Parking** 50

DOLGELLAU — Map 14 SH71

Dolserau Hall Hotel

◎ Traditional

Country-house cooking with a local flavour

☎ 01341 422522 ▤ 01341 422400
LL40 2AG
e-mail: welcome@dolserau.co.uk
dir: 1.5m from Dolgellau on unclassified road between A470/A494 to Bala

Situated amid the magnificent scenery of the Snowdonia National Park close to Cader Idris Mountain, this lovely 19th-century country-house hotel has 5 acres of grounds, including a Victorian walled garden. The Winter Garden Restaurant is attractively decorated in red and gold and enjoys stunning views of Snowdonia. The daily-changing menu focuses on local and seasonal meat, fruit and vegetables, and fish from a private fleet in Anglesey. A platter of crayfish tails as a starter might be followed by

pan-fried sea bream served with Pernod lemon butter and quenelles of swede. Finish with mango brûlée.

Times 7-9 Closed Nov-Feb, L all week

Penmaenuchaf Hall Hotel

◎◎ Modern British ⚫NOTABLE WINE LIST

Imaginative cooking in an elegant conservatory-style dining room

☎ 01341 422129 ▤ 01341 422787
Penmaenpool LL40 1YB
e-mail: relax@penhall.co.uk
dir: From A470 take A493 (Tywyn/Fairbourne), entrance 1.5m on left by sign for Penmaenpool

The impressive stone mansion, built in 1860 as a summer house for a Lancashire cotton magnate, stands in 20 acres of terraced gardens and woodland, with glorious views over the Mawddach estuary to Snowdonia beyond. Gothic windows frame the view in the formal garden room restaurant, with its slate floor, oak-panelled walls and high ceiling. It has a fresh, contemporary feel and provides an elegant backdrop for a modern British menu with Mediterranean and French influences featuring dishes such as confit duck with poached pear and aged balsamic, or pepper-crusted lemon sole with red pepper relish and pesto dressing. Expect confidence, flair and plenty of fresh local produce. A sensibly priced wine list sourced with considerable care by the proprietors and an alfresco area for summer dining completes the package.

Chef J Pilkington, T Reeve **Owner** Mark Watson, Lorraine Fielding **Times** 12-2/7-9.30 **Prices** Fixed L 2 course fr £15.95, Fixed D 4 course fr £40, Starter £8.75-£9.50, Main £22-£26, Dessert £8.25-£9.50, Service optional **Wines** 65 bottles over £20, 37 bottles under £20, 6 by glass **Notes** Sunday L, Vegetarian available, Dress restrictions, Smart casual, no jeans or T-shirts, Civ Wed 50 **Seats** 36, Pr/dining room 16 **Children** Portions **Parking** 36

PORTMEIRION — Map 14 SH53

Castell Deudraeth

◎ Modern Welsh

Stylish hotel dining in the North Wales fantasy village

☎ 01766 772400 ▤ 01766 771771
LL48 6ER
e-mail: castell@portmeirion-village.com
dir: Off A487 at Minffordd. Between Porthmadog & Penryndeudraeth

Sir Clough Williams-Ellis' eccentric Italianate fantasy village of Portmeirion needs no introduction for fans of cult 60s series *The Prisoner*. Castell Deudraeth is - from the outside at any rate - a slice of Victorian Gothic camp worthy of a Hammer Horror film, but inside - wow! - the designers have been let loose, combining original textures of slate and oak with a voguish décor to impress the most demanding of style slaves. The light-flooded conservatory-style brasserie is casually chic with pine

continued

PORTMEIRION *continued*

tables, leather banquettes and a chatty buzz. With the estuary on the doorstep, local seafood is big here, as in scallops from the Lleyn Peninsula that appear with sweetcorn purée and truffle cream in a typical starter, followed by, perhaps, stout-braised oxtail with creamed potatoes and roasted root vegetables. Efficient, smiling staff who don't treat you like a number are the icing on the cake.

Chef Peter Hedd Williams **Owner** Portmeirion Ltd
Times 12-2.30/6.30-9.30 **Prices** Food prices not confirmed for 2010. Please telephone for details.
Notes Sunday L, Vegetarian available, Civ Wed 40, Air con **Seats** 80, Pr/dining room 40 **Children** Portions, Menu
Parking 40

Hotel Portmeirion

◎◎ Modern Welsh

Stunning, unique setting for imaginative cooking

☎ 01766 770000 & 772440 📄 01766 771331
LL48 6ET
e-mail: hotel@portmeirion-village.com
dir: Off A487 at Minffordd

The immaculately restored hotel in the unique conservation area was saved from dereliction by Clough Williams-Ellis in the 1920s and retains several period details, quality antiques, art and memorabilia. Located beneath the wooded slopes of the famous Italianate village and overlooking the sandy estuary towards Snowdonia, the elegant conservatory restaurant setting is surely one of the most spectacular in Wales. With wonderful seafood on the doorstep, as well as locally reared Welsh lamb, beef and game, the fact the local bounty appears on the bi-lingual menu is a no-brainer. These fine products are handled with flair and flavours are considerably balanced. A delicious tomato bread has a firm crust and light tomato flavour, then comes seared scallops with pan-fried potato, artichoke and chorizo, followed by Glasfryn pork with confit belly, pommes purée, ceps and crackling in a technically top-notch dish. The mainly Welsh-speaking staff are warm, hospitable and efficient.

Chef Wayne Roberts **Owner** Portmeirion Ltd
Times 12-2.30/6.30-9 **Closed** 11-22 Jan **Prices** Food prices not confirmed for 2010. Please telephone for details. **Wines** 60 bottles over £20, 40 bottles under £20, 8 by glass **Notes** Sunday L, Civ Wed 130 **Seats** 100, Pr/dining room 36 **Children** Portions, Menu **Parking** 130

PWLLHELI Map 14 SH33

Plas Bodegroes

◎◎ Modern British

Attractive restaurant with rooms dedicated to top local produce

☎ 01758 612363 📄 01758 701247
Nefyn Rd LL53 5TH
e-mail: gunna@bodegroes.co.uk
dir: On A497, 1m W of Pwllheli

On the wild Llyn Peninsula, replete with rugged cliffs and sandy coves, Plas Bodegroes is a true destination restaurant. It's a beautifully restored Georgian manor house with the stylish décor of soft greens and subtle lighting enhanced with original art by local artists. A polished floor and crisp linen-draped tables add to the feeling that this is a restaurant where the finer points are important, a fact which is reflected in the knowledgeable and personable service. Outside you'll find secluded gardens and an avenue of two-hundred-year-old beeches with wisterias and roses lending their scent to the verandah. Chef Chris Chown takes advantage of many of the fine regional ingredients to create well judged and intelligently balanced dishes. Arbroath smokie tart, for example, with shaved fennel salad and lemon dressing might precede roast tenderloin of Llyn pork with bacon and leek crumble and mustard sauce, with bara brith-and-butter pudding with Penderyn whisky ice cream to finish.

Chef Chris Chown, Aled Williams & Hugh Bracegirdle **Owner** Mrs G Chown & Chris Chown
Times 12.30-2.30/7-9.30 **Closed** Dec-Feb, Mon, L Tue-Sat, D Sun **Prices** Fixed D 4 course £42.50-£50, Service optional **Wines** 261 bottles over £20, 72 bottles under £20, 4 by glass **Notes** Sunday L, Vegetarian available **Seats** 40, Pr/dining room 14 **Parking** 30

MONMOUTHSHIRE

ABERGAVENNY Map 9 SO21

Angel Hotel

◎ Modern British, European

Popular venue with broad appeal

☎ 01873 857121 📄 01873 858059
15 Cross St NP7 5EN
e-mail: mail@angelhotelabergavenny.com
dir: Follow town centre signs from rdbt, S of Abergavenny, past rail & bus stations. Turn left by hotel

This Georgian coaching inn has long been satisfying travellers making the long journey between London and Fishguard, whilst satisfying hungry locals to boot. There's a touch of contemporary chic about the place these days, with a relaxed bar, attractive courtyard and a smart restaurant providing plenty of options; on Friday and Saturday nights a pianist helps set the mood. The menu is split into sections - pasta and rice, fish and shellfish and more - and offers a range of broadly European-

---

focused dishes, including plenty of brasserie classics. Mussels marinière, perhaps, followed by crayfish risotto with mascarpone, or 28-day aged local rib-eye with hand-cut chips. There's an impressive children's menu and afternoon tea is a bit of a speciality.

Chef Mark Turton **Owner** Caradog Hotels Ltd
Times 12-2.30/7-10 **Closed** 25 Dec, D 24 & 26 Dec **Prices** Starter £4.80-£9.80, Main £9.60-£19.80, Dessert £4.80-£5.20, Service optional **Wines** 70 bottles over £20, 32 bottles under £20, 8 by glass **Notes** Sunday L, Vegetarian available, Civ Wed 200 **Seats** 80, Pr/dining room 120 **Children** Portions, Menu **Parking** 40

The Foxhunter

◎◎ Modern European ♦ NOTABLE WINE LIST ✷

Fine food and service in a delightful setting

☎ 01873 881101
Nantyderry NP7 9DN
e-mail: info@thefoxhunter.com
dir: Just off A4042 between Usk & Abergavenny

A remote former stationmaster's house next to the railway line from Newport to Abergavenny, this Victorian building is now a beautifully restored and stylish place. The Foxhunter has an excellent reputation both locally and beyond for its deceptively simple modern European food, charming service and excellent wine list. Fresh local ingredients come to the fore in dishes with well-defined flavours and stunning presentation. The menus change twice a day and might start with pigeon and smoked eel bruschetta with red wine sauce, followed by loin of Middlewhite pork with choucroute and black pudding. Finish with apple and quince polenta crumble with clotted cream. Two adjacent cottages provide overnight accommodation for those wishing to extend their stay.

Chef Matt Tebbutt **Owner** Lisa & Matt Tebbutt
Times 12-2.30/7-9.30 **Closed** Xmas, 1 Jan, Mon (exceptions apply), D Sun **Prices** Fixed L 2 course fr £18.95, Starter £5.95-£9.95, Main £12.95-£20.95, Dessert £5.95-£8.95, Service optional, Groups min 8 service 10% **Wines** 50 bottles over £20, 26 bottles under £20, 5 by glass **Notes** Sunday L, Vegetarian available **Seats** 50, Pr/dining room 30 **Children** Portions **Parking** 25

The Hardwick

◎◎ Modern British

Hearty but classy cooking based on great regional produce

☎ 01873 854220
Old Raglan Rd NP7 9AA
e-mail: info@thehardwick.co.uk

Chef-proprietor Stephen Terry has a great pedigree having worked with Marco back in the day and more recently at The Walnut Tree in Abergavenny and these days, courtesy of *The Great British Menu*, his talents can be seen on TV. The Hardwick is a pub inasmuch as you

continued on page 558

Walnut Tree Inn

Modern British NOTABLE WINE LIST

Legendary Welsh restaurant back at the top

☎ 01873 852797   📠 01873 859764
Llandewi Skirrid NP7 8AW
e-mail: mail@thewalnuttreeinn.com
web: www.thewalnuttreeinn.com
dir: 3m NE of Abergavenny on B4521

Shaun Hill is one of only a few chefs for whom the mere mention of his name can bring a smile to the face of even the most hardened food critic. The Walnut Tree is a restaurant with a formidable past, once celebrated for its honest, simple and robust cooking. Put the respected chef in the much-loved restaurant and you have a recipe for success. The setting on a B road in the Black Mountains is splendidly rural and seemingly isolated (Abergavenny is only a couple of miles away), adding further to the impression of it as a culinary oasis, and the cream-painted former inn is a study in understated charm. It's all relaxed and unpretentious on the inside, too, with bare-wood tables and neutral colours, and staff who know the menu and keep everything ticking along in an unstuffy manner. Shaun's menus are based around top-notch produce and sound technical skills, showing allegiance only to good sense and the seasons. There's an excellent value set lunch menu and a carte which extends

to 10 or so choices per course, with a selection of desserts which would surely bring a smile to the face of Franco Taruschio. Crab cakes with anchovy and garlic mayonnaise or calves' brains with brown butter are starters to set pulses racing, before saddle of hare with celeriac purée and Savoy cabbage, and finishing with buttermilk pudding with rhubarb or a board of English and French cheeses to share. The intelligently annotated wine list has good selections by the glass and half-bottle.

Chef Shaun Hill **Owner** Shaun Hill, William Griffiths **Times** 12-2.30/7-10 Closed Sun-Mon **Prices** Fixed L 2 course £15, Starter £6-£9, Main £9-£20, Dessert £7 **Wines** 65 bottles over £20, 8 bottles under £20, 8 by glass **Notes** Vegetarian available, Air con **Seats** 70, Pr/dining room 26 **Children** Portions, Menu **Parking** 30

ABERGAVENNY *continued*

can just pop in for pint (there's a great selection of local hand-pulled ales), but, really, that would be a shame - this is a food-focused establishment and Stephen's honest and intelligent food should not be missed. There's a copper topped bar and wooden tables, a relaxed and unstuffy atmosphere, and a display of cookery books if you're looking for ideas. The menu is broadly modern British in tone, showing a dedication to good local Welsh produce. Grilled ox tongue, served with salsa verde, soft-boiled organic egg and grilled sourdough bread, is a fine and hearty first course, followed, perhaps, by a substantial roast loin of pedigree Welsh Black pork with creamy haricot beans, purple sprouting broccoli, dandelion and pancetta.

Times 12-3/6.30-10 Closed Mon (exc BHs), D Sun

Llansantffraed Court Hotel

◉◉ Modern British

Good views and accomplished cooking in elegant country-house hotel

☎ 01873 840678 ▤ 01873 840674
Llanvihangel Gobion, Clytha NP7 9BA
e-mail: reception@llch.co.uk
dir: M4 junct 24/A449 to Raglan. At rdbt take last exit to Clytha. Hotel on right in 0.5m

On the old Abergavenny to Raglan road, this elegant Georgian country-house hotel is set in 20 acres of landscaped grounds complete with trout lake and offers breathtaking views of the Brecon Beacons. A Grade II listed former manor house, the Court Restaurant is located in the oldest part of the building and is traditionally decorated with exposed beams, warm colours, country-style furniture and pretty floral prints. The south-facing terrace is just the ticket for alfresco dining in summer. Service is friendly and attentive and adds to the relaxed atmosphere. The cooking style here is Modern British, with classical dishes presented simply and without fussy garnishes. Local produce is handled well, as in spiced terrine of Llanarth Estate rabbit, mango relish and toasted ciabatta and belly of Usk Valley Middlewhite pork, Chantenay carrots, dauphinoise potatoes and crisp shallots. There's a very good wine list, too.

Chef Steve Bennett **Owner** Mike Morgan **Times** 12-2/7-9 **Prices** Fixed L 2 course £14.50, Fixed D 4 course £29.50, Starter £6-£8.50, Main £15-£19.50, Dessert £6-£8, Service optional **Wines** 65 bottles over £20, 22 bottles under £20, 65 by glass **Notes** Tasting menu with matched wines, Sunday L, Vegetarian available, Civ Wed 150 **Seats** 50, Pr/dining room 35 **Children** Portions, Menu **Parking** 300

Restaurant 1861

◉◉ Modern British

Country restaurant with well-crafted menu

☎ 0845 388 1861
Cross Ash NP7 8PB
web: www.18-61.co.uk
dir: On B4521, 9m from Abergavenny, 15m from Ross-on-Wye, on outskirts of Cross Ash

Simon and Kate King's restaurant in a quiet hamlet a few miles outside Abergavenny can be considered a serious destination in the region. Lunch and dinner includes everything from an excellent home-made loaf (complete with mini carving knife), to amuse-bouche and pre-dessert, all revealing the culinary ambition of this experienced couple. The building, dating from 1861 of course, resembles a Victorian station and is surrounded by a white picket fence. Inside it is simply decorated, with wooden beams, whitewashed walls and unclothed dark-wood tables. Excellent value fixed-price menus and a separate carte feature plenty of local produce, and the dishes are well-judged in terms of balance of flavours and textures. That amuse-bouche might be a tomato and chive jelly, bursting with flavour, before twice-baked cheese soufflé with onion marmalade. Main-course fillet of gurnard comes with bouillabaisse sauce, and iced apple parfait with apple and Calvados sorbet is a splendid finish to a meal.

Chef Simon King **Owner** Simon & Kate King **Times** 12-2/7-9 Closed 1st 2 wks Jan, Mon, D Sun **Prices** Fixed L 2 course £16.50, Fixed D 3 course £28, Starter £6-£8.50, Main £16-£18.50, Dessert £5.50-£7.50, Service optional **Wines** 37 bottles over £20, 14 bottles under £20, 6 by glass **Notes** Tasting menu 7 course, Sunday L, Vegetarian available **Seats** 32 **Children** Portions **Parking** 20

Walnut Tree Inn

◉◉◉ — *see page 557*

— *see page 557*

The Beaufort Arms Coaching Inn & Restaurant

◉ Modern British **NEW**

Historic Welsh Marches inn with modern style and food to match

☎ 01291 690412 ▤ 01291 690935
High St NP15 2DY
e-mail: enquiries@beaufortraglan.co.uk
dir: M4 junct 24 (Newport/Abergavenny) A449 then A40 to Raglan. Opposite church in Raglan

The Beaufort Arms has been at the heart of Raglan village life since the 16th century. Roundhead soldiers dropped by for a pint whilst besieging medieval Raglan castle, from where it's said the grand stone fireplace in the lounge was 'recycled', and Prime Ministers have stayed. Energetic owners have carefully preserved the character of ancient beams, slate floors and wood panelling to blend with a stylish contemporary design. The Brasserie restaurant is airily modern in shades of cappuccino and cherry that strike the right note to accompany the kitchen's accurate cooking in the modern British idiom. Fresh local produce is used intelligently, as in a tian of crab with lime and ginger sorbet and chilli crème fraîche, followed by rump of welsh lamb with creamed leeks, lamb heart pie, fondant potato and lavender-infused jus.

Chef Stuart Spicer **Owner** Eliot & Jana Lewis **Times** 12-3/6-9 **Prices** Starter £4.50-£7.95, Main £12.50-£18.50, Dessert £5-£6.50, Service optional **Wines** 10 bottles over £20, 25 bottles under £20, 12 by glass **Notes** Sunday L, Vegetarian available, Air con **Seats** 60, Pr/dining room 26 **Children** Menu **Parking** 30

The Stonemill & Steppes Farm Cottages

◉◉ British, French

Modern, flavour-driven cooking in a converted 16th-century mill

☎ 01600 716273
NP25 5SW
e-mail: enquiries@thestonemill.co.uk
dir: A48 to Monmouth, B4233 to Rockfield. 2.6m from Monmouth town centre

In a hamlet west of Monmouth near the Wye Valley and Forest of Dean, the Stonemill Restaurant occupies a tastefully converted mill dating from the 16th century. Inside it's a riot of oak beams and vaulted ceilings, with chunky rustic tables around an ancient stone cider press. The kitchen takes a modern route with its Mediterranean-influenced dishes and thinks local in its approach to sourcing excellent seasonal materials. Chargrilled tuna loin with guacamole, herb salad and lime dressing might start the ball rolling, followed by rack of Welsh lamb with mustard mash and local asparagus. Interesting desserts might toss in a sugar ring doughnut with hot chocolate soup and peanut parfait. Six smart cottages are available on a self-catering or bed and breakfast basis if you want to stay over.

Owner Mrs M L Decloedt **Times** 12-2/6-9 Closed 25-26 Dec, 2 wks Jan, Mon, D Sun **Prices** Food prices not confirmed for 2010. Please telephone for details. **Wines** 15 bottles over £20, 28 bottles under £20, 8 by glass **Notes** Civ Wed 60 **Seats** 56, Pr/dining room 12 **Children** Portions **Parking** 40

SKENFRITH
Map 9 SO42

WINE AWARD WINNER FOR WALES

The Bell at Skenfrith

Modern British

Restaurant with rooms and all-round appeal

☎ 01600 750235 🖹 01600 750525
NP7 8UH
e-mail: enquiries@skenfrith.co.uk
dir: N of Monmouth on A466 for 4m. Left on B4521 towards Abergavenny, 3m on left

Set beside the River Monnow in glorious Monmouthshire countryside, this beautifully restored 17th-century inn impresses on many counts. It oozes all the charming allure of an old Welsh inn, with slate walls, oak beams and blazing log fires, yet offers all the modern-day comforts of a chic country hotel, with sumptuous sofas and beautifully appointed bedrooms. It's the quality food and drink that really steal the show. A commitment to local produce, as seen in the list of suppliers on the daily menus and ingredients from their own organic kitchen garden, results in some seriously good cooking that displays great technical skill. Take a confident, well balanced starter of crab and dill risotto with roasted peppers, marinated tiger prawns and seared red mullet, followed by breast of Tidenham Chase duck with confit duck spring roll and redcurrant jus, and a well textured and flavoured iced praline parfait with dark chocolate fondant and peppermint ice cream. A large walk-in wine cellar and award-winning wine list completes the picture.

Chef David Hill **Owner** Mr & Mrs W Hutchings **Times** 12-2.30/7-9.30 Closed last wk Jan, 1st wk Feb, Tue (Nov-Mar) **Prices** Fixed L 2 course fr £15, Starter £4.95-£9.50, Main £14.50-£19, Service optional **Wines** 254 bottles over £20, 34 bottles under £20, 14 by glass **Notes** Sunday L, Vegetarian available, Dress restrictions, Smart casual **Seats** 60, Pr/dining room 40 **Children** Portions, Menu **Parking** 35

USK
Map 9 SO30

The Newbridge

Modern British NEW

Good local produce in a riverside country inn

☎ 01633 451000 🖹 01633 451001
Tredunnock NP15 1LY
dir: Please telephone for directions

A few minutes' drive out of Usk, and perched on the banks of the river of the same name, the Newbridge is an attractive country inn. Handy for any number of activities in the surrounding parts, from golf to fishing, the place is filled with a relaxed, easy-going ambience, and outdoor tables by the river will look tempting on a sunny day. The emphasis of the menus is on local game, fish and meats, and dishes are simply conceived and based on intelligent flavour combinations. A small piece of sea bass fillet is bedded on crayfish risotto for an effective starter, while a main course might be a roast chicken breast with diced chorizo, sauté potatoes and an artichoke velouté.

Times 12-6/7-10

Raglan Arms

Modern British

Unpretentious atmosphere and good, honest food

☎ 01291 690800 🖹 01291 690155
Llandenny NP15 1DL
e-mail: raglanarms@aol.com
dir: M4 junct 26. Turn off A449 towards Usk, then immediately right towards Llandenny

In deepest Monmouthshire farming country this flagstoned, flint-built pub in a gorgeous village has moved upmarket from a traditional boozer to a more food-oriented hostelry. If you prefer a pubby vibe, seat yourself in the bar, where well-kept ales are on tap, otherwise most activity centres on the conservatory extension. There's a clear Gallic flavour to the modern British dishes; the menu mixes old favourites with inventive options, and daily blackboard specials take advantage of the season. Expect unaffected presentation and sound, clean flavours. Start with comforting pea and ham soup with crème fraîche, followed by local bangers and mash with rich gravy, white onion sauce and spinach, then crème caramel with boozy prunes and shortbread.

Chef Giles Cunliffe **Owner** Giles Cunliffe & Charlott Fagergard **Times** 12-2.30/7-9.30 Closed 25-26 Dec & BHs, Mon, D Sun **Prices** Fixed L 2 course £14.50-£18.50, Fixed D 3 course £19.25-£35, Starter £4.75-£8.50, Main £10-£19, Dessert £4.50-£7.50, Service optional **Wines** 26 bottles over £20, 35 bottles under £20, 13 by glass **Notes** Sunday L, Vegetarian available **Seats** 65 **Children** Portions **Parking** 30

WHITEBROOK
Map 4 SO50

Crown at Whitebrook

Modern British

Stylish restaurant with rooms with first-class cooking

☎ 01600 860254 🖹 01600 860607
NP25 4TX
e-mail: info@crownatwhitebrook.co.uk
dir: From Monmouth take B4293 towards Trellech, in 2.7m left towards Whitebrook, continue for 2m

The location in the beautiful Wye Valley gives this restaurant with rooms a real sense of tranquillity, and everything about the place, from the 17th-century features of the building to the impressive modern cooking, combines to create a jewel in Wales's culinary crown. The dining room has a contemporary feel, despite the old beams whitewashed with lime ash, where elegantly dressed tables help create a suitably refined setting for what follows. And what follows is some skilfully prepared, eye-catching dishes of real appeal. Serious intent is shown in the canapés and amuse-bouche that kick things off (langoustine with leek and fennel topped with a white chocolate foam, for example), and in the superb breads. First-rate produce is used, much of it local, in modern British dishes of considerable flair: roast monkish is perfectly partnered with capers, salted turnip and a cucumber sorbet in an impressive first course, and main-course oven-roasted loin of venison with chestnuts and celeriac is finished with a well-judged espresso and chocolate sauce. The balance of flavours is spot-on throughout, and the excellent wine list does justice to the kitchen's output. The Crown at Celtic Manor (see entry) is a new stable-mate at the famous golfing resort.

Chef James Sommerin **Owner** The Crown Hotels & Restaurants Ltd **Times** 12-2/7-9.30 Closed 2 wks Xmas, New Year, D Sun **Prices** Fixed L 2 course £25, Fixed D 3 course £45, Tasting menu £70, Service optional, Groups min 8 service 12.5% **Notes** Tasting menu 8 course, Sunday L, Vegetarian available, Dress restrictions, Smart casual, No T-shirts, shorts or sandals **Seats** 30, Pr/dining room 12 **Parking** 20

| NEWPORT | Map 9 ST38 |

The Chandlery

◉◉ Modern, Traditional

Skilful cooking in historic maritime surroundings

☎ 01633 256622 🖷 01633 256633
77-78 Lower Dock St NP20 1EH
e-mail: food@thechandleryrestaurant.com
dir: On A48, 0.5m from Royal Gwent Hospital at foot of George St Bridge

No prizes for guessing what this listed Georgian building in the heart of Newport was used for before money from the Heritage Lottery Fund and the Welsh Assembly helped restore it into a very shipshape restaurant. The interior blends original Georgian elegance with dark wood floors, white walls and bare wooden tables for a classy contemporary look. Quality Welsh produce is the cornerstone of the kitchen's output, but its carefully prepared modern dishes take their inspiration from much further afield. Flavours are kept clean and not overworked, as in a starter of marinated fish and shellfish with fennel salad. Spiced pork meat balls with home-made linguine makes for a faultlessly tasty main course, while a dark chocolate tart with vanilla ice cream finishes on a decadently rich note.

Chef Simon Newcombe, Ryan Mitchel **Owner** Simon Newcombe, Jane Newcombe **Times** 12-2/7-10 Closed 1 wk Xmas, Mon, L Sat, D Sun **Prices** Fixed L 2 course £11.95, Starter £4.50-£6.95, Main £11.95-£17.95, Dessert £4.95-£6.50, Service optional, Groups min 6 service 10% **Wines** 19 bottles over £20, 21 bottles under £20, 8 by glass **Notes** Tasting & pre-post theatre menus available on request, Sunday L, Vegetarian available, Air con **Seats** 80, Pr/dining room 60 **Children** Portions **Parking** 20

The Crown at Celtic Manor

◉◉◉ – **see below**

Rafters

◉ Modern European NEW ◔

Good modern food alongside good golfing views

☎ 01633 413000 🖷 01633 431523
Celtic Manor, Usk Valley NP18 1HQ
dir: M4 junct 24. At rdbt take the B4237 towards Newport, after 100mtrs turn right at Celtic Manor sign

Rafters is in the clubhouse of the '2010' golf course, some way from the hotel itself. The clubhouse has been built especially for the 2010 Ryder Cup, and Rafters restaurant, so named for its lofty ceiling with exposed cedar beams, is a large, open space with magnificent vistas over the course. It is smart and contemporary, but not overstated, with well-set cloth-less wooden tables adding to the relaxed tone. The cooking is broadly Pan-European with starters such as Cornish crab linguini, followed by excellent 10oz Usk Valley rib-eye steak with hand-cut chips, and finishing with a trio of sponge puddings or Welsh cheeses.

Chef Simon Searle **Owner** Celtic Manor Resort **Times** 12-6/6-10 Closed Oct-Mar Mon-Wed from 6pm **Prices** Fixed L 2 course £13.45, Fixed D 3 course £19.95, Starter £4.95-£10.50, Main £10.95-£20.95, Dessert £4.95-£9, Service optional **Wines** 34 bottles over £20, 4 bottles under £20, 6 by glass **Notes** Sunday L, Dress restrictions, Smart casual (no jeans, trainers, flip-flops), Air con **Seats** 80, Pr/dining room 96 **Children** Portions **Parking** 115

The Crown at Celtic Manor

| NEWPORT | Map 9 ST38 |

Modern European NEW

Fine restaurant in Welsh landmark hotel

☎ 01633 410262 & 413000 🖷 01633 412910
Coldra Woods NP18 1HQ
e-mail: reservations@celtic-manor.com
dir: From M4 junct 24 take B4237 towards Newport, turn right after 300mtrs

It is impossible to write about Celtic Manor without mentioning the Ryder Cup, which is being held at the resort in the autumn of 2010. So, if you want to eat like a top golfer, and maybe even earwig on Colin Montgomerie's tactics, book a table for late September or early October. There are plenty of dining options at the Celtic Manor Resort, but The Crown, a partnership between the resort and the award-winning Crown at

Whitebrook (see entry), is undoubtedly the star of the show. The dining room is chic and smart with high-backed leather chairs, well-spaced, stylishly set tables, and mood lighting to add to the sense of glamour. The menu makes good use of Welsh produce, delivering punchy flavours in refined and elegantly presented dishes. Things get off to a good start with a fine range of canapés, including langoustine and salmon beignet, good bread, and amuse-bouche. Roasted quail with superb ravioli of the meat, consommé flavoured with jasmine and morel garnish is an impressive starter, and main-course loin of Welsh venison (pink and tender) is served with hazelnuts, crosnes, pancetta and a light watercress velouté. This is modern European food, broadly speaking, with desserts ranging from bitter chocolate mousse with basil and orange sorbet to mango and passionfruit soufflé with coconut ice cream. Service is both discreet and personal, and the sommelier is on hand with good advice on the excellent wine list.

Times 12-2/7-10.30 Closed 1-12 Jan, Sun

PEMBROKESHIRE

HAVERFORDWEST   Map 8 SM91

Wolfscastle Country Hotel

British, International 🕲

Enjoyable food in peaceful country hotel

☎ 01437 741225 & 741688 📠 01437 741383
Wolf's Castle SA62 5LZ
e-mail: info@wolfscastle.com
dir: From Haverfordwest take A40 towards Fishguard.
Hotel in centre of Wolf's Castle

A stone-built former vicarage nestling in the lush mid-Pembrokeshire countryside, this 19th-century building is still known locally by its original name of Allt-yr-Afon ('Hill by the River'). The hotel is very much a family affair, in ambience and character, and it has a good reputation locally for its food. The same menu is offered in the bar and restaurant and is divided into a choice of traditional dishes, like salmon duo with crème fraîche and walnut toast, and a more international selection such as pan-seared sea bass with gingered leeks and spring onions, crispy potatoes and chive crème fraîche. Round things off with a traditional lemon meringue pie.

Chef Owen Hall **Owner** Mr A Stirling **Times** 12-2/6.30-9 Closed 24-26 Dec **Prices** Fixed L 2 course £10.95, Starter £4.95-£8.95, Main £8.95-£19.95, Dessert £4.95, Service optional **Wines** 33 bottles over £20, 15 bottles under £20, 9 by glass **Notes** Sunday L, Vegetarian available, Civ Wed 60, Air con **Seats** 55, Pr/dining room 32 **Children** Portions, Menu **Parking** 75

NEWPORT   Map 8 SN03

Llys Meddyg

British **NEW** 🕲

Impressive cooking in elegant townhouse

☎ 01239 820008 & 820753
East St SA42 0SY
e-mail: contact@llysmeddyg.com
dir: A487 to Newport, located on the Main Street, through the centre of town

Originally a coaching house and later a doctor's residence, this splendid Georgian townhouse on the high street is now a fine dining restaurant with rooms. Enjoy a pre-dinner drink in front of the wood-burning fire in the cosy bar before moving into the light and airy dining room with its sea green walls, sisal carpet and leather-seated wooden chairs. In the kitchen, the modern British cooking is heavily influenced by the seasons and the local produce available. Expect accurate cooking and well-balanced flavours in dishes such as smoked haddock Scotch egg with wholegrain mustard hollandaise followed by roast pork belly with grilled plums and salty caramel.

Chef Scott Davis **Owner** Ed & Louise Sykes **Times** 12-2/7-9 Closed Mon, L Tue, D Sun **Prices** Fixed L 2 course £12.95-£15.95, Fixed D 3 course £21, Starter £6.95-£9.95, Main £17.50-£29.50, Dessert £4.50-£9.50,

Service optional **Wines** 27 bottles over £20, 16 bottles under £20, 6 by glass **Notes** Sunday L, Vegetarian available **Seats** 30, Pr/dining room 14 **Parking** 8

PORTHGAIN   Map 8 SM83

The Shed

Traditional British, Mediterranean 🕲

Local seafood dining in sea-going surroundings

☎ 01348 831518
SA62 5BN
e-mail: caroline@theshedporthgain.co.uk
dir: 7m from St David's. Off A40

Smack on the quayside in the delightful fishing village of Porthgain, this former carpenter's workshop and fisherman's lock-up draws seafood lovers in their droves for own-caught crab and lobster and squeaky-fresh fish landed outside the door. Expect a rustic, beach hut feel about the place, with slate floors, chequered tablecloths, local landscapes on whitewashed walls, and a relaxed atmosphere. Start with red mullet and red wine soup or sautéed Swansea Bay crevettes with lashings of garlic, parsley and butter, before steamed lemon sole with crab soufflé and a brown crab, ginger and lemongrass butter sauce.

Chef Caroline Jones **Owner** Rob & Caroline Jones **Times** 11-4.30/6-11.30 Closed Nov-Apr open only wknds (except half term & Xmas hols), D Mon **Prices** Starter £4.95-£8.50, Main £12.50-£24.95 **Wines** 26 bottles under £20, 6 by glass **Notes** Sunday L, Vegetarian available **Seats** 36 **Children** Portions **Parking** On village street

ST DAVID'S   Map 8 SM72

Cwtch

Modern Welsh, European **NEW**

Good use of local produce in high street restaurant

☎ 01437 720491
22 High St SA62 6SD
e-mail: info@cwtchrestaurant.co.uk

Pronounced 'cutsh', non-Welsh speakers please note (it means 'hug'), this restaurant is recognisable by its two-tone blue frontage on the high street of Britain's smallest city. A two-part ground-floor dining room is served by a dumb waiter from the first-floor kitchen, and there is more seating upstairs too. A big, rough wooden beam support and stone walls create an agreeably rustic appearance, reinforced by bare wood tables, and there

are shelves of cookery books for you to browse (good for solo diners). The small kitchen brigade produces classy food, based on sound local supplies. A chunky chowder of smoked haddock and Penclawdd cockles is a fine opener, and might be followed by remarkably tender Pembrokeshire lamb shoulder with smoked bacon, Puy lentils and dressed with salsa verde. Desserts will fill up any spare corners with the likes of clotted cream rice pudding, garnished with a Marsala-soaked plum.

Times 6pm Closed Sun-Tues (Nov-Mar)

Morgan's

Modern British 🕲

Inventive modern cooking in a converted schoolhouse

☎ 01437 720508 📠 01437 720508
20 Nun St SA62 6NT
e-mail: eat@morgans-restaurant.co.uk
web: www.morgans-restaurant.co.uk
dir: Haverfordwest 16m. On A487 to Fishguard, just off main square, 100mtrs from cathedral

A small, brightly furnished restaurant in Wales' pint-sized city is home to a locally focused, unpretentious operation. It was once a schoolhouse, as well as having done time as a dentist and a launderette. Bare wooden tables, good pictures on the walls and discreet lighting set a relaxing tone for the gastronomic business now undertaken, with cooking in the modern idiom. Caerfai cheese goes into a twice-baked soufflé, with apple and plum compôte for tangy bite. Lobster sauce and saffron oil are the medium for a main-course serving of sea bass, which comes with crisped skin and a wealth of flavour. Nor do meals end on a downbeat, as witness perfectly formed pannacotta of hazelnut and Frangelico, with espresso and chocolate truffle jelly and light, buttery hazelnut shortbread.

Chef Tara Pitman **Owner** David & Tara Pitman **Times** 6.30-11.30 Closed Jan, Tue, L all week, D Wed (Oct-Jun) **Prices** Starter £5.50-£8.75, Main £12.95-£19.95, Dessert £4.50-£6.50, Service optional **Wines** 10 bottles over £20, 31 bottles under £20, 5 by glass **Notes** Vegetarian available **Seats** 36, Pr/dining room 12 **Children** Portions **Parking** Car park opposite

ST DAVID'S *continued*

Warpool Court Hotel

◉◉ Modern British

Enjoyable dining with impressive coastal scenery

☎ 01437 720300 📠 01437 720676
SA62 6BN
e-mail: info@warpoolcourthotel.com
dir: From Cross Sq in centre of St David's, left by HSBC
bank into Goat St, at fork follow hotel signs

Smack beside the Pembrokeshire Coast Path and built in
the 1860s as St David's Cathedral School, Warpool Court
stands in glorious grounds amid spectacular scenery,
with panoramic views across St Brides Bay. Equally eye-
catching within is the Ada Williams collection of unique
armorial and ornamental hand-painted tiles which
bedeck the public areas. The spacious dining room
overlooks the gardens towards the sea and offers a daily-
changing set dinner menu that focuses on fresh local
ingredients used in an innovative fashion to allow the key
flavours to shine through. A typical meal may begin with
roast squab pigeon with wild mushroom and Puy lentil
stew, or carrot and coriander soup, with cannon of local
lamb with tomato and herb jus to follow. Round off with
vanilla pannacotta with spiced baby figs or a plate of
Welsh cheeses.

Chef Barry Phillips **Owner** Peter Trier
Times 12-1.45/7-9.15 Closed Jan **Prices** Food prices not
confirmed for 2010. Please telephone for details.
Wines 101 bottles over £20, 21 bottles under £20, 4 by
glass **Notes** Sunday L, Vegetarian available, Civ Wed 120
Seats 50, Pr/dining room 22 **Children** Portions, Menu
Parking 100

TENBY | Map 8 SN10

Penally Abbey Hotel

◉ Traditional, Modern

Modern British cuisine with Carmarthen Bay views

☎ 01834 843033 📠 01834 844714
Penally SA70 7PY
e-mail: penally.abbey@btinternet.com
dir: From Tenby take A4139 to Penally

A gothic-style country-house hotel set in 5 acres of
grounds on the western promontory of Wales, Penally
Abbey has splendid views of Carmarthen Bay. Renovation
and upgrading has resulted in an attractive mix of

---

classic and contemporary styles. The spacious restaurant
offers a menu of traditional and modern British dishes
created from local produce. Service is pleasant and
unhurried and diners can enjoy garden and sea views.
Starters might include mushrooms and bacon with garlic
cream in a filo pastry parcel, followed by fillet of Welsh
lamb filled with spinach, wrapped in bacon and served
with a red wine jus.

Times 12.30-2/7.30-9.30 Closed L (ex by arrangement
only)

POWYS

BRECON | Map 9 SO02

The Felin Fach Griffin

◉◉ British 🍷

**Exemplary rural gastro-pub with top-notch unshowy
cooking**

☎ 01874 620111
Felin Fach LD3 0UB
e-mail: enquiries@eatdrinksleep.ltd.uk
dir: 3.5m N of Brecon on A470. Large terracotta building
on left, on edge of village

The Griffin is exactly the kind of rural foodie pub you
dream of ending up in after a day's hiking in the
wilderness of the Brecon Beacons and Black Mountains.
Inside, it is the very picture of rustic chic, with thick
beams, warm colours, open fires and nicely scuffed
leather sofas. But it's not just about looking good: this is
a place that gets it right on so many levels - locals are
regulars at the bar, menus are pitched at keen prices -
without sacrificing quality - and the switched-on owners
now serve around 20 excellent wines by the glass or
carafe to let diners find the best match for each course.
The kitchen works with a top-class network of local
suppliers, and fruit, salads and vegetables come from
the first organically-certified kitchen garden in Wales.
Fresh local goats' cheese is teamed with tomato tartare,
black olive dressing and focaccia to start, with slow-
braised ox cheeks with creamed girolles and leek and
pancetta colcannon to follow.

Chef Ricardo Van Ede **Owner** Charles Inkin, Edmund Inkin
Times 12.30-2.30/6.30-9.30 Closed 24-25 Dec, few days
Jan **Prices** Fixed L 2 course fr £15.90, Fixed D 3 course fr
£27.50, Starter £8.50-£12.50, Main £17.50-£20, Dessert
£6-£8.50, Service optional **Wines** 100 bottles over £20,
30 bottles under £20, 20 by glass **Notes** Sunday L,
Vegetarian available **Seats** 45, Pr/dining room 20
Children Portions **Parking** 60

Peterstone Court

◉◉ Modern British, European 🍷 ☺

Excellent local food on the edge of the Brecon Beacons

☎ 01874 665387 📠 01874 665376
Llanhamlach LD3 7YB
e-mail: info@peterstone-court.com
web: www.peterstone-court.com
dir: 1m from Brecon on A40 to Abergavenny

This fine Georgian Manor sits in its own grounds just
outside the market town of Brecon, with stunning views
over the River Usk. Eclectically styled with the traditional
blending with the contemporary, the restaurant boasts
high, decorative ceilings, crystal chandeliers and 2 open
fireplaces. Quality local produce, good technical skills and
eye-catching presentation make for a memorable meal in
the restaurant, which prides itself on sourcing 90% of the
meat and poultry direct from the family farm 7 miles
away. The modern British cooking is underpinned by
French influences - seared breast of pigeon with braised
Puy lentils and crispy parsnips could be followed by confit
of lamb shoulder, roasted root vegetables and creamed
potatoes.

Chef Sean Gerrard, Robert Taylor **Owner** Jessica & Glyn
Bridgeman, Sean Gerrard **Times** 12-2.30/7-9.30
Prices Fixed L 2 course fr £13.50, Starter £4.95-£9.95,
Main £10.95-£18.95, Dessert £5.50-£6.95, Service
optional **Wines** 30 bottles over £20, 31 bottles under £20,
12 by glass **Notes** Sunday L, Vegetarian available, Civ
Wed 120 **Seats** 45, Pr/dining room 120 **Children** Portions,
Menu **Parking** 40

The Usk Inn

◉ British, French

Hearty cuisine at a traditional inn

☎ 01874 676251 📠 01874 676392
Station Rd, Talybont-on-Usk LD3 7JE
e-mail: dine@uskinn.co.uk
dir: 250yds off A40, 6m E of Brecon

The tranquil village of Talybont-on-Usk is a handy base
for taking on the rigours of the Brecon Beacons National
Park. The Usk Inn has traded up from its origins as a spit
and sawdust village pub with a refurb that has more the
ambience of a smart country inn, with open log fires,
polished wooden tables and flagstone floors. Rag-rolled
terracotta walls give the restaurant a bright and cheery
Mediterranean feel, while the bar stays resolutely
traditional. Local Welsh suppliers are name-checked on a
well-balanced menu of down-to-earth dishes backed by
daily blackboard specials. Pheasant confit with pearl

barley and berry sauce is a suitably rustic starter, while mains might offer pork tenderloin with apple sauce and black pudding.

Times 12-3/6.30-9.30 Closed 25-27 Dec

CAERSWS Map 15 SO09

The Talkhouse

◉◉ British, European

Seasonal cooking at a former coaching inn

☎ 01686 688919 & 07876 086183 📠 01686 689134
Ty Siarad, Pontdolgoch SY17 5JE
e-mail: info@talkhouse.co.uk
dir: 1.5m W of Caersws on A470 (Machynlleth road)

This stone-built 17th-century inn - once a typical pub - retains bags of original character, while delivering smart décor and furnishings and a warm, friendly and relaxed atmosphere. The restaurant, enhanced by Laura Ashley fabrics, has French windows opening on to a secluded garden for summer dining, while the sitting room comes with deep sofas and armchairs and the beamed bar with a log fire. The kitchen's frequently-changing menu of traditional dishes, served in generous portions, keeps things simple and fresh allowing prime local ingredients centre stage. Take Welsh lamb rump simply served with cream potatoes, or Bryn Drew free-range chicken breast stuffed with Snowdonia cheddar and leeks.

Times 12-1.30/6.30-8.45 Closed 25-26 Dec, Mon (only open for group booking of 15 or more), L Sat, D Sun

---

CRICKHOWELL Map 9 SO21

The Bear Hotel

◉ Modern British

Convivial dining in a late-medieval inn

☎ 01873 810408 📠 01873 811696
High St NP8 1BW
e-mail: bearhotel@aol.com
dir: Town centre, off A40 (Brecon road). 6m from Abergavenny

The Hindmarsh family has been running The Bear for over thirty years, and that long service has resulted in a wonderfully smooth operation. It's one of the more venerable former coaching inns, dating from the mid-15th century, and the ambience of crackling log fires and exposed stone walls creates a convivial appeal. Keeping abreast with changing food fashions, the kitchen offers dishes such as scallops with Ireland's Clonakilty black pudding and pea purée, followed perhaps by grilled bream with crab tagliatelle and prawn bisque, or glazed ham hock with spring onion mash, apple purée and honey jus. Finish with a home-style pudding like rhubarb crumble and custard.

Chef Stephen Hodson, John Ganeiu **Owner** Mrs J Hindmarsh, Stephen Hindmarsh **Times** 12-2/7-9.30 Closed 25 Dec, Mon, L Tue-Sat, D Sun **Prices** Starter £4.95-£7.95, Main £10.50-£14.95, Dessert £5-£5.95, Service optional **Wines** 47 bottles over £20, 22 bottles

---

under £20, 10 by glass **Notes** Sunday L, Vegetarian available, Dress restrictions, Smart casual **Seats** 60, Pr/dining room 30 **Children** Portions, Menu **Parking** 40

See advert below

Gliffaes Country House Hotel

◉ Modern British

Commitment to local produce in idyllic Welsh setting

☎ 01874 730371 📠 01874 730463
Gliffaes Rd NP8 1RH
e-mail: calls@gliffaeshotel.com
dir: 1m off A40, 2.5m W of Crickhowell

Tucked under the stunning uplands in a magical part of the Brecon Beacons National Park, this imposing Italianate country-house hotel has featured in films and TV programmes. It also has a reputation for fly fishing, being ideally situated by the River Usk in 33 acres of gardens and woods. The work of Welsh artists hangs on the walls of the panelled dining room where the modern British menu features plenty of local produce. As a member of the 'Slow Food Movement', the hotel attempts to source 65% of its fresh produce from within a radius of 75 miles, and aims to use only fish approved by the Marine Conservation Society. The daily-changing dinner menu features starters such as smoked duck filo parcel with julienne of vegetables, green beans and sesame soy and main-course seared haunch of venison with buttered spinach, carpaccio of beetroot, potato rösti and a rich venison kidney sauce.

Chef Karl Cheetham **Owner** Mr & Mrs Brabner & Mr & Mrs Suter **Times** 12-2.30/7.30-9.15 Closed 2-31 Jan, L Mon-Sat **Prices** Fixed D 3 course fr £35, Service included **Wines** 45 bottles over £20, 33 bottles under £20, 8 by glass **Notes** Sunday L, Vegetarian available, Dress restrictions, Smart casual preferred, Civ Wed 40 **Seats** 60, Pr/dining room 18 **Children** Portions, Menu **Parking** 30

CRICKHOWELL *continued*

Manor Hotel

◉ Traditional, International

Dramatic mountain backdrop with good simple cooking

☎ 01873 810212 📠 01873 811938
Brecon Rd NP8 1SE
e-mail: info@manorhotel.co.uk
web: www.manorhotel.co.uk
dir: 0.5m W of Crickhowell on A40 (Brecon road)

The hotel's claim on posterity is that Sir George Everest, after whom the mount is named, was born here in 1790. A gleaming white frontage stands out against the dramatic Black Mountain backdrop and the River Usk, and in a comfortable, well-run dining room, the cooking keeps things simple. Pheasant and pistachio terrine is one way to begin, with mains such as Parma ham-wrapped hake with garlic mash, or roast duck with braised red cabbage and redcurrant jus, to follow. Passionfruit mousse with watermelon granita will leave you feeling suitably refreshed.

Chef Mr G Bridgeman **Owner** Mr G Bridgeman
Times 12-2.30/6.30-9.30 **Prices** Fixed L 2 course fr £10.95, Fixed D 3 course fr £13.95, Starter £3.95-£5.95, Main £9.50-£16.95, Dessert £4.50, Service optional **Wines** 31 bottles over £20, 35 bottles under £20, 15 by glass **Notes** Sunday L, Vegetarian available, Civ Wed 250 **Seats** 54, Pr/dining room 26 **Children** Portions, Menu **Parking** 200

The Old Black Lion

◉ Modern British

Honest cooking on the Welsh borders

☎ 01497 820841 📠 01497 822960
26 Lion St HR3 5AD
e-mail: info@oldblacklion.co.uk
web: www.oldblacklion.co.uk
dir: 1m off A438. From TIC car park turn right along Oxford Rd, pass NatWest Bank, next left (Lion St), hotel 20yds on right

Personally managed by the resident proprietor, this whitewashed 17th-century inn, parts of which date back to the 1300s, is situated close to what was known as the Lion Gate, one of the original entrances to the old walled town of Hay-on-Wye. The inn is brimful of historical charm and atmosphere and it is reputed that Oliver Cromwell stayed here when the Roundheads busied themselves besieging Hay Castle. Well supported by locals and visitors alike, the smart dining room has access to a patio for alfresco dining in summer. The traditional, carefully cooked food includes simple starters such as oven-baked fresh crab topped with Caerphilly cheese, and main courses like Gressingham duck breast on parsnip purée with pink peppercorn sauce.

Chef Peter Bridges **Owner** Dolan Leighton
Times 12-2/6.30-9 Closed 24-26 Dec **Prices** Starter £4.95-£7.50, Main £11.25-£18.95, Service optional **Wines** 16 bottles over £20, 23 bottles under £20, 6 by glass **Notes** Vegetarian available **Seats** 60, Pr/dining room 20 **Parking** 20

Milebrook House

◉◉ Modern, Traditional British

Good food in a beautiful setting

☎ 01547 528632 📠 01547 520509
Milebrook LD7 1LT
e-mail: hotel@milebrook.kc3ltd.co.uk
dir: 2m E of Knighton on A4113 (Ludlow)

Situated in the Teme Valley about a mile and a half from the border town of Knighton, this sensitively restored stone building is set in a truly beautiful area. The rolling hills of the Marches surround this 18th century dower house, with the mountains and moorlands of Wales to the west. The former home of explorer Sir Wilfred Thesiger, the beautiful formal gardens include a productive kitchen garden which provides virtually all the vegetables served in the restaurant. Food is presented with real flair and panache in the traditional, comfortable dining room. Start with pan-seared Cornish scallops, beetroot purée, crisp pancetta and herb oil, and for mains perhaps choose pan-roasted rack and slow roasted shoulder of Welsh lamb with Savoy cabbage, rosemary potato cake and red wine jus.

Chef Christopher Marsden **Owner** Mr & Mrs R T Marsden **Times** 12-2/7-9 Closed Mon (open for residents D), D Sun (open for residents) **Prices** Fixed L 2 course £11.95-£15.50, Fixed D 3 course £33.50, Starter £5-£8, Main £15-£20.50, Service optional **Wines** 40 bottles over £20, 25 bottles under £20, 4 by glass **Notes** Sunday L, Vegetarian available **Seats** 40, Pr/dining room 16 **Children** Portions **Parking** 24

LLANDRINDOD WELLS Map 9 SO06

The Metropole

◉ Modern British **V**

Stylish dining room with well-balanced menus

☎ 01597 823700 📄 01597 824828
Temple St LD1 5DY
e-mail: info@metropole.co.uk
dir: In centre of town off A483

Run by the same family for over 100 years, this imposing Victorian hotel dominates the famous spa town. Spencers Bar and Brasserie is an informal dining option, or relax in the elegant lounge before heading into the smart Radnor Restaurant, which cuts a dash with its contemporary leather and suede high-backed chairs complemented by classic ivory and white linen. It's a relaxed and upbeat atmosphere for some simple, honest cooking based on quality ingredients. The modern repertoire extends to game terrine with beetroot jelly, rack of Welsh lamb with aubergine caviar and thyme sauce, and Valrhona chocolate tart with vanilla sauce.

Chef Nick Edwards **Owner** Justin Baird-Murray
Times 12.30-1.45/7-9.30 **Prices** Fixed D 4 course £25.50, Starter £4.95-£7.50, Main £12.50-£18.95, Dessert £4.95-£7.50, Service optional **Wines** 24 bottles over £20, 54 bottles under £20, 7 by glass **Notes** Sunday L, Vegetarian menu, Civ Wed 200, Air con **Seats** 200, Pr/dining room 250 **Children** Portions, Menu **Parking** 150

LLANFYLLIN Map 15 SJ11

Seeds

◉ Modern British

Accurate cooking in an intimate, relaxed setting

☎ 01691 648604
5-6 Penybryn Cottages, High St SY22 5AP
dir: In village centre. Take A490 N from Welshpool, follow signs to Llanfyllin

A truly intriguing setting, Seeds is a low-ceilinged parlour with an intimate dinner-party atmosphere. Set within a 500-year-old terrace, this intimate restaurant boasts original beams and slate floors combined with curios, maps, books and original works of art. Jazz music plays in the background and friendly staff provide relaxed service, while the menu offers up unfussy modern British fare. Try king prawn and mango salad with honey and poppy seed dressing or smoked mackerel paté and toast, followed by grilled skate wing with cider and cream sauce or sautéed lamb's kidneys with mustard, sherry and cream sauce. Comforting puddings include apple and oat crumble with vanilla ice cream or crème brûlée.

Chef Mark Seager **Owner** Felicity Seager, Mark Seager
Times 11-2.15/7-8.30 Closed 25 Dec, 2 wks Mar, 1 wk Oct, Sun-Mon, L Tue-Wed **Prices** Fixed D 3 course £25.75-£29.25, Service optional **Wines** 30 bottles over £20, 81 bottles under £20, 3 by glass **Notes** Vegetarian available **Seats** 20 **Children** Portions **Parking** Free car park in town, street parking

LLANGAMMARCH WELLS Map 9 SN94

Lake Country House Hotel & Spa

◉◉ British, European **V**

Traditional and luxurious country-house dining

☎ 01591 620202 & 620474 📄 01591 620457
LD4 4BS
e-mail: info@lakecountryhouse.co.uk
dir: 6m from Builth Wells on A483 from Garth, turn left for Llangammarch Wells & follow signs to hotel

Set in attractive and secluded grounds, recent investment has seen this splendid Victorian property increase its number of rooms and the spa and leisure centre have been refurbished. The property exudes an air of bygone luxury with spacious, well-appointed lounges and an old-fashioned level of hospitality. Short menus offer 3 choices per course, including perhaps a salad of roast guinea fowl with black truffle, artichoke, green asparagus and walnut vinaigrette, or a main course of vanilla-roasted silver mullet with wild mushrooms, mashed potato and a star anise reduction. Finish with lemon crème brûlée with lime sorbet and vanilla shortbread. A well thought out vegetarian menu is also available and afternoon tea by the fire is a particular draw.

Times 12.30-2/7.30-9.15

LLANWDDYN Map 15 SJ01

Lake Vyrnwy Hotel & Spa

◉ Modern British

Seasonally based cooking in an incomparable Welsh landscape

☎ 01691 870692 📄 01691 870259
Lake Vyrnwy SY10 0LY
e-mail: info@lakevyrnwyhotel.co.uk
web: www.lakevyrnwyhotel.co.uk
dir: on A4393, 200yds past dam turn sharp right into drive

The sumptuous views over lake and mountains, best enjoyed from the conservatory restaurant, are a powerful lure here, and the Victorian house itself is furnished with an eye to classical elegance, right down to the fine paintings. Top-notch seasonal Welsh produce finds its way into cooking that doesn't stint on either quality or quantity (there are hungry walkers to be fed). Lamb from the surrounding estate is full of sweet flavour and tenderness, and might be served as roast shoulder, braised liver and a noisette, with spinach, lentils and rosemary mash for company. Start enterprisingly, perhaps with sea trout on dill risotto with coconut and lemongrass velouté, and finish indulgently with apricot cheesecake and satsuma compôte.

Chef David Thompson **Owner** The Bisiker family
Times 12-2/6.45-9.15 **Prices** Food prices not confirmed for 2010. Please telephone for details. **Wines** 9 by glass **Notes** Sunday L, Vegetarian available, Dress restrictions, Smart casual preferred, Civ Wed 220 **Seats** 85, Pr/dining room 220 **Children** Portions **Parking** 80

LLANWRTYD WELLS — Map 9 SN84

Carlton Riverside

◉◉◉ – *see below*

Lasswade Country House Restaurant with Rooms

◉◉ Modern British 🍴

Organically minded Edwardian country-house dining

☎ 01591 610515   📠 01591 610611
Station Rd LD5 4RW
e-mail: info@lasswadehotel.co.uk
dir: On A483, follow signs for station, opposite Spar shop, adjacent to tourist info office, 400yds on right before station

This unpretentious and welcoming Edwardian house on the edge of the Victorian spa town of Llanwrtyd Wells is run with aplomb by a husband-and-wife-team who treat their diners as house guests. The idyllic Welsh Marches setting plays its part, too, in providing that much sought-after commodity - complete relaxation, which together with accomplished modern Welsh cuisine, adds up to a tempting package. There's a strong commitment to organic local produce here, like smoked organic salmon from the Welsh borders, fish fresh from Milford Haven, or mutton reared on wild herbs and heather in the Elan Valley. Cooking from the skilled chef-patron is confident, simple and down-to-earth, as in a starter of home-smoked Welsh trout with a poached duck's egg and pea sprouts, or a main course of Welsh Black beef fillet with parsnip mash, wild mushrooms and grain mustard hollandaise with a red wine reduction. Finish with poached plums in mulled wine with tea jelly and organic crème fraîche.

Chef Roger Stevens **Owner** Roger & Emma Stevens **Times** 7.30-9.30 Closed 25 Dec, L all week **Prices** Fixed D 3 course £32, Service optional **Wines** 9 bottles over £20, 17 bottles under £20, 2 by glass **Notes** Dress restrictions, Smart casual **Seats** 20, Pr/dining room 20 **Parking** 6

MONTGOMERY — Map 15 SO29

Dragon Hotel

◉ Traditional 🍴

Historic inn serving traditional food in restaurant and bar

☎ 01686 668359 & 668287   📠 0870 011 8227
Market Square SY15 6PA
e-mail: reception@dragonhotel.com
dir: Behind town hall

The Welsh Marches market town of Montgomery is well-placed for sourcing fine produce, so you can expect soundly-prepared, hearty Welsh dishes at this handsome 17th-century coaching inn. The Dragon has been rooted into local life for centuries - in fact, beams and timbers in the lounge and bar were recycled from the ruined castle after it was destroyed by Cromwell. Traditional décor, then, is what you can expect in its beamed restaurant, and a menu of old favourites majoring on solid meaty fare delivered in belt-busting portions and presented without fussiness - perhaps crispy-crumbed haddock and cod fishcakes to start, then liver and bacon with rich onion gravy and mash.

Dragon Hotel

Chef Thomas Fraenzel **Owner** M & S Michaels **Times** 12-2/7-9 **Prices** Fixed D 3 course £25-£27, Starter £4.25-£6.50, Main £11.25-£23, Dessert £3.25-£4.50, Service optional **Wines** 7 bottles over £20, 43 bottles under £20, 12 by glass **Notes** Sunday L, Vegetarian available **Seats** 42, Pr/dining room 50 **Children** Portions **Parking** 20

Carlton Riverside

LLANWRTYD WELLS — Map 9 SN84

Modern British

Good honest cooking in delightful family-run riverside restaurant

☎ 01591 610248
Irfon Crescent LD5 4ST
e-mail: info@carltonriverside.com
web: www.carltonriverside.com
dir: In town centre beside bridge

The River Irfon runs through the town - Llanwrtyd Wells is the smallest town in Britain, by all accounts - and Alan and Mary Ann Gilchrist's restaurant is set beside the bridge in the centre of town. The stone-built building isn't difficult to spot with its light blue paintwork and you can expect a warm welcome on arrival. The restaurant is attractively decorated in soothing tones of cream, beige and brown, and looks contemporary without resorting to overt style statements; comfort is provided by high-backed leather chairs and linen napery, and the diligent and attentive service of Alan Gilchrist. Wife Mary Ann looks after the cooking, her confident, one-woman act undertaken with panache, underlining her obvious passion and talent. Her à la carte menu (there's also fixed-price Menu Surprise) makes a virtue of simplicity, the wonderful straightforward approach driven by stunningly fresh, local seasonal produce. Tagliolini with a spicy tomato and olive sauce is a simple and enjoyable first course, perhaps followed by Carmarthenshire beef fillet with potato rösti, garlic spinach and a red wine jus. There's a bar-bistro in the basement.

Chef Mary Ann Gilchrist **Owner** Dr & Mrs Gilchrist **Times** 7-9 Closed L all week, D Sun (ex BH) **Prices** Fixed D 3 course £22.50-£25, Starter £5-£9.50, Main £13.95-£25, Dessert £6-£9.50, Service optional **Wines** 60 bottles over £20, 15 bottles under £20, 4 by glass **Notes** Chef's menu £40, Vegetarian available **Seats** 20 **Children** Portions, Menu **Parking** Car park opposite

WELSHPOOL · Map 15 SJ20

Royal Oak Hotel

◉ Welsh

Sympathetically refurbished former coaching inn with enjoyable, imaginative food

☎ 01938 552217 ◻ 01938 556652
The Cross SY21 7DG
e-mail: relax@royaloakhotel.info

The traditional, sympathetically renovated market town hotel dates back over 350 years and was once a popular coaching inn. Today's travellers exploring the Welsh border country will find a warm welcome and a contemporary, minimalist décor that blends well with the hotel's historic features – exposed beams, polished wood floors and crackling log fires. Expect friendly and attentive service in the red and green dining rooms and imaginative seasonal menus that make good use of fresh local produce. Dishes are accurately cooked, achieving a clarity of flavour, such as chicken liver parfait with red onion jam, seared sea bass with shellfish bisque, and bread-and-butter pudding.

Times 6.30-9.30

RHONDDA CYNON TAFF

MISKIN · Map 9 ST08

Miskin Manor Country Hotel

◉◉ Modern British V ✍

Innovative cuisine in romantic setting

☎ 01443 224204 ◻ 01443 237606
Pendoylan Rd CF72 8ND
e-mail: info@miskin-manor.co.uk
dir: M4 junct 34, exit onto A4119, signed Llantrisant, hotel 300yds on left

Parts of this traditional manor house date back to the 15th century, and it combines many features - minstrels' gallery and an oak-panelled restaurant with grand fireplace and decorative ceiling - with up-to-the-minute modern facilities such as a handy helicopter landing pad. Its setting in 22 acres of gardens, with a stream running through the grounds and beautiful woodland walks, makes the hotel an idyllic rural retreat. The kitchen prides itself on using farm-fresh seasonal ingredients to produce traditional British cuisine while still keeping up with modern trends. Expect accomplished cooking of ravioli of cod cheek, carrot purée, chiffonade of crispy pig's ear and white truffle oil preceding a trio of lamb main course with pan-fried loin, pea purée, sautéed kidney and mini faggot, drizzled with caper jus.

Chef Mark Beck, Ian Presgrave **Owner** Mr & Mrs Rosenberg **Times** 12-2.30/7-10 **Prices** Fixed L 2 course £15.95, Fixed D 3 course £19.95, Starter £5.95-£8.10, Main £16.20-£22.50, Dessert £5.95-£6.20 **Wines** 13 bottles over £20, 33 bottles under £20, 12 by glass **Notes** Sunday L, Vegetarian menu, Dress restrictions, Smart casual, Civ Wed 120 **Seats** 50, Pr/dining room 30 **Children** Portions, Menu **Parking** 200

PONTYCLUN · Map 9 ST08

Brookes Restaurant & Private Dining Room

◉ Modern International

Vibrant modern eatery with a global cocktail of cuisine

☎ 01443 239600 ◻ 01443 239654
79-81 Talbot Rd, Talbot Green CF72 8AE
e-mail: staffbrookes@btconnect.com
dir: M4 junct 34, follow signs for Llantrisant, turn left at 2nd lights

A bold blue canopied façade announces Brookes, a buzzy eatery with a bright contemporary look. Inside, it's a chic spot - all mirrored and whitewashed walls hung with vibrant modern art, and bare wooden tables. The kitchen goes for a modern international style, cooked and presented simply; the wide-ranging menu changes with the seasons, and delves freely into the cuisines of the Mediterranean and Asia. Daily-changing tapas-style specials offer casual grazing and sharing options. Griddled belly pork brushed with rock salt, chilli and rosemary served on a Greek-style feta salad with sweet-and-sour hoi sin dressing shows the style.

Times 12-2.30/7-10.30 Closed 24 Dec, 1 Jan & BHs, Mon, L Sat, D Sun

PONTYPRIDD · Map 9 ST08

Llechwen Hall Hotel

◉ Modern Welsh

Country retreat with imaginative food in relaxed surroundings

☎ 01443 742050 & 743020 ◻ 01443 742189
Llanfabon CF37 4HP

Overlooking four valleys from its hilltop perch, this 17th-century Welsh longhouse is now run as an impressive country-house hotel. The approach is stunning and the 6 acres of gardens are beautiful. Victorian-styled with deep-red furniture and traditional appointments, its dining-room's well-spaced tables come dressed in their best whites, while service is typically relaxed and efficient. The kitchen's modern approach takes its cue from fresh, local ingredients, so expect clean, simple, not overworked dishes that allow the main ingredient centre stage. Think warm stilton tart with a compôte of sweet-and-sour shallots, lamb shank with Puy lentils and thyme jus, and apricot and almond tart with home-made ice cream.

Times 12-2/7-9

SWANSEA

BISHOPSTON · Map 8 SS58

Winston Hotel

◉ Modern, Traditional NEW ✍

Gower hotel and restaurant with good, honest cooking

☎ 01792 232074
11 Church Ln SA3 3JT
dir: A4067 from Swansea onto B4436 signed Bishopston. In 2.7m turn left to Bishopston & immediately right into Church Lane

Situated in the lower valley of the Gower Peninsular, Churchill's restaurant is located in a family-run hotel that boasts a swimming pool and spa. Service is relaxed and friendly, adding to the unpretentious atmosphere, the tone set by the use of lots of natural dark wood. Winston Churchill's Anglo-American heritage and travels are the somewhat tenuous inspiration for the menu, so crab cakes with home-made tartare sauce precedes accurately cooked sea bass with herb crust and creamy white wine sauce, with chocolate fondant tart set in sweet pastry for dessert. Presentation is straightforward and good Welsh produce is to the fore.

Chef Katrina Stewart **Owner** Keith Eaton **Times** 12-2/7-9 **Prices** Fixed L 2 course £9.95-£14.95, Fixed D 3 course £14.95-£26.95, Starter £3-£5.75, Main £9.95-£19.95, Dessert £4.50-£5.50, Service optional **Wines** 1 bottle over £20, 14 bottles under £20, 4 by glass **Notes** Sunday L, Vegetarian available, Civ Wed 100 **Seats** 50, Pr/dining room 120 **Children** Portions, Menu **Parking** 38

LLANRHIDIAN · Map 8 SS49

The Welcome to Town

◉◉ British, French

Country inn serving excellent local produce

☎ 01792 390015 ◻ 01792 390015
SA3 1EH
dir: 8m from Swansea on B4231. M4 junct 47 towards Gowerton. From Gowerton take B4295

Just inland from the wild salt marshes of the gorgeous North Gower peninsula, this 300-year-old whitewashed coaching inn once served time as the local jail. Happily, the accomplished cooking from the modern kitchen now brings visitors who are eager to stay of their own free will. Sound classical roots and pride in sourcing the pick of

continued

LLANRHIDIAN *continued*

local produce are the foundations of the house repertoire. Expect starters such as chicken and wild mushroom ravioli on braised cabbage and sauce Albufera, followed by fresh, moist fillets of line-caught sea bass with sweet parsnip purée, wilted spinach and vanilla saffron. The final note might be a perfectly-cooked fondant that yields to the spoon, releasing hot chocolate to mingle with caramel ice cream and pistachio croquant.

Times 12-2/7-9.30 Closed 25-26 Dec, 1 Jan, last 2 wks Feb, 1 wk Oct, Mon, D Sun

REYNOLDSTON
Map 8 SS48

Fairyhill

◎◎ Modern British **V** ⭐

Elegant country-house hotel with real local flavour

☎ 01792 390139 📄 01792 391358
SA3 1BS
e-mail: postbox@fairyhill.net
dir: M4 junct 47, take A483 then A484 to Llanelli, Gower, Gowerton. At Gowerton follow B4295 for approx 10m

From the terrace, when the famously temperate climate of the Gower Peninsula allows, the house and gardens can be fully appreciated; this delightful 18th-century house sits hidden away in 24 acres of grounds with mature woodland, a trout stream and a beautiful lake. Inside is comfortably done out in a traditional manner, with smartly dressed, well-spaced tables in the two adjoining dining rooms. Local produce, with particular attention paid to food miles, is the driving force in the kitchen. Herbs and vegetables come from the garden, the Gower provides fish, cockles and laverbread, and Carmarthenshire supplies Black beef and salt marsh lamb. Smoked haddock and Caerphilly soufflé is a well-made beginning to a meal, followed by cannon of local lamb stuffed with confit tomatoes and mint and finished with a cawl jus. An excellent wine list and efficient service completes the picture.

Chef Paul Davies, James Hamilton **Owner** Mr Hetherington, Mr Davies **Times** 12-2/7-9 Closed 26 Dec, 1-25 Jan **Prices** Fixed L 2 course £15.95, Fixed D 3 course £45, Starter £5.75-£12.50, Main £9.95-£24.50, Dessert £5.50-£6.25, Service optional **Wines** 400 bottles over £20, 50 bottles under £20, 10 by glass **Notes** Sunday L, Vegetarian menu, Civ Wed 32 **Seats** 60, Pr/dining room 32 **Children** Portions **Parking** 45

SWANSEA
Map 9 SS69

The Dragon Hotel

◎ Modern European

Modern European-style cuisine in the heart of Swansea

☎ 01792 657100 & 0870 4299 848 📄 01792 456044
The Kingsway Circle SA1 5LS
e-mail: enquiries@dragon-hotel.co.uk
dir: M4 junct 42. At lights (after supermarket) turn right. Left into Kings Ln. Hotel straight ahead

The contemporary Dragon Hotel is within walking distance of the main city-centre attractions and offers all the spa services you might require following a day or night on the town. The Piano Bar and Restaurant, up on the first floor with great views over the city, is the place to go on Sunday lunchtimes for the traditional carvery (breakfast is also served here), otherwise head for the Dragon Brasserie, with its floor-to-ceiling windows and modern menu which draws inspiration from across Europe and sometimes a little further afield. Start with pork croquette with creamed Savoy cabbage and pine nuts, followed by grilled spatchcocked poussin served with an aromatic couscous salad.

Chef Sam Thomas **Owner** Dragon Hotel Ltd **Times** 12-2.30/6-9.30 **Prices** Fixed L 2 course £9.95-£15.95, Fixed D 3 course fr £19.95, Starter £4.95-£7.95, Main £9.95-£19.95, Dessert £5.50-£6.95, Service optional **Wines** 5 bottles over £20, 24 bottles under £20, 10 by glass **Notes** Sunday L, Vegetarian available, Civ Wed 220, Air con **Seats** 65, Pr/dining room 80 **Children** Menu **Parking** 50

Hanson at the Chelsea Restaurant

◎ Modern Welsh, French

Quality cooking in relaxed surroundings

☎ 01792 464068 & 07971 163 148
17 St Mary St SA1 3LH
e-mail: andrew_hanson@live.co.uk
dir: In small lane between St Mary Church & Wine St

Tucked away down a peaceful side street in Swansea's city centre, this handsome modern restaurant brings a touch of the Mediterranean to South Wales with its sunny-hued wood-panelled walls. It is an easy-going, cheery place that has built its reputation on using the pick of local ingredients, and a particular passion for fish and seafood that is obvious from the blackboard touting daily specials. The modern Welsh menu shows a kitchen

that is at home with French-influenced classics. A starter of home-made fishcakes incorporates prawns and cockles into the mix, served simply with tartare sauce and tomato relish, while a slow-cooked steak and kidney pie in rich Burgundy sauce stays firmly in the comfort zone. To finish, a trio of crème brûlées brings flavours of vanilla, passion fruit and orange Grand Marnier.

Chef Andrew Hanson **Owner** Andrew & Michelle Hanson **Times** 12-2/7-10 Closed 25-26 Dec, BHs, Sun **Prices** Fixed L 2 course £11.95-£16.50, Fixed D 3 course £28-£35, Starter £4.50-£7.50, Main £9.95-£21.95, Dessert £4.50-£5.50 **Wines** 20 bottles over £20, 20 bottles under £20, 8 by glass **Notes** Vegetarian available, Dress restrictions, Smart casual **Seats** 50, Pr/dining room 20 **Children** Portions, Menu

VALE OF GLAMORGAN

BARRY
Map 9 ST16

Egerton Grey Country House Hotel

◎ Modern, Traditional British

Modern British cooking in a former rectory

☎ 01446 711666 📄 01446 711690
Porthkerry, Rhoose CF62 3BZ
e-mail: info@egertongrey.co.uk
dir: M4 junct 33 follow airport signs, left at rdbt for Porthkerry, 500yds left down lane between thatched cottages

In a wooded valley not far from Cardiff airport lurks this handsome greystone hotel that was a rectory in Victorian times. Its cosy restaurant is half-panelled in oak, with a homely-looking, green-tiled fireplace. Efficient and friendly staff serve forth the modern British food, which might take in a roulade of poached and smoked salmon with cucumber vinaigrette, roasted rump of Brecon lamb with dauphinoise in a well-judged reduction of red wine and smoked garlic, and a fruitily garnished pistachio and praline parfait with shortbread biscuits and whipped cream. The reasonably priced wine list starts at £15.

Chef Andrew Lawrance **Owner** Mr R Morgan-Price & Huw Thomas **Times** 12-2.30/6-9 **Prices** Fixed L 2 course £12-£27, Fixed D 3 course £33-£36, Service optional **Wines** 40 bottles over £20, 25 bottles under £20, 10 by glass **Notes** Sunday L, Vegetarian available, Dress restrictions, Smart casual, Civ Wed 40 **Seats** 40, Pr/dining room 16 **Children** Portions **Parking** 60

HENSOL — Map 9 ST07

Vale Grill

◉ Modern British NEW ☺

Multi-purpose hotel in the valleys with good brasserie menu

☎ 01443 667800 🗎 01443 667801
Vale Hotel, Golf & Spa Resort, Hensol Park CF72 8JY
e-mail: sales@vale-hotel.com
dir: M4 junct 34, exit signed Pendoylan, turn 1st right twice, then 1st left before white house on bend. Hotel on right

The hotel has it all. With golf, spa treatments, facilities for conferences and registration for weddings, it's hard to see what else you might want to do here. Other than eat, of course, which is where the Vale Grill comes in. Modern brasserie design with dark wood tables, good glassware, an open-plan kitchen and a glass-fronted wine cellar make for an elegant atmosphere, and the full-length windows look out on to a patio for outdoor dining. Simply written menus announce the modern European fare, which achieves some notable successes. Gently browned scallops come with shaved fennel and a sardine-based dressing, while main course might be rump of lamb with boulangère potatoes, colourfully accompanied by spinach and a swede and carrot purée.

Chef James Bumpass **Owner** Leekes Family **Times** 7-11 Closed L all week **Prices** Fixed D 3 course £24.95, Starter £5-£8, Main £14-£16, Dessert £6-£7 **Wines** 60 bottles over £20, 27 bottles under £20, 10 by glass **Notes** Sunday L, Vegetarian available, Dress restrictions, Smart casual, Civ Wed 700, Air con **Seats** 80, Pr/dining room 350 **Children** Menu **Parking** 500

LLANTWIT MAJOR — Map 9 SS96

Illtud's 216

◉ Modern Welsh

Historic, atmospheric restaurant utilising fresh, locally-sourced produce

☎ 01446 793800
Church St CF61 1SB
e-mail: info@illtuds216.co.uk
web: www.illtuds216.co.uk
dir: Please telephone for directions

Chef-proprietor Georg Fuchs set up shop with wife Einar in this 16th-century malt house after making a name for himself at St David's Hotel in Cardiff. Illtud was a medieval monk who once brewed beer on the property, as medieval monks were wont to do - there's a picture of him looking down from the stonewashed walls in a rustic, medieval banquet-style setting with ceiling canopies and rugs scattered on stone floors. Georg's cooking is modern Welsh, but there are hints of his Austrian origins too; dishes follow the seasons and pull in excellent materials from the coasts and valleys. Cockle and smoked haddock chowder with dry sherry, streaky bacon lardons and rosemary croûtons might precede Brecon Beacon venison in juniper berry sauce on home-made noodles tossed with onion, smoked bacon and Cadog mature cheddar. Pedigree Austrian apple strudel with vanilla ice cream is a must for pudding.

Chef Georg Fuchs **Owner** Georg & Einar Fuchs **Times** 12-2.30/6-9.30 Closed Mon, D Sun **Prices** Fixed L 2 course £8.25-£16, Starter £4-£8, Main £8-£16, Dessert £4-£7.50, Service optional **Wines** 11 bottles over £20, 15 bottles under £20, 7 by glass **Notes** Sunday L, Vegetarian available **Seats** 65, Pr/dining room 12 **Children** Portions, Menu **Parking** Town Hall car park

WREXHAM

LLANARMON DYFFRYN CEIRIOG — Map 15 SJ13

The Hand at Llanarmon

◉ Welsh ☺

Good local produce in a hidden village inn

☎ 01691 600666 🗎 01691 600262
Ceiriog Valley LL20 7LD
e-mail: reception@thehandhotel.co.uk
dir: Leave A5 at Chirk onto B4500 signed Ceiriog Valley, continue for 11m

Llanarmon Dyffryn Ceiriog, shortened to Llanarmon DC, is a sleepy Welsh Marches village beneath the Berwyn mountains. The 16th-century Hand oozes all the charm and character you'd expect of a country pub where local farmers rub shoulders with visitors among the gnarled beams and gleaming brasses in the rustic bar. The food aims to please with its daily-changing menus of honest, down-to-earth dishes; the kitchen buys carefully from the mind-boggling abundance of local produce, and has the confidence not to mess about with it. Take home-made chicken liver pâté with dark fruit chutney and hot toast to start, then a slow-braised shoulder of Ceiriog Valley lamb with redcurrant and red wine sauce and roasted plums.

Chef Grant Mulholland **Owner** Gaynor & Martin De Luchi **Times** 12-2.20/6.30-8.45 **Prices** Fixed L 2 course fr £15, Starter £5-£7, Main £10-£20, Dessert £3.50-£5.50, Service optional **Wines** 5 bottles over £20, 19 bottles under £20, 4 by glass **Notes** Sunday L, Vegetarian available, Civ Wed 50 **Seats** 40 **Children** Portions **Parking** 15

LLANARMON DYFFRYN CEIRIOG *continued*

West Arms Hotel

◉◉ British, French ✆

Great local food in historic drovers' inn

☎ 01691 600665 & 600612 📠 01691 600622
LL20 7LD
e-mail: gowestarms@aol.com
dir: Exit A483 (A5) at Chirk (mid-way between Oswestry &
Llangollen). Follow signs for Ceiriog Valley (B4500), 11m

Centuries ago, this charming 16th-century inn in the
stunning Ceiriog Valley would have been the watering
hole of choice for hungry and tired cattle drivers coming
down from the Welsh hills en route to Oswestry, Chirk and
Wrexham markets. The pub still retains its character with
original exposed beams, flagged floors, inglenooks and
elaborate fireplaces. The traditional bar with its alluring
menu is popular with locals, and you might find a
shooting party tucking into the traditional food. The menu
is classically-inspired with a bit of a modern edge and
there is a passionate use of local and Welsh produce.
Breast of local pigeon wrapped in bacon roasted on a bed
of thyme is served with watercress and poached pear
salad and finished with a walnut vinaigrette. A main
course of fillet of Welsh lamb is pan-fried and arrives
with mint and rosemary crust and a tarragon sauce.

Chef Grant Williams **Owner** Mr & Mrs Finch & Mr G
Williams **Times** 12-2/7-9 Closed L Mon-Sat **Prices** Fixed
D 3 course £32.90, Service added but optional 10%
Wines 16 bottles over £20, 21 bottles under £20, 9 by
glass **Notes** Sunday L, Vegetarian available, Civ Wed 70
Seats 34, Pr/dining room 10 **Children** Portions, Menu
Parking 20

WREXHAM   Map 15 SJ35

The Lanes Bar Restaurant

◉ British

Friendly hotel brasserie in beautiful grounds

☎ 01978 780555 📠 01978 780568
**Best Western Cross Lanes Hotel, Cross Lanes,
Bangor Rd, Marchwiel LL13 0TF**
e-mail: guestservices@crosslanes.co.uk
web: www.crosslanes.co.uk
dir: On A525 (Wrexham to Whitchurch road), between
Marchwiel & Bangor-on-Dee

Built as a country house in 1890, this popular hotel
stands in 6 acres of beautiful grounds in a rural setting 3
miles south east of Wrexham. The Lanes is a relaxed and
friendly brasserie-style restaurant, with slate and oak
floors, rustic tables, log fires in winter and patio dining in
summer. The extensive modern British menu draws
inspiration from around the globe, the food simply cooked
using fresh local ingredients. Start with red onion and
tomato tart with cucumber and lime salsa, then perhaps
Welsh sirloin steak with peppercorn sauce, and apple and
sultana crumble for dessert.

Chef Mr Vinnie Williams **Owner** Michael Kagan
Times 12-3/6.30-9.30 Closed D 25-26 Dec **Prices** Food
prices not confirmed for 2010. Please telephone for
details. **Wines** 34 bottles over £20, 29 bottles under £20,
20 by glass **Notes** Sunday L, Vegetarian available, Dress
restrictions, Smart casual, Civ Wed 140 **Seats** 50, Pr/
dining room 60 **Children** Portions, Menu **Parking** 70

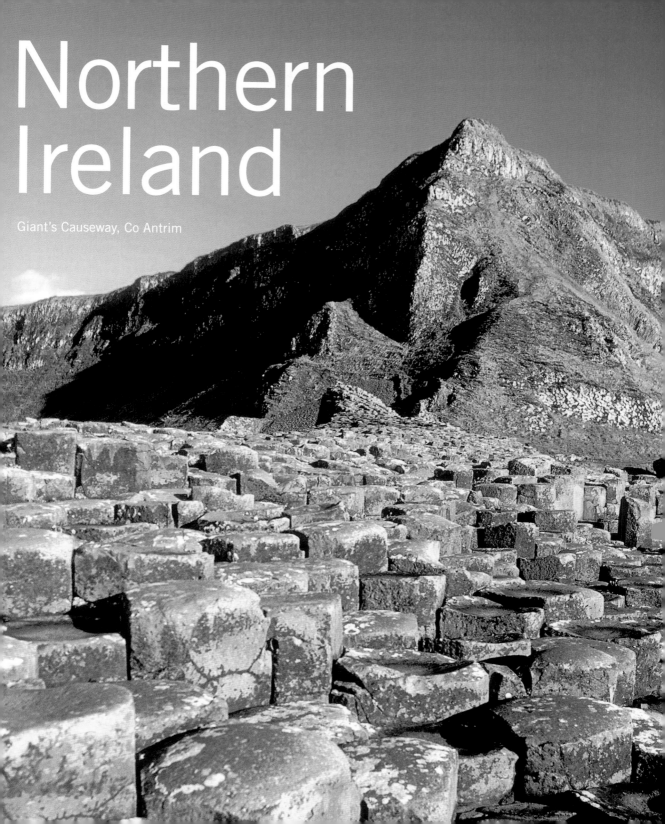

Northern Ireland

Giant's Causeway, Co Antrim

CO ANTRIM

BALLYMENA — Map 1 D5

Galgorm Manor

◉◉ International NEW

Fine dining with river views at luxury resort

☎ 028 2588 1001 ▤ 028 2588 0080
BT42 1EA
e-mail: info@galgorm.com

This country manor house-turned resort hotel is set in 163 acres of parkland and forest beside the beautiful River Maine. Horse riding and fishing are available on the estate, but if that sounds like too much hard work, there's an award-winning spa to relax in. The hotel's main restaurant is the fine-dining River Room, which looks out over the river through floor-to-ceiling windows. It's an attractive space, with striking floral displays, booth seating and well-dressed tables with crisp linen and fine glassware. The innovative modern European menu draws on top-quality local produce and is supported by a serious wine list. Dinner might begin with accurately cooked pan-seared scallops with veal sweetbreads and pickled sultanas, followed by excellent roasted fillet of John Dory with blood orange beurre blanc and ratte potatoes. A light and moist warm gingerbread pudding with cardamom sorbet and syrup rounds things off nicely.

Times 12-2.30/79.30 Closed Mon-Tue, L Wed-Sat

CARNLOUGH — Map 1 D6

Frances Anne Restaurant

◉ Modern, Traditional

Unfussy modern Irish dishes in historic coastal hotel

☎ 028 2888 5255 ▤ 028 2888 5263
Londonderry Arms Hotel, 20 Harbour Rd BT44 0EU
e-mail: ida@glensofantrim.com
dir: 14m N of Larne on Causeway coastal route

The Londonderry Arms Hotel was built in the pretty fishing village of Carnlough on the glorious Antrim coast in 1848 as a coaching inn for Lady Londonderry. Her great grandson, Sir Winston Churchill, also owned the property at one time, and there's a solid feel of the past in its carved oak fireplaces, antiques and driftwood sculptures. The kitchen takes a modern route with its unfussy contemporary cooking founded on pedigree produce from the local larder. Meals in the Frances Anne Restaurant might start with oak-smoked Atlantic salmon with beetroot and chive dressing, moving on to oven-roasted supreme of County Down chicken with champ and wild mushroom cream.

Times 12.30-2.45/7-8.15 Closed 24-25 Dec, L Mon-Sat

BELFAST

BELFAST — Map 1 D5

Aldens

◉ Modern

Hearty food in slick modern restaurant

☎ 028 9065 0079 ▤ 028 9065 0032
229 Upper Newtownards Rd BT4 3JF
e-mail: info@aldensrestaurant.com
dir: At x-rds with Sandown Rd

A short walk from the city centre, this stylish and recently refurbished contemporary restaurant offers a varied modern menu including traditional favourites alongside seasonal and more complex offerings. Hearty dishes include starters of rabbit and herb risotto or roast duck with saffron pear and Parma ham, followed by pot-roast shoulder of lamb with best end and butternut squash purée or braised venison shank with baby vegetables and onion compôte. Finish with chocolate and banana loaf with chocolate sauce or raspberry and orange syllabub trifle. Friendly staff and attentive service ensure a loyal local following.

Times 12-2.30/6-10 Closed 1 wk Jul, BHs, Sun, L Sat

Beatrice Kennedy

◉ Modern International

Imaginative food in listed Victorian building

☎ 028 9020 2290 ▤ 028 9020 2291
44 University Rd BT7 1NJ
e-mail: reservations@beatricekennedy.co.uk
web: www.beatricekennedy.co.uk
dir: Adjacent to Queens University

In a handsome townhouse building a short walk from Queens University, Beatrice Kennedy (named for an erstwhile owner) is a romantic venue with a touch of the French bistro about it. A bold colour scheme works well with wooden floors, chocolate brown leather chairs, lazy colonial ceiling fans and a big-band jazz soundtrack to take you on a nostalgia trip back to the 1940s. Smartly-dressed, clued-up young staff serve an excellent value menu of creative modern European cuisine: venison carpaccio with rocket and beetroot oil, and fillets of sea bass with fennel and potato rösti show the style.

Times 12.30-3/5-10.30 Closed 24-26 Dec, 1 Jan, Etr, Mon, L Mon-Sat

Cayenne

◉ Modern International Ⅴ ☺

Globally-influenced food in relaxed, hip and friendly surroundings

☎ 028 9033 1532 ▤ 028 9026 1575
7 Ascot House, Shaftesbury Square BT2 7DB
e-mail: belinda@rankingroup.co.uk
dir: Top of Great Victoria St

Cayenne is the flagship of TV chef Paul Rankin, a funky, voguish place with a vivid colour scheme and intriguing, interactive artworks by local-born artist Peter Anderson that make you sit up and pay attention. The food is pretty eye-catching stuff, too, influenced by the chef's globe-trotting past, so expect a fusion of Pacific, Indian and Mediterranean touches applied to well-sourced Irish ingredients. Typical offerings include salt and chilli squid with chilli jam and aïoli, followed by roast breast of duck au poivre with mushroom risotto cakes, mushrooms and spring greens, or blackened monkfish with roast aubergine, Indian rösti and spicy lemon dressing.

Chef Paul Rankin **Owner** Paul & Jeanne Rankin **Times** 12-2.15/6-late Closed 25-26 Dec, Etr Mon, May Day BH, 12-13 Jul, L Sun-Wed **Prices** Fixed L 2 course £12-£20, Fixed D 3 course £20-£25, Starter £4.50-£10.50, Main £10.50-£22.50, Dessert £5.95, Service optional, Groups min 6 service 10% **Wines** 60 bottles over £20, 20 bottles under £20, 15 by glass **Notes** Vegetarian menu, Air con **Seats** 150, Pr/dining room 16 **Children** Portions **Parking** On street, NCP

Deanes Restaurant

◉◉◉◉ – *see opposite page*

Green Door Restaurant

◉ Modern European

Fine dining in a stylish city-centre hotel

☎ 028 9038 8000 ▤ 028 9038 8088
Malone Lodge Hotel, 60 Eglantine Av, Malone Rd BT9 6DY
e-mail: info@malonelodgehotel.com
dir: At hospital rdbt exit towards Bouchar Rd. At 1st rdbt, right at lights onto Lisburn Rd, 1st left into Eglantine Ave

Situated in a leafy suburb of South Belfast, within the refurbished Malone Lodge Hotel, which occupies an attractive row of Victorian townhouses, the Green Door Restaurant is an intimate and atmospheric dining venue that reflects the boutique style of the hotel. Expect aubergine coloured walls, high-backed chairs, crisp linen, subdued lighted, and an innovative seasonal menu that champions quality local suppliers. Typical dishes may include stilton brûlée with oatcakes and caramelised onions, rack of lamb with confit sweet potato, and monkfish wrapped in proscuitto with saffron potatoes and tomato and chilli jam.

continued on page 574

Deanes Restaurant

Modern French, Irish NOTABLE WINE LIST

Exemplary modern cooking from star of the Northern Ireland restaurant scene

☎ 028 9033 1134 📄 028 9056 0001
36/40 Howard St BT1 6PF
e-mail: info@michaeldeane.co.uk
dir: At rear of City Hall. Howard St on left opposite Spires building

Michael Deane's fertile culinary imagination keeps him up there in the top flight of Ireland's chefs. The refurbished flagship of Deane's Belfast empire occupies a prime city centre spot, and there's no missing it: his name stands two metres high on steely blue columns fronting the ground floor of the Howard Street building. Conveniently round the corner is the Deane's Vin Café, a bistro and deli in Bedford Street, and the Deanes at Queens bar and grill is a 10-minute walk away opposite the university. Perfect, then, for a hands-on approach to overseeing all three operations. The open-plan interior of Deanes goes for a cool metropolitan look in gunmetal greys and charcoal, with wooden floors, tasteful modern art, black leather and dark wood seating and crisp linen to complete the picture. The modish open kitchen keeps diners entertained as the brigade goes about its business: calm and discipline reign, while smartly-attired staff deliver well-informed, relaxed service. The cooking lets high quality ingredients speak for themselves, with serious levels of skill that draw out amazing flavours in innovative, thoughtful combinations. The menu reads well and steers clear of fads to deliver consistent quality. Rare roast Irish veal is the star in a salad of wild mushrooms, butternut squash and truffle pecorino, with all flavours standing clearly to attention. Next up, free-range chicken breast is served in ballotine form with macaroni gratin, deeply-flavoured cep cream, braised cos lettuce and herby roasting juices. Desserts end on a high note - take, for example, the flavours and textures of mango mousse and jelly with pink peppercorn meringue and lime ice cream. Deanes has carved a niche for itself as one of the city's places to be seen, so advance booking is a sound idea.

Chef Michael Deane, Derek Creagh **Owner** Michael Deane, Derek Creagh **Times** 12-2.30/6-9.30 Closed 25 Dec, BHs, 12-13 Jul, Sun-Mon **Prices** Fixed L 2 course £17.50-£28, Fixed D 3 course £31.50-£50, Tasting menu £60, Starter £8-£9.50, Main £15.50-£25, Dessert £8-£9, Service added but optional 10% **Wines** 99 bottles over £20, 8 bottles under £20, 9 by glass **Notes** Vegetarian available, Air con **Seats** 70, Pr/dining room 40 **Children** Portions, Menu **Parking** On street (after 6pm), car park Clarence St

BELFAST *continued*

Chef Dean Butler **Owner** Brian & Mary Macklin **Times** 12-3/6.30-10 Closed D Sun **Prices** Starter £4-£8, Main £9.50-£23, Dessert £4-£8, Service optional **Wines** 7 bottles over £20, 28 bottles under £20, 4 by glass **Notes** Sunday L, Vegetarian available, Civ Wed 130, Air con **Seats** 60, Pr/dining room 130 **Children** Portions, Menu **Parking** 35

James Street South Restaurant & Bar

◎◎ European ♥

Intimate city-centre restaurant offering imaginative cooking

☎ 028 9043 4310 🖹 028 9043 4310
21 James St BT2 7GA
e-mail: info@jamesstreetsouth.co.uk
dir: Located between Brunswick St & Bedford St

This popular restaurant in Belfast city centre is handy for the shops and the business district. The design and décor are modern, sophisticated and minimalist, with white walls adorned with colourful artwork, and a small contemporary bar at the entrance. The classical French cooking draws on European influences to create clean and fresh dishes, cooked with flair, which make full use of high-quality local produce. Good value two- and three-course fixed-price menus are offered for lunch, with a pre-theatre dinner menu available alongside the carte. Typical starters might include carpaccio of venison with pickled tomato and truffled honey, followed by loin of Antrim lamb with white asparagus and garlic and saffron jus. Finish with a dessert of pear tarte Tatin and vanilla bean ice cream.

Chef Niall McKenna **Owner** Niall & Joanne McKenna **Times** 12-2.45/5.45-10.45 Closed 25-26 Dec, 1 Jan, Etr Sun & Mon, 12 Jul, L Sun **Prices** Fixed L 2 course fr £14.50, Fixed D 3 course fr £18.50, Starter £4.50-£9.50, Main £12.50-£19.50, Dessert £4.50-£9.50, Service optional **Wines** 90 bottles over £20, 6 bottles under £20, 8 by glass **Notes** Pre-theatre menu Mon-Fri 2/3 course £16.50-£18.50, Vegetarian available, Air con **Seats** 60 **Parking** On street

Malmaison Belfast

◎ British

Contemporary-style converted seed mill offering satisfying dishes

☎ 028 9022 0200 🖹 028 9022 0220
34-38 Victoria St BT1 3GH
e-mail: mdavies@malmaison.com

Stylish, contemporary and just a little quirky, the Belfast branch of the Malmaison family is housed in a converted seed mill close to the city centre. Step beyond the striking, tastefully embellished and rather ornate exterior to find a hotel that exudes quality with a funky style found in fun furnishings and interesting artefacts. With plain bistro-style tables, the brasserie delivers simple, enjoyable dishes with friendly service, and the 'home-grown and local' menu features excellent local produce. Carefully prepared dishes include game terrine with home-made piccalilli, followed by grilled halibut with smoked salmon beurre blanc, and chocolate truffle cake with pistachio ice cream. Try the funky bar and don't miss the excellent wine list.

Times 12-2.30/6-12.30

The Merchant Hotel

◎ Traditional Irish, French NEW

Rustic cooking in a grand and opulent setting

☎ 028 9023 4888 🖹 028 9024 7775
35-39 Waring St BT1 2DY
e-mail: info@themerchanthotel.com
dir: Please telephone for directions

The Great Room Restaurant in the former headquarters of the Ulster Bank, built in 1860 in Italian style and now a stylish hotel, conveys the architectural grandeur and opulence of this impressive building. A high-domed ceiling, detailed sculptures, Corinthian columns, and a rich red and gold décor provide a stunning backdrop for some rustic, modern British cooking using good quality produce. Simply presented dishes may include smoked haddock tortellini with pea velouté, pan-roasted halibut with lobster-crushed potatoes and cucumber vièrge, and saddle of Lough Erne lamb stuffed with morels and served with minted hollandaise for two. For pudding, try the caramelised lemon tart with clove ice cream.

Times 12-2.30/6-10 Closed L Sat (afternoon tea only) **Prices** Food prices not confirmed for 2010. Please telephone for details.

Shu

◎◎ Modern European V

Irish food with a French accent

☎ 028 9038 1655 🖹 028 9068 1632
253-255 Lisburn Rd BT9 7EN
e-mail: eat@shu-restaurant.com
dir: From city centre take Lisburn Rd (lower end). Restaurant in 1m, on corner of Windsor Ave

The Shu referenced in the name of this fashionable Belfast address is the Egyptian god of the air, a deity responsible for wafting calming cool breezes over us. Looking about at the relaxing open-plan ambience of the place, you'll easily get the point. In the well-appointed environs of the Lisburn Road, it's a magnetic draw for a smart, laid-back crowd, who come in for the French-inspired modern Irish cooking. A risotto of summer vegetables with mascarpone is a well-seasoned, flavourful spirits-raiser to start. Mains run a gamut from roast sea bass with beetroot and horseradish purée to robustly flavoured crisp pork belly with potato gratin, puréed cauliflower and cider-soaked raisins. Light, moist steamed lemon pudding with vanilla ice cream is a good finale.

Chef Brian McCann **Owner** Alan Reid **Times** 12-2.30/6-10 Closed 25-26 Dec, Sun **Prices** Fixed L 2 course £12, Fixed D 3 course £27, Starter £4.25-£8.75, Main £11.25-£19.75, Dessert £5.50-£6.50, Service optional, Groups min 6 service 10% **Wines** 44 bottles over £20, 18 bottles under £20, 17 by glass **Notes** Vegetarian menu, Air con **Seats** 100, Pr/dining room 24 **Children** Portions **Parking** On street

CO DOWN

BANGOR Map 1 D5

Clandeboye Lodge Hotel

◉ Modern

Creative cooking in a contemporary country setting

☎ 028 9185 2500 🖷 028 9185 2772
10 Estate Rd, Clandeboye BT19 1UR
e-mail: info@clandeboyelodge.co.uk
dir: M3 follow signs for A2 (Bangor). Before Bangor, turn
right at junct signed Newtownards/Clandeboye Lodge
Hotel & Blackwood Golf Course

A few miles from the seaside resort of Bangor, and easily
reached from Belfast, Clandeboye is a modern country-
house-style hotel with a Swiss chalet feel, set beside the
Clandeboye Estate's 200 acres of woodland and gardens.
Spiralling chandeliers, wood panelling, leather chairs and
wood- and marble-topped tables make for a smart
designer look in the Clanbrasserie Restaurant, ably
supported by a well-drilled and courteous waiting team. A
contemporary menu of straightforward dishes suits the
setting: kick off with carpaccio of Craigantlet Hills beef
with wholegrain mustard dressing. Braised shoulder of
lamb with roasted root vegetables might follow.

Chef Ian Lyttle **Owner** Pim Dalm **Times** 12-9.30
Closed 25-26 Dec **Prices** Starter £3.75-£7.25, Main
£9.25-£19.50, Dessert £4.95-£7.20, Service optional
Wines 7 bottles over £20, 24 bottles under £20, 6 by
glass **Notes** Sunday L, Vegetarian available, Dress
restrictions, Smart casual, Civ Wed 250 **Seats** 60, Pr/
dining room 300 **Children** Portions, Menu **Parking** 250

1614

◉◉ Modern, Traditional British

Atmospheric inn serving seasonal food

☎ 028 9185 3255 🖷 028 9185 2775
The Old Inn, 15 Main St, Crawfordsburn BT19 1JH
e-mail: info@theoldinn.com
web: www.theoldinn.com
dir: Take A2 E from Belfast. In 5-6m turn left at
Ballyrobert lights, 400yds to Crawfordsburn. Inn on left

Owned and run by the Rice family for over 23 years, this
17th-century inn retains its historic character with oak
panelling, chandeliers and local coats of arms. The
elegant 1614 restaurant is the fine-dining option here
and frequently changing and keenly priced menus rely on
seasonal ingredients, notably seafood from County Down

ports and local beef, lamb, game and vegetables. Typical
dishes include tian of fresh crab served with guacamole,
rocket, red chard, coriander, peppers and pickled girolles,
and tenderloin of pork fillet with spiced apple, honey,
spring cabbage, thyme and green peppercorns. Food is
also served in The Churn Bistro and the Parlour Bar.
Committed staff provide friendly and helpful service.

Chef Alex Taylor **Owner** Danny Rice
Times 12.30-2.30/7-9.30 Closed 25 Dec, L Mon-Sat, D
Sun **Prices** Fixed L 3 course £30-£35, Fixed D 4 course
£30-£35, Service optional **Wines** 22 bottles under £20, 23
by glass **Notes** Sunday L, Vegetarian available, Dress
restrictions, Smart casual, Civ Wed 85 **Seats** 64, Pr/
dining room 25 **Children** Portions, Menu **Parking** 100

DUNDRUM Map 1 D5

Mourne Seafood Bar

◉ Seafood

Vibrant fish restaurant 30 minutes from Belfast

☎ 028 4375 1377 🖷 028 4375 1161
10 Main St BT33 0LU
e-mail: bob@mourneseafood.com
dir: On main road from Belfast to The Mournes, on village
main st

The Mourne Mountains create an impressive backdrop to
this picturesque fishing village within easy reach of
Belfast. Housed in a Georgian building, the informal
restaurant is simply presented with wood floors and
rustic wooden tables, and you can expect a cracking
atmosphere and a menu bristling with fresh local
seafood, including oysters and mussels from their own
beds. Uncomplicated seafood dishes are simply presented
without fuss or elaboration, the emphasis being on the
quality main ingredient. Take salt and chilli squid with
garlic mayonnaise, seafood pasta, sea bass with lemon
cream, grilled lobster and, for meat-eaters, rib-eye steak
with pepper sauce.

Chef Wayne Carville **Owner** Bob & Joanne McCoubrey
Times 12-9.30 Closed 25 Dec, Mon-Wed, L Thu
Prices Fixed L 2 course £8.95, Fixed D 3 course fr £23.95,
Starter £4-£7, Main £8.95-£17.95, Dessert fr £4.50,
Service optional, Groups min 6 service 10% **Wines** 18
bottles over £20, 22 bottles under £20, 5 by glass
Notes Fixed D menu Sat only, Sunday L, Vegetarian
available **Seats** 75, Pr/dining room 16 **Children** Portions,
Menu **Parking** On street

CO FERMANAGH

ENNISKILLEN Map 1 C5

The Catalina Lough Erne Golf Resort

◉◉ Modern, Traditional NEW V

**Modern waterside golf and spa resort with
contemporary classic cuisine**

☎ 028 6632 3230 🖷 028 6634 5758
Belleek Rd BT93 7ED
e-mail: info@lougherneogolfresort.com
dir: A46 from Enniskillen towards Donegal, hotel in 3m

Golfing legend Nick Faldo may have put his name to the
championship course, but he probably won't be too put
out if you'd rather get all holistic in the luxurious Thai
Spa than play a round of golf. Pictures on the Catalina
Restaurant's walls commemorate the seaplanes that
were based on the lough during the Second World War; it
is an open, airy place with vaulted ceilings, arched
windows looking over the lake, and a classic décor. The
talented home-grown chef puts a modern spin on classic
dishes founded on top-quality local materials, kicking off
with a simple tian of Kilkeel crab teamed with vanilla
beetroot pickle and avocado purée, followed by the
signature mixed grill of pork belly, chop, fillet and kidney
with poached egg, hollandaise sauce and Pont-Neuf
potatoes.

Chef Noel McMeel **Times** 1-2.30/6.30 Closed L Mon-Sat
Prices Fixed L 2 course fr £24, Fixed D 3 course fr £39.50,
Service added but optional 10% **Wines** 120 bottles over
£20, 8 bottles under £20, 3 by glass **Notes** Sunday L,
Vegetarian menu, Air con **Seats** 75, Pr/dining room 30
Children Portions, Menu

CO LONDONDERRY

LIMAVADY
Map 1 C6

The Lime Tree

◎ Traditional Mediterranean ✪

Reliable neighbourhood restaurant with a welcoming atmosphere

☎ 028 7776 4300
60 Catherine St BT49 9DB
e-mail: info@limetreerest.com
web: www.limetreerest.com
dir: Enter Limavady from Derry side. Restaurant on right on small slip road

The Lime Tree has hit on a winning formula of down-to-earth atmosphere and equally unaffected cooking founded on French and Mediterranean classics that keeps loyal supporters coming back time and again. The menus ring frequent changes and showcase excellent local fish and seafood; themed evenings might put together a Spanish menu offering pan-fried hake with garlic cream sauce and Mallorcan-style slow-roasted rabbit with sherry, onions and almonds. Otherwise, Malin Head crabcakes with balsamic dressing are a perennial success, as is the seafood thermidor - brill, hake, monkfish and cod glazed with cheese and brandy sauce.

Chef Stanley Matthews **Owner** Mr & Mrs S Matthews **Times** 6-9 Closed 25-26 Dec, Sun-Mon, L all week (except by prior arrangement) **Prices** Starter £4.50-£7.95, Main £14.50-£22, Dessert £4.95-£7.50, Service optional **Wines** 11 bottles over £20, 31 bottles under £20, 5 by glass **Notes** Early bird menu Tue-Fri 6-7pm 2-3 course £13.50-£16.50, Vegetarian available **Seats** 30 **Children** Portions, Menu **Parking** 15, On street

Radisson Blu Roe Park Resort

◎ Modern

Good food in golf and leisure resort setting

☎ 028 7772 2222 📠 028 7772 2313
BT49 9LB
e-mail: reservations@radissonroepark.com
dir: On A6 (Londonderry-Limavady road), 0.5m from Limavady. 8m from Derry airport

Self-styled as 'Northern Ireland's premier golf, leisure and conference resort', this impressive, modern hotel and golf course complex occupies a 150-acre estate on the banks of the River Roe. For accomplished modern European cooking choose Greens, a stylish, well-appointed and informal restaurant, where the carte takes in duck liver parfait with Cumberland sauce, venison Wellington, roast rack of lamb with pea and mint hollandaise, and chilled white chocolate cheesecake. A lighter dining experience is available in the Coach House Brasserie, which overlooks the golf course.

Chef Emma Gormley **Owner** Mr Conn, Mr McKeever, Mr Wilton **Times** 12-3/6.30-10 Closed Tue-Thu in Jan, Mon, L Tue-Sat, D Sun (Oct-May) **Prices** Starter £4-£6.25, Main £10.50-£19.50, Dessert £5.95-£6.95, Service optional **Wines** 8 bottles over £20, 23 bottles under £20, 8 by glass **Notes** Sunday L, Vegetarian available, Dress restrictions, Smart casual, Civ Wed 250, Air con **Seats** 160, Pr/dining room 50 **Children** Portions, Menu **Parking** 250

MAGHERA
Map 1 C5

Ardtara Country House

◎◎ Modern International

Modern cuisine in a period country-house setting

☎ 028 7964 4490 📠 028 7964 5080
8 Gorteade Rd BT46 5SA
e-mail: valerie_ferson@ardtara.com
dir: Take A29 to Maghera/Coleraine. Follow B75 (Kilrea) to Upperlands. Past sign for W Clark & Sons, next left

Built in 1896 as the Clark Linen Factory, the building then moonlighted as a family home before being turned into today's traditional country-house hotel. Appearances can be deceptive, however, and the classic décor of the dining room (a unique hunting frieze and large skylight are features) conceals some skilful modern cooking. The concisely scripted, fixed-price dinner menu is rightly driven by prime local produce; take a rack of Sperrins Irish lamb served with a grilled onion sauce, or perhaps grilled Irish salmon accompanied by a coconut sauce and traditional champ, while desserts might be headed up by an Armagh apple Tatin with vanilla ice cream.

Times 12.30-2.30/6.30-9

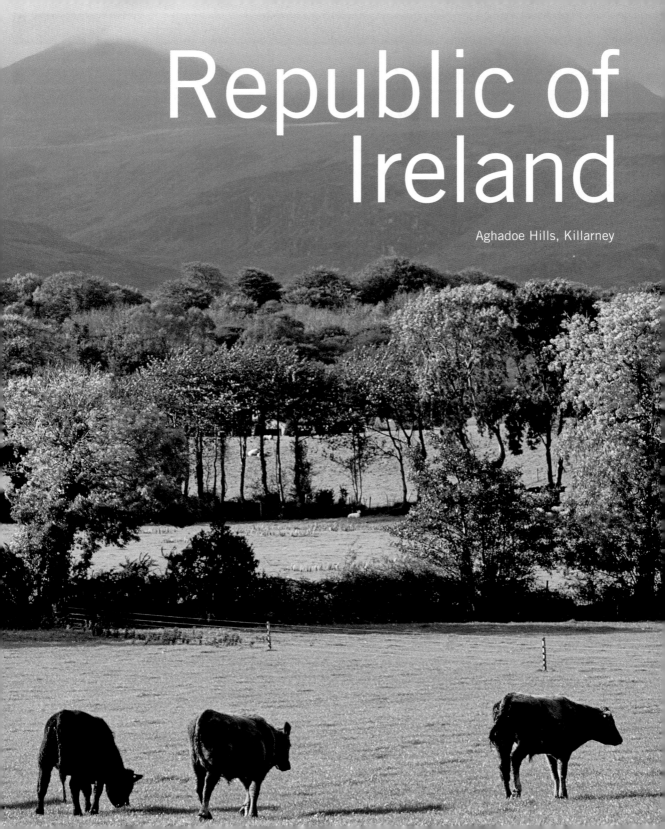

Republic of
Ireland

Aghadoe Hills, Killarney

CO CARLOW

TULLOW
Map 1 C3

Mount Wolseley Hotel, Spa & Country Club

◉ Modern European NEW

Sound modern European cooking at a luxury golf resort

☎ 059 9180100 ▤ 059 9152123
e-mail: sales@mountwolseley.ie
dir: South on N81 to Tullow. Left before bridge onto Mill Street

Frederick York Wolseley - the man behind the famous Wolseley car marque - would probably barely recognise his family's Irish estate today. The luxurious Mount Wolseley resort occupies 200 acres and is a must-visit course for golfers from all over the world. The hotel's light and airy main restaurant, named Frederick's in honour of the estate's former owner, caters well to an international clientele with its modern European menu. Seared scallops on a spring asparagus and roasted squash salad with a yogurt and pistachio dressing gets things off to a good start, while main-course Irish fillet of beef is tender and full of flavour, and comes with a gutsy roasted meatloaf, wild mushrooms, spinach purée and a red wine jus.

Times 6.30-9.30 Closed L all week **Prices** Food prices not confirmed for 2010. Please telephone for details.

CO CAVAN

CAVAN
Map 1 C4

Cavan Crystal Hotel

◉◉ Modern

Innovative cooking in contemporary hotel

☎ 049 4360600 ▤ 049 4360699
Dublin Rd
e-mail: info@cavancrystalhotel.com
dir: Approach Cavan on N3, straight over rdbt, hotel immediately on left

Cavan Crystal is the second oldest crystal manufacturer in Ireland, and the Cavan Crystal Hotel is the company's contemporary new hotel, built on the same site as the factory; there's a new gift shop, too. As you might expect, crystal crops up quite a bit in the hotel, in the form of chandeliers, plus glasses and dishes in the modern Opus One restaurant. The cuisine is innovative in style and presentation, the cooking confident and using quality local and seasonal ingredients with integrity. A ravioli of crab with an apple jelly and foam and a celeriac purée shows accuracy and a good balance of flavours, while saddle of local lamb is meltingly tender, and pineapple tarte Tatin has the lightest of puff pastry and is complemented by a well-made five-spice ice cream.

Times 12.30-3.30/6-10 Closed 24-25 Dec

KINGSCOURT
Map 1 C4

Courtroom Restaurant

◉ Modern Irish NEW

Elegant and intimate dining in a castle setting

☎ 042 9667030 ▤ 042 9667039
Cabra Castle
e-mail: sales@cabracastle.com
dir: 2m outside Kingscourt on Carrickmacross road

An elegant and intimate restaurant on the first floor of imposing Cabra Castle Hotel, a magnificent turreted building set in 100 acres of garden and parkland, with glorious views over the Cavan countryside. Consistent, modern Irish cooking makes sound use of well-sourced seasonal ingredients, which are carefully presented by a dedicated kitchen team. A typical meal may commence with light ricotta cheese and sage tartlet served with a tomato and chive salsa, followed by plump, caramelised scallops with lime butter, and grilled strawberries with ginger and Pimms for pudding.

Times 12.30-2/7-9 Closed L Mon-Sat Closed 24-27 Dec

VIRGINIA
Map 1 C4

The Park Hotel

◉ European, International

Estate-fresh produce served in a former hunting lodge

☎ 049 8546100 ▤ 049 8547203
Virginia Park
e-mail: reservations@parkhotelvirginia.com
dir: exit N3 in Virginia onto R194. Hotel 500yds on left

The Marquis of Headfort got a superb location for his 18th-century hunting lodge. This impressive pile sits in 100 acres of mature gardens and woodland with walking trails and a golf course to ensure a keen appetite. The formal Marquis restaurant is packed with period features and antiques, making a fine setting for fuss-free classic country-house cuisine with global influences. The chefs keep food miles to a minimum with home-grown organic produce from the estate's orchards, greenhouses and kitchen garden. Try duck leg confit with glazed plum sauce to start, followed by braised lamb shank with tomato and rosemary sauce and champ mash.

Chef Colm Kieran **Owner** Baltimore International College **Times** 12.30-3.30/6.30-9.30 Closed Jan, Xmas, Mon, L Tue-Sat, D Sun **Prices** Starter €6.95-€8.95, Main €12.95-€29.95, Dessert €6.95-€8.95, Service optional **Wines** 7 bottles over €20, 19 bottles under €20, 6 by glass **Notes** Pre-theatre D available, Sunday L, Vegetarian available, Dress restrictions, Smart casual, Civ Wed 100 **Seats** 45, Pr/dining room 35 **Children** Portions, Menu **Parking** 160

CO CLARE

BALLYVAUGHAN
Map 1 B3

Gregans Castle

◉◉ Modern Irish ✿

Enchanting surroundings and skilful cooking

☎ 065 7077005 ▤ 065 7077111
e-mail: stay@gregans.ie
dir: On N67, 3.5m S of Ballyvaughan

The pretty 18th-century Georgian house turned hotel enjoys a commanding position overlooking the breathtaking valley of the limestone Burren hills; be lucky and bag yourself a window table. Delightful public rooms are furnished with antiques and welcoming open fires. The dining room is elegantly furnished with crisp linen on the tables and excellent silver and glassware. Cooking is skilful and uses the best local and organic ingredients to create modern French and Irish dishes on the weekly-changing menu. The new Finnish chef has oodles of experience in French and Irish kitchens and delivers a satisfying tortellini of local lobster with sweetbread and shellfish espuma, followed by wild Wicklow venison loin rolled in ash and served with crispy shin, pumpkin, confit turnip, fondant potato and pear.

Chef Mickael Viljanen **Owner** Simon Haden **Times** 6-9 Closed seasonal, L all week **Prices** Fixed L 2 course €21, Fixed D 3 course €39-€50, Tasting menu €80, Service included **Wines** 95 bottles over €20, 14 by glass **Notes** Early bird €35, Sunday L, Vegetarian available, Dress restrictions, No shorts, Civ Wed 45 **Seats** 50, Pr/dining room 36 **Children** Portions, Menu **Parking** 20

ENNIS
Map 1 B3

Temple Gate

◉ Modern International

Modern dining in a Gothic-style building

☎ 065 6823300 ▤ 065 6823322
The Square
e-mail: info@templegatehotel.com
dir: Exit N18 onto Tulla Rd for 0.25m, hotel on left

The Temple Gate hotel delivers a generous slice of Victorian Gothic flavour in a charming townhouse built on the site of the former Convent of Mercy. But while the medieval-styled arches fit in seamlessly with the historic centre of Ennis, this hotel is not stuck in the past: a refurbishment in April 2008 has installed all the gizmos and contemporary style you'd expect in the 21st century. The Legends restaurant is a light conservatory-style space with clean lines and an eclectic menu of European-accented dishes that takes in starters like steamed mussels in lemongrass, ginger and coconut broth, followed by pan-fried monkfish wrapped in Parma ham and parmesan breadcrumbs with tomato and chive beurre blanc.

Chef Paul Shortt **Owner** John Madden **Times** 12.30-3/6-10 Closed 25-26 Dec, L ex by request only Mon-Sat **Prices** Fixed L 2 course €17.95, Starter €6-

€8.50, Main €18-€28.50, Dessert €6.95 **Wines** 19 bottles over €20, 4 bottles under €20, 3 by glass **Notes** Sunday L, Vegetarian available, Civ Wed 200 **Seats** 90 **Children** Portions, Menu

LISDOONVARNA Map 1 B3

Sheedy's Country House Hotel

◉◉ Modern Irish

Country-house cooking with classic and modern influences

☎ 065 7074026 ▤ 065 7074555
e-mail: info@sheedys.com
dir: 20m from Ennis on N87

The oldest property in the village, close to Lahinch golf course, Doolin and the Cliffs of Moher, this small but delightful family-owned and managed country-house hotel has been in the Sheedy family since the 18th century. The restaurant has a relaxing colour scheme and friendly, professional service, while chef-patron John Sheedy cooks with skill and flair and a strong emphasis on classic dishes, though with some modern influences. Well-sourced local ingredients and home-grown vegetables and herbs from the hotel's potager drive dishes; perhaps a rack of Burren lamb, roasted and served with pearl barley, baby onions and smoked bacon, or Irish chicken breast teamed with confit pork belly and wild mushrooms.

Times 6.45-8.30 Closed mid Oct-mid Mar, 1 day a week Mar-Apr

NEWMARKET-ON-FERGUS Map 1 B3

Dromoland Castle

◉◉ Traditional Irish, European **V**

Impressive cooking in historic castle

☎ 061 368144 ▤ 061 363355
e-mail: sales@dromoland.ie
dir: From Ennis take N18, follow signs for Shannon/ Limerick. 7m follow Quin. Newmarket-on-Fergus sign. Hotel 0.5m. From Shannon take N18 towards Ennis

Set on the shore of Lough Dromoland, surrounded by 410 acres of breathtaking scenery, Dromoland is one of Ireland's finest castles. Dating back to the 16th century, the magnificent public rooms are warmed by log fires, while the fine-dining restaurant boasts elegant silk wall hangings, crystal chandeliers and Irish linen. The traditional Irish cuisine has a classical edge and the ambitious kitchen creates some stunning dishes from high quality ingredients. You might start with warm salad of spiced tuna, red onion and sweet chilli dressing, and follow with a main course of pork cutlet with apple, spinach, mushrooms, spiced aubergine compôte and Madeira sauce.

Chef David McCann **Owner** Earl of Thomond **Times** 7-10 Closed 24-27 Dec, L all week **Prices** Fixed L 3 course €25-€40, Fixed D 4 course €65, Starter €12-€23, Main €29-€45, Dessert €9-€13, Service added 15% **Wines** 10

bottles under €20, 10 by glass **Notes** Vegetarian menu, Dress restrictions, Jacket **Seats** 80, Pr/dining room 40 **Children** Portions, Menu **Parking** 140

CO CORK

BALLYCOTTON Map 1 C2

Bay View Hotel

◉◉ Modern Irish, French 🌑

Accomplished cuisine in comfortable country house with dramatic views

☎ 021 4646746 ▤ 021 4646075
e-mail: res@thebayviewhotel.com
web: www.thebayviewhotel.com
dir: At Castlemartyr on N25 (Cork-Waterford road) turn onto R632 to Garryvoe, then follow signs for Shanagarry & Ballycotton

As its name implies, the Bayview offers breathtaking coastal views, perched on the clifftop overlooking the unspoilt fishing harbour of Ballycotton. The views prove an irresistible draw for diners (with window tables much sought after), and, not surprisingly given the location, locally-landed seafood is a speciality, though there is plenty more besides. The kitchen's modern Irish approach is underpinned by classic French themes and international influences, while making good use of local meats and produce. Expect skilful cooking and clear flavours in the balanced and well-executed repertoire. Grilled fillet of turbot, perhaps, accompanied by chargrilled fennel, saffron mash and an olive oil and lemon dressing, or roast rack and loin of lamb served with Provençale vegetables, fondant potato, aubergine caviar and gremolata.

Chef Ciaran Scully **Owner** John & Carmel O'Brian **Times** 1-2/7-9 Closed Nov-Apr, L Mon-Sat **Prices** Food prices not confirmed for 2010. Please telephone for details. **Wines** 6 bottles over €20 **Notes** Lighter meals served in lounge & on terrace, Dress restrictions, Smart casual **Seats** 65, Pr/dining room 30 **Children** Portions **Parking** 40

BALLYLICKEY Map 1 B2

Sea View House

◉◉ Traditional

Impressive Irish cooking in a delightful country house

☎ 027 50073 & 50462 ▤ 027 51555
e-mail: info@seaviewhousehotel.com
dir: 3m N of Bantry towards Glengarriff, 70yds off main road, N71

Secluded in colourful gardens, offering views of Bantry Bay and the mountains beyond, this friendly hotel has earned a reputation for high standards over many years. The dining area consists of several rooms, decorated in warm tones of green and elegantly furnished with antiques and fresh flowers, and includes a delightful garden room. Cooking is classic country-house style and shows consistency and skill, keeping things simple and fresh and allowing top-quality produce to shine. Fresh, locally-landed fish is a feature on the daily, fixed-price dinner menu; perhaps scallops Parisienne (local hand-dived scallops poached in court-bouillon and served in a cream and wine reduction with seasonal vegetables), while to finish, perhaps a perfect quivering pannacotta with poached rhubarb.

Times 12.30-1.45/7-9.30 Closed Nov-Mar, L Mon-Sat

BALTIMORE Map 1 B1

Casey's of Baltimore Hotel

◉ Traditional, Seafood

Fresh fish, coastal views and a warm welcome

☎ 028 20197 ▤ 028 20509
e-mail: info@caseysofbaltimore.com
dir: from Cork take N71 to Skibbereen, then take R595. Hotel on right

With breathtaking views over Roaring Water Bay to the islands beyond, this family-run hotel with pub attached is a local institution and renowned for its hospitality. Expect open fires, a simple, rustic décor, traditional music at weekends, and a bustling atmosphere in the bistro-style restaurant. Naturally, seafood is a speciality, the exceptionally fresh selection landed within a mile of the kitchen, which also utilises locally-sourced vegetables and traceable meats. Cooking is straightforward and runs to lemon sole with lemon and caper butter, seafood chowder, lobster thermidor, and meat options like Angus fillet steak with peppercorn sauce. ***continued***

BALTIMORE *continued*

Chef Victoria Gilshenan **Owner** Ann & Michael Casey **Times** 12.30-2.30/6.30-9 Closed 21-26 Dec **Prices** Fixed L 3 course fr €30, Fixed D 3 course fr €42, Starter €8-€15, Main €15-€45, Dessert fr €6, Service optional **Wines** 5 bottles over €20, 15 bottles under €20, 2 by glass **Notes** Sunday L, Vegetarian available, Air con **Seats** 100 **Children** Portions, Menu **Parking** 50

BLARNEY Map 1 B2

Blarney Golf Resort

Modern European **NEW**

Accomplished cooking in luxurious golf resort

☎ 021 4384477 📄 021 4516453
Kerry Rd, Tower
e-mail: reservations@blarneygolfresort.com
dir: Exit N20 for Blarney, 4km to Tower, turn right onto Old Kerry Road. Hotel 2km on right

Set amongst 170 acres of the beautiful wooded Shournagh valley, close to the historic town of Blarney, this luxury golf hotel boasts a glorious location. The spacious Inniscarra Restaurant occupies a split-level room with contemporary décor and the small kitchen team use seasonal local produce in the Modern European food (with strong Italian and French influences). Start with local scallops served with pork belly and follow with a crown of roast pheasant with polenta, sautéed wild mushrooms and toasted hazelnut vinaigrette. Valrhona chocolate tart rounds things off.

Times 6-9 Closed L all week

CLONAKILTY Map 1 B2

Inchydoney Island Lodge & Spa

Modern French

Fresh West Cork food in a glorious coastal setting

☎ 023 8833143 & 8821100 📄 023 8835229
Inchydoney
e-mail: reservations@inchydoneyisland.com
dir: From Cork take N71 following West Cork signs. Through Innishannon, Bandon & Clonakilty, then follow signs for Inchydoney Island

After splashing a cool €3 million on refurbishment, this luxurious spa hotel's position in the top flight of Ireland's resort destinations is assured. The setting is to die for, bracketed by fabulous beaches with sublime views of the Atlantic, and the designer interior ticks all the right style-slave boxes. The Gulfstream Restaurant has a chic contemporary look and glorious sea views as befits its name. French and Mediterranean influences underpin the menu, with plenty of fresh local seafood and organic produce to the fore, as in a tian of local crab with saffron-scented aïoli, ginger and coriander. A main course teams baked halibut with mussels and oysters in a vermouth sauce, seared scallops, pearl barley risotto and prawn bisque.

Chef Adam Medcalf **Owner** Des O'Dowd **Times** 1-3/6.30-9.45 Closed 24-26 Dec, L Mon-Sat **Prices** Food prices not confirmed for 2010. Please telephone for details. **Wines** 56 bottles over €20, 5 by glass **Notes** Vegetarian available, Dress restrictions, Smart casual, Civ Wed 250, Air con **Seats** 90, Pr/dining room 250 **Children** Portions, Menu **Parking** 250

CORK Map 1 B2

Maryborough Hotel & Spa

Modern International **V**

Enjoyable dining in a popular hotel restaurant

☎ 021 4365555 📄 021 4365662
Maryborough Hill
e-mail: info@maryborough.ie
dir: Please telephone for directions

The Maryborough Hotel is a fine old Georgian country house in 14 acres of listed gardens and woodland on the leafy outskirts of Cork. A modern extension houses a glitzy spa and leisure centre, while the restaurant offers an extensive contemporary European menu with a broad appeal. The dining room is a smart split-level affair with a fashionable look and a showpiece walk-in wine cellar. Go for chicken liver and foie gras terrine with Sauternes jelly to start, followed by roast rump of Kerry lamb with braised Puy lentils, parsnip gratin and rosemary jus, and end with a luscious double chocolate brownie baked Alaska with butterscotch sauce.

Chef Gerry Allen **Owner** Dan O'Sullivan **Times** 12.30-2.30/6.30-10 Closed 24-26 Dec, L Sat, D Sun-Mon **Prices** Fixed L 2 course €20-€25, Starter €6.50-€9.50, Main €19-€27, Dessert €7.50-€9, Service optional, Groups min 10 service 10% **Wines** 44 bottles over €20, 11 bottles under €20, 4 by glass **Notes** Sunday L, Vegetarian menu, Dress restrictions, Smart casual, Civ Wed 100, Air con **Seats** 120, Pr/dining room 60 **Children** Portions, Menu **Parking** 300

GARRYVOE Map 1 C2

Garryvoe Hotel

Modern Irish

Seafood-rich menu with Bay views

☎ 021 4646718 📄 021 4646824
Ballycotton Bay, Castlemartyr
e-mail: res@garryvoehotel.com
web: www.garryvoehotel.com
dir: From N25 at Castlemartyr (Cork-Rosslare road) take R632 to Garryvoe

There has been a hotel on this site since the Edwardian era, although none quite so bright and trim-looking as the present interior. Views over Ballycotton Bay and the 5 miles of sandy beach are a constant, and make a sumptuous backdrop to dining. The cooking keeps things simple, with a logical emphasis on seafood and no gilding the lily. Prawns Marie Rose is an effective rendition, with sweetly fresh shellfish and pickled cucumber for contrast, while baked hake is a well-timed main, served with an equally accurate leek and chorizo risotto. Crème brûlée is set a little lighter than the norm, with a note of anise for extra kick.

Chef Kevin O'Sullivan **Owner** Carmel & John O'Brien **Times** 1-2.30/6.45-8.45 Closed 24-25 Dec, L Mon-Sat **Prices** Fixed L 3 course €28-€33, Fixed D 3 course €35, Starter €6.50-€9.50, Main €24-€29, Dessert €6.50-€9.50, Service optional **Wines** 6 by glass **Notes** Vegetarian available, Civ Wed 100 **Seats** 80, Pr/dining room 40 **Children** Portions, Menu **Parking** 80

GOUGANE BARRA Map 1 B2

Gougane Barra Hotel

Irish, French

Distinguished cooking in spectacular lakeside setting

☎ 026 47069 📄 026 47226
e-mail: gouganebarrahotel@eircom.net
dir: Off R584 between N22 at Macroom & N71 at Bantry. Take Keimaneigh junct for hotel

This friendly, family-run hotel is set in the picturesque glen of Gougane Barra, overlooking the lake and St Finbarr's 6th-century hermitage. The restaurant has stunning views and well-appointed tables decorated with local wild flowers. The menu delivers traditional dishes presented in a contemporary fashion, using top-quality local ingredients. Expect starters such as traditional potato cakes given a modern twist with the addition of whipped egg whites and served with Clonakilty pudding and a salad of dressed garden leaves. A simply prepared, well-flavoured main course might be cutlets of Cork lamb served on a rich reduction of juices and red wine accompanied by steamed root vegetables.

Times 12.30-2.30/5.30-8.45 Closed 18 Oct-10 Apr, L Mon-Sat

KINSALE   Map 1 B2

Pier One

◉ Modern, Traditional

Waterfront hotel with modern cuisine and harbour views

☎ 021 4779300 📄 021 4774173
Trident Hotel, Worlds End
e-mail: info@tridenthotel.com
dir: From Cork take R600 to Kinsale. Hotel at end of Pier Rd

You couldn't ask for a better spot for dining in historic Kinsale than Pier One's brilliant pitch overlooking the waterfront. The interior goes for a bright modern look with rustic stone walls and artwork by well-known Irish artists, and huge windows looking out from its 2nd-floor perch over the comings and goings in the harbour below. The kitchen takes a modern route based on French and European influences, and cherry picks the best of local seasonal produce from land and sea. Seafood terrine made with salmon and haddock makes a fine starter, followed by medallions of pork loin served with creamy cider sauce, colcannon and apple fritters.

Chef Frank O'Reilly **Owner** Trident Dawncross Ltd **Times** 1-2.30/7-9.30 Closed 24-26 Dec, L Mon-Sat **Prices** Food prices not confirmed for 2010. Please telephone for details. **Wines** 24 bottles over €20, 30 bottles under €20, 6 by glass **Notes** Sunday L, Vegetarian available, Dress restrictions, Smart casual **Seats** 90, Pr/dining room 200 **Children** Portions, Menu **Parking** 60

The White House

◉ Traditional, International

Lively restaurant and bar serving local Irish food

☎ 021 4772125 📄 021 4772045
Pearse St, The Glen
e-mail: whitehse@indigo.ie

The White House is a family-run restaurant and bar with rooms in the centre of the medieval town of Kinsale. There is a busy bar adjacent to the stylishly rustic Restaurant d'Antibes and there is live music each night. The bistro-style menu features traditional Irish cuisine given a modern twist, using vegetables from their own garden and the best of the local fresh fish catch. A typical starter might be Oysterhaven hot oysters baked in the oven with garlic and chilli breadcrumbs, followed by fresh fish and shellfish wrapped in a crêpe then glazed with melted cheese and served with salad, or medallions of beef fillet on a bed of rosemary vegetables served with brandy and black pepper sauce and mustard mash.

Times 12-10 Closed 25 Dec

MACROOM   Map 1 B2

Castle Hotel

◉ Modern Mediterranean 🍷

Friendly, family-run hotel on the tourist route

☎ 026 41074 📄 026 41505
Main St
e-mail: castlehotel@eircom.net
dir: On N22, midway between Cork & Killarney

On the route between Blarney and Killarney, the hotel is perfectly placed to benefit from those on the tourist itinerary through beautiful Cork. It's a town-centre venue with an art deco-style, split-level restaurant, where staff are friendly and professional and the menus make the most of the southern larder. Herb-crusted crab and prawn bake, chargrilled pork medallions with parmesan risotto and mushroom sauce, or Cajun salmon in balsamic dressing are the kinds of dishes to expect, and the rhubarb crumble, served with a little jug of custard, is little short of delicious.

Chef Pat Ryan **Owner** The Buckley Family **Times** 12-3/6-9.30 Closed 24-28 Dec, D Mon **Prices** Fixed L 3 course €27.50-€29.50, Starter €5.95-€8.50, Main €16.95-€27, Dessert €5.95-€7.95, Service included **Wines** 2 bottles over €20, 10 bottles under €20, 3 by glass **Notes** Sunday L, Vegetarian available, Civ Wed 150, Air con **Seats** 50, Pr/dining room 150 **Children** Portions, Menu **Parking** 30

YOUGHAL   Map 1 C2

Aherne's

◉ Irish, Seafood NEW

Seaside hotel restaurant well known for its local seafood

☎ 024 02424 📄 024 93633
163 North Main St
e-mail: ahernes@eircom.net
dir: Exit N25 at Youghal. Pass the lighthouse and under the clock gate. Continue until one-way system ends, Aherne's is 50yds on right.

Situated in the historic walled seaside resort of Youghal, on the south coast, this smart townhouse hotel has a huge reputation for serving some of the finest seafood around. The menu changes everyday but it always features a number of dishes using the best fish and shellfish from that day's catch in Youghal harbour. Locally-reared beef and lamb are also available but there is no better advertisement for local produce than the bay prawns cooked in garlic butter followed by grilled John Dory with seafood risotto.

Times 6.30-9 Closed L all week **Prices** Food prices not confirmed for 2010. Please telephone for details.

CO DONEGAL

DONEGAL   Map 1 B5

Harvey's Point Country Hotel

◉◉ Modern, Traditional V

High-impact cooking in a soothing lakeside location

☎ 074 9722208 📄 074 9722352
Lough Eske
e-mail: sales@harveyspoint.com
dir: From Donegal 2m towards Lifford, left at Harvey's Point sign, follow signs, take 3 right turns to hotel gates

A haven of unruffled tranquillity on the shores of Lough Eske, the hotel makes the most of its location, affording diners soothing lakeside views from the dining room, although a helicopter may occasionally be seen alighting on the landing-pad just outside. Well-spaced tables and relaxing service add allure to a culinary operation that achieves great things. Mussels from Donegal Bay are presented in garlic- and herb-scented Chardonnay with vegetable julienne, while the familiarly trendy root purée - in this case parsnip - is the vehicle for a brace of accurately seared scallops. Continue with roast rump and slow-cooked breast of local lamb, served with a stew of white beans, crushed carrots and rosemary gravy. Sour cherry parfait with apple ice cream is a dessert with some tang.

Chef Paul Montgomery **Owner** Marc Gysling, Deirdre McGlone **Times** 12.30-2.30/6.30-9.30 Closed Mon-Tue (Nov-Etr) **Prices** Fixed L 2 course €14-€22, Fixed D 2 course fr €29, Fixed D 4 course fr €59, Starter fr €4.50, Main fr €18.50, Dessert fr €6.50, Service included **Wines** 51 bottles over €20, 38 bottles under €20, 2 by glass **Notes** Sunday L, Vegetarian menu, Dress restrictions, Smart casual, Civ Wed 250, Air con **Seats** 100, Pr/dining room 100 **Children** Menu **Parking** 200

DUNKINEELY   Map 1 B5

Castle Murray House and Restaurant

◉ Traditional French

Great local seafood in hotel with sea views

☎ 074 9737022 📄 074 9737330
St Johns Point
e-mail: info@castlemurray.com
dir: From Donegal take N56 towards Killybegs. Left to Dunkineely

This clifftop hotel enjoys a fabulous location with stunning sea and coastal views across to the ruins of Castle Murray. Sometimes called Rahan Castle, this landmark has a storey dating back to the 15th century and to the McSwynes, a Donegal clan. In the comfortable restaurant, enjoy fresh seafood landed that day on a French-influenced menu that changes with the seasons and depending on what's at its best; prawns and monkfish in garlic butter, followed by roast halibut with crabmeat, prawn and dill lemon dressing.

continued

DUNKINEELY *continued*

Chef Remy Dupuy **Owner** Marguerite Howley
Times 1.30-3.30/6.30-9.30 Closed mid Jan-mid Feb, L
Mon-Sat **Prices** Fixed D 4 course €51-€67 **Wines** 24 bottles
over €20, 28 bottles under €20, 5 by glass **Notes** Fixed L 4
course €31, Sunday L, Vegetarian available, Civ Wed 30
Seats 80 **Children** Portions, Menu **Parking** 25

RATHMULLAN   Map 1 C6

Fort Royal Hotel

◉ Modern Irish, Seafood

**Country-house dining in mature gardens sloping down
to the sea**

☎ 074 9158100 📄 074 9158103
Fort Royal
e-mail: fortroyal@eircom.net
dir: Please telephone for directions

There's no excuse for not coming to the table with an
appetite at this welcoming hotel: with 18 acres of
grounds to wander in, a tennis court, a 9-hole pitch and
putt course, and endless walking on a glorious sandy
beach and the shores of Lough Swilly. The Fletcher family
have run Fort Royal for more than fifty years, giving the
classic country house a sense of deep-rooted solidity and
well-oiled hospitality. In the dining room, huge floor-to-
ceiling windows overlook the garden, which supplies
fresh fruit, vegetables and herbs, while award-winning
local suppliers provide the fish and meat. Set dinner
menus change daily and might offer grilled fresh
asparagus with parmesan gratin to start, then grilled
turbot fillet with leek and Sauternes sauce.

Times 7.30-8.30 Closed L all week

Rathmullan House

◉◉ Modern Irish **V** ⊙

Classy cooking using top-quality Donegal produce

☎ 074 9158188 📄 074 9158200
e-mail: info@rathmullanhouse.com
dir: R245 Letterkenny to Ramelton, over bridge right onto
R247 to Rathmullan. On entering village turn at Mace
shop through village gates. Hotel on right

Perched above the shores of Lough Swilly, with a
sparkling beach a few steps away, this lovely old country
house is set in beautiful gardens with fabulous Donegal
views on all sides. Three hexagon-shaped sunrooms make
up the Weeping Elm Restaurant, giving it the appearance
of an Arabian tent, only with views of lawns sweeping
down to the seashore. Chef Ian Orr (ex River Café) is a
supporter of the 'slow food' movement and uses organic
fresh fruit, vegetables and herbs from the hotel's walled
garden, local farmland produce such as Donegal lamb,
and an abundance of fresh fish and seafood in his
cooking. Expect the likes of fritto misto of Portavogie
prawns and halibut with garden salad, sundried
tomatoes and chilli mayo for starters, followed by
Rathmullan House 21-day aged fillet of beef or roast
breast of Silverhill duck.

Chef Ian Orr **Owner** Wheeler Family **Times** 7.30-8.45
Closed Jan-Mid Feb **Prices** Fixed D 3 course fr €52.50,
Starter €12.50-€17.50, Main €29.50-€34, Dessert
€12.50-€14.50, Service added 10% **Wines** 3 bottles
under €20, 10 by glass **Notes** Vegetarian menu, Dress
restrictions, Smart casual, Civ Wed 70 **Seats** 70, Pr/
dining room 30 **Children** Portions, Menu **Parking** 40

ROSSNOWLAGH   Map 1 B5

Sandhouse Hotel

◉ Traditional

Fine food in stunning Donegal Bay location

☎ 071 9851777 📄 071 9852100
e-mail: info@sandhouse-hotel.ie
dir: 10m S of Donegal & 7m from Ballyshannon on coast
road

Close by the shore at Rossnowlagh, this splendid hotel has
sweeping vistas across miles of secluded coves and sandy
beaches. The erstwhile fishing lodge has grown up into a
rather more sybaritic affair with a classy spa and smartly
refurbished, split-level restaurant. The kitchen makes fine
use of wonderful produce from the verdant hinterland and
pristine coastal waters in a menu that is firmly rooted in
the classics, but doesn't turn its back on more modern
trends. Given the location, a tian of Donegal Bay seafood
with saffron mayonnaise is a fine way to start, while among
main courses might be roast rack of local lamb with a
fresh herb crust and apple and mint jelly.

Times 12.30-2.30/7-9.30 Closed Nov-Feb, L Mon-Sat

DUBLIN

DUBLIN   Map 1 D4

Dylan

◉ Modern Irish **NEW**

Ambitious cooking in stylish boutique hotel

☎ 01 6603000 📄 01 6603005
Eastmoreland Ln
e-mail: justask@dylan.ie
dir: From St Stephen's Green take Baggot St, over canal
bridge, second left. Dylan is on left

Located in a leafy and affluent area of Dublin, this stylish
boutique hotel is just minutes away from the heart of the
city centre. Enjoy cocktails in the sophisticated bar before
moving into the elegant restaurant which is very much a
place to be seen. The contemporary food has Italian and
French influences and flavours are bold and seasonal. A
starter of St Maure goats' cheese with Granny Smith
apple beignet might be followed by Atlantic halibut with
braised scallions, shitake mushrooms and spiced broth.
Classic bread-and-butter pudding with caramel sauce,
sauce anglaise and vanilla ice cream rounds things off.

Times 12.30-2.30/6-10 Closed L Sat **Prices** Food prices
not confirmed for 2010. Please telephone for details.

Finnstown Country House

◉ European, International

Traditional cuisine in grand country house

☎ 01 6010700 📄 01 6281088
Newcastle Rd
e-mail: manager@finnstown-hotel.ie
dir: From M1 take 1st exit onto M50 southbound. 1st exit
after Toll Bridge. At rdbt take 3rd left (N4 W). Left at
lights. Over next 2 rbts, hotel on right

This magnificent 18th-century country house stands in 45
acres of splendid grounds complete with elegant
peacocks. Just a short drive from the centre of Dublin, the
house has fine period details throughout, with the
Georgian-style Peacock Restaurant particularly
impressive. An octagonal sunroom extension has been
added to the side. The kitchen focuses on fresh local
produce in traditional and international dishes, cooked in
a simple, straightforward way. Starters might include
steamed Bantry Bay mussels with celery, shallots,
parsley, white wine and cream, followed by a main course
of roast Silverhill duckling with fruit stuffing, glazed with
an orange and Cointreau sauce.

Times 12.30-2.30/7.30-9.30 Closed 24-26 Dec, D Sun

The Park Restaurant

◉ Traditional, International **NEW**

Modern bistro in country club setting

☎ 01 6406300 📄 01 6406303
**Castleknock Hotel & Country Club, Porterstown Rd,
Castleknock**
e-mail: info@chcc.ie
dir: M50 exit 3 to Castleknock village, left at Myos junct &
follow signs

The picturesque country setting of this hotel belies the
fact that it is only 9km from Dublin city centre. With an
18-hole golf course, leisure centre and beauty salon, this
contemporary hotel is the base for the All Blacks rugby
squad when they play in Europe. Guests have a wide
choice of dining options, including The Brasserie and The
Park Restaurant, a modern bistro and steak house with
stunning views of the golf course. Classic dishes include
West Coast mussels cooked with shallots, white wine and
cream, followed by crispy beer-battered chicken or a
selection of aged Irish steaks with traditional
accompaniments.

Chef Lewis Bannerman **Owner** FBD Group
Times 12.30-3/5.30-10 Closed 24-26 Dec **Prices** Fixed L
2 course €15.95, Fixed D 4 course €20-€55, Starter €6-
€13.50, Main €16-€38.50, Dessert €7.50-€10, Service
optional **Wines** 12 by glass **Notes** Early bird set menu
available, Sunday L, Vegetarian available, Civ Wed 150,
Air con **Seats** 65, Pr/dining room 400 **Children** Portions,
Menu **Parking** 200

Restaurant Patrick Guilbaud

◉◉◉◉ – *see opposite page*

Restaurant Patrick Guilbaud

Modern French **V**

Ireland's premier dining experience

☎ 01 6764192   📄 01 6610052
Merrion Hotel, 21 Upper Merrion St
e-mail: restaurantpatrickguilbaud@
eircom.net
dir: Opposite government buildings,
next to Merrion Hotel

Reservations are essential at Dublin's premier temple of gastronomy, a place that attracts the wealthy, the famous and Ireland's high-fliers, all eager to sample food delivered with panache. Before descending the steps to the dining room, there's also a small - but equally stylish - bar-lounge for aperitifs. And, while the restaurant's location in the opulent Georgian splendour of the Merrion Hotel is equally fitting, it does have its own street entrance as well as access through the hotel lobby itself. The impressive collection of modern Irish art blends well with the colourful carpet and the swish Italian leather chairs, while the former inner courtyard garden terrace has been enclosed with a glass roof to create a second lounge for diners, the perfect space for post-dinner drinks. Immaculate napery graces well-spaced tables, while impressive service is precise and measured, without losing that friendly touch. Patrick Guilbaud's modern interpretation of classic French cuisine more than lives up to the billing,

and focuses on the very best seasonal Irish produce. His intricate cooking is delivered via an impressive array of menu options that includes a good-value fixed-price lunch, extensive and enticing carte (including a vegetarian menu) as well as a tasting offering. Expect plenty of sophisticated flair and innovation, immaculate attention to detail, silky technical skills and luxury. Think traditional crubeens - thinly sliced pig's trotters - served with a maris piper and sour cream salad, crispy pork, poached quail's egg and Meaux mustard, or veal sweetbread slowly caramelised and glazed with liquorice sauce with a light parsnip sauce and lemon confit. To finish, perhaps caramelised Granny Smith apple tart with sesame croquant and vanilla ice cream.

Chef Guillaume Lebrun **Owner** Patrick Guilbaud **Times** 12.30-2.15/7.30-10.15 Closed 25 Dec, 1st wk Jan, Sun-Mon **Prices** Fixed L 2 course €38, Tasting menu €180, Starter €25-€42, Main €46-€60, Dessert €22-€25, Service optional **Wines** 1000 bottles over €20, 12 by glass **Notes** Tasting menu 7 course, Vegetarian menu, Dress restrictions, Smart casual, Air con **Seats** 80, Pr/dining room 25 **Children** Portions **Parking** Parking in square

DUBLIN *continued*

The Shelbourne

European, Irish NEW

Comforting classics in luxurious Dublin hotel

☎ 01 6634500 ▤ 01 6616006
27 St Stephen's Green
dir: In city centre

Built in 1824, the luxury Shelbourne Hotel overlooks St Stephen's Green in the heart of Dublin, one of Europe's grandest garden squares. The hotel has been magnificently restored and is ideally situated close to the city's cultural and historic buildings. Enjoy a cocktail or Dublin's own Guinness at the Horseshoe Bar and try the Oyster Bar before moving into The Saddle Room Restaurant with its open kitchen. The food is traditional, classically based with some more modern ideas on show. Start with scallops with chicken wings and move on to rib-eye beef with fondant potato, turnip and prune gratin and béarnaise sauce.

Times 12.30-2.30/6-10.30 **Prices** Food prices not confirmed for 2010. Please telephone for details.

Stillorgan Park Hotel

Traditional International

Stylish hotel with contemporary international menus

☎ 01 2881621 & 2001800 ▤ 01 2831610
Stillorgan Rd
e-mail: sales@stillorganpark.com
web: www.stillorganpark.com
dir: Please telephone for directions

You can indulge in a bit of celeb-spotting at this eye-catching design-led hotel as its neighbour is RTE, the national broadcasting institution, so you never know who might drop in for a snifter or a bite to eat. The atmospheric Turf Club Bar is a favourite watering hole before moving into the striking Purple Sage restaurant, where bold colours, hand-painted frescoes, mosaic tiles and modern artwork combine in a striking décor. The contemporary menu has a broad-ranging international remit, founded on pedigree Irish ingredients. Lamb shank in red wine and mint jus with creamy garlic potatoes and roasted root vegetables shows the style.

Times 12.30-3/5.45-10.15 Closed 25 Dec, L Sat, D Sun

The Tea Room @ The Clarence

Irish, French 🍷

Designer hotel with distinctive ballroom restaurant

☎ 01 4070800 ▤ 01 4070820
6-8 Wellington Quay
e-mail: tearoom@theclarence.ie
dir: from O'Connell Bridge, W along Quays, through 1st lights (at Ha'penny Bridge) hotel 500mtrs

Situated in the heart of city, overlooking the Liffey in the Temple Bar district, this handsome 19th-century building

is owned by U2's Bono and The Edge, who have successfully given the hotel a cool contemporary makeover. Traditional features remain, the perfect example being the lofty and sophisticated Tea Room restaurant, originally the ballroom, which is flooded with natural light from huge windows. Bustling with diners, it's the perfect place for people watching, as is the hotel's famous Octagonal Bar. The kitchen's modern approach - underpinned by a classical French theme - delivers with consistency and style, driven by high-quality seasonal Irish produce; take crab ravioli with truffled fennel salad and soya sauce beurre blanc, and cannon of lamb with curried clams and mussels and lamb jus.

Chef Mathieu Melin **Owner** Bono, The Edge & Quinlan Private **Times** 7-10.30 Closed 25-26 Dec, L all week **Prices** Fixed D 3 course €34, Starter €13, Main €22-€42, Dessert €12-€16, Service optional, Groups min 8 service 12.5% **Wines** 100 bottles over €20, 20 by glass **Notes** Vegetarian available, Dress restrictions, Smart casual **Seats** 80, Pr/dining room 70 **Children** Portions **Parking** Valet Parking

CO DUBLIN

KILLINEY   Map 1 D4

PJ's Restaurant

Traditional, International

Fine dining overlooking Dublin Bay

☎ 01 2305400 ▤ 01 2305430
Fitzpatrick Castle Hotel
e-mail: reservations@fitzpatricks.com
dir: Please telephone for directions or see website

The beautiful location alone is worth the 9-mile drive from Dublin - the imposing Fitzpatrick Castle Hotel stands on Killiney Hill with stunning views across Dublin Bay. At the heart of this 18th-century property is PJ's, the elegant fine-dining restaurant, with crystal chandeliers, well-spaced tables, crisp linen and good quality glass and silverware. Fresh local produce is a feature of the seasonal menu, which might offer wild game terrine with plum and spiced apple chutney, grilled turbot with tomato and coriander salsa, and dark and white chocolate bavarois with raspberry purée.

Chef Sean Dempsey, John Bueno **Owner** Eithne Fitzpatrick **Times** 12.30-2.30/6-10 Closed 25 Dec, Mon, Tue, L Wed-Sat, D Sun **Prices** Fixed L 3 course €35-€39, Fixed D 3 course €45-€50, Service added 10% **Wines** 25 bottles over €20, 14 bottles under €20, 2 by glass **Notes** Sunday L, Vegetarian available, Air con **Seats** 65, Pr/dining room 50 **Children** Portions **Parking** 200

PORTMARNOCK   Map 1 D4

Osborne Brasserie

Modern International

Creative cuisine in a superb seaside location

☎ 01 8460611 ▤ 01 8462442
Portmarnock Hotel & Golf Links, Strand Rd
e-mail: sales@portmarnock.com
dir: N1 towards Drogheda. Take R601 to Malahide. In 2m left at T-junct, through Malahide, 2.2m hotel on left. Off M1 take Malahide junct, then onto Portmarnock

The handsome Victorian mansion that was once home to the Jameson family (of Irish whiskey fame) is bracketed by the sea and an impressive Bernhard Langer-designed 18-hole golf course. The sophisticated Osborne Brasserie is named for the artist who painted the very view of the gardens and hills that form a scenic backdrop to the culinary endeavours. The menu takes a modern European route using the area's best ingredients, so expect innovative cooking with plenty of flair; fresh fish and seafood from Howth turns up in a starter of seared scallops, smoked pork, Carrageen moss, fennel and orange, followed by sea bream with pommes Parmentier, tomato fondue and Pernod beurre blanc. End with apple crème brûlée with hazelnut ice cream.

Chef Ivo Dewitt **Owner** Natworth Ltd **Times** 6-9.45 Closed Sun-Mon, L all week **Prices** Fixed D 3 course €25-€38, Starter €8-€12, Main €22-€34, Dessert €9-€11.50, Service added but optional 1% **Wines** 50 bottles over €20, 9 by glass **Notes** Vegetarian available, Dress restrictions, Smart casual, Civ Wed 100, Air con **Seats** 100, Pr/dining room 20 **Children** Portions, Menu **Parking** 100

SKERRIES   Map 1 D4

Redbank House & Restaurant

Modern European 🍷

Reliable cooking in a picturesque village

☎ 01 8491005 ▤ 01 8491598
5-7 Church St
e-mail: info@redbank.ie
dir: From Dublin, M1 N to Lissenhall interchange, take exit to Skerries

Squeaky-fresh seafood from local boats is the draw at this popular, well-respected restaurant with rooms housed in a former bank in a fishing village north of Dublin. Expect an imaginative range of menus to suit all tastes and budgets and a skilful, modern approach that allows the fresh flavours to shine through. Take a simple, full flavoured starter dish of Loughshinny crab, blended with sherry and baked in the oven with cream, followed by monkfish with leek and smoked bacon sauce, and a light orange and almond gâteau to finish. The former vault houses the well-stocked cellar and service is friendly and professional.

Chef Terry McCoy **Owner** Terry McCoy **Times** 12.30-4/6-10 Closed 24-26 Dec, L Mon-Sat, D Sun **Prices** Fixed D 4 course €25-€50, Starter €12-€19.95, Main €23-€45,

Dessert €10, Service included **Wines** 50 bottles over €20, 2 bottles under €20, 2 by glass **Notes** Sunday L, Vegetarian available, Dress restrictions, Smart casual, Civ Wed 55 **Seats** 60, Pr/dining room 10 **Parking** On street

CO GALWAY

CASHEL Map 1 A4

Cashel House

◉◉ Traditional International **V**

Food without fuss and a wealth of seafood in a heavenly location

☎ 095 31001 📄 095 31077
e-mail: res@cashel-house-hotel.com
dir: S of N59. 1m W of Recess

The McEvilly family have run this well-established Victorian country-house hotel since 1968, so you can be sure that every aspect of service is polished. Cashel House stands at the head of Cashel Bay in 50 acres of delightful, award-winning gardens with woodland walks to hone the appetite. The original restaurant offers a traditional setting amid antiques and artworks, or there's a bright conservatory extension where you can put the French-influenced menu through its paces. The kitchen is lucky to have superb produce to hand from Connemara's lakes, rivers, hillsides and the waters of the bay. You might start simply with a half-dozen local oysters, or Cleggan mussels with chilli, garlic and tomato, then move on to roast rack of the renowned Connemara lamb with champ potatoes, minted peas and pan juices.

Chef Arturo Amit, Arturo Tillo **Owner** Kay McEvilly & family **Times** 12.30-2.30/7-8.30 Closed 2 Jan-2 Feb **Prices** Fixed D 4 course €60, Starter €14, Main €30, Dessert €12, Service added 12.5% **Wines** 90 bottles over €20, 4 bottles under €20, 5 by glass **Notes** Sunday L, Vegetarian menu, Dress restrictions, Smart casual **Seats** 70, Pr/dining room 20 **Children** Portions, Menu **Parking** 30

CLIFDEN Map 1 A4

Abbeyglen Castle Hotel

◉ French, International

Elegant restaurant in a hospitable country-house hotel

☎ 095 21201 📄 095 21797
Sky Rd
e-mail: info@abbeyglen.ie
dir: N59 from Galway towards Clifden. Hotel 1km from Clifden on Sky Rd

Crenallations, towers and pointed-arch windows give an individual air to the exterior of this striking 19th-century manor house, which stands in glorious landscaped grounds overlooking Clifden Bay. Daily menus champion local seasonal ingredients, including shellfish from the bay, locally-caught salmon, and Connemara lamb. Begin with duck confit with black pudding, served with a spicy fruit salsa, follow with a fabulously fresh turbot fillet, landed at nearby Cleggan, crab or lobster from the seawater tank, or fillet steak au poivre, then finish with white chocolate bread-and-butter pudding. The elegant restaurant overlooks the gardens and has a relaxed, informal atmosphere.

Chef Kevin Conroy **Owner** Mr P Hughes **Times** 7-9 Closed 10 Jan-5 Feb, L Mon-Sun **Prices** Fixed D 3 course €43-€48, Starter €6.50-€11.50, Main €19.95-€39, Dessert €8, Service added 12.5% **Wines** 60 bottles over €20, 8 by glass **Notes** Vegetarian available **Seats** 75 **Parking** 40

Ardagh Hotel & Restaurant

◉◉ French, Mediterranean

Assured cooking of local produce in a stunning setting

☎ 095 21384 📄 095 21314
Ballyconneely Rd
e-mail: ardaghhotel@eircom.net
dir: Galway to Clifden on N59. Signed in Clifden, 2m on Ballyconneely road

The views across Ardbear Bay, particularly at sunset, are reason enough to book yourself a table in the restaurant at this charming family-run hotel. Located on the first-floor of the modern-fronted building, the restaurant has large windows all around, with a terracotta-tiled floor and simple wooden furniture lending an almost Mediterranean feel. As you'd expect, the menu centres around the fruits of the local seas, so starters include salt lake oysters and seafood chowder, while mains could be fillet of wild turbot with home-grown organic spinach and a light saffron sauce, or grilled lobster from the hotel's own tank. Meaty alternatives might include rack of spring lamb on celeriac mash with thyme and lamb jus, or Irish fillet steak with wild mushrooms and pepper sauce.

Times 7.15-9.30 Closed end Nov-end Mar, L all week

GALWAY Map 1 B3/4

Camilaun Restaurant

◉ Modern International

Modern Irish cooking in restaurant with garden views

☎ 091 521433 📄 091 521546
The Ardilaun Hotel, Taylor's Hill
e-mail: info@theardilaunhotel.ie
dir: 1m from city centre, towards Salthill on west side of city, near Galway Bay

This 19th-century building may have started life as home to a prominent Galway family, but it opened as the Ardilaun Hotel on St Patrick's Day 1962 and it's still run by the Ryan family. Overlooking 5 acres of landscaped grounds on the edge of Galway city, the restaurant and terrace have a sense of occasion and the internationally-influenced dishes are prepared from high-quality local ingredients and presented with flair. Start with tartare of Connemara smoked salmon with citrus and fennel pickle with aïoli dressing and move on to braised rack of lamb with lavender and roasted garlic with cassoulet of winter beans and rosemary. A carvery lunch is served on Sundays.

Chef David O'Donnell **Owner** John Ryan **Times** 1-2.15/6.30-9.15 Closed 23-27 Dec, L Sat **Prices** Fixed L 2 course €12.50, Fixed D 3 course €31.50, Starter €8.75-€10.50, Main €17.25-€52, Dessert €6.95-€7.95, Service added 10% **Wines** 62 bottles over €20, 2 bottles under €20, 11 by glass **Notes** Sunday L, Vegetarian available, Dress restrictions, Smart dress, Civ Wed 650, Air con **Seats** 180, Pr/dining room 380 **Children** Portions, Menu **Parking** 300

Galway Bay Hotel

◉ Modern International, Seafood

Light, contemporary hotel restaurant with sea views and fresh Irish produce

☎ 091 520520 📄 091 520530
The Promenade, Salthill
e-mail: info@galwaybayhotel.com
dir: 2m from Galway city centre

The Lobster Pot restaurant enjoys magnificent triple-aspect views over Galway Bay from its elegant, contemporary-styled dining room, decked out in soothing colours, stylish furnishings and high-backed chairs. The cuisine style is modern Irish with international influences and there's a strong emphasis on fresh, local produce like Connemara lamb, but notably fish and seafood, including fresh lobster from the tank, perhaps served simply grilled or thermidor. Otherwise, a pink grapefruit and peppercorn sauce might provide the accompaniment for a blackened fillet of monkfish 'Cajun style', while a tangy, citrusy lemon tart might provide the finale.

Times 1.30-3.30/6.30-9.15 Closed 25 Dec (residents only), L Mon-Sat

GALWAY *continued*

Park House Hotel & Park Room Restaurant

◉ International

Appealing menu in bustling city-centre hotel

☎ 091 564924 ▤ 091 569219
Forster St, Eyre Square
e-mail: parkhousehotel@eircom.net
dir: In city centre, off Eyre Sq

Park House started out over 30 years ago as a restaurant in what was once a Victorian grain store with a splendid stone façade. Although it has evolved into a busy hotel, the Park Room Restaurant is still at the heart of the enterprise, bustling with a loyal local following at lunch, and mellowing into a more romantic softly-lit vibe in the evening. The cooking sticks to classical French roots and offers a broad choice of well-executed dishes founded on local materials, particularly fish and seafood. Kinvara organic smoked salmon with caper vinaigrette and home-made brown bread is a good way to start, followed by pan-fried supreme of sea trout with shrimp and dill butter.

Times 12-3/6-10 Closed 24-26 Dec

River Room

◉ Modern Irish, International

Modern cuisine in an 18th-century country residence

☎ 091 526666 ▤ 091 527800
Glenlo Abbey Hotel, Bushypark
e-mail: info@glenloabbey.ie
dir: Approx 2.5m from centre of Galway on N59 to Clifden/Connemara

Glenlo was built in 1740, and has gone from the abbey home of Galway's tribal elders to today's luxurious hotel in a 138-acre lakeside golf estate. Meticulously restored to its original glory, it is a magnificent place, with lofty ceilings and sculpted cornices, stained glass and fine antique furniture. The River Room restaurant continues the theme and everyone gets glorious views over Lough Corrib through its 5 walls of soaring windows. The kitchen showcases the best of Irish ingredients in creative modern cuisine. Try pan-fried scallops, chive gnocchi and crisp pancetta millefeuille with saffron foam and caviar potato for starters, then medallions of monkfish fillet wrapped in nori seaweed with squid ink noodles, wasabi sabayon and radish salsa.

Times 6.30-9.30 Closed 24-27 Dec, L all week

RECESS (SRAITH SALACH)   Map 1 A4

Ballynahinch Castle

◉◉ Modern International **V**

Fine dining in a castle overlooking the river

☎ 095 31006 & 31086 ▤ 095 31085
e-mail: bhinch@iol.ie
dir: Take N59 from Galway. Turn right after Recess towards Roundstone (R331) for 2m

Stunningly located in the heart of Connemara, this grand crenellated Victorian mansion stands in 350 acres of woodland rivers and lakes and overlooks the famous Ballynahinch river. A renowned fishing hotel, it offers high levels of comfort and friendliness in elegantly furnished lounges, drawing rooms, and the inviting restaurant with its crisp linen, gleaming glassware and soothing river views. Dinner is a fixed-price affair offering French-Irish cooking based on excellent local produce, including seafood landed at nearby Cleggan and wild salmon and game from the estate. A typical meal may kick off with smoked salmon with apple and celeriac remoulade and Tabasco mayonnaise, with seared breast of wild mallard and port wine braised leg with shallot and prune tart to follow. Round off with warm chocolate fondant with pistachio ice cream.

Chef Xin Sun **Owner** Ballynahinch Castle Hotel Inc
Times 6.30-9 Closed 2 wks Xmas, Feb, L all week
Prices Food prices not confirmed for 2010. Please telephone for details. **Wines** 42 bottles over €20, 20 bottles under €20, 5 by glass **Notes** Fixed D 5 course, Vegetarian menu, Dress restrictions, Smart casual
Seats 90 **Parking** 55

Lough Inagh Lodge

◉ Irish, French

Fabulous setting for Irish country fare

☎ 095 34706 & 34694 ▤ 095 34708
Inagh Valley
e-mail: inagh@iol.ie
dir: From Galway take N344. After 3.5m hotel on right

Set amidst the most spectacular Connemara scenery on the shore of the beautiful Lough Inagh, this former 19th-century fishing lodge offers modern comforts in a delightful old-world atmosphere. Guests can enjoy wonderfully relaxed hospitality in the comfortable lounges with turf fires, cosy oak-panelled bar, and an intimate dining room. The simple country-house cooking focuses on flavour and makes good use of local produce; seafood and wild game are specialities of the house. Start with Connemara oysters on ice with lemon, then Irish fillet steak with braised red cabbage and onion jus, finishing with lemon and passionfruit tart with cream.

Times 7-8.45 Closed mid Dec-mid Mar

ROUNDSTONE   Map 1 A4

Roundstone House Hotel

◉ Modern Irish

Stunning sea and mountain views and cracking seafood

☎ 095 35864 ▤ 095 35944
dir: Please telephone for directions

You can feast your eyes on the natural beauty of Bertraghboy Bay and the Connemara Mountains from this cosy hotel in the heart of the fishing village of Roundstone. And you can feast on seafood landed just a few hundred feet from the hotel's door, too. Roundstone House is run by the Vaughan family and Siobhan Vaughan's modern Irish cooking makes the most of the abundant local larder. Take a seat at one of the attractive, linen-dressed tables in Vaughan's Restaurant and tuck into the likes of salmon and crab cakes - brimful of fresh fish - followed by fillet of turbot with fresh prawns in a white wine and cream sauce.

Times 7-9 Closed Nov-Feb

CO KERRY

CAHERDANIEL (CATHAIR DÓNALL)   Map 1 A2

Derrynane Hotel

◉ Irish, European

Enjoyable dining with spectacular Atlantic backdrop

☎ 066 9475136 ▤ 066 9475160
e-mail: info@derrynane.com

Derrynane is a welcoming family-run hotel in a perfect spot for enjoying the great outdoors. Perched on a spectacular clifftop on the Ring of Kerry, jaw-dropping views of Kenmare Bay and the ocean are truly memorable, and with all the outdoor activities on the doorstep you're sure to come to dinner with a keen appetite. With full-length picture windows on two sides of the airy dining room, you get those stunning views of the rugged Atlantic shoreline as a backdrop to the kitchen's repertoire of straightforward modern Irish dishes. Toasted local goats' cheese with pesto dressing might start things off, followed by a thick slab of 36-day hung Hereford beef with béarnaise sauce and Lyonnaise potatoes.

Times 7-9 Closed Oct-mid Apr

Cascade

◉◉ European **V**

Imaginative cooking with a soundtrack of rushing water

☎ 06466 41600 📄 06466 41386
Sheen Falls Lodge
e-mail: info@sheenfallslodge.ie
dir: From Kenmare take N71 to Glengarriff. Take 1st left after suspension bridge. 1m from Kenmare

An elegantly designed, split-level dining room in a peach-hued modern hotel has for a backdrop the floodlit falls on the River Sheen. It makes for a simultaneously fascinating and relaxing ambience, and is a fine setting for the racy modern cuisine. Start as you mean to go on with a serving of lobster in beurre blanc, with gnocchi, artichokes, shiitakes and black truffle, pause for a sorbet, and then proceed in style with spiced pork fillet in a Guinness jus, with stir-fried Chinese leaves and apple and raisin compôte, or caramelised Bantry Bay scallops on langoustine risotto with citrus zests and sprouting broccoli. Rosemary cream custard with Jameson's ice cream and an apple muffin is a dessert to gladden the senses.

Chef Philip Brazil **Owner** Sheen Falls Estate Ltd
Times 7-9.30 Closed 2 Jan-1 Feb, L all week **Prices** Food prices not confirmed for 2010. Please telephone for details. **Wines** 817 bottles over €20, 6 bottles under €20, 21 by glass **Notes** Tasting menu available, Vegetarian menu, Dress restrictions, Smart casual (jacket), No jeans or T-shirts **Seats** 120, Pr/dining room 20
Children Portions, Menu **Parking** 75

The Brehon Restaurant

◉ Modern International

Enchanting setting for fine dining experience

☎ 06466 30700 📄 06466 30701
The Brehon Hotel, Muckross Rd
e-mail: info@thebrehon.com
dir: Enter Killarney follow signs for Muckross Road (N71). Hotel on left 0.3m from town centre

This modern hotel is located across from Killarney National Park with its 25,000 acres (10,000 hectares) of woodlands, moorland, mountains, lakes and gardens. Service is friendly and efficient in the stylish split-level dining room, which has floor-to-ceiling windows giving panoramic views of the surrounding park. Intimate seating is available in private alcoves. The menu offers modern Irish and international cuisine, with fresh seasonal produce from the abundant local larder featuring prominently. Valentia Island prawns and crab is served with caramelised scallop and fennel jam, and fillet of Munster beef with crisp pancetta and pea purée on wilted baby gem with red wine and shallot jus.

Chef John Drummond **Owner** O'Donoghue Family

Times 6-9.30 Closed L bookings only **Prices** Fixed D 3 course €30-€40, Starter €8-€16, Main €18-€35, Dessert €7-€10, Service optional **Wines** 53 bottles over €20, 23 bottles under €20, 13 by glass **Notes** Pre-show menu available, Vegetarian available, Dress restrictions, Smart casual, Civ Wed 200, Air con **Seats** 120, Pr/dining room 100 **Children** Portions, Menu **Parking** 100

Cahernane House Hotel

◉◉ Modern European, International **V**

Uncomplicated cooking in an elegant lakeside setting

☎ 06466 31895 📄 06466 34340
Muckross Rd
e-mail: marketing@cahernane.com
dir: From Killarney follow signs for Kenmare, then from Muckross Rd over bridge. Hotel signed on right. Hotel 1m from town centre

Set in the heart of the Killarney National Park, surrounded by towering mountain ranges, Cahernane is a three-storeyed house that was once the residence of the Earls of Pembroke. The gracious, elegant dining room has fine views over park and lake, and the cooking is all about treating well-sourced ingredients with respect and a minimum of culinary engineering. Start with a terrine of smoked salmon and anchovy butter, dressed in chive crème fraîche and lemon oil, and then try rack of lamb, its flavour and tenderness unimpeachable, served with sweet potato fondant and a thyme jus. An intermediate course offers a choice of soup, sorbet or salad, while desserts might take in excellent brown bread ice cream and red berry compôte with a not entirely successful rhubarb crème brûlée.

Chef Maurice Prendiville **Owner** Mr & Mrs J Browne
Times 7-9.30 Closed Jan, L all week ex by arrangement **Prices** Fixed D 3 course €40, Starter €7-€12, Main €27-€32, Dessert €7-€9, Service optional **Wines** 98 bottles over €20, 22 bottles under €20, 20 by glass **Notes** Tasting menu available, Sunday L, Vegetarian menu, Dress restrictions, Smart casual, no shorts, Civ Wed 60 **Seats** 50, Pr/dining room 18 **Children** Portions, Menu **Parking** 50

Killeen House Hotel

◉ Modern International

Accomplished cooking in charming country-house hotel

☎ 06466 31711 & 31773
Aghadoe, Lakes of Killarney
e-mail: charming@indigo.ie
web: www.killeenhousehotel.com
dir: 4m from Killarney town centre, in Aghadoe, just off Dingle Road

Set in enchanting gardens, this appealing Victorian country-house hotel located on the edge of town offers style and elegance in its relaxed sitting rooms and restaurant. Spread over 2 rooms, the dining room has lovely table settings and fresh flower displays. The kitchen's country-house cooking suits the surroundings

and is driven by prime seasonal local ingredients. Good technical skills and flavour shine in dishes like open ravioli of seared scallops and prawns with leek and courgette served with garlic cream, followed by pan-fried fillet of beef with oyster mushrooms, seasonal greens, red onion jam and port wine sauce. To finish, perhaps peach and strawberry crème brûlée with hazelnut cookie.

Chef Paul O'Gorman **Owner** Michael and Geraldine Rosney **Times** 6.30-9.30 Closed 20 Oct-20 Apr **Prices** Fixed D 4 course €55, Starter €8-€10, Main €24-€30, Dessert €9, Service optional, Groups min 8 service 10% **Wines** 20 bottles over €20, 10 bottles under €20, 6 by glass **Notes** Vegetarian available, Dress restrictions, Smart casual **Seats** 50, Pr/dining room 28 **Children** Portions **Parking** 30

Carrig House Country House & Restaurant

◉ Modern Irish, European

Fine dining in country house overlooking lake

☎ 066 9769100 📄 066 9769166
Caragh Lake
e-mail: info@carrighouse.com

Beautiful lakeland and mountain scenery and stunning woodland gardens, which contain 935 plant species, provide a dramatic backdrop for this handsome Victorian country manor. Furnished in period style, it has log fires in the public rooms, formal linen tablecloths and delightfully friendly service. Well-sourced seasonal produce is cooked with care allowing the flavour of the main ingredient to shine through. A typical meal may start with home-cured Kerry salmon with mustard and dill sauce, followed by saddle of rabbit stuffed with apricots and thyme with grain mustard cream, and rice pudding with marinated figs for pudding.

Times 7-9

TRALEE
Map 1 A2

The Walnut Room

◉ Modern, Traditional

Smart, modern hotel restaurant using fresh local produce

☎ 066 7194500 & 066 7194505 ▤ 066 7194545
Manor West Hotel, Killarney Rd
e-mail: info@manorwesthotel.ie
dir: On main Killarney road next to Manor West Retail Park

Part of Kerry's largest retail park close to the town centre, the smart, modern Manor West Hotel is a stylish place to rest and refuel after a hard day's shopping. Relax over a drink in the cocktail lounge before heading to the fine-dining Walnut Room, a comfortable contemporary restaurant with rich, warm décor. High quality ingredients, cooked with flair and due attention without the need for over-embellishment, feature on the seasonal menu, which includes fish from Dingle Bay and a carvery option at lunch. A starter of seafood chowder might be followed by pan-fried beef fillet with basil mash, red onion marmalade and natural jus.

Chef Bart O'Sullivan **Owner** Boyle Brothers **Times** 6-11 Closed 25 Dec, L all week **Prices** Fixed D 3 course €25-€35, Starter €5.25-€10.50, Main €19.50-€28, Dessert €5.50-€8, Service added but optional 10% **Wines** 30 bottles over €20, 20 bottles under €20, 8 by glass **Notes** Vegetarian available, Air con **Seats** 70, Pr/dining room 50 **Children** Portions, Menu **Parking** 150

WATERVILLE
Map 1 A2

Butler Arms Hotel

◉ European, Seafood

Enjoyable cuisine in snug dining room overlooking the ocean

☎ 066 9474144 ▤ 066 9474520
e-mail: reservations@butlerarms.com
dir: Telephone for directions

There's a comforting sense of continuity at the Butler Arms as the Huggard family's seaside hotel has passed into the hands of its 5th generation since 1915. The pretty honey-pot of Waterville has been drawing in golf-struck celebs to some of Ireland's top courses around the Ring of Kerry since Charlie Chaplin holidayed here, and it's all embraced by mountains and lakes with splendid views of the wild Atlantic coast. The restaurant comes with ocean views as a backdrop to daily-changing modern menus showcasing prime local ingredients, especially seafood, as in a starter of seafood linguine generously loaded with local crab and langoustines. Loin of lamb might follow, served with red wine and thyme sauce and a croquette of potato, goats' cheese and leeks.

Chef Barry Wallace **Owner** Peter Huggard **Times** 7-9.30 Closed 31 Oct-4 Apr, L all week **Prices** Starter €5-€15, Main €10-€35, Dessert €3-€9, Service optional **Wines** 7 bottles over €20, 1 bottles under €20, 2 by glass **Notes** Sunday L **Seats** 80 **Children** Portions, Menu **Parking** 40

CO KILDARE

LEIXLIP
Map 1 D4

Leixlip House

◉ Modern Irish

Fine dining in charming Georgian hotel

☎ 01 6242268 ▤ 01 6244177
Captains Hill
e-mail: info@leixliphouse.com

Leixlip is a splendid Georgian house on the fringes of the eponymous village, just a short drive from Dublin city centre. Resurrected after a disastrous fire in 1985, the interior keeps it traditional with antique furniture and a classically elegant décor. The Bradaun Restaurant is a bright, airy venue for the kitchen's unpretentious modern Irish output; there's a real passion here for sourcing top-notch produce and keeping as much production in-house as possible - all fish and meats, for example, are now smoked on-site. Baked Clonakilty black pudding is teamed with apple and vanilla, cider jelly and Black Forest ham to start, while main courses include seared rack of Slaney Valley lamb with celeriac and parsnip purée and rosemary jus.

Times 12.30-4/6.30-9.45 Closed 25-26 Dec, Mon, L Tue-Sat

NAAS
Map 1 D4

Killashee House Hotel & Villa Spa

◉ Irish

Elegant dining in magnificent surroundings

☎ 045 879277 ▤ 045 879266
e-mail: sales@killasheehouse.com
dir: 1m from Naas on old Kilcullen road. On left past Garda (police station)

After many decades of enforced abstinence and discipline during its time as a convent and boys' preparatory school, this Victorian manor house now offers its inmates a rather more indulgent time amid 200 acres of well-tended grounds with views of the Wicklow mountains. After a thorough de-stress in the sybaritic spa, Turner's restaurant is a palatial venue with chandeliers, ornate plasterwork, painted panelling and plush seating, complete with a harpist to boost the romance on Friday and Saturday nights. Classic country-house dishes are given some inventive modern twists on menus founded on great local produce. Boneless quail is served with home-made houmous and game jus, while monkfish fillets are teamed with horseradish mash, spinach purée and tomato and onion salsa.

Times 1-2.45/7-9.45 Closed 24-25 Dec, L Sat

Virginia Restaurant at Maudlins House Hotel

◉◉ Modern French NEW V ☜

Comfort and good cooking in Kildare

☎ 045 896999 ▤ 045 906411
Dublin Rd
e-mail: info@maudlinshousehotel.ie
dir: Exit N7 approaching large globe, at rdbt head towards Naas, restaurant 200mtrs on right

Creepers cover the façade of this early-Victorian country house on the outskirts of Naas. Inside, plenty of original features have been retained following a sensitive restoration, with the Virginia Restaurant occupying a series of elegantly appointed rooms. Tables are laid with white linen cloths and the service is friendly rather than fussy. Irish cooking with a French classical influence is the order of the day: chicken and mushroom crêpe enriched with foie gras and main-course loin of lamb is wrapped in Parma ham and served with fondant potato, aubergine caviar and confit tomato. Sound technical skill is shown throughout, including the lemon tart dessert.

Chef Rossa Fathey **Owner** Dominic Fagan **Times** 12.30-9.30 **Prices** Fixed L 2 course €19.50-€25.50, Fixed D 3 course €29-€55, Starter €6.50-€11.50, Main €19.50-€33.50, Dessert €8.50-€10.50, Service optional **Wines** 25 bottles over €20, 2 bottles under €20, 10 by glass **Notes** Early bird menu available, Sunday L, Vegetarian menu, Civ Wed 75, Air con **Seats** 86, Pr/dining room 72 **Children** Portions, Menu **Parking** 350

The Byerley Turk

STRAFFAN Map 1 C/D4

Modern, Traditional Irish

Fine dining in a country hotel with championship golf courses

 01 6017200 📠 01 6017299
The K Club
e-mail: hotel@kclub.ie
dir: 30 minutes from Dublin. From Dublin Airport follow M4 to Maynooth, turn for Straffan, just after village on right

The well-endowed K Club hotel is a golfing and spa establishment, expansive, calm and civilised, and decorated throughout with bold, vivid colour schemes. As well as golf on the doorstep, a thoroughbred racing theme pervades, and the flagship Byerley Turk dining room is named after a legendary thoroughbred. With walls upholstered in rich brocade, and marble columns to surround you, the tone is certainly grand. A pianist plays to accompany dinner, tableware is of the highest quality, and the mood is sealed with a jacket-and-tie dress code for gentlemen diners. The cooking is modern Irish, and seriously impressive, making the most of some of the Republic's natural bounty, and achieving an awe-inspiring degree of technical proficiency. Luxuries abound. Start with seared Dordogne foie gras, accompanied by a marbled terrine of the same, with celeriac foam and a five-spice tuile, and continue perhaps

with a heavenly risotto containing Périgord truffle. Beef Tuach is a signature dish of beef fillets with wild mushrooms and mead sauce created to commemorate the holding of the Ryder Cup golf tournament in the grounds here in 2006. An assiette of chocolate variations should round things off in style, and there are also pedigree Irish cheeses with home-made chutneys.

Chef Finbarr Higgins **Owner** Michael Smurfit **Times** 7-9 Closed L all week, D Sun-Fri **Prices** Food prices not confirmed for 2010. Please telephone for details, Service added but optional 10% **Wines** 600 bottles over €20, 8 by glass **Notes** Gastronomic menu €85, Vegetarian available, Dress restrictions, Jacket & tie, Air con **Seats** 36, Pr/dining room 16 **Children** Portions **Parking** 100

Barberstown Castle

◎◎ Irish, French

Fine dining in a 13th-century castle with attractive grounds

☎ 01 6288157 📠 01 6277027
e-mail: barberstowncastle@ireland.com
dir: From Dublin take M50, exit for M4 at rdbt, follow signs for castle

A one-time castle turned country-house hotel, Barberstown features a series of elegant Victorian and Elizabethan dining rooms in the extensions to its original battlements, which come decked out with period furniture and overlook the gardens. Lunch can be taken in the airy conservatory tearoom, and aperitifs in the elegant drawing room, but dinner is an atmospheric occasion by candlelight. Service is appropriately professional, and the cooking firmly rooted in the classics while making the best of quality local produce. Presentation may be rather traditional, but flavours shine; take Gressingham duck two ways (seared breast and confit leg), perhaps delivered with wilted spinach, gratin potato and a melange of organic vegetables, while dessert might feature a nougat and mascarpone parfait.

Times 12.30-2.30/7-9.30 Closed 24-28 Dec, Jan, Mon-Tue, L Wed-Sat

The Byerley Turk

◎◎◎ — *see page 589*

Riverside Restaurant

◎ Traditional, Mediterranean

International cuisine next to Kilkenny Castle

☎ 056 7723388 📠 056 7723389
Kilkenny River Court Hotel, The Bridge, John St
e-mail: reservations@kilrivercourt.com
dir: Please telephone for directions

With Kilkenny Castle as a neighbour, views from this modern riverside hotel are always going to be good. Whether you're inside the elegant Georgian-styled restaurant looking through a wall of picture windows, or dining alfresco on the terrace, the 12th-century fortress lords it over the surrounding area. The wide-ranging menu takes an international approach to its cuisine, but thinks local in showcasing the best seasonal materials. Beech-smoked salmon teamed with Scandinavian potato salad might start things off, with mains running to a crown of duck from nearby Glenesk with olive oil mash, apple and sultana compôte and Calvados jus, or Bannow Bay sea bass with ginger and coriander marmalade, smoked paprika rice and lemongrass dressing.

Chef Gerrard Dunne **Owner** Xavier McAuliffe
Times 12.30-2.30/6-9.30 Closed 24-26 Dec, 25-26 Jan, L

Mon-Sat, D Sun (excl BH's) **Prices** Fixed L 3 course €16.50-€29.95, Fixed D 4 course €29.95-€49.95, Starter €6.50-€12.50, Main €18.25-€33, Dessert €8.50-€10.50 **Wines** 40 bottles over €20, 20 bottles under €20, 10 by glass **Notes** Sunday L, Vegetarian available, Dress restrictions, Smart casual preferred, Air con **Seats** 90, Pr/dining room 200 **Children** Portions, Menu **Parking** 70, NCP

Kendals Restaurant

◎ French NEW

A taste of France beside the golf course

☎ 056 7773000 📠 056 7773019
Mount Juliet Conrad Hotel
e-mail: info@mountjuliet.ie
dir: Just outside Thomastown, south on N9

It may not be a very Gallic-sounding name, but this - the second restaurant at the luxurious Mount Juliet Conrad resort - is designed as a French brasserie. Away from the main hotel in the golf clubhouse, it's a light and airy room with large windows looking out over the Jack Nicklaus-designed course. France dominates on the wine list and the menu is mainly made up of brasserie classics. Ingredients are fresh, locally sourced and often organic. A starter of haddock risotto is accurately cooked and topped with a soft hen's egg, a mousseline sauce and shavings of fennel, while organic spatchcocked poussin comes with a warm salad of Parmentier potatoes, spring onion and orange.

Times 6-9.30 Closed Sun & Tue

The Lady Helen Restaurant

◎◎ Modern French

Impressive mansion and country-house cooking

☎ 056 7773000 📠 056 7773019
Mount Juliet Conrad Hotel
e-mail: info@mountjuliet.ie
dir: Just outside Thomastown, south on N9

Standing in 1,500 acres of parkland overlooking the River Nore, this elegant 18th-century Georgian mansion hotel is a haven of gracious living and retains many original features. This extends to the formal and classically elegant Lady Helen Restaurant, which is decorated in grand country-house style and has lovely views. The cooking is likewise classical, Irish country-house cooking using local and organic produce, with fresh vegetables and herbs from the kitchen garden and game (perhaps venison) from the estate in season. Otherwise, look out for a glazed rump of Kilkenny lamb served with confit shoulder, potato fondant and a thyme jus, while from the sea, perhaps steamed John Dory teamed with a forest mushroom duxelle and smoked bacon broth.

Times 7-9.30 Closed Mon, Wed, L all week

The Landmark Hotel

◎ Modern International

Modern dining in a waterfront setting

☎ 071 9622222 📠 071 9622233
e-mail: reservations@thelandmarkhotel.com
dir: From Dublin on N4 approaching Carrick-on-Shannon, take 1st exit at rdbt, hotel on right

Facing the marina overlooking the River Shannon, the Landmark Hotel has a glorious waterside location. The fine dining evening restaurant CJ's is formally stylish with a Wedgwood blue and gold colour scheme and an antique fireplace as its centrepiece. The kitchen deals in creative modern dishes founded on classical French techniques, and served by affable staff. Start with home-made chicken liver pâté with cracked black pepper and warm onion bread, then move on to oven baked fillet of pork en croûte with sautéed asparagus, new potatoes, tarragon and cider cream. Finish with a fashionably retro knickerbocker glory.

Owner Ciaran & John Kelly **Times** 12-4/5-9 Closed 24-25 Dec **Prices** Starter €5-€9.50, Main €12-€21, Dessert €6, Service optional **Wines** 12 bottles over €20, 24 bottles under €20, 8 by glass **Notes** Sunday L, Vegetarian available, Civ Wed 300, Air con **Seats** 180, Pr/dining room 50 **Children** Portions, Menu **Parking** 150

The Sandstone Restaurant

◎ Modern French V ♨

Big flavours and a secluded setting

☎ 071 9632700 & 071 9632714 📠 071 9632710
Lough Rynn Castle
e-mail: enquiries@loughrynn.ie
dir: N4 Dublin to Sligo, Lough Rynn is located 8km off N4 & 2km from Mohill

Set in 300 acres of splendidly tranquil loughside scenery, this delightful country-house hotel has plenty to offer, including a brand new championship golf course and a charming walled garden. The Sandstone Restaurant, in the converted stables, is a comfortable and elegant space, with exposed stonework, high backed chairs and white-clothed tables. The kitchen are proud of their sourcing, with many of the ingredients coming from within County Leitrim. Begin with loin of rabbit, red pepper polenta, crispy chorizo and truffle oil sauce, followed by Leitrim loin of lamb, flageolet beans ragout and basil cream sauce. Lough Rynn's own take on the classic Jaffa cake should round things off nicely.

Chef Jean Michel Chevet **Owner** Hanly Group **Times** 12-2.30/6-9.45 Closed L Mon-Fri (open for private bookings only) **Prices** Fixed L 2 course €24-€28, Fixed D 3 course €42.50, Starter €8.50-€12, Main €25.50-€35, Dessert €8.50-€22, Service optional **Wines** 90+ bottles over €20, 8 by glass **Notes** Sunday L, Vegetarian menu, Civ Wed 450, Air con **Seats** 65, Pr/dining room 10 **Children** Portions, Menu **Parking** 100

CO LIMERICK

ADARE   Map 1 B3

Dunraven Arms

◎◎ Modern European

Traditional Irish cooking in charming village hotel

☎ 061 605900   ▤ 061 396541
e-mail: reservations@dunravenhotel.com
dir: Telephone for directions

A charming thatched coaching inn in a picture postcard village, the Dunraven Arms has a country-house feel. Expect comfort and plenty of atmosphere in this smart hotel with its lovely open fires, delightful garden and large windows looking over the handsome village. The elegant dining room offers modern European cuisine, with extensive use of fresh local produce. Local beef is one of the signature dishes here, carved from the trolley and served with red wine jus and horseradish sauce. Fish arrives daily from local boats and a suprême of Irish chicken might turn up roasted with scallion crushed potatoes and mushroom cream. Irish farmhouse cheeses jostle for attention alongside comforting puddings such as warm Bakewell tart with vanilla ice cream.

Chef Laurent Chabert **Owner** Bryan & Louis Murphy
Times 12.30-2.30/7-9.30 Closed L Mon-Sat
Prices Starter €6-€10, Main €11-€26, Dessert €5-€6.50,
Service added 12.5% **Wines** 25 bottles over €20, 25 bottles under €20, 6 by glass **Notes** Sunday L, Vegetarian available, Dress restrictions, Smart casual, Air con
Seats 80, Pr/dining room 30 **Children** Portions
Parking 60

CO MAYO

BALLINA   Map 1 B4

The Kitchen Restaurant

◎◎ Modern V ✋

A French interpretation of Ireland's natural bounty

☎ 096 74472   ▤ 096 74473
Mount Falcon Country, House Hotel, Foxford Rd
e-mail: info@mountfalcon.com
dir: On N26, 6m from Foxford & 3m from Ballina. Hotel on left

On the west bank of the river Moy, the Victorian greystone hotel sits in 100 acres of splendid woodland. Dining goes on in a very comfortable, elegantly appointed series of rooms that were once the kitchens and outhouses of the manor house. Service is informal and yet highly polished, and the cooking marries French expertise to the pick of Ireland's natural larder, not forgetting freshwater fish from the river. A seafood tasting plate featuring gravad lax, sea trout tartare and a crab beignet with horseradish cream might be one way to begin, or there could be quail breasts on lentils in red wine, a dish of great, powerful flavours. Loin of veal dusted with powdered ceps, served with potato dumplings and girolles, is a carefully timed, impressive main dish. Excellent breads and a trolley of petits fours add to the allure.

Chef Philip Farineau **Owner** Alan Maloney
Times 12.30-2/6.30-9.30 Closed 25-26 Dec **Prices** Food prices not confirmed for 2010. Please telephone for details. **Wines** 140 bottles over €20, 12 by glass
Notes Sunday L, Vegetarian menu, Civ Wed 200 **Seats** 80, Pr/dining room 14 **Children** Portions, Menu

CONG   Map 1 B4

The George V Dining Room

◎ Modern European V ✋

Lavish castle dining room serving classical cuisine

☎ 094 9546003   ▤ 094 9546260
Ashford Castle
e-mail: ashford@ashford.ie
dir: From Galway take N84 through Headford & Glencorrib towards Cross. Turn left for Cong. Ashford Castle gates in approx 5km

The Guinness family no longer live in the fairytale 13th-century Ashford Castle, but they are probably not bitter. The luxurious George V Room was originally designed to impress the eponymous royal when he visited and there's still a timeless opulence in its oak panelling, high plasterwork ceilings and palatial chandeliers. The formal table service (jacket and tie for gentlemen, if you please) and classical cooking style are in keeping with the sybaritic surroundings. The kitchen's repertoire is founded on French traditions, but lightened for modern tastes, so you might begin with chargrilled scallops on steamed barley and black pudding, and follow with pan-fried local turbot fillet, Killary harbour prawns and preserved apricot risotto, or a classic roast of the day carved at the table.

Chef Stefan Matz **Owner** Edward Holdings
Times 1-2/7-9.30 Closed L Mon-Sat **Prices** Fixed L fr €39, Fixed D 4 course €63-€65, Tasting menu €80-€95, Starter €18-€25, Main €28-€35, Dessert €12, Service added 15% **Wines** 600 bottles over €20, 12 by glass **Notes** Tasting menu 5-7 course, Sunday L, Vegetarian menu, Dress restrictions, Jacket & tie, Civ Wed 166 **Seats** 170, Pr/dining room 44 **Children** Portions, Menu **Parking** 115

Lisloughrey Lodge Hotel

◎◎ Modern Irish

Modern Irish cooking with spectacular lake views

☎ 094 9545400   ▤ 094 9545424
The Quay
e-mail: lodge@lisloughrey.ie
dir: Please telephone for directions

Overlooking Lough Corrib, this elegant lakeside country house is set in 10 acres of grounds and enjoys spectacular panoramic views of the lake, quay and surrounding woodland. Dating from 1824, it was once part of the Ashford estate and has been a boutique hotel since 2007, combining contemporary style and facilities with fine country-house tradition. The first floor has been restored to create the Salt Restaurant in 4 intimate rooms with a spectacular view of Lisloughrey Quay and the lake. Here you can enjoy modern Irish cuisine featuring top-

notch, fresh local ingredients and friendly, attentive service. Expect intelligent, simply-cooked dishes such as grilled baby calamari with white bean cassoulet and chilli oil, followed by pan-roasted Irish Angus beef tenderloin with red onion purée and wild chanterelles, sautéed foie gras and lemon thyme jus.

Chef Wade Murphy **Owner** Lisloughrey Lodge Trading
Times 6.30-10 Closed 24-26 Dec **Prices** Food prices not confirmed for 2010. Please telephone for details.
Wines 112 bottles over €20, 8 bottles under €20, 8 by glass **Notes** Vegetarian available, Civ Wed 180 **Seats** 56, Pr/dining room 14 **Children** Portions, Menu **Parking** 100

MULRANY   Map 1 A4

Nephin Restaurant

◎◎ Modern

Atlantic views and contemporary cooking

☎ 098 36000   ▤ 098 36899
Park Inn Hotel
e-mail: info@parkinnmulranny.ie
web: www.parkinnmulranny.ie
dir: From Westport take N59 throught Newport. R311 to Mulrany, hotel on right

A smart, bright and contemporary affair, the Nephin comes with stunning views over the Atlantic. It's set in an imposing and recently restored Victorian former railway hotel in 42 acres of grounds. The menus tread a classical path driven on by fresh, high-quality local and seasonal produce with the cooking displaying skill and an eye for presentation on a repertoire of carte, fixed-price and tasting options. Expect fillet of Irish beef with Carrowholly herb cheese glaze, shallot mousseline, mushroom pithivier and Madeira cream or perhaps Atlantic halibut teamed with spinach, cauliflower cream and a lemongrass and vanilla froth.

Times 7-9

WESTPORT Map 1 B4

Bluewave Restaurant

⊚ Modern European

Fine local produce and spectacular views

☎ 098 29000 ▤ 098 29111
Carlton Atlantic Coast Hotel, The Quay
e-mail: info@atlanticcoasthotel.com
dir: From Westport take coast road towards Louisburgh
for 1m. Hotel on harbour on left

A rooftop restaurant located in a modern hotel in a
converted woollen mill on Westport Harbour, Bluewave
has stunning views of the islands of Clew Bay. Sitting
under the shadow of Croagh Patrick, the 18th-century
building has been carefully restored to preserve the
original stonework façade. The daily-changing menu
makes good use of the finest local produce, especially
fresh fish, so expect dishes such as steamed Clew Bay
mussels in a tomato and basil sauce, followed by
chargrilled sirloin of beef with a carrot and coconut
purée, herb butter and thyme jus.

Times 6.30-9.15 Closed 20-27 Dec, L all week

Knockranny House Hotel

⊚ Modern, Traditional

Ambitious cooking and fabulous views

☎ 098 28600 ▤ 098 28611
e-mail: info@khh.ie
dir: On N5 (Dublin to Castlebar road), hotel on left before
entering Westport

A magical landscape surrounds this modern hotel, with
breathtaking views of Clew Bay and Croagh Patrick.
Tables in the elegant, split-level restaurant, La Fougère,
are dressed with white linen and fine silverware, and
large windows offer great views. There's a choice of table
d'hôte, à la carte and tasting menus, featuring modern
and traditional cuisine, with a huge emphasis on top-
quality local and seasonal ingredients, including smoked
products from the hotel's own kiln. Typically complex
dishes might include Irish beef fillet served with a
braised shin ravioli, nettle glaze, brisket, mushroom
paste, celeriac and horseradish velouté.

Chef Seamus Commons **Owner** Adrian & Geraldine
Noonan **Times** 6.30-9.30 Closed Xmas **Prices** Tasting
menu €74, Service optional **Wines** 6 by glass **Notes** Fixed
D 6 course €54, Sunday L, Vegetarian available, Dress

restrictions, Smart casual, Civ Wed 300, Air con
Seats 140 **Children** Portions **Parking** 200

CO MEATH

KILMESSAN Map 1 D5

The Station House Hotel & Signal Restaurant

⊚ European, Mediterranean

Country-house cooking in a converted railway station

☎ 046 9025239 & 9025586 ▤ 046 9025588
e-mail: info@thestationhousehotel.com
dir: From Dublin N3 to Dunshaughlin, R125 to Kilmessan

Surrounded by acres of tranquil gardens and woodland,
the former railway station is now a quirky, family-run
hotel, noted for its charming atmosphere and as a venue
for family celebrations. Expect good country-house
cooking with a touch of French flair in the cosy Signal
Restaurant. Top quality local ingredients are sourced and
skilfully treated, and the menus are truly seasonal.
Typical dishes are seared scallops with black pudding
and apple chutney, followed by rack of lamb with
ratatouille and rosemary jus. Bar food is served in the
Platform Bar and Lounge.

Chef David Mulvihill **Owner** Chris & Thelma Slattery
Times 12.30-3/4.30-10.30 **Prices** Fixed L 2 course €10-
€30, Fixed D 3 course €15-€45, Starter €7-€15, Main
€12-€40, Dessert €5-€10, Service optional **Wines** 8
bottles over €20, 29 bottles under €20, 4 by glass
Notes Sunday L, Vegetarian available, Civ Wed 120
Seats 90, Pr/dining room 180 **Children** Portions, Menu
Parking 200

CO MONAGHAN

CARRICKMACROSS Map 1 C4

Restaurant at Nuremore

⊚⊚⊚ – *see opposite page*

CO SLIGO

SLIGO Map 1 B5

The Glasshouse

⊚ Modern

Contemporary cuisine overlooking the Garavogue River

☎ 071 9194300 ▤ 071 9194301
Swan Point
e-mail: info@theglasshouse.ie
web: www.theglasshouse.ie

Relax with an aperitif in the striking Glasshouse hotel's
View Bar - so-named because of its fantastic setting
looking out over the Garavogue River - before settling
down to dinner in The Kitchen. The bright restaurant is
intimate and colourful with a Mediterranean vibe and
those same great river views. Contemporary
interpretations of classic dishes are on offer, with some
unusual but effective combinations. Lissadell mussels
with lemongrass, basil and wine makes a fine starter,
followed by pork fillet wrapped in Parma ham with
Clonakilty black pudding cake and shallot jus. Finish with
After Eight cheesecake or summer fruit mousse.

Times 12-5/6.30-9.30

Restaurant at Nuremore

Modern French **V**

Innovative cuisine with bold combinations at country-house hotel

☎ 042 9661438 📄 042 9661853
e-mail: info@nuremore.com
web: www.nuremore.com
dir: 11m from M1, junct 14 Ardee exit (N33)

Nuremore is a golfer's paradise with its championship course surrounded by gently undulating Monaghan countryside. But it's not all about golf: the country-house hotel is a classy bolthole for anyone who fancies a spot of pampering in the spa complex and a bit of peace and quiet in its acres of parkland. The refurbished dining room is a smartly formal venue with a conservatory extension and lovely views over gardens to the lake. Chef Ray McArdle brings a wealth of pedigree experience to the kitchen and has a go-ahead approach to keeping his brigade's skills sharp by sending them to top London restaurants to see how things are done there. It's a policy that clearly pays off as there are great things happening here: imagination and solid technique are evident in contemporary dishes founded on meticulously-sourced materials put together in well-balanced combinations that look great on the plate. A well-motivated and attentive front-of-house team keeps things ticking over with effortless efficiency. Waffle-free menu descriptions belie the intricate work that goes into each dish. Classical French foundations are clear in starters such as seared Wexford scallops with braised beef daube and broccoli pannacotta, or a riff on rabbit that serves up sautéed loin of Anjou rabbit with rabbit tortellini and velouté. For main course, try a celebration of Old Spot pork from Fermanagh with Bulmer's candy, choucroute and Calvados jus, and finish with caramelised pear terrine with almond milk ice cream.

Chef Raymond McArdle **Owner** Gilhooly Family **Times** 12.30-2.30/6.30-9.45 Closed L Sat **Prices** Fixed L 2 course €20-€30, Fixed D 4 course €52.50-€60, Service optional **Wines** 153 bottles over €20, 18 by glass **Notes** Prestige menu, Sunday L, Vegetarian menu, Civ Wed 200, Air con **Seats** 120, Pr/dining room 50 **Children** Portions, Menu **Parking** 200

CO TIPPERARY

CASHEL
Map 1 C3

Bishops Buttery Restaurant

Traditional French

Country-house cuisine set in former ecclesiastical kitchens

☎ 062 62707 ▤ 062 61521
Cashel Palace Hotel, Main St
e-mail: reception@cashel-palace.ie
dir: On main street in town centre

Once home to archbishops, earls and lords, this elegant hotel in a Queen Anne house in the centre of Cashel truly deserves the palace epithet. It oozes history from its magnificent red pine staircases, wood panelling and grand rooms; the Bishop's Buttery Restaurant lies in an atmospheric flagstoned basement with vaulted ceilings. The cooking is French in inspiration, and Irish in provenance of the ingredients it is built upon. Seared Dublin Bay prawns are served with broccoli purée, herb gnocchi, lemon and saffron oil for starters, while mains might be veal cutlet marinated in herb oil with a fricassée of veal sweetbreads and spinach, and redcurrant jus.

Chef Shane McGonigle **Owner** Patrick & Susan Murphy **Times** 12-2.30/6-9.30 Closed 24-27 Dec **Prices** Fixed L 2 course €14-€24, Fixed D 3 course fr €30, Starter €6-€13.50, Main €24-€34, Dessert €8-€11, Service optional **Wines** 2 bottles over €20, 2 bottles under €20, 6 by glass **Notes** Sunday L, Vegetarian available, Dress restrictions, Smart casual, Civ Wed 130 **Seats** 60, Pr/dining room 20 **Children** Portions, Menu **Parking** 60

CO WATERFORD

WATERFORD
Map 1 C2

Athenaeum House Hotel

Modern European

Innovative food in a luxury boutique hotel

☎ 051 833999 ▤ 051 833977
Christendom, Ferrybank
e-mail: info@athenaeumhousehotel.com
dir: From station on N25 towards Rosslare, through lights, then right, next right

Sympathetically restored in contemporary style, this 18th-century house stands in 10 acres of parkland on the banks of the River Suir, with views across Waterford. Offering comfort and luxury, the impressive boutique hotel offers chic bedrooms and Zaks, a bright and airy conservatory-style restaurant with period furnishings, contemporary art and innovative, modern European food. Local and seasonal foods from artisan suppliers are cooked with care and consistency, as seen in a well-flavoured smoked ham hock rillette, served with red onion marmalade, and a meltingly tender braised daube of beef accompanied by fondant potato and rustic braised carrots.

Chef James Crawford **Owner** Stan & Mailo Power **Times** 12.30-3.30/7-9.30 Closed 25-27 Dec **Prices** Fixed L 3 course €23, Fixed D 3 course €29, Starter fr €5.50, Main €8-€12, Dessert €8-€11.50, Service optional **Wines** 7 bottles over €20, 9 bottles under €20, 10 by glass **Notes** Sunday L, Vegetarian available, Civ Wed 70, Air con **Seats** 100, Pr/dining room 30 **Children** Portions, Menu **Parking** 40

Faithlegg House Hotel

Irish

Country-house cooking in elegant dining room

☎ 051 382000 ▤ 051 382010
Faithlegg
e-mail: reservations@fhh.ie

This 18th-century mansion - a former stately home and school - has been sensitively restored to form the centrepiece of this hotel and golf course overlooking the River Suir estuary. Its elegant, spacious Roseville Rooms Restaurant reflects its past, with original high ceilings and decorative plasterwork, furnished in classic country-house style and with views of the gardens. The cooking follows the theme, solid country house with some European influences, classically presented (if a tad on the old-fashioned side) but admirably taking its cue from quality local ingredients; perhaps a roast rack of Commeragh mountain lamb served with pommes dauphinoise and a claret jus.

Times 6.30-9.30 Closed Xmas, L Mon-Sat

Waterford Castle - Munster Dining Room

Modern, Traditional

Modern interpretations of the classics in romantic castle setting

☎ 051 878203 ▤ 051 879316
The Island
e-mail: info@waterfordcastle.com
dir: Please telephone for directions

You know you're going somewhere a bit special when the ferry meets you for the short hop to this 800-year old castle on its own 310-acre island complete with an 18-hole championship golf course. The Elizabethan oak-panelled Munster Dining Room is a suitably lordly setting for seasonal set menus that showcase superb seafood landed nearby at Dunmore East, as well as local meats and cheeses and organic vegetables. Modern country-house cooking is the order of the day, with well-handled sauces and creatively-married flavours. Beef tongue and cheek salad is served with horseradish mayonnaise, salsa verde and shavings of Glebe Brethan cheese in a typical starter; up next might be a Mediterranean-tinged roast cod with peperonata, aïoli, tapenade and parmesan crisp.

Times 12.30-1.45/7-9 Closed Xmas, early Jan, L Mon-Sat

CO WESTMEATH

ATHLONE
Map 1 C4

Hodson Bay

Traditional, International

Loughside hotel with fine dining

☎ 090 6442000 ▤ 090 6442020
Hodson Bay
e-mail: info@hodsonbayhotel.com
dir: From Athlone follow Roscommon signs. Approx 2.5m, on entering Hodson Bay follow hotel signs. Hotel on right

Situated on the shore of Lough Ree, this attractive modern spa hotel is full of contemporary comforts. A range of dining rooms and bars is on hand, with L'Escale being the smart option. Service is friendly, and the cooking distinguished by clear flavours and well-sourced ingredients. A seafood and mozzarella tart has a succulent filling of prawns and mussels in wine and tarragon. Main course might be roast leg of lamb, carved at the table, served on a bed of shallots in sauce Robert, with a nutty butternut squash purée. Seasonal strawberries make a fine dessert, sandwiched between discs of meringue and whipped cream.

Times 12.30-2.15/7-9.30

Wineport Lodge

Modern, Classical

Modern Irish cuisine in glorious lakeside setting

☎ 090 6439010 ▤ 090 6485471
Glasson
e-mail: lodge@wineport.ie

Forget country house chintz: Wineport is a new breed of contemporary lodge, clad in cedar and with huge windows and long balconies designed to make the most of its glorious pitch on the shores of Lough Ree on the Shannon. Turn up by boat or by car, and dine on the deck or in the airy dining room to uplifting views and friendly service. Modern Irish cooking is the kitchen's forté, seen at its best in the wild and organic tasting menu. Sea bass and scallops with piquillo peppers, raisin and capers and roast chorizo oil show the style. In keeping with its name - a nod to the ancient wine trade with early Christian monasteries at Clonmacnoise - there's a serious approach to quality wine here.

Times 3-10/6-10 Closed 24-26 Dec, L Mon-Sat

CO WEXFORD

GOREY   Map 1 D3

Marlfield House

◎◎ Classic

Elegant restaurant in a country-house setting

☎ 053 9421124   📠 053 942 1572
Courtown Rd
e-mail: info@marlfieldhouse.ie
dir: N11 junct 23, follow signs to Courtown. Turn left for Gorey at Courtown Road Rdbt, hotel 1m on the left

Glorious Regency grandeur oozes from this luxurious family-run country-house hotel. The opulent Wexford home of the Earls of Courtown has been receiving guests in style since it opened its doors for grand house parties in 1830, and still delivers top-drawer service with aplomb. Cocktails served in the elegant library are a prelude to dining in the flower-filled conservatory restaurant, where frescoed walls and manicured gardens make a memorable backdrop for its Mediterranean-influenced French cuisine. Vegetables and herbs from the kitchen garden supplement locally-sourced ingredients as the basis for succinct four-course menus. Ravioli of braised ham and foie gras with butternut squash broth and sage beurre noisette, and crab-crusted halibut fillet with watercress purée, roasted ratte potatoes, tomato ragout and beurre blanc are typical examples of the style.

Chef Conor MacCann **Owner** The Bowe Family
Times 12.30-2/7-9 Closed 1 Jan-28 Feb, L Mon-Sat
Prices Fixed L 2 course €22-€28, Fixed D 4 course €67-€70, Groups min 6 service 10% **Wines** 200 bottles over €20, 20 bottles under €20, 6 by glass **Notes** Sunday L, Vegetarian available, Dress restrictions, Smart dress, no jeans, Civ Wed 130, Air con **Seats** 70, Pr/dining room 50 **Parking** 100

The Rowan Tree Restaurant

◎ Modern, International

Enjoyable dining in modern spa hotel

☎ 053 9480500   📠 053 9480777
Ashdown Park Hotel, The Coach Rd
e-mail: info@ashdownparkhotel.com
dir: On approach to Gorey town take N11 from Dublin. Take left signed for Courtown. Hotel on left

The Ashdown Park Hotel is a swish modern spa and leisure retreat on the fringes of the pretty town of Gorey, handy for beaches and golf courses to hone the appetite.

The Rowan Tree Restaurant is a stylish place looking over the rooftop garden, with a classical pianist tinkling away to boost the sense of occasion. The kitchen makes use of prime local produce in a repertoire that embraces uncomplicated European and international dishes. You might start with a chorizo and feta cheese tartlet with red pepper salsa and follow with crispy pork belly, sautéed potatoes with smoked pancetta and apple sauce, or braised Wicklow venison shank on leek mash with juniper sauce.

Times 12.30-2.30/6-9.30 Closed 24-25 Dec, L Mon-Sat

ROSSLARE   Map 1 D2

Beaches

◎ Traditional European

Classic country-house cooking in a family-run seafront hotel

☎ 053 9132114   📠 053 9132222
Kelly's Resort Hotel & Spa
e-mail: kellyhot@iol.ie

The resort hotel on a stretch of unspoiled sandy beach in Rosslare has been in the same family ownership since the late Victorian era. Its principal restaurant, Beaches, is restful on the eye, with a light colour palette, potted plants and crisp linen. Fixed-price menus offer plenty of choice, from a range of classic Irish country-house dishes. Expect local seafood terrine with sauce verte, and then something like grilled Wicklow venison steak with wild mushrooms in Madeira jus, followed up by passionfruit bavarois, colourfully adorned with summer berries. Simpler fare is on offer in La Marine bistro and bar.

Times 1-2/7.30-9 Closed mid Dec-mid Feb

La Marine Bistro

◎ Modern

Bistro-style cooking at a smart seaside resort hotel

☎ 053 9132114   📠 053 9132222
Kelly's Resort Hotel & Spa
e-mail: kellyhot@iol.ie

Kelly's Resort is a seriously smart hotel beside Rosslare's vast sandy beach and the maritime décor within La Marine Bistro, the stand-alone restaurant in the complex, reflects its location. Expect a relaxed and informal atmosphere, views of the bustling kitchen, and competently cooked bistro-style food. Dishes are uncomplicated, with fresh ingredients cooked with care and simplicity. Local seafood is a feature, for example creamy seafood and saffron chowder and pan-fried plaice with tomato and brandy butter. Meaty options include rib-eye steak with garlic and red wine jus, with sticky toffee crème brûlée to finish.

Times 12.30-2/6.30-9

WEXFORD   Map 1 D3

Newbay Country House & Restaurant

◎ Modern European 🖵

Popular country-house dining with excellent, simply-prepared dishes

☎ 053 9142779   📠 053 9146318
Newbay, Carrick
e-mail: newbay@newbayhouse.com
dir: Take Cork road from Wexford, left after Citroen garage, at x-rds turn right, restaurant on right

A short drive from Wexford town, Newbay is a handsome late-Georgian country house in 25 acres of mature gardens and parkland with a brace of Wexford's top tables. The Cellar Bistro, done out in yellow ochre and blond wood floors is the more casual option where you can breeze between the bar and heated outdoor terrace. Upstairs is the fine-dining restaurant, where the kitchen deals in top-quality ingredients handled simply and with confidence to let the flavours do the talking. The hotel's own trawler brings in the fish, so piscine pleasures have to be high on the hit-list. A hotpot of mussels with leek and vermouth cream is a sound way to start, then follow with cannon of monkfish with forest mushroom and rocket fettuccine.

Times 12-3/6-9.30 Closed Xmas, New Year, L Mon-Thu

WEXFORD *continued*

Seasons Restaurant

◉ Modern International

Friendly hotel with imaginative menu

☎ 053 9143444 ▤ 053 9146399
Whitford House Hotel, New Line Road
e-mail: info@whitford.ie
dir: From Rosslare ferry port take N25. At Duncannon Rd
rdbt right onto R733, hotel immediately on left. 1.5m
from Wexford

The Whitford House Hotel is a well-established family-run
hotel and leisure club, hugely popular in the Wexford area
as a base for breaks to the sandy beaches and golf
courses of Ireland's sunny South East. Live classical
piano or guitar music accompanies dinner in the Seasons
Restaurant at weekends. The menu descriptions of the
modern Irish and European dishes are refreshingly
simple, and belie the careful preparation and sound
technical skills that have gone into the likes of braised
loin of lamb with rustic vegetables, roast Cajun monkfish
with cumin cream, or confit of duck leg on warm potato
salad.

Chef Siobhan Devereux **Owner** The Whitty Family
Times 12.30-3/7-9 Closed 24-27 Dec, L Mon-Sat
Prices Fixed L 2 course €21-€24.95, Fixed D 3 course
€31.50, Starter €5-€12.50, Main €17.50-€24.50, Dessert
€7.50-€8.50, Service optional **Wines** 15 bottles over €20,
42 bottles under €20 **Notes** Sunday L, Vegetarian
available, Air con **Seats** 100 **Children** Portions, Menu
Parking 150

MACREDDIN Map 1 D3

The Strawberry Tree Restaurant

◉◉ Modern Irish ✿

**Dramatic dining venue specialising in organic and wild
food**

☎ 0402 36444 ▤ 0402 36580
Brooklodge Hotel & Wells Spa
e-mail: info@brooklodge.com
dir: From Dublin take N11, turn off at Rathnew for
Rathdrum, then through Aughrim to Macreddin (2m)

Ireland's first certified organic restaurant is situated in
the luxurious country-house Brooklodge Hotel, part of the
purpose-built Macreddin Village, which includes a
country pub and brewery, café, bakery, smokehouse,
Italian restaurant, equestrian centre, 18-hole golf course
and spa. Strawberry Tree's dining area occupies 3 grand
rooms, each with mirrored ceilings, modern lighting and
dark blue décor. The kitchen takes a modern approach,
but with the sourcing of ingredients - both organic and
wild, combined with seasonality - at the heart of
everything. Creativity and skill is evident throughout; beef
fillet is served with buttered beetroot and balsamic jus,
while guinea fowl comes with a dried-fruit compôte, and
from the sea, perhaps pan-fried John Dory with Swiss
chard and saffron cream.

Chef Tim Daly, Evan Doyle **Owner** The Doyle Family
Times 7-9.30 Closed L all week **Prices** Food prices not
confirmed for 2010. Please telephone for details.
Wines 10 bottles under €20, 21 by glass
Notes Vegetarian available, Dress restrictions, Smart
casual, Civ Wed 200, Air con **Seats** 90, Pr/dining room 50
Children Portions **Parking** 200

RATHNEW Map 1 D3

Hunter's Hotel

◉ Traditional French

Beautiful views and 300 years of history

☎ 0404 40106 ▤ 0404 40338
e-mail: reception@hunters.ie
dir: N11 exit at Wicklow/Rathnew junct. 1st left onto
R761. Restaurant 0.25m before village

Ireland's oldest coaching inn set in lovely gardens on the
banks of the River Varty has been in the same family for
5 generations since 1820. Hunter's Hotel has an
inimitable charm that only comes from such stability and
a healthy disinterest in the ephemeral vagaries of
fashion, bolstered by excellent staff who have a well-
earned reputation for friendliness and hospitality. The
kitchen sticks resolutely to its repertoire of classic
country-house cooking, letting first-class local and
seasonal produce speak for itself in accurately-cooked
dishes. Typical starters include Moroccan lamb salad on
couscous, followed by pan-fried sea bass with sundried
tomato tapenade, and a simple rhubarb fool for dessert.

Times 12.45-3/7.30-9 Closed 3 days Xmas

WOODENBRIDGE Map 1 D3

Redmond Restaurant

◉ Irish

Traditional Irish cooking in a charming setting

☎ 0402 35146 ▤ 0402 35573
Woodenbridge Hotel
e-mail: info@woodenbridgehotel.com
dir: 7km from Arklow

The Woodenbridge Hotel, in the green and wooded Vale of
Avoca, has just celebrated its 400th birthday. Although
it's gained a few modern extensions since opening as a
coaching inn on the old Dublin to Wexford highway back
in 1608, the hotel has retained its traditional charm. For
traditional Irish cooking, head to The Redmond
Restaurant. The menu features plenty of fresh fish and
local game and lamb in season. Start with the home-
made chicken and vegetable soup, following on with a
fresh and accurately cooked salmon steak simply
presented with fresh vegetables, all accompanied by
plenty of excellent wheaten soda bread and butter.

Times 12.30-3/7-9

Book into AA rated hotels from the comfort of your home. How very accommodating

If you're looking for a hotel or B&B visit theAA.com/travel first. You can book hundreds of AA rated establishments there and then

- All accommodation is rated from one to five stars with detailed listings
- 5% discount available for AA Members at many hotels – look for the Members' 5% off – book it buttons
- Fantastic offers also available on the hotel and B&B homepage

AA Route Planner – guides you through every step of your journey

If you're planning on going on a long journey and need to find a stop over or two on the way, simply go to the AA's new and improved Route Planner. With its new mapping powered by Google™, you just scroll over your route to find available hotels at every step of your journey.

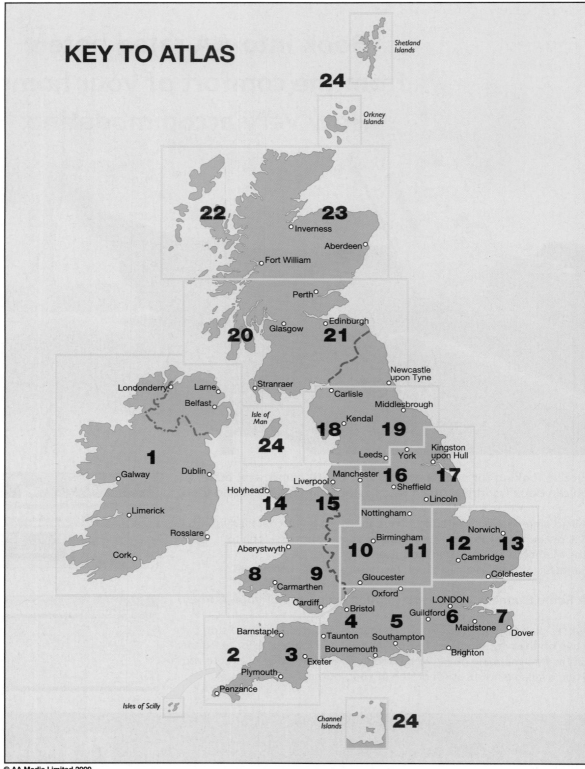

KEY TO ATLAS

Shetland Islands

24

Orkney Islands

22 **23**

Inverness

Aberdeen

Fort William

Perth

20 Edinburgh

Glasgow **21**

Newcastle upon Tyne

Stranraer

Londonderry Larne Carlisle Middlesbrough

Belfast **18** Kendal **19**

Isle of Man

1 **24** Leeds York Kingston upon Hull

Galway Dublin Manchester **16** **17**

Liverpool Sheffield

Limerick Holyhead **14** **15** Lincoln

Rosslare Nottingham

Cork Aberystwyth Birmingham Norwich

10 **11** **12** **13**

8 **9** Cambridge

Carmarthen Gloucester Colchester

Cardiff Oxford LONDON

Bristol **4** **5** Guildford **6** **7**

Barnstaple Taunton Southampton Maidstone Dover

2 **3** Bournemouth Brighton

Exeter

Plymouth

Penzance

Isles of Scilly

Channel Islands **24**

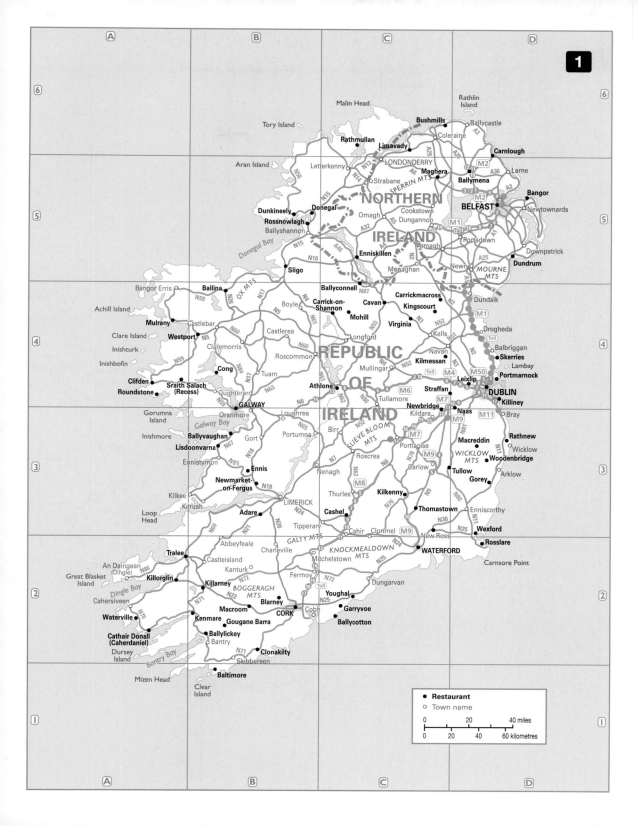

Legend:

M6 — Motorway/toll motorway
Motorway junction full/restricted. Service area
A33 — Primary route single/dual carriageway
A34 — Other A road single/dual carriageway
B3400 — B road
Unclassified road
V — Vehicle ferry
C — Fast vehicle ferry or catamaran
●Spalding — Restaurant
○Oundle — Town/Village name
National boundary
ESSEX — English county name & boundary
CONWY — Welsh county name & boundary
MORAY — Scottish county name & boundary
National Park

Isles of Scilly inset:

ISLES OF SCILLY
Bryher, Tresco, St Martin's, Higher Town
New Grimsby, Hugh Town, St Mary's, Old Town, St Agnes
Middle Town
ISLES OF SCILLY (ST MARY'S)
SV

Main map place names:

Lundy
Hartland Point
Hartland
Morwenstow
Kilkhampton
Bude
Bude Bay
Widemouth Bay
Crackington Haven
Week St Mary
Boscastle
Tintagel
Delabole
Camelford
Port Isaac
Polzeath
Harlyn
Rock
Padstow
Porthcothan
Wadebridge
St Tudy
Bolventor
BODMIN MOOR
Blisland
St Clee
CORNWALL
Bodmin
Dobwalls
Liskeard
Mawgan Porth
St Mawgan
St Columb Major
Lanivet
St Keyne
Watergate Bay
Newquay
West Pentire
Roche
Bugle
St Blazey
Lostwithiel
Golant
Pelynt
Perranporth
Summercourt
St Austell
Tywardreath
Polperro
St Agnes
Ladock
St Stephen
Fowey
Polruan
Tallar Bay
Porthtowan
Marazanvose
Grampound
Pentewan
Portreath
St Day
Tregony
Mevagissey
St Ives Bay
Gwithian
Redruth
Carnon Downs
Truro
Gorran Haven
St Ives
Zennor
Lelant
Hayle
Camborne
Ruan High Lanes
Portloe
Veryan
St Just-in-Roseland
Portscatho
St Just
Penryn
Portscatho
St Mawes
PENZANCE
Marazion
Falmouth
Penzance
Perranuthnoe
Constantine
Mawnan Smith
Newlyn
Praa Sands
Helston
LAND'S END
Sennen
St Buryan
Porthleven
Gweek
Manaccan
Porthcurno
Treen
Mousehole
St Keverne
Mullion
Coverack
Lizard
Cadgwith
Lizard Point

SW

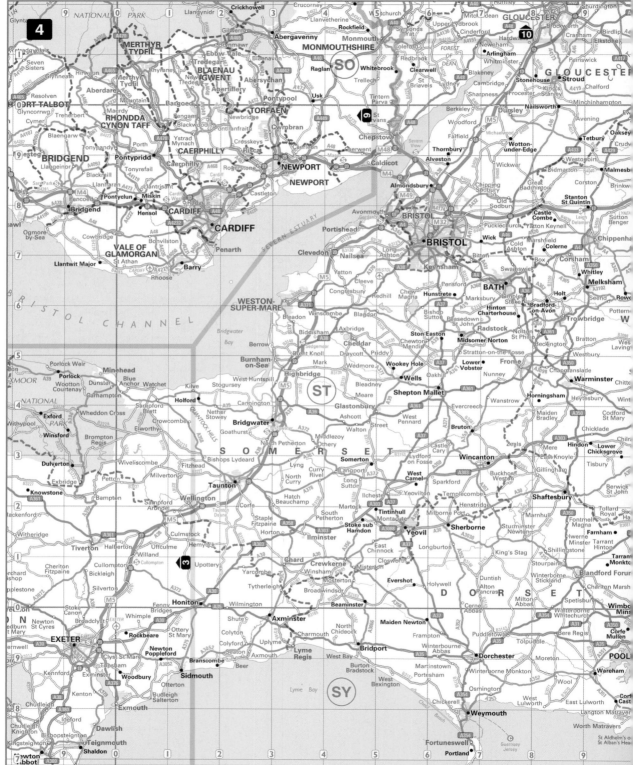

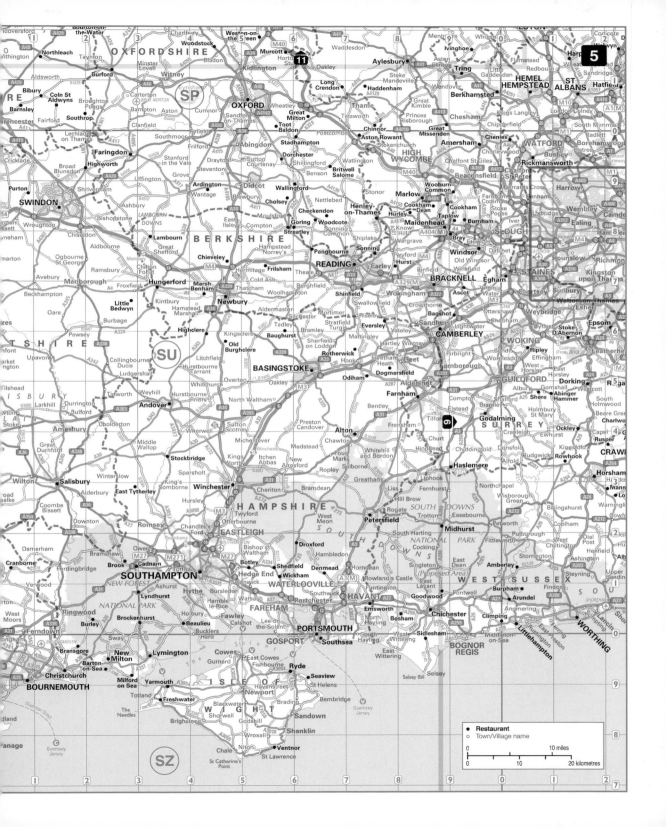

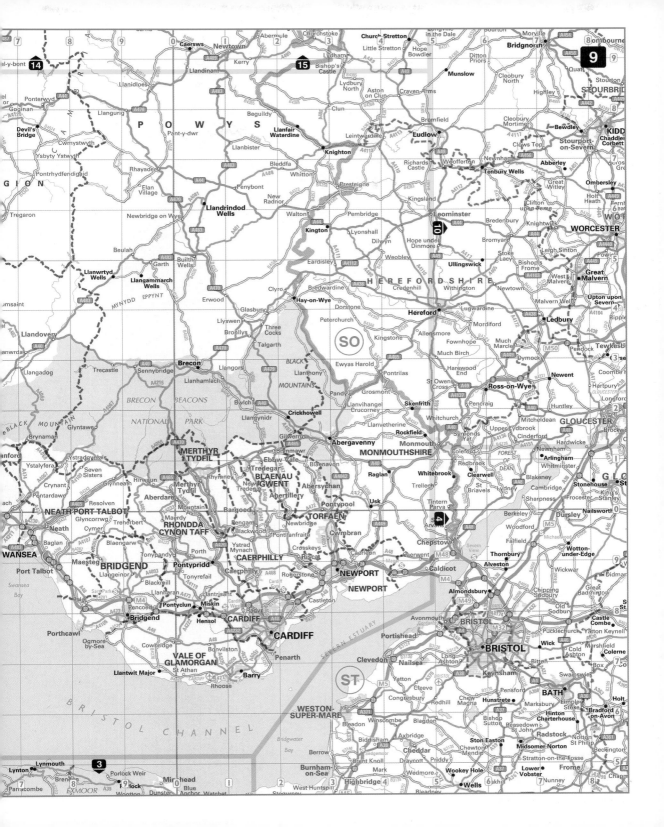

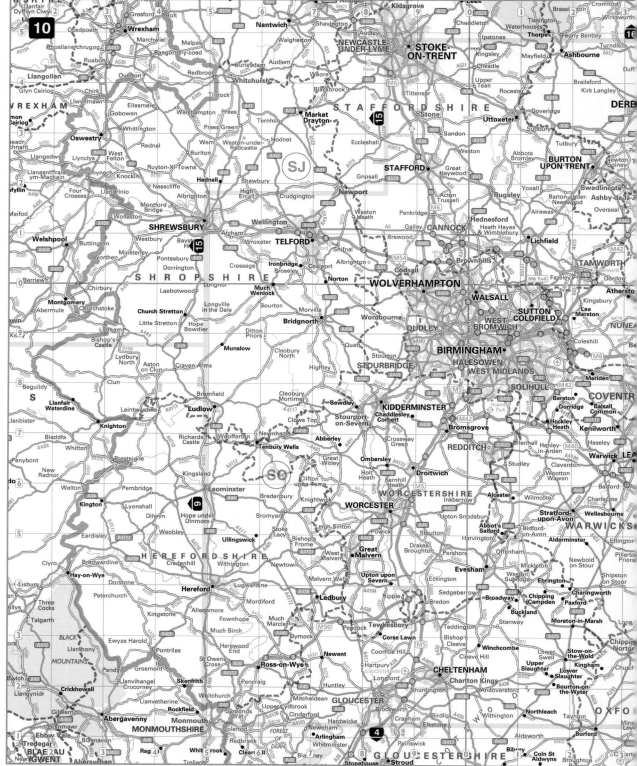

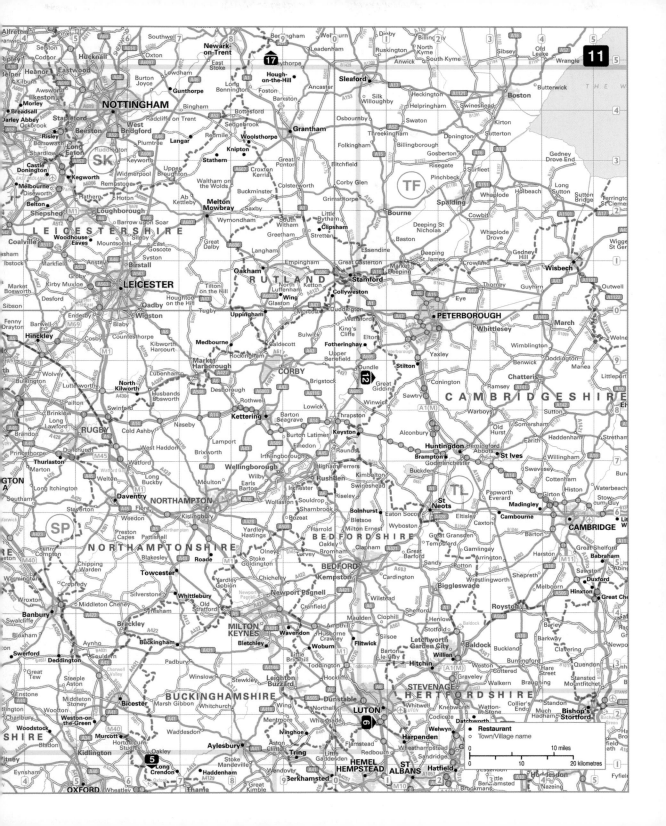

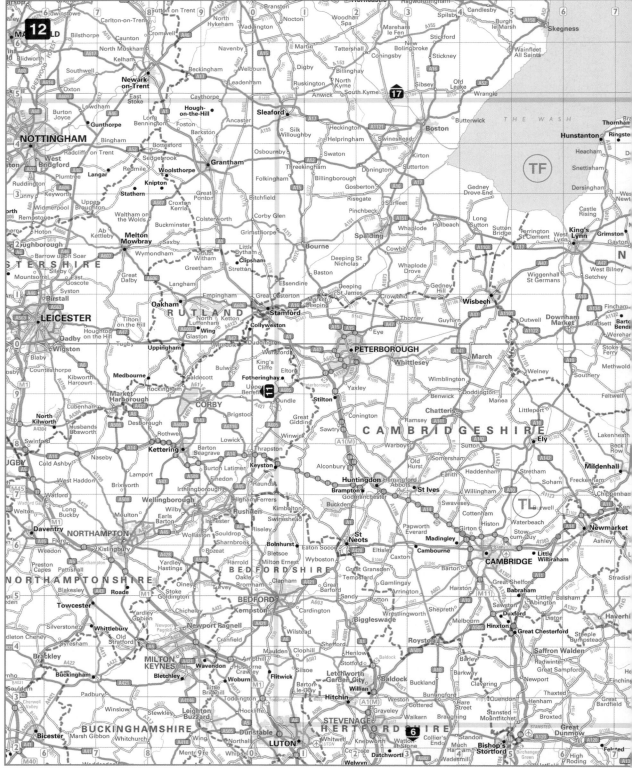

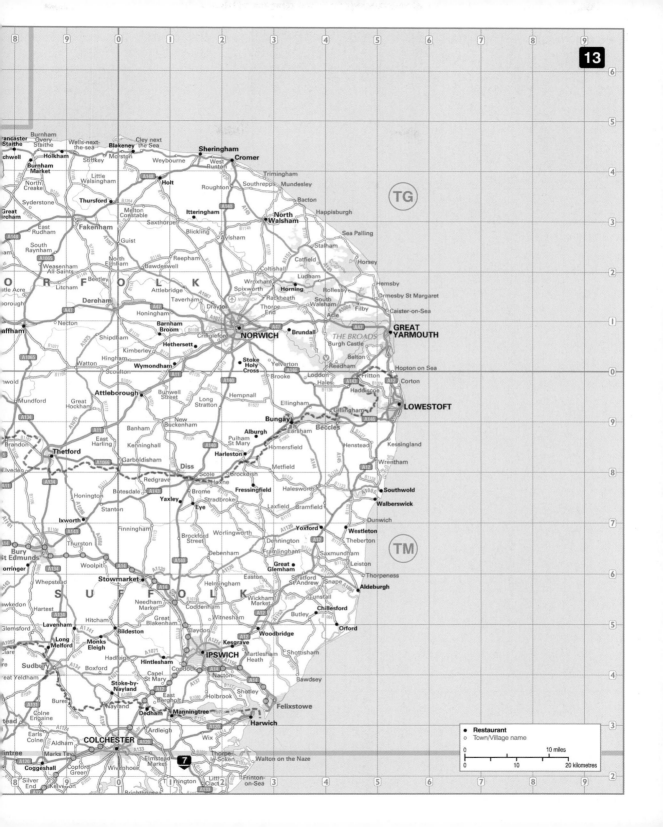

14

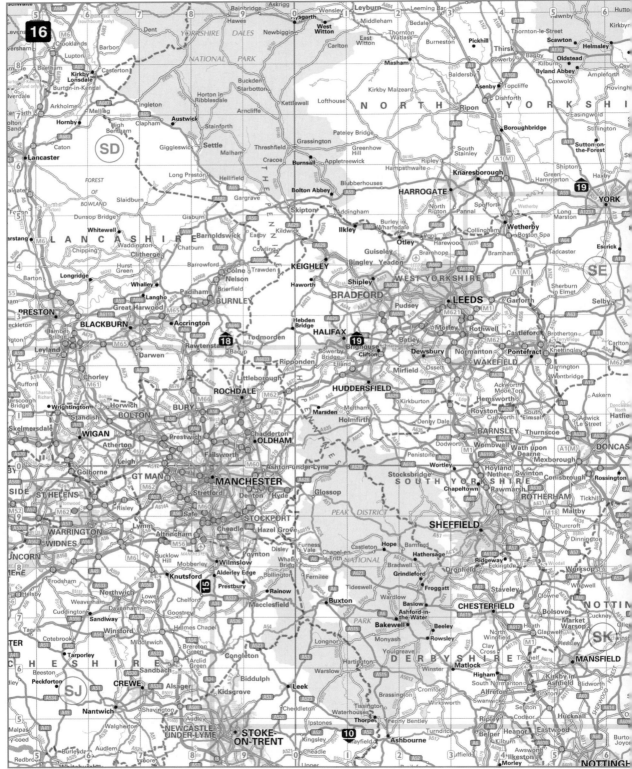

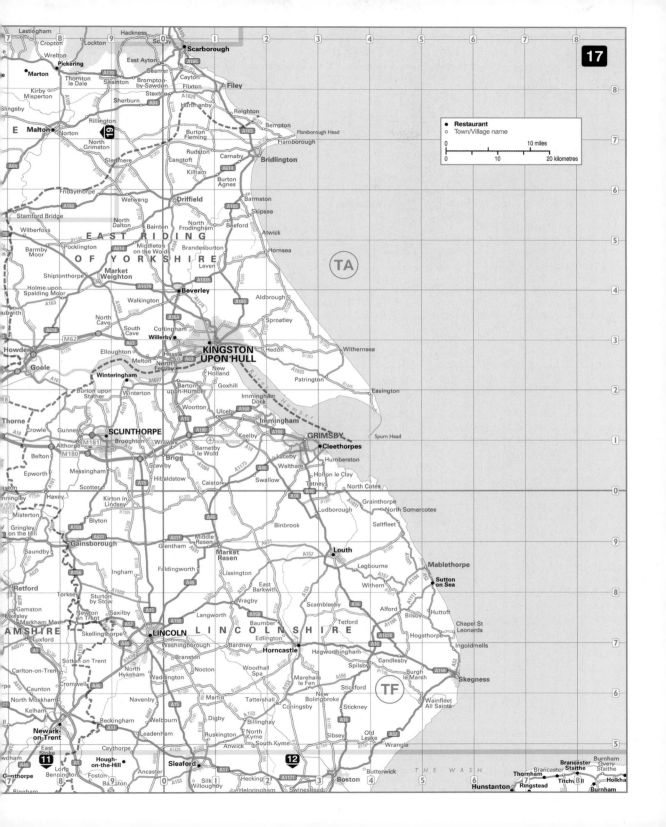

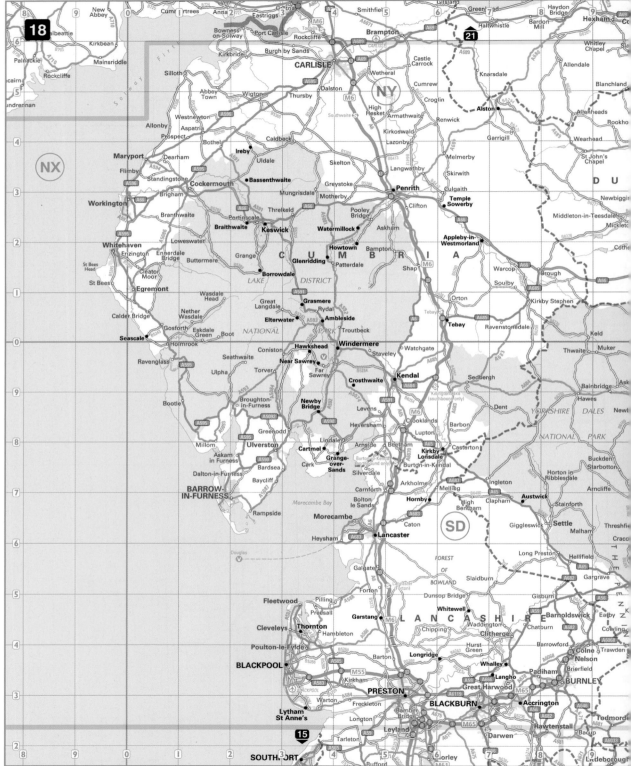

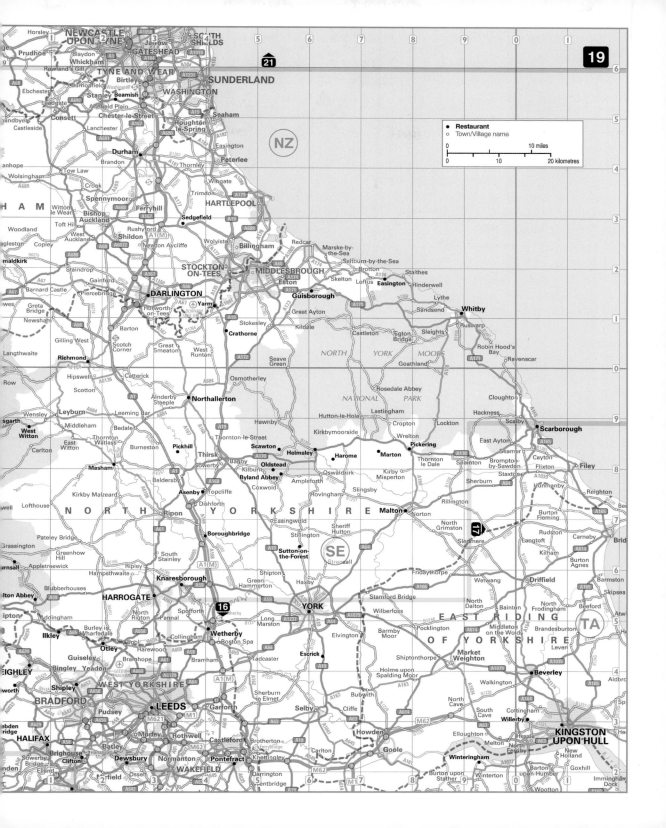

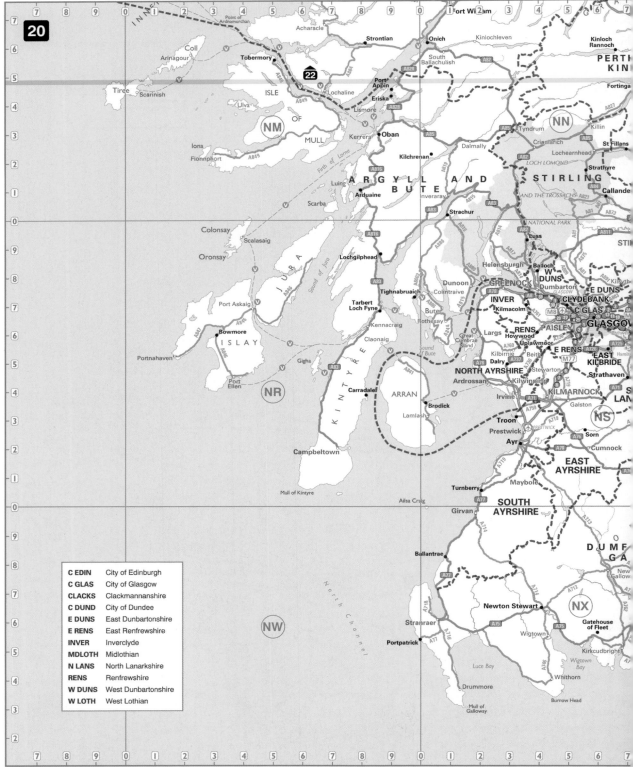

C EDIN	City of Edinburgh
C GLAS	City of Glasgow
CLACKS	Clackmannanshire
C DUND	City of Dundee
E DUNS	East Dunbartonshire
E RENS	East Renfrewshire
INVER	Inverclyde
MDLOTH	Midlothian
N LANS	North Lanarkshire
RENS	Renfrewshire
W DUNS	West Dunbartonshire
W LOTH	West Lothian

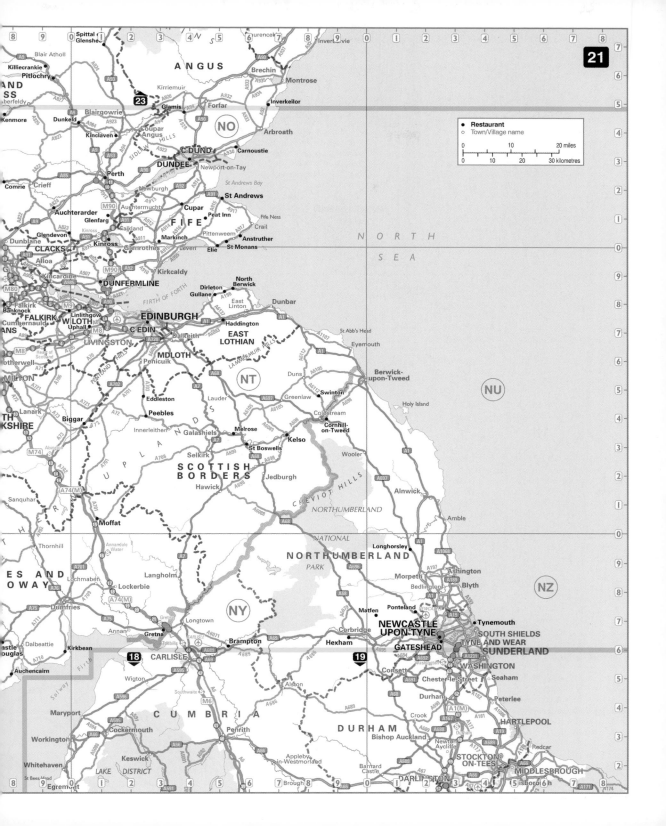

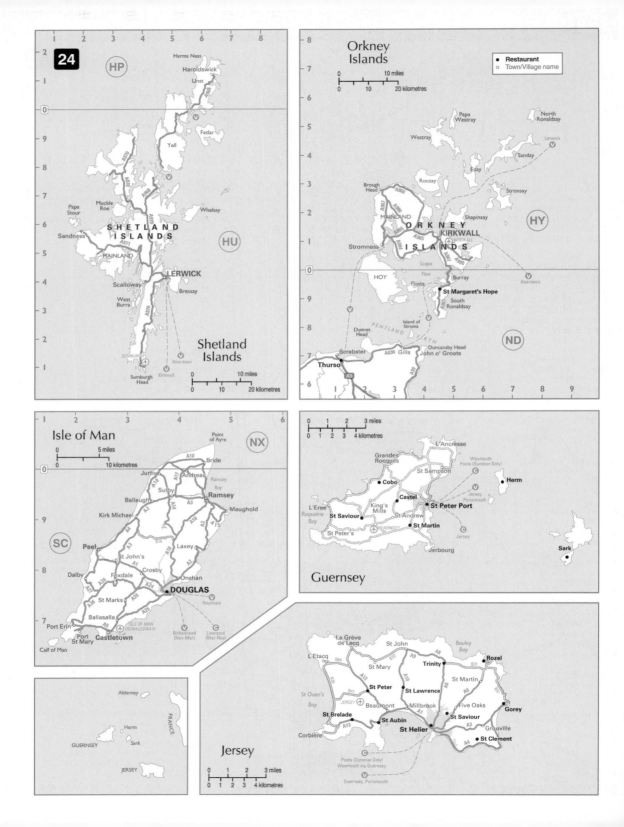

Index of Restaurants

The Automobile Association would like to thank the following photographers and companies for their assistance in the preparation of this book.

Abbreviations for the picture credits are as follows: (t) top; (b) bottom; (l) left; (r) right; (c) centre (AA) AA World Travel Library.

1 Cellar Restaurant, Anstruther; 2 Exclusive Hotels; 3 VonEssen Hotels; 4 Sarah Montgomery; 5 The Three Chimneys, Colbost; 8 L'Esgargot, The Ground Floor Restaurant, London; 11, 12, 13t. 13c, 13b Le Manoir Aux Quat'Saisons; 14l; 14r Corrigan's Mayfair; 15l Plumed Horse, Edinburgh; 15r Y Polyn, Nantgaredig; 18 AA/S Montgomery; 19l The Old Bridge Hotel, Huntingdon; 19c The Cross at Kingussie; 19r The Bell at Skenfrith; 20 Exclusive Hotels; 21 Exclusive Hotels; 22 VonEssen Hotels; 23 VonEssen Hotels; 24t Exclusive Hotels; 24bl Claridges; 24br Exclusive Hotels; 25 Exclusive Hotels; 26/7 AA/N Setchfield; 28 Rex Features; 29 To Come; 30 Lucknham Park; 31 Photolibrary Group; 32/3 AA/C Sawyer; 33 Three Choirs Winery; 34 Tenterden Vineyard; 35 English Wines Producers; 36 Three Choirs Winery; 37 Camel Valley Winery; 42 Exclusive Hotels; 45 Exclusive Hotels; 46/7 AA/J A Tims; London AA/C Sawyer; Scotland AA/J Smith; Wales AA/I Burgum

Every effort has been made to trace the copyright holders, and we apologise in advance for any accidental errors. We would be happy to apply the corrections in the following edition of this publication.

Readers' Report Form

Please send this form to:–
Editor, The Restaurant Guide,
Lifestyle Guides,
AA Publishing,
13th Floor, Fanum House,
Basingstoke RG21 4EA

or fax: 01256 491647
or e-mail: lifestyleguides@theAA.com

Please use this form to tell us about any restaurant you have visited, whether it is in the guide or not currently listed. Feedback from readers helps us to keep our guide accurate and up to date. Please note, however, that if you have a complaint to make during a visit, we strongly recommend that you discuss the matter with the restaurant management there and then, so that they have a chance to put things right before your visit is spoilt. The AA does not undertake to arbitrate between you and the restaurant management, or to obtain compensation or engage in correspondence.

Date

Your name (BLOCK CAPITALS)

Your address (BLOCK CAPITALS)

Post code

E-mail address

Restaurant name and address: (If you are recommending a new restaurant please enclose a menu or note the dishes that you ate.)

Comments

(please attach a separate sheet if necessary)

We may use information we hold about you to write, e-mail or telephone you about other products and services offered by us and our carefully selected partners, but we can assure you that we will not disclose it to third parties.

Please tick here ☐ if you DO NOT wish to receive details of other products or services from the AA.   PTO

Readers' Report Form *continued*

Have you bought this guide before? ☐ YES ☐ NO

Please list any other similar guides that you use regularly

_____

_____

What do you find most useful about The AA Restaurant Guide?

_____

_____

Please answer these questions to help us make improvements to the guide
What are your main reasons for visiting restaurants (tick all that apply)
Business entertaining ☐ Business travel ☐ Trying famous restaurants ☐ Family celebrations ☐
Leisure travel ☐ Trying new food ☐ Enjoying not having to cook yourself ☐
To eat food you couldn't cook yourself ☐ Because I enjoy eating out regularly ☐
Other (please state)

_____

How often do you visit a restaurant for lunch or dinner? (tick one choice)
Once a week ☐ Once a fortnight ☐ Once a month ☐ Less than once a month ☐
Do you use the location atlas ☐ YES ☐ NO?
Do you generally agree with the Rosette ratings at the restaurants you visit in the guide?
(If not please give examples)

_____

Who is your favourite chef?

_____

Which is your favourite restaurant?

_____

Which type of cuisine is your first choice e.g. French

_____

Which of these factors is most important when choosing a restaurant?
Price ☐ Service ☐ Location ☐ Type of food ☐ Awards/ratings ☐ Décor/surroundings ☐
Other (please state)

_____

Which elements of the guide do you find most useful when choosing a restaurant?
Description ☐ Photo ☐ Rosette rating ☐ Price ☐
Other (please state)

_____

Readers' Report Form

Please send this form to:–
Editor, The Restaurant Guide,
Lifestyle Guides,
AA Publishing,
13th Floor, Fanum House,
Basingstoke RG21 4EA

or fax: 01256 491647
or e-mail: lifestyleguides@theAA.com

Please use this form to tell us about any restaurant you have visited, whether it is in the guide or not currently listed. Feedback from readers helps us to keep our guide accurate and up to date. Please note, however, that if you have a complaint to make during a visit, we strongly recommend that you discuss the matter with the restaurant management there and then, so that they have a chance to put things right before your visit is spoilt. The AA does not undertake to arbitrate between you and the restaurant management, or to obtain compensation or engage in correspondence.

Date

Your name (BLOCK CAPITALS)

Your address (BLOCK CAPITALS)

Post code

E-mail address

Restaurant name and address: (If you are recommending a new restaurant please enclose a menu or note the dishes that you ate.)

Comments

(please attach a separate sheet if necessary)

We may use information we hold about you to write, e-mail or telephone you about other products and services offered by us and our carefully selected partners, but we can assure you that we will not disclose it to third parties.

Please tick here ☐ if you DO NOT wish to receive details of other products or services from the AA.   PTO

Readers' Report Form *continued*

Have you bought this guide before? ☐ YES ☐ NO

Please list any other similar guides that you use regularly

_____

_____

What do you find most useful about The AA Restaurant Guide?

_____

_____

Please answer these questions to help us make improvements to the guide
What are your main reasons for visiting restaurants (tick all that apply)
Business entertaining ☐ Business travel ☐   Trying famous restaurants ☐   Family celebrations ☐
Leisure travel ☐   Trying new food ☐   Enjoying not having to cook yourself ☐
To eat food you couldn't cook yourself ☐   Because I enjoy eating out regularly ☐
Other (please state)

_____

How often do you visit a restaurant for lunch or dinner? (tick one choice)
Once a week ☐   Once a fortnight ☐   Once a month ☐   Less than once a month ☐
Do you use the location atlas ☐ YES ☐ NO?
Do you generally agree with the Rosette ratings at the restaurants you visit in the guide?
(If not please give examples)

_____

Who is your favourite chef?

_____

Which is your favourite restaurant?

_____

Which type of cuisine is your first choice e.g. French

_____

Which of these factors is most important when choosing a restaurant?
Price ☐   Service ☐   Location ☐   Type of food ☐   Awards/ratings ☐   Décor/surroundings ☐
Other (please state)

_____

Which elements of the guide do you find most useful when choosing a restaurant?
Description ☐   Photo ☐   Rosette rating ☐   Price ☐
Other (please state)

_____

Readers' Report Form

Please use this form to tell us about any restaurant you have visited, whether it is in the guide or not currently listed. Feedback from readers helps us to keep our guide accurate and up to date. Please note, however, that if you have a complaint to make during a visit, we strongly recommend that you discuss the matter with the restaurant management there and then, so that they have a chance to put things right before your visit is spoilt. The AA does not undertake to arbitrate between you and the restaurant management, or to obtain compensation or engage in correspondence.

Date

Your name (BLOCK CAPITALS)

Your address (BLOCK CAPITALS)

Post code

E-mail address

Restaurant name and address: (If you are recommending a new restaurant please enclose a menu or note the dishes that you ate.)

Comments

(please attach a separate sheet if necessary)

PTO

Readers' Report Form *continued*

Have you bought this guide before? ☐ YES ☐ NO

Please list any other similar guides that you use regularly

_____

_____

What do you find most useful about The AA Restaurant Guide?

_____

_____

Please answer these questions to help us make improvements to the guide

What are your main reasons for visiting restaurants (tick all that apply)

Business entertaining ☐ Business travel ☐   Trying famous restaurants ☐   Family celebrations ☐

Leisure travel ☐   Trying new food ☐   Enjoying not having to cook yourself ☐

To eat food you couldn't cook yourself ☐   Because I enjoy eating out regularly ☐

Other (please state)

_____

How often do you visit a restaurant for lunch or dinner? (tick one choice)

Once a week ☐   Once a fortnight ☐   Once a month ☐   Less than once a month ☐

Do you use the location atlas   ☐ YES   ☐ NO?

Do you generally agree with the Rosette ratings at the restaurants you visit in the guide?

(If not please give examples)

_____

Who is your favourite chef?

_____

Which is your favourite restaurant?

_____

Which type of cuisine is your first choice e.g. French

_____

Which of these factors is most important when choosing a restaurant?

Price ☐   Service ☐   Location ☐   Type of food ☐   Awards/ratings ☐   Décor/surroundings ☐

Other (please state)

_____

Which elements of the guide do you find most useful when choosing a restaurant?

Description ☐   Photo ☐   Rosette rating ☐   Price ☐

Other (please state)

_____

PURE DECK-ADENCE

A Guide to Beautiful Decks

PURE DECK-ADENCE

A Guide to Beautiful Decks

TINA SKINNER

4880 Lower Valley Road, Atglen, PA 19310

ACKNOWLEDGMENTS

This book was made possible by the Hickson Corporation, which supplied all the photos herein. The dozens of deck photographs were taken by the Hickson Corporation at the suggestion of builders and architects who used Wolmanized® pressure-treated wood, a brand-name product of Hickson.

We have tried to present as diverse a sampling of deck styles and features as possible to help homeowners who are planning additions to their homes. However, it is important to note that regional building codes vary greatly. Some of the decks featured might not be permitted in your area, particularly with regard to railings. Local codes may dictate the size of railing gaps for the safety of children.

Skinner, Tina.
   Pure deck-adence / Tina Skinner.
      p.   cm.
   ISBN 0-7643-0445-3 (pbk.)
   1. Decks (Architecture, Domestic)   I. Title.
TH4970.S55   1998
690'.893--dc21   97-35940
                                         CIP

Book design by Blair R.C. Loughrey

ISBN: 0-7643-0445-3
Printed in Hong Kong

Published by Schiffer Publishing Ltd.
4880 Lower Valley Road
Atglen, PA 19310
Phone: (610) 593-1777; Fax: (610) 593-2002
Email: schifferbk@aol.com
Please write for a free catalog.
This book may be purchased from the publisher.
Please include $3.95 for shipping.

Try your bookstore first.

We are interested in hearing from authors with book ideas on related subjects.

TABLE OF CONTENTS

INTRODUCTION

Wooden decks mirror the American dream.

They stand as symbols of our increasing affluence. Surveys have found that one-quarter of all American homes have a deck of some size. Not only are decks becoming more commonplace, they are increasing in size and scope, incorporating more screened-in areas, more hot tubs, more pools, more gardens, ...

More importantly, though, decks reflect the appeal of the great outdoors in this New World country. They appeal to a desire for outdoor adventure and a closeness to nature. And they reflect the popularity of activities like sunbathing and adventures in the great outdoors.

Innovative technology has helped bolster the popularity of decks, too. The development of pressure-treating processes has made pine and other locally grown woods viable for such projects. A chemical treatment, known as CCA, or chromated copper arsenate, makes the wood resistant to insects and to rot for decades. And because this preservative is most effective with fast-growing and relatively inexpensive woods, fewer dollars can create more expansive home additions.

Treatments to make wood last are not new. In fact, they've been used since the turn of the century to preserve railroad ties, utility poles, and the like. Though the process was invented in 1933, CCA treated wood didn't really become popular as decking material until the 1970s.

It caught on in a big way, however. Home remodeling is one of the fastest growing segments of our economy, says Rick Provost, president of Archadeck in Richmond, Virginia. That company has been building decks since 1980 and has franchises in 21 states and Japan.

In Japan, Provost says, decks are a new phenomenon and are generally built on the front of new houses as a way to demonstrate the owner's affluence via this all-American icon. Japanese decks average 60 square feet. In America, particularly east of the Rocky Mountains where decks made from pressure-treated wood are most popular, these additions average 250 square feet, according to Provost, and are typically placed on the backs of homes.

Decks vary from owner to owner. Some homeowners are simply looking for a small, private place to enjoy the outdoors while others want a lavish spread for entertaining. There is an increasing movement toward creating transitional environments, where the outdoors can be enjoyed from a sheltered, screened-in area, or visually captured from a sunroom. These, in turn, spill onto decks, down stairs, onto lawns and into gardens—creating a direct walkway from your home to Mother Nature's. On the way you can enjoy the obvious esthetic advantages of wood—the cushioning thud and the warmth radiated to bare feet. It's that boardwalk cadence, remembered from seaside vacations, now made possible in your very own backyard.

Chapter One

STEPPING INTO
THE GREAT OUTDOORS

MAKING THE TRANSITION

Decks expand our homes, and our horizons, providing a place in nature custom built for relaxation. They serve as an invitation to enjoy quiet, to escape phones and appliances, to bask in sunshine, or to breathe the night air.

Painted an opaque color to allow the grain to show through while tying in with roof shingles and door trim, this simple deck was made elegant with subtle touches—a matching bench, a small railing accent by the window, and the contrast of wood against brick.

This suburban home has staked a piece of the outdoors in an open, suburban environment. While giving occupants access to the fresh air, it also provides some privacy via screens and some shade via the slatted boards overhead.

10

A home is greatly expanded by a big deck, which allows
the occupants to take full advantage of the outdoors.

This deck gives pause to a
quick transition between
home and lawn. The slatted
roof provides shade and a
natural transition from
indoors to full sun. Boards
that sit on the ground, as
opposed to those raised
higher, have been treated
differently to preserve them.

In this case, the transition from lawn to indoor carpeting is a bit more pronounced with this raised platform. A solid, bench railing provides for full use of this added-on space.

Here various levels and seating areas create virtual rooms outdoors: places to sit and read, work on crafts, or simply socialize. Matching chairs built from the same wood as the deck lend harmony to the atmosphere.

BRINGING THE GARDEN CLOSER

Summer's blooms have to wait for the season's sun to come,
but still they seem almost indoors when they border a deck.
And gardening seems such a clean undertaking.

Potted plants punctuate this rounded, multi-level deck.

Plants colonize a new deck, with the sun-lovers climbing the
perimeter, the woodland plants taking shelter under a lattice roof.

Right:
Narrow flower boxes house geraniums on a narrow porch, improving the view from both sides. Note that the placement of boards perpendicular to the house, instead of the traditional parallel construction, also helps create an illusion of width.

Below:
A more established deck is surrounded by greenery. Slatted boards form a narrow bower.

Opposite:
Pots create an above-ground
garden, at a height just right for
enjoyment from lounge-chair level.

Left:
A walkway leads away from home, toward a hot tub bubbling in the distance and a shaded area created by a slatted roof.

Below:
This deck draws people as far as possible from the home, to a corner made appealing by a fan-like structure of slats above and wide benches below.

A roofed pavilion creates a secluded environment, attached and yet remote and private.

A remote place is created mere steps from the home—a platform made private by a small stretch of fencing.

Below:
Unique in its separateness, this deck is not attached to a home, but sits far off in the yard, a separate place one must journey to. Though not far, the setting is nevertheless remote and secluded.

RISING ABOVE IT ALL

Some decks provide a crow's nest, a point of observation far from the madding crowd where one can relax and contemplate the world below. Here a couple enjoys their private view of an inlet near Jacksonville, Florida.

Above:
This home has a perch almost as high as the tree canopy.

Left:
That first step would be a big one if this small deck didn't provide a place to walk out and take in this California view.

21

This home in Pennsylvania has decks on two levels, but
the upper decks are clearly the place to be for the view.

Even an apartment
dweller can rise
above it all.

Left:
It's human nature to gravitate to high ground. This raised deck sits high enough to let the grass remain green underneath, so there's no need for the heavy plastics and mulches generally used beneath deck structures.

Below:
Though only a few feet off the ground, this deck's position at the top of the hill gives those standing on it an impressive view.

Chapter 2

LEVELING THE ODDS

ON DIFFERENT LEVELS

As decks have grown in both popularity and size, they've evolved a trickle-down-like effect. The result is a layered playground, with infinite invitations to pause, rest, and reflect.

A wooden deck spills down and surrounds a brick patio, where
summer geraniums add a softer texture to the two building materials.

Changes in the
boards' direc-
tions mark the
subtle settling of
this deck as it
moves away
from the house.

Two levels of deck add interest to the journey from house to lawn.

LEVELING THE PLAYING FIELD

One of a deck's greatest advantages is its ability to smooth uneven plots of land. Frequently a deck is used to help recapture sloped land and to ease that first step from back door to bottom of yard.

Here a deck provides a level space beside the house where previously there was none. It also offers a great view.

A deck helps smooth the way down a steep, rocky hillside.

Left:
A steep staircase illustrates the perilous drop this platform deck has covered up.

Below:
This deck is the final crowning touch to the hill which this house commands.

A deck works well over a partially submerged basement.

A small deck serves as both a back porch and
as a transition from the first floor to the ground.

Two doorways from the first floor
lead onto a deck, which sits above
a partially submerged basement.

Here is a more drastic example of the need for a transition between the living level of a home and the backyard.

Large decks form people-friendly terracing, complemented by a large retaining wall—all built to conquer and utilize a hilly backyard.

TAKING THE PLUNGE

For those fortunate enough to own waterfront property, a deck is often the first step to a day on the beach, or the first step toward hoisting the sails.

This deck sets the context for a soothing lakefront view.

This house sits so close to the water that only the deck and its railings keep one from rolling straight in.

A spacious deck provides an above-water beach and a spectacular
view, while a staircase lures one off to the waterside.

35

Right:
While making the transition from house to water level, this deck also provides beach where nature couldn't.

Below:
A sprawling deck spills slowly toward a cliff before offering a staircase and a route straight down. Descending levels maximize the view so a railing never blocks it. Indeed, the only railing is actually a bench, inviting people to sit and fully enjoy the view beyond.

Not all decks descend. Some climb. Both of these decks
reward those who ascend with a maximized view.

Staircases and steps, whether rising or
falling, are beautiful in and of themselves.

RALLY AROUND THE WATER

POOLSIDE PARADISES

Wood has replaced the traditional cement skirting around indoor pools. It doesn't heat up like concrete surfaces, and it's not as hard on bathing suits either.

A wooden surface blends with railings and a back porch for a seamless transition.

Wood flooring creates an enormous play area around this pool. Besides providing an easy path for bare feet traversing between water and the dining/seating areas, the wood helps ensure that mud and other debris aren't being carried to the water.

Again, nature is neatly contained in planters and behind railings, helping to prevent dirt from being tracked into the pool. White paint adds to the clean feeling of this pool-side deck and walkway.

Natural tones of wood, stone, and canvas are a foil to brilliant blue water.

Wood forms a neat frame around this pool. Note the tidy corner formed by changing board directions.

A herringbone floor pattern lends interest to this pool-side decking. Above, a slatted roof provides shade.

Floorboard patterns form a nice frame for this pool and a small,
raised platform improves the view for those out of the water.

Lights in planter beds make a deck more inviting by night.

IN HOT WATER

A frothy, steamy hot tub makes a deck useable any time of the year, at any latitude.

On the other hand, this hot tub is tucked in a corner
and nestled by trees, creating a private nook.

Opposite:
Raised up and clear of trees
and a nearby slatted roof, this
hot tub's position offers great
views for occupants.

This sunken tub sits amidst a sunburst pattern, overlooking a small pond.

Opposite:
A low roof makes this a more private place for a soak.

This enormous hot tub lures people out into the open.

A small area enclosed with railing gives a semi-secluded feel to this hot tub.

BEST OF BOTH WORLDS

Then there are those who have both on one deck—hot tub and pool. A brick lip around the tub and variations in board direction give this deck texture and appeal.

A hot tub overlooks the pool. An inviting walk
between the two is lined with wooden flower beds.

Chapter 4

ALMOST OUTDOORS

Screened-in porches and sun rooms combined with outdoor decking are one of the hottest trends in home remodeling today. They form the perfect transition between indoors and out, and provide a fresh refuge when the weather, or the mosquitoes, are not quite conducive to sitting under the open sky.

Above:
Matching roof shingles tie this porch into the darker, painted wood of the home.

Right:
Skylights and a fan make this porch feel almost indoors.

This porch provides a smooth transition from indoors to out—a path that is no doubt worn smooth by these two North Carolina children.

Note how, on the left, this porch addition incorporates a door leading to a crawl space. A matching roof ties it into the house, while the new wood creates a beautiful contrast against brick.

Raising the porch or lowering the deck surrounding it helps to create unobstructed views. Matching wood helps lend harmony to this entire house addition.

This screened-in porch and adjacent deck are part of the home's entryway, providing a perfect mud room for taking off dirty shoes.

Likewise, this narrow, screened-in porch forms an entryway for the home.

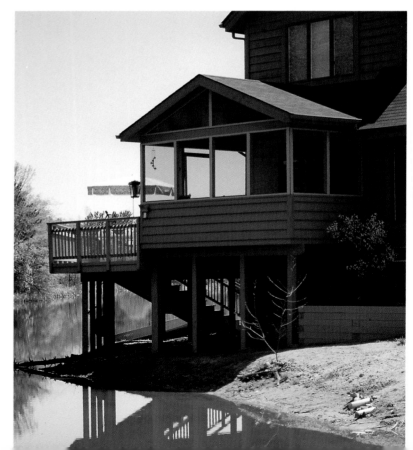

The screened walls on this porch provide mosquito protection in the summer months.

This screened-in porch stands on its own,
reached by a walkway from the house.

AN ILLUSION OF WALLS

Natural boundaries and indoor fixtures can leave visitors in doubt, visually, about their location indoors or out.

The roof over this hot tub leaves an impression
of confinement when, in fact, there are no walls.

Above and left:
Ceiling fans, skylights, and chandeliers bring all the comforts of home indoors, but there are no walls, screens, or glass between this space and the greater outdoors.

Chapter 5

GREAT SPREADS

This spread near the North Carolina/Virginia border uses wood to form a bridge between garden and home. Notice how the consistent, rich color of the wood stain provides a feeling of warmth while lending itself to the landscaping. The same color is carried throughout, in details like furnishings, rails, and arbors.

70

An almost identical stain to that used in the previous house is used here, though a more formal feeling is created through contrasts with the brick home and clean, white fencing, and by geometrical forms like those of the staircase and bench.

Here a semi-transparent stain lightens and leaves the
deck neutral, in contrast to bold color punctuation.

Flowing stretches of wood flooring and short strips of benches create a Zen garden feel for this massive deck in Berlin, New York.

The wood ties indoors to out in a gentle transition to the lawn
and the woods beyond this Raleigh, North Carolina home.

Here a deck ties an entire household together, as well as providing the first step to the backyard. Notice the unique rail pattern which lends uniformity to the entire project.

A private, outdoor compound is formed with tall fences surrounding open stretches of flooring and water. Even the family dog is included in this extension of a Pennsylvania home.

A Pennsylvania home is surrounded by decking, which acts as an invitation to move outdoors and into the greenery beyond.

Long stretches of decking link a hillside home
with a boathouse on a lake in North Carolina.

White paint dresses up the rear view of a house, while natural wood flooring on the deck adds visual warmth to this home in the mountains of North Carolina. Radiating floorboards on the front porch mimic the painted boards above in the roof.

91

An alluring environment in Plantation, Florida,
was sculpted from wood around this pool.

Pool and waterfront are linked using a combination
of wood and brick in Pompano Beach, Florida.

Spiral staircases end decks on either side of a house in Ohio. This deck is now almost fifteen years old, and the owner says it still looks as good as the day it was finished.

97

Chapter 6

THE FINE DETAILS

FLOORING

Typically, floorboards are put down parallel to the house. However, this pattern is varied as often as not, both for esthetic and for practical reasons.

Above:
Putting the floor-boards perpendicular to the house helps make a narrow deck appear wider.

Left:
Diagonally placed floorboards give a jaunty look to this small deck.

Parquet flooring is a typical and easy variation for squared
decks. Many home improvement stores and lumber retailers
sell pre-made parquet that can be simply installed for flooring.

A herringbone pattern is created where opposed
diagonal boards meet, creating an intriguing line.

A radiating square creates a beautiful, geometric pattern.

103

Arranging boards in different directions helps to define areas and warns pedestrians about upcoming changes in floor levels.

A slight curvature invites one for a quick
climb, however slight the view enhancement.

Varying the length of boards as they form steps for
a staircase makes the staircase seem to flow or spill.

LOOKING UP

Wood can be used to create shade above decks where trees fall short. Here lattice on one side and slats above protect a dining area.

A small sunscreen can enhance a sitting area and provide a frame from which plants can be hung and protected from direct sunlight.

A Roman bath effect is created with capped columns and classically finished beams and joists above this hot tub.

Retractable awnings allow deck dwellers a choice of sun or shade, and provide rain protection and beautiful color.

In a wooded location, screens help keep out leaves and other tree debris.

A conical roof creates a gazebo effect over one area of a deck.

An unfinished ceiling gives more of
a room-like feel to this deck area.

111

Above:
Though open, this circle
of spoke-like beams
creates a detached area.

Left:
An open grid of beams
provides beauty and form.

THE OPEN RAILS

Railings serve many roles, primarily helping to prevent people from tumbling off decks and hurting themselves. They also form a support one can lean against while enjoying the view beyond and, when wide enough, a work space and even a seat. The most common rails are sections of vertical balusters—those rails which don't support the deck, but may protect the occupants and provide decoration.

Vertical balusters are often beveled to sit flush against the top rail.

Vertical balusters lend themselves to circular railings
and other twists and turns these barriers might take.

Vertical balusters are interspersed with panels containing a diamond-shaped cutout pattern.

Horizontal rails have a much different appearance and help create an illusion of length in walkways.

Lattice is another popular form of railing. It creates a semi-private enclosure and a safety net for small children and animals. Here the appearance of a lattice rail is enhanced by a white rope under the top rail.

Here lattice is set in a sturdy frame and punctuated
by capped posts, which lend themselves to displays.

117

Another popular railing is a sunburst pattern, often sold in sections by lumber retailers.

118

Above:
Spindles are another option in railings, infinite in their variety.

Right:
Likewise, deck posts can be transformed by lathe into all manner of shapes, or be adorned with pre-made caps, like this post with a post cap and a ball top.

119

Contrasts are one of the easiest ways to introduce interest and beauty to decks. Here a straight rail fence, a solid board wall, and lattice provide a visual feast of styles.

A half-lattice, half-solid board railing creates a quiet nook.

A long railing is broken at the junction of two staircases by a geometric design.

There are infinite varieties of railing styles. However, regional building codes vary. Many regions restrict open railings, allowing spacing between rails of no more than six or eight inches. It is important to check local codes before building.

DUAL DESIGNS

Building benches into railings saves space, plus it gives one a perch as close to the outdoors as possible without stepping off the deck.

127

OTHER FURNISHINGS

Wood can be used to build everything imaginable on a deck.

Besides helping to form barriers, benches can also double with planter boxes to enhance the environment, or with end tables to add comfort.

139

Matching tables can be constructed for decks.

Built-in barbecues are one of the most
popular features on decks today.

A handy table or buffet was built on to this deck.

Wet or dry bars can be constructed on a deck for those who entertain often.

Chapter 7

ON ENTERING AND EXITING

Though often placed on the back of the house, decks are frequently the family member's main entrance and exit. Wherever they are placed, decks help to define the character of the house.

159